S0-DVC-326

S0-DVC-326

LABOR
IN AMERICA

Clio Bibliography Series No. 18

LABOR IN AMERICA

A Historical Bibliography

ABC-Clio Information Services

Santa Barbara, California
Denver, Colorado
Oxford, England

Library of Congress Cataloging in Publication Data
Main entry under title:

Labor in America.

   (Clio bibliography series; no. 18)
   Includes index.
   1. Labor and laboring classes—United States—History
—Bibliography. I. ABC-Clio Information Services.
II. Series.
Z7164.L1L3   1985   016.331'0973   83-26640
[HD8066]
ISBN 0-87436-397-7

©1985 by ABC-Clio, Inc.

All rights reserved. No part of this publication may be reproduced, stored in a retrieval
system, or transmitted, in any form or by any means, electronic, mechanical, photo-copying
recording, or otherwise, without the prior written permission of ABC-Clio, Inc.

ABC-Clio Information Services, Inc.
2040 Alameda Padre Serra
Santa Barbara, California

ABC-Clio Information Services, Inc.
The Consulate
700 East Ninth Avenue
Denver, Colorado

Clio Press Ltd.
55 St. Thomas St.
Oxford 0X1 1JG, England

Printed and bound in the United States of America

TABLE OF CONTENTS

LIST OF ABBREVIATIONS

A.	Author-prepared Abstract
Acad.	Academy, Academie, Academia
Agric.	Agriculture, Agricultural
AIA	Abstracts in Anthropology
Akad.	Akademie
Am.	America, American
Ann.	Annals, Annales, Annual, Annali
Anthrop.	Anthropology, Anthropological
Arch.	Archives
Archaeol.	Archaeology, Archaeological
Art.	Article
Assoc.	Association, Associate
Biblio.	Bibliography, Bibliographical
Biog.	Biography, Biographical
Bol.	Boletim, Boletin
Bull.	Bulletin
c.	century (in index)
ca.	circa
Can.	Canada, Canadian, Canadien
Cent.	Century
Coll.	College
Com.	Committee
Comm.	Commission
Comp.	Compiler
DAI	Dissertation Abstracts International
Dept.	Department
Dir.	Director, Direktor
Econ.	Economy, Econom-.
Ed.	Editor, Edition
Educ.	Education, Educational
Geneal.	Genealogy, Genealogical, Genealogique
Grad.	Graduate
Hist.	History, Hist-.
IHE	Indice Historico Espanol

Illus.	Illustrated, Illustration
Inst.	Institute, Institut-.
Int.	International, Internacional, Internationaal, Internationaux, Internazionale
J.	Journal, Journal-prepared Abstract
Lib.	Library, Libraries
Mag.	Magazine
Mus.	Museum, Musee, Museo
Nac.	Nacional
Natl.	National, Nationale
Naz.	Nazionale
Phil.	Philosophy, Philosophical
Photo.	Photograph
Pol.	Politics, Political, Politique, Politico
Pr.	Press
Pres.	President
Pro.	Proceedings
Publ.	Publishing, Publication
Q.	Quarterly
Rev.	Review, Revue, Revista, Revised
Riv.	Rivista
Res.	Research
RSA	Romanian Scientific Abstracts
S.	Staff-prepared Abstract
Sci.	Science, Scientific
Secy.	Secretary
Soc.	Society, Societe, Sociedad, Societa
Sociol.	Sociology, Sociological
Tr.	Transactions
Transl.	Translator, Translation
U.	University, Universi-.
US	United States
Vol.	Volume
Y.	Yearbook

Abbreviations also apply to feminine and plural forms.
Abbreviations not noted above are based on *Webster's Third New International Dictionary*
and the *United States Government Printing Office Style Manual*.

PREFACE

The history of labor in America is replete with examples of violence and misery, as well as collectivism and camaraderie. A multifaceted story, it encompasses the struggle for better wages and working conditions and the individual human toll of mechanization and automation. Recently expanded beyond traditional definitions of the field, American labor history is now understood to include far more than mere examination of the institutions and economics of organized labor. While narratives of local and national unions and their industrial relations are still an important part of labor history, they no longer form the entire basis for research on labor in the United States.

In contraposition to the old labor economists, the "new" labor historians have, since the early 1970's, posed new socio-psychological and quantitative frameworks for examining what Herbert Gutman described as the "beliefs and behaviors of ordinary working Americans." This new generation of scholars, greatly influenced by the work of English social historian E. P. Thompson on the English working class, has started to question the assumptions of the Wisconsin School proponents of the "old" labor historiography. Pioneering studies of working-class consciousness in America have discarded or modified the intellectual framework of a "job conscious" working class; these new approaches have begun to integrate a variety of disciplines and to examine the factors that have contributed to the unique class consciousness of the American worker—from the so-called Protestant work ethic to the influences of immigration and ethnicity and the effects of geographical and social mobility. New investigations into labor politics have followed from the new approaches, raising questions about the transformation of economic demands into political ones through democratic socialism, anarchism, and communism.

A major survey of this scholarship, *Labor in America: A Historical Bibliography* provides access, in a single reference work, to over a decade of research, coinciding with the emergence of the new labor historiography, as well as following traditional developments within the study of labor-management relations. Drawn from ABC-Clio's vast history data base—which covers over 2,000 journals published in some 90 countries—the volume contains 2,865 abstracts of articles published from 1973 to 1983 in the periodical literature of history and the related social sciences and humanities.

In order to create this unique tool, the editors reviewed the many thousands of abstracts of articles published during 1973-1983 and selected every abstract that relates to American labor, within both the old and new delineations of its scope. Thus, this volume represents an in-depth summary of the scholarship in the world's periodical literature and far exceeds in accuracy and economy what one could expect to retrieve through an online search or even through a manual search of the subject index of ABC-Clio Information Services' history data base.

The chapters in this bibliography are organized in a chronological and topical arrangement. The chronological divisions are 1) early American labor, including the colonial, antebellum, and Civil War eras; 2) the post-Civil War period, 1865-1900; 3) the new century, 1900-1945; 4) the contemporary period, 1945-1982; and 5) multiperiod, where the dates span two or more of the chronological categories.

Within each of these chapters, there are several topical divisions. The earliest period, to 1865, includes one section for professional, indentured, and organized labor, and one devoted to the conditions of slave labor. All other chapters have the following subheadings: general information; attitudes, behavior, and working conditions of the individual worker; the rise and decline of the labor movement; particular locals and strikes; government programs and policies and labor politics; racial, ethnic, and sex discrimination; and the economics and statistics of labor. The 1900-1945 and the 1945-1982 chapters also include a separate category for white collar, professional, and technical workers. Article abstracts are arranged alphabetically by author within each of these sections. Differences in the size of the chapters represents no editorial predisposition, but rather the relative volume of scholarship in the periodical literature produced during 1973-1983.

Additional access to the abstracts and citations in *Labor in America* is through ABC-SPIndex (Subject Profile Index), a highly specific subject index developed by ABC-Clio Information Services. Key subject terms are linked with the historical dates to form a complete profile of the article. Each set of index terms is rotated alphabetically so that the complete profile appears under each of the subject terms. Thus, the accuracy and specificity of subject access is enhanced as compared to conventional, hierarchical indexes. Great care has been taken to eliminate inconsistencies that might have appeared in the subject index as a result of merging over a decade of data base material. A large number of cross-references has been included to ensure fast and thorough searching. The explanatory note at the beginning of the subject index provides further information for using ABC-SPIndex.

This volume represents the collaboration of a skilled group of professionals. Pamela R. Byrne, Executive Editor of the Clio Bibliography Series, had overall responsibility for the creation of this volume and provided the guidance for its production. The Data Base Products staff—Managing Editor, Jessica S. Brown and Assistant Editor, Susan K. Kinnell—were responsible for developing the chapter headings, selecting and organizing the entries, reviewing the subject index, devising the numerous helpful cross-references in the index, and planning and carrying out all major phases of editorial production. The Data Processing Services Department, under the supervision of Ken Baser, Director, and Deborah Looker, Production Supervisor, ably manipulated the data base to fit the editorial specifications of this bibliography. David R. Blanke, Applications Programmer, provided essential design support in assuring high-quality photocomposition.

And, finally, a heartfelt thanks to the community of scholars throughout the world who wrote the abstracts that comprise this volume and whose continuing commitment to quality bibliographic tools made possible the publication of this volume.

1. LABOR IN AMERICA: MULTIPERIOD

General

1. Alanen, Arnold R. and Peltin, Thomas J. KOHLER, WISCONSIN: PLANNING AND PATERNALISM IN A MODEL INDUSTRIAL VILLAGE. *J. of the Am. Inst. of Planners 1978 44(2): 145-159.* Although it never achieved the infamy of Pullman, Illinois, nor the size of Gary, Indiana, the company town of Kohler, Wisconsin, stands out as an interesting example of community planning and corporate paternalism. Walter J. Kohler, Sr., the company president from 1905 to 1940 and the primary force behind the model village, hired several nationally known planners to guide the early development of the community. These activities brought a considerable amount of fame to Kohler, but two bitter strikes (1934 and 1954-1960) tarnished the image of systematic order and seeming harmony which the company sought to maintain. While the company still plays an important role in community affairs, current residents appear to be quite satisfied with village-corporate relationships and evaluate the community's physical planning features highly. J

2. Alanen, Arnold R. THE PLANNING OF COMPANY COMMUNITIES IN THE LAKE SUPERIOR MINING REGION. *J. of the Am. Planning Assoc. 1979 45(3): 256-278.* In Michigan, Wisconsin, and Minnesota community and social welfare plans did provide housing and services to employees and residents, however, the intent of these company towns was to increase labor productivity and thus the profits of enterprise. The evolution of the region, therefore, has been characterized by conflicts between the interests of corporations and those of the community. J/S

3. Alston, Lee J. TENURE CHOICE IN SOUTHERN AGRICULTURE, 1930-1960. *Explorations in Econ. Hist. 1981 18(3): 211-232.* Analyzes the decline in agricultural tenant contracts in 10 southern states from Texas to the Carolinas during 1930-60. Mechanization and crop choice reduced supervision costs and the type of labor needed. Wage labor became more cost efficient, reducing tenancy contracts. 3 tables, app., 16 notes, 41 ref. P. J. Coleman

4. Altenbaugh, Richard J. "OUR CHILDREN ARE BEING TRAINED LIKE DOGS AND PONIES": SCHOOLING, SOCIAL CONTROL, AND THE WORKING CLASS. *Hist. of Educ. Q. 1981 21(2): 213-222.* Discusses Walter Feinberg and Henry Rosemont, Jr., *Work, Technology, and Education: Dissenting Essays in the Intellectual Foundations of American Education* (1975) and Paul C. Violas, *The Training of the Urban Working Class: A History of Twentieth Century American Education* (1978). The reviewer agrees with the common point of the two books that public schooling has been "a mechanism of social control," but he adds that workers have recognized that fact and have developed their own alternatives to public schooling. 18 notes. D. B. Marti

5. Ankarloo, Bengt. AGRICULTURE AND WOMEN'S WORK: DIRECTIONS OF CHANGE IN THE WEST, 1700-1900. *J. of Family Hist. 1979 4(2): 111-121.* Compares the roles of women in Sweden and the United States in agriculture as commercial farming replaced subsistence agriculture. Women's labor was usually confined to the family. Based mainly on statistics from the American Midwest, 1870-1900; 4 tables, fig., biblio. S

6. Antler, Joyce. "AFTER COLLEGE, WHAT?": NEW GRADUATES AND THE FAMILY CLAIM. *Am. Q. 1980 32(4): 409-434.* Describes the postgraduate experiences of the first generation of women college graduates, 1880-1910. Most found that their families reasserted control over their lives once they graduated. Aspirations of these women for achievement outside the home were largely unfulfilled, leaving many with a feeling of worthlessness. Those who did manage to establish a career either were fortunate to have supportive parents or broke away from their families. An analysis of the experience of some notable women graduates predicts well the pattern found among a larger group of college women, the Wellesley class of 1897. Based on classbooks of the Wellesley College class of 1897 and other primary sources; table, 34 notes. D. K. Lambert

7. Arroyo, Luis Leobardo. NOTES ON PAST, PRESENT AND FUTURE DIRECTIONS OF CHICANO LABOR STUDIES. *Aztlán 1976 6(2): 137-149.* Early studies of Chicano labor were of the impact of Mexican immigrants on the US economy. Paul Taylor and Manuel Gamio pioneered a new approach which enlarged the field. Recent studies view Mexican Americans as active rather than passive agents in labor history. A critique of articles contained in this issue reveals that Chicano labor history is weak in conceptualization and too narrow in scope. 11 notes. R. Griswold del Castillo

8. Bach, Robert L. MEXICAN IMMIGRATION AND THE AMERICAN STATE. *Int. Migration Rev. 1978 12(4): 536-558.* Discusses illegal aliens during 1867-1977, in reference to the economic needs and strengths of organized labor in the United States.

9. Bailey, Kenneth R. A JUDICIOUS MIXTURE: NEGROES AND IMMIGRANTS IN THE WEST VIRGINIA MINES, 1880-1917. *West Virginia Hist. 1973 34(2): 141-161.* Ethnic and racial changes in West Virginia from the 1870's to the 1920's resulted from the expansion of the coal mining industry. Until 1890 few foreigners came to the mines, but by 1915 they constituted more than half of the work force. Recruitment by mining interests, with its accompanying abuses and efforts to check them, largely accounts for the influx. The introduction of Negroes, generally as an effort to check unionism, was only partly successful, as ties of common economic problems often overcame racial and ethnic differences. Based on newspapers; 81 notes. C. A. Newton

10. Banks, Alan J. THE EMERGENCE OF A CAPITALISTIC LABOR MARKET IN EASTERN KENTUCKY. *Appalachian J. 1980 7(3): 188-198.* Traces the development of capitalist modes of production (CMP) in Kentucky, from the preindustrial, agricultural economy of 1787 through the 1890's, focusing on the labor and economic policies of Kentucky politicians.

11. Barr, Thomas P. THE POTTAWATOMIE BAPTIST MANUAL LABOR TRAINING SCHOOL. *Kansas Hist. Q. 1977 43(4): 377-431.* Recounts the founding of the Pottawatomie Baptist Manual Labor Training School in Kansas following the signing of the Pottawatomie Indian treaties of 1846. Directed by the Baptist minister and physician Johnston Lykins (1800-76), the school was built in a style unusual for the time. The attic is the most unusual feature of the school and is classified as a flush-gable monitor, thus placing the school apart from nearly all known 19th-century structures. Describes the school's method of operation and cites evidence of its success, in the face of severe health problems and a worsening financial condition. The school ceased operation after the Pottawatomie Indians were moved to the Indian Territory in 1867. In 1873 the school property was sold to a breeder of nationally known trotting horses. 122 notes. W. F. Zornow

12. Barral, Pierre and Tavernier, Yves. MOUVEMENTS PAYSANS VISANT À ADAPTER L'AGRICULTURE À L'ECONOMIE [Peasant movements concerning the adaptation of agriculture to the market economy]. *Cahiers Int. d'Hist. Écon. et Sociale [Italy] 1976 6: 36-51.* Synthesizes reports at the International Colloquium (Naples, 1969) on peasant movements in the industrialized societies of Europe and North America in the late 19th and 20th centuries. The evolution of "capitalistic agriculture" added to the old peasant struggle for land, new problems created by salaried employees, technical equipment, and transport. World War II brought the peasant into direct encounter with the technical revolution of the 19th century and thereby altered the history of peasants. Peasant movements developed from pressure groups to political parties, and peasant voters forced all political groups to formulate policies for agricultural problems. F. X. Hartigan

13. Bell, Daniel. WORK, ALIENATION, AND SOCIAL CONTROL. *Dissent 1974 21(2): 207-212.* First published in the Summer 1959 *Dissent*. One of 21 articles on *Dissent*'s 20 years of publication. S

14. Benedict, Michael Les. FREE LABOR IDEOLOGY AND THE MEANING OF THE CIVIL WAR AND RECONSTRUCTION. *Rev. in Am. Hist.* 1981 9(2): 179-185. Review essay of Eric Foner's *Politics and Ideology in the Age of the Civil War* (1980), a collection of essays on the Civil War and Reconstruction era that support the author's interpretation of the period based on the free labor ideology of the North and the "hierarchical, paternal, organic society" of the South.

15. Berch, Bettina. THE DEVELOPMENT OF HOUSEWORK. *Int. J. of Women's Studies [Canada]* 1978 1(4): 336-348. The development of housework, 1840's-1970's, includes the "servant crisis," scientific management, technological revolution, and present-day task- and time-oriented housework.

16. Blatt, Martin; Green, Jim; and Reverby, Susan. A REUNION OF SHOEWORKERS: THE FIRST MASSACHUSETTS HISTORY WORKSHOP. *Radical Am.* 1980 14(1): 67-73. A report on the Saturday Workshop conducted on 27 October 1979 at Hibernian Hall in West Lynn, Massachusetts, and attended by 70 former Lynn shoeworkers, plus historians, journalists, labor unionists, and some strikers from the adjacent General Electric River Works. It was patterned somewhat after history workshops organized by Raphael Samuel and students of Ruskin College, Oxford. It attempted to bring together working people in a community with historians who have studied that community, an effort "to break out of our own isolation as radical historians and work together with people who have an important story to tell." The experiment was successful at many levels: as a reunion for the workers, as a recreation of an old union meeting, and as a means of stimulating further research. The workshop was financed by the Essex Institute, and demonstrated that workers are anxious to work with historians. 4 photos.   R. V. Ritter

17. Bodnar, John. IMMIGRATION, KINSHIP, AND THE RISE OF WORKING CLASS REALISM IN INDUSTRIAL AMERICA. *J. of Social Hist.* 1980 14(1): 45-66. Class formulation rather than class conflict needs attention in understanding the attitudes and actions of immigrant workers and their children. After reviewing the literature stressing the shift from idealistic militancy in the late 19th century and the greater realism of the 1920's and 30's, the author examines the family ties of immigrant workers in various industries. Job security for several family members was a key goal. This often outweighed concern about power relationships, work routines, occupational advancement, or social transformation. Based on oral interviews conducted in Pittsburgh and other sources in 1976; 31 notes.   C. M. Hough

18. Bourg, Carroll J. WORK AND/OR JOB IN ADVANCED INDUSTRIAL SOCIETIES. *Soundings* 1974 57(1): 113-125. Work time, once associated through the Protestant work ethic with moral duty, has been drastically reduced following industrialization, forcing a reevaluation of values and redefinition of leisure.

19. Braverman, Harry. THE DEGRADATION OF WORK IN THE TWENTIETH CENTURY. *Monthly Rev.* 1982 34(1): 1-13. Analyzes the theme of work in 20th-century capitalist society, by considering the production process, its outcome, its effect on labor and the worker, and the results of an accumulation of wealth at one end of society matched at the other by an accumulation of misery.

20. Braverman, Harry. LABOR AND MONOPOLY CAPITAL: THE DEGRADATION OF WORK IN THE TWENTIETH CENTURY. *Monthly Rev.* 1974 26(3): 1-134. Presents excerpts from Braverman's forthcoming book, *Labor and Monopoly Capital: The Degradation of Work in the Twentieth Century* (New York: Monthly Review Press, 1974), which describe capitalism's impact in industrialized countries on occupational duties and occupational shifts by labor.

21. Bringhurst, Newell G. THE "NEW" LABOR HISTORY AND HARD ROCK MINERS IN NEVADA AND THE WEST. *Nevada Hist. Soc. Q.* 1981 24(2): 170-175. Reviews Ronald C. Brown's *Hard Rock Miners: The Intermountain West, 1860-1920* (1979) and Mark Wyman's *Hard Rock Epic: Western Miners and the Industrial Revolution, 1860-1910* (1979). Both books reflect the influence of the new labor history methodologies in which union and nonunion people receive fair billing, and the socioeconomic aspirations and experiences of both

groups are related interpretatively to the social milieu. 10 notes.
                                                            H. T. Lovin

22. Brody, David. LABOR HISTORY IN THE 1970'S: TOWARD A HISTORY OF THE AMERICAN WORKER. Kammen, Michael, ed. *The Past Before Us: Contemporary Historical Writing in the United States* (Ithaca, N.Y.: Cornell U. Pr., 1980): 252-269. Until well after World War II, labor history remained primarily the concern of institutional economists. Initial historical research focused on the labor movement: its leaders, strikes, organizations, and politics. In the 1970's, Herbert Gutman's *Work, Culture, and Society in Industrializing America* (Knopf, 1976) heralded a shift in emphasis aimed at capturing the totality of working-class experience. New areas of research utilized quantitative and social history approaches to examine ethnicity, family, technology, and tradition in relation to the labor experience. 32 notes.
                                                                      S

23. Brody, David. THE OLD LABOR HISTORY AND THE NEW: IN SEARCH OF AN AMERICAN WORKING CLASS. *Labor Hist.* 1979 20(1): 111-126. Reviews labor historiography, the stimuli for the "new" labor history, and current methodological and conceptual questions. A "useable framework for our particular labor history" is called for. Secondary sources; 22 notes.   L. L. Athey

24. Brody, David. PHILIP TAFT: LABOR SCHOLAR. *Labor Hist.* 1978 19(1): 9-22. Offers a tribute to the scholarly activities of Philip Taft (1902-76), whose death marks the end of the Wisconsin school of labor scholarship. An institutionalist and empiricist, Taft's work identified with the trade-union perspective and had a sure grasp of job-conscious trade unionism. Based on Taft's writings; 12 notes.
                                                            L. L. Athey

25. Brody, David. RADICAL LABOR HISTORY AND RANK-AND-FILE MILITANCY. *Labor Hist.* 1975 16(1): 117-126. A review article prompted by Alice and Staughton Lynd's *Rank and File: Personal Histories by Working Class Organizers* (Boston: Beacon Press, 1973). An example of current radical labor history, the work advances rank and file oral history but lacks critical analysis and rigorous method. 13 notes.   L. L. Athey

26. Browning, Harley L. and Singelmann, Joachim. THE TRANSFORMATION OF THE U.S. LABOR FORCE: THE INTERACTION OF INDUSTRY AND OCCUPATION. *Pol. and Soc.* 1978 8(3-4): 481-509. Proposes an alternative six-sector industrial-allocation scheme for the widely used Fisher-Clark three-sector (primary, secondary, and tertiary) model. The alternative model is subsequently used to examine distributive changes in the US labor force over the past century, and to speculate on possible trends in occupation distribution over the next three decades. Secondary sources; 4 tables, 28 notes.
                                                            D. G. Nielson

27. Brownlee, W. Elliot, Jr. HOUSEHOLD VALUES, WOMEN'S WORK, AND ECONOMIC GROWTH, 1800-1930. *J. of Econ. Hist.* 1979 39(1): 199-209. This essay explores the state of economic knowledge regarding the development of household economic life in the United States since early industrialization by examining explanations for the low labor-force participation of middle-class married women prevailing until the 1940's. These explanations, including those emerging from fertility studies and resting on market forces, imprecisely specify the domestic roles of housewives. Interdisciplinary specification of these roles, drawing on social and cultural historians, and rigorous measurement of time allocation within the household would help resolve the various interpretations and assist in estimating the contribution of household work to social product.   J

28. Buhle, Paul. ANARCHISM AND AMERICAN LABOR. *Int. Labor and Working Class Hist.* 1983 (23): 21-34. Reviews recent historiography of American anarchism of the 1880's-1920's, focusing on the ethnic foundations of anarchist movements and the co-option of anarchism by international Communism after the Russian Revolution of 1917.

29. Cantor, Milton. INTRODUCTION [TO AMERICAN WORKING-CLASS CULTURE]. Cantor, Milton, ed. *American Workingclass Culture: Explorations in American Labor and Social History* (Westport,

Conn.: Greenwood, 1979): 3-30. The need for studies of specific industries and communities on the effect of industrialization on the community and working-class culture has inspired this collection of essays which emphasize the interrelationship between economic forces and popular attitudes. Based on the premise that class identity is shaped as much by shared values and traditions as by one's economic relations to the means of production, traces the evolution of the American working-class culture since the onset of industrialization in the 1820's emphasizing some factors such as leisure time, relations between the sexes, religious institutions, immigration, and the family. Secondary sources; 88 notes.   S

30. Cassity, Michael J. SOUTHERN WORKERS AND SOCIAL CHANGE: CONCEPTS AND PROSPECTS. *Georgia Hist. Q. 1978 62(3): 200-212.* Histories of American labor have usually concentrated on the economic aspects and the labor unions. Suggests that many questions about the social implications of labor which have been asked by European labor historians should be applied to the American labor movement and particularly workers in the South. Secondary sources; 17 notes.   G. R. Schroeder

31. Castillo, Pedro; Krauze, Enrique, commentator. THE MAKING OF THE MEXICAN WORKING CLASS IN THE UNITED STATES: LOS ANGELES, CALIFORNIA: 1820-1920. Frost, Elsa Cecilia; Meyer, Michael C.; and Zoraida Vázquez, Josefina, ed. *El Trabajo y los Trabajadores en la Historia de México* (Mexico City: Colegio de México, 1979): 506-517. From the end of the Mexican War in 1848 to 1880 there was a gradual transition in Los Angeles from a rural to an urban way of life, in which the Mexican Americans sank to the bottom of the social structure: during the quickening of industrial development down to 1920, they remained there as the poorest of the laboring communities, to be Americanized or eradicated according to one's point of view. Their numbers increased after 1920: but apart from living in their own quarters, they showed little coherence as a group, or much interest in labor politics. Commentary on pp. 529-532. Secondary sources; table, 33 notes.   J. P. H. Myers

32. Chudacoff, Howard P. INTEGRATING WORKING CLASS HISTORY. *Rev. in Am. Hist. 1979 7(4): 535-541.* Review essay of Susan E. Hirsch's *Roots of the American Working Class: The Industrialization of Crafts in Newark, 1800-1860* (Philadelphia: U. of Pennsylvania Pr., 1978), and Daniel J. Walkowitz's *Worker City, Company Town: Iron and Cotton-Worker Protest in Troy and Cohoes, New York, 1855-84* (Urbana: U. of Illinois Pr., 1978).

33. Ciporen, Marvin. LABOR'S USE OF HISTORY. *Public Hist. 1980 2(2): 66-69.* Discusses the importance of knowledge of labor history for labor leaders and the rank and file in building up unions.

34. Clecak, Peter. NOTES ON WORK. *Antioch Rev. 1978 36(4): 397-421.* The author examines his personal experience as a third-generation immigrant seeking assimilation as an academic within the context of the changing character of and assumptions about work in 19th- and 20th-century America.

35. Clifford, Geraldine Joncich. "DAUGHTERS INTO TEACHERS": EDUCATIONAL AND DEMOGRAPHIC INFLUENCES ON THE TRANSFORMATION OF TEACHING INTO "WOMEN'S WORK" IN AMERICA. *Hist. of Educ. Rev. [Australia] 1983 12(1): 15-28.* Two factors may have been important in drawing large numbers of women into teaching: the salaries women would accept and their predilection for the work.

36. Cole, Paul. REVITALIZING THE STUDY OF LABOR. *Social Educ. 1982 46(2): 102-104.* Discusses material appropriate for a high school course on labor, considering whether it is an elective course or a component of another course.

37. Conk, Margo. ACCURACY, EFFICIENCY AND BIAS: THE INTERPRETATION OF WOMEN'S WORK IN THE US CENSUS OF OCCUPATIONS, 1890-1940. *Hist. Methods 1981 14(2): 65-72.* In correcting data sets, the building in of biases might happen. The Census Office in 1890 introduced machine tabulation procedures for counting the census. The physical size of the punch card (much smaller than today's model) meant that specification fields were neither numerical

nor regular. The use of existing ideals of sexual differentiation of the labor on verification procedures compounded the problem. The New Dealer's demand for data on the dislocations of the Great Depression put great pressure on the Census Bureau which was not up to this task. Bureaucratic pride and status continued the bias during World War II. Statisticians are human and in moments of scholarly uncertainty they used preconceived notions. 2 tables, 22 notes.   D. K. Pickens

38. Conk, Margo. IMMIGRANT WORKERS IN THE CITY, 1870-1930: AGENTS OF GROWTH OR THREATS TO DEMOCRACY? *Social Sci. Q. 1981 62(4): 704-720.* Uses US Census data on occupations to analyze the role that immigrant workers played in the labor force of large northeastern cities; assesses the assimilation process for these immigrants.

39. Conk, Margo. OCCUPATIONAL CLASSIFICATION IN THE UNITED STATES CENSUS: 1870-1940. *J. of Interdisciplinary Hist. 1978 9(1): 111-130.* Review of the history of occupational classification in the US census statistics. The limitations imposed on the form and quality of these occupational statistics are explicable in terms of general events in the career of the Census Bureau. The Bureau's efforts to describe and classify the manufacturing population show a fundamental confusion beginning in 1910 in how the information was used. This confusion derives from the Bureau's treatment of occupational statistics as both social and economic indicators. Printed sources; 41 notes.   R. Howell

40. Conley, John A. PRISONS, PRODUCTION, AND PROFIT: RECONSIDERING THE IMPORTANCE OF PRISON INDUSTRIES. *J. of Social Hist. 1980 14(2): 257-275.* Analysis of Oklahoma prisons suggests that historians of 19th- and early 20th-century prison development have ignored the role of prison industries run for profit. The usual emphasis on a struggle over punishment or reform, or between the solitary or congregate system of prison industries as modes of rehabilitation gives inadequate attention to the centrality of prison industries. Information on adjoining states and on the New York prison system buttresses the argument. 48 notes.   C. M. Hough

41. Corn, Jacqueline Karnell. "DARK AS A DUNGEON": ENVIRONMENT AND COAL MINERS' HEALTH AND SAFETY IN NINETEENTH CENTURY AMERICA. *Environmental Rev. 1983 7(3): 257-268.* Ignorance and out-of-sight, out-of-mind attitudes were instrumental in the continuance of unhealthful and hazardous 19th-century mine conditions, which were not addressed legally until 1870.

42. Cornelius, Wayne A. LA MIGRACIÓN ILEGAL MEXICANA A LOS ESTADOS UNIDOS: CONCLUSIONES DE INVESTIGACIONES RECIENTES, IMPLICACIONES POLÍTICAS Y PRIORIDADES DE INVESTIGACIÓN [Illegal Mexican immigration to the United States: conclusions of recent research, political implications, and research priorities]. *Foro Int. [Mexico] 1978 18(3): 399-429.* Examines illegal Mexican aliens in the United States, their impact on both countries, and research needed to obtain data for dealing with the problem. Concludes that little can be done until conditions in Mexico make emigration for employment unattractive. Covers 1930-70's. Based on interviews and secondary sources; notes, biblio.   D. A. Franz

43. Cumbler, John T. THE CITY AND COMMUNITY: THE IMPACT OF URBAN FORCES ON WORKING CLASS BEHAVIOR. *J. of Urban Hist. 1977 3(4): 427-442.* Compares the impact of industrialization on the working class in shoemaking Lynn and textile spinning Fall River, Massachusetts (1850-1930). In Lynn the shoe industry and the working class clustered together, while in Fall River centrifugal forces waxed. This arrangement led to significant differences in the formation of working-class institutions and behavior. Greater centralization of institutions created greater solidarity among the workers. Based on oral histories; 42 notes.   T. W. Smith

44. Cybriwsky, Roman A. and Hardy, Charles, III. THE STETSON COMPANY AND BENEVOLENT FEUDALISM. *Pennsylvania Heritage 1981 7(2): 14-19.* Discusses the hat-making John B. Stetson Company of Philadelphia from its founding in 1865 to 1976, with special attention to the boom years of 1870 through 1929, when the firm functioned under a labor-management system in many ways reminiscent

of European feudalism, and which provided health care, education, recreation, banking and other employee benefits.

45. Dawley, Alan. AMERICAN WORKERS/WORKERS AMERICA: A REVIEW OF RECENT WORKS BY DAVID BRODY AND JAMES GREEN. *Int. Labor and Working Class Hist. 1983 (23): 35-44.* Reviews David Brody's *Workers in Industrial America: Essays on the Twentieth Century Struggle* (1980) and James Green's *The World of the Worker: Labor in Twentieth-Century America* (1980), which reveal that the history of the working class is essential to understanding the major directions of 20th-century American development.

46. Dawley, Alan and Faler, Paul. WORKINGCLASS CULTURE AND POLITICS IN THE INDUSTRIAL REVOLUTION: SOURCES OF LOYALISM AND REBELLION. Cantor, Milton, ed. *American Workingclass Culture: Explorations in American Labor and Social History* (Westport, Conn.: Greenwood, 1979): 61-76. Reprint of an article published in the *Journal of Social History* .

47. Dawson, Andrew. THE PARADOX OF DYNAMIC TECHNOLOGICAL CHANGE AND THE LABOR ARISTOCRACY IN THE UNITED STATES, 1880-1914. *Labor Hist. 1979 20(3): 325-351.* Paradoxically, in a period of rapid mechanization in the United States, a labor aristocracy was maintained who held an ideology distinct from either the middle or the lower class. Although some skilled workers declined in wages and social status, the labor aristocracy held relatively constant, 1880-1914. Based on the census and US government documents; 4 tables, 24 notes. L. L. Athey

48. Dawson, Andy. HISTORY AND IDEOLOGY: FIFTY YEARS OF "JOB CONSCIOUSNESS." *Literature and Hist. [Great Britain] 1978 (8): 223-241.* Examines the influence of Selig Perlman's *Theory of the Labor Movement* (New York: 1928) on the teaching of labor history in the United States since the late 1930's. Perlman contended that the working class was uniquely job conscious as opposed to class conscious, which in the American context accounted for the absence of working-class radicalism and a labor party. Perlman's exponents worked at the University of Wisconsin on the economic, psychological, and institutional determinants of the labor union movement. From 1945, his writings influenced national attitudes about the social role and responsibilities of labor. Based on secondary sources; 46 notes. M. Smith

49. Debouzy, Marianne. LA CLASSE OUVRIÈRE AMÉRICAINE: RECHERCHES ET PROBLÈMES [The American working class: Research and problems]. *Mouvement Social [France] 1978 (102): 3-8.* The American working class has always struck European observers, particularly leftists, as distinguished chiefly by negatives: lack of cohesion, lack of class consciousness, lack of revolutionary ideology, and absence of a workers' party. But it exists, nonetheless, and its discontent seems to be growing. The history of the working class in the United States defies schematization; its historians must create new theories to explain its course. 4 notes. J. C. Billingmeier

50. Demeter, John. INDEPENDENT FILM & WORKING CLASS HISTORY: A REVIEW OF "NORTHERN LIGHTS" AND "THE WOBBLIES." *Radical Am. 1980 14(1): 16-26.* This review of the two latest additions to the growing number of independent, leftist, labor history films, *Northern Lights* (1978) and *The Wobblies* (1979), gives an opportunity to give consideration also to the problems and potential for a continued relationship of the American Left and independent cinema. Both are essentially documentaries of early 20th-century left-wing working-class history and help in eradicating this blind spot in radical worker history and preserving some of the material our persistent amnesia in that area could otherwise have eliminated from the record. Primary sources, especially oral history; 8 photos, 11 notes. R. V. Ritter

51. Dersch, Virginia Jonas. COPPER MINING IN NORTHERN MICHIGAN: A SOCIAL HISTORY. *Michigan Hist. 1977 61(4): 290-321.* The automobile industry image associated with Michigan has obscured the fact that the first US mining boom occurred in the remote Keweenaw Peninsula during the early 1840's. Primitive conditions, lack of experience, the region's remoteness, and transportation problems spelled failure for virtually every entrepreneur until 1866. In that year, the Calumet and Hecla Mining Company pioneered a new approach to

locating and mining copper, and the social and economic development of the area accelerated markedly. Soon the company possessed monopoly control, and despite efforts by organized labor, prevented unionization until 1943. But a 1913 miners' strike dealt the industry a blow from which it never recovered. Secondary sources; 16 photos, table, glossary, 53 notes. D. W. Johnson

52. Dinwiddie, Robert C. and Hough, Leslie S. THE SOUTHERN LABOR ARCHIVES. *Labor Hist. 1982 23(4): 502-512.* Chronicles the creation and collecting history of the Southern Labor Archives at Georgia State University in Atlanta. The archives collects the records of all labor organizations in the southeastern United States at the international, state, and local levels. The collections, for which detailed descriptions are provided, include the records of the United Textile Workers of America, District Four of the International Woodworkers of America, Stanton E. Smith, Atlanta Typographical Union Number 48, and the Atlanta lodge of the International Association of Machinists. L. F. Velicer

53. Dixon, Marlene; Martinez, Elizabeth; and McCaughan, Ed. CHICANAS AND MEXICANAS WITHIN A TRANSNATIONAL WORKING CLASS: THEORETICAL PERSPECTIVES. *Rev. (Fernand Braudel Center) 1983 7(1): 109-150.* Looks first at the various processes of colonization and recolonization that have led to the Chicano/Mexicano population as a transnational and exploited sector of the working class. Imperialism's integration of Mexico and the Southwest was a brutal, degrading process, particularly for women and the family. In this context, machismo is not strictly a cultural phenomenon but rather primarily a form of male supremacist ideology serving capital accumulation. Ref. L. V. Eid

54. Donno, Antonio. LABOR HISTORY: DALLA STORIA DEL SINDACATO ALLA STORIA OPERAIA [Labor history: from the history of labor unions to the history of labor]. *Nuova Riv. Storica [Italy] 1982 66(3-4): 319-341.* Since the mid 1960's British and American social historians have brought new perspectives and methods to the study of working class history. In contrast to earlier schools, especially the Wisconsin school which denied the existence of a working class in America due to ethnic heterogeneity and constant immigration, and concentrated on the history of labor unions, the new historians focus on the contribution each ethnic group made to the labor movement and class consciousness. Inspired by Marxist concepts they argue that labor history is the history of a social movement and not merely of the struggles of market unionism. 82 notes. J. V. Coutinho

55. Dubofsky, Melvyn. ADAM'S CURSE: OR THE DRUDGERY OF WORK. *Rev. in Am. Hist. 1978 6(4): 429-434.* Review article prompted by James B. Gilbert's *Work without Salvation: America's Intellectuals and Industrial Alienation, 1880-1910* (Baltimore, Md.: Johns Hopkins U. Pr., 1977) and Daniel T. Rodgers's *The Work Ethic in Industrial America, 1850-1920* (Chicago: U. of Chicago Pr., 1974).

56. Dubofsky, Melvyn. HOLD THE FORT: THE DYNAMICS OF TWENTIETH-CENTURY AMERICAN WORKING CLASS HISTORY. *Rev. in Am. Hist. 1981 9(2): 244-251.* Review essay of David Brody's *Workers in Industrial America: Essays on the Twentieth Century Struggle* (1980) and David Montgomery's *Workers' Control in America: Studies in the History of Work, Technology, and Labor Struggles* (1979).

57. Dubofsky, Melvyn. NEITHER UPSTAIRS, NOR DOWNSTAIRS: DOMESTIC SERVICE IN MIDDLE-CLASS AMERICAN HOMES. *Rev. in Am. Hist. 1980 8(1): 86-91.* Review essay of Robert Hamburger and Susan Fowler-Gallagher's *A Stranger in the House* (New York: Macmillan, 1978), and David M. Katzman's *Seven Days a Week: Women and Domestic Service in Industrializing America* (New York: Oxford U. Pr., 1978); 1870-1920.

58. Dubofsky, Melvyn. THE "NEW" LABOR HISTORY: ACHIEVEMENTS AND FAILURES. *Rev. in Am. Hist. 1977 5(2): 249-254.* Review article prompted by Herbert G. Gutman's *Work, Culture, and Society in Industrializing America: Essays in American Working-Class and Social History* (New York: Alfred A. Knopf, 1976).

59. East, Dennis. LABOR HISTORY RESOURCES IN THE OHIO HISTORICAL SOCIETY. *Labor Hist. 1982 23(4): 513-515.* Describes the work of the Ohio Labor History Project of 1975-79 and surveys the labor-related records, personal papers, microfilmed collections, oral histories, and microfilmed newspapers and publications available at the Ohio Historical Society in Columbus, Ohio. L. F. Velicer

60. Edson, C. H. SOCIOCULTURAL PERSPECTIVES ON WORK AND SCHOOLING IN URBAN AMERICA. *Urban Rev. 1979 11(3): 127-148.* Concentrates on attitudes during 1880-1920. By not appreciating how the varied social and cultural backgrounds of American workers contributed to their behavior on the job, "managers and industrialists often misunderstood the complexity of the problems they faced and increased the tension between the worker and the factory." School administrators also faced problems, mainly of organization and personnel, and attempted to have their educational organizations follow the administrative leads of industrial empires. "Thus, problems faced by industry were doubly problems facing the public schools: urban schools needed to prepare children for industrial society, and schools themselves needed to run as efficiently as industrial enterprises. Thus, it largely fell to the urban educational reformers of the early twentieth century to translate industrial problems into specific educational strategies." R. J. Wechman

61. Elder, Peyton K. and Miller, Heidi D. THE FAIR LABOR STANDARDS ACT: CHANGES OF FOUR DECADES. *Monthly Labor Rev. 1979 102(7): 10-16.* Discusses the changes in the Fair Labor Standards Act (US, 1938) when Franklin Roosevelt signed it into law, and offers some insights as to the future of the Act.

62. Ericksen, Eugene P. and Yancey, William L. WORK AND RESIDENCE IN INDUSTRIAL PHILADELPHIA. *J. of Urban Hist. 1978 5(2): 147-182.* The Burgess zonal model of spatial organization for cities does not represent the general pattern of modern cities but rather characterizes cities during only a brief and bygone era of urban development. The major force ordering the residential pattern of cities is the location of work places. The Central Business District (CBD) is seen as nothing more than "a particularly large workplace concentration." With the subsequent decline of the CBD as a primary work place the zonal model has increasingly become an inadequate description of urban spatial organization. 8 tables, 4 fig., 46 notes. T. W. Smith

63. Fee, Terry. DOMESTIC LABOR: AN ANALYSIS OF HOUSEWORK AND ITS RELATION TO THE PRODUCTION PROCESS. *Rev. of Radical Pol. Econ. 1976 8(1): 1-8.* Housework (1930's-70's) does not fit into common categories in labor analysis, but is integral in the smooth flow of labor production, and is cheap labor and a socializing agent.

64. Feichtmeir, Karl. DEFENDING THE BILL OF RIGHTS: THE ACLU ARCHIVES AT CHS. *California History 1979-80 58(4): 362-364.* Reports on the opening of the first record group of the American Civil Liberties Union (ACLU) of northern California in the California Historical Society Archives. Established on a permanent basis in 1934, the northern California ACLU was involved in many issues of civil rights and liberties, including the general strike of 1934, IWW activities, McCarthyism, and other controversies. Longtime director Ernest Besig collected a wide variety of miscellaneous literature, including 40 volumes of indexed newspaper articles. More than 90% of the ACLU collection still awaits cataloging and processing. 2 photos, 6 notes. A. Hoffman

65. Feller, Irwin. THE DIFFUSION AND LOCATION OF TECHNOLOGICAL CHANGE IN THE AMERICAN COTTON-TEXTILE INDUSTRY, 1890-1970. *Technology and Culture 1974 15(4): 569-593.* New England cotton-textile manufacturers lost the competitive struggle with new plants opening in the South, not because they failed to invest in innovations like the Draper automatic loom, but because of labor costs and other disadvantages. By contrast, the textile-machine industry remained in the North until the 1950's, when enough skilled labor became available in the South. Based on secondary sources; 56 notes. C. O. Smith

66. Fellman, Anita Clair. HAPLESS HOUSEWIVES IN HAVENLESS HOMES. *Can. Rev. of Am. Studies [Canada] 1983 14(3): 297-308.* Reviews *Homemakers: The Forgotten Workers* (1981), by Rae Andre, *The Grand Domestic Revolution: A History of Feminist Designs for American Homes, Neighborhoods, and Cities* (1981), by Delores Hayden, and *Building a Dream: A Social History of Housing in America* (1981), by Gwendolyn Wright. Unlike traditional histories, these volumes picture their subject as primarily expressions of the American political order. H. T. Lovin

67. Fennell, Dodee. BENEATH THE SURFACE: THE LIFE OF A FACTORY. *Radical Am. 1976 10(5): 21-41.* The small-town location of a manufacturer of electrical connectors was reflected in its early years when it was a liberal place to work, with flexible hours designed to meet the needs of part-time employees earning pay inferior to other plants in the industry. Successive changes in ownership resulted in its present position as part of a large-scale conglomerate. A company-dominated union worsened labor relations, resulting in the creation of an informal social network presenting opposition to the dictates of company and union alike. Based on 14 months of participant-observation by the author. N. Lederer

68. Filippelli, Ronald L. and Hoffman, Alice. LABOR SOURCES AT PENN STATE UNIVERSITY. *Labor Hist. 1982 23(4): 516-519.* Key labor collections in the Pennsylvania Historical Collections and Labor Archives of the Pennsylvania State University in University Park, Pennsylvania, include the records of the United Steelworkers of America, personal papers of steelworker officials, printing trades records, the papers of Darlington Hoopes (a long-time activist in the Socialist Party of Reading, Pennsylvania), and a large oral history collection. L. F. Velicer

69. Fink, Gary M. THE FOURTH SOUTHERN LABOR CONFERENCE. *Int. Labor and Working Class Hist. 1983 (23): 62-64.* Discusses recent trends in Southern labor relations historiography as revealed at the 1982 "Southern Labor Studies" conference in Atlanta, Georgia; institutional and social history covering the late 19th-20th centuries have achieved a recent synthesis and reconciliation.

70. Finkel, Alvin. THE "WORK ETHIC" AND CONTROL OF THE WORKFORCE. *Can. Rev. of Am. Studies [Canada] 1980 11(3): 371-379.* Reviews Bruno Ramirez's *When Workers Fight: The Politics of Industrial Relations in the Progressive Era, 1898-1916* (Westport, Conn.: Greenwood Pr., 1978) and Daniel T. Rodgers's *The Work Ethic in Industrial America, 1850-1920* (Chicago: U. of Chicago Pr., 1978). The books examine the partial displacement of Americans' traditional work ethic beliefs by consumerism and idealization of big corporations for their economic efficiency during the post-Civil War industrial revolution. 2 notes. H. T. Lovin

71. Fones-Wolf, Kenneth. SOURCES FOR THE STUDY OF LABOR HISTORY IN THE URBAN ARCHIVES, TEMPLE UNIVERSITY. *Labor Hist. 1982 23(4): 520-525.* Describes the labor resources of the Urban Archives at Temple University in Philadelphia, Pennsylvania. Some of the more important collections are the records of the Upholsterers' International Union, the Federation of Telephone Workers of Pennsylvania, the Amalgamated Clothing Workers of America Philadelphia Joint Board, the Philadelphia Teachers' Union, and the Metal Manufacturers' Association of Philadelphia. L. F. Velicer

72. Form, William. SOCIOLOGICAL RESEARCH AND THE AMERICAN WORKING CLASS. *Sociol. Q. 1983 24(2): 163-184.* The American working class was seldom the subject of sociological study before the 1930's; research since then has yielded many conclusive insights.

73. Gamble, Robert A. and Green, George. LABOR ARCHIVES AT THE UNIVERSITY OF TEXAS AT ARLINGTON. *Labor Hist. 1982 23(4): 526-527.* Provides a brief introduction to the Texas Labor Archives at the University of Texas at Arlington and lists the major collections or groups of collections held by the archives.

L. F. Velicer

74. Garraty, John A. TO BE JOBLESS IN AMERICA. *Am. Heritage 1978 30(1): 64-69.* Discusses attitudes toward unemployment shown by those involved and by government. Keynesian theories led to a change in feelings whereby the unemployed no longer felt responsible for his own

situation. This subtle attitudinal change is at the root of many of the problems of the working force in the 1970's. Covers 18th century-present.   J. F. Paul

75. Gersuny, Carl. NEW ENGLAND MILL CASUALTIES: 1890-1910. *New England Q. 1979 52(4): 467-482.* Factory owners and insurance companies did everything possible to limit what they had to pay to injured workmen. When possible, they invoked the common law principles of contributory negligence, assumption of risk, and the fellow-servant rule to deny obligation. Delaying tactics were employed until victims settled for minimal amounts, and the judicial process was undermined by influencing judicial appointments and conspiring with attorneys behind their clients' backs. Based on Dwight Manufacturing Company, Lyman Mills, and Hamilton Manufacturing Company papers in Baker Library, Harvard; 45 notes.   J. C. Bradford

76. Gillespie, Angus K. FOLKLORE AND LABOR: AN INTELLECTUAL CONTEXT FOR THE WORK OF GEORGE KORSON. *Keystone Folklore 1979 23(3): 11-27.* Discusses the work of folklorist George Korson among Pennsylvania miners during the 1920's-60's in the context of the developing discipline of folk studies.

77. Goldman, Robert and Wilson, John. THE RATIONALIZATION OF LEISURE. *Pol. and Soc. 1977 7(2): 157-187.* The organization of workers' leisure time was as much a part of the rationalization of industries, of Taylorism and scientific management, as the organization of the work place. Organized recreation programs found their justification in their contribution to the general social welfare and sometimes came to resemble a moral crusade. Little attempt was made during the growth of welfare capitalism (1890-1920's), however, to conceal that the goal of these programs was to enhance production and efficiency, stabilize the class structure, and maintain the legitimacy of control. Primary and secondary sources; 97 notes.   D. G. Nielson

78. Gómez-Quiñones, Juan; Krause, Enrique, commentator. THE ORIGINS AND DEVELOPMENT OF THE MEXICAN WORKING CLASS IN THE UNITED STATES: LABORERS AND ARTISANS NORTH OF THE RÍO BRAVO, 1600-1900. Frost, Elsa Cecilia; Meyer, Michael C.; and Zoraida Vázquez, Josefina, ed. *El Trabajo y los Trabajadores en la Historia de México* (Mexico City: Colegio de México, 1979): 463-505. Traces the development of the Mexican Far North, the American Southwest, from 1600 to 1900, across the divide produced by the Texas revolution, 1836, and the Mexican War, 1846-48. Far Northern enterprises in mining, textiles, and commercial agriculture provide early examples of capitalist development, drawing on Mexico's own resources and population. The 1848 peace cost Mexico half of its territory, three-quarters of its national resources, and over 100,000 people. But the trek north continued, though industrial development was now large-scale and financed from overseas; and, whatever their origins, Mexican Americans were relegated to the lower stratum of society, forced to defend their culture against a new racism. Commentary on pp. 529-532. Secondary sources; 6 notes.   J. P. H. Myers

79. Grandjean, Burke D. THE DIVISION OF LABOR, TECHNOLOGY, AND EDUCATION: CROSS-NATIONAL EVIDENCE. *Social Sci. Q. 1974 55(2): 297-309.* "... offers data on 29 countries to test the hypothesis of Durkheim, Marx, and Adam Smith that the division of labor and technological development lead to expanded education ... Finds that age-specific school attendance rates correlate positively with a measure of labor-force dispersion among industries, and with energy consumption. Further analysis suggests that the effect of technology on primary and secondary education is mediated by the division of labor, and that advanced education is associated only weakly or not at all with technology and the division of labor when the effects of lower educational levels are controlled."   J

80. Green, Archie. INDUSTRIAL LORE: A BIBLIOGRAPHIC-SEMANTIC QUERY. *Western Folklore 1978 37(3): 213-244.* Surveys the development and history of occupational and industrial folklore, and discusses basic sources for the study of occupational culture. Primary and secondary sources.   S. L. Myres

81. Green, James R. L'HISTOIRE DU MOUVEMENT OUVRIER ET LA GAUCHE AMÉRICAINE [Labor history and the American left]. *Mouvement Social [France] 1978 (102): 9-40.* Originally Ameri-

can labor history was shaped by the "progressive" economists of the Wisconsin school. It was limited mainly to the development of the trade union as an institution and its place in a changing labor market. Though they questioned the Wisconsin School's defense of business unionism, Old Left historians writing from the 1930's on through the 1950's did not really challenge Commons' conceptual approach. The narrow "economic" approach to labor history adopted by the Commons school and the orthodox Marxist school failed to deal with the larger questions that would be posed about culture and society by the historians who studied the working class itself rather than simply its organizations. The 1960's witnessed the emergence of new kinds of labor history which offer new points of departure for Marxist students of the working class. Some labor historians following the lead of C. Wright Mills took a more critical approach to labor unions; others, influenced by E. P. Thompson and other European social historians, shifted from an institutional approach to a more cultural one. Finally, historians focused more on the creativity involved in union organizing and in labor struggles as the process of workers making their own history.   J

82. Green, Jim. CULTURE, POLITICS AND WORKERS' RESPONSE TO INDUSTRIALIZATION IN THE US. *Radical Am. 1982 16(1-2): 101-128.* Reviews four works on particular communities and three on distinct ideas or subjects that continue the themes already established by Herbert Gutman, David Montgomery, and E. P. Thompson. The overriding question followed here is whether or not the "populist" interpretation of the new generation of social historians showing a left-wing approach based on sharp breaks with the past has been discredited. Examines studies by Faler and Dawley on Lynn, Laurie on Philadelphia, Dublin on Lowell, Cott on New England women workers, Foner on Tom Paine, and Ridgers on the work ethic. Other works are discussed as well. 37 notes, 9 illus.   C. M. Hough

83. Green, Jim. WORKER EDUCATION AND LABOUR HISTORY IN AMERICA. *Hist. Workshop J. [Great Britain] 1982 (14): 168-170.* Some recent changes in the AFL-CIO and some individual unions are helping to legitimize socialist activity within American trade unions and opening up possibilities for collaboration between workers and historians involved in worker education in producing working-class history. Excellent educational material is now available, and meetings and workshops have been successful and are leading to publications. The elimination or drastic reduction of federal funding possibilities will require historians to gain much more direct support from working people and their organizations and may make radical efforts at producing and presenting people's history less ambitious, but the collaboration will continue.   D. J. Nicholls

84. Greenberg, Edward S. THE CONSEQUENCES OF WORKER PARTICIPATION: A CLARIFICATION OF THE THEORETICAL LITERATURE. *Social Sci. Q. 1975 56(2): 191-209.* Contributions from management, humanistic psychology, democratic theory, and the participatory left are summarized and synthesized. Clarifies the theoretical issues involved in decisional participation at the workplace.   J

85. Hartland-Thonberg, Penelope. PHILIP TAFT, THE TEACHER. *Labor Hist. 1978 19(1): 24-30.* Offers a tribute to labor historian Philip Taft, (1902-76), the teacher of economic history, based on views of former students at Brown University. 2 notes.   L. L. Athey

86. Havira, Barbara. AT WORK IN BELDING: MICHIGAN'S SILK MILL CITY. *Michigan Hist. 1981 65(3): 33-41.* Examines the development of Belding, Michigan, as a silk factory town from 1885 to 1932. Belding attracted women laborers from all over the Midwest because of the type of work required and relatively high wages. 12 illus., 28 notes.   L. E. Ziewacz

87. Havira, Barbara S. MANAGING INDUSTRIAL AND SOCIAL TENSIONS IN A RURAL SETTING: WOMEN SILK WORKERS IN BELDING, MICHIGAN, 1885-1932. *Michigan Acad. 1981 13(3): 257-273.* Investigates the character of industrial labor in a rural setting, focusing on the undramatic experiences of women who worked at the silk thread and fabric mills in Belding, Michigan, between 1885-1932.

88. Henry, James. HOW PENSION FUND SOCIALISM DIDN'T COME TO AMERICA. *Working Papers for a New Soc. 1977 4(4): 78-87.* Review article prompted by Peter F. Drucker's *The Unseen*

Revolution: How Pension Fund Socialism Came to America (New York: Harper and Row, 1976).

89. Herbst, Jurgen. WHITE COLLAR, BLUE COLLAR, AND NO COLLAR: COMPARISON, ANYONE? *Rev. in Am. Hist. 1978 6(4): 562-569.* Review article prompted by Jurgen Kocka's *Angestellte zwischen Faschismus und Demokratie. Zur politischen Sozialgeschichte der Angestellten: USA 1890-1940 im internationalen Vergleich* [White Collar Salaried Employees under Fascism and Democracy. The political Social History of White Collar Employees: USA 1890-1940 in international perspective] (Gottingen: Vandenhoeck & Ruprecht, 1977) and Hans-Jurgen Puhle's *Politische Agrarbewegungen in kapitalistischen Industriegesellschaften: Deutschland, USA und Frankreich im 20. Jahrhundert* [Political Agrarian Movements in Capitalist Industrial Societies: Germany, the United States and France in the 20th Century] (Gottingen: Vandenhoek & Ruprecht, 1975).

90. Hobsbawm, E. J. LABOR HISTORY AND IDEOLOGY. *J. of Social Hist. 1974 7(4): 371-381.* Studies the changes which have taken place in the historiography of labor and labor ideologies There has been a growing academicism and "radicalization has produced a substantial crop of new labor historians." There needs to be a fresh realization that labor history is concerned with changing as well as with interpreting the world, but also to know what is meant by changing people. "For many of us the final object of our work is to create a world in which working people can make their own life and their own history, rather than to have it made for them by others, including academics." 8 notes.
R. V. Ritter

91. Hogan, David. EDUCATION AND THE MAKING OF THE CHICAGO WORKING CLASS, 1880-1930. *Hist. of Educ. Q. 1978 18(3): 227-270.* Examines why children enrolled in Chicago schools between 1880 and 1930 stayed in school for a longer time, particularly those over the age of 14, regardless of ethnic background.

92. Hogeboom, Willard L. LABOR STUDIES IN THE AMERICAN HISTORY CURRICULUM. *Social Studies 1975 66(3): 118-120.* Stresses the need for labor studies in the history curriculum since man is essentially an economic being. The larger number of his activities center on earning a living. 4 notes.
L. R. Raife

93. Howell, David. DOCILE DIGGERS AND RUSSIAN REDS: CONTRASTS IN WORKING-CLASS POLITICS. *Pol. Studies [Great Britain] 1981 29(3): 455-463.* Reviews John Gaventa's *Power and Powerlessness: Quiescence and Rebellion in an Appalachian Valley* (1980), and Stuart Macintyre's *Little Moscows: Communism and Working Class Militancy in Inter-War Britain* (1980), both valuable contributions to the study of the diversities of working-class politics in the late 19th and early 20th centuries. Generalizations are almost impossible to make, but radical politics are facilitated by critical standards inherited from an industrial past, demographic mobility, the possibility of active trade unionism, and the existence of political "space" to exploit potential radicalism within the preexisting culture. 13 notes.
D. J. Nicholls

94. Imhoff, Kathleen and Brandwein, Larry. LABOR COLLECTIONS AND SERVICES IN PUBLIC LIBRARIES THROUGHOUT THE UNITED STATES, 1976. *RQ 1977 17(2): 149-158.* "Public libraries in communities of more than 10,000 and having a central labor council were surveyed in the spring of 1976 by the Joint Committee on Library Services to Labor Groups (American Federation of Labor/Congress of Industrial Organizations-ALA [Reference and Adult Services Division]) to ascertain the status of existing labor collections and services . . ." Reports a decline since 1967 in the number of special labor collections, a mistrust of unions by librarians, and a reported lack of assistance from unions. 3 tables, 4 notes, 2 appendixes.
S

95. Isserman, Maurice. "GOD BLESS OUR AMERICAN INSTITUTIONS:" THE LABOR HISTORY OF JOHN R. COMMONS. *Labor Hist. 1976 17(3): 309-328.* John R. Commons possessed a rebellious social vision which was profoundly conservative. His central desire was to preserve the capitalist system by granting organized labor its rights as a cooperative group within the system. The central themes of Commons' works reveal historical influences leading him to develop a theory of labor history which emphasized a conservative institutionalism embrac-

ing change led by experts. His belief that workers would sacrifice long-term goals for "bread and butter" gains has not yet proved mistaken in the United States. Based on Commons' published works; 39 notes.
L. L. Athey

96. Javersak, David T. LABOR DAY IN WHEELING. *Upper Ohio Valley Hist. Rev. 1979 9(1): 31-35.* Traces the history of Labor Day celebrations in the United States since the first was held in New York City in 1882, particularly the celebration of the holiday in Wheeling, Ohio, beginning in 1886.

97. Jeffreys-Jones, Rhodri. THEORIES OF AMERICAN LABOUR VIOLENCE. *J. of Am. Studies [Great Britain] 1979 13(2): 245-264.* Historians disagree when attempting to explain those outbreaks of labor violence plaguing America during the Gilded Age and early 20th century. Some emphasized environmental forces; others stressed the impacts of race and heredity. A third group focused on clashing cultural elements, while another attributed the violence to "biological-instinctual imperatives." A fifth group claimed that ideology had insured such turmoil. 49 notes.
H. T. Lovin

98. Kortum, Karl. HARRY LUNDEBERG HAS BEEN HEARD FROM: THE PART PLAYED BY A SEAFARING LABOR LEADER IN THE RESCUE OF CERTAIN SHIPS, LEADING TO THE ESTABLISHMENT OF THE HISTORIC FLEET AT SAN FRANCISCO. *Sea Hist. 1980 (18): 36-38.* Presents a few of the situations in which Harry Lundeberg (1901-57), sailor and militant union organizer, intervened to save and preserve old vessels, now part of the historic fleet in the San Francisco Maritime Museum.

99. Kramnick, Isaac. EQUAL OPPORTUNITY AND "THE RACE OF LIFE." *Dissent 1981 28(2): 178-187.* Discusses the notion of equal opportunity with respect to the social and economic sectors of bourgeois liberal nations in the writings of French dramatist Pierre Augustin Caron de Beaumarchais, Thomas Mann, Thomas Hobbes, and other European as well as American authors since the 17th century, from the perspective of the debate in the United States over affirmative action in 1981.

100. Kravchenko, A. I. SOTSIALNYE FAKTORY ORGANIZATSII TRUDA V SISTEME TEILORA [Social factors of labor management in the Taylor system]. *Sotsiologicheskie Issledovaniia [USSR] 1981 (3): 182-189.* Frederick W. Taylor's social philosophy laid the foundations for US labor management, which had been adopted in many other countries.

101. Kriuchkova, O. V. DISSERTATSII PO ISTORII SSHA, ZASHCHISHCHENNYE V SSSR V 1971-1979 GG. [Dissertations on US history defended in the USSR, 1971-79]. *Amerikanskii Ezhegodnik [USSR] 1980: 338-348.* Lists 32 dissertations and 217 theses on American foreign and domestic affairs since colonial times and recent developments in the civil rights and labor movements, trade unions, party politics, etc.
N. Frenkley

102. Laurie, Bruce; Hershberg, Theodore; and Alter, George. IMMIGRANTS AND INDUSTRY: THE PHILADELPHIA EXPERIENCE, 1850-1880. *J. of Social Hist. 1975 9(2): 219-248.* Attempts to provide more secure categories of occupational status for 19th-century activities beyond the ahistorical reach of sociological studies in this century. Examines 14 manufacturing industries in Philadelphia, 1850-80, and attempts to explain changes in the job status, and how the changes affected the distribution to different ethnic groups. Little change is seen in the ethnic distribution because of disadvantages different groups brought with them, and because industrialization did not necessarily equal mechanization. 11 tables, 5 figs., 30 notes.
M. Hough

103. Law, Gordon T., Jr. RECENT PUBLICATIONS. *Industrial and Labor Relations Rev. 1981 35(1): 115-125.* Bibliography of publications in the fields of labor management relations; labor organizations; labor law; politics, government and industrial relations; international and comparative industrial relations; labor market; income security, insurance and benefits; labor conditions; human resources; personnel management; organization; and work performance and satisfaction. Covers the 19th and 20th centuries.
J. Powell

104. Lazar, Robert E. THE INTERNATIONAL LADIES' GARMENT WORKERS' UNION ARCHIVES. *Labor Hist. 1982 23(4): 528-533.* Describes the labor records at the Archives of the International Ladies' Garment Workers' Union (ILGWU) in New York City, emphasizing the materials from the ILGWU president's office and especially the papers of David Dubinsky (1892-1982). Note.

L. F. Velicer

105. Lipset, Seymour Martin. RADICALISM OR REFORMISM: THE SOURCES OF WORKING-CLASS POLITICS. *Am. Pol. Sci. Rev. 1983 77(1): 1-18.* By utilizing categories elaborated by Marxists and others to explain the weakness of left-wing radical movements in the United States, examines comparatively socialist and working-class movements abroad emphasizing the importance of the nature of the social-class system before industrialization and the way in which the economic and political elites respond to the demands of workers for the right to participate in the polity and the economy. %HD Biblio.

J. V. Coutinho

106. Marable, Manning. A. PHILIP RANDOLPH & THE FOUNDATIONS OF BLACK AMERICAN SOCIALISM. *Radical Am. 1980 14(2): 6-32.* A study of the views and contributions of Asa Philip Randolph (d. 1979), black trade unionist, radical journalist, and socialist leader to black America. His career has been controversial and difficult to understand because he was often seen as compromising the very positions he had supported. Yet his accomplishments in black union organizing, militant journalism, and political protest were unequaled for many decades. Although a Marxist, he resisted Communist Party control of his cherished black causes and broke with Bolshevism. He fell into a habit of political compromise and reconciliation, and, in the end, "his ambiguous hostility toward the Negro's nationalism negated the full potential of his efforts." 7 photos, 75 notes. R. V. Ritter

107. Martin, Albro. POVERTY, UNEMPLOYMENT, AND THE ANGUISH OF THE INTELLECTUALS. *Rev. in Am. Hist. 1979 7(1): 31-36.* Review article prompted by John A. Garraty's *Unemployment History: Economic Thought and Public Policy* (New York: Harper & Row, 1978).

108. Mason, Philip P. THE ARCHIVES OF LABOR AND URBAN AFFAIRS, WALTER P. REUTHER LIBRARY, WAYNE STATE UNIVERSITY. *Labor Hist. 1982 23(4): 534-545.* Discusses the resources, collecting policies, and services of the Archives of Labor and Urban Affairs, Walter P. Reuther Library, Wayne State University in Detroit, Michigan. The archives is the depository for the records of the United Automobile, Aerospace, and Agricultural Workers of America; the Industrial Workers of the World; the Newspaper Guild; the American Federation of Teachers; the Airline Pilots' Association; the American Federation of State, County, and Municipal Employees; and the United Farm Workers of America. 4 notes. L. F. Velicer

109. Mason, Philip P. LABOR ARCHIVES IN THE UNITED STATES: ACHIEVEMENTS AND PROSPECTS. *Labor Hist. 1982 23(4): 487-497.* Reviews the progress made in collecting labor union and worker records in the United States since 1950, discusses current problems of labor archives, and suggests areas of concern for labor archives in the future. 3 notes. L. F. Velicer

110. McQuillan, D. Aidan. FARM SIZE AND WORK ETHIC: MEASURING THE SUCCESS OF IMMIGRANT FARMERS ON THE AMERICAN GRASSLANDS, 1875-1925. *J. of Hist. Geography 1978 4(1): 57-76.* In America farm size is often seen as an indicator of farming success. To test this assumption, colonies of French Canadians, Mennonites, and Swedish Americans were studied in Kansas. Although the Swedish farms were largest, they were the least productive, while the Mennonites with the smallest farms were the most productive because they were the most labor-intensive farmers of the three groups. The poor reputation of French Canadian farmers in Canada was not repeated in Kansas. Based on Kansas township records and on secondary sources; map, 3 tables, 6 graphs, 32 notes. F. N. Egerton

111. Miller, Harold L. LABOR RECORDS AT THE STATE HISTORICAL SOCIETY OF WISCONSIN. *Labor Hist. 1982 23(4): 546-552.* Highlights the labor history resources in the Archives Division of the State Historical Society of Wisconsin in Madison, Wisconsin.

The Archives Division's holdings include collections on 19th-century labor, national labor organizations, labor historians and economists, workers' lives and the nature of work, labor attorneys, socialists and other reformers, Wisconsin state and local labor organizations, and Wisconsin state government agencies. 3 notes. L. F. Velicer

112. Montgomery, David. LABOR AND THE REPUBLIC IN INDUSTRIAL AMERICA: 1860-1920. *Mouvement Social [France] 1980 (111): 201-215.* The common roots of the many sectoral struggles of workers in the deflationary phase of capitalist development, which followed the Civil War, enabled militants to inspire a sense of moral universality among *the producers,* which challenged both the ethic of acquisitive individualism and *monopoly corruption* of the republic. The changing structure of American capitalism, the recomposition of the working class, and new bourgeois strategies at the turn of the century failed to destroy working-class militancy, but they did disrupt the moral universality of the movement. In its place emerged a dominant *pure and simple* trade unionism, challenged by the Socialist Party and by direct action ideologies—minority movements which were necessarily both American and nationalist. J

113. Nelson, Daniel. SCIENTIFIC MANAGEMENT, SYSTEMATIC MANAGEMENT, AND LABOR, 1880-1915. *Business Hist. Rev. 1974 48(4): 479-500.* An examination of the implementation of scientific management in industry reveals that it bore only a superficial resemblance to the system developed by Frederick W. Taylor. Rather than a "partial solution of the labor problem," the Taylor system was "a comprehensive answer to the problems of factory coordination, a refinement and extension of the earlier ideas known as systematic management." Table, 78 notes. R. V. Ritter

114. Osterman, Paul. EDUCATION AND LABOR MARKETS AT THE TURN OF THE CENTURY. *Pol. and Soc. 1979 9(1): 103-122.* Explores the relationship of American economic and technological developments in the late 19th and early 20th centuries, and the emergence of modern compulsory education. A dramatic drop over the four decades (1890-1930) in the need for the young in the labor market, produced by the second industrial revolution and migration, removed the last resistance to progressive reformers' demands for expanded educational opportunities. This resulted in legislation providing for extended mandatory education, and a coercive bureaucracy to enforce attendance, but little corresponding change in the class structure. 60 notes. D. G. Nielson

115. Ozanne, Robert. TRENDS IN AMERICAN LABOR HISTORY. *Labor Hist. 1980 21(4): 513-521.* Defends "old" American labor historians John R. Commons (1862-1945) and Selig Perlman (1888-1959) from the attacks of "new" American labor historians David Brody (b. 1930), Alan Dawley (b. 1943), and David Montgomery (b. 1927). 26 notes. L. F. Velicer

116. Parham, Groesbeck and Robinson, Gwen. "IF I COULD GO BACK . . ." *Southern Exposure 1976 4(1-2): 16-20.* Dobbie Sanders, a steel worker, tells about his life working in steel mills throughout the South, 1922-59.

117. Ramirez, Bruno. LABOUR AND THE LEFT IN AMERICA: A REVIEW ESSAY. *Labour [Canada] 1981 7(Spr): 165-172.* Reviews six books published from 1978 to 1979 about why socialism failed to become a permanent alternative for a radical transformation of American society. American socialism had its greatest success from the latter part of the 19th century until the 1920's. An entire generation of American socialists lived and fought with a belief in radical social transformation, but that did not come about. J. Powell

118. Riegelhaupt, Joyce F. WOMEN, WORK, WAR, AND FAMILY: SOME RECENT WORKS IN WOMAN'S HISTORY. A REVIEW ARTICLE. *Comparative Studies in Soc. and Hist. [Great Britain] 1982 24(4): 660-672.* Reviews Thomas Dublin's *Women at Work: The Transformation of Work and Community in Lowell, Massachusetts, 1826-1860* (1979); Susan Kennedy's *If All We Did Was to Weep at Home: A History of White Working-Class Women in America* (1979); Carl N. Degler's *At Odds: Women and the Family in America from the Revolution to the Present* (1980); Darlene G. Levy, Harriet B. Applewhite, and Mary D. Johnson's *Women in Revolution-*

ary Paris, 1789-1795 (1979); and *Women, War and Revolution,* edited by Carol R. Berkin and Clara M. Lovett (1980). Examining the social organization of relations among men is crucial to understanding both relations between men and women and the roles available to women in a society. Gender construction is a key element in all social systems.

S. A. Farmerie

119. Schwantes, Carlos A. WASHINGTON STATE'S PIONEER LABOR-REFORM PRESS: A BIBLIOGRAPHICAL ESSAY AND ANNOTATED CHECKLIST. *Pacific Northwest Q. 1980 71(3): 112-126.* Newspapers played an important role in the Washington labor movement from the 1880's through World War I. The earliest of these was the Seattle *Daily Call,* which set the tone for early anti-Chinese agitation. It soon gave way to successive types of labor newspapers: 1) communitarianism, 2) Knights of Labor, 3) Populist, 4) anarchist, 5) socialist, and 6) Industrial Workers of the World. An annotated checklist provides the names, publication years, frequency, political orientation, present repositories, and other information on each of these newspapers. Based on newspapers and secondary sources; 15 photos, 18 notes.

M. L. Tate

120. Scully, Michael Andrew. WOULD "MOTHER" JONES BUY *MOTHER JONES? Public Interest 1978 (53): 100-108.* A study of the career, ideas, methods, problems, and accomplishments of Mary Harris Jones (1830-1930), Irish American socialist and labor organizer, reveals considerable disparity with those of her namesake radical magazine *Mother Jones* and its readers. It has become the largest-selling radical magazine of the decade. It has "something for everyone who feels put-out with American life; each issue treats the themes of corporate corruption, political atrophy, small-is-beautiful, communal living, and feminism." In contrast to the journal with its antimodernity and tendency to prescribe various guarantees to society, Mother Jones had an understanding of what can be obtained from modernity, something the counterculture generally lacks. Likewise, Mother Jones fought for very real issues of decent living and working conditions, whereas the readers of *Mother Jones* in comparison are not actually deprived and fight for less substantial causes.

R. V. Ritter/S

121. Simpson, Ida Harper; Simpson, Richard L.; Evers, Mark; and Poss, Sharon Sandomirsky. OCCUPATIONAL RECRUITMENT, RETENTION, AND LABOR FORCE COHORT REPRESENTATION. *Am. J. of Sociol. 1982 87(6): 1287-1313.* Traces the recruitment and retention of four male and four female cohorts in 63 occupations during 1920-40 and 1950-70, concluding that young cohorts are more likely to be recruited than older cohorts, that high qualifications and wide opportunities influenced recruitment favorably, that job security and rewards did not favor retention, and that sex-differentiated labor markets structured the recruitment of male and female labor forces similarly.

122. Sivachev, N. V. and Savel'eva, I. M. MEZHDUNARODNOE RABOCHEE DVIZHENIE: VOPROSY ISTORII I TEORII [American labor in recent Soviet historiography]. *Labor Hist. 1977 18(3): 407-432.* Surveys recent developments in the history of American labor by Soviet scholars. Based on publications in the USSR; 43 notes.

L. L. Athey

123. Strassberg, Richard. LABOR HISTORY RESOURCES IN THE MARTIN P. CATHERWOOD LIBRARY OF THE NEW YORK STATE SCHOOL OF LABOR AND INDUSTRIAL RELATIONS AT CORNELL UNIVERSITY. *Labor Hist. 1982 23(4): 553-561.* Surveys the labor history materials at the Martin P. Catherwood Library of the New York State School of Labor and Industrial Relations at Cornell University in Ithaca, New York, emphasizing the archival collections in the Labor-Management Documentation Center of the Library. 2 notes.

L. F. Velicer

124. Swanson, Dorothy. ANNUAL BIBLIOGRAPHY OF PERIODICAL ARTICLES ON AMERICAN LABOR HISTORY, 1973. *Labor Hist. 1974 15(4): 543-558.* Presents a bibliography from 1973 in two general categories and 31 subcategories grouped chronologically and topically.

L. L. Athey

125. Swanson, Dorothy. ANNUAL BIBLIOGRAPHY ON AMERICAN LABOR HISTORY, 1980: PERIODICALS, DISSERTATIONS,

AND RESEARCH IN PROGRESS. *Labor Hist. 1981 22(4): 545-572.*

L. F. Velicer

126. Swanson, Dorothy. ANNUAL BIBLIOGRAPHY OF AMERICAN LABOR HISTORY, 1975: PERIODICALS, DISSERTATIONS, AND RESEARCH IN PROGRESS. *Labor Hist. 1976 17(4): 586-605.* Lists 210 articles, dissertations, and research in progress in 1975; organized chronologically and topically.

L. L. Athey

127. Swanson, Dorothy. ANNUAL BIBLIOGRAPHY ON AMERICAN LABOR HISTORY, 1979: PERIODICALS, DISSERTATIONS, AND RESEARCH IN PROGRESS. *Labor Hist. 1980 21(4): 570-596.* A bibliography arranged by period and subject.

L. F. Velicer

128. Swanson, Dorothy. ANNUAL BIBLIOGRAPHY ON AMERICAN LABOR HISTORY, 1981: PERIODICALS, DISSERTATIONS, AND RESEARCH IN PROGRESS. *Labor Hist. 1982 23(4): 582-598.* The bibliography is arranged by period and subject.

L. F. Velicer

129. Swanson, Dorothy. TAMIMENT INSTITUTE/BEN JOSEPHSON LIBRARY AND ROBERT F. WAGNER LABOR ARCHIVES. *Labor Hist. 1982 23(4): 562-567.* Reviews the history and collections of the Tamiment Institute/Ben Josephson Library and the Robert F. Wagner Labor Archives at New York University. The Tamiment Institute/Ben Josephson Library contains a wide variety of materials on the history of American radicalism and working class reform, including the personal library and scrapbooks of Eugene V. Debs. The Robert F. Wagner Labor Archives maintains the noncurrent records of a number of unions in the New York City area as well as the personal papers of labor leaders.

L. F. Velicer

130. Synnott, Marcia G. "REPLACING 'SAMBO': COULD WHITE IMMIGRANTS SOLVE THE LABOR PROBLEM IN THE CAROLINAS?" *Pro. of the South Carolina Hist. Assoc. 1982: 77-89.* Between 1865 and 1925, immigrant labor was periodically recruited in an attempt to solve the labor shortage in the Carolinas. Recruitment of immigrants was especially attractive in South Carolina, where it was hoped that European immigrants would balance the growing Negro population. The recruitment policies failed due to partisan politics, growing national support for immigration restriction, and lack of money. 22 notes.

J. W. Thacker, Jr.

131. Tomlins, Christopher L. GETTING INDUSTRIAL RELATIONS RIGHT. *Rev. in Am. Hist. 1982 10(3): 413-418.* Reviews Howell John Harris's *The Right to Manage: Industrial Relations Policies of American Business in the 1940's* (1982), which examines the various reactions of businesses toward the entrenchment of industrial unionism.

132. Tomlins, Christopher L. NEW DIRECTIONS IN AMERICAN LABOR HISTORY. *Labour Hist. [Australia] 1982 (43): 90-103.* Details the emergence of the scientific study of labor problems. The solution to the weakness of labor is its own awareness and its willingness to reexamine its history. 49 notes.

S. L. Solomon

133. Tyler, Gus. THE UNIVERSITY AND THE LABOR UNION: EDUCATING THE PROLETARIAT. *Change 1979 11(1): 32-37.* The author, a veteran of 50 years in labor education, discusses the evolution of his views concerning the best relationship between the education of workers and higher education in the United States.

134. Tyree, Andrea and Smith, Billy G. OCCUPATIONAL HIERARCHY IN THE UNITED STATES: 1789-1969. *Social Forces 1978 56(3): 881-899.* The degree of change in the hierarchy of occupations over long periods is the focus of this paper. Our concern is with the mechanism by which the hierarchy changes. Taxable wealth of incumbents of detailed occupations from 1789 Philadelphia is related to income data from the last three dicennial censuses. Several models of how change might occur are evaluated. We conclude that (1) change in occupational reward differentials is slower than previous estimates, and (2) the first-order causal mechanism by which change in the hierarchy has been presumed to take place is implausible. We also note within-occupation variability in assets of approximately the same magnitude in the two periods.

J

135. Vaudagna, Maurizio. CAPITALE MONOPOLISTICO E LAVORO NELL'AMERICA DEL XX SECOLO [Monopolistic capital and labor in 20th-century America]. *Movimento Operaio e Socialista [Italy] 1978 1(4): 443-446.* Harry Braverman has produced a book, *Labor and Monopoly Capital: The Degradation of Work in the Twentieth Century* (Monthly Rev. Pr., 1975), which has now appeared in Italian translation *(Lavoro e capitale monopolistico. La degradazione del lavoro nel XX secolo)* (Torino, Einaudi: 1978). It is a Marxist analysis of the relationship between "monopolistsic" capital and labor in the 20th-century United States, which contributes much to the overcoming of the backwardness of Marxist thought in its approach to American society, which has always been so resistent to Marxism and to a sociology based on class struggle. 3 notes.   J. C. Billigmeier

136. Vecoli, Rudolph J. LABOR RELATED COLLECTIONS IN THE IMMIGRATION HISTORY RESEARCH CENTER. *Labor Hist. 1982 23(4): 568-574.* Describes the labor-related collections at the Immigration History Research Center of the University of Minnesota in St. Paul. The center collects materials related to United States immigrants from Eastern, Central, and Southern Europe and the Near East. Some of the strengths of the collection are the runs of leftist, non-English immigrant newspapers and the manuscript holdings for Finnish, Italian, and South Slavic immigrants. 11 notes.   L. F. Velicer

137. Vittoz, Stan. WORLD WAR I AND THE POLITICAL ACCOMMODATION OF TRANSITIONAL MARKET FORCES: THE CASE OF IMMIGRATION RESTRICTION. *Pol. and Soc. 1978 8(1): 49-78.* The assumption that continued labor migration would affect labor-capital power relationships in the American political economy, and was therefore partly responsible for the coming of restrictive immigration legislation in the post-World War I period, will not stand close scrutiny. Investigation of migration patterns, industrial growth, and capital's demands for labor from the 1870's to the 1920's shows that by the latter period, the structure of the economy was such that both labor and capital required changes that would enhance stability and predictability in both sectors of the economy. Any continued influx of foreign labor would not have altered the power structure. Primary and secondary sources; 75 notes.   D. G. Nielson

138. Wallerstein, Immanuel; Martin, William G.; and Dickinson, Torry. HOUSEHOLD STRUCTURES AND PRODUCTION PROCESSES: PRELIMINARY THESES AND FINDINGS. *Rev. (Fernand Braudel Center) 1982 5(3): 437-458.* Most households in the world capitalist system receive income from wages, subsistence activities, petty commodity production, rent, and gifts. The labor force in South Africa in the 19th and 20th centuries and the black labor force in 19th and 20th century Philadelphia steel mills both relied upon more forms of income than wages during the initial stages of their incorporation into the capitalist labor force. Secondary sources; 3 fig., 21 notes, ref.
J. Powell

139. Warner, Malcolm and Edelstein, J. David. FACTIONS IN BRITISH AND AMERICAN UNIONS—A COMPARATIVE STRUCTURAL APPROACH. *Relations Industrielles/Industrial Relations [Canada] 1973 28(1): 166-198.* "In this paper, the authors attempt to discuss the relationship between intra-organizational conflict and factionalism, and how this manifests itself in different ways in British and American unions. They start with a discussion of conflict, then attempt to set out the characteristics of factions. They next look at factionalism comparatively, and finally attempt an analytical framework which looks at the dimensions of factionalism."   J

140. Wason, James R. AMERICAN WORKERS AND AMERICAN STUDIES. *Am. Studies (Washington, D.C.) 1974 13(2): 10-36.* A lengthy bibliographical essay on labor history and its relationship to American Studies; the bibliographies are presented in eleven categories divided topically and chronologically.   L. L. Athey

141. Weber, Edward C. THE LABADIE COLLECTION IN THE UNIVERSITY OF MICHIGAN LIBRARY. *Labor Hist. 1982 23(4): 575-581.* Joseph Antoine Labadie, a labor activist and anarchist, donated his library of radical labor materials to the University of Michigan at Ann Arbor in 1911, providing the foundation of the Labadie Collection. Agnes Ann Inglis, a labor radical and anarchist, organized and enhanced the original Labadie Collection. The collection is richest in radical labor periodicals, pamphlets, and ephemera. The most important manuscript collections are the papers of Labadie and Inglis.   L. F. Velicer

142. Weber, Michael P. and Boardman, Anthony E. ECONOMIC GROWTH AND OCCUPATIONAL MOBILITY IN NINETEENTH CENTURY URBAN AMERICA. *J. of Social Hist. 1977 11(1): 52-74.* An analysis of the horizontal and vertical mobility of one Pennsylvania community in the 19th century reveals that "individual success was determined more by the structure of the city than by individual ethnic and cultural background." More importantly the "time one entered a city, the skill level of one's occupation at that time, one's industrial occupation and whether one switched occupations were crucial determinants of one's success in America." 5 tables, 29 notes, appendix.   L. E. Ziewacz

143. Westermeier, Clifford P. BLACK RODEO COWBOYS. *Red River Valley Hist. Rev. 1978 3(3): 4-26.* Describes the participation of black men in the range and ranch cattle industry and rodeos, 1880's-1970's.

144. Zeiger, Robert H. MEMORY SPEAKS: OBSERVATIONS ON PERSONAL HISTORY AND WORKING CLASS STRUCTURE. *Maryland Hist. 1977 8(2): 1-12.* Labor history and social history are being merged by American historians. Comments on the social history available in four labor publications: Victor Reuther's *The Brothers Reuther and The Story of U.A.W.: A Memoir* (1976), Frank Marquart's *An Auto Worker's Journal* (1975), Wyndham Mortimer's *Organize! My Life As A Union Man* (Boston, 1971) and Claude Hoffman's *Sit-Down in Anderson: U.A.W. Local 663, Anderson, Indiana* (1968). Each of the studies sheds light on working class social history as well as on the United Auto Workers. Based on secondary sources; 22 notes.
G. O. Gagnon

145. —. [INDUSTRIALIZATION, REGIONAL CHANGE, AND THE SECTORAL DISTRIBUTION OF THE U.S. LABOR FORCE, 1850-1880]. *Econ. Development and Cultural Change 1975 23(4): 739-750.*
Vatter, Harold G. INDUSTRIALIZATION, REGIONAL CHANGE, AND THE SECTORAL DISTRIBUTION OF THE U.S. LABOR FORCE, 1850-1880, *pp. 739-747.* Examines the proportion of the labor force devoted to agriculture in the United States 1850-80 in order to ascertain the reason for it remaining relatively stable despite the dramatic increase in industrialization. Using some of the work of Stanley Lebergott, the author attempts to show that the constancy of the farm labor force proportion is deceptive because "the total growth process is likely to be discontinuous and . . . more importantly, because regional disaggregation reveals quite opposing economic tendencies in the South and the non-South." Based on published sources; 3 tables, 20 notes, appendix.
Lebergott, Stanley. A REPLY TO HAROLD G. VATTER, *pp. 749-750.* Maintains the validity of his earlier work, but does suggest that additional research into regional economic changes for the period would be helpful. 4 notes.   J. W. Thacker, Jr.

146. —. LABOR HISTORY BIBLIOGRAPHY. *Southern Exposure 1976 4(1-2): 160-169.* Lists books, articles, and dissertations on southern labor history, 1900-75.

The Worker

147. Abbott, Collamer M. CORNISH MINERS IN APPALACHIAN COPPER CAMPS. *Rev. Int. d'Hist. de la Banque [Italy] 1973 (7): 199-219.* Although they did not constitute a majority, Cornish miners represented a significant part of the work force in the copper mines of Appalachia, 1830-90. Sources for development in the mining regions, especially those for Orange County in Vermont and Polk County in Tennessee, indicate that mine owners looked to the Cornishmen for the skills necessary for hardrock, underground mining. They also were sought out as foremen. Both the methods of working the mines and the systems of payment reflected the traditional practices of the Cornish miners in the old country. Based on US Census, mining company records, newspapers, and secondary sources; 51 notes.   D. McGinnis

148. Bahr, Howard M. THE DECLINING DISTINCTIVENESS OF UTAH'S WORKING WOMEN. *Brigham Young U. Studies 1979 19(4): 525-543.* A comparative study of the nature of Utah's working women with working women nationally since 1900. Utah women were slower to enter the work force, but their numbers increased rapidly after 1940; today there is little difference. Utah women formerly were better educated, but much of that margin has also been erased. When compared with men, both in Utah and nationally, women have experienced an actual decline in their position since 1940; the number of college-educated women has increased, but the number of men much more so. Today, the former distinctiveness of Utah women has virtually disappeared.   V. L. Human

149. Barton, Josef J. LAND, LABOR, AND COMMUNITY IN NUECES: CZECH FARMERS AND MEXICAN LABORERS IN SOUTH TEXAS, 1880-1930. Luebke, Frederick C., ed. *Ethnicity on the Great Plains* (Lincoln: U. of Nebraska Pr., for the Center for Great Plains Studies, 1980): 190-209. Discusses the similarities and contrasts between Czech farmers and Mexican laborers, and the relationships of land and family in Nueces County, Texas, early in the 20th century. Both groups were highly transient, but each was united by bonds of common origin and kinship. Whereas Czechs were linked by generational lines, Mexicans were united by lateral ties among kinfolk. Among the Czechs landownership quickly became the mode, but Mexican tenant farmers were reduced to a migrant, landless rural proletariat. Both groups attempted to use familiar forms as they faced new and altered circumstances. Out of such confrontations emerged ethnic cultures that shaped and sustained their lives. Religion became the bond of community in both groups, as cooperative efforts were transformed into institutions and ritual associations into resources for collective action. Secondary sources; 31 notes.   J. Powell

150. Bennett, Mary. WOMEN AT HOME. *Palimpsest 1982 63(2): 42-51.* Discusses and provides photographs of Iowa women working at home, ca. 1890-1910.

151. Benson, Susan Porter. "THE CLERKING SISTERHOOD" RATIONALIZATION AND THE WORK CULTURE OF SALESWOMEN IN AMERICAN DEPARTMENT STORES, 1890-1960. *Radical Am. 1978 12(2): 41-55.* Unlike the contemporary trends in male-dominated crafts and skills, the impact of managerial involvement in department store sales work in the 20th century was to upgrade skills, enhance the position of the saleswoman, and contribute to the creation of a thoroughgoing work culture in the department store. The increasing emphasis on the selling skills of the work force on the part of management heightened the status of saleswomen and further impelled managers to find ways of enhancing the work setting to spur production. Saleswomen in the various selling areas of the department store developed an *esprit d'corps* and sense of togetherness that managers ignored at their own peril.   N. Lederer

152. Bernard, Jessie. HISTORICAL AND STRUCTURAL BARRIERS TO OCCUPATIONAL DESEGREGATION. *Signs 1976 1(3, Part 2): 87-94.* To balance the emphasis on negative consequences for women of occupational segregation, the author comments that 1) occupational segregation has, at some times and places, been valued by women, such as Catharine Beecher's espousal of the cult of domesticity, 2) occupational segregation can have noneconomic and nontechnological aspects such as homosociality, 3) occupational desegregation may enhance productivity, for example in group decisionmaking, and 4) occupational desegregation may result in sex-fairness rather than sex-equality in occupational distribution. Based on sociological experiments and secondary sources; 23 notes.   S. E. Kennedy

153. Biola, Heather. THE BLACK WASHERWOMEN IN SOUTHERN TRADITION. *Tennessee Folklore Soc. Bull. 1979 45(1): 17-27.* Analyzes historical ideals, folklore images, and literary characterizations of laundry and black laundresses as a folklore image in southern tradition, 17th-20th centuries.

154. Blanchard, David. HIGH STEEL! THE KAHNAWAKE MOHAWK AND THE HIGH CONSTRUCTION TRADE. *J. of Ethnic Studies 1983 11(2): 41-60.* The role of the Mohawk ironworker has been compared to the traditional role that Iroquois men enjoyed as warriors. Such role continuity is especially evident in the relationship between men and women, and expresses a social tradition important in Kahnawake for 300 years. Ironwork provides three important rituals: it is a rite of passage for young Mohawk men, it symbolically keeps the Mohawk in touch with their history and traditions, and it serves to define male-female relationships and enhances the self-esteem of the men in a female-dominated society. As an adaptive strategy, ironwork has helped the Mohawks to maintain their culture in a white society. 5 notes, ref.   G. J. Bobango

155. Blitz, Rudolph C. WOMEN IN THE PROFESSIONS, 1870-1970. *Monthly Labor Rev. 1974 97(5): 34-39.* The proportion of women in the professions in the United States rose until 1930 and then steadily declined as the job structure shifted toward professions dominated by men.

156. Bodnar, John E. THE IMPACT OF THE "NEW IMMIGRATION" ON THE BLACK WORKER: STEELTON, PENNSYLVANIA, 1880-1920. *Labor Hist. 1976 17(2): 214-229.* Black workers in Steelton entered unskilled and semiskilled trades during 1880-1905, but with the rapid influx of Slavic and Italian immigrants Negroes suffered a devastating decline in occupational mobility until after World War I. Based on interviews and local records; 8 tables, 16 notes.
                                                         L. L. Athey

157. Boone, Richard W. CREATING JOBS FOR MINORITY YOUTH. *Social Policy 1982 12(4): 29-36.* Discusses the role of youth in American labor from the 18th century to the 20th century with special attention to the problems of large-scale unemployment of minority youth.

158. Carter, Susan B. and Prus, Mark; with commentary by Margo, Robert A. THE LABOR MARKET AND THE AMERICAN HIGH SCHOOL GIRL 1890-1928. *J. of Econ. Hist. 1982 42(1): 163-171.* Girls far outnumbered boys in American high schools at the turn of the century. Despite the fact that women on average spent far fewer years than men in the paid labor force, a high school education was a better investment for girls than for boys. This was because formal education offered the only opportunity for girls to obtain job-related skills, whereas it was but one of many such opportunities for boys. Comments pp. 187-189.   J

159. Collins, D. Cheryl. WOMEN AT WORK IN MANHATTAN, KS, 1890-1910. *J. of the West 1982 21(2): 33-40.* By 1914, almost half the 929 women graduates during 1890-1910 from Kansas State Agricultural College gave their occupation as "housewife." The next largest group, 270, were teachers at all levels. "At home" were 118 unmarried women, while fewer than 10 each were dressmakers, nurses, farmers, physicians, and other professional or skilled workers. The 1900 Manhattan City Directory reflected these figures, with teaching and dressmaking listed as the leading occupations. Some women helped in their family businesses, keeping accounts, or working in photography, journalism, and sales. Based on a 1914 Kansas State Agricultural College (now Kansas State University) occupations survey; 19 photos, 3 notes.
                                                         B. S. Porter

160. Douglass, William A. THE VANISHING BASQUE SHEEPHERDER. *Am. West 1980 17(4): 30-31, 59-61.* Although others were involved, Basques were the ethnic backbone of the sheepherders of the western sheep industry for its century of prominence. They were eager to escape the economic deprivation of their native land. This began to change in the 1970's because of American labor regulations and improved conditions at home. Today, Basques constitute only about one-sixth of the herders of the American West. 2 illus., biblio. note.
                                                         D. L. Smith

161. Duke, David C. ANNA LOUISE STRONG AND THE SEARCH FOR A GOOD CAUSE. *Pacific Northwest Q. 1975 66(3): 123-137.* Committed to humanitarian causes throughout her life, Anna Louise Strong initially received inspiration from Industrial Workers of the World activities and the Seattle General Strike of 1919. But it was in the USSR of the 1920's and 1930's that she found a new sense of achievement as organizer and writer. Never a doctrinaire Marxist and never fully recognized for her achievements in the Soviet Union, Ms. Strong gradually developed an affection for the Maoist brand of communism. Her praise of the Chinese model led to deportation from

the Soviet Union in 1948. Though subsequently exonerated of the charges, she chose life in China as an activist writer until her death in 1970. Based on primary and secondary sources; 2 photos, 67 notes.

M. L. Tate

162. Dunnigan, Kate; Roberts, Laura B.; Kebabian, Helen; and Taylor, Maureen. WORKING WOMEN: IMAGES OF WOMEN AT WORK IN RHODE ISLAND, 1880-1925. *Rhode Island Hist. 1979 38(1): 3-23.* Women are portrayed in a wide range of occupations, from farming and domestic labor to nursing and factory work. The essay serves as an introduction to a photographic exhibit at the Rhode Island Historical Society in 1979. Published documents and secondary accounts; 18 illus., 16 notes.

P. J. Coleman

163. Ehrenreich, Barbara and English, Deirdre. REFLECTIONS ON THE "WOMAN QUESTION." *Working Papers for a New Soc. 1978 6(4): 72-81.* The disappearance of women's traditional role as producer under the old patriarchal system with the advent of 19th-century industrialization and modern capitalism gave birth to the problem, both on an individual crisis level and as a sociological concern, of defining the place of women in the new masculinist order.

164. Epstein, Cynthia Fuchs. WOMEN WHO WORK. *Dissent 1983 30(2): 267-269.* Reviews Alice Kessler-Harris's *Out to Work: A History of Wage-Earning Women in the United States* (1983), which emphasizes the "interplay between ideology, job opportunity, and economic conditions as it has affected women from colonial times to World War II."

165. Fink, Leon. INDUSTRIAL AMERICA'S RANK AND FILE: RECENT TRENDS IN AMERICAN LABOR HISTORY. *Social Educ. 1982 46(2): 92-99.* During the past 15 years the focus of labor historiography has shifted from "a fairly tightly-constructed subsection of economic and political history" to "the changing nature of work and the workplace, the forms and logic of working-class organization, and the impact of labor history—or 'the workers' presence'—on American history in general."

166. Friggens, Paul. THE CURIOUS "COUSIN JACKS": CORNISH MINERS IN THE AMERICAN WEST. *Am. West 1978 15(6): 4-7, 62-63.* With tin and copper ores virtually exhausted, Cornish miners left their homeland and made "monumental contributions" to mining in other parts of the world. Thousands came to the United States to pioneer mining in several states from Pennsylvania to California, especially in the West. These "Cousin Jacks" ranked among the greatest hard-rock miners in the world. They have indelibly stamped the West with their curious language, culture, and customs. 3 illus., note, biblio.

D. L. Smith

167. Garcia, Mario T. THE CHICANA IN AMERICAN HISTORY: THE MEXICAN WOMEN OF EL PASO, 1880-1920: A CASE STUDY. *Pacific Hist. Rev. 1980 49(2): 315-337.* Mexican women accompanied their husbands who immigrated into the western United States to work, and the nuclear family prevailed among Chicanos. At El Paso, Texas, Mexican wives did not work outside the home. Because of poverty and exploitation and neglect by landlords and city officials, Mexicans lived in overcrowded and unsanitary conditions. Mexican wives guarded Mexican cultural traditions in the family, thereby retarding American assimilation. Unmarried women who worked outside the home were employed mostly as servants and laundresses, although some were production workers. Their wages were lower than non-Mexican Americans', and Mexican women were involved in major labor strikes in the Southwest. Based on census reports, US Senate documents, contemporary newspapers, and secondary sources; 47 notes.

R. N. Lokken

168. Gedicks, Al. ETHNICITY, CLASS SOLIDARITY, AND LABOR RADICALISM AMONG FINNISH IMMIGRANTS IN MICHIGAN COPPER COUNTRY. *Pol. and Soc. 1977 7(2): 127-156.* Case study of the growth of class consciousness among Finnish immigrants to the Michigan copper region. Examines the antecedents of labor radicalism among the Finnish miners during 1890-1920 and the strategies of the mining companies for the maintenance of a stable labor force. Primary and secondary sources; map, 106 notes.

D. G. Nielson

169. Glenn, Evelyn Nakano. OCCUPATIONAL GHETTOIZATION: JAPANESE AMERICAN WOMEN AND DOMESTIC SERVICE, 1905-1970. *Ethnicity 1981 8(4): 352-386.* Examines how the concentration of Japanese women in domestic work was established and why it persisted across time, considering both push and pull factors. The major push toward employment in general was the low wages earned by Japanese males, too low to support a family. Pull factors included the flexibility of domestic work and its closeness to traditional domestic roles. 7 tables, 15 notes, biblio.

T. W. Smith

170. Goldin, Claudia. THE WORK AND WAGES OF SINGLE WOMEN, 1870 TO 1920. *J. of Econ. Hist. 1980 40(1): 81-88.* Single women dominated the US female labor force from 1870 to 1920. Data on the home life and working conditions of single women in 1888 and 1907 enable the estimation of their earnings functions. Work in the manufacturing sector for these women was task-oriented and payment was frequently by the piece. Earnings rose steeply with experience and peaked early; learning was mainly on-the-job. Occupational segregation by sex was a partial product of the method of payment, and the early termination of human capital investment was a function of the life-cycle labor force participation of these women, although the role of the family was also critical.

J

171. Goode, Bill. THE SKILLED AUTO WORKER: A SOCIAL PORTRAIT. *Dissent 1976 23(4): 392-397.* Discusses the position, attitudes, problems, and work of skilled workers in the automobile industry's auto shops since their unionization with the advent of the Congress of Industrial Organizations (CIO).

172. Gotto, Baron. ETHNIC GROUPS AND THE COFFEE INDUSTRY IN HAWAII. *Hawaiian J. of Hist. 1982 16: 112-124.* Chronicles the progress of the industry, including technological improvements and the important role played by ethnic groups, such as the Chinese, Japanese, and Filipinos. The coffee laborers worked 12-hour days for 25 cents. Some were treated cruelly and ran away while others, among them many Chinese, bought their own farms. The Chinese came to own the better lands while the Japanese and native Hawaiians owned the poorer growing fields. %HD 38 notes.

S. L. Solomon

173. Graziosi, Andrea. COMMON LABORERS, UNSKILLED WORKERS: 1880-1915. *Labor Hist. 1981 22(4): 512-544.* Explores the conditions of common laborers in the steel mills and machine shops of the United States in the late 19th and early 20th centuries. During this period the work performed by laborers changed from hauling materials and cleaning up to being directly involved in production. The laborer became the unskilled worker tending a machine, while the role of the skilled worker became less important. US Immigration Commission Reports and other primary sources; 75 notes.

L. F. Velicer

174. Green, James. WORKING-CLASS HISTORY IN THE 1940'S: A BIBLIOGRAPHICAL ESSAY. *Radical Am. 1975 9(4-5): 206-213.* The dearth of research on the working class is "partially due to the fact that the labor movement seemed to be on the 'offensive' in the Depression and in a 'defensive' position during and after World War II."

S

175. Greene, Victor. THE POLISH AMERICAN WORKER TO 1930: THE "HUNKY" IMAGE IN TRANSITION. *Polish Rev.1976 21(3): 63-78.* Examines the evolution in thought, 1920's-60, among historians and intellectuals studying the image of Polish immigrant labor, 1860-1930, from one in which the laborer was portrayed as a naive illiterate bumbler to a more widely accepted contemporary image of the Polish American worker as one who was able to socially, psychologically, and intellectually adjust to the new socioeconomic system encountered in the United States.

176. Groneman, Carol. WORKING-CLASS IMMIGRANT WOMEN IN MID-NINETEENTH-CENTURY NEW YORK: THE IRISH WOMAN'S EXPERIENCE. *J. of Urban Hist. 1978 4(3): 255-274.* Despite the disruption of immigration to the United States, kinship and cultural ties to the old country continued during 1840-60. As a result, the work, family, and leisure activities of the Irish immigrants were continuations or modifications of established Irish practices. 37 notes.

T. W. Smith

177. Groniowski, Krzysztof. SOCJALISTYCZNA EMIGRACJA POLSKA W STANACH ZJEDNOCZONYCH (1883-1914) [Polish socialist emigrants in the United States of America 1883-1914]. *Z Pola Walki [Poland] 1977 20(1): 3-35.* Polish Socialist activity in New York City in 1883 was contemporaneous with the first Marxist working-class party, Proletariat, in Poland. In 1886 the Association Równość [Equality] was founded in New York. In that same year the first Polish groups in the Knights of Labor were founded; their center was in Milwaukee. By 1890 the first Polish section of the American Socialist Labor Party was established; Polish centers developed in major cities and established contacts with the Socialist movement in the Prussian sector of Poland. Leadership conflicts developed within the American party over the national question. During the Revolution of 1905, a Polish Revolutionary Committee was established in the United States. It collected funds for the Polish Socialist Party. The influx of Poles after the revolution increased the splintering of the Polish Socialist movement over the issue of the home parties. The closest collaboration with the US movement took place in Milwaukee where in 1910 Socialists won the municipal elections.   J/S

178. Grover, Mary Anne. PREPARING TEACHERS FOR HOMESTEAD PAROCHIAL SCHOOLS, 1888-1921: A STUDY OF EARLY CATHOLIC TEACHER EDUCATION. *Pennsylvania Heritage 1983 9(4): 14-18.* The young postulants teaching at Catholic schools in Homestead, Pennsylvania, received mostly on-the-job training from older associates, but many later used their spare time to earn advanced degrees.

179. Hamilton, Stephen F. WORKING TOWARD EMPLOYMENT. *Society 1982 19(6): 19-29.* Work experience programs have a beneficial effect on subsequent employability for disadvantaged youth; adults who were usually unemployed as youths continue that pattern in adult work years.

180. Hartmann, Heidi I. WOMEN'S WORK IN THE UNITED STATES. *Current Hist. 1976 70(416): 215-219, 229.* Discusses the division of labor between women and men in social stratification, 1789-1970's, emphasizing the influence of the ideology of the feminine mystique in current women's responsibilities of child care and housework.

181. Hartmann, Susan M. WOMEN'S WORK AMONG THE PLAINS INDIANS. *Gateway Heritage 1983 3(4): 2-9.* Contrary to popular impressions perpetuated by some manuscript and oral history materials, the line for dividing labor by sex was not uniform among Indians of the Great Plains. Tribal social mores, polygynous marriage customs, and different economic systems dictated work assignments. Whatever the particular feminine duties, women at first enjoyed prestige and wielded power in the tribes because of their economic contributions. But male deaths in 19th-century Indian wars altered Indian social organization. The relative dearth of males placed women in disadvantaged bargaining positions, forcing them to surrender powers they once exercised. Secondary sources; 15 photos, biblio.   H. T. Lovin

182. Harvey, Donald G. UNCLE CHARLIE WAS A RAILROADER: BEGAN AS AN APPRENTICE, EARNING $4.50 A WEEK. *Pacific Northwesterner 1978 22(4): 61-64.* Charles Prescott discusses his lifetime career in the railroad industry in Massachusetts and Montana, 1873-1932.

183. Hill, Peter J. RELATIVE SKILL AND INCOME LEVELS OF NATIVE AND FOREIGN BORN WORKERS IN THE UNITED STATES. *Explorations in Econ. Hist. 1975 12(1): 47-60.* Challenges the widely held view that immigrants were overwhelmingly unskilled, that they almost always entered the job market at the bottom, and that their economic position was generally much lower than that of the native-born. In the period 1870-1920, native- and foreign-born were comparable in economic status, annual earnings and savings were nearly equal, the foreign-born had a higher rate of home ownership than the native-born, and there were no very significant differences between the two groups in job skills. Based on published statistics and secondary accounts.   P. J. Coleman

184. Hilton, Mike. THE SPLIT LABOR MARKET AND CHINESE IMMIGRATION, 1848-1882. *J. of Ethnic Studies 1979 6(4): 99-108.*

A case study of West Coast Chinese immigration demonstrates the usefulness of Edna Bonacich's Split Labor Market theory of ethnic antagonism, and urges expansion of the model in analyzing the Chinese situation, to include the importance of fluctuations in the economy in the antagonism-generating process, the role of the ethnic bourgeoisie and the hostilities to which it gives rise, and the potential caste resolutions to a split labor market, which the numerous combinations of native capital and labor and immigrant capital and labor may effect. 28 notes.
G. J. Bobango

185. Hirata, Lucie Cheng. FREE, INDENTURED, ENSLAVED: CHINESE PROSTITUTES IN NINETEENTH-CENTURY AMERICA. *Signs 1979 5(1): 3-29.* When Chinese prostitution developed in 19th-century America, it provided a double economic benefit. Cheap labor in California was guaranteed, while economic benefits were transmitted to China. Families of the laborers in China were supported, and the problem of an over-abundance of nonproductive women was remedied. The Chinese patriarchal system supported prostitution because daughters had no choice except to submit. In America, conditions ranged from concubinage to ruthless slavery. A period of competition during 1849-54 was followed by the creation of a rigorous and corrupt trade network, which lasted until 1925, although prostitution had begun to decline by 1880. Based on California and US census records and secondary sources; 4 tables, 126 notes.   S. P. Conner

186. Hofferth, Sandra L. and Moore, Kristin A. WOMEN'S EMPLOYMENT AND MARRIAGE. Smith, Ralph E., ed. *The Subtle Revolution: Women at Work* (Washington: Urban Inst., 1979): 99-124. Discusses the changing ideas about traditional marriage and how women working outside the home have affected these, using statistics on marriage and divorce since 1890, focusing on how women's employment affects marital relations and the domestic power structure, and assesses the implications.

187. Hunt, Vilma R. A BRIEF HISTORY OF WOMEN WORKERS AND HAZARDS IN THE WORKPLACE. *Feminist Studies 1979 5(2): 274-285.* History of health hazards to women workers in industry in the United States and Europe from 1869, when Charles Dickens described conditions in a lead mill in East London, until the mid-1970's, when research on the potential health hazards of exposure to dangerous substances to workers, especially women, showed that exposure to lead, benzene, and ionizing radiation causes numerous illnesses and death. Focuses on the efforts of individuals active in improving conditions for women workers, such as Alice Hamilton, Marie Curie, and George Bernard Shaw. Instead of improving conditions for workers exposed to lead, benzene, and ionizing radiation, society excludes women workers from the workplace.   G. Smith

188. Jensen, Joan M. CLOTH, BUTTER AND BOARDERS: WOMEN'S HOUSEHOLD PRODUCTION FOR THE MARKET. *Rev. of Radical Pol. Econ. 1980 12(2): 14-24.* Women moved into the capitalist mode of production when they stopped household production of cloth, butter, and boarders. Marx's concept of simple community production can accommodate the development of women's work if it is expanded to include services produced in the home, but Marx's theory needs to be expanded to incorporate all types of women's work and the transition from rural home production to urban factory labor; ca. 1790-1910. 2 tables, 34 notes.   D. R. Stevenson

189. Justin, Meryl S. THE ENTRY OF WOMEN INTO MEDICINE IN AMERICA: EDUCATION AND OBSTACLES 1847-1910. *Synthesis 1978 4(3): 31-46.* Although Elizabeth Blackwell was admitted to the Geneva Medical School in western New York in 1847, and received an M. D. degree two years later, barriers to the admission of women to medical schools, to practice, and to professional societies were lowered only slowly and grudgingly. The American Medical Association did not admit women until 1915, although in 1900 there were over 7,300 female doctors in the United States. 40 notes.   M. M. Vance

190. Kealey, Linda. WOMEN'S WORK IN THE UNITED STATES: RECENT TRENDS IN HISTORICAL RESEARCH. *Atlantis [Canada] 1979 4(2): 133-142.* Discusses trends in the study of women's history, particularly of the 19th-century woman's role, and the interest in Marxism as an analytical tool for research on the history of working

women; reviews books, essays, and articles on working women in US history published in the 1970's.

191. Kessler-Harris, Alice. OUT TO WORK. *Society 1983 20(2): 63-66.* Photographic essay composed of text and photos from *Out to Work: A History of Wage-Earning Women in the United States* (1982) by Alice Kessler-Harris; covers the 20th century.

192. Kessler-Harris, Alice. "WHERE ARE THE ORGANIZED WOMEN WORKERS?" *Feminist Studies 1975 3(1/2): 92-110.* Women were only a tiny percentage of the membership of trade unions as late as 1925, although the A.F.L. had been organizing for more than 40 years. Despite traditional views, the question is not why women did not organize themselves, but rather how and why they were prevented from becoming union members. Women provided a large pool of unskilled labor in the late 19th and early 20th centuries, with the added advantage of accepting low pay and poor working conditions in work situations that were often temporary. Unionists considered women a threat to their jobs and argued that they belonged at home tending to children and kitchen, not competing in the labor force. Labor committed itself to equal pay for women to protect male workers from female competition at lower wages. On the whole unions saw women as a threat to jobs and did little to promote their participation in trade unionism. Primary and secondary sources; 79 notes.   S. R. Herstein

193. Kessler-Harris, Alice. WOMEN, WORK, AND THE SOCIAL ORDER. Carroll, Berenice A., ed. *Liberating Women's Hist.* (Chicago: U. of Illinois Pr., 1976): pp. 330-343. Explores women's work outside the home in the context of the interaction between the fluctuations of the economy and the need for social order contingent upon the family. Traces women's participation in the labor force from colonial New England to present and contends that varying needs of the labor market determine changes in family structure and women's roles. Because the ideology of the family has always been considered crucial to the social order, the enormous number of women presently employed prompts questions about whether working women undermine family structure, and, even more importantly, whether the role of the family is to maintain the social order. 46 notes.   B. Sussman

194. Kessner, Thomas. JOBS, GHETTOES AND THE URBAN ECONOMY, 1880-1935. *Am. Jewish Hist. 1981 71(2): 218-238.* Statistically compares Russian Jewish with Italian immigrants to New York City in the late 19th and early 20th centuries. Coming with greater urban and industrial skills, and intending to remain in their new homeland, Russian Jews more quickly became citizens and voters, took greater advantage of educational opportunities, and sought higher skilled and white collar occupations, thus rising economically more rapidly and surviving better the Great Depression. Based on US and New York state censuses, and US Immigration Commission Reports; 4 tables, 56 notes.   R. A. Keller

195. Kiffer, Theodore E. DRIVING TEAM IN THE BIG WOODS. *Pennsylvania Heritage 1983 9(1): 13-17.* Portrays the teamsters of the Pennsylvania lumber industry, ca. 1885-1930, with excerpts from interviews with men once employed by the Wheeler and Dusenberry Lumber Company of Forest and Warren counties.

196. Kilar, Jeremy W. BLACK PIONEERS IN THE MICHIGAN LUMBER INDUSTRY. *J. of Forest Hist. 1980 24(3): 142-149.* After the Civil War blacks arrived in the Michigan lumber towns of Bay City, Saginaw, and Muskegon and took jobs in the sawmills (particularly as firemen and salt-packers) and in other occupations. In 1880 about half were categorized as skilled, semiskilled, self-employed, or professional. As long as the timber supply held out, black workers operated in an atmosphere of relative tolerance. With economic decline in the 1890's, however, opportunities disappeared, prejudice was expressed in housing and employment, and many blacks moved away. Few black men worked in the woods, although two, William Q. Atwood and John H. Freeny, were successful entrepreneurs who owned timberland and sawmills. A brief companion essay titled "The Goodridge Brothers: Lumbering's Photographic Historians" (pp. 150-151) is about William, Wallace, and Glenalvin Goodridge, black photographers who recorded Saginaw's "white pine era" from 1864 to 1922. Based on census data and other sources; 7 photos, 2 tables, 11 notes.   R. J. Fahl

197. Knight, Oliver. WESTERN SADDLEMAKERS, 1865-1920. *Montana 1983 33(2): 16-29.* Traces the history of saddles and saddlemakers in the West. Saddlemakers were a vital part of the West but left few written records. The American stock saddle incorporated a variety of improvements on earlier Mexican horned saddles, so that American saddlemakers' products were distinct from Hispanic saddle styles. Saddlemakers were highly mobile, and moved from town to town as conditions or fancy demanded. Based on primary materials in the Panhandle-Plains Museum, the Colorado State Historical Society, the Denver Public Library, and the University of Wyoming Library; 7 illus., 48 notes.   R. C. Myers

198. LaBrack, Bruce. OCCUPATIONAL SPECIALIZATION A-MONG RURAL CALIFORNIA SIKHS: THE INTERPLAY OF CULTURE AND ECONOMICS. *Amerasia J. 1982 9(2): 29-56.* Traces the history of rural Sikhs in California during 1904-82. Finds that a combination of culture, a desire for land and an extended family (both formal and informal), and of economics such as frugal lifestyles and dual-employment, have led the rural Sikhs to concentrate on specialty orchard crops. Secondary sources; 2 tables, 37 notes.   E. S. Johnson

199. Lapitskii, M. I. BOLSHOI BILL: WILLIAM HAYWOOD (1869-1928) [Big Bill: William Haywood (1869-1928)]. *Novaia i Noveishaia Istoriia [USSR] 1974 (2): 77-97.* William Dudley Haywood held an important place in the history of the workers' and socialist movements in the late 19th and early 20th centuries in the United States. As a revolutionary he fought with reformism, took an active part in workers' movements, including the creation of trade unions, and became a prominent leader of the American proletariat. Gives an account of Haywood's ancestry and life from his birth in the far west, the development of his political ideas and activity, his emigration to the USSR in March 1921, to his death in March 1928. Primary and secondary sources; 70 notes.   L. Smith

200. Leighow, Susan R. JOANNA FURNACE WOMEN: 1881-1925, A STUDY OF WOMEN'S ROLES IN INDUSTRIAL SOCIETY. *Pennsylvania Heritage 1982 8(4): 13-16.* Describes the lives of surviving women who grew up in the Berks County industrial complex known as Joanna Furnace between 1881 and 1925, where ironworkers and their families worked and lived.

201. Levine, Susan. HIDDEN HISTORIES: SOUTHERN LABOR AND THE WOMAN WORKER. *Rev. in Am. Hist. 1978 6(3): 288-292.* Review article prompted by *Class, Sex, and the Woman Worker* (Westport, Conn.: Greenwood Pr., 1977), edited by Milton Cantor and Bruce Laurie, and *Essays in Southern Labor History: Selected Papers, Southern Labor History Conference, 1976* (Westport, Conn.: Greenwood Pr., 1977), edited by Gary M. Fink and Merl E. Reed.

202. Litoff, Judy Barrett and Litoff, Hal. WORKING WOMEN IN MAINE: A NOTE ON SOURCES. *Labor Hist. 1976 17(1): 88-95.* Surveys sources for the study of working women in Maine, including published works, articles, dissertations and theses, government publications, and unpublished papers. 5 notes.   L. L. Athey

203. Maldonado, Edwin. CONTRACT LABOR AND THE ORIGINS OF PUERTO RICAN COMMUNITIES IN THE UNITED STATES. *Int. Migration Rev. 1979 13(1): 103-121.* Describes the rise of Puerto Rican communities in the United States before, during, and after World War II as a result of the need for cheap agricultural and industrial labor.

204. Marcum, John P. and Radosh, Mary. RELIGIOUS AFFILIATION, LABOR FORCE PARTICIPATION AND FERTILITY. *Sociol. Analysis 1981 42(4): 353-362.* Different teachings on family and procreation make balancing the demands of church and career more difficult for Catholic than Protestant women. For Catholics, fertility is high and similar to that of women who have never worked; for Protestants, fertility is low and similar to that of currently employed women. This pattern occurs because lower contraceptive efficacy leads more Catholic women to leave the labor force. Based on the 1965 National Fertility Survey.   J/S

205. May, Elaine Tyler. THE PRESSURE TO PROVIDE: CLASS, CONSUMERISM, AND DIVORCE IN URBAN AMERICA 1880-1920. *J. of Social Hist.* 1978 12(2): 180-193. Compares and examines the effects of heightened material aspirations on white-collar and blue-collar Americans at the turn of the century. While a rising standard of living may have enhanced family life for some classes, it often wreaked havoc on those homes which could not afford the fruits of abundance. The emergence of an affluent society paralleled the skyrocketing of American divorce rate. A sample of 500 litigations in Los Angeles in the 1880's and another 500 from 1920 compared with a sample of 250 divorces filed throughout New Jersey in 1920 can show effects of economic change over time. Issues involving money became increasingly important. For the affluent couples tension arose over how the family's resources should be spent; for lower white-collar ranks status consideration clashed with limited incomes; and for working class couples, mass consumption remained out of reach thus contributing to a greater sense of economic insecurity and heightened frustrations. Primary and secondary sources; 5 tables, 22 notes.   R. S. Sliwoski

206. McBane, Margo and Winegarden, Mary. LABOR PAINS: AN ORAL HISTORY OF CALIFORNIA WOMEN FARMWORKERS. *California History* 1979 58(2): 179-181. The California Women Farmworkers Project is producing a radio program and multimedia slide and tape show relating the contributions of women to California farm labor. More than 70 interviews have been conducted under various oral history projects, with funding from the California Council for the Humanities in Public Policy. The project investigates a topic neglected by historians and public officials. Women comprise more than 40% of the agricultural labor force, yet their efforts remain largely unknown. Questions such as poor union representation, job discrimination, medical care, and problems of working mothers are now being examined. The project focuses on the work of women in fields and packing sheds. Photo.   A. Hoffman

207. Melosh, Barbara. WOMEN'S WORK. *Rev. in Am. Hist.* 1980 8(3): 351-359. Review essay of Thomas Dublin's *Women at Work: The Transformation of Work and Community in Lowell, Massachusetts, 1826-1860* (New York: Columbia U. Pr., 1979) and Susan Estabrook Kennedy's *If All We Did Was to Weep at Home: A History of White Working-class Women in America* (Bloomington: Indiana U. Pr., 1979); 1600-1970's.

208. Metzler, William H. MEXICAN AMERICANS AND THE ACQUISITIVE SYNDROME. *J. of Mexican Am. Hist.* 1973 3(1): 1-12. In Mexico, with an extremely diverse culture, the acquiring of new knowledge and techniques has varied greatly. The stratified culture of the Aztec was merely replaced by the Spanish, and when the Spanish were removed village patrons assumed the autocratic role. Much of this submissive nature has fit all too well into American labor requirements in agricultural areas. Mexican American organizations in America are now becoming effective in countering this native submissiveness. Secondary sources; 31 notes.   R. T. Fulton

209. Montgomery, David. THE PAST AND FUTURE OF WORKERS' CONTROL. *Radical Am.* 1979 13(6): 6-23. Traces the history of the struggle for workers' control over at least part of the production process in the 19th and 20th centuries, which became increasingly difficult as mechanization and large-scale production increased labor productivity and increased the number of supervisors to overlook the workers; and briefly compares and contrasts the struggles of the 19th and 20th centuries.

210. Mormino, Gary. "WE WORKED HARD AND TOOK CARE OF OUR OWN": ORAL HISTORY AND ITALIANS IN TAMPA. *Labor Hist.* 1982 23(3): 395-415. Italian immigrants migrated to Tampa, Florida, from three Sicilian villages in the southwestern province of Agrigento. The Italians first worked as cigar makers (as did Spanish and Cuban immigrants), though many more Italians later became owners of small stores and fruit stands than did the Spaniards or Cubans. The impact of migration was mitigated by mutual aid societies and a close family structure, but the surprisingly few Catholic churches in Ybor City, the Italian section of Tampa, attest to the anticlericalism of these immigrants. Based on interviews with Tampa's Italian immigrants and their children, contemporary newspaper accounts, and other primary sources; 3 tables, 70 notes.   L. F. Velicer

211. Mormino, Gary R. and Pozzetta, George E. IMMIGRANT WOMEN IN TAMPA: THE ITALIAN EXPERIENCE, 1890-1930. *Florida Hist. Q.* 1983 61(3): 296-312. Italian women played a significant role in the cigar industry of Tampa, Florida. The Italian family structure was able to adjust to New World conditions. Italian women demonstrated frugality, hard work, and a retention of family bonds in coping with the new conditions of Florida. Based on personal interviews and other sources; 4 fig., 57 notes.   N. A. Kuntz

212. Moseley, Russell. FROM AVOCATION TO JOB: THE CHANGING NATURE OF SCIENTIFIC PRACTICE. *Social Studies of Sci.* [Great Britain] 1979 9(4): 511-522. Review article traces the professionalization of scientific work, 19th-20th centuries, and scientists' perception of their changing roles.

213. Mullings, Leith. ON WOMEN, WORK AND SOCIETY. *Freedomways* 1980 20(1): 15-24. This anthropological perspective questions the assumption that the division of labor in early society was based on male and female anatomical differences and is likely to persist, based on 1970's studies on the evolution of the family and the history of women's roles in the labor force and society in Europe and the United States since colonial times.

214. Perlmann, Joel. WORKING CLASS HOMEOWNERSHIP AND CHILDREN'S SCHOOLING IN PROVIDENCE, RHODE ISLAND, 1880-1925. *Hist. of Educ. Q.* 1983 23(2): 175-193. Working-class families usually did not take their children out of school and put them to work in order to buy homes. Statistical examination of homeownership and schooling patterns in Providence suggests that while sacrifice of a child's education to homeownership was a possible strategy open to families, it was not an important one. Alternatives like taking in boarders, delaying home buying, or restricting family size were more likely strategies. Homeownership was more likely to be associated with greater school attendance than with less. Based on US Census Bureau reports and Providence school records; 19 notes.

J. T. Holton

215. Pred, Allen. PRODUCTION, FAMILY AND FREE-TIME PROJECT: A TIME-GEOGRAPHIC ON THE INDIVIDUAL AND SOCIETAL CHANGE IN NINETEENTH-CENTURY U.S. CITIES. *J. of Hist. Geography* 1981 7(1): 3-36. Examines individual and family experience in artisan and factory modes of production. Factory workers lost the self-determination in their working conditions, which accounted for 10 or more hours daily. Life became more regimented and disciplined at work, but those traits were lost in the home where women were required to make more decisions and perform more duties. Other family members with jobs became more independent and self-centered with their income. These conditions led to a minimum of extra money and a consequent reduction in average family size. Free-time activities centered on those taking place on Sunday with little cost. Attendance at major league baseball games by industrial wage earners illustrates these constraints. Based on US Census and other sources; 3 tables, 2 graphs, 122 notes.   A. J. Larson

216. Quinlan, Daniel C. and Shackelford, Jean A. LABOR FORCE PARTICIPATION RATES OF WOMEN AND THE RISE OF THE TWO-EARNER FAMILY. *Am. Econ. Rev.* 1980 70(2): 209-212. The rise of the two-earner family comes from a double demand model encouraged first in nonprimary industries and second, since 1950, in clerical occupations. Maryann O'Hagan Keating's discussion (p. 213) questions the conclusion while remaining sympathetic because the data did not explore the occupations with strong quasi-monopolistic licensing where sex-typing has been historically prevalent. Covers 1900-78. Table, 6 ref.   D. K. Pickens

217. Rapone, Anita. WOMEN'S WORK: OFFICES AND OPPORTUNITY. *AHA Perspectives* 1983 21(1): 13-15. Clerical work during the 1870's-1920's offered women high wages, paid benefits, and many career opportunities, but since the 1920's changes in the organization of clerical work have blocked occupational mobility and have reduced women's wages.

218. Reverby, Susan. THE SEARCH FOR THE HOSPITAL YARDSTICK: NURSING AND THE RATIONALIZATION OF HOSPITAL WORK. Reverby, Susan and Rosner, David, ed. *Health Care in*

America: Essays in Social History (Philadelphia: Temple U. Pr., 1979): 206-225. Examines the relationship between nurses and hospital administration from the establishment of the first nursing school in 1873 through the 1950's. By the 1920's human relations and psychological techniques from industry were introduced to instill loyalty to the institution. By the Depression, the use of nurse trainees rather than nurses who had graduated from the schools and the rapid turnover of employees were perceived as financial and professional liabilities rather than assets. With the introduction of scientific management, nurses lost the one-to-one relationship with patients as they became more task-oriented. 67 notes.   S

219. Robertson, Paul L. EMPLOYERS AND ENGINEERING EDUCATION IN BRITAIN AND THE UNITED STATES, 1890-1914. *Business Hist. [Great Britain] 1981 23(1): 42-58.* After the 1880's the number of engineers educated annually in Britain dropped rapidly behind the number in the United States and Germany. This has been ascribed to the attitudes of British businessmen. The author compares attitudes toward higher technical education by British and American businessmen at meetings of engineering societies, and shows that from about 1900 employers expressed similar opinions. Differences in the structure of industry made it less necessary for British firms to employ graduate engineers. Differences in social structure and aspirations made it more expensive for the British to obtain educated personnel. Therefore it may have been economically rational for British businessmen to emphasize practical training. Secondary sources; 49 notes.
                                                              B. L. Crapster

220. Rotella, Elyce J. THE TRANSFORMATION OF THE AMERICAN OFFICE: CHANGES IN EMPLOYMENT AND TECHNOLOGY. *J. of Econ. Hist. 1981 41(1): 51-57.* Between 1870 and 1930 production methods in American offices changed substantially as mechanical devices were introduced and work was subdivided and routinized. A close correspondence is found between the timing of changes in the sex composition of clerical employment and the adoption of new techniques. The new technology led to increased hiring of female clerical workers by reducing the firm-specific skill requirements for clerical jobs.   J

221. Rotella, Elyce J. WOMEN'S LABOR FORCE PARTICIPATION AND THE DECLINE OF THE FAMILY ECONOMY IN THE UNITED STATES. *Explorations in Econ. Hist. 1980 17(2): 95-117.* The standard household-production-oriented model of female labor explains the behavior of single women in 1890 and married women in 1930. Their actions reflected the development of the modern pattern of labor force participation in which single women become less responsive to household variables and married women more responsive. This is consistent with the decline of the family economy as it existed in the 19th century. Based on published statistics and reports, the author's unpublished dissertation, and secondary accounts; 6 tables, 24 notes, 27 ref., appendix.   P. J. Coleman

222. Rowland, Andrew. TANNING LEATHER, TANNING HIDES: HEALTH AND SAFETY STRUGGLE IN A LEATHER FACTORY. *Radical Am. 1980 14(6): 23-37.* Notes the circumstances in a California tannery and the 20th-century history of the industrial safety and insurance industry theory designed to place responsibility for accidents almost exclusively on the "careless" worker, and the lack of accountability for poor industrial design. The division of safety into short-run physical safety and long-run health considerations becomes even more questionable with the growing introduction of exotic chemicals into virtually every industrial process. Based on six months on site as a safety researcher; 4 illus., 22 notes.   C. M. Hough

223. Schlissel, Lillian. WOMEN'S DIARIES ON THE WESTERN FRONTIER. *Am. Studies [Lawrence, KS] 1977 18(1): 87-100.* Women suffered sharp dislocations in western travel, and traditional work patterns were overturned. Women worked like men. This challenged traditional gender role, class orientation, and self-evaluation, and split women's world. Women as well as men became civilizing elements; but did the frontier perhaps also work against the pioneers, rendering them more primitive? Did it set women against men? Primary and secondary sources; 53 notes.   J. Andrew

224. Schneider, John C. OMAHA VAGRANTS AND THE CHARACTER OF WESTERN HOBO LABOR, 1887-1913. *Nebraska Hist. 1982 63(2): 255-272.* Careful analysis of a 26-year sample of vagrancy arrest records in Omaha suggests, among other things, that the transient population became almost exclusively native born; that those who tramped were usually unskilled, but included the skilled during depressions; that some men were more likely to tramp at certain times of the year; and that as early as 1900 the full-time hobo was becoming less visible among migrant and seasonal laborers. Based on manuscript Omaha police arrest ledgers, other official documents, newspapers, and secondary sources; 37 notes.   R. Lowitt

225. Schwendinger, Robert J. SEA SHANTIES: FLIGHTS OF SPIRIT BEFORE THE MAST. *Am. West 1977 14(3): 50-55.* Sea shanties (chanteys, chaunteys) are folk songs of the sea that helped to establish and to maintain the pace of labor. Each one was used for a particular activity on shipboard: the short drag or short haul, the long drag or halyard, the capstan or windlass, the forecastle song, walkaways, hand-over-hand, and pumping shanties. A good shantyman was usually paid more than a common sailor because he could spur the sailors on in their work. 4 illus.   D. L. Smith

226. Schwieder, Dorothy. ITALIAN-AMERICANS IN IOWA'S COAL MINING INDUSTRY. *Ann. of Iowa 1982 46(4): 263-278.* Italians who came to work in the coal mines of Iowa did not undergo the shattering, alienating experiences of the "new" immigrants described by Oscar Handlin and other writers. Instead, they adjusted to life in the new world with a minimum of difficulty. Based on interviews and other primary sources; 4 photos, 21 notes.   P. L. Petersen

227. Segal, David R.; Lynch, Barbara Ann; and Blair, John D. THE CHANGING AMERICAN SOLDIER: WORK-RELATED ATTITUDES OF U.S. ARMY PERSONNEL IN WORLD WAR II AND THE 1970'S. *Am. J. of Sociol. 1979 85(1): 95-108.*

228. Selavan, Ida Cohen. JEWISH WAGE EARNERS IN PITTSBURGH, 1890-1930. *Am. Jewish Hist. Q. 1976 65(3): 272-285.* The formation of a Jewish proletariat in Pittsburgh began after the influx of a large number of Jews from Eastern Europe. During the 40 years under discussion Jewish wage earners were found in large numbers among stogy makers, the needle trades, and the bakery trade, which was unionized in 1906. These three industries, each different in conditions, wages, and work force, are described on the basis of oral interviews, contemporary journals, newspapers, etc. Attempts to unionize tailors and seamstresses were successful only in the larger shops before 1914. 39 notes.   F. Rosenthal.

229. Shofner, Jerrell H. FORCED LABOR IN THE FLORIDA FORESTS, 1880-1950. *J. of Forest Hist. 1981 25(1): 14-25.* Two institutions—convict leasing and debt peonage—developed in Florida after Reconstruction to replace slavery as labor systems. Both were commonly employed in the lumber and turpentine industries to keep labor costs low. Although sanctioned by state law and local custom, these labor practices were sporadically threatened by federal officials from about 1900 until finally eradicated in the late 1940's by changing technology and reduced employment levels in the forest industries. Convict leasing and debt peonage, involving both blacks and whites, are illustrated through examples of federal investigations and court cases. Based on federal archival records and other primary and secondary sources; 9 photos, 39 notes.   R. J. Fahl

230. Smith, Dorothy E. WOMEN AND TRADE UNIONS: THE U.S. AND BRITISH EXPERIENCE (REVIEW ESSAY). *Resources for Feminist Res. [Canada] 1981 10(2): 53-59.* Discusses six books (1977-80), with different themes and approaches, that build a basis for the understanding of the relation of women's struggle within the labor movement to the common struggle of the working class of men and women; 18th century-1980.

231. Smith, Joan. THE WAY WE WERE: WOMEN AND WORK. *Feminist Studies 1982 8(2): 437-456.* Reviews Philip Foner's *Women and the American Labor Movement: From Colonial Times to the Eve of World War I* (1979), Leslie Woodcock Tentler's *Wage-Earning Women: Industrial Work and Family Life in the United States, 1900-1930* (1979), Thomas Dublin's *Women at Work: The Transformation of Work and*

Community in Lowell, Massachusetts, 1826-1860 (1979), David Katzman's *Seven Days a Week: Women and Domestic Service in Industrializing America* (1978), and *Class, Sex and the Woman Worker* (1977), edited by Milton Canter and Bruce Laurie. Each work is assessed for its ability to illuminate the relationship between paid and unpaid work in women's lives. 8 notes.   S. Hildenbrand

232. Smith, Ralph E. THE MOVEMENT OF WOMEN INTO THE LABOR FORCE. Smith, Ralph E., ed. *The Subtle Revolution: Women at Work* (Washington: Urban Inst., 1979): 1-29. Introduces this collection of essays by tracing the entrance of women into the paid labor force over the past century, focusing on what types of work women do, the context in which women's roles are changing and how the women's movement has effected the changes, and attempts to forecast the increase of women in the labor force through 1990.

233. Spier, William. A SOCIAL HISTORY OF MANGANESE MINING IN THE BATESVILLE DISTRICT OF INDEPENDENCE COUNTY. *Arkansas Hist. Q. 1977 36(2): 130-157.* Cushing, Arkansas, was a manganese mining center which was developed in the late 1840's and reached its peak production during the 1890's-1930's. Most workers were either local farmers wishing to earn extra money during slack seasons or migrants from nearby states. Pay was only $1.50 per day or $4.00 per ton of coal mined and delivered to Batesville, the nearest railroad terminus. Workers enjoyed simple, but often rowdy, lives. There was little food, clothing, or shelter for their families, and only the hope for a big strike tomorrow kept them going. Based on interviews with former miners; 4 illus., 94 notes.   T. L. Savitt

234. Stern, Marjorie. AN INSIDER'S VIEW OF THE TEACHERS UNION AND WOMEN'S RIGHTS. *Urban Rev. 1973 6(5-6): 46-49.* The American Federation of Teachers was among the first organizations, with its foundation in 1916, to promote equal rights for women; includes a description of the structure of the union.

235. Stoddard, Ellwyn R. ILLEGAL MEXICAN LABOR IN THE BORDERLANDS: INSTITUTIONALIZED SUPPORT OF AN UNLAWFUL PRACTICE. *Pacific Sociol. Rev. 1976 19(2): 175-210.* Analysis of the use of illegal Mexican labor since the 1820's reveals that US social institutions support the practice in Texas and other areas in the Southwest.

236. Strasser, Susan M. MISTRESS AND MAID, EMPLOYER AND EMPLOYEE: DOMESTIC SERVICE REFORM IN THE UNITED STATES, 1892-1920. *Marxist Perspectives 1978 1(4): 52-67.* Describes the rise of employment of servants during 1892-1920 in the United States and the resultant reforms.

237. Sutton, Susan Buck. LIFE ON THE ROAD: MIDWESTERN MIGRANT FARMWORKER SURVIVAL SKILLS. *Migration Today 1983 11(1): 24-31.* Describes the migrant farmworker population in Indiana, 1930's-83, contradicts several misconceptions about this group, and finds that approximately 90% are from Mexico; this farmworker group is basically a family-organized population engaged in a vital industry as they adjust their lives to the conditions of seasonal work.

238. Sylvers, Malcolm. SULLA STORIA DEL MOVIMENTO OPERAIO AMERICANO [On the history of the American workers' movement]. *Studi Storici [Italy] 1977 18(4): 153-162.* An examination of the problem of the apparent lack of a working class in America. Studies of workers in the United States have traditionally focused on the labor movement or unions rather than on the laborers. To unearth the working class, the author recommends a methodological inquiry that incorporates the historical peculiarity of the experience of American laborers but is informed by a knowledge of world capitalism and the organized, self-conscious working class. The strict ties between proletarian leadership and class, for example, reveal the political importance of the working class as a threat to capitalism resulting in a policy of welfarism. Secondary sources; 16 notes.   J. R. Banker

239. Tedebrand, Lars-Göran. STRIKES AND POLITICAL RADICALISM IN SWEDEN AND EMIGRATION TO THE UNITED STATES. *Swedish-American Hist. Q. 1983 34(3): 194-210.* Approximately 1.3 million Swedes immigrated to North America between 1851 and 1930, mostly between 1880 and World War I. Emigration was initially prompted by a growth in the rural population combined with the slow growth of industry. As industry and the labor force grew, class tension intensified, resulting in labor organization and strikes. Case studies of strikes and socialist activity in Sweden between 1879 and 1906 indicate that strike failures were followed by noticeable increases in the emigration of laborers. Swedish immigrants arrived with some knowledge of the labor situation in the United States and a critical attitude toward American capitalism. Based partly on Swedish government statistics; 2 photos, 2 tables, 37 notes.   K. E. Ford

240. Thomas, Patricia J. WOMEN IN THE MILITARY: AMERICA AND THE BRITISH COMMONWEALTH: HISTORICAL SIMILARITIES. *Armed Forces and Soc. 1978 4(4): 623-646.* A historical survey of women in the military in the United States, Great Britain, Canada, and Australia in World War I, World War II, and after World War II. In each nation military and political leaders used women volunteers in wartime in narrowly defined categories as nonsoldiers and nonsailors. Only after the World War II era has the military leadership, and only then under the pressure of societal and court rulings, altered attitudes and policies toward women. In general, women in the United States have progressed further toward full integration into the military as soldiers and sailors, although several major questions remain unresolved. Secondary works; 12 notes.   J. P. Harahan

241. Tomes, Nancy. 'LITTLE WORLD OF OUR OWN': THE PENNSYLVANIA HOSPITAL TRAINING SCHOOL FOR NURSES, 1895-1907. *J. of the Hist. of Medicine and Allied Sci. 1978 33(4): 507-530.* Lucy Walker was superintendent of the Pennsylvania Hospital Training School for Nurses in Philadelphia from 1895 to 1907. She improved discipline and improved the quality of nursing care. She established a strict hierarchical system, and insisted on absolute discipline from her students. By 1899 she had replaced the untrained nurses at the hospital with her own graduates. Most of the students were from small towns, and they were Protestant. They had a wide range of educational background. For those who were educated, nursing was a respectable alternative to medical school. For others, it was a livelihood rather than a profession. The school did not attract or accept urban working class women. One problem was class conflict between the middle class students and the working class patients. Lucy Walker sought to improve the nursing profession. She transmitted to American hospitals British methods which were the beginning of professionalization. American nurses followed her in adapting those forms to the 20th-century hospital. 66 notes.   M. Kaufman

242. Tornquist, Elizabeth. A WOMAN'S WORK... *Southern Exposure 1976 4(1-2): 125-127.* Examines statistics concerning women workers, 1920-70, especially those pertaining to women in the South and minorities; changes are necessary in pay equality, work conditions, and advancement opportunities.

243. Urban, Wayne. ORGANIZED TEACHERS AND EDUCATIONAL REFORM DURING THE PROGRESSIVE ERA: 1890-1920. *Hist. of Educ. Q. 1976 16(1): 35-52.* Examines attitudes of teachers' organizations toward educational reform in Atlanta, Georgia, New York City, and Chicago, Illinois, during 1890-1920.

244. Ury, Claude M. WOMEN IN TRADE UNIONS: AN HISTORICAL OVERVIEW. *Social Studies 1981 72(6): 280-283.* Presents a historical analysis of women's role in the trade unions, indicating that women must remain productive in the US labor force. Significant changes in family life are being brought about as a result of this participation. Biblio.   L. R. Raife

245. Vanek, Joann. HOUSEHOLD TECHNOLOGY AND SOCIAL STATUS: RISING LIVING STANDARDS AND STATUS AND RESIDENCE DIFFERENCES IN HOUSEWORK. *Technology and Culture 1978 19(3): 361-375.* In 1900 American housework varied greatly according to social status. The contrast between urban and rural families was especially sharp. Between 1930 and 1970, the mass production of electrical appliances made possible the standardization of housework across class and geographical lines. Concomitantly, the advertising media propagated a common "ideology of housework." Based on social surveys; 4 tables, 38 notes.   C. O. Smith

246. Vanek, Joann. WORK, LEISURE, AND FAMILY ROLES: FARM HOUSEHOLDS IN THE UNITED STATES, 1920-1955. *J. of Family Hist. 1980 5(4): 422-431.* There appears to have been little change in the work and leisure time of farmers and farm wives between the 1920's and the 1950's. In addition, the work and leisure patterns of these two groups were quite similar. Much leisure time was shared, and separate activities were similar. Table, 3 notes, biblio.   T. W. Smith

247. Walker, Samuel. THE RISE AND FALL OF THE POLICE-WOMEN'S MOVEMENT, 1905-1975. Hawes, Joseph M., ed. *Law and Order in American History* (Port Washington, N.Y.: Kennikat Pr., 1979): 101-111. Traces efforts to include women on police forces to 1905 when the first known woman to have full police powers was hired by the Portland, Oregon, police department, until 1975 when women were still being hired mostly as clerical workers or in juvenile divisions.

248. Watts, Eugene J. PATTERNS OF PROMOTION: THE ST. LOUIS POLICE DEPARTMENT, 1899-1975. *Social Sci. Hist. 1982 6(2): 233-258.* Major determinants for bureaucratic promotions include seniority, merit, and social background. This case study examines promotion among a sample of 1,954 men on the St. Louis Police Department to assess the relative importance of each factor. Seniority was a critical factor, but merit also played a significant role. There is little evidence that preservice social background had a major effect on promotion. Basic promotion patterns remained surprisingly stable through the study. Based on the personnel files of the St. Louis Police Department; 13 notes, 9 tables, biblio.   L. K. Blaser

249. Weber, Michael P. RESIDENTIAL AND OCCUPATIONAL PATTERNS OF ETHNIC MINORITIES IN NINETEENTH CENTURY PITTSBURGH. *Pennsylvania Hist. 1977 44(4): 317-334.* Focuses on occupational and residential patterns of ethnic groups in four Pittsburgh industrial wards during 1880-1920. In comparison to native-born workers, Irish and German immigrants were not disadvantaged in occupational mobility. Blue-collar workers who remained in Pittsburgh experienced considerable upward mobility. Age had little influence on transiency or persistence, but place of birth and occupation did influence residential persistence. Based on census data; 3 illus., map, 3 tables, 16 notes.   D. C. Swift

250. White, Lynn K. and Brinkerhoff, David B. THE SEXUAL DIVISION OF LABOR: EVIDENCE FROM CHILDHOOD. *Social Forces 1981 60(1): 170-181.* Sex typing begins very early in work roles and, by the time children reach adolescence, sharp differences exist between "boys' work" and "girls' work." Multiple classification analysis indicates that family background characteristics and family structure have relatively little impact compared to sex and age of child determinants of sex typing.   J/S

251. Wirth, Arthur G. ISSUES AFFECTING EDUCATION AND WORK IN THE EIGHTIES: EFFICIENCY VERSUS INDUSTRIAL DEMOCRACY, A HISTORICAL SURVEY. *Teachers Coll. Record 1977 79(1): 55-67.* A continuing philosophical debate about the relation between work and education, first formulated in the United States in the early 1900's, is likely to intensify in the next decade. On one side, Charles Prosser (1860-1916) and David Snedden (1868-1951) felt that the purpose of education was to fit future workers to precise roles in the industrial economy. John Dewey, however, believed that students should be educated for self-fulfillment through work and that businesses should adjust to workers' needs. Primary and secondary sources; 24 notes.   E. Bailey

252. Zieger, Robert H. WOMEN'S WORK. *Rev. in Am. Hist. 1983 11(2): 186-189.* Reviews Alice Kessler-Harris's *Out to Work: A History of Wage-Earning Women in the United States* (1982), which argues that working women have suffered from segmentation in the job market, erosion of working skills, and confining ideologies from the 18th century to 1970.

253. —. [PAY GAPS AND WOMEN]. *J. of Econ. Hist. 1982 42(2): 423-439.*

Niemi, Albert W., Jr. THE INCREASING PAY GAP FOR WOMEN IN TEXTILE AND CLOTHING INDUSTRIES: A REEX-AMINATION, *pp. 423-426.* Suggests that the conclusion by Paul F. McGouldrick and Michael B. Tannen in their earlier (December 1980) article analyzing the male-female gap should be rejected because evidence shows stability in wages during 1910-70, not an increasing gap.

Thornton, Robert J. and Hyclak, Thomas. THE INCREASING PAY GAP FOR WOMEN IN THE TEXTILE AND CLOTHING INDUSTRIES, 1910 TO 1970: AN ALTERNATIVE EXPLA-NATION, *pp. 427-431.* Rejects McGouldrick and Tannen's conclusions as statistical illusions.

McGouldrick, Paul F. and Tannen, Michael B. THE RISING MALE-FEMALE PAY GAP: CONTRARY EVIDENCE AND NEW FINDINGS, *pp. 432-439.* Finds the criticisms inconsistent with statistical evidence but agrees more evidence is needed. 26 notes, 6 tables.   N. A. Newhouse

The Labor Movement

254. Aronowitz, Stanley. TRADE UNIONS IN AMERICA. *Can. Dimension 1976 11(6): 48-59.* Examines the bureaucratization of labor unions, their cooperation with business through such instruments as collective bargaining, their conservative political ideology, the failure of the CIO since the 1930's, and the necessity for 1970's radicals to develop a revolutionary consciousness among workers.

255. Askol'dova, S. M. RELIGIIA I AMERIKANSKII TRED-IUNIONIZM V KONTSE XIX-NACHALE XX VEKA [Religion and American trade unionism at the turn of the 20th century]. *Voprosy Istorii [USSR] 1973 (9): 89-104.* The article is devoted to the ideological rapprochement between the church seeking to "modernize" its programme and American trade unionism which renounced socialist demands and became an instrument for exerting bourgeois influence on the American proletariat. This rapprochement was aimed at achieving coordinated action in the struggle against the socialist movement in the U.S.A. The collaboration of the AFL with the Catholic Church and the various Protestant trends was adroitly used by the bourgeoisie when it resorted to the ill-famed New Deal for the sake of salvaging capitalism.   J

256. Barbash, Jack. LABOR MOVEMENT THEORY AND THE INSTITUTIONAL SETTING. *Monthly Labor Rev. 1981 104(9): 34-37.* Briefly describes the utopian, Marxist, Leninist, Wisconsin, neo-Marxist, and social contract labor movement theories, concluding with the author's theory about labor movement goals since the 19th century.

257. Berger, Henry W. UNIONS AND EMPIRE: ORGANIZED LABOR AND AMERICAN CORPORATIONS ABROAD. *Peace and Change 1976 3(4): 34-48.* Discusses the AFL's (and later AFL-CIO's) role in, and attitudes toward, US multinational corporations 1880's-1970's, emphasizing employment, economic expansionism, and foreign policy.

258. Berkowitz, Monroe. "ECONOMIC ASPECTS OF COMPULSO-RY TRADE UNIONISM": A NOTE. *Oxford Econ. Papers [Great Britain] 1955 7(2): 221-225.* Criticizes V. L. Allen's "Some Economic Aspects of Compulsory Trade Unionism" *Oxford Econ. Papers 1954 6(1): 69-81,* and states the differences between 20th-century managerial attitudes toward compulsory trade unionism in the United States and Great Britain.

259. Boccaccio, Mary. LABOR RESOURCES AT THE UNIVERSI-TY OF MARYLAND AT COLLEGE PARK. *Labor Hist. 1982 23(4): 498-501.* Describes four labor union collections held by the University of Maryland, College Park Archives: the records of the Cigar Makers International Union, the Tobacco Workers International Union, the Industrial Union of Marine and Shipbuilding Workers of America, and the Bakery and Confectionary Workers International Union.   L. F. Velicer

260. Cacciatore, Giuseppe. SU UNA LETTURA STORICA DELLA QUESTIONE SINDACALE [On an historical reading of the union question]. *Pensiero Pol. [Italy] 1978 11(3): 406-410.* Review article

prompted by Giuseppe Acocella's *Teorie dello Stato e questione sindacale. Appunti per una storia delle idee politiche* (Salerno: Consorzio Provinciale per l'Istruzione tecnica, 1976), which precisely delineates the role of the union in countries including France, Germany, and the United States that are dominated by liberal democratic economic models. In such countries, the union is not a transforming power, but a political agent which influences the state and renders social and structural reform a problem of general concern rather than a specific goal.   S. Ruffo-Fiore

261. Chaison, Gary N. A NOTE ON UNION MERGER TRENDS, 1900-1978. *Industrial and Labor Relations Rev. 1980 34(1): 114-120.* This paper examines 143 union mergers that have occurred since the turn of the century, identifying the frequency and forms of mergers (106 absorptions and 37 amalgamations) and the affiliations of merger partners. The data for three broad time periods and for five-year intervals indicate, among other trends, a long-term decline in the proportion of amalgamations and an increase in merger activity since the formation of the AFL-CIO in 1955. The author also discusses the frequency and forms of mergers between affiliates of the AFL, CIO, AFL-CIO, and unaffiliated unions.   J

262. Davies, J. Kenneth. THE SECULARIZATION OF THE UTAH LABOR MOVEMENT. *Utah Hist. Q. 1977 45(2): 108-134.* In the 1850's, the Mormon church encouraged a religiously oriented worker movement. The 1860's brought nonreligious influences: war induced inflation, large numbers of non-Mormon workers, and association with national unions. Church cooperatives, United Orders, and the Board of Trade movement reduced Mormon influence on the budding unions. Nonintercourse with Gentiles, union violence, and closed shops induced some to leave unions. Political and business secularization of the 1890's ended the church's economic program. By 1896 labor secularization was accomplished. Primary and secondary sources; 5 illus., 51 notes.
J. L. Hazelton

263. Davis, Mike. THE AFL-CIO'S SECOND CENTURY. *New Left Rev. [Great Britain] 1982 (136): 43-54.* Discusses the history of the AFL-CIO from the establishment of its antecedents in 1881, with special attention to its relationship with the Carter and Reagan administrations.

264. Ferrer, Juan de la Cruz. USA: LOS SINDICATOS SE QUEDAN ATRÁS [USA: the unions lag behind]. *Nuestro Tiempo [Spain] 1978 49(284): 68-72.* Recent conventions of the AFL-CIO give the impression that its leaders are old and tired, and that after the great victories of the golden age of the unions they are incapable of adapting to a system that has undergone profound changes; 1935-77.

265. Grant, Jim. THE ORGANIZED UNORGANIZED. *Southern Exposure 1976 4(1-2): 132-135.* Examines unionization movements in the South since the 1920's; mentions northern industries which moved south to avoid organization and members' and organizers' stepped-up efforts to maintain union organization, 1968-74.

266. Green, George N. THE UNION MOVEMENT IN THE SOUTHWEST. *Dissent 1980 27(4): 485-492.* Recounts the history of the union movement in Texas and the rest of the Sun Belt, accounts for the fact that over the past 40 years Southern workers have unionized at only half the rate of the national average, lists trends identified by Ray Marshall as favoring union growth in the South at present, and predicts that the attitudes, laws, and economic conditions that hinder southern and southwestern unions will change significantly within a generation.

267. Haines, Randall A. WALTER LANFERSIEK: SOCIALIST FROM CINCINNATI. *Cincinnati Hist. Soc. Bull. 1982 40(2): 124-144.* Biography of Walter Lanfersiek (1873-1962), later known as Walter B. Landell, who served as national executive secretary of the Socialist Party of America from 1913 to 1916; he was active in the labor and peace movements, particularly prior to World War I.

268. Harap, Louis. IRVING HOWE AND JEWISH AMERICA. *J. of Ethnic Studies 1977 4(4): 95-104.* Review article prompted by Irving Howe's *World of Our Fathers* (New York: Harcourt Brace Jovanovich, 1976). The book was written so that the receding culture of Yiddish America would be adequately chronicled for future generations in a single, readable work. A central theme is the role of the socialist and

labor movements on New York City's East Side. An avowed "democratic socialist," Howe's chief criticisms of contemporary society are against those he regards as a false left, rather than the right. His "abstract, perfectionist approach to socialism" occasionally brings him to tactics of omission and emphasis which he would condemn in totalitarians. Howe's qualifications for writing this work, his treatment of Yiddish scholarship, theater, literature, the European *shtetl* , and the social and mutual benefit organizations of the *landsmanshaften* are compelling and readable. The book is a comprehensive account of the origin and life-course of the massive Jewish immigration. 13 notes.   G. J. Bobango

269. Haynes, John E. COMMUNISTS AND ANTI-COMMUNISTS IN THE NORTHERN MINNESOTA CIO, 1936-1949. *Upper Midwest Hist. 1981 1: 55-73.* In Minnesota the Communist Party's moderate program found favor with some liberals and radicals, creating the so-called Popular Front, and becoming a powerful force in the Farmer-Labor Party and the local Congress of Industrial Organizations. Forces outside the region, the Hitler-Stalin pact, German invasion of Russia, and the Cold War, forced the Popular Front into less popular positions after 1948, permitting anti-Communists to gain power. Based on labor records in the Minnesota Historical Society; 55 notes.
G. L. Olson

270. Holt, James. TRADE UNIONISM IN THE BRITISH AND U.S. STEEL INDUSTRIES, 1888-1912: A COMPARATIVE STUDY. *Labor Hist. 1977 18(1): 5-35.* Compares the development of labor unions in the steel industry in the United States and Great Britain. The weakness of US industrial and political labor organizations is found in the structure and policies of the steel industry's business organizations and not in a lack of class solidarity, new immigration, etc. Based on union membership rolls, government reports, and newspapers; 64 notes.
L. L. Athey

271. Kawada, Hisashi. AMERIKA RŌDŌ UNDŌ KEIZAI ENO EIKYŌ [The impact of labor unionism on the economic growth of the United States]. *Mita Gakkai Zasshi [Japan] 1970 63(3): 1-19.* Covers 1918-62.

272. Kenneally, James J. WOMEN AND TRADE UNIONS 1870-1920: THE QUANDARY OF THE REFORMER. *Labor Hist. 1973 14(1): 42-55.* Surveys the changing role of women in the trade union movement 1870-1920, focusing primarily upon the Women's Trade Union League's struggle with the A.F.L. Trade unionists believed that women should be organized, but at the same time held that women belonged at home. Based on publications of the A.F.L. and W.T.U.L., manuscripts, and the Gompers Letterbooks; 60 notes.   L. L. Athey

273. Koch, Lene. MODERNE AMERIKANSK FAGBEVAEGELSE: EN BIBLIOGRAFI [The modern American trade union movement: a bibliography]. *Årbog for Arbejderbevaegelsens Hist. [Denmark] 1978 8: 286-295.* A selective bibliography of works published in English, German, and Danish on trade unions in the United States from 1963 to 1977.

274. LeGrande, Linda H. WOMEN IN LABOR ORGANIZATIONS: THEIR RANKS ARE INCREASING. *Monthly Labor Rev. 1978 101(8): 8-14.* Discusses women's activism in the American labor movement since the 1920's, the disparity between women's membership and leadership within unions, and women's issues as dealt with by unions.

275. Levinson, Arlene. THE JEWISH LABOR BUND: FORGOTTEN REVOLUTIONARIES. *Present Tense 1981 8(4): 37-41.* Describes Bundism as "democratic socialism coupled with concern for perpetuating secular Yiddish culture" and traces the history of the Jewish Labor Bund from its founding in Russia in 1897, focusing on its presence in the United States since the early 20th-century influx of East European Jews.

276. Lichtenstein, Nelson. AUTO WORKER MILITANCY AND THE STRUCTURE OF FACTORY LIFE, 1937-1955. *J. of Am. Hist. 1980 67(2): 335-353.* Analyzes United Automobile Workers of America (UAW) worker militancy concerning production standards and workplace discipline during 1937-55 and stresses the centralization of power in the UAW itself after World War II. Militancy in the 1930's

arose from efforts by semiskilled workers to assert some control over the conditions of their labor. Changes in both the workforce and the factory itself spawned additional militancy during World War II at Detroit, Michigan. In attempting to influence production standards and factory discipline, UAW locals found themselves at odds with both industry management and the national union's leadership and goals. Based on personal interviews and other primary sources from the Archives of Labor History, Wayne State University, Detroit; 62 notes.

T. P. Linkfield

277. Liski, Ilkka. AMERIKAN SUOMALAINEN TYÖVÄEN YHDISTYS IMATRA I (1890-1921) [The Finnish American Workingmen's Association "Imatra I" (1890-1921)]. *Turun Hist. Arkisto [Finland] 1981 35: 7-69.* A history of the Finnish American Workingmen's Association "Imatra I" active in Brooklyn from 1890 until 1921, when the association ceased to have an ideological program. Observers have disagreed over the extent to which the association was a part of the workers' movement. Finnish American clerical and conservative groups viewed the association as virtually socialist, but after 1904 radical Finnish American socialists criticized the Brooklyn Imatra, and the nationwide federation of the same name, for their failure to accept official socialist affiliation. An examination of debates and activities within the organization suggests that the function of Imatra was to create and preserve a supportive, liberal, and nationalistic subculture for Finnish immigrants who did not wish to join either the conservative church congregations or the radical Finnish American socialist parties. Based on the archives of the Imatra Association, on Finnish American newspapers, on memoirs, and on recent monographs; 3 tables, 259 notes. English summary.

R. G. Selleck

278. Logue, John; Peterson, Martin; and Schiller, Bernt. INDUSTRIAL DEMOCRACY YESTERDAY AND TODAY. *Scandinavian Rev. 1977 65(2): 4-11.* Discusses the background of and current developments in industrial democracy in Scandinavian countries, including a larger European perspective, and contrasting it with organized labor activities in the United States. Industrial democracy includes consultation on production, job revision, and worker participation in management and ownership. Charts.

J. G. Smoot

279. Martin, Andrew. WORKERS' PARTICIPATION: CONTRASTING UNION STRATEGIES. *Scandinavian Rev. 1977 65(2): 15-20.* Contrasts industrial democracy developments such as production consultation, job revision, and worker participation in management and ownership in Sweden and the United States and concludes that traditional labor bargaining practices will continue in the United States whereas Sweden's full-employment has led to broader labor bargaining efforts. Chart.

J. G. Smoot

280. Mergen, Bernard. "ANOTHER GREAT PRIZE": THE JEWISH LABOR MOVEMENT IN THE CONTEXT OF AMERICAN LABOR HISTORY. *Yivo Ann. of Jewish Social Sci. 1976 (16): 394-423.* Emphasizes the uniqueness of the American Jewish labor movement within the context of American labor history. Shows the various relationships between the Jewish labor movement and the American labor movement, demonstrating similarities, differences, and influences.

R. J. Wechman

281. Miller, Eugene. LEO KRZYCKI: POLISH AMERICAN LABOR LEADER. *Polish Am. Studies 1976 33(2): 52-64.* Leo Krzycki (1881-1966) contributed in no small measure to the history of political radicalism in the United States. He was vice-president of the Amalgamated Clothing Workers for 25 years. At one time he was national chairman of the executive committee of the Socialist Party. He was also active in the early organizing drives of the CIO. His fiery speeches resounded throughout Pennsylvania's Schuylkill Valley during the Depression. As a Polish American leader he dared support the Yalta agreement and the pro-Soviet regime following the end of World War II. Based on Polish and English sources; 46 notes.

S. R. Pliska

282. Miller, Richard U. AMERICAN RAILROAD UNIONS AND THE NATIONAL RAILWAYS OF MEXICO: AN EXERCISE IN NINETEENTH-CENTURY PROLETARIAN MANIFEST DESTINY. *Labor Hist. 1974 15(2): 239-260.* Analyzes the effects of the involvement of the American Railroad Brotherhoods in Mexico during 1880-1912. American unions provided the model for Mexican railway unions during 1912-33. The existence of American unions in Mexico promoted the development of railroads, affected the Mexican labor movement, fostered the adoption of business unionism until 1933, and may have lengthened the Mexican Revolution by increasing tension between Mexico and the United States. Based upon the *Mexican Herald*, labor publications, and Mexican sources; 3 tables, 57 notes.

L. L. Athey

283. Montgomery, David. THE IRISH AND THE AMERICAN LABOR MOVEMENT. Doyle, David Noel and Edwards, Owen Dudley, ed. *America and Ireland, 1776-1976: The American Identity and the Irish Connection* (Westport, Conn.: Greenwood Pr., 1980): 205-218. Discusses how Irish Americans rose to prominence in the labor movement in 19th-century America, what changes in their own attitudes and behavior were involved in that process, and what distinctive qualities they imparted to the movement as a whole. Considers two eras: that of rapid economic development between the 1820's and the 1860's and that in which the modern labor movement took shape when Irish Americans became so prominent in its leadership from the 1870's to the great depression of the 1890's. Lists suggestions for further reading.

J. Powell

284. Moyers, Bill. THE ADVENTURES OF A RADICAL HILLBILLY: AN INTERVIEW WITH MYLES HORTON. *Appalachian J. 1982 9(4): 248-285.* Reprints the text of the interview between Bill Moyers and hillbilly organizer Myles Horton, founder of the Highlander Folk School, union organizer, and civil rights activist in the Chattanooga area of Tennessee, during 1932-81.

285. Nissen, Bruce. U.S. WORKERS AND THE U.S. LABOR MOVEMENT. *Monthly Rev. 1981 33(1): 17-30.* Discusses the 20th-century working class from the viewpoint of the labor movement and of trade-union activity.

286. Pratt, Norma Fain. ARCHIVAL RESOURCES AND WRITING IMMIGRANT AMERICAN HISTORY: THE BUND ARCHIVES OF THE JEWISH LABOR MOVEMENT. *J. of Lib. Hist. 1981 16(1): 166-176.* One of the most rare immigrant collections in the United States is the Archives of the Jewish Labor Bund in New York City. It is exceptional because of its age, comprehensiveness, and history. Originally established in 1899 in Geneva, Switzerland, to serve as the archive-library of the then illegal social democratic organization, the Jewish Labor Bund of Russia, Poland and Lithuania, the archives were transported to New York in the late 1940's. Within a few years of settling in New York, the Bund's archivists began to collect material relating to American Jewish history, particularly to trade unionism, socialist and communist movements, and Yiddish culture. Based on secondary sources; 14 notes.

J. Powell

287. Rimlinger, Gaston. LABOR AND THE GOVERNMENT: A COMPARATIVE HISTORICAL PERSPECTIVE. *J. of Econ. Hist. 1977 37(1): 210-225.* Compares the development of the workers' right to organize and bargain collectively in England, France, and the U.S. Starting with a common repressive policy, each country followed a different path toward establishing the workers' rights. The main ultimate difference lies in the extent to which the state became involved in industrial relations. In England the state remained aloof after securing very broad legal rights of collective action. The workers were left to do their own battling. In France the state came to look upon collective agreements as an aspect of public policy and became the dominant partner in labor negotiations. The American pattern lies in between: state protection extends to procedural but not to substantive issues.

J

288. Segers, Mary C. EQUALITY AND CHRISTIAN ANARCHISM: THE POLITICAL AND SOCIAL IDEAS OF THE CATHOLIC WORKER MOVEMENT. *Rev. of Pol. 1978 40(2): 196-230.* The Catholic Worker Movement since 1933 has "consistently adopted controversial positions on contemporary social issues and has challenged Americans to think through the implications of public policy." The key to the success of the movement has been on its emphasis on "the fundamental equality and constant humanity of all men and women." The "personalism" of the Catholic Workers serves as a lesson to capitalistic society that all the "civil rights laws and all the affirmative action policies—will have relatively little impact unless there are

fundamental changes in capitalist society and unless, on an attitudinal level, equality is believed and accepted as a rule of practical action." 55 notes.   L. E. Ziewacz

289.   Skakkebaek, Mette. OVERSIGTER: AMERIKANSK SOCIAL-ISME OG FAGBEVAEGELSE I BEGYNDELSEN AF DET 20. ARHUNDREDE: AN HISTORIOGRAFISK OVERSIGT [Surveys: American socialism and the labor movement at the beginning of the 20th century: a historiographical survey]. *Hist. Tidsskrift [Denmark] 1980 80(2): 479-499.* Details the development of the socialist parties in the United States, and their relationship with the American labor movement at the beginning of the 20th century, and looks at contemporary historical studies. Marxist socialism of the 1860's led to the dogmatic Socialist Labor Party in 1876, and to the more popular Socialist Party of America in 1901. Farmer-labor parties followed as did the Communist Party from the 1930's. Relations between the socialist parties and the labor movement, particularly the American Federation of Labor (AFL) founded in 1896, were never good, with the latter never wishing to be anything other than a "labor union." 80 notes.   P. D. Walton

290.   Troy, Bill and Williams, Claude. THE PEOPLE'S INSTITUTE OF APPLIED RELIGION. *Southern Exposure 1976 4(3): 46-53.* The People's Institute of Applied Religion was established by Claude Williams and his wife Joyce Williams to train religious leaders of the cotton belt in labor unionism, 1940-75.

291.   Trunk, Isaiah. THE CULTURAL DIMENSION OF THE AMERICAN JEWISH LABOR MOVEMENT. *Yivo Ann. of Jewish Social Sci. 1976 (16): 342-393.* Divides the cultural history of the American Jewish labor movement into three periods. The first period, 1880's-90's, was characterized by socialism, a desire for educational achievement, and a tendency toward assimilation. The second period, 1900-20's, was caused by a new influx of immigrants coming after the Dreyfus trial and the Kishinev pogrom. As a result, they were disillusioned with socialism and tended toward cultural autonomy, radical nationalism, and Zionist socialism. A growth of the Hebrew and Yiddish press and literature characterized the Jewish labor movement during this period. The last period, extending from the 1930's to the end of World War II, saw a rise of national solidarity through such groups as the Workmen's Circle and the Jewish Labor Committee who worked against anti-Semitism.   R. J. Wechman

292.   Wolkinson, Benjamin W. LABOR AND THE JEWISH TRADI-TION—A REAPPRAISAL. *Jewish Social Studies 1978 40(3-4): 231-238.* Responds to Michael S. Kogan's "Liberty and Labor in the Jewish Tradition," *(Ideas, A Journal of Contemporary Jewish Thought,* Spring, 1975). Argues that union efforts to compel workers to join a union or to pay dues as a condition of employment do not conflict with biblical and talmudic principles concerning the rights of workers. Kogan, supported by Rabbi Jakob J. Petuchkowski, also stated that such union demands were opposed by leading Jewish figures in the trade union movement, including Samuel Gompers. Gompers supported voluntarism in the formulation of AFL policies, but he was very concerned about union security. Even Louis D. Brandeis, an opponent of the closed shop, favored preferential employment of union members. The thesis that union security is antagonistic to Jewish law and tradition regarding freedom of choice ignores the fact that throughout Jewish history freedom of choice has been subordinated to the well-being of the group.   N. Lederer

Individual Locals, Strikes, and Lockouts

293.   Asher, Robert. UNION NATIVISM AND THE IMMIGRANT RESPONSE. *Labor Hist. 1982 23(3): 325-348.* Labor unions and organizations in the United States exhibited nativistic responses toward the new immigrants from Eastern and Southern Europe in the late 19th and early 20th centuries. This nativism receded when new immigrant numbers in an industry forced the union either to organize them or to lose viability. Industrial unions, such as the United Mine Workers of America, were the first to accept the immigrants into the unions, while the old craft unions restricted or completely ignored them much longer. Ethnic organizers of the radical Left played a key role in bringing the new immigrant workers into the unions. Based on the David Saposs Papers, contemporary union periodicals, and other primary sources; 55 notes.   L. F. Velicer

294.   Bowers, Mollie H. THE DILEMMA OF IMPASSE PROCE-DURES IN THE PUBLIC SAFETY SERVICES. *Arbitration J. 1973 28(3): 167-174.* "In virtually all jurisdictions, policemen and fire fighters are forbidden to strike. But the ban against stoppages does not guarantee labor peace. The alternatives offered—mediation, fact-finding and arbitration—frequently leave employees dissatisfied, and their restlessness is expressed in illegal strikes and in varient forms of stoppages which may or may not be in violation of the law. A chief reason present alternatives to the strike prove unacceptable is that they do not provide the 'clout' needed by unions to achieve a settlement on their terms. But this need not be so, the author believes. A form of 'legislated arbitration' or compulsory arbitration could be made suffi-ciently 'costly' to both parties as to provide pressures toward settlement which are roughly analogous to those that eventually bring strikes to a conclusion."   J

295.   Gould, William B. SUBSTITUTES FOR THE STRIKE WEAP-ON. *Arbitration J. 1973 28(2): 111-118.* "American observers of the labor scene in England have often found it odd that grievance disputes in that country are more likely to result in strikes than in arbitration—a reversal of the customary procedure here. On the other hand, British trade unionists and employers have not been as reluctant as have Americans to arbitrate wage and new contract issues. A change may be in the offing in England in the light of its new Industrial Disputes Act. Against this background, the author, a law professor and arbitrator in the United States, was invited to read a paper at the Royal Institute of International Affairs in London last February. Although his comments on American experience were intended for British consumption, they will also be instructive for Americans, who are equally preoccupied with finding substitutes for the strike."   J

296.   Hadsell, Richard M. and Coffey, William E. FROM LAW AND ORDER TO CLASS WARFARE: BALDWIN-FELTS DETECTIVES IN THE SOUTHERN WEST VIRGINIA COAL FIELDS. *West Virginia Hist. 1979 40(3): 268-286.* William G. Baldwin and Thomas L. Felts formed Baldwin-Felts Detectives in the 1890's and for 30 years provided a private police and guard service for West Virginia coal mines. Their agents infiltrated unions, evicted undesirables, guarded nonstrik-ers, and kept order on mine property. Their antiunion activities became paramount and many were killed in gun battles or ambushes. By the 1930's they were outmoded and even illegal. Based on Justus Collins papers and other primary sources; 72 notes.   J. H. Broussard

297.   Hicken, Victor. MINE UNION RADICALISM IN MACOU-PIN AND MONTGOMERY COUNTIES. *Western Illinois Regional Studies 1980 3(2): 173-191.* Describes coal miners in Illinois ca. 1870-1930's, focusing on protests by the miners in Macoupin and Montgomery Counties, particulary the United Mine Workers of Ameri-ca coal strike of 1897, which resulted in what became known as the Virden Massacre when goons from the Chicago-Virden Company and miners participated in a mass shootout resulting in the deaths of 12 and the wounding of about 40, and other attempts at unionization led by Socialists, Progressives, and Communists.

298.   Holmes, Joseph J. RED BAITING AS USED AGAINST STRIKING WORKINGMEN IN THE UNITED STATES, 1871-1920. *Studies in Hist. and Soc. 1974 5(2): 1-19.* An attempt to determine the degree and extent of validity of Socialist influence charges behind labor unrest at the turn of the 20th century, and some reasons for it. The charges were widely disseminated, but are not borne out by facts. Socialists exploited unrest, but poor working conditions and economic depression were the causes. The economic overlords and their allies used the charge of Socialist influence with success because it was suited to the ideals of middle-class persons whose success in the cities had not made them happy. 91 notes.   V. L. Human

299.   Kaufman, Bruce E. THE DETERMINANTS OF STRIKES IN THE UNITED STATES, 1900-1977. *Industrial and Labor Relations Rev. 1982 35(4): 473-490.* Assesses the recent debate over the "eco-nomic" and "organizational-political" models of strikes, and tests a synthesis of those models as an explanation for the pattern of US strike

activity since 1900. The paper begins with a review of strike activity in the post-1900 period, then develops a conceptual framework incorporating six factors—the size of union membership, economic conditions, political events, institutional arrangments, psychological variables, and the extent of rival unionism—to explain this historical pattern. Regression analysis shows that both the economic factors of unemployment and inflation and various noneconomic factors, such as changes in union membership, the outbreak of World War II, and enactment of New Deal legislation, explain variations in strike activity. The results also show that economic and noneconomic factors have worked together to cause a marked reduction in the variation in strike activity in the post-1948 period.

           J/S

300. Loose, John Ward Willson. PROTECTIONISM, WAGES, AND STRIKES IN THE ANTHRACITE IRON INDUSTRY OF LANCASTER COUNTY: 1840-1900. *J. of the Lancaster County Hist. Soc. 1982 86(1): 2-23.*

301. Masson, Jack and Guimary, Donald. ASIAN LABOR CONTRACTORS IN THE ALASKAN CANNED SALMON INDUSTRY: 1880-1937. *Labor Hist. 1981 22(3): 377-397.* Describes the functioning and end of the labor contract system in the Alaskan salmon industry. This risky, seasonal industry functioned with a cannery operator, a labor contractor, and a work crew recruited by the contractor, with a labor contract binding the three groups for a season. Oriental laborers gave way to Mexicans, Negroes, and Filipinos, with native foremen hired to supervise them. The contractors fed and paid them poorly; growing nativism and hostility toward one another also thrived. The lucrative labor contractor system fell after the murder of the first president of the Cannery Workers and Farm Laborers Union. Based on interviews, federal publications, and other primary sources; 35 notes.

           L. F. Velicer

302. McBride, James D. GAINING A FOOTHOLD IN THE PARADISE OF CAPITALISM: THE WESTERN FEDERATION OF MINERS AND THE UNIONIZATION OF BISBEE. *J. of Arizona Hist. 1982 23(3): 299-316.* Chronicles the struggle of the Western Federation of Miners to organize the mine workers of Bisbee, Arizona. Despite an unsuccessful strike and intense antiunion actions, Local 106 was organized and its members provided union leaders for the state. Covers 1893-1909. Secondary sources, 2 photos, 49 notes.

           G. O. Gagnon

303. Melzer, Richard. A DEATH IN DAWSON: THE DEMISE OF A SOUTHWESTERN COMPANY TOWN. *New Mexico Hist. Rev. 1980 55(4): 309-330.* The factors which led to the closing in 1950 of the coal mining town of Dawson, New Mexico, were different from those which contributed to the demise of the typically run-down coal camps in the East after World War II. While economic problems and modern technology were the basic reasons for Dawson's decline, other factors such as the growth of the miners' union and its escalating demands, the frustration over strikes, and the steady loss of the younger aged population, were also important. Since some of Dawson's problems began in the 1920's it is a wonder that the town survived as long as it did. Newspapers and other primary sources; 2 photos, table, 111 notes.

           P. L. McLaughlin

304. Metcalf, Fay D. THE TRANSFORMATION OF THE WORKING PLACE: ITS IMPACT ON THE SHOEMAKERS. *Social Educ. 1982 46(2): 100-101.* Presents a lesson for teaching high school students about the shoe industry, based on Norman Ware's *The Industrial Worker, 1840-1860* (1964), Leon Litwack's *The American Labor Movement* (1962), and Studs Terkel's *Working* (1972), and presents questions for discussion on union organizing and its effects on the industry, and the changes in the industry, 1830-1972.

305. Meyerhuber, Carl I., Jr. ORGANIZING ALCOA: THE ALUMINUM WORKERS' UNION IN PENNSYLVANIA'S ALLEGHENY VALLEY, 1900-1971. *Pennsylvania Hist. 1981 48(3): 195-219.* History of the Aluminum Workers' Union in New Kensington, Pennsylvania, from 1901 to 1981, emphasizing the 1930's and 1940's. Based upon interviews, union archives, and newspapers; 74 notes.

           D. C. Swift

306. Mitchell, Harry Leland. THE FOUNDING AND EARLY HISTORY OF THE SOUTHERN TENANT FARMERS UNION. *Arkansas Hist. Q. 1973 32(4): 342-369.*

307. Powell, William E. EUROPEAN SETTLEMENT IN THE CHEROKEE-CRAWFORD COAL FIELD OF SOUTHEASTERN KANSAS. *Kansas Hist. Q. 1975 41(2): 150-165.* Underground coal mining started in southeastern Kansas during the 1870's reached a peak during 1890-1920. Adverse conditions in Europe, coupled with economic opportunity and lax immigration laws, drew large numbers of immigrants from Europe and Canada to Kansas coal fields, where they settled in existing towns or company mining camps. When the mines declined after 1920 many immigrants moved to northern industrial cities. Based on primary and secondary sources; 3 photos, 2 tables, fig., 51 notes.

           W. F. Zornow

308. Reutter, Clifford J. THE PUZZLE OF A PITTSBURGH STEELER: JOE MAGARAC'S ETHNIC IDENTITY. *Western Pennsylvania Hist. Mag. 1980 63(1): 31-36.* Reviews several articles about the Slavic ethnic identity of folklore character Joe Magarac, the Paul Bunyan of steelworkers; linguistic evidence suggests that his surname is Croatian.

309. Simon, Roger. LOOKING BACKWARD AT STEEL. *Antioch Rev. 1978 36(4): 441-462.* Two interviews with retired workers from the Bethlehem Steel Corporation reflect a wide range of responses about life histories, working conditions, life during the Depression, and union activity, 1910's-50's.

310. Snyder, David. EARLY NORTH AMERICAN STRIKES: A REINTERPRETATION. *Industrial and Labor Relations Rev. 1977 30(3): 325-341.* Most studies of aggregate strike activity in the United States and Canada have stressed the importance of economic determinants such as the stage of the business cycle and the rate of change in real wages. This study tests the hypothesis that such economic models are most appropriate for explaining fluctuations in strike activity during the post-World War II period, when bargaining was well established in both countries, but an expanded model—including measures of the political environment and of labor's organizational strength—is necessary to explain strike behavior in the years prior to 1948. This hypothesis is supported by an analysis of data for 1900-71 for the United States and for 1912-71 for Canada.

           J

311. Snyder, David. INSTITUTIONAL SETTING AND INDUSTRIAL CONFLICT: COMPARATIVE ANALYSES OF FRANCE, ITALY AND THE UNITED STATES. *Am. Sociol Rev. 1975 40(3): 259-278.* Economic models and interpretations have dominated empirical studies of industrial conflict. However, recent investigations of French work stoppages assign more importance to organizational and political than to economic determinants of strike activity. These apparent contradictory results and conclusions are ignored by previous work, almost all of which examines a single country and/or limited time span. In this paper, we argue that existing findings differ according to the institutional context of labor relations. Specifically, we identify assumptions underlying each line of argument; argue that the extent to which these assumptions hold influences results and conclusions of various analyses; and show that each set of assumptions holds best within different types of institutional setting. We test this argument with regression analyses of yearly timeseries data for France (1876-1966), Italy (1901-1970) and the United States (1900-1970). Results of these analyses correspond to our hypotheses concerning the influence of institutional setting on fluctuations in aggregate strike activity. We then consider implications of these findings for investigations of other forms of collective protest.

           J

312. Swetnam, George. LABOR-MANAGEMENT RELATIONS IN PENNSYLVANIA'S STEEL INDUSTRY, 1800-1959. *Western Pennsylvania Hist. Mag. 1979 62(4): 321-332.* Traces the labor-management relations in the ferrous metals industry from paternalism in the early 19th century to the development of strong unions in the 1950's.

313. Thornton, Robert J. U.S. TEACHERS' ORGANIZATIONS AND THE SALARY ISSUE: 1900-1960. *Res. in Econ. Hist. 1982 (Supplement 2): 127-143.* Discusses the efforts by teacher organizations, such as the Chicago Teachers Federation, the American Federa-

tion of Teachers (AFT), the National Teachers Association (NTA), and the National Education Association (NEA), to have a voice in salary determination. The first organization was the Chicago Teachers Federation, established in 1897. Before 1945, although considerable activity toward improvement of teacher welfare was evident at the local level, no major victories were achieved. After 1945, teachers became increasingly militant, participated in strikes, and benefitted from increasing support by the AFT and the NEA. Primary sources; table, 2 notes.   J. Powell

314. —. MOTHER JONES, 1830-1930. *J. of the Illinois State Hist. Soc. 1980 73(3): 235-237.* Prints Duncan McDonald's previously unpublished autobiography which recalls impressions of socialist and labor organizer Mary Harris "Mother" Jones on the occasion of the dedication of a monument in her honor at the Union Miners Cemetery in Mount Olive, Illinois, in 1936.   J. Powell

315. —. TWO VIEWS OF THE KNIGHTS OF LABOR CENTENNIAL SYMPOSIUM, CHICAGO, MAY 1979. *Labour [Canada] 1980 5(Spr): 185-192.*
Dick, W. M. THE KNIGHTS OF LABOR AND THE MAKING OF THE AMERICAN WORKING CLASS, *pp. 185-190.* During the May 1979 Knights of Labor Centennial Symposium in Chicago, the papers presented illustrated the essential fluidity of American society at the turn of the century.
Reilly, Nolan. THE KNIGHTS IN CHICAGO, *pp. 190-192.* Reviews the Centennial Symposium briefly; most participants felt that historians needed to broaden their horizons beyond the Knights of Labor's institutional development.   G. P. Cleyet

Government Programs, Policies, and Politics

316. Berger, Harriet F. APPOINTMENT AND CONFIRMATION TO THE NATIONAL LABOR RELATIONS BOARD: DEMOCRATIC CONSTRAINTS ON PRESIDENTIAL POWER? *Presidential Studies Q. 1978 8(4): 403-417.* Using the National Labor Relations Board (NLRB) as a case study, examines the presidential power of appointment to independent regulatory commissions and the effectiveness of the Senate's power of confirmation as a restraint on the President. Since the establishment of the NLRB in 1935, members have enjoyed long tenure and frequent reappointment with only perfunctory review by the Senate. While the Boards tend to reflect the orientation of the President, the absence of deep ideological differences and the influence of the regulated parties ensures stability and limited Senate review. Chart, 59 notes.   S. C. Strom

317. Brand, Horst. THE EVOLUTION OF FAIR LABOR STANDARDS: A STUDY IN CLASS CONFLICT. *Monthly Labor Rev. 1983 106(8): 25-28.* Reviews Ronnie Steinberg's *Wages and Hours: Labor Reform in the Twentieth Century* (1982) which tracks the growth of legislation concerning minimum wage and maximum hours and examines the social rights incorporated in the wage and hour standards.

318. Candela, Joseph L., Jr. THE STRUGGLE TO LIMIT THE HOURS AND RAISE THE WAGES OF WORKING WOMEN IN ILLINOIS, 1893-1917. *Social Service Rev. 1979 53(1): 15-34.* Discusses the reform attitudes of Illinois during 1893-1917, focusing on the outcome of attempted labor legislation to protect women.

319. Easterbrook, Gregg. HOW BIG LABOR BRINGS HOME THE BACON. *Washington Monthly 1971 12(11, i.e. 12): 40-47.* The Davis-Bacon Act (US, 1931) ordered federal building projects to pay the prevailing wage so contractors, particularly in the South, could not underbid jobs; the Davis-Bacon Act costs taxpayers two billion dollars a year in federal construction wages and "indirectly inflates the cost of private construction, by 'importing' high union wages into non-union areas, and driving small, cost-conscious contractors out of business."

320. Fulton, Tom. AGRICULTURAL LABOR LEGISLATION IN THE UNITED STATES: A REVIEW OF THE MAJOR NEW DEAL LEGISLATION, THE EMERGENCY FARM LABOR SUPPLY PROGRAM, AND THE AGRICULTURAL LABOR RELATIONS ACT OF CALIFORNIA. *J. of NAL Assoc. 1979 4(3-4): 49-58.* The

above agricultural labor law shows that until recently farmworkers in the United States were not aided by government and did not enjoy a good relationship with American farmers; also gives a brief history of the rights and privileges of land ownership since 17th-century European settlement in North America.

321. Gordon, Lynn. WOMEN AND THE ANTI-CHILD LABOR MOVEMENT IN ILLINOIS, 1890-1920. *Social Service Rev. 1977 51(2): 228-248.* A small group of women concerned about child labor 1890-1903 aided in the passage of three major laws against child labor and the establishment of a State Department of Factory Inspection.

322. Graebner, William. RETIREMENT IN EDUCATION: THE ECONOMIC AND SOCIAL FUNCTIONS OF THE TEACHERS' PENSION. *Hist. of Educ. Q. 1978 18(4): 397-418.* Discusses how teachers' pensions were accepted in the economic and social world of education. It began with discussions of the proposal published as a symposium in the April 1891 issue of the *Journal of Education.* W. T. Harris, US Commissioner of Education, opened the symposium with his article in opposition. The first state legislation based on actuarial data was enacted by Massachusetts in 1913. Pensions seemed congruous to secure growth and order in society, but efficiency and community behind teachers' pensions were revealed as ultimately destructive of each other. 64 notes.   R. V. Ritter

323. Grossman, Jonathan. THE ORIGIN OF THE U.S. DEPARTMENT OF LABOR. *Monthly Labor Rev. 1973 96(3): 3-7.* Labor leaders campaigned for the creation of a federal Labor Department in the United States from 1864 until their aim was achieved in 1913.

324. Guzda, Henry P. SOCIAL EXPERIMENT OF THE LABOR DEPARTMENT: THE DIVISION OF NEGRO ECONOMICS. *Public Hist. 1982 4(4): 7-37.* Discusses the origins, development, and goals of the Division of Negro Economics, a unit of the US Department of Labor during 1884-1921.

325. Guzda, Henry P. THE U.S. EMPLOYMENT SERVICE AT 50: IT TOO HAD TO WAIT ITS TURN. *Monthly Labor Rev. 1983 106(6): 12-19.* Chronicles the development of free public employment services from 1890 to the establishment of the US Employment Service in 1933.

326. Holloway, Wilfred B. YOUTH EMPLOYMENT EDUCATION PROGRAMS: WHERE ARE WE HEADED? *Educ. and Urban Soc. 1981 14(1): 33-54.* Traces such federal youth employment-education programs since the 1930's as the National Youth Administration, the Civilian Conservation Corps, the Economic Opportunity Act (US, 1964), the Neighborhood Youth Corps, the Job Corps, the Youth Conservation Corps, and the Comprehensive Employment and Training Act (US, 1973).

327. Overton, Craig E. CRITERIA IN GRIEVANCE AND INTEREST ARBITRATION IN THE PUBLIC SECTOR. *Arbitration J. 1973 28(3): 159-166.* "If arbitration is to be used more than it has been for new contract terms in public employment, there will have to be much more understanding of criteria arbitrators use in setting wages and other basic conditions of employment. Usually accepted as relevant are: ability to pay; cost of living; wages paid to comparable classifications within the same community; and the 'welfare of the public.' In the final analysis, however, parties will not be able to rely upon a fixed formula, for 'each case has different facts presented in a different way by different persons.' Moreover, despite basic criteria, arbitrators will be called upon to make value judgments. In the final analysis, 'the criteria used by the arbitrator will vary not only from case to case, but from arbitrator to arbitrator.'
      J

328. Poulson, Barry W. IDEOLOGY AND LABOR LAW IN AMERICA. *J. of Social, Pol. and Econ. Studies 1983 8(1): 43-79.* Traces ideological trends that have affected the attitudes of judges and politicians involved in the creation and enforcement of labor-relations law since the 1780's.

329. Rosenbloom, David H. PUBLIC PERSONNEL REFORMS. *Policy Studies J. 1980-81 9(8): 1227-1237.* Discusses the relationship between civil service reforms and political change using examples from the 19th and 20th centuries.

330. Schacht, John N. THE DEPRESSION AND AFTER. *Palimpsest 1982 63(1): 12-29.* Examines the expertise and opinions of President Herbert C. Hoover, United Mine Workers President John L. Lewis, Secretary of Agriculture Henry A. Wallace, and New Deal administrator and presidential advisor Harry Hopkins.

331. Spalding, Hobart A., Jr. U.S. AND LATIN AMERICAN LABOR: THE DYNAMICS OF IMPERIALIST CONTROL. *Latin Am. Perspectives 1976 3(1): 45-69.* Analyzes the history of US labor involvement in Latin American labor movements. Organized labor (first the AFL, then the AFL-CIO) has consistently supported US foreign policy in supporting unions which are pro-capitalist. Emphasis is given to the role of the American Institute for Free Labor Development. Labor's role has been to hold back independent forces in Latin America and has facilitated its domination by foreign and domestic capital.
J. L. Dietz

332. Stevenson, James A. LETTERS TO DANIEL DE LEON: THE INTRA-PARTY CONSTITUENCY FOR HIS POLICY OF STRICT PARTY DISCIPLINE, 1896-1904. *Labor Hist. 1977 18(3): 382-396.* Daniel De Leon's position in the Socialist Labor Party of America as a strict party disciplinarian arose from within the party rather than from De Leon's personal preference. Based on the De Leon correspondence and the S.L.P.'s National Executive Committee papers; 61 notes.
L. L. Athey

333. Thompson, J. A. THE "AGE OF REFORM" IN AMERICA. *Hist. J. [Great Britain] 1976 19(1): 257-274.* A review article on reform and reformers 1890-1930, prompted by: William M. Dick's *Labor and Socialism in America: The Gompers Era* (Port Washington, N.Y. and London: Kennikat Pr., 1972); Warren R. Van Tine's *The Making of the Labor Bureaucrat: Union Leadership in the United States* (Amherst, Mass.: U. of Massachusetts Pr., 1973); Julian F. Jaffe's *Crusade Against Radicalism: New York During the Red Scare, 1914-1924* (Port Washington, N.Y. and London: Kennikat Pr., 1972); Samuel T. McSeveney's *The Politics of Depression: Political Behavior in the Northeast, 1893-1896* (New York: Oxford U. Pr., 1972); James Edward Wrights' *The Politics of Populism: Dissent in Colorado* (New Haven and London: Yale U. Pr., 1974); Peter H. Argersinger's *Populism and Politics: William Alfred Peffer and the People's Party* (Lexington, Kentucky: The U. Pr. of Kentucky, 1974); and Arthur A. Ekirch, Jr.'s *Progressivism in America: A Study of the Era from Theodore Roosevelt to Woodrow Wilson* (New York: New Viewpoints, 1974). Sees less dominance of the politics of their era by reformers, including Progressives, than their latter-day critics have assumed. 34 notes.
L. A. McGeoch/S

334. Wetzel, Kurt. RAILROAD MANAGEMENT'S RESPONSE TO OPERATING EMPLOYEES ACCIDENTS, 1890-1913. *Labor Hist. 1980 21(3): 351-368.* American railroads consistently opposed attempts to legislate and administer stricter safety standards in the late 19th and early 20th centuries. The industry delayed installation of safety equipment mandated by the Safety Appliances Act (US, 1893) until the courts found the companies liable for accidents caused by inoperative or missing safety equipment. Only after the Federal Employers' Liability Act (US, 1908) increased the railroads' liability for accidents did management develop a constructive program to make the operating employees' work safer. Based on articles in contemporary railroad management and union publications, and other primary sources; 41 notes.
L. F. Velicer

Racial, Ethnic, and Sex Discrimination

335. Amsterdam, Susan. THE NATIONAL WOMEN'S TRADE UNION LEAGUE. *Social Service Rev. 1982 56(2): 259-272.* Traces the history of the National Women's Trade Union League from 1903 through the 1950's, with relevant biographical data illustrating the backgrounds of prominent women in the league, concluding with an analysis of the current status of women in the labor force.

336. Baker, Ross K. ENTRY OF WOMEN INTO FEDERAL JOB WORLD—AT A PRICE. *Smithsonian 1977 8(4): 82-91.* Women had worked at menial federal jobs before 1833 when the Civil Service Act became law. Real equality was a long way off. Clara Barton worked at the Patent Office during 1854-61. The Civil War accelerated the trend toward female employment because the war had eliminated many men from the civilian labor force. World War I caused a surge in female employment but peacetime retrenchment obliterated most of the gains. Today nearly three fourths of the women have clerical and technical jobs that pay less than $10,000 a year, and equality is still a long way off. Illus.
E. P. Stickney

337. Barrera, Mario. COLONIAL LABOR AND THEORIES OF INEQUALITY: THE CASE OF INTERNATIONAL HARVESTER. *Rev. of Radical Pol. Econ. 1976 8(2): 1-19.* At International Harvester Company, 1831-1976, attitudes toward minorities have been consistently oppressive; treatment of minorities as subordinates is due to a basic belief in racial inequality fostered by a colonial concept in race relations.

338. Boskin, Joseph. "O BROTHER, GET BACK, GET BACK, GET BACK": BLACK LABORERS IN WHITE AMERICA. *Rev. in Am. Hist. 1979 7(2): 273-280.* Review article prompted by William B. Gould's *Black Workers in White Unions: Job Discrimination in the United States* (Ithaca, N.Y.: Cornell U. Pr., 1977) and Herbert Hill's *Black Labor and the American Legal System* Vol. 1, *Race, Work and the Law* (Washington, D.C.: the Bureau of National Affairs, 1977).

339. Brown, Catherine and Ganschow, Thomas. THE AUGUSTA, GEORGIA, CHINESE: 1865-1980. *West Georgia Coll. Studies in the Social Sci. 1983 22: 27-41.* Immediately after the Civil War, the concept of cheap Chinese labor was favored in Augusta, but discrimination took root by the 1880's and did not abate until the mid-20th century.

340. Bularzik, Mary. SEXUAL HARASSMENT AT THE WORKPLACE: HISTORICAL NOTES. *Radical Am. 1978 12(4): 24-43.* Describes sexual harassment and its implications for women who work, and provides a history of sexual harassment, primarily of working-class white women in northern cities since the 18th century.

341. Fraundorf, Martha Norby. RELATIVE EARNINGS OF NATIVE- AND FOREIGN-BORN WOMEN. *Explorations in Econ. Hist. 1978 15(2): 211-220.* Sees little difference in wages in the United States between native- and foreign-born women during 1890-1911, though there were some differences between single and married women. If anything, foreign-born women encountered the same or less discrimination than their husbands. Based on published documents and secondary accounts; 6 tables, 37 notes, biblio.
P. J. Coleman

342. Freeman, Richard B. DECLINE OF LABOR MARKET DISCRIMINATION AND ECONOMIC ANALYSIS. *Am. Econ. Rev. 1973 63(2): 280-286.* Examines the changes in labor market discrimination against Negroes between 1890 and 1970.

343. Glanz, Rudolph. SOME REMARKS ON JEWISH LABOR AND AMERICAN PUBLIC OPINION IN THE PRE-WORLD WAR I ERA. *Yivo Ann. of Jewish Social Sci. 1976 (16): 178-202.* Shows how the Jewish labor movement influenced American and Jewish American public opinion about the popular conception of a Jew and how it influenced the entire American labor movement.
R. J. Wechman

344. Greer, Edward. RACISM AND U.S. STEEL, 1906-1974. *Radical Am. 1976 10(5): 45-66.* Discrimination against Negroes in the Gary works of the US Steel Corporation was initiated and controlled by the company rather than as the result of the racist attitudes of white workers. Before the CIO, prejudice against blacks was engendered by company officials to keep the working force disunited and to maintain a marginal labor force at inferior pay for the worst jobs in the plant. This discriminatory policy is still partially in being, owing to departmental seniority regulations and to company control over the hiring of supervisory personnel. Based on primary and secondary sources.
N. Lederer

345. Hartley, Shirley Foster. AMERICAN WOMEN AS "MINORITY." *Int. J. of Women's Studies [Canada] 1978 1(2): 108-132.* Comparisons of the earnings, educational levels, occupational categories, and union status of men and women of six racial-ethnic groups since the 1900's indicate that women not only share the experience of minority groups but are at a greater disadvantage in the work force.

346. Hartmann, Heidi. CAPITALISM, PATRIARCHY, AND JOB SEGREGATION BY SEX. *Signs 1976 1(3, Part 2): 137-169.* Capitalists, male workers, and centuries of patriarchal social relations have produced sex-segregation of jobs and women's current status in the labor market. Capitalism extended male-female dominance-dependence relations to the wage-labor market; and the mutual accommodation of patriarchy and capitalism has resulted in a vicious circle for women. Women's subordination will end and men will begin to escape class oppression and exploitation only when men are forced to relinquish their favored positions in the labor market and at home. Based on secondary sources; 105 notes. S. E. Kennedy

347. Hill, Ann Corinne. PROTECTION OF WOMEN WORKERS AND THE COURTS: A LEGAL CASE HISTORY. *Feminist Studies 1979 5(2): 247-273.* History of labor law pertaining to women's job protection in the United States, focusing on four periods: from 1876 (when the Massachusetts Supreme Court upheld the first piece of protective legislation for women workers) until 1923; from 1935 to 1948, when unemployment during the Depression and women working at traditionally male-held jobs during World War II raised contradictory questions in the courts about equality in the work force; from 1964 to 1971, when women challenged labor laws; and from 1974 to 1979, characterized by more Supreme Court cases on discrimination against women in the labor force than in any other period in American labor history. Examines specific court cases and legislation. G. Smith

348. Huckle, Patricia. THE WOMB FACTOR: PREGNANCY POLICIES AND EMPLOYMENT OF WOMEN. *Western Pol. Q. 1981 34(1): 114-126.* Examines the historical treatment of pregnant or potentially pregnant women from 1908 to 1978, describes the process of amending the Civil Rights Act (US, 1964) to include pregnancy discrimination as sex discrimination, and analyzes the central arguments postulated. The resulting Pregnancy Discrimination Act (US, 1978), while barring discrimination in employment benefits based on the capacity to reproduce, and while responsive to the problem of equity for women workers, does little to restructure employment for women who must fill dual roles of worker and mother. Government sources; table, 53 notes. J. Powell

349. Mamiya, Lawrence H. and Kaurouma, Patricia A. YOU NEVER HEAR ABOUT THEIR STRUGGLES: BLACK ORAL HISTORY IN POUGHKEEPSIE, NEW YORK. *Afro-Americans in New York Hist. and Life 1980 4(2): 55-70.* Data from oral history interviews about labor, racial discrimination, leadership structure, social change, internal tensions, Ku Klux Klan operations, and the role of black churches and support organizations, 1880-1980.

350. Mandelbaum, Dorothy Rosenthal. WOMEN IN MEDICINE. *Signs 1978 4(1): 136-145.* Reviews literature published since 1973 dealing with women in the medical profession, citing two noteworthy research tools: Sandra L. Chaff, et al., *Women in Medicine: A Bibliography of the Literature on Women Physicians* (Metuchen, N.J.: Scarecrow Pr., 1977) and Mary Roth Walsh, *"Doctors Wanted: No Women Need Apply": Sexual Barriers in the Medical Profession, 1835-1975* (New Haven, Conn.: Yale U. Pr., 1977). After the formation of the AMA in 1847, barriers against women had risen. However, in 1976 there were signs of a "critical mass" of female students developing which may make further discrimination impossible. Other studies suggest that women now view their roles differently; adopting longer hours, fewer and shorter withdrawals even if married, and preferences for other specialties. Secondary sources; 67 notes. S. P. Conner

351. McGouldrick, Paul and Tannen, Michael. THE INCREASING PAY GAP FOR WOMEN IN THE TEXTILE AND CLOTHING INDUSTRIES, 1910 TO 1970. *J. of Econ. Hist. 1980 40(4): 799-814.* This multiple regression study of male and female wages in the clothing and textile industries finds that the standardized pay gap has changed against women from 1910 to 1970. The cross-section study of wages in 1909-10 finds a very small residual in favor of men; but when the English-speaking variable is interpreted as screening many able women (but not men) from manufacturing, the residual shifts to one slightly favoring women. The cross-section study of pay in substantially the same industry group during 1969 finds very substantial residuals in favor of men after standardizing earnings. Hypotheses suggested for explaining these contrary findings include a decline in women's investment in

human capital relative to that of men, and changing government and union tax and benefit patterns that discriminate against female investment in human capital. J

352. McGouldrick, Paul F. and Tannen, Michael B. DID AMERICAN MANUFACTURERS DISCRIMINATE AGAINST IMMIGRANTS BEFORE 1914? *J. of Econ. Hist. 1977 37(3): 723-746.* Fits wage functions to two distinct data sources: US Immigration Commission surveys of 1908-10, supplemented by the 1909 Census of Manufactures, and a Department of Labor survey of production costs in nine protected industries, directed by the US Commissioner of Labor, Carroll D. Wright. Regression analysis applied to both sets of data concludes that there was moderate discrimination against southern and eastern European immigrants. Based on census data, Department of Labor statistics, and secondary sources; 3 tables, 34 notes.
D. J. Trickey

353. Ment, David. CORPORATIONS, UNIONS, AND BLACKS: THE STRUGGLE FOR POWER IN AMERICAN INDUSTRIAL CITIES. *J. of Urban Hist. 1981 7(2): 247-254.* This review essay examines three books dealing with the three-sided struggle between unions, blacks, and corporations in large 20th-century cities: Linda Ann Ewen's *Corporate Power and Urban Crisis in Detroit,* Edward Greer's *Big Steel,* and August Meier and Elliott Rudwick's *Black Detroit and the Rise of the UAW.* One important question considered by each group is why the problems faced by the working class in general and black workers in particular did not lead to more militant action or even revolt. Note. T. W. Smith

354. Moore, Howard. BLACK LABOR: SLAVERY TO FAIR HIRING. *Black Scholar 1973 4(4): 22-31.* Discusses black labor and the practices of both slave drivers and businessmen hiring wage labor, 17th-20th centuries; focuses on the evolution in labor situations and the move which began in the mid-1940's to equalize hiring and wages; discusses the Civil Rights Act (1964) and the Equal Employment Opportunity Commission.

355. Niemi, Albert W., Jr. THE MALE-FEMALE EARNINGS DIFFERENTIAL: A HISTORICAL OVERVIEW OF THE CLERICAL OCCUPATIONS FROM THE 1880S TO THE 1970S. *Social Sci. Hist. 1983 7(1): 97-108.* Differences in earnings by sex have often been explained by sexual differences in occupational structure. A study of clerical workers from 1880 to 1970 reveals that intraoccupational differences in wages is the more critical factor in explaining sexual earnings differences. Male stenographers, bookkeepers, and clerks earned significantly more than females in the same jobs through the entire period. Based on the Department of Labor's *Occupational Wage Surveys;* table, 2 notes, appendix. L. K. Blaser

356. Paulsen, Darryl. MASTERS OF IT ALL: BLACK BUILDERS IN THIS CENTURY. *Southern Exposure 1980 8(1): 9-10.* Jim Crow kept black construction workers out of many white unions, denying them lucrative jobs in the white community, but black builders—in their own unions, in a few integrated unions, and outside unions—continued to ply their trades with superior skills based on years of antebellum experience. Today blacks comprise 8.8% of building trades union members. Further, integrated construction unions may be able to pursue a more aggressive organizing drive against New South open-shop employers, appealing to black workers as well as white. 3 photos.
H. M. Parker, Jr.

357. Peake, Charles F. RACIAL POLICIES OF AMERICAN INDUSTRY. *New Scholar 1978 5(2): 351-364.* Review article prompted by William E. Fulmer's *The Negro in the Furniture Industry* (Philadelphia: U. of Pennsylvania Pr., 1973), Lester Rubin, *The Negro in the Longshore Industry* (Philadelphia: U. of Pennsylvania Pr., 1973), and Elaine Gale Wrong *The Negro in the Apparel Industry* (Philadelphia: U. of Pennsylvania Pr., 1973). These are three additions to 30 volumes published in the Racial Policies of American Industry Series by the University of Pennsylvania Press. The result is a brief and clear picture of the series' achievement. Good statistical analysis illustrates the traditional discriminatory employment but it also shows the potential for reform that the 1960's promised if the economy continues in a pattern of growth. 34 notes. D. K. Pickens

358. Philips, Peter; with commentary by Margo, Robert A. GENDER-BASED WAGE DIFFERENTIALS IN PENNSYLVANIA AND NEW JERSEY MANUFACTURING, 1900-1950. *J. of Econ. Hist. 1982 42(1): 181-186.* This multiple regression study of women's and men's wages in New Jersey and Pennsylvania manufacturing finds that the average pay gap has changed in favor of women from 1900-50 in several industries and in the aggregate. Technological homogenization of jobs is suggested as a possible explanation of gender-based wage convergence. An overall framework of forces and relations of production is outlined, and future work on this newly introduced body of data is suggested. Comments pp. 187-189.   J

359. Radzialowski, Thaddus. THE COMPETITION FOR JOBS AND RACIAL STEREOTYPE: POLES AND BLACKS IN CHICAGO. *Polish Am. Studies 1976 33(2): 5-18.* The struggle for jobs, not hunger for status, produced Polish prejudice against blacks in Chicago, ca. 1890-1919. Blacks from the South threatened the jobs of the settled Polish immigrants. In no time, blacks found themselves serving as strikebreakers and even killing Polish workers. For these prejudices and racial antagonisms much blame rests with American industry. Based on newspaper accounts and Polish and English secondary sources; 28 notes.
                                S. R. Pliska

360. Sales, William, Jr. CAPITALISM WITHOUT RACISM: SCIENCE OR FANTASY. *Black Scholar 1978 9(6): 23-34.* A capitalistic system like that in the United States cannot endure without the subjugation of workers; in the US case this is manifest in racist attitudes toward blacks (both domestic and foreign).

361. Shofner, Jerrell H. THE LEGACY OF RACIAL SLAVERY: FREE ENTERPRISE AND FORCED LABOR IN FLORIDA IN THE 1940S. *J. of Southern Hist. 1981 47(3): 411-426.* Despite its modern image, Florida in the 1940's was still dominated by the Jim Crow system and its related labor policies. The contract-labor law, originating in the farm tenancy and crop-lien system that replaced slavery, enabled employers like the United States Sugar Corporation to practice debt peonage with impunity. Vagrancy legislation, on the books since the 19th century, allowed white law enforcement officers, despite the efforts of organizations such as the Workers' Defense League, to deprive blacks of their civil rights. In northern Florida where forced labor originated, decades of abuse culminated in the Payne lynching of 1945, the surrounding publicity helped convince Florida it needed to improve its race-relations image. Based on Governors' Correspondence (Florida State Archives, Tallahassee) and other primary sources; 43 notes.   E. L. Keyser

362. Shofner, Jerrell H. POSTSCRIPT TO THE MARTIN TABERT CASE: PEONAGE AS USUAL IN THE FLORIDA TURPENTINE CAMPS. *Florida Hist. Q. 1981 60(2): 161-173.* Legislation resulting from the Martin Tabert case was thought to end peonage in the Turpentine camps in 1923. Analysis reveals that the statutes changed little, and brings into question the effectiveness of statute law versus custom. There were numerous cases of peonage in the camps after 1923. The burden of proof was shifted to the laborer to disprove any allegation of debt to an employer. Peonage remained in the camps as late as 1949. Based on records in the National Archives, Florida newspapers, court records and other sources; 28 notes.   N. A. Kuntz

363. Sowell, Thomas. ARE QUOTAS GOOD FOR BLACKS? *Commentary 1978 65(6): 39-43.* Discusses the validity of the quota system for blacks, finding it fallacious as a measurement of discrimination. Affirmative Action hiring does not take into account such variables as age distribution and educational contrasts. Preferential admissions policies work against the talented black student, reflecting instead a concern over image and government subsidies on the part of institutions of higher learning. Finally, blacks oppose these measures, as they frequently do school busing, which often heightens racism among the young.   J. Tull

364. Spivey, Donald. THE AFRICAN CRUSADE FOR BLACK INDUSTRIAL SCHOOLING. *J. of Negro Hist. 1978 63(1): 1-17.* Industrial arts education was utilized in the maintenance of subordination and exploitation of black people in the US South and in Africa. It was a negative aspect of the Pan-African movement. Both white Europeans and white Southerners put industrial schooling to effective use in pursuing a world order based upon white rule. Primary materials in the Rockefeller archives and domestic and foreign secondary materials; covers 1879-1940. 82 notes.   N. G. Sapper

365. Spivey, Donald. BLACKS AND ORGANIZED LABOR. *New Scholar 1978 5(2): 365-368.* Cites numerous historians and notes that American scholarship lags behind that of Europeans. New Left historians of Latin America and Africa are exploring models of a cultural-psychological nature which would be informative if applied to the American history of the black working class. 5 notes.   D. K. Pickens

366. Storey, Anne; Crouch, Henry; and Storey, John. "THE LITTLE WOMAN" SYNDROME AN ANALYSIS OF SOME CULTURAL DETERMINANTS OF PAY DIFFERENTIALS. *Int. J. of Women's Studies [Canada] 1981 4(3): 289-303.* Discusses how the British Victorian novel has nurtured the "little woman" image of women in Great Britain and the United States and contributed to the inequality in pay for women, which is 60% of men's compensation; 19th-20th centuries.

367. Szymanski, Al. TRENDS IN ECONOMIC DISCRIMINATION AGAINST BLACKS IN THE U.S. WORKING CLASS. *Rev. of Radical Pol. Econ. 1975 7(3): 1-21.* Discusses the exploitive nature of racism and capitalism in the 19th and 20th centuries, the decreasing of employment discrimination, and the difficulties of inculcating radical socialist ideology in the working class as a whole, 1950's-70's.

368. Thomas, Richard W. INDUSTRIAL CAPITALISM, INTRA-CLASS RACIAL CONFLICT AND THE FORMATION OF BLACK WORKING CLASS POLITICAL CULTURE. *J. of African-Afro-American Affairs 1979 3(1): 11-45.* Traces the rise of industrial capitalism during the 19th century, emphasizing the fostering of racial tension and provides a survey of the development of black labor unions during the 20th century.

369. Tuttle, William M., Jr. AMERICA'S BLACK WORKERS: A TOUCHSTONE OF DEMOCRACY'S PROGRESS AND RETREAT. *Rev. in Am. Hist. 1983 11(2): 181-185.* Reviews William H. Harris's *The Harder We Run: Black Workers since the Civil War* (1982), which studies the patterns of racism that have prevented black workers from full participation in social and economic life.

370. Williams, Gregory. A RESEARCH NOTE ON TRENDS IN OCCUPATIONAL DIFFERENTIATION BY SEX. *Social Problems 1975 22(4): 543-547.* Replicates and extends the research of Edward Gross on the measurement of long-term trends in occupational differentiation by sex in the US labor force, taking into account methodological problems that Gross faced. The result is a substantial and consistent decline in differentiation as opposed to Gross' findings of little or no decline during 1900-60. The data suggest some but not rapid progress toward reducing segregation of women in occupations. Notes, biblio.
                                A. M. Osur

371. Withey, Lynne. WOMEN AND WORK IN THE EARLY TWENTIETH CENTURY. *Rev. in Am. Hist. 1982 10(1): 109-114.* Review essay of Maurine Weiner Greenwald's *Women, War, and Work: The Impact of World War I on Women Workers in the United States* (1980) and Nancy Schrom Dye's *As Equals and As Sisters: Feminism, the Labor Movement, and the Women's Trade Union League of New York* (1980), covering 1870-1920.

Economics and Statistics of Labor

372. Adams, Donald R., Jr. ONE HUNDRED YEARS OF PRICES AND WAGES: MARYLAND, 1750-1850. *Working Papers from the Regional Econ. Hist. Res. Center 1982 5(4): 90-129.* Shows that rural Americans remained a powerful influence on total US expenditures throughout the antebellum period.

373. Benz, George A. THE THEORETICAL BACKGROUND OF JOHN M. CLARK AND HIS THEORY OF WAGES. *Rev. of Social Econ. 1981 39(3): 307-321.* Discusses social economist John M. Clark's

theory of wages as determined by the form of structure of institutional forces.

374. Boyd, Marjorie. A PRIMER ON THE ECONOMY: HOW WE CAN BRING BACK QUALITY—SHARING A PIECE OF THE ACTION. *Washington Monthly 1974 5(12): 23-31.* Labor quality would rise with increased participation in management and profit sharing. S

375. Brack, John and Cowling, Keith. ADVERTISING AND LABOUR SUPPLY: WORKWEEK AND WORKYEAR IN U.S. MANUFACTURING INDUSTRIES, 1919-76. *Kyklos [Switzerland] 1983 36(2): 285-303.* Advertising and the resulting consumerism are responsible for the stability of the 40-hour workweek, despite increases in real wages.

376. Burkhauser, Richard V. and Turner, John A. SOCIAL SECURITY, PRERETIREMENT LABOR SUPPLY, AND SAVING: A CONFIRMATION AND A CRITIQUE. *J. of Pol. Econ. 1982 90(3): 643-646.* Reevaluates earlier research performed with Martin Feldstein's social security wealth variable, in view of errors pointed out by Dean R. Leimer and Selig D. Lesnoy. Burkhauser and Turner's original regressions dealing with the impact of social security on the market work of adult males in the United States during 1929-42 and 1946-71 are reestimated.

377. Cameron, Rondo. COMPARATIVE ECONOMIC HISTORY. *Res. in Econ. Hist. 1977 (supplement 1): 287-305.* Reviews the history and development of comparative economic history. This subdiscipline, though still not extensive, is growing rapidly. Early literature is decidedly sparse, but the recent variety is too abundant to cope with. Some favorite subjects include multinational macroeconomic comparisons, organized labor and the working classes, agriculture, and banking and finances. Covers major problems in methodology, as well as other difficulties. 80 notes, ref., appendix. V. L. Human

378. Clark, Kim B. UNIONIZATION AND PRODUCTIVITY: MICRO-ECONOMETRIC EVIDENCE. *Q. J. of Econ. 1980 95(4): 613-639.* Studies the effect of unionization upon productivity, using establishment level data from the US cement industry, and finds a positive union effect on the order of 6%-8% in both cross-section and time series data; 1920-80.

379. DuBoff, Richard. UNEMPLOYMENT IN THE UNITED STATES: AN HISTORICAL SUMMARY. *Monthly Rev. 1977 29(6): 10-24.* Challenges the notion that high-level employment has characterized economic performance since the foundations of US industrial capitalism; questions the validity of statistics for 1896-1976 showing that when comprehensively measured, unemployment has affected large numbers of people for significant periods.

380. Edwards, Richard C. THE SOCIAL RELATIONS OF PRODUCTION IN THE FIRM AND LABOR MARKET STRUCTURE. *Pol. and Soc. 1975 5(1): 83-108.* Asserts the inadequacy of concentrating on labor market processes in examining unemployment, poverty, etc., and provides an analysis of capitalist production which differentiates the workplace control of large monopolistic firms (bureaucratic control) from that of small, competitive companies (hierarchical control). The former, rising after the 1890's, resulted in "internal labor markets" and changed worker traits, while the latter, dependent upon the 'external' labor market, has carried forward the employer and employee practices of earlier capitalist development. Based on secondary sources; 2 tables, 25 notes, biblio. D. G. Nielson

381. Friedmann, Harriet. SIMPLE COMMODITY PRODUCTION AND WAGE LABOUR IN THE AMERICAN PLAINS. *J. of Peasant Studies [Great Britain] 1978 6(1): 71-100.* Households which exclusively produce a single commodity have a dual character as enterprises and as families. Competition establishes a constant requirement for labour, while demographic variation prevents its continuous supply within the household. Using data from a county in the heart of the American wheat plains to illustrate the analysis, this paper applies a modified version of Marx's theory to the circuits of reproduction of simple commodity production, focusing on their intersection with markets in labour power. The analysis requires elaboration of the Marxist definition of class, in order to differentiate members of specialized commodity production households who work for wages as a temporary phase in the life-cycle, from a permanent class of wage labourers. It concludes that simple commodity production, although it differs from capitalist production as well as from peasant households, requires for its reproduction a well-developed market in labour-power and thus an essentially capitalist economy. J

382. Gordon, Robert J. WHY U.S. WAGE AND EMPLOYMENT BEHAVIOUR DIFFERS FROM THAT IN BRITAIN AND JAPAN. *Econ. J. [Great Britain] 1982 92(365): 13-44.* A comparative historical-theoretical analysis of wages and employment behavior in Great Britain, Japan, and the United States since the late 19th century. The author considers the connection between wage stickiness and employment fluctuations, evidence on the responsiveness of wages, hours, and employment, the organization of labor markets, and the origins of labor market institutions. Based on statistical data from the US Department of Commerce, OECD Historical Statistics for Great Britain and Japan, and secondary sources; 5 tables, 22 notes, biblio. G. L. Neville

383. Grossman, Allyson Sherman. WOMEN IN DOMESTIC WORK: YESTERDAY AND TODAY. *Monthly Labor Rev. 1980 103(8): 17-21.* Provides statistics on women in domestic service since 1870 when over half of female workers were private household workers, and concludes that the demand for professional domestics with higher job status may increase from the less than 3% of women employed in 1980.

384. Haber, Sheldon. TRENDS IN WORK RATES OF WHITE FEMALES, 1890 TO 1950. *Industrial and Labor Relations Rev. 1973 26(4): 1122-1134.* "The dramatic increase over the years in the labor force participation rate of women has been the subject of considerable speculation and research, with most analysts stressing the effect on this rate of changes that have occurred on the supply side of the market. Using census data for 1890, 1920, and 1950, this study tests the relationship between the participation rates of white females and a major demand variable—the industrial structure of the economy—as well as supply variables such as educational attainment. The author concludes that changes in industrial structure have been far more significant than previously realized as a determinant of the increase in the work rates of women." J

385. Harrison, William B. and Yoo, Jang H. LABOR IMMIGRATION IN 1890-1914: WAGE RETARDATION VS. GROWTH-CONDUCIVE HYPOTHESIS. *Social Sci. J. 1981 18(2): 1-12.*

386. Hayghe, Howard. SPECIAL LABOR FORCE REPORTS: SUMMARIES. *Monthly Labor Rev. 1979 102(10): 62-64.* Analyzes the changes in wives' contributions to family income with respect to work experience and percentage of family income, using 1977 data, and compares it to the situation in the 1920's.

387. Humphrey, David Burras and Moroney, J. R. SUBSTITUTION AMONG CAPITAL, LABOR, AND NATURAL RESOURCE PRODUCTS IN AMERICAN MANUFACTURING. *J. of Pol. Econ. 1975 83(1): 57-82.* This paper presents estimates of partial elasticities of substitution among reproducible capital, labor, and an input aggregate of natural resource products. We are specifically interested in two hypotheses: i) Are natural resource products strictly complementary in production with either capital or labor? ii) Are resource products typically less substitutable with capital than with labor? To both questions the answer is, generally, no. Two modes of investigation are used, one based on a translog production function and the other making use of a translog cost function. For most industry groups, the estimated substitution elasticities obtained from the cost function are somewhat lower than those based on the translog production function. J

388. James, John A. SOME EVIDENCE ON RELATIVE LABOR SCARCITY IN 19TH-CENTURY AMERICAN MANUFACTURING. *Explorations in Econ. Hist. 1981 18(4): 376-388.* Examines the thesis that an abundance of natural resources leads to more intensive techniques in manufacturing and a more rapid technical progress. Manufacturing records of 19th-century industries indicate that the hypothesis that the ratio of land to available labor raised wages, and thus the wage-rental ratio, is not as sound as previously believed. Based on

censuses for 1850-80 and secondary sources; 3 tables, ref., appendix.
J. Powell

389. Kerppola, Klaus. PARTICIPATORY ADMINISTRATION AND TEAMWORK IN LABOR-MANAGEMENT COOPERATION. *Am. J. of Econ. and Sociol. 1974 33(1): 19-31.* Various organization motivation theories are examined, along with some empirical data pertaining to them. Primary and secondary sources; fig., 25 notes. W. L. Marr

390. Kniesner, Thomas J. THE FULL-TIME WORKWEEK IN THE UNITED STATES, 1900-1970. *Industrial and Labor Relations Rev. 1976 30(1): 3-15.* The average workweek of full-time workers declined by 35 percent between 1900 and 1940, but has not changed significantly since then. The author of this study first shows that even when one carefully corrects household survey data for underreporting of paid vacations and holidays, the recent secular rigidity of the full-time workweek remains. Next, the author shows that the "traditional" model of labor supply adequately explains the prewar decline in the full-time workweek, but fails to capture the post-1940 rigidity. An expanded model, however, which incorporates the effects of growth in education and in the female wage, does explain the secular trend quite well. This model assumes that an individual's labor supply choice depends on the work-leisure decisions of his family. J

391. Lindert, Peter H. and Williamson, Jeffrey G. THREE CENTURIES OF AMERICAN INEQUALITY. *Res. in Econ. Hist. 1976 1: 69-123.* Analyzes income inequality throughout American history. No overall pattern emerges; income inequality has sporadically increased and declined. Contemporary explanatory theories and cures are far from convincing. Government efforts to reduce income extremes have certainly not been more efficacious than the informal controls of the marketplace. Inequality increases when the labor supply is plentiful but skilled labor is scarce, as does a plethora of technological imbalance. The question as to whether industrialization necessarily requires early income inequality remains unanswered. Table, 4 fig., 45 notes. V. L. Human

392. Lowenstern, Henry. ADJUSTING WAGES TO LIVING COSTS: A HISTORICAL NOTE. *Monthly Labor Rev. 1974 97(7): 21-26.* Reviews the use of the cost-of-living factor in adjustment of wages in the United States from 1919 to 1974, and traces the emergence of the cost-of-living escalator in two key contracts between General Motors and the United Automobile Workers of America in 1948 and 1950.

393. Orton, Eliot S. CHANGES IN THE SKILL DIFFERENTIAL: UNION WAGES IN CONSTRUCTION, 1907-1972. *Industrial and Labor Relations Rev. 1976 30(1): 16-24.* This study examines the year-to-year movement in the wage differential between skilled and unskilled workers, 1907-72, using union contract rates in the construction industry. The author examines a number of hypotheses that have been suggested as explanations for changes in the skill differential. He finds that changes in the price level (a demand factor) best explain cyclical changes and that the level of foreign immigration (a supply factor) best explains secular changes. Although the author's model predicts a narrowing of the skill differential since the early 1960's, the differential has remained essentially unchanged in recent years, leading the author to conclude that the increasing level of illegal immigrants, not recorded in official statistics, has served to retard the expected decrease in the premium paid to skilled workers. J

394. Parsley, C. J. LABOR UNION EFFECTS ON WAGE GAINS: A SURVEY OF RECENT LITERATURE. *J. of Econ. Literature 1980 18(1): 1-31.* Examines recent literature on the union-nonunion wage differential in the United States and Great Britain; 1920's-70's.

395. Perskey, Joseph and Tsang, Herbert. PIGOUVIAN EXPLOITATION OF LABOR. *Rev. of Econ. and Statistics 1974 56(1): 52-57.* An econometric testing of a neoclassicist economic theory of labor exploitation.

396. Ramsett, David E. and Heck, Tom R. WAGE AND PRICE CONTROLS: A HISTORICAL SURVEY. *North Dakota Q. 1977 45(4): 5-22.* Compares wage-price controls during World War I, World

War II, the Korean War, and 1971; assesses success, impact, decision-making, and administration.

397. Ratner, Ronnie Steinberg. THE SOCIAL MEANING OF INDUSTRIALIZATION IN THE U.S.: DETERMINANTS OF THE SCOPE OF COVERAGE UNDER WAGE AND HOUR STANDARDS LEGISLATION, 1900-1970. *Social Problems 1980 27(4): 448-466.* Examines two perspectives on the meaning and characteristics of work in the tertiary sector—Daniel Bell's postindustrial model and Harry Braverman's monopoly capital model—especially the applicability of these frameworks for understanding variations in employee coverage under wage and hour standards legislation between 1900 and 1970.

398. Reiff, Janice L. and Hirsch, Susan. RECONSTRUCTING WORK HISTORIES BY COMPUTER: THE PULLMAN SHOP WORKERS, 1890-1967. *Hist. Methods 1982 15(3): 139-142.* When Pullman ceased operations in 1967, the company left a history of labor conflict and rich, well-organized archives. The Scientific Information Retrieval System was selected as the computer program to express employment statistics into a usable form for social scientists. The project has detailed and voluminous data about complex historical issues. 10 notes. D. K. Pickens

399. Roberts, Charles A. INTERREGIONAL PER CAPITA INCOME DIFFERENTIALS AND CONVERGENCE: 1880-1950. *J. of Econ. Hist. 1979 39(1): 101-112.* In several recently published works Richard A. Easterlin has shown that per capita incomes as measured in current dollars have tended to converge over time. In this paper the per capita income estimates have been adjusted for interregional differences in prices. In adjusting the regional per capita income estimates for interregional differences in both urban and rural-urban prices it was found that no significant differences occurred in either the levels of differences or in the rates of convergence from the original estimates. In addition, no significant correlation was found between interregional per capita incomes and price levels. J

400. Rockoff, Hugh. PRICE AND WAGE CONTROLS IN FOUR WARTIME PERIODS. *J. of Econ. Hist. 1981 41(2): 381-401.* The debate over wage and price controls has taken a highly stylized form. Advocates of controls stress the direct effect on the obvious problem, inflation, whereas critics stress the side effects. This paper measures and compares the effects of controls during the four periods when controls have been used in the United States in the 20th century. Although tentative conclusions are drawn concerning the price effects, the size of the administrative bureaucracies, and so forth, the clearest lesson, as usual, is that the issue warrants further investigation by economic historians because it is important, and because the historical record is surprisingly rich. J

401. Rodgers, Daniel T. TRADITION, MODERNITY, AND THE AMERICAN INDUSTRIAL WORKER: REFLECTIONS AND CRITIQUE. *J. of Interdisciplinary Hist. 1977 7(4): 655-681.* Analyzes the hypothesis of initial shock and gradual acculturation as the theoretical model for explicating the history of workers experiencing the process of industrialization. The modernization hypothesis is seen as suspect and "a de-escalation of levels of generalization" is urged. Recasting labor history as collective working-class biography would indicate the variety of subcultures within the working class and would reveal continuities and divergences. 34 notes. R. Howell

402. Sachs, Jeffrey. THE CHANGING CYCLICAL BEHAVIOR OF WAGES AND PRICES: 1890-1976. *Am. Econ. Rev. 1980 70(1): 78-90.* This analysis of the long-term changes in the Phillips curve (the level of unemployment influences the rate of inflation) demonstrates that, theoretically, monetary and fiscal authorities would intervene to prevent price deflations and unemployment. Since 1945, counter-cyclical macroeconomic policy changed the cyclical behavior of price and wage setters aided by creation of implicit and explicit long-term contracts, thereby creating cyclical rigidity. 4 tables, 22 ref. D. K. Pickens

403. Solow, Robert M. WHAT HAPPENED TO FULL EMPLOYMENT? *Q. Rev. of Econ. and Business 1973 13(2): 7-20.* This article, the David Kinley Lecture at the University of Illinois at Urbana-Champaign in December 1972, reviews some of the vicissitudes of the

concept of full employment as it is affected by alternative views of the structure of the labor market. In particular, the older 'structural employment' theory is compared with a newer view that concentrates more on the nature of jobs than on the characteristics of workers, and more on turnover than on the scarcity of jobs.   J

404. Sweezy, Alan and Owens, Aaron. THE IMPACT OF POPULATION GROWTH ON EMPLOYMENT. *Am. Econ. Rev. 1974 64(2): 45-50.* Evaluates economic theory since the 1930's on the impact of low population growth on labor and economic conditions.

405. Williams, Vergil L. and Fish, Mary. ECONOMIC POLICY AND DISTRIBUTION OF INCOME. *Midwest Q. 1971 13(1): 47-64.* A study of the changes in economic theories of distribution of income,

mentioning Adam Smith and his followers, known as Classical Economists, Karl Marx, John Stuart Mill, and Herbert Spencer. The Depression of the 1930's, in which unemployment spread to hard-working people, drove home the point that poverty is not necessarily related to lack of ambition and willful idleness. The authors report on the New Jersey Graduated Work Incentive Experiment and the current welfare reform movement.   G. H. G. Jones

406. Wright, Gavin. CHEAP LABOR AND SOUTHERN TEXTILES, 1880-1930. *Q. J. of Econ. 1981 96(4): 605-629.* The delay in the South's capture of the American cotton textile market was due to the slow process of capital accumulation and the rapid increase in real wages that occurred in the South as well as in the North.

2. EARLY AMERICAN LABOR, TO 1865

General

407. Adams, Donald R., Jr. EARNINGS AND SAVINGS IN THE EARLY 19TH CENTURY. *Explorations in Econ. Hist. 1980 17(2): 118-134.* Records of E. I. Du Pont de Nemours in Delaware, Maryland, from 1813 to 1860 show that the firm did not exploit its workers, that real wages increased significantly over time, and that all employees, even those in the lowest wage categories, were able to save on a regular basis. The highest paid workers saved a larger percentage of their wages than did the lowest paid, but a substantial proportion of all workers succeeded in accumulating savings equal to or higher than their annual incomes. Based on manuscript records, published statistics, and secondary accounts; 9 tables, 19 notes, 13 ref. P. J. Coleman

408. Adams, Donald R., Jr. THE STANDARD OF LIVING DURING AMERICAN INDUSTRIALIZATION: EVIDENCE FROM THE BRANDYWINE REGION, 1800-1860. *J. of Econ. Hist. 1982 42(4): 903-917.* The question of whether tangible economic growth occurred during the American industrial revolution has been aggravated by the lack of reliable data. A rich source of evidence on worker earnings and savings in the Brandywine River Valley, a center of 19th-century industrial activity, is found in the records of the E. I. DuPont and Company. These indicate that these workers shared in the antebellum process of American economic growth. Based on records of the E. I. DuPont and Company; 8 tables, 14 notes, appendix. J. Powell

409. Aiken, John R. NEW NETHERLANDS ARBITRATION IN THE 17TH CENTURY. *Arbitration J. 1974 29(3): 145-160.* "Early mercantile arbitration on the American continent is usually assumed to have been derived from English common law and the experience of English merchants and guilds. But there were also Dutch colonies during the 17th century, and their tradition was traceable to Roman law, by way of The Netherlands. In the course of exhaustive research, the author may have found the earliest example of a woman serving as an arbitrator. It appears that back in 1662, a dispute arose as to whether a woman had been paid properly for making linen caps. The issue turned on whether she had performed her job without excessive spoilage. A court appointed another women as an expert arbitrator 'to inspect the linen caps' and 'settle the parties' case.' The history of arbitration among Dutch colonies convinces the author that it was superior to that of the English common law." J

410. Anderson, Terry L. and Thomas, Robert Paul. THE GROWTH OF POPULATION AND LABOR FORCE IN THE 17TH-CENTURY CHESAPEAKE. *Explorations in Econ. Hist. 1978 15(3): 290-312.* New population estimates suggest that the major influx of immigrants to the American plantation colonies occurred after 1650; Negroes constituted only a small proportion of the total population and labor force; the population began to reproduce itself in the last third of the century; and the tobacco colonies enjoyed rapid extensive growth and perhaps intensive growth. Published records and secondary accounts; 15 tables, 58 notes, 24 ref., appendix. P. J. Coleman

411. Archibald, Robert. INDIAN LABOR AT THE CALIFORNIA MISSIONS: SLAVERY OR SALVATION? *J. of San Diego Hist. 1978 24(2): 172-182.* The mission system in California set out to institute social change and transformation of cultural values, often with force which unintentionally resulted in virtual slavery for the Indians; covers 1775-1805.

412. Blewett, Mary H. I AM DOOM TO DISAPOINTMENT: THE DIARIES OF A BEVERLY, MASSACHUSETTS, SHOEBINDER, SARAH E. TRASK, 1849-51. *Essex Inst. Hist. Collections 1981 117(3): 192-212.* The diaries of Sarah E. Trask, rediscovered in the Beverly Historical Society, reveal that common work in domestic manufacture provided an additional bond of womanhood for working-class women. The diary entries from January 1849-August 1849 and May 1851, included here, describe Sarah Trask's work as a shoebinder from which she was unable to support herself and lonely in the absence of a prospective male provider. Based on Sarah E. Trask's diaries; 14 notes. R. S. Sliwoski

413. Boyer, Lee R. LOBSTER BACKS, LIBERTY BOYS, AND LABORERS IN THE STREETS: NEW YORK'S GOLDEN HILL AND NASSAU STREET RIOTS. *New York Hist. Soc. Q. 1973 57(4): 280-308.* Numerous clashes between British troops and colonials took place earlier than the well-publicized Boston Massacre in 1770. One of these was a bloody, two-day confrontation in New York City in January 1770 known as the Battle of Golden Hill. No deaths occurred there nor in a riot on Nassau Street a short time later. In both, merchant seamen were prominent, both money and labor problems were involved, and the outbreak was apparently spontaneous. Both were indications of deeper problems which would culminate in Lexington and Concord five years later. Based on contemporary correspondence, newspapers, and other primary sources; 9 illus., 44 notes. C. L. Grant

414. Breen, T. H. A CHANGING LABOR FORCE AND RACE RELATIONS IN VIRGINIA 1660-1710. *J. of Social Hist. 1973 7(1): 3-25.* Prior to 1660, Negroes in Virginia were indiscriminately grouped with poor whites and indentured servants as a generally untrustworthy class. The 1660's witnessed the rise of tobacco as a money crop, which helped pull the poor whites out of poverty but left the Negro behind. After this the poorest whites allied with the wealthy against the Negro. 110 notes. V. L. Human

415. Brigham, Loriman S., ed. AN INDEPENDENT VOICE: A MILL GIRL FROM VERMONT SPEAKS HER MIND. *Vermont Hist. 1973 41(3): 142-146.* A Clinton, Massachusetts, textile operative in 1851 writes her schoolmarm cousin at "the Harbor" of her hard work weaving the cloth around wagon cushions; also of her reading and her disdain for church-going hypocrites. Editor's foreword. T. D. S. Bassett

416. Chambers-Schiller, Lee. THE SINGLE WOMAN REFORMER: CONFLICTS BETWEEN FAMILY AND VOCATION, 1830-1860. *Frontiers 1978 3(3): 41-48.* Studies the lives and attitudes of unmarried women reformers, 1830-60, as they faced the conflicts between their work and their unmarried social status.

417. Cometti, Elizabeth. THE LABOR FRONT DURING THE REVOLUTION. *West Georgia Coll. Studies in the Social Sci. 1976 15: 79-90.* Describes the economic and labor situation in the American colonies during the American Revolution.

418. Constantin, Charles. THE PURITAN ETHIC AND THE DIGNITY OF LABOR: HIERARCHY VS. EQUALITY. *J. of the Hist. of Ideas 1979 40(4): 543-561.* The Puritan conception of "calling" changed in the 18th century as thinkers in that tradition became familiar with the "Great Chain of Being." Calling, as Puritans had the idea from Martin Luther and John Calvin, was potently equalitarian; all labor, if offered to God as a "living sacrifice," in faith, had high spiritual value. Some Puritans, such as William Perkins, insisted that various labors were more and less honorable, but others, including John Cotton, emphasized the equalitarian implication of calling. In the 18th century Jonathan Edwards and his followers Joseph Bellamy and Samuel Hopkins conceived the "infinite diversity" of the creation, including men, in terms of the hierarchical chain, but continued to insist on the spiritual value of all faithful labor. Their rationalistic contemporaries Charles Chauncey and Jonathan Mayhew derived a less spiritual and equalitarian view from the chain. Based on published primary and secondary sources; 45 notes. D. B. Marti

419. Dobbs, Jeannine. AMERICA'S FIRST ALL WOMEN'S MAGAZINE. *New-England Galaxy 1977 19(2): 44-48.* Describes the first magazine written, edited, and published by women, *The Operatives' Magazine,* in 1841. Women employed in the Lowell Mills kept this magazine and, later, *The Lowell Offering,* going until 1845. Lucy Larcom, who later wrote for the *Atlantic,* was first published in this journal. P. C. Marshall

420. Dodd, Jill Siegel. THE WORKING CLASSES AND THE TEMPERANCE MOVEMENT IN ANTE-BELLUM BOSTON. *Labor Hist. 1978 19(4): 510-531.* The working classes of ante-bellum Boston divided over temperance movements; some used "traditional"

forms of collective violence to resist, others supported temperance. The evidence is analyzed in "pre-industrial" and "industrializing" terms which cut across class lines. Based on quantitative data from newspapers; 5 tables, 46 notes.   L. L. Athey

421. Dublin, Thomas. THE HODGDON FAMILY LETTERS: A VIEW OF WOMEN IN THE EARLY TEXTILE MILLS, 1830-1840. *Hist. New Hampshire 1978 33(4): 283-295.* In the mid-19th century many young New Englanders migrated from rural areas to urban centers. Sarah and Elizabeth Hodgdon, whose letters are reproduced here, left Rochester, New Hampshire, to work in a Lowell, Massachusetts, textile factory. Typical of female mill workers of the period, they apparently migrated not from economic necessity but because of rural overcrowding. Their letters reveal their strong family bonds, adjustment problems, and their economic independence. 20 notes.   D. F. Chard

422. Dublin, Thomas. WOMEN, WORK, AND PROTEST IN THE EARLY LOWELL MILLS: "THE OPPRESSING HAND OF AVARICE WOULD ENSLAVE US." *Labor Hist. 1975 16(1): 99-116.* The organization of work and the nature of housing in Lowell promoted the development of a sense of community among the women workers. The women relied upon the element of community in strikes in 1834 and 1836, and in the political action of the 1840's. The cultural traditions emergent involved preindustrial and industrial values. Based on records of the Hamilton Manufacturing Co. and on the *Lowell Offering;* 36 notes.   L. L. Athey

423. Dublin, Thomas. WOMEN, WORK, AND THE FAMILY: FEMALE OPERATIVES IN THE LOWELL MILLS, 1830-1860. *Feminist Studies 1975 3(1/2): 30-39.* Between 1830 and 1860 Lowell, Massachusetts, was a leading center of textile manufacture in the United States. From 1830 to 1845 women operatives formed a majority of the mill workforce. They were native-born and lived in company-owned boarding houses, which became centers of community life, and which provided the organizational base for the Lowell labor movement. After 1845 Irish immigrant men and women became an increased portion of the mill population. Immigrant women tended to live with their families (usually parents) rather than in boarding houses. Family dependence on the income of these female children meant greater caution in strike action and discouraged labor activity in Lowell during the 1850's. Primary and secondary sources; 33 notes.   S. R. Herstein

424. Dublin, Thomas. WOMEN, WORK, AND PROTEST IN THE EARLY LOWELL MILLS: "THE OPPRESSING HAND OF AVARICE WOULD ENSLAVE US." Cantor, Milton, ed. *American Workingclass Culture: Explorations in American Labor and Social History* (Westport, Conn.: Greenwood, 1979): 167-188. Reprint of an article originally published in *Labor History* .

425. Dublin, Thomas. WOMEN WORKERS AND THE STUDY OF SOCIAL MOBILITY. *J. of Interdisciplinary Hist. 1979 9(4): 647-665.* Studies the careers of women operatives in the cotton textile mills of the Hamilton Manufacturing Company in Lowell, Massachusetts, between 1836 and 1860. Simple correlations between economic opportunity and the existence of labor protest are contradicted by the evidence. For women operatives in Lowell, the existence of real opportunities for occupational mobility and wage gains did not undermine the growth of collective protest. At the end of the period the forces which kept women in the mills despite narrowing prospects made it more difficult for them to engage in collective protest. The changing circumstances also generated a different set of expectations among operatives, making mill work by the 1850's more a drab necessity than an exciting opportunity. Printed sources and the records of the Hamilton Manufacturing Company, housed in the Baker Library, Harvard Business School; 5 tables, 27 notes.   R. Howell

426. Dublin, Tom. WORKING WOMEN AND THE "WOMEN'S QUESTION." *Radical Hist. Rev. 1979-80 (22): 93-98.* During 1830-60, some women challenged the then-occurring articulation of women's place in American society; reprints a letter written in 1850 to feminist Caroline Dall by Harriet Farley, former textile mill worker and former coeditor of the textile companies-subsidized periodical, the *Lowell Offering.*

427. Dubnoff, Steven. GENDER, THE FAMILY, AND THE PROBLEM OF WORK MOTIVATION IN A TRANSITION TO INDUSTRIAL CAPITALISM. *J. of Family Hist. 1979 4(2): 121-136.* Using data from the payrolls of a Lowell, Massachusetts, factory and the 1860 federal manuscript census, studies the adaptation of the largely preindustrial labor force to the strictures of factory labor. Men were absent from work less than women and that family position influenced one's work orientation. 3 tables, 18 notes, biblio.   T. W. Smith

428. Earle, Carville and Hoffman, Ronald. THE FOUNDATION OF THE MODERN ECONOMY: AGRICULTURE AND THE COSTS OF LABOR IN THE UNITED STATES AND ENGLAND, 1800-60. *Am. Hist. Rev. 1980 85(5): 1055-1094.* A comparative analysis of the availability and cost of labor in the grain belt of the northern United States, the cotton of the South, and the English countryside. Includes a review of the literature on scarce and expensive American labor as a cause of technological change, presentation of an alternative model of development based on low-priced labor incorporating the mechanism of agricultural seasonality and its market imperfections, and, to test this model, an examination of labor costs as determinants in the process of capital accumulation, urbanization, and industrialization. Mainly secondary sources; 2 graphs, 3 tables, 7 fig., 82 notes.   J. Powell

429. Early, Francis H. A REAPPRAISAL OF THE NEW ENGLAND LABOUR-REFORM MOVEMENT OF THE 1840'S: THE LOWELL FEMALE LABOR REFORM ASSOCIATION AND THE NEW ENGLAND WORKINGMEN'S ASSOCIATION. *Social Hist. [Canada] 1980 13(25): 33-54.* Fifteen women operatives formed the Lowell Female Labor Reform Association in 1845, after 20 years of ephemeral associations devoted to working-class causes. The Association concentrated on bread-and-butter issues, but supported other reforms, ignoring the controversy between workers and Associationists in order to advance its own objectives. In 1847 the LFLRA was absorbed by the Lowell Female Industrial Reform and Mutual Aid Society. It never had more than 500 members out of over 7,000 Lowell women mill workers, but the labor-reform mentality did not disappear. 123 notes.
                                                             D. F. Chard

430. Ewart, Shirley. CORNISH MINERS IN GRASS VALLEY: THE LETTERS OF JOHN COAD, 1858-1860. *Pacific Hist. 1981 25(4): 38-45.* A brief history of Cornish miners and their search for gold in Grass Valley, California. John Coad (1819-81) emigrated from Cornwall to Wisconsin in 1844 and then to Grass Valley hoping to improve his fortune. His experiences are detailed in letters to his wife, who returned to Wisconsin in 1858. 6 illus.   H. M. Evans

431. Faler, Paul. CULTURAL ASPECTS OF THE INDUSTRIAL REVOLUTION: LYNN, MASSACHUSETTS, SHOEMAKERS AND INDUSTRIAL MORALITY, 1826-1860. *Labor Hist. 1974 15(3): 367-394.* The Industrial Revolution was accompanied by a cultural revolution emphasizing an "industrial morality" which stressed self-discipline, work, and sobriety. Promoted by religious revivals, the changing economy, and the emergent manufacturing class who first accepted the industrial morality, the new value code was applied stringently to the poverty stricken, drunkards, and malingerers. Forms of recreation and leisure were modified, and three distinct responses appeared among workmen: traditionalists who clung to past customs, loyalists who accepted the new morality with deference to employers, and rebels who accepted the new morality but promoted collective self-help against employers. The division promoted discord and prevented the development of a class consciousness. Based on the Lynn *Mirror* , unpublished dissertations, and governmental reports.   L. L. Athey

432. Faler, Paul. CULTURAL ASPECTS OF THE INDUSTRIAL REVOLUTION: LYNN, MASSACHUSETTS, SHOEMAKERS AND INDUSTRIAL MORALITY, 1826-1860. Cantor, Milton, ed. *American Workingclass Culture: Explorations in American Labor and Social History* (Westport, Conn.: Greenwood, 1979): 121-148. Reprint of an article originally published in *Labor History* .

433. Faragher, John Mack. "MEN AND WOMEN'S WORK ON THE OVERLAND TRAIL" FROM *FAMILIES ON THE OVERLAND TRAIL. Pacific Hist. 1979 23(1): 4-23.* Graphic account of the everyday tasks of pioneers in getting ready to make the trek westward (raising the money, soapmaking, selecting and mending clothing, making

out diets, getting the necessary foodstuffs, and packing) as well as necessary work while on the trail (droving, getting ready for the night, cooking, and grazing). All work and responsibilities were apportioned in strict adherence to the traditional sexual division of labor, with the work of women structured around the men's. When men became sick, women often filled their places. Covers 1840's-50's. Based on many published primary accounts of people involved in wagon trains; 110 notes.

H. M. Parker, Jr.

434. Foner, Philip S. DIE ROLLE DER HANDWERKER UND LOHNARBEITER BEI DER VORBEREITUNG DER AMERI-KANISCHEN REVOLUTION [The role of the artisans and day laborers in the preparations of the American Revolution]. *Zeitschrift für Geschichtswissenschaft [East Germany] 1977 25(6): 676-687.* Even when American artisans had the franchise, they were intimidated and dominated by the colonial economic elite, while poor wage laborers were generally denied the ballot. Thus, the artisans and the wage laborers who joined the Sons of Liberty had two goals: to terminate British political and economic oppression, and to end political dominance by the colonial economic elite. The Sons of Liberty actually provided the impetus for the revolutionary struggle for independence. Primary and secondary sources; 67 notes. J. T. Walker

435. Fullard, Joyce. ANN PRESTON: PIONEER OF MEDICAL EDUCATION AND WOMEN'S RIGHTS. *Pennsylvania Heritage 1982 8(1): 9-14.* Describes Doctor Ann Preston's struggle to be admitted to medical schools in Philadelphia, Pennsylvania, in the late 1840's, her eventual acceptance by Dr. Nathaniel R. Mosely as a student at his private clinic, and her training at the Female Medical College of Pennsylvania, founded by William Mullen in 1850, which led her to work for "the improvement of women's medical education and for the acceptance of women physicians as fully qualified professionals."

436. Gilman, Amy. "COGS TO THE WHEELS": THE IDEOLOGY OF WOMEN'S WORK IN MID-NINETEENTH-CENTURY FIC-TION. *Sci. & Soc. 1983 47(2): 178-204.* In both popular and serious fiction, writers portrayed women workers in ways that illuminated a middle-class ideology of female work. For all writers, the idealized female work role contained a plethora of humanistic and traditional values that were counterpoised against a new industrial, male, material-istic, and individualistic arena. Only in the fiction of Melville was the issue of social class joined, and only Melville and Hawthorne portrayed women workers without sentimentality. The sentimental novelists avoid-ed understanding the causes or consequences of female poverty and exploitation, and ended by creating myths about industrial capitalism that masked social problems and their causes. 41 notes.

R. E. Butchart

437. Goldin, Claudia and Sokoloff, Kenneth L. WOMEN, CHIL-DREN, AND INDUSTRIALIZATION IN THE EARLY REPUB-LIC: EVIDENCE FROM THE MANUFACTURING CENSUSES. *J. of Econ. Hist. 1982 42(4): 741-774.* Manufacturing firm data for 1820 to 1850 are employed to investigate the role of women and children in the industrialization of the American Northeast. The principal findings include: 1) Women and children composed a major share of the entire manufacturing labor force; 2) their employment was closely associated with production processes used by large establishments, both mecha-nized and nonmechanized; 3) the wage of females (and boys) increased relative to that of men with industrial development; and 4) female labor force participation in industrial counties was substantial. These findings bear on the nature of technical change during early industrialization and why American industrial development was initially concentrated in the Northeast. J

438. Gundersen, Joan R. THE SEARCH FOR GOOD MEN: RE-CRUITING MINISTERS IN COLONIAL VIRGINIA. *Hist. Mag. of the Protestant Episcopal Church 1979 48(4): 453-464.* Challenges the thesis that, in colonial Virginia, the Anglican Church failed to find good men to serve its churches, or lacked quality among its candidates. Focuses on how Virginians, including George Washington, did find enough suitable men for a greatly expanding church. By 1776, in contrast to 1726, the number of priests had increased to 109 from 42, and more than half were colonial-born, in contrast to none 50 years earlier. Based on author's doctoral dissertation; the Fulham Palace Manuscripts, Virginia Colonial Records Project microfilm; published

collections of letters and secondary sources; 2 fig., 58 notes.

H. M. Parker, Jr.

439. Hardy, Melissa A. OCCUPATIONAL MOBILITY AND NA-TIVITY-ETHNICITY IN INDIANAPOLIS, 1850-60. *Social Forces 1978 57(1): 205-221.* Rates and patterns of occupational mobility in Indianapolis during the 1850's are analyzed using data from manuscript federal census schedules. Between 1850 and 1860, nearly half the working males who remained in the city were mobile, most of them within the nonmanual or manual categories. Analysis by age cohorts revealed that the young were more likely to be upwardly mobile and less likely to be downwardly mobile than older cohorts of workers. This differential mobility was almost totally a result of the different origin distributions of the cohorts. An analysis of nativity-ethnicity indicated that immigrant males occupied favorable positions in the occupational hierarchy in 1850, which led to considerable upward mobility. Once structural conditions were taken into account, however, differences between the mobility rates of native-born and foreign-born were small, with the native-born somewhat more likely to cross the manual-nonmanual boundary. Basic findings from this study are compared with those from studies of Boston, Philadelphia, and Houston. J

440. Harvey, Katherine A. BUILDING A FRONTIER IRON WORKS: PROBLEMS OF TRANSPORT AND SUPPLY, 1837-1840. *Maryland Hist. Mag. 1975 70(2): 149-166.* Discusses "the major logistical problems and ... solutions" of the George's Creek Coal and Iron Company in building a sizable complex of blast furnaces, foundry, and rolling mill on land southwest of Cumberland, Maryland, at today's Lonaconing. Distance from manufacturing centers and labor supplies required the fullest possible use of materials from company lands. Technical problems of hauling stone, brickmaking for lime-kilns, building quarry railroads and tramways, and lifting blocks into place on the stack are reported from journals kept by superintendents. The first run-out of iron came in May 1839, by which time workers and their families brought the population to 700 in what had been "almost a wilderness." Miners were recruited from Pennsylvania and the scarcity of finished lumber for houses led to erecting a company sawmill, while housing materials were purchased from far and wide. The entire venture was predicated on access to eastern markets via the Chesapeake and Ohio Canal, but by June 1839 the canal was still 50 miles from Cumberland. The problems of transporting heavy goods to and from the region otherwise were insuperable, so the big furnace was blown out and the staff reduced. Only years later did the business resume; but in coal, not iron. Primary sources; 3 illus., 89 notes. G. J. Bobango

441. Henretta, James A. COMMUNITY STUDIES IN THE MID-ATLANTIC: A COMMENTARY. *Working Papers from the Regional Econ. Hist. Res. Center 1980 3(2): 58-65.* Commentary on two articles in this issue (Billy G. Smith's "Struggles of the 'Lower Sort' in Late Eighteenth-Century Philadelphia" and Elizabeth Moyne Homsey's "Free Blacks in Kent County, Delaware, 1790-1830") discusses the usefulness of quantitative and literary data in interpreting and analyzing social class and racial goals, and in political history.

442. Hirata, Lucie Cheng. CHINESE IMMIGRANT WOMEN IN NINETEENTH-CENTURY CALIFORNIA. Berkin, Carol Ruth and Norton, Mary Beth, ed. *Women of America: A History* (Boston: Houghton Mifflin Co., 1979): 223-244. In 1850, the ratio of men to women was 12 to 1 in California; because the supply of labor lagged behind demand, Chinese women were given more opportunities in the labor force. Because of the many bachelors, women performed services usually reserved for family women: they were domestic servants, laundresses and prostitutes. Many Chinese prostitutes were able to earn enough money to quit the profession. The second Chinese female resident of San Francisco was Ah-Choi, a Chinese prostitute who arrived in 1848. Tong members were frequently owners of brothels and there were few free agents. Map, table, 18 notes. K. Talley

443. Hurtado, Albert L. CONTROLLING CALIFORNIA'S INDIAN LABOR FORCE: FEDERAL ADMINISTRATION OF CALIFORNIA INDIAN AFFAIRS DURING THE MEXICAN WAR. *Southern California Q. 1979 61(3): 217-238.* Examines the formation of federal Indian policy in California during 1846-49. During this period California operated under a succession of military governors who were less observant of Indian rights than of landholder complaints

of Indian raids on livestock. Indians were categorized as 1) those who worked for Anglo and Mexican landholders, and 2) "horsethief" Indians who aroused fear and hostility from the ranchers. Military governors such as Kearny appointed subagents to deal with Indian affairs, and soon Indians were expected to obey a series of restrictive vagrancy regulations. Few attempts were made to assist California Indians who were expected to remain passive and to work for Anglo and Mexican employers. 71 notes.　　　　　　　　　　A. Hoffman

444. Huzel, James P. THE FAMILY, WORK AND CAPITALISM. *Can. J. of Hist.* [Canada] 1980 15(2): 249-251. Reviews David Levine's *Family Formation in an Age of Nascent Capitalism* (1977) and Thomas Dublin's *Women at Work: The Transformation of Work and Community in Lowell, Massachusetts, 1826-1869* (1979), the first of which undertakes family reconstitution, selecting four English parishes, spanning the years 1550 through 1850, each representing distinct socioeconomic types. The thesis is that employment creates population. Thomas Dublin in his study of women workers goes beyond the economic structure to examine questions of ideology. His aim is to explore the degree to which changes in the composition, family structure, residential patterns, and work situation of the labor force in the Lowell textile mills affected the intensity of protest, 1826-69.　　　　　　J. Powell

445. Janiewski, Dolores. ARCHIVES: MAKING COMMON CAUSE: THE NEEDLEWOMEN OF NEW YORK, 1831-69. *Signs* 1976 1(3, Part 1): 777-786. Women laborers in New York City's garment trades between 1831 and 1869 tried to deal with subsistence-level wages, exploitative homework, piecework, ruinous competition, and chronic unemployment by varying modes of organization and expression such as trade unions, producers' cooperatives dependent on public patronage, mutual aid societies, and feminist pressure groups. Some developed an analysis of class and sex oppression while others eschewed theory for publicity campaigns to attract public support. All failed to change the economic and social system, but each group in its own way tried to resist oppression. Primary sources; 5 notes.
　　　　　　　　　　　　　　　　　　　　　　S. E. Kennedy

446. Jordan, Jean P. WOMEN MERCHANTS IN COLONIAL NEW YORK. *New York Hist.* 1977 58(4): 412-439. Customs records and post-1730 newspaper advertisements reveal that there were numerous women merchants in New York City during the 17th and 18th centuries. Women merchants were not allowed to participate in political decision-making. Economic opportunities for women declined after the American Revolution, and only now are women regaining the status in business they enjoyed in the colonial period. 2 illus., 68 notes.　　R. N. Lokken

447. Kauffman, Henry J. HANDCRAFTS IN LANCASTER COUNTY. *J. of the Lancaster County Hist. Soc.* 1982 86(2): 57-68. Traces the development of crafts industries in 18th-century Lancaster, Pennsylvania.

448. Kaufman, Polly Welts. A WIDER FIELD OF USEFULNESS: PIONEER WOMEN TEACHERS IN THE WEST, 1848-1854. *J. of the West* 1982 21(2): 16-25. A group of highly motivated and unusually self-sufficient New England women went west during 1848-54 as schoolteachers. In many cases economic necessity, as well as a sense of mission, drove these women to undertake alone the difficult journeys and endure frontier living conditions. Many of them remained in the West beyond their two-year teaching commitments. Their professional standing enabled them to attain a degree of autonomy unavailable to other women of their time. Based on letters and a diary in the National Popular Education Board papers, Connecticut Historical Society, Hartford; 2 maps, photo, table.　　　　　　　　　B. S. Porter

449. Keller, Kenneth W. THE PHILADELPHIA PILOTS' STRIKE OF 1792. *Labor Hist.* 1977 18(1): 36-48. Ship pilots in Philadelphia organized a work stoppage in 1792 which resulted in higher wages, and also in a law which outlawed similar actions by any labor organization in Pennsylvania. The pilots were not motivated by radical social thought. Based on Pennsylvania statutes and newspapers; 18 notes.
　　　　　　　　　　　　　　　　　　　　　　L. L. Athey

450. Klein, Maury. FROM UTOPIA TO MILL TOWN. *Am. Hist. Illus.* 1981 16(6): 34-41, 48, (7): 36-43. Part I: THE ASSOCIATES. Chronicles the failure of the Boston Associates, a group of male elite of Boston society who founded the mill town of Lowell, Massachusetts, to establish a planned community beautifully landscaped and peopled by happy workers; between 1810 and 1860 the "industrial utopia" fell to typical mill town squalor. Part II: THE MILL GIRLS. During 1833-50 the labor force of the cotton mills in Lowell consisted of mostly undemanding, hardworking farm women, who expected only half men's wages; this changed when economic difficulties and industrialization made the women militant, convincing the associates to hire desperate immigrants, a practice followed by firms in other mill towns by 1860.

451. Lasser, Carol S. A "PLEASINGLY OPPRESSIVE" BURDEN: THE TRANSFORMATION OF DOMESTIC SERVICE AND FEMALE CHARITY IN SALEM, 1800-1840. *Essex Inst. Hist. Collections* 1980 116(3): 156-175. The Salem Female Charitable Society, founded in 1801, directed its efforts toward providing for indigent female children: first in a semi-institutional setting, then in homes, as legally bound domestic servants. The society assisted 82 girls before the mercantile base of New England's economy eroded, necessitating dissolution of the society in 1837. Both incipient industrialization and changes in domestic service, where the structured relations of employer and employee were replacing personal bonds of benevolence and gratitude, forced the society to abandon its placement program. Extensive records provide the necessary materials for a case study of this transformation and for follow-up histories of half the girls bound out by the society. Primary sources; 45 notes.　　　　　R. S. Sliwoski

452. Lightner, David L. CONSTRUCTION LABOR ON THE ILLINOIS CENTRAL RAILROAD. *J. of the Illinois State Hist. Soc.* 1973 66(3): 285-301. As many as 10,000 men labored for the Illinois Central in the 1850's. Particularly in southern Illinois, Asiatic cholera was responsible for a scarcity of laborers. Wages had to be high for the hard work at long hours. The railroad and its contractors showed little interest in the personal comfort of their laborers but were prompt in paying wages in cash. The workers suffered from mistrust by local residents, and from drunkenness and rioting among themselves. Many, unable to save money, moved on to other labor camps, although a few managed to buy farms. Based on the Illinois Central Archives, Newberry Library; 3 illus., 72 notes.　　　　　　　　A. C. Aimone

453. McGaw, Judith A. "A GOOD PLACE TO WORK." INDUSTRIAL WORKERS AND OCCUPATIONAL CHOICE: THE CASE OF BERKSHIRE WOMEN. *J. of Interdisciplinary Hist.* 1979 10(2): 227-248. In 1848 Mrs. Amy Fuller of Sheffield, Berkshire County, Massachusetts, wrote to the owners of a paper mill in nearby Dalton and applied for a position. She had heard that their mill was "a good place to work." The terminology might mean that 19th-century workers exercised occupational choice. Research shows that women in paper mills usually had obtained their positions themselves, many times moving to accept them. They also chose their particular jobs. Nineteenth-century workers were active shapers of their employment instead of victims of it. Based on US Census records, Massachusetts government documents, letters, and newspapers; 41 notes.　　　　　E. R. Campbell

454. McGaw, Judith A. TECHNOLOGICAL CHANGE AND WOMEN'S WORK: MECHANIZATION IN THE BERKSHIRE PAPER INDUSTRY, 1820-1855. Trescott, Martha Moore, ed. *Dynamos and Virgins Revisited: Women and Technological Change in History* (Metuchen, N.J.:Scarecrow Pr., 1979): 77-99. Mechanization in the Massachusetts paper industry in the 19th century did not greatly affect sex segregation on the job. Women essentially continued doing the same jobs before and after the introduction of various machines which were typically tended by men. Women's work continued to be unskilled, but, because it was not generally involved with machines, the working conditions of women improved relative to the men's. 16 fig., 20 notes.
　　　　　　　　　　　　　　　　　　　　　　J. Powell

455. Miller, Randall M. LOVE OF LABOR: A NOTE ON DANIEL PRATT'S EMPLOYMENT PRACTICES. *Alabama Hist. Q.* 1975 37(2): 146-150. Discusses working conditions and attitudes of labor from the Piney Woods toward textile factory work, and reproduces a letter by Shadrach Mims in which conditions at Daniel Pratt's mill at Prattsville are described. The letter was in part a protest to Colonel Price Williams over a representative of his who was attempting to attract (with extravagant inducements) Pratt's factory workers. Mims did not feel

that this procedure was in the best interest of any party involved. 7 notes.   E. E. Eminhizer

456. Miner, H. Craig. THE CAPITOL WORKMEN: LABOR POLICY ON A PUBLIC PROJECT. *Capitol Studies 1975 3(1): 45-52.* Examines the responses of the federal government to labor difficulties in the construction of the wings of the Capitol Building during the 1850's.

457. Monkkonen, Eric H. CLASS OR CULTURE? *Rev. in Am. Hist. 1981 9(1): 62-66.* Review essay of Bruce Laurie's *Working People of Philadelphia, 1800-1850* (1980).

458. Muller, Edward K. and Groves, Paul A. THE EMERGENCE OF INDUSTRIAL DISTRICTS IN MID-NINETEENTH CENTURY BALTIMORE. *Geographical Rev. 1979 69(2): 159-178.* The prevalent view of land use in large, mid-nineteenth century North American cities is one of high density and of a chaotic intermixture of activities. The evolution of large-scale and new organizational forms of industrial production created centrifugal and localization forces among some manufacturing activities and resulted in industrial districts distinguished by product type, production mode, and labor-force composition. In Baltimore by 1860, despite the persistence of some elements of manufacturing location from the older mercantile city, the new locational tendencies formed six functionally differentiated and spatially separated industrial districts. In the context of population growth, peripheral urban expansion, and predominantly pedestrian journeys-to-work, industrial localization imparted a cellular structure to the organization of work and residence. Based on US manufacturing censuses, contemporary published reports, and secondary sources; 5 maps, 6 tables, graph, 59 notes.   J

459. Nash, Gary B. THE FAILURE OF FEMALE FACTORY LABOR IN COLONIAL BOSTON. *Labor Hist. 1979 20(2): 165-188.* Poverty, the escalating costs of poor relief, and the effects of war resulted in the first experiment in the American colonies, undertaken by Boston leaders in their organization of the United Society for Manufactures and Importation, to involve large numbers of women in a linen manufactory during the 1750's. Women resisted; officials were reluctant to use coercion; and the effort collapsed. Based on records of the Society for Encouraging Industry and the Employment of the Poor; 40 notes.
                                                                L. L. Athey

460. Nellis, Eric G. WORK AND SOCIAL STABILITY IN PRE-REVOLUTIONARY MASSACHUSETTS. *Hist. Papers [Canada] 1981: 81-100.* The study of working conditions and labor status in Massachusetts demonstrates that the society was stable and without appreciable changes in socioeconomic and cultural conditions. This conclusion contradicts current historiography and returns to earlier appraisals. Based on the Public Archives of Massachusetts and official documents; 58 notes, appendixes.   G. P. Cleyet

461. Nellis, Eric Guest. LABOR AND COMMUNITY IN MASSACHUSETTS BAY: 1630-1660. *Labor Hist. 1977 18(4): 525-544.* Wage controls and labor law in early Massachusetts Bay Colony were part of a coordinated community effort to survive and to develop. English legislation separated labor as a distinctive social unit. The proper function of labor in Massachusetts was participation in attaining stability and permanence. Based on *Massachusetts Bay Records* and actions of the General Court; 63 notes.   L. L. Athey

462. Neufeld, Maurice F. THE PERSISTENCE OF IDEAS IN THE AMERICAN LABOR MOVEMENT: THE HERITAGE OF THE 1830S. *Industrial and Labor Relations Rev. 1982 35(2): 207-220.* In creating the first US labor movement, the craftsmen of Andrew Jackson's time advanced several ideas that challenged the emergent doctrine of extreme laissez-faire. Six of those ideas—such as the beliefs that excessive inequality of wealth and widespread monopoly existed—provided support for the idea and practice of trade unionism. These ideas have continued to be espoused by leaders and members of successive labor federations, including those of the AFL-CIO. The persistence in some form of the political, social, and economic inequities that first evoked the ideas may explain this.   J

463. Nickless, Pamela J. A NEW LOOK AT PRODUCTIVITY IN THE NEW ENGLAND COTTON TEXTILE INDUSTRY,

1830-1860. *J. of Econ. Hist. 1979 39(4): 889-910.* The antebellum cotton textile industry has been characterized as experiencing rising labor productivity despite technological stagnation. Explanations of this phenomenon often emphasize the role of changes in labor quality. New data on skilled workers make it possible to construct a labor input index that accounts for changes in skill mix. Labor productivity is then analyzed in the context of changes in total-factor productivity. A very different picture of productivity change in the textile mills emerges, casting doubt on the hypothesis of technological stagnation and emphasizing the importance of an increasing capital-labor ratio in maintaining productivity advance. 6 tables, 35 notes, appendix.   J

464. Nisonoff, Laurie. BREAD AND ROSES: THE PROLETARIANISATION OF WOMEN WORKERS IN NEW ENGLAND TEXTILE MILLS, 1827-1848. *Hist. J. of Massachusetts 1981 9(1); 3-14.* Examines female textile workers' resistance to the changes introduced as the textile industry grew. 2 illus., 39 notes. Comment by Carl Siracuse, pp. 27-29.   W. H. Mulligan, Jr.

465. O'Day, Edward J. CONSTRUCTING THE WESTERN RAILROAD: THE IRISH DIMENSION. *Hist. J. of Massachusetts 1983 11(1): 7-21.* Examines the work of Irish immigrants in constructing the Western Railroad and the impact of the temporary labor camps on the population history of the Massachusetts towns along the railroad route. %HD Based on Western Railroad letter books, local records, published contemporary reports, and secondary sources.   W. H. Mulligan, Jr.

466. Pessen, Edward. LABOR FROM THE REVOLUTION TO THE CIVIL WAR. *Monthly Labor Rev. 1976 99(6): 17-24.* Discusses the situation of the American labor force 1790's-1860's, showing the effect on American workers of technological, economic, and social changes during that period.

467. Riley, Glenda. 'NOT GAINFULLY EMPLOYED': WOMEN ON THE IOWA FRONTIER, 1833-1870. *Pacific Hist. Rev. 1980 49(2): 237-264.* Iowa women, grouped in 19th-century census reports as "not gainfully employed," performed many household tasks economically significant in the history of a western state. The Bureau of the Census erred in equating gainful employment with paid work. Iowa women processed foodstuffs and made garments, soap, home medicines, and other products necessary to life on the frontier. Based on census reports, memoirs, reminiscences, and diaries of 19th-century Iowa women, personal correspondence, and contemporary newspapers; 79 notes.
                                                                R. N. Lokken

468. Ríos-Bustamante, Antonio José. NEW MEXICO IN THE EIGHTEENTH CENTURY: LIFE, LABOR AND TRADE IN LA VILLA DE SAN FELIPE DE ALBUQUERQUE, 1706-1790. *Aztlán 1976 7(3): 357-389.* A caste-class system developed in Albuquerque, in which there was considerable social mobility.

469. Rock, Howard B. THE PERILS OF LAISSEZ-FAIRE: THE AFTERMATH OF THE NEW YORK BAKERS' STRIKE OF 1801. *Labor Hist. 1976 17(3): 372-387.* The 1801 bakers' strike in New York City arose from complaints about the city council's regulations of profits. The effect was to promote formation of a large manufactory of bread which endangered the economic existence of small bakeries. Based upon New York City newspapers and municipal archives; 35 notes.
                                                                L. L. Athey

470. Sainsbury, John A. INDIAN LABOR IN EARLY RHODE ISLAND. *New England Q. 1975 48(3): 378-393.* By the end of King Philip's War (1675-76) the Indians of Rhode Island were scattered and many became dependent on whites for employment; by the end of the colonial period over 35% of the Indians in Rhode Island were living with white families. Rhode Island settlers, especially during the 17th century, employed Indians on a voluntary, short-term basis. Local governments also hired Indians for construction work, and some Indians became indentured servants for stated lengths of time. Many Indians, however, became servants involuntarily as a punishment for felony, in payment for debts, or for participating in King Philip's War. Despite a strain of humanitarianism, the perpetual bondage of Indians was established and legally acceptable in 18th-century Rhode Island. Legislation against the import of Indian slaves, however, prevented Indian slavery from reaching the proportions of Negro slavery. The government

was against the expansion of Indian labor, which was generally unskilled, consisting mainly of construction work and military service. "Indian employment by white colonists in Rhode Island was the result . . . of Indian social disintegration. . . ." Based on primary and secondary sources; 69 notes, appendix.   B. C. Tharaud

471. Salinger, Sharon V. ARTISANS, JOURNEYMEN, AND THE TRANSFORMATION OF LABOR IN LATE EIGHTEENTH-CENTURY PHILADELPHIA. *William and Mary Q. 1983 40(1): 62-84.* Labor relations shifted from that of owners and bound laborers to employers and wage earners. Craft organizations appeared—chiefly groups of master craftsmen. At mid-century, bound labor had accounted for a half of the labor force. Discusses the changing composition of labor in the various trades. Accounts for the decline in the use of bound labor. Because of difficulties in setting up as independent artisans, most Philadelphia workers became permanent wage earners. Lack of vertical mobility caused tension within the shops and also contributed to exploitation. Based on newspapers and histories of labor; 3 tables, 93 notes.   H. M. Ward

472. Salinger, Sharon V. "SEND NO MORE WOMEN": FEMALE SERVANTS IN EIGHTEENTH-CENTURY PHILADELPHIA. *Pennsylvania Mag. of Hist. and Biog. 1983 107(1): 29-48.* Female indentures rose in proportion to those of males indicating a demand for domestics. The women arrived impoverished, worked at demeaning duties, and frequently ended in the poor house. Based on the Historical Society of Pennsylvania's Servant Lists and the Elizabeth Drinker Diary, court records, Guardians of the Poor Admissions Records from the City Archives of Philadelphia, newspapers, and secondary works; 32 notes.   T. H. Wendel

473. Shelton, Cynthia. LABOR AND CAPITAL IN THE EARLY PERIOD OF MANUFACTURING: THE FAILURE OF JOHN NICHOLSON'S MANUFACTURING COMPLEX: 1793-1797. *Pennsylvania Mag. of Hist. and Biog. 1982 106(3): 341-364.* The failure of Nicholson's Falls-of-Schuylkill manufactory near Philadelphia resulted from a diversification which disabled Nicholson from paying regular wages to his skilled workmen who therefore struck. Blurred distinctions between laborer, manager, and capitalist circumscribed early manufacturing enterprise. Based on the Nicholson Papers, Pennsylvania State Archives, Harrisburg; other manuscript sources, and secondary works; 76 notes.   T. H. Wendel

474. Shelton, Cynthia J. TEXTILE PRODUCTION AND THE URBAN LABORER: THE PROTO-INDUSTRIALIZATION EXPERIENCE OF PHILADELPHIA, 1787-1820. *Working Papers from the Regional Econ. Hist. Res. Center 1982 5(4): 46-89.* Shows that urban textile manufacturing was based on the labor of the poor and that manufactories were modelled on English and colonial workhouses.

475. Shepherd, Rebecca A. RESTLESS AMERICANS: THE GEOGRAPHIC MOBILITY OF FARM LABORERS IN THE OLD MIDWEST, 1850-1870. *Ohio Hist. 1980 89(1): 25-45.* Discusses the motivations of agricultural laborers who migrated westward from the Midwest, based on analysis of the entire farm labor population of six townships in Ohio, Indiana, and Illinois. The availability of cheap or free land, the opportunity to escape from undesirable circumstances, and the general freedom offered by the move were important factors. Primary sources; 8 tables, 46 notes.   J. Powell

476. Silvia, Philip T., Jr. THE POSITION OF WORKERS IN A TEXTILE COMMUNITY: FALL RIVER IN THE EARLY 1800S. *Labor Hist. 1975 16(2): 230-248.* Examines employer-dominance in the textile industry of Fall River, Massachusetts. Although a critique of labor conditions was led by Robert Howard, a muleskinner, the policies of the employers regarding grievances, wages, work conditions and company housing were maintained as a part of a laissez-faire philosophy hostile to organized labor in the 1880's. Based upon reports of the Massachusetts Bureau of Labor Statistics and Senate committees, newspapers and secondary sources; 32 notes.   L. L. Athey

477. Sisson, William A. FROM FARM TO FACTORY: WORK VALUES AND DISCIPLINE IN TWO EARLY TEXTILE MILLS. *Working Papers from the Regional Econ. Hist. Res. Center 1981 4(4): 1-26.* Discusses numerous studies of the changes in work habits and attitudes of workers who experienced the transformation from preindustrial to industrial society in the 19th century, and presents a study of two textile mills operating in the 1810's, the Duplanty, McCall and Company in Delaware and the Antietam Woolen Manufacturing Company in Funkstown, Maryland, in which workers and owners retained their preindustrial working habits and attitudes even after their experiences in the industrial workplace; 1814-19.

478. Smith, Billy G. STRUGGLES OF THE "LOWER SORT" IN LATE EIGHTEENTH-CENTURY PHILADELPHIA. *Working Papers from the Regional Econ. Hist. Res. Center 1980 3(2): 1-30.* Analysis of living standards and career patterns among cordwainers, tailors, laborers, and merchant seamen in Philadelphia, 1754-1800, indicates that they accounted for a good percentage of the lower economic echelons and, contrary to previously published data, that they had a marginal existence.

479. Thomas, Robert Paul and Anderson, Terry L. WHITE POPULATION, LABOR FORCE AND EXTENSIVE GROWTH OF THE NEW ENGLAND ECONOMY IN THE SEVENTEENTH CENTURY. *J. of Econ. Hist. 1973 33(3): 634-667.* The authors critically review existing population series and present new population and labor force estimates for each decade. Because land was abundant and capital was relatively unimportant, labor trends provide substantial information where normal measures of economic growth are lacking. A stable population model, developed by Alfred J. Lotka, is applied to New England. Findings on the average size of a completed family are given (7.13 children), and two estimates for the natural increase rate of the white population are presented. Based on primary and secondary sources; 9 tables, graph, 36 notes, 2 appendixes.   W. R. Hively

480. Thompson, Agnes L. NEW ENGLAND MILL GIRLS. *New-England Galaxy 1974 16(2): 43-49.* Describes life in the woolen and cotton mills of Lowell, Massachusetts, in the 1840's and 1850's. Farm girls gained economic independence by working for a few years before marriage, but were closely supervised in the mill, boarding house, and community, and had to cope with long hours, low wages, and limited social and educational opportunities. By 1857 competition forced their replacement by a permanent industrial working class of Irish and French Canadians. 6 illus.   P. C. Marshall

481. Tjarks, Alicia V. DEMOGRAPHIC, ETHNIC AND OCCUPATIONAL STRUCTURE OF NEW MEXICO, 1790. *Americas (Acad. of Am. Franciscan Hist.) 1978 35(1): 45-88.* The best census of colonial New Mexico, prepared in 1790, showed the slow demographic growth of the province, which was almost wholly vegetative. Spanish and caste towns grew, whereas Indian villages were in decline. About half the population was Spanish, though ethnic definitions were not precise. Outside the primary rural sector, occupations were relatively unimportant and undifferentiated. Primary sources; 16 tables, 64 notes.

D. Bushnell

482. Tucker, Barbara M. THE FAMILY AND INDUSTRIAL DISCIPLINE IN ANTE-BELLUM NEW ENGLAND. *Labor Hist. 1980 21(1): 55-74.* Analyzes the role of the family in industrial discipline in factories in Slatersville, Rhode Island, and Webster, Massachusetts, 1790-1840. The family assumed part of the responsibility for industrial training and discipline in these factory towns, which were modeled in a way to preserve tradition. Old practices dissolved in the 1840's as factories shifted to an individual-based work force and new immigration disrupted traditional patterns. Labor conflict accompanied the change. Based on the Samuel Slater collection, Harvard U.; 46 notes.

L. L. Athey

483. Tucker, Barbara M. OUR GOOD METHODISTS: THE CHURCH, THE FACTORY AND THE WORKING CLASS IN ANTE-BELLUM WEBSTER, MASSACHUSETTS. *Maryland Hist. 1977 8(2): 26-37.* Describes the appeal of Methodism to owners and workers in Webster's textile industry. The church provided the "moral foundation of a work effort" which provided owners with a disciplined work force and allowed workers to adjust to industrialism while having their social needs met. Illus., 39 notes.   G. O. Gagnon

484. Ulrich, Laurel Thatcher. "A FRIENDLY NEIGHBOR": SOCIAL DIMENSIONS OF DAILY WORK IN NORTHERN COLO-

NIAL NEW ENGLAND. *Feminist Studies 1980 6(2): 392-405.* Examines the role which the relative economic position of women, servants, and husbands had on women's social status in Essex County, Massachusetts, and New Hampshire from 1650 to 1750. Women were largely excluded from the more formal types of colonial trade, but predominated in the less formal networks, where they acted as agents for their husbands or rarely for themselves by selling the surplus produced by their cottage industries. Based on 17th- and 18th-century account books, probate inventories, and court records; 35 notes.

G. V. Wasson

485. Vedder, Richard K.; Gallaway, Lowell E.; and Klingaman, David. DISCRIMINATION AND EXPLOITATION IN ANTEBELLUM AMERICAN COTTON TEXTILE MANUFACTURING. *Res. in Econ. Hist. 1978 3: 217-262.* A "pessimistic" school of historians has argued that antebellum American cotton textile workers were "exploited" and female workers discriminated against, while some "optimistic" scholars argue that workers shared in an expected fashion in productivity gains over time. By statistically estimating production functions from data from the McLane Report (1833) and 1860 Census manuscripts, marginal products of the factors of production are obtained and compared with their factor prices. Workers were paid roughly their marginal products and other productive factors were likewise rewarded. It is concluded that the "optimists" are more likely correct and that neoclassical theory is consistent with observed wage and profit levels. Some job entry discrimination against females probably existed, however.

J

486. Vogel, Lise. ARCHIVES: THEIR OWN WORK: TWO DOCUMENTS FROM THE NINETEENTH-CENTURY LABOR MOVEMENT. *Signs 1976 1(3, Part 1): 787-802.* Deteriorating conditions of factory work and wages in the 1840's led to efforts by labor reformers and organizers to mobilize women workers. "The Factory Bell," a poem by an unknown mill woman, contrasts the measurement of time by the relentless ringing of the factory bell with the warm rhythms of nature. *Factory Life as It is, by an Operative* sums up grievances of women textile workers and suggests solutions such as reform and organization to achieve the goals of republicanism, liberty, and equality. Based on primary and secondary works; 10 notes. S. E. Kennedy

487. Wagman, Morton. LIBERTY IN NEW AMSTERDAM: A SAILOR'S LIFE IN EARLY NEW YORK. *New York Hist. 1983 64(2): 101-119.* Authorities in New Amsterdam imposed restrictions on seamen who were believed to disturb law and order while on shore. The Dutch West India Company protected its monopoly rights by prohibiting sailors from selling duty-free goods from their own sea chests, thereby ending in New Amsterdam a very old custom of the sea. Seamen employed by the Dutch West India Company were required to do extra work while in port and were subject to impressment into military service. Nevertheless, their rights and privileges were protected by courts in New Amsterdam, especially in wage disputes. Many seamen made New Netherland their home. A few became rich burghers in New Amsterdam, but most were plain folk in the city. Based on *New York Historical Manuscripts: Dutch* and other primary sources; 5 illus., 34 notes. R. N. Lokken

488. Walker, Joseph. LABOR-MANAGEMENT RELATIONS AT HOPEWELL VILLAGE. *Labor Hist. 1973 14(1): 3-18.* Traces the development of labor-management relations at the Hopewell Village iron furnace 1800-50. Relations were relatively stable with few wage changes. There were few strikes or lockouts, and no evidence of a trend toward unionism. A system of fines was used to keep workers in line, and paternalism and self-interest prevailed as a guide to relations. Based on the Hopewell Village recordbooks, documents, and other manuscript collections; 87 notes. L. L. Athey

489. Walker, Juliet E. K. OCCUPATIONAL DISTRIBUTION OF FRONTIER TOWNS IN PIKE COUNTRY: AN 1850 CENSUS SURVEY. *Western Illinois Regional Studies 1982 5(2): 146-171.*

490. Weiner, Lynn. "WHO ARE WANTED IN MINNESOTA": WORKERS AS DESCRIBED IN ANTEBELLUM "BOOSTER LITERATURE." *Labor Hist. 1977 18(3): 403-406.* Presents an historical document from the newspaper, *St. Anthony Express,* which illustrates

local "class and gender" dimensions of work in 1851. 4 notes.

L. L. Athey

491. —. LABOR IN THE ERA OF THE AMERICAN REVOLUTION: AN EXCHANGE. *Labor Hist. 1983 24(3): 414-454.* Nash, Gary B.; Smith, Billy G.; and Hoerder, Dirk. LABORING AMERICANS AND THE AMERICAN REVOLUTION, pp. 414-439. Critiques Hermann Wellenreuther's "Labor in the Era of the American Revolution: A Discussion of Recent Concepts and Theories" (see following entry). Wellenreuther negates the importance of material factors in the origins of the American Revolution, while restoring the importance of ideological factors. Wellenreuther, Hermann. REJOINDER, pp. 440-454. Nash, Smith, and Hoerder read 19th- and 20th-century economic concepts and developments into the origins of the American Revolution, ignoring the importance of religious and political factors. 2 tables, graph, appendix, 127 notes. L. F. Velicer

492. Wellenreuther, Hermann. LABOR IN THE ERA OF THE AMERICAN REVOLUTION: A DISCUSSION OF RECENT CONCEPTS AND THEORIES. *Labor Hist. 1981 22(4): 573-600.* Recent work on American Revolutionary society assumes that a large segment of the colonial urban population consisted of laborers moved to political activity by an increasing maldistribution of wealth, and rising unemployment. The number of laborers in colonial society was not as large as many authors have suggested, nor were these laborers in such dire economic straits. Factors other than economic deprivation need to be assessed when explaining the laborers' participation in the American Revolution. Table, fig., 72 notes. L. F. Velicer

493. Wiggins, David K. WORK, LEISURE, AND SPORT IN AMERICA: THE BRITISH TRAVELERS IMAGE, 1830-1860. *Can. J. of Hist. of Sport [Canada] 1982 13(1): 28-60.* British travel accounts reveal perceptions of the role and types of sports and other leisure activities in America; unlike the British, Americans considered work of utmost importance and were "preoccupied with the pursuit of wealth."

494. Wolfe, Allis Rosenberg, ed. LETTERS OF A LOWELL MILL GIRL AND FRIENDS: 1845-1846. *Labor Hist. 1976 17(1): 96-102.* Presents five letters of a Lowell mill girl, Harriet Hanson Robinson, as a reflection of the upbringing, attitudes, and desires of working women in 1845-46. Letters are from the Robinson collection in the Schlesinger Library, Radcliffe College. 3 notes. L. L. Athey

495. Wright, Helena. THE UNCOMMON MILL GIRLS OF LOWELL. *Hist. Today [Great Britain] 1973 23(1): 10-19.* Describes the life and working conditions of women textile workers at the Boston Manufacturing Company at Lowell, an outgrowth of the Waltham experiment, 1813-50.

496. —. [LOW-SKILLED LABOR FOR SOUTHERN TEXTILE INDUSTRY]. *J. of Econ. Hist. 1976 36(1): 84-101.* Terrill, Tom E. EAGER HANDS: LABOR FOR SOUTHERN TEXTILES, 1850-1860, pp. 84-99. Was there an ample supply of low-skilled, free labor in the antebellum Southeast to develop a textile industry producing coarser goods? Using county-level data from the 1850 and 1860 manuscript censuses and other historical sources, we found there was a surplus of low-skilled, free (mostly white) labor in Edgefield County, South Carolina, where the textile industry was firmly established before the Civil War. If Edgefield County was not a unique case, then potential investors in southern textiles were probably not restrained by an inadequate labor force. Moreover, our Edgefield study reinforces other analyses which indicate that many whites hovered on the margins of southern society even in its most prosperous decade before the Civil War. Gitelman, H. M. DISCUSSION, pp. 100-101. J

497. —. [MECHANIZATION IN THE SHOE INDUSTRY: LYNN, MASSACHUSETTS]. *J. of Econ. Hist. 1981 41(1): 59-64.*

Mullian, William H., Jr. MECHANIZATION AND WORK IN THE AMERICAN SHOE INDUSTRY: LYNN, MASSACHUSETTS, 1852-1883, pp. 59-63. Between 1852 and 1883 the nature and organization of work in the American shoe industry changed due to the introduction of machinery and the factory system. For generations before 1852, shoes had been made by hand in small workshops organized through a putting out system. Each artisan possessed the skill and tools to make an entire shoe by hand, and work was intertwined with family life. With the introduction of machinery, making a shoe was divided into many distinct tasks, each performed by a different worker, and work was moved into a factory where it came under closer supervision.
Blewett, Mary H. DISCUSSION, p. 64.   J

498. —. [WAGES IN THE IRON INDUSTRY].

498. Zabler, Jeffrey F. FURTHER EVIDENCE ON AMERICAN WAGE DIFFERENTIALS, 1800-1830. Explorations in Econ. Hist. 1972 10(1): 109-117.
Adams, Donald R., Jr. WAGE RATES IN THE IRON INDUSTRY: A COMMENT, Explorations in Econ. Hist. 1973 11(1): 89-94. Prompted by Zabler's article, "Further Evidence on American Wage Differentials, 1800-1830"
Zabler, Jeffrey F. MORE ON WAGE RATES IN THE IRON INDUSTRY: A REPLY, Explorations in Econ. Hist. 1973 11(1): 95-99. Both disagree on the interpretation of the evidence and whether or not it confirms the "Habakuk hypothesis." Based on documents and secondary sources.   P. J. Coleman

Professional, Indentured, and Organized Labor

499. Benson, Susan Porter. BUSINESS HEADS & SYMPATHIZING HEARTS: THE WOMEN OF THE PROVIDENCE EMPLOYMENT SOCIETY. J. of Social Hist. 1978 12(2): 302-312. Recent work on women's history has led to new questions regarding "the warp of affectional and kin ties on which the fabric of daily life was woven." To answer these questions the author focuses upon the 52 women managers of the Providence (Rhode Island) Employment Society (PES) from 1837 to 1858, which was a typical meliorist urban reform organization devoted to aiding self-supporting seamstresses. Most of the managers were members of the social and economic elite of Providence. Concludes that there emerged a sex-based culture among the women on the PES, which was an amalgam of their class and gender position. Their female culture distanced them from men with whom they lived and their class-based style of life distanced them from their working-class sisters. The society in which they lived, however, did not exacerbate these contradictions. Primary and secondary sources; 34 notes.   R. S. Sliwoski

500. Breen, T. H.; Lewis, James H.; and Schlesinger, Keith. MOTIVE FOR MURDER: A SERVANT'S LIFE IN VIRGINIA, 1678. William and Mary Q. 1983 40(1): 106-120. On 24 May 1678 Thomas Hellier, a 28-year-old indentured servant, murdered with an axe Cuthbert Williamson, Williamson's wife, and a young servant girl at a Charles City County plantation, known as Hard Labour. Immediately captured, he confessed. The night before his execution Hellier told his life story to an Anglican minister, presumed to have been Paul Williams. The narrative of Hellier's life, the minister's comments, and the condemned man's final speech at the gallows were published as The Vain Prodigal Life (1680), and sections of the pamphlet are reprinted here. Surprisingly the minister's reflections are sociological, and the Williamsons were much to be blamed themselves for the tragedy because of their abusive treatment of servants. Cites works on servants; 39 notes.   H. M. Ward

501. Carr, Lois Green and Menard, Russell R. IMMIGRATION AND OPPORTUNITY: THE FREEDMAN IN EARLY COLONIAL MARYLAND. Tate, Thad W. and Ammerman, David L., ed. The Chesapeake in the Seventeenth Century: Essays on Anglo-American Society (Chapel Hill: U. of North Carolina Pr. for the Inst. of Early Am. Hist. and Culture, 1979): 206-242. For much of the 17th century, freed indentured servants who had emigrated from England provided the major labor force in Maryland and were the source of the planters. At the end of the century, however, their economic and social position

declined. This potentially volatile situation was defused as the number of freed servants declined, and as slaves took over their role. 9 tables, 79 notes.   S

502. Char, Tin-Yuke and Char, Wai Jane. THE FIRST CHINESE CONTRACT LABORERS IN HAWAII, 1852. Hawaiian J. of Hist. 1975 9: 128-134. Discusses the need for contract laborers and uses newspaper reports and ships' logs to show that the first contract laborers came from Amoy in Fukien.   R. Alvis

503. Clunie, Margaret B. FURNITURE CRAFTSMEN OF SALEM, MASSACHUSETTS, IN THE FEDERAL PERIOD. Essex Inst. Hist. Collections 1977 113(3): 191-203. The Reverend William Bentley's diary is only a starting point for a study of Salem's craftsmen, because he commented upon them as individuals and did not describe their work. The salient quality of cabinetmaking in Federalist Salem was the cooperative nature of the work. Furniture shops employed specialists whose pieces made up the final product. This symbiotic relationship was due to the nature of the apprenticeship system, family traditions, shop locations, and designs. Based on the diary (1784-1819) of William Bentley and on primary and secondary sources; 50 notes.
                                                           R. S. Sliwoski

504. Davis, Hugh H. THE AMERICAN SEAMEN'S FRIEND SOCIETY AND THE AMERICAN SAILOR, 1828-1838. Am. Neptune 1979 39(1): 45-57. Studies the origins and early years of the American Seamen's Friend Society (ASFS), "when its broad strategy was developed and refined and many of its major projects were first undertaken." This benevolent organization's "foremost objectives—to persuade the sailor to avoid the manifold vices which tempted him and to advance the cause of evangelical Christianity—were scarcely accomplished." However, a "vital part of what was done in these years to improve the lot of American seamen resulted from the efforts of the ASFS." Baed on published sources; 54 notes.   G. H. Curtis

505. Dublin, Thomas. A PERSONAL PERSPECTIVE ON THE TEN HOUR MOVEMENT IN NEW ENGLAND. Labor Hist. 1983 24(3): 398-403. Presents two letters of Daniel Spencer Gilman, a Canadian who worked in Lowell, Massachusetts, during 1840-49. The letters provide a personal glimpse of organized labor activities in New England, especially the drive for the 10-hour working day. Based on the Daniel Spencer Gilman letters; 15 notes.   L. F. Velicer

506. Dunn, Durwood. APPRENTICESHIP AND INDENTURED SERVITUDE IN TENNESSEE BEFORE THE CIVIL WAR. West Tennessee Hist. Soc. Papers 1982 36: 25-40. During 1800-60, the state of Tennessee sought through its county courts to deal both with the social problems of indentured servants, most of whom were orphans, and the administration of the medieval apprenticeship program. Both institutions underwent dramatic and irreversible alterations before the Civil War. Many judicial cases illustrate the wide variety of legal problems handled by the courts, and show that judges consistently handed down decisions benefiting the poor and the disinherited. Such consensus against white bondage unified to a surprising degree these otherwise divergent magistrates in a state early noted for sectional conflict. Based on county court records and compilations of the Tennessee Code; 43 notes.   H. M. Parker, Jr.

507. Foner, Philip S. RABOCHIE I AMERIKANSKAIA REVOLIUTSIIA XVIII VEKA [Labor and the American Revolution in the 18th century]. Voprosy Istorii [USSR] 1978 1: 73-91. Mechanics, artisans, tradespeople, artificers, labourers, journeymen and seamen—the entire colonial working class in short—played a vital role in the American revolution. The colonial workers conducted their resistance to British policies through organizations such as the Sons and Daughters of Liberty, and it was they that took the leadership in the resistance to independence. As the colonies marched down the road from resistance to revolution, the representatives of the mechanics played an increasingly influential role. They advocated not merely the freeing of American economic life from the restrictions of British mercantile policy, but also a reform in the society in Colonial America so that the masses could obtain more benefits from the society and participate in its political activities to a greater extent than heretofore.   J

508. Galenson, David W. BRITISH SERVANTS AND THE COLONIAL INDENTURE SYSTEM IN THE EIGHTEENTH CENTURY. *J. of Southern Hist. 1978 44(1): 41-66.* Examines British indentured servitude, using the quantitative methodology Fogel and Engerman used in analyzing the economics of American Negro slavery. Due to lack of surviving records, this research is based on close study of a collection of more than 3,000 indenture records for 1718-59 from the Guildhall in London. Compiles statistical profiles of the servants' personal characteristics, destinations in the New World, education and skills, and the determining factors in their indentures. Concludes that the British indentures possessed a high literacy rate and valuable occupational skills this contradicts much previous work and should stimulate further research. Disputes the common view that the servants were human cargo shipped and sold only under the profit motive. Instead, it appears that many young people sought better opportunities under the system, that the length of indenture varied by age, training, and skills, and that colonial laws protected them against discrimination in relation to other servants without indentures.   M. S. Legan

509. Galenson, David. IMMIGRATION AND THE COLONIAL LABOR SYSTEM: AN ANALYSIS OF THE LENGTH OF INDENTURE. *Explorations in Econ. Hist. 1977 14(4): 360-377.* Records covering 2,049 servants who emigrated to the American colonies, 1718-59, show that the length of indenture depended on age, sex, literacy, professional skills, and destination. The overwhelming majority of British servants emigrated voluntarily. The length of the contract reflected the market demand for servants in the colony of destination. Based on manuscripts in London and Scotland, published documents and records, and secondary accounts; table, 32 notes, 92 ref.
P. J. Coleman

510. Gersuny, Carl. A BIOGRAPHICAL NOTE ON SETH LUTHER. *Labor Hist. 1977 18(2): 239-248.* Discusses Seth Luther (1795-1863), an important labor leader in Rhode Island in the 1830's. An articulate carpenter, Luther moved from a perception of oppression to defeat in rebellion and then to retreat from reality. A radical, Luther was involved in the labor movement, the free suffrage movement, and the Dorr Rebellion. Based on the writings of Seth Luther; 27 notes.
L. L. Athey

511. Glick, Clarence E. THE VOYAGE OF THE "THETIS" AND THE FIRST CHINESE CONTRACT LABORERS BROUGHT TO HAWAII. *Hawaiian J. of Hist. 1975 9: 135-139.* Using documents from the Public Records Office in London, argues that the first Chinese contract laborers came from Amoy in Fukien.   R. Alvis

512. Gray, Ralph and Wood, Betty. THE TRANSITION FROM INDENTURED TO INVOLUNTARY SERVITUDE IN COLONIAL GEORGIA. *Explorations in Econ. Hist. 1976 13(4): 353-370.* The shift to slavery was caused by the comparatively higher labor costs of indentured servants. Experience also showed that a buffer colony strong enough to deter Spain would not be economically viable if based on indentured white labor. However, a colony dominated by black slave labor would not be an effective military buffer either. Based on manuscripts at the University of Georgia (Athens), published diaries, documents, journals, and secondary accounts.   P. J. Coleman

513. Hancock, Harold B. THE INDENTURE SYSTEM IN DELAWARE, 1681-1921. *Delaware Hist. 1974 16(1): 47-59.* Dutch, Swedish, and English colonists practiced indenture to repay transportation costs to America (or other debts), and later used it "to provide for poor children and to see that they learned a trade." Debtors found indenture "a convenient means by which to work off their obligations," and the British used it to dump "undesirables" in the colony. Terms of indenture became fixed and formalized and gave overwhelming supervisory and disciplinary powers to the master. Negroes found that apprenticeship laws discriminated against them, but in time indenture enabled beneficent masters to manumit their slaves. In the 19th century apprenticeship generally served to introduce youths to useful trades and especially to provide workers for industry. Indenture declined after the Civil War but was not formally abolished until 1921. Based largely on court records; 39 notes.   R. M. Miller

514. Heavner, Robert O. INDENTURED SERVITUDE: THE PHILADELPHIA MARKET, 1771-1773. *J. of Econ. Hist. 1978 38(3):* 701-713. In the 1770's Philadelphia had a well developed indentured servant market which served the city and the surrounding region. This market had many attributes of rational labor and physical capital markets and provided a means for financing migration and education. This study is of indenture records which include prices, term lengths, employer-provided amenities, and servant attributes to test hypotheses based on a rational buyer model. Results indicate that in response to the riskiness of a servant, the buyer used indexes of servant productivity and reliability; that the servant paid for amenities offered by the master, such as general education; and that there was a seasonal pattern of prices corresponding to seasonal activities of agriculture.   J

515. Horn, James P. P. THE LETTERS OF WILLIAM ROBERTS OF ALL HALLOWS PARISH, ANNE ARUNDEL COUNTY, MARYLAND, 1756-1769. *Maryland Hist. Mag. 1979 74(2): 117-132.* These seven letters, reprinted in full, are the only known examples of correspondence from an 18th-century former indentured servant. William Roberts (born ca. 1735 and possibly still living in 1790) migrated from England to Anne Arundel County as an indentured servant in 1756. After serving a good master for three years, he lived the marginal life of a landless wage laborer and tenant farmer. The letters, written during 1756-59 to Roberts's uncle, John Broughton, request financial help, and spell out purposes to which the money will be put. One character-reference letter from Thomas Hunt to Broughton concludes the series of letters, now in the London Public Record Office. Based on manuscript materials in the Maryland Hall of Records, British Public Record Office, and other primary sources; 53 notes.   C. B. Schulz

516. Huston, James L. FACING AN ANGRY LABOR: THE AMERICAN PUBLIC INTERPRETS THE SHOEMAKERS' STRIKE OF 1860. *Civil War Hist. 1982 28(3): 197-212.* Describes the circumstances of the event as well as the responses of the Republicans, Democrats, antislavery advocates, and miscellaneous other persons to the shoemakers' strike in Lynn, Massachusetts, during February-April 1860. Based on newspapers and secondary sources; 56 notes.
G. R. Schroder

517. Jones, James Boyd, Jr. THE MEMPHIS FIREFIGHTERS' STRIKES, 1858 AND 1860. *East Tennessee Hist. Soc. Publ. 1977 49: 37-60.* There were two major firefighters' strikes among the volunteer companies of antebellum Memphis. The first strike of 1858 was the result of the problems of the fire companies in traveling the city's muddy streets when they were denied access to the plank walkways. The second action was more complex, but it was precipitated by the unruliness of the firefighters and was related to the viability of decentralized and seemingly uncontrollable volunteer companies. 120 notes.
D. A. Yanchisin

518. Kriebel, Martha B. WOMEN, SERVANTS AND FAMILY LIFE IN EARLY AMERICA. *Pennsylvania Folklife 1978 28(1): 2-9.* A view of German female immigrants who settled in colonial Pennsylvania and their status in the family, using statistical data on the households of members of the Schwenkfelder sect, wills, and indentured servant agreements; religion was to be at the center of family life and a woman's duties in this regard.

519. Kulik, Gary. PAWTUCKET VILLAGE AND THE STRIKE OF 1824: THE ORIGINS OF CLASS CONFLICT IN RHODE ISLAND. *Radical Hist. Rev. 1978 (17): 5-37.* Describes the textile workers' strike of 1824 in Pawtucket, Rhode Island, in a discussion of the tradition of labor conflicts between mill owners and workers in Rhode Island.

520. Kulik, Gary B. PATTERNS OF RESISTANCE TO INDUSTRIAL CAPITALISM: PAWTUCKET VILLAGE AND THE STRIKE OF 1824. Cantor, Milton, ed. *American Workingclass Culture: Explorations in American Labor and Social History* (Westport, Conn.: Greenwood, 1979): 209-240. Focuses on the 1824 strike among textile workers at the Pawtucket, Rhode Island, weaving and spinning mills to demonstrate local resistance to industrialization in the textile industry and working-class opposition to the mill owners.

521. Laurie, Bruce. "NOTHING ON COMPULSION": LIFE STYLES OF PHILADELPHIA ARTISANS, 1820-1850. Cantor, Milton, ed. *American Workingclass Culture: Explorations in American*

Labor and Social History (Westport, Conn.: Greenwood, 1979): 91-120. Reprint of an article originally published in *Labor History* .

522. Mayer, Stephen. *PEOPLE V. FISHER:* THE SHOEMAKERS' STRIKE OF 1833. *New York Hist. Soc. Q. 1978 62(1): 6-21.* Court decisions such as *People* v. *Fisher* (New York, 1832) adversely affected the position of the journeyman in the shoemaking industry, but were not the primary cause for the breakdown of the apprentice system. Times were changing, and the merchant-capitalist was becoming more important. His influence, in addition to the manufacture of shoes in the state's prisons, made the position of the New York journeyman untenable. This change, which soon would be felt in all American industry, is illustrated by the experiences of Geneva, New York, during the 1820's-30's. Thus the *Fisher* case was both "a product and a symptom" of the changes in the apprentice system. Primary and secondary sources; 46 notes.
C. L. Grant

523. Melder, Keith. WOMEN IN THE SHOE INDUSTRY: THE EVIDENCE FROM LYNN. *Essex Inst. Hist. Collections 1979 115(4): 270-287.* When craftsmen began to specialize in making women's shoes, after 1750, women became vital parts of the family manufacturing unit. By the 1830's in Lynn, Massachusetts, women believed in equal rights for all producers and in organizations to obtain a fair share for the proceeds of their work. Examines the development of women's involvement from the formation of the Female Society of Lynn and Vicinity for the Protection and Promotion of Female Industry in 1833 to the role of Lynn's women in the great shoe strike of 1860. Based on primary sources; 40 notes.
R. S. Sliwoski

524. Menard, Russell R. FROM SERVANT TO FREEHOLDER: STATUS MOBILITY AND PROPERTY ACCUMULATION IN SEVENTEENTH-CENTURY MARYLAND. *William and Mary Q. 1973 30(1): 37-64.* Analyzes the mobility and material success of 275 men who entered Maryland as servants before 1642. Acquisition of land came rapidly for them and most of them became small planters. Draws a composite statistical picture from inventories of estates. Comments on the extent of political service of people who gained their freedom. Discusses the overall institution of white bond labor in Maryland and relates to conditions of free labor and land tenancy. Comments on social patterns such as marriage and education. Compares the level of attainment with the fortunes of the second generation. Manuscript material at the Maryland Hall of Records, the *Maryland Archives* , and secondary sources; 87 notes.
H. M. Ward

525. Montgomery, David. LES ARTISANS ET LA CONSCIENCE DE CLASSE OUVRIÈRE: NOUVELLES RECHERCHES AUX ÉTATS-UNIS [Artisans and working-class consciousness: new research in the United States]. *Labour [Canada] 1978 3: 233-242.* Discusses recent studies of American artisans which have focused on the effects of the development of capitalism on artisans, the role of artisans as transmitters of 18th-century radical ideas to 19th-century workers, worker resistance to the imposition of new controls, and analyses of popular attitudes as seen in the composition and behavior of crowds. 21 notes.
W. A. Kearns

526. Neufeld, Maurice F. THE SIZE OF THE JACKSONIAN LABOR MOVEMENT: A CAUTIONARY ACCOUNT. *Labor Hist. 1982 23(4): 599-607.* The size of trade union membership in the 1830's remains uncertain and unverifiable. Membership estimates range from 26,250 in 1834 to 300,000 in 1836. An analysis of the ratio of organized workers to the total nonagricultural labor force from 1830 to 1978 suggests that the 1836 figure of 300,000 trade unionists is much too high, as it results in a ratio that was never exceeded until 1940. 2 tables, 13 notes.
L. F. Velicer

527. Parsons, William T. and Parsons, Phyllis Vibbard. "BE IT REMEMBERED THAT THESE INDENTURED SERVANTS AND APPRENTICES. . . ." *Pennsylvania Folklife 1978 28(1): 10-24.* A look at indentured servants in Pennsylvania, using indentures from 1785-90, to show that most indentured servants came to America with the consent of their parents or by their own will.

528. Preston, Jo Anne. "TO LEARN ME THE WHOLE OF THE TRADE": CONFLICT BETWEEN A FEMALE APPRENTICE AND A MERCHANT TAILOR IN ANTE-BELLUM NEW EN-GLAND. *Labor Hist. 1983 24(2): 259-273.* Presents the 1830's letters of Mary Adams from Derry, New Hampshire, illustrating her attempts to secure a position as an apprentice tailor and the difficulties in acquiring all of the tailor's skills once apprenticed. Based on the author's collection of Adams's letters; 13 notes.
L. F. Velicer

529. Rich, David. THE TOLEDO MECHANICS' ASSOCIATION: THE CITY'S FIRST LABOR UNION. *Northwest Ohio Q. 1973-74 46(1): 25-31.* Austin Willey's Toledo Mechanics'. Association was a short-lived effort before the municipal elections of 1843 to unite local workingmen in an effort to protect them from exploitation and to assure a better reward for their labor. The union faded after the elections, because after the workingmen captured most of the positions they turned to regular political processes to achieve their ends. Based on newspapers; 25 notes.
W. F. Zornow

530. Rinn, Jacqueline A. SCOTS IN BONDAGE: FORGOTTEN CONTRIBUTORS TO COLONIAL SOCIETY. *Hist. Today [Great Britain] 1980 30(July): 16-21.* Among members of other ethnic groups, Scots willingly became indentured servants to emigrate to America, where they became the major part of the labor force in several colonies.

531. Rosemont, Henry P. BENJAMIN FRANKLIN AND THE PHILADELPHIA STRIKERS OF 1786. *Labor Hist. 1981 22(3): 398-429.* This posthumously published article describes the association of Benjamin Franklin with Philadelphia printers who struck for wages in 1786. Brief biographical information on some strikers is followed by a longer discussion of wage rates. The 1754 Philadelphia scale had been written by Franklin. Phildelphia's printing business and events preceding the strike demonstrated the solidarity of the printers; in 1793, this culminated in the first Franklin Society. Franklin's "radical" ideas and the formation of other printers' societies (labor organizations) all helped secure established wages for printers and led to the 1852 founding of the International Typographical Union. Based on newspaper accounts, federal publications, and other primary sources; 87 notes.
L. F. Velicer

532. Salinger, Sharon V. COLONIAL LABOR IN TRANSITION: THE DECLINE OF INDENTURED SERVITUDE IN LATE EIGHTEENTH-CENTURY PHILADELPHIA. *Labor Hist. 1981 22(2): 165-191.* Contrary to earlier assumptions concerning the use of indentured servants in the American colonies, bound white laborers were utilized more extensively in Philadelphia than in the rural areas of Pennsylvania. The number of indentured servants, however, declined in the last half of the 18th century when an ample supply of free labor, along with changes in production and the beginning of a market economy, created a free labor system in Philadelphia. Based on tax assessors' reports and other primary sources; 7 tables, 37 notes.
L. F. Velicer

533. Shammas, Carole. INDENTURED SERVITUDE AND THE FIRST SUNBELT MIGRATION. *Rev. in Am. Hist. 1983 11(1): 43-46.* Reviews David Galenson's *White Servitude in Colonial America: An Economic Analysis* (1982), which examines economic reasons for the high immigration rate of indentured servants from Europe to the American colonies, especially to Virginia, Maryland, and the West Indies.

534. Shammas, Carole. THE RISE OF THE COLONIAL TENANT. *Rev. in Am. Hist. 1978 6(4): 490-495.* Review article prompted by Gregory A. Stiverson's *Poverty in a Land of Plenty: Tenancy in Eighteenth-Century Maryland* (Baltimore, Md.: Johns Hopkins U. Pr., 1978).

535. Souden, David. 'ROGUES, WHORES AND VAGABONDS'? INDENTURED SERVANT EMIGRANTS TO NORTH AMERICA, AND THE CASE OF MID-SEVENTEENTH-CENTURY BRISTOL. *Social Hist. [Great Britain] 1978 3(1): 23-41.* The majority of young emigrants to North America and the West Indies during the 17th century were indentured servants. Contemporaries regarded these peoples as the dregs of English lower classes, but evidence shows that despite humble backgrounds, they were enterprising enough to make emigration arrangements. Many congregated in Bristol, coming from various parts of southern England, in the hope of finding employment in the new world. 2 illus., map, 6 tables, 3 fig., 55 notes.

536. Steffen, Charles G. CHANGES IN THE ORGANIZATION OF ARTISAN PRODUCTION IN BALTIMORE, 1790 TO 1820. *William and Mary Q. 1979 36(1): 101-117.* The artisan crafts of Baltimore had varied development: some held to the handicraft system while others changed substantially. Analyzes the distribution and kinds of wealth among members of different crafts. Emphasizes slaveholding and the uses of slave labor in certain crafts. Discusses problems of indentured and apprenticed service. Growing numbers of apprentices and slaves in some of the crafts threatened the status of journeymen. Based on account books, indenture contracts, and court documents; 9 tables, 42 notes. H. M. Ward

537. Steffen, Charles G. THE PRE-INDUSTRIAL IRON WORKER: NORTHAMPTON IRON WORKS, 1780-1820. *Labor Hist. 1979 20(1): 89-110.* The Northampton Iron Works of Baltimore County, Maryland provides data for understanding the pre-industrial iron worker. The structure prevented development of a worker consciousness of shared interest; the complexity of the work force divided laborers; the police system discouraged collective action; and the institutional arrangements inculcated values of deference among workers. Records of the Northampton Iron Works; 3 tables, 75 notes. L. L. Athey

538. Turbin, Carole. AND WE ARE NOTHING BUT WOMEN: IRISH WORKING WOMEN IN TROY. Berkin, Carol Ruth and Norton, Mary Beth, ed. *Women of America: A History* (Boston: Houghton Mifflin Co., 1979): 202-222. Examines the foundation of the Collar Laundry Union of Troy, New York, in 1864 in an age when woman had little leverage to bargain with employers. During 1864-69, the lifespan of the union, the laundresses were able to raise their wages to nearly equal those of working men. They formed close alliances with the male labor movement, and their three-month strike in 1869 was highly successful. Secondary sources; 19 notes, ref. K. Talley

539. Winpenny, Thomas R. CULTURAL FACTORS IN THE PERSISTENCE OF HAND TECHNOLOGY IN LANCASTER, PENNSYLVANIA. *Pennsylvania Hist. 1983 50(3): 218-228.* Disputes the contention that artisans suffered whenever the factory system was introduced. In Lancaster, each of 22 craft occupations grew and prospered in the years 1820-80 despite the emergence of the factory system. A comparison is made with Newark, New Jersey, where the opposite situation prevailed. Based on census data and other materials; table, 33 notes. D. Swift

540. Wolf, Stephanie G. ARTISANS AND THE OCCUPATIONAL STRUCTURE OF AN INDUSTRIAL TOWN: 18TH-CENTURY GERMANTOWN, PA. *Working Papers from the Regional Econ. Hist. Res. Center 1977 1(1): 33-56.* Through the case of Germantown, Pennsylvania, studies the basic economic conditions and occupational structure of the artisans of that community, 1767-91; manufacturing and preindustrial activity was greater than often suspected by historians, and required development of complex local production networks and economic infrastructures.

541. Wright, Helena. SARAH G. BAGLEY: A BIOGRAPHICAL NOTE. *Labor Hist. 1979 20(3): 398-413.* Provides biographical details about New Hampshire born Sarah G. Bagley (b. 1806), the founder and first president of the Female Labor Reform Association of Lowell, Massachusetts. After 1848, there is no record available. Based on company records, tax lists, and probate records; 34 notes. L. L. Athey

Slave Labor

542. Africa, Philip. SLAVEHOLDING IN THE SALEM COMMUNITY, 1771-1851. *North Carolina Hist. Rev. 1977 54(3): 271-307.* Between the founding of Salem in 1771 as a congregation town and the outbreak of Civil War, Moravians altered their attitudes toward slaveholding. The communal sense of *gemeinschaft* slowly changed during the 19th century to a more business-like attitude of *gesellschaft*. Moravians came to regard slaves not as persons but as property. Secular pressures eroded opposition to slavery on religious and moral grounds, and by the 1850's slaves were used in a variety of pursuits. Based on papers in the Moravian Archives and on published primary sources; 8 illus., map, 101 notes. T. L. Savitt

543. Armstrong, Thomas F. FROM TASK LABOR TO FREE LABOR: THE TRANSITION ALONG GEORGIA'S RICE COAST, 1820-1880. *Georgia Hist. Q. 1980 64(4): 432-447.* Describes the antebellum task labor system of the slaves of the rice plantations in Chatham, Bryan, Liberty, McIntosh, Glynn, and Camden Counties, Georgia. Altered conditions after the Civil War are also discussed. Primary and secondary sources; 46 notes. G. R. Schroeder

544. Aufhauser, R. Keith. SLAVERY AND SCIENTIFIC MANAGEMENT. *J. of Econ. Hist. 1973 33(4): 811-824.* The recent debate between Marxist and "new economic" historians has obscured "some striking, if discouraging, similarities which modern capitalist-wage-labor economies bear to slavery." The author shows how George Fitzhugh's philosophy (Genovese's "ideal type" of slaveholder) corresponds with and even anticipates F. W. Taylor's school of scientific management. Large-scale enterprises and intensified division of labor account for the planters' "precocious" worker discipline. An account of disciplinary methods used on Louisiana and Caribbean plantations supplements the conceptual comparison. Based on secondary sources; 40 notes. W. R. Hively

545. Barzel, Yoram. AN ECONOMIC ANALYSIS OF SLAVERY. *J. of Law and Econ. 1977 20(1): 87-110.* Slavery was practiced differently in each society where it flourished, therefore, generalizations are difficult. It was economically most successful where policing was minimal, and climate permitted year-round utilization of slaves. Voluntary slaves were more able to buy freedom, whereas forced slaves had few opportunities. Primary and secondary sources; table, 2 graphs, 79 notes. C. B. Fitzgerald

546. Bellamy, Donnie D. SLAVERY IN MICROCOSM: ONSLOW COUNTY, NORTH CAROLINA. *J. of Negro Hist. 1977 62(4): 339-350.* A study of slavery in Onslow County, North Carolina shows it was not one of the state's large plantation counties. Slavery did provide the foundation for the turpentine industry and thereby committed the white population to uphold the institution since 1790. In 1861, the voters of Onslow County supported secession even though few secessionists were plantation owners. Based on the records of Onslow County, North Carolina and secondary sources; 3 tables, 53 notes. N. G. Sapper

547. Bonacich, Edna. ABOLITION, THE EXTENSION OF SLAVERY, AND THE POSITION OF FREE BLACKS: A STUDY OF SPLIT LABOR MARKETS IN THE UNITED STATES, 1830-1863. *Am. J. of Sociol. 1975 81(3): 601-628.* Using the "split labor market" theory of ethnic and racial antagonism, this paper analyzes race relations in the pre-Civil War United States. Both slaves and free blacks are found to have been lower-priced sources of labor than whites, to whom they therefore posed a threat of displacement. Slavery was a system which gave southern capitalists total control of a cheap labor force, permitting extensive displacement. It also put the South in conflict with northern capital, because the latter depended on higher-priced (white) labor. Abolition threatened to increase competition between black and white labor, spreading the problem to all regions and segments of the economy. But manumission also made blacks more vulnerable to counterattacks by white labor in the form of either exclusion or caste. The various class interests of the three parties to split labor markets are presented for the North, South, and West on the issues of abolition, the extension of slavery, and the position of free blacks. It is argued that an understanding of the interests of the white working class and its power to implement them is of major importance for untangling race relations before the Civil War. J

548. Brownlee, W. Elliot. THE ECONOMICS OF URBAN SLAVERY. *Rev. in Am. Hist. 1977 5(2): 230-235.* Review article prompted by Claudia Dale Goldin's *Urban Slavery in the American South 1820-1860: A Quantitative History* (Chicago: U. of Chicago Pr., 1976).

549. Burnham, Dorothy. THE LIFE OF THE AFRO-AMERICAN WOMAN IN SLAVERY. *Int. J. of Women's Studies [Canada] 1978 1(4): 363-377.* Surveys the life of slave women (from narratives, interviews, and written observations), including sexual treatment by slavemasters, family and living conditions, work (both field and household), treatment of the elderly, and psychological effects, 17th century-1865.

550. Calderhead, William. THE ROLE OF THE PROFESSIONAL SLAVE TRADER IN A SLAVE ECONOMY: AUSTIN WOOLFOLK, A CASE STUDY. *Civil War Hist. 1977 23(3): 195-211.* Austin Woolfolk was a prosperous Baltimore-based slave trader. He dominated the border-state trade during 1819-30's. Manumission and emigration contributed equally to Maryland slave losses. Traders slowed slave population growth by changing age and sex ratios. Antislave trader sentiment strengthened resistance to selling south. Based on newspapers, federal censuses, city and county records, manifest lists, and secondary sources; 67 notes.   R. E. Stack

551. Campbell, Randolph. HUMAN PROPERTY: THE NEGRO SLAVE IN HARRISON COUNTY, 1850-1860. *Southwestern Hist. Q. 1973 76(4): 384-396.* The high percentage of slaveholding families and of the total population that was slave, and the availability of good county records, along with federal census data, make East Texas' Harrison County an excellent case study for the Negro slave's role in society. Examines the ways in which the slave was involved in day-to-day economic affairs and social arrangements, the degree to which his many roles depended on his humanity, and what it meant to him and his master when he was recognized as a human in situations where he was defined as property. 28 notes.   D. L. Smith

552. Campbell, Randolph. LOCAL ARCHIVES AS A SOURCE OF SLAVE PRICES: HARRISON COUNTY, TEXAS AS A TEST CASE. *Historian 1974 36(4): 660-669.* An inquiry into the best sources for estimates of the economics of slavery, especially the individual cost of slaves. Most studies have relied on the work of Ulrich B. Phillips (works published during 1905-29), based largely on auction records, which were often unanalyzed group figures. Shows how such figures can be double-checked through the use of local archival records, concentrating the study on slave labor in Harrison County, Texas, having the largest slave population of any Texas county. Bases the study largely on estate inventories of 40 slaveholders from the probate records of 1849-60, which listed slaves individually and with considerable detail. These prices are consistently lower than Phillips' prices, though on the whole not to a marked degree. 20 notes.   R. V. Ritter

553. Campbell, Randolph. THE PRODUCTIVITY OF SLAVE LABOR IN EAST TEXAS: A RESEARCH NOTE. *Louisiana Studies 1974 13(2): 154-172.* The question of the profitability of slave labor hinges on the accuracy of the methods used to compute productivity. Surveys the studies made thus far and the questions which have been raised regarding their methods of computing productivity. Reports a current "microcosmic" study in which a different and untested procedure is employed, determining the productivity of slave labor by dealing with the entire farming and slaveholding population of Harrison County, Texas, a major cotton-producing area. The results suggest that "there is room for adjustment of the consensus concerning the profitability of slave labor." There is need for studies in various regions and among various size slaveholders. 8 tables, 30 notes.   R. V. Ritter

554. Canarella, Giorgio and Tomaske, John A. THE OPTIMAL UTILIZATION OF SLAVES. *J. of Econ. Hist. 1975 35(3): 621-629.* Examines the brutality of plantation slavery in the South, using the neoclassical theory to explore the implications of competitive market forces and the profit motive. The findings of Robert William Fogel and Stanley L. Engerman that slaves held skilled jobs and received goods above the biological subsistance level "are consistent with the proposition that masters were capable of extracting labor services from slaves effectively," but they do not "provide evidence bearing on the joint issues of the welfare of slaves and the brutality of the plantation slavery." Based on primary and secondary sources; 17 notes.
                                                     D. J. Trickey

555. Clifton, James M. THE RICE DRIVER: HIS ROLE IN SLAVE MANAGEMENT. *South Carolina Hist. Mag. 1981 82(4): 331-354.* Drivers on antebellum rice plantations supervised daily work routines and disciplined slaves in the fields and slave quarters, making drivers unpopular with fellow slaves. As a reward for his work, the driver enjoyed a higher standard of living than that of other slaves: better housing and clothes, more food, and a personal servant. Unfortunately the job required long hours, conflicting demands from owners and slaves, and the possibility of instant demotion. When slavery came to an end, Southern whites failed to use the many talents and experiences of the former drivers. Based on primary sources, mainly for South Carolina, including observations of Frederick Law Olmstead, J. B. DeBow, and Fanny Kemble; 39 notes.   R. H. Tomlinson

556. Cody, Cheryll Ann. A NOTE ON CHANGING PATTERNS OF SLAVE FERTILITY IN THE SOUTH CAROLINA RICE DISTRICT, 1735-1865. *Southern Studies 1977 16(4): 457-463.* Presents evidence on slave fertility on Ball plantation in Cooper River rice district of South Carolina, 1735-1865. Indicates that sexual intercourse was delayed beyond puberty for many women, although motherhood came early for others. Median age at first birth for slave mothers grew from 19.0 to 20.0. After 1800 the number of early teen-aged mothers declined. A seasonal distribution of births suggests the importance of the labor demands of the plantation. Based on the John and Keating S. Ball Plantation Books in the Southern Historical Collection at the University of North Carolina, and secondary sources; 2 tables, graph, 7 notes.
                                                     J. Buschen

557. David, Paul A. and Temin, Peter. SLAVERY: THE PROGRESSIVE INSTITUTION? *J. of Econ. Hist. 1974 34(3): 739-783.* Reviews Robert William Fogel and Stanley L. Engerman's *Time on the Cross*, Vol. I: *The Economics of American Negro Slavery*, and Vol. II: *Evidence and Methods—A Supplement* (Boston: Little, Brown and Company, 1974). Problems of methodology, economic theory, and bias make questionable Fogel and Engerman's favorable assessments of slave performance and welfare, and southern agricultural efficiency. Based on official statistics, and secondary sources; fig., 54 notes.
                                                     O. H. Reichardt

558. DeCanio, Stephen. A NEW ECONOMIC HISTORY OF SLAVERY IN THE UNITED STATES. *Rev. in Am. Hist. 1974 2(4): 474-487.* Review article prompted by Robert William Fogel and Stanley L. Engerman's *Time on the Cross: The Economics of American Negro Slavery* (Boston: Little, Brown and Co., 1974) and *Time on the Cross: Evidence and Methods: A Supplement* (Boston: Little, Brown and Co., 1974) which asserts the fundamental importance of the books for future investigations of the economics of slavery. Outlines the books' contents and major theses concerning occupational structure of slavery, mobility of slaves, impact of slavery upon the black family, sexual exploitation of slave women, profitability of slave system, exploitation of slavery, and the "myth of black incompetence." Also critiques the books' methodology and conclusions and suggests aspects which need additional investigation. Based on secondary sources; 6 notes.
                                                     A. E. Wiederrecht

559. Deverre, Christian. LA "NOUVELLE HISTOIRE" AMERICAINE ET L'ESCLAVAGE [The new American history and slavery]. *Cahiers d'Etudes Africaines [France] 1982 22(1-2): 179-183.* Reviews Sidney Mintz, ed., *Esclave-Facteur de Production: L'Economie Politique de l'Esclavage* (1981), translated by Jacqueline Rouah, a series of articles by American authors dealing with slavery and racism in the Americas.

560. Dew, Charles B. BLACK IRONWORKERS AND THE SLAVE INSURRECTION PANIC OF 1856. *J. of Southern Hist. 1975 41(3): 321-338.* A review of events of the slave-uprising panic of 1856. The panic originated among Negro ironworkers in mills along the Kentucky-Tennessee border and spread from there over much of the South. Retribution was swift and harsh; the insurrection was put down before it ever got underway. There is no evidence that an uprising was even planned. These fears apparently developed as a consequence of election-year excitements and the sudden emergence of the strongly anti-slavery Republican Party. 35 notes.   V. L. Human

561. Dew, Charles B. DAVID ROSS AND THE OXFORD IRON WORKS: A STUDY OF INDUSTRIAL SLAVERY IN THE EARLY NINETEENTH CENTURY. *William and Mary Q. 1974 31(2): 189-224.* David Ross, a wealthy merchant, planter, and industrialist, owned and operated Oxford Iron Works during and after the Revolution. Located eight miles southeast of Lynchburg, the works was operated by slave labor. Discusses division of work force, occupational trends, slave life (family, runaways), Ross' attitude toward slavery, and economics and technology of iron making. Based on Ross' Letter Book, contemporary materials, and monographs; table, 116 notes.   H. M. Ward

562. Dew, Charles B. DISCIPLINING SLAVE IRONWORKERS IN THE ANTEBELLUM SOUTH: COERCION, CONCILIATION AND ACCOMMODATION. *Am. Hist. Rev. 1974 79(2): 383-418.* Finds the Southern ironmen willing to give their slaves considerable influence over their working conditions, their family arrangements, and the course of their everyday life. Suggests that the material is available for studies in microcosm of this sort. Iron-masters needed to increase their labor force and therefore needed to avoid the reputation that they abused slaves in their employ. Men who did more than they were required were rewarded with payment, and as a result large numbers of slave workers made a smooth and rapid conversion to a free labor situation in 1865. Illus., 59 notes.   E. P. Stickney

563. Dibble, Ernest F. SLAVE RENTALS TO THE MILITARY: PENSACOLA AND THE GULF COAST. *Civil War Hist. 1977 23(2): 101-113.* Slavery was not extensive from New Orleans to Key West, until the military arrived. Without a supply of white laborers, Commandant Lewis Warrington of Pensacola's new Navy Yard began slave hiring in 1826. Before that, the Army Corps of Engineers under Captain William H. Chase had been important to the slave market all along the Gulf Coast. Slave owners came to depend on the rentals. The extension of slavery was accompanied by the expansion of slavery's defense. A majority of free, colored creoles finally were forced to depart Pensacola. Primary and secondary sources; 53 notes.   R. E. Stack

564. Dormon, James H. THE PERSISTENT SPECTER: SLAVE REBELLION IN TERRITORIAL LOUISIANA. *Louisiana Hist. 1977 18(4): 389-404.* Whites in the Louisiana Territory, 1801-12, feared black insurrection. There were several rumored and threatened slave revolts, but not until 1811 was there an actual rebellion, beginning at the Manuel Andry plantation, near present-day Norco. Regular and militia forces quickly suppressed it; nearly all the rebel slaves were massacred or subsequently executed. The legislature compensated owners whose slaves had been killed. In general, whites refused to believe that it was a true slave rebellion. They preferred to believe that outsiders were responsible, and rewarded blacks who had opposed the rebels. This was "the largest slave insurrection in U.S. history," but it had little chance of succeeding and represented only a small portion of the region's slaves. Yet the spectre of slave revolt persisted and "fear of revolt lay at the heart of the relationship between slaves and masters and was thus fundamental to the creation of distrust by whites, even as the whites created for their own psychic salvation the myth of the contented bondsman." Primary sources; 2 photos, map, 48 notes.
     R. L. Woodward, Jr.

565. Earle, Carville V. A STAPLE INTERPRETATION OF SLAVERY AND FREE LABOR. *Geographical Rev. 1978 68(1): 51-65.* The geography of slavery and free labor in the pre-1860 United States is interpreted as a rational economic response to the prevailing regional staples and the costs and returns of slave and free labor. Northern farmers rejected slavery because slaves were more expensive than hired day labor in producing the wheat staple, not on grounds of moral-ideological repugnance, as some have suggested. Regions of staple change invited pressures for labor adjustment. Free labor displaced slaves in the colonial Chesapeake, and slavery threatened free labor in the antebellum Midwest. The imminence of slavery in the 1850's Midwest sheds new light on regional politics and on the urgency of the Civil War.   J

566. Egnal, Marc. AMERICAN SLAVERY: THE NEWER EXEGESIS. *Can. Rev. of Am. Studies 1975 6(1): 110-117.* Review article on two contradictory publications about slavery in the United States. In *Time on the Cross: The Economics of American Negro Slavery* (Boston: Little, Brown, 1974), Robert Fogel and Stanley Engerman contend that the material well-being of slaves in the antebellum South equalled that of Northern free labor. Eugene Genovese, in *Roll, Jordan, Roll: The World the Slaves Made* (New York: Pantheon, 1974), has little praise for slavery, treating at length the unique behavior, culture, and institutions that developed in the slave communities of the pre-Civil War South.   H. T. Lovin

567. Elbert, Sarah. GOOD TIMES ON THE CROSS: A MARXIAN REVIEW. *Rev. of Radical Pol. Econ. 1975 7(3): 55-66.* Robert William Fogel's and Stanley L. Engerman's *Time on the Cross* (New York, 1974) asserts that slavery in the South, 1840-60, "was a

scientifically managed, profitable system of capital investment which left a proud record of efficient work to the descendants of American Negro slaves," and ignores the paternalistic, exploitive nature of the system.

568. Elkins, Stanley M. THE SLAVERY DEBATE. *Commentary 1975 60(6): 40-54.* Discusses recent writings about the economics of slavery in the early- to mid-19th century.

569. Emmer, P. C. PROLETARIAAT OF KLEINE BOURGEOISIE? NIEUWE LITERATUUR OVER DE SLAVERNIJ IN DE V.S. [Proletariat or petty bourgeoisie? New literature on slavery in the U.S.]. *Tijdschrift voor Geschiedenis [Netherlands] 1978 91(2): 263-269.* Review article prompted by Robert William Fogel and Stanley L. Engerman, *Time on the Cross: The Economics of American Negro Slavery* (2 vols; Boston, London, 1974), Paul A. David *et al.*, *Reckoning with Slavery* (New York, 1976), Herbert G. Gutman, *Slavery and the Numbers Game* (Urbana, 1975), Eugene D. Genovese, *Roll Jordan, Roll* (London, 1974), and Herbert G. Gutman, *The Black Family in Slavery and Freedom, 1750-1925* (Oxford, 1976). Fogel and Engerman contended that slavery was profitable and efficient, stimulated economic growth, and provided slaves with a measure of economic security not enjoyed by many free urban and industrial workers. They were to some degree petty bourgeoisie. This work provoked considerable discussion and critique. Critics such as Gutman, David *et al.*, pointed out that Fogel and Engerman's sample of big plantations was too small. Genovese discusses the paternalistic aspects of master and slave and slave culture. Gutman contends that slave and black marriages were stable until the 1920's-30's when the economic crisis did great harm to the black family structure.
     G. D. Homan

570. Engerman, Stanley L. MARXIST ECONOMIC STUDIES OF THE SLAVE SOUTH. *Marxist Perspectives 1978 1(1): 148-165.* Broad overview of Marxist interpretations of social and economic life in the South before the Civil War.

571. Fleisig, Heywood. SLAVERY, THE SUPPLY OF AGRICULTURAL LABOR, AND THE INDUSTRIALIZATION OF THE SOUTH. *J. of Econ. Hist. 1976 36(3): 572-597.* This article assumes that the only effect of slavery was the relief of a labor constraint facing individual farmers, and shows the conditions under which slavery would increase the share of agriculture in total output, reduce the size of the market for, and the incentive to invent and innovate, new farm machinery. Two farm models are developed, one with a fixed labor-constraint, the other with a rising labor supply-curve; these are contrasted with a third model of an unconstrained farm. The constrained (free labor) and unconstrained (slave labor) models successfully predict several salient differences between northern and southern agriculture and industry.   J

572. Fogel, Robert William and Engerman, Stanley L. EXPLAINING THE RELATIVE EFFICIENCY OF SLAVE AGRICULTURE IN THE ANTEBELLUM SOUTH. *Am. Econ. Rev. 1977 67(3): 275-296.* Claims, with a great deal of statistical evidence, that slaves were more efficient than free workers because slavery was organized around the gang which functioned as a type of antebellum assembly line. This increased productivity was only on farms that specialized in certain crops. 10 tables.   D. K. Pickens

573. Fohlen, Claude. L'ESCLAVAGE AUX ETATS-UNIS: DIVERGENCES ET CONVERGENCES [Slavery in the United States: Divergences and Convergences]. *Rev. Hist. [France] 1977 257(2): 345-360.* American historians neglected the subject of slavery before 1918 when Ulrich B. Phillips published *American Negro Slavery* and in 1929, when he published *Life and Labor in the Old South*. Since then regional studies by Ralph B. Flanders, Charles S. Sydnor, G. G. Johnson, James B. Sellers, and Joe G. Taylor and general interpretations by Kenneth M. Stampp and Stanley Elkins have been published. In 1974 Robert William Fogel and Stanley L. Engerman published *Time on the Cross: The Economics of American Negro Slavery*, which applies the statistical approach referred to as Cliometrics. This book stirred up debate on slavery and the value of quantification in all fields of history. 16 notes.   G. H. Davis

574. Fohlen, Claude. UN DÉBAT HISTORIOGRAPHIQUE: L'ESCLAVAGE AUX ÉTATS-UNIS [A historiographical debate:

Slavery in the United States]. *Bull. de la Soc. d'Hist. Moderne [France]* 1977 76(18): 8-16. Studies the 1974 controversy about slavery as an economically sound and efficient institution which brought prosperity to the South and good working and living conditions for slaves as opposed to free laborers.

575. Forness, Norman O. THE MASTER, THE SLAVE, AND THE PATENT LAWS: A VIGNETTE OF THE 1850S. *Prologue 1980 12(1): 23-28.* Oscar J. E. Stuart, a lawyer in Pike City, Mississippi, tried to get a patent on an invention created by his slave Ned. According to Stuart, the master owned the manual and intellectual fruits of his slave's labor and this satisfied the requirement of the law that patents only be issued to persons who could swear that the inventions were products of their own genius. The patent application was submitted to Commissioner of Patents Joseph Holt. The merits of the application were judged against the patent legislation of 4 July 1836, and Attorney General Jeremiah S. Black denied the patent application for "a double cotton scraper." Undaunted in his efforts, Stuart proceeded to manufacture cotton scrapers in Mississippi and published a broadside offering them for sale. Based on Patent Office Records, Records of the Office of the Secretary of the Interior, Oscar J. E. Stuart papers and correspondence; 3 illus., 2 photos, 9 notes.   M. A. Kascus

576. Fox-Genovese, Elizabeth. POOR RICHARD AT WORK IN THE COTTON FIELDS: A CRITIQUE OF THE PSYCHOLOGI-CAL AND IDEOLOGICAL PRESUPPOSITIONS OF *TIME ON THE CROSS*. *Rev. of Radical Pol. Econ. 1975 7(3): 67-83.* Compares the findings in Robert William Fogel's and Stanley L. Engerman's *Time on the Cross* (New York, 1974) with other historians' conclusions on 19th-century slavery in the South.

577. Gallman, Robert E. SLAVERY AND SOUTHERN ECONOM-IC GROWTH. *Southern Econ. J. 1979 45(4): 1007-1022.* Discusses slavery and its effects on economic growth in the South during 1840-60 by examining various theories of economic historians.

578. Gallman, Robert E. and Anderson, Ralph V. SLAVES AS FIXED CAPITAL: SLAVE LABOR AND SOUTHERN ECONOM-IC DEVELOPMENT. *J. of Am. Hist. 1977 64(1): 24-46.* Begins with Eugene Genovese's assumption that "Slavery requires all hands to be occupied at all times" to show how slavery converted black labor into fixed capital in the South. Planters developed a diversified production system to occupy slaves between harvest and planting time of their primary cash crops, and fulfilled most of their basic food requirements. Compares this situation with the socioeconomic conditions of the South after Emancipation, when planters became specialists. This required only seasonal labor, so extensive unemployment appeared. The effects of the intensive use of resources under the slave system obscured southern underdevelopment. 44 notes.   J. B. Reed

579. Glickstein, Jonathan A. "POVERTY IS NOT SLAVERY": AMERICAN ABOLITIONISTS AND THE COMPETITIVE LABOR MARKET. Perry, Lewis and Fellman, Michael, ed. *Antislavery Reconsidered: New Perspectives on the Abolitionists* (Baton Rouge: Louisiana State U. Pr., 1979): 195-218. Although some abolitionists such as William I. Bowditch believed that the economic system of the industrialized North created a slavery almost as terrible as that of the South, most people in the antislavery movement—especially those who came from evangelical Christianity—believed that, on the positive side, marketplace competition in the United States was so fair that willing workers would not be exploited, and, on the negative side, fear of poverty and poverty itself would act as a spur to industriousness and as proof against indolence. 38 notes.   S

580. Goodfriend, Joyce D. BURGHERS AND BLACKS: THE EVO-LUTION OF A SLAVE SOCIETY AT NEW AMSTERDAM. *New York Hist. 1978 59(2): 125-144.* The development of a slave population in New Netherland was prompted by the Dutch West India Company to deal with the perpetual problem of underpopulation in the Dutch settlements, and to assure prosperity by increasing agricultural production. At first slavery in New Netherland was institutionalized on a corporate basis, an unusual case in American colonial experience. By 1664, as the result of company practices, slavery had become a widespread mode of labor exploitation among the settlers in the colony. 4 illus., 44 notes.   R. N. Lokken

581. Graham, Richard. SLAVERY AND ECONOMIC DEVELOP-MENT: BRAZIL AND THE UNITED STATES SOUTH IN THE NINETEENTH CENTURY. *Comparative Studies in Soc. and Hist. [Great Britain] 1981 23(4): 620-55.* Analyses of slavery in Brazil and the US South have compared these areas with nonslavery areas, hence painting an illusory image. A more valid comparison would be with slaveholding areas. In comparing the US South and Brazil, the former surged far ahead in rate of development. An important factor accounting for this was the value of the South's cotton in comparison to Brazil's coffee. The social structure inherited from different mother countries was a contributing factor. Parameters set by historical development over a long period of time can be considered to accurately depict relationships between economic development and slavery. 84 notes, 7 tables, 2 maps.   S. A. Farmerie

582. Green, Barbara L. SLAVE LABOR AT THE MARAMEC IRON WORKS, 1828-1850. *Missouri Hist. Rev. 1979 73(2): 150-164.* Recent historians have been interested in the political and economic ramifications of industrial slavery. Samuel Massey and Thomas James, the founders of the company, used little slave labor, preferring to recruit skilled white ironworkers from Ohio. Their limited experience with black workers and the knowledge gleaned from their contact with industrialists, who extensively used black labor, show that the slave workers were not the lazy, shiftless, childish, and dishonest workers portrayed by Ulrich B. Phillips and Stanley Elkins. Illus., 56 notes.   W. F. Zornow

583. Hall, Mark. THE PROSLAVERY THOUGHT OF J. D. B. DEBOW: A PRACTICAL MAN'S GUIDE TO ECONOMICS. *Southern Studies 1982 21(1): 97-104.* Antebellum proslavery writer James Dunwoody Brownson DeBow supported slavery for practical reasons. The South could gain economic independence from the North by the effective use of slavery. He avoided the morality issue by supporting the polygenesist argument that slaves were inherently a lower species than the whites. Blacks could not survive in a capitalist society but were protected in the South and enjoyed greater physical comfort and good health than their fellow blacks in the North or Africa. Because so many people were involved directly or indirectly, it was in the best interests of the whole South to maintain slavery. 24 notes.   J. J. Buschen

584. Harper, C. W. HOUSE SERVANTS AND FIELD HANDS: FRAGMENTATION IN THE ANTEBELLUM SLAVE COMMUNI-TY. *North Carolina Hist. Rev. 1978 55(1): 42-59.* House servants comprised a separate class of slaves from field hands in white and black antebellum society. They lived in the "big house" or in better facilities, had more personal contact with the master and mistress, wore better clothes, did less menial labor, and ate the same food as their owners. Their attitude toward field hands was one of superiority in both social and occupational dealings. Most house servants were mulattoes, further highlighting differences with black field hands. Based on slave narratives, former slave interviews, plantation records, published letters, and secondary sources; 8 illus., 109 notes.   T. L. Savitt

585. —. [RELATIVE EFFICIENCY OF SLAVE AGRICULTURE]. *Am. Econ. Rev. 1979 69(1): 206-226.*
Haskell, Thomas L. EXPLAINING THE RELATIVE EFFICIENCY OF SLAVE AGRICULTURE IN THE ANTEBELLUM SOUTH: A REPLY TO FOGEL-ENGERMAN, *pp. 206-207.* In Fogel-Engerman's latest scholarship, Haskell maintains that they have quietly abandoned their thesis of the achievement-oriented slave, a central theme of *Time On the Cross* (1974). Haskell rejects their latest model of labor efficiency regarding American slavery.
Schaefer, Donald F. and Schmitz, Mark D. THE RELATIVE EFFI-CIENCY OF SLAVE AGRICULTURE: A COMMENT, *pp. 208-212.* Argues that Fogel and Engerman combined and confused scale and the number of slaves and therefore the increased number of slaves were one means of creating a larger scale of operation which in turn contributed to increased amount of productivity.

David, Paul A. and Temin, Peter. IN EXPLAINING THE RELATIVE EFFICIENCY OF SLAVE AGRICULTURE IN THE ANTE-BELLUM SOUTH: A COMMENT, *pp. 213-218.* The nature of cotton growing contributed to "efficiency" (a questionable concept in this scholarly context). According to David and Temin, Fogel-Engerman's data supports David and Temin's conclusion.

Wright, Gavin. THE EFFICIENCY OF SLAVERY, *pp. 219-226.* Concludes, after observing the unusually good cotton crop of 1860, that it was the combination of female field work and the crop mix which gave slavery its distinctive advantage. Wright sees slavery's economic essence as the use of family labor in market activity.   D. K. Pickens

586. Hine, William C. AMERICAN SLAVERY AND RUSSIAN SERFDOM: A PRELIMINARY COMPARISON. *Phylon 1975 36(4): 378-384.* Perhaps because of the overriding considerations of race, the similarities between Russian serfdom and American slavery have only occasionally been noted. Examines the development, treatment, and status of the two servile labor groups and concludes that Russian serfdom was equally oppressive and as physically and psychologically debilitating as American slavery. Serfs and slaves alike were without rights and were regarded only as an exploitable labor force that anchored an economic system and a whole way of life as well. Secondary sources; 33 notes.   K. C. Snow

587. Homsey, Elizabeth Moyne. FREE BLACKS IN KENT COUNTY, DELAWARE, 1790-1830. *Working Papers from the Regional Econ. Hist. Res. Center 1980 3(2): 31-57.* Though legally manumitted according to state laws, free blacks in Kent County (and in all Delaware, as well), through a series of prohibitive laws were kept in a limbo of quasislavery; eventually they were declared to still be slaves, so that a steady black work force could be maintained.

588. Hughes, Sarah S. SLAVES FOR HIRE: THE ALLOCATIONS OF BLACK LABOR IN ELIZABETH CITY COUNTY, VIRGINIA, 1782 TO 1810. *William and Mary Q. 1978 35(2): 260-286.* Hiring out slaves in Elizabeth City County was a frequent practice. Comments on the demography of the county, which by 1810 had 3,600 persons, 1,734 of whom were slaves. Discusses occupations, labor division, hiring patterns, rates for hire, and in particular the cases of several individuals and families involved in the hiring of slaves. The hiring system was flexible and was engaged in by both property and tenant classes. Mentions the effects on master-slaves relations. Based on slaveowners' property tax records; 4 tables.   H. M. Ward

589. Jackson, Harvey H. THE CALM BEFORE THE STORM: A LOUISIANA OVERSEER'S WORLD ON THE EVE OF THE CIVIL WAR. *Southern Studies 1979 18(2): 241-246.* Reprints a letter in the author's possession from Henry A. Thigpen (b. 1820) to a friend in 1862 describing his new job as overseer on a plantation in northeastern Louisiana. Thigpen worked for a widow whose husband had been killed in the war. He described the plantation, its size, soil fertility, machinery, slaves, and daily work routine. His life was fairly easy, the slaves disciplined and obedient. Union troops occupied the plantation within a year, and he was forced to leave. The overseer's job was no longer needed. 12 notes.   J. J. Buschen

590. Jacobs, Donald M. TWENTIETH-CENTURY SLAVE NARRATIVES AS SOURCE MATERIALS: SLAVE LABOR AS AGRICULTURAL LABOR. *Agric. Hist. 1983 57(2): 223-227.* Slave narratives recorded by Works Progress Administration interviewers during 1936-38 often depict positive aspects of the slavery experience, perhaps because many of the former slaves interviewed were still young children at the time of emancipation. The narratives provide useful information on the economic and agricultural diversity of Southern plantations. 8 notes.   D. E. Bowers

591. Johnson, Harry G. THE ANTE-BELLUM SOUTH: NEGRO SLAVERY. *Encounter [Great Britain] 1975 44(1): 56-59.* Discusses the economics of slavery in the South in the early- to mid-19th century, emphasizing its relation to the Industrial Revolution.

592. Jones, Jacqueline. "MY MOTHER WAS MUCH OF A WOMAN": BLACK WOMEN, WORK AND THE FAMILY UNDER SLAVERY. *Feminist Studies 1982 8(2): 235-269.* The burdens of slave women represented, in extreme form, the productive and reproductive work required of all women in a patriarchal society. While masters made little gender distinction, delicately balancing the desire for maximum output from each against the need for healthy new slaves, the slaves defiantly maintained gender distinctions in their households. These latter often reflected the African heritage. 63 notes.   S. Hildenbrand

593. Kosarev, B. M. GENEZIS PLANTATSIONNOI RABOVLA-DEL'CHESKOI SISTEMY V S.SH.A. [The genesis of the slaveowning plantation system in the U.S.A.]. *Voprosy Istorii [USSR] 1978 (5): 62-73.* The author investigates the rise and development of the slaveowning plantation system in the U.S.A. In the 17th-18th centuries the markets for the sale of tobacco and other export crops grown by the labour of Negro slaves were extremely unstable. The development of the plantation system in Britain's North American colonies proceeded at a relatively slow rate. The system of slavery which existed there constituted one of the economic forms. By the end of the 18th century the industrial revolution in the cotton production of England, which subsequently spread to a number of other European countries and to North America, led to the emergence of a steadily expanding market for the sale of cotton—the chief product of slave labour; in the 19th century the slaveholding economy in the South of the U.S.A. became transformed into the plantation system proper.   J

594. Kosarev, B. M. O ROLI AMERIKANSKOGO PRANTATSI-ONNOGO RABSTVA PERVOI POLOVINY XIX V. V GENEZISE KAPITALIZMA [Employment of slave labor on the American plantations in the first half of the 19th century and its role in the genesis of capitalism]. *Voprosy Istorii [USSR] 1970 (8): 57-71.* Stresses that the intensive development of the system of slavery in the South undoubtedly presented a serious obstacle to its social, economic, political and cultural progress. At the same time, the slaves played an immense part in creating material values, and in laying the groundwork for the rapid industrial development of the United States, Britain, and, to a certain extent, of a number of other countries. In the case of Britain, for instance, Negro slavery, up to the outbreak of the Civil War, was the mainstay of the cotton industry and an important source of profits. Slavery exerted a multiform and contradictory influence. From the economic point of view, as a "method of enrichment" and capital accumulation, it was an important prerequisite of the industrial revolution, although it exerted a negative influence on the country's political and ideological life. With the beginning of a swift transition from manufacture to factory production in the mid-19th century, slavery as a whole became a formidable obstacle to the further progress of the country and was bound to end.   J/S

595. Kotlikoff, Laurence J. THE STRUCTURE OF SLAVE PRICES IN NEW ORLEANS, 1804 TO 1862. *Econ. Inquiry 1979 17(4): 496-518.* Analyzes the structure of slave prices in New Orleans to shed light on the competitive nature of the market, desirable attributes of slaves, the separation of families, and relationships between slaves and owners.

596. Kress, Sylvia H. WILL THE FREEDMEN WORK? WHITE ALABAMIANS ADJUST TO FREE BLACK LABOR. *Alabama Hist. Q. 1974 36(2): 151-163.* "Will the freedman work?" was a central question in the South following the end of the Civil War. There was concern in Alabama when many freedmen refused to go back to the plantations in the spring of 1865. Rumors of free land kept men idle until early 1866, when no division of land was made. Paying freed laborers and keeping them until after the harvest was difficult. Hard money was scarce. What developed in Alabama and much of the rest of the South was a system of share-cropping. This became the pattern of economic arrangement between former slave and former master. The new system was in full operation by 1867. 35 notes.   E. E. Eminhizer

597. Krouse, Rita M. THE GERMANTOWN STORE. *North Louisiana Hist. Assoc. J. 1977 8(2): 53-64.* There must have been hundreds of country stores in the South before the Civil War, although little has been written about them. "Because of their isolation it is very probable that many of the country stores played a multiplicity of roles," and this was certainly true for the Germantown store which opened for business in 1851. Germantown was about seven miles north of Minden, and the surviving records from that store "provide a wealth of information apart from the names of customers and the prices which they paid for goods

and services." Many of the store's customers were slaves, and quite a few products of the slaves' leisure-time labor were sold to the store. Contains extracts from a slave account; a list of the typical articles bought by the slaves; and a comparison of the prices charged at the store for certain products during the 1850's. 18 notes. A. N. Garland

598. Kulikoff, Allan. BLACK SOCIETY AND THE ECONOMICS OF SLAVERY. *Maryland Hist. Mag. 1975 70(2): 203-210.* Criticizes Robert W. Fogel and Stanley L. Engerman's *Time on the Cross* (Boston: Little, Brown & Co., 1974, 2 vols.) for viewing slaves "almost exclusively from the vantage point of the masters" and for being "remarkably insensitive to temporal and geographical variations in slave life and treatment." Since almost all the book's data are confined to 1850-60, a nearly static picture of slave life is presented, which ignores the growing awareness today of secular and generational changes in slave society. The book further "greatly underestimates the impact of migration on slave families" and data on this topic exclude many migrants and give a distorted and overly stable view of slave family life, which was in fact severely disrupted during 1810-40. The major problem with *Time on the Cross* , though, is not the authors' "manipulation of data but their conceptual framework," which ignores vital questions on the cultural and social context of slave family life. Nevertheless, Fogel and Engerman admit their analysis is still incomplete and conclusions are tentative, while the book suggests "new directions for the study of slavery." 2 tables, 11 notes. G. J. Bobango

599. Lewis, Ronald L. "THE DARKEST ABODE OF MAN": BLACK MINERS IN THE FIRST SOUTHERN COAL FIELD, 1780-1865. *Virginia Mag. of Hist. and Biog. 1979 87(2): 190-202.* Discusses eastern Virginia coal field development. Although free workers were employed in the mines, slave labor was essential to these enterprises, in high- and low-skill jobs. Relates the nature of and the response to mine safety problems, including insurance on the miners. The mines declined when capital investments shifted to the Appalachian area. 2 tables, 60 notes. P. J. Woehrmann

600. Lewis, Ronald L. SLAVE FAMILIES AT EARLY CHESAPEAKE IRONWORKS. *Virginia Mag. of Hist. and Biog. 1978 86(2): 169-179.* Despite a widespread belief that the institution of slavery destroyed the black family, the evidence indicates that this was not true with industrial slavery. In ironworks, the opportunity for overwork provided male slaves with money to buy additional food or clothing for their families and helped to preserve the family unit. For the majority of slave ironworkers, the family was a viable patriarchal institution. Drawn from primary material in the Maryland Historical Society, the College of William and Mary, the Library of Congress, the University of Virginia, the State Historical Society of Wisconsin, the Virginia Historical Society, and Duke University; 33 notes. R. F. Oaks

601. Lewis, Ronald L. SLAVERY ON CHESAPEAKE IRON PLANTATIONS BEFORE THE AMERICAN REVOLUTION. *J. of Negro Hist. 1974 59(3): 242-254.* Until 1783 the Chesapeake area iron industry produced the vast bulk of the iron in North America, with a labor force of black bondsmen. Based on primary and secondary sources; 55 notes. N. G. Sapper

602. Lewis, Ronald L. THE USE AND EXTENT OF SLAVE LABOR IN THE CHESAPEAKE IRON INDUSTRY: THE COLONIAL ERA. *Labor Hist. 1976 17(3): 388-405.* Analyzes the number and occupations of slaves in colonial Chesapeake's iron works. Although exact percentages are unavailable, slaves held skilled positions as well as unskilled. The colonial iron works adapted slavery to an industrial setting. Based on travel accounts, account books, and newspapers; 43 notes. L. L. Athey

603. Lewis, Ronald L. THE USE AND EXTENT OF SLAVE LABOR IN THE VIRGINIA IRON INDUSTRY: THE ANTEBELLUM ERA. *West Virginia Hist. 1977 38(2): 141-156.* Slaves were the chief labor force in southern ironworks before 1865. Most were hired, not owned. Virginia had about 80 ironworks with perhaps 7,000 hands at any one time, about 70 percent of them blacks. Slavery was flexible and expanding into industry. Primary sources; 5 tables, 63 notes. J. H. Broussard

604. Luraghi, Raimondo. WAGE LABOR IN THE "RICE BELT" OF NORTHERN ITALY AND SLAVE LABOR IN THE AMERICAN SOUTH: A FIRST APPROACH. *Southern Studies 1977 16(2): 109-127.* Agricultural wage laborers in northern Italy, the most advanced capitalistic area of Europe, 1876-81, were much worse off than black slaves in America before the Civil War. The Italian peasants received less income, were more poorly fed, had a higher mortality rate, had worse living and working conditions and higher taxes, and had no interpersonal relations with their employers. Based on the Jacini Inquiry and secondary sources; 7 tables, 3 graphs, 20 notes. J. Buschen

605. McGettigan, James William. BOONE COUNTY SLAVES: SALES, ESTATE DIVISIONS AND FAMILIES, 1820-1865. *Missouri Hist. Rev. 1978 72(2): 176-197; (3): 271-295.* Part I. In *Slave Trading in the Old South,* Frederic Bancroft said Missouri exported many slaves to the deep South, a position reasserted by Kenneth Stampp in *The Peculiar Institution.* Slavery apparently was not dying in Boone County, Missouri. An examination of census data, the probate court records, and the subscription lists of the Columbia *Missouri Statesman* reveal that very few slaves were traded out of the county and that there was a marked tendency for the slaves of a deceased owner to pass to family members in the county. Primary and secondary sources. Illus., 4 tables, 48 notes. Part II. Newspapers, personal correspondence, and estate sale records show that slave hiring was popular in Boone County, because it made a pool of labor available to men who did not want to own slaves themselves. The same records show that most slaves tended to pass to other owners in Boone County by sale or by estate distribution. Most of the slaves might have remained in Boone County, but this did not mean that slave families remained together. Few slaveowners responded to humanitarian sentiments when there were economic and legal pressures that made it seem more advantageous to break family ties. Illus., table, 59 notes. W. F. Zornow

606. McGowan, James T. PLANTERS WITHOUT SLAVES: ORIGINS OF A NEW WORLD LABOR SYSTEM. *Southern Studies 1977 16(1): 5-26.* The institutionalization of African slavery as the dominant form of labor organization in Louisiana arose in response to a fundamental class conflict within the life of the colony during 1790-1820. The unrelenting refusal of craftsmen, hunters, and soldiers, the men recruited in Europe, to be tied to the land paved the way for the rejection of white labor on staple-producing plantations. These men had neither the experience nor the inclination for the responsibilities of farming or marriage, preferring adventure and Indian mistresses. Their life style brought about the failure to create agricultural communities based on white labor in Louisiana, and led, after 1717, to the importation of African slaves. Based on Archives of the Ministry of Colonies in Paris, other primary and secondary sources; 56 notes. J. Buschen

607. Meier, August. SLAVERY: A DIFFERENT VIEW OF THE "CROSS." *Rev. in Am. Hist. 1975 3(2): 206-212.* Eugene D. Genovese's *Roll, Jordan, Roll: The World the Slaves Made* (New York: Pantheon Books, 1974) examines the ambiguities in the paternalistic slave system in the South in the 19th century.

608. Menard, Russell. FROM SERVANTS TO SLAVES: THE TRANSFORMATION OF THE CHESAPEAKE LABOR SYSTEM. *Southern Studies 1977 16(4): 355-390.* The transition from indentured servants to slaves at the end of the 17th century in the Chesapeake area cannot be explained by the superior profitability of slavery. Rather, a decline in the traditional labor supply from England forced planters to recruit workers from new sources, principally but not exclusively from Africa. Changing demographic patterns and economic forces in England and the colonies produced fewer young white males available for service. Only after this supply dwindled in the late 17th century did large-scale importation of slaves begin. Primary and secondary sources; 8 tables, 3 graphs, 63 notes. J. Buschen

609. Miller, Randall M. THE FABRIC OF CONTROL: SLAVERY IN ANTEBELLUM SOUTHERN TEXTILE MILLS. *Business Hist. Rev. 1981 55(4): 471-490.* Most slaves employed in textile mills were women and children, and they were less skilled than their adult male counterparts in other industries. Nevertheless, through sabotage or carelessness, they could still disrupt production. To prevent such activities, most employers preferred to insure good performance by

adopting a policy of accomodation rather than by using force and intimidation. Incentives in the form of holidays, overpayments, and internal mobility were concessions used to encourage continued operation of the mill machinery. Only after these failed was punishment inflicted. Based on periodical sources of the period and some private papers and business records; 33 notes.   C. J. Pusateri

610. Miller, Randall M. THE MAN IN THE MIDDLE: THE BLACK SLAVE DRIVER. *Am. Heritage 1979 30(6): 40-49.* Sympathizes with the intermediaries between the slave owner and the slave community, the black slave drivers.

611. Mintz, Sidney W. THE DIGNITY OF HONEST TOIL: *A REVIEW ARTICLE. Comparative Studies in Soc. and Hist. [Great Britain] 1979 21(4): 558-566.* Review article based on Graham W. Irwin's *Africans Abroad* (New York: Columbia U. Pr., 1977), Leslie Howard Owens's *The Species of Property* (New York: Oxford U. Pr., 1976), Vera Rubin and Arthur Tuden's *Comparative Perspectives on Slavery in New World Plantation Societies* (New York: New York Academy of Sciences, 1977), J. Thorsten Sellin's *Slavery and the Penal System* (New York: Elsevier, 1976), and James E. Smith's *Slavery in Bermuda* (New York: Vantage Pr., 1976).

612. Myers, John B. THE ALABAMA FREEDMEN AND THE ECONOMIC ADJUSTMENTS DURING PRESIDENTIAL RECONSTRUCTION, 1865-1867. *Alabama Rev. 1973 26(4): 252-266.* The Bureau of Refugees, Freedmen, and Abandoned Lands began operating in Alabama under the direction of General Wager Swayne in July 1865. Relief measures (food rations, shelter, and medical care) proved inadequate, due to the poverty of the state and the burden of general economic conditions. Exploitation was controlled and freedmen's response to labor was commendable, but working conditions did not widely improve, because of racial antagonism, coercive rules, and penalties adopted by the bureau. Little abandoned land was available for blacks, and the Homestead Act of 1866 proved unworkable because most public land was unsuited to agriculture. The Freedmen's Savings Bank was a limited success where it operated, but it could not overcome contemporary difficulties. The freedmen's transition from slavery to freedom required more "sincere and sustained assistance" than was available 1865-67. Based on primary and secondary sources; 46 notes.   J. F. Vivian

613. Nash, Gary B. SLAVES AND SLAVEOWNERS IN COLONIAL PHILADELPHIA. *William and Mary Q. 1973 30(2): 223-256.* Slaveholding reached a peak during the decade following the outbreak of the Seven Years War. Analyzes the slave population 1767-75. Offers reasons for the decline of the slave population after 1767. Mentions labor conditions and considers the correlation between slave ownership with wealth and religious affiliation. 8 tables, 69 notes.   H. M. Ward

614. Newton, James E. SLAVE ARTISANS AND CRAFTSMEN: THE ROOTS OF AFRO-AMERICAN ART. *Black Scholar 1977 9(3): 35-44.* The overwhelmingly anonymous black artisans and craftspeople maintained a high level of skill and artistry which was inherited largely from West African tradition and provided a basis for postemancipation florescence of black art.

615. O'Brien, John T. FACTORY, CHURCH, AND COMMUNITY: BLACKS IN ANTEBELLUM RICHMOND. *J. of Southern Hist. 1978 44(4): 509-536.* Recent studies have shed much light upon the culture of plantation slaves. Yet neglect of urban slaves have left historians with no way to explain such phenomena as the blacks of Richmond successfully organizing and petitioning President Johnson in mid-1865 to ease the US military's control on their lives. Studying and analyzing the social skills which developed from slave labor in the tobacco factories and the well-organized black Christian churches permit us to understand the surfacing of these work habits, and the revelation of firm family and community structures in the months after the Civil War. Manuscripts and printed primary and secondary sources; 99 notes.   T. D. Schoonover

616. Otto, John Solomon. SLAVERY IN A COASTAL COMMUNITY: GLYNN COUNTY (1790-1860). *Georgia Hist. Q. 1979 64(4): 461-468.* Traces the rise and decline of slaveholding in Glynn County. Changes in the proportion of slave to white inhabitants occurred as

agricultural labor needs changed and as occupations became more diversified. Based on 1850 and 1860 Censuses and on secondary sources; 2 tables, 36 notes.   G. R. Schroeder

617. Otto, John Solomon. SLAVERY IN THE MOUNTAINS: YELL COUNTY, ARKANSAS, 1840-1860. *Arkansas Hist. Q. 1980 39(1): 35-52.* Statistical analysis of slaveholding small farmers. Most of those who held a few slaves seem to have done so in order to increase the farm's self-sufficiency. Based on 1850 and 1860 censuses and on secondary sources; 6 tables, 3 fig., 39 notes.   G. R. Schroeder

618. Perdue, Theda. CHEROKEE PLANTERS, BLACK SLAVES, AND AFRICAN COLONIZATION. *Chronicles of Oklahoma 1982 60(3): 322-331.* Although they had owned black slaves since the 1790's, most Cherokees felt uncomfortable with the institution and hoped for its gradual demise. Apart from the demand upon their labor and some restrictions on marriage rights, the slaves enjoyed a fairly independent life. This relatively lenient treatment carried over into Cherokee support for a "back to Africa movement" for freed slaves. This pattern changed after the forced removal of Cherokees to Indian Territory during the 1830's. The greater demand for labor in a frontier environment hardened Cherokee attitudes toward blacks, and a harsh slave code resulted. Harsher treatment and total collapse of the African colonization scheme compelled slaves to become more defiant and to run away more frequently. Based on the *Cherokee Phoenix, Cherokee Advocate,* and archival sources; 20 notes.   M. L. Tate

619. Perkins, William E. TIME ON THE CROSS: A CRITIQUE AND COUNTERPROPOSAL. *J. of Ethnic Studies 1975 3(3): 102-112.* Discusses selection and use of data in Robert William Fogel's and Stanley Engerman's *Time on the Cross* , but emphasizes the ideological nature of the book. The theme of this book is a preservation of the old 'neo-abolitionist' mythology rather than a refutation of it. Slaves were receivers, not actors, and their family life, sexual mores, and Protestant work-ethic were the results of planter-induced stimuli, the book suggests, which disproves the slave-initiated independence which Fogel and Engerman seek to demonstrate. "*Time on the Cross* ends in failure. It confuses rather than helps us unravel the complexity and uniqueness of the Afro-American experience." The coauthors have created a new myth of their own: "The Jolly Institution." "The book is useless to anyone writing and understanding the real history of Afro-Americans." It is the liberal "laissez faire" interpretation of slavery, to be expected from economists. Includes notes on other reviews and secondary works; 9 notes.   G. J. Bobango

620. Rankin, David. BLACK SLAVEHOLDERS: THE CASE OF ANDREW DURNFORD. *Southern Studies 1982 21(3): 343-347.* There were more than 3,700 black slaveholders in 1830 in the South. One of them, Andrew Durnford, owned 77 slaves and a large sugar plantation in Louisiana. Son of a white slaveholder and a mulatto woman, Durnford had a good education and purchased various farms during his lifetime. He was a tough and tight-fisted master; he freed only four slaves during his lifetime. He was very much like white slaveholders of the time in his attitudes and behavior. Based on David Whitten's *Andrew Durnford: A Black Sugar Planter in Antebellum Louisiana* (1981); 14 notes.   J. J. Buschen

621. Ratcliffe, Donald. THE *DAS KAPITAL* OF AMERICAN NEGRO SLAVERY? *TIME ON THE CROSS* AFTER TWO YEARS. *Durham U. J. [Great Britain] 1976 69(1): 103-130.* Robert William Fogel and Stanley L. Engerman's *Time on the Cross* (Boston, 1974) attempts to reverse traditional views of American slavery by suggesting that it was less moribund, more flexible, and more humane. The general argument of the book coincides with the conclusions that scholars are now coming to accept, but it exaggerates or overlooks complexities. Fogel and Engerman are soundest on economics. Criticizes their conclusions on the social aspects of slavery. Quantitative methods such as those of Fogel and Engerman have much less to offer historians than has been suggested, and are dangerously deceptive because of their ability to create an illusion of certainty without the reality. 101 notes.   C. A. McNeill

622. Rivers, Larry. "DIGNITY AND IMPORTANCE": SLAVERY IN JEFFERSON COUNTY, FLORIDA—1827 TO 1860. *Florida Hist. Q. 1983 61(4): 404-430.* The ownership of slaves was a key to obtaining

status in Jefferson County, Florida. Land ownership combined with slavery and sound business practices produced profits. Slaves realized that they were a necessary commodity for the achievement of "dignity and importance." Based on the William Wirt Papers, census returns, and other sources; 5 tables, 98 notes.　　　　　　　N. A. Kuntz

623. Sandin, Bengt. SLAVEN SOM MEDELKLASSAMERIKAN. FOGEL OCH ENGERMAN OCH DEBATTEN OM SLAVERIET I USA [The slave as a middle-class American: Fogel and Engerman and the discussion of slavery in the USA]. *Hist. Tidskrift [Sweden] 1977 (1): 39-70.* Analyzes Robert William Fogel and Stanley L. Engerman's, *Time on the Cross* (Boston: Little, Brown, 1974), which describes slavery as benefiting slaves materially and socially. Fogel and Engerman use quantitative methods in attempting to be objective and to produce a study unrelated to a particular school of thought. They have failed in both, as their work implies approval of the social structure and continues the consensus tradition in American historiography. Moreover, the book has implications for present American society in suggesting a sound social structure in which the individual can advance through hard work, as the slave could in the institution of slavery as they depict it. 70 notes, ref.　　　　　　　P. A. Hegstad

624. Savitt, Todd L. SLAVE LIFE INSURANCE IN VIRGINIA AND NORTH CAROLINA. *J. of Southern Hist. 1977 43(4): 583-600.* During 1840-60 life insurance blossomed in the North and to a lesser extent in the South. In the South few whites purchased life insurance on themselves, but slave owners often purchased life insurance on slaves loaned out or insisted that the lessee do so, particularly when the slaves were being loaned out for dangerous work. By the outbreak of the Civil War, slave insurance companies were providing a small measure of support to the "peculiar institution." Based on manuscript and primary and secondary sources; 2 tables, 62 notes.　　　　　　　T. D. Schoonover

625. Scarpino, Philip V. SLAVERY IN CALLAWAY COUNTY, MISSOURI: 1845-1855. PART 2. *Missouri Hist. Rev. 1977 71(3): 266-283.* Continued from a previous article. Slaveowners often preferred to settle in places like Callaway County where there was easy access to the river. Slaveholders in Callaway County regarded their slaves as both human beings and property. Slaves worked to increase their masters' wealth, but were also given an opportunity to perform voluntary and self-rewarding work. As a result, the county boasted an expanding agricultural production that buttressed the local economy. Slaveholders convinced themselves that slavery was the best arrangement for both races. County slaveholders in the 1850's looked forward to prosperous times; there was no thought that slavery was dying. Illus., 43 notes.　　　　　　　W. F. Zornow

626. Schmitz, Mark D. and Schaefer, Donald F. SLAVERY, FREEDOM, AND THE ELASTICITY OF SUBSTITUTION. *Explorations in Econ. Hist. 1978 15(3): 327-337.* The empirical findings strongly suggest that slave agricultural labor was characterized by a low degree of substitutability and was quantitatively different in this respect from the free sector. Manuscript census records and secondary accounts; 3 tables, 27 ref., appendix.　　　　　　　P. J. Coleman

627. Schweninger, Loren. THE FREE-SLAVE PHENOMENON: JAMES P. THOMAS AND THE BLACK COMMUNITY IN ANTEBELLUM NASHVILLE. *Civil War Hist. 1976 22(4): 293-307.* Quasi-free bondsmen comprised a significant southern Negro group. They have received scant historical attention because of their precarious, secretive existence. Numbering perhaps many thousands throughout the South, they achieved large measures of independence. James P. Thomas, a free-slave barber, illustrates these wide possibilities, available particularly in the urban setting. Through contrivance, deception, and intelligent hard work, he and many others successfully compromised the slave system. Their condition resulted in resiliency and strength, not infantilization nor demoralization. Primary and secondary sources; 71 notes.　　　　　　　R. E. Stack

628. Shofner, Jerrell H. NEGRO LABORERS AND THE FOREST INDUSTRIES IN RECONSTRUCTION FLORIDA. *J. of Forest Hist. 1975 19(4): 180-191.* Florida's forests provided the most extensive employment for ex-slaves when cotton production declined in the late 19th century. A wage-labor system evolved to ease the accommodation of ex-slaves to free labor and to compensate for the short supply of fluid capital. Despite limited success in organizing for collective bargaining, Florida timber workers were as well off as average wage earners of their time. 5 illus., map, 38 notes.　　　　　　　L. Johnson

629. Steirer, William F., Jr. SLAVE OR SUPER-SLAVE: WHO REALLY DID LABOR IN THE SOUTHERN COTTON FIELDS? *Pro. of the South Carloina Hist. Assoc. 1979: 14-27.* Examines the historical literature on slavery since Kenneth Stampp's *The Peculiar Insitution* in 1956, characterizing most of the more recent writers as studying the "super-slaves," those who escaped slavery relatively unscathed. Suggests that a better treatment would discard both the old "Sambo" and the more recent "super-slave" images and treat slaves as human beings. 32 notes.　　　　　　　J. W. Thacker, Jr.

630. Sutherland, Daniel E. A SPECIAL KIND OF PROBLEM: THE RESPONSE OF HOUSEHOLD SLAVES AND THEIR MASTERS TO FREEDOM. *Southern Studies 1981 20(2): 151-166.* After emancipation, blacks responded in different ways to their new freedom and former masters. House servants, especially, differed in their reactions from field hands. During slavery, house servants had been closer to their masters. After freedom, they tended to act more decisively about their condition than other blacks. Thus some were arrogant and resentful and immediately abandoned their masters; others, however, were the most loyal blacks and worked for their former masters during Reconstruction. Eventually most Southerners resumed employing black adults in their homes because the hiring of white servants proved unsatisfactory. Primary sources; 59 notes.　　　　　　　J. J. Buschen

631. Tansey, Richard. BERNARD KENDIG AND THE NEW ORLEANS SLAVE TRADE. *Louisiana Hist. 1982 23(2): 159-178.* The trade was dominated by men born in the South Atlantic states who imported slaves from that region and from the Upper South. Bernard Kendig was atypical: he was a Pennsylvanian and relied on the local market, buying three-quarters of his slaves from Louisiana (mostly New Orleans) residents and selling primarily to buyers living in the city. While his rivals sold to large rural slaveholders, his customers were small farmers and shopkeepers. Cheap prices and a liberal credit policy contributed to his success, but he also made fraudulent sales of defective slaves, stolen slaves, and kidnapped free blacks. Based primarily on New Orleans civil court and notarial records; 2 tables, map, 55 notes.　　　　　　　R. E. Noble

632. Temperley, Howard. CAPITALISM, SLAVERY AND IDEOLOGY. *Past and Present [Great Britain] 1977 (75): 94-118.* Revisionist arguments that in a capitalist economy slavery was uneconomical can be shown to be wrong. That procapitalist arguments were effectively used by abolitionists is explained by their linking of abolitionism with the ideological views (originating with Adam Smith and repeated by J. E. Cairnes) that free labor and the humanitarian treatment of labor brings greater productivity. Southern polemicists saw that capitalist ideology was inimical to slave-holding. The abolition controversy centered on a conflict of values which was not related to economic advantage at all; slavery was perfectly suited to a ruthless capitalistic interest in highest profits. Based on primary sources, Parliamentary papers, and secondary sources.　　　　　　　D. Levy

633. Tipton, Frank B., Jr. and Walker, Clarence E. *TIME ON THE CROSS*. *Hist. & Theory 1975 14(1): 91-121.* Review article prompted by Robert William Fogel and Stanley L. Engerman, *Time on the Cross: The Economics of American Negro Slavery* (Boston: Little, Brown and Co., 1974). Fogel and Engerman used quantitative methods to question the "traditional interpretation" (first propagated by the abolitionists) of slavery as an unworkable economic system. The reviewers examine Fogel and Engerman's alternative, finding it incomplete and their authority questionable, which problems illustrate "some of the difficulties of an attempt to apply systematic quantitative methods to historical data." But traditional methods of research are also unsatisfactory. The reviewers offer some suggestions for future research when the crucial questions "will be the impact of slavery on the economy and social structure of the south." 61 notes.　　　　　　　D. A. Yanchisin

634. Vedder, Richard K. and Stockdale, David C. THE PROFITABILITY OF SLAVERY REVISITED: A DIFFERENT APPROACH. *Agric. Hist. 1975 49(2): 392-404.* Using production functions involving output, labor and capital, the authors have calculat-

ed that slavery was indeed profitable for cotton production, yielding a 9.95 percent rate of return, approximately equal to the return on land and agricultural capital without slave labor. Changing assumptions about price, cost, depreciation, etc., still leaves the rate of return on labor roughly equal to that on capital. 2 tables, 17 notes.   D. E. Bowers

635. Wallerstein, Immanuel. AMERICAN SLAVERY AND THE CAPITALIST WORLD-ECONOMY. *Am. J. of Sociol. 1976 81(5): 1199-1213.* Reviews Robert William Fogel and Stanley L. Engerman's *Time on The Cross* , Vol. I: *The Economics of American Negro Slavery Slavery* , Vol. 2: *Evidence and Methods—A Supplement* (Boston, 1974), and Eugene D. Genovese's *Roll Jordan Roll: The World the Slaves Made* (New York, 1974).

636. White, Deborah G. FEMALE SLAVES: SEX ROLES AND STATUS IN THE ANTEBELLUM PLANTATION SOUTH. *J. of Family Hist. 1983 8(3): 248-261.* Slave families were matrifocal. Work and social roles were sufficiently sex-stratified so that female slaves operated quite independently of male slaves. 20 notes.   T. W. Smith

637. Whitten, David O. MEDICAL CARE OF SLAVES: LOUISI-ANA SUGAR REGION AND SOUTH CAROLINA RICE DIS-TRICT. *Southern Studies 1977 16(2): 153-180.* Slaves on unhealthful rice and sugar plantations had better medical attention than cotton slaves because of the owners' recognition of the capital value in slave investments. Proof is found in detailed instructions to overseers on care of slaves, contracting of medical personnel for professional attendance when necessary, maintenance of hospitals and nursehouses, and appoint-ment of full time personnel to care for sick slaves. Slave sales, not a heavy death rate, explain an abnormal loss of slaves in the rice and sugar areas during the antebellum period. Based on letters at Tulane U. and Louisiana State Museum: US Census Reports, unpublished thesis, and secondary sources; 6 tables, 58 notes.   J. Buschen

638. Whitten, David O. SUGAR SLAVERY: A PROFITABILITY MODEL FOR SLAVE INVESTMENTS IN THE ANTEBELLUM LOUISIANA SUGAR INDUSTRY. *Louisiana Studies 1973 12(2): 423-442.* Uses an equation involving slave prices, cost of implements and machinery, cost of livestock, land, and housing, rate of interest, and the longevity of the slave, to determine whether slavery was profitable to the sugar planter. Equation, 4 tables, 26 notes.   G. W. McGinty

639. Wilson, William J. SLAVERY, PATERNALISM, AND WHITE HEGEMONY. *Am. J. of Sociol. 1976 81(5): 1190-1198.* Reviews Robert William Fogel and Stanley L. Engerman's *Time on The Cross* , Vol. 1: *The Economics of American Negro Slavery* , and Vol. 2: *Evidence and Methods—A Supplement* (Boston, 1974) and Eugene D. Genovese's *Roll Jordan Roll: The World the Slaves Made* (New York, 1974).

640. Wood, Peter H. "IT WAS A NEGRO TAUGHT THEM," A NEW LOOK AT AFRICAN LABOR IN EARLY SOUTH CAROLI-NA. *J. of Asian and African Studies [Netherlands] 1974 9(3/4): 160-179.* Slaves made an important series of contributions to 17th- and 18th-century South Carolina through the introduction of African crops and methods of agriculture. 11 notes, biblio.   R. T. Brown

641. Yetman, Norman R. THE RISE AND FALL OF *TIME ON THE CROSS. Rev. in Am. Hist. 1976 4(2): 195-202.* Review article prompted by Herbert G. Gutman's *Slavery and the Numbers Game: A Critique of Time on the Cross* (Urbana: U. of Illinois Pr., 1975) which discusses Robert William Fogel and Stanley L. Engerman's conceptual-ization of slave behavior and personality and their assessment and use of collected data.

3. LABOR IN POST-BELLUM AMERICA, 1865 TO 1900

General

642. Ansley, Fran and Bell, Brenda, eds. MINERS' INSURREC-TIONS/CONVICT LABOR. *Southern Exposure 1974 1(3/4): 144-159.* Coal mining companies leased convicts from the state of Tennessee to replace miners and to break strikes. During 1891-93, miners waged strikes and armed resistance against the mining companies involved, especially Tennessee Coal Mining Company. Battles against the state militia, destruction of mining company equipment, and the freeing of convicts from the mines stemmed from the imposition of anti-union oaths required for employment. Eventually the state stopped leasing convicts to the highest bidder, purchasing its own mines and using convict labor. Based on oral interviews, primary and secondary sources; 11 illus., 10 notes, biblio.   G. A. Bolton

643. Applen, Allen G. LABOR CASUALIZATION IN GREAT PLAINS WHEAT PRODUCTION: 1865-1902. *J. of the West 1977 16(1): 5-9.* Examines the mechanization of wheat farming in the midwest and its effect on the labor force. It necessitated a migratory work force and demanded fewer skills among the farm workers than before. A labor vacuum existed in the Plains states but the labor was needed only about 15 weeks a year. This casualization of labor, and the lower skill level required, lowered the worker's status.   R. Alvis

644. Brush, Ted. CHINESE LABOR IN NORTH JERSEY 1870-1895. *North Jersey Highlander 1973 9(1): 13-21.* Chinese labor was excluded from California in 1870 after being used to build transcontinental railroads, but New Jersey companies used Chinese laborers as strike-breakers against the Knights of Labor. James B. Hervey, owner of the Passaic Steam Laundry, contracted Chinese laborers from San Francisco despite strong local protest, especially from Irish laundresses. Eventually the Chinese laundresses also went on strike and other ethnic groups were tried. 4 illus.   A. C. Aimone

645. Cohen, Lucy M. ENTRY OF CHINESE TO THE LOWER SOUTH FROM 1865 TO 1870: POLICY DILEMMAS. *Southern Studies 1978 17(1): 5-37.* Immediately after the Civil War, to alleviate labor problems planters in some southern states tried to introduce Chinese laborers from Cuba and China. The movement lasted only a few years and involved only a few thousand people. The federal government disapproved for fear of reviving the coolie trade, prohibited since 1862. A few hundred Chinese were brought from China after signing affidavits to the American consul that they came of their own free will. Most of the Chinese soon became sharecroppers or tenant farmers and left the ranks of employees. Primary and secondary sources; 91 notes, appendix.   J. Buschen

646. Daniel, Pete. THE TENNESSEE CONVICT WAR. *Tennessee Hist. Q. 1975 34(3): 273-292.* During 1891-93 a violent struggle occurred in the coal mines of eastern Tennessee between free laborers and their employers who sought to enlarge the existing system of convict labor. Involved in the conflict were incompetent state leaders, especially Governor John P. Buchanan, powerful mine owners who espoused a system of "free enterprise" supported by a conservative court system, mostly black convicts caught in the middle, and tough Tennessee mountain people who took up arms to eliminate convict labor competition. In the end, the conflict solved none of the inherent problems. Primary and secondary sources; 42 notes.   M. B. Lucas

647. DuBois, Ellen, ed. ON LABOR AND FREE LOVE: TWO UNPUBLISHED SPEECHES OF ELIZABETH CADY STANTON. *Signs 1975 1(1): 257-268.* Stanton (1815-1902) was the chief ideologue and theoretician of suffragism from the 1850's to the 1890's. During Reconstruction, she and other suffragists broke with their former allies, the abolitionists, and integrated the enfranchisement of women with other reforms such as labor and free love. Departing from her upper-class background in "On Labor" (1868), Stanton called poverty and wage slavery social, not natural, phenomena and advocated strikes; yet she saw "the educated classes" as the source of social change. In "On

Marriage and Divorce" (1870) she criticized "external regulation of private affections" and commented favorably on the freedom in her marriage to Henry Stanton. Based on primary and secondary sources; 8 notes.   T. Simmerman

648. Duggan, Edward P. MACHINES, MARKETS, AND LABOR: THE CARRIAGE AND WAGON INDUSTRY IN LATE-NINE-TEENTH-CENTURY CINCINNATI. *Business Hist. Rev. 1977 51(3): 308-325.* Tests H. J. Habakkuk's labor supply hypothesis which asserts that a labor shortage stimulated rapid technological change. Carriage and wagon producers in Cincinnati did not appear to suffer from such a shortage. They sought production techniques to increase output, not to save on labor costs. They also invested more capital in developing markets than in manufacturing, indicating a belief that there was more to gain from marketing innovations than from production. Based on governmental records and periodical sources; 30 notes.

C. J. Pusateri

649. Early, Frances H. THE FRENCH-CANADIAN FAMILY ECONOMY AND STANDARD OF LIVING IN LOWELL, MASSA-CHUSETTS, 1870. *J. of Family Hist. 1982 7(2): 180-199.* One of the lesser known rural-to-urban migrations of the 19th century was the influx of French-Canadian farmers to the mills of New England. While traditionally seen as a negative experience (driven from the land to the slums, diverted from simple rural virtues to chaotic urban vices), the French Canadians successfully managed to adapt and some prospered. Yet success was only possible through the continued use of child labor. 3 tables, 23 notes, appendix.   T. W. Smith

650. Fink, Leon. POLITICS AS SOCIAL HISTORY: A CASE STUDY OF CLASS CONFLICT AND POLITICAL DEVELOP-MENT IN NINETEENTH-CENTURY NEW ENGLAND. *Social Hist. [Great Britain] 1982 7(1): 43-58.* The political and institutional transformation of the marble-quarrying town of Rutland, Vermont, 1880-95, shows the inadequacy of accepted views of urban political development in the United States, and the intimate connections between politics and social history. The key to change was the organized working-class challenge to the elite in the 1880's, involving Knights of Labor and United Labor election slates. This led to the division of Rutland into three: the company town of Proctor run through paternalistic consensus; a democratic consensus in West Rutland where the Democrats gained the support of ethnic working-class voters; and the rest of Rutland where a dominant Republican machine was challenged by a Democrat minority with labour support. Thus class conflict broke the political edifice and forced its reconstruction in new forms. Based on documents in the Proctor Free Library and Vermont State Library, newspapers, and other printed sources; 28 notes.   D. J. Nicholls

651. Frank, Miriam and Glaberman, Martin. FRIEDRICH A. SORGE ON THE AMERICAN LABOR MOVEMENT. *Labor Hist. 1977 18(4): 592-606.* Translates Friedrich A. Sorge's article on the American labor movement, 1866-76, which first appeared in *Neue Zeit*, Vol. Ax, Band 7, 1891-92, pp. 69-76. 2 notes.   L. L. Athey

652. Fryman, Mildred L. CAREER OF A "CARPETBAGGER": MALACHI MARTIN IN FLORIDA. *Florida Hist. Q. 1978 56(3): 317-338.* Malachi Martin (1822-84) is associated primarily with Florida's notorious convict-lease system, in which he served from 1868-77 as chief administrator of the Chattahoochee Penitentiary. Martin first came to Florida with the Army of the Potomac and stayed to pursue farming. Eventually he enjoyed moderate success in state Republican politics and in his vineyards and wine producing. His record as warden was not exemplary, but it was not as barbarous as his critics claimed. Based mainly on government documents, primary and secondary sources; 94 notes.   P. A. Beaber

653. Gordon, Michael A. THE LABOR BOYCOTT IN NEW YORK CITY, 1880-1886. *Labor Hist. 1975 16(2): 184-229.* The labor boycotts in New York City originated primarily in the previous agricultural experiences of Irish immigrants in their struggle for land reforms. Thus,

the labor boycott was a pre-industrial mode of protection adapted to industrial conditions. The mass arrests and trials of immigrants during 1880-86 are examined. Based upon newspapers, reports of the New York Bureau of Labor Statistics and secondary sources; 79 notes.

L. L. Athey

654. Grant, H. Roger. PORTRAIT OF A WORKERS' UTOPIA: THE LABOR EXCHANGE AND THE FREEDOM, KANSAS, COLONY. *Kansas Hist. Q. 1977 43(1): 56-66.* G. B. De Bernardi's Labor Exchange was a popular panacea for the depression of 1893. It provided members with "labor checks" issued against their products which could be used to purchase other goods from the exchange's depositories. The Freedom Colony in Bourbon county went beyond De Bernardi's plan to show that a utopian community drawing workers out of the cities and dedicated to Labor Exchange principles was workable. The colony failed with a return of good times. Primary and secondary sources; illus., 23 notes.

W. F. Zornow

655. Grindle, Roger L. BODWELL BLUE: THE STORY OF VINALHAVEN'S GRANITE INDUSTRY. *Maine Hist. Soc. Q. 1976 16(2): 51-112.* Recounts the rise and fall of the granite industry in Maine 1851-1919, especially the Bodwell Granite Company of Vinalhaven. Notes the types of granite quarried, numbers of cutters at work, buildings and monuments using Vinalhaven granite, daily wages, and piece work rates.

P. C. Marshall

656. Holmes, William F. THE DEMISE OF THE COLORED FARMERS' ALLIANCE. *J. of Southern Hist. 1975 41(2): 187-200.* The Colored Farmers' Alliance urged hard work, sacrifice, land ownership, and other typical farm positions to improve the lot of the Negro farmer. The Alliance spread throughout the South, during the 1880's-90's but failed because of racism, competition with other farm organizations, and divisiveness in its own leadership. A Cotton Pickers' League was formed and called a strike for higher wages. The strike failed, but whites equated it with the Alliance. Alliance members were farmers, and therefore hardly supporters of the strike. This position cost the Alliance support in Negro areas and it consequently faded away. 52 notes.

V. L. Human

657. Holmes, William F. LABOR AGENTS AND THE GEORGIA EXODUS, 1899-1900. *South Atlantic Q. 1980 79(4): 436-448.* Labor agents played an active, but little-known, role in southern economic life during the late 19th century. They urged black laborers to move from one southern state to another, or from one part of a state to another, basically to meet temporary labor shortages. Examination of an exodus in a region of eight counties in central Georgia, 1899-1900, provides insight into the work of these labor agents and the movement of black laborers within the South. The agents' methods, the reasons many blacks responded to their enticements and the reactions of whites to the resulting exodus are considered. A controversy has recently developed among historians concerning the degree of freedom and economic gains that blacks experienced in the postbellum South. Based largely on contemporary regional newspaper accounts and secondary works; 24 notes.

H. M. Parker, Jr.

658. Loose, John Ward Willson. THE ANTHRACITE IRON INDUSTRY OF LANCASTER COUNTY: ROLLING MILLS 1850-1900. *J. of the Lancaster County Hist. Soc. 1982 86(4): 129-144.* The native anthracite coal attracted a number of rolling mills to Lancaster County, which operated mostly with Welsh owners and labor.

659. Lynd, Staughton. WHY IS THERE NO SOCIALIST MOVEMENT IN THE UNITED STATES? *Rev. in Am. Hist. 1974 2(1): 115-120.* Reviews Gerald Roseblum's *Immigrant Workers: Their Impact on American Labor Radicalism* (New York: Basic Books, 1973) and suggests that the failure of American socialism resulted from immigrant labor's narrow economic motivation and ethnic fragmentation, while Harold V. Aurant, *From the Molly Maguires to the United Mine Workers: The Social Ecology of an Industrial Union, 1869-1897* (Philadelphia: Temple U. Pr., 1973) argues that union membership transformed ethnic consciousness to worker consciousness. 3 notes.

W. D. Piersen

660. McMullin, Thomas A. LOST ALTERNATIVE: THE URBAN INDUSTRIAL UTOPIA OF WILLIAM D. HOWLAND. *New En-*

gland Q. 1982 55(1): 25-38. Investigates the labor practices of New Bedford, Massachusetts cotton yarn manufacturer William Dillwyn Howland. Unique to Howland was a family commitment to social and religious causes that led him to pursue a policy of labor relations different from that of his colleagues. Howland believed he could avoid the prevalent adversary relationship between the workers and management, but, in the end, failed because his dreams succumbed to the industrial reality of late 19th-century America, and he committed suicide rather than face the financial collapse of the company. Primary sources; 34 notes.

R. S. Sliwoski

661. Piątkowska, Danuta. POLACY W AMERYKAŃSKIM RUCHU ROBOTNICZYM W ŚWIETLE PRASY ŚLĄSKIEJ (1880-1900) [Poles in the American labor movement in light of the Silesian press, 1880-1900]. *Z Pola Walki [Poland] 1979 22(4): 21-42.* Traces the assimilation of Polish immigrants in the US labor movement through reports of their activities appearing in the press in Silesia and describes the beginnings of organized socialist activity among Poles in the United States in the 1890's. Based on Silesian newspapers and other periodicals; table, 93 notes. Russian and English summaries.

J/S

662. Reid, Joseph D., Jr. THE EVALUATION AND IMPLICATIONS OF SOUTHERN TENANCY. *Agric. Hist. 1979 53(1): 153-169.* Tenancy, sharecropping and renting, were rungs on an agricultural ladder "to coordinate owned with unowned inputs into agriculture." The data on post-bellum tenancy support the idea that the effect was more rapidly and efficiently to restore productivity to southern agriculture. "The legacy of ante-bellum slavery in agriculture was post-bellum tenancy." That this did not lead to prosperity was not the fault of tenancy. 58 notes.

R. V. Ritter

663. Roediger, David. RACISM, RECONSTRUCTION, AND THE LABOR PRESS: THE RISE AND FALL OF THE *ST. LOUIS DAILY PRESS*, 1864-1866. *Sci. and Soc. 1978 42(2): 156-177.* The *Daily Press* originated during a period of class struggle in St. Louis, Missouri, as striking printers established the organ either as a means of winning their strike or as a beginning towards a permanent major labor voice in the city. The newspaper continued its existence after the strike as a medium for exploited white labor and was supported on an international basis. It endeavored to attract Irish workers through its espousal of the cause of Fenianism. It also tried to advocate the cause of female labor equality. It failed to become a permanent part of the St. Louis newspaper scene owing to fragmentation in labor's political ranks between the conservative Johnsonian Democrats exhibiting racism and the adherents of Radical Republicanism, many of whom were German workers. During its last days, it tried to reverse its field on racism and Radical Republicanism by championing black rights and the Republican cause, but to no avail. Its history illustrated the corroding influence of racism on labor.

N. Lederer

664. Ross, Steven J. THE CULTURE OF POLITICAL ECONOMY: HENRY GEORGE AND THE AMERICAN WORKING CLASS. *Southern California Q. 1983 65(2): 145-166.* Assesses the political ideology of Henry George (1839-94), author of *Progress and Poverty* (1879) and advocate of the single tax on land monopoly. Having lived in extreme poverty, George went to California in 1858 but found land monopolists there already controlled the wealth of the state. In his book he argued for a tax on unearned wealth. The book was a best-seller, and many working-class people who never read books bought *Progress and Poverty.* In 1886 George formed the United Labor Party and was only narrowly defeated in his attempt to win the mayoralty in New York City. Two years later his party collapsed, due to George's attempt to attract middle-class support for a working-class movement and to his belief that land monopoly, not capitalism itself, was the workers' main problem. Still, his movement had purely American roots, and George deserves recognition for making the working class aware of what they might gain from an industrial America. Primary and secondary sources; 39 notes.

A. Hoffman

665. Samedov, V. Yu. RUSSKAIA RABOCHAIA GAZETTA V AMERIKE [Russian workers' newspaper in America]. *Istoriia SSSR [USSR] 1973 (5): 172-179.* In 1889 a Russian group of socialists published the first issue of *Znamia* (Banner) and called it a workers' newspaper. It criticized the capitalist system, pointed out the shortcomings of the bourgeoisie, and called on the workers to liberate themselves.

It published K. Marx's "Civil War in France" and some articles by the members of the group "Liberation of Labor." Its own writers published "Ownership, Religion and Family," based on Engels' work on the same topics. Other interesting articles were "March Anniversary," which celebrated the 18th anniversary of the Paris commune; "Paris Congress," which informed its readers of the International Workers' Congress which was being held in Paris in the summer of 1889; and "Russian Review," which told about uprisings and difficult conditions in Russia. This newspaper came to a halt in June 1889 and was not published for half a year. When it again started to come out, it was somewhat different—it had lost its vitality, and by its content and dry style it resembled a periodical or a literary journal. In its sixth issue, the editors informed their readers that *Znamia* was being changed from a weekly newspaper into a monthly periodical. However, the periodical *Znamia* was never published. Primary and secondary sources; 23 notes.

L. Kalinowski

666. Scharnau, Ralph. ELIZABETH MORGAN, CRUSADER FOR LABOR REFORM. *Labor Hist. 1973 14(3): 340-351.* Elizabeth Chambers Morgan (b. 1850), Chicago trade unionist and social reformer, rose from unskilled labor to prominence in Chicago reform and union circles. With a power base in the Ladies' Federal Labor Union and the Illinois Women's Alliance, Mrs. Morgan was partly instrumental in extending compulsory education for children, updating child labor laws, and the attack on sweatshops which resulted in the Factory and Workshop Inspection Act of 1893 in Illinois. Working with Hull House reformers and others, Mrs. Morgan helped explore detrimental health and labor conditions—for which exploration she has not received due credit. Based on the Thomas J. Morgan collection, Chicago newspapers, government reports, and secondary sources; 63 notes.   L. L. Athey

667. Schleppi, John R. "IT PAYS": JOHN H. PATTERSON AND INDUSTRIAL RECREATION AT THE NATIONAL CASH REGISTER COMPANY. *J. of Sport Hist. 1979 6(3): 20-28.* During the industrial decline of the 1890's, John H. Patterson came to realize that skilled workers were needed to build cash registers, and he initiated programs affecting the welfare of his workers. He built a factory that was lighted and that could be easily ventilated in summer; it became a model for future factories. He brought John C. Olmsted to his National Cash Register Company in Dayton, Ohio, to landscape the grounds. Physical fitness and health programs became part of the workers' lives. In 1897, an athletic club and a bicycle club were formed. In 1905, a company baseball team was formed. Patterson's work improved working and living conditions in Dayton. Based on company publications; 24 notes.   M. Kaufman

668. Schwantes, Carlos A. LABOR UNIONS AND SEVENTH-DAY ADVENTISTS; THE FORMATIVE YEARS, 1877-1903. *Adventist Heritage 1977 4(2): 11-19.* The opposition of the Seventh-Day Adventists to organized labor was a reaction to strikes and violence and to the presence of Catholics and Socialists in labor unions and organizations.

669. Tripp, Joseph F. KANSAS COMMUNITIES AND THE BIRTH OF THE LABOR PROBLEM, 1877-1883. *Kansas Hist. 1981 4(2): 114-129.* Historians once assumed that Americans in the Gilded Age were generally unsympathetic with workers and uniformly opposed to strikes. This was rarely true in urban industrial centers and never true in small communities, where social and political ties brought workers and nonworkers close together. Strikes involving mostly railroaders and miners in Kansas during 1877-83 show that small-town Kansans reacted in sharply divergent ways to the disputes and the issues raised. To some extent the ambivalence reflected a slightly awkward attempt to assess the costs and benefits of industry to Kansas communities. Governor George T. Anthony and Adjutant General correspondence, Kansas State Historical Society, newspapers; illus., 68 notes.   W. F. Zornow

670. Wright, Gavin. CHEAP LABOR AND SOUTHERN TEXTILES BEFORE 1880. *J. of Econ. Hist. 1979 39(3): 655-680.* Labor costs historically have been decisive in determining the location of cotton textile production. Despite an apparent advantage in wage rates, however, the southern industry did not achieve *sustained* relative progress before about 1875. This study argues that in most times and places the region did not have "cheap labor" before this date. What matters is not just the level of wages in any year, but the quality of labor attracted at this wage and the geographic scope of the labor market

within which firms operate. The scope of the labor market depends in turn on property rights and incentives toward recruitment activity. 5 tables, 3 fig., 66 notes.   J

The Worker

671. Agnew, Brad. HENRY VOGEL: A WHITE LABORER IN INDIAN TERRITORY. *Chronicles of Oklahoma 1981 59(3): 320-334.* In 1887 Henry Vogel began a career as a construction worker that would take him all across eastern Oklahoma and eventually lead to a successful contracting business in Muskogee. His descriptions of towns such as Tahlequah and Muskogee, Oklahoma, and Fort Smith, Arkansas, provide brief glimpses of their rugged frontier nature during the 1890's. Vogel further described his role in building a number of prominent structures in those towns. Based on Henry Vogel's handwritten "autobiography"; 4 photos.   M. L. Tate

672. Aron, Cindy S. "TO BARTER THEIR SOULS FOR GOLD": FEMALE CLERKS IN FEDERAL GOVERNMENT OFFICES, 1862-1890. *J. of Am. Hist. 1981 67(4): 835-853.* Investigates the 19th-century phenomenon of young women from white, middle-class families, working as clerks in the federal bureaucracy in Washington, D.C. Most of these female clerks were single, and the motivation that drove them from their homes into the work force was economic. These women sought to minimize the contradictions between their traditional domestic roles and their new roles as workers by presenting their clerical jobs as extensions of their domestic responsibilities. Whether single or married, female clerks worked to support their families. 59 notes.

T. P. Linkfield

673. Aurand, Harold W. THE ANTHRACITE MINER: AN OCCUPATIONAL ANALYSIS. *Pennsylvania Mag. of Hist. and Biog. 1980 104(4): 462-473.* An occupational rather than a class analysis of miners reveals differences in status among a group usually described as uniformly servile. Covers ca. 1870-97. Based on official records, newspapers, and secondary works; 39 notes.   T. H. Wendel

674. Barnes, Joseph W. KATHARINE B. DAVIS AND THE WORKINGMAN'S MODEL HOME OF 1893. *Rochester Hist. 1981 43(1): 1-20.* Brief biography of Katharine Bement Davis of Rochester, New York, focusing on her exhibit, the New York State Workingman's Model Home, at the World's Columbian Exposition (Chicago, 1893), and gives some background on the exposition itself.

675. Baron, Ava. WOMEN AND THE MAKING OF THE AMERICAN WORKING CLASS: A STUDY OF THE PROLETARIANIZATION OF PRINTERS. *Rev. of Radical Pol. Econ. 1982 14(3): 23-42.* Changes in the sex-structuring of occupations are shaped by the uneven development of capitalism and the strategies that define class relations. Male newspaper compositors' strategies were to establish cooperative relations with female printers and to fight for equal pay for equal work, but their strategies were undermined by internal contradictions within their culture, namely male chauvinism. Secondary sources; 27 notes, ref.   D. R. Stevenson

676. Baxandall, Rosalyn; Gordon, Linda; and Reverby, Susan. ARCHIVES: BOSTON WORKING WOMEN PROTEST, 1869. *Signs: J. of Women in Culture and Soc. 1976 1(3, Part 1): 803-808.* Increasing numbers of women found employment in garment manufacturing in Boston during the Civil War because of the demand for military uniforms and the absence of male workers. But, by 1869, return of men and the end of war production reduced job opportunities for women despite increasing numbers of females who were dependent on their own earnings because of war casualties. Women, therefore, expressed anger at low wages and terrible working conditions, but they also railed against the degradation of their own labor and skill through the factory system's mechanization and division of labor. Primary sources.

S. E. Kennedy

677. Black, Paul V. EMPLOYEE ALCOHOLISM ON THE BURLINGTON RAILROAD, 1876-1902. *J. of the West 1978 17(4): 5-11.* The management of the Chicago, Burlington & Quincy Railroad (CB&Q) tried several means to eliminate alcohol-related incidents. The initial policy, formed in the 1860's, was to prohibit liquor sales in

company-owned facilities, and to discourage employees' patronage of saloons. The second major policy was enforced temperance, both on and off duty, under threat of dismissal. A meeting of the CB&Q Superintendents' Association in 1883 established a policy that survived 20 years, but gave enforcement power to local authorities rather than to the board of directors. Based on Chicago, Burlington & Quincy Railroad Papers, Newberry Library, Chicago, Illinois; 3 photos, 37 notes.

B. S. Porter

678. Cohen, William. NEGRO INVOLUNTARY SERVITUDE IN THE SOUTH, 1865-1940: A PRELIMINARY ANALYSIS. *J. of Southern Hist. 1976 42(1): 31-60.* Even after the 13th amendment, bondage stubbornly persisted, sustained by state and local laws and custom which continued to extract labor from Negroes. Despite the bondage systems, blacks were permitted a fair amount of mobility. The apparent contradiction stems from the willingness of the white power structure to permit black movement from areas of surplus labor to areas in need of labor, even during good times, and to make virtually no effort to restrict black mobility during depressions. Legal structure gave legitimacy to the bondage system, but the system was rooted in whites' assumption of their right to use Negro labor as they wished to. Based on manuscripts and primary and secondary sources; 63 notes.

T. D. Schoonover

679. Compton, Stephen C. EDGAR GARDNER MURPHY AND THE CHILD LABOR MOVEMENT. *Hist. Mag. of the Protestant Episcopal Church 1983 52(2): 181-194.* The strength of the child labor movement was greatly enhanced by Edgar Gardner Murphy (b. 1869), an Episcopal priest who has been credited with having done more than any other person to awaken the South to the wrongs of child labor. Murphy was greatly influenced by his mentor at the University of the South, Wiliam Porcher DuBose, who emphasized unity of persons to God, to themselves, and to each other as the key to life. Murphy was quite active in race and education in Alabama before he became involved in the child labor movement. Traces Murphy's role in getting the Child Labor Act enacted in Alabama in 1907, which ended the horrible conditions under which children worked in Southern cotton mills. Based largely on the published works of Murphy and the Edgar Gardner Murphy Papers in the Southern Historical Collection, University of North Carolina Library; photo, 60 notes.   H. M. Parker, Jr.

680. Daily, Christie. A WOMAN'S CONCERN: MILLINERY IN CENTRAL IOWA, 1870-1880. *J. of the West 1982 21(2): 26-32.* Several thousand women had careers as milliners in Iowa in the 1870's. Millinery was one of the few socially acceptable occupations for women, and it was important to all the female residents of the community. The milliner's shop provided essential fashion accessories, including collars, gloves, ribbons, dress patterns, and "hair goods." It was a conduit for the latest news and fashions from the "civilized" East and was frequently the town's only outlet for spontaneous socializing. Based on advertisements and news items in period newspapers; 5 photos, 2 tables.

B. S. Porter

681. Davis, Ronald L. F. THE U.S. ARMY AND THE ORIGINS OF SHARECROPPING IN THE NATCHEZ DISTRICT: A CASE STUDY. *J. of Negro History 1977 62(1): 60-80.* Investigating the apparent contradiction between the war to end slavery and the origins of sharecropping, examines the role of the US Army in the transition from slavery to sharecropping. In the Mississippi Valley and other areas it supervised the economic treatment of blacks as refugees and free men for six years or more in the 1860's. Although no official policy launched sharecropping, the Army and the Freedmen's Bureau contributed indirectly to its emergence, as demonstrated by the Natchez district experience. Based mainly on government records; 70 notes.

P. J. Taylorson

682. DeCanio, Stephen J. ACCUMULATION AND DISCRIMINATION IN THE POSTBELLUM SOUTH. *Explorations in Econ. Hist. 1979 16(2): 182-206.* The freedman's initial lack of property was the most important cause of race-related income differences in the postbellum American South. Discrimination then slowed the rate of wealth accumulation for blacks as compared to whites. Based on published statistics, reports, and secondary accounts; 5 tables, 22 notes, 33 ref.

P. J. Coleman

683. Early, Frances H. MOBILITY POTENTIAL AND THE QUALITY OF LIFE IN WORKING-CLASS LOWELL, MASSACHUSETTS: THE FRENCH CANADIANS CA. 1870. *Labour [Canada] 1977 2: 214-228.* Preliminary findings for a social history of French Canadians in Lowell (1870-1900) seem to indicate the "inaccuracy of the romantic portrayal of the French-Canadian experience" in New England. In 1870, at least, life for Lowell's French Canadians was "rather grim." Most were in working-class occupations; there was no Quebec-born lay *classe dirigeante;* the vast majority of children 10 and over held jobs outside the home. Evidence suggests French Canadians "would be slow to experience occupational mobility;" neither was it possible for most to accumulate savings for a return to Quebec. Census reports, other primary and secondary sources; 44 notes.

W. A. Kearns

684. Everett, Robert B. LEGAL PEONAGE IN SOUTH CAROLINA. *Res. Studies 1973 41(1): 56-60.*

685. Finn, Barbara R. ANNA HOWARD SHAW AND WOMEN'S WORK. *Frontiers 1979 4(3): 21-25.* Describes feminist activist Anna Howard Shaw's life from 1865, when, at 18, she became a schoolteacher, until her death in 1919, focusing on the issue of equal opportunity in employment for women which she considered more important than suffrage, and her relationship with Lucy Anthony, niece of Susan B. Anthony, from their meeting in 1888, which lasted 30 years until Shaw's death; 1870's-1919.

686. Fishbane, Richard B. "THE SHALLOW BOAST OF CHEAPNESS": PUBLIC SCHOOL TEACHING AS A PROFESSION IN PHILADELPHIA, 1865-1890. *Pennsylvania Mag. of Hist. and Biog. 1979 103(1): 66-84.* Census manuscript data reveal the teachers' age (young), socioeconomic background (advantaged), household composition (lived with familes), training and recruitment (poor), remuneration (inadequate), feminization, and persistence (12 years). Based on 1870 census manuscripts, official records, newspapers, and secondary works; 33 notes.   T. H. Wendel

687. Flynt, J. Wayne. SPINDLE, MINE, AND MULE: THE POOR WHITE EXPERIENCE IN POST-CIVIL WAR ALABAMA. *Alabama Rev. 1981 34(4): 243-286.* Four occupations—tenant farming, textiles, mining, and timbering—accounted for the overwhelming majority of the state's poor whites. The reality of their lives, the grinding poverty, the desire to better themselves, and, too often, the realization that they would not escape poverty are vividly portrayed in several case studies. Based on Federal Writers Project interviews in the Southern Historical Collection, University of North Carolina, and personal interviews located in the Samford University Archives; 78 notes.

C. R. Gunter, Jr.

688. Foner, Philip S. THE FRENCH TRADE UNION DELEGATION TO THE PHILADELPHIA CENTENNIAL EXPOSITION, 1876. *Sci. and Soc. 1976 40(3): 257-287.* The delegation of French workers, subsidized by public subscription and the Paris municipal government, reported that America was not a land of promise and opportunity for the worker compared with Europe. Workers from France would not benefit by emigrating to the United States. The French observers felt that American workers dissipated their efforts in futile strikes instead of concentrating on the more rewarding goals of building producer cooperatives. Based on French and American printed primary sources.   N. Lederer

689. Gasinski, Tadeusz Z. POLISH CONTRACT LABOR IN HAWAII, 1896-1899. *Polish Am. Studies 1982 39(1): 14-27.* The key word in the title is "contract" rather than "Polish." Despite an ethnic connotation, the article basically deals with contract labor relations between certain sugar plantation owners on Oahu and imported European laborers. However, the author corrects the misconception of countless immigration statisticians who have invariably labeled immigrant Poles prior to 1918 as "political" Austrians and Germans. Toward the end of the 19th century, Hawaii received hundreds of these Polish immigrants, and no doubt could have become home for thousands more if it were not for the abusive reception accorded the first comers, who shortly after arrival found themselves involved in a bitter strike in 1898. Based on periodicals and official reports; 21 notes.   S. R. Pliska

690. Gersuny, Carl. INDUSTRIAL CASUALTIES IN LOWELL, 1890-1905. *Labor Hist. 1979 20(3): 435-442.* Documents industrial accidents in Lowell, Massachusetts. Safety was not a major concern, and workers were held responsible. Based on Hamilton Co. records, Lowell Manufacturing Co. records, and the Lowell Hospital Register; 2 tables, 14 notes.   L. L. Athey

691. Gitelman, H. M. NO IRISH NEED APPLY: PATTERNS OF AND RESPONSES TO ETHNIC DISCRIMINATION IN THE LABOR MARKET. *Labor Hist. 1973 14(1): 56-68.* Surveys ethnic discrimination against the Irish in the Waltham, Massachusetts, labor market 1850-90. With on-the-job training and formal education blocked, Irishmen received the lowest-paying, unskilled jobs, establishing a vicious cycle which tended to keep the Irish in unskilled positions. The experience in Waltham probably differs from large cities or one-industry towns, and generalizations are dangerous. Based on state and federal manuscript census returns, corporate records, public registers, and city directories; 2 tables, 19 notes.   L. L. Athey

692. Goldin, Claudia. FEMALE LABOR FORCE PARTICIPATION: THE ORIGIN OF BLACK AND WHITE DIFFERENCES, 1870 AND 1880. *J. of Econ. Hist. 1977 37(1): 87-108.* Although white women have only recently entered the work force, their black counterparts have participated throughout American history. Differences between their rates of participation have been recorded only for the post-1890 period and analyzed only for the post-1940 period due to a lack of available data. To remedy this deficiency my work explores female labor supply at the dawn of emancipation, 1870 and 1880, in seven southern cities, using data drawn from the manuscripts of the population census. Probit regression techniques demonstrate that economic and demographic variables explain only part of the difference between black and white women and, as in the findings of contemporary research, race is shown to be an important factor. Several explanations are discussed, in particular one relying on socialization differences which are termed a "legacy of slavery."   J

693. Goldin, Claudia. HOUSEHOLD AND MARKET PRODUCTION OF FAMILIES IN A LATE NINETEENTH CENTURY AMERICAN CITY. *Explorations in Econ. Hist. 1979 16(2): 111-131.* Apart from the male head of household, urban families relied upon children as an important source of labor income. An examination of Philadelphia, Pennsylvania, in 1880 shows substitution between mothers and their daughters and the role of comparative advantage in family decisions concerning the allocation of their members' time. Ethnic differences were important only for daughters. Based on published documents and secondary accounts; 4 tables, 29 notes, 23 ref.
                                                     P. J. Coleman

694. Gottlieb, Amy Zahl. IMMIGRATION OF BRITISH COAL MINERS IN THE CIVIL WAR DECADE. *Int. Rev. of Social Hist. [Netherlands] 1978 23(3): 357-375.* Immigration of British coal miners to the United States was greatly accelerated during the Civil War decade and reached its peak in 1869. Profitable employment opportunities in the United States, punitive measures by mine owners against labor unions, encouragement from British unions to emigrate in order to reduce excess supply of miners, the rise of fatalities in mining explosions in Great Britain, and the prospect of earning a livelihood from inexpensive land in the United States all induced thousands of British miners to scrape their resources into a passage to the New World. Based on newspapers and other published sources; table, 112 notes.   G. P. Blum

695. Griego, Andrew, ed. REBUILDING THE CALIFORNIA SOUTHERN RAILROAD: THE PERSONAL ACCOUNT OF A CHINESE LABOR CONTRACTOR, 1884. *J. of San Diego Hist. 1979 25(4): 324-337.* Introduction to and excerpts from the journal of Ah Quin, a Chinese merchant and labor contractor who supervised Chinese workers in the building and rebuilding of the California Southern Railroad; covers 1868-1914.

696. Haber, Carole. MANDATORY RETIREMENT IN NINE-TEENTH-CENTURY AMERICA: THE CONCEPTUAL BASIS FOR A NEW WORK CYCLE. *J. of Social Hist. 1978 12(1): 77-96.* Although mandatory retirement is a relatively new phenomenon in American society, in the late 19th century companies began to demand that workers automatically retire at a predetermined age. Retirement, as

a concept, did not arise from the employed but from charity reformers, large industralists, and social and economic analysts. Traces the beliefs, motives, and decisions that transformed retirement from a measure of ad hoc charity for some of the elderly into a mandatory prescription for all aged workers. Mandatory retirement provided many solutions: "providing work for the young, seniority to unions, efficiency to the engineer, stability and discipline to the employer." Primary and secondary sources; 72 notes.   R. S. Sliwoski

697. Hannon, Joan Underhill. ETHNIC DISCRIMINATION IN A 19TH-CENTURY MINING DISTRICT: MICHIGAN COPPER MINES, 1888. *Explorations in Econ. Hist. 1982 19(1): 28-50.* Michigan copper miners were predominantly foreign-born, unskilled, and residents of isolated company towns. Thus they began their careers at a disadvantage. They found it difficult to acquire skills or failed to do so because of potential wage discrimination against skilled ethnics. Based on published documents and statistics, newspapers, and unpublished dissertations; 4 tables, 29 notes, 35 ref.   P. J. Coleman

698. Harmon, Sandra D. FLORENCE KELLEY IN ILLINOIS. *J. of the Illinois State Hist. Soc. 1981 74(3): 162-178.* Florence Kelley was a major force in the struggle for protection of laboring children and women throughout her career as a resident of Hull House, the first Illinois factory inspector, and general secretary of the National Consumers' League. A graduate of Cornell University, she was introduced to socialism at the University of Zurich. The abuses of sweatshops led Governor John P. Altgeld to appoint her factory inspector on 12 July 1893. She exposed widespread illiteracy, poor hygiene, and unsafe working conditions. Her work relied on the use of trained inspectors, collection of reliable statistics, issuance of public reports, and legislative lobbying. 6 illus., 82 notes.   A. W. Novitsky

699. Harris, William. WORK AND THE FAMILY IN BLACK ATLANTA, 1880. *J. of Social Hist. 1976 9(3): 319-330.* Investigates whether slavery or conditions in the post civil war environment affected the opportunities of blacks and the nature of the black family. Lack of advancement was not as much a result of a poverty of skills, which could be blamed on slavery, as the lack of political opportunities in the post civil war situation. Limitations in the census information make analysis of the slight differences in fatherless families difficult. Attempts are made to enlighten the subject with comparisons with other data and conclusions about different ethnic groups in urban situations in the late 19th century. Based on a sample of 400-500 blacks and the same number of whites in Atlanta from the censuses of 1870 and 1880.   M. Hough

700. Hellwig, David J. BLACK ATTITUDES TOWARD IMMI-GRANT LABOR IN THE SOUTH, 1865-1910. *Filson Club Hist. Q. 1980 54(2): 151-168.* Maintains that black concern about immigrant labor competition was strongest during 1865 to 1875 and 1900 to 1907. Most blacks felt that white southerners would use the Chinese to force blacks to accept even more degraded working and social conditions. Notes that many blacks did not address themselves to this question—particularly after few immigrants settled in the south. Based on contemporary black newspapers and the published papers and memoirs of black leaders; 43 notes.   G. B. McKinney

701. Hellwig, David J. BLACK REACTIONS TO CHINESE IMMI-GRATION AND THE ANTI-CHINESE MOVEMENT 1850-1910. *Amerasia J. 1979 6(2): 25-44.* The attitude of Afro-Americans toward Chinese immigration was ambivalent. Frederick Douglass and John M. Langstrom wrote that the "coolie" labor would threaten their own rise from slavery to economic opportunity and guaranteed civil rights. D. Augustus Straker and some black journalists believed that Orientals would enrich the US economy and culture. From the debates concerning the Exclusion Act (US, 1882) through the early 20th century, most blacks deplored the economic threat and extreme cultural differences but insisted that discrimination against Chinese only was a threat to American ideals of democracy. 54 notes.   H. F. Thomson

702. Humphrey, George D. THE FAILURE OF THE MISSISSIPPI FREEDMEN'S BUREAU IN BLACK LABOR RELATIONS, 1865-1867. *J. of Mississippi Hist. 1983 45(1): 23-27.* Labor practices in Mississippi refute Herman Belz's argument that the bureau effectively supported black interests in the South. The Mississippi bureau was unable or unwilling to provide necessary aid for blacks. The bureau,

despite its enlightened racial attitudes, sought to serve the planter interest with the maintenance of a docile labor force. The government's failure to provide land for the freedmen, the imposition of the contract labor system, and the propensity for Southern whites to use violence against newly freed slaves were contributory factors toward the bureau's general impotence. Indeed, the bureau's ineptness created disharmony within the black laboring force, even when blacks demonstrated a willingness to labor when treated fairly by Mississippi planters. Based on the Records of the Assistant Commissioner for the State of Mississippi, Bureau of Refugees, Freedmen, and Abandoned Lands and secondary sources; 66 notes.   M. S. Legan

703. Jones, Jacqueline. WOMEN WHO WERE MORE THAN MEN: SEX AND STATUS IN FREEDMEN'S TEACHING. *Hist. of Educ. Q. 1979 19(1): 47-59.* Tests stereotypes of 19th-century female teachers, particularly the idea that females were only able to offer nurturing qualities, and that they were very submissive to male authority. Discusses northern teachers who went south after the Civil War to work in freedmen schools for the American Missionary Association. Research indicates that some females questioned male authority and that their strong sense of professionalism led to some challenges in matters of curriculum. Based on extensive research in the American Missionary Association archives at Dillard University in New Orleans, LA.; 30 notes.   L. C. Smith

704. Kartman, Lauraine Levy. JEWISH OCCUPATIONAL ROOTS IN BALTIMORE AT THE TURN OF THE CENTURY. *Maryland Hist. Mag. 1979 74(1): 52-61.* Studies the immigrant Polish-Russian Jewish working class community of Baltimore between 1895 and 1916 as to country of origin, occupations, and demographic features, based on a local midwife's records for a 19-year period, and a Workmen's Circle Insurance Ledger Book, a source which included women in its tabulations. Evidence suggests that upward occupational and geographical mobility for the original immigrant generation were minimal. Heavy stress on education for Jewish children meant, however, that the second generation would fulfill the community's aspirations for upward socio-economic mobility. 4 tables, 3 notes.   G. J. Bobango

705. Katz, Harriet. WORKERS' EDUCATION OR EDUCATION FOR THE WORKER? *Social Service Rev. 1978 52(2): 265-274.* Jane Addams's Hull House educational programs for the working class in Chicago stressed humanities, fine arts, and folk handicrafts and reflected her educational philosophy of enrichment of social relations and human existence, 1890's.

706. Keil, Hartmut and Jentz, John. A SOCIAL HISTORY OF THE GERMAN WORKERS OF CHICAGO 1850-1910. *Hist. Social Res. [West Germany] 1980 (16): 57-63.* Reports on a study in progress, a social history of German immigrant workers in Chicago, which will analyze censuses and Chicago German newspapers from 1850 to 1900.

707. Keil, Thomas J. CAPITAL ORGANIZATION AND ETHNIC EXPLOITATION: CONSEQUENCES FOR MINER SOLIDARITY AND PROTEST (1850-1870). *J. of Pol. and Military Sociol. 1982 10(2): 237-255.* Examines the effects of capital organization and ethnicity on the levels of property ownership among mineworkers in two anthracite coal producing regions of Pennsylvania. It was found that where production was competitive and dominated by small entrepreneurs, the Irish were a superexploited subgroup. Under conditions of oligopolistic production, there were no significant differences among mineworkers. The role of the Irish as a superexploited group is examined to explain the presence of ethnic communal terrorism in one production region and its absence in the other. Based on the census manuscripts of 1850, 1860, and 1870.   J

708. Kelley, Don Quinn. IDEOLOGY AND EDUCATION: UPLIFTING THE MASSES IN NINETEENTH CENTURY ALABAMA. *Phylon 1979 40(2): 147-158.* Discusses education for blacks in Alabama, 1870's-90's, detailing black frustrations, disappointments, and the success of industrial training schools run by blacks for blacks, such as Booker T. Washington's Tuskegee Institute. 41 notes.
     G. R. Schroeder

709. Kessner, Thomas and Caroli, Betty Boyd. NEW IMMIGRANT WOMEN AT WORK: ITALIANS AND JEWS IN NEW YORK CITY, 1880-1905. *J. of Ethnic Studies 1978 5(4): 19-31.* Statistical analysis of first and second generation Italian and Jewish women shows that "gender proved less significant than ethnicity in shaping the occupational distribution of wives" in lower Manhattan, Brooklyn, and Harlem. Upward mobility is demonstrable from unskilled blue-collar to skilled blue-collar jobs outside the home for Italian daughters, but none reached professional status. Jewish women started at higher status levels and continued to move up rapidly. Attitudes toward education among the two groups, willingness to defer to brothers, familial values as to suitable work for women, and Italian girls' acceptance of homework on garments and artificial flowers, which Jewish girls by 1905 had abandoned, explain the divergent occupational priorities and objectives flowing from different cultural and historical perspectives. Primary and secondary data; 4 tables, 23 notes.   G. J. Bobango

710. Kleinberg, S. J. DEATH AND THE WORKING CLASS. *J. of Popular Culture 1977 11(1): 193-209.* Explores attitudes toward death in their social and economic context among working-class residents of Pittsburgh during the 1890's. Use of both quantitative and qualitative approaches in studies of popular culture overcomes in part the possibility of placing too much emphasis on the unusual or unrepresentative, as is the case where conventional sources alone are employed. Primary and secondary sources; 3 tables, 50 notes.   D. G. Nielson

711. Kleinberg, Susan J. TECHNOLOGY AND WOMEN'S WORK: THE LIVES OF WORKING CLASS WOMEN IN PITTSBURGH, 1870-1900. Trescott, Martha Moore, ed. *Dynamos and Virgins Revisited: Women and Technological Change in History* (Metuchen, N.J.: Scarecrow Pr., 1979): 185-204. Changes in domestic and municipal technology, such as, in the former, washing machines, and, in the latter, the spread of sewers, public water supplies, and paved roads, did not reach the working classes nearly as quickly as the middle and upper classes in 1900 in America. There, the lives and labors of the working-class housewives were still quite onerous compared to their wealthier counterparts. Mainly secondary sources; 35 notes.   J. Powell

712. Kleinberg, Susan J. TECHNOLOGY AND WOMEN'S WORK: THE LIVES OF WORKING CLASS WOMEN IN PITTSBURGH, 1870-1900. *Labor Hist. 1976 17(1): 58-72.* Pittsburgh's economic structure relied primarily on male labor which prevented working-class women from an industrial role, thus reinforcing the traditional segregation of men and women. Working-class women continued time-consuming housework without technological advantages well into the 20th century, because of the political priorities of the city. For example, the decision to lay only small water pipes in working-class neighborhoods meant that only the middle and upper classes and heavy industry got enough water and sewage facilities. Working-class women were forced to perform all their household cleaning chores without adequate water. Domestic, technological inventions such as washing machines and gas stoves were also beyond the means of the working class. Based upon Pittsburgh government publications and secondary sources; 35 notes.
     L. L. Athey

713. Krebs, Sylvia. THE CHINESE LABOR QUESTION: A NOTE ON THE ATTITUDES OF TWO ALABAMA REPUBLICANS. *Alabama Hist. Q. 1976 38(3): 214-217.* The question of using cheap Chinese agricultural labor in the South was discussed at a convention in Memphis, Tennessee, in July 1869. Governor William H. Smith and Commissioner of Industrial Resources, John C. Keffer, both of Alabama, were opposed to the idea. Their arguments are summarized here. 16 notes.   E. E. Eminhizer

714. Lynch, Joseph P. BLACKS IN SPRINGFIELD, 1868-1880: A MOBILITY STUDY. *Hist. J. of Western Massachusetts 1979 7(2): 25-34.* Springfield's small black population experienced little upward occupational mobility during 1868-80, although the city was expanding rapidly. A few blacks did accumulate some real property and this economic mobility was more available than either residential or social improvement. Based on city directories and state censuses; 2 illus., 3 tables, 39 notes.   W. H. Mulligan, Jr.

715. Marks, Carole. SPLIT LABOR MARKETS AND BLACK-WHITE RELATIONS, 1865-1920. *Phylon 1981 42(4): 293-308.* After emancipation, two classes of black workers emerged, agrarian and industrial. At the turn of the century, the black industrial workers

increased in number and created a racially split labor market. It developed partly due to antagonism between black and white workers but mainly due to the deliberate manipulation by employers who benefitted from cheaper black laborers.   A. G. Belles

716. Montgomery, David. WORKERS' CONTROL OF MACHINE PRODUCTION IN THE NINETEENTH CENTURY. *Labor Hist. 1976 17(4): 485-509.* Patterns of behavior among workers in the second or third generations of industrial experience became a form of workers' control of production, a chronic struggle which assumed three forms in the late 19th century: functional autonomy of the craftsman; the union work rule; and mutual support of diverse trades in rule enforcement and sympathetic strikes. The scientific management movement of the 20th century fundamentally disrupted the development of workers' control. Based on union minute books, labor newspapers, and secondary sources; 57 notes.   L. L. Athey

717. Morain, Thomas. THE DEPARTURE OF MALES FROM THE TEACHING PROFESSION IN NINETEENTH-CENTURY IOWA. *Civil War Hist. 1980 26(2): 161-170.* Schoolteaching in Iowa was mainly an occupation of young men beginning their careers and young women awaiting marriage. Around 1880 state standards began to require more preparation for teachers while salaries remained low. Therefore, fewer young men chose to enter teaching unless they planned to make it a career, while women, who had limited occupational choices, came to dominate the profession. Based on Annual Reports of the Iowa Superintendent of Schools, and other sources; 20 notes.
G. R. Schroeder

718. Moulder, Rebecca Hunt. CONVICTS AS CAPITAL: THOMAS O'CONNOR AND THE LEASES OF THE TENNESSEE PENITENTIARY SYSTEM, 1871-1883. *East Tennessee Hist. Soc. Publ. 1976 48: 40-70.* Thomas O'Connor, gambler, lieutenant in the Civil War who claimed the postwar title of major, entrepreneur, and Democratic standard bearer, became involved in the Tennessee convict lease system. His operation of the system not only became involved in politics but also became a focus of corruption, undermining a good idea gone bad. The convict details went from work in the coal mines to operations on the railroads. They were always compounded by brutality and Reconstruction mismanagement. Based on secondary sources, original documents, and state reports; 71 notes.   D. A. Yanchisin

719. Murphy, Miriam B. THE WORKING WOMEN OF SALT LAKE CITY: A REVIEW OF THE *UTAH GAZETTEER, 1892-93. Utah Hist. Q. 1978 46(2): 121-135.* A review of Stenhouse's *Utah Gazetteer, 1892-93* indicates that almost 2,000 working women played important roles in Utah's economy as employees and employers. Factories, mills, and laundries provided jobs. Women created jobs for themselves as milliners, dress makers, and lodging house keepers. They worked at jobs requiring different levels of education, experience, mental and manual dexterity, management and leadership skills, business acumen, and physical endurance. A significant number entered the professions or owned or managed businesses. Primary and secondary sources; 8 illus., 20 notes.   J. L. Hazelton

720. Nelli, Humbert S. THE PADRONE SYSTEM: AN EXCHANGE OF LETTERS. *Labor Hist. 1976 17(3): 406-412.* Reprints letters to the editor in a Chicago paper, *L'Italia* , November-December 1886, a complaint against a padrone and two replies. These letters represent two sides to the padrone system of using Italian immigrant labor in the United States.   L. L. Athey

721. Nelson, Daniel. TAYLORISM AND THE WORKERS AT BETHLEHEM STEEL, 1898-1901. *Pennsylvania Mag. of Hist. and Biog. 1977 101(4): 487-505.* Introducing time study and the differential piece rate, Frederick W. Taylor's scientific management and supposed labor force reorganization was a modest affair. It nevertheless yielded impressive results, showing how aggressive executives forced marginal employees to work harder. Based on Taylor Papers, Stevens Institute of Technology, published sources and secondary works; 56 notes.
T. H. Wendel

722. Noel, Tom. "THE CHEAPEST AND EASIEST WAY TO BECOME AN INFLUENTIAL MAN": OCCUPATIONAL MOBILITY OF DENVER'S PIONEER SALOONKEEPERS. *Red River Valley Hist. Rev. 1980 5(3): 40-53.* Saloonkeeping was a common avenue of attempted upward social mobility for Denver's poorly paid manual workers during 1858-85.

723. Ong, Paul M. CHINESE LABOR IN EARLY SAN FRANCISCO: RACIAL SEGMENTATION AND INDUSTRIAL EXPANSION. *Amerasia J. 1981 8(1): 62-92.* Partly due to their lack of skills, their perceived transitory status, and discrimination by both white labor and white management, Chinese labor was employed in the lowest paying industrial jobs. This low-cost labor allowed Chinese manufacturers in San Francisco to be competitive with the more capital-intensive white entrepreneurs. 3 tables, 88 notes.   E. S. Johnson

724. Ong, Paul. AN ETHNIC TRADE: THE CHINESE LAUNDRIES IN EARLY CALIFORNIA. *J. of Ethnic Studies 1981 8(4): 95-113.* One of the most significant minority ventures in ethnic entrepreneurship was the Chinese laundry trade in urban California during the latter part of the 19th century. A descriptive outline of these multifarious washhouses provides insight into the process of ethnic (and racial) divisions of the urban economy. Ethnic culture, however, was not the sole or even determining factor in the developmental process. Equally important were the structural context, the emergence of a racially and hierarchically segmented labor market in a surplus labor society, and the rise of institutional racism generating discriminatory practices beyond those normally found in a simple racial division of labor. Primary archival material, secondary studies; 6 tables, 69 notes.
G. J. Bobango

725. Pozzetta, George E. IMMIGRANTS AND RADICALS IN TAMPA, FLORIDA. *Florida Hist. Q. 1979 57(3): 337-348.* Reprints five articles from Italian-language newspapers revealing a rich cultural and intellectual life for Italian immigrants in Tampa, Florida. The immigrant workers were influenced in Sicily by "worker leagues." Such sotialistic or anacharistic concepts were influencial in the development of Tampa. Primary and secondary sources; 14 notes.   N. A. Kuntz

726. Reid, Joseph D., Jr. SHARECROPPING IN HISTORY AND THEORY. *Agric. Hist. 1975 49(2): 426-440.* Develops a market equilibrium model of sharecropping for the post-Civil War South and elsewhere. Sharecropping was successful because the system gave both landlord and tenant an interest in cooperating to produce a large crop. Sharecropping was preferred by new immigrants, the poor, and unskilled tenants because of managerial aid from the landlord. 34 notes, appendix.
D. E. Bowers

727. Rohe, Randall E. AFTER THE GOLD RUSH: CHINESE MINING IN THE FAR WEST, 1850-1890. *Montana 1982 32(4): 2-19.* Chinese miners in the American West came primarily from Kwangtung Province and worked principally in placer deposits. Heavy concentrations of Chinese miners occurred in California and Oregon in the 1850's, and in Idaho and Montana in the 1860's, with smaller concentrations in Nevada and British Columbia in the same decade, and in Washington, Colorado, the Black Hills area, Arizona, and New Mexico in the 1870's and later. By 1890, most Chinese had abandoned mining, having made a significant contribution. Based on secondary works, contemporary newspapers, as well as US and state census records; 12 illus., map, 104 notes.   R. C. Myers

728. Rosenzweig, Roy. MIDDLE-CLASS PARKS AND WORKING-CLASS PLAY: THE STRUGGLE OVER RECREATIONAL SPACE IN WORCESTER, MASSACHUSETTS, 1870-1910. *Radical Hist. Rev. 1979 (21): 31-46.* A demographically typical manufacturing city, Worcester, Massachusetts, serving the various interests of political figures, social reformers, industrialists, and the working class, created public parks to solve the social problem of leisure; 1870-1910.

729. Scarpaci, Jean Ann. IMMIGRANTS IN THE NEW SOUTH: ITALIANS IN LOUISIANA'S SUGAR PARISHES, 1880-1910. *Labor Hist. 1975 16(2): 165-183.* In the late 19th century the scarcity of labor during the sugar cane harvest in Louisiana attracted thousands of Italian immigrants to the sugar parishes. The immigrants were a temporary element in the state's population, yet the Italians were the largest immigrant group in Louisiana in 1900. Italians and Negroes apparently tolerated one another while on the same occupational level, but as Italians became more successful racial prejudice became more

dominant. Based upon population censuses and government reports; 42 notes.   L. L. Athey

730. Schwendinger, Robert J. CHINESE SAILORS: AMERICA'S INVISIBLE MERCHANT MARINE, 1876-1905. *California History* 1978 57(1): 58-69. Describes the role played by Chinese in the American merchant marine in the late 19th century. Chinese sailors filled a variety of positions, including seamen, boatswains, firemen, coal passers, cooks, and other jobs. The Pacific Mail Steamship Company and the Occidental and Oriental Steamship Company (under British flag) employed largely Chinese crews, but officers were white. The total number of Chinese serving these companies 1876-1906 was over 80,000; the number of crewmen cannot be calculated because rehiring policies caused duplicated counts. Despite pressures from American seamen's unions, the Chinese Exclusion Act, and prejudice against Chinese, sea captains and employers found Chinese sailors hardworking and reliable. Eventually restrictive regulations and legislation caused the decline of Chinese sailors in the US merchant marine. Little research has been done on the topic. Notes that their numbers and contributions have gone unrecognized to the point of their being inaccurately considered of minor importance in the era, an "invisible merchant marine." Primary and secondary sources; illus., photos, charts, 33 notes.   A. Hoffman

731. Scott, Rebecca. THE BATTLE OVER THE CHILD: CHILD APPRENTICESHIP AND THE FREEDMEN'S BUREAU IN NORTH CAROLINA. *Prologue* 1978 10(2): 101-113. Studies the contending forces claiming rights over indentured black children: the former slave owners, parents, and relatives. Agents of the Freedmen's Bureau generally ruled on the disputes, often using subjective factors in reaching their decision. A ruling by the North Carolina Supreme Court in 1867 strengthened the freedmen's position somewhat. 4 photos, 42 notes.   J. Tull

732. Shlomowitz, Ralph. THE ORIGINS OF SOUTHERN SHARECROPPING. *Agric. Hist.* 1979 53(3): 557-575. The author examined the records of the Bureau of Refugees, Freedmen, and Abandoned Lands, usually referred to as the Freedmen's Bureau. The Bureau approved and enforce southern labor contracts between planters and freedmen. Notable for their wide variety of terms, the contracts offered as many as seven forms of compensation: standing wages, share of the crop, sharing of time, standing rent, wages in kind, money payment per task, and explicit incentive schemes. In most of these agreements the planter contracted his labor force as a group. In this study a 5% sample of labor contracts for South Carolina was taken. Primary and secondary sources; 2 tables, 32 notes.   R. T. Fulton

733. Shumsky, Neil L. FRANK RONEY'S SAN FRANCISCO—HIS DIARY: APRIL, 1875-MARCH, 1876. *Labor Hist.* 1976 17(2): 245-264. Presents a diary of an Irish immigrant iron molder. Poverty, unemployment, money problems, and part-time labor dominated his life struggle. 30 notes.   L. L. Athey

734. Shumsky, Neil L. SAN FRANCISCO'S WORKINGMEN RESPOND TO THE MODERN CITY. *California Hist. Q.* 1976 55(1): 46-57. Provides a reinterpretation of workingmen in San Francisco in the 1870's. Having come to California in search of opportunity and wealth, workingmen found neither. Skilled craftsmen found an industrialized economy operating machinery with unskilled labor and employing and exploiting Chinese immigrants. Workingmen labored long hours for low wages and lived in such areas as the district south of Market Street, where overcrowding, poor housing, and disease were part of everyday life. Tensions in home life, disillusionment with organized religion, and traditional support of the Democratic Party contributed to the frustration of workingmen. In 1877 the Workingmen's Party of California was organized, providing a new social and political outlet. The WPC proposed radical reforms from Chinese exclusion to creation of independent businesses. Although the WPC never fully grasped the fundamental changes created by modernization in their lives, it provided a new sense of vitality and meaning to the lives of workingmen. For a brief time they became a potent political force and were integrated into the new urban life through participation in social, religious, and political affairs. Based on primary and secondary sources; illus., photos, 43 notes.   A. Hoffman

735. Silvia, Philip T., Jr. THE POSITION OF "NEW" IMMIGRANTS IN THE FALL RIVER TEXTILE INDUSTRY. *Int. Migration Rev.* 1976 10(2): 221-232. Discusses the reception of Portuguese and Polish immigrants by French Canadians in textile industries and trade unions in Fall River, Massachusetts, 1890-1905.

736. Silvia, Philip T., Jr. THE POSITION OF WORKERS IN A TEXTILE COMMUNITY: FALL RIVER IN THE EARLY 1880S. Cantor, Milton, ed. *American Workingclass Culture: Explorations in American Labor and Social History* (Westport, Conn.: Greenwood, 1979): 189-208. Reprint of an article originally published in *Labor History* .

737. Smallwood, James. PERPETUATION OF CASTE: BLACK AGRICULTURAL WORKERS IN RECONSTRUCTION TEXAS. *Mid-America* 1979 61(1): 5-23. At the end of the Civil War, Texas whites sought to maintain the pre-war caste status of the former slaves. In spite of work by the Freedmen's Bureau and the Army in enforcing Reconstruction laws, the former slaves were kept in a sharecropper status or as low-paid field hands. A partial reason was lack of black economic resources, but the evidence indicates that white racism was the major factor. Primary and secondary sources; 64 notes.   J. M. Lee

738. Smythe, Ted Curtis. THE REPORTER, 1880-1900: WORKING CONDITIONS AND THEIR INFLUENCE ON THE NEWS. *Journalism Hist.* 1980 7(1): 1-10. Describes the working conditions of newspaper reporters, which included low pay, job insecurity, office intrigue, long hours, and bill cutting (reduction of total inches of published space of a reporter within a pay period), that resulted in reporters padding their writing, moonlighting, payola, combination reporting to reduce competition among reporters, and sensationalism, a result of pay based on column-inches produced and working conditions.

739. Stephens, Lester D. A FORMER SLAVE AND THE GEORGIA CONVICT LEASE SYSTEM. *Negro Hist. Bull.* 1976 39(1): 505-507. Lancaster LeConte (1812-1889), a 75-year-old former slave, was convicted of receiving stolen goods in 1887 and leased to the Dale Coal Company of Georgia for three years, where he faced inadequate rations and 12-hour days in a cold, damp mine. LeConte's pathetic letter to his former owner, Joseph LeConte, begged for legal assistance. Joseph LeConte had been known for his paternalism, but that benevolence was apparently reserved for slaves. Lancaster LeConte died a forgotten prisoner, another example of the callous convict lease system. Based on primary and secondary sources; photo, 17 notes.   W. R. Hively

740. Tank, Robert M. MOBILITY AND OCCUPATIONAL STRUCTURE ON THE LATE NINETEENTH-CENTURY URBAN FRONTIER: THE CASE OF DENVER, COLORADO. *Pacific Hist. Rev.* 1978 47(2): 189-216. Quantitative study of occupational and geographic mobility in Denver, 1870-92, finds that Denver resembled long-established urban communities in some ways and frontier communities in others. Like urban communities, Denver's occupational structure in 1870 favored native whites over immigrants and blacks and between 1870 and 1890 blacks and immigrants without skills were less likely to advance than similarly low skilled native whites. However, unlike urban communities, but like frontier communities, skilled and white-collar immigrants were able to experience considerable upward mobility. Geographical mobility was high in Denver and varied inversely with social status. Based on census manuscript schedules and city directories; 7 tables, 29 notes.   W. K. Hobson

741. Vecoli, Rudolph J. EMIGRATI ITALIANI E MOVIMENTO OPERAIO NEGLI USA [Italian immigrants and the workers' movement in the United States]. *Movimento Operaio e Socialista [Italy]* 1976 22(1-2): 153-167. The history of Italian Americans in the American labor movement either has been ignored totally or has represented the Italian worker as a scab or the cause of salary reductions. Attracted by hopes of saving money, Italians from Central and Southern Italy flocked to America from about 1880. Many came only for brief periods and, because they did not speak English, understand American customs, or belong to the unions, found themselves isolated and often with the worst jobs. Without formal means to protest their situation, they often staged spontaneous strikes. These had no lasting effects, but definitely prove the fallacy of the stereotypical submissive Italian worker. After 1900, Italian radicals played organizational roles in the Industrial Workers of the

World and the formation of the garment workers' unions.

M. T. Wilson

742. Walker, Samuel. TERENCE V. POWDERLY, MACHINIST: 1866-1877. *Labor Hist. 1978 19(2): 165-184.* An examination of Terence V. Powderly's early years in Carbondale and Scranton, Pennsylvania, reveals that he was well-acquainted with the realities of working-class life. His years as a machinist were successful, and they show that Powderly diligently practiced thrift, hard work, temperance, and self-improvement. Powderly's fundamental outlook on life was shaped in the essentially prebureaucratic age; he never changed that outlook. Based on the Powderly diaries in the Powderly Archives, Catholic University of America; 53 notes.   L. L. Athey

743. Walker, Samuel. VARIETIES OF WORKINGCLASS EXPERIENCE: THE WORKINGMEN OF SCRANTON, PENNSYLVANIA, 1855-1885. Cantor, Milton, ed. *American Workingclass Culture: Explorations in American Labor and Social History* (Westport, Conn.: Greenwood, 1979): 361-376. Examines the transformation of Scranton, once a small village, into a major center of the anthracite coal industry to demonstrate the more generalized working-class experiences of rapid industrialization, urbanization, ethnic conflict, and industrial conflict in the 19th century.

744. Walkowitz, Daniel J. STATISTICS AND THE WRITING OF WORKINGCLASS CULTURE: A STATISTICAL PORTRAIT OF THE IRON WORKERS IN TROY, NEW YORK, 1860-1880. Cantor, Milton, ed. *American Workingclass Culture: Explorations in American Labor and Social History* (Westport, Conn.: Greenwood, 1979): 241-286. Reprint of an article published originally in *Labor History* (see abstract in this bibliography).

745. Ward, Robert David and Rogers, William Warren. RACIAL INFERIORITY, CONVICT LABOR, AND MODERN MEDICINE: A NOTE ON THE COALBURG AFFAIR. *Alabama Hist. Q. 1982 44(3-4): 203-210.* Discusses the report of the Jefferson County, Alabama, Board of Health, by Dr. Thomas D. Parke, on working conditions at the Sloss-Sheffield coal mine, where the mortality rate of prisoners used for labor was 90 per 1,000. In other states where prison labor was sold, the death rate was between 18 and 25 per 1,000. Parke held that race had nothing to do with the high rate. The blacks working there died because of inferior health conditions at the mine and its prison, not because blacks were inferior. Based on the report of Dr. Parke; 24 notes.

E. E. Eminhizer

746. Weiner, Lynn. "OUR SISTER'S KEEPERS": THE MINNEAPOLIS WOMAN'S CHRISTIAN ASSOCIATION AND HOUSING FOR WORKING WOMEN. *Minnesota Hist. 1979 46(5): 189-200.* In the late 19th century, many young women made their way to Minneapolis to find work, coming from rural areas and from Europe. The paucity of inexpensive boardinghouses available to these women and the consequent fear that poverty would drive the women into prostitution and other forms of criminal behavior, generated an effort on the part of middle and upper class Minneapolis women to provide suitable, safe and cheap housing for women. Various buildings were donated to the Women's Christian Association (WCA) for this purpose, and both long-term and temporary housing arrangements were made available. The boardinghouses sponsored by the WCA were run along rather puritanical lines but seemed to fill the needs of generations of female sojourners in the city. The WCA also sponsored Travelers' Aid efforts in which young women arriving via train were met by agents and were given advice and assistance. By the end of World War I large-scale migration into Minneapolis had ended and the efforts of the WCA tapered off but did not die out.   N. Lederer

747. Wharton, Leslie. HERBERT N. CASSON AND THE AMERICAN LABOR CHURCH, 1893-1898. *Essex Inst. Hist. Collections 1981 117(2): 119-137.* In response to the social and economic tensions generated by the labor unrest of the late 19th century, a young Methodist seminary graduate and Socialist from Ontario, Canada, Herbert N. Casson, founded a Labor Church in Lynn, Massachusetts. Modeled after the English Labor Church, Casson's church was for the laboring poor, providing them with ideals and methods to lift themselves out of industrial slavery. Casson also tried to give his church a religious philosophy: Christian history was a struggle between the working class

and the aristocrats. In the end, the church succumbed to the tensions of the labor movement, returning prosperity, and nationalist enthusiasm fostered by the Spanish-American War. Primary sources; 34 notes.

R. S. Sliwoski

748. —. [LABOR SUPPLY, THE ACQUISITION OF SKILLS, AND THE LOCATION OF SOUTHERN TEXTILE MILLS, 1880-1900]. *J. of Econ. Hist. 1981 41(1): 65-73.*
Carlson, Leonard A. LABOR SUPPLY, THE ACQUISITION OF SKILLS, AND THE LOCATION OF SOUTHERN TEXTILE MILLS, 1880-1900, *pp. 65-71.* The development of the textile industry in the South was shaped by the fact that by 1870 most experienced workers lived in the Piedmont. Thus, a firm which wished to hire experienced workers would have been led to choose the Piedmont Plateau, similarly, mills producing more difficult finer count cloth would have chosen the Piedmont in order to hire experienced workers. Finally, the persistence of a virtually all white work force may be explained by the fact that most experienced workers were white and would have resisted working in integrated mills.
Oates, Mary J. DISCUSSION, *pp. 72-73.*   J

The Labor Movement

749. Amsden, Jon and Brier, Stephen. COAL MINERS ON STRIKE: THE TRANSFORMATION OF STRIKE DEMANDS AND THE FORMATION OF A NATIONAL UNION. *J. of Interdisciplinary Hist. 1977 7(4): 583-616.* There is a consistent relationship between the growth and impact of trade unionism among American mine workers and the pattern of strikes in the industry in the same period. Strikes over the reordering of productive relations in mining increase as a proportion of the total, despite fluctuations in business activity. During 1881-94 miners transformed the strike into an aggressive and more broadly class-conscious tactic. Printed and manuscript sources; 3 tables, 6 figs., 53 notes.   R. Howell

750. Baskett, Thomas S., Jr. *MINERS STAY AWAY!* W. B. W. HEARTSILL AND THE LAST YEARS OF THE ARKANSAS KNIGHTS OF LABOR, 1892-1896. *Arkansas Hist. Q. 1983 42(2): 107-133.* Describes the role of Willie Blount Wright Heartsill (1840-1913) and the Greenwood, Arkansas, Local 239 of the Knights of Labor in the mining disputes which marked the end of the Knights in Arkansas. Based on correspondence, other primary and secondary sources; 3 photos, 133 notes.   G. R. Schroeder

751. Becnel, Thomas. LOUISIANA SENATOR ALLEN J. ELLENDER AND IWW LEADER COVINGTON HALL: AN AGRARIAN DICHOTOMY. *Louisiana Hist. 1982 23(3): 259-275.* Ellender and Hall had like backgrounds: both grew up on sugar plantations on Bayou Terrebonne under similar family and peer influences. But in later life Ellender was a thorough conservative, critic of organized labor, and segregationist opponent of every civil rights bill, while Hall became an Industrial Workers of the World spokesman, a champion of blacks, a socialist opponent of World War I, and an active radical throughout his life. It is not clear why they developed so differently, but Hall's family's loss of their land when he was 20 contributed to his radicalization. Based on interviews, Ellender's papers, Hall's writings, parish records, and secondary sources; 31 notes.   R. E. Noble

752. Bennett, Sari J. and Earle, Carville V. LABOUR POWER AND LOCALITY IN THE GILDED AGE: THE NORTHEASTERN UNITED STATES, 1881-1894. *Social Hist. [Canada] 1982 15(30): 383-405.* Some sources view the 1880's as a period in which modernization destroyed the fabric of a preindustrial culture congenial to the worker. Labor power did decline in smaller communities as the population grew and the preindustrial culture disappeared. In larger cities, however, labor power increased, mainly because a convergence of the wage ratio of skilled and unskilled workers brought their economic interests together, creating a broader base for agitation. 2 tables, 7 maps, 14 notes.   D. F. Chard

753. Buhle, Paul. THE KNIGHTS OF LABOR IN RHODE ISLAND. *Radical Hist. Rev. 1978 (17): 39-73.* The Knights of Labor rose dramatically to power in the 1880's and practically disappeared by

1887 in Rhode Island; discusses labor and politics in Rhode Island from the Civil War to the turn of the century.

754. Cassity, Michael J. MODERNIZATION AND SOCIAL CRISIS: THE KNIGHTS OF LABOR AND A MIDWEST COMMUNITY, 1885-1886. *J. of Am. Hist. 1979 66(1): 41-61.* Examines two railroad strikes in Sedalia, Missouri, to illustrate the impact of modernization on the Knights of Labor. Both strikes involved the Jay Gould system and demonstrated local antagonisms toward centralized authority. The first strike, in early 1885, motivated by the railroad's harsh economic policy, was spontaneous and local in origin. Because the Gould system represented a harsh, alien, and monopolistic central authority, the strikers and their union won local sympathy. The second strike, a year later, however, produced the opposite effect. The Knights shifted their goals from equality, fraternity, and community responsibility to goals which would increase workers' power in a broader, more centralized, institutional concept. This strike upheld the pattern of modernization in society and alienated the Knights from the local level. 52 notes.   T. P. Linkfield

755. Cotkin, George B. THE SPENCERIAN AND COMTIAN NEXUS IN GOMPERS' LABOR PHILOSOPHY: THE IMPACT OF NON-MARXIAN EVOLUTIONARY THOUGHT. *Labor Hist. 1979 20(4): 510-523.* Samuel Gompers's ideology was affected by the Spencerian views of Frank K. Foster and the Comtian views of Hugh McGregor, both important trade unionists. Gompers's pragmatism is more explicable from non-Marxian evolutionary thought, although some Marxian influence need not be denied. Based on the Gompers Letter Books and Files of the Tamiment Library; 25 notes.   L. L. Athey

756. Dancis, Bruce. SOCIAL MOBILITY AND CLASS CONSCIOUSNESS: SAN FRANCISCO'S INTERNATIONAL WORKMEN'S ASSOCIATION IN THE 1880'S. *J. of Social Hist. 1977 11(1): 75-98.* Examines the social characteristics of the class conscious members of the International Workmen's Association revealing that they differ from the general working population of San Francisco because they were "both more stable and prosperous." This is because they were older and were more skilled workers which enabled them "to overcome ethnic differences within their own ranks." More research needs to be done, however, in regard to marital status and background of descent. 16 tables, 52 notes.   L. E. Ziewacz

757. Downey, Dennis B. THE CONGRESS ON LABOR AT THE 1893 WORLD'S COLUMBIAN EXPOSITION. *J. of the Illinois State Hist. Soc. 1983 76(2): 131-138.* Chicago's Columbian Exposition occurred in the midst of a depression, adding to the interest in the Congress on Labor held from 28 August to 4 September 1893. Speakers at the Congress included Samuel Gompers, Terence V. Powderly, Eugene V. Debs, Florence Kelley, Clarence Darrow, Archbishop John Ireland, Frederick Douglass, Booker T. Washington, Henry George, and Edward McGlynn. Topics discussed were the condition of labor, labor and wages of women and children, statistics, literature and philosophy, legislation, arbitration, and strategy and tactics. Most participants, except Ireland, who defended Pope Leo XIII's *Rerum Novarum,* agreed that class conflict was the basic characteristic of society. Denunciations of the maldistribution of wealth, support of the single tax, and participation in mass rallies dominated the proceedings. 5 illus., 24 notes.   A. W. Novitsky

758. Foner, Eric. CLASS, ETHNICITY, AND RADICALISM IN THE GILDED AGE: THE LAND LEAGUE AND IRISH-AMERICA. *Marxist Perspectives 1978 1(2): 6-55.* During 1880-83 the American Land League introduced Irish Americans to modern reform and labor ideologies, helped integrate them into the broader context of reform, and shaped the traditions of the Irish working class.

759. Fones-Wolf, Elizabeth and Fones-Wolf, Kenneth. VOLUNTARISM AND FACTIONAL DISPUTES IN THE AFL: THE PAINTERS' SPLIT IN 1894-1900. *Industrial and Labor Relations Rev. 1981 35(1): 58-69.* Some students of the American Federation of Labor (AFL) have argued that voluntarism evolved into an ideology used to justify, among other things, the stifling of rank-and-file protest within federation affiliates. Examination of the behavior of Samuel Gompers and other AFL leaders in the face of a rank-and-file movement against the leadership of the Brotherhood of Painters and Decorators during

1894 to 1900 shows that voluntaristic principles actually afforded AFL leaders a good deal of flexibility, allowing the dissident group to grow while Gompers worked to obtain a negotiated settlement between the factions. Those efforts culminated in a federation-sponsored unity conference in 1900 that set the stage for the dissident faction to assume control of the painters' union.   J/S

760. Fones-Wolf, Kenneth. BOSTON EIGHT HOUR MEN, NEW YORK MARXISTS AND THE EMERGENCE OF THE INTERNATIONAL LABOR UNION: PRELUDE TO THE AFL. *Hist. J. of Massachusetts 1981 9(2): 47-59.* Discusses the influence of Ira Steward and George McNeill, leaders in the Boston Eight Hour League, on the International Workingmen's Association (IWA) of New York during 1860-89. The IWA moved from independent political action and took up more general issues such as the eight-hour day, which was central to the emergence of the American Federation of Labor. Based on contemporary newspapers, the Ira Steward Papers (Wisconsin State Historical Society), and secondary literature.   W. H. Mulligan, Jr.

761. Garlock, Jonathan. THE KNIGHTS OF LABOR DATA BANK AND U.S. SOCIAL HISTORY. Raben, Joseph and Marks, Gregory, ed. *Data Bases in the Humanities and Social Sciences* (Amsterdam: North-Holland Publ., 1980): 35-39. Information in the Knights of Labor Data Bank on the membership of the union calls into question the traditional view that the movement peaked during 1869-79 and steadily declined during 1889-1921.

762. Garlock, Jonathan. THE KNIGHTS OF LABOR DATABANK. *Hist. Methods Newsletter 1973 6(4): 149-160.* Although the author consulted many sources, the Knights of Labor's official *Journal of United Labor* and the annual *Proceedings* of the Order's General Assembly provided the majority of material for his data bank. Explains the code used in this University of Rochester project. The Knights of Labor was heavily rural throughout its existence, regarding the number of locals; yet the membership was concentrated in metropolitan areas. The result was a major problem in organization. Maps, charts.

        D. K. Pickens

763. Gildemeister, Glen A. THE FOUNDING OF THE AMERICAN FEDERATION OF LABOR. *Labor Hist. 1981 22(2): 262-268.* The American Federation of Labor-Congress of Industrial Organizations (AFL-CIO) designated its founding date as 15 November 1881, the date of the founding of the AFL's predecessor, the Federation of Organized Trades and Labor Unions (FOTLU), but the latter organization had ceased to exist before the AFL came into existence. A conference of trade unionists within the Knights of Labor, joined by FOTLU members who had dissolved their organization two days earlier, created the AFL on 10 December 1886 in Columbus, Ohio. Based on contemporary newspaper accounts and other primary sources; 27 notes.

        L. F. Velicer

764. Goldberg, Joseph P. and Moye, William T. THE AFL AND A NATIONAL BLS: LABOR'S ROLE IS CRYSTALLIZED. *Monthly Labor Rev. 1982 105(3): 21-29.* Traces the beginnings of the American Federation of Labor (AFL) and the Bureau of Labor Statistics (BLS), founded in 1881 and 1884 respectively, focusing on their relationship until 1913, which was based on "the needs of the times and the personalities of the leaders, AFL President Samuel Gompers and BLS commissioners Carroll D. Wright and Charles P. Neill."

765. Holt, James. THE TRADE UNIONS AND SOCIALISM IN THE UNITED STATES. *J. of Am. Studies [Great Britain] 1973 7(3): 321-327.* Reviews William M. Dick's *Labor and Socialism in America: The Gompers Era* (Port Washington, N.Y.: Kennikat Press, 1972) and John Laslett's *Labor and the Left: A Study of Socialist and Radical Influences in the American Labor Movement, 1881-1924* (New York: Basic Books, 1970). The books provide a "clearer picture" of Samuel Gompers (1850-1924) and of native-born Socialists in the labor movement. 10 notes.   H. T. Lovin

766. Kaufman, Stuart Bruce. BIRTH OF A FEDERATION: MR. GOMPERS ENDEAVORS "NOT TO BUILD A BUBBLE." *Monthly Labor Rev. 1981 104(11): 23-26.* Based on excerpts from the Pittsburgh *Commercial Gazette* in 1881, traces Samuel Gompers's role in the formation of the Federation of Organized Trades and Labor Unions of

the United States and Canada, the predecessor of the American Federation of Labor.

767. Kaufman, Stuart Bruce. THE SAMUEL GOMPERS PAPERS AS LITERATURE: TOWARD A STREAM-OF-CONSCIOUSNESS HISTORY. *Maryland Hist. 1977 8(2): 54-59.* Explains the Samuel Gompers Papers Project and the intent to provide continuous history as perceived by Samuel Gompers and his correspondents. This permits the reader to empathize with the period covered by the papers. 5 notes, ref.
G. O. Gagnon

768. Lane, A. T. AMERICAN LABOUR AND EUROPEAN IMMIGRANTS IN THE LATE NINETEENTH CENTURY. *J. of Am. Studies [Great Britain] 1977 11(2): 241-260.* During the 1890's, American labor unions argued about curbing immigration to America through alien contract labor laws, literacy test acts, and other exclusionary measures. In 1897, the national convention of the American Federation of Labor finally adopted a measure supporting literacy test legislation. That act, however, conflicted with rank and-file opinion and remained a minority view within the Federation for another decade. Federation leaders obtained approval of literacy tests in 1897 by persuasive campaigning, by maneuvering by the "literacy test lobby" at the 1897 convention, and by Samuel Gompers' artful use of personal influence over trade unionists. Based on labor union documents, government publications, and secondary sources; 44 notes.
H. T. Lovin

769. McLaurin, Melton A. KNIGHTS OF LABOR: INTERNAL DISSENSIONS OF THE SOUTHERN ORDER. Fink, Gary M. and Reed, Merl E., eds. *Essays in Southern Labor History: Selected Papers, Southern Labor History Conference, 1976.* (Westport, Conn.; London, England: Greenwood Pr., 1977): 3-17. Weakness within the Knights of Labor contributed to its early decline, ca.1885-88, after an initial show of great strength. Most significant were the ill-defined membership requirements leading to great diversity of motives, and hence a scattering of efforts, poor leadership (often they were not actually laborers, and often they were from areas other than their areas of leadership effort), extensive internal feuding, and (equally destructive) racial polarization. 51 notes.
R. V. Ritter

770. Mendelsohn, Ezra. THE RUSSIAN ROOTS OF THE AMERICAN JEWISH LABOR MOVEMENT. *Yivo Ann. of Jewish Social Sci. 1976 (16): 150-177.* The large emigration of Russian Jews to the United States following the pogroms of 1881-82 was mainly a movement of poor artisans and traders who came looking for an opportunity to work, grow prosperous, and live without fear. In addition, there were Russian Jewish intellectuals who felt themselves mentally superior to the masses. From the Russian Jewish intellectuals grew the Jewish US labor movement. 74 notes.
R. J. Wechman

771. Oestreicher, Richard. SOCIALISM AND THE KNIGHTS OF LABOR IN DETROIT, 1877-1886. *Labor Hist. 1981 22(1): 5-30.* Joseph Labadie and Judson Grenell, radical labor leaders in Detroit, Michigan, worked for the advancement of socialism through the Socialist Labor Party (SLP) in 1877. They and other Detroit socialists joined the Knights of Labor after 1878 to spread socialism to a wider audience. Labadie and Grenell abandoned the SLP in the early 1880's because it advocated doctrinal purity over immediate political and economic gains. Based on the Joseph Labadie Papers and other primary sources; 63 notes.
L. F. Velicer

772. Ostrander, Gilman M. THE REVOLUTION MISLAID: SOCIALISM AND THE TRADE UNIONS REVISITED. *Can. Rev. of Am. Studies 1973 4(1): 107-112.* Reviews William M. Dick's *Labor and Socialism in America: The Gompers Era* (Port Washington, N.Y.: Kennikat Press, 1972). Dick argues that socialism was once an important force in America, but ultimately failed because of opposition from the American Federation of Labor and its head, Samuel Gompers (1850-1924). Socialists and the AFL leaders clashed over dissimilar goals, especially the issue of socialist insistence that labor organize industrial unions. Socialism also faltered when it failed to win the hearts of "radical intellectuals" except some in academia.
H. T. Lovin

773. Perrier, Hubert. THE SOCIALISTS AND THE WORKING CLASS IN NEW YORK: 1890-1896. *Labor Hist. 1981 22(4): 485-511.*

Examines the relationship between the Socialist Labor Party (SLP) and the workers in New York City in the 1890's. While placing political considerations above short-term material gains, the SLP-dominated Central Labor Federation of New York recognized the need to assist workers achieve immediate gains in order to win their allegiance. However, difficult economic conditions, a change in the ethnic composition of the city's workers, and the growing power of the American Federation of Labor doomed the SLP's efforts at being the uniting force for New York City's workers. Socialist Labor Party publications and primary sources; 49 notes.
L. F. Velicer

774. Schappes, Morris U. THE POLITICAL ORIGINS OF THE UNITED HEBREW TRADES, 1888. *J. of Ethnic Studies 1977 5(1): 13-44.* Details the origins, planning, and organizational meetings which produced the United Hebrew Trades (UHT) organization in New York City, a product of Branch 8 and Branch 17 of the Socialist Labor Party. The leaders were Yiddish-speaking workingmen such as Jacob Magidow, Lev Bandes, and Bernard Weinstein, who were products of the Jewish working class rather than the older middle-class composition of American Jewry. Demonstrates the close contacts and clearly imitative nature of the UHT and the older *Vereinigte Deutsche Gewerkschaften* (German Central Labor Union). The UHT faced opposition by Jewish middle class organs such as *The Jewish Messenger* and the *American Hebrew,* who called the Farein anarchistic. The opposition of Samuel Gompers, who objected to the socialist nature of the group's program and its religious basis, also took several years to overcome. Gompers' writings later falsely claimed him as one of the organizers of the UHT. For 25 years this union was a vital factor in organizing Jewish workers and bringing them into the American labor movement. Primary and secondary sources, 88 notes.
G. J. Bobango

775. Schwantes, Carlos A. THE CHURCHES OF THE DISINHERITED: THE CULTURE OF RADICALISM ON THE NORTH PACIFIC INDUSTRIAL FRONTIER. *Pacific Hist. 1981 25(4): 54-65.* Reviews the economic and social conditions that preceded 19th-century socialism and presents a brief history of the movement, comparing it with a religious revolution. The Knights of Labor played a significant part in Pacific Northwest radicalism, combining social events with labor reform and education. The American Federation of Labor supplanted the Knights of Labor and similar organizations and put an end to the movement. 5 illus., 28 notes.
H. M. Evans

776. Walker, Samuel. TERENCE V. POWDERLY, THE KNIGHTS OF LABOR AND THE TEMPERANCE ISSUE. *Societas 1975 5(4): 279-293.* This study uses temperance as a focus but raises larger issues. It argues that for Terence V. Powderly and other leaders of the Knights of Labor, temperance was not simply a middle-class oriented, moralistic reform but was adopted as a limited policy only and was motivated in large part by pragmatic considerations having to do with the organization's stability and strength. This leads the author to support other historians (specifically David Montgomery and Warren Van Tine) in their attack on the prevailing view in 19th-century labor historiography that there existed a significant dichotomy between utopian reform unionism and pragmatic business unionism. Based on the proceedings and constitutions of the national and some local Knights of Labor organizations, Powderly's papers, and other primary and secondary sources; 56 notes.
J. D. Hunley

Individual Locals, Strikes, and Lockouts

777. Andersen, Arlow W. AMERICAN LABOR UNREST IN NORWAY'S PRESS: THE HAYMARKET AFFAIR AND THE PULLMAN STRIKE. *Swedish Pioneer Hist. Q. 1974 25(3/4): 208-219.* The labor movement in 19th-century America was paralleled in Norway, where it was sparked by Marcus Thrane. The Norwegian press closely followed the Haymarket affair and the Pullman strike. The reaction was generally antisocialist. The Norwegian press lacked the anti-alien prejudice and the emotionalism of the American press. Primary and secondary sources; 12 notes.
K. J. Puffer

778. Birtle, Andrew. GOVERNOR GEORGE HOADLY'S USE OF THE OHIO NATIONAL GUARD IN THE HOCKING VALLEY

STRIKE OF 1884. *Ohio Hist. 1982 91: 37-57.* While many governors during the late 19th century called out the national guard in order to suppress strikes rather than to maintain peace and order, Ohio Governor George Hoadly used the guard in the Hocking Valley strike of June 1884-March 1885 in an admirable example of the intervention of state forces that was not designed to subvert labor. The strike—one of the worst in Hocking Valley history—erupted into violence following a flood of evictions of miners from company-owned housing in late August, an act that sparked the miners' growing frustrations over the owners' use of strikebreakers and private guards. Under Governor Hoadly's efficient management, the guard's brief deployment in the valley restored peace, order, and civil authority, and succeeded in keeping violence and property damage to a minimum, while demonstrating that the governor was not a tool of business but a judicious, sympathetic, and moderate man whose primary goal was to restore order to an inflammatory situation. Based on the papers of Governor George Hoadly in the Ohio Historical Society, the Ohio General Assembly *Proceedings of the Hocking Valley Investigation,* the records and reports of the Ohio Adjutant General's Office, and other primary sources; photo, 2 illus., 82 notes.   L. A. Russell

779. Black, Paul V. EXPERIMENT IN BUREAUCRATIC CENTRALIZATION: EMPLOYEE BLACKLISTING ON THE BURLINGTON RAILROAD, 1877-1892. *Business Hist. Rev. 1977 51(4): 444-459.* On the Chicago, Burlington & Quincy Railroad the use of a blacklist to screen future employees was "a significant feature of the institutional experimentation" that developed with the rise of bureaucratic organization. Traces the origins of the blacklist, the types of discharge causes cited, and the reasons for its abolition. The abandonment of blacklisting reflected legislative pressure and the internal and external costs of the use of artitrary power. Based on corporate records; 3 tables, 29 notes.   C. J. Pusateri

780. Blewett, Mary H. THE UNION OF SEX AND CRAFT IN THE HAVERHILL SHOE STRIKE OF 1895. *Labor Hist. 1979 20(3): 352-375.* Female stitchers, skilled workers, were among the most militant strikers against the Haverhill, Massachusetts, shoe factories in 1895. Skill, consciousness of class, and personal mobility underlaid the organizational effort which fostered a tradition of union activity among female shoeworkers in the 19th century. Based on newspapers; 49 notes.   L. L. Athey

781. Bombardini, Lorenzino. IL *NATIONAL WORKMAN* DI NEW YORK CITY (1866-67) E L'"EDUCAZIONE" DELLA CLASSE OPERAIA NEGLI USA [The *National Workman* of New York City (1866-67) and the "education" of the working class in the United States]. *Movimento Operaio e Socialista [Italy] 1981 4(3): 223-246.* The machine inside the plant and "welfare work" regarding housing, health, and education outside were the two means by which capitalist control over manpower was exercised in the 19th century. This control and the reaction to it can be seen not merely as aspects of the extraction of surplus value by the capitalist but as moments of the formation of a "body" and a "soul" of the working class. The article describes some of the functions which New York trade unions had in the creation of the moral atmosphere of the working class of that city, as seen through the files of the trade union paper *National Workman.* %HD 81 notes.   J. V. Coutinho

782. Bonney, Richard J. THE PULLMAN STRIKE OF 1894: POCATELLO PERSPECTIVE. *Idaho Yesterdays 1980 24(3): 23-28.* The Pullman Strike of 1894 lasted nine days in July in Pocatello, Idaho. A major railroad center, Pocatello was affected in many ways. Although there was no violence, 69 men lost their jobs. The most noticeable effect of the strike was the delay in mail and supplies. Three newspapers presented a cross-section of opinions about the strike. Based on newspapers; 2 photos, 22 notes.   B. J. Paul

783. Bularzik, Mary J. THE BONDS OF BELONGING: LEONORA O'REILLY AND SOCIAL REFORM. *Labor Hist. 1983 24(1): 60-83.* Explores the ethnic, feminist, and trade union influences on the life of Leonora O'Reilly (1870-1927), while focusing on her work with the New York branch of the Women's Trade Union League during the Progressive Era. Based on the Leonora O'Reilly Papers; 49 notes.   L. F. Velicer

784. Carvalho, Joseph, III. THE BAUGHMAN BOYCOTT AND ITS EFFECT ON THE RICHMOND, VIRGINIA LABOUR MOVEMENT, 1886-1888. *Social Hist. [Canada] 1979 12(24): 409-417.* The American labor movement employed strikes and boycotts as two basic tools in the 1880's. The Richmond Typographical Union was formed and included every printing office by early 1886 except for Baughman Brothers. A boycott of Baughmans severely restricted business. During this period, labor also scored numerous political victories, but a court ruling defining boycotts as a criminal conspiracy deprived labor of a powerful tool, and sounded the death-knell for the Knights of Labor in Richmond. Based on primary and secondary sources, including records of Typographical Union, No. 90, Richmond, Virginia; 54 notes.   D. F. Chard

785. Cary, Lorin Lee. ADOLPH GERMER AND THE 1890'S DEPRESSION. *J. of the Illinois State Hist. Soc. 1975 68(4): 337-343.* Coal miners in a heavily German-populated area of southern Illinois, Adolph Germer and his father were active members of the early United Mine Workers of America. Germer was a participant in the strikes of 1894 and 1897. These strikes, culminating in the killing of seven miners by company guards at Virden, Illinois, in 1898, alonq with the depression of the 1890's, made Germer a staunch believer in unionism and Socialism. Based on primary and secondary sources.   N. Lederer

786. Chapin, John R. THE INFAMOUS PULLMAN STRIKE AS REVEALED BY THE ROBERT TODD LINCOLN COLLECTION. *J. of the Illinois State Hist. Soc. 1981 74(3): 179-198.* The Robert Todd Lincoln Collection of the Illinois State Historical Library contains letters telling of the Pullman Palace Car Company during May-November 1894. The strike of that year was caused by a decrease in wages with no corresponding decrease in rents in the company town. By early May, 35% of the work force had joined the American Railway Union (ARU), leading the company to attempt to improve employee relations. On 20 July, Pullman began accepting applications from both strikers and strikebreakers, leading to the collapse of the strike on 2 August. A federal investigating commission supported the ARU and chastised the company and the General Managers Association. It found that rents should have been reduced with wages and that the company should have submitted to arbitration. Reprints some letters. Based on the Robert Todd Lincoln Collection in the Illinois State Historical Library; 8 illus., 38 notes.   A. W. Novitsky

787. Cohen, Steven R. STEELWORKERS RETHINK THE HOMESTEAD STRIKE OF 1892. *Pennsylvania Hist. 1981 48(2): 155-177.* John A. Fitch's study of steelworkers in Pittsburgh was part of the famous *Pittsburgh Survey* of 1909. This article is based on Fitch's field notes on 145 interviews; 45 of those interviewed participated in the Homestead Strike. In addition to illuminating the union's internal problems during the strike, these notes demonstrate how the Carnegie Steel Company reduced workers' security and compensation while destroying the Amalgamated Association of Iron and Steel Workers movement in its mills and extracting more work from its employees. Based on the Fitch notes and other materials; 33 notes.   D. C. Swift

788. Cooper, Jerry M. THE ARMY AS STRIKE BREAKER—THE RAILROAD STRIKES OF 1877 AND 1894. *Labor Hist. 1977 18(2): 179-196.* Describes the role of the Army in the strikes of 1877 and 1894. Although officers justified Army intervention as a restoration of order, the act of restoring order worked against labor. The Army's officers actually identified with middle class values on property and order. Based on Army correspondence in the National Archives and other primary sources; 28 notes.   L. L. Athey

789. Corcoran, Thomas F. LABOR UNIONS IN THE COEUR D'ALENE MINING DISTRICT, 1887-1900. *Pacific Northwesterner 1982 26(2): 17-32.* Traces the beginning of miners' unions in the silver-lead mines along the Coeur d'Alene River in Idaho during 1887-1900 and the mine owners' response which instigated a strike, violence, and the eventual victory of the unions.

790. Cotkin, George B. STRIKEBREAKERS, EVICTIONS AND VIOLENCE: INDUSTRIAL CONFLICT IN THE HOCKING VALLEY, 1884-1885. *Ohio Hist. 1978 87(2): 140-150.* Examines the absence of violence toward strikebreakers in the Hocking Valley coal strike of 1884-85 in Ohio. Immigrant strikebreakers were brought to the

coal mines by the operators and armed guards were posted on the properties, but violence against the strikebreakers was rare. When violence did appear, it was directed against the coal companies' property. Lasting over nine months, the strike ended in defeat for the miners. The strikers clearly had imposed limitations on the forms and objects of their violence. Based on manuscripts, archives, newspapers, and secondary sources; 2 illus., 43 notes.   N. Summers

791. Cumbler, John T. ACCOMMODATION AND CONFLICT: SHOE WORKERS IN TWENTIETH-CENTURY LYNN. *Essex Inst. Hist. Collections 1979 115(4): 232-255.* In the late 19th century, American labor was recovering from a series of defeats. To counteract further losses of membership, labor leaders sought a strategy to protect the organizations that still existed and provide a basis for future growth. They developed a policy of accommodation known as bread-and-butter unionism. The Boot and Shoe Workers Union struggle in Lynn, Massachusetts, illustrates the contradictions inherent in accommodation and the tensions between the interests of the working class and the unions. The workers' struggle demonstrates that they perceived bread-and-butter unionism as beneficial to the unions and not to the workers. Based on primary sources; 66 notes.   R. S. Sliwoski

792. Cumbler, John T. LABOR, CAPITAL, AND COMMUNITY: THE STRUGGLE FOR POWER. Cantor, Milton, ed. *American Workingclass Culture: Explorations in American Labor and Social History* (Westport, Conn.: Greenwood, 1979): 149-166. Reprint of an article originally published in *Labor History* .

793. Cumbler, John T. LABOR, CAPITAL AND COMMUNITY: THE STRUGGLE FOR POWER. *Labor Hist. 1974 15(3): 395-415.* Discusses the eight-month leatherworkers' strike in Lynn, Massachusetts, in 1890. Although Lynn was a strong union town with a tradition of solidarity and close relationships with the community, the labor-community solidarity and community support was no match for an effectively organized group of employers, and the strike failed. Based on the Lynn *Daily Item* and other newspapers, and minutes of Lynn unions; 84 notes.   L. L. Athey

794. Debouzy, Marianne. GRÈVE ET VIOLENCE DE CLASSE AUX ETATS-UNIS EN 1877 [US strikes and class violence in 1877]. *Mouvement Social [France] 1978 (102): 41-66.* By their extent, by the original forms of working-class resistance and solidarity which they produced, the 1877 strikes are a unique social phenomenon in the history of industrial conflicts in nineteenth century America. This mass movement brought to light both the deep class cleavages that divided American society at the time and the existence of circumstantial alliances between the working class and that part of the bourgeoisie which was hostile to railroad companies. These strikes raise the question of what accounts for such a high level of combativity and solidarity. The uprising involved challenge to authority, organized resistance to repression and controlled violence aimed at very precise targets. In this uprising the American working-class expressed a form of class consciousness which it would never reach again.   J

795. Dodd, Martin H. MARLBORO, MASSACHUSETTS AND THE SHOEWORKERS' STRIKE OF 1898-1899. *Labor Hist. 1979 20(3): 376-397.* The shoeworkers' strike of 1898-99 yielded a shift in Marlboro sentiment from support of labor to support for industry, thus forcing the shoeworkers to rely more on unions and less on support from other groups. The local unions were broken. Based on city directories and newspapers; 2 tables, 42 notes.   L. L. Athey

796. Doherty, William T., Jr. BERKELEY'S NON-REVOLUTION: LAW AND ORDER AND THE GREAT RAILWAY STRIKE OF 1877. *West Virginia Hist. 1974 35(4): 271-289.* During the Railway Strike of 1877, strikers seized the Baltimore and Ohio rail yard at Martinsburg, West Virginia, and halted service during July 16-19. Local militia were ineffective and federal troops were finally sent in to clear out the strikers. During and after the event, local newspapers took a moderate position, criticizing the actions of Governor Henry M. Mathews and the federal government as too pro-railroad. Local opinion sympathized with the strikers and thought the railroad was greedy, but objected to violence. Based chiefly on local newspapers; 56 notes.   J. H. Broussard

797. Eggert, Gerald G. GUNFIRE AND BRICKBATS: THE GREAT RAILWAY STRIKES OF 1877. *Am. Hist. Illus. 1981 16(2): 16-25.* Tells of the bloody railway strike that began in West Virginia in July 1877 and spread to rail centers in all parts of the country leading to disorders that "produced the first near-national emergency strike in the country's history, led to massive governmental intervention in a labor dispute, established important precedents for dealing with later strikes, aned opend a new epoch in American labor history."

798. Ehrlich, Richard L. IMMIGRANT STRIKE BREAKING ACTIVITY: A SAMPLING OF OPINION EXPRESSED IN THE NATIONAL LABOR TRIBUNE, 1878-1885. *Labor Hist. 1974 15(4): 529-542.* Investigates the question of the strikebreaking activity of immigrants as found in the *National Labor Tribune* from 1878-85. The lack of evidence for widespread use of immigrants to break strikes suggests that the traditional interpretation of unskilled immigrants relationship to the strike needs severe modification. 23 notes.   L. L. Athey

799. Erlich, Mark. PETER J. MCGUIRE'S TRADE UNIONISM: SOCIALISM OF A TRADES UNION KIND? *Labor Hist. 1983 24(2): 165-197.* Peter J. McGuire, founder and first general-secretary of the United Brotherhood of Carpenters and Joiners of America (UBCJA), tried to combine "benefits unionism" with the conviction that labor organizations should prepare the way for a new socialist society. Conservative forces within the UBCJA, more concerned with the power of their own union than in cooperating with other unions, forced McGuire from office in 1902 and established the conservatism characteristic of the building crafts unions in the United States ever since. Based on *The Carpenter,* UBCJA *Proceedings,* and other primary sources; 79 notes.   L. F. Velicer

800. Fahey, John. ED BOYCE AND THE WESTERN FEDERATION OF MINERS. *Idaho Yesterdays 1981 25(3): 18-30.* Edward Boyce served as president of the Western Federation of Miners from 1896 to 1902. During that time he traveled around the West, organizing new locals, supporting strikes, and urging support for his union from Samuel Gompers and the American Federation of Labor. He declined reelection at the 1902 convention of the Western Federation of Miners convention. The union had developed argumentative factions, wages had decreased in many mining districts, governmental authorities were siding with the mineowners in conflicts, and the union refused to adopt Socialism as a long-range objective. Boyce gave up his intense involvement in union activities after 1902. Based on Boyce's diary; 50 notes, 3 photos.   B. J. Paul

801. Foner, Philip S. RABOCHAIA PARTIIA SOEDINENNYKH SHTATOV I VELIKAIA ZABASTOVKA 1877 G [The workingmen's party of the United States and the railroad strike of 1877]. *Novaia i Noveishaia Istoriia [USSR] 1978 (5): 64-82.* The author offers a detailed analysis of the first national strike in the history of the United States, describes the participation in it of the Workingsmen' Party of the USA and the specifics of its tactics as well as the significance of the strike for the US working-class movement.

802. Foner, Philip S.|ZUR|ROLLE|DER|WORKINGMEN'S|PARTY OF THE U.S.A. IM EISENBAHNERSTREIK VON 1877 [On the role of the Workingmen's Party of the U.S.A. in the railroad strike of 1877]. *Zeitschrift für Geschichtswissenschaft [East Germany] 1978 26(4): 325-335.* The 1877 railroad strike, coming near the end of the depression which followed the 1873 panic, was a true workers' revolt, similar in many ways to the 1871 Paris Commune. The US Workingmen's Party, a federation founded in Philadelphia in 1876, fused the nation's growing Marxist elements. Initially the Party was divided over support for the strike, but when workers were repeatedly attacked by army and national guard troops, it moved to support the striking railroad workers. It fought to gain decent working and living conditions for the oppressed workers and to gain reasonable wages and job security for workers continually threatened with unemployment. 73 notes.   G. H. Libbey

803. Fones-Wolf, Elizabeth and Fones-Wolf, Kenneth. KNIGHTS VERSUS THE TRADE UNIONISTS: THE CASE OF THE WASHINGTON, D.C. CARPENTERS, 1881-1896. *Labor Hist. 1981 22(2): 192-212.* Chronicles the struggle between the Brotherhood of Carpen-

ters and Joiners of America (BCJA) and the Knights of Labor carpenters' assembly in Washington, D.C., during the last two decades of the 19th century. The BCJA won the allegiance of more carpenters nationally, but the Knights assembly dominated the carpentry trade in Washington, D.C., for more than a decade. Based on the Gabriel Edmonston Papers, the Terence V. Powderly Papers, and other primary sources; 50 notes.   L. F. Velicer

804. Frisch, Paul A. LABOR CONFLICT AT EUREKA, 1886-97. *Utah Hist. Q. 1981 49(2): 145-156.* The 1893 labor strike in Eureka was caused by declining silver prices, which prompted Bullion-Beck, mine owners, to lower miner weekly wages to $2.50. Most miners, led by John Duggan and members of the Western Federation of Miners, struck. Peaceful conflicts ensued between operators, supported by the Mormon Church, and workers, most of whom were referred to as non-Mormons. Marshals came to support the company's position. Many Eureka proprietors supported the strikers. In the end, the union capitulated and accepted the weekly wage reduction. 2 photos, 40 notes.   K. E. Gilmont

805. Gersuny, Carl. ELEANOR MARX IN PROVIDENCE. *Rhode Island Hist. 1978 37(3): 85-87.* Karl Marx's daughter Eleanor, with her companion Edward Aveling and Wilhelm Liebknecht, a Socialist deputy in the Reichstag, toured the United States at the invitation of the Labor Party. She spoke in Providence under the sponsorship of the Rhode Island Central Labor Union on 22 October 1886 as part of the effort to expand American socialism beyond the confines of German-speaking groups. Based on newspapers and secondary accounts; illus., 17 notes.   P. J. Coleman

806. Gordon, Michael A. THE LABOR BOYCOTT IN NEW YORK CITY, 1880-1886. Cantor, Milton, ed. *American Workingclass Culture: Explorations in American Labor and Social History* (Westport, Conn.: Greenwood, 1979): 287-332. Reprint of an article originally published in *Labor History* (see abstract in this bibliography).

807. Gowaskie, Joseph M. FROM CONFLICT TO COOPERATION: JOHN MITCHELL AND BITUMINOUS COAL OPERATORS. *Historian 1976 38(4): 669-688.* During 1898-1907 bituminous coal fields consisted of thousands of individually owned mines competing for profit and new markets. Relations between operators and unions were turbulent. After profits plunged in 1897 many operators agreed that recognition of the United Mine Workers of America, led by John Mitchell, would provide order. Employers overcame their resistance to unionization because further conflict in the soft coal industry would lead to their economic destruction. Notes.   M. J. Wentworth

808. Grant, H. Roger. THE LABOR EXCHANGE MOVEMENT: AN EPISODE IN SELF-HELP. *Midwest Q. 1983 24(2): 138-151.* Besides helping to fuel the reform politicians, the depression of 1893 caused many individuals to seek immediate solutions for agrarian problems through different self-help remedies. The Labor Exchange, founded by Giovanni Battista De Bernardi in 1890, sought to organize warehouses in agrarian communities to buy supplies and market goods in a communal fashion. Expanding rapidly after the 1893 panic, this secular experiment in communitarism thrived. However, due to a lack of strong, continuous management and to hostility from the outside society to what was conceived to be a utopian threat, most branches failed soon after De Bernardi's death in 1901. Biblio.   D. H. Cline

809. Harahan, Joseph P., ed. " 'POLICE FORCE' IN THE ARSENAL SHOPS": A DOCUMENT ON THE 1899 MACHINISTS' STRIKE AT ROCK ISLAND ARSENAL. *J. of the Illinois State Hist. Soc. 1981 74(2): 119-129.* In October 1897, arsenal machinists petitioned commanding officer Captain Stanhope E. Blunt for higher wages. Wages were cut on 1 January 1898, while piecework and a requirement that each machinist operate two machines were introduced. Labor unrest was interrupted by the Spanish-American War, but revived as the war ended and new work rules were imposed. The machinists' demands were supported by area senators and representatives as well as by unanimous resolutions in the Illinois house and senate. A report to the Secretary of War by Brigadier General A. R. Buffington, reprinted here, asserted that military officers were not authorized to negotiate with civilian employees and that participation in an international union could be treasonable. The secretary exonerated Blunt, but decided that

workers could form committees to petition the commanding officer. 7 illus., 22 notes.   A. W. Novitsky

810. Holmes, William F. THE ARKANSAS COTTON PICKERS STRIKE OF 1891 AND THE DEMISE OF THE COLORED FARMERS'S ALLIANCE. *Arkansas Hist. Q. 1973 32(2): 107-119.*

811. Javersak, David T. ONE PLACE ON THIS GREAT GREEN PLANET WHERE ANDREW CARNEGIE CAN'T GET A MONUMENT WITH HIS MONEY. *West Virginia Hist. 1979 41(1): 7-19.* In 1903, in Wheeling, West Virginia, as a bitter legacy of the Homestead Strike of 1892, the Ohio Valley Trades and Labor Assembly, which held Andrew Carnegie personally responsible for the violence of that strike, successfully opposed the bond issue necessary to raise the money needed for a matching grant for a Carnegie Library. In 1911, Wheeling built a library from its own resources. 55 notes.   J. D. Neville

812. Javersak, David T. RESPONSE OF THE O.V.T. & L.A. TO INDUSTRIALISM. *J. of the West Virginia State Hist. Assoc. 1980 4(1): 35-45.* The Ohio Valley Trades and Labor Assembly, an independent, centralized labor assembly of Ohio County, West Virginia, responded to industrialism with humanitarian, social, and relief services, political activism, and aggressive advocacy for its member locals, 1882-1914.

813. Jebsen, Harry, Jr. THE ROLE OF BLUE ISLAND IN THE PULLMAN STRIKE OF 1894. *J. of the Illinois State Hist. Soc. 1974 67(3): 275-293.* On 29 June 1894 Eugene V. Debs delivered a strike appeal to the workers of Blue Island, a town 16 miles southwest of Chicago. The next day a striking switchman purposely derailed a Rock Island locomotive, blocking the main track out of the town and marking the first damage to railroad property in the Chicago region. Citizens, police, and town officials united behind the workers' boycott, responding to a federal injunction against the strike with jeers, violence, and the overturning of boxcars. Accounts of this incident by federal marshal John W. Arnold and a biased Chicago press convinced President Cleveland and much of the public that federal intervention was necessary in the Pullman Strike. Primary and secondary sources; 4 illus., 5 photos, 40 notes.   L. Woolfe

814. Jentz, John B. BREAD AND LABOR: CHICAGO'S GERMAN BAKERS ORGANIZE. *Chicago Hist. 1983 12(2): 24-35.* Studies the growth of German-American bakers' unions in Chicago during 1880-1910.

815. Kerr, K. Austin. LABOR-MANAGEMENT COOPERATION: AN 1897 CASE. *Pennsylvania Mag. of Hist. and Biog. 1975 99(1): 45-71.* A review of the 1897 strike of the United Mine Workers in western Pennsylvania and its consequences. The harsh depression of the 1890's hit the coal industry severely, and owners competed ruthlessly for markets. The workers struck without warning, hoping to catch the owners off guard. The ploy worked fairly well, with a convention of worker and management representatives producing a satisfactory settlement. The impetus of the time was toward resolving disputes harmoniously, but it failed to survive the severe challenges of the decades to come. 105 notes.   V. L. Human

816. Kilar, Jeremy W. COMMUNITY AND AUTHORITY RESPONSE TO THE SAGINAW VALLEY LUMBER STRIKE OF 1885. *J. of Forest Hist. 1976 20(2): 67-79.* In 1885 the community of Bay City, Michigan, supported striking lumbermen politically and legally against absentee millowners. The industrial diversification of the neighboring community of Saginaw precluded such community support. Industrial relationships in the two communities seemed similar, but social, ideological, and economic structures determined the different responses to the strike. 5 illus., map, graph, 65 notes.   L. F. Johnson

817. Lazerow, Jama. "THE WORKINGMAN'S HOUR": THE 1886 LABOR UPRISING IN BOSTON. *Labor Hist. 1980 21(2): 200-220.* In the 1886 labor uprising in Boston, Massachusetts, the Knights of Labor gained much influence and many members, and the Central Labor Union waged an unsuccessful strike for the eight-hour day. The labor movement was full of ambiguity in organization and ideology because it sought power and respectability while being conciliatory. However, a viable workers' movement was created in Boston. Based on local newspapers; 52 notes.   L. L. Athey

818. Levine, Susan. "HONOR EACH NOBLE MAID": WOMEN WORKERS AND THE YONKERS CARPET WEAVERS' STRIKE OF 1885. *New York Hist. 1981 62(2): 153-176.* A prolonged strike at the Alexander Smith and Sons Carpet Company in Yonkers, New York, in 1885 revealed sources of conflict between a new, mostly female work force and an expanding industrial management. Wage cuts, the firing of Knights of Labor union members, and management interference with work rhythms and social behavior in the mills brought on the strike. Management did not recognize the union and considered strikers former employees. The strikers, however, had community support. The arrest of women strikers outraged the town. The strike ended when the company made concessions to the workers. However, the company resumed antiunion activity in 1886. Based on contemporary newspapers and other primary sources; 8 illus., table, 36 notes.   R. N. Lokken

819. Levstik, Frank R. THE HOCKING VALLEY MINERS' STRIKE, 1884-1885: A SEARCH FOR ORDER. *Old Northwest 1976 2(1): 55-65.* Discusses the miners' strike in the coal field of Hocking Valley, Ohio, during 1884-85, emphasizing the actions of Governor George Hoadly.

820. Lopez, David E. COWBOY STRIKES AND UNIONS. *Labor Hist. 1977 18(3): 325-340.* Although there were no enduring unions and no labor organizers of cowboys, they did strike. Most prominent among cowboy strikes were the Texas Panhandle Strike of 1883 and the Wyoming Strike of 1885. Contrary to the mythology about cowboys, their working conditions promoted a dependency upon employers; therefore unionization was not a realistic alternative. Based on newspapers and the archives of the Western History Research Center in Laramie, Wyoming; 35 notes.   L. L. Athey

821. Luning Prak, N. PULLMAN. *Spiegel Historiael [Netherlands] 1977 12(4): 236-241.* George M. Pullman (1831-97) invented the famous sleeping car in 1858 and in 1880 established the city of Pullman near Chicago. Here his workers lived in company homes and sent their children to company schools. In 1885 and again in 1893 wages were reduced, but not rents. A strike in 1894 was supported by the American Railway Union. The strike was broken because President Cleveland called out federal troops, invoking the Sherman Anti-Trust act of 1890. Illus., biblio.   G. D. Homan

822. Marsh, John L. CAPTAIN FRED, CO. I, AND THE WORKERS OF HOMESTEAD. *Pennsylvania Hist. 1979 46(4): 291-311.* The 16th Regiment of the National Guard of Pennsylvania was among the units that were ordered to service during the Homestead strike of 1892. Essentially auxiliary borough constables, these men from the oil region relieved their boredom and frustration through athletic contests, musical evenings, and similar diversions. Based on *Annual Report of the Adjutant General of Pennsylvania, 1892,* newspaper accounts, and the photograph collection of Captain Fred E. Windsor, now held by the Warren County Historical Society; 4 photos, 30 notes.   D. C. Swift

823. McMath, Robert C., Jr. AGRARIAN PROTEST AT THE FORKS OF THE CREEK: THREE SUBORDINATE FARMERS' ALLIANCES IN NORTH CAROLINA. *North Carolina Hist. Rev. 1974 51(1): 41-63.* The strength of the Farmers' Alliance in the late 1880's was based on its local chapters. Farmers and rural professionals were attracted by a program of economic relief, cooperative enterprise, and fraternal organization. Statewide decline of the Alliance in 1891 was associated with increased political activity. Primary and secondary sources; illus., map, 75 notes.   W. B. Bedford

824. Montgomery, David. STRIKES IN NINETEENTH-CENTURY AMERICA. *Social Sci. Hist. 1980 4(1): 81-104.* Surveys patterns of strike behavior in 19th-century America and examines what these patterns reveal of workers' changing consciousness and culture. The applicability of various generalized theories of strikes and labor protest is then tested against these specific American materials. Most of the theories are rejected as too mechanistic and positivistic. Based partly on published materials of the US Census Bureau, the Commission of Labor, and the state of Pennsylvania; 2 tables, 6 notes.   L. K. Blaser

825. Mormino, Gary R. TAMPA AND THE NEW URBAN SOUTH: THE WEIGHT STRIKE OF 1899. *Florida Hist. Q. 1982 60(3): 337-356.* The 1890's witnessed significant change in Tampa.

Gradually the old Latin manner of cigar-making was replaced by the machine, and the paternalism of the owners gave way to the corporation. The "Huelga de Pesa" (the weight strike) of 1899 marks a transition between the old Latin factory system and corporate organization. By 1900 racial friction and industrial difficulties marked the path of the future for Tampa. Based on oral histories, the Federal Writers' Project (WPA), *Tampa Morning Tribune,* and other sources; 83 notes.   N. A. Kuntz

826. Papanikolas, Helen Z. UTAH'S COAL LANDS: A VITAL EXAMPLE OF HOW AMERICA BECAME A GREAT NATION. *Utah Hist. Q. 1975 43(2): 104-124.* The discovery of vast coal fields in eastern Utah in 1875 and the resulting railroad competition ended pioneer Utah's fuel problems. Mines also brought immigrants. Each major immigrant group came as strike-breakers during Utah's struggling labor movement. Each group contributed its own nationalism, folk culture, and animosities. The coal fields brought together pioneer hardiness, American individualism, immigrant brawn, and bountiful resources to form a unique blend of cultures. Based on primary and secondary sources; 10 illus., 34 notes.   J. L. Hazelton

827. Peterson, Richard H. CONFLICT AND CONSENSUS: LABOR RELATIONS IN WESTERN MINING. *J. of the West 1973 12(1): 1-17.* An analytical account of the instability in the mining industry in eight western states during 1892-1904 and the labor priorities, policies, and attitudes of the most successful mining capitalists. Some bonanza kings preferred to cut labor costs and relied on military and judicial power to enforce and defend their policies.... However, other Western mining entrepreneurs, recognizing that a hard line policy could sometimes result in a considerable loss of life and property and build a heritage of conflict between workers and owners, adopted policies to prevent rather than to suppress the grievances of organized labor." 66 notes, appendix.   D. D. Cameron

828. Pozzetta, George E. A PADRONE LOOKS AT FLORIDA: LABOR RECRUITING AND THE FLORIDA EAST COAST RAILWAY. *Florida Hist. Q. 1975 54(1): 74-84.* Discusses the Florida East Coast Railway's use of the padrone, or labor boss, as a means of securing immigrant labor for railroad construction. Padroni were responsible for the recruiting and transporting of men to the job site, for which they collected a fee from the worker himself. On the job site, padroni ran the commissary and handled other financial matters for the workers, often doing so in a larcenous manner. However, the padrone system, with its faults, did provide a way for immigrants to make a living around the turn of the century. Reprints a letter written by a padrone, an advertisement from a New York Italian-language paper. Based on newspaper and secondary sources; 25 notes.   J. E. Findling

829. Ray, William W. CRUSADE OR CIVIL WAR? THE PULLMAN STRIKE IN CALIFORNIA. *California History 1979 58(1): 20-37.* Describes the effect of the 1894 Pullman strike in California. Historians have overlooked events in California which highlighted public disaffection with the Central Pacific-Southern Pacific's economic and political dominance, the regional variations in the strike, and the relative effectiveness of the American Railway Union. The ARU's boycott of Pullman cars and trains which used them was most effective in Sacramento, disappointing in the Bay area, and minimal in Los Angeles. However, the strike persisted in California after the dispute ended in Pullman, Illinois, where the strike had originated. The strike brought out longstanding grievances over wage reductions but it also indicated the degree to which Californians disliked the Southern Pacific. The impact of the strike in California included the calling out of federal and state troops for the first time to maintain order, electoral successes by Populist candidates, and violence and sabotage by desperate ARU members. Railroads viewed ARU agitation as civil war; ARU supporters considered it a crusade for the rights of unskilled workers. Primary and secondary sources; 7 photos, 44 notes.   A. Hoffman

830. Reed, Merle E. THE AUGUSTA TEXTILE MILLS AND THE STRIKE OF 1886. *Labor Hist. 1973 14(2): 228-246.* Surveys the conditions of textile mills and workers before and during the 1886 strike. Working conditions in Augusta were among the best in the South, but wage cuts during depression generated union activity led by the Knights of Labor. The strike and lockout in the summer of 1886 were significant to the region and were part of the pattern of labor strife in the nation.

The strike was broken largely because labor was in great supply. Based on newspapers and owner and labor publications; 35 notes.

L. L. Athey

831. Salvatore, Nick. RAILROAD WORKERS AND THE GREAT STRIKE OF 1877: THE VIEW FROM A SMALL MIDWEST CITY. *Labor Hist. 1980 21(4): 522-545.* The railroad workers' strikes of 1877 did not create greater class consciousness among the railroad workers in Terre Haute, Indiana. The ethnic composition, decentralized industrial structure, and good employment opportunities with the Vandalia Railroad contributed to Terre Haute's railroad workers continuing their prestrike political and union attitudes long after the July 1877 strike ended. Primary sources; 38 notes.

L. F. Velicer

832. Schneider, Linda. THE CITIZEN STRIKER: WORKERS' IDEOLOGY IN THE HOMESTEAD STRIKE OF 1892. *Labor Hist. 1982 23(1): 47-66.* Workers at the Carnegie Company's Homestead steel mills in Pennsylvania utilized the rhetoric of republicanism to link unionism to the preservation of American national values during the strike of 1892. The union, the Amalgamated Association of Iron and Steel Workers, protected the workers' rights as independent citizens and homeowners from being undermined by the employer. At the same time, the workers' perception of the government as a neutral force embodying national ideals prevented the workers from resisting the state militia's intervention in the strike, leading directly to the workers' defeat. Based on contemporary newspaper accounts and congressional testimony; 25 notes.

L. F. Velicer

833. Schneirov, Richard. CHICAGO'S GREAT UPHEAVAL OF 1877. *Chicago Hist. 1980 9(1): 2-17.* During the national railroad strike of 1877, unskilled laborers (mainly Irish, German, Bohemian, and Polish) in Chicago during 23-26 July went on strike, went about in crowds to enlist other workers, and fought bloody battles with the police and the state militia; many workers won restoration of their recently cut wages.

834. Schwantes, Carlos A. COXEY'S MONTANA NAVY: A PROTEST AGAINST UNEMPLOYMENT ON THE WAGEWORKERS' FRONTIER. *Pacific Northwest Q. 1982 73(3): 98-107.* On 5 June 1894 an expedition of 340 unemployed miners departed Fort Benton, Montana, on 10 flatboats. They intended to float down the Missouri River to St. Louis and then continue overland to Washington, D.C., where they would join other members of Jacob Coxey's Army to protest national economic policies. Weather and sandbars made the trip somewhat difficult, but the greater problems arose from shortage of food and clothing. In Dakota towns, such as Pierre and Chamberlain, they received considerable aid, but city officials in Kansas City physically opposed their landing. The expedition broke up in St. Louis after three leaders absconded with the remaining funds. Based on Western newspapers; 3 illus., map, 44 notes.

M. L. Tate

835. Schwantes, Carlos A. LAW AND DISORDER: THE SUPPRESSION OF COXEY'S ARMY IN IDAHO. *Idaho Yesterdays 1981 25(2): 10-26.* The Coxeyite army that tried to move across southern Idaho in May of 1894 was arrested for commandeering Union Pacific rolling stock. After a trial, federal judge James H. Beatty sentenced 184 men to prison for 30 to 60 days. A special compound was built, and the army helped guard it. Based on letters and newspaper accounts; 6 photos, 51 notes.

B. J. Paul

836. Schwantes, Carlos A. PROTEST IN A PROMISED LAND: UNEMPLOYMENT, DISINHERITANCE, AND THE ORIGIN OF LABOR MILITANCY IN THE PACIFIC NORTHWEST, 1885-1886. *Western Hist. Q. 1982 13(4): 373-390.* Anti-Chinese agitation in the Pacific Northwest in the mid-1880's began as a popular response to the Caucasian-Chinese competition for jobs in the depression years. The Chinese had been imported to build the Pacific railroads, but these were now completed. Seattle and Tacoma, Washington, building booms collapsed and released whites who were now job hungry. The Knights of Labor militantly exploited the discontent, joining racism and radicalism. Gradually vague resentments were recast into a set of specific demands and an ideology of disinheritance evolved, insinuating a relationship between unemployment and political and economic power in Oregon and Washington. 38 notes.

D. L. Smith

837. Shotliff, Don A. THE 1894 TARIFF AND THE POTTERY STRIKE: THE REBIRTH OF THE NATIONAL BROTHERHOOD OF OPERATIVE POTTERS. *Western Pennsylvania Hist. Mag. 1975 58(3): 307-326.* Discusses the origin of the National Brotherhood of Operative Potters as a result of lowered wages because of cheap foreign labor which brought about a strike of both union and nonunion potters in 1894.

838. Skaggs, Julian C. and Ehrlich, Richard L. PROFITS, PATERNALISM, AND REBELLION: A CASE STUDY IN INDUSTRIAL STRIFE. *Working Papers from the Regional Econ. Hist. Res. Center 1978 1(4): 1-30.* Analysis of labor unrest and an 1886 strike at the Lukens Iron Works in Coatesville, Pennsylvania, indicates that management objected not to increased wages and benefits but to the potential for worker independence and the ensuing threat to paternalism and rights of ownership.

839. Skaggs, Julian C. and Ehrlich, Richard L. PROFITS, PATERNALISM, AND REBELLION: A CASE STUDY IN INDUSTRIAL STRIFE. *Business Hist. Rev. 1980 54(2): 155-174.* In the strike against the Lukens Iron Works in Coatesville, Pennsylvania, in 1886, the management's intransigence was due more to a desire to reaffirm a traditional paternalism than to the dollar cost of the workers' demands. The cause of many such confrontations of the period was a conflict over control of the firm; management saw labor's demands as threatening its own legitimate authority. Based on the Lukens Collection in the Eleutherian Mills Library; 6 graphs, 36 notes.

C. J. Pusateri

840. Stout, Steve. TRAGEDY IN NOVEMBER: THE CHERRY MINE DISASTER. *J. of the Illinois State Hist. Soc. 1979 72(1): 57-69.* Reviews antecedents of the fire disaster in the coal mine at Cherry, Illinois, in 1909. The disaster could easily have been prevented had anyone taken it seriously soon enough. An electrical failure had caued kerosene torches to be used for light; they ignited some bales of hay used to feed the mine mules. Miners passed the fire when it could easily have been extinguished, thinking it was under control. When finally the fire was fought, the effort was so incompetent that it actually spread the blaze. Rescue efforts were not ideal, either. Altogether, 259 miners lost their lives. 8 photos, 45 notes.

V. L. Human

841. Ullmo, Sylvia. THE GREAT STRIKES OF 1877. *Rev. Française d'Etudes Américaines [France] 1976 (2): 49-56.* Studies the radical aspects of the massive railroad and industrial strikes of 1877 in Baltimore, Chicago, St. Louis, and Pittsburgh.

842. Waksmundski, John. WILLIAM MC KINLEY AND THE RAILROAD WORKERS: INSIGHT INTO POLITICAL STRATEGY. *West Virginia Hist. 1974 36(1): 37-39.* A letter to William McKinley from West Virginia labor leader S. W. Murphy asking McKinley's help in an 1893 labor dispute shows that at least one labor group viewed him as its friend. Primary sources; 3 notes.

J. H. Broussard

843. Waugh, Joan. FLORENCE KELLEY AND THE ANTI-SWEATSHOP CAMPAIGN OF 1892-1893. *UCLA Hist. J. 1982 3: 21-35.* Describes the campaign led by Florence Kelley for legislation regulating Illinois sweatshop conditions. A Hull House activist working with Jane Addams, Kelley rejected radical tactics in favor of a coalition of broadly based groups seeking remedial legislation. Kelley argued against sweatshop labor but also warned consumers of the dangers of disease in the garments made by unhealthy workers. This approach gained widespread support. Passage of the State Factory Inspection Law of 1893 gave Illinois prominence in the campaign to protect workers and consumers and was a landmark in social welfare legislation. 52 notes.

A. Hoffman

844. Weaver, Bill L. LOUISVILLE'S LABOR DISTURBANCE, JULY, 1877. *Filson Club Hist. Q. 1974 48(2): 177-186.* On 24 July 1877, a small mob of disorganized workers caused some minor property damage in Louisville, Kentucky. Unlike the situation in other cities, Louisville's problems did not grow into a major conflict. Railway workers, the backbone of labor unrest in other areas in 1877, had just prevented a wage cut in Louisville and did not take part in the violence. In addition, Louisville had escaped the full force of the depression of the 1870's, which, combined with the prompt action of police, prevented

continuation of the protest. Documentation from contemporary newspapers and memoirs; 54 notes.   G. B. McKinney

845. Wyman, Mark. INDUSTRIAL REVOLUTION IN THE WEST: HARD-ROCK MINERS AND THE NEW TECHNOLOGY. *Western Hist. Q. 1974 5(1): 39-57.* Technological improvements which included the machine drill, the power hoist, dynamite, electricity, complex timbering systems, pumps, and related developments constituted a revolution in the mining industry, 1860-1910. Hard-rock miners, company owners, and stockholders alike welcomed these new developments as beneficial, but miners' enthusiasm waned when faced with wage cuts, importation of Chinese workers, company stores, blacklists, and increased dangers to health and safety. Miners were kept weak by their status as wage laborers and common law legal traditions. To overcome these obstacles, the hard-rock miners formed labor unions and turned increasingly to state legislation. 63 notes.   D. L. Smith

846. Yellowitz, Irwin. SKILLED WORKERS AND MECHANIZATION: THE LASTERS IN THE 1890S. *Labor Hist. 1977 18(2): 197-213.* Lasters, one of few remaining handcraft trades in the shoe industry in the 1890's, responded to mechanization of their craft in two basic ways: 1) conciliation toward machine introduction with some preservation of traditional practices, and 2) union action to restrain the economic impact of mechanization. Both responses were designed to protect lasters from too-rapid innovation. Based on the records of the Lynn, Massachusetts, Lasters, government reports, and union publications; 38 notes.   L. L. Athey

Government Programs, Policies, and Politics

847. Asher, Robert. FAILURE AND FULFILLMENT: AGITATION FOR EMPLOYERS' LIABILITY LEGISLATION AND THE ORIGINS OF WORKMEN'S COMPENSATION IN NEW YORK STATE, 1876-1910. *Labor Hist. 1983 24(2): 198-222.* Traces the long struggle of organized labor in New York State to obtain state laws making employers liable for accidents in the work place. Only when organized labor gained enough political power to influence state legislators was any meaningful employers' liability legislation enacted. The increased amounts of money won by injured workers and the threat of even tougher employers' liability legislation then made employers receptive to workmen's compensation legislation, under which injured workers were automatically compensated without resorting to the courts. Based on Workingmen's Federation of the State of New York *Proceedings,* New York State Assembly and Senate *Journals,* and other primary sources; 73 notes.   L. F. Velicer

848. Finn, J. F. AF OF L LEADERS AND THE QUESTION OF POLITICS IN THE EARLY 1890'S. *J. of Am. Studies [Great Britain] 1973 7(3): 243-265.* Unionists have debated the merits of an American "Labor Party." One faction led by Samuel Gompers (1850-1924) resisted a labor party. The other faction, heavily Socialists and "philosophical anarchists," demanded a labor party but disagreed about a "collectivist" platform for the party. Based on labor publications and manuscript sources; 117 notes.   H. T. Lovin

849. French, John D. "REAPING THE WHIRLWIND": THE ORIGINS OF THE ALLEGHENY COUNTY GREENBACK LABOR PARTY IN 1877. *Western Pennsylvania Hist. Mag. 1981 64(2): 97-119.* Discusses the alliance of labor and currency reformers in July 1877 in Pittsburgh that resulted in the formation of the Greenback Labor Party to express opposition to the government's suppression of the great strike of railroad workers in July 1877, the national banking system, and the contraction of currency.

850. Gottlieb, Amy Zahl. THE INFLUENCE OF BRITISH TRADE UNIONISTS ON THE REGULATION OF THE MINING INDUSTRY IN ILLINOIS, 1872. *Labor Hist. 1978 19(3): 397-415.* English and Scots immigrant miners settling in Illinois brought with them experience in political action and mining legislation. Their organizations supported legislation based on experience in Great Britain, and succeeded in 1872. Based on newspapers, periodicals, and legislative records; 36 notes.   L. L. Athey

851. Grant, H. Roger. BLUEPRINTS FOR CO-OPERATIVE COMMUNITIES: THE LABOR EXCHANGE AND THE COLORADO CO-OPERATIVE COMPANY. *J. of the West 1974 13(3): 74-82.* Discusses the Labor Exchange and the Colorado Co-operative Company as movements in response to the depression in the 1890's. The Labor Exchange, founded by G. B. DeBernardi, was most successful in small towns and cities in the Midwest. It stressed cooperative reform in towns already existing. The Colorado Co-operative Community was organized in Denver by socialists, unemployed miners, railroad employees, artisans, and farmers. It organized a self-contained agricultural community. Both movements were plagued by internal dissension and declined when prosperity returned to the American economy. Based on contemporary newspaper, pamphlet, and journal reports, and secondary sources; 28 notes.   N. J. Street

852. Grossman, Jonathan and MacLaury, Judson. THE CREATION OF THE BUREAU OF LABOR STATISTICS. *Monthly Labor Rev. 1975 98(2): 25-31.* Details the 20 years of legislative crusading by American labor organizations which preceded the establishment of the first national labor statistics agency in 1885.   S

853. Harring, Sidney L. POLICE REPORTS AS SOURCES IN LABOR HISTORY. *Labor Hist. 1977 18(4): 585-591.* Presents eight documents from the Board of Police of Buffalo, New York, which reveal the cooperation between police and industrialists during strikes. Police reports are important sources for the social history of immigrant labor. Based on annual reports of the Buffalo, New York Board of Police; 14 notes.   L. L. Athey

854. Hunt, Richard P. THE FIRST LABOR DAY. *Am. Heritage 1982 33(5): 109-112.* Although Grover Cleveland signed an act of Congress in 1894 making Labor Day a national holiday, workingmen in New York actually began celebrating in 1882, when Matthew Maguire, secretary of the Central Labor Union, suggested a public show of organized strength. The proposal, not without making difficulties, resulted in success and led to concerted efforts to create such a holiday two years later. Massachusetts became the first state to recognize Labor Day, and by the time that President Cleveland made it a national event, 25 states were observing some form of Labor Day. Photo, 2 illus.   J. F. Paul

855. Hurt, R. Douglas. JOHN R. ROGERS: THE UNION LABOR PARTY, GEORGISM AND AGRARIAN REFORM. *J. of the West 1977 16(1): 10-15.* Reviews John R. Rogers, concentrating on his years in Kansas. As a member of the Greenback Party, and as a leader of the Union Labor Party, he attacked both major parties for unwillingness to deal with problems. While in Kansas he published the Newton *Kansas Commoner.* He left Kansas in 1890 and moved to Washington, where in 1896 he was elected governor.   R. Alvis

856. Hurt, R. Douglas. POPULIST-ENDORSED JUDGES AND THE PROTECTION OF WESTERN LABOR. *J. of the West 1978 17(1): 19-26.* Though commonly associated with agrarianism, the Populist movement also supported urban laborers (both out of philosophy and necessity) as shown by the pro-labor rulings of populist-endorsed judges of state supreme courts in Kansas, Nebraska, Colorado, Washington, and Montana, 1893-1902.

857. James, Edward T. BEN BUTLER RUNS FOR PRESIDENT: LABOR, GREENBACKERS, AND ANTI-MONOPOLISTS IN THE ELECTION OF 1884. *Essex Inst. Hist. Collections 1977 113(2): 65-88.* Before the 1954 accession by the Library of Congress of Benjamin F. Butler's (1818-1893) papers, scholars inadequately understood his campaign as a third-party presidential candidate in 1884. Even with support from the Anti-Monopoly Convention, Greenbackers, and labor, Butler's People's Party failed to stop Grover Cleveland's nomination at the Democratic convention and subsequent election. Discusses causes for failure, chiefly the Republican subsidy. Based on the Butler Papers, primary and secondary sources; 3 illus., photo, 78 notes.   R. S. Sliwoski

858. Kanter, Elliot J. CLASS, ETHNICITY, AND SOCIALIST POLITICS: ST. LOUIS, 1876-1881. *UCLA Hist. J. 1982 3: 36-60.* Examines the rise and decline of the Socialistic Labor Party in St. Louis, Missouri, following a major railroad strike that revealed class discontent

among the city's working class. Although many German immigrants supported the socialists, a German background in St. Louis did not necessarily indicate homogeneity in status. Voting patterns demonstrate that the socialists had to compete with other issues for working-class votes, such as the Greenback movement. Factionalism also disrupted the socialists; and the labor movement rejected doctrinaire socialism. Other factors influencing voters included age, occupation, and economic status. With the end of the depression of the 1870's and renewed economic growth, the party went into decline even as labor discontent grew in the 1880's. Map, 5 tables, 31 notes.   A. Hoffman

859. MacLaury, Judson. THE SELECTION OF THE FIRST US COMMISSIONER OF LABOR. *Monthly Labor Rev. 1975 98(4): 16-19.* Examines President Chester A. Arthur's problems in choosing the first US Commissioner of Labor, and how his eventual choice, Carroll Wright, performed successfully for 20 years.

860. McKinney, Gordon B. THE POLITICS OF PROTEST: THE LABOR REFORM AND GREENBACK PARTIES IN NEW HAMPSHIRE. *Hist. New Hampshire 1981 36(2-3): 149-170.* In 1870, rapid industrialization and rural population decline led to the formation of the Labor Reform Party of New Hampshire, which received 10.6% of the popular vote in the 1870 state elections, making it the most successful third party in New Hampshire between 1856 and 1912. But it failed to achieve any of its objectives, as its support came from disaffected Democrats, allowing Republicans to sweep into power. In the late 1870's the Greenback Party began organizing in New Hampshire, and workers alienated by the two major parties turned to it with great interest. It also failed to provide an effective vehicle for reform and amounted only to a protest party. 57 notes.   D. F. Chard

861. Scharnau, Ralph William. THOMAS J. MORGAN AND THE UNITED LABOR PARTY OF CHICAGO. *J. of the Illinois State Hist. Soc. 1973 66(1): 41-61.* In the 1880's the press depicted industrial strikers as lawless radicals and "reds." The Illinois General Assembly was particularly antilabor. Thomas J. Morgan, a socialist labor leader, favored political action to curb unfavorable political pressure. His United Labor Party worked as a labor coalition with local trade unions and Knights of Labor assemblies nationally. He helped write the 1886 national platform of the new party and made nightly speeches to workers to support the party ticket. Several state Labor Party legislature victories in Democratic districts in 1886 resulted in Democratic patronage lures to infiltrate Morgan's party. Women's suffrage, the eight-hour day for city employees, better school accommodations, and an equitable taxation system were popular party platforms. Morgan continued to spread socialist ideas through the early 1890's by his organizing genius, political interests, and speaking abilities. Based on the Morgan collection at the University of Illinois and on newspapers; 5 illus., 68 notes.   A. C. Aimone

862. Schewel, Michael J. LOCAL POLITICS IN LYNCHBURG, VIRGINIA, IN THE 1880'S. *Virginia Mag. of Hist. and Biog. 1981 89(2): 170-180.* Narrates attempt of populist groups to gain control of local government and use it for purposes more egalitarian than practiced by dominant conservative Democrats. Using the names Regulators, Coalitionists, and Republicans, biracial working-class voters achieved a narrow success in the mid-1880's in controlling the city council by subsuming themselves within the Knights of Labor. Their biggest success was building a public school for black children. City expenses overall increased only marginally while the coalition was in power. After the national failure of the Knights, racial animosity split the ranks and the Democrats returned to power. The principle cause of division was competition for jobs in the local tobacco industry, which in prosperity had brought liberally inclined voters to Lynchburg, but was now in decline. Based primarily on local newspapers of the period and secondary sources; 32 notes.   P. J. Woehrmann

863. Waksmundski, John. GOVERNOR MC KINLEY AND THE WORKING MAN. *Historian 1976 38(4): 629-647.* Unlike earlier Republican Party leaders, Ohio governor William McKinley (1843-1901) sought to align himself and his party with the working class. Elected in 1891, McKinley asked the legislature to enact laws on railroad worker safety, right of employees to join labor organizations, and arbitration. McKinley was reelected in 1893 with improved Republican vote totals in counties with a substantial worker voting bloc.

McKinley's careful actions dealing with striking coal miners during the 1893 depression enabled him to keep labor support. Notes.
                    M. J. Wentworth

864. Wyman, Roger E. AGRARIAN OR WORKING-CLASS RADICALISM? THE ELECTORAL BASIS OF POPULISM IN WISCONSIN. *Pol. Sci. Q. 1974/75 89(4): 825-848.* "Demonstrates that Populism in Wisconsin arose out of socialist-oriented labor radicalism rather than from agricultural distress and that urban workers, not agrarians, provided the largest component of Populist supporters. His findings thus challenge the commonly held belief that Wisconsin had a long tradition of agrarian radicalism in the late nineteenth century."
                    J

865. —. THE WORKINGMEN'S PARTY OF CALIFORNIA, 1877-1882. *California Hist. Q. 1976 55(1): 58-73.* Presents a portfolio of 20 illustrations depicting the Workingmen's Party of California. Founded by Denis Kearney and others, the party opposed the competition of Chinese labor, called for regulation of banks and railroads, and demanded labor reforms. The Workingmen's Party participated in the framing of the 1879 State Constitution. Most of the reproductions are taken from the San Francisco *Illustrated Wasp* , which held a critical view of the movement.   A. Hoffman

Racial, Ethnic, and Sex Discrimination

866. Bloch, Herman D. and Banks, Carol M. THE NATIONAL LABOR UNION AND BLACK WORKERS. *J. of Ethnic Studies 1973 1(1): 13-21.* Since the rise of trade unions in the 1850's, the American labor movement has discriminated against blacks. Motivated by a belief in white supremacy and a fear of job competition, white workers attempted to keep or drive blacks from the skilled trades and bar them from union membership. The National Labor Union (1866-72), a reform-orientated federation of trades assemblies, national trade unions, and other labor and labor-reform bodies, considered the problem of the black worker and adopted the intermediate position of inviting black unions to affiliate, without openly opposing the racist practices of its constituent bodies. Blacks elected instead to form the National Colored Labor Union (1869-72). The "half-hearted reformism" of the National Labor Union and its neglect of labor solidarity contributed to its limited success and early demise. Based largely on primary sources with major secondary sources also cited; 48 notes.   T. W. Smith

867. Brier, Stephen. INTERRACIAL ORGANIZING IN THE WEST VIRGINIA COAL INDUSTRY: THE PARTICIPATION OF BLACK MINE WORKERS IN THE KNIGHTS OF LABOR AND THE UNITED MINE WORKERS, 1880-1894. Fink, Gary M. and Reed, Merl E., eds. *Essays in Southern Labor History: Selected Papers, Southern Labor History Conference, 1976.* (Westport, Conn.; London, England: Greenwood, Pr., 1977): 18-43. A study of national unionism in the coal fields, but especially the relationship of the growth of militant, interracial local unions among southern West Virginia mine workers. Focuses on the Flat-Top Pocahontas field, 1880-94. In the latter part of the period a decline in local organization set in, largely the result of intensified economic and political repression on the part of the coal operators. For more than a decade, however, West Virginia mine workers, black and white, had flocked to the banner of trade unionism, and there was demonstrated the possibility of cooperation between black and white workers. 44 notes.   R. V. Ritter

868. Dann, Martin. BLACK POPULISM: A STUDY OF THE COLORED FARMERS' ALLIANCE THROUGH 1891. *J. of Ethnic Studies 1974 2(3): 58-71.* Describes the efforts of post-Civil War blacks to break the deadlock of oppression and exploitation by organized action. The Colored Farmers' Alliance may have evolved out of secret rural societies, some of them founded by Knights of Labor organizers sent South during the 1880's. Reviews the career of Colonel R. M. Humphrey, and the spread of the Alliance from Texas into South Carolina under T. E. Pratt of Cheraw, and to Virginia under C. W. Macune. The turning point for the CFA came between the Ocala Convention and the Cincinnati Conference, when fears of whites increased in the face of cotton pickers' strikes and CFA support for a

third political party. The failure of Humphrey's general strike call of September 1891 discredited the militant wing of the Alliance and brought on direct confrontation with the White Alliance which generally encouraged the brutal repression of black labor agitation, forgetting the political expediency which had originally produced limited support for black agrarianism. Based on primary news accounts, periodicals, secondary works; 43 notes.   G. J. Bobango

869. Fink, Leon. "IRRESPECTIVE OF PARTY, COLOR OR SOCIAL STANDING": THE KNIGHTS OF LABOR AND OPPOSITION POLITICS IN RICHMOND, VIRGINIA. *Labor Hist. 1978 19(3): 325-349.* The Knights of Labor in Richmond turned to political action in 1886 by supporting a reform slate in municipal elections. A coalition with Negro Republicans threatened existing Democratic control, but racial divisions generated by the meeting of the 10th General Assembly of the Knights helped divide the coalition and ensured defeat. By 1888 the reform movement vanished, and Negroes steadily lost political influence. Based on newspapers; 50 notes.   L. L. Athey

870. Foner, Philip S. A LABOR VOICE FOR BLACK EQUALITY: THE *BOSTON DAILY EVENING VOICE,* 1864-1867. *Sci. and Soc. 1974 38(3): 304-325.* Unique among labor publications, the *Boston Daily Evening Voice* championed unification of black and white workers and considered strong labor organization a means toward union hegemony.

871. Kann, Kenneth. THE KNIGHTS OF LABOR AND THE SOUTHERN BLACK WORKER. *Labor Hist. 1977 18(1): 49-70.* Surveys attempts 1880-87 by the Knights of Labor to organize southern blacks into unions. The racial issue was divisive, but the Knights demonstrated that southern workers of both races could be united on common interests and goals. Based on reports of the Knights of Labor and newspapers; 60 notes.   L. L. Athey

872. Kremm, Thomas W. and Neal, Diane. CHALLENGES TO SUBORDINATION: ORGANIZED BLACK AGRICULTURAL PROTEST IN SOUTH CAROLINA, 1886-1895. *South Atlantic Q. 1978 77(1): 98-112.* In spite of their hopeless situation, during 1886-95 black agricultural laborers in South Carolina attempted to improve their economic position by organizing to plan boycotts and strikes. These actions were not isolated or unique to the Palmetto State, but were a part of a much larger black protest movement of the late 19th century. Although unsuccessful, these efforts were significant and afford an excellent insight into race relations in the rural South and the methods employed by blacks to improve their declining position in society. Newspaper accounts; 31 notes.   H. M. Parker, Jr.

873. Kremm, Thomas W. and Neal, Diane. CLANDESTINE BLACK LABOR SOCIETIES AND WHITE FEAR: HIRAM F. HOOVER AND THE "COOPERATIVE WORKERS OF AMERICA" IN THE SOUTH. *Labor Hist. 1978 19(2): 226-237.* Hiram F. Hoover, a white northerner and former member of the Knights of Labor, attempted to form a clandestine society, the Cooperative Workers of America, in South Carolina and Georgia during 1886-87. Local residents responded violently; Hoover was shot and the CWA was crushed. Although a reform group, the CWA was perceived as revolutionary. Based on local newspapers; 24 notes.   L. L. Athey

874. Leonard, Henry B. ETHNIC CLEAVAGE AND INDUSTRIAL CONFLICT IN LATE 19TH CENTURY AMERICA: THE CLEVELAND ROLLING MILL COMPANY STRIKES OF 1882 AND 1885. *Labor Hist. 1979 20(4): 524-548.* Examines two strikes against the Cleveland Rolling Mill Company in Ohio. Ethnic cleavages between British skilled workers, who led the 1882 Strike, and Poles and Bohemians, who led the 1885 Strike, promoted weaknesses which, when combined with technological change, adamant employers, and a hostile public, doomed the strikes. Misunderstood ethnic cleavages were important to labor in the late 19th century. Based on newspapers, diocesan records, and Polish and Bohemian sources; 34 notes.   L. L. Athey

875. Levine, Susan. LABOR'S TRUE WOMAN: DOMESTICITY AND EQUAL RIGHTS IN THE KNIGHTS OF LABOR. *J. of Am. Hist. 1983 70(2): 323-339.* The Knights of Labor offered working-class women a significant alternative to the new role demanded by the

capitalist wage system of the Gilded Age. The organization appealed to both housewives and wage earners, emphasizing cooperation as a viable alternative to "wage slavery." The Knights held two seemingly contradictory goals for working-class women: secure homes and family structures and equality of the sexes. The Knights' reform vision linked women's industrial concerns with two important issues of the late 19th-century women's movement: suffrage and temperance. Based on the *Journal of United Labor,* and *John Swinton's Paper,* and other primary sources; 77 notes.   T. P. Linkfield

876. Lewis, Ronald L. RACE AND THE UNITED MINE WORKERS' UNION IN TENNESSEE: SELECTED LETTERS OF WILLIAM R. RILEY, 1892-1895. *Tennessee Hist. Q. 1977 36(4): 524-536.* William R. Riley emerged during 1892-95 as a black labor leader in Tennessee. He understood the delicate position of blacks in the southern labor market and spoke pointedly in their behalf through letters to the *United Mine Workers' Journal.* Primary and secondary sources; 26 notes.   M. B. Lucas

877. McLaurin, Melton A. THE RACIAL POLICIES OF THE KNIGHTS OF LABOR AND THE ORGANIZATION OF SOUTHERN BLACK WORKERS. *Labor Hist. 1976 17(4): 568-585.* The Knights of Labor developed a paradoxical strategy in race relations in organizing attempts in the South. The K. of L. tried both to circumvent the race issue by emphasizing economic grievances and to solve the issues by compromising its antebellum reform heritage with southern prejudices. Although the K. of L. was the first serious attempt to organize southern blacks, racial prejudice slowly forced it to become a black union—which sounded its death knell in the South. Based on the Powderly papers and newspapers; 65 notes.   L. L. Athey

878. McMath, Robert C., Jr. SOUTHERN WHITE FARMERS AND THE ORGANIZATION OF BLACK FARM WORKERS: A NORTH CAROLINA DOCUMENT. *Labor Hist. 1977 18(1): 115-119.* Presents a document from North Carolina illustrating an attempt by a white farmer to infiltrate a black assembly of the Knights of Labor in 1889. Based on the John Bryon Grimes Papers; 14 notes.

L. L. Athey

879. —. DID SOUTHERN FARMERS DISCRIMINATE? AN EXCHANGE. *Agric. Hist. 1975 49(2): 441-447.*
Roberts, Charles A. THE EVIDENCE REEXAMINED, pp. 441-445. Contends that Higgs' recent article in *Agricultural History* on comparative wage rates for southern white and black agricultural workers in 1898-99 understates the difference between wage rates because it doesn't compare the value of board and rations given white and black workers, respectively.
Higgs, Robert. INTERPRETIVE PROBLEMS AND FURTHER EVIDENCE, pp. 445-447. Replies that many white workers did not receive board, whereas most blacks did receive rations, and offers further evidence that real wages were about the same regardless of race. Table, 16 notes.   D. E. Bowers

880. Schweninger, Loren. JAMES RAPIER AND THE NEGRO LABOR MOVEMENT, 1869-1872. *Alabama R. 1975 28(3): 185-201.* James T. Rapier, Alabama-born black politician, was vice-president of the short-lived National Negro Labor Union and leading founder of the Labor Union of Alabama. He sought creation of a federal land bureau in the interests of freedmen and reform of the public school system, but opposed westward migration as a solution to the plight of blacks. White resistance and Republican indifference precluded any favorable results. As a congressman (1872-75), he hoped for a political solution to black grievances and supported the Civil Rights Act of 1875. Based on primary and secondary sources, including the Rapier papers at Howard Univ.; 43 notes.   J. F. Vivian

881. Shofner, Jerrell H. MILITANT NEGRO LABORERS IN RECONSTRUCTION FLORIDA. *J. of Southern Hist. 1973 39(3): 397-408.* Discusses the efforts of Negroes in Reconstruction Florida to form labor unions, often coming into conflict with white unions. Florida blacks were active in the Colored National Labor Union and the National Union of Negro Labor as well as local organizations. Agricultural labor organizations were not successful but those in the lumber and shipping industries were. The use of strikes and overt violence was common, especially in Pensacola where Canadian lumbermen were

edging blacks out, and in Monroe County, where Bahamian laborers would work for lower pay. The Florida legislature often responded to union actions and passed laws to improve the workers' position. Based on contemporary newspaper reports, state and Federal government documents, primary and secondary sources; 42 notes.   N. J. Street

882. Smith, John David. MORE THAN SLAVES LESS THAN FREEDMEN: THE "SHARE WAGES" LABOR SYSTEM DURING RECONSTRUCTION. *Civil War Hist. 1980 26(3): 256-266.* Distinguishes the "share wages" labor system during Reconstruction from sharecropping and "share tenancy," and illustrates the first from the records of Dr. J. Rhett Motte's (1811-68) Exeter Plantation in St. John's Parish, Berkeley District, South Carolina. Prints and analyzes the labor agreement between Dr. Motte and 28 freedmen signed on 1 February 1867. Based on plantation records, census schedules, and secondary sources; 45 notes.   G. R. Schroeder

883. Stern, Mark. BLACK STRIKEBREAKERS IN THE COAL FIELDS: KING COUNTY, WASHINGTON: 1891. *J. of Ethnic Studies 1977 5(3): 60-70.* Relates the activities of the Oregon Improvement Company's recruitment and use of Negroes from Iowa and Illinois at its Newcastle and Franklin mines during the Knights of Labor-inspired strike of 1891. Contrary to the white miners' stereotypes, the blacks involved were not "collected from the slums" or "unconscious tools of the company," but were for the most part experienced coal miners who had gone through industrial conflicts before, were conscious of their role, and had some ideological justification for their actions. Local black leaders preached a philosophy of self-help and racial pride, and saw the managers of the corporation as allies against the Knights and the white workers. Events in King County contradict the dominant interpretation of the phenomenon of the black strikebreaker, and show that Booker T. Washington's creed was less a rationalization of racism than a stress on cultural pride and separateness. Primary and secondary sources; 29 notes.   G. J. Bobango

884. Woodman, Harold D.; Fite, Gilbert C., (commentary). POST-BELLUM SOCIAL CHANGE AND ITS EFFECTS ON MARKETING THE SOUTH'S COTTON CROP. *Agric. Hist. 1982 56(1): 215-230, 244-248.* Class as well as race separated Southern black farmers from white farmers for generations after the Civil War. Many white landowners and tenants slipped in status as they became indebted to furnishing merchants and lost control of the marketing of their crop. Many black tenants by the 20th century were working on centralized plantations, like the Delta and Pine Land Company in Mississippi, which controlled every aspect of their work and left them little better off than laborers. These differences as well as racial differences made it impossible for the two groups to become closer allies. Comments, pp. 244-248; 24 notes.   D. E. Bowers

885. —. *[ONE KIND OF FREEDOM:* A SYMPOSIUM]. *Explorations in Econ. Hist. 1979 16(1): 3-108.*
Parker, William N. INTRODUCTORY REMARKS, *pp. 3-7.* An introduction to a symposium on *One Kind of Freedom: The Economic Consequences of Emancipation* (1977) by Roger Ransom and Richard Sutch, held at Duke University on 11 February 1978.
Goldin, Claudia. "N" KINDS OF FREEDOM: AN INTRODUCTION TO THE ISSUES, *pp. 8-30.* Two of the basic arguments in *One Kind of Freedom* (1977) by Roger Ransom and Richard Sutch are either not substantiated or are overdrawn. First, the decline in Southern income and agricultural production can be explained only partly by a reduction in the black labor supply and by the fact that the 1860 cotton crop was unusually large; second, rural merchants were more competitive than Ransom and Sutch argue and that interest rates reflected risk rather than monopoly. Published documents and secondary sources; 3 tables, 24 notes, 42 ref.

Reid, Joseph D., Jr. WHITE LAND, BLACK LABOR, AND AGRICULTURAL STAGNATION: THE CAUSES AND EFFECTS OF SHARECROPPING IN THE POSTBELLUM SOUTH, *pp. 31-55.* A close examination of agricultural trends in the postbellum American South shows considerable diversity of forms and terms of tenure. These differences reflected variations in skill, capital resources, and corn-cotton price ratios. As suppliers of credit, market information, and goods, country stores were competitive, with prices reflecting costs rather than debt peonage. Published reports and secondary accounts; 5 tables, 19 notes, 39 ref.
Temin, Peter. FREEDOM AND COERCION: NOTES ON THE ANALYSIS OF DEBT PEONAGE IN *ONE KIND OF FREEDOM, pp. 56-63.* Coercion did exist in the postbellum American South, but Ransom and Sutch, *One Kind of Freedom* (1977), have overestimated its extent. Secondary accounts; 9 ref.
Ransom, Roger and Sutch, Richard. COTTON MERCHANDISING IN THE POST-EMANCIPATION SOUTH: STRUCTURE, CONDUCT, AND PERFORMANCE, *pp. 64-89.* The authors restate and amplify the interpretation advanced in *One Kind of Freedom: The Economic Consequences of Emancipation* (1977) and respond to their critics. Published reports and secondary accounts; table, 2 fig., 36 notes, 37 ref.
Wright, Gavin. FREEDOM AND THE SOUTHERN ECONOMY, *pp. 90-108.* A reexamination of the postbellum labor supply, land, wealth, tenancy, crop mix, farm size, and tenure arrangements indicates that *One Kind of Freedom* (1977) by Ransom and Sutch provides only a partial explanation of Southern poverty and that students should look at much larger questions, including the determinants of population growth, obstacles to industrialization, and migration to Northern jobs. Secondary accounts; 2 fig., 27 notes, 38 ref.

Economics and Statistics of Labor

886. Aldrich, Mark. STATE REPORTS ON WOMEN AND CHILD WAGE EARNERS, 1870-1906. *Labor Hist. 1980 21(1): 86-90.* Lists state labor reports on women and child wage earners published during 1897-1902 and not usually found in standard bibliographies. Based on RG. 257, B.L.S., National Archives; 2 notes.   L. L. Athey

887. Coelho, Philip R. P. and Shepherd, James F. REGIONAL DIFFERENCES IN REAL WAGES: THE UNITED STATES, 1851-1880. *Explorations in Econ. Hist. 1976 13(2): 203-230.* Sets out, year by year, real wages for each of the nine census regions. Shows that regional differences were substantial and that real wages were higher in the Midwest than in New England. Such differences may help explain 19th-century migration patterns. Based on congressional documents and secondary sources.   P. J. Coleman

888. Ermisch, John and Weiss, Thomas. THE IMPACT OF THE RURAL MARKET ON THE GROWTH OF THE URBAN WORKFORCE: UNITED STATES, 1870-1900. *Explorations in Econ. Hist. 1973/74 11(2): 137-153.* The rural market had little effect on the acceleration of urban growth through the substitution of urban production of nonagricultural goods and services. A mathematical analysis based on published statistics and secondary sources.   P. J. Coleman

889. Glassberg, Eudice. WORK, WAGES, AND THE COST OF LIVING, ETHNIC DIFFERENCES AND THE POVERTY LINE, PHILADELPHIA, 1880. *Pennsylvania Hist. 1979 46(1): 17-58.* A family of five in Philadelphia in 1880 needed $643 per year for an adequate income. Even workers in most skilled trades could not earn that much, and unskilled laborers were far worse off. Children had to work and wives had to earn money, often through "home work." Male white Americans had the best prospects of earning nearly enough money. Germans held more skilled jobs than did Irishmen. Blacks encountered the most occupational difficulties. Based on Philadelphia Social History Project data and other materials; 2 photos, 10 tables, 87 notes.   D. C. Swift

890. Haines, Michael R. INDUSTRIAL WORK AND THE FAMILY LIFE CYCLE, 1889-1890. *Res. in Econ. Hist. 1979 4: 289-356.* This paper provides an analysis of the 1889-1890 Commissioner of Labor Survey of budgets for 8544 families in nine industries in the United States and five European countries. The focus is the composition of family income over the life cycle and its relationship to family expenditures. It was found that earnings of the principal male wage earner peaked early in the life cycle whereas expenditures peaked later. The gap was made up by secondary wage earners, particularly children, entering the labor market. The pattern was same for both the U.S. and Western European families and is in marked contrast to the mid-20th century, when mostly married women reenter the labor market later in the life cycle. Finally, some analysis of the determinants of labor force participation and earnings of married women and children was conducted. 10 tables, 22 notes, biblio.   J

891. Higgs, Robert. RACIAL WAGE DIFFERENTIALS IN AGRICULTURE: EVIDENCE FROM NORTH CAROLINA IN 1887. *Agric. Hist. 1978 52(2): 308-311.* The first annual report of the North Carolina Bureau of Labor Statistics in 1887 contained the results of a questionnaire which gives evidence that white and black agricultural laborers were paid almost equal wages. Disputes Frenise A. Logan's conclusions drawn from the report. 8 notes.   D. E. Bowers

892. Kousser, J. Morgan; Cox, Gary W.; and Galerison, David W. LOG-LINEAR ANALYSIS OF CONTINGENCY TABLES: AN INTRODUCTION FOR HISTORIANS WITH AN APPLICATION TO THERNSTROM ON THE "FLOATING PROLETARIAT." *Hist. Methods 1982 15(4): 152-169.* Using Stephan Thernstrom's *The Other Bostonians* (1973) as a case in point, this study via a log-linear analysis reveals a richer range of conclusions than Thernstrom's findings. The floating proletariat concept is modified toward youthful mobility, suggesting patterned searches for opportunity by rational people. The result was the accumulation of physical and human capital over a lifetime. 13 tables, 41 notes.   D. K. Pickens

893. Lewis, Frank D. EXPLAINING THE SHIFT OF LABOR FROM AGRICULTURE TO INDUSTRY IN THE UNITED STATES: 1869 TO 1899. *J. of Econ. Hist. 1979 39(3): 681-698.* Focuses on the effects of productivity growth in agriculture and industry, and of increases in the supply of land (safety-valve theory). A two-sector general equilibrium model is used in the analysis. Many of the results hinge on whether the economy is assumed to be open or closed to foreign trade. In order to determine the appropriate specification, each issue is analyzed in terms of its equivalent counterfactual-conditional proposition. An important conclusion is that increases in agricultural

productivity and the level of supply of land likely reduced the proportion of workers in agriculture even though the United States economy was open. 6 tables, fig., 29 notes.   J

894. Meeker, Edward and Kau, James. RACIAL DISCRIMINATION AND OCCUPATIONAL ATTAINMENT AT THE TURN OF THE CENTURY. *Explorations in Econ. Hist. 1977 14(3): 250-276.* Presents data on the occupational distribution of workers by race and sex for 1890 and 1910. Estimates the dollar value of differences by race and sex within occupations and the extent to which these differences reflected racial discrimination. White males and females reached higher levels of occupational attainment than their black counterparts. Discusses the economics underlying occupational distribution patterns. 12 tables, 28 notes, 43 ref., 2 appendixes.   P. J. Coleman

895. Parker, William N. LABOR PRODUCTIVITY IN COTTON FARMING: THE HISTORY OF A RESEARCH. *Agric. Hist. 1979 53(1): 228-244.* Attempts to estimate labor productivity regionally in cotton farming in the postbellum South by statistical analysis, based on quantitative methods research carried on for 20 years by several people. 5 tables, 14 notes, biblio.   R. V. Ritter

896. Smith, Billy G. THE BEST POOR MAN'S COUNTRY: LIVING STANDARDS OF THE "LOWER SORT" IN LATE EIGHTEENTH-CENTURY PHILADELPHIA. *Working Papers from the Regional Econ. Hist. Res. Center 1979 2(4): 1-770.* Discusses the income, working conditions, and standard of living including food, rent, fuel, and clothing, of the working class in Philadelphia, Pennsylvania during the late 18th century.

897. Strober, Myra H. and Best, Laura. THE FEMALE/MALE SALARY DIFFERENTIAL IN PUBLIC SCHOOLS: SOME LESSONS FROM SAN FRANCISCO, 1879. *Econ. Inquiry 1979 17(2): 218-236.* Seeks to explain the differences between men's and women's salaries in San Francisco public schools, 1879.

898. Walkowitz, Daniel J. STATISTICS AND THE WRITING OF WORKINGCLASS CULTURE: A STATISTICAL PORTRAIT OF THE IRON WORKERS IN TROY, NEW YORK, 1860-1880. *Labor Hist. 1974 15(3): 416-460.* Provides a statistical profile of the iron workers of Troy, New York, as a vehicle for examining the relationship between class and culture. Census data can illuminate cultural and class configurations which shape working-class behavior, but it is necessary to integrate statistics with more traditional sources to encompass all dimensions of culture. Based on census schedules for 1860 and 1880 and secondary sources; 11 statistical tables, 66 notes.   L. L. Athey

4. LABOR IN THE NEW CENTURY, 1900 TO 1945

General

899. Drescher, Nuala McGann. THE WORKMEN'S COMPENSATION AND PENSION PROPOSAL IN THE BREWING INDUSTRY, 1910-1912: A CASE STUDY IN CONFLICTING SELF-INTEREST. *Industrial and Labor Relations Rev. 1970 24(1): 32-46.* "The United States Brewers' Association in 1910 proposed a plan for workmen's compensation and pensions for employees of the brewing industry. After negotiation over some features of the proposed plan, the leadership of the United Brewery Workers enthusiastically urged approval of the plan by union members. To the surprise of the union officials and the management of the industry, the proposal was overwhelmingly rejected by the workers. This article tells the story of the Schram plan and discusses why the industry made this proposal, unusual for its time, and the probable reasons for its rejection." J

900. Fickle, James E. MANAGEMENT LOOKS AT THE LABOR PROBLEM: THE SOUTHERN PINE INDUSTRY DURING WORLD WAR I AND THE POSTWAR ERA. *J. of Southern Hist. 1974 40(1): 61-76.* Surveys management's view of labor conditions in the southern pine industry during 1910-20's. Troubled relations between labor and management in the pine industry before World War I continued during the war. Management would not admit the validity of labor's complaints regarding hours, wages, and working conditions, and used patriotic slogans to extract more production from the pine workers during the war. By the end of the war and afterwards, the lumber company operators sought to stem the migration of Negroes out of the South, and through the creation of an employment bureau in Chicago, actually attempted to reverse the flow of workers. Despite labor conditions, management continued to talk of the "contented workers." The views of the southern lumber operators, whether realistic or not, reflect the attitudes of influential and powerful figures toward social and economic issues during this period. Based on manuscript materials and published primary and secondary sources; 54 notes.

T. D. Schoonover

901. Fink, Gary M. THE REJECTION OF VOLUNTARISM. *Industrial and Labor Relations Rev. 1973 26(2): 805-819.* "'Voluntarism' is a term used to describe the philosophy said to characterize American unionism prior to the New Deal era under which the labor movement committed itself to work within the laissez-faire capitalist economy, relying on its economic power to protect and promote the interests of workers and rejecting government aid and intervention. Examination of the actual response of unions to proposed legislation to establish workmen's compensation, unemployment insurance, and so forth reveals, however, sharp divergence in behavior at the national and local levels. While national union officials rigidly opposed such government measures to assist workers, local officers and members strongly supported them. In rejecting the philosophy of voluntarism, local labor was much closer to the immediate economic and political realities of working class America." J

902. Fishbein, Leslie. A LOST LEGACY OF LABOR FILMS. *Film and Hist. 1979 9(2): 33-40.* Films were made of the Communist-led mass marches of the unemployed, battles of eviction, milk strikes, and workers fighting against police and company thugs during the Depression by the Workers' Film and Photo League, a section of Workers' International Relief, when commercial filmmakers were avoiding controversy.

903. Galvin, Miles. THE EARLY DEVELOPMENT OF THE ORGANIZED LABOR MOVEMENT IN PUERTO RICO. *Latin Am. Perspectives 1976 3(3): 17-35.* Analyzes the role of the American Federation of Labor in the early Puerto Rican labor movement. Emphasizes the importance of both Samuel Gompers and Santiago Iglesias Pantín on the changing thrust and militancy of unions and offers an explanation for the early conservatism of early unionization. The intellectual opportunism and reformist politics of both Gompers and Iglesias—as the sole paid union organizer on the island—were extremely important in diverting the thrust of the unions away from radical positions.

J. L. Dietz

904. Herbst, John. A SLICE OF THE EARTH... THE BOTTO HOUSE, HOME OF THE AMERICAN LABOR MUSEUM IN HALEDON, NEW JERSEY. *New Jersey Hist. 1981 99(1-2): 32-48.* In 1892 Pietro and Maria Botto emigrated to America from Biella, Italy, and found jobs as workers in the textile industry in Paterson, New Jersey. They built a house in nearby Haledon 15 years later and, in addition to residing there, operated it as an inn. During the 1913 silk workers' strike in Paterson, the Botto's house served as one of the headquarters for the Industrial Workers of the World and other representatives of labor. The house has recently been turned into a museum to commemorate labor's struggle over the years. Secondary sources; 24 illus.

E. R. McKinstry

905. Jeffreys-Jones, Rhodri. MASSACHUSETTS LABOUR AND THE LEAGUE OF NATIONS CONTROVERSY IN 1919. *Irish Hist. Studies [Ireland] 1975 19(76): 396-416.* Criticizes the view that the Irish American vote was decisive in defeating Wilson's peace treaty. Taking Massachusetts as an example of Irish influence, shows that labor there generally favored the League in 1918, as likely to offer solutions to problems of high prices and high unemployment. In 1919 a militant faction pressed for rejection of any settlement which did not provide for Irish independence. Argues, however, that the eventual conversion of Massachusetts labor to opposition to the treaty rested not so much on ethnic factors as on apathy toward the League, generated by recent economic recovery, achievement of stable prices, and nearly full employment. Based on the Lodge Papers (Massachusetts Historical Society), League to Enforce Peace Papers (Harvard), and Walsh Papers (Holy Cross College); 65 notes.

P. H. Hardacre

906. Koistinen, Paul A. C. MOBILIZING THE WORLD WAR II ECONOMY: LABOR AND THE INDUSTRIAL-MILITARY ALLIANCE. *Pacific Hist. Rev. 1973 42(4): 443-478.* Examines the junior partnership role of organized labor during World War II through agencies such as the War Production Board and the War Manpower Commission. Challenges the theory that big labor became the equal of the business community or the military establishment. War production set records, but industrial unrest increased as the industrial and military complex successfully maintained the status quo. The Roosevelt administration avoided supporting changes not only because they might interfere with the overseas war effort, but also because the administration was committed to preserving the corporate capitalist system. Labor was no match for its opponents. 66 notes.

C. W. Olson

907. Lanza, Aldo. TEATRO OPERAIO E "LABOR CHAUTAUQUAS" AL BROOKWOOD LABOR COLLEGE [Workers' theater and "Labor Chautauquas" at Brookwood Labor College]. *Movimento Operaio e Socialista [Italy] 1980 3(2-3): 199-220.* Brookwood Labor College, 40 miles north of New York City, was the first training school for union organizers. Its founders believed that labor unions should be more than instruments in an economic struggle and that its leaders should lay more stress on social thinking than on business psychology. In its curriculum was a course on Labor Dramatics to "quicken the spirit which animates tha labor movement." But lacking a basis of theoretical analysis and a political strategy the course did not contribute much to the task of transformation as distinguished from a stance of opposition to the status quo. In this sense the school shared in the failure of the Socialist Party and other third parties in the United States. 32 notes.

J. V. Countinho

908. Marquart, Frank. FROM A LABOR JOURNAL: UNIONS & RADICALS IN THE DEPRESSION YEARS. *Dissent 1974 21(3): 421-430.* Discusses the development of labor organizations in Detroit during the 1920's-30's. S

909. Neufeld, Maurice F., ed. PORTRAIT OF THE LABOR HISTORIAN AS BOY AND YOUNG MAN. *Labor Hist. 1978 19(1): 39-71.* Excerpts from the interviews of Philip Taft (1902-76) by Margot Honig, tape-recorded in 1975-76 and deposited at the Oral History Research Office, Columbia University. The excerpts emphasize Taft's early years, 1902-28.

L. L. Athey

910. Palmer, Bryan. CLASS, CONCEPTION AND CONFLICT: THE THRUST FOR EFFICIENCY, MANAGERIAL VIEWS OF LABOR AND THE WORKING CLASS REBELLION, 1903-1922. *Rev. of Radical Pol. Econ. 1975 7(2): 31-49.* Considers managerial efforts to implement scientific management techniques, and to maximize efficiency at the expense of the workers, and the workers' response, such as the Illinois Central and Harriman lines Railroad Carmen's Strike (1911-15).

911. Rivers, Larry E. THE PITTSBURGH WORKSHOP FOR THE BLIND, 1910-1939: A CASE STUDY OF THE BLINDED SYSTEM IN AMERICA. *Western Pennsylvania Hist. Mag. 1978 61(2): 135-150.* Surveys historical attitudes toward blind persons during the 19th century, the movement toward education of the blind, and a specific case, the Pittsburgh Workshop for the Blind in western Pennsylvania which sought, 1910-39, to provide employment for the blind.

912. Rosenzweig, Roy. RADICALS AND THE JOBLESS: THE MUSTEITES AND THE UNEMPLOYED LEAGUES, 1932-1936. *Labor Hist. 1975 16(1): 52-77.* The Unemployed Leagues (UL), formed under the direction of Abraham J. Muste, illustrate the dilemmas faced by radicals in efforts to build mass organizations of the jobless. Initial growth of the UL was fostered by the emphasis upon meeting local needs for jobs, relief, etc. When the radical leaders shifted to revolutionary tactics, the leagues split along ideological lines because the rank and file were not prepared for revolution. Besides organizational problems, the leagues demonstrate some limited successes of the radical movement in the 1930's. Based on papers and publications of the UL and Musteites, and on interviews; 45 notes. L. L. Athey

913. Seretan, L. Glen. THE "NEW" WORKING CLASS AND SOCIAL BANDITRY IN DEPRESSION AMERICA. *Mid-America 1981 63(2): 107-117.* The US working class did not suffer the depression without engaging in criminal activity. Admiration for and cooperation with bank robbers, kidnappers, and shooters of public officials, encouraged by the mass media, was a form of striking at an oppressive society. The phenomenon withered with New Deal era reforms of federal police operations, and with the attack on those social problems that had led to identification with Robin Hood-like criminals. %HD 21 notes. P. J. Woehrmann

914. Sternsher, Bernard. GREAT DEPRESSION LABOR HISTORIOGRAPHY IN THE 1970S: MIDDLE-RANGE QUESTIONS, ETHNOCULTURES, AND LEVELS OF GENERALIZATION. *Rev. in Am. Hist. 1983 11(2): 300-319.* Trends in Great Depression labor historiography since the 1970's include closer examination of the relationship between labor activism and ethnicity and greater emphasis on the "history from the bottom up" perspective of the new social historians.

915. Throckmorton, H. Bruce. A NOTE ON LABOR BANKS. *Labor Hist. 1979 20(4): 573-575.* Discusses the existence of labor banks in the 1920's. Most failed or merged in the 1930's. Presents a table of labor banks, 1920-31. 8 notes. L. L. Athey

916. Tselos, George. SELF-HELP AND SAUERKRAUT: THE ORGANIZED UNEMPLOYED, INC., OF MINNEAPOLIS. *Minnesota Hist. 1977 45(8): 306-320.* The Reverend George H. Mecklenburg founded the Organized Unemployed, Inc. in 1932. In this organization, individuals, through self-help, could lift themselves out of economic adversity. Headquartered in an old girls' high school in Minneapolis, the organization harvested, processed, and canned produce, operated a cafeteria and stores, cut wood for fuel, made clothing, and provided housing and employment services. It lasted until 1935 when superseded by government efforts. Scrip money was used as a medium of exchange, awarded in return for services to the organization. The organization's slogan, "Work Not Dole," indicated that its efforts represented a backward attempt to alleviate poverty through private endeavors rather than through organizing the poor to exert pressure on the government to provide jobs and sustenance. Primary sources. N. Lederer

917. Weber, Devra. ORAL SOURCES AND THE HISTORY OF MEXICAN WORKERS IN THE UNITED STATES. *Int. Labor and Working Class Hist. 1983 (23): 47-50.* The paucity of written records on Mexican-American laborers and labor relations during the 1920's-30's requires that scholars use oral history approaches to the subject.

918. Weir, Stan. AMERICAN LABOR ON THE DEFENSIVE: A 1940'S ODYSSEY. *Radical Am. 1975 9(4-5): 163-186.* A personal narrative illustrating the elimination of working-class power in industrial labor unions before, during, and after World War II. S

The Worker

919. Aldrich, Mark. DETERMINANTS OF MORTALITY AMONG NEW ENGLAND COTTON MILL WORKERS DURING THE PROGRESSIVE ERA. *J. of Econ. Hist. 1982 42(4): 847-863.* Multiple regression analysis reveals that work in New England cotton textile mills during 1905-12 raised age-adjusted mortality rates over those of non-millworkers, and that worker mortality increased with years of mill experience. Mortality varied among groups because of differential self selection. Central age group native males with broad occupational choices had lower mortality rates than control groups. Young males, women, and the foreign born had restricted occupational choices. Hence they were less self selected and experienced higher mortality. Death rates were highest among married women workers who bore children. The combination of homework and millwork worsened their health and raised their mortality rates. J

920. Alexander, Mary and Childress, Marilyn, ed. THREE PHOTOGRAPHS OF CHILDREN AT WORK, CIRCA 1908. *Social Educ. 1982 46(2): 106-109.* Presents three photographs of children working in factories around 1908 as a topic for discussion in high school classes about child labor conditions and contemporary labor reform efforts.

921. Altenbaugh, Richard J. and Paulston, Rolland G. WORK PEOPLE'S COLLEGE: A FINNISH FOLK HIGH SCHOOL IN THE AMERICAN LABOR COLLEGE MOVEMENT. *Paedagogica Hist. [Belgium] 1978 18(2): 237-256.* The folk education traditions and the radical orientation of many Finnish immigrants in 1903 precipitated Work People's College, a forerunner of the American Labor College Movement. That the school (first in Minneapolis and later in Duluth, Minnesota) reached its apex when the American workers' education movement was just beginning and continued producing leaders and activists longer than its counterparts attests to its significance and vitality. Attacks on the school's ideology demonstrate that nonformal education which opposes prevailing social groups will not be tolerated in the United States. Based on newspaper and magazine articles, college publications, and secondary sources; 90 notes. J. M. McCarthy

922. Aurand, Harold W. SELF-EMPLOYMENT: LAST RESORT FOR THE UNEMPLOYED. *Int. Social Sci. Rev. 1983 58(1): 7-11.* Upward mobility is attributed to a conscious effort at self-improvement. But not all movement between socioeconomic strata can be explained by the internalization of the success ethos. In desperate times the will to survive propels wage earners into the ranks of the self-employed. Such mobility reflects a passive "I'll get by" attitude rather than the dynamic "I'll get ahead" mentality associated with the American doctrine of success. Covers efforts to establish independent coal mines in Pennsylvania during 1920-44. J/S

923. Babow, Irving. DOING TIME AT THE PALACE. *Western States Jewish Hist. Q. 1981 13(4): 351-360.* The author worked with his parents at the Palace Hotel in San Francisco in the late 1920's. His father had a job as baggage room attendant; but the operation of this service seven days a week required the help of all family members. The glamour and celebrity of the Palace did not make up for the low wages and poor working conditions, and the family found another occupation after three years of "urban peonage." B. S. Porter

924. Bauman, John F. ETHNIC ADAPTATION IN A SOUTHWESTERN PENNSYLVANIA COAL PATCH, 1910-1940. *J. of Ethnic Studies 1979 7(3): 1-23.* Focuses on the mining community of Daisytown, Pennsylvania, and the mobility patterns of the eastern and southern Europeans who immigrated to that area and attained social and economic stability in spite of strikes, evictions, and mine town living.

925. Beeten, Neil. POLISH AMERICAN STEELWORKERS: AMERICANIZATION THROUGH INDUSTRY AND LABOR. *Polish Am. Studies 1976 33(2): 31-42.* The United States Steel Corporation in Gary, Indiana, manipulated immigrant workers under the guise of Americanization. In a final analysis, both immigrants and the employers profited from the corporation programs. Unplanned and unnoticed during the process, however, was a steady exposure of the immigrant workers to the merits of unionization, the potential benefits of organized strikes, and the necessary techniques of survival in a hard economic world. Covers ca. 1906-20. Based primarily on English newspaper accounts; 21 notes.   S. R. Pliska

926. Blackwelder, Julia Kirk. WOMEN IN THE WORK FORCE: ATLANTA, NEW ORLEANS, AND SAN ANTONIO, 1930 TO 1940. *J. of Urban Hist. 1978 4(3): 331-358.* By studying women in three ethnically distinct communities (Atlanta—white, New Orleans—black, and San Antonio—Hispanic), compares the work experiences and motivations of different cultural groups of women. Matriarchy does not appear to be the main explanation for black women entering the labor force, and was actually higher among the supposedly close-knit Hispanics. 12 tables, 20 notes.   T. W. Smith

927. Blatt, Martin. FROM BENCH LABORER TO MANUFACTURER: THE RISE OF JEWISH OWNERS IN THE DECLINING SHOE INDUSTRY IN LYNN. *Essex Inst. Hist. Collections 1979 115(4): 256-269.* In the early 20th century, many Jewish immigrants from Poland and Russia settled in Lynn to work in the shoe factories. Oral interviews with seven immigrants involved in the shoe industry present a composite picture of the characteristics of Jewish manufacturers in Lynn, Massachusetts. Traces the course by which these enterprising shoe workers, in particular, Cecil Weinstein (b. 1913), became factory owners. Based on oral interviews; 35 notes.   R. S. Sliwoski

928. Bodnar, John E. THE PROCUREMENT OF IMMIGRANT LABOR: SELECTED DOCUMENTS. *Pennsylvania Hist. 1974 41(2): 189-206.* Presents 23 letters during 1915-23 dealing with the Robesonia Iron Company's efforts to recruit immigrant and black laborers. The greatest efforts were made to obtain Italian and Slavic laborers, and company officials corresponded with a Russian lawyer in Philadelphia that specialized in the recruitment of foreign laborers. Efforts to recruit Negroes were made through a labor agent in Tennessee. The Robesonia Iron Company was located near Reading and operated a quarry, furnace, and mines. The company correspondence is part of the Colemen Collection held by the Pennsylvania Historical and Museum Commission; 9 notes.   D. C. Swift

929. Bolin, Winifred D. Wandersee. THE ECONOMICS OF MIDDLE-INCOME FAMILY LIFE: WORKING WOMEN DURING THE GREAT DEPRESSION. *J. of Am. Hist. 1978 65(1): 60-74.* Despite the traditionally conservative attitude among whites regarding working wives, the depression decade witnessed an increase in both the number and the proportion of married women in the labor force. With many families this was necessary just for survival. But with middle-income families, those earning at least $1,000 a year, this increase is attributable not to absolute economic need, but to a change in values. Wives from middle-income families entered the labor force not to procure necessities like food and clothing for their families, but to purchase items such as refrigeration, modern plumbing, and lighting. They worked to enable their families to pursue a higher standard of living, a value acquired during the late 1920's. 5 tables, 21 notes.   T. P. Linkfield

930. Brandes, Joseph. FROM SWEATSHOP TO STABILITY: JEWISH LABOR BETWEEN TWO WORLD WARS. *Yivo Ann. of Jewish Social Sci. 1976 (16): 1-149.* Traces the growth of the Jewish labor movement from its inception, with particular emphasis on the period between World War I and World War II. Stresses the uniqueness of the Jewish labor movement and puts particular emphasis on the growth of the Jewish labor movement within the garment industry. Describes the roles of such notable labor leaders as David Dubinsky and Sidney Hillquit. Particular stress is put on the International Ladies' Garment Workers' and the United Hebrew Trades' role in the development of Jewish labor in the 1920's-30's.   R. J. Wechman

931. Brodski, R. M. RUSSKIE IMMIGRANTY NA GAVAIIAKH [Russian immigrants in Hawaii]. *Novaia i Noveishaia Istoriia [USSR] 1981 (3): 172-177.* Relates the story of about 10,000 Russian laborers recruited in 1909 to work on the rice, cotton, and sugar plantations in Hawaii in place of the Japanese labor force, which had gone on strike. The Russians were recruited largely under false pretenses, and the experiment collapsed. By 1947 few families survived. Primary sources from Moscow archives; 29 notes.   J. P. H. Myers

932. Buhle, Paul. ITALIAN-AMERICAN RADICALS AND LABOR IN RHODE ISLAND, 1905-1930. *Radical Hist. Rev. 1978 (17): 121-151.*

933. Burns, Anna C. THE GULF LUMBER COMPANY, FULLERTON: A VIEW OF LUMBERING DURING LOUISIANA'S GOLDEN ERA. *Louisiana Hist. 1979 20(2): 197-207.* Samuel Holmes Fullerton (1852-1939), an Irish immigrant and entrepreneur, developed the Gulf Lumber Co. on some 106,000 acres of exceptionally productive virgin timberland near Leesville, Louisiana. The company town of Fullerton grew to a population of about 5,000 during the huge mill's peak years, 1917-22. As in other mill towns, the company owned everything; unlike the others, however, Gulf Lumber demonstrated keen interest in its employees' welfare—offering numerous fringe benefits and fair prices at the company store. Once the timber was harvested, the town disappeared and the land was sold. Partially based on contemporary newspapers and journals; 51 notes.   D. B. Touchstone

934. Butler, Joseph T., Jr. PRISONER OF WAR LABOR IN THE SUGAR CANE FIELDS OF LAFOURCHE PARISH, LOUISIANA, 1943-44. *Louisiana Hist. 1973 14(3): 283-296.* Discusses the use of German prisoners of war to farm sugar cane fields in 1943-44.

935. Calvi, Giulia. LO SPAZIO DEL PADRONE E IL TEMPO DELL'OPERAIO: ALCUNE IPOTESI DI LAVORO SULL'AMERICA DEL PRIMO NOVECENTO [The boss's space and the worker's time: some working hypotheses on early 20th century America]. *Movimento Operaio e Socialista [Italy] 1980 3(1): 81-90.* Compares the massive reorganization of production and management, especially in the industrial centers of the east coast of the United States, during World War I, and the cultural context and behavior as a class of the agricultural proletariat of the western states, roughly during the same period. The author attributes the difference in the organizational forms of the workers' resistance to the presence in one area and absence in the other of a significant element: the factory. The author also discusses neutralization of workers' resistance. Covers 1913-18. Based on government reports and unpublished records in the National Archives; 21 notes.   J. V. Coutinho

936. Casillas, Mike. MEXICAN LABOR MILITANCY IN THE U.S.: 1896-1915. *Southwest Econ. and Soc. 1978 4(1): 31-42.* Mexican Americans' militancy in the Southwestern states resulted from desire for economic parity and from perceived social, cultural, and ethnic prejudice.

937. Ciro, Sepulveda. UNA COLONIA DE OBREROS: EAST CHICAGO, INDIANA. *Aztlán 1976 7(2): 327-336.* A history of the colonia in the Indiana Harbor district of East Chicago, from the first large-scale arrival of Mexicanos (as strikebreakers) in 1919 to the mass deportations of 1932. During the 1920's, Inland Steel Co. of Indiana Harbor was the largest single employer of Mexicanos in the United States, and the colonia grew up on Block and Pennsylvania Avenues near the Inland Steel plant. Living conditions here were extremely bad, while working conditions were hazardous and a worker in the blast furnaces averaged approximately 60 hours/week. Rivalry for the best jobs caused some friction within the colonia, but relations with non-Mexicano neighbors were generally good. Primary (mainly press) and secondary sources; map, 41 notes.   L. W. Van Wyk

938. Cox, J. Robert. "THE RHETORIC OF CHILD LABOR REFORM: AN EFFICACY-UTILITY ANALYSIS." *Q. J. of Speech 1974 60(3): 359-370.* "Two variables influenced the rhetorical choices of Progressive leaders in their fight against harsh working conditions of children: the ability of auditors to affect the aggrieved conditions (efficacy); and the valuation associated with the object of protest (utility). Success in achieving the movement's goal depended upon the

adaptation of desirable objectives to groups that possessed the necessary power to induce change."   J

939. Crouse, Joan M. PRECEDENTS FROM THE PAST: THE EVOLUTION OF LAWS AND ATTITUDES PERTINENT TO THE "WELCOME" ACCORDED TO THE INDIGENT TRANSIENT DURING THE GREAT DEPRESSION. Plesur, Milton, ed. *An American Historian: Essays to Honor Selig Adler* (Buffalo: State U. of N.Y., 1980): 191-203. History of the negative attitudes toward the transient poor in the United States during the Depression, derived from attitudes toward the wandering poor of medieval England, particularly the Statute of Labourers of the 14th century (in effect, a vagrancy law) and the Elizabethan Poor Law of 1572.

940. Cumbler, John T. THREE GENERATIONS OF POVERTY: A NOTE ON THE LIFE OF AN UNSKILLED WORKER'S FAMILY. *Labor Hist.* 1974 15(1): 78-85. Reviews the need for more information and new methods of approach to the study of the life of the everyday laborer. The remnants of a case history of a family in Lynn from 1915-40 are published as an example of the types of material needed to understand poverty. Based on a case history from the files of the Associated Charities of Lynn, Massachusetts. 4 notes.   L. L. Athey

941. Deutsch, James L. THE RISE AND FALL OF THE HOUSES OF USHERS: TEENAGE TICKET-TAKERS IN THE TWENTIES THEATERS. *J. of Popular Culture* 1980 13(4): 602-608. Platoons of magnificently garbed ushers served the public in movie theaters after World War I. Competition for these positions was keen among lower and middle class adolescents of the time. Once they were within the ranks, their behavior had to be above reproach. The Great Depression decimated them. 39 notes.   D. G. Nielson

942. Ellis, William E. LABOR-MANAGEMENT RELATIONS IN THE PROGRESSIVE ERA: A PROFIT SHARING EXPERIENCE IN LOUISVILLE. *Register of the Kentucky Hist. Soc.* 1980 78(2): 140-156. An account of the early profit sharing experience of the Louisville Varnish Company, headed by Patrick Henry Callahan. Callahan, a paternalist, viewed his plan as a viable alternative to labor-management conflict. The plan worked well during prosperity, but not during the Great Depression. Prosperity (and profit sharing) returned for the company in 1936, but with Callahan's death in 1940, no one in the company was as committed to the plan. Covers 1908-40. Based on personal manuscript collections and other sources; 2 illus., 32 notes.   J. F. Paul

943. Esval, Orland E. MEMBER OF THE CREW. *Montana* 1977 27(4): 64-71. Reminiscences of experiences in 1921 as a 16 year old "bundle hauler" on a threshing crew near Peerless, Daniels County, Montana. Long days and exhausting work provided a proving ground where a boy became a man if he was equal to demands of the job. After suffering through the rigors of the first week, he became an accepted member of the crew and worked continually through the harvest season. Primary sources; 4 illus.   R. C. Myers

944. Finger, Bill. TEXTILE MEN: LOOMS, LOANS AND LOCK-OUTS. *Southern Exposure* 1976 3(4): 54-65. Presents biographies of southern textile industry figures, 1918-40: J. Spencer Love, a mill owner, Lacy Wright, a mill hand, and Joe Pedigo, a labor organizer.

945. Franke, Richard Herbert and Kaul, James D. THE HAWTHORNE EXPERIMENTS: FIRST STATISTICAL INTERPRETATIONS. *Am. Sociol. Rev.* 1978 43(5): 623-643. A guide is provided to the proceedings of the Hawthorne experiments, and experimental data are now made readily available. Data from the main experiment (that in the first relay assembly test room at Western Electric [Company in Chicago, Illinois, 1924-33, concerning illumination levels]) are interpreted statistically for the first time. Quantitative analysis of this quasi experiment is accomplished by time-series multiple regression using nearly five years of data. This analysis demonstrates that experimental variables account for some 90% of the variance in quantity and quality of output, both for the group and for individual workers. Imposition of managerial discipline, economic adversity, and quality of raw materials provide most explanation, obviating the need to draw upon less clearly definable human relations mechanisms. For decades the Hawthorne studies have provided a rationale for humane approaches in the

organization of work by suggesting that considerate or participative treatment of workers led to better economic performance. The present analysis suggests, to the contrary, that humanitarian procedures must provide their own justification.   J

946. Fraundorf, Martha Norby. THE LABOR FORCE PARTICIPATION OF TURN-OF-THE-CENTURY MARRIED WOMEN. *J. of Econ. Hist.* 1979 39(2): 401-418. The standard modern model of married women's labor force participation is modified because turn-of-the-century families had the alternatives of substituting children for the mother in the labor force and of taking in paying boarders. The modified model explained 1901 participation rates quite well. Participation rates were significantly related (negatively) to the number of older children (potential workers) but not to the number of young children. In addition, the availability of jobs was more important than high wages in inducing women to seek work. Other family income, the male unemployment rate, and literacy also were significant.   J

947. Frederickson, Mary. THE SOUTHERN SUMMER SCHOOL FOR WOMEN WORKERS. *Southern Exposure* 1977 4(4): 70-75. From 1927 until World War II a group of middle class southern white women, led by Louise McLaren and Lois MacDonald, drew support from the Young Women's Christian Association and other agencies to run regular summer schools for southern white working women. These schools, held in Virginia and North Carolina, were designed to provide women with analytical tools necessary to understand their situation, to provide means of interrelationships between working women and to develop labor organizing skills for the southern labor movement. Participants acknowledged that their role in the school had a significant impact on their lives and thinking. Primary sources.   N. Lederer

948. Garraty, John A. UNEMPLOYMENT DURING THE GREAT DEPRESSION. *Labor Hist.* 1976 17(2): 133-159. Comparing the impact of unemployment in western Europe and the United States, the effects were almost identical. Interests of workers and the unemployed were separated, political pressure on governments to solve unemployment increased, and the psychological impact of prolonged joblessness resulted in apathy and despair rather than revolutionary action. Based on published sources and governmental reports; 40 notes.
                                                           L. L. Athey

949. Gersuny, Carl. WORK INJURIES AND ADVERSARY PROCESSES IN TWO NEW ENGLAND TEXTILE MILLS. *Business Hist. Rev.* 1977 51): 326-340. Describes work injuries in New England mills during 1895-1916 and "the patterns of imputing contributory negligence." Concludes that after the no-fault workmen's compensation law went into effect, the number of injuries changed little but there was a sharp reduction in injuries blamed on employee carelessness. Negligence charges before the law's enactment were often economic expediency for the mill owner. Based on company records; 38 notes.
                                                           C. J. Pusateri

950. Gibson, Arrell Morgan. POOR MAN'S CAMP: LABOR MOVEMENT VICISSITUDES IN THE TRI-STATE DISTRICT. *Chronicles of Oklahoma* 1982 60(1): 4-21. The Tri-State District, which includes Ottawa County, Oklahoma, Jasper and Newton counties in Missouri, and part of Cherokee County, Kansas, continually resisted unionization throughout the first half of the 20th century, despite its economic dependence on mining. The main reason for lack of interest in unions rests with the wide range of opportunities for the miners. Most operations were small and subject to considerable control by the workers. Furthermore, agricultural jobs beckoned those who became dissatisfied with poor working conditions. Although strikes did occur, they were generally aimed at specific grievances and did not become widespread. Only the management-recognized Tri-State Union maintained any power, and it was used to keep the American Federation of Labor from organizing workers. Based on *Engineering and Mining Journal* and newspapers; 4 photos, 41 notes.   M. L. Tate

951. Gluck, Sherna Berger. INTERLUDE OR CHANGE: WOMEN AND THE WORLD WAR II WORK EXPERIENCE: A FEMINIST ORAL HISTORY. *Int. J. of Oral Hist.* 1982 3(2): 92-113. As a consequence of their wartime work experience, their work force status, family status, and age, some 43 women who worked in the aircraft industry during World War II in Los Angeles, California, experienced

only pleasure from participating in wartime work settings while others gained a sense of control over their lives, a feeling of accomplishment, and a sense of self-confidence.

952. Gottlieb, Peter. MIGRATION AND JOBS: THE NEW BLACK WORKERS IN PITTSBURGH, 1916-1930. *Western Pennsylvania Hist. Mag.* 1978 61(1): 1-16. Discusses the internal migration of 1.5 million job-seeking Negroes from the South to the Pittsburgh iron and steel mills during 1916-30; assesses job mobility, wage increases, and educational possibilities juxtaposed to preference for rural lifestyles.

953. Hallagan, William S. LABOR CONTRACTING IN TURN-OF-THE-CENTURY CALIFORNIA AGRICULTURE. *J. of Econ. Hist.* 1980 40(4): 757-776. This paper examines in detail a case in which vertical relations between buyers and suppliers of labor services changed over a short span of time. The case in point involves the provision of harvest labor to California orchards where contractural arrangements changed over a five-year interval from wage contracting to leasing. The results of this study suggest that tenancy represents an institutional response to the risks and costs associated with worker opportunism experienced under wage contracting during times of economic prosperity and labor shortages.   J

954. Hareven, Tamara K. FAMILY TIME AND INDUSTRIAL TIME: FAMILY AND WORK IN A PLANNED CORPORATION TOWN 1900-1924. *J. of Urban Hist.* 1975 1(3): 365-389. Cumulative individual employee files 1910-36 of the Amoskeag Manufacturing Company of Manchester, New Hampshire, coupled with marriage and insurance records and oral histories, reveal a pervasive family influence in working. Vacancies were discovered via word-of-mouth, family members substituted for each other, family finances postponed marriages and caused babies to be dropped off so women could return to work. Young children found summer jobs in the mills, and many met their future spouses there. 45 notes.   S. S. Sprague

955. Higgs, Robert. THE WEALTH OF JAPANESE TENANT FARMERS IN CALIFORNIA IN 1909. *Agric. Hist.* 1979 53(2): 488-494. The first significant number of Japanese began arriving in the US mainland around 1890. They first took jobs as laborers on the railroads and in mining camps. At the turn of the century a number of them turned to agriculture for a vocation. By 1909 approximately 30,000 Japanese were working in California fields. Many eventually became land owners, and although there were some failures, most of them succeeded. 2 tables, 6 notes.   C. L. Harvey

956. Hofsommer, Donovan L. WORKING ON THE (BRANCH LINE) RAILROAD. *Railroad Hist.* 1977 (137): 80-93. Examines the employees who worked the branch lines of the Missouri-Kansas-Texas Railroad's Northwestern District in Texas and Oklahoma, 1906-75.

957. Ichioka, Yuji. JAPANESE IMMIGRANT LABOR CONTRACTORS AND THE NORTHERN PACIFIC AND THE GREAT NORTHERN RAILROAD COMPANIES, 1898-1907. *Labor Hist.* 1980 21(3): 325-350. Discusses the role of two labor contractors in providing immigrant Japanese laborers for the Northern Pacific and the Great Northern railroad companies in the Pacific Northwest during the late 19th and early 20th centuries. The labor contractors profited at the expense of these laborers, taking a percentage of each one's wages. The principal beneficiaries were the railroads, who reduced labor costs by employing the Japanese section hands at a low wage rate. The system declined sharply after 1907, when President Theodore Roosevelt stopped the migration of Japanese laborers from Hawaii, and Japan agreed to curtail emigration. Based on Northern Pacific Railroad Company records and other primary sources; 35 notes.   L. F. Velicer

958. Isserman, Maurice. INHERITANCE LOST: SOCIALISM IN ROCHESTER, 1917-1919. *Rochester Hist.* 1977 39(4): 1-24. Details the socialist movement among laborers in Rochester, New York, 1917-19.

959. Katsanevas, Michael, Jr. THE EMERGING SOCIAL WORKER AND THE DISTRIBUTION OF THE CASTLE GATE RELIEF FUND. *Utah Hist. Q.* 1982 50(3): 241-254. Following the Number 2 Mine at Castle Gate explosion of 8 March 1924, Governor Charles R. Mabey began a monetary relief program. The Utah Fuel Company, the mine operators, offered assistance to all families. Mrs. Annie Palmer, experienced in Red Cross relief activities, was hired to direct and establish relief systems and performed a major role in social work before trained professionals were available. 5 photos, 43 notes.

     K. E. Gilmont

960. Keuchel, Edward F. THE POLISH AMERICAN MIGRANT WORKER: THE NEW YORK CANNING INDUSTRY 1900-1935. *Polish Am. Studies* 1976 33(2): 43-51. In New York state the early canning industry was primarily rural. By 1900, when local sources could no longer meet the expanding labor demands, migrant workers, including many Polish Americans, were introduced. An investigation by the New York State Factory Investigating Commission in 1912 described jobs, wages, and living conditions. Polish Americans continued in canning through World War II, but by then in the canneries; blacks and Puerto Ricans succeeded them in the field. Based chiefly on the 1912 report and on other secondary sources, all in English; 21 notes.
     S. R. Pliska

961. Korrol, Virginia Sánchez. ON THE OTHER SIDE OF THE OCEAN: THE WORK EXPERIENCES OF EARLY PUERTO RICAN MIGRANT WOMEN. *Caribbean Rev.* 1979 8(1): 22-28. Examines the employment history of Puerto Rican women in New York from the 1920's to the 1940's and finds that piece work, child care, the taking-in of lodgers and employment in the garment, tobacco, and candy-making industries were the chief areas of employment for the vast majority of both married and unmarried working women of Puerto Rican origin.

962. Kostiainen, Auvo. WORK PEOPLE'S COLLEGE: AN AMERICAN IMMIGRANT INSTITUTION. *Scandinavian J. of Hist. [Sweden]* 1980 5(4): 295-309. The Finns, part of the later wave of immigrants to the United States, have proved more active in the American labor movement than most other ethnic groups. One of the key developments in the Finnish American community was the Work People's College at Smithville, Minnesota, during the 1900's; the college's links with socialism resulted in a radical and educational role, although it also facilitated the adjustment of recent immigrants to American society. Based partly on the Work People's College collection at the University of Minnesota; 48 notes.   P. J. Beck

963. LaGumina, Salvatore J. REFLECTIONS OF AN ITALIAN-AMERICAN WORKER. *J. of Ethnic Studies* 1975 3(2): 65-77. Presents excerpts from the writings of Saverio Rizzo, an 87-year-old Italian American worker who settled in the United States in 1903. Deals with the padrone system of labor recruitment, unionization, and the Triangle Waist Company fire of 1911. Based on primary and secondary sources; 7 notes.   T. W. Smith

964. Leonard, Olen E. and Cleland, Courtney B. OCCUPATIONAL CHANGES IN NORTH CENTRAL NEW MEXICO: A RESPONSE TO SOCIAL AND ECONOMIC ALTERATIONS IN A TRADITIONAL AGRICULTURE AREA. *Social Sci. J.* 1976 13(2): 95-102. Observes the increased trend among young farm workers in a sample of North Central New Mexican rural and agricultural villages towards migration or commuting to the cities in an effort to improve social and economic lifestyle, ca. 1930-50.

965. Luodesmeri, Varpu. AMERIKANSUOMALAISTEN TYÖVÄENJÄRJESTÖJEN SUHTAUTUMINEN SUOMESTA VUODEN 1918 SODAN JÄLKEEN TULLEISIIN SIIRTOLAISIIN: "HILJAN SUOMESTA TULLEITTEN TUTKIJAKOMITEAT" [The attitudes of the Finnish American workers' movement toward immigrants coming from Finland after the 1918 war: the "Committees of examination of recent arrivals from Finland"]. *Turun Hist. Arkisto [Finland]* 1974 29: 63-113. Describes radical labor organizations of Finnish immigrants in the United States and Canada. Recent immigrants were screened to determine their roles in the 1918 Finnish civil war before that person was allowed to join the local organization. At least 68 local committees were established, ceasing in the United States after 1924, but continuing longer in Canada. Based on newspapers, manuscripts and interviews collected at Turku University, Finland; map, 195 notes, English summary.   R. G. Selleck

966. Mannard, Joseph G. BLACK COMPANY TOWN: A PECU-LIAR INSTITUTION IN PIERCE, FLORIDA. *Tampa Bay Hist. 1979 1(1): 61-66.* Reprints an essay written in 1938 by Paul Diggs under the auspices of the Federal Writers' Project which described daily life, social organization, and employment in Pierce, Florida, an all-black company town operated by the American Agricultural Chemical Community.

967. Marshall, James R. and Dowdall, George W. EMPLOYMENT AND MENTAL HOSPITALIZATION: THE CASE OF BUFFALO, NEW YORK, 1914-55. *Social Forces 1982 60(3): 843-853.* Explores the connection between employment trends and state mental hospital admissions, using employment data for the Buffalo area and admissions to the only major public psychiatric hospital in the area during 1914-55. Employment is positively related to admissions. Hospital capacity is also important in predicting admissions.   J/S

968. Matthies, Susan A. FAMILIES AT WORK: AN ANALYSIS BY SEX OF CHILD WORKERS IN THE COTTON TEXTILE INDUS-TRY. *J. of Econ. Hist. 1982 42(1). 173-180.* Differences in the school and work experience of young girls and boys are explained by factors related to the demand for household production including the presence of young children, boarders and lodgers, and home ownership. Gender-based differences in job characteristics and hourly earnings associated with occupational segregation contributed to the observed pattern of higher schooling investment by girls and earlier work experience by boys.   J

969. May, Martha. THE HISTORICAL PROBLEM OF THE FAMI-LY WAGE: THE FORD MOTOR COMPANY AND THE FIVE DOLLAR DAY. *Feminist Studies 1982 8(2): 399-424.* Examination of a specific case of the institution of the family wage challenges previous interpretations. Neither nasty patriarchal attitudes desiring female subordination, nor working-class adaptation of the ideology of domestic-ity explains the five dollar day at Ford. The auto company used this wage rate, double the going rate, to combat high turnover, to forestall unionization and an imminent strike, and to reflect production changes. A more complex mediation between the productive and reproductive aspects of labor is suggested than has been previously offered. 73 notes.   S. Hildenbrand

970. McLoughlin, William G. BILLY SUNDAY AND THE WORK-ING GIRL OF 1915. *J. of Presbyterian Hist. 1976 54(3): 376-384.* Introduces and contains a letter which a Philadelphia working girl wrote to her mother about hearing a sermon which Billy Sunday preached to a "women only" service in 1915. Sunday was not a feminist. It is questionable whether he sympathized with the suffrage movement. He viewed the working girl as a target for unscrupulous young men, and his sermon warned and cautioned them about the temptations they faced on the one hand, and encouraged them to maintain their virtue on the other. According to Sunday, woman's place was in the home. Although the sermon was addressed to a metropolitan women's group, he was merely reaffirming the old rural evangelical beliefs and values of American life. 4 notes.   H. M. Parker, Jr.

971. Mercier, Laurie. "I WORKED FOR THE RAILROAD": ORAL HISTORIES OF MONTANA RAILROADERS, 1910-1950. *Montana 1983 33(3): 34-59.* Publishes interviews discussing all aspects of railroad operations in Montana. Rail lines mentioned include the Northern Pacific; Great Northern; Chicago, Milwaukee and St. Paul; Butte, Anaconda and Pacific; and various branch lines. Based on taped interviews in the Montanans at Work Oral History Project, Montana Historical Society; 15 illus., 58 notes.   R. C. Myers

972. Meyer, Stephen. ADAPTING THE IMMIGRANT TO THE LINE: AMERICANIZING IN THE FORD FACTORY, 1914-1921. *J. of Social Hist. 1980 14(1): 67-82.* The Ford Motor Company's Americanization Program, carried on by the Ford Sociological Depart-ment and the Ford English School, was a paternalistic effort to insure that the workers were worthy of remaining Ford employees and receiving the benefits of the Ford Profit Sharing Plan and the Five Dollar Day initiated in 1914. The company sought to train diligent, clean, and thrifty workers. By 1920 the company's high profits had been undercut by changes in the industry and the Americanization programs were dropped, as was the financial incentive of offering the inflated

equivalent of the 1914 five dollar a day wage. 38 notes.
C. M. Hough

973. Miller, Robert K., Jr. INITIAL POSTMIGRATION EMPLOY-MENT AMONG EUROPEAN IMMIGRANTS: 1900-1935. *Int. Mi-gration Rev. 1981 15(3): 529-542.* Examination of European immigrant workers in Philadelphia who entered skilled and semiskilled manual manufacturing occupations, focusing on the cultural determinants of their work choices; evidence is lacking to support the theory that the difficulties in gaining employment among native migrants, nonmigrants, and immigrants were related to cultural heritage.

974. Nordstrom, Byron J. EVELINA MÅNSSON AND THE MEM-OIR OF AN URBAN LABOR MIGRANT. *Swedish Pioneer Hist. Q. 1980 31(3): 182-195.* An account of the life of Evelina Månsson in the United States, 1901-07. She was born and raised in Sweden, emigrated to America in 1901, and returned to Sweden in 1907 to live out her life. Based on Månsson's memoirs; 22 notes.   C. W. Ohrvall

975. Oblinger, Carl D. INVESTIGATING THE CONSCIOUSNESS OF LABOR IN A COMMUNITY SETTING: CORNWALL, PENN-SYLVANIA, AS A CASE STUDY. *Maryland Hist. 1982 13(2): 23-31.* Working-class attitudes in Cornwall, Pennsylvania, during 1900-20 reflected a "decline of a work-centered culture" and a "rise of a defensive, inward-turning culture." Offers several explanations for the transformation of the consciousness of labor in this area. Based on oral histories and secondary sources; 2 photos, 11 notes.   G. O. Gagnon

976. Olien, Diana Davids. KEEPING HOUSE IN A TENT: WOM-EN IN THE EARLY PERMIAN BASIN OIL FIELDS. *Permian Hist. Ann. 1982 22: 3-14.* Describes the social conditions and the difficulties faced by homemakers in the oil fields of the Permian Basin, Texas, 1920's-30's.

977. Papanikolas, Helen. GREEK WORKERS IN THE INTER-MOUNTAIN WEST: THE EARLY TWENTIETH CENTURY. *J. of the Hellenic Diaspora 1977 4(3): 4-13.* Greek Americans living in the western US were part of the groups agitating for labor organization among the working classes (railroad and mine), 1897-1924.

978. Papanikolas, Helen. GREEK WORKERS IN THE INTER-MOUNTAIN WEST: THE EARLY TWENTIETH CENTURY. *Byz-antine and Modern Greek Studies [Great Britain] 1979 5: 187-215.* Discusses the large-scale immigration of Greeks to the American West in the early 20th century, their employment in mines, mills, and railroad gangs, their living conditions, the attitudes of Americans toward Greeks, and their gradual assimilation.

979. Pérez, Louis A., Jr. REMINISCENCES OF A *LECTOR:* CUBAN CIGAR WORKERS IN TAMPA. *Florida Hist. Q. 1975 53(4): 443-449.* Describes from personal experience the *lector*'s (reader's) function and influence among the Cuban illiterate workers in a Tampa cigar factory. "A highly developed proletarian consciousness and a long tradition of trade union militancy accompanied the Cuban tobacco workers to the United States." They embraced a variety of radical ideologies. The *lector* often served as a disseminator of the proletarian tradition, as well as a broad variety of written materials. Conflicts arose between the workers and factory owners over the *lector*'s pay and pro-labor materials. 13 notes.   R. V. Ritter

980. Pessen, Edward. A YOUNG INDUSTRIAL WORKER IN EARLY WORLD WAR II IN NEW YORK CITY. *Labor Hist. 1981 22(2): 269-281.* The author relates his personal experiences as an industrial worker in New York City from 1940 to 1944. Discusses his role as a steward for the International Brotherhood of Electrical Workers. Based on a luncheon address at the annual meeting of the New York State Labor History Association, New York City, 7 June 1980.
L. F. Velicer

981. Peterson, Joyce Shaw. AUTO WORKERS AND THEIR WORK, 1900-1933. *Labor Hist. 1981 22(2): 213-236.* Examines the changes in factory life and the nature of work in the automobile industry of the United States from 1900 to 1933. Relatively high wages and the ability to change employers easily made these early decades a time of labor passivity. The nature of work changed as unskilled workers operating newly developed machines performed the tasks done earlier by

craftsmen. The perfection of the assembly line took control of the pace of work away from the worker. Based on records from the Ford Motor Company Archives, the Wayne State University Archives of Labor and Urban Affairs, and other primary sources; 49 notes. L. F. Velicer

982. Pierce, Virgil Caleb. UTAH'S FIRST CONVICT LABOR CAMP. *Utah Hist. Q. 1974 42(3): 245-257.* A convict labor law was passed in Utah in 1911 to make extensive use of prisoners on state road projects. The first camp was established near Willard, Box Elder County. It proved successful, and saved the state much money. After 1920 the use of convict labor declined; by the 1930's it was nearly unknown. "Opposition to convict labor came because of the competition it brought to wage laborers." Convict labor served as an important step in the development of an effective prison vocational training program in Utah. Illus., 42 notes. E. P. Stickney

983. Piott, Steven. THE LESSON OF THE IMMIGRANT: VIEWS OF IMMIGRANTS IN MUCKRAKING MAGAZINES, 1900-1909. *Am. Studies (Lawrence, KS) 1978 19(1): 21-33.* Immigrants brought with them an undefiled sense of morality. Many early muckraking authors used this, and depicted innocent immigrants as victims of an industrial capitalism devoid of ethics or a sense of community. They argued for the reestablishment of a moral responsibility. A differentiated society had blinded citizens to corporate malefactors. Ordinary people could not perceive industrial patterns, and reform writers sought to implant a sense of guilt. Industrial capitalists, not the immigrants, were the true enemies. Primary and secondary sources; 36 notes. J. Andrew

984. Quinney, Valerie. TEXTILE WOMEN: THREE GENERATIONS IN THE MILL. *Southern Exposure 1976 3(4): 66-72.* Interviews three women of the same family on their experiences in the southern textile industry; discusses changes in working conditions, lifestyles, textiles, and union organization, 1908-52.

985. Rosenblum, Naomi L. THE HOUSING OF LYNN'S SHOE WORKERS IN 1915. *Essex Inst. Hist. Collections 1979 115(4): 221-231.* Lynn, Massachusetts, was not a company town and had no company housing. Lynn developed a dense residential ring around its industrial core. Central to this residential ring was the triple-decker, an architectural phenomenon developed for working classes in and around Boston. Based on primary sources; table, 19 notes. R. S. Sliwoski

986. Ruckman, Jo Ann. "KNIT, KNIT, AND THEN KNIT": THE WOMEN OF POCATELLO AND THE WAR EFFORT OF 1917-1918. *Idaho Yesterdays 1982 26(1): 26-36.* During World War I, several women's civic and social clubs in Pocatello, Idaho, were called upon to contribute to the war effort. Despite the florid exhortations, there was little for the women to do. They conserved food and knitted clothing, but made few substantial contributions. Based on newspapers, primarily the Pocatello *Tribune;* 3 photos, 53 notes. B. J. Paul

987. Sanders, Bernard, ed. VERMONT LABOR AGITATOR. *Labor Hist. 1974 15(2): 261-270.* Presents a memoir of Mose Cerasoli (1898-), a Vermont granite worker who tells the story of attempts to organize granite workers and of the brutal resistance encountered in the "pastoral state." The oral memoir covers 1913-38. L. L. Athey

988. SanJuan, E., Jr. CARLOS BULOSAN: AN INTRODUCTION. *Asian and Pacific Q. of Cultural and Social Affairs [South Korea] 1978 10(2): 43-48.* Carlos Bulosan (1913-56) emigrated from the Philippines to the United States in 1931. His dreams of a better life under American democracy soon crumbled before the presence of repressive monopoly capitalism and the Great Depression years. Moving progressively to the left, Bulosan actively contributed to the expanding labor movement in the 1930's. His literary works embody the twin Marxist goals of criticizing bourgeois culture and creating a proletarian literary tradition. Secondary sources; 2 notes. A. C. Migliazzo

989. Scriabine, Christine. UPTON SINCLAIR AND THE WRITING OF *THE JUNGLE. Chicago Hist. 1981 10(1): 26-37.* Focuses on how Upton Sinclair amassed material for his muckraking exposé of the Chicago meatpacking industry, *The Jungle* (1906); the book resulted in investigations of the industry and in the Meat Inspection Amendment (US, 1906).

990. Sharpe, William D. THE NEW JERSEY RADIUM DIAL PAINTERS: A CLASSIC IN OCCUPATIONAL CARCINOGENESIS. *Bull. of the Hist. of Medicine 1978 52(4): 560-570.* During 1917-24, 1000 persons worked at radium extraction and dial painting in northern New Jersey, mostly in Orange. From 1922-25, cases of jaw necrosis, anemia, and cancer began to appear, and the Essex County Medical Examiner, Dr. Harrison S. Martland, defined radium intoxication as a new occupational disease. 24 notes. M. Kaufman

991. Smiley, Gene. RECENT UNEMPLOYMENT RATE ESTIMATES FOR THE 1920'S AND 1930'S. *J. of Econ. Hist. 1983 43(2): 487-493.* Reviews Robert Coen's estimates of unemployment rates in the 1920's and 1930's and Michael Darby's estimates of unemployment rates in the 1930's. Both scholars revise Stanley Lebergott's estimates, done in 1950. Coen's estimates, while making allowance for "the discouraged worker" phenomenon, overestimate its effect. Darby's estimates are preferable or not to Lebergott's depending on their intended use. Secondary sources; table, 15 notes. J. Powell

992. Smith, Duane A. TWO LITERARY MINERS: THE WEST OF NOVELIST FRANK NASON AND POET ALFRED KING. *Colorado Heritage 1982 (1): 64-77.* Frank Lewis Nason and Alfred Castner King were miners in Colorado's San Juan area about 1900 and wrote about it. Nason, a geologist and engineer published *To the End of the Trail* (1902) and *The Blue Goose* (1903), while King wrote *Mountain Idylls* (1901) and *The Passing of the Storm* (1907). They discuss reasons people came to mining camps, labor unions, prospectors and burros, mining processes, and other aspects of the mining frontier. Important themes were the East-West dichotomy and the free youthful West. Based upon works of Nason and King and secondary works; 10 photos. O. H. Zabel

993. Smith, Michael M. BEYOND THE BORDERLANDS: MEXICAN LABOR IN THE CENTRAL PLAINS, 1900-1930. *Great Plains Q. 1981 1(4): 239-251.* A general spatial, occupational and distributional survey of Mexican migrant labor in Oklahoma, Kansas, Nebraska, South Dakota and North Dakota, 1900-30, offering economic reasons for migration; Mexicans today remain an "invisible minority" in the northern and central plains, whose role in the economic development of these plains areas should be incorporated into the history of the region.

994. Stein, Walter J. THE "OKIE" AS FARM LABORER. *Agric. Hist. 1975 49(1): 202-215.* During the 1930's, more than 300,000 white Protestant Americans from Oklahoma, Missouri, Texas, and Arkansas moved to California, where they displaced Mexican and Oriental agricultural laborers. Union officials thought that these people would provide the catalyst necessary for the complete unionization of farm workers, but this was unsuccessful. Suggests that as former tenant farmers "Okies" were accustomed to low wages and hard stoop labor and thus resisted unionization. Based on primary and secondary sources; 41 notes. R. T. Fulton

995. Sternsher, Bernard. VICTIMS OF THE GREAT DEPRESSION: SELF-BLAME/NON-SELF BLAME, RADICALISM, AND THE PRE-1929 EXPERIENCE. *Social Sci. Hist. 1977 1(2): 137-177.* There was little political radicalism during the Great Depression in America despite the existence of what some might consider ideal conditions. A review of several thousand welfare cases from the 1920's to the 1950's indicates that though many complained about the relief system, most felt the government had not let them starve. There were two groups of unemployed workers, the lower of which resembled the culture of poverty described in Michael Harrington's *The Other America.* They were used to poverty and became non-self blamers. Behavioralist theories help explain the upper culture. Based on welfare records and primary studies of Depression workers; 2 tables, fig., 107 notes. T. L. Savitt

996. Stricker, Frank. AFFLUENCE FOR WHOM? ANOTHER LOOK AT PROSPERITY AND THE WORKING CLASSES IN THE 1920S. *Labor Hist. 1983 24(1): 5-33.* The 1920's were not years of mass affluence as many historians have believed. Unemployment was higher and although wages were higher than before World War I, many workers received meager increases, if any, after 1923. Many workers did not earn enough to support basic needs and the number of poor may have been as high as 40% of the population. Based on tables from

Historical Statistics of the United States and contemporary studies of income and consumption; 7 tables, 2 graphs, 63 notes.   L. F. Velicer

997. Verba, Sidney and Schlozman, Kay Lehman. UNEMPLOY-MENT, CLASS CONSCIOUSNESS, AND RADICAL POLITICS: WHAT DIDN'T HAPPEN IN THE THIRTIES. *J. of Pol. 1977 39(2): 291-323.* The failure of socialism in the United States has been attributed to lack of class consciousness and alienation from political and economic institutions among workers. Even during the Depression of the 1930's, the working class supported the New Deal rather than more radical changes. Two national surveys conducted by Elmo Roper for *Fortune Magazine* in 1939 reveal working class attitudes. Although class consciousness and alienation increased from upper white collar, lower white collar, wage worker to unemployed, they remained fully developed in only a small minority. This seems to be attributable to the acceptance of the American Dream of rugged individualism and optimism. Based on primary and secondary sources; 14 tables, 24 notes.
                                                          A. W. Novitsky

998. Virtanen, Keijo. THE INFLUENCE OF THE AUTOMOTIVE INDUSTRY ON THE ETHNIC PICTURE OF DETROIT, MICHIGAN, 1900-1940. *U. of Turku. Inst. of General Hist. Publ. [Finland] 1977 9: 71-88.* During 1910-30 the automotive industry drew the labor it needed largely from outside areas rather than from the immigrant communities already established in Detroit. The foreign-born population underwent its most vigorous increase at this time. Social activity among the Finns living in Detroit, despite its late start, developed fairly vigorously; its inception was clearly bound up with the progress of the automotive industry. Statistics show that half of the Finns who had arrived in the United States after 1916 and resided in Detroit had made the journey from Finland straight to Detroit, the others having first lived in some other locality in the United States. Map, fig., 5 tables, 36 notes.   E. P. Stickney

999. Weinberg, Sydney Stahl. THE WORLD OF OUR MOTHERS: FAMILY, WORK, AND EDUCATION IN THE LIVES OF JEWISH IMMIGRANT WOMEN. *Frontiers 1983 7(1): 71-79.* Analyzes the experiences of 40 Jewish women who immigrated to the United States, emphasizing issues of cultural adaptation.

1000. White, Bruce M. WORKING FOR THE RAILROAD: LIFE IN THE GENERAL OFFICES OF THE GREAT NORTHERN AND NORTHERN PACIFIC, 1915-21. *Minnesota Hist. 1978 46(1): 24-30.* The records of the Northern Pacific and Great Northern Railroads as preserved in the Minnesota Historical Society provide informative data on the daily work lives of the white collar employees in the railroads' St. Paul headquarters. Despite being located in the same building, the management of the companies kept their employees deliberately apart through physical and bureaucratic means, in an effort to prevent employee comparisons of working conditions, salaries, etc. The Great Northern set up a cafeteria in 1916 to which employees were lured by the staging of employee-rendered entertainments. Memoranda reproduced indicate that company officials were disturbed by employee neglect and/or damage of company property, excessive noise and boisterous behavior, and by the throwing of objects from company windows, endangering and even injuring passers-by. Primary sources.
                                                          N. Lederer

1001. Zamora, Emilio, Jr. CHICANO SOCIALIST LABOR ACTIVI-TY IN TEXAS 1900-1920. *Aztlán 1976 6(2): 221-236.* Many Chicano workers in central and south Texas organized and joined socialist labor unions influenced by Mexican and Anglo radicals. In Laredo, due to ethnic conflicts, Mexican Americans did not follow strict socialist trade union principles and engaged in numerous railway strikes. In central and south Texas Chicano organizers worked within the Renter's Union of America and the Land League. They were more concerned with bread and butter issues than the Laredo group. 55 notes.
                                                R. Griswold del Castillo

1002. —. HUMANIZING THE WORKPLACE: THEN AND NOW. *Society 1977 15(1): 112-115.* Discusses experiments, 1924-33, by the Western Electric Co. in collaboration with Harvard University, Graduate School of Business, to determine the ideal environment for maximum production and worker satisfaction; includes photos of work areas.

1003. —. [THE "NEW UNIONISM"]. *J. of Social Hist. 1974 7(4): 509-535.*
Montgomery, David. THE "NEW UNIONISM" AND THE TRANS-FORMATION OF WORKERS' CONSCIOUSNESS IN AMERICA 1909-1922, *pp. 509-529.* By 1920 new vistas had been opened to millions of workers through the struggles of skilled workers and the wage strikes of laborers and machine tenders. It was only after a decade of continuous struggle that great masses had been enrolled in the unions and there had been infused into their consciousness a widespread aspiration to direct the operation of railroads, mines, shipyards, and factories collectively. This "new unionism" with "syndicalist tendencies" still did not have formal connections with the Industrial Workers of the World or the Socialist Party. 80 notes.
Green, James R. COMMENTS ON THE MONTGOMERY PAPER, *pp. 530-535.* Raises questions concerning Montgomery's careful dissociation of the IWW from "new unionism," and develops more fully the reasons for the limitations on the growth of the IWW, especially in employment with high immigrant worker concentrations.   R. V. Ritter

The Labor Movement

1004. Arroyo, Luis Leobardo. CHICANO PARTICIPATION IN ORGANIZED LABOR: THE CIO IN LOS ANGELES 1938-1950. *Aztlán 1976 6(2): 277-313.* During 1938-50 Chicanos were active leaders in the Los Angeles Congress of Industrial Organizations locals and the CIO Council. They worked in close association with community organizations to help solve *Mexicano* problems, among them the Sleepy Lagoon incident and the Zoot Suit Riots. After 1943 Chicano unionists lost an effective voice in the CIO Council but continued to work on the local level. Based on newspapers, oral interviews and labor union proceedings; 101 notes.   R. Griswold del Castillo

1005. Asher, Robert. JEWISH UNIONS AND THE AMERICAN FEDERATION OF LABOR POWER STRUCTURE 1903-1935. *Am. Jewish Hist. Q. 1976 65(3): 215-227.* Jewish unions, i.e., those with a substantial number of Jewish members and led by Jewish officers, until the 1930's were largely in, but not of, the mainstream of the American labor movement. Recognizing their differences with the AFL, the Jewish unions cooperated with the AFL when they could, but went their own way politically in their attempt to build a welfare state through union institutions and trade agreements with employers. By the late 1920's the Jewish unions, especially the International Ladies' Garment Workers' Union, had drifted slowly to the right and the American Federation of Labor had moved toward the left, so that the Amalgamated Clothing Workers of America could be admitted into the AFL, and the ILGWU could be allowed into the AFL power structure (executive council and resolutions committee). The accomplishments of the New Deal Democratic Party accelerated this process. 23 notes.   F. Rosenthal

1006. Barkey, Fred A. SOCIALIST INFLUENCE IN THE WEST VIRGINIA STATE FEDERATION OF LABOR: THE JOHN NU-GENT CASE. *West Virginia Hist. 1977 38(4): 275-290.* Challenges the common view that organized labor in the early 20th century was purely pragmatic and rejected radical class-conscious proposals to change American society. Socialists in the West Virginia State Federation of Labor showed surprising strength during 1901-14, and tried to oust state president John Nugent in 1907-08 for being insufficiently militant. By 1912 Socialists were a majority in the state labor convention. Primary and secondary sources; 64 notes.   J. H. Broussard

1007. Bercuson, David Jay. THE ONE BIG UNION IN WASHING-TON. *Pacific Northwest Q. 1978 69(3): 127-134.* Traces the development of the One Big Union movement in the Pacific Northwest (particularly in Washington) whereby laborers in Canada and the United States would join hands in a common effort. While leftist groups such as the Industrial Workers of the World branded the movement as nonrevolutionary, leaders of the mainstream American Federation of Labor attempted to undercut its influence during 1919. The AFL's secretary Frank Morrison worked behind the scenes in the state of Washington and successfully discredited the movement which never established strong grass roots support. Primary sources; 2 photos, 26 notes.   M. L. Tate

1008. Burki, Mary Ann Mason. THE CALIFORNIA PROGRESSIVES: LABOR'S POINT OF VIEW. *Labor Hist. 1976 17(1): 24-37.* Reviews and reassesses the interpretations of the relationship between Progressives and organized labor in California. Although labor made gains during the Progressive Era, they were not a result of the benevolent, middle-class reformer actions, but of a powerful lobbying activity on the part of organized labor with its solid base in the San Francisco area. Based on California labor publications; 4 tables, 22 notes.   L. L. Athey

1009. Carter, David A. THE INDUSTRIAL WORKERS OF THE WORLD AND THE RHETORIC OF SONG. *Q. J. of Speech 1980 66(4): 365-374.* The Industrial Workers of the World members sang extensively in their union meetings and demonstrations from 1906 to 1917. This investigation of the lyrics and uses of the songs examines their rhetorical importance and suggests that they contributed significantly to the formation of the IWW's image.   J

1010. Cary, Lorin Lee. THE BUREAU OF INVESTIGATION AND RADICALISM IN TOLEDO, OHIO: 1918-1920. *Labor Hist. 1980 21(3): 430-440.* A series of US Bureau of Investigation reports on the activities of the Industrial Workers of the World and other radical groups in Toledo, Ohio, between 1918-20, illustrates the importance of the Bureau's files for future studies of early 20th-century radicalism in Toledo and elsewhere. 14 notes.   L. F. Velicer

1011. Cary, Lorin Lee. THE REORGANIZED UNITED MINE WORKERS OF AMERICA, 1930-1931. *J. of the Illinois State Hist. Soc. 1973 66(3): 244-270.* The Reorganized United Mine Workers of America was founded in 1930 by a coalition of traditionalists and radicals dissatisfied with the leadership of United Mine Workers of America president John L. Lewis. The reorganized union lasted for only one year, in which it illustrated the unusual problems of labor unions during the Depression. Inadequate funds, personality clashes, and membership distrust particularly hindered the establishment of a strong anti-Lewis union. 5 illus., 72 notes.   A. C. Aimone

1012. Conlin, Joseph R. INTRODUCTION. Conlin, Joseph R., ed. *At the Point of Production: The Local History of the I.W.W.* (Westport, Conn.: Greenwood Pr., 1981): 3-24. Surveys the histories and the historians of the Industrial Workers of the World (IWW), especially Paul F. Brissenden's *The I.W.W.: A Study of American Syndicalism* (1919), which succeeded as a comprehensive, definitive history of the IWW. Also discusses the works of Fred Thompson, Joyce Kornbluh, Philip S. Foner, Patrick Renshaw, and Melvyn Dubofsky. These illustrate various perspectives whhich supplement Brissenden's classic. The articles in this collection are introduced as examples of what needs to be done in the field of IWW history. Secondary sources.   J. Powell

1013. Conlin, Joseph R. L'ORGANIZZAZIONE DEGLI I.W.W. E I SUOI STORICI: RASSEGNA BIBLIOGRAFICA [The organization of the I.W.W. and its historians: a bibliographical summary]. *Movimento Operaio e Socialista [Italy] 1976 22(1-2): 111-131.* The common bind between historians studying the American Labor Movement is that they have centered their attention on the successes: the ever-triumphant order, the adaptability of corporate liberalism, and the all-powerful and unparalleled American Federation of Labor. Radical movements have been described by sympathetic historians as passive victims, powerless in front of an insidious and impregnable culture or destroyed by repression. In light of these assertions, reviews the major works concerning the Industrial Workers of the World. Primary and secondary sources; 39 notes.   M. T. Wilson

1014. Cortner, Richard C. THE WOBBLIES AND *FISKE* V. *KANSAS*: VICTORY AMID DISINTEGRATION. *Kansas Hist. 1981 4(1): 30-38.* Attacks on the Industrial Workers of the World (IWW) after World War I led to arrests, trials and several precedent-setting appeals. Harold B. Fiske's conviction in 1923 for violating Kansas's Criminal Syndicalism law was reviewed by the US Supreme Court in 1927. The court's unanimous decision in his favor contributed to the contemporary efforts to establish freedom of speech as a right protected against state interference under the 14th amendment. The IWW's Legal Defense Committee could not capitalize on this victory, because many Wobblies believed their organization should concentrate on economic rather than political and judicial tactics. US Reports, Kansas Reports, ACLU

Archives, Princeton University, newspapers; illus., 46 notes.
                                                       W. F. Zornow

1015. Dadà, Adriana. I RADICALI ITALO-AMERICANI E LA SOCIETA ITALIANA [Italo-American radicals and the Italian society]. *Italia Contemporanea [Italy] 1982 (146-147): 131-140.* Studies the activities of radicals in the United States during 1916-26. Italian-Americans and other radical groups were active in the Industrial Workers of the World. These groups refused to join the American Federation of Labor in entering into agreements to aid the war effort during World War I. Though the groups were subject to harassment in America, they won support among similar groups in Italy. Both Italian and American radical groups opposed the coming to power of Fascism in Italy. Based on primary sources, including archival material from the Central State Archives, Rome; 56 notes.   E. E. Ryan

1016. Damiani, Alessandro. I COMMUNISTI E IL MOVIMENTO OPERAIO DENTRO LA CRISI: LA LIQUIDAZIONE DEI SINDACATI ROSSI, 1933-1935 [The communists and the workers' movement during the crisis: the liquidation of the red unions, 1933-1935]. *Movimento Operaio e Socialista [Italy] 1976 22(1-2): 87-110.* The year 1933 signaled the growth of worker agitation in the United States. The communist Trade Union Unity League (TUUL), which grew rapidly and proportionately more than the American Federation of Labor, was unable to keep in step with the increased radicalism of its members and the leadership necessary for a true revolutionary party of the masses. By late 1933 the Communist Party was vigorously supporting its old policy of "bore from within." The National Executive Committee of the TUUL proposed in October of 1934 to unify all unions, ultimately leading to the dissolution of the TUUL and many other independent unions. The entrance of large numbers of Communists into the AFL was undoubtedly an important cause of the breakup of the union movement and the eventual formation of the Committee for Industrial Organization, thus representing the first determining role ever played by the Communist Party in the workers' movement. Primary and secondary sources; 44 notes.   M. T. Wilson

1017. Davis, Mike. THE STOP WATCH AND THE WOODEN SHOE: SCIENTIFIC MANAGEMENT AND THE INDUSTRIAL WORKERS OF THE WORLD. *Radical Am. 1975 9(1): 69-95.* Discusses the conflict between the concept of scientific management of labor, as exemplified in the writings of Frederick W. Taylor, and the Industrial Workers of the World (IWW), the American Federation of Labor, and the Congress of Industrial Organizations, 1900-13.

1018. Dubofsky, Melvyn. FILM AS HISTORY: HISTORY AS DRAMA—SOME COMMENTS ON "THE WOBBLIES," A PLAY BY STEWART BIRD AND PETER ROBILOTTA, AND "THE WOBBLIES," A FILM BY STEWARD BIRD AND DEBORAH SHAFFER. *Labor Hist. 1981 22(1): 136-140.* Reviews the film and play of the same name, *The Wobblies,* documentaries on the Industrial Workers of the World in the United States. Both the film and the play fail to present "the complex processes of historical change and growth." Note.   L. F. Velicer

1019. Dye, Nancy Schrom. FEMINISM OR UNIONISM? THE NEW YORK WOMEN'S TRADE UNION LEAGUE AND THE LABOR MOVEMENT. *Feminist Studies 1975 3(1/2): 111-125.* The Women's Trade Union League of New York was founded in 1903. Made up of female social reformers and female workers, the WTUL tried, with little success, to organize women and make them part of the labor movement. The WTUL supported A.F.L. principles and patterned women's locals on that craft style model, although it was inappropriate for the majority of unskilled female workers, simply because the A.F.L. was the only successful trade union model in the United States. Separate women's unions or women's federal unions might have promoted feminist goals more successfully, but from the trade union point-of-view these models were unacceptable, because they would not have the necessary economic power base for demands to warrant serious consideration. Primary and secondary sources; 50 notes.   S. R. Herstein

1020. Fasce, Ferdinando. GLI INDUSTRIAL WORKERS OF THE WORLD E IL MOVIMENTO SOCIALISTA AMERICANO (1905-1913) [The Industrial Workers of the World and the American Socialist movement (1905-1913)]. *Movimento Operaio e Socialista*

[Italy] 1976 22(1-2): 23-50. Examines the relationships among the Industrial Workers of the World, the Socialist Party of America, and the Socialist Labor Party, during 1905-13. Delineates three phases in the history of these interactions: the origins of the IWW and the role of the socialists in its foundation; from 1905 to the expulsion of Daniel De Leon and to the affirmation of a nonpolitical line; the IWW success in entering the reality of the American working class, whose initiatives were followed and supported. Primary and secondary sources; 63 notes.
M. T. Wilson

1021. Ficken, Robert E. THE WOBBLY HORRORS: PACIFIC NORTHWEST LUMBERMEN AND THE INDUSTRIAL WORKERS OF THE WORLD, 1917-1918. *Labor Hist. 1983 24(3): 325-341.* The owners of logging camps and lumber mills in Oregon and Washington persuaded the federal government to intercede following a July 1917 strike for the eight-hour day by lumber industry workers, led by the Industrial Workers of the World (IWW) and the American Federation of Labor's timberworker and shingleweaver unions. The government's intervention in October 1917, coordinated by Colonel Brice P. Disque, destroyed IWW influence among the lumber industry workers by barring IWW members from employment and by utilizing soldiers to reduce the labor shortage and subdue IWW organizers. Based on the Weyerhaeuser Timber Company Papers, records of other Pacific Northwest lumber companies, the Brice P. Disque Papers, and other primary sources; 71 notes.
L. F. Velicer

1022. Fickle, James E. RACE, CLASS, AND RADICALISM: THE WOBBLIES IN THE SOUTHERN LUMBER INDUSTRY, 1900-1916. Conlin, Joseph R., ed. *At the Point of Production: The Local History of the I.W.W.* (Westport, Conn.: Greenwood Pr., 1981): 97-113. Details the conflict between lumber workers and mill operators in eastern Texas and western Louisiana, especially from 1911 to 1912. Central to the conflict was Arthur L. Emerson, who formed his first local union at Carson in western Louisiana in 1910, leading to the founding of the Brotherhood of Timber Workers in 1911. The conflict with the mill operators reached violent proportions, as the BTW was backed by the Industrial Workers of the World and other organizations. On 7 July 1912, a gun battle erupted at an Emerson speech. Emerson and other unionists were jailed, and the operators were successful in breaking the financial and psychological strength of the union. By 1914 the BTW was practically destroyed. Mainly secondary sources; 70 notes. Portions of this chapter previously appeared in *Louisiana History* in 1975.
J. Powell

1023. Fox, Maier Bryan. LABOR ZIONISM IN AMERICA: THE CHALLENGE OF THE 1920'S. *Am. Jewish Arch. 1983 35(1): 53-71.* Describes the struggle between various labor Zionist groups. The Poale Zion (Workers of Zion) was a left-wing movement led by Nachman Syrkin, following the principles of Moses Hess. The Poale Zion ideology called for spiritual support to the nationalistic endeavor. Zeire Zion (Youth of Zion) was more doctrinaire and lacked the large following of Poale Zion. Poale Zion raised funds and shipped equipment to Palestine throughout the 1920's and frequently acted independently of the Zionist Organization of America and its philanthropies. By late in the decade, the Poale Zion and Zeire Zion were near merger, and the Jewish Agency was still developing. The stage was set for the important Zionist events of the 1930's. Based on the Labor Zionist Organization Archives (Cincinnati) and various Jewish and Zionist newspapers of the period; 75 notes.
T. Koppel

1024. Freeman, Joshua. DELIVERING THE GOODS: INDUSTRIAL UNIONISM DURING WORLD WAR II. *Labor Hist. 1978 19(4): 570-593.* Discusses historiography on industrial unionism during World War II which argues that militancy and conservatism coexisted in a dynamic relationship. Unions became dependent on decisions by government agencies, notably the WLB, but the activity of industrial unionists often had a spontaneous, even reactionary, quality to it. Widespread support for the war effort helps explain the dichotomy. Based on published works; 46 notes.
L. L. Athey

1025. Galloni, Nino. EVOLUZIONE TECNOLOGICA E ORGANIZZAZIONE DELLA CLASSE OPERAIA AMERICANA NEGLI ANNI VENTI [Technological development and American working class organization in the 20's]. *Movimento Operaio e Socialista [Italy] 1982 5(2): 165-185.* Technological development in the 20's quantita-

tively and qualitatively modified the composition of the American working class: directly by creating a new type of worker and indirectly by affecting the programs, forms of organization, and resistance of the working class. Examines aspects of the anticapitalist nature of certain unions affiliated with the American Federation of Labor and the connections between technological development, changes in productivity, working-class composition, and union organization. Based on the proceedings of various trade union congresses and industrial management bulletins and other specialized reviews; 99 notes.
J. V. Coutinho

1026. Genini, Ronald. INDUSTRIAL WORKERS OF THE WORLD AND THEIR FRESNO FREE SPEECH FIGHT, 1910-1911. *California Hist. Q. 1974 53(2): 100-114.* After several victorious free-speech fights, the IWW clashed with authorities in Fresno, where there coexisted conservative agricultural interests and the most militant IWW local in the state. The free speech fight in Fresno consisted of confrontations from April 1910 to March 1911 between Wobblies and police over the issue of soap box speeches on street corners. Wobblies journeyed to Fresno from all parts of the country, answering the challenge of another free speech issue. More than 100 arrested Wobblies crammed the jails, demanded separate jury trials, and challenged prospective jurors. In December 1910, IWW leader Frank Little was freed after he pointed out that Fresno had no ordinance prohibiting street speaking. The city trustees instituted such a ban, but the impending influx of hundreds of additional Wobblies caused them to reconsider the move. On 2 March 1911 the ban was rescinded and all IWW prisoners were released. Most Wobblies went on to new battles elsewhere, losing the chance to build a labor organization in Fresno. Although the IWW had won its battle, the confrontations caused conservatives to view the IWW with growing concern, especially in agricultural regions. Based on contemporary articles and newspapers, interviews, and secondary sources; 61 notes.
A. Hoffman

1027. Ghetti, Sandra. DALL'AZIONE DIRETTA ALL *"ORGANIZING TO GO BACK TO WORK": LA SVOLTA E IL DECLINO DEGLI INDUSTRIAL WORKERS OF THE WORLD NEGLI ANNI VENTI* [From direct action to "organizing to go back to work": the turnabout and decline of the Industrial Workers of the World in the 20's]. *Movimento Operaio e Socialista [Italy] 1982 5(2): 147-163.* Increased sophistication in the Taylorization and organization of factory work exposed the Wobblies to new technology, to the work ethic, to planning, to factory management problems, and the conception of the single big union. The new configuration of capital imposed on the movement radical political and strategic changes that corresponded less and less to the immediate needs of the mass of American workers. This is a fundamental question in any critical understanding of the decline of the Wobblies. 57 notes.
J. V. Coutinho %L Italian.

1028. Gomez, Joseph A. HISTORY, DOCUMENTARY, AND AUDIENCE MANIPULATION: A VIEW OF "THE WOBBLIES." *Labor Hist. 1981 22(1): 141-145.* Reviews *The Wobblies,* a film about the Industrial Workers of the World (IWW) in the United States. *The Wobblies* falls short of being a good documentary because of the clever cinematic manipulations and the failure to present enough background on the formation and growth of the IWW as well as on the fates of the IWW members interviewed in the film. 3 notes.
L. F. Velicer

1029. Goodman, Walter. THE SAD LEGACY OF JOHN L. LEWIS. *Dissent 1972 19(1): 91-98.* A brief history of the United Mine Workers of America and the influence of John L. Lewis which brought about abuses of power.

1030. Grubbs, Frank L., Jr. ORGANIZED LABOR AND THE LEAGUE TO ENFORCE PEACE. *Labor Hist. 1973 14(2): 247-258.* At first the A.F.L. ignored the L.T.E.P. and tried to use it to enhance the A.F.L. position after war erupted in 1917. Conversely, the league tried to use the A.F.L. to increase its own influence. The effect was to advance a form of conservative internationalism in both organizations. Based on the minutes of the L.T.E.P. and on the Gompers letterbooks; 53 notes.
L. L. Athey

1031. Helfand, Barry. LABOR AND THE COURTS: THE COMMON-LAW DOCTRINE OF CRIMINAL CONSPIRACY AND ITS APPLICATION IN THE BUCK'S STOVE CASE. *Labor Hist. 1977*

18(1): 91-114. Details the origins and development of the legal fight between the Buck's Stove and Range Co. and the American Federation of Labor during 1907-11. The decision continued the anti-labor tendency of the courts and utilized the common-law doctrine of criminal conspiracy to refute labor's defense of freedom of speech. Based upon legal records and court reports; 66 notes.   L. L. Athey

1032. Hobby, Daniel T., ed. "WE HAVE GOT RESULTS": A DOCUMENT ON THE ORGANIZATION OF DOMESTICS IN THE PROGRESSIVE ERA. *Labor Hist. 1976 17(1): 103-108.* Presents a 1917 letter from Jane Street, Industrial Workers of the World organizer of domestics, as a reflection of philosophy and tactics of organizing unskilled workers. The letter, intercepted by the Post Office and sent to the Justice Department, was found in the National Archives.   L. L. Athey

1033. Howlett, Charles F. BROCKWOOD LABOR COLLEGE AND WORKER COMMITMENT TO SOCIAL REFORM. *Mid-America 1979 61(1): 47-66.* Brockwood Labor College was founded in 1919 by William Fincke, a pacifist minister. Its main aims were the training of labor leaders and education for social reform. It was opposed to the conservative leadership of the American Federation of Labor, calling for the unionization of all industrial workers and emphasizing reform ideology. The differences in philosophy with traditional unions led to a great decrease in funding and eventual dissolution of Brockwood in 1937. Primary and secondary sources; 44 notes.   J. M. Lee

1034. Jemnitz, János. AZ AMERIKAI EGYESÜLT ÁLLAMOK MUNKÁSMOZGALMA AZ ELSŐVILÁGHÁBORÚ ÉVEIBEN (1914-1917) [The labor movement in the United States of America during the years of the First World War (1914-1917)]. *Párttörténeti Közlemények [Hungary] 1974 20(2): 88-128.* The outbreak of the war took the American Socialist Party by surprise. They went on the wrong track by addressing the US Government to mediate for peace. The anarchists also agitated against the war. The small Socialist Labor Party (SLP) attempted to coordinate action with radicals and pacifists. The left wing of the SP, Hillquit and Lee, remained pacifist even after the sinking of the *Lusitania* , while the right wing, Upton Sinclair, Herron and A. M. Simmons, turned vehemently anti-German. Many immigrants and political exiles took active parts in these propaganda campaigns. The AFL, led by Gompers, isolated itself from the pacifists and drifted closer to the Wilson administration. When the USA entered the War in 1917 the AFL joined the National Defense Council and worked out a *modus vivendi* with Washington. The leftist union, the IWW, refused to suspend the labor struggle for the duration of the war. This union opposed the war, but allowed its members to enlist. The SP demanded that the President organize a referendum on US participation in the war. Meanwhile, the government turned on the antiwar agitators with the newly passed Espionage Law. Many SP and IWW leaders were jailed. The courts dealt severely with the anarchists who encouraged draft dodging. 146 notes.   P. I. Hidas

1035. Johnson,Clyde. CIO OIL WORKERS' ORGANIZING CAMPAIGN IN TEXAS, 1942-1943. Fink, Gary M. and Reed, Merl E., eds. *Essays in Southern Labor History: Selected Papers, Southern Labor History Conference, 1976.* (Westport, Conn.; London, England: Greenwood Pr., 1977): 173-188. A narrative (by an ex-organizer) of strategies and results in the efforts of the Congress of Industrial Organizations to organize oil workers in Texas in the early years of World War II. Covers the campaigns in Port Arthur, the Pan American campaign in Texas City, the Southport campaign, the Ingleside Humble campaign, the Baytown Humble Oil campaign, and the Gulf oil campaign. Notable were the company's exploitation of race issues and its appeals to "patriotism."   R. V. Ritter

1036. Klehr, Harvey. LENIN ON AMERICAN SOCIALIST LEADERS AND ON SAMUEL GOMPERS. *Labor Hist. 1976 17(2): 265-270.* Notes Lenin's views on Eugene Debs, "Big Bill" Haywood, Samuel Gompers, and others. Lenin was hostile to Gompers and misrepresented him. Based on Lenin's writings; 34 notes.   L. L. Athey

1037. Koppes, Clayton R. THE INDUSTRIAL WORKERS OF THE WORLD AND COUNTY-JAIL REFORM IN KANSAS, 1915-1920. *Kansas Hist. Q. 1975 41(1): 63-86.* A nationwide effort to jail the leaders of the Industrial Workers of the World (IWW) during World War I led to the arrest of 26 men in Kansas. They were held for two years before being brought to trial. The county jails in which they were held pending trial were antiquated pestholes. The campaign to bring about their modernization, led by the IWW, is described in detail. Based on manuscripts in the National Archives, Library of Congress, Kansas State Historical Society, and Federal Records Center, Kansas City, Missouri, and other primary and secondary sources; 4 photos, 67 notes.   W. F. Zornow

1038. Koppes, Clayton R. THE KANSAS TRIAL OF THE I. W. W., 1917-1919. *Labor Hist. 1975 16(3): 338-358.* Although the Chicago trial of 1918 has often been cited as a major cause of the Industrial Workers of the World's decline, the Kansas trials, especially the Wichita trial of 1919, were viewed as crucial by the IWW. The trial dramatized radicals' problems in achieving justice during the Red Scare, especially when they were beset by financial woes and bereft of an effective political defense. Based on court records, newspapers, and secondary sources; 47 notes.   L. L. Athey

1039. Krueger, Thomas A. ANOTHER REFLECTION ON THE FAILURE OF SOCIALISM IN AMERICA: THE CASE OF THE CIO. *Rev. in Am. Hist. 1977 5(2): 269-274.* Review article prompted by Peter Losche's *Industriegewerkschaften im Organisierten Kapitalismus; Der CIO in der Roosevelt-Ara* (Opladen, West Germany: Westdeutscher Verlag, 1975), which discusses the Congress of Industrial Organizations.

1040. Lane, Tony. A MERSEYSIDER IN DETROIT. *Hist. Workshop J. [Great Britain] 1981 (11): 138-153.* Stan Coulthard (b. 1898) describes his emigration from Birkenhead, near Liverpool, to the United States in 1922, his dreams of going to college to become a dentist, his experiences in the Detroit car plants and dairies, his activities as a union organizer, his return to Merseyside in 1935, and his activities in the British Communist Party, 1935-50. The author's introduction examines Coulthard's life and career, the background to emigration from Liverpool, 1820-1950, the links between Liverpool and labor organizations in the United States, and other British union organizers in Detroit, 1930's-40's. Secondary sources; 41 notes.   G. L. Neville

1041. Larson, Simeon. THE AMERICAN FEDERATION OF LABOR AND THE PREPAREDNESS CONTROVERSY. *Historian 1974 37(1): 67-81.* Although Samuel Gompers, president of the American Federation of Labor, staunchly supported Woodrow Wilson's military preparedness policies, the rank and file of American labor did not. Withstanding all pressures from the AFL organization as well as from the administration, the workers remained convinced that their stake in the American economic system was small, that wars are fought mainly for economic or imperialistic goals, and that the true struggle is that of the poor against the rich. Opposition to Wilson's defense program continued to the point of US entry into the war. Based mainly on AFL annual reports, procedures of AFL conventions, the published writings of Gompers, and trade union journals; 76 notes.   N. W. Moen

1042. Larson, Simeon. OPPOSITION TO AFL FOREIGN POLICY: A LABOR MISSION TO RUSSIA, 1927. *Historian 1981 43(3): 345-364.* The American Federation of Labor (AFL), opposed to all foreign intercourse and fraternization with the Bolshevik government in Russia, reacted vigorously against the formation of an American labor mission to visit Russia in 1926. The AFL saw the Communist government as an evil that had to be destroyed at any cost. This opposition became a cornerstone of AFL foreign policy and influenced domestic policy. Examines the individuals behind the visit, its discussion at the 1926 convention, the mission itself, and its report, which recommended US recognition of the USSR. The mission failed to divert the AFL from its foreign policy since its supporters refused to challenge the federation openly and forcefully. It did have some effect on affiliates who saw closer relations between the United States and the Soviet Union as beneficial. Primary sources; 61 notes.   R. S. Sliwoski

1043. Levenstein, Harvey. LENINISTS UNDONE BY LENINISM: COMMUNISM AND UNIONISM IN THE UNITED STATES AND MEXICO, 1935-1939. *Labor Hist. 1981 22(2): 237-261.* The Communist Party in the United States and Mexico during the Popular Front period (1935-39) encouraged its members to cooperate with other leftists and moderates in the organizing of workers in the two countries. The Communist Party's leadership, however, actively discouraged Communists from gaining and maintaining powerful positions in such US unions as the United Steelworkers and United Automobile Workers and in the *Confederación de Trabajadores Mexicanos* in Mexico. The restraint preached by its leadership weakened the Communist Party's position in union activities enough to facilitate a purge of all Communists from these unions in the 1940's. Based on the Earl Browder Papers and other primary sources; 44 notes.   L. F. Velicer

1044. Levine, Arthur. AN UNHERALDED EDUCATIONAL EXPERIENCE: BROOKWOOD REMEMBERED. *Change 1981 13(8): 38-42.* Describes Brookwood Labor College in Katonah, New York, 1921-37, and its success in educating labor leaders; focuses on its nontraditional education as an example to struggling liberal arts colleges today.

1045. LeWarne, Charles P. ON THE WOBBLY TRAIN TO FRESNO. *Labor Hist. 1973 14(2): 264-289.* Presents Edward M. Clyde's account of the 1911 trek toward Fresno by the Industrial Workers of the World to support the free-speech fight. The struggle was over, and the group never reached its destination. Based on the Clyde manuscript; 9 notes.   L. L. Athey

1046. Licht, Walter and Barron, Hal Seth. LABOR'S MEN: A COLLECTIVE BIOGRAPHY OF UNION OFFICIALDOM DURING THE NEW DEAL YEARS. *Labor Hist. 1978 19(4): 532-545.* Analyzes labor leadership during the New Deal years from the 1940 edition of *Who's Who in Labor*. A sample of 400 officials reveals that labor leaders were predominantly male, white, and middle-aged. Ideological factors were more important to the labor movement. 7 tables, 19 notes.   L. L. Athey

1047. Lichtenstein, Nelson. AMBIGUOUS LEGACY: THE UNION SECURITY PROBLEM DURING WORLD WAR II. *Labor Hist. 1977 18(2): 214-238.* Mass industrial unions gained in membership during World War II and solidified their position, but the wartime experience represents a transition from the aggressive period of the 1930's to a quiescent postwar stage. The unions achieved security at the expense of the rank-and-file and union democracy. Based on union records and reports of the National War Labor Board; 45 notes.
L. L. Athey

1048. Lichtenstein, Nelson. DEFENDING THE NO-STRIKE PLEDGE: CIO POLITICS DURING WORLD WAR II. *Radical Am. 1975 9(4-5): 49-76.* Discusses the Congress of Industrial Organizations' cooperation with government and industry in forcing its members to forego strike activity during the war.   S

1049. Listikov, S. V. IDEINOE VLIIANIE SOTSIALISTICHESKOGO DVIZHENIIA V S.SH.A. NA PROFSOIUZY (1916-1919 GG.) [The socialist movement's ideological influence on trade unions, 1916-19]. *Amerikanskii Ezhegodnik [USSR] 1981: 209-229.* The socialist movement strongly influenced trade unions during World War I. This was mainly because the working class was inspired by the socialist experience of European countries and by the successes of the Communists in Russia and the Labour Party in Britain. The socialist movement's ideological influence was one of the main factors behind the trade unions' antimilitarism. The working class became convinced that it should concentrate on fighting the class enemy within the country, but the influence of socialism waned after the war. 100 notes.   J. Bamber

1050. Lorence, James J. THE MILWAUKEE CONNECTION: THE URBAN-RURAL LINK IN WISCONSIN SOCIALISM, 1910-1920. *Milwaukee Hist. 1980 3(4): 102-111.* Focuses on the largely ignored struggle by "rural, small town" Socialists in Wisconsin, such as farm organizer Oscar Ameringer of Oklahoma, who recruited farmers in Wisconsin during 1911-12, Leo Krzycki, and others, who helped send Victor L. Berger to Congress and Emil Seidel to the Milwaukee mayor's office in 1910; their efforts resulted in Socialist dominance in Wisconsin for a long period.

1051. Lovin, Hugh T. THE CIO AND THAT "DAMNABLE BICKERING" IN THE PACIFIC NORTHWEST 1937-1941. *Pacific Hist.*

1979 23(1): 66-79. In 1937, the Congress of Industrial Organizations (CIO) successfully invaded the AFL-dominated Pacific Northwest. But in spite of the initial success, national CIO officers were increasingly concerned about disputes among the CIO unionists. In 1940, John L. Lewis reprimanded them for their "damnable bickering." Two factions gradually emerged in the CIO ranks: the Opposition (rightists) and the Left. The latter favored America's isolation posture in the late 1930's, and was definitely pro-Soviet in its attitudes. However, after Germany attacked the USSR in 1941, the Left renounced the isolationism it had so fervently advocated. Gradually the Left lost its dominance and the "pork chop" unionists emerged triumphant on the eve of America's entry into World War II, to the relief of the Washington CIO leaders. Based largely on union publications such as the *Timberworker, Voice of the Federation,* and *Tacoma Labor Advocate,* on collections of personal papers as well as union archives, and on secondary sources; photo, 53 notes.   H. M. Parker, Jr.

1052. Lovin, Hugh T. CIO INNOVATORS, LABOR PARTY IDEOLOGUES, AND ORGANIZED LABOR'S MUDDLES IN THE 1937 DETROIT ELECTIONS. *Old Northwest 1982 8(3): 223-243.* Discusses the attempt by militant Congress of Industrial Organizations unionists to elect a labor slate in the Detroit city elections of 1937. Disenchanted with the failure of the Democratic Party to carry out campaign promises, the more radical unionists demanded independent political action and the possible formation of a labor party. The disappointing election results actually led to closer ties with the Democratic Party. Primary sources; 52 notes.   P. L. McLaughlin

1053. Lovin, Hugh T. IDAHO AND THE "REDS," 1919-1926. *Pacific Northwest Q. 1978 69(3): 107-115.* The collapse of the 1919 Seattle general strike alarmed Idaho citizens who feared that the Industrial Workers of the World and other leftist groups would soon flood their state. Idaho Governor David W. Davis mobilized public opinion and organized a roundup of Wobblies. Idaho's Socialist Party and Nonpartisan League also received pressure, but the "red-baiting" gradually declined during the early 1920's. Primary sources; 4 photos, 37 notes.   M. L. Tate

1054. Lovin, Hugh T. THE PERSISTENCE OF THIRD PARTY DREAMS IN THE AMERICAN LABOR MOVEMENT, 1930-1938. *Mid-America 1976 58(3): 141-157.* Reviews attempts of a faction of the American Federation of Labor (AFL) to form a labor- or farmer-labor-based third party in the 1930's. These attempts were discouraged by AFL leaders during the 1920's and 1930's, especially after Franklin D. Roosevelt's election and the ensuing New Deal. After 1934 a progressive faction began to promote the idea again, particularly in the garment unions, because the Democrats and Republicans were considered unreliable. There were too many obstacles to overcome, especially the opposition of union leaders. Based on contemporary news accounts, letters, and secondary sources; 70 notes.   J. M. Lee

1055. Mal'kova, V. L. IZ ARKHIVA TOMA MUNI [The Tom Mooney papers]. *Amerikanskii Ezhegodnik [USSR] 1981: 259-273.* Tom Mooney (1882-1942) was an American trade union activist and champion of the left wing of the socialist movement. Mooney was a miner's son, born in Indiana. He became politically active at the beginning of World War I, when he was working in a foundry. Mooney was persecuted for his anti-imperialist and antimilitarist stance and the authorities in California conspired to accuse him wrongfully of murder. He was convicted and sentenced to death, this later being commuted to life imprisonment. He was not released until the eve of World War II, when he again became active in American union politics. Translates Mooney's correspondence with the Soviet press and other American trade union activists after his release from prison. 4 notes, translation of 6 documents held by the Bancroft Library.   J. Bamber

1056. Martin, Charles H. SOUTHERN LABOR RELATIONS IN TRANSITION: GADSDEN, ALABAMA, 1930-1943. *J. of Southern Hist. 1981 47(4): 545-568.* A review of labor organizing and the rise of unionism in Gadsden, Alabama. The town was dominated by three industries, which acted in concert to oppose all unionization efforts. Covers the early failures of organizers, the accompanying violence, and the influence of big wartime contracts in enabling the federal government to force the industries to comply. The Southern story was not very different from the Northern variety, except that Southern workers were mildly less enthusiastic about unionization, and the local "establishment" worked the "outsider" and "Northern carpetbagger" themes intensively, and to considerable effect. 47 notes.   V. L. Human

1057. McLaughlin, Doris B. THE SECOND BATTLE OF BATTLE CREEK: THE OPEN SHOP MOVEMENT IN THE EARLY TWENTIETH CENTURY. *Labor Hist. 1973 14(3): 323-339.* Assesses the career of Charles William Post, the cereal magnate, and his activities in promoting the open shop movement in Battle Creek, Michigan. Post fought for the open shop on local and national levels, and as Battle Creek grew in population he led the effort to maintain a nonunion industrial town by paternalism and "welfare capitalism." The A.F.L. unsuccessfully tried to organize in Battle Creek in 1910-12. The experience there was the historical forerunner of the resurgence of the open shop movement in the 1920's. Based on records of Post's companies, his official publication, *The Square Deal,* and the *American Federationist;* 33 notes.   L. L. Athey

1058. Miles, Dione. SOURCES FOR THE LOCAL HISTORY OF THE I.W.W. Conlin, Joseph R., ed. *At the Point of Production: The Local History of the I.W.W.* (Westport, Conn.: Greenwood Pr., 1981): 237-318. Provides a bibliography for the local history of the Industrial Workers of the World, including primary sources, IWW publications, doctoral dissertations, master's essays and theses, articles, and books.   J. Powell

1059. Miller, Sally M. FROM SWEATSHOP WORKER TO LABOR LEADER: THERESA MALKIEL, A CASE STUDY. *Am. Jewish Hist. 1978 68(2): 189-205.* Theresa Serber Malkiel (1874-1949) is an example of a female Jewish leader in the labor movement and in a minor political party (Socialist Labor Party, and later the Socialist Party of America). On the Women's National Committee of the Socialist Party in the decade before 1914 she gave her greatest attention to women and the party, unionization of women workers, foreign-born women, woman suffrage, and the party commitment to sexual equality. Her most lasting accomplishment was the establishment of the Brooklyn Adult Students Association. 20 notes.   F. Rosenthal

1060. Morris, James O. THE ACQUISITIVE SPIRIT OF JOHN MITCHELL, UMW PRESIDENT (1899-1908). *Labor Hist. 1979 20(1): 5-43.* Documents the "acquisitive spirit" of John Mitchell who used his position for personal profit, squeezed the miners, and joined coal operators in business and financial deals which constituted conflicts of interest. Five specific ventures where Mitchell profited directly from miners are detailed, and his financial benefits from the National Civic Federation are delineated. Mitchell was bothered by these activities; a conscience-ridden man, he may have turned to alcohol as a result of his dilemma of wanting to move farther and faster financially than his position would allow. Based upon the Mitchell papers; table, 76 notes.   L. L. Athey

1061. Nelson, Daniel. THE COMPANY UNION MOVEMENT, 1900-1937: A REEXAMINATION. *Business Hist. Rev. 1982 56(3): 335-357.* Company unions have traditionally fared poorly in scholarly interpretation, a view that has oversimplified their role in industrial history. There were actually three different types of company unions: those that came into existence because of external pressure from government or the threat of independent unionism; those that were founded simply because a businessman wanted to be in fashion; and those that were associated with innovative plant management theories and with modern personnel practices. The last group was the backbone of the movement during the 1920's-30's. Based on company archives and government records; 4 tables, illus., 45 notes.   C. J. Pusateri

1062. Palmer, Bryan D. "BIG BILL" HAYWOOD'S DEFECTION TO RUSSIA AND THE IWW: TWO LETTERS. *Labor Hist. 1976 17(2): 271-278.* Presents two letters from John Grady, Secretary-Treasurer of the IWW, to Mont Schuyler, Haywood's US agent, which reveal the financial and social disruption of the IWW caused by Haywood's defection. Letters are from the Archives of Labor History and Urban Affairs at Wayne State University. 11 notes.   L. L. Athey

1063. Petterchak, Janice A. CONFLICT OF IDEALS, SAMUEL GOMPERS V. "UNCLE JOE" CANNON. *J. of the Illinois State Hist. Soc. 1981 74(1): 31-40.* Joseph Gurney Cannon, a conservative Republican from Danville, Illinois, served as Speaker of the US House of Representatives from 1903 to 1911. He did not share the good relationship with labor leader Samuel Gompers enjoyed by his predecessor Thomas B. Reed. Cannon's obstruction of labor legislation led Gompers to merge unionism with politics and issue, in 1906, a labor blacklist. Cannon was reelected in that year despite strong labor support in his district for Socialist John H. Walker. In the 1908 campaign, the American Federation of Labor endorsed the Democratic ticket. Cannon shared in the Republican victory of that year and was reelected in every campaign but one until his retirement in 1923. 6 illus., 38 notes.   A. W. Novitsky.

1064. Polishook, Sheila Stern. THE AMERICAN FEDERATION OF LABOR, ZIONISM, AND THE FIRST WORLD WAR. *Am. Jewish Hist. Q. 1976 65(3): 228-244.* The period of World War I brought with it recognition of organized labor as an essential element in the nation's development, whose support the Wilson administration sought and needed. Thus, even though the AFL leadership readily accepted the principle of national self-determination, its endorsement of a Jewish national state in Palestine came as a surprise which Samuel Gompers was able to push through against vociferous opposition by the pacifist and socialist spokesmen of the ILGWU. Labor's commitment to a Jewish homeland has strengthened over the years. 39 notes.   F. Rosenthal

1065. Rosenzweig, Roy. ORGANIZING THE UNEMPLOYED: THE EARLY YEARS OF THE GREAT DEPRESSION, 1929-1933. *Radical Am. 1976 10(4): 37-60.* The unemployed councils formed by the Communists, Socialists, and Musteites after 1929 failed to create a mass revolutionary movement of the unemployed. The movement was, however, a significant example of locally based, grassroots organization under radical leadership that worked creatively and militantly to meet the concrete, immediate needs of the unemployed. Based on oral and printed primary sources.   N. Lederer

1066. Schwantes, Carlos A. LEFTWARD TILT ON THE PACIFIC SLOPE: INDIGENOUS UNIONISM AND THE STRUGGLE AGAINST AFL HEGEMONY IN THE STATE OF WASHINGTON. *Pacific Northwest Q. 1979 70(1): 24-34.* Analyzes the problems faced by the American Federation of Labor (AFL) in its attempt to organize workers in the Pacific Northwest. Its problems came not so much from conservative management as from leftist unions which had begun in the 1880's. The Western Federation of Miners and its offshoot, the American Labor Union, proved especially troublesome to the AFL. By 1920, however, the nationally organized AFL was able to displace the regional influence of the smaller indigenous unions of the Pacific Northwest. Primary and secondary sources; 6 photos, 51 notes.   M. L. Tate

1067. Seraile, William. BEN FLETCHER, I.W.W. ORGANIZER. *Pennsylvania Hist. 1979 46(3): 213-232.* Benjamin Harrison Fletcher (1890-1949) was an extraordinarily successful organizer of dockworkers for the Industrial Workers of the World in Philadelphia, Baltimore, and Boston. He was particularly effective in appealing to fellow blacks who were dockworkers. Sentenced to prison in 1918 with other IWW leaders for alleged violations of the Selective Service Act and Espionage Act of 1917, he was released in 1922 with a conditional commutation of his sentence. In 1933, President Franklin D. Roosevelt granted him a full pardon. Based upon Pardon Attorney files, Haywood et al. vs. U.S., and other sources; illus., 24 notes.   D. C. Swift

1068. Seretan, L. Glen. THE PERSONAL STYLE AND POLITICAL METHODS OF DANIEL DE LEON: A RECONSIDERATION. *Labor Hist. 1973 14(2): 163-201.* Reviews the literature about the "uncompromising" Daniel De Leon. De Leon was intransigent in intraparty affairs, but he was willing to compromise in working with other organizations. De Leon was no more vituperative in oral and written communications than were other contemporary labor leaders, nor was he more dictatorial. The general picture of De Leon is far too stereotyped, and a comprehensive reexamination of him is needed. Based on De Leon's writings and on secondary sources; 156 notes.   L. L. Athey

1069. Shanks, Rosalie. THE I.W.W. FREE SPEECH MOVEMENT: SAN DIEGO, 1912. *J. of San Diego Hist. 1973 19(1): 25-33.* During

1911 a "socialist army" dominated by the Industrial Workers of the World (I.W.W.) took over Tijuana, Mexico, for a time. Soon San Diegans feared violence and perhaps even pillage at the hands of the I.W.W. The city council prohibited free speech in a six-block area, resulting in mob action and arrests. To most people there was a tie between the red scare and the I.W.W., making restriction of civil rights respectable. Police brutality and vigilante tactics won the day and influenced laws to contain syndicalism. Based on interviews, San Diego newspapers, and secondary accounts; 3 illus., 78 notes.

S. S. Sprague

1070. Shapiro, Stanley. THE PASSAGE OF POWER: LABOR AND THE NEW SOCIAL ORDER. *Pro. of the Am. Phil. Soc. 1976 120(6): 464-474.* Discusses left-wingers' predictions of the imminent victory of socialism at the outbreak of World War I and the lack of uniformity in the political results of the aftermath in Great Britain and the United States. Describes how a similar set of forces eased the passage of power to the left in Britain but retarded it in the United States. The crucial factor is seen to lie in organized labor, because in contrast to the United States, Britain had an established evolutionary instrument of change. 68 notes.

P. J. Taylorson

1071. Sims, Robert C. IDAHO'S CRIMINAL SYNDICALISM ACT: ONE STATE'S RESPONSE TO RADICAL LABOR. *Labor Hist. 1974 15(4): 511-527.* Analyzes Idaho's criminal syndicalism acts which were part of the campaign against the Industrial Workers of the World (I.W.W.). The act was passed as a result of pressure from lumber and mining interests in 1917, and it was vigorously enforced from 1918 to 1920. During the 1920's there were attempts to revive the law, but opposition from organized labor helped make the law a dead issue. The I.W.W. was effectively suppressed through its use. Based upon Idaho statutes, the Moses Alexander Papers, and the *Idaho Statesman* . 50 notes.

L. L. Athey

1072. Skakkebaek, Mette. CONCERNS OF ORGANIZED LABOR, 1902-19: THE BELLEVILLE TRADES AND LABOR ASSEMBLY, ILLINOIS. *Am. Studies in Scandinavia [Norway] 1981 13(2): 81-92.* The Belleville, Illinois, Trades and Labor Assembly experienced a change in concern, emphasis and political alignment, 1902-18. Earlier concerns centered on the political and social welfare of labor. By 1918 the assembly accepted American war participation and had shifted from a Socialist stance, willing to collaborate within the two-party system to advance trade union goals. Based on Belleville Trades and Labor Assembly Minutes of Meetings, 1902-22, Illinois State Historical Library, Springfield; 30 notes.

E. E. Krogstad

1073. Tomlins, Christopher L. AFL UNIONS IN THE 1930S: THEIR PERFORMANCE IN HISTORICAL PERSPECTIVE. *J. of Am. Hist. 1979 65(4): 1021-1042.* Challenges traditional interpretations and suggests a new analytic framework to explain American Federation of Labor (AFL) successes. Historically, AFL unions had adapted to the changing industrial environment; this tendency continued in the 1930's when the AFL faced Congress of Industrial Organizations (CIO) competition. AFL unions made major contributions to the growth of the organized labor movement in the 1930's, especially in transport, communications, service trades, and retail trades. 4 tables, 50 notes.

T. P Linkfield

1074. Toth, Charles. BULWARK FOR FREEDOM: SAMUEL GOMPERS' PAN AMERICAN FEDERATION OF LABOR. *Revista/Review Interamericana [Puerto Rico] 1979 9(3): 455-491.* Samuel Gompers's Pan American Federation of Labor was formed to promote trade unionism in Latin America. Its success was limited, partly because the organization faced difficult political issues. In its brief career, this labor organization tried to curtail German influence in Latin America during World War I, attempted to stop the tide of revolutionary socialism in the New World, and opposed US intervention in Latin American political affairs. Covers 1918-27. 116 notes, biblio.

J. A. Lewis

1075. Toth, Charles W. SAMUEL GOMPERS, EL COMUNISMO Y LA FEDERACIÓN PANAMERICANA DEL TRABAJO [Samuel Gompers, Communism, and the Pan American Federation of Labor]. *Rev. de Ciencias Sociales [Puerto Rico] 1973 17(1): 95-101.* The threat of radical socialism was less dangerous than people thought in the

1920's, but it had some potential; Samuel Gompers saw the Pan American Federation of Labor as a bulwark against leftist dictatorships.

1076. Wagaman, David G. THE INDUSTRIAL WORKERS OF THE WORLD IN NEBRASKA, 1914-1920. *Nebraska Hist. 1975 56(3): 295-337.* Narrates the problems of the Industrial Workers of the World in Nebraska during the Wilson era. The organization was not numerically strong in Nebraska, but its presence was felt and many of its members were prosecuted.

R. Lowitt

1077. Wagaman, David G. "RAUSCH MIT": THE I.W.W. IN NEBRASKA DURING WORLD WAR I. Conlin, Joseph R., ed. *At the Point of Production: The Local History of the I.W.W.* (Westport, Conn.: Greenwood Pr., 1981): 115-142. Details the Industrial Workers of the World's organizational campaigns in Nebraska during World War I, and examines the Justice Department's raids in September and November 1917 on the important Omaha headquarters of the union. On 15 April 1915, an IWW conference of representatives of local agricultural workers' unions in Kansas City created the Agricultural Workers Organization. After some success in Kansas, they began their campaign in Nebraska, where they were not warmly welcomed. Nebraska's agriculture-dominated economy made organization difficult for the union. The IWW was identified as a pro-German, antiwar organization engaged in sabotage. Public opinion was thus swayed against them, and made the raids of 1917 possible. By 1920 the IWW in Nebraska was practically destroyed by the ability of the federal government, along with oil, mining, and lumber interests, to sway public opinion against them. Based largely on newspaper and journal articles of the period; 79 notes.

J. Powell

1078. White, Earl Bruce. *THE UNITED STATES* V. *C. W. ANDERSON ET AL.: THE WICHITA CASE, 1917-1919.* Conlin, Joseph R., ed. *At the Point of Production: The Local History of the I.W.W.* (Westport, Conn.: Greenwood Pr., 1981): 143-164. When the United States entered World War I, the Industrial Workers of the World was reorganizing itself into industrial organizations which could be controlled from Chicago headquarters. The unions were making some progress in the northern timber regions and the western copper mines, and with maritime, construction, and oil workers, when wartime legislation, patriotism, and hysteria were turned against them. They were increasingly harassed, culminating in the federal raids on IWW locals in 1917, one of which was in Wichita, Kansas. Charles W. Anderson was secretary-treasurer of the Agricultural Workers Industrial Union and the Oil Workers Industrial Union, branches of the IWW. The author details the complex events of the case of the federal government against the Wichita union. Based on court transcripts and journal articles of the period; 105 notes.

J. Powell

1079. Whittaker, William G. SAMUEL GOMPERS, LABOR, AND THE MEXICAN-AMERICAN CRISIS OF 1916: THE CARRIZAL INCIDENT. *Labor Hist. 1976 17(4): 551-567.* Analyzes the actions of Samuel Gompers in appealing to President Carranza of Mexico to release American prisoners taken at Carrizal in 1916, and presents the evidence for the conclusion that Gompers and the American Federation of Labor helped prevent a war between the United States and Mexico. Based on the AFL collection of the Wisconsin State Historical Society and the Gompers Copy Books; 44 notes.

L. L. Athey

1080. Wortman, Roy T. THE RESURGENCE OF THE IWW IN CLEVELAND: A NEGLECTED ASPECT OF LABOR HISTORY. *Northwest Ohio Q. 1974/75 47(1): 20-29.* Discusses the Industrial Workers of the World in Cleveland 1918-50, especially resurgence 1934-50 due to growth in the Metal and Machinery Workers' Industrial Union (440).

1081. Wyche, Billy H. SOUTHERN INDUSTRIALISTS VIEW ORGANIZED LABOR IN THE NEW DEAL YEARS, 1933-1941. *Southern Studies 1980 19(20): 151-171.* Although the NIRA, or National Industrial Recovery Act (US, 1933), was at first greeted with enthusiasm by southern industrialists, they soon came to attack Section 7(a), which provided for collective bargaining. The general textile strike of 1934 and the emergence of the CIO (Congress of Industrial Organizations) aroused great fear and anger among the industrialists, who opposed the NLRA, or National Labor Relations Act (US, 1935), from the beginning. Economic rather than ideological factors played the leading role in shaping these views. Textiles, the leading industry of the South, had overexpanded and overproduced for many years, and costs had to be reduced. Union and management journals and other primary sources; 88 notes.   J. J. Buschen

1082. Wyche, Billy H. SOUTHERN NEWSPAPERS VIEW ORGANIZED LABOR IN THE NEW DEAL YEARS. *South Atlantic Q. 1975 74(2): 178-196.* Southern newspapers presented a full spectrum of opinion on labor problems during the 1930's. Most of them broadly supported the New Deal in principle, but were sometimes less enthusiastic when its programs were put into practice. Strikes were almost unanimously abhorred, especially when violent, but violence against strikers was seldom condemned. The Congress of Industrial Organizations was generally disliked. The fulcrum of newspaper opinion moved more and more to an antilabor position as the decade advanced. 90 notes.   V. L. Human

1083. Yellowitz, Irwin. JEWISH IMMIGRANTS AND THE AMERICAN LABOR MOVEMENT, 1900-1920. *Am. Jewish Hist. 1981 71(2): 188-217.* Investigation of attitudes and practices among clothing, bookbinding, building trades, meat cutters, and cigar makers unions toward new Jewish immigrants at the turn of the 20th century show that, though each trade differed, anti-Semitic were less important than anti-immigrant attitudes, and both were less significant than trade interests in determining union policies. American labor leaders, usually representing skilled craftsmen, often excluded both skilled and unskilled immigrants until the welfare of their own unions demanded inclusion. Anti-Semitic sentiment, though used to support exclusion, seldom if ever was the determining factor. Based on interviews with labor leaders in the David B. Saposs Papers, State Historical Society of Wisconsin, and other primary sources; 113 notes.   R. A. Keller

1084. Zieger, Robert H. NOBODY HERE BUT US TRADE UNIONISTS: COMMUNISM AND THE CIO. *Rev. in Am. Hist. 1982 10(2): 245-249.* Review essay on Harvey A. Levenstein's *Communism, Anticommunism, and the CIO* (1981), which contends that Communist influence in the American labor movement during the 1930's and 1940's was "largely salutary."

1085. —. SEATTLE GENERAL STRIKE, 1919: CAN WE DO BETTER NEXT TIME? *Progressive Labor 1973 9(2): 32-44.* The ability of Seattle workers to successfully carry out the duties of government without the 'help' of the ruling class or its flunkeys in government and business proved the working class can run society and in fact will use their combined forces to seize power. This terrified the rulers. They defused the threat by relying on the weakness of the strike leadership, which lacked a communist core. How would a real communist party conduct such a struggle?   J

Professional, Technical, and White Collar Workers

1086. Finison, Lorenz J. AN ASPECT OF THE EARLY HISTORY OF THE SOCIETY FOR THE PSYCHOLOGICAL STUDY OF SOCIAL ISSUES: PSYCHOLOGISTS AND LABOR. *J. of the Hist. of the Behavioral Sci. 1979 15(1): 29-37.* This article traces briefly the roots of the Society for the Psychological Study of Social Issues in the movement to combat unemployment among psychologists during the mid-1930's. The principal topic is one aspect of the Society's history: the manner in which the Society responded to the issue of labor. There were two attempts to deal with this issue in the context of the Depression: the Society's Committee on Trade Union Affiliation and its Yearbook Committee on Industrial Conflict. These committees are described in the context of prolabor sympathies among academics during the period, and in the context of industrial conflict occurring at that time. The continuing conflict within the Society over its role as an "activist" organization versus its role as a research-supporting organization is shown to have its roots in the very earliest efforts to organize the Society.   J

1087. Graebner, William. THE ORIGINS OF RETIREMENT IN HIGHER EDUCATION: THE CARNEGIE PENSION SYSTEM. *Acad.: Bull. of the AAUP 1979 65(2): 97-103.* The origins of the

retirement system in higher education date to 1901 when Andrew Carnegie retired, leaving $5 million in bonds to the Carnegie Company to be spent on, among other things, pensions for loyal, long-term employees; in later years, he focused on college professors.

1088. Gratton, Brian. SOCIAL WORKERS AND OLD AGE PENSIONS. *Social Service Rev. 1983 57(3): 403-415.* The popular 1920's demand for old age pensions was resisted by social workers in Massachusetts for several reasons, including fears for their own security.

1089. Kritzberg, Barry. AN UNFINISHED CHAPTER IN WHITE-COLLAR UNIONISM: THE FORMATIVE YEARS OF THE CHICAGO NEWSPAPER GUILD, LOCAL 71, AMERICAN NEWSPAPER GUILD, A.F.L.-C.I.O. *Labor Hist. 1973 14(3): 397-413.* The Chicago Newspaper Guild spearheaded the drive toward unionization in a strike against the Hearst newspapers, the *Examiner* and the *American.* The strike (November 1938-April 1940) was initially successful as a result of an N.L.R.B. decision, but the effect was to shift union leadership to the A.F.L. The A.F.L. had hotly contested the guild, which was affiliated with the C.I.O.; so although the American Newspaper Guild was strengthened nationally, it was sharply weakened in Chicago. Based on oral interviews, C.N.G. files, and Chicago newspapers; 78 notes, appendix.   L. L. Athey

1090. McColloch, Mark. WHITE COLLAR UNIONISM, 1940-1950. *Sci. & Soc. 1982-83 46(4): 405-419.* A study of early and briefly successful efforts to unionize white-collar workers among three groups: bank workers, public welfare employees, and white-collar electrical machinery workers. Groups such as the United Office and Professional Workers of America; State, County and Municipal Workers of America; Federation of Westinghouse Independent Salaried Unions; United Public Workers of America; United Electrical, Radio and Machine Workers of America; and others organized thousands of workers in the 1940's. Late in the decade employers and the federal government launched a vigorous assault on these unions, and, with the collaboration of the Congress of Industrial Organizations, effectively crushed the organizations. 30 notes.   R. E. Butchart

1091. Milden, James W. WOMEN, PUBLIC LIBRARIES, AND LIBRARY UNIONS: THE FORMATIVE YEARS. *J. of Lib. Hist. 1977 12(2): 150-158.* Presents histories of several of the unions which began and ended during 1917-20, including the New York Public Library Employee's Union and the Library Workers' Union of Boston Public. Discussion of the controversies of library employees over unionization. Primary and secondary sources; 24 notes.

A. C. Dewees

1092. Murphy, Marjorie. TAXATION AND SOCIAL CONFLICT: TEACHER UNIONISM AND PUBLIC SCHOOL FINANCE IN CHICAGO, 1898-1934. *J. of the Illinois State Hist. Soc. 1981 74(4): 242-260.* In 1898, the Chicago Board of Education debated the priority of educational and building accounts in the school system's budget resulting in the greatest contemporary public works project. Revenue reforms permitted reduction of all taxes except those for the building fund. In 1899, Catharine Goggin and Margaret A. Haley of the Chicago Teachers' Federation investigated tax evasion by various corporations, especially streetcar and utility companies. While the board attributed educational deficits to unionization of teachers and required disaffiliation in 1917, the real causes included explosive growth in school attendance, expecially at the secondary level; increased competition with road construction for tax dollars; and a reassessment campaign led by the federation, which reduced revenues. Payrolls for public schools could not be met by December 1929. 6 illus., table, 3 graphs, 47 notes.

A. W. Novitsky

1093. Scriabine, Christine Brendel. THE FRAYED WHITE COLLAR: PROFESSIONAL UNEMPLOYMENT IN THE EARLY DEPRESSION. *Pennsylvania Hist. 1982 49(1): 3-24.* Among the unemployed and underemployed professionals discussed are architects, engineers, physicians, professors, teachers, and lawyers. Their numbers increased during the 1930's. Based on government documents, other primary sources, and a variety of secondary materials; 83 notes.

D. C. Swift

1094. Sholes, Elizabeth. WOMEN IN THE MEDIA: A REPORT ON FEMALE PROFESSIONALISM DURING THE AMERICAN DEPRESSION. *Modernist Studies [Canada] 1974-75 1(3): 27-38.* Professional women in journalism, radio, and film were able to improve their economic and personal status during the depression because of their personal styles and because the media was less affected by hard times in the 1930's.

Individual Locals, Strikes, and Lockouts

1095. Allen, John E. EUGENE TALMADGE AND THE GREAT TEXTILE STRIKE IN GEORGIA, SEPTEMBER 1934. Fink, Gary M. and Reed, Merl E., eds. *Essays in Southern Labor History: Selected Papers, Southern Labor History Conference, 1976.* (Westport, Conn.; London, England: Greenwood Pr., 1977): 224-243. Studies the history of the southern textile industry before and during the early years of the National Recovery Administration (NRA) as the setting for the strike of 1934, the course of the strike, and Governor Eugene Talmadge's role in getting the strike settled. That role was based philosophically in his staunchly conservative opposition to the whole NRA concept. The strike was an unmitigated disaster for Georgia's textile workers; no union men were rehired. Talmadge's duplicity regarding his intentions and "the brutality and flamboyance with which he suppressed the strike" was unprecedented. The workers were not fooled as to where his real loyalties lay, but the damage had been done. 74 notes.   R. V. Ritter

1096. Ansley, Fran and Bell, Brenda. DAVIDSON-WILDER 1932: STRIKES IN THE COAL CAMP. *Southern Exposure 1974 1(3/4): 113-136.* After World War I, the coal mining companies in eastern Tennessee whittled away the gains won by the United Mine Workers. When the miners struck the companies retaliated with yellow dog contracts, injunctions, National Guard troops, black lists, and deputized gunmen. Harrassment and violence were waged by both sides. The murder in 1933 of the local union president Barney Graham, along with the acquittal of his assailant, brought the turbulence to a climax. Leaderless, tired, and hungry, the miners went back to the mines without contracts. Based on oral interviews with participants and primary and secondary sources; 10 illus., 10 notes, biblio.
                                                G. A. Bolton

1097. Asher, Robert. PAINFUL MEMORIES: THE HISTORICAL CONSCIOUSNESS OF STEELWORKERS AND THE STEEL STRIKE OF 1919. *Pennsylvania Hist. 1978 45(1): 61-86.* Most skilled steelworkers in the Pittsburgh district remained at work during the Steel Strike of 1919. Many factors influenced their defection, but none was more important than their recollection of earlier unsuccessful confrontations with the companies. Many of the skilled steelworkers had participated in those strikes, and others had been told of the events by "old timers" in the steel towns. The skilled steelworkers who did not support the 1919 strike doubted the ability of the union leadership, respected the power and wealth of the companies, and understood the relationship between paternalism and repression. Based on interviews undertaken by David Saposs and others in 1920, US Senate hearings, recent oral history interviews, and other materials; 3 tables, 56 notes.
                                                D. C. Swift

1098. Aurand, Harold W. and Gudelunas, William. THE MYTHICAL QUALITIES OF MOLLY MAGUIRE. *Pennsylvania Hist. 1982 49(2): 91-105.* The significance of the Molly Maguires and labor violence in the coal fields lies in the myths that developed. The various interpretations of the Molly Maguire episode in Schuylkill County are reviewed and critiqued. There is no solid evidence of the guilt or innocence of the reputed Mollies. The myth of the Molly Maguires served interests of nativists, Irish ethnicity, and the Philadelphia and Reading Railroad; it also gave labor a credible method of protest. Based on newspapers, legislative hearings, and other materials; 68 notes.
                                                D. C. Swift

1099. Aurand, Harold W. SOCIAL MOTIVATION OF ANTHRACITE MINE WORKERS: 1901-1920. *Labor Hist. 1977 18(3): 360-365.* Argues that anthracite miners in Pennsylvania were strongly motivated toward individual economic and social success contrary to traditional

images of miners. Based on statistical reports of the Pennsylvania Department of Mines; 4 tables.   L. L. Athey

1100. Austin, Mary. PETRILLO'S WAR. *J. of Popular Culture 1978 12(1): 11-18.* Discussion of the causes and outcome of the 27 month strike by union musicians against recording companies called by American Federation of Musicians president James Caesar Petrillo in June 1942. Primary and secondary sources; 22 notes.   D. G. Nielson

1101. Bailey, Kenneth R. "GRIM VISAGED MEN" AND THE WEST VIRGINIA NATIONAL GUARD IN THE 1912-13 PAINT AND CABIN CREEK STRIKE. *West Virginia Hist. 1980 41(2): 111-125.* In the 1912-13 Paint and Cabin Creek strike, because of violence between coal mine guards and members of the United Mine Workers of America, Governor William E. Glasscock declared martial law and sent in the National Guard to keep order. Based on newspaper accounts, mine workers' reports, and West Virginia government papers; 49 notes.   J. D. Neville

1102. Barnhill, John. TRIUMPH OF WILL: THE COAL STRIKE OF 1899-1903. *Chronicles of Oklahoma 1983 61(1): 80-95.* Frequent accidents, long hours, and low wages prompted a general strike by Oklahoma's United Mine Workers during March 1899. Strikes soon spread into Missouri and Kansas as the use of violence increased, but the mine owners entered into an agreement that concessions would not be made. Intense resolve by the owners and successful utilization of "scab miners" endangered the strike to such an extent that many felt it would collapse. Pete Hanraty became president of the union's District 21 and orchestrated a successful struggle that led to victory for the strikers by mid-1903. Based on Oklahoma newspapers and the Hanraty Collection in the Oklahoma Historical Society; 5 photos, 40 notes.   M. L. Tate

1103. Baughman, James L. CLASSES AND COMPANY TOWNS: LEGENDS OF THE 1937 LITTLE STEEL STRIKE. *Ohio Hist. 1978 87(2): 175-192.* Examines events in Canton, Youngstown, and Warren (Ohio) during the 1937 "Little Steel" strike, the first major strike since 1919. Discusses the relationship of the communities to the month-long labor-management conflict. After the strike of the Youngstown Sheet and Tube, Inland Steel, and Republic Steel, not solidarity but demoralization and internal division characterized the employees. The union never came close to victory—after four weeks the laborers began filing back into the mills and the managers had halted the impressive advance for CIO organization in the nation's basic industries. Through examination of the communities involved, discusses why the union lost. Based on primary and secondary sources; 3 illus., 48 notes.   N. Summers

1104. Benson, Jackson J. and Loftis, Anne. JOHN STEINBECK AND FARM LABOR UNIONIZATION: THE BACKGROUND OF *IN DUBIOUS BATTLE*. *Am. Literature 1980 52(2): 194-223.* Analyzes the degree of realism in Steinbeck's *In Dubious Battle*, which portrays agricultural strikes in southern California during the early 1930's. The novel's main characters, strike, and strike location were all composites of actual people, events, and locations in California in 1933. Steinbeck may have created realistic (true to life) human speech, situations, and events, but he did not realistically portray the human motives and feelings that accompanied the people and events he used as composites. *In Dubious Battle* is too brutal to be considered a realistic portrayal of an agricultural strike in California in 1933. Based on personal interviews and secondary sources; 77 notes.   T. P. Linkfield

1105. Bernhardt, Debra. BALLAD OF A LUMBER STRIKE. *Michigan Hist. 1982 66(1): 38-43.* A strike by lumberjacks in Michigan's Upper Peninsula in 1937 resulted in one-third of the Upper Peninsula's lumberjacks being organized into an industrial union, which resulted in an eight-hour day and improved living conditions. However, depletion of the timber and the introduction of the one-man power saw radically altered timbering so that most lumberjack camps were phased out.
                                                L. E. Ziewacz

1106. Bishop, Bill. 1931: THE BATTLE OF EVARTS. *Southern Exposure 1976 4(1-2): 92-103.* Coal miners attempting to organize for the United Mine Workers of America in Harlan County, Kentucky, went on strike and encountered evictions, hunger, violence, imprisonment, and abandonment by the union.

1107. Blatz, Perry K. THE ALL-TOO-YOUTHFUL PROLETARI-ANS. *Pennsylvania Heritage 1981 7(1): 13-14, 16-17.* Discusses working conditions in the anthracite coal mines of Pennsylvania in the late 19th and early 20th centuries for boys who were often younger than the legally required age; focuses on a 1902 strike by 50 boys protesting brutal treatment by their supervisor.

1108. Bonthius, Andrew. ORIGINS OF THE INTERNATIONAL LONGSHOREMEN'S AND WAREHOUSEMEN'S UNION. *Southern California Q. 1977 59(4): 379-426.* Traces the organization of longshoremen and warehousemen on the Pacific Coast from the founding of the International Longshoremen's Association in 1934 to the merger of their union and warehousemen's union into the International Longshoremen's and Warehousemen's Union in 1937. Longshoremen had been neglected by American Federation of Labor leadership for decades; they endured company unions, low wages, and wretched working conditions. Under radical and Communist leadership, the ILA made dramatic gains in the mid-1930's, eventually achieving affiliation with the Congress of Industrial Organizations. Finding duplication in their work, the ILA and the warehousemen's union worked for common goals and eventual merger. Opposition came from the AFL hierarchy and the International Brotherhood of Teamsters. In an era filled with strikes, violence, and internecine labor struggles, the ILWU emerged as a powerful, militant union which successfully achieved a working relationship with the forces of capital. Primary and secondary sources; 131 notes.   A. Hoffman

1109. Boryczka, Ray. MILITANCY AND FACTIONALISM IN THE UNITED AUTO WORKERS UNION, 1937-1941. *Maryland Hist. 1977 8(2): 13-25.* Traces the impact of factionalism on United Automobile Workers of America efforts to generate consistent rank and file militancy. Concludes that pragmatic, self-serving factionalism prevented organized militancy. Based on oral and printed primary sources and secondary sources; illus., 33 notes.   G. O. Gagnon

1110. Boryczka, Ray. SEASONS OF DISCONTENT: AUTO UNION FACTIONALISM AND THE MOTOR PRODUCTS STRIKE OF 1935-1936. *Michigan Hist. 1977 61(1): 3-32.* The Motor Products Corporation strike during 1935-36 illustrated conditions in automobile unionism between *Schechter* in 1935 and the major union upheavals of 1936. Factionalism, bred by conservatism within the United Auto Workers of America (UAW), produced a three-way contest between the corporation, the UAW, and the more militant independent unions. UAW president Francis Dillon vacillated constantly. Violence, scabbing, and employer belligerence further discouraged striking workers who became increasingly unwilling to support a seemingly futile endeavor. Although the UAW won exclusive recognition and a contract from Motor Products in 1937, the overall impact of the strike was ambiguous. But factionalism was unquestionably the cause of defeat. Primary sources; illus., 7 photos, 98 notes.   D. W. Johnson

1111. Botting, David C., Jr. BLOODY SUNDAY. *Pacific Northwest Q. 1958 49(4): 162-172.* An account of the bloody confrontation between police and adherents of the Industrial Workers of the World at Everett, Washington, on 5 November 1916, with comments on the litigation which followed.

1112. Brody, David. WORKING CLASS HISTORY IN THE GREAT DEPRESSION. *Rev. in Am. Hist. 1976 4(2): 262-267.* Review article prompted by Peter Friedlander's *The Emergence of a UAW Local, 1936-1939: A Study in Class and Culture* (Pittsburgh: U. of Pennsylvania Pr., 1975), which documents the growth of a Detroit local of the United Automobile Workers of America.

1113. Broyles, Glen J. THE SPOKANE FREE SPEECH FIGHT, 1909-1910: A STUDY IN IWW TACTICS. *Labor Hist. 1978 19(2): 238-252.* The free speech fight in Spokane, contrary to recent historical interpretation, was a victory not for the Industrial Workers of the World but for the city and Mayor Pratt. Based on Spokane newspapers; 27 notes.   L. L. Athey

1114. Brune, Lester H. "UNION HOLIDAY—CLOSED TILL FURTHER NOTICE": THE 1936 GENERAL STRIKE AT PEKIN, ILLINOIS. *J. of the Illinois State Hist. Soc. 1982 75(1): 29-38.* By February 1936, two years of antagonism at the American Distillery

Company made Pekin the site of the fourth city-wide general strike in US history. In May 1934, American Federation of Labor organization efforts led to a strike at the distillery. The resulting one-year contract ended in July 1935, and the company refused to renegotiate, took action against employees who testified before the National Labor Relations Board, and supported a rival Pekin Distillery Employees Association. Antiunion speeches by Mayor William E. Schurman and violent confrontations with police led the Pekin Trades and Labor Assembly to declare a labor holiday for 5 February. Violence was avoided as 1,500 workers participated in the two day demonstration, which effectively shut down the town and led the company to concede. 4 illus., 35 notes.
                                                        A. W. Novitsky

1115. Buhle, Mari Jo. SOCIALIST WOMEN AND THE "GIRL STRIKERS," CHICAGO, 1910. *Signs 1976 1(4): 1039-1051.* The 1910 Chicago garment workers' strike showed a new determined spirit in the American labor movement. The "new immigrants," especially young women, militantly opposed the United Garment Workers' conciliations with factory owners. Contemporary newspaper articles by Nellie M. Zeh and Mary O'Reilly represented Socialist women's responses to the strike and their efforts to publicize the implications of the struggle. Their perspective was rooted in their interpretation of the historic position of women workers. They themselves had given their girlhood to commodity production and felt a sisterhood with the young strikers. They saw the actions of the "girl strikers" as a symbol of the larger tendency in the industrial working class to determine their own destiny. Based on newspaper articles; 11 notes.   J. Gammage

1116. Buhle, Paul and Celenza, James, eds. "BORN OUT OF STRIKES": AN INTERVIEW WITH LUIGI NARDELLA. *Radical Hist. Rev. 1978 (17): 153-160.* Luigi Nardella recounts his experiences in the textile strike of 1922 in Rhode Island.

1117. Bulosan, Carlos. AMERICA IS IN THE HEART, AN EXCERPT. *Amerasia J. 1975 3(1): 1-15.* Presents excerpts from the author's autobiography dealing with his attempts to organize Filipino Americans' labor unions in California 1934-38, including activities of leftist political factions.

1118. Burran, James A. LABOR CONFLICT IN URBAN APPALACHIA: THE KNOXVILLE STREETCAR STRIKE OF 1919. *Tennessee Hist. Q. 1979 38(1): 62-78.* In the period of demobilization and search for normalcy following World War I, a streetcar strike occurred in October 1919 in conservative, typically Republican, Knoxville, Tennessee. It was part of a larger movement of the American Federation of Labor which was aimed at organizing, among others, the Knoxville police. When violence broke out after strike breakers were hired, the governor called in Federal troops. The presence of troops broke the strike. Primary and secondary sources; 35 notes.   M. B. Lucas

1119. Byrkit, James W. THE IWW IN WARTIME ARIZONA. *J. of Arizona Hist. 1977 18(2): 149-170.* The Industrial Workers of the World (IWW) struck the three mining companies in Bisbee, Arizona, in summer 1917. Company-hired *agents provocateurs* infiltrated the union. Although there was no proof of overt IWW violence, the agents played upon popular fear which labeled the union as radical. Company officials prevailed upon a sheriff's posse to arrest some 2000 strikers and to send them by railway freight cars to southwestern New Mexico. The Bisbee Deportation was the most effective effort to purge Arizona of all labor influence. Other bona fide unions disintegrated and organized labor ceased to be "a substantial force in Arizona political affairs." Derived from a graduate dissertation; 5 illus., 76 notes.   D. L. Smith

1120. Carpenter, Gerald. PUBLIC OPINION IN THE NEW ORLEANS STREET RAILWAY STRIKE OF 1929-1930. Fink, Gary M. and Reed, Merl E., eds. *Essays in Southern Labor History: Selected Papers, Southern Labor History Conference, 1976.* (Westport, Conn.; London, England, Greenwood Pr., 1977): 191-207. Studies the New Orleans Street Railway Strike of 1929-30 as an illustration of the incorrectness of the usual stereotype of southern public opinion as united against trade unionism. This is seen both in company (New Orleans Public Service, Inc.) appeals which reflected the public's acceptance of unionism and in union (Street and Electric Railway Employees of America) appeals for support resting on "positive concern for the principles of organized labor and negative objections to outside control."

The usual generalizations therefore must be examined more critically. 65 notes.   R. V. Ritter

1121. Carr, Joe Daniel. LABOR CONFLICT IN THE EASTERN KENTUCKY COAL FIELDS. *Filson Club Hist. Q. 1973 47(2): 179-192.* Analyzes the industrial conflict in Harlan and Bell counties in eastern Kentucky during the 1930's, providing graphic examples of the exploitation of miners by the mining corporations. Violent confrontations at Evarts in 1931 and at Stanfill in 1939 are investigated in depth, and the roles of the United Mine Workers, the National Recovery Administration, and the National Labor Relations Board are also explored. Exposes the failure of the judicial system and the corruption of Harlan County sheriff Theodore Middleton. Based on the Louisville *Courier-Journal* and the New York *Times* ; 58 notes.
                                                  G. B. McKinney

1122. Chiles, Frederic. GENERAL STRIKE: SAN FRANCISCO, 1934—AN HISTORICAL COMPILATION FILM STORYBOARD. *Labor Hist. 1981 22(3): 430-465.* Dramatizes the 1934 West Coast waterfront strike in photographs. Because no funding has been forthcoming to complete this project, an outline (narration and photographs) paired with directions for filming and recording is presented. Reminiscences of strikers convey the spirit which has been preserved by the camera. Based on interviews, several photographic collections, and other primary sources; 78 photos, 41 notes.   L. F. Velicer

1123. Cole, Merle T. MARTIAL LAW IN WEST VIRGINIA AND MAJOR DAVIS AS "EMPEROR OF TUG RIVER." *West Virginia Hist. 1982 43(2): 118-144.* Coal mine strikes during 1912-22 led West Virginia governors to invoke martial law in order to keep order in the southern counties. Thomas Boyd Davis, an officer in the West Virginia militia, acted as agent for a succession of state governors in suppressing the activities of labor activists and enforcing martial law. Based mostly on correspondence, government documents, newspapers, and other primary sources; photo, 99 notes.   J. D. Neville

1124. Condon, Richard H. BAYONETS AT THE NORTH BRIDGE: THE LEWISTON-AUBURN SHOE STRIKE, 1937. *Maine Hist. Soc. Q. 1981 21(2): 75-98.* Details the events of the Auburn and Lewiston, Maine, shoe workers' strike led by the United Shoe Workers of America (USWA), a Congress of Industrial Organizations affiliate. The USWA, attempting to gain union recognition and raise wages, organized a strike that lasted from 25 March to 28 June 1937. Although the USWA was generally successful in other locations, this strike essentially failed. This was due to the opposition of community leaders, including the French Roman Catholic priests, and to the fact that the leaders of the strike were outsiders, that local people had little militant labor experience, and that the strikers were quite poor. Based on local newspapers and interviews; 142 notes.   C. A. Watson

1125. Conlin, Joseph R. GOLDFIELD HIGH GRADE. *Am. West 1983 20(3): 38-44.* The principle that "gold belongs to him who finds it and digs it and no one else," a carry-over from the days of placer mining, continued to be held by miners after they began to work for gold mining corporations. Goldfield, Nevada, yielded fabulous amounts after the rush began in 1904, and the theft, or "high-grading," of the extraordinarily high-grade ore reached incredible proportions. Everyone participated or benefitted. The efforts of mine operators to stop high-grading and the resistance of miners to changes bringing them under scrutiny and regulation finally involved the Western Federation of Miners, the Industrial Workers of the World, and the sending in of federal troops. 8 illus., biblio.   D. L. Smith

1126. Cook, Bernard A. COVINGTON HALL AND RADICAL RURAL UNIONIZATION IN LOUISIANA. *Louisiana Hist. 1977 18(2): 227-238.* Covington Hall, a socialist organizer in the Louisiana lumber industry, promoted militant labor organizations and edited radical rural labor publications in Louisiana during 1907-16. His organization of the Forest and Farm Workers Union of the Industrial Workers of the World in 1916 was a failure, and socialism in Louisiana declined thereafter. The decline resulted from national causes, the exploitation of racial issues by lumber operators, the poverty and apathy of the workers, the earlier failure of the rural labor movement in Louisiana, the organized opposition of the companies and their political adjuncts, and the prosperity of World War I. Based on Hall's

unpublished manuscript, "Labor Struggles in the Deep South," in the Tulane University Library, and on published primary and secondary sources; 49 notes.   R. L. Woodward, Jr.

1127. Cook, Bernard A. and Watson, James R. THE SAILORS AND MARINE TRANSPORT WORKERS' 1913 STRIKE IN NEW ORLEANS: THE AFL AND THE IWW. *Southern Studies 1979 18(1): 111-122.* Two major types of divisions among workers in New Orleans, Louisiana, traditionally have prevented them from working together and improving their lot: racial differences and antagonism between skilled and unskilled workers. Although several attempts were made to unite the workers, and brief periods of cooperation took place, antagonism has been the general attitude. The dock strike of June-July 1913 by the Sailors' Union (American Federation of Labor) and the Marine Transport Workers (Industrial Workers of the World) against the United Fruit Company in New Orleans failed because of these antagonisms, lack of cooperation, scabbing by members, and betrayals by leadership. 47 notes.   J. J. Buschen

1128. Cooper, Patricia A. WHAT EVER HAPPENED TO ADOLPH STRASSER? *Labor Hist. 1979 20(3): 414-419.* Discusses the behavior and death of the Cigar Makers' International Union of America's leader, Adolph Strasser (1834-1938), who disappeared from the labor scene after 1910, and was initially buried at public expense. Based on the CMIU collection and Strasser's will; 12 notes.   L. L. Athey

1129. Corbin, David A. BETRAYAL IN THE WEST VIRGINIA COAL FIELDS: EUGENE V. DEBS AND THE SOCIALIST PARTY OF AMERICA, 1912-1914. *J. of Am. Hist. 1978 64(4): 987-1009.* Even though Eugene V. Debs has enjoyed a favorable historical image in America's labor movement, his attitudes and actions concerning local affiliates and rank-and-file members actually hurt the development of the Socialist Party of America. Nowhere is this more apparent than in the West Virginia coal strike of 1912-14. Not only did the national office of the SPA ignore the strike for a year, but when Debs finally intervened with an investigating committee, he urged coal miners to accept a questionable compromise. He also exonerated Governor Hatfield of charges of having abused his power, even though a US congressional committee reached the opposite conclusion. By ignoring the wishes of the miners and by betraying local Socialist affiliates, Debs did considerable damage to Socialist solidarity in West Virginia's coal fields. 89 notes.   T. P. Linkfield

1130. Corbin, David A. "FRANK KEENEY IS OUR LEADER, AND WE SHALL NOT BE MOVED": RANK-AND-FILE LEADERSHIP IN THE WEST VIRGINIA COAL FIELDS. Fink, Gary M. and Reed, Merl E., eds. *Essays in Southern Labor History: Selected Papers, Southern Labor History Conference, 1976.* (Westport, Conn.; London, England: Greenwood Pr., 1977): 144-156. A study of the career of Frank Keeney as a labor leader in the West Virginia coal fields. His career in the United Mine Workers of America began in 1912. In 1916 he led a "rump" organization and was elected president. He forced investigation and correction of corruption among local union district leaders. He was convinced of the importance and value of indigenous leadership and acted accordingly. His independence alienated him from UMW leaders, including John L. Lewis. In 1931 his last important move, the organization of an independent union and the calling of a strike, was a failure and resulted in his ostracism by the UMW. 49 notes.
                                                  R. V. Ritter

1131. Corbin, David A. *THE SOCIALIST AND LABOR STAR:* STRIKE AND SUPPRESSION IN WEST VIRGINIA, 1912-1913. *West Virginia Hist. 1973 34(2): 168-186.* The Socialist newspaper *The Socialist and Labor Star* reported the Paint Creek-Cabin Creek Strike of 1912-13 and articulated union interests in a radical fashion. Critical of labor and government establishments, it even assailed Eugene Debs for sacrificing the workers to Socialist Party solidarity. Editor Wyatt Hamilton Thompson spoke out so harshly that the military, under orders of Governor Henry D. Hatfield, destroyed the newspaper's plant and arrested Thompson. 57 notes.   C. A. Newton

1132. Corcoran, Theresa. VIDA SCUDDER AND THE LAWRENCE TEXTILE STRIKE. *Essex Inst. Hist. Collections 1979 115(3): 183-195.* During the 1912 Lawrence, Massachusetts, textile strike the Progressive Women's Club of Lawrence invited prominent speakers to address them on 4 March. No outsider stirred the conservatives more than Vida Dutton Scudder, professor at Wellesley College. A founder of the College Settlements Association and Denison House, a distinctively Boston settlement for women, a member of the Socialist Party in 1911, and author of *Socialism and Character* (1912), Scudder had moved into settlements in hopes that they might play their part in radical propaganda. In this she was discouraged, but later became convinced that Christianity offered the one solution to industrialized society, and after 1912 moved into various Christian groups for social reform. Examines Scudder's speech and the reaction to it, the Progressive Women's Club, and the textile strike. Primary and secondary sources; 30 notes.   R. S. Sliwoski

1133. Daniel, Cletus E. IN DEFENSE OF THE WHEATLAND WOBBLIES: A CRITICAL ANALYSIS OF THE IWW IN CALIFORNIA. *Labor Hist. 1978 19(4): 485-509.* Analyzes the "hop pickers riot" in Wheatland, California, in August 1913. IWW action in Wheatland reinforced ideological and tactical deficiencies among California Wobblies and increased their powerlessness. The incident occurred in spite of IWW organizational policies and produced many more failures than successes. Based on newspapers; 50 notes.   L. L. Athey

1134. Daniel, Cletus E. WOBBLIES ON THE FARM: THE IWW IN THE YAKIMA VALLEY. *Pacific Northwest Q. 1974 65(4): 166-175.* A study of the 1933 efforts of the reactivated Industrial Workers of the World ("Wobblies") to organize the fruit workers of the Yakima Valley. When picket lines were formed to enforce a strike the farmers organized into vigilante groups. The most notable and violent confrontation was at Congdon's Orchard, in the course of which a large number of strikers were turned over to county authorities for arrest and trial. The farmers gained the sympathies of the area on "patriotic" grounds as a mask for their antiunionism, and the "Wobblies" were never again able to successfully revive their efforts. 51 notes.   R. V. Ritter

1135. Dembo, Jonathan. JOHN DANZ AND THE SEATTLE AMUSEMENT TRADES STRIKE, 1921-1935. *Pacific Northwest Q. 1980 71(4): 172-182.* Due to a recession and decline in movie attendance, Seattle movie theater owner John Danz laid off a number of employees in 1921. Orchestra members belonging to a musicians' union retaliated with strikes. Legal maneuvering by both sides left the issue unresolved. Confrontations became violent. Danz's automobile was destroyed by a bomb blast. Negotiations dragged on into the 1930's, when the National Recovery Administration ruled that Danz owed $20,000 in back salaries to some employees dismissed in 1929 for their union activity. In 1935 the issue was finally resolved outside the courts. Though the settlement favored the union position, the original musicians' group profited little from the compromise. Based on newspapers and Seattle Central Labor Council Papers; 5 photos, 47 notes.   M. L. Tate

1136. DeWitt, Howard A. THE FILIPINO LABOR UNION: THE SALINAS LETTUCE STRIKE OF 1934. *Amerasia J. 1978 5(2): 1-21.* The Salinas, California, lettuce strike of 1934, though easily broken, was "a seminal turning point" in the evolution of organized Filipino labor. For the first time, a Filipino organization, the Filipino Labor Union, retained its structure and cohesion throughout the conflict. Despite the Salinas defeat, Filipino labor became more militant afterward, and destroyed the stereotype of the happy immigrant content to labor long hours at menial tasks for low wages. 68 notes.   T. L. Powers

1137. Dorsey, George. THE BAYONNE REFINERY STRIKE OF 1915-1916. *Polish Am. Studies 1976 33(2): 19-30.* This strike started on 15 July 1915 at "Jersey Standard's great refinery in Bayonne" when about 100 still cleaners demanded a 15% pay increase justified by a work speedup and publicly announced anticipated company profits. When other workers joined in, the company answered by hiring armed guards from P. J. Berghoff, a New York City "industrial service." The strike, of unorganized workers, spread to other companies. In confrontations, one Pole was killed and four others were wounded. The strike ended by the end of July after promises of pay increases, a change of a foreman, and an appeal to wartime patriotism. Fifteen months later, another strike erupted to improve upon the two dollars-per-day wages. Though not apparent in 1915 and 1916, a new industrialism, one of concern for the worker, was beginning to play a recognizable role in the

American economic world. Based primarily on newspaper accounts; 27 notes.   S. R. Pliska

1138. Dunnigan, Kate and Quinney, Richard. WORK AND COMMUNITY IN SAYLESVILLE. *Radical Hist. Rev. 1978 (17): 173-180.* Describes the sense of community and worker solidarity in Saylesville, Rhode Island, with excerpts from the cotton manufacturing company, Sayles Finishing Plants' company magazine, which contributed to the success of the 1934 strike.

1139. Dyson, B. Patricia and Dyson, Lowell K. AN HONEST LIGHT. *Labor Hist. 1982 23(3): 422-423.* Reviews *Northern Lights,* a film by John Hanson and Rob Nilsson, which focuses on the organizing of the Nonpartisan League in North Dakota during 1915-16. Note.   L. F. Velicer

1140. Ebner, Michael H. STRIKES AND SOCIETY: CIVIL BEHAVIOR IN PASSAIC, 1875-1926. *New Jersey Hist. 1979 97(1): 7-24.* Puts into historical perspective the 1926 textile strike in Passaic. Soon after the mills began operating in that city, questions arose about working conditions. Low wages, seasonal employment fluctuations, and unhealthy plant surroundings were concerns. Labor attempted to organize the industry, and strikes occurred. Local officials succeeded in quelling these disturbances, though the Red Scare, a post-World War I phenomenon, and suspicions of left-wing influences made them put constraints on labor's activities. The textile industry was at first thought of as a constructive and integral part of Passaic's life, but by 1926 these suppositions were being questioned. Based on government records, contemporary newspaper accounts, manuscript collections, and secondary sources; 9 illus., 33 notes.   E. R. McKinstry

1141. Eklund, Monica. MASSACRE AT LUDLOW. *Southwest Econ. and Soc. 1978 4(1): 21-30.* A strike of coal miners in 1913-14 in Ludlow, Colorado (against the Colorado Fuel and Iron Company), elicited attempted strike-breaking; mine guards, detectives, and the National Guard attacked and burned the strikers' tent city and at least 13 women and children died.

1142. Engelmann, Larry D. "WE WERE THE POOR PEOPLE": THE HORMEL STRIKE OF 1933. *Labor Hist. 1974 15(4): 483-510.* Narrates the formation of a union in the Hormel packinghouse in Austin, Minnesota, the conflict with the "benevolent dictatorship" of Hormel management and the violent strike of 1933. The union was sparked by an insurance proposal, issued as an edict, which would cost workers 20 cents per week. A strike ensued and peaked in November 1933 when workers seized the plant. The strike was successfully arbitrated after intervention by Governor Floyd B. Olson. Pay increases were granted, but union recognition was not achieved. The company shifted to a policy of "welfare capitalism." Based upon Austin, Minnesota, newspapers and personal interviews; 67 notes.   L. L. Athey

1143. Fairclough, Adam. THE PUBLIC UTILITIES INDUSTRY IN NEW ORLEANS: A STUDY IN CAPITAL, LABOR AND GOVERNMENT, 1894-1929. *Louisiana Hist. 1981 22(1): 45-65.* Chronicles municipal efforts to regulate New Orleans's public utilities, and the efforts on behalf of transit workers of the Amalgamated Association of Street and Electric Railway Employees of America (AASEREA) from the 1894 founding of the Citizens' Protective Association to the AASEREA's decisive defeat in the transit strike of 1929. In 1902 all local transit, gas, and electric companies were consolidated as the New Orleans Railways Company which later became New Orleans Public Service Inc. (NOPSI). Also in 1902, the AASEREA won partial recognition through a strike which, despite some union violence, enjoyed much public support. During this period both city and union were handicapped in their dealings with NOPSI by the attitude of the courts. Contemporary press and secondary sources; 46 notes.   L. Van Wyk

1144. Feldberg, Roslyn L. "UNION FEVER": ORGANIZING AMONG CLERICAL WORKERS, 1900-1930. *Radical Am. 1980 14(3): 53-70.* As recently as 1977 only 8.2% of the clerical workers in the United States were organized. Among women, the proportion was even lower. In a period when clerical workers were not considered real workers, (because they were clerical), and not considered organizable (because they were women), difficulties were pervasive. Women moved into stenographic and typing positions during the 1890's. The job was gradually redefined. It lost its status as a career entry point for men. Collective efforts by women workers to form unions emerged many times during 1900-29. Scattered offices, close ties with employers, social views of women's role, and labor movement indifference all accounted for the difficulties in major victories. The more positive work of the Women's Trade Union League is traced. 52 notes.   C. M. Hough

1145. Fickle, James E. THE LOUISIANA-TEXAS LUMBER WAR OF 1911-1912. *Louisiana Hist. 1975 16(1): 59-85.* Ruthless exploitation of workers in the early 20th century in the lumber industry of western Louisiana and eastern Texas led to labor strife, culminating in the "Louisiana-Texas Lumber War of 1911-1912." During the lumber mill strikes of 1906-07 around Lake Charles, Louisiana, mill operators formed the Southern Lumber Operators Association, headed by Houston lumber magnate John Henry Kirby, to resist labor organization. Arthur Emerson and Jay Smith led the workers, but William ("Big Bill") Haywood also played an active role in the 1911-12 dispute, amid growing Socialist sympathies of the region's workers. Worker layoffs and a decline in economic conditions stimulated the dispute. Violence on both sides escalated, as the "War" attracted national attention. The operators, however, generally enjoyed greater support from government authorities; and in the end the strikes failed and labor organization declined. Primary sources, 90 notes.   R. L. Woodward, Jr.

1146. Filippelli, Ronald L. DIARY OF A STRIKE: GEORGE MEDRICK AND THE COAL STRIKE OF 1927 IN WESTERN PENNSYLVANIA. *Pennsylvania Hist. 1976 43(3): 253-266.* The bituminous coal strike that began in 1925 involved most of the nation's fields, but its greatest impact was felt in Pennsylvania. The United Mine Workers were severely damaged as operators were often successful in forcing the union from their mines. By 1929 most of the Pennsylvania bituminous coal industry was nonunion. U.M.W.A. membership in the nation stood at about one-fourth of what it had been in 1920. The 1927 diary entries presented here are those of George Medrick, then a U.M.W.A. agent active in the Pittsburgh area. Based on the George Medrick Papers; illus., 18 notes.   D. C. Swift

1147. Findlay, James F. THE GREAT TEXTILE STRIKE OF 1934: ILLUMINATING RHODE ISLAND HISTORY IN THE THIRTIES. *Rhode Island Hist. 1983 42(1): 17-29.* The significance of the strike lay in the way in which it dramatized the crisis in the textile industry, which had long been the base of the Rhode Island economy. In addition, Governor Theodore Francis Green's skillful handling of the crisis consolidated the power of the Democratic Party, confirmed the hegemony of the New Deal in state politics, and brought urban, ethnic, and working class Rhode Islanders to challenge the traditional influence of rural, Yankee Republicans. Based on manuscripts, published documents, and newspapers; 4 illus., 39 notes.   P. J. Coleman

1148. Fine, Sidney, ed. JOHN L. LEWIS DISCUSSES THE GENERAL MOTORS SIT-DOWN STRIKE: A DOCUMENT. *Labor Hist. 1974 15(4): 563-570.* Presents a document about John L. Lewis discussing the General Motors sit-down strike of 1936-37. Lewis apparently hoped to place the problem in the lap of President Roosevelt. Document in the Heber Blankenhorn Papers in the Archives of Labor History and Urban Affairs of Wayne State University. 16 notes.   L. L. Athey

1149. Fogelson, Nancy. THEY PAVED THE STREETS WITH SILK: PATERSON, NEW JERSEY SILK WORKERS, 1913-1924. *New Jersey Hist. 1979 97(3): 133-148.* In 1913, Paterson silk workers staged one of a long series of strikes that culminated in 1924 with a violent outbreak that received extensive coverage in New York newspapers. During this decade, laborers in the silk industry were unable to secure beneficial changes for themselves because so many of their number left to form their own businesses and because mill owners deserted the city in search of cheap labor available elsewhere in abundance. In addition, management did not modernize machinery or production systems, but relied on antiquated business practices that eventually led to the death of the industry in Paterson. Based on interviews, contemporary newspaper accounts, ACLU papers, and secondary sources; 3 illus., 46 notes.   E. R. McKinstry

1150. Foner, Philip S. *A MARTYR TO HIS CAUSE:* THE SCENARIO OF THE FIRST LABOR FILM IN THE UNITED STATES. *Labor Hist. 1983 24(1): 103-111.* During 1907-10, antilabor films were numerous, often portraying strike leaders as dynamiters and killers and scabs as social heroes. The first film produced under labor auspices appeared in 1911 and was part of the McNamara defense movement. *A Martyr to His Cause* portrayed the life of John J. McNamara, the secretary-treasurer of the International Association of Bridge and Structural Iron Workers, who had been indicted with his brother, James B. McNamara, for the 1910 dynamiting of the *Los Angeles Times* building. 9 notes.   L. F. Velicer

1151. Fones-Wolf, Kenneth. REVIVALISM AND CRAFT UNIONISM IN THE PROGRESSIVE ERA: THE SYRACUSE AND AUBURN LABOR MOVEMENTS OF 1913. *New York Hist. 1982 63(4): 389-416.* Local craft union leaders organized the Labor Forward Movement, drawing on local religious culture to reassure middle-class reformers of the movement's devotion to American capitalism. In Syracuse and Auburn, New York, the growth of industries owned by outside manufacturers, a large population of immigrants, the Men and Religion Forward social gospel revival, and progressivism set the stage for the Labor Forward Movement. Labor Forward represented an alternative to socialism, and labor evangelists persuaded immigrant workers to join unions. Labor Forward's struggle for higher wages and better working conditions was resisted by employers. Strike riots involving newly organized unions of immigrant workers alarmed the middle class. Labor leaders, fearing loss of community status, abandoned the immigrant workers, thereby disrupting labor solidarity. Based on contemporary periodicals and newspapers, and other primary sources; 3 illus., 59 notes.   R. N. Lokken

1152. Foster, James C. AFL, IWW AND NOME: 1905-1908. *Alaska J. 1975 5(2): 66-77.* Describes the beginning of union organization in Nome. The first successful union was the AFL-Federal Labor Union, which had a strike for longshoremen in 1905. The Western Federation of Miners followed. Describes the conflict in the area between the American Federation of Labor and the Industrial Workers of the World. Reviews union interest and action in local politics. 11 illus., 37 notes.   E. E. Eminhizer

1153. Foster, James C. THE TEN DAY TRAMPS. *Labor Hist. 1982 23(4): 608-623.* The Western Federation of Miners (WFM), recognizing the institutional threat inherent in the high turnover rates among miners in the western United States and British Columbia, tried various methods to keep the itinerant miner within the union. The union-at-large system, in which the itinerant miner paid dues directly to the WFM's Denver headquarters, proved the most successful. A regression analysis comparing the success rates of locals with high itinerant or tramp membership and locals with stable membership, however, reveals that the number of itinerant miners in a local had little effect on the union's performance. Based on the Western Federation of Miners Collection, the Vernon Jensen Collection, the Patrick Callahan Collection, interviews with retired miners, and other primary sources; 3 tables, 34 notes.   L. F. Velicer

1154. Foster, James C. THE TREADWELL STRIKES, 1907 AND 1908. *Alaska J. 1976 6(1): 2-11.* In the early 20th century the Western Federation of Miners attempted to organize in Alaska. The mines at Douglas Island across from Juneau were a part of the effort. Failure of the WFM in Goldfield, Nevada, stimulated the interest in Alaska. Details the tactics of both sides in the strike against the Treadwell Mines. Suggests reasons for the union's failure. 10 photos., 38 notes.   E. E. Eminhizer

1155. Foster, James C. THE WESTERN FEDERATION COMES TO ALASKA. *Pacific Northwest Q. 1975 66(4): 161-173.* During 1905 the Western Federation of Miners (WFM) launched an effective campaign for support among Alaskan miners. Within 10 months it had gained enough members to join with the Nome Federal Labor Union to create a labor party and win elections in Nome. Strikes for higher wages and better working conditions followed, only to be met by mine owners' outcries against radicalism. But the WFM adopted moderate reformist tactics and won public support. Success ended, however, when a few WFM hotheads used force to keep strikebreakers out of the mines. After 1908 the Alaskan WFM quickly declined as its leaders were jailed and its public credibility was undermined. Based on primary and secondary sources; 2 photos, 48 notes. M. L. Tate

1156. Fry, Joseph A. RAYON, RIOT, AND REPRESSION: THE COVINGTON SIT-DOWN STRIKE OF 1937. *Virginia Mag. of Hist. and Biog. 1976 84(1): 3-18.* The attempt by the Textile Workers Organizing Committee to organize the Industrial Rayon Corporation's plant in Covington, Virginia, illustrates the problems which faced union leaders in the South. Though the movement did result in Virginia's first significant sit-down strike, the support of state officials and police for the management produced violence and ultimate failure. Based on the George C. Peery Papers, Virginia State Library, interviews with participants, newspapers, and additional primary sources; 55 notes. R. F. Oakes

1157. Gerstle, Gary. THE MOBILIZATION OF THE WORKING CLASS COMMUNITY: THE INDEPENDENT TEXTILE UNION IN WOONSOCKET, 1931-1946. *Radical Hist. Rev. 1978 (17): 161-172.* Gives the history and purpose of the Independent Textile Workers, an industrial trade union founded in 1931 by Belgians in Woonsocket, Rhode Island; during 1934-43 they organized Woonsocket's French-Canadian workers.

1158. Ginger, Ann Fagan. WORKERS' SELF-DEFENSE IN THE COURTS. *Sci. & Soc. 1983 47(3): 257-284.* Traces the activities of Carol Weiss King and the organizations in which she worked—the International Labor Defense and the International Juridical Association—in early Depression-era efforts to provide legal defense for radical workers, aliens, and unemployed people who were arrested in large numbers before the New Deal began. King's co-workers and associates included William Z. Foster, Joseph R. Brodsky, William L. Patterson, David Freeman, Isaac Shorr, and others. King and her co-workers provided direct legal aid to workers, published an International Labor Defense pamphlet on worker self-defense in the courts, and helped to free Georgi Dimitrov from Nazi courts. Primary sources; appendix. R. E. Butchart

1159. Glaser, Martha. PATERSON, 1924: THE A.C.L.U. AND LABOR. *New Jersey Hist. 1976 94(4): 155-172.* Loom assignments and low wages caused the Paterson silk strike of 1924. The American Civil Liberties Union (ACLU) involved itself on behalf of labor after the strike committee of the Associated Silk Workers Union asked for assistance. By taking legal action, by publicizing events in Paterson throughout the country, and by confronting the owners of the factories and local authorities who made it difficult to assemble for strike meetings, the ACLU demonstrated its tactics in handling the problems of free speech and assembly that arose from labor-management clashes. Although the owners were victorious in this instance, the ACLU won the right to assemble and to listen to any speaker desired for the union. Primary and secondary sources; 3 illus., 47 notes. E. R. McKinstry

1160. Golin, Steve. DEFEAT BECOMES DISASTER: THE PATERSON STRIKE OF 1913 AND THE DECLINE OF THE IWW. *Labor Hist. 1983 24(2): 223-248.* The Industrial Workers of the World (IWW) never recovered from its defeat in the Paterson, New Jersey, silk workers strike of 1913. Rather than concede defeat at the hands of the powerful manufacturers, the IWW and other radical groups blamed the IWW strike leaders and the organization of the IWW for the Paterson defeat. The internal criticism and the attempts to more tightly control the organization led to the decline of the IWW in the East long before the massive federal repression directed against the IWW from 1917 to 1919. Based on accounts in *Solidarity*, IWW *Proceedings*, and other primary sources; 74 notes. L. F. Velicer

1161. Gordon, Max. THE COMMUNISTS AND THE DRIVE TO ORGANIZE STEEL, 1936. *Labor Hist. 1982 23(2): 254-265.* Reproduces a report to John Stachel, the Communist Party's national trade union secretary by John Steuben, a Communist organizer in charge of the Steel Workers Organizing Committee's drive in Youngstown, Ohio. Steuben comments on the union drive in Youngstown, organizers and methods of organization, "partial struggles" resulting in some immediate worker victories, subversion of company unions, steel company policies, and the status of the local Communist Party. Based on the Nelson Frank papers; 19 notes. L. F. Velicer

1162. Gottlieb, Peter. THE COMPLICATED EQUATION: WORKER REBELLION AND UNIONIZATION. *Appalachian J. 1979 6(4): 321-325.* Analyzes the growth of unions and workers' organizations in the United States during the 1930's despite the Depression and high unemployment; discusses John W. Hevener's *Which Side Are You On? The Harlan County Coal Miners, 1931-39* (Urbana: U. of Illinois Pr., 1978), an account of the Kentucky workers' struggle to organize.

1163. Green, Ben. "IF WE'D STUCK TOGETHER": ORGANIZING FISHERS IN FLORIDA. *Southern Exposure 1982 10(3): 69-76.* The attempts from 1930 to 1958 of Bob Knowlton and United Packinghouse Workers of America national organizer Ed Beltrame to organize Cortez mullet fishermen into a union failed because the fishermen and fish dealers were in the same families.

1164. Green, James R. THE BROTHERHOOD OF TIMBER WORKERS 1910-1913: A RADICAL RESPONSE TO INDUSTRIAL CAPITALISM IN THE SOUTHERN U.S.A. *Past and Present [Great Britain] 1973 (60): 161-200.* Analyses factors behind the struggle of the Brotherhood of Timber Workers (BTW) and Industrial Workers of the World (IWW) with the lumber companies of Louisiana and Texas, 1910-13. Both black and white workers and farmers cooperated out of hatred for the northern syndicates, which was greater than any fear of the IWW agitators' revolutionary ideas. The BTW and IWW created a radical, collective response to industrial capitalism, remarkable in an era of racial segregation. US Labor Department documents, censuses, Kirby Papers, newspapers. E. M. Sirriyeh

1165. Green, Jim. THE BROTHERHOOD. *Southern Exposure 1976 4(1-2): 21-29.* The Brotherhood of Timber Workers was founded 1911-13, in western Louisiana and eastern Texas by white and black workers who hoped to combat the repressive Southern Lumber Operators' Association.

1166. Harris, William H. A. PHILIP RANDOLPH AS A CHARISMATIC LEADER, 1925-1941. *J. of Negro Hist. 1979 64(4): 301-315.* A. Philip Randolph emerged as a national figure in organizing the Brotherhood of Sleeping Car Porters. His later disavowal of the Communist tendencies in the National Negro Congress and his abortive March on Washington Movement made Randolph one of the best known and widely respected Afro-American leaders. Primary materials; 49 notes. N. G. Sapper

1167. Herring, Neill and Thrasher, Sue. UAW SITDOWN STRIKE: ATLANTA, 1936. *Southern Exposure 1974 1(3/4): 63-83.* Analysis of the labor strike at General Motor's Lakewood plant in Atlanta, one of a series of strikes that spread through the General Motors plants across the nation during 1935-37. Local conditions influenced the workers to strike while the United Auto Workers Executive Board played only a peripheral role. The workers and community cooperated to provide the necessities of life for the strikers. Job security resulted from the Atlanta strike. Based on oral interviews; 21 illus. G. A. Bolton

1168. Hield, Melissa. "UNION-MINDED": WOMEN IN THE TEXAS ILGWU, 1933-1950. *Frontiers 1979 4(2): 59-70.* Details the prounion struggles of black, Mexican American, and Anglo women in the Texas garment industry during 1933-50, based on interviews with eight women then active in the International Ladies' Garment Workers' Union.

1169. Hill, Charles. FIGHTING THE TWELVE-HOUR DAY IN THE AMERICAN STEEL INDUSTRY. *Labor Hist. 1974 15(1): 19-35.* Reviews the movement against the twelve-hour day in the steel industry and details the intricate maneuvering of a diverse group of opponents and supporters ranging from John A. Fitch, President Harding, Secretary of Commerce Herbert Hoover, Paul Kellogg, and others during 1923. The reform was achieved, and the steel companies had little difficulty in making the changeover to the eight-hour day. Based on the files of the War Labor Policies Board, the Samuel McCune Lindsay papers, the Herbert Hoover papers, and *The Survey.* 96 notes. L. L. Athey

1170. Hoffman, Abraham. THE EL MONTE BERRY PICKERS' STRIKE, 1933: INTERNATIONAL INVOLVEMENT IN A LOCAL LABOR DISPUTE. *J. of the West 1973 12(1): 71-84.* A detailed account of the 1933 berry pickers' strike in El Monte, California, which involved "Mexican laborers, Communist agitators, Japanese employers, Los Angeles Chamber of Commerce and business representatives, and state and federal mediators . . . over issues of wages, hours, and working conditions. . . . The El Monte strike, however, claimed the distinction of direct involvement by the government of Mexico, in the form of diplomatic pressure, monetary assistance, and consular intervention. . . . In contrast to the active assistance of the Mexican consuls, the Japanese consul maintained a low profile, probably because of his awareness that excessive publicity would raise questions about Japanese leasing of property in a state that had already endorsed two alien land laws." 44 notes.   D. D. Cameron

1171. Horstman, Ronald. TRADE UNIONS IN THE BANKING FIELD: A FOOTNOTE ON THE HISTORY OF ST. LOUIS. *Missouri Hist. Soc. Bull.* 1978 34(2): 104-105. Describes the Telegraphers National Bank in St. Louis during 1922-42. Owned by the Brotherhood of Railway Telegraphers, the bank flourished under the leadership of Edward J. Manion and Vernon O. Gardner. 2 photos.   H. T. Lovin

1172. Hudson, James J. THE ROLE OF THE CALIFORNIA NATIONAL GUARD DURING THE SAN FRANCISCO GENERAL STRIKE OF 1934. *Military Affairs* 1982 46(2): 76-83. On 5 July 1934, the California National Guard was called upon in one of the most serious labor disputes of the 20th century, the San Francisco maritime and general strike of that year. This strike was part of a larger one that affected the entire west coast of the United States. During its 3-week tour, the guard took control of the waterfront and established law and order, without trying to usurp the powers and duties of the civil authorities. Its performance was exemplary. Based on California National Guard and other primary sources; 55 notes.   A. M. Osur

1173. Hutchinson, John. JOHN L. LEWIS: TO THE PRESIDENCY OF THE UMWA. *Labor Hist.* 1978 19(2): 185-203. Surveys the life of John L. Lewis from his birth in 1880 to his appointment as president of the United Mine Workers of America in 1920. Lewis, an itinerant miner from a mining family, emerged as a leader in the UMWA through his activities in Illinois District 12. Based on interviews and *Proceedings of UMWA District 12 conventions*; 30 notes.   L. L. Athey

1174. Hyser, Raymond M. DISCORD IN UTOPIA: THE ELLSWORTH STRIKE OF 1904. *Pennsylvania Mag. of Hist. and Biog.* 1982 106(3): 393-410. When James William Ellsworth abandoned a sincere paternalism for profit by initiating a wage reduction, bitter strife and the unionization of his coal-mining company at Ellsworth, Pennsylvania, resulted. Based on the Ellsworth Papers, Western Reserve Academy Archives, Hudson, Ohio, other MSS, newspapers, and secondary works; 84 notes.   T. H. Wendel

1175. Jensen, Billie Barnes. WOODROW WILSON'S INTERVENTION IN THE COAL STRIKE OF 1914. *Labor Hist.* 1974 15(1): 63-77. Assesses the factors which caused Woodrow Wilson to intervene with federal troops in the Colorado coal fields strikes of 1914. All parts of the country pressured President Wilson to intervene. His mediation attempts failed, partly as a result of mineowners obstinacy. Union and congressional outcries also increased pressure, while newspapers were generally in favor of sending federal troops. After the "Ludlow Massacre" pressure became so intense that Governor Elias Ammons finally requested federal intervention, and Wilson ordered troops in. Wilson and Ammons are characterized as men "pushed by the events." Based on the Woodrow Wilson papers in the Library of Congress. 59 notes.   L. L. Athey

1176. Johnson, James P. THEORIES OF LABOR UNION DEVELOPMENT AND THE UNITED MINE WORKERS, 1932-1933. *Register of the Kentucky Hist. Soc.* 1975 73(2): 150-170. Analyzes the resurgence of the United Mine Workers from October 1932 to mid-1933. General theories are examined, including strategic position, changing governmental attitudes, employer resistance, union leadership, dramatic discontent, and momentum, with examples from Alabama and Kentucky. Primary and secondary sources; 68 notes.   J. F. Paul

1177. Jordan, Daniel P. THE MINGO WAR: LABOR VIOLENCE IN THE SOUTHERN WEST VIRGINIA COAL FIELDS, 1919-1922. Fink, Gary M. and Reed, Merl E., eds. *Essays in Southern Labor*

History: Selected Papers, Southern Labor History Conference, 1976. (Westport, Conn.; London, England: Greenwood Pr., 1977): 102-143. Chronicles the Mingo War, discusses the major adversaries' views of issues, their strategy, tactics, and weapons, and analyzes the war's effects and significance. The fundamental issue was unionization or "the right to belong to a labor union," but also included many related issues. The United Mine Workers of America operated under serious handicaps. Though largely typical, the conflict had several distinctive elements: its single issue, the exceptionally great amount of violence, the lack of radical issues despite a fairly large number of blacks in both camps, and the lack of outside radical participants. 129 notes.   R. V. Ritter

1178. Kahn, Lawrence M. UNIONS AND INTERNAL LABOR MARKETS: THE CASE OF THE SAN FRANCISCO LONGSHOREMEN. *Labor Hist.* 1980 21(3): 369-391. West Coast longshoremen's unions transformed longshoring in San Francisco, California, in the 1930's from a secondary job characterized by low earnings and poor working conditions, to a primary job offering high relative earnings, job stability, and improved working conditions. The key to this transformation was the 1934 West Coast longshoremen's strike. Based on Bureau of Labor Statistics data, Works Progress Administration surveys, and other primary sources; 6 tables, 48 notes.   L. F. Velicer

1179. Kanarek, Harold K. DISASTER FOR HARD COAL: THE ANTHRACITE STRIKE OF 1925-1926. *Labor Hist.* 1974 15(1): 46-62. Details the struggle between the mine owners, the U.M.W.A., and the federal government during the anthracite strike of 1925-26. The owners and the unions lacked foresight and precipitated a strike which disastrously affected the whole industry. Only Gifford Pinchot, among public officials, consistently tried to protect the interests of the public and the worker. The federal government did not support this view. Based on the Gifford Pinchot, Coolidge, and W. Jett Lauck papers, and on the *Congressional Record.* 83 notes.   L. L. Athey

1180. Kanarek, Harold K. THE PENNSYLVANIA ANTHRACITE STRIKE OF 1922. *Pennsylvania Mag. of Hist. and Biog.* 1975 99(2): 207-225. Studies the way mining operators met the miners' demands and their failure to understand their own best interests, which opened the way for competitors (gas, oil, and electricity) to capture the market. Various factors were involved: the dangers of an unregulated monopoly, the operators concentration on weakening the union, preoccupation with wages on the part of the United Mine Workers, and total disinterest on the part of both Congress and the White House. 73 notes.
                                                              R. V. Ritter

1181. Keeran, Roger R. COMMUNIST INFLUENCE IN THE AUTOMOBILE INDUSTRY, 1920-1933: PAVING THE WAY FOR AN INDUSTRIAL UNION. *Labor Hist.* 1979 20(2): 189-225. Although small in number, the Communists formed a nucleus in the auto industry in the 1920's which challenged "welfare capitalism." Through shop activity, newspapers, strike support, and fraternal society meetings, the Communists spread the idea of industrial unionism and established the base for success of unionism in the 1930's. Based on the records of the Auto Workers Union, newspapers, and oral history; 58 notes.
                                                              L. L. Athey

1182. Keeran, Roger R. THE COMMUNISTS AND UAW FACTIONALISM, 1937-39. *Michigan Hist.* 1976 60(2): 115-135. Prevailing views distorted Communist responsibility for United Auto Workers' (UAW) factionalism in Michigan during the late 1930's. Throughout the period Communists worked to maintain unity within the UAW and with the Congress of Industrial Organizations. Only after UAW President Homer Martin thoroughly alienated rank and file unionists and their leaders did open, but reluctant, Communist opposition develop. Martin himself caused the factionalism, blamed the Communists, made them his unwilling adversaries, and brought about his own downfall. Primary and secondary sources; 2 photos, 36 notes.   D. W. Johnson

1183. Keeran, Roger R. EVERYTHING FOR VICTORY: COMMUNIST INFLUENCE IN THE AUTO INDUSTRY DURING WORLD WAR II. *Sci. and Soc.* 1979 43(1): 1-28. The decline of Communist influence within the United Automobile Workers of America during World War II can only partially be traced to the group's support for incentive pay and the no-strike clause; both of which were highly popular among many workers. In these matters the Communists were acting in accordance with the "win-the-war" philosophy of the UAW and CIO leadership. The waning of Communist power owed a great deal to the general anti-labor and rightwing political influences that gained strength during the war and to the confusion within Party ranks over Earl Browder's post-Teheran policies. Communists remained influential among black workers and despite the election of Walter Reuther in 1946 were by no means a negligible force in the UAW in the immediate postwar period. Printed primary and secondary sources.　　N. Lederer

1184. Keeran, Roger R. HIS BROTHER'S KEEPER. *Rev. in Am. Hist. 1977 5(1): 100-105.* Review article prompted by Victor G. Reuther's *The Brothers Reuther and the Story of the UAW: A Memoir* (Boston: Houghton Mifflin Co., 1976), which discusses the brothers' involvement in organizing the United Automobile Workers of America (UAW) in the mid-30's.

1185. Kessler-Harris, Alice. ORGANIZING THE UNORGANIZA-BLE: THREE JEWISH WOMEN AND THEIR UNION. *Labor Hist. 1976 17(1): 5-23.* Surveys the lives and work of Pauline Newman, Fannia Cohn, and Rose Pesotta of the International Ladies' Garment Workers' Union. Their experience as women and their tasks as union officers persistently conflicted, but their class consciousness took precedence over their identification as women. Based upon the Pesotta, Schneiderman, and Cohn papers; 84 notes.　　L. L. Athey

1186. Klehr, Harvey. AMERICAN COMMUNISM AND THE UNITED AUTO WORKERS: NEW EVIDENCE ON AN OLD CONTROVERSY. *Labor Hist. 1983 24(3): 404-413.* Communist Party members within the United Automobile Workers of America (UAW) were responsible for encouraging wildcat strikes and undermining the more moderate leadership of the UAW in the 1930's. While the Communist Party Politburo favored alliances and cooperation with non-Communists in organized labor during the Popular Front era, it could not always control the activities of individual Communist members working with the UAW. Attempts to undermine the UAW leadership led to the expulsion of all Communists from the UAW, destroying any hope of furthering Communist influence in the UAW or other American unions. Based on minutes of Communist Party Politburo meetings and on other primary sources; 19 notes.　　L. F. Velicer

1187. Lawler, Pat. IN BOOM TOWN ANCHORAGE: RAILROAD WORKERS BATTLE "CAPITALIST WAGE SLAVERY." *Alaska J. 1980 10(3): 22-27.* Recounts the rise and fall of the socialist movement in Anchorage. When the Alaska Railroad began its activities the socialist movement was gaining strength, and in 1916 the Alaska Labor Union was founded. Many immigrants participated; the union prospered and started the *Alaska Labor News.* Lena Morrow Lewis joined its staff and through her the paper became a radical, socialist, feminist voice. The Alaska Engineering Commission began to erode the influence of the union and paper by hiring workers by contracts for specific jobs and not by an hourly wage. Then World War I nationalism made the socialist position less popular. Finally the conservative forces in the union actually came out in favor of the Allies; this helped fragment the party. By 1918 the Socialist Party was dead in Alaska. 3 photos, 9 notes.　　S

1188. Leab, Daniel J. WRITING HISTORY WITH FILM: TWO VIEWS OF THE 1937 STRIKE AGAINST GENERAL MOTORS BY THE UAW. *Labor Hist. 1980 21(1): 102-112.* Reviews two films: *The Great Sitdown* (1976) by British filmmaker Stephen Peet and *With Babies and Banners* (1978) by Lorraine Gray and Lynn Goldfarb. The films rewrite history from the United Automobile Workers of America (UAW) strikers' and women's perspectives. 20 notes.　　L. L. Athey

1189. Leon, Arnoldo de. *LOS TASINQUES* AND THE SHEEP SHEARERS' UNION OF NORTH AMERICA: A STRIKE IN WEST TEXAS, 1934. *West Texas Hist. Assoc. Year Book 1979 55: 3-16.* Chronicles the attempted unionization and unsuccessful strike of Mexican *tasinques* (sheep shearers), and the numerous racial, economic, and political factors which doomed their cause.

1190. Levi, Steven C. THE BATTLE FOR THE EIGHT-HOUR DAY IN SAN FRANCISCO. *California History 1978-79 57(4): 342-353.* From July 1916 to January 1917 the structural steel workers of San Francisco conducted a strike for the eight-hour working day. Fifty-four out of sixty-four companies agreed to the request; the ten who

refused, along with other members of the business community under the blessing of the San Francisco Chamber of Commerce, organized the Law and Order Committee to maintain the nine-hour day and recreate the open shop. The Committee employed a budget of $1 million against the union and conducted an anti-union propaganda campaign. However, several of the companies found it difficult to continue with nonunion labor and capitulated to the union. The union boycotted the remaining companies. Eventually Mayor James Rolph became exasperated by Law and Order Committee tactics and sided with the union. The companies admitted defeat and accepted the eight-hour day. The Committee lasted another two years before disbanding, having alienated much of its support through endorsement of extralegal measures. Primary and secondary sources; 4 photos, 37 notes.　　A. Hoffman

1191. Lichtenstein, Nelson. ANOTHER TIME, ANOTHER PLACE: BLACKS, RADICALS AND RANK AND FILE MILITANCY IN AUTO IN THE 30S & 40S. *Radical Am. 1982 6(1-2): 131-137.* Reviews three works with slightly different political viewpoints but that share a focus on the secondary leadership level of policymaking in the forming of the United Auto Workers: Roger Keeran's *The Communist Party and the Auto Workers Unions* (1980), Martin Glabermann's *The Struggle against the No-Strike Pledge during World War II* (1980), August Meier and Elliot Rudwick's *Black Detroit and the Rise of the UAW* (1979). Note, 5 illus.　　C. M. Hough

1192. Listikov, S. V. PROFSOIUZY I IDEINO-POLITICHESKAIA BOR'BA VOKRUG PLANA PLAMBA [Trade unions and the ideological and political struggle over the Plumb Plan]. *Amerikanskii Ezhegodnik [USSR] 1980: 92-117.* Railroad union demands, 1917-19, were of an economic and sociopolitical nature, expressing a strange mixture of socialist and traditional ideas. The so-called Plumb Plan drafted by the railroad brotherhoods' legal counsel Glenn Edward Plumb in 1919 called, among other things, for the nationalization of railroads with reimbursement of investors, workers' participation in management and profits, and the right of workers to join the union of their choice. The plan was rejected by financiers, right-wing radicals, and even by some trade unions. A temporary compromise, indirectly reflecting some of the Plumb Plan demands, was reached with the Watson-Parker bill of 1926. 122 notes.　　N. Frenkley

1193. Lovin, Hugh T. MOSES ALEXANDER AND THE IDAHO LUMBER STRIKE OF 1917: THE WARTIME ORDEAL OF A PROGRESSIVE. *Pacific Northwest Q. 1975 66(3): 115-122.* Representing the reformist impulse of the Progressive Era, Moses Alexander won the governorship of Idaho in 1914 and was reelected two years later. World War I disrupted his legislative programs and placed him in the arena of conflict between "patriotic" groups and the Industrial Workers of the World. The State Council of Defense, supported by Idaho industrial interests, chided Alexander for protecting the IWW and other alleged pro-German interests, but he remained steadfast in their defense. Yet when the IWW threatened violence, he cracked down on their activities and promoted compromise at the conference table. Violence was averted and some of the barriers to labor reform were gradually overcome. Based on primary sources; photo, 34 notes.　　M. L. Tate

1194. Lynch, Patrick. PITTSBURGH, THE I.W.W., AND THE STOGIE WORKERS. Conlin, Joseph R., ed. *At the Point of Production: The Local History of the I.W.W.* (Westport, Conn.: Greenwood Pr., 1981): 79-94. During the summer of 1909 a significant strike began in McKees Rocks, near Pittsburgh, Pennsylvania. The workers of the Pressed Steel Car Company demanded higher wages, the positing of wage rates, the end of a wage-pool system, and the creation of an acceptable grievance procedure. The strikers soon enlisted the help of the Industrial Workers of the World. Some historians have described the McKees Rocks strike as the incident that inspired the revival of the IWW in the East. The IWW activities in the area from 1909 through 1913 caused important developments in the Pittsburgh area, especially the stogie workers' strike of 1913. These cigar makers demanded better wages and working conditions. They won the strike, establishing the union shop and worker control of shop conditions. Based on magazine, newspaper, and journal articles of the period; 86 notes.　　J. Powell

1195. Maroney, James C. THE INTERNATIONAL LONGSHORE-MEN'S ASSOCIATION IN THE GULF STATES DURING THE PROGRESSIVE ERA. *Southern Studies 1977 16(2): 225-232.* The

International Longshoremen's Association, Gulf Coast District, maintained a conservative attitude in the early 20th century. Despite its moderation, the union movement was strongly opposed by well organized management. A powerful drive by management to promote the open shop rule almost eradicated union power by 1920. In race relations, separate and segregated locals but equal work for blacks and whites became standard. Blacks thus received more work and more opportunities for union officeholding. The black workers' gains resulted from economic rather than humanitarian factors; strikes and violence hurt white workers. Based on union records, unpublished M.A. theses, secondary sources; 19 notes.   J. Buschen

1196. Maroney, James C. THE TEXAS-LOUISIANA OIL FIELD STRIKE. Fink, Gary M. and Reed, Merl E., eds. *Essays in Southern Labor History: Selected Papers, Southern Labor History Conference, 1976.* (Westport, Conn.; London, England: Greenwood Pr., 1977): 161-172. Studies of the 1917 strike of Texas and Louisiana oil field workers as an illustration of some employers' inexorable opposition to organized labor and great resentment of all concessions made to labor by the Wilson administration. Producers gained a clear victory in opposition to the findings of the President's Mediation Commission. Union effectiveness was not to be regained before the 1930's. It all ended in employer unity, but continued division in the ranks of union members. 32 notes.   R. V. Ritter

1197. Maroney, James C. THE UNIONIZATION OF THURBER, 1903. *Red River Valley Hist. Rev. 1979 4(2): 27-32.* An account of efforts to unionize the mine workers of Thurber, Texas, in 1903, which remained a union stronghold until mining operations ended in the 1920's; also discusses the establishment of coal mining in Thurber since the 1880's.

1198. Masson, Jack K. and Guimary, Donald L. PILIPINOS AND UNIONIZATION OF THE ALASKAN CANNED SALMON INDUSTRY. *Amerasia J. 1981 8(2): 1-30.* Describes the working conditions in the Alaskan salmon industry in the early 1900's and the entrance of Filipino labor into the canneries. First efforts to unionize the Filipinos occurred in 1933 and continued with both inter- and intraunion disputes until 1938 when the industry finally recognized the Congress of Industrial Organizations' United Cannery, Agricultural, Packing and Allied Workers of America as the bargaining agent for the laborers. Secondary sources; 71 notes.   E. S. Johnson

1199. McMahan, Ronald L. "RANG-U-TANG": THE I.W.W. AND THE 1927 COLORADO COAL STRIKE. Conlin, Joseph R., ed. *At the Point of Production: The Local History of the I.W.W.* (Westport, Conn.: Greenwood Pr., 1981): 191-212. Employs the historical record, ethnographic accounts, and scholarly works in an attempt to get at the heart of the issues raised by the 1927 Colorado coal strike. Examines the conditions that created the environment enabling the Industrial Workers of the World to organize a massive strike, the goals of the IWW, the success of their activities in achieving those goals, and the decline and virtual disappearance of Socialist influence within the American labor movement. The IWW failed to establish and maintain a viable organization in Colorado because of the anarcho-syndicalist ideology and strategy they employed. Based on ethnographic accounts, newspaper and journal articles; 49 notes.   J. Powell

1200. Meyerhuber, Carl I., Jr. BLACK VALLEY: PENNSYLVANIA'S ALLE-KISKI AND THE GREAT STRIKE OF 1919. *Western Pennsylvania Hist. Mag. 1979 62(3): 251-265.* Analyzes the antiunion activities and violence in the Allegheny-Kiskiminetas Valley during the Great Steel Strike of 1919.

1201. Mohl, Raymond A. THE GREAT STEEL STRIKE OF 1919 IN GARY, INDIANA: WORKING-CLASS RADICALISM OR TRADE UNION MILITANCY? *Mid-America 1981 63(1): 36-52.* The 1919 Gary, Indiana, steel strike was notable for the absence of widespread radicalism, the lack of violence, and the moderation of the steel workers in the face of antiunion propaganda and martial law. The workers wanted better wages, shorter hours, and improved working conditions. Steel industry leaders successfully portrayed the strikers as bolshevists which alarmed the civic leaders and the local press. The US Army, led by General Leonard Wood, was called in to impose martial law on Gary. Notes.   M. J. Wentworth

1202. Molloy, Scott. RHODE ISLAND COMMUNITIES AND THE 1902 CARMEN'S STRIKE. *Radical Hist. Rev. 1978 (17): 75-98.* Provides a brief history of transportation workers in Rhode Island, specifically discussing the streetcar workers' strike of 1902.

1203. Monroy, Douglas. ANARQUISMO Y COMUNISMO: MEXICAN RADICALISM AND THE COMMUNIST PARTY IN LOS ANGELES DURING THE 1930S. *Labor Hist. 1983 24(1): 34-59.* Mexican workers in Los Angeles during the 1930's had an anarcho-syndicalist tradition stemming from the Partido Liberal Mexicano, the Mexican Revolution of 1910-14, and Industrial Workers of the World influence. While the Communist Party welcomed Mexican workers to its union organizing and political activities in the 1930's, the Party failed to keep the allegiance of Mexican workers because it did not understand the revolutionary traditions and nationalist aspirations of Mexicans in the United States. Based on interviews with participants, contemporary accounts in union and Communist Party periodicals, the Dorothy Healey Papers, and other primary sources; 54 notes.   L. F. Velicer

1204. Monroy, Douglas. LA COSTURA EN LOS ANGELES, 1933-1939: THE ILGWU AND THE POLITICS OF DOMINATION. Mora, Magdalena and DelCastillo, Adelaida R., ed. *Mexican Women in the United States: Struggles Past and Present* (Los Angeles: U. of California Chicano Studies Res. Center, 1980): 171-178. Describes the situation which Mexicanas in Los Angeles confronted in la costura during the Depression, the enthusiastic union organization drives, and the ideology and political philosophy of the International Ladies' Garment Workers' Union as related to the Mexicana rank and file. From this can be seen some negative effects of successful union organizing. Often another layer of authority, the union leadership, rarely Mexicano or female, burdened Mexicanas. In this case, while making crucial gains in wages and hours, the union did not significantly increase the power and control which rank and file women exercised over their work. Secondary sources; 33 notes.   J. Powell

1205. Moore, John H. JACK LONDON: STRIKE METHODS: AMERICAN AND AUSTRALIAN. *Politics [Australia] 1973 8(2): 356-359.* Reprints an article by Jack London based on his personal visit to Sydney in 1908. London used the Broken Hill mining strike to demonstrate the contrasts in US and Australian disputes, with particular reference to strike-breaking, picketing, and the attitude of civil and military authorities. He also discussed the fundamental nature of labor disputes and how to achieve industrial peace. Reprinted from the *Australian Star* of 14 January 1909.   C. A. McNeill

1206. Morton, Michael. NO TIME TO QUIBBLE: THE JONES FAMILY CONSPIRACY TRIAL OF 1917. *Chronicles of Oklahoma 1981 59(2): 224-236.* During the summer of 1917 a group of farmers from central Oklahoma were arrested on charges of sedition. Dubbed the "Green Corn Rebellion," this insurrection resulted from the desperate economic plight of tenant farmers who had been inflamed by leftist spokesmen within the Working Class Union (WCU). The superpatriotism of World War I created an intolerant climate toward these "antiwar radicals," and resulted in a kangaroo court for the seven men arrested in Cleveland and Pottawatomie counties. Collectively known as the Jones Family, the seven were convicted on flimsy evidence. Based on Oklahoma newspapers; photo, 42 notes.   M. L. Tate

1207. Moye, William T. THE END OF THE 12-HOUR DAY IN THE STEEL INDUSTRY. *Monthly Labor Rev. 1977 100(9): 21-26.* Discusses attempts 1890's-1923 to reduce the work day in the steel industry from 12-hour shifts; examines the American Iron and Steel Institute's 1923 concession in light of the Harding Administration and groups which lobbied for the reduction in work hours.

1208. Nash, Al. THE LOCAL UNION: CENTER OF LIFE IN THE UAW. *Dissent 1978 25(4): 398-408.* Relates the history of Local 7, the representative of the Detroit Chrysler Kercheval-Jefferson plant workers in the United Auto Workers since 1937.

1209. Nash, Al. A UNIONIST REMEMBERS: MILITANT UNIONISM AND POLITICAL FACTIONS. *Dissent 1977 24(2): 181-189.* Author reminisces about his militancy during World War II in the United Automobile Workers of America and working at the Brewster

Aeronautical Corporation which was building Brewster Buffalos and Corsairs in Long Island City, New York, for the Army and Navy.

1210. Nelson, Daniel. A CIO ORGANIZER IN ALABAMA: 1941. *Labor Hist. 1977 18(4): 570-584.* Presents 19 documents authored by John D. House, a member of the United Rubber Workers who led the third attempt to unionize the Goodyear Tire and Rubber Company plant in Gadsden, Alabama, in 1941. The effort failed. Based on the John D. House Papers, University of Akron; 16 notes.   L. L. Athey

1211. Nelson, Daniel. THE NEW FACTORY SYSTEM AND THE UNIONS: THE NATIONAL CASH REGISTER COMPANY DISPUTE OF 1901. *Labor Hist. 1974 15(2): 163-178.* Assesses the impact of the new factory system, based on "welfare work," on the workers and the unions in the National Cash Register Company. "Welfare work" did not prevent the maintenance of the old autocratic foreman methods. The latter caused the dispute of 1901 which provoked criticism of "welfare work" practices, set back the attempt to organize mass production industries, and began a new phase in the emerging "new factory system." The N.C.R. Labor Department became the first modern personnel department in American industry. Based upon the McCormick Papers, the Gompers Letterbooks, unpublished correspondence, and the Dayton Daily Journal; 55 notes.   L. L. Athey

1212. Nelson, Daniel ORIGINS OF THE SIT-DOWN ERA: WORKER MILITANCY AND INNOVATION IN THE RUBBER INDUSTRY, 1934-38. *Labor Hist. 1982 23(2): 198-225.* Workers in the rubber industry of Akron, Ohio, pioneered the sit-down strike between mid-1934 and late 1936. The sit-down was not a creation of United Rubber Workers (URW) leaders, but an expression of rank and file militancy. While the early sit-down strikes yielded changes in factory operation, the sit-downs of 1937-38 were less effective, as management regained its initiative and URW officials diverted labor militancy to more "positive" ends. Based on National Labor Relations Board Files and newspaper accounts; 81 notes.   L. F. Velicer

1213. Nelson-Cisneros, Victor B. UCAPAWA AND CHICANOS IN CALIFORNIA: THE FARM WORKER PERIOD, 1937-1940. *Aztlán 1976 7(3): 453-477.* The United Cannery, Agricultural, Packing and Allied Workers of America (UCAPAWA), began as primarily a farm workers' union before it became mainly concerned with food processing.

1214. Nelson-Cisneros, Victor B. UCAPAWA ORGANIZING ACTIVITIES IN TEXAS, 1935-50. *Aztlán 1978 9: 71-84.* A study of the activities of the United Cannery, Agricultural, Packing and Allied Workers of America, which changed its name in 1944 to Food, Tobacco, Agricultural and Allied Workers Union of America (FTA), to include the tobacco workers, as it sought to organize Mexican Americans in Texas, 1937-50. Agricultural and packing shed workers on the one hand, and grain and cotton process workers on the other, are considered. The unions lost influence and membership for reasons which included possible communist infiltration and the deportation of Mexican citizens. Based on primary sources, viz., the union newspaper, labor archives at the University of Texas, Arlington, and other sources. 52 notes.   R. V. Ritter

1215. Newbill, James G. FARMERS AND WOBBLIES IN THE YAKIMA VALLEY, 1933. *Pacific Northwest Q. 1977 68(2): 80-87.* During August 1933 farm workers struck the Congdon Orchards in the Yakima Valley of Washington. Led by the Industrial Workers of the World (IWW), the workers sought higher wages, amounting to between 35 and 50 cents per hour. Farm owners, receiving close cooperation from the sheriff's department, resisted and a bloody fight broke out. State police and National Guardsmen restored order, but not before the power of the IWW had been totally destroyed in Yakima Valley. Owners ultimately raised wages slightly, but economic difficulties made it impossible for them to fully meet the strikers' demands. Based on interviews and newspapers; 3 photos, 33 notes.   M. L. Tate

1216. Newbill, James G. YAKIMA AND THE WOBBLIES, 1910-1936. Conlin, Joseph R., ed. *At the Point of Production: The Local History of the I.W.W.* (Westport Conn.: Greenwood Pr., 1981): 167-190. Describes confrontations between the Industrial Workers of the World and ranchers and farmers in Yakima before 1933, the combination of depression economics and racism which led to mass meetings and

eventual violence, fruit rancher-laborer difficulties in July and August 1933, and the "Congdon orchards battle" of 24 August 1933, and its aftermath. The major confrontation at Congdon resulted from a distorted image the IWW held of their own strength, and the fear of the farming community of the union. The confrontation and legal actions against the union in 1933 resulted in the collapse of the union's power in the Yakima Valley. Based on newspaper, journal, and personal accounts; 53 notes.   J. Powell

1217. Nolan, Dennis R. and Jonas, Donald E. TEXTILE UNIONISM IN THE PIEDMONT, 1901-1932. Fink, Gary M. and Reed, Merl E., eds. *Essays in Southern Labor History: Selected Papers, Southern Labor History Conference, 1976.* (Westport, Conn.; London, England: Greenwood Pr., 1977): 48-79. A study designed to round out the argument previously developed which attributes to outside forces the failure of the textile unions to form stable local organizations and negotiate improvements in wages and working conditions. The workers and unions also brought on problems themselves, by "rash and poorly planned strikes, internal feuds, poor leadership, and the failure of interested groups to provide financial aid." The textile industry in the Piedmont Plateau is the locale for the study. Whatever the strength of outside forces, the workers and their organizations often were their own worst enemies. 75 notes.   R. V. Ritter

1218. O'Brien, Larry D. THE OHIO NATIONAL GUARD IN THE COAL STRIKE OF 1932. *Ohio Hist. 1975 84(3): 127-144.* "The most interesting characteristic of the National Guard's participation in the 1932 strike was the balance which existed in the attitudes of the guard officers and the moderating influence they exercised." What gains the miners could claim were due to this moderating influence. Governor George White's decision to send in troop units reduced the level of violence during the strike. Illus., 73 notes.   E. P. Stickney

1219. O'Connell, Lucille. THE LAWRENCE TEXTILE STRIKE OF 1912: THE TESTIMONY OF TWO POLISH WOMEN. *Polish Am. Studies 1979 36(2): 44-62.* A personal account of two participants in the textile strike against the Everett Mill in Lawrence, Massachusetts, as revealed in testimony before the Committee on Rules of the House of Representatives on 2-7 March 1912. In their testimony, 14-year-old Victoria Winiarczyk and the older, more experienced Josephine Liss describe the hardships, deprivations, and dire poverty of their fellow immigrant workers. The strike radicalized many of the mill women and led them to militancy, collective action, and even membership in the Industrial Workers of the World. This strike was the first victory in the United States by unskilled, immigrant wage earners. Documented sources in English; 14 notes.   S. R. Pliska

1220. O'Farrell, M. Brigid and Kleiner, Lydia. ANNA SULLIVAN: TRADE UNION ORGANIZER. *Frontiers 1977 2(2): 29-36.* Anna Sullivan (b. 1904), who in 1936 began organizing the Massachusetts textile industry for the Textile Workers Union of America (TWUA), recalls her career in labor and politics; part of a special issue on women's oral history.

1221. Ollila, Douglas J., Jr. THE EMERGENCE OF RADICAL INDUSTRIAL UNIONISM IN THE FINNISH SOCIALIST MOVEMENT. *U. of Turku. Inst. of General Hist. Publ. [Finland] 1975 7: 25-54.* Examines the growing radicalism in the Finnish socialist movement in the United States, which culminated in a split within the Finnish Socialist Federation, 1903-14.

1222. Ollila, Douglas J., Jr. A TIME OF GLORY: FINNISH-AMERICAN RADICAL INDUSTRIAL UNIONISM, 1914-1917. *U. of Turku. Inst. of General Hist. Publ. [Finland] 1977 9: 31-53.* The industrial unionists in 1916 became heavily involved in the great Mesabi Iron Range strikes in Minnesota which Finnish radicals viewed as "a time of glory." But instead of ushering in the destruction of American capitalism, it was short-lived. Describes the stabilization of the Finnish-American radical industrial union movement, the evolution of its political-economic Marxist orientation to pure economic Marxism, and "an analysis of the ethnic factors related to the Mesabi strike and the ensuing challenge to the lumber industry which precipitated the eventual downfall of the IWW." Primary sources; 87 notes.   E. P. Stickney

1223. Osborne, James D. PATERSON: IMMIGRANT STRIKERS AND THE WAR OF 1913. Conlin, Joseph R., ed. *At the Point of Production: The Local History of the I.W.W.* (Westport, Conn.: Greenwood Pr., 1981) 61-78. Details the history of the textile strike of 1913 in Paterson. Police, city government, and the local judiciary combined to back local manufacturers against strikers. Almost 2,000 mill hands were arrested, picket lines broken up, and workers' processions dispersed. Even strike headquarters were closed down. The Industrial Workers of the World attracted attention to the strike, bringing it before a national audience, and for a time seemed near prompting federal intervention and a favorable settlement. The central incident of the strike was the death of Valentino Modestino, an Italian metal worker who lived in Paterson's Riverside section. The strike resulted in the partial emigration of the industry, the changed ethnic composition of the workforce, and the reform of local government, particularly the police department. Based on US Bureau of Census data, journal articles; 60 notes.   J. Powell

1224. Overstreet, Daphne. ON STRIKE! THE 1917 WALKOUT AT GLOBE, ARIZONA. *J. of Arizona Hist. 1977 18(2): 197-218.* Globe, Arizona, was plagued with labor-management problems which made it a center for radical labor agitation in the state. Soaring copper prices in the midst of World War I were not accompanied by improved wages and working conditions for the workers, who were locally organized by the Western Federation of Miners. Describes the walkout strike in July 1917 and its settlement. 3 illus., 57 notes.   D. L. Smith

1225. Papanikolas, Helen Z. UNIONISM, COMMUNISM, AND THE GREAT DEPRESSION: THE CARBON COUNTY COAL STRIKE OF 1933. *Utah Hist. Q. 1973 41(3): 254-300.* In 1933 the United Mine Workers of America and the National Miners Union attempted to unionize the bituminous coal fields of Carbon County. Immigrant laborers were attracted to the NMU. A strike set for Labor Day spread unrest, protests, and violence throughout the county. Mine operators called for the National Guard, maintaining that strikers were anarchists and communists. Many strikers were arrested and placed in bullpens at a ball park. While the NMU was involved with the strike the UMWA negotiated with operators on a coal code, which was adopted in October. The NMU declined in importance thereafter. Significant gains for labor did occur in Carbon County in 1933. Map, illus., 147 notes.   H. S. Marks

1226. Parker, Russell D. ALCOA, TENNESSEE: THE EARLY YEARS, 1919-1939. *East Tennessee Hist. Soc. Publ. 1976 48: 84-103.* During its first 20 years, Alcoa, Tennessee, was a typical company town relatively free of social tensions with few efforts at unionization run by paternalistic officials, Victor J. Hultquist and Arthur B. Smith, who retired before the economic boom and altered the community situation brought about by World War II. Based on the Alcoa Company archives and oral interviews; 108 notes.   D. A. Yanchisin

1227. Perry, Elisabeth Israels. INDUSTRIAL REFORM IN NEW YORK CITY: BELLE MOSKOWITZ AND THE PROTOCOL OF PEACE, 1913-1916. *Labor Hist. 1982 23(1): 5-31.* Examines the role of Belle Moskowitz (1887-1933) as a labor mediator and industrial reformer in New York City's garment industry during the era of protocols—agreements between the garment workers' unions and manufacturers' associations. Employed by the Dress and Waist Manufacturers' Association (DWMA), Moskowitz represented the manufacturers' interests in disputes with the workers, who were represented by the International Ladies' Garment Workers' Union (ILGWU). The protocols attempted to deal rationally and scientifically with employer-employee differences through a grievance system and an arbitration board. The protocol system collapsed by the end of 1916, and increased labor unrest followed. Based on ILGWU-DWMA board meeting transcripts, the Belle Moskowitz Papers, the Louis Brandeis Papers, *Women's Wear Daily* accounts, and other primary sources; 57 notes.   L. F. Velicer

1228. Phillips, Cabell. THE WEST VIRGINIA MINE WAR. *Am. Heritage 1974 25(5): 58-61, 90-94.* Violence erupted as Logan and Mingo County, West Virginia coal miners attempted to join the United Mine Workers' Union.

1229. Piott, Steven L. MODERNIZATION AND THE ANTI-MONOPOLY ISSUE: THE ST. LOUIS TRANSIT STRIKE OF 1900. *Missouri Hist. Soc. Bull. 1978 35(1): 3-16.* As permitted by new state legislation passed in 1899, the United Railways Company took control of the transit lines serving St. Louis. That monopoly angered employees who organized a union, and the new corporation named the St. Louis Transit Company, signed an agreement with the union in March, 1900. The March pact only postponed a major transit employees strike for two months. The strike, accompanied by violence and killing, lasted two months and ended with reverses for the union. The strike also focused attention on the ills of monopolies. Manuscript and newspaper sources; 3 photos, 45 notes.   H. T. Lovin

1230. Powell, Allan Kent. THE "FOREIGN ELEMENT" AND THE 1903-4 CARBON COUNTY COAL MINERS' STRIKE. *Utah Hist. Q. 1975 43(2): 125-154.* Finnish, Slavic, and Italian miners provided the strength behind a serious labor confrontation in Carbon County, Utah, in 1903. The Utah Fuel Company refused union recognition. The Utah National Guard was called out. Charles DeMolli, Con Kelliher, Mother Mary Jones, and Samuel H. Gilson involved themselves in the strike. The strike failed because the union lacked internal and external support and the company played on antiforeign sentiments in defending its position. Based on primary and secondary sources; 9 illus., 65 notes.   J. L. Hazelton

1231. Powell, Allan Kent. UTAH AND THE NATIONWIDE COAL MINERS' STRIKE OF 1922. *Utah Hist. Q. 1977 45(2): 135-157.* Union organizers felt union strength in Carbon County, Utah, was too weak to be included in the nationwide strike of the United Mine Workers of America in 1922. Utah miners protesting a 30 percent wage reduction struck anyway. Shooting incidents forced Governor Charles R. Mabey to call in the National Guard. Although the strikers gained a temporary restoration of the pay scale, the strike failed to achieve union recognition. Primary and secondary sources; 3 illus., 67 notes.   J. L. Hazelton

1232. Pozzetta, George E. ¡ALERTA TABAQUEROS! TAMPA'S STRIKING CIGARWORKERS. *Tampa Bay Hist. 1981 3(2): 19-30.* The 1910 general strike in Tampa, Florida was led by thousands of Cuban, Italian, and Spanish immigrants who worked in the community's single major industry, the manufacture of cigars; 1901-11.

1233. Prickett, James R. COMMUNIST CONSPIRACY OR WAGE DISPUTE?: THE 1941 STRIKE AT NORTH AMERICAN AVIATION. *Pacific Hist. Rev. 1981 50(2): 215-233.* The strike at the North American Aviation plant in Inglewood, California, in the summer of 1941 resulted from an attempt to bring aircraft workers into the United Automobile Workers of America (UAW) and to increase wages. The union's negotiating committee twice postponed the strike while trying to work out a settlement with the National Defense Mediation Board, but the union voted to strike when the board proved to be dilatory. US Army forces broke the strike, and the UAW organizer of aircraft workers, a Communist, advised the strikers to return to work. There is no evidence that the strike was Communist-inspired. Communist leaders in the UAW in southern California had tried to prevent the strike. Based on oral history interviews, labor union records and publications, and other primary sources; 76 notes.   R. N. Lokken

1234. Prickett, James R. COMMUNISTS AND THE AUTOMOBILE INDUSTRY IN DETROIT BEFORE 1935. *Michigan Hist. 1973 57(3): 185-208.* Traces the trade union activities of the Communist Party USA in Detroit automobile unionism before the formation of the United Automobile Workers in 1935. Such Communist leaders as Philip Raymond and Anthony Gerlach dominated the Automobile Workers Union in the 1920's and early 1930's. The AWU was particularly active in the wave of strikes of 1933. Communist rhetoric was tempered by pragmatism. 4 illus., 86 notes.   D. L. Smith

1235. Reed, Merl E. SOME ADDITIONAL MATERIAL ON THE COAL STRIKE OF 1943. *Labor Hist. 1982 23(1): 90-104.* Presents two memoranda from Richard Lawrence-Grace Deverall to Interior Secretary Harold Ickes describing the deplorable working and living conditions found in a tour of the coal mines of Welch, West Virginia, in June 1943. Deverall, an employee of the Office of War Information, had been selected by Ickes as a special consultant on the United Mine

Workers' strike of 1943. Based on US Fair Employment Practices Committee Records and other primary sources; 8 notes.

L. F. Velicer

1236. Remele, Larry. THE NORTH DAKOTA FARM STRIKE OF 1932. *North Dakota Hist. 1974 41(4): 4-19.* Discusses farmers' strike for higher prices through the withholding of crops and livestock in North Dakota in 1932.

1237. Remele, Larry. NORTH DAKOTA'S FORGOTTEN FARMERS UNION 1913-1920. *North Dakota Hist. 1978 45(2): 4-21.* During 1913-20, the first North Dakota branch of the Farmers Educational and Cooperative Union of America played a significant role in the state's economic and political affairs. However, the organization passed so rapidly from the scene after 1920 that within a few years organizers of the second and lasting Farmers Union were almost completely unaware of the existence of their predecessor. The first Farmers Union was organized in Bismarck, largely as a result of the activity of Howard P. Knappen, editor of a local weekly. The original purposes of the Union included economic moves to end corporate control over marketing and distribution of farm goods; establishment of cooperative buying and selling agencies; discouragement of the credit and mortgage systems; and fraternal aims. Cooperatives were founded to enter into the grain elevator, flour milling, warehousing, and grocery store businesses. Some of the elevators are still in business. The Union became entangled with the political actions of the Non-Partisan League and by 1920 was defunct as a state group.

N. Lederer

1238. Reverby, Susan. *WITH BABIES AND BANNERS: A REVIEW. Radical Am. 1979 13(5): 63-69.* Discusses the award-winning political documentary film made by the Women's Labor History Film Project, which details the key role of women in the 1937 United Auto Workers of America victory in Flint, Michigan.

1239. Riell, Robert B. THE 1917 COPPER STRIKE AT GLOBE, ARIZONA. *J. of Arizona Hist. 1977 18(2): 185-196.* The Western Federation of Miners and the Industrial Workers of the World were receptive to membership that was militant socialist. On 2 July 1917, all copper mines in the country were struck, precipitating crises all over the West. Describes the strike in Globe, Arizona from the viewpoint of a company man, the paymaster. 3 illus.

D. L. Smith

1240. Rocha, Guy Louis. THE I.W.W. AND THE BOULDER CANYON PROJECT: THE DEATH THROES OF AMERICAN SYNDICALISM. Conlin, Joseph R., ed. *At the Point of Production: The Local History of the I.W.W.* (Westport, Conn.: Greenwood Pr., 1981): 213-234. Reprinted from an earlier article (see preceding abstract). Nevada was the site of the birth and death of the Industrial Workers of the World. The first major organizational campaigns took place within the state, in 1905. On 16 August 1931, the final significant organizational activity of the IWW in the state terminated with an unsuccessful strike at the Boulder Canyon Project, one of the last important IWW activities in America. The working conditions at the Boulder Canyon Project, constructing Hoover Dam, were extremely hazardous. In 1930 President Herbert C. Hoover felt it necessary to 1) employ some of the vast number of jobless Americans on the project and 2) rush the project. The Six Companies, Inc., of San Francisco, exploited the workers, leading to the IWW-backed strike, 7-16 August. Based on newspaper and journal articles; 59 notes.

J. Powell

1241. Rocha, Guy Louis. THE IWW AND THE BOULDER CANYON PROJECT: THE FINAL DEATH THROES OF AMERICAN SYNDICALISM. *Nevada Hist. Soc. Q. 1978 21(1): 2-24.* Construction began in 1931 on the Boulder Canyon project (later, Hoover Dam) on the Colorado River, a project that Bureau of Reclamation officials speeded to create employment. Genuine grievances about living and working conditions developed among the workers. Industrial Workers of the World (IWW) organizers fanned the discontent and provoked repressive measures by Las Vegas townsmen and civil authorities. The workers went on strike 8-14 August 1931 and obtained redress of part of their grievances. Despite IWW aid and leadership of the strike, most workers never joined the IWW and (in 1933) ignored a second IWW strike call on the Boulder Canyon project. Newspaper and secondary sources; 4 photos, 59 notes.

H. T. Lovin

1242. Rocha, Guy Louis. RADICAL LABOR STRUGGLES IN THE TONOPAH-GOLDFIELD MINING DISTRICT, 1901-1922. *Nevada Hist. Soc. Q. 1977 20(1): 2-45.* Analyzes labor-management relations in one Nevada mining district during 1901-22. Stresses the expansion role of the Industrial Workers of the World (IWW) in the district. The IWW advocated better wages, hours, and working conditions, but also predicted a "revolutionary apocalypse" at Tonopah and Goldfield. Consequently, it alienated more conservative miners and helped employers to win support for governmental repression of the IWW. Economic reverses and the post-World War I Red Scare further weakened the IWW in Nevada, but IWW unions functioned in the area until 1924. Based on newspaper and secondary sources; 3 illus., 133 notes.

H. T. Lovin

1243. Rosales, Francisco A. and Simon, Daniel T. CHICANO STEEL WORKERS AND UNIONISM IN THE MIDWEST, 1919-1945. *Aztlán 1976 6(2): 267-275.* Chicano and Mexican workers comprised a large portion of the labor force in Chicago (Illinois), Gary (Indiana), and East Chicago (Indiana). Racial discrimination motivated them to actively participate in labor union organization. They played prominent roles in major strikes in the steel industry during the 1930's. Based on newspapers and secondary sources; 27 notes.

R. Griswold del Castillo

1244. Rosenzweig, Roy. *UNITED ACTION MEANS VICTORY: MILITANT AMERICANISM ON FILM. Labor Hist. 1983 24(2): 274-288.* Analyzes the making of the United Automobile Workers' 1940 film, *United Action Means Victory*, which portrayed the story of the 1939 strike of 7,600 tool and die makers against General Motors. Based on interviews and correspondence with participants in the film's production and other primary sources; 24 notes.

L. F. Velicer

1245. Rousmaniere, Kate. THE MUSCATINE BUTTON WORKERS' STRIKE OF 1911-12. *Ann. of Iowa 1982 46(4): 243-262.* The unsuccessful strike of more than 2,000 workers, many of them female, against most of the 43 fresh-water pearl button factories in Muscatine, Iowa, is an example of the chaos and conflict that often developed when a historically rural community underwent the process of industrialization. Based on correspondence in the papers of Iowa Governor Beryl F. Carroll, interviews, and other primary sources; 2 photos, 35 notes.

P. L. Petersen

1246. Rubenstein, Harry R. THE GREAT GALLUP COAL STRIKE OF 1933. *New Mexico Hist. Rev. 1977 52(3): 173-192.* As a result of the depression, union membership in New Mexico declined. AFL craft unions began to reorganize and the mine workers became the most active in regard to strikes. The Gallup mining community was involved in the most serious strikes. The coal miners were affected most by the depression. The National Guard was used against the strikers. The eastern mining districts had more serious strikes than those in New Mexico. The Gallup strike was not isolated, but a part of the turmoil of the 1930's. 65 notes.

J. H. Krenkel

1247. Scatamacchia, Cristina. LO SCIOPERO DI ST. LOUIS DEL 1900 [The 1900 St. Louis strike]. *Ann. della Facoltà di Scienze Politiche: Materiali di Storia [Italy] 1978-79 15(3): 177-200.* The strike by streetcar workers in St. Louis, Missouri, in 1900, one of the most important moments in the US labor movement, has been neglected by American historians; based chiefly on contemporary press reports.

1248. Schacht, John N. TOWARD INDUSTRIAL UNIONISM: BELL TELEPHONE WORKERS AND COMPANY UNIONS, 1919-1937. *Labor Hist. 1975 16(1): 5-36.* Development of company unions in the Bell Telephone System helped prepare the way for the emergence of industrial unions after 1935. The structure of the company union helped erase distinctions between workers, and leadership and organizational skills were learned by workers. Success in converting the Bell Company union into an industrial union may help explain why other company unions failed to make the transformation. Based on oral history interviews, company publications, dissertations, and government reports; 43 notes.

L. L. Athey

1249. Schatz, Ronald. UNION PIONEERS: THE FOUNDERS OF LOCAL UNIONS AT GENERAL ELECTRIC AND WESTINGHOUSE, 1933-1937. *J. of Am. Hist. 1979 66(3): 586-602.* Analyzes the sociological backgrounds of 35 union pioneers during the 1930's in four plants owned by Westinghouse Electric Corp. and General Electric Co. in Pennsylvania, Massachusetts, and New York. Both male and female pioneers in the electrical union were atypical workers. Male pioneers tended to be skilled, over 35, and either native-born or from northern European stock. Though the female pioneers came from a lower stratum of the labor force than that of the male pioneers, these women were even outside the normal sociological relationships for their class. Both males and females tended to have union or radical backgrounds. 44 notes.

T. P. Linkfield

1250. Scopino, A. J., Jr. COMMUNITY, CLASS, AND CONFLICT: THE WATERBURY TROLLEY STRIKE OF 1903. *Connecticut Hist. 1983 (24): 29-46.* Waterbury's strike by 80 motormen and conductors of the Connecticut Railway and Lighting Company from 11 January to 10 August 1903 was initially effective but eventually failed when public support waned due to violence.

1251. Sears, Stephen W. "SHUT THE GODDAM PLANT!" *Am. Heritage 1982 33(3): 49-64.* The sit-down strike at the General Motors Corporation's Fisher Body plant in Flint, Michigan, began 30 December 1936. Other plants were also involved. For six weeks, the conflict continued. Tension led to violence and brought quick action from Governor Frank Murphy who sent National Guardsmen to Flint. The end came on 11 February with a negotiated settlement accepting the presence of the United Automobile Workers of America. 18 illus.

J. F. Paul

1252. Shannon, Michael C. FIRST NATIONAL ORGANIZATION FOR EMPLOYEE-PHARMACISTS 1910-1934. *Pharmacy in Hist. 1975 17(2): 58-68.* Peter A. Mandabach was the principal founder of the National Association of Drug Clerks, which was active in organizing employee-pharmacists as early as 1910.

1253. Shiner, John F. THE 1937 STEEL DISPUTE AND THE OHIO NATIONAL GUARD. *Ohio Hist. 1975 84(4): 182-195.* Governor Martin L. Davey contemplated using the National Guard to curb the growing violence in the strike area. Troops acted as a screen behind which it was easier to operate a struck plant. Davey was not anti-labor, but wanted the National Guard merely to restore order. Unintentionally, however, he employed the guard as a strikebreaking force, and "the overwhelming majority of the people of the state supported him in that action." 72 notes.

E. P. Stickney

1254. Skeels, Jack W. THE ECONOMIC AND ORGANIZATIONAL BASIS OF EARLY UNITED STATES STRIKES, 1900-1948. *Industrial and Labor Relations Rev. 1982 35(4): 491-503.* Examines whether economic factors played an important role in determining strike activity in the first half of the twentieth century. Recently David Snyder concluded that economic conditions mattered little during that period and that union organization and political variables explained much more. P. K. Edwards concluded the opposite. A retest of these authors' analyses, employing ordinary least squares regression and a variety of measures, suggests that Snyder's position is more sound. However, Edwards was correct in claiming that economic factors are major determinants of the extent of unionism as well as of strike activity, and thus one needs to apply a two-stage least squares test of the Snyder hypothesis. When that is done, the results show that economic variables are highly significant determinants of strike activity throughout the pre-1949 period, but for the subperiod 1921-29 noneconomic factors also played a role.

J/S

1255. Snyder, Robert E. WOMEN, WOBBLIES, AND WORKER'S RIGHTS: THE 1912 TEXTILE STRIKE IN LITTLE FALLS, NEW YORK. *New York Hist. 1979 60(1): 29-57.* The 1912 textile strike in Little Falls, New York, shows how immigrant women workers, Schenectady socialists, the Industrial Workers of the World, Helen Keller, and a visiting tuberculosis nurse overcame the hostility of Little Falls authorities and mill management and the indifference of native American labor to achieve reforms in wages, hours, and working conditions. 6 illus., 57 notes.

R. N. Lokken

1256. Snyder, Robert E. WOMEN, WOBBLIES, AND WORKERS' RIGHTS: THE 1912 TEXTILE STRIKE IN LITTLE FALLS, NEW YORK. Conlin, Joseph R., ed. *At the Point of Production: The Local*

History of the I.W.W. (Westport, Conn.: Greenwood Pr., 1981): 27-48. The Little Falls textile strike lasted from 9 October 1912 until 4 January 1913. This overview sheds light on Industrial Workers of the World strike activities, Socialist participation in working-class radicalism, and immigrant disenchantment and disillusionment. Some 70% of the strikers were women (inarticulate Poles, Slavs, Austrians, and Italians) who saw their actions only as a protest over a reduction in wages; yet the movement for protective labor legislation for women was actually the backdrop to the strike. Based on primary sources, including newspaper, magazine and journal articles of the period; 57 notes. Portions previously published in *New York History* in 1979 (see preceding entry).

J. Powell

1257. Sprague, Stuart Seely. UNIONIZATION STRUGGLES ON PAINT CREEK, 1912-1913. *West Virginia Hist. 1977 38(3): 185-213.* When the United Mine Workers of America tried to organize the Kanawha region coal fields in West Virginia in 1912-13, they met adamant resistance from the mine operators, who brought in guards and strike breakers. The miners responded with violence, and Governor William E. Glasscock sent in the national guard to restore order. Public opinion, which had been tolerant of the union, swung against it by early 1913 and the new Governor, Harry D. Hatfield, forced an end to the dispute. The union won recognition and a pay raise for workers. Primary and secondary sources; 163 notes.

J. H. Broussard

1258. Straw, Richard. AN ACT OF FAITH: SOUTHEASTERN OHIO MINERS IN THE COAL STRIKE OF 1927. *Labor Hist. 1980 21(2): 221-238.* Studies the living conditions of miners in the Hocking Valley during the strike of 1927. Although miners were feverishly loyal to the United Mine Workers of America (UMW), the union lost the strike, a severe blow to the local and the national UMW, led by John L. Lewis. Based on government documents and local newspapers; 56 notes.

L. L. Athey

1259. Straw, Richard A. THE COLLAPSE OF BIRACIAL UNIONISM: THE ALABAMA COAL STRIKE OF 1908. *Alabama Hist. Q. 1975 37(2): 92-114.* The United Mine Workers of America was the only large biracial union during the period 1840-1920. This policy came out of the use of Negroes as strike-breakers. The failure of the UMW in the Alabama strike of 1908 was southern racial attitudes, not the operators' actions. Details the strike, including the violence and racial conflict caused by the union's racial attitude. 64 notes.

E. E. Eminhizer

1260. Straw, Richard A. THE UNITED MINE WORKERS OF AMERICA AND THE 1920 COAL STRIKE IN ALABAMA. *Alabama Rev. 1975 28(2): 104-128.* The United Mine Workers ordered a general strike in Alabama in September, 1920 for higher wages and collective bargaining rights. Coal operators refused to negotiate, persuaded Governor Thomas E. Kilby to call out troops, and won a court injunction against the union. Strike forces weakened by February, 1921, with public opinion and state officials taking an anti-union stand, although the Birmingham press was more moderate and tried to promote a compromise. As in 1904 and 1908, the union failed in its objectives; only one United Mine Workers local functioned in Alabama by 1929, allowing mine operators to maintain open shop. Based on primary and secondary sources; 59 notes.

J. F. Vivian

1261. Street, Richard Steven. "WE ARE NOT SLAVES": THE PHOTOGRAPHIC RECORD OF THE WHEATLAND HOP RIOT: THE FIRST IMAGES OF PROTESTING FARM WORKERS IN AMERICA. *Southern California Q. 1982 64(3): 205-226.* Examines photographs allegedly depicting the Wheatland "strike" of 3 August 1913 and finds them incorrectly identified. Offers previously unpublished photographs as more accurately depicting conditions on the Durst ranch at Wheatland, California, the farm laborers and their children, and the protest over working conditions that led to the riot. Identifies the probable photographers and argues for historians to pay greater attention to the documentary value of photographs. 14 photos, 32 notes.

A. Hoffman

1262. Sturm, Phillip. MOTHER JONES AND THE IRON JUDGE. *J. of the West Virginia Hist. Assoc. 1981 5(1): 18-26.* Discusses the careers of United Mine Workers activist Mother Jones (Mary Harris Jones) and Federal District Judge John Jay Jackson, Jr., of the Western

District of Virginia, and their meeting in court after her arrest in the coal strike of 1902 in West Virginia.

1263. Suggs, George G., Jr. THE COLORADO COAL MINERS' STRIKE, 1903-1904: A PRELUDE TO LUDLOW? *J. of the West 1973 12(1): 36-52.* Describes the deplorable conditions in the coal mines of southern Colorado prior to the miners' strike of 1903-04 in Las Animas and Huerfano Counties. "The strike was a tragic mistake, not because there was insufficient justification, but because it was launched when neither the district nor national unions were powerful enough to guarantee its success. . . . Secondly, although state intervention undoubtedly assured the breaking of the strike, other causes more adequately explain the failure of the United Mine Workers of America in the southern fields." The failure of this strike paved the way for the struggle between the United Mine Workers and the coal companies that led to the "Ludlow massacre" in 1913-14. 59 notes.   D. D. Cameron

1264. Supina, Philip D. HERNDON J. EVANS AND THE HARLAN COUNTY COAL STRIKE. *Filson Club Hist. Q. 1982 56(3): 318-335.* Herndon J. Evans, editor of the Pineville *Sun,* tried to present a balanced account of the coal miners' strike in Harlan County, Kentucky, during 1931-32. Evans, a local booster, deeply resented the efforts of Theodore Dreiser, Waldo Frank, and John Dos Passos in portraying Harlan County as a violent area. His efforts won some national recognition, but they did little to alleviate the suffering of the local population or to restore civil rights to miners who tried to join labor unions. Based on the Evans collection at the Univeristy of Kentucky Library.   G. B. McKinney

1265. Taft, Philip. THE LIMITS OF LABOR UNITY: THE CHICAGO NEWSPAPER STRIKE OF 1912. *Labor Hist. 1978 19(1): 100-129.* Analyzes the internal division generated by the strike-lockout of Chicago newspapers in 1912. Begun by pressmen in a dispute over crew reduction on Hearst newspapers, the strike led to sympathetic walkouts by stereotypers, delivery men, and newsboys. George L. Berry of the pressman's union attempted to obtain support from Chicago newspaper unions and to broaden the strike against the Hearst chain. His efforts failed as the limits of labor unity were reached when opposition to sympathy strikes and lack of support for a National Strike, led by typographers, split labor organizations in the newspaper industry. Based on union publications, conference proceedings, and newspapers; 92 notes.   L. L. Athey

1266. Thrasher, Sue and Wise, Leah. THE SOUTHERN TENANT FARMERS' UNION. *Southern Exposure 1974 1(3/4): 5-32.* During the Depression, black and white sharecroppers organized the Southern Tenant Farmers' Union which became a mass movement. Explores the plight of the tenants and the union's relationships with the Communist Party, American Federation of Labor, Congress of Industrial Organizations, and black and white sharecroppers. The Agricultural Adjustment Administration caused the eviction of thousands of sharecroppers who then sought work in industrial plants outside the South during World War II. Based on papers in Southern Historical Collection, University of North Carolina, and oral interviews; 12 illus., 3 notes, biblio.   G. A. Bolton

1267. Thurner, Arthur W. WESTERN FEDERATION OF MINERS IN TWO COPPER CAMPS: THE IMPACT OF THE MICHIGAN COPPER MINERS' STRIKE ON BUTTE LOCAL NO. 1. *Montana 1983 33(2): 30-45.* Western Federation of Miners members struck the Calumet and Hecla copper mining operations in Michigan from July 1913 to April 1914. Initially, they received substantial philosophical and financial support from Western Federation of Miners Local No. 1 in Butte, Montana, but as the strike dragged on unsuccessfully and economic conditions deteriorated, the Butte miners came to resent their financial support for the strikers. The Butte miners' recalcitrance ultimately crippled Local No. 1 and the Western Federation of Miners as a whole. Based on the Western Federation of Miners Archives at the University of Colorado, government documents, and secondary sources; 12 illus., 65 notes.   R. C. Myers

1268. Toy, Eckard, V., Jr. THE OXFORD GROUP AND THE STRIKE OF THE SEATTLE LONGSHOREMEN IN 1934. *Pacific Northwest Q. 1978 69(4): 174-184.* Traces the development of the Oxford Group from its founding in 1921 as a Christian mediation group

devoted to settling labor and international problems. During the 1934 longshoremen's strike in Seattle, Oxford Group leaders George Light, James Clise, and Walter Horne worked themselves into a mediating role which helped end the deadlock by June. Throughout the negotiations, they unabashedly supported management over labor which was consistent with the entire Oxford Group movement. Primary and secondary sources; 2 photos, 41 notes.   M. L. Tate

1269. Warrick, Sherry. RADICAL LABOR IN OKLAHOMA: THE WORKING CLASS UNION. *Chronicles of Oklahoma 1974 52(2): 180-195.* Describes the Oklahoma activities of the Working Class Union, an agrarian labor organization, during 1914-17, pointing out how such radical organizations exploited workers for their own ends. By 1916 the union used violent and illegal methods to indoctrinate fellow workers and to frighten bankers and government officials. Anti-draft agitation was included in the union's program and culminated in the abortive 1917 Green Corn Rebellion. Primary and secondary sources; 3 photos, 71 notes.   N. J. Street

1270. Watson, Fred. STILL ON STRIKE: RECOLLECTIONS OF A BISBEE DEPORTEE. *J. of Arizona Hist. 1977 18(2): 171-184.* Fred Watson worked as a tool nipper at the Shattuck Mine in Bisbee, Arizona, when it was struck by the Industrial Workers of the World in 1917. He recalls the confusion of the workers over the issues, the contending forces, and his experiences as one of the several hundred who were summarily arrested and deported to New Mexico by a railway freight train. 11 illus.   D. L. Smith

1271. Weiler, N. Sue. WALKOUT: THE CHICAGO MEN'S GARMENT WORKERS' STRIKE, 1910-1911. *Chicago Hist. 1979-80 8(4): 238-249.* Examines the men's garment industry in Chicago which began growing rapidly after the Chicago Fire of 1871, particularly the division of the manufacturing process into operations performed at sweatshops for the large Chicago clothing firms such as Hart, Schaffner & Marx, The House of Kuppenheimer, the Scotch Wollen Mills, Royal Tailors, and Society Brand; focuses on the 1910-1911 men's garment workers' strikes which started when 18 year old Hannah Shapiro walked out on her sewing job.

1272. Weisbord, Vera Buch. GASTONIA 1929: STRIKE AT THE LORAY MILL. *Southern Exposure 1974 1(3/4): 185-203.* The author, a labor organizer, views the textile workers' strike in which she was harassed, jailed, and tried on charges stemming from her participation in the strike. The National Textile Workers Union organized the strike which also was supported by International Labor Defense and the Young Communist League. Tension between white and black workers was exploited, while the National Guard were used as strikebreakers. The mills had not been unionized by 1974. Based on unpublished autobiography and oral interviews; 8 illus.   G. A. Bolton

1273. White, Earl Bruce. MIGHT IS RIGHT: UNIONISM AND GOLDFIELD, NEVADA, 1904 TO 1908. *J. of the West 1977 16(3): 75-84.* In 1904 the Western Federation of Miners (WFM) and the American Federation of Labor (AFL), rival unions, organized in Goldfield. The militant WFM had suffered a major defeat at Cripple Creek, Colorado, in 1903-04 and agreed to unite with the Industrial Workers of the World (IWW) under the leadership of Vincent St. John. The opponents of the IWW were newspaper editor Lindley C. Branson and mine owners George Wingfield, Jack Davis, and Senator George Nixon. Disputes during 1906-07 between the WFM/IWW and the mine owners, who backed the AFL, were marked by increasing hostility. Finally in December 1907 federal troops came to Goldfield at the request of Governor John Sparks and Senator Nixon. Later, a presidential commission found that the troops were not needed and that the mine owners took advantage of the military presence by reducing wages and banning the WFM. The use of the troops badly hurt the cause of industrial unionism, which was not revived until the 1930's. Based on government documents, union archival material, and other primary and secondary sources; 5 photos, 54 notes.   B. S. Porter

1274. Williams, William J. BLOODY SUNDAY REVISITED. *Pacific Northwest Q. 1980 71(2): 50-62.* On 5 November 1916, the steamship *Verona* carried approximately 250 members of the Industrial Workers of the World (IWW) from Seattle to a rally at Everett, Washington. A large number of Everett's deputized citizens attempted to stop the landing and gunshots were fired by unidentified assailants. Seven people were killed and 47 wounded in the "Everett Massacre" before the *Verona* could escape and return to Seattle. Documents recently uncovered at the Seattle Federal Archives and Records Center offer new eyewitness testimony about the event, but fail to answer the ultimate question of who fired the initial shots. 5 photos, map, 13 notes.

M. L. Tate

1275. Wold, Frances. STILL: THE "UNION CITY." *North Dakota Hist. 1978 45(3): 4-15.* Despite its size of fewer than a dozen buildings and a population never in excess of 25, Still, North Dakota, exerted a considerable social, political, and economic influence on Burleigh County and its environs. Still became the headquarters of Estherville Local 11 in 1913, a flourishing chapter of the Farmers Educational and Cooperative Union, influential in the state before and during World War I. The Local became involved in the establishment of a cooperative store, a cooperatively owned grain elevator and warehouse, as well as providing a forum for political activity and for social affairs attracting farmers from a large area around the tiny hamlet. Even following the demise of the Farmer's Union in the early 1920's. Still, dubbed "Union City," continued to influence the surrounding region through mercantile activities, the existence of a grain elevator and the presence of a meeting hall and a school. Today Still is abandoned.   N. Lederer

1276. Wold, Frances. THE WASHBURN LIGNITE COAL COMPANY: A HISTORY OF MINING AT WILTON, NORTH DAKOTA. *North Dakota Hist. 1976 43(4): 4-20.* W. D. Washburn, Minnesota politician and railroad entrepreneur, founded the Washburn Lignite Coal Company in 1900 to exploit lignite coal found in large quantities on the extensive land acreage owned by the Washburn Land Co. in North Dakota. The company prospered during the early 20th century. It drew upon the part-time labor of local farmers. Gradually it increasingly depended on imported fulltime miners, many of them immigrants. The company's paternalistic attitudes toward its employees were seriously shaken by the advent of the United Mine Workers of America during and after World War I and by the long strike of 1924. By 1930 the successor owners of the Washburn interests converted the operation to strip mining and threw hundreds of miners out of work. Based on oral interviews and on newspaper and secondary sources.

N. Lederer

1277. Wollenberg, Charles. WORKING ON EL TRAQUE: THE PACIFIC ELECTRIC STRIKE OF 1903. *Pacific Hist. Rev. 1973 42(3): 358-369.* Discusses the pre-1910 migration of Mexican railroad workers and the Pacific Electric Railroad strike of 1903 in Los Angeles, California, which are largely ignored by scholars of Mexican American history. Mexicans were considered the most tractable workers by the railroads, primarily because they worked for lower wages than other ethnic groups, and with the aid of the railroads the Mexican-born population of Los Angeles reached nearly 20,000 in 1910. The Pacific Electric strike was "one of the first major labor disputes between Mexican workers and Anglo employers." Although the Mexican Federal Union was effective in organizing track workers to strike for higher wages, the strike was squelched when Anglo carmen affiliated with the Amalgamated Association of Street Car Employees failed to walk out, which would have shut down the entire electric railroad system owned by Henry E. Huntington. The railroad did raise wages on the Main Street line, which had highest priority, but did not rehire strikers. The tracks were completed in time for the Los Angeles fiesta, as planned, but the failure of the strike did not end conflict between Huntington and the workers on *el traque*. 47 notes.   B. L. Fenske

1278. Wortman, Roy T. THE I.W.W. AND THE AKRON RUBBER STRIKE OF 1913. Conlin, Joseph R., ed. *At the Point of Production: The Local History of the I.W.W.* (Westport, Conn.: Greenwood Pr., 1981): 49-60. The 1913 rubber industry strike in Akron was precipitated by long working hours, depersonalized working conditions, and low wages. The attempts of the workers to unionize were thwarted until 11 February 1913, when a group of 25 tire finishers walked off the job, protesting Firestone's policy of introducing new machines which produced more tires, but with a reduction in pay scale to the workers. The Industrial Workers of the World were called in to organize the strike. By 18 February the IWW claimed 12,000 members out of a total of 20,000 rubber workers. A schism developed between workers who wanted compromise with management and the more militant strike

position espoused by the IWW. This led to the general failure of the strike on 25 March 1913. Based on journal articles of the period; 60 notes.   J. Powell

1279. Zeigler, Robert E. THE LIMITS OF POWER: THE AMALGAMATED ASSOCIATION OF STREET RAILWAY EMPLOYEES IN HOUSTON, TEXAS, 1897-1905. *Labor Hist. 1977 18(1): 71-90.* Studies the Amalgamated Association of Street Railway Employees and supports the thesis that a community often supported local labor organizations in opposition to corporations. The union failed in a lengthy, violent strike because of employer recalcitrance, not public hostility. Based on newspapers and union records; 44 notes.

L. L. Athey

1280. Zieger, Robert H. THE LIMITS OF MILITANCY: ORGANIZING PAPER WORKERS, 1933-1935. *J. of Am. Hist. 1976 63(3): 638-657.* Analyzes efforts to organize workers in the converted paper industry in the early years of the New Deal. The mid-1930's form a discrete segment of transitional trial-and-error organizational techniques in which grass roots militancy played a major role. This early militancy lacked staying power and represented a false start. The claims of militancy conflicted with those of permanent organization and erratic, ineffective local unions quarreled with the international organization, the International Brotherhood of Pulp, Sulphite, and Paper Mill Workers, AFL. Primary and secondary sources; 44 notes.

W. R. Hively

1281. Zieger, Robert H. OLDTIMERS & NEWCOMERS: CHANGE AND CONTINUITY IN THE PULP, SULPHITE UNION IN THE 1930'S. *J. of Forest Hist. 1977 21(4): 188-201.* The International Brotherhood of Pulp, Sulphite, and Paper Mill Workers was organized in 1909, but it failed to expand as rapidly as did the paper industry. In the mid-1930's, however, it did expand rapidly to include urban workers, many of whom were European immigrants and women. When it expanded into the South, it had to establish separate charters for black and white workers at the paper mills. Its new locals in the Pacific Northwest "exhibited a remarkable degree of suspicion and even contempt for the international union." Based on the IBPSPMW Papers and on primary and secondary sources; 12 illus., 27 notes.

F. N. Egerton

1282. Zieger, Robert H. THE UNION COMES TO COVINGTON: VIRGINIA PAPERWORKERS ORGANIZE, 1933-1952. *Pro. of the Am. Phil. Soc. 1982 126(1): 51-89.* Discusses the events which led after a score of years to the unionization of the West Virginia Pulp and Paper Company, Covington, Virginia. Their long encounter with an employer that resisted organization reflected the difficulty with which unions gained acceptance even in this period of success. Involved was the issue of rivalry between the AFL and the CIO. The importance of noneconomic issues, the struggle of the workers to gain regular and predictable conditions of employment, and their willingness to resort to sitdown and wildcat strikes to gain their goals demonstrated the continuance of the shop floor activism of the 1930's and 40's into the allegedly placid 50's. The role of black workers proved that in Covington, as well as in Detroit, black workers were vital to the success of industrial unionism. The working out of these central themes in a small Southern city reflected the depth and scope of the upheaval of American workers in the two decades after the birth of the New Deal. Based on papers of the International Brotherhood of Pulp, Sulphite, and Paper Mill Workers, State Historical Society of Wisconsin; Westvaco Papers, Dept. of Manuscripts and University Archives, Cornell University; National Labor Board Records (Record Group 25), National Archives; files of *The Covington Virginian;* oral interviews; 104 notes, biblio.

H. M. Parker, Jr.

1283. —. STRIKE FOR LIBERTY! SONGS, POETRY, AND COMMENTS BY WORKERS OF THE WESTERN FEDERATION OF MINERS: 1900-1907. *Southwest Econ. and Soc. 1979-80 51(1-2): 1-139.* Double issue entirely devoted to reprinting material originally published in *Miners' Magazine.*

1284. —. TEXTILE RESOURCES. *Southern Exposure 1976 3(4): 80-85.* The Institute for Southern Studies here provides a bibliography of books on the Southern textile industry and two famous strikes, 1929 and 1934; includes three diagrams on corporate interconnections.

1285. —. "WE WANT INTEGRITY": AN INTERVIEW WITH AL SISTI. *Radical Hist. Rev. 1978 (17): 181-190.* Al Sisti, an employee of the Atlantic Mills in Rhode Island, describes his work as a labor activist while at the textile mills and later as a steel organizer.

Government Programs, Policies, and Politics

1286. Asher, Robert. THE ORIGINS OF WORKMEN'S COMPENSATION IN MINNESOTA. *Minnesota Hist. 1974 44(4): 142-153.* The inefficiency and the litigation involved in employers' liability insurance, and the friction it caused, led some large companies to favor no fault workmen's compensation by 1909, the year that Governor Johnson called for an investigating commission to look into the problem. Uncertainty as to rates led to hesitancy, but by 1912 15 states approved such plans and in 1913 Minnesota passed a weak bill, a consensus reform measure. 13 illus.; 67 notes.   S. S. Sprague.

1287. Asher, Robert. RADICALISM AND REFORM: STATE INSURANCE OF WORKMEN'S COMPENSATION IN MINNESOTA, 1910-1933. *Labor Hist. 1973 14(1): 19-41.* The struggle for state insurance of workmen's compensation was spearheaded by the Minnesota State Federation of Labor in alliance with the Non-Partisan League. The attempt failed for numerous reasons including the antimonopolistic stance of Minnesota agrarians, the conservative defense of private plans, the growing disenchantment with government after World War I, and opposition on the grounds that reform was a socialist measure. Agitation from the left, however, did produce improvements which otherwise would not have succeeded. Based on publications of the Minnesota State Federation of Labor, legislative reports, manuscripts, and newspapers; 58 notes.   L. L. Athey

1288. Attoe, Wayne and Latus, Mark. THE FIRST PUBLIC HOUSING: SEWER SOCIALISM'S GARDEN CITY FOR MILWAUKEE. *J. of Popular Culture 1976 10(1): 142-149.* Garden Homes, a product of Milwaukee's applied socialist principles ("sewer socialism"), was constructed when private building failed to meet the housing crisis that followed World War I. Built equal to or exceeding private standards, this publicly supported venture of cooperatively owned housing for low income workers was based on "model workers villages" developed earlier in Germany and England. It failed in 1925 when the residents desired private ownership. Primary and secondary sources; fig., 9 notes.   D. G. Nielson

1289. Babu, B. Ramesh. UNEMPLOYMENT INSURANCE IN THE UNITED STATES: AN ANALYSIS OF THE BEGINNING. *J. of the U. of Bombay [India] 1975-76 44-45(80-81): 139-172.* The Social Security Act (US, 1935), which provided for unemployment insurance, was part of Franklin D. Roosevelts second New Deal. Although intended to counter criticism from the left, the Act was in fact a middle-of-the-road policy. It was preceded in 1934 by two attempts at unemployment insurance which failed to secure Congressional approval: the Wagner-Lewis Bill, intended to encourage the states to provide benefits, and the Lundeen Bill, which proposed coverage for persons who had been unable to secure employment for a minimum period. The Committee on Economic Security, appointed in 1934 to advise Roosevelt on social security, placed more emphasis on job creation than on unemployment insurance. They recommended a federal-state system based on tax credits. The Social Security Act, based on their recommendations but modified somewhat by the House of Representatives and the Senate, became law on 14 August 1935. Although the unemployment insurance provisions, criticized by the left and the right, were less impressive than some of its others, the Act as a whole was a major development in the evolution of the United States as a welfare state. Published government documents, contemporary newspapers and journals and secondary works; 87 notes.   J. F. Hilliker

1290. Bailey, Robert J. THEODORE G. BILBO AND THE FAIR EMPLOYMENT PRACTICES CONTROVERSY: A SOUTHERN SENATOR'S REACTIONS TO A CHANGING WORLD. *J. of Mississippi Hist. 1980 42(1): 27-42.* During World War II, President Franklin Roosevelt, in an effort to integrate minority groups into the war effort, created the Fair Employment Practices Committee by executive order in 1941, and enlarged its responsibilities in 1943. However, only congressional action could extend its life beyond the war years. Senator Dennis Chavez of New Mexico introduced a bill to establish a permanent FEPC in 1945 which set off a national controversy over how much control the federal government should have in employment practices. Some members of Congress, especially southern Democrats, viewed the bill as a step toward social equality of the races. Leading the opposition was Senator Theodore G. Bilbo of Mississippi who vowed he would beat the "damnable, unAmerican and unconstitutional" FEPC to death. Describes Bilbo's arguments and efforts to defeat the bill as well as the bill's supporters' criticisms of the Mississippian's race-baiting. Although the bill was withdrawn from consideration after a 24-day filibuster, concludes that Bilbo had become an anachronism, for by 1946 racism was becoming more subtle in American politics.   M. S. Legan

1291. Berkowitz, Monroe. OCCUPATIONAL SAFETY AND HEALTH. *Ann. of the Am. Acad. of Pol. and Social Sci. 1979 (443): 41-53.* Work accidents became a matter of societal concern in the Progressive era of Woodrow Wilson. When other contingencies of modern life were brought under social security in the New Deal reforms of the 1930's, work accident legislation remained separate. One possible reason was that work accidents can be controlled within industrial and chance limits. But control does not imply elimination since a risk-free environment would paralyze production. In spite of imperfections caused by low benefits and imperfect insurance arrangements, the workers' compensation legislation does help internalize the costs of accidents, but internalization of costs is only one remedy. Regulation and a much broader community responsibility are others. It is argued that regulation poses greater problems and that broader community responsibility may evade the issues involved in choosing the appropriate tradeoff point between production and health which will maximize social welfare.   J

1292. Best, Gary Dean. PRESIDENT WILSON'S SECOND INDUSTRIAL CONFERENCE, 1919-20. *Labor Hist. 1975 16(4): 505-520.* The most important proposal of the second Industrial Conference was for representation of employees through shop committees. No action was taken in the legislature, but industrialists transformed this "progressive idea" into company unions in the 1920's. Yet the idea of industrial democracy was advanced. Based on the second Industrial Conference archives, Wilson papers, and periodicals. 34 notes.   L. L. Athey

1293. Borisiuk, V. I. OT ZAKONA VAGNERA K ZAKONU TAFTA-KHARTLI: POVOROT K REAKTSII V TRUDOVOM ZAKONODATEL'STVE SSHA (1935-1947 GG.) [From the Wagner Act to the Taft-Hartley Act: the shift to reactionary labor legislation in the United States, 1935-47]. *Vestnik Moskovskogo U., Seriia 9: Istoriia [USSR] 1971 26(5): 15-31.* The Wagner Act (US, 1935), considered the most radical piece of labor legislation of the New Deal, generated sharp opposition from the right, manufacturers, and capital, and from their representatives in Congress. At first they sought to prove it unconstitutional; failing this they tried to amend it. They called the power of unions "un-American." During World War II there was a reactionary shift under the guise of protecting the war effort. After the war, with controls lifted, the number of strikes increased sharply. This set the stage for the victory of the right, the Taft-Hartley Act (US, 1947), which strictly regulated union activities. Based on published sources; 67 notes.   G. E. Munro

1294. Bremer, William W. ALONG THE "AMERICAN WAY": THE NEW DEAL'S WORK RELIEF PROGRAMS FOR THE UNEMPLOYED. *J. of Am. Hist. 1975 62(3): 636-652.* Describes the ideal of a constructive and psychologically supportive work relief program formulated by New Deal administrators and social workers, including Harry Hopkins, William Matthews, and Homer Folks, and its partial and temporary implementation in the Civil Works Administration of 1933-34. Political and budgetary pressures soon ended the CWA experiment. Instead, more traditional relief practices were adopted which kept work relief less attractive than private employment and retained the animus of charity. New Dealers did not view work relief as a permanent policy which guaranteed a "right to work." Based on collected papers, journals, and secondary works; 70 notes.   J. B. Street

1295. Brown, Lorraine. FEDERAL THEATRE: MELODRAMA, SOCIAL PROTEST, AND GENIUS. *Q. J. of the Lib. of Congress 1979 36(1): 18-37.* Recounts the history of the Federal Theatre Project of the Works Progress Administration from its establishment in 1935 until its demise in 1939. Implemented by Harry L. Hopkins, director of the WPA, and directed by Hallie Flanagan, the Federal Theatre Project was begun to relieve unemployed theater people during the depression. Theatre centers nationwide produced a wide variety of plays independently and simultaneously, including works by Sinclair Lewis, George Bernard Shaw, and Eugene O'Neill. The Federal Theatre Project produced both regional and national projects and struggled against censorship and cuts in funds for four years before it was ended for political reasons. Based on the Federal Theatre Project Collection at the Library of Congress; 15 photos, 39 notes.   A. R. Souby

1296. Capeci, Dominic J., Jr. FIORELLO H. LA GUARDIA AND EMPLOYMENT DISCRIMINATION, 1941-1943. *Italian Am. 1983 7(2): 49-67.* World War II broadened Fiorello La Guardia's liberalism and his concept of government's relationship to private enterprise, and it affected his policies on employment discrimination.

1297. Cuff, Robert D. THE POLITICS OF LABOR ADMINISTRATION DURING WORLD WAR I. *Labor Hist. 1980 21(4): 546-569.* The US Department of Labor was more effective in resisting bureaucratic invasions from the emergency war agencies during World War I than many other executive departments. The department won a major political victory when President Woodrow Wilson named the Secretary of Labor head of the government's wartime administration for labor policies in January 1918; yet, the Labor Department never really succeeded in acquiring actual administrative control of the government's labor policies. Based on the William B. Wilson Papers and other primary sources; 48 notes.   L. F. Velicer

1298. Daniel, Cletus E. AGRICULTURAL UNIONISM AND THE EARLY NEW DEAL: THE CALIFORNIA EXPERIENCE. *Southern California Q. 1977 59(2): 185-215.* Argues that the Franklin D. Roosevelt administraton, in the first phase of its New Deal policies, undercut the development of agricultural unionism in California. New Deal economic planners at first envisioned a harmonious relationship between employers and workers brought about through active federal mediation under the National Industrial Recovery Act (NIRA). Although New Deal labor policy dramatically changed after the end of the NIRA and the passage of the Wagner Act, California's agricultural labor movement suffered irreparably from the involvement of George Creel, self-styled NIRA mediator, in the San Joaquin cotton strike of October 1933. Creel effected a compromise which the Communist-led union accepted, and the chance to create an effective agricultural workers' union was lost. The Department of Labor sent Pelham Glassford to mediate labor disputes in the Imperial Valley. In 1934 he undercut the union by endorsing a company union, only to find that employers rejected both federal involvement and the company union. Thus the New Deal, remembered for its liberalism and reform, promoted the destruction of a vigorous effort to organize California agriculture. Primary and secondary sources; 68 notes.   A. Hoffman

1299. Davin, Eric Leif and Lynd, Staughton. PICKET LINE AND BALLOT BOX: THE FORGOTTEN LEGACY OF THE LOCAL LABOR PARTY MOVEMENT, 1932-1936. *Radical Hist. Rev. 1979-80 (22): 43-63.* Using Berlin, New Hampshire, as a case study, discusses the widespread working-class participation in state and local politics through the formation of independent labor and farmer-labor parties during 1932-36, and the destruction of the movement in 1936 by the Congress of Industrial Organizations through the Non-Partisan League.

1300. Dinwoodie, D. H. DEPORTATION: THE IMMIGRATION SERVICE AND THE CHICANO LABOR MOVEMENT IN THE 1930S. *New Mexico Hist. Rev. 1977 52(3): 193-206.* During the 1930's, Chicanos were the object of much investigation as to whether they had entered the United States illegally. The investigations generally took place when the immigrants organized labor unions. In 1935, Julio Herrera was deported on charges that he had entered the United States illegally. The following year Jesus Pallares was deported, after subversion charges were brought against him. Actually he was deported as a result of his activities in organizing the *Liga Obrera de Habla Español.* Chicanos were encouraged to organize labor unions by the policies of the New Deal, although local authorities were opposed to these policies. 39 notes.   J. H. Krenkel

1301. Dratch, Howard. THE POLITICS OF CHILD CARE IN THE 1940'S. *Sci. and Soc. 1974 38(2): 167-204.*

1302. Duram, James C. THE LABOR UNION JOURNALS AND THE CONSTITUTIONAL ISSUES OF THE NEW DEAL: THE CASE FOR COURT RESTRICTION. *Labor Hist. 1974 15(2): 216-238.* Assesses the editorial position of labor union periodicals on the constitutional issues posed by the New Deal between 1935 and 1937. A liberal interpretation of the constitution was demanded which would allow comprehensive economic and social legislation. The journals reacted to specific court decisions and carried general articles on judicial reform. During the court fight of 1937, labor union journals favored reorganization of the judiciary. The editorials reflect a relationship between the group's economic and constitutional positions and the fact that labor gave up its traditional independent approach to politics in the 1930's. 70 notes, appendix.   L. L. Athey

1303. Fowler, James H., II. CREATING AN ATMOSPHERE OF SUPPRESSION, 1914-1917. *Chronicles of Oklahoma 1981 59(2): 202-223.* Although the United States endorsed a policy of neutrality toward World War I, Americans increasingly developed an intolerance toward Germany and toward unpatriotic persons. The level of intolerance boiled over in Oklahoma as both vigilantes and respected newspapers harangued pacifists, labor union organizers, and political leftists. President Woodrow Wilson's frequent outbursts against the same groups seemingly gave legitimacy to local vigilante groups such as the Oklahoma State Council of Defense. Freedom of speech evaporated in this poisoned atmosphere. Based on Oklahoma newspapers; 3 illus., 85 notes.   M. L. Tate

1304. Gaffield, Chad. BIG BUSINESS, THE WORKING-CLASS, AND SOCIALISM IN SCHENECTADY, 1911-1916. *Labor Hist. 1978 19(3): 350-372.* Analyzes the record of George Lunn, Socialist mayor of Schenectady, New York, and the voting patterns in the city. Socialism had its greatest strength in working-class wards, and business leaders were not unduly upset by the party victory. The demise of the Socialist Party may be more attributable to a hostile judicial system than to other factors. Based on city directories, census reports, and newspapers; 7 tables, 43 notes.   L. L. Athey

1305. Gengarelly, W. Anthony. SECRETARY OF LABOR WILLIAM B. WILSON AND THE RED SCARE, 1919-1920. *Pennsylvania Hist. 1980 47(4): 311-330.* During the red scare of 1919-20, Secretary of Labor William B. Wilson permitted subordinates and Attorney General A. Mitchell Palmer to violate the rights of immigrants in deportation procedures. Legislation placed deportation matters under Secretary Wilson, who previously had established just guidelines for them. While Wilson was on a brief leave of absence in 1920, Assistant Secretary Louis F. Post cancelled 1,140 deportation warrants and moved to rectify earlier abuses of power. Upon his return, Wilson backed Post in these efforts. Based on Wilson papers, Labor Department archives, other government documents, and secondary sources; 2 photos, 51 notes.   D. C. Swift

1306. Gordon, Linda. ARE THE INTERESTS OF MEN AND WOMEN IDENTICAL? *Signs 1976 1(4): 1011-1018.* During the early 20th century the Socialist Party organized women's branches in 156 party locals. At that time it was the only political party to allow women's participation and to endorse equal rights and woman suffrage. The Socialists appealed to all working-class women, not just those employed. The attempt to create a socialist feminism anchored in the working-class experience failed, in part due to the reluctance of socialist men to incorporate feminism into their program, and in part due to the legalistic middle-class women's rights movement which could not offer much to working class or radical women. The attempt to create a mass movement, however, advanced the analysis of women's situation. Based on three newspaper articles; 6 notes.   J. Gammage

1307. Gould, William B. RACIAL PROTEST AND SELF-HELP UNDER TAFT-HARTLEY: THE WESTERN ADDITION CASE. *Arbitration J. 1974 29(3): 161-175.* Under federal labor law, a bargaining unit employee who, ignoring grievance and arbitration procedure available to him, engages in 'self-help' by a work stoppage or a refusal to obey reasonable orders, runs the risk of discharge or other forms of discipline. He thereby loses the protection of the Taft-Hartley law. But there is now pending before the U.S. Supreme Court a case involving employees who are arguing that, as the purpose of their self-help was to vindicate rights guaranteed by Title VII of the Civil Rights Act, they did not lose the protection of law by choosing not to stay within the limits prescribed by the collective agreement.... Suggests that courts must decide such cases in the light of the union's policies not only with respect to the particular grievance but of its total record with respect to minority races.   J

1308. Graebner, William. EFFICIENCY, SECURITY, COMMUNITY: THE ORIGINS OF CIVIL SERVICE RETIREMENT. *Prologue 1980 12(3): 116-133.* Discusses the historical background (ca. 1897-1920) of the first general piece of retirement legislation for federal civil servants, passed in May 1920. The function of retirement legislation was to help rationalize the bureaucracy so that relations would be conducted on an impersonal rather than a personal basis. The 1920 legislation was intended to induce bureaucratic efficiency while providing a measure of security to the prospective retiree, but allowed for such small pensions that it served to prolong the old system of community that existed in most federal agencies for dealing with older employees. The law was amended in 1926 to increase the size of the pension and has been further amended since that time, but the 1920 legislation remains the core of federal civil service retirement. Based on correspondence, newspapers, Treasury Department Records, Bureau of the Budget Records, Office of the Secretary of Interior Records, National Civil Service League Papers; 9 photos, chart, 56 notes.   M. A. Kascus

1309. Grossman, Jonathan. THE COAL STRIKE OF 1902—TURNING POINT IN U.S. POLICY. *Monthly Labor Rev. 1975 98(10): 21-28.* Describes the settlement of Pennsylvania's 1902 coal strike, in which President Theodore Roosevelt, with the Commissioner of Labor, represented the federal government while acting as an arbitrator between labor and management.

1310. Guzda, Henry P. FRANCES PERKINS' INTEREST IN A NEW DEAL FOR BLACKS. *Monthly Labor Rev. 1980 103(4): 31-35.* Discusses Secretary of Labor Frances Perkins's commitment to making blacks' welfare a top priority of the Labor Department, 1933-45.

1311. Guzda, Henry P. LABOR DEPARTMENT'S FIRST PROGRAM TO ASSIST BLACK WORKERS. *Monthly Labor Rev. 1982 105(6): 39-44.* The Division of Negro Economics was formed in 1917 as part of the Department of Labor to recruit black workers for the war effort at the state and local levels, particularly in the Northern industrial cities where the division met with the greatest success; the program ended in 1921 when a new administration and a new head of the Labor Department without interest in promoting equal opportunity employment took over.

1312. Harring, Sidney L. THE POLICE INSTITUTION AS A CLASS QUESTION: MILWAUKEE SOCIALISTS AND THE POLICE, 1900-1915. *Sci. & Soc. 1982 46(2): 197-221.* The role of Milwaukee police in managing the late 19th-century labor crises of that city shows that the roots of police professionalism lie in the need of a ruling bourgeois to isolate public institutions from working-class power. In opposition to a police force operating as a class institution enforcing class law, the Milwaukee Social Democratic Party offered a real alternative for the working class. Milwaukee Municipal Reference Bureau.   L. V. Eid

1313. Harris, William H. FEDERAL INTERVENTION IN UNION DISCRIMINATION: FEPC AND WEST COAST SHIPYARDS DURING WORLD WAR II. *Labor Hist. 1981 22(3): 325-347.* Describes the effects of the Fair Employment Practices Committee (FEPC) to eliminate racial discrimination by unions and shipbuilding companies against blacks who came west during World War II. An auxiliary union membership system kept blacks separated from white union members, and the West Coast Master Agreement gave AFL (American Federation of Labor) unions a nearly closed shop in the shipyards. Blacks' complaints to the FEPC eventually spurred investigations, a reorganization of the FEPC, hearings before the FEPC, and

lawsuits in state courts. The California Supreme Court's right to work decision reinforced the FEPC findings of racial discrimination and led to an end of that practice by unions. Covers 1939-46. Based on FEPC West Coast Hearings and other primary sources; table, 48 notes.
L. F. Velicer

1314. Haughton, Virginia. JOHN W. KERN: SENATE MAJORITY LEADER AND LABOR LEGISLATION, 1913-1917. *Mid-America 1975 57(3): 184-194.* Though of a rural background, John W. Kern was an early champion of labor. He ran on the defeated Bryan ticket in 1908, entered the Senate in 1911, and became Senate Majority Leader in 1913. Kern obtained Senate investigation of deplorable labor conditions in West Virginia. His most lasting achievement was the Kern-McGillicuddy Workman's Compensation Act (1916). He was instrumental in passage of the La Follette Seaman's Bill and much other prolabor legislation. Based on official records, newspapers, and secondary works; 38 notes.   T. H. Wendel

1315. Head, Faye E. THE THEATRICAL SYNDICATE VS. THE CHILD LABOR LAW OF LOUISIANA. *Louisiana Studies 1974 13(4): 365-374.* The Theatrical Syndicate's monopoly was opposed by the Child Labor Law (Louisiana, 1908), which had a costly though not immediate effect upon New Orleans theaters. In 1912, after a battle by Jean Gordon and a small group of women, the theatrical interests were the victors: the Child Labor Law was amended by the pressure of New York interests to permit children under 16 to act on the stages of Louisiana. Note.   E. P. Stickney

1316. Heinemann, Ronald L. BLUE EAGLE OR BLACK BUZZARD? THE NATIONAL RECOVERY ADMINISTRATION IN VIRGINIA. *Virginia Mag. of Hist. and Biog. 1981 89(1): 90-100.* Interprets the rise and fall of the National Recovery Administration (NRA). Initial enthusiasm for this New Deal program in mid-1933 faded when resistance to enforcement of many of its codes developed, mostly over wage and hour violations. The NRA simultaneously fought the customary southern versus northern wage differential, cut hours and discharges instead of wage rates, a mixed reaction from business, and a generally hostile press. In May 1935 the US Supreme Court declared the NRA unconstitutional. 29 notes.   P. J. Woehrmann

1317. Hendrickson, Kenneth E., Jr. THE CIVILIAN CONSERVATION CORPS IN SOUTH DAKOTA. *South Dakota Hist. 1980 11(1): 1-20.* Discusses the administration, organization, and achievements of the Civilian Conservation Corps (CCC) in South Dakota between 1933 and 1942. The CCC was one of the most effective federal relief programs in South Dakota. The program provided employment for more than 26,000 men and distributed over six million dollars to their families. The program also improved the South Dakota environment, particularly through soil conservation, timber stand improvement, and control of forest fires. Based on the records of the Civilian Conservation Corps-South Dakota in the National Archives, Washington, D.C., and other primary sources; 12 photos, 37 notes.   P. L. McLaughlin

1318. Hendrickson, Kenneth E., Jr. THE NATIONAL YOUTH ADMINISTRATION IN SOUTH DAKOTA: YOUTH AND THE NEW DEAL, 1935-1943. *South Dakota Hist. 1979 9(2): 130-151.* The National Youth Administration (NYA), between its creation in 1935 and its demise in 1943, provided part-time employment for needy high school and college students and relief work for youth not in school. Although often caught up in political and bureaucratic difficulties, the NYA in South Dakota experienced its greatest success and popularity between 1937 and 1940 under Anna C. Struble as State Youth Director. The NYA program in South Dakota gave assistance and relief to thousands of youngsters and their families and demonstrated that the federal system can work effectively for the welfare of all the people. Primary sources; 6 photos, 35 notes.   P. L. McLaughlin

1319. Hendrickson, Kenneth E., Jr. RELIEF FOR YOUTH: THE CIVILIAN CONSERVATION CORPS AND THE NATIONAL YOUTH ADMINISTRATION IN NORTH DAKOTA. *North Dakota Hist. 1981 48(4): 17-27.* The Civilian Conservation Corps and the National Youth Administration were both initially well received by officials and citizens of North Dakota. They provided work relief and assistance to needy families, performed conservation services, built recreation facilities, and provided practical training and education.

World War II brought changes in purpose to both agencies, from need to aptitude and defense preparedness, and it reduced the number of applicants. Agencies functioned until funding was eliminated by Congress. Based on official records and published sources; 59 notes, 9 illus.

G. L. Olson

1320. Hoffman, Abraham. EL CIERRE DE LA PUERTA TRASERA NORTEAMERICANA: RESTRECCIÓN DE LA INMIGRACIÓN MEXICANA [The closure of the North American back door: restriction of Mexican immigration]. *Hist. Mexicana [Mexico] 1976 25(3): 302-422.* On the eve of the Depression various groups sought to reduce immigration into the United States. Racists, some unions, and small-scale agriculturalists wished to reduce Mexican immigration, while larger-scale agricultural and industrial concerns needing labor were less hostile. The 1924 Immigration Bill was vigorously enforced and the State Department advised consulates to restrict the issuance of visas; by September 1929 a 30% reduction in visas granted had occurred. Based on State department documents, the press, and memoirs; 39 notes.

S. P. Carr

1321. Hurd, Rick. NEW DEAL LABOR POLICY AND THE CONTAINMENT OF RADICAL UNION ACTIVITY. *Rev. of Radical Pol. Econ. 1976 8(3): 32-43.* New Deal labor policies were designed to impart support for working class movements to discourage activism and militance on the part of labor radicals, 1930's.

1322. Hurwitz, Haggai. IDEOLOGY AND INDUSTRIAL CONFLICT: PRESIDENT WILSON'S FIRST INDUSTRIAL CONFERENCE OF OCTOBER 1919. *Labor Hist. 1977 18(4): 509-524.* The First Industrial Conference of 1919 reveals the underlying ideological conflict between labor and management. Instead of pragmatic business unionism, labor delegates representing major unions argued for a broad transformation of the role of labor based on human rights. Industrialists attacked unions on the basis of property rights and managerial prerogatives designed to destroy unions. The complete ideological division represented the irreconciliable social views of labor and industry; the Conference was doomed to fail. Based on the *Proceedings* of the Conference; 41 notes.

L. L. Athey

1323. Jackson, Joy J. PROHIBITION IN NEW ORLEANS: THE UNLIKELIEST CRUSADE. *Louisiana Hist. 1978 19(3): 261-284.* Presidential address, 20th Annual Meeting of the Louisiana Historical Association, Alexandria, Louisiana, 10 March 1978. The Louisiana legislature ratified the 18th Amendment in August 1918 by a narrow margin, as north and central Louisiana "dry" interests defeated the "wet" votes of southern Louisiana and New Orleans. New Orleans opposed prohibition and was a center for bootlegging to dry regions throughout the Gulf South. Many establishments in the city secretly and openly defied the ban on alcoholic beverages. Despite heavy enforcement efforts, wine, beer, and liquor remained widely available throughout the period, and prohibition violation contributed to the rise of organized crime, gangsterism and bribery of public officials in New Orleans as in other large cities. Details enforcement efforts as well as popular opposition and flaunting of prohibition. Primary sources; 86 notes.

R. L. Woodward, Jr.

1324. Khan, Mohammad Mohabbat. EVOLUTION OF MANAGEMENT-LABOUR RELATIONS IN TENNESSEE VALLEY AUTHORITY: AN OVERVIEW. *Dacca U. Studies Part A [Bangladesh] 1979 (30): 70-77.* The Tennessee Valley Authority was created in 1933 to stimulate economic development in Appalachia. In 1935 the TVA Board of Directors issued the Employee Relationship Policy, which gave TVA employees the right to form unions and to negotiate collectively with the management. Responding to the policy, the American Federation of Labor organized the TVA workers along craft lines, a situation that has held since. In general, labor relations have tended to be harmonious and there has been an openness that operates even at the lowest levels in the TVA. Public documents and secondary works; 8 notes.

J. V. Groves

1325. Lauderbaugh, Richard A. BUSINESS, LABOR, AND FOREIGN POLICY: U.S. STEEL, THE INTERNATIONAL STEEL CARTEL, AND RECOGNITION OF THE STEEL WORKERS ORGANIZING COMMITTEE. *Pol. and Soc. 1976 6(4): 433-457.* "Private" foreign diplomacy led to the US Steel Corp.'s collective bargaining agreement with the Steel Workers Organizing Committee (SWOC) in early 1937. The agreement with the SWOC depended upon a verbal commitment to join the Entente Internationale de L'Acier (International Steel Cartel). In contravention of New Deal policies and US antitrust laws, the agreement included import restrictions, thereby controlling competition in the international steel market, and in turn protecting the US market. The agreement with SWOC served to camouflage the international aspects of the "invisible tariff" protecting the US steel market from the eyes of Roosevelt's New Dealers. 48 notes.

D. G. Nielson

1326. Lea, Arden J. COTTON TEXTILES AND THE FEDERAL CHILD LABOR ACT OF 1916. *Labor Hist. 1975 16(4): 485-494.* Cotton textile industrialists shifted their position on federal regulation of child labor during 1907-16 as a result of increased competition and a desire for uniformity and stability. The Keating-Owen Act, conservative in nature, served the interests of large industrialists who promoted use of the Federal government to stabilize the economy, although the Act was levied against business interests in a particular section of the country. Child labor and voting tables presented on pp. 492-493. Based on census reports and the *Congressional Record*; 20 notes.

L. L. Athey

1327. Levi, Steven C. THE MOST EXPENSIVE MEAL IN AMERICAN HISTORY. *J. of the West 1979 18(2): 62-73.* In the summer of 1916 Charles Evans Hughes, Republican candidate for president, attempted to bring disaffected Progressives back into the Republican Party. His campaign in California coincided with a period of labor unrest in San Francisco. Hughes unwisely followed the advice of conservative Republicans and attended a banquet in an antiunion restaurant on 19 August 1916. This act marked Hughes as an enemy of labor and was a major cause of his failure to carry California in the presidential election. Based on newspapers and other published sources; 4 photos, 59 notes.

B. S. Porter

1328. Levi, Steven C. THE TRIAL OF WILLIAM MC DEVITT. *Southern California Q. 1977 59(3): 289-312.* The San Francisco Chamber of Commerce created the Law and Order Committee (LAOC) to support the open shop and to oppose labor unions, Socialists, and radicals. The committee attempted to force the dismissal of Socialist William McDevitt from the Board of Election Commissioners. McDevitt had delivered an indiscreet speech at a public meeting two days before the 22 July 1916 Preparedness Day Parade and its tragic bombing; the Law and Order Committee insisted the speech had been inflammatory. The "trial" was actually a hearing before Mayor James J. Rolph, who tried to remain neutral. The proceeding was marred by numerous irregularities, not the least of which was confusion over whether it was a judicial trial or a civil hearing. After hearing evidence, much of which was verbose and irrelevant, Rolph refused to dismiss McDevitt. The limits of LAOC influence were thus shown. 51 notes.

A. Hoffman

1329. Longin, Thomas C. COAL, CONGRESS, AND THE COURTS: THE BITUMINOUS COAL INDUSTRY AND THE NEW DEAL. *West Virginia Hist. 1974 35(2): 101-130.* The depressed coal industry became a case study of New Deal economic policy. The National Recovery Administration Bituminous Coal Code temporarily boosted wages and prices. The Guffey Act (1935), supported by labor and small operators against the large companies, imposed wage price controls and collective bargaining. Struck down by the Supreme Court, it was replaced by a milder Coal Act (1937). Although these measures raised wages and reduced hours, they never solved the basic long-term problem of over-capacity; only World War II did that. Based on newspapers, congressional debates, and court cases; 47 notes.

J. H. Broussard

1330. Lovin, Hugh T. AGRARIAN RADICALISM AT EBB TIDE: THE MICHIGAN FARMER-LABOR PARTY, 1933-1937. *Old Northwest 1979 5(2): 149-166.* During Franklin Delano Roosevelt's first term as president (1933-37), agrarian rebel groups in Michigan, such as the Farmers' Educational and Cooperative Union, the Farmers' Holiday Association, and the Farmer-Laborites of Wisconsin Congressman Thomas Amlie, cooperated to form a Farmer-Labor Party to oppose New Deal programs. Party secretary D. D. Alderdyce, however, tried to sever ties with Amlie's national movement, and although his demotion and the support of the United Automobile Workers helped, Committee for Industrial Organization President John L. Lewis's support for Roosevelt hurt. The presidential candidacy of Union Party member William Lenke made party unity impossible. Based on the Thomas R. Amlie Papers, State Historical Society of Wisconsin, Madison, the Howard Y. Williams Papers, Minnesota Historical Society, St. Paul, and other primary sources; 41 notes.   E. L. Keyser

1331. Lovin, Hugh T. THE AUTOMOBILE WORKERS UNIONS AND THE FIGHT FOR LABOR PARTIES IN THE 1930S. *Indiana Mag. of Hist. 1981 77(2): 123-149.* When the automobile workers began to organize unions in the mid-1930's there were strong disputes about whether these industrial unions should join one of the new labor-liberal parties or continue to reflect the nonpolitical bread and butter issues of the American Federation of Labor. After many experiments and some indecision the United Automobile Workers of America in Indiana and Ohio went along with the Democratic New Deal, but without much enthusiasm. Based on official proceedings, monographs, manuscripts, and newspapers; 2 illus., 57 notes.   A. Erlebacher

1332. Lovin, Hugh T. THE "FARMER-LABOR" MOVEMENT IN IDAHO, 1933-1938. *J. of the West 1979 18(2): 21-29.* The Farmer-Labor movement spread through the Middle West but failed to take hold in Idaho. The movement's failure in the election of 1934 was due to the lack of local groups to assist the campaign, and to the ill-conceived alliance with the fundamentally conservative Prohibition Party. Prospects in 1935 and 1936 seemed to improve until the defection of Ray McKaig, a controversial Farmer-Labor leader. The Townsend movement and John L. Lewis's Congress of Industrial Organization (CIO) drew away many followers. In 1936 Farmer-Labor leaders joined a coalition with the Union Party, a move that destroyed its identity and its prospects for survival in Idaho. It struggled along for two more years in other states. Based on documents in the Minnesota Historical Society, the Idaho State Historical Society, and contemporary news articles; 7 photos, 31 notes.   B. S. Porter

1333. Lovin, Hugh T. THE OHIO "FARMER-LABOR" MOVEMENT IN THE 1930'S. *Ohio Hist. 1978 87(4): 419-437.* Discusses Thomas Amlie and Herbert Hard's attempts to build a viable farmer-labor coalition as a third party to the left of the New Deal. Ohio Farmer-Labor Progressive Federation (1933-36) leaders viewed Ohio as a crucial state in their movement and hoped to draw on the well-organized movement of the unemployed and the rebellious union consciousness of the industrial worker to combat the conservative and intractable records of Governors White and Davey. The subsequent failure of the movement resulted not only from the personal popularity of FDR, the power of the CIO, the New Deal support of the AFL, Grange, and Farm Bureau, and the party schism created by the Communist-sponsored 1935 Popular Front, but from the leadership's inability to work with or appeal to the ethnic and urban laborites who dominated Ohio's work force. Based on the archives of Wayne State University, the Minnesota Historical Society, the State Historical Society of Wisconsin, and other primary sources; 44 notes.   L. A. Russell

1334. Lovin, Hugh T. TOWARD A FARMER-LABOR PARTY IN OREGON, 1933-38. *Oregon Hist. Q. 1975 76(2): 135-151.* Analyzes the failure of attempts to establish a branch of the Farmer-Labor Party in Oregon. This party was composed of agrarians and labor unionists discontented with the New Deal's failure to combat the depression. It proposed as a cure an "economy of abundance" achieved by government encouragement of cooperatives and legislation ensuring the production of goods "for use" rather than "for profit." In 1937 opponents of the New Deal formed the Oregon Commonwealth Federation but the new party failed because of its radical reputation, weak backing from agrarians and the American Federation of Labor, and a disinclination toward third parties. Many of the reform-oriented goals were ultimately achieved through political activities within the Oregon Democratic Party. Based on manuscript collections, newspapers, unpublished theses, and secondary sources; 57 notes.   J. D. Smith

1335. Martin, George. HOW MISS PERKINS LEARNED TO LOBBY. *Am. Heritage 1976 27(3): 64-71.* Frances Perkins, FDR's Secretary of Labor for 12 years, learned much about lobbying when she represented the Consumers League of New York before the New York state legislature in 1911. The experience in getting a bill passed in Albany served her well in Washington. Excerpted from *Madam*

Secretary: Frances Perkins (Houghton Mifflin, 1976). 5 illus.
                                        B. J. Paul

1336. McLaughlin, Doris B. PUTTING MICHIGAN BACK TO WORK. *Michigan Hist. 1982 66(1): 30-37.* William Haber, professor emeritus, University of Michigan, was Michigan relief administrator, deputy Works Progress administrator and state National Youth administrator during the Depression. As a part of a larger oral history project, he gave his reflections of his work during the Depression. 19 pictures.
                                        L. E. Ziewacz

1337. Mitchell, Virgil L. LOUISIANA HEALTH AND THE CIVIL WORKS ADMINISTRATION. *Red River Valley Hist. Rev. 1982 7(1): 22-32.* The Civil Works Administration, created as a temporary agency to alleviate the problems of the unemployed in 1933-34, did complete a variety of lasting projects that benefited the state of Louisiana; discusses the health and sanitation projects of rodent extermination, mosquito control, the construction of sanitary toilets, and cattle tick eradication.

1338. Mitchell, Virgil L. THE LOUISIANA UNEMPLOYED AND THE CIVIL WORKS ADMINISTRATION. *Red River Valley Hist. Rev. 1980 5(3): 54-67.* Because federal relief programs instituted in 1932 in Louisiana to offset the effects of the Depression had failed to produce the desired results, President Roosevelt created the Civil Works Administration to aid the destitute through the winter of 1933-34 or until they could be absorbed by the Public Works Administration then being formed.

1339. Moorhouse, John C. COMPULSORY UNIONISM AND THE FREE-RIDER DOCTRINE. *Cato J. 1982 2(2): 619-635.* Examines the free-rider provision (Section 9a) of the National Labor Relations Act of 1935; it fails because it provides an incentive to vote for the establishment of a union but provides no incentives for workers to support a union.

1340. Mullins, William H. SELF-HELP IN SEATTLE, 1931-1932: HERBERT HOOVER'S CONCEPT OF COOPERATIVE INDIVIDUALISM AND THE UNEMPLOYED CITIZENS' LEAGUE. *Pacific Northwest Q. 1981 72(1): 11-19.* The Unemployed Citizens' League (UCL) of Seattle, Washington, created in 1931, closely paralleled President Herbert C. Hoover's call for voluntary, self-help programs to solve the problems of the Depression. Mayor Robert Harlin agreed with the program and appointed I. F. Dix to coordinate public and private relief efforts. Initial UCL success in creating jobs was shortlived, however, as internal strife, local politics, loss of funding sources, and the leftward turn of UCL leaders undermined its efforts. By the end of 1932 the organization had lost its popular following and its power. Primary sources; 3 photos, 39 notes.   M. L. Tate

1341. Narber, Gregg R. and DeLong, Lea Rosson. THE NEW DEAL MURALS IN IOWA. *Palimpsest 1982 63(3): 86-96.* Reproduces some of the 50 public murals, painted in Iowa as part of the New Deal's efforts to put people to work through agencies such as the Works Progress Administration, the Public Works of Art Project, and the Treasury Relief Art Project.

1342. Nye, Ronald L. THE CHALLENGE TO PHILANTHROPY: UNEMPLOYMENT RELIEF IN SANTA BARBARA, 1930-1932. *California Hist. Q. 1977-78 56(4): 310-327.* Santa Barbara met the challenge of unemployment relief during the first two years of the Great Depression. Led by philanthropist Max Fleischmann, the community attempted to provide work relief, create jobs, and solicit private funds to subsidize public works projects. These goals were implemented through citizens' committees, especially the Emergency Unemployment Fund Committee, created in December 1930. Wealthy residents were urged to contribute. With conditions worsening by fall 1931, a second campaign raised almost $115,000. Santa Barbarans endorsed job creation, work relief, and priority aid to the city's jobless residents, including singles and Mexican Americans. Transients were encouraged to move on, and Mexican noncitizens were advised to return to Mexico. By mid-1932 the magnitude of the problem was recognized, and funding shifted to public agencies. Primary sources and secondary studies; illus., 59 notes.
                                        A. Hoffman

1343. Ober, Michael J. THE CCC EXPERIENCE IN GLACIER NATIONAL PARK. *Montana 1976 26(3): 30-39.* During its existence between 1933 and 1942, the Civilian Conservation Corps maintained camps in Glacier National Park and engaged in projects of construction and protection. The supervisors reported that the work was beneficial to the Park and to the members of the Corps. Based on official correspondence in the Park archives at the University of Montana, and on newspaper accounts. Illus.   S. R. Davison

1344. Olssen, Erik. THE MAKING OF A POLITICAL MACHINE: THE RAILROAD UNIONS ENTER POLITICS. *Labor Hist. 1978 19(3): 373-396.* The railroad unions, traditionally conservative in politics, entered into a course of political action in 1919 which led to their participation in 1922 in the Conference for Progressive Political Action (CPPA). The CPPA initially functioned as a successful political machine, particularly in the congressional elections of 1922. However, the unions avoided presidential politics after the failure of the La Follette candidacy in 1924. Based on the La Follette Family papers and union periodicals; 46 notes.   L. L. Athey

1345. Ortquist, Richard T. UNEMPLOYMENT AND RELIEF: MICHIGAN'S RESPONSE TO THE DEPRESSION DURING THE HOOVER YEARS. *Michigan Hist. 1973 57(3): 209-236.* During the Depression, Michigan had the largest proportion of unemployment of industrial workers in the United States. Governor Wilber M. Brucker held traditional attitudes toward unemployment and believed that local and private resources were sufficient to alleviate the crisis. On the other hand, Mayor Frank Murphy of Detroit became one of the nation's leading advocates of federal aid. The Lansing-Detroit conflict continued even after Brucker was defeated for reelection. 4 illus., 48 notes.
                    D. L. Smith

1346. Ostrower, Gary B. THE AMERICAN DECISION TO JOIN THE INTERNATIONAL LABOR ORGANIZATION. *Labor Hist. 1975 16(4): 495-504.* Support for American membership in the International Labor Organization arose from the Department of Labor under Frances Perkins. With the support of the Department of State and Franklin D. Roosevelt, opposition from isolationist sentiment and financial conservatives was overcome by 1934. Suggests that the New Deal may have been less isolationist than generally characterized. Based on archives of Departments of Labor and State; 23 notes.
                    L. L. Athey

1347. Patterson, James T., ed. LIFE ON RELIEF IN RHODE ISLAND, 1934: A CONTEMPORARY VIEW FROM THE FIELD. *Rhode Island Hist. 1980 39(3): 79-91.* Reproduces, with editorial annotations, two letters to Harry L. Hopkins, head of the Federal Emergency Relief Administration, from Robert Washburn and Martha Gellhorn. Based on documents in the Roosevelt Library, Hyde Park, New York, and published documents and statistics; 11 illus., 9 notes.
                    P. J. Coleman

1348. Platschek, Hans. ROOSEVELTS MALER [Roosevelt's painters]. *Frankfurter Hefte [West Germany] 1975 30(7): 49-64.* During the New Deal, thousands of artists were given jobs painting public buildings; the style, which can still be seen on the walls of post offices and courthouses throughout the land, is a heroic, historical one, reminiscent of contemporary Russia's Socialist Realism.

1349. Read, Dennis M. TALKING IT UP. *Am. Scholar 1981 50(4): 555-558.* Reviews *First-Person America* (1980), edited by Ann Banks, which consists of interviews of members of the working class acquired by the Federal Writers' Project. It is oral history once removed from the storyteller. A methodological problem exists in that the procedure for selecting interviewees is not known. *First-Person America* is not quite history but is better than storytelling.   F. F. Harling

1350. Reagan, Patrick D. THE IDEOLOGY OF SOCIAL HARMONY AND EFFICIENCY: WORKMEN'S COMPENSATION IN OHIO, 1904-1919. *Ohio Hist. 1981 90(4): 317-331.* From 1912 through the early 1920's, Progressive reformers tried to enact social insurance legislation through a state-by-state and step-by-step strategy to ameliorate the industrial conditions of work accidents, sickness, unemployment, and premature old age. Discusses the six general stages of this process of reform as manifested in the 1910 Metzger Act, the creation of

the Employers' Liability Commission in 1910, the Workmen's Compensation Act of 1911, the creation of the State Liability Board of Awards in 1911, the Green Compulsory Workmen's Compensation Act of 1913, and the 1913 creation of the Industrial Commission. The success of reform efforts in Ohio stemmed from the growth and implementation of a conservation ideology of mutual accommodation between the Ohio State Federation of Labor (OSFL) and the Ohio Manufacturer's Association (OMA), which encompassed an interlocking set of concepts to create a new "organizational society." In the main, the Ohio developments followed the pattern set by earlier compensation laws and set the precedent for later systems. Based on the records of the Ohio Employers' Liability Commission, the Ohio State Federation of Labor, the Ohio General Assembly, the Ohio State Liability Board of Awards, the Ohio Industrial Commission, and other primary sources; 2 photos, 27 notes.   L. A. Russell

1351. Reed, Merl E. THE FEPC, THE BLACK WORKER, AND THE SOUTHERN SHIPYARDS. *South Atlantic Q. 1975 74(4): 446-467.* The outbreak of World War II led to a great upsurge of work activity in the southern shipyards. Labor was scarce, but Negroes were employed only in manual positions. President Franklin D. Roosevelt succumbed to pressure and created the Fair Employment Practices Commission. The FEPC acted to give black workers equal job opportunities. A riot in Mobile, Alabama forced the army to move in and some changes were made. The FEPC, its power weakened, was less active in other southern shipyards, and thus has left a mixed record. 31 notes.   V. L. Human

1352. Rice, Hazel F. A MEMO FROM MEMORY: WORKING WITH THE NORTH DAKOTA WORKMEN'S COMPENSATION BUREAU, 1919-1922. *North Dakota Hist. 1979 46(2): 22-29.* The author became the first Secretary of the North Dakota Minimum Wage Department in 1919. Her bureau was created by the state government brought into power through the successful electoral efforts of the Non-Partisan League. The author had sporadic contacts with officials of the Bureau, especially Board Member Laureas J. Wehe, but she basically worked alone in journeying throughout the state to investigate working conditions. Her letters to her family in New England during her tenure of service describe the arduous efforts necessary to travel from place to place in a state served by three railroads but ill-served by any other rapid transportation. The author's work was greatly inconvenienced by abysmal weather conditions and by the lack of adequate lodging for women in towns and villages.   N. Lederer

1353. Rosenstone, Robert A. THE FEDERAL (MOSTLY NON-) WRITERS' PROJECT. *Rev. in Am. Hist. 1978 6(3): 400-404.* Review article prompted by Monty Noam Penkower's *The Federal Writers' Project: A Study in Government Patronage of the Arts* (Urbana: U. of Illinois, 1977).

1354. Rosenzweig, Roy. "SOCIALISM IN OUR TIME": THE SOCIALIST PARTY AND THE UNEMPLOYED, 1929-1936. *Labor Hist. 1979 20(4): 485-509.* Socialists played an important role, especially after 1932, in organizing the unemployed. Led by young socialists, practical action for relief was important in Chicago, New York, Baltimore, and other cities. The practical focus, when combined with external events such as the rise of the Nazis, led socialists toward being absorbed into New Deal liberalism. Their Depression activism should not be forgotten. Based on the Norman Thomas manuscript, Socialist Party manuscript, and files in the Tamiment Library; 39 notes.
                    L. L. Athey

1355. Ross, Hugh. JOHN L. LEWIS AND THE ELECTION OF 1940. *Labor Hist. 1976 17(2): 160-189.* The breach between John L. Lewis and Franklin D. Roosevelt in 1940 originated from domestic and foreign policy concerns. The struggle to organize the steel industry, and after 1938, business attempts to erode Walsh-Healy and the Fair Labor Standards Act provided the backdrop for the feud. But activities of Nazi agents, working through William Rhodes Davis, increased Lewis' suspicions of Roosevelt's foreign policy and were important in the decision to support Wendell Willkie. Based on correspondence, German foreign policy documents, and published sources; 63 notes.
                    L. L. Athey

1356. Sautter, Udo. NORTH AMERICAN GOVERNMENT LABOR AGENCIES BEFORE WORLD WAR ONE: A CURE FOR UNEMPLOYMENT? *Labor Hist. 1983 24(3): 366-393.* Public employment bureaus were established by state governments in the United States and provincial governments in Canada prior to World War I as a result of the pleadings of progressive reformers for a humanitarian, efficient, labor-distribution system. Labor unions and manufacturers' associations were ambivalent. Insufficient funding, a poor public image, and incompetent superintendents were responsible for the failure of public employment bureaus. The creation of these agencies was an example of government's half-hearted attempt to ease the ills of industrializing society as Canada and the United States hesitatingly abandoned laissez-faire. Based on state bureaus of labor reports, provincial bureaus of labor reports, and other primary sources; table, 67 notes.   L. F. Velicer

1357. Schwartz, Bonnie Fox. NEW DEAL WORK RELIEF AND ORGANIZED LABOR: THE CWA AND THE AFL BUILDING TRADES. *Labor Hist. 1976 17(1): 38-57.* The Civil Works Administration, a first attempt at work relief, faced immediate problems of hiring and wage practices in their relationship to the American Federation of Labor's building trades. Under the leadership of John Carmody federal regulations attempted to protect labor's right to organize and uphold the prevailing wage rates, while mollifying the opposition of local employers. The CWA provided a "first forum" to alleviate organized labor's suspicions of work relief. Based on the CWA papers and the oral memoir of John Carmody; 41 notes.   L. L. Athey

1358. Segur, W. H. and Fuller, Varden. CALIFORNIA'S FARM LABOR ELECTIONS: AN ANALYSIS OF THE INITIAL RESULTS. *Monthly Labor Rev. 1976 99(12): 25-30.* Analyzes the provisions of California's National Labor Relations Act (1935) and of the powers of the controversial board that has served to solve jurisdictional disputes between the Teamsters and United Farmworkers by monitoring union elections.

1359. Severson, Robert F., Jr. THE CIVILIAN CONSERVATION CORPS: A WORKFARE SOLUTION. *Res. in Econ. Hist. 1982 (Supplement 2): 121-126.* Income data for 1937-81 of former members of the Civilian Conservation Corps shows that the enrollees had higher income levels compared to the total working population. The Civilian Conservation Corps was a success in terms of the human investment value of giving young men jobs and skills. Primary sources; table, 7 notes.   J. Powell

1360. Shapiro, Herbert. THE MC NAMARA CASE: A CRISIS OF THE PROGRESSIVE ERA. *Southern California Q. 1977 59(3): 271-287.* Reasssesses the *Los Angeles Times* dynamiting case's impact on reformers and the labor movement in the Progressive Era. The American Federation of Labor rejected militancy and violence in favor of legalistic approaches to labor issues. Progressives urged capital and labor to reject extreme methods because of the possibility of class conflict. Militant unionists left the American Federation of Labor and the Socialist Party, making it possible for the labor movement to achieve moderate goals without extreme methods. The McNamara case, overlooked by labor historians, thus stands as a turning point for the labor movement and as a repudiation of violence. The case itself invites further investigation, because evidence indicates that the McNamara brothers were influenced by *agents provocateurs.* Based on primary sources and on contemporary and secondary sources; 53 notes.   A. Hoffman

1361. Sivachev, N. V. RABOCHAIA POLITIKA PRAVITEL'STVA SSHA V NACHALE VTOROI MIROVOI VOINY (SENTIABR' 1939 G.-DEKABR' 1941 G.) [The labor policy of the US government at the beginning of World War II, September 1939-December 1941]. *Vestnik Moskovskogo U., Seriia 9: Istoriia [USSR] 1971 26(6): 18-37.* During this 27-month period the liberal-progressive labor policy of the 1930's (Wagner Act, etc.) began a reactionary shift led by Congressman Smith of Virginia. The large corporations sought strict limitations on the rights of labor unions, all in the interest of national defense. The National Labor Relations Board was instituted to handle disputes. When strikes continued to occur, President Franklin D. Roosevelt called out military forces on two occasions to work in defense-related industries in the absence of striking workers. In 1940 the National Defense Advisory Commission (NDAC) and in 1941 the Office of Production Manage-

ment (a branch of the NDAC) were created. By 7 December 1941, the reactionary forces had won. 106 notes.   G. E. Munro

1362. Spencer, Thomas T. "LABOR IS WITH ROOSEVELT": THE PENNSYLVANIA LABOR NON-PARTISAN LEAGUE AND THE ELECTION OF 1936. *Pennsylvania Hist. 1979 46(1): 3-16.* In Pennsylvania, the Labor Non-Partisan League contributed much to Franklin D. Roosevelt's 1936 victory through its contributions, voter canvassing drives, and propaganda. Organized at the national level by John L. Lewis and Sidney Hillman, the league was comprised largely of C.I.O. unions and was intended to assure the president's reelection and function as a spokesman for liberalism. In 1943, it became the C.I.O.'s Political Action Committee. Based on the Pennsylvania Non-Partisan League Papers and other materials; 3 photos, 32 notes.   D. C. Swift

1363. Stetson, Frederick W. THE CIVILIAN CONSERVATION CORPS IN VERMONT. *Vermont Hist. 1978 46(1): 24-42.* Most Vermont politicians opposed New Deal programs, but "Vermonters found the C. C. C. both justifiable and popular." It provided steady jobs for disproportionately large numbers in Vermont, poured millions into the depressed Vermont economy, developed skills useful in World War II, and helped lay the foundations of Vermont's postwar recreation industry. 9 illus., table, 73 notes.   T. D. S. Bassett

1364. Tripp, Joseph F. TOWARD AN EFFICIENT AND MORAL SOCIETY: WASHINGTON STATE MINIMUM-WAGE LAW, 1913-1925. *Pacific Northwest Q. 1976 67(3): 97-112.* Though numerous states adopted minimum wage legislation and eight-hour days for women during the Progressive Era, the state of Washington produced the most effective and lasting statutes. Reformers met only minimal resistance from Washington businessmen who recognized the small percentage of women within the labor force. Additional support for the legislation and its enforcement agency, the Industrial Welfare Commission, came from Senator George Piper and belatedly from Governor Lewis Hart who extended the commission's powers. By the mid-1920's, however, the policies were reversed by a more conservative state government. Primary sources; 4 photos, 59 notes.   M. L. Tate

1365. Valerina, A. F. ROL' BESPARTIINOI RABOCHEI LIGI VO VNUTRENNEI POLITICHESKOI BOR'BE S. SH. A. (1936-1938 GG.) [The role of the Labor Non-Partisan League in the internal political struggle in the US, 1936-38]. *Vestnik Moskovskogo U., Seriia 9: Istoriia [USSR] 1975 30(6): 38-57.* Outlines the activities of the League, the most progressive labor organization in the United States during the 1930's. It represented the true feelings of the workers, tried to provide them with independent political representation, and stimulated important legislation which improved working conditions in the country. 129 notes.   N. Dejevsky

1366. Wagaman, David G. THE EVOLUTION OF SOME LEGAL-ECONOMIC ASPECTS OF COLLECTIVE BARGAINING BY PUBLIC EMPLOYEES IN NEBRASKA SINCE 1919. *Nebraska Hist. 1977 58(4): 475-490.* The Nebraska State Constitution (1919) empowered the legislature to create the Nebraska Court of Industrial Relations, which was established in 1946. Favorably surveys the court's subsequent history, including its prohibition of strikes by public employees.
                                                               R. Lowitt

1367. Wallis, John Joseph and Benjamin, Daniel K. PUBLIC RELIEF AND PRIVATE EMPLOYMENT IN THE GREAT DEPRESSION. *J. of Econ. Hist. 1981 41(1): 97-102.* The unemployment relief programs introduced by the federal government in the 1930's were the largest single factor in the growth of the federal budget over the decade. Cross-sectional data bearing on the operation of the Federal Emergency Relief Administration rejects the hypothesis that the federal relief programs reduced private employment. Individuals did respond to the incentives of relief benefits, but only by moving between relief and nonrelief unemployment.   J

1368. Warren-Findley, Jannelle. MUSICIANS AND MOUNTAINEERS: THE RESETTLEMENT ADMINISTRATION'S MUSIC PROGRAM IN APPALACHIA, 1935-37. *Appalachian J. 1979-80 7(1-2): 105-123.* Led by left-winger Charles Seeger of the Composers' Collective in New York City, the New Deal Resettlement Administration's music program in Appalachia intended "to integrate music, participation in the arts, and political education into a coherent whole which would enable resettled farmers, unemployed miners, impoverished lumbermen, and their families to take control of their own lives and situations."

1369. Watson, Thomas. THE PWA COMES TO THE RED RIVER VALLEY: PHASE I, NON-FEDERAL PROJECTS IN TEXAS, JUNE 1933-FEBRUARY 1934. *Red River Valley Hist. Rev. 1974 31(2): 146-164.* The Public Works Administration did not create a boom in the Texas economy, but it did create many nonfederal jobs and projects.

1370. Wolfle, Lee M. HISTORICAL RECONSTRUCTION OF SO-CIALIST VOTING AMONG COAL MINERS, 1900-1940. *Hist. Methods 1979 12(3): 111-121.* Produces a quantitative, time series measure of voting behavior using regression techniques and data from Illinois. Estimates the percent of coal miners who voted for the Socialist Party of America. Fig., 4 tables, 24 notes.

1371. York, Hildreth. THE NEW DEAL ART PROJECTS IN NEW JERSEY. *New Jersey Hist. 1980 98(3-4): 132-174.* Describes the Public Works of Art Project—the Section of Painting and Sculpture of the Treasury Department later to become the Section of Fine Arts, the Treasury Relief Art Project, and the WPA art program. Considers the kinds of art work produced, the participants, locations of the work, and the administration of the programs. Included is a list of artists along with the type of work each did and a list of murals, reliefs, and public sculptures. Based on government records, material in the Archives of American Art, newspaper articles, and secondary sources; 10 illus., 19 notes, biblio.   E. R. McKinstry

1372. Zieger, Robert H. THE CAREER OF JAMES J. DAVIS. *Pennsylvania Mag. of Hist. and Biog. 1974 98(1): 67-89.* James John Davis' (1873-1947) career as US Secretary of Labor and senator from Pennsylvania (1930-45) has been largely neglected by historians. As Secretary of Labor under Presidents Harding, Coolidge, and Hoover, Davis earned a reputation for moderation, although he was rarely consulted as an advisor and thus had little impact on economic policy. As a moderately liberal Republican Senator for 15 years, Davis was noted by his colleagues for "his uncanny ability to maintain himself in public office rather than for intellectual distinction, legislative prowess, or political courage." Based on primary and secondary sources; 42 notes.   E. W. Carp

1373. Zieger, Robert H. HERBERT HOOVER, THE WAGE-EARN-ER, AND THE "NEW ECONOMIC SYSTEM," 1919-1929. *Business Hist. Rev. 1977 51(2): 161-189.* Herbert Hoover regarded the labor issue as the greatest challenge facing American capitalism, feared union militancy as "wasteful and authoritarian," and favored employee representation systems in industry. During the 1920's, however, he was "curiously silent" on the subject, apparently unwilling to seriously examine the real nature of representation plans. Attributes this inaction in large part to Hoover's natural affinity for the new corporate managers who were the sponsors of welfare capitalism and company-sponsored unions. Based on Hoover papers and writings as well as other contemporary sources; 62 notes.   C. J. Pusateri

1374. —. [BUSINESS AND BUREAUCRACY: THE AMERICAN SOCIAL WELFARE SYSTEM, 1900-1940]. *J. of Econ. Hist. 1978 38(1): 120-147.*
Berkowitz, Edward D. and McQuaid, Kim. BUSINESSMAN AND BUREAUCRAT: THE EVOLUTION OF THE AMERICAN SOCIAL WELFARE SYSTEM, 1900-1940, *pp. 120-142.* Around the turn of the century private businesses began social welfare programs for their employees. It was only because these ideas prospered that the public welfare reforms of the New Deal were passed by a receptive Congress. Throughout the first half of the 20th century business and government cooperated to increase the level of social services for the poor and infirm. 46 notes, appendix.

DeCanio, Stephen J. COMMENT, *pp. 143-147.* Economists must take care before imputing economic motives to political actions. Often both ideas are mixed, and hasty differentiation obscures the truth. Similarly, economic policy does not always have the intended effect forecast by its authors; side-effects are not, therefore, less real or important. Berkowitz and McQuaid, for instance, sometimes fail to see beneath the propaganda of the policies which obscures the motives of the main characters in American welfare history. 5 notes.   J. W. Leedom

1375. —. CIVILIAN CONSERVATION CORPS AND THE FARM ISLAND CAUSEWAY. *South Dakota Hist. 1978 8(4): 312-326.* An annotated photographic documentary of the building of the rock causeway between the north bank of the Missouri River and Farm Island, South of Pierre, South Dakota, by CCC Company 796. The photographs were taken by Paul J. Hogan of New Rockford, North Dakota, one of the leaders of the company. 27 photos, map.   R. V. Ritter

1376. —. [THE COMMUNIST PARTY AND ELECTORAL POLI-TICS IN THE 1930'S]. *Radical Hist. Rev. 1980 (23): 104-135.*
Waltzer, Kenneth. THE PARTY AND THE POLLING PLACE: AMERICAN COMMUNISM AND AN AMERICAN LABOR PARTY IN THE 1930'S, *pp. 104-129.* The Communist Party tried to deal with electoral politics during the 1930's by forming a labor party made up of united front alliances and by adopting a low profile in the American Labor Party and elsewhere.
Gordon, Max. THE PARTY AND THE POLLING PLACE: A RESPONSE, *pp. 130-135.* Critique of Waltzer's article on the Communist Party and the American Labor Party during the 1930's, based on author Gordon's experience as a Communist Party organizer during the 1930's and as a Party journalist during the 1940's and 1950's; although the Popular Front lasted only four years, it nevertheless served as an example "for socialist tactics in a strongly capitalist society."

Racial, Ethnic, and Sex Discrimination

1377. Aldrich, Mark and Albelda, Randy. DETERMINANTS OF WORKING WOMEN'S WAGES DURING THE PROGRESSIVE ERA. *Explorations in Econ. Hist. 1980 17(4): 323-341.* Progressives were deeply troubled by the low wages earned by women but could not agree on the causes or solutions. Education was not the problem, nor were youth and inexperience true explanations. Rather the causes were in the choice of occupations with low investment potential, physical differentials precluding women from skilled but arduous jobs, and occupational segregation. Geographic immobility and nativist prejudices were also factors. 5 tables, fig., 41 notes, 20 ref.   P. J. Coleman

1378. Anderson, Karen Tucker. LAST HIRED, FIRST FIRED: BLACK WOMEN WORKERS DURING WORLD WAR II. *J. of Am. Hist. 1982 69(1): 82-97.* Although black women entered the American labor force in large numbers during World War II, discriminatory practices by both management and unions confined them to low-paying service and other unskilled catagories. Despite the existence of Roosevelt's Fair Employment Practices Commission, discrimination persisted against minority women. During the postwar period, female workers in general and black women in particular became victims of industrial discrimination as employers reverted to prewar policies of hiring and firing. Based on U. S. Labor Department statistics and reports by the Committee on Fair Employment Practice; 37 notes.   T. P. Linkfield

1379. Bennett, Sheila Kishler and Elder, Glen H., Jr. WOMEN'S WORK IN THE FAMILY ECONOMY: A STUDY OF DEPRES-SION HARDSHIP IN WOMEN'S LIVES. *J. of Family Hist. 1979 4(2): 153-176.* Drawing on the Berkeley Guidance Study that covers a group of families from 1928-29 to the present (the most recent panel wave was 1969-71). Examines the impact of the Great Depression on the lives on mothers and daughters. They find that the Great Depression had perhaps as much impact on increased female employment as World War II did. They show that Depression-caused changes in the employment status of mothers influenced the employment pattern of their daughters. 5 tables, 3 fig., 9 notes, biblio.   T. W. Smith

1380. Benson, Susan Porter. THE CINDERELLA OF OCCUPATIONS: MANAGING THE WORK OF DEPARTMENT STORE SALESWOMEN, 1900-1940. *Business Hist. Rev. 1981 55(1): 1-25.* By 1900 department store managers, recognizing a need to increase sales volumes in order to cover high fixed costs, attempted to develop a more effective salesforce of the working class shopgirls employed as clerks. In the following decades management emphasized training in skilled selling and later the resocialization of the saleswomen themselves. The program failed because of an inherent contradiction in managerial philosophy; the saleswomen were expected to behave as skilled professionals in dealing with customers, but they were treated as low-paid and unskilled employees in all other ways by store owners. Based primarily on industry and trade association periodicals; 73 notes.   C. J. Pusateri

1381. Betten, Neil and Mohl, Raymond A. FROM DISCRIMINATION TO REPATRIATION: MEXICAN LIFE IN GARY, INDIANA, DURING THE GREAT DEPRESSION. *Pacific Hist. Rev. 1973 42(3): 370-388.* Relates the social, economic, and political discrimination faced by Mexican Americans in the 1920's-30's in Gary, Indiana, culminating in the forced exodus of a large segment of the Mexican population during the early 1930's. The economic tensions generated by the Depression produced a new wave of nativism throughout the United States, and were fostered by antiethnic sentiments expressed in the *Saturday Evening Post* aimed particularly at Mexican Americans. "Undoubtedly the Mexican's darker skin, his Catholicism, and the usual problems and vices associated with the poor affected national opinion as well." From 1931 to May 1932 repatriation was voluntary, supported by most local institutions in Gary, including US Steel Co. and the International Institute, an immigrant-oriented welfare agency. However, "after May 1932, when the township trustee's office assumed direction of repatriation, repressive measures were used to force the return of reluctant voyagers." The organized efforts in Gary against Mexicans reflected the xenophobia present throughout American society during the early 1930's. 33 notes.   B. L. Fenske

1382. Bodnar, John; Weber, Michael; and Simon, Roger. MIGRATION, KINSHIP, AND URBAN ADJUSTMENT: BLACKS AND POLES IN PITTSBURGH, 1900-1930. *J. of Am. Hist. 1979 66(3): 548-565.* Analyzes the adaptation of Poles and blacks to Pittsburgh, 1900-30, by comparing their migration experiences, socialization practices, and occupational mobility patterns. The analysis relies heavily on 94 oral history interviews of Polish immigrants and black migrants. For both groups, adaptation involved strategic reactions to specific conditions in Pittsburgh. Adjustment to the new urban setting was a product of the interaction of premigration culture and urban racism. 4 tables, 42 notes..   T. P. Linkfield

1383. Bonacich, Edna. ADVANCED CAPITALISM AND BLACK/WHITE RELATIONS IN THE UNITED STATES: A SPLIT LABOR MARKET INTERPRETATION. *Am. Sociol. Rev. 1976 41(1): 34-51.* A distinguishing feature of the black position in advanced capitalism lies in relatively high unemployment and underemployment, a phenomenon that emerged in the 1930s and became firmly entrenched in the mid-1950s. To explain this we examined the black/white split labor market between World War I and the New Deal, showing how blacks were used to undermine white workers and their unions. The conflict was resolved with New Deal Labor legislation, protecting the unions and outlawing undercutting. This permitted a coalition to emerge between black and white workers. But in the long run the rising cost of labor drove capital to seek cheaper labor overseas, to make use of internal pockets of unprotected labor or to automate. All three processes hurt black industrial workers disproportionately, leaving a group of hardcore unemployed in the ghettos.   J

1384. Brier, Stephen. LABOR, POLITICS, AND RACE: A BLACK WORKER'S LIFE. *Labor Hist. 1982 23(3): 416-421.* Presents the transcript of a 1937 autobiographical interview with Henry Johnson, a black labor organizer who had lived in various parts of the country and witnessed race riots. Included in the records of the WPA's "Negro in Illinois" survey.   L. F. Velicer

1385. Cardosa, Lawrence A. LA REPATRIACIÓN DE BRACEROS EN ÉPOCA DE OBREGÓN: 1920-1923 [The repatriation of laborers in the epoch of Obregón: 1920-23]. *Hist. Mexicana [Mexico] 1977 26(4): 576-595.* A grave problem was faced by the Álvaro Obregón administration when 100,000 Mexicans lost their jobs in the United States during the depression following World War I. The government attempted to help and to avoid a similar event by discouraging emigration, but the events of the 1930's highlighted the failure of these plans. Based on Obregón's presidential papers, and American and Mexican archives; 39 notes.   S. P. Carr

1386. Carper, N. Gordon. SLAVERY REVISITED: PEONAGE IN THE SOUTH. *Phylon 1976 37(1): 85-99.* During 1903-25 peonage developed culturally and legally in the South as a method of retaining forced labor without slavery.

1387. Christiansen, John B. THE SPLIT LABOR MARKET THEORY AND FILIPINO EXCLUSION: 1927-1934. *Phylon 1979 40(1): 66-74.* Uses a theory presented by Edna Bonacich in "A Theory of Ethnic Antagonism: The Split Labor Market," *American Sociological Review* 1972 37(5): 547-559, to discuss economic conditions contributing to the exclusion of Filipino immigrants by the United States. Secondary sources; 30 notes.   G. R. Schroeder

1388. Clive, Alan. WOMEN WORKERS IN WORLD WAR II: MICHIGAN AS A TEST CASE. *Labor Hist. 1979 20(1): 44-72.* Examines women and World War II in Michigan to test national-level generalizations, tracing changes in the work force, attitudes of industry, labor organizations, and government, and the experience of women. Details resistance to working mothers and provision for day-care for children, which largely failed. The war created no revolution in attitudes, just a series of expedient measures as the traditional concept of womanhood was reaffirmed. Census data, state and federal documents, and newspapers; 61 notes.   L. L. Athey

1389. Conn, Sandra. THREE TALENTS: ROBINS, NESTOR, AND ANDERSON OF THE CHICAGO WOMEN'S TRADE UNION LEAGUE. *Chicago Hist. 1980-81 9(4): 234-247.* Margaret Dreier Robins, Agnes Nestor, and Mary Anderson pooled their talents to improve working conditions for women throughout the nation from 1903 to 1920; focuses on their involvement in the National Women's Trade Union League.

1390. Corbett, Katharine T. ST. LOUIS WOMEN GARMENT WORKERS: PHOTOGRAPHS AND MEMORIES. *Gateway Heritage 1981 2(1): 18-25.* Describes a project of the Women's Center at the University of Missouri, St. Louis. Using photohistory and oral history methods, researchers secured and interpreted the responses of female garment industry workers to strikes in the 1930's. Among the results have been an exhibit, "Dollar Dresses: St. Louis Women in the Garment Industry," comprised of 38 photographs and oral history comments solicited from seven retired garment workers. 17 photos, 9 notes.   H. T. Lovin

1391. Critchlow, Donald T. COMMUNIST UNIONS AND RACISM. *Labor Hist. 1976 17(2): 230-244.* Studies the responses of the United Electrical Radio and Machine Workers and the National Maritime Union to the "Black Question" during World War II. The U.E. ignored Negroes while the N.M.U. prided itself on its black members. This ambiguity of policy casts doubt on the assumption that "Communist-dominated" unions were essentially identical in interests. Based on proceedings of the U.E. and the N.M.U.; 38 notes.
                                                     L. L. Athey

1392. Gamboa, Erasmo. MEXICAN LABOR IN THE PACIFIC NORTHWEST, 1943-1947: A PHOTOGRAPHIC ESSAY. *Pacific Northwest Q. 1982 73(4): 175-181.* Presents 13 photographs of life in the migrant labor camps of Washington and Oregon during World War II. Life for the young Mexican laborers proved harsh as they faced culture shock, racial discrimination, spartan camp conditions, lack of social activities, and the threat of continuous transfer between camps. Yet the federally organized program provided them with steady employment and solved the critical labor shortage in the Pacific Northwest.   M. L. Tate

1393. Garcia, Mario T. ON MEXICAN IMMIGRATION, THE UNITED STATES, AND CHICANO HISTORY. *J. of Ethnic Studies 1979 7(1): 80-88.* Review essay of Mark Reisler's *By the Sweat of Their Brow: Mexican Immigrant Labor in the United States, 1900-1940* (Greenwood Pr., 1976).

1394. Glenn, Evelyn Nakano. THE DIALECTICS OF WAGE WORK: JAPANESE-AMERICAN WOMEN AND DOMESTIC SERVICE, 1905-1940. *Feminist Studies 1980 6(3): 432-471.* Examines the role of working as domestics in creating group solidarity and a sense of self-reliance among Issei Japanese-American women in the San Francisco Bay area. Describes the early racism directed against Japanese immigrants, which barred them from competing with whites for white-collar jobs and relegated the Issei to menial domestic and gardening labor. A detailed account explores working conditions, employer-employee relations, and the interaction between Issei women's household duties and the jobs outside the home. Based on US censuses from 1900 to 1940; 2 tables, 63 notes.   G. V. Wasson

1395. Greene, Rebecca S. THE UNITED STATES: WOMEN IN WORLD WAR II. *Trends in Hist. 1981 2(2): 71-82.* Reviews books and articles on the new role of women in the labor force during World War II, which illustrate the disagreement among scholars on the extent of change in the status of women during and after the war.

1396. Greenwald, Maureen. WOMEN WORKERS AND WORLD WAR I: THE AMERICAN RAILROAD INDUSTRY, A CASE STUDY. *J. of Social Hist. 1975 9(2): 154-177.* World War I records of the railroad industry shows women moved into jobs already identified as women's jobs. During 1917-30 the number of women workers increased 42%. 55 notes.   M. Hough

1397. Hammett, Hugh B. LABOR AND RACE: THE GEORGIA RAILROAD STRIKE OF 1909. *Labor Hist. 1975 16(4): 470-484.* Union and management used race to further their respective position in the Georgia Railroad strike of 1909. Wage differentials based on race were used by the company to justify black employment economically. As the strike progressed, violence against black firemen was committed and the Brotherhood of Locomotive Firemen and Enginemen campaigned to remove all black firemen. Only a courageous decision by a board of arbitration led by Hilary A. Herbert which established the principle of equal pay for equal work and rejected union demands for dismissal of black firemen prevented closing of job opportunities for black firemen. Based on newspapers, union publications, and the Hoke Smith papers; 36 notes.   L. L. Athey

1398. Hemminger, Carol. LITTLE MANILA: THE FILIPINO IN STOCKTON PRIOR TO WORLD WAR II. *Pacific Hist. 1980 25(1): 21-34, (2): 207-220.* Part I. The attractions of a promised education, a job, and a lot of money drew thousands of Filipinos to the United States in the 1920's and 1930's. Stockton, California, located in the agriculturally rich San Joaquin Valley, became the center for the largest population of Filipinos in the United States. Field labor was the only work open to the immigrants. The white landowners and foremen and the Oriental or Filipino crew bosses took advantage of the workers. Discrimination in Stockton forced the Filipino community into a small area of Chinatown. The Chinese hotel owners, barkeepers, and gamblers tried to separate Filipinos from their money. New arrivals were warned to avoid the Chinese gambling houses and the American dance halls and brothels. Based on interviews; 3 photos, 63 notes. Part II. During the heavy immigration of Filipinos, 1920-29, women immigrants were discouraged and men could only bring their wives. However, most wives stayed in the Philippines because they were needed with their families and because it was too expensive to immigrate. Therefore, there were few Filipino women to act as a settling agent for the men who came to Stockton. Mixed marriages and relationships were not accepted. Dance-hall girls, prostitutes, drinking, and gambling were the recreational outlets for the Filipino men. Several Christian missions tried to serve the needs of the people. Filipinos were openly discriminated against. They had a reputation for causing crime and violence, although the record does not support it. Filipinos were labeled as ignorant, illiterate, and different because they were only farm laborers. Based on oral interviews; photo, table, 50 notes, biblio.   G. L. Lake

1399. Henderson, Alexa B. FEPC AND THE SOUTHERN RAILWAY CASE: AN INVESTIGATION INTO DISCRIMINATORY PRACTICES DURING WORLD WAR II. *J. of Negro Hist. 1976 61(2): 173-187.* For the first time, hearings into discrimination by railroad employers, all members of the Southeastern Carriers Conference, were held by the Fair Employment Practice Committee during World War II. Hundreds of black rail workers cooperated with the field investigators in building the FEPC's case against the railroads and all-white unions. However, the resolve of the FEPC was undermined by presidential vacillation. Based on the records of the FEPC; 45 notes.   N. G. Sapper

1400. Hendrick, Irving G. EARLY SCHOOLING FOR CHILDREN OF MIGRANT FARMWORKERS IN CALIFORNIA: THE 1920'S. *Aztlán 1977 8: 11-26.* As State Superintendent of Schools, Georgiana Carden worked diligently to enforce legislation funding mandatory elementary education for the children of Mexican American farmworkers in order to encourage assimilation and guarantee equality of education in California.

1401. Honey, Maureen. THE "WOMANPOWER" CAMPAIGN: ADVERTISING AND RECRUITMENT PROPAGANDA DURING WORLD WAR II. *Frontiers 1981 6(1-2): 50-56.* Advertisers, particularly the War Advertising Council, played an important role in supporting government wartime campaigns, including the drive to bring women into defense jobs; thus, they created an ideological framework for the employment of women in male-identified blue-collar jobs, a framework that simultaneously acknowledged that women were capable of filling jobs requiring "male" characteristics and preserved essential features of the feminine role.

1402. Ichioka, Yuji. ASIAN IMMIGRANT COAL MINERS AND UNITED MINE WORKERS OF AMERICA: RACE AND CLASS AT ROCK SPRINGS, WYOMING, 1907. *Amerasia J. 1979 6(2): 1-23.* Numerically analyzes, by nationalities, men employed in the coal mines of Wyoming at the turn of the century. The United Mine Workers of America (UMW) did well in organizing locals in the northern counties, but in the south, Orientals were refused membership. The racial discrimination was abandoned in 1907. After the companies' lockout of miners who had enrolled in the UMW on 21 May, the Orientals had been employed to keep one mine working. John Mitchell, president of the national UMW, reversed his racist stand in the interest of solidarity among all miners in future crises, and Japanese Americans were admitted to the locals in Wyoming. 81 notes.   H. F. Thomson

1403. Imhoff, Clem. THE RECRUITER. *Southern Exposure 1976 4(1-2): 83-87.* D. W. Johnson tells of his work as a labor recruiter who encouraged Negroes to move from the South to Wisconsin and Illinois, 1917-22.

1404. Jacoby, Robin Miller. FEMINISM AND CLASS CONSCIOUSNESS IN THE BRITISH AND AMERICAN WOMEN'S TRADE UNION LEAGUE, 1890-1925. Carroll, Berenice A., ed. *Liberating Women's History* (Chicago: U. of Illinois Pr., 1976): pp. 137-160. Discusses the influence of class consciousness on British and American trade union women when union goals for women conflicted with an ideology of class loyalty. Analyzes the different relationships of both trade union leagues to the women's suffrage movement, and the effect these differences had on the International Federation of Working Women. Despite the priority given by the British to class-based issues, and by the American to interaction between women of all classes, the British and American women were participants in the same struggle. 64 notes.   B. Sussman

1405. Jacoby, Robin Miller. THE WOMEN'S TRADE UNION LEAGUE AND AMERICAN FEMINISM. *Feminist Studies 1975 3(1/2): 126-140.* The Women's Trade Union League, founded in 1903 by a group of women workers and middle-class female social reformers, emphasized the power of lobbying increasingly during 1903-20. This increased reliance on the legislative process reflected the unenthusiastic support of organized labor for women workers. The WTUL supported women's suffrage and the activities of the National American Woman Suffrage Association (NAWSA) because the vote promised influence on the activities of lawmakers on state and federal levels and therefore was in itself a tool for improving working conditions for female workers.

Middle-class feminists were for the most part fairly insensitive to the problems of working women, and it must be concluded that the WTUL did more for middle-class feminism than it gained from that movement. Primary and secondary sources; 49 notes.   S. R. Herstein

1406. Johnson, Jerah. MARCUS B. CHRISTIAN AND THE WPA HISTORY OF BLACK PEOPLE IN LOUISIANA. *Louisiana Hist. 1979 20(1): 113-115.* Referring to a previous article on the Louisiana Federal Writers' Project at Dillard University, discusses the efforts of the project's director, Marcus B. Christian (1898-1976), to compile and write the history of blacks in Louisiana. All of his note cards and poems, as well as his unfinished history, are now deposited in the archives of the University of New Orleans. The University is also presently establishing a Marcus B. Christian Lectureship in Christian's honor.

L. N. Powell

1407. Jones, Allen W. THOMAS M. CAMPBELL: BLACK AGRI-CULTURAL LEADER OF THE NEW SOUTH. *Agric. Hist. 1979 53(1): 42-59.* A record of the training, ideals, and methods used to improve agricultural techniques and personal attitudes of the black small farmers of Macon and the surrounding counties of Alabama. In 1906 Thomas M. Campbell was hired by the Agriculture Department as its first black farm agent to operate a traveling agricultural wagon and conduct farm demonstration work. His career spanned nearly half a century and established him as one of the most effective and highly recognized black agricultural leaders in the United States, coming ultimately to reach out in his influence to all of southern agriculture. He tried "to help the masses of black people in the South achieve economic independence, a higher standard of living, and a better home and family life." 58 notes. Comment by William Scarborough, pp. 60-61.

R. V. Ritter

1408. Kennedy, Susan Estabrook. "THE WANT IT SATISFIES DEMONSTRATES THE NEED OF IT": A STUDY OF *LIFE AND LABOR* OF THE WOMEN'S TRADE UNION LEAGUE. *Int. J. of Women's Studies [Canada] 1980 3(4): 391-406.* Analyzes the contents of the monthly journal published by the Women's Trade Union League from 1911 to 1921, *Life and Labor,* which focused on the union's activities, efforts to educate women workers on trade unions, and gain public support.

1409. Kesselman, Amy; Tau, Tina; and Wickre, Karen. *GOOD WORK SISTER!* THE MAKING OF AN ORAL HISTORY PRO-DUCTION. *Frontiers 1983 7(1): 64-70.* Discusses the making of a slide show, *Good Work, Sister!,* by the Northwest Women's History Project (1978-82) about the women who worked in the shipyards in Portland, Oregon, and Vancouver, Washington, during World War II, including their subsequent experiences.

1410. Kessler-Harris, Alice. JOBS FOR WOMEN IN WAR AND DEPRESSION. *Rev. in Am. Hist. 1982 10(3): 419-423.* Reviews Karen Anderson's *Wartime Women: Sex Roles, Family Relations, and the Status of Women during World War II* (1981), Winifred D. Wandersee's *Women's Work and Family Values: 1920-1940* (1981), and Susan Ware's *Beyond Suffrage: Women in the New Deal* (1981), which examine the cultural transformations concomitant on women's increasing participation in the work force during 1920-45.

1411. Kessler-Harris, Alice. "ROSIE THE RIVETER": WHO WAS SHE? *Labor Hist. 1983 24(2): 249-253.* Reviews Connie Field's *The Life and Times of Rosie the Riveter,* questioning how closely the women interviewed in the movie represent the majority of American women who went into the labor force during World War II.   L. F. Velicer

1412. Klaczynska, Barbara. WHY WOMEN WORK: A COMPARI-SON OF VARIOUS GROUPS—PHILADELPHIA, 1910-1930. *Labor Hist. 1976 17(1): 73-87.* Analyzes the reasons for women working by comparing patterns of Italian, Polish, Irish, Jewish, black, and native-born white women. Central determinants were strong ethnic familial traditions, the lack of strong familial ties, and class consciousness. Italian and Polish women worked least often, and blacks, native-born whites, and Irish most often. Jewish women tended to move from a work tradition to a nonwork position as they moved into the middle class. Based on government publications and periodicals; 20 notes.

L. L. Athey

1413. Kruman, Marie W. QUOTAS FOR BLACKS: THE PUBLIC WORKS ADMINISTRATION AND THE BLACK CONSTRUC-TION WORKER. *Labor Hist. 1975 16(1): 37-51.* Harold Ickes instituted quotas for hiring skilled and unskilled blacks in construction financed through the Public Works Adminstration (PWA). Resistance from employers and unions was partially overcome by negotiations and implied sanctions. Although results were ambiguous, the plan helped provide blacks with employment, especially among unskilled workers. Based on files of the PWA in the National Archives; tables of compliance, 30 notes.   L. L. Athey

1414. Landes, Elisabeth M. THE EFFECT OF STATE MAXIMUM-HOURS LAWS ON THE EMPLOYMENT OF WOMEN IN 1920. *J. of Pol. Econ. 1980 88(3): 476-494.* Strict enforcement of state maxi-mum hours laws in 1920 led to reduced work hours and employment among women and was most dramatically felt among foreign-born females, indicating a hostility toward immigration and immigrants within the American labor movement.

1415. Lemons, J. Stanley. SOCIAL FEMINISM IN THE 1920S: PROGRESSIVE WOMEN AND INDUSTRIAL LEGISLATION. *Labor Hist. 1973 14(1): 83-91.* Surveys the continuing struggle for industrial legislation in the 1920's. A group of women's organizations pressed for many reforms including the elimination of child labor, maternity and infant care, nightwork laws, and labor legislation. Although attacked bitterly, the groups kept alive the hope for industrial legislation which was finally realized under the impetus of the Depres-sion. Based on periodicals, proceedings of organizations, and a doctoral dissertation; 21 notes.   L. L. Athey

1416. Martelet, Penny. THE WOMAN'S LAND ARMY, WORLD WAR I. Deutrich, Mabel E. and Purdy, Virginia C., ed. *Clio Was a Woman: Studies in the History of American Women* (Washington, D.C.: Howard U. Pr., 1980): 136-146. The Woman's Land Army helped broaden the role of US women in the work force during World War I. It was organized by private women's organizations because of the man-power shortages in agricultural areas during the war. Attesting to women's deep patriotic spirit and dynamic organizational ability, the Land Army also signaled the growing desire of many women for new avenues of employment. Their adaptability to farm work demonstrated their capacity for hard physical labor. The clothing, living arrangements and nature of the work were considered inappropriate to standards of feminine behavior. The Land Army proved to be a small part of a larger movement that would involve millions of women during World War II. A discussion summary follows. 26 notes.   J. Powell

1417. Martin, Charles H. WHITE SUPREMACY AND BLACK WORKERS: GEORGIA'S "BLACK SHIRTS" COMBAT THE GREAT DEPRESSION. *Labor Hist. 1977 18(3): 366-381.* In Georgia during the 1930's the "Black Shirts," the American Order of Fascisti, tried to become a political force. Its major premise was white supremacy rather than a philosophy of fascism, and its main objective was employment for whites. Based on newspapers in Atlanta and Macon, Georgia; 41 notes.   L. L. Athey

1418. Matthews, John Michael. THE GEORGIA RACE STRIKE OF 1909. *J. of Southern Hist. 1974 40(4): 613-630.* Eighty white union firemen struck the Georgia Railroad in May 1909, charging that the railroad was replacing white firemen with black firemen at lower pay and also granting Negroes seniority over whites. The strike became violent when the Georgia Railroad attempted to continue operating with black firemen. Soon receiving national attention, the confrontation forced federal arbitration, but not before Governor Hoke Smith had revealed the prevailing racism of the era by declaring that Negroes were dangerous to whites as voters and as social equals, but that they must be permitted to work anywhere. To the railroad, the strike indicated the limits of pitting one race against another in economic competition, and for the union it demonstrated the advantages of marshalling public opinion to support its views. Based on manuscripts and published primary and secondary sources; 51 notes.   T. D. Schoonover

1419. McCain, Johnny M. TEXAS AND THE MEXICAN LABOR QUESTION, 1942-1947. *Southwestern Hist. Q. 1981 85(1): 45-64.* Since 1920, the annual trek of Mexican workers into the US southwest has caused one of the most persistent and perplexing problems in relations between Mexico and the United States because of the low wages and discrimination against workers. During World War II, Mexico attempted to prohibit its migrant labor force from entering Texas. Mexican policy failed, however, because Texas could not guarantee an end to discrimination, and because migrant workers entered the state illegally. Mexico made no attempt to stop that migration, preferring to have its surplus labor force working while avoiding the responsibility of rectifying discrimination complaints which the illegal migrants levied against Texans. Labor records in the National Archives, newspapers, and secondary sources; 44 notes.   R. D. Hurt

1420. Meier, August and Rudwick, Elliott. COMMUNIST UNIONS AND THE BLACK COMMUNITY: THE CASE OF THE TRANS-PORT WORKERS UNION, 1934-1944. *Labor Hist. 1982 23(2): 165-197.* Examines how the Transport Workers Union (TWU), a Committee for Industrial Organization affliate run by a Communist-dominated leadership, attacked job bias in the transit industry in New York City and Philadelphia, Pennsylvania. The TWU leadership refrained from pushing the interests of black workers because of the racial prejudices of its white members. Only after prodding by a strong black community response in New York City and the forceful presence of the President's Fair Employment Practices Committee in Philadelphia did TWU leaders advance the interests of black members. Baed on the TWU Archives, FEPC Archives, NAACP papers, and other primary sources; 116 notes.   L. F. Velicer

1421. Mergen, Bernard. THE PULLMAN PORTER: FROM "GEORGE" TO BROTHERHOOD. *South Atlantic Q. 1974 73(2): 224-235.* "The organization of the Brotherhoood of Sleeping Car Porters (BSCP) in the 1900's coincided with the destruction of the 'George' stereotype in the minds of management, the American Federation of Labor (AFL), and the traveling public." A. Philip Randolph, editor of a radical Negro magazine and organizer of the BSCP, regarded the success of the BSCP and the creation of black pride and race consciousness as inextricably united. Climaxing years of struggle, Randolph succeeded in getting the AFL to grant the BSCP full equality. 42 notes.   E. P. Stickney

1422. Milkman, Ruth. REDEFINING "WOMEN'S WORK": THE SEXUAL DIVISION OF LABOR IN THE AUTO INDUSTRY DURING WORLD WAR II. *Feminist Studies 1982 8(2): 337-372.* Large-scale employment of women in the auto industry during World War II represented no shift in attitudes toward women and work by management, unions, or workers of either sex. It stemmed from wartime shortages of male labor and government pressure and was generally viewed as a temporary measure. The United Automobile Workers of America was torn between gender interests and class interests, but the former prevailed and sexual segregation was maintained. Based on materials at the National Archives, Wayne State University Archives of Labor History and Urban Affairs, and the Ford Archives; 59 notes.
S. Hildenbrand

1423. Milkman, Ruth. WOMEN'S WORK AND THE ECONOMIC CRISIS: SOME LESSONS FROM THE GREAT DEPRESSION. *Rev. of Radical Pol. Econ. 1976 8(1): 73-97.* Investigates work roles of women, both paid and unpaid, during the 1930's; though women readily entered the labor force during economic expansion, sexual segregation of labor created an inflexibility which did not allow for expulsion during economic contraction.

1424. Monroy, Douglas. AN ESSAY ON UNDERSTANDING THE WORK EXPERIENCE OF MEXICANS IN SOUTHERN CALI-FORNIA, 1900-1939. *Aztlán 1981 12(1): 59-74.* During 1900-39 Mexicans were relegated to a secondary low wage sector of the labor force. With social mobility limited, job advancement over seasonal agricultural employment was found not only in skilled work but in jobs that offered a measure of stability. Such employment, however, came at the price of disruption of Mexican families through work schedules, exposure to American customs, and generational conflicts. But the challenges of American urban life also brought Mexican participation in labor unions and the benefits gained through union activities. Theses and dissertations, contemporary and secondary published studies; 24 notes.
A. Hoffman

1425. Monteleone, Renato. SAM GOMPERS: PROFILO DI UN JINGO AMERICANO [Sam Gompers: profile of an American jingo]. *Movimento Operaio e Socialista [Italy] 1976 22(1-2): 133-152.* Defines "jingo" in its American context and says it accurately describes Samuel Gompers, founder of the American Federation of Labor. Gompers openly supported and initiated racist policies; AFL exclusion of nonqualified workers coincided with an influx of immigrant workers. Gompers fought hard to stop immigration, particularly of Orientals, because he feared for American independence and security. Along with the industrialists and financiers of his day, Gompers refused to acknowledge a connection between capitalism and imperialism and failed to recognize what was occurring in international politics. Protesting Bolshevism, he failed to comprehend the threat of a reactionary crisis of the democratic bourgeoisie and thus later suggested to American workers that fascism was a model for the reconciliation of the classes. Primary and secondary sources.   M. T. Wilson

1426. Murphy, Miriam B. WOMEN IN THE UTAH WORK FORCE FROM STATEHOOD TO WORLD WAR II. *Utah Hist. Q. 1982 50(2): 139-159.* The history of women in Utah's labor force followed the general pattern of the United States. Females, who earned less than men, became secretaries, teachers, nurses, and low-wage factory assem-blers. Accompanied by discrimination (wages, sexual abuse, and promo-tion), women were denied opportunities to compete with men until World War II, when demand changed employment opportunities. 10 photos, 53 notes.   K. E. Gilmont

1427. Nelson-Cisneros, Victor B. LA CLASE TRABAJADORA EN TEJAS, 1920-1940 [The working class in Texas, 1920-1940]. *Aztlán 1976 6(2): 239-265.* In Texas Mexican Americans were relegated to the lowest-paid jobs and worked in subhuman conditions. They were unable to organize stable agricultural or industrial unions due to the geographic mobility of membership, failures of leadership, poverty, and the AFL's racist policies. Some short-lived, successful Chicano unions engaged in strikes, among them the Associación de journaleros, U.C.A.P.A.W.A., and the Pecan Shelling Workers of San Antonio. Based on interviews and secondary sources; 125 notes.   R. Griswold del Castillo

1428. Nuechterlein, James A. THE POLITICS OF CIVIL RIGHTS: THE FEPC, 1941-46. *Prologue 1978 10(3): 171-191.* Despite his lack of a strong political commitment to civil rights, Roosevelt bent to black pressures in 1941 to establish the Fair Employment Practices Committee through Executive Order 8802. The FEPC had no direct enforcement powers to curb job discrimination in war industries and was therefore forced to rely on other governmental agencies to cancel the war contracts of offenders. The principal weapon of the committee was publicity generated through media exposure of their hearings. Placing the FEPC under the supervision and control of hostile Paul V. McNutt, director of the War Production Board, in 1942 brought tensions between the committee and other government agencies to a head. An explosion resulted from McNutt's cancellation of committee hearings into railroad employment discrimination. Roosevelt was forced to step in, reconstitut-ing the FEPC with a larger budget but still without enforcement powers. Between 1943 and the committee's demise in 1946, the body was under continual Congressional attack from conservative Southern Democrats who ended the FEPC in 1946. Based on research in the National Archives.   N. Lederer

1429. Nyden, Linda. BLACK MINERS IN WESTERN PENNSYL-VANIA, 1925-1931: THE NATIONAL MINERS UNION AND THE UNITED MINE WORKERS OF AMERICA. *Sci. and Soc. 1977 41(1): 69-101.* The National Miners Union kept the spirit of unionism in the coal fields alive during the late 1920's and early 1930's when open shop efforts by operators, coupled with poor and dispirited leadership of the United Mine Workers of America, threatened to drive collective bargaining from the region. The NMU was a class struggle trade union which organized the unorganized, fought wage cuts, and led mass picket lines. It successfully organized and elevated blacks to leadership positions in the union at a time when the UMW segregated them from a meaningful role in its ranks and operators employed huge numbers of blacks as strikebreakers. Without the efforts of the NMU, conditions for the miners would have been far worse and the situation would not have been readied for the later resurgence of the UMW.   N. Lederer

1430. —. COMMENT ON BONACICH. *Am. Sociol. Rev. 1979 44(2); 339-344.*

Oehler, Kay. ANOTHER LOOK AT THE BLACK/WHITE TREND IN UNEMPLOYMENT RATES, *pp. 339-341.* A critique of an article by Edna Bonacich, who argues that the black American enjoyed a lower rate of unemployment than the white until the 1930's. She has erred in mixing census data that do not necessarily measure the same groups, in not considering sexual differences in employment rates, and in not considering all of the variables. A brief effort to do so suggests that blacks had lower rates of unemployment until the 1940's; the change may have occurred because of the increasing mechanization of southern farms. 3 tables, 3 notes, ref.

Bonacich, Edna. STILL ANOTHER LOOK AT BLACK/WHITE UNEMPLOYMENT: REPLY TO OEHLER, *pp. 342-344.* Oehler's assertion that sex differences might alter the shift in black/white rates of employment is true, but figured either way the shift remains. Her comment that two different sets of statistics, not necessarily comparable, have been used is true, but that was explained, and Oehler is guilty of it herself. Her substantive charge to the effect that the shift occurred during the 1940's rather than the 1930's was explained in the article as a temporary shift due to federal administrative policies. In sum, Oehler's criticisms are without foundation. Table, ref.   V. L. Human

1431. Parker, Russell D. THE BLACK COMMUNITY IN A COMPANY TOWN: ALCOA, TENNESSEE, 1919-1939. *Tennessee Hist. Q. 1978 37(2): 203-221.* Alcoa, Tennessee, was a company town, not conducive to community leadership, black or white. Unskilled blacks were recruited to work in the Aluminum Company of America (Alcoa) plant, and blacks moved in almost as fast as whites. Blacks were allowed to purchase their homes in the Negro section. John T. Arter, a black man, was brought in as principal of the black school, and became the leader of the Negro community. His closest associates were John Brice and T. P. Marsh, but neither managed to wield influence after Arter's death. Leadership within the black community eventually fell to Hendrika Tol, a white woman, who had attended nearby Maryville College. Tol started a library for blacks and attempted to create a health plan for blacks, but without success. "Unionization in the mid-1930's reduced the vulnerability of black workers." Primary and secondary sources; 91 notes.   M. B. Lucas

1432. Peterson, Joyce Shaw. BLACK AUTOMOBILE WORKERS IN DETROIT, 1910-1930. *J. of Negro Hist. 1979 64(3): 177-190.* In the two decades after 1910, the black population of Detroit tripled as the Great Migration brought thousands of black workers into the auto industry. The auto industry offered black workers some of the best industrial jobs available in terms of wages. Most black auto workers viewed life in Detroit as an improvement, but with reservations. Based upon materials in the Ford Motor Company Archives and public records; table, 38 notes.   N. G. Sapper

1433. Potter, Barrett G. THE CIVILIAN CONSERVATION CORPS AND NEW YORK'S "NEGRO QUESTION": A CASE STUDY IN FEDERAL-STATE RACE RELATIONS DURING THE GREAT DEPRESSION. *Afro-Americans in New York Life and Hist. 1977 1(2): 183-200.* Discusses employment discrimination against Negroes in the Civilian Conservation Corps in New York, 1933-42.

1434. Quinney, Valerie. CHILDHOOD IN A SOUTHERN MILL VILLAGE. *Int. J. of Oral Hist. 1982 3(3): 167-192.* Recounts growing up in Carrboro, North Carolina, and discusses such issues as child labor and rigidly defined sex roles.

1435. Reed, Merl E. FEPC AND THE FEDERAL AGENCIES IN THE SOUTH. *J. of Negro Hist. 1980 65(1): 43-56.* Despite the emergency of World War II, employment discrimination on the basis of race was a way of life in the South. The efforts of the Fair Employment Practices Commission (FEPC) in behalf of nondiscrimination were revolutionary, but a quarter of a century would pass before those efforts were enforced by later agencies. Based on primary materials in the Archives of the U.S. and the Atlanta Federal Records Center; 37 notes.   N. G. Sapper

1436. Reisler, Mark. ALWAYS THE LABORER, NEVER THE CITIZEN: ANGLO PERCEPTIONS OF THE MEXICAN IMMIGRANT DURING THE 1920S. *Pacific Hist. Rev. 1976 45(2): 231-254.* A systematic study of how Americans viewed Mexican workers in the 1920's. Popular perceptions were translated into public policy, and pressure groups were able to influence federal action on the Mexican immigration issue. Two themes were stressed: "the Mexican's Indian blood would pollute the nation's genetic purity, and his biologically determined degenerate character traits would sap the country's moral fiber and corrupt its institutions." He might be a good laborer, but he could never become a potential citizen. 86 notes.   R. V. Ritter

1437. Rupp, Leila J. WOMAN'S PLACE IS IN THE WAR: PROPAGANDA AND PUBLIC OPINION IN THE UNITED STATES AND GERMANY, 1939-1945. Berkin, Carol Ruth and Norton, Mary Beth. *Women of America: a History* (Boston: Houghton Mifflin Co., 1979): 342-359. Compares US and German exhortations for women to join in the war effort. Though both societies encouraged women to participate, neither altered traditional concepts of women's roles. The American female labor force increased by 32% during the war, the German only 1%, although many women were mobilized before the war. Both countries took a patriotic approach, particularly seen in the American Office of War Information campaigns. Primary sources; 12 notes.   K. Talley

1438. Ryon, Roderick M. AN AMBIGUOUS LEGACY: BALTIMORE BLACKS AND THE CIO, 1936-1941. *J. of Negro Hist. 1980 65(1): 18-33.* Black people in Baltimore largely were left untouched by the Congress of Industrial Organizations (CIO) membership campaigns. Despite its shortcomings, the CIO was perceived as a friend of black workers by white workers who feared integrated unions. As World War II approached, the character of the CIO changed with beginning of the war boom. Large numbers of black migrants swelled the ranks of the CIO and were vital ingredients to its success. 49 notes.
          N. G. Sapper

1439. Sharpless, John and Rury, John. THE POLITICAL ECONOMY OF WOMEN'S WORK: 1900-1920. *Social Sci. Hist. 1980 4(3): 317-346.* Examines the impact of different cultural environments in shaping women's collective responses to traditional labor issues and activities. Women lacked the formal and informal contacts outside their work situation that fostered worker mobilization among men. Women's work was mostly intermittent and a temporary life phase, furthering difficulties of organization. Finally, ethnic groups restricted women's roles outside the family. All of this limited the appeal of labor organizations and feminist groups to New York's working women in the early 20th century. Based on published federal materials on women and labor; 2 tables, 7 notes, biblio.   L. K. Blaser

1440. Smith, Alonzo N. BLACKS AND THE LOS ANGELES MUNICIPAL TRANSIT SYSTEM, 1941-1945. *Urbanism Past & Present 1980-81 6(1): 25-31.* During World War II equal opportunity employment became a national issue. Government officials in the President's Committee on Fair Employment Practices and black civil rights leaders recognized that residential segregation and inadequate transportation were factors in black unemployment and poverty. Upgrading the transit system would enhance employment opportunities for Negroes, but a rigid system of segregation dominated municipal transit systems even though there were severe labor shortages. Railway companies became a major target for black activists during the war. Through directives from the FEPC, the mayor's office, as well as black pressure groups, municipal transit discrimination was solved. Based on records of the President's Committee on Fair Employment Practice, and records of the Los Angeles City Council; map, 2 tables, 25 notes.
          B. P. Anderson

1441. Smith, Elaine M. MARY MCLEOD BETHUNE AND THE NATIONAL YOUTH ADMINISTRATION. Deutrich, Mabel E. and Purdy, Virginia C., ed. *Clio Was a Woman: Studies in the History of American Women* (Washington, D.C.: Howard U. Pr., 1980): 149-177. The National Youth Administration existed during 1935-44 primarily to assist youth aged 16 to 24 in getting work. Mary McLeod Bethune persuaded the agency to recognize Negro leadership both by expanding the Office of Negro Affairs and by employing black administrative assistants in more than 25 states. Under her aegis, too, it addressed blacks' needs notably through the Special Graduate and Negro College Fund. She also promoted a policy which assured blacks the same defense training and placement opportunities as whites. A discussion summary follows. 107 notes.   J. Powell

1442. Straub, Eleanor F. WOMEN IN THE CIVILIAN LABOR FORCE. Deutrich, Mabel E. and Purdy, Virginia C., ed. *Clio Was a Woman: Studies in the History of American Women* (Washington, D.C.: Howard U. Pr., 1980): 206-226. The establishment of the War Manpower Commission (WMC) in April 1942 allowed the development of a unified approach to the problems of civilian labor supply. The mobilization of women workers became a pressing chore. The United States, however, never adopted compulsory measures or sanctions to force women to work during World War II. The mobilization of women depended on effective publicity, special promotions, and public relations techniques. A discussion summary follows. 105 notes.   J. Powell

1443. Strom, Sharon Hartman. OLD BARRIERS AND NEW OP-PORTUNITIES: WORKING WOMEN IN RHODE ISLAND, 1900-1940. *Rhode Island Hist. 1980 39(2): 43-55.* Rhode Island women gravitated into the same occupational patterns characteristic of other industrialized and urbanized American states: clerical, nursing, and sales positions. But even when they achieved professional status as doctors or lawyers, the overall position of females remained what it traditionally had been, one of dependence and powerlessness. Based on material in the Women's Biography Project, University of Rhode Island, published documents, reports, and statistics, and secondary accounts; 7 illus., 46 notes.   P. J. Coleman

1444. Tanaka, Stefan. THE TOLEDO INCIDENT: THE DEPORTA-TION OF THE NIKKEI FROM AN OREGON MILL TOWN. *Pacific Northwest Q. 1978 69(3): 116-126.* During the mid-1920's the Pacific Spruce Corporation of Toledo, Oregon, began to import Japanese Americans for lumber mill work. Local white citizens established a nativist organization to stop the Oriental influx and this led to a riot during July, 1925. Though the Japanese were driven from Toledo, they received financial compensation for damages a year later. Based on newspapers and interviews; map, 4 photos, 43 notes.   M. L. Tate

1445. Tannen, Michael B. WOMEN'S EARNINGS, SKILL, AND NATIVITY IN THE PROGRESSIVE ERA. *Explorations in Econ. Hist. 1982 19(2): 128-155.* Both measured and unmeasured skill varied according to nativity and industry. Female immigrants in manufacturing received a higher return on their measured skill than many of their more Americanized counterparts. However, for manufacturing and retailing combined, the native-born had higher standardized earnings. Based on published statistics and secondary accounts; 7 tables, 24 notes, ref.   P. J. Coleman

1446. Taylor, Paul S. MEXICAN WOMEN IN LOS ANGELES INDUSTRY IN 1928. *Aztlán 1980 11(1): 99-131.* Compiled in 1928, this analysis of Mexican women in Los Angeles industry is now published for the first time. Mexican women from upper, middle, and lower class backgrounds were interviewed. Places of employment for most of the 110 women interviewed included clothing and needle trades, packing houses, canneries, laundries, and other places. Mexican women undertook employment primarily because of economic necessity. The women in the family who went to work experienced changes in social attitudes, especially since such employment was contrary to Mexican custom. When young girls went to work, family conflicts often resulted. Some employers found Mexican women poor workers, while others said they were as good as or better than other nationalities. Distinctions were noted between women born in Mexico and those born in the United States. Primary sources.   A. Hoffman

1447. Walter, John C. FRANK R. CROSSWAITH AND LABOR UNIONIZATION IN HARLEM. *Afro-Americans in New York Life and Hist. 1979 3(2): 35-49; 1983 7(2): 47-58.* Part 1. 1925-1939. Frank R. Crosswaith (1892-1965) founded the Negro Labor Committee in Harlem in 1935. Part 2. 1939-1945. Crosswaith, one of the most prominent labor leaders of the World War II era, was instrumental in reducing discriminatory hiring practices in defense industries.

1448. Wiggins, David K. WENDELL SMITH, THE *PITTSBURGH COURIER-JOURNAL* AND THE CAMPAIGN TO INCLUDE

BLACKS IN ORGANIZED BASEBALL, 1933-1945. *J. of Sport Hist. 1983 10(2): 5-29.* Beginning in 1933, Wendell Smith, sports editor of the largest and most radical black newspaper in America, wrote articles and editorials and worked behind the scenes to see that blacks were allowed to play major league baseball. Building on support for blacks by Westbrook Pegler, Heywood Broun, and Jimmy Powers, Smith informed major league executives of promising black players and interviewed white players, like Dizzy Dean, who declared that black players were certain to show that whites were not the best players. Smith called on blacks to boycott major league games, and pointed out similarities between the Nazi treatment of minorities and the major-league treatment of blacks. World War II gave Smith a chance to demonstrate the difference between America's creed and reality. Based primarily on newspapers; 93 notes.   M. Kaufman

1449. Wise, Leah. THE ELAINE MASSACRE. *Southern Exposure 1974 1(3/4): 9-10.* In 1919 black sharecroppers and tenant farmers in Arkansas organized themselves to protest for equitable wages. Racial tensions were already heightened by race riots in Washington, D. C., Chicago, and East St. Louis during the summer. When the black community armed itself, whites assumed they would be attacked. The violence was started when a drunken white terrorized the black community, resulting in state and federal troops being called in to quell the violence. Based on published accounts and oral interviews.   G. A. Bolton

1450. Wollenberg, Charles. JAMES VS. MARINSHIP: TROUBLE ON THE NEW BLACK FRONTIER. *California History 1981 60(3): 262-279.* Describes the efforts of black shipyard workers to become full members in the International Brotherhood of Boilermakers, Iron Shipbuilders and Helpers of America. During World War II, thousands of blacks came to the San Francisco Bay area to work at skilled jobs for good wages. At the Marinship shipyard in Sausalito the boilermakers granted union clearances to black workers for employment but limited their union affiliation to auxiliary status. Led by Joseph James, a shipyard welder and NAACP leader, blacks argued for their right to full union membership. The issue went to court and in *James v. Marinship* (California, 1945), Negroes' right to full union membership was upheld. Ironically, the end of the war marked a decline in shipyard work, with the growing black population finding only unskilled employment at low wages in the postwar years. 10 photos, 54 notes.   A. Hoffman

1451. —. WORKING WOMEN AND THE WAR: FOUR NARRA-TIVES. *Radical Am. 1975 9(4-5): 133-162.*
—. INTRODUCTION, *pp. 133-134.*
Clawson, Augusta. SHIPYARD DIARY OF A WOMAN WELDER, *pp. 134-138.*
Archibald, Katherine. WOMEN IN THE SHIPYARD, *pp. 139-144.*
Sonnenberg, Mary. TWO EPISODES, *pp. 145-155.*
Stein, Anne. POST-WAR CONSUMER BOYCOTTS, *pp. 156-162.* Personal narratives include examples of sex discrimination, betrayals by labor unions, and the 1946 meat boycott in Washington, D.C.   S

Economics and Statistics of Labor

1452. Goldberg, Joseph P. FRANCES PERKINS, ISADOR LUBIN, AND THE BUREAU OF LABOR STATISTICS. *Monthly Labor Rev. 1980 103(4): 22-30.* Secretary of Labor Frances Perkins's influence on the Bureau of Labor Statistics was evidenced by her initiating a review of the Bureau's statistics and choosing Isador Lubin as Commissioner of Labor Statistics under Franklin Roosevelt's New Deal, both of which improved and modernized the Bureau; covers 1920's-40's.

1453. Hoffman, Abraham. AN UNUSUAL MONUMENT: PAUL S. TAYLOR'S *MEXICAN LABOR IN THE UNITED STATES* MONOGRAPH SERIES. *Pacific Hist. Rev. 1976 45(2): 255-270.* Reviews the series of 11 monographs, produced by Paul S. Taylor of the University of California during 1926-34, on *Mexican Labor in the United States.* The study used every research technique then available and was altogether new in the field. It remains a monument to Taylor's skill, care, and judicious use of materials. With the renewed interest in

Chicano history, the series recently was reprinted. 37 notes.

R. V. Ritter

1454. Kesselman, Jonathan R. and Savin, N. E. THREE-AND-A-HALF MILLION WORKERS NEVER WERE LOST. *Econ. Inquiry 1978 16(2): 205-225.* The 3.5 million people working on US emergency relief projects should be counted as employed during 1934-41; including this population seriously undermines earlier theories of employment during the depression.

1455. Rees, Albert. DOUGLAS ON WAGES AND THE SUPPLY OF LABOR. *J. of Pol. Econ. 1979 87(5, pt. 1): 915-922.* Outlines the American economist Paul H. Douglas's work on wage theory and the labor supply.

1456. Rockoff, Hugh. INDIRECT PRICE INCREASES AND REAL WAGES DURING WORLD WAR II. *Explorations in Econ. Hist. 1978 15(4): 407-420.* If adjustments are made to reflect such factors as shortages of goods, deterioration of quality, and reclassification of workers into higher wage categories even though no additional work or responsibility was involved, real wages may not have been higher in June 1946 than in August 1948. Based on published documents and reports and secondary accounts; 4 tables, fig., 6 notes, 30 ref.   P. J. Coleman

1457. Schmitt, Robert C. UNEMPLOYMENT RATES IN HAWAII DURING THE 1930'S. *Hawaiian J. of Hist. 1976 10: 90-101.* Examines unemployment statistics during the 1930's, comparing those of Hawaii with the continental United States. Unemployment in Hawaii never reached the magnitude that it did on the mainland. Tables.

R. Alvis

1458. Shergold, Peter R. WAGE DIFFERENTIALS BASED ON SKILL IN THE UNITED STATES, 1889-1914: A CASE STUDY. *Labor Hist. 1977 18(4): 485-508.* Contrary to traditional interpretations wage differentials based on skill did not widen in Pittsburgh during 1889-1914. A locality rather than an industry provides a more effective data base for generalizations. Managerial action and changes in industrial techniques help account for narrowing wage differentials, but more study of local data over an extended time period is required. Based on

government statistics and census reports; 4 tables, graph, 56 notes.

L. L. Athey

1459. Shergold, Peter R. WAGE RATES IN PITTSBURGH DURING THE DEPRESSION OF 1908. *J. of Am. Studies [Great Britain] 1975 9(2): 163-188.* Assesses statistical and qualitative evidences to explain the phenomenon of wage rates declining less drastically in Pittsburgh during the depression of 1908 than in earlier recessions of considerably less severity. The depression of 1908 encouraged emigration from Pittsburgh, discouraged immigration from Europe to the United States, and produced "relative tightness" in the Pittsburgh labor market. Hence, wage rates remained higher than depression conditions otherwise warranted. Based on newspaper and secondary sources; 75 notes.   H. T. Lovin

1460. Stricker, Frank. THE WAGES OF INFLATION: WORKER'S EARNINGS IN THE WORLD WAR ONE ERA. *Mid-America 1981 63(2): 93-105.* Analyzes the effects of inflation on American worker wages and purchasing power, 1910's-20's. Consumer prices grew to an unprecedented level during 1914-20 and fell slightly during 1920-26. In effect, low-salaried and public workers financed US participation in World War I through real pay cuts and reduced consumption. By contrast, even lower-paid factory workers' wages rose during the war. After the conflict, wage differentials between the poorly- and well-paid tended to return to prewar disparities. Based in part on National Industrial Conference Board and Bureau of Labor Statistics reports; 3 tables, 27 notes.   P. J. Woehrmann

1461. Tripp, Joseph F. AN INSTANCE OF LABOR AND BUSINESS COOPERATION: WORKMEN'S COMPENSATION IN WASHINGTON STATE (1911). *Labor Hist. 1976 17(4): 530-550.* Enactment of a compulsory workmen's compensation law in Washington state in 1911, was achieved through cooperation of the lumber industry and labor unions. Frequency of accidents, resultant damage suits, animosity toward casualty companies, and an inadequate legal machinery promoted the cooperation which led to a compromise between industrial and labor interests. Based on trade journals, court reports, and manuscript sources; 58 notes.   L. L. Athey

5. MODERN LABOR, 1945 TO 1982

General

1462. Aho, C. M. and Orr, J. A. TRADE-SENSITIVE EMPLOY-MENT: WHO ARE THE AFFECTED WORKERS? *Monthly Labor Rev. 1981 104(2): 29-35.* While the one in eight manufacturing jobs now related to exports have created openings for workers with above-average skills, imports have displaced job prospects in industries with less-skilled labor and more women and minorities.

1463. Aries, Nancy R. ABORTION CLINICS AND THE ORGANI-ZATION OF WORK: A CASE STUDY OF CHARLES CIRCLE. *Rev. of Radical Pol. Econ. 1980 12(2): 53-62.* Harry Braverman's hypothesis of degradation of work is exemplified by organization of abortion clinics. Idealistic women clashed with the male management profit motive. Conflict leads to struggle to unionize. Covers 1973-77. 10 notes.　　　　　　　　　　　　　　　　　　D. R. Stevenson

1464. Bornstein, Leon. INDUSTRIAL RELATIONS IN 1978: SOME BARGAINING HIGHLIGHTS. *Monthly Labor Rev. 1979 102(1): 58-64.*

1465. Bowers, Norman. YOUTH AND MARGINAL: AN OVER-VIEW OF YOUTH EMPLOYMENT. *Monthly Labor Rev. 1979 102(10): 4-18.* Presents an overview of historical trends for selected labor market indicators: unemployment rates, labor force participation rates and employment-population ratios for teenagers and young adults in the United States, with an analysis of these trends by race and sex.

1466. Bowles, Samuel and Gintis, Herbert. CLASS POWER AND ALIENATED LABOR. *Monthly Rev. 1975 26(10): 9-25.* Analyzes alienation during the 1970's as a social problem resulting from the structure of technology and examines the labor process from a radical perspective.

1467. Briggs, Vernon M., Jr. ILLEGAL IMMIGRATION AND THE AMERICAN LABOR FORCE: THE USE OF "SOFT" DATA FOR ANALYSIS. *Am. Behavioral Scientist 1976 19(3): 351-363.* Examines the knowledge crisis surrounding the issue of illegal immigration into the United States, focusing on the critical social issues which are influenced by the type of data used for analysis.

1468. Bulmer, Charles and Carmichael, John L., Jr. LABOR AND EMPLOYMENT POLICY: AN OVERVIEW OF THE ISSUES. *Policy Studies J. 1977 6(2): 255-262.* Reviews issues currently affecting labor and employment policy, including labor law reform, labor standards, public sector, and workmen's benefits.

1469. Carlson, Alvar W. SEASONAL FARM LABOR IN THE SAN LUIS VALLEY. *Ann. of the Assoc. of Am. Geog. 1973 63(1): 97-108.* "Specialty agriculture has been the mainstay of the agricultural economy of the San Luis Valley, Colorado. The dependence of Valley farmers upon thousands of local, intrastate, and interstate seasonal farm laborers is important in understanding the evolution of this agricultural region. Spanish-surname people have been available for farm labor since the early settlement of the Valley."　　　　　　　　　　　　　　J

1470. Chen, Yung-Ping. THE GROWTH OF FRINGE BENEFITS: IMPLICATIONS FOR SOCIAL SECURITY. *Monthly Labor Rev. 1981 104(11): 3-10.* Traces the actual and projected distribution of cash pay and fringe benefits, focusing on the fringe benefits, of American workers from 1950.

1471. Cherry, Robert. CLASS STRUGGLE AND THE NATURE OF THE WORKING CLASS. *Rev. of Radical Pol. Econ. 1973 5(2): 47-86.* Defines a leftist political program based on analysis of the working class's standard of living and their demands for reform from the late 1950's to 1973.

1472. Chinloy, Peter. SOURCES OF QUALITY CHANGE IN LA-BOR INPUT. *Am. Econ. Rev. 1980 70(1): 108-119.* Labor input (the product of total hours worked and average labor quality per hour) indicates that the contribution of education to US productivity growth

has declined between 1959-63 and 1971 and 1974. Employment for the relatively educated has failed to maintain the rise in this growth for the postwar era. 5 tables, 15 ref.　　　　　　　　　　　D. K. Pickens

1473. Clark, Earl. WHEN LITTLE BANDS WERE BIG. *Am. Heritage 1974 25(4): 38-40, 96-97.* Reminiscences of the author's days as member of a small dance band in the 1920's in Columbus, Ohio.
　　　　　　　　　　　　　　　　　　　　　　　　　　S

1474. Colman, William G. SCHOOLS, HOUSING, JOBS, TRANS-PORTATION: INTERLOCKING METROPOLITAN PROBLEMS. *Urban Rev. 1978 10(2): 92-107.* The indissoluble linkage among income, health, education, employment, and crime in metropolitan areas must be broken to begin solving the inner cities' problems. Two possible solutions are "central city revitalization" and "central city depopulation and disinvestment." The latter strategy, providing housing or jobs in and transportation to the suburbs for inner city residents, seems to be more politically feasible. Primary and secondary sources; 2 tables, 8 notes, biblio.　　　　　　　　　　　　　　　　　　R. G. Sherer

1475. Cox, Robert W. LABOR AND THE MULTINATIONALS. *Foreign Affairs 1975 54(2): 344-365.* "...the expansion of the multina-tional corporation is a major, perhaps *the* major, phenomenon of the international economy today...labor today has managed to generate only a confused, partial and lopsided response..." in exercising its options in this critical situation. 12 notes.　　　　　　　R. Riles

1476. Danziger, Sheldon H. and Lampman, Robert J. GETTING AND SPENDING. *Ann. of the Am. Acad. of Pol. and Social Sci. 1978 (435): 23-39.* The selected time series on income and consumption appear to give a clear picture of postwar change along the following lines: family incomes have grown substantially; consumption patterns have shifted away from necessities; income inequality has not increased; and poverty and intergroup income differences have declined. However, the broad indicators on which these conclusions are based do not illuminate the processes by which income is generated, consumption is shared, and costs are borne. The authors raise a set of questions related to the measurement and interpretation of the indicators. The answers to these questions suggest that a time series does not speak for itself and that a careful analysis of postwar changes awaits specification of the socioeconomic processes that generate the indicators.　　　　J

1477. Deering, Dorothy. EGALITARIAN HISTORY AND STUDS TERKEL'S *WORKING* . *J. of General Educ. 1976 28(2): 103-113.* As did his 19th-century predecessor Henry Mayhew, Studs Terkel has presented in his moving, contemporary history, *Working* , the lives of men and women described in their own words from within their own consciousness. Their interviews air the problems of recognition, isola-tion, unfulfilled aims, and dreams of finding meaningful, purposeful work. Based on secondary sources; note.　　　　　　N. A. Williamson

1478. Derber, Milton. COLLECTIVE BARGAINING: THE AMER-ICAN APPROACH TO INDUSTRIAL DEMOCRACY. *Ann. of the Am. Acad. of Pol. and Social Sci. 1977 (431): 83-94.* Collective bargaining is the American route to industrial democracy. Some unionists and others, however, have advocated a widening and deepen-ing of the participative role of workers and unions in managerial decisionmaking. Examples of union-management cooperation outside of the conventional collective bargaining boundaries can be found as far back as the 1920s. But only a small number of cases have survived to the present day. Since 1970 the federal government has encouraged joint union-management committees and autonomous work group experi-ments to improve productivity and the quality of working life. A National Center for Productivity and Quality of Working Life has been established by Congress. A number of companies have, independently or in cooperation with unions, introduced job enrichment programs, flexible work schedules, and semi-autonomous work groups. Many companies have taken advantage of tax law benefits to adopt profit-sharing and employee stock ownership plans. Union leaders have generally been suspicious of such management schemes as well as productivity plans unless safeguards are provided for worker job security and employment conditions. They have rejected the German codetermination system of worker-directors. There appears to be little prospect of dramatic change during the foreseeable future although collective bargaining may gradually extend worker participation in managerial decisionmaking.   J

1479. Diacon, Barry. THE SPECTRE OF THE SILICON CHIP: THE THIN EDGE OF THE NEXT WAVE OF UNEMPLOYMENT. *Can. Dimension [Canada] 1981 15(8)-16(1): 21-25.* Discusses the growing computerization and robotization of industry in the United States and Canada over the last two decades, and argues that continued acceleration of this trend will result in the elimination or downgrading of millions of workers.

1480. Dutka, Anna B. and Freedman, Marcia. WHERE THE JOBS ARE. *New York Affairs 1980 6(2): 20-36.* Examines New York City's labor force, the types of jobs available, the training programs available, their effectiveness, and the correlation among jobs, labor force, and training programs, based on data from the 1970 US Census and on employment data for New York City during 1974-76 and reports during 1977-78, concluding that the situation is not as dismal as it was thought to be.

1481. Dwyer, Richard E. UNION-UNIVERSITY COOPERATION: THE EDUCATION OF ORGANIZED LABOR AT THE UNIVERSITY. *J. of General Educ. 1976 28(2): 145-158.* This review of the Rutgers University experience in union-university cooperation describes one university's successful attempt to establish a structure for cooperation in the development of educational programs for organized labor, and indicates ways to alleviate some of the difficulties in labor education. Based on primary and secondary sources; 41 notes.

N. A. Williamson

1482. Dymmel, Michael D. TECHNOLOGY IN TELECOMMUNICATIONS: ITS EFFECT ON LABOR AND SKILLS. *Monthly Labor Rev. 1979 102(1): 13-19.* Discusses technological advances in the US telecommunications industry and future productivity in that industry.

1483. Feldstein, Martin. THE ECONOMICS OF THE NEW UNEMPLOYMENT. *Public Interest 1973 (33): 3-42.* Discusses causes and remedies of unemployment in the 1970's.

1484. Form, William. SELF-EMPLOYED MANUAL WORKERS: PETTY BOURGEOIS OR WORKING CLASS? *Social Forces 1982 60(4): 1050-1069.* This national study investigates whether self-employed manual workers form an economic class and status group that is recognizably distinct from manual employees and whether the distinctions have political consequences. The findings show that manual proprietors are a higher status group and earn demonstrably more than employees. Though political cleavages between proprietors and employees are small, along with other factors they may be large enough to destabilize working-class political loyalties.   J

1485. Foster, Howard G. THE LABOR MARKET IN NONUNION CONSTRUCTION. *Industrial and Labor Relations Rev. 1973 26(4): 1071-1085.* This article reports on one of the few systematic studies done of the labor market in nonunion construction, a sector currently expanding very rapidly in scope and importance. Relying primarily on interviews with 143 nonunion builders in the Buffalo area, the author examines hiring practices, worker training, wages and benefits, and seasonality of employment. He concludes that the nonunion market does perform well in several aspects of wage setting and manpower utilization, but it probably does not function as effectively as the union sector in the hiring and training of workers.   J

1486. Freeman, Richard B. INDIVIDUAL MOBILITY AND UNION VOICE IN THE LABOR MARKET. *Am. Econ. Rev. 1976 66(2): 361-368.* In discussing the relation between exit-voice (quitting a job) and unionization, notes that when quitting is nonviable, unionization has greater appeal. Trade unionism makes the median or some other average the determinant of the labor contract. By encouraging expressions of discontent and keeping unhappy workers from leaving, unions may increase dissatisfaction even when factors of wages and working conditions are constant. Notes.   D. K. Pickens

1487. Freeman, Richard B. THE NEWCOMERS. *Wilson Q. 1980 4(1): 113-125.* Surveys the evolving shape of the US labor force,

especially the emergence of the female worker, the youth unemployment problem, the overeducated underemployed, and the growth of the white collar work force during 1950-1970.

1488. Freeman, Richard B. UNION WAGE PRACTICES AND WAGE DISPERSION WITHIN ESTABLISHMENTS. *Industrial and Labor Relations Rev. 1982 36(1): 3-21.* The dispersion of wages is significantly narrower in unionized than in nonunionized establishments, due in large part to unions' wage practices, such as single rate or automatic-progression modes of wage payment as opposed to merit reviews and individual wage determination. Dispersion in average wages is narrower among organized plants, but by more modest amounts. Overall, the evidence suggests a major role for explicit union wage policies in explaining the dispersion of wages within firms and in the economy as a whole.   J/S

1489. Gallotta, Vito. LOTTE SINDACALI E ISTITUTI DI *INDUSTRIAL RELATIONS* NELL'IMMEDIATO DOPOGUERRA IN AMERICA [Labor union struggles and institutes of Industrial Relations in the immediate post-war period in America]. *Nuova Riv. Storica [Italy] 1976 60(5-6): 619-627.* The American myth always has been that the United States is a classless society. Immediately after World War II, when the country faced an expanding Communist bloc abroad and wide labor unrest at home, numerous institutes of labor management and industrial relations were set up. They played a key role in removing elements of class struggle from the labor-management confrontations and reduced them to power struggles between two different interest groups, rather than between two opposing social forces. 11 notes.

J. C. Billigmeier

1490. Goldblatt, Louis. LABOR AND OVERDUE SOCIAL CHANGE. *Monthly Rev. 1981 33(4): 60-64.* Comments on Bruce Nissen's 1981 essay applauding its clarity and value in further analyzing both internal developments within unions, and objective factors that will play a major role in determining the labor movement's future.

1491. Greene, Richard. EMPLOYMENT TRENDS IN ENERGY EXTRACTION. *Monthly Labor Rev. 1981 104(5): 3-8.* Discusses the increase in exploration for and extraction of oil and natural gas in the United States since the 1973-74 Arab oil embargo, which has in turn increased employment in these industries.

1492. Hailstones, Thomas J. TRANSFER PAYMENTS AND THE WORK ETHIC. *Rev. of Social Econ. 1976 34(1): 71-79.* Discusses the relationship between the work ethic and the contemporary American expenditure on transfer payments as a means of financing social welfare expenditures.

1493. Hall, Paul. A UNION LEADER LOOKS AT THE MERCHANT MARINE. *US Naval Inst. Pro. 1974 100(5): 178-189.* The economic, political, and military challenges facing the United States indicate the need to develop a stronger and more versatile merchant marine. The US merchant marine can become a naval auxiliary in peace as well as war by adapting the Navy's peacetime operations to the full-time use of merchant vessels to provide part of the fleet's logistic support. The merchant marine could also meet the country's emergency shipping needs, and carry a major share of US energy imports. 12 photos, table.   A. N. Garland

1494. Hall, Richard H. THEORETICAL TRENDS IN THE SOCIOLOGY OF OCCUPATIONS. *Sociol. Q. 1983 24(1): 5-23.* Recent research in the sociology of occupations has concentrated on status, income, women and sex roles, job redesign and satisfaction, and job alienation; and there has been a big decline in papers on the professions, 1976-82.

1495. Hedges, Janice Neipert. NEW PATTERNS FOR WORKING TIME. *Monthly Labor R. 1973 96(2): 3-8.* New patterns of worktime and worklife are being considered in the United States and Europe.

1496. Hedges, Janice Neipert and Sekscenski, Edward S. WORKERS ON LATE SHIFTS IN A CHANGING ECONOMY. *Monthly Labor Rev. 1979 102(9): 14-22.* Reviews the history of shift work in the United States from 1960 to 1978, covering organization, demographics, differential pay, workers' attitudes, etc., and notes that the ratio of workers doing such work has remained fairly constant (approximately one in six) from 1973 to 1978, but that energy and job satisfaction factors may influence future use of evening and night shifts.

1497. Heron, Craig. THE ANATOMY OF WORK: A REVIEW ESSAY. *Labour [Canada] 1982 10(Aut): 151-157.* Reviews Michael Burawoy's *Manufacturing Consent: Changes in the Labor Process under Monopoly Capitalism* (1979); Richard Edwards's *Contested Terrain: The Transformation of the Workplace in the Twentieth Century* (1979); Richard M. Pfeffer's *Working for Capitalism* (1979); and *Case Studies in the Labour Process* (1979) edited by Andrew Zimbalist. Analyzes capitalist work processes and capitalist work relations, their implications for the social order, and the possibilities for changing it. Attempts to explain working-class life in North America since World War II, especially in the 1970's.   J. V. Coutinho

1498. Hildebrand, George H. PROBLEMS AND POLICIES AFFECTING LABOR'S INTERESTS. *Am. Econ. Rev. 1974 64(2): 283-288.* Examines the impact of multinational corporations on labor in the world economy.

1499. Hirsch, Barry T. THE INTERINDUSTRY STRUCTURE OF UNIONISM, EARNINGS, AND EARNINGS DISPERSION. *Industrial and Labor Relations Rev. 1982 36(1): 22-34.* The estimated equalizing effects of unionism on within-industry earnings distributions are significant both in the manufacturing and nonmanufacture sectors. In addition, the dispersion in earnings does appear to affect the level of unionism.   J/S

1500. Hoerder, Dirk. AMERICAN LABOR & IMMIGRATION HISTORY: REPORTS ON THE STATE OF THE HISTORIOGRAPHY SINCE 1945 IN THE EUROPEAN COUNTRIES. *Labor Hist. 1980 21(2): 261-276, (3): 392-419.* In two parts. A preliminary survey of research published or in progress.   L. L. Athey

1501. Howard, Robert. BRAVE NEW WORKPLACE. *Working Papers for a New Soc. 1980 7(6): 21-31.* Discusses the negative effects new technology has on workers, such as automatic pacing, oversupervision, fragmented and downgraded jobs, the obsolescence of traditional skills, focusing on the experience of telephone workers since 1968 when the Federal Communications Commission deregulated key sectors in the telephone industry.

1502. Howe, Carolyn. MULTINATIONALS AND LABOR UNITY: BOTH SIDES. *Southwest Econ. and Soc. 1978 4(1): 43-74.* Examines theoretical and objective bases for labor solidarity in American-Mexican border areas; discusses multinational corporations and the Mexican Border Industry Program, 1966-78.

1503. Ickowitz, Allan. THE ROLE OF THE INTERNATIONAL TELECOMMUNICATION UNION IN THE SETTLEMENT OF HARMFUL INTERFERENCE DISPUTES. *Columbia J. of Transnat. Law 1974 13(1): 82-97.*

1504. Johnson, Doyle P. SOCIAL ORGANIZATION OF AN INDUSTRIAL WORK GROUP: EMERGENCE AND ADAPTATION TO ENVIRONMENTAL CHANGE. *Sociol. Q. 1974 15(1): 109-126.* "This is a participant observation study of a small work group on the night shift in a food processing plant. Although in the Human Relations tradition, this study focuses explicitly upon the interrelations between the group and salient aspects of the organizational and technical environment. The analysis is guided by the small group theory of George C. Homans. Attention is focused first upon the *development* of an informal social organization which was functional both in meeting formal organizational goals and group members' socioemotional needs. This informal organization was disrupted by supervisory style changes, however, after which both job commitment and group morale declined dramatically. This was followed by two technical changes; as the group informally and collectively adapted to these changes, a new informal social organization emerged. This new organization clearly reflected the group members' desire for autonomy. Clear support is claimed for the general proposition that commitment to formal organizational goals, group morale, and individual satisfaction is positively related to a lenient supervisory style and high autonomy."   J

1505. Kanter, Rosabeth Moss. A GOOD JOB IS HARD TO FIND. *Working Papers for a New Soc. 1979 7(1): 44-50.* Examines trends in the makeup and expectations of the US labor force since World War II with respect to the new pressures of these trends on companies and unions.

1506. Krueger, Thomas A. REVIEW ESSAY: LABOR IN CONTEMPORARY AMERICA. *J. of Social Hist. 1977 10(3): 346-353.* Suggests that an alliance of academic radicals and labor intellectuals with the labor movement for social change needs careful forethought. Andrew Levison's *The Working Class Majority* (1974) disputes the Marxian and procapitalist views that US industrialists have succeeded in domesticating a significant share of the labor movement. Poverty, boredom, fear, and poor services are realities. Unions serve real needs. The gulf between the workers and the McGovernites is no stronger than the logic of their common goals. Notes Levison's brief and unrevealing treatment of women and his failure to pay sufficient attention to the anti-Communism of the labor unions. 7 notes.   M. Hough

1507. Kuhn, James W. THE LABOR FORCE. *Pro. of the Acad. of Pol. Sci. 1979 33(3): 101-112.* Surveys the role of the labor force in the changing structure of the economy, 1960-79. Controversy over the minimum wage is at the center of labor's concern. Concludes that control of inflation will adversely affect many interest groups, labor among them.   K. N. T. Crowther

1508. Lazer, Charles and Dier, S. THE LABOR FORCE IN FICTION. *J. of Communication 1978 28(1): 174-182.* Popular fiction does not describe the actual occupational distribution of men and women (as drawn from census reports, 1940-70).

1509. Leigh, Duane E. UNIONS AND NONWAGE RACIAL DISCRIMINATION. *Industrial and Labor Relations Rev. 1979 32(4): 439-450.* Finds that unionism lengthens tenure and reduces quits for Negroes and whites, and that unions' positive impact on black-to-white ratios is not negated by bargaining on nonwage working conditions; covers 1969-73.   J/S

1510. Levenstein, Aaron. WORK—WHAT IS ITS FUTURE? *Freedom at Issue 1974 (26): 5-10.* Discusses intellectuals' and laborers' attitudes toward the institution of work in the 1960's and 70's, emphasizing the factors of social status and job satisfaction.

1511. Levenstein, Harvey. SINDICALISMO NORTEAMERICANO, BRACEROS Y "ESPALDAS MOJADAS" [North American trade unionism, Mexican contract laborers, and wetbacks]. *Hist. Mexicana [Mexico] 1978 28(2): 153-184.* Analyzes the attitude of US trade unions to the issue of imported Mexican labor during 1945-74. North American unions have traditionally regarded Mexico's large population of migrant laborers as a threat to the economic livelihood of their membership. For this reason, the unions were lukewarm to the bracero program which, beginning in 1943, permitted the legal importation of temporary Mexican labor. Official opposition surfaced only in 1950 when a slump in agricultural prices produced widespread unemployment. Reacting to adverse economic conditions, the unions joined with other political sectors to mount a campaign against the Bracero Program. In 1964 their efforts culminated in the termination of the program. Frustrating the objectives of the unions, termination of the contract labor movement brought a flood of illegal aliens. Based on documents in the Archives of Labor History and Urban Affairs, Wayne State University, Detroit, official minutes, and secondary works; 76 notes.   F. J. Shaw, Jr.

1512. Lovell, Frank. THE STATE OF THE UNIONS. *Int. Socialist Rev. 1974 35(6): 10-15.*

1513. Luebke, Paul; McMahon, Bob; and Risberg, Jeff. SELECTIVE RECRUITMENT IN NORTH CAROLINA. *Working Papers for a New Soc. 1979 6(6): 17-20.* Describes the current growing practice in the South of discouraging companies from establishing new plants because of decent wage rates and/or unionization, and efforts to reach a single state economic development policy in each southern state.

1514. McConville, Ed. WILL HE OR WON'T HE. *Southern Exposure 1976 4(1-2): 128-131.* Examines factors influencing labor unions' ability to organize southern laborers, including the southern mind, individualism, and external working conditions, 1970's.

1515. Meany, George. DÉTENTE AND THE WORKINGMAN. *Atlantic Community Q.* *1974 14(1): 37-41.* A hard-hitting attack on "détente" as he sees it being carried out.   J

1516. Merrill, Michael. SELLING SOCIALISM DOOR TO DOOR. *Radical Hist. Rev.* *1978 (18): 109-115.* Describes the efforts of the Institute for Labor Education and Research to teach classes on political economy and working class history to members of industrial unions in New York and New Jersey, July 1976-September 1977.

1517. Miller, Ann R. CHANGING WORK LIFE PATTERNS; A TWENTY-FIVE YEAR REVIEW. *Ann. of the Am. Acad. of Pol. and Social Sci.* *1978 (435): 83-101.* Over the past 25 years there have been substantial changes in the proportion of population engaged in market work and in the age and sex composition of the work force. The nonworker-worker ratio has fluctuated widely, primarily as a reflection of the dramatic fluctuations in birth rates, while the long-term trends of increasing participation by women and declining years of work by men have accelerated. Recent developments indicate that this acceleration of long-term trends has taken on certain new characteristics: young women appear to be returning to the labor market much more quickly after the birth of children, with a consequent reduction of time out of the work force; and the customary retirement age of men is falling. As a result, work life patterns are becoming increasingly similar for men and women and much higher proportions of the population in the age range 20-54 are working than has been true in the past. In a broader context, it is suggested that the rapid decline in average annual worker hours characteristic of the first part of the twentieth century may be transformed into a decline in average worker years in the last part.   J

1518. Mitchell, Daniel J. B. RECENT CHANGES IN THE LABOR CONTENT OF U.S. INTERNATIONAL TRADE. *Industrial and Labor Relations Rev.* *1975 28(3): 355-375.* "Focuses on the changes in the composition of US exports and imports, and the effect of these changes on labor, during the 1965-70 period."   S

1519. Moles, Jerry A. WHO TILLS THE SOIL? MEXICAN-AMERICAN WORKERS REPLACE THE SMALL FARMER IN CALIFORNIA: AN EXAMPLE FROM COLUSA COUNTY. *Human Organization* *1979 38(1): 20-27.* Data collected 1950-69 in Colusa County, California, indicate that small farmers forced out of agriculture by rising costs incommensurate with increased production have been replaced by labor provided by Mexican Americans.

1520. Morales, Rebecca. UNIONS AND UNDOCUMENTED WORKERS. *Southwest Econ. and Soc.* *1982 6(1): 3-11.* Discusses the relationship between illegal aliens, labor unions and organizations, and federal policy.

1521. Moy, Joyanna and Sorrentino, Constance. UNEMPLOYMENT IN NINE INDUSTRIAL NATIONS, 1973-75. *Monthly Labor Rev.* *1975 98(6): 9-18.* Examines recent trends, finding that joblessness rose in all countries studied except Sweden, with postwar highs in the US, Australia, and France.

1522. Moylan, Maurice P. EMPLOYMENT IN THE ATOMIC ENERGY FIELD, 1973. *Monthly Labor Rev.* *1974 97(9): 23-27.* Surveys employment in atomic energy in the United States between 1963 and 1973, showing the impact of the gradual replacement of government by private industry in peaceful atomic activities.

1523. Noble, David F. PRESENT TENSE TECHNOLOGY. *Democracy* *1983 3(2): 8-24, (3): 70-82.* Part 1. Considers the dislocations caused by mechanization on the British textile industry during the 1st Industrial Revolution and the various responses to the changing technology. Part 2. Discusses labor militancy in response to the threat of automation-induced unemployment of the 2d Industrial Revolution.

1524. Noble, David F. SOCIAL CHOICE IN MACHINE DESIGN: THE CASE OF AUTOMATICALLY CONTROLLED MACHINE TOOLS, AND A CHALLENGE FOR LABOR. *Pol. and Soc.* *1978 8(3-4): 313-347.* Case study of the design of numerical control (N.C.) machine tools, managerial imperatives involved in their deployment, and labor's response to this technological advancement. Employment of technological innovations has demonstrated continuing acceptance of a technological determinism, which excludes the social dimensions of

technology and its employment. Based on survey and interview data, and other primary and secondary sources; 69 notes.   D. G. Nielsen

1525. O'Rand, Angela M. and Henretta, John C. DELAYED CAREER ENTRY, INDUSTRIAL PENSION STRUCTURE, AND EARLY RETIREMENT IN A COHORT OF UNMARRIED WOMEN. *Am. Sociol. Rev.* *1982 47(3): 365-373.* The effects of early family and work patterns and industrial pension structures on the timing of retirement among unmarried women are examined within a life course perspective. The retirement process is viewed in a longitudinal framework with similar combinations of factors influencing successive stages of final withdrawal from work. Having children and delayed career entry along with late life family, pension, and health status affect retirement schedules.   J/S

1526. Oswald, Rudy. LABOR LOOKS AT THE AMERICAN ECONOMY. *Social Educ.* *1983 47(1): 22-27.* The five biggest problems for labor in today's economy are high taxes, government spending, inflation, high interest rates, and unemployment.

1527. Parker, Ruth Rose. COMPARAISON INTERNATIONALE DE L'UTILISATION DE LA MAIN D'OEUVRE DANS L'INDUSTRIE: UN PROGRAMME LINÉARE [International comparison of use of manpower in industry: a linear program]. *Actualité Écon.* *[Canada] 1974 50(1): 47-62.* Presents a model for a linear program (implicitly for computer use), to identify the contribution of workers and manpower to production. An effort is made to separate this from the influence of demand, and to allow for variation between the various factors of production while so doing. Presents various models and suggests an optimum road to a solution of the problem, and the resultant model. Mentions the limits and significance of the model. 2 graphs, table, 8 notes.   W. B. Whitham

1528. Patry, Bill. RETAIL: A WORKER'S OBSERVATIONS. *Monthly Rev.* *1978 29(11): 23-31.* During the 1970's, chain retailers introduced merchandising methods and electronic equipment which reduced labor needs, provided constant checks and surveillance on workers, made workers interchangeable, and kept workers docile and poorly paid by employing part-time labor who frequently requested more hours.

1529. Ruben, George. INDUSTRIAL RELATIONS IN 1980 INFLUENCED BY INFLATION AND RECESSION. *Monthly Labor Rev.* *1981 104(1): 15-20.* Review of industrial relations in 1980, focusing on large losses by General Motors, Ford, Chrysler, and American Motors, and United States Steel, the companies' turn to the government and the United Auto Workers for help, collective bargaining, internal union affairs, the truce between J. P. Stevens & Co. and the Clothing and Textile Workers after a 17-year battle, and union wage increases.

1530. Salins, Peter D. CAN ECONOMIC DEVELOPMENT HELP NEW YORK CITY's UNEMPLOYED? *New York Affairs* *1976 3(2): 80-93.* Recession or no, there is a long-term problem of finding jobs for the less-skilled residents of large, central cities. Efforts to create new jobs for them within New York City or to "export" them to suburban jobs have not had encouraging results.   J

1531. Sassen-Koob, Saskia. IMMIGRANT AND MINORITY WORKERS IN THE ORGANIZATION OF THE LABOR PROCESS. *J. of Ethnic Studies* *1980 8(1): 1-34.* Accelerating immigration to northeastern cities of workers from Latin America indicates a shift in the labor market. Jobs which have traditionally gone to Negroes in the United States recently have not been filled by them, due to the refusal of inner city minorities to take low wage, dead-end jobs. The new immigrants are filling these positions. 12 notes, biblio.   S

1532. Saxenian, AnnaLee. OUTGROWING THE VALLEY. *Working Papers Mag.* *1981 8(5): 24-27.* Discusses the environmental, economic, and social problems that resulted from the concentration of highly trained professionals and poorly educated minority workers in the Silicon Valley electronics industry of Santa Clara County, California, during the 1950's-70's.

1533. Schiavello, Piero. VIAGGIO NEGLI USA: SPOSTERANNO LA STATUA DELLA LIBERTÀ [Travel in the United States: they will move the Statue of Liberty]. *Ponte [Italy] 1981 37(1): 36-46.* An

Italian comments on the fascinating, many-sided, multiracial life of New York City, especially its violence; the American labor movement; and the remnants of youth unrest on American campuses; 1968-79.

1534. Schonberger, Howard. AMERICAN LABOR'S COLD WAR IN OCCUPIED JAPAN. *Diplomatic Hist. 1979 3(3): 249-272.* American labor leaders participated actively in the administration of Occupied Japan, 1945-52. Their major goal was the creation of an American-style Japanese labor movement which could offset the economic dominance of the great Zaibatsu businesses, forcing them to attend more to domestic economic needs and less to foreign trade in competition with American interests, and which could serve as a political bulwark against both supernationalism and communism. A large labor movement did arise in Japan, but its leaders, even the non-Communists, generally opposed American policies, considering them contrary to the interests of Japanese workers. Based on English-language primary sources; 67 notes.
                                                                    T. L. Powers

1535. Sharpston, Michael. INTERNATIONAL SUB-CONTRACT-ING. *Oxford Econ. Papers [Great Britain] 1975 27(1): 94-135.* Surveys the process of subcontracting manufacturing by developed countries such as Great Britain, Japan, and the United States, to developing nations, 1966-76, and analyzes the reasons for its growth. Economic and political effects of this practice are widespread. Overall high profits to the contracting firms have not resulted. Protectionist lobbying against imported subcontracted goods is confined to unions and hence is less effective than combined lobbying against direct imports from developing countries. Unskilled labor tends to experience a net loss from international subcontracting, though the latter may be an alternative to legal or illegal immigration of workers. Labor's hostility to the practice is chiefly concerned with possible unemployment effects. International subcontracting by retailing interests creates adjustment problems for both labor and small, backward firms with the developed countries, where government assistance may be ill-organized. 7 tables.   D. H. Murdoch

1536. Singelmann, Joachim and Browning, Harley L. INDUSTRIAL TRANSFORMATION AND OCCUPATIONAL CHANGE IN THE U.S., 1960-70. *Social Forces 1980 59(1): 246-264.* Increasingly, sociologists concerned with occupational mobility and the changes in the occupational distribution are turning their attention to the structural conditions for such changes. One important change has been industry shifts, particularly the decline of agriculture and the growth of services. In this paper we argue that industry shifts have an important effect on changes in the occupational structure. Using a shift-share approach, changes in the occupational structure of the United States between 1960 and 1970 are decomposed into an industry shift effect, an occupational composition effect, and an interaction effect. These effects vary for major occupational categories, but for total US employment the industry shift effect accounted for about two-thirds of the change in occupational structure, the composition effect for one-third, and the interaction effect was negligible. It is not likely that there will be as important shifts in the industry structure during the next 30 years as in the last 30 years. But it has been the industry shifts that have mostly contributed to an expansion of the higher status occupations, particularly professionals and managers. Therefore, unless the occupational composition changes in such a way as to compensate for the diminishing effects of the industry structure, structural opportunities will either remain at current levels or even decline in the years to come.   J

1537. Sommers, Dixie and Eck, Alan. OCCUPATIONAL MOBILITY IN THE AMERICAN LABOR FORCE. *Monthly Labor Rev. 1977 100(1): 3-19.* Analyzes occupational mobility in the American labor force between 1965 and 1970, using data collected in the 1970 Census. Makes comparisons between the census data and other data sources to further examine the transfer and labor force separation rates.

1538. Stahura, John M. THE EVOLUTION OF SUBURBAN FUNCTIONAL ROLES. *Pacific Sociol. Rev. 1978 21(4): 423-440.* Persisting stable socioeconomic characteristics (housing, employment opportunities, incomes) differentially select out suitable replacement populations for suburban areas, and maintain a constant socioeconomic atmosphere.

1539. Stradley, Scott A. A DESCRIPTION OF THE DETERMINANTS OF THE AVERAGE PHYSICAL PRODUCT OF LABOR IN UNDERGROUND COAL MINING. *North Dakota Q. 1977 45(4):*

128-141. Geological conditions and federal regulations determine the yield of underground coal mines; covers 1969-77.

1540. Swanson, Dorothy. ANNUAL BIBLIOGRAPHY ON AMERICAN LABOR HISTORY: 1976. *Labor Hist. 1977 18(4): 545-569.* A bibliography of periodical articles, dissertations, and works-in-progress in labor history. There are 301 entries organized chronologically and topically.   L. L. Athey

1541. Swanson, Dorothy. ANNUAL BIBLIOGRAPHY ON AMERICAN LABOR HISTORY, 1974. *Labor Hist. 1975 16(4): 521-540.* A bibliography of articles, dissertations and works in progress. There are 267 entries organized chronologically and topically.   L. L. Athey

1542. Swartz, Katherine. HELPING THE JOBLESS: THEORIES AND PRACTICE. *Wilson Q. 1980 4(1): 138-149.* Describes the difficulties of defining and alleviating joblessness in the United States from 1946 to 1980, especially the difficulty of finding the causes of unemployment.

1543. Thomas, June Manning. THE IMPACT OF CORPORATE TOURISM ON GULLAH BLACKS: NOTES ON ISSUES OF EMPLOYMENT. *Phylon 1980 41(1): 1-11.* The Negroes living on the Hilton Head, Johns, and Wadmalaw islands of South Carolina are undergoing a transition from a relatively quiet farm life, as a developing and sophisticated tourist industry uses them as a low-skilled labor force. 15 notes.   N. G. Sapper

1544. Van der Speck, Peter G. MEXICO'S BOOMING BORDER ZONE: A MAGNET FOR LABOR-INTENSIVE AMERICAN PLANTS. *Inter-Am. Econ. Affairs 1975 29(1): 33-47.* Discusses advantages and disadvantages of locating US plants along the border, in Mexico, to take advantage of low wages in Mexico. Map, 3 figs.
                                                                    D. A. Franz

1545. Vickery, Clair. WOMEN'S ECONOMIC CONTRIBUTION TO THE FAMILY. Smith, Ralph E., ed. *The Subtle Revolution: Women at Work* (Washington: Urban Inst., 1979): 159-200. Discusses how women working in the paid labor force affect their families' standard of living, focusing on what a wife's employment adds to her family's security and well-being, and how it changes housework patterns; 1950-73.

1546. Wertheim, Edward G. WORKER PARTICIPATION AND INDUSTRIAL RELATIONS: THE TREND TOWARD DECENTRALIZATION. *Industrial Relations [Canada] 1976 31(1): 98-110.* Examines worker participation and industrial relations, concluding that in the United States and Canada where much decentralization has already taken place, worker control is not so badly needed, unlike Europe, where employee input appears as a complement to traditional worker-management relations, 1960's-70's.

1547. Westin, Alan and Wurf, Jerry. ONCE THEY JOIN THIS DAMN UNION, WE PROTECT THEIR RIGHTS. *Civil Liberties Rev. 1975 2(3): 105-124.* A conversation with labor leader Jerry Wurf.
                                                                    J

1548. Whyte, William Foote. IN SUPPORT OF VOLUNTARY EMPLOYEE OWNERSHIP. *Society 1978 15(6): 73-82.* Discusses the advantages, conditions for success, and means of achieving employee-community ownership of plants that would otherwise be shut down, and gives a history of cooperatively owned plants in the United States and Mondragon, Spain, during 1943-77, in a presentation in support of the Voluntary Job Preservation and Community Stabilization bill introduced to the House of Representatives in 1978.

1549. Zuboff, Shoshanah. PROBLEMS OF SYMBOLIC TOIL. *Dissent 1982 29(1): 51-61.* US labor is under attack on at least two fronts: the Reagan administration is using the power of the state to dismantle decades of protective regulations; and, taking new initiative and courage from their friends in Washington, the corporations are accelerating the pace of automation, plant closings and the export of jobs; explores the many ways workers are coping with these attacks, particularly with the computer revolution.

1550. —. AMERICAN LABOR'S STAKE IN A CHANGING WORLD ECONOMY. *Monthly Labor Rev. 1977 100(3): 34-50.* Provides excerpts from several of the papers presented at the international conference "American Labor's Stake and Voice in a Changing World Economy" held 14-16 December 1976 at Port Chester, N.Y.

1551. —. BIBLIOGRAPHIC ESSAY. Cantor, Milton, ed. *American Workingclass Culture: Explorations in American Labor and Social History* (Westport, Conn.: Greenwood, 1979): 423-427. Traces the rise of American labor historiography since the 1960's, emphasizing the influence of E. P. Thompson and Eric Hobsbawn on the more recent scholarship.

1552. —. CAPITAL'S FLIGHT: THE APPAREL INDUSTRY MOVES SOUTH. Mora, Magdalena and DelCastillo, Adelaida R., ed. *Mexican Women in the United States: Struggles Past and Present* (Los Angeles: U. of California Chicano Studies Res. Center, 1980): 95-104. The garment industry provides a clear illustration of capital's mobility and its effect on the working class. Since World War II, thousands of jobs in the apparel sector were exported. Domestic production has dramatically shifted its geographic locus, as the firms have abandoned their birthplaces in the large industrial cities of the Northeast and Midwest in favor of the rural South. The reasons for this exodus and its effects on the working class, particularly in the Northeast and the South, are discussed. Reprinted from *NACLA Report on the Americas* formerly *NACLA's Latin America and Empire Report* 1977, 11(3): 2-9; 2 tables, 32 notes. J. Powell

1553. —. LA INDUSTRIA NORTEAMERICANA Y LA EMIGRACIÓN DE TRABAJADORES [North American industry and the emigration of workers]. *Bol. del Archivo General de la Nación [Mexico] 1980 4(4): 53-56.* Three documents from the Manuel Avila Camacho papers in the National Archives of Mexico denounce the activities of certain American companies in exporting products to Mexico. Photo. J. A. Lewis

1554. —. [METHODS OF IMPROVING THE CONDITION OF THE POOR]. *Social Problems 1978 26(2): 160-178.*
Roach, Jack L. and Roach, Janet K. MOBILIZING THE POOR: ROAD TO A DEAD END, *pp. 160-171.* Discusses Frances Fox Piven's and Richard Cloward's assertion that the poor should improve their position by using socially disruptive tactics, and suggests that activity toward improvement should be implemented within organized labor. Covers 1960-78.
Piven, Frances Fox and Cloward, Richard A. SOCIAL MOVEMENTS AND SOCIETAL CONDITIONS: A RESPONSE TO ROACH AND ROACH, *pp. 172-178.* The authors defend their position, arguing that Roach and Roach considered only one aspect of a complex issue.

1555. —. THE WORKING AMERICAN. *Am. Heritage 1980 31(4): 8-21.* Describes Gallery 1199, established by District 1199, National Union of Hospital and Health Care Employees in New York City; the paintings depict the American laborer, and are part of the Union's two-year "Bread and Roses" cultural project.

The Worker

1556. Aronowitz, Stanley. AMERICAN WORKING CLASS CONSCIOUSNESS TODAY: AN INTERVIEW. *Rev. Française d'Etudes Américaines [France] 1976 (2): 97-106.* In an interview with Marianne Debouzy and John Atherton, Stanley Aronowitz discusses the American working class and its current problems, such as occupational hierarchy, labor conditions, working-class consciousness, and radicalization of the American labor movement.

1557. Arroyo, Laura E. INDUSTRIAL AND OCCUPATIONAL DISTRIBUTION OF CHICANA WORKERS. Sánchez, Rosaura and Martinez Cruz, Rosa, eds. *Essays on la Mujer* (Los Angeles, Ca.: Chicano Studies Center Publ., 1977): 150-187. Compiles and analyzes statistics on the labor force participation of Chicanas, or Mexican American women, in Texas and California. The overwhelming majority of Chicana workers are found in the lowest paid categories of the labor force. In 1969 their average annual wage was estimated at $3,000. A case

study of the Farah strike in El Paso, Texas adds insights into the specific conditions of Chicana garment workers and their success in organizing. Based primarily on statistics from the Equal Employment Opportunity Report of 1969; 9 tables, 17 notes. M. T. Wilson

1558. Asher, Robert. CONNECTICUT WORKERS AND TECHNOLOGICAL CHANGE, 1950-1980. *Connecticut Hist. 1983 (24): 47-62.* Interviews with Connecticut manually-skilled factory workers during 1950-80 demonstrate that technological advances have increased job satisfaction for some while decreasing it for other workers.

1559. Atchley, Robert C. RETIREMENT: LEAVING THE WORLD OF WORK. *Ann. of the Am. Acad. of Pol. and Social Sci. 1982 (464): 120-131.* Currently, high levels of desire for retirement and poor health cause most retirements to occur at or near the minimum age for retirement. Those who retire voluntarily have little or no difficulty adjusting. Those who are forced out by mandatory retirement policies tend to be dissatisfied at first, but eventually they adjust. And those who retire because of poor health are the most dissatisfied. Retirement itself has no predictable negative effect on physical health, self-esteem, or life satisfaction. A good adjustment to retirement depends on having a secure income, good health, meaningful activities, and high marital satisfaction. Given income and health, most retired persons adjust well. J/S

1560. Attinasi, John J. LANGUAGE ATTITUDES AND WORKING CLASS IDEOLOGY IN A PUERTO RICAN BARRIO OF NEW YORK. *Ethnic Groups 1983 5(1-2): 55-78.* Two groups of Puerto Ricans studied exhibit strong loyalties to both the Spanish language and Puerto Rican culture. The lack of a rigorous ideology defending Spanish and the culture against bilingualism with English is not a negative characteristic, but a pragmatic reaction to a bilingual social situation. An "interpenetrating bilingualism" constitutes the first element of a bilingual working class consciousness in which positive attitudes reflect a recognition of change on the part of the working class, but a refusal to give up a distinctly Puerto Rican identity. J/S

1561. Baca, Reynaldo and Bryan, Dexter. MEXICAN UNDOCUMENTED WORKERS IN THE BINATIONAL COMMUNITY: A RESEARCH NOTE. *Int. Migration Rev. 1981 15(4): 737-748.* Discusses research on undocumented restaurant workers in Los Angeles who work in the United States and reside in both the United States and in Mexico, including information from a 1979 survey of undocumented workers regarding "citizenship aspirations and residency rights preferences," and "settlement patterns, employment histories, occupational aspirations, and resettlement plans."

1562. Baca-Ramirez, Reynaldo and Bryan, Dexter Edward. THE UNDOCUMENTED MEXICAN WORKER: A SOCIAL PROBLEM? *J. of Ethnic Studies 1980 8(1): 55-70.* Undocumented laborers from Mexico form a permanent force in the United States. Immigration has been stimulated by the desire for social mobility. A class structure is emerging with a new middle class of Mexican American professionals, a brown collar lower middle class, and an underclass of recent undocumented workers. Biblio. S

1563. Bach, Robert L. and Bach, Jennifer B. EMPLOYMENT PATTERNS OF SOUTHEAST ASIAN REFUGEES. *Monthly Labor Rev. 1980 103(10): 31-38.* The main goal of the Refugee Act (US, 1980) is to locate and obtain employment for refugees from South Vietnam, Laos, and Cambodia since they began arriving in the United States in 1975; data from 1975 and 1979 indicate that each year of residence increases the likelihood of employment, that arrivals after 1978 face more difficulty adjusting and finding employment due to US economic conditions, and that in general the occupational profiles of Southeast Asian refugees and US workers are similar.

1564. Bach, Robert L. THE NEW CUBAN IMMIGRANTS: THEIR BACKGROUND AND PROSPECTS. *Monthly Labor Rev. 1980 103(10): 39-46.* Describes Cuban immigrants who arrived in Miami, Florida, from the sealift in 1980; the early arrivals in general had above-average education and job skills, and although many refugees were ex-offenders, many had been political prisoners; compares the 1980 arrivals with a group that entered the United States in 1973-74.

1565. Baker, Katharine Gratwick. MOBILITY AND FOREIGN SERVICE WIVES. *Foreign Service J. 1976 53(2): 12-14, 27-29.* Discusses the views held by the wives of Foreign Service officers primarily in 1974 on the impact of their husband's occupational mobility on themselves and their families.

1566. Baker, Mary Holland. MOTHER'S OCCUPATION AND CHILDREN'S ATTAINMENTS. *Pacific Sociol. Rev. 1981 24(2): 237-254.* Using data collected from families in a midwestern city, analyzes the effect of mother's occupation on children's attainments, finding that in dual-employment families the mothers' occupation had a significant effect on both daughters' and sons' academic achievements.

1567. Barnes, William F. THE WILLINGNESS OF UNEMPLOYED JOBSEEKERS TO BE OCCUPATIONALLY FLEXIBLE DOWNWARD OR TO BE RETRAINED. *Q. Rev. of Econ. and Business 1974 14(2): 75-84.* "Investigates variables which affect the unemployed individual's willingness to be occupationally flexible downward or to be retrained. Income maximizing behavior for investment in job search and retraining predicts explanatory variables of flexibility and retraining. Data for this study were provided by a questionnaire survey covering 2,476 unemployed jobseekers registered at employment service offices in 12 cities in 6 states. Since the measures of dependent behavior in this study are binary, linear discriminant analysis is used to test predictions." J

1568. Barrett, Nancy S. WOMEN IN THE JOB MARKET: OCCUPATIONS, EARNINGS, AND CAREER OPPORTUNITIES. Smith, Ralph E., ed. *The Subtle Revolution: Women at Work* (Washington: Urban Inst., 1979): 31-61. Focuses on the employment and income patterns of American women in the labor force, reflecting on the implications of the changes of the past decade.

1569. Bartlett, Robin L. and Poulton-Callahan, Charles. CHANGING FAMILY STRUCTURES AND THE DISTRIBUTION OF FAMILY INCOME, 1951-1976. *Social Sci. Q. 1982 63(1): 28-38.* The recent increase in the proportion of families with employed wives has tended to decrease income inequality among male-headed families; concurrently, the recent increases in female-headed families has tended to increase overall family income inequality, offsetting the former trend and creating an illusion of distributional stability.

1570. Bassett, W. Bruce. DOES IT PAY TO LEARN? *Labor Hist. 1983 24(2): 254-258.* Reviews Russell W. Rumberger's *Overeducation in the U.S. Labor Market* (1981). The educational requirements for the American work force were lower than the educational attainments of the working population, leaving many workers overqualified for the jobs they held. Note.   L. F. Velicer

1571. Beck, Scott H. THE ROLE OF OTHER FAMILY MEMBERS IN INTERGENERATIONAL OCCUPATIONAL MOBILITY. *Sociol. Q. 1983 24(2): 273-285.* Data from the 1960's and 70's indicate that the occupations of mothers and paternal grandfathers, as well as fathers, significantly affect the choice of sons' occupations.

1572. Beckett, Joyce O. and Smith, Audrey D. WORK AND FAMILY ROLES: EGALITARIAN MARRIAGE IN BLACK AND WHITE FAMILIES. *Social Service Rev. 1981 55(2): 314-326.* Using statistical data collected in a 1976 survey, presents evidence that although whites are more egalitarian in theory, blacks tend in fact to devise egalitarian arrangements in employment and household duties; black husbands share domestic and child-care roles more often than their white counterparts.

1573. Bednarzik, Robert W. SHORT WORKWEEKS DURING ECONOMIC DOWNTURNS. *Monthly Labor Rev. 1983 106(6): 3-11.* Part-time employment during the 1982 recession increased both because of cutbacks in weekly hours due to slack work conditions and because many workers could not find full-time jobs.

1574. Bednarzik, Robert W. WORKSHARING IN THE U.S.: ITS PREVALENCE AND DURATION. *Monthly Labor Rev. 1980 103(7): 3-12.* Examines worksharing arrangements (pay and working hour reductions so all workers can continue working), and provides statistics on the number of worksharers, how long before they return to full-time status, their transition to part-time or unemployed status, and other

information from the Current Population Survey of 1976-77, and discusses worksharing as it relates to business cycles since the 1950's.

1575. Bell, Carolyn Shaw. AGE, SEX, MARRIAGE, AND JOBS. *Public Interest 1973 (30): 76-87.* Discusses whether unemployment during 1950-72 was related to the entrance of more women and teenage youths into the labor market.

1576. Benson, Charles S. and Lareau, Annette P. THE UNEASY PLACE OF VOCATIONAL EDUCATION. *Educ. and Urban Soc. 1982 15(1): 104-124.* Vocational education programs in the United States are more effectively located in special vocational education schools than in secondary high schools; focuses on the experiences of minorities and women in California, Colorado, Illinois, and Florida during 1979-81.

1577. Berger, Brigitte. PEOPLE WORK: THE YOUTH CULTURE AND THE LABOR MARKET. *Public Interest 1974 (35): 55-66.* Young people continue to demand high-paying and personally fulfilling employment, although there is no current expansion in the labor market at the white-collar level. The government should respond by creating jobs ("people work") which meet this demand.   S

1578. Blackwell, James E. and Haug, Marie. RELATIONS BETWEEN BLACK BOSSES AND BLACK WORKERS. *Black Scholar 1973 4(4): 36-43.* There is a need to update theories of intraracial group and intraethnic group relations in light of new developments, 1960's-70's, of the black liberation movement; uses a case study of black workers and their relations with black bosses in Cleveland, Ohio, as the basis for such a model.

1579. Blasi, Joseph R. and Whyte, William Foote. WORKER OWNERSHIP AND PUBLIC POLICY. *Policy Studies J. 1981 10(2): 320-337.* Examines the development of expanding support for worker ownership in the United States, providing a brief review of various types of state and federal legislation; also presents a discussion of the problems in establishing and maintaining a worker-owned firm as well as various requirements for implementing wide-scale worker ownership.

1580. Blitz, Rudolph C. AN INTERNATIONAL COMPARISON OF WOMEN'S PARTICIPATION IN THE PROFESSIONS. *J. of Developing Areas 1975 9(4): 499-510.* Analyzes the role of women in the professions and the labor market in 49 countries in various stages of economic development. Historically the percentage of women in the professions has increased just as per capita income has increased. Using equally weighted indicators of per capita energy consumption and percentage of male labor force in non-agricultural pursuits, it was discovered that female labor force participation increases with advancing economic development. In the early stages of development where conservative values predominate, women were employed primarily in the lower skill strata. Based on 1950-67 censuses of 49 nations; 3 tables, 24 notes.   O. W. Eads, Jr.

1581. Blostin, Allan P. IS EMPLOYER-SPONSORED LIFE INSURANCE DECLINING RELATIVE TO OTHER BENEFITS? *Monthly Labor Rev. 1981 104(9): 31-33.* Compares changes in 56 life insurance plans provided by 44 large employers or "multi-employer associations" between 1971 and 1980, concluding that life insurance plans changed very little compared to health and retirement plans, but life insurance payments did increase.

1582. Borjas, George J. THE EARNINGS OF MALE HISPANIC IMMIGRANTS IN THE UNITED STATES. *Industrial and Labor Relations Rev. 1982 35(3): 343-353.* There are major differences in the rate of economic mobility of the various Hispanic groups. In particular, the rate of economic progress by Cuban immigrants exceeds that of other Hispanic groups, the result in part of the fact that Cuban immigrants have invested more heavily in US schooling than other Hispanic immigrants arriving in this country at the same time. These findings are consistent with the hypothesis that political refugees are likely to face higher costs of return immigration than do "economic" immigrants, and therefore the former have greater incentives to adapt rapidly to the US labor market.   J

1583. Bould, Sally. BLACK AND WHITE FAMILIES: FACTORS AFFECTING THE WIFE'S CONTRIBUTION TO THE FAMILY

INCOME WHERE THE HUSBAND'S INCOME IS LOW TO MODERATE. *Sociol. Q. 1977 18(4): 536-547.* The economic role of the black wife in contrast to her husband's weak economic position is a key assumption in Moynihan's thesis of a black matriarchy. Using the National Longitudinal Survey of women, aged 30 to 44, in 1967, this paper examines the factors affecting the wife's contribution to the family income for both black and white families where the husband's income is below the median of all male-headed families. The results suggest that black wives and white wives respond similarly with respect to their overall contribution, the demand for female labor, and the effect of children. There is no support, moreover, for Moynihan's assumption that black wives are compensating for their husband's weak economic position. It appears, however, that the definition of the provider may differ among black families and white families.   J

1584. Bould, Sally. UNEMPLOYMENT AS A FACTOR IN EARLY RETIREMENT DECISIONS. *Am. J. of Econ. and Sociol. 1980 39(2): 123-136.* Is retiring early a way for older workers to cope with the stigma and discouragement of unemployment? A regression analysis using the National Longitudinal Survey sample of American men age 52-64 in 1973 shows that weeks of previous unemployment is significantly related to early retirement for both black and white males. This relationship holds when controlling for social security and pension eligibility, assets, health limitations, family responsibilities, occupation, changes in the unemployment rate and urban residence. The results suggest that social policy concerning retirement prior to age 65 should take into account the important role of unemployment in pushing workers out of the labor force into early retirement. 4 tables, 34 notes, biblio.   J

1585. Bowers, Norman. TRACKING YOUTH JOBLESSNESS: PERSISTENT OR FLEETING? *Monthly Labor Rev. 1982 105(2): 3-15.* High turnover, seasonality, and work-school transitions are some reasons for high unemployment among young people; recurrent and extensive joblessness among a relatively few persons is an important aspect of the labor market.

1586. Bowman, James S. WHISTLE-BLOWING IN BUSINESS AND GOVERNMENT. *Policy Studies Rev. 1983 2(4): 810-812.* Bibliography on the topic of challenging abuses at work.

1587. Bradshaw, Benjamin Spencer. POTENTIAL LABOR FORCE SUPPLY, PLACEMENT, AND MIGRATION OF MEXICAN-AMERICAN AND OTHER MALES IN THE TEXAS-MEXICO BORDER REGION. *Int. Migration Rev. 1976 10(1): 29-45.* Discusses the migration and potential labor force supply of Mexican American males in the Texas-Mexico border region in the 1960's and 70's.

1588. Brand, H. ON THE ECONOMIC CONDITION OF AMERICAN WORKERS. *Dissent 1981 28(3): 331-338.* Cites three reasons for the economic demise of US labor: 1) the demise of the unions in industries, 2) the retreat of government from promoting full employment, and 3) the drive for a subminimum wage.

1589. Braverman, Miriam. YOUTH, UNEMPLOYMENT, AND WORK WITH YOUNG ADULTS. *J. of Lib. Hist. 1981 16(2): 353-364.* Explores the consistently high and stubbornly persistent unemployment rate of youth since 1954, with a view to developing an approach that will serve as a model for an extended study in this and other areas seriously affecting the lives of youth. Discusses the evolution of government programs developed to deal with it, including Job Corps, the Neighborhood Youth Corps, and notes the role of the library in providing career materials. Secondary sources; 41 notes.   J. Powell

1590. Brecher, Jeremy and Costello, Tim. WAGE LABOR IN THE U.S. TODAY. *Radical Am. 1976 10(4): 7-24.* Interviews with working class men and women obtained during a tour of the United States, excluding the South, in the summer of 1973 provide the basis for a review of the existing structure of social relations. Concludes that most current members of the working class have shared expanding aspirations that make a steady job and income inadequate definitions of a good life and that they now face sharp deterioration of real incomes and general social conditions.   N. Lederer

1591. Briar, Katherine Hooper. LAY-OFFS AND SOCIAL WORK INTERVENTION. *Urban & Social Change Rev. 1983 16(2): 9-14.* Examines ways in which social workers can help to ease the social and economic impact of layoffs, and aid the jobless in finding new employment.

1592. Brown, Gary D. DISCRIMINATION AND PAY DISPARITIES BETWEEN WHITE MEN AND WOMEN. *Monthly Labor Rev. 1978 101(3): 17-22.* Surveys employment discrimination against white women; wages differed between white men and women, based on return to investment in human capital, rate of employment, type of employer, and return of experience, 1970's.

1593. Burawoy, Michael. THE FUNCTIONS AND REPRODUCTION OF MIGRANT LABOR: COMPARATIVE MATERIAL FROM SOUTHERN AFRICA AND THE UNITED STATES. *Am. J. of Sociol. 1976 81(5): 1050-1087.* For a capitalist economy to function, its labor force must be maintained; that is, workers must receive a historically determined minimal day-to-day subsistence. It must also be renewed; that is, vacancies must be filled. A system of migrant labor is characterized by the institutional differentiation and physical separation of the processes of renewal and maintenance. Accordingly, migrant labor entails a dual dependence upon employement in one place and an alternate economy and/or state in another. In addition, the separation of migrant workers from their families is implied. It is enforced through specific legal and political mechanisms which regulate geographical mobility and impose restrictions on the occupational mobility of migrants. These mechanisms in turn are made possible by the migrant workers' powerlessness in the place of employment, in the labor market, and under the legal and political systems where they are employed. One consequence of a system of migrant labor is the externalization, to an alternate economy and/or state, of certain costs of labor-force renewal—costs normally borne by the employer and/or state of employment. This framework is developed and applied to migrant farm workers in California and migrant mine workers in South Africa. The differences between the two systems are highlighted and analyzed in terms of the broader features of the respective social structures. Finally, the implications of the theoretical scheme are discussed and extended to an interpretation of race relations.   J

1594. Bustamante, Jorge. "ESPALDAS MOJADAS," MATERIA PRIME PARA LA EXPANSIÓN DEL CAPITAL NORTEAMERICANO ["Wet-backs," raw material for the expansion of US capital]. *Cahiers des Amériques Latines [France] 1975 (12): 275-314.* Focuses on the attractiveness of labor in the United States to Mexicans.

1595. Bustamante, Jorge A. and Cockroft, James D. ONE MORE TIME: THE "UNDOCUMENTED." *Radical Am. 1981 15(6): 7-15.* Increased unemployment in Mexico, caused by US dominated multinational corporations and by a growing lack of unskilled labor in parts of the US labor market, insures a continued presence of the "undocumented." The size of this population and the costs to the United States are frequently exaggerated by the press and by organized labor. However, governmental negotiations to structure the flow of illegal aliens will be mingled with concern for oil concessions and for a common market arrangement with Mexico. 4 notes, 7 illus.   C. M. Hough

1596. Bustamante, Jorge A. EL ESPALDA MOJADA, REPORTE DE UN OBSERVADOR PARTICIPANTE [The wetback: notes of a participating observer]. *Rev. Mexicana de Ciencia Pol. [Mexico] 1973 19(71): 81-107.* Though it is considered illegal in the United States, to become a wetback is a socially accepted means of entering the United States in order to seek work, and carries no stigma in Mexico.

1597. Cannon, Lynn Weber. NORMATIVE EMBOURGEOISEMENT AMONG MANUAL WORKERS: A REEXAMINATION USING LONGITUDINAL DATA. *Sociol. Q. 1980 21(2): 185-195.* Using national surveys between 1956 and 1975, verifies the assumption that manual workers are becoming middle class in their cognitive orientation and further finds that this rate is greater than for nonmanual workers; longitudinal data are crucial for such studies.

1598. Chadwick, Bruce A. and Bahr, Howard M. FACTORS ASSOCIATED WITH UNEMPLOYMENT AMONG AMERICAN INDIANS IN THE PACIFIC NORTHWEST. *Phylon 1978 39(4):*

356-368. Examines several factors in correlation with high rates of unemployment among American Indians in Umatilla County in northeast Oregon, including education, traditionalism, achievement motivation, discrimination, and others, based on statistics from the 1970 US Census.

1599. Chao Ling Wang. OCCUPATIONAL SKIN DISEASE CONTINUES TO PLAGUE INDUSTRY. *Monthly Labor Rev. 1979 102(2): 17-22.* Though incidence of occupational skin disease has fallen since 1976, lost work time remains high with agricultural and manufacturing workers being most susceptible to dermatosis, 1978.

1600. Chavkin, Wendy. OCCUPATIONAL HAZARDS TO REPRODUCTION: A REVIEW ESSAY AND ANNOTATED BIBLIOGRAPHY. *Feminist Studies 1979 5(2): 310-325.* Reviews Andrea Hricko and Melanie Brunt's *Working For Your Life: A Woman's Guide to Job Health Hazards* (Berkeley, California: Labor Occupational Health Project and Public Citizen's Health Research Group, U. of California, 1976) and Jeanne Mager Stellman's *Women's Work, Women's Health: Myths and Realities* (New York: Pantheon Books, 1977) covering 1970-77; and provides an annotated bibliography of articles, journals, pamphlets, and books on the effects of hazardous occupations and exposure to dangerous substances at the workplace on the reproductive systems of men and women; 1974-78.   G. Smith

1601. Chelius, James R. ECONOMIC AND DEMOGRAPHIC ASPECTS OF THE OCCUPATIONAL INJURY PROBLEM. *Q. Rev. of Econ. and Business 1979 19(2): 65-70.* The increase in industrial accidents from 1964 to 1970 was actually due to the influx of younger workers into the labor market; the compulsory safety rules and regulations of the Occupational Safety and Health Act (US, 1970), while well-intentioned, are too rigid to be truly meaningful and effective in preventing accidents, penalizing employers, and assuring proper compensation to injured employees.

1602. Chelte, Anthony F.; Wright, James; and Tausky, Curt. DID JOB SATISFACTION REALLY DROP DURING THE 1970'S? *Monthly Labor Rev. 1982 105(11): 33-36.* The significant drop in job satisfaction nationwide found by Graham Staines and Robert Quinn in 1979 is not repeated in other surveys.

1603. Chiswick, Barry R. THE EFFECT OF AMERICANIZATION ON THE EARNINGS OF FOREIGN-BORN MEN. *J. of Pol. Econ. 1978 86(5): 897-922.* Analyzes the earnings of immigrant men compared with native born and among foreign born according to their country of origin, years in the United States, and citizenship; uses 1970 census data.

1604. Chiswick, Barry R. IMMIGRANTS IN THE U.S. LABOR MARKET. *Ann. of the Am. Acad. of Pol. and Social Sci. 1982 (460): 64-72.* Relative to the population, immigration has increased fivefold since the trough of the 1930's, and in recent years the annual legal inflow has been about 2.2 immigrants per year per thousand population. In the past 15 years, Europe and Canada have declined in importance as sources of immigrants, while Asia, Latin America, and the Caribbean have increased in importance. Illegal immigration has also increased. Overall, adult male immigrants earn about the same as the adult male native-born population, but important differences among the foreign born are attributable to duration of residence in the United States, reason for migrating, and country of origin. On arrival, immigrants have low earnings compared with native born, but with increased length of U.S. residence, their earnings rise. Economic migrants reach earnings equality with the native born when they have been in the United States for about 11 to 15 years. Refugees and tied movers have lower earnings than those who move for economic reasons. Illegal aliens from Mexico have labor market characteristics very similar to those of legal immigrants from Mexico.   J

1605. Clemente, Frank and Summers, Gene F. THE JOURNEY TO WORK OF RURAL INDUSTRIAL EMPLOYEES. *Social Forces 1975 54(1): 212-219.* In previous research on the journey to work several variables have consistently emerged as correlates of distance commuted. Unfortunately, virtually all previous analyses have been confined to metropolitan areas. Thus, there is a question of the generalizability of these findings to less urbanized regions. The present research examines the commuting patterns of 959 white male employees of a large manufacturing facility in rural Illinois. Hypotheses regarding the impact of (1) SES, (2) age, and (3) length of employment upon distance between place of residence and place of work are tested by least-squares analysis. The results indicate no support for any of the hypotheses derived from the model of metropolitan commuting. Further, the composite effect of the independent variables accounts for only one percent of the variation in distance traveled to work. These findings strongly indicate that the model of metropolitan commuting is not applicable to nonmetropolitan regions.   J

1606. Cohen, Joan. THE CULTURE OF THE BLACKLIST. *Mankind 1978 6(3): 16-20.* For over 15 years, scores of Hollywood performers, writers, producers, and directors were forbidden from working in their craft owing to their real or alleged previous contacts with left-wing ideologies. Their condition resulted in many personal tragedies, including broken friendships and marriages and the destruction of careers. Only in recent years have some of those victimized been able to return to their professions. Many of those "blacklisted" emigrated to Europe or Mexico where they either participated in native entertainment enterprises or continued to write for the Hollywood market under assumed names. Excerpts from the correspondence of screen writer Dalton Trumbo illustrate the problems inherent in the latter. Others remained in the United States and either retired or assumed other occupations.   N. Lederer

1607. Connette, Woody. WORKER OWNED: SOME SOUTHERN BEGINNINGS. *Southern Changes 1982 4(6): 11-15.* Discusses the problems and aspirations of modern worker-owned businesses, focusing on examples in the Deep South.

1608. Conte, Michael and Tannenbaum, Arnold S. EMPLOYEE-OWNED COMPANIES: IS THE DIFFERENCE MEASURABLE? *Monthly Labor Rev. 1978 101(7): 23-28.* A recent study of 98 firms reveals the likelihood of a positive correlation between employee ownership and higher productivity, profitability, and motivation.

1609. Conway, Mimi. COTTON DUST KILLS, AND IT'S KILLING ME. *Southern Exposure 1978 6(2): 29-39.* Byssinosis, "brown lung disease," is a prevalent problem among long term employees of Southern cotton mills. The mill owners, including Burlington Industries, Inc. which enjoys an excellent reputation in the safety field, have strenuously endeavored to avoid payment of compensation for workers' claims of disability caused by byssinosis. The Carolina Brown Lung Association has been organized to forward workers' claims for compensation. Burlington's insurance agent, Liberty Mutual Insurance Co., has by and large to date successfully thwarted payments for byssinosis-caused illnesses through the workmen's compensation system. Liberty Mutual is probably liable to third party suits resulting from possible negligence in serving as safety inspectors for the mills. Based on personal interviews.   N. Lederer

1610. Critchlow, Robert V. TECHNOLOGY AND LABOR IN ELECTRIC POWER AND GAS INDUSTRY. *Monthly Labor Rev. 1978 101(11): 18-22.* Discusses the effects of new technology on the occupational structure of the electric power and natural gas industry, 1960-77.

1611. Cuthbert, Richard W. and Stevens, Joe B. THE NET ECONOMIC INCENTIVE FOR ILLEGAL MEXICAN MIGRATION: A CASE STUDY. *Int. Migration Rev. 1981 15(3): 543-550.* Studies Mexican farm workers in the Hood River Valley in Oregon during the fall apple harvest to determine the "net earnings differential" between wages earned in the United States and those earned in Mexico; net earnings in the United States were three times those in Mexico, less than usually stated by researchers.

1612. Dabrowski, Irene. WORKING-CLASS WOMEN AND CIVIC ACTION: A CASE STUDY OF AN INNOVATIVE COMMUNITY ROLE. *Policy Studies J. 1983 11(3): 427-435.* Women in the working-class neighborhood of Carondelet in St. Louis, Missouri, participated extensively in civic and political action projects in the 1970's, and comprised three-fourths of all volunteers and half of the leadership positions in community organizations.

1613. Dalia, Joan Talbert and Guest, Avery M. EMBOURGEOISE-MENT AMONG BLUE-COLLAR WORKERS? *Sociol. Q. 1975 16(3): 291-304.* This paper examines the notion that blue-collar workers have been converting from working-class to middle-class orientations as a consequence of gains in income and education over the past few decades. Cross-sectional analysis of survey data for white workers and spouses reveals that a considerable manual-nonmanual subjective class schism persists when remaining differences in income and education are taken into account. The gap is maintained both by an adherence to working-class identification among blue-collar workers at all socioeconomic levels and by a weaker tendency for these workers, compared with white-collar workers, to use income and educational status as criteria for self-placement in the class system. Longitudinal analysis further indicates that embourgeoisement among blue-collar workers has been slight and suggests that the manual-nonmanual gap in class orientations is widening.   J

1614. Daly, Patricia A. UNPAID FAMILY WORKERS: LONG-TERM DECLINE CONTINUES. *Monthly Labor Rev. 1982 105(10): 3-5.* Discusses demographic changes in the number of unpaid family members working in family businesses, which has dropped by more than 50% from 1950 to 1981, with special attention to occupational trends, and hours worked.

1615. Darian, Jean C. FACTORS INFLUENCING THE RISING LABOR FORCE PARTICIPATION RATES OF MARRIED WOMEN WITH PRE-SCHOOL CHILDREN. *Social Sci. Q. 1976 56(4): 614-630.* Investigates factors influencing the rising labor force participation rates of married women with pre-school children.   J

1616. Davis, King E. JOBS, INCOME, BUSINESS AND CHARITY IN THE BLACK COMMUNITY. *Black Scholar 1977 9(4): 2-11.* Examines black income, spending patterns, income sources, philanthropy, and fundraising, 1944-74.

1617. DeFleur, Lois B. and Menke, Ben A. LEARNING ABOUT THE LABOR FORCE: OCCUPATIONAL KNOWLEDGE AMONG HIGH SCHOOL MALES. *Sociology of Educ. 1975 48(3): 324-345.* Assesses occupational knowledge among high school males from urban and rural areas in eastern Washington, 1958-72.

1618. DeFronzo, James. FEMALE LABOR FORCE PARTICIPATION AND FERTILITY IN 48 STATES: CROSS-SECTIONAL AND CHANGE ANALYSES FOR THE 1960-1970 DECADE. *Sociol. and Social Res. 1980 64(2): 263-278.* Investigates the relationship between fertility and labor force participation of married women, using a nonrecursive model. The findings provide at least tentative support for the hypothesis of reciprocal negative effects between the fertility and the labor force participation of young married women.   J/S

1619. Derber, Charles and Schwartz, William. TOWARD A THEORY OF WORKER PARTICIPATION. *Sociol. Inquiry 1983 53(1): 61-78.* Discusses the implications for management theory of the emergence since the 1970's of "relative worker autonomy," which preserves the authority of management over the labor process while assigning limited control over production to the workers.

1620. Derber, Charles. UNDEREMPLOYMENT AND THE AMERICAN DREAM: "UNDEREMPLOYMENT-CONSCIOUSNESS" AND RADICALISM AMONG YOUNG WORKERS. *Sociol. Inquiry 1979 49(4): 37-44.* Analyzes the work attitudes and political views of educated young workers unable to find jobs commensurate with their education and skills, on the basis of a survey conducted in Massachusetts in 1977; by suggesting that the optimistic promise of the American Dream to some degree offsets discontent, modifies the assumption that such workers tend to hold radical political views.

1621. Deutermann, William V., Jr. and Brown, Scott Campbell. VOLUNTARY PART-TIME WORKERS: A GROWING PART OF THE LABOR FORCE. *Monthly Labor Rev. 1978 101(6): 3-10.* Chronicles the rise in part-time employment during 1954-77, mainly of women and youth.

1622. De Vise, Peter. THE SUBURBANIZATION OF JOBS AND MINORITY EMPLOYMENT. *Econ. Geog. 1976 52(4): 348-362.* Analyzes journey-to-work data among black workers in Chicago, Illinois, 1960-70.

1623. Dowdall, Jean A. STRUCTURAL AND ATTITUDINAL FACTORS ASSOCIATED WITH FEMALE LABOR FORCE PARTICIPATION. *Social Sci. Q. 1974 55(1): 121-130.* "Finds that for a sample of married women with children, the prediction of employment status is improved by the inclusion of the attitude measure. Moreover, the strength of the attitude measure is greater at higher income levels."   J

1624. Dowdall, Jean A. WOMEN'S ATTITUDES TOWARD EMPLOYMENT AND FAMILY ROLES. *Sociol. Analysis 1974 35(4): 251-262.* "Greeley has argued that not enough is known about American ethnic group differences but that such differences exist primarily in the 'common core of assumptions' about familial role expectations. A measure of women's attitudes toward questions of female employment and family responsibilities is taken as an index of such expectations. Using a sample of 673 white, native born, married Rhode Island women, nationality, religious affiliation and social class are explored in relation to attitudes. Significant nationality-linked differences in attitudes were found. Religion was not significantly associated with attitudes, but among Catholic respondents there were significant differences associated with nationality. Taking social class into consideration, nationality group differences in attitudes were significant only among non-high school graduates and among those from non-white collar families. As Greeley predicted, there is considerable nationality-linked attitudinal variation among working class women; the reasons for it require further research."   J

1625. Ewing, David W. EMPLOYEE RIGHTS: TAKING THE GAG OFF. *Civil Liberties Rev. 1974 1(4): 54-61.* "The corporate world's First Amendment reads: 'This company will not tolerate words or acts of hostility.' "   J

1626. Ewing, David W. THE EMPLOYEE'S RIGHT TO SPEAK OUT: THE MANAGEMENT PERSPECTIVE. *Civil Liberties Rev. 1978 5(3): 10-15.* Discusses nine instances from the late 1960's-77 where the reluctance of corporate executives to use dissidents protesting practices or products dangerous to society as a useful resource in decisionmaking, resulted in disaster for their company.

1627. Ewing, David W. WINNING FREEDOM ON THE JOB: FROM ASSEMBLY LINE TO EXECUTIVE SUITE. *Civil Liberties Rev. 1977 4(2): 8-22.* Examines a serious lack of civil liberties in employment, especially freedom of speech, guarantees of job safety, and secrecy; a new worker's bill of rights is needed to erase the totalitarianism of work situations, 1960's-70's.

1628. Farber, Henry S. and Saks, Daniel H. WHY WORKERS WANT UNIONS: THE ROLE OF RELATIVE WAGES AND JOB CHARACTERISTICS. *J. of Pol. Econ. 1980 88(2): 349-369.* Examination of National Labor Relations Board (NLRB) representation elections indicates that the perceived advantage of unionization was inversely related to the worker's position in the firm's earning distribution. Nonwage aspects, job security, and the age and race of the worker also were factors in determining how a worker would vote on labor representation during the early 1970's.

1629. Fennell, Mary L.; Rodin, Miriam B.; and Kantor, Glenda K. PROBLEMS IN THE WORK SETTING, DRINKING, AND REASONS FOR DRINKING. *Social Forces 1981 60(1): 114-132.* Despite the familiarity of the expression "My job is driving me to drink," very little research has focused on the effects of work setting induced stress on increased alcohol consumption. The authors tested two hypotheses linking the perception of various work-setting problems to the frequency of drinking and reasons proffered for drinking. Results on the first hypothesis were mixed but indicated that a worker is much more likely to state a particular reason for drinking is important if he or she experiences any one of eight different work-setting problems.   J/S

1630. Feree, Myra Marx. EMPLOYMENT WITHOUT LIBERATION: CUBAN WOMEN IN THE UNITED STATES. *Social Sci. Q. 1979 60(1): 35-50.* Tests the hypothesis that women's participation in the paid labor force changes sex-role attitudes and behavior. Observation of middle-class Cuban women who immigrated to the United States after 1959 indicates that there is no necessary conflict between employment and traditional values. Traditionally, women in Cuban society had to be subservient to the needs of the family. This central role has continued in the United States, while the means have changed: the woman must work outside the family for the family's honor and upward mobility. 4 tables, biblio.   S

1631. Ferree, Myra Marx. WORKING CLASS FEMINISM: A CONSIDERATION OF THE CONSEQUENCES OF EMPLOYMENT. *Sociol. Q. 1980 21(2): 173-184.* Based on a 1974-75 Boston survey, argues that the standard view of working-class women as traditional and domestic has become inaccurate, and that they are more feminist-oriented than full-time housewives.

1632. Finegan, T. Aldrich. DISCOURAGED WORKERS AND ECONOMIC FLUCTUATIONS. *Industrial and Labor Relations Rev. 1981 35(1). 88 102.* Both the incidence of discouragement and its sensitivity to labor market conditions vary widely across demographic groups. The number of persons discouraged for job-market reasons has shown marked cyclical swings, but not the number discouraged for personal reasons. The findings illumine one of the social costs of a slack economy and are relevant to the continuing controversy over the classification of discouraged workers as not in the labor force. Many persons who decide to enter the labor force when unemployment is low are not reported as discouraged workers—or even as wanting jobs—when unemployment is high.   J/S

1633. Finn, Peter. THE EFFECTS OF SHIFT WORK ON THE LIVES OF EMPLOYEES. *Monthly Labor Rev. 1981 104(10): 31-35.* One out of six workers employed on evening or night shifts suffers from sleep fatigue, health problems, on the job safety hazards, and impaired marital and social life.

1634. Fisher, Robert W. WHEN WORKERS ARE DISCHARGED—AN OVERVIEW. *Monthly Labor Rev. 1973 96(6): 4-17.* Discusses legal and contractual aspects in the discharging of employees by employers 1930's-70's, emphasizing dismissal cases and the implications of the National Labor Relations Act (1935).

1635. Foner, Nancy and Napoli, Richard. JAMAICAN AND BLACK-AMERICAN MIGRANT FARM WORKERS: A COMPARATIVE ANALYSIS. *Social Problems 1978 25(5):491-503.* Comparative study of Jamaican and black migrant farm workers in a New York state camp based on data from the 1960's-70's. The Jamaicans are more productive and save most of their earnings because to them their wages have more value and they perceive more opportunity for social mobility. The impact of race greatly affected Negroes and caused low productivity. Foreign seasonal farm laborers are likely to be industrious on US farms. Primary and secondary sources; 9 notes; refs.
                                                                          A. M. Osur

1636. Form, William H. AUTO WORKERS AND THEIR MACHINES: A STUDY OF WORK, FACTORY, AND JOB SATISFACTION IN FOUR COUNTRIES. *Social Forces 1973 52(1): 1-15.* Social scientists have warned about the deadening effects of increasing mechanization and job routinization on the lives of industrial workers. Three areas of work satisfaction were studied for four operations which varied in amount of worker control. Respondents were auto workers in four countries which varied in extent of industrialization. Most workers believe that their work integrates their lives, they prefer to work in the industrial sector, and they report that their jobs are satisfying. Nowhere did assemblyline workers dwell upon monotony. Small and inconsistent differences were found in the three areas of satisfaction according to the degree of worker control over the job and degree of plant mechanization. From Marx to Marcuse, ideas about the deadening impact of mechanized and routinized work need serious reconsideration.   J

1637. Form, William H. AUTOMOBILE WORKERS IN FOUR COUNTRIES: THE RELEVANCE OF SYSTEM PARTICIPATION FOR WORKING-CLASS MOVEMENTS. *British J. of Sociol. 1974 25(4): 442-460.* Examines the impact of industrialization on how workers live and with regard to the politicization of workers. Considers automobile workers in India, Argentina, Italy, and the United States. Maintains that in every case they "become involved in a series of social

systems extending from the family to the nation." It is possible for an independent workers' movement to emerge during the first stages of industrialization. Primary and secondary sources; 7 tables, 42 notes.
                                                                          R. G. Neville

1638. Fottler, Myron D. EMPLOYER SIZE AND SUCCESS IN MANPOWER TRAINING FOR THE DISADVANTAGED: A DUAL LABOR MARKET ANALYSIS. *Industrial Relations [Canada] 1974 29(4): 685-708.* Manpower training programs for the disadvantaged in the United States have been shifting in emphasis over time from institutional to on-the-job training. As a result, it has become increasingly important for program administrators to place trainees in the private sector. Yet little is known about employer characteristics which are conducive or not conducive to a successful experience. The data presented here indicates that larger companies are significantly more successful in these programs than are small companies.   J

1639. Fox, Marion B. WORKING WOMEN AND TRAVEL: THE ACCESS OF WOMEN TO WORK AND COMMUNITY FACILITIES. *J. of the Am. Planning Assoc. 1983 49(2): 156-170.* Because the existing infrastructure no longer fits the travel demands of women with multiple roles at work and in the family, there may be consequences for access to employment and to community facilities. While comparisons of travel patterns of women to those of other groups have shown fewer and shorter trips, and a lesser use of automobiles, a newer indicator, travel time over the 24-hour day, reveals that working women with children may have shorter time durations for work, household, and leisure trips. Travel is traded off as a discretionary activity in favor of obligatory time requirements.   J/S

1640. Frederickson, Mary. FOUR DECADES OF CHANGE: BLACK WORKERS IN SOUTHERN TEXTILES, 1941-1981. *Radical Am. 1982 16(6): 27-44.* During and since the 1960's, blacks have doubled their proportion of the work force in Southern textile mills from one-tenth to one-fifth. This change laid the ground work in many communities for the local civil rights movement. Blacks, for a variety of reasons, were more likely to be involved in supporting unionization. They are now more involved in direct production activity and even in white-collar jobs than before. Still the textile workers of the South earn 60% of the national manufacturing average pay, and they face automation, threats to gains in wages and working conditions, and plant closings. Based in part on interviews with Georgia workers; 32 notes, 6 illus.   C. M. Hough

1641. Freedman, Marcia. THE LABOR MARKET FOR IMMIGRANTS IN NEW YORK CITY. *New York Affairs 1983 7(4): 94-111.* Discusses New York City's employment structure during 1979-82, focusing on penetration and integration of immigrants into the city economy.

1642. Fullerton, H. N., Jr. and Byrne, J. J. LENGTH OF WORKING LIFE FOR MEN AND WOMEN, 1970. *Monthly Labor Rev. 1976 99(2): 31-35.* Worklife expectancy increased for women, especially married women with children, and decreased slightly for men.

1643. Gannon, Martin J. A PROFILE OF THE TEMPORARY HELP INDUSTRY AND ITS WORKERS. *Monthly Labor Rev. 1974 97(5): 44-49.* Available data from 1966 to 1973 show that the majority of employees in the temporary help industry in the United States are women and that most are in clerical jobs.

1644. Garkovich, Lorraine. VARIATIONS IN NONMETRO PATTERNS OF COMMUTING TO WORK. *Rural Sociol. 1982 47(3): 529-543.* Examines differences in how often and what patterns are involved in commuting for "nonmetro persons" in various employment situations in Kentucky and how these situations, along with better transportation and communication systems, have changed the context of migration decisions.

1645. Garson, G. David. AUTOMOBILE WORKERS AND THE RADICAL DREAM. *Pol. and Soc. 1973 3(2): 163-177.* Reports on working class attitudes based on 50 interviews with auto workers in Framingham, Massachusetts. The Marxian view of "multiple" layers of general political consciousness is demonstrated but not the class consciousness argument that the American worker has been absorbed into the middle classes. Finds little support for charge that workers are politically alienated, but considerable evidence that there is a strong workplace alienation, and a desire for more worker control on the job. 12 tables, 7 notes.   D. G. Nielson

1646.   Garvey, Edward R. FROM CHATTEL TO EMPLOYEE: THE ATHLETE'S QUEST FOR FREEDOM AND DIGNITY. *Ann. of the Am. Acad. of Pol. and Social Sci. 1979 (445): 91-101.* Sports owners in America have always played by different rules than other corporate entities. Gives examples of exemptions provided by Congress and various practices to enable them. The US Supreme Court has ruled that such practices are exempt from federal antitrust laws. The professional athlete has had no choice but to accept the system imposed by management. However, the courts have started to change and athletes now have unions to help them gain dignity and freedom from the reserve system. Questions whether the athletes will continue to make progress in the 1980's.   J/S

1647.   Gellert, Dan. WHISTLE BLOWER: DAN GELLERT, AIRLINE PILOT. *Civil Liberties Rev. 1978 5(3): 15-19.* Dan Gellert, a pilot for Eastern Airlines, describes his 1972-78 struggle with the airline protesting a safety hazard in their Lockheed 1011 aircraft.

1648.   Gerson, Kathleen. CHANGING FAMILY STRUCTURE AND THE POSITION OF WOMEN: A REVIEW OF THE TRENDS. *J. of the Am. Planning Assoc. 1983 49(2): 138-148.* Slowly gathering trends have crystallized into new patterns of household composition and female labor force participation. Alongside traditional families, a variety of alternative household forms have emerged. Women's positions in the paid labor force have also increased significantly. These developments are interrelated, have long-term roots, and promise to continue.   J/S

1649.   Gerstein, Ira. DOMESTIC WORK AND CAPITALISM. *Radical Am. 1973 7(4/5): 101-130.* A Marxist view of the role of the domestic laborer working for families in a capitalistic economic system, 1970-73.

1650.   Ginger, Ray. AMERICAN WORKERS: VIEWS FROM THE LEFT. *Labor Hist. 1973 14(3): 425-428.* Reviews Len De Caux's *Labor Radicals: From the Wobblies to CIO* (Boston: Beacon Press, 1970), Wyndham Mortimer's *Organize: My Life as a Union Man* (Boston: Beacon Press, 1971), Alexander Saxton's *The Indispensible Enemy: Labor and the Anti-Chinese Movement in California* (Berkeley: U. of California Press, 1971), and Howard Zinn's *The Politics of History* (Boston: Beacon Press, 1970).   L. L. Athey/S

1651.   Ginzberg, Eli. FULL EMPLOYMENT: THE NEW YORK PERSPECTIVE. *New York Affairs 1977 4(1): 55-63.* Advocates a national youth employment program in New York City.

1652.   Giraldo, Fernando Urrea. LIFE STRATEGIES AND THE LABOR MARKET: COLOMBIANS IN NEW YORK IN THE 1970S. *Migration Today 1982 10(5): 28-32.* Discusses the socioeconomic conditions of the labor market in New York City for immigrants from Colombia.

1653.   Glaberman, Martin. THE WORKING CLASS. *Radical Am. 1976 10(1): 23-40.* A working class definitely exists in America despite many arguments to the contrary. This class manifests its unhappiness with the alienation and oppression of the workplace through sabotage, absenteeism, and indifference to conservative unionism. The revolutionary impulse of the working class was revealed through the spontaneous uprisings of the Hungarian workers in 1956 and the French workers in 1968. American workers lack a clear-cut sense of class consciousness but will use any means at their disposal to oppose alienation and oppression.   N. Lederer

1654.   Glenn, Norval D. and Weaver, Charles N. ENJOYMENT OF WORK BY FULL-TIME WORKERS IN THE U.S., 1955 AND 1980. *Public Opinion Q. 1982 46(4): 459-470.* Two questions concerning enjoyment of work asked on a 1955 American Gallup Poll were asked on a 1980 US national survey to gauge the net change. Indicated enjoyment of work was substantially lower in 1980 than in 1955. The difference was especially great for manual workers, Protestants, and older persons. The change resulted from cohort succession and from

orientations and attitudes members of younger cohorts brought to their work rather than from changes in work conditions which affected workers of all ages and in all birth cohorts.   J/S

1655.   Goldstein, Neal; Brody, Ralph; and Buckman, Rilma O. THE PHANTOM POPULATION: A STUDY OF GENERAL RELIEF REJECTEES OF THE CUYAHOGA COUNTY WELFARE DEPARTMENT. *Public Welfare 1975 33(3): 26-32.* Report of a 1974-75 study to identify the employable childless adult welfare rejectees of Cuyahoga County, Ohio, and to discover why they are rejected and how they live when unable to find employment or collect welfare.

1656.   Gonzalez, Rosalinda Mendez. MEXICAN WOMEN AND FAMILIES: RURAL-TO-URBAN, AND INTERNATIONAL MIGRATION. *Southwest Econ. and Soc. 1978-79 4(2): 14-27.* Discusses the labor activities of Mexican women and their families after immigration to the United States from Mexico, specifically the ability of immigrants to fit into the American capitalist system from a rural labor system, 1970's.

1657.   Gordon, Suzanne. HALF-TIME BLUES. *Working Papers for a New Soc. 1981 8(3): 36-41.* Examines the growing number of part-time workers, a fact reflected in the Federal Employees Part Time Career Employment Act (US, 1978), and argues that part-time work as it now exists in the United States simply provides a source of cheap labor for exploitative companies.

1658.   Gordon, Suzanne. WORKPLACE FANTASIES. *Working Papers for a New Soc. 1980 7(5): 36-41.* The individual stress reduction programs suggested by industrial psychologists, which are being applied to both white- and blue-collar workers, should not only teach employees to deal with work-related stress individually, but also to "examine their work-place, to evaluate the objective conditions that cause job stress, and to seek collective remedies"; 1920's-80.

1659.   Gottlieb, David and Bell, Mary Lou. WORK EXPECTATIONS AND WORK REALITIES: A STUDY OF GRADUATING COLLEGE SENIORS. *Youth and Soc. 1975 7(1): 69-83.* Women experience less career fulfillment than do men. Both men and women, after some experience, tend to emphasize personal satisfaction over security or stability in job goals, and to realize that hard work is not necessarily a way of reaching those goals. Based on a study of five Pennsylvania colleges and universities in 1972 and 1973; 6 tables, 1 note.

J. H. Sweetland

1660.   Gover, Kathryn R. and McEaddy, Beverly J. JOB SITUATION OF VIETNAM-ERA VETERANS. *Monthly Labor Rev. 1974 97(8): 17-26.* Employment of Vietnam War veterans rose steadily in 1973 and the first half of 1974, but the jobless rate of young veterans remained high.

1661.   Greenberg, Edward S. PARTICIPATION IN INDUSTRIAL DECISION MAKING AND WORK SATISFACTION: THE CASE OF PRODUCER COOPERATIVES. *Social Sci. Q. 1980 60(4): 551-569.* Compares the levels of expressed work satisfaction among workers in four producer-owned cooperative plywood plants with that of workers in a neighboring, conventional plywood plant in the Pacific Northwest. Based on a mail survey of the workers and interviews; 4 tables, 29 notes, biblio.   L. F. Velicer

1662.   Greene, Richard. TRACKING JOB GROWTH IN PRIVATE INDUSTRY. *Monthly Labor Rev. 1982 105(9): 3-9.* "Small young firms are very important to the process of job generation, according to three recent studies of the behavior of individual employers"; 1969-82.

1663.   Greene, William H. and Quester, Aline O. DIVORCE RISK AND WIVES' LABOR SUPPLY BEHAVIOR. *Social Sci.Q. 1982 63(1): 16-27.* Investigates the risk of marital dissolution in affecting human capital accumulation, labor market supply patterns, savings, and fertility and hypothesizes that wives subject to high probabilities of marital dissolution will be more likely to be working in the labor market; since individual wives subject to high probabilities of marital dissolution have hedged in the past by working in the labor market, they have accumulated more years of labor market experience than have other wives.

1664. Guest, Avery M. JOURNEY TO WORK, 1960-70. *Social Forces 1975 54(1): 220-225.* In general, most metropolitan dwellers continue both to work and live within either central city or suburban rings of metropolian areas. Nevertheless, travel across central city boundaries, inward and outward, was increasing slightly in the 1960-70 decade. And tendencies to live and work in central city or suburban rings vary clearly by the age and population size of the metropolitan area.   J

1665. Guest, Avery M. OCCUPATION AND THE JOURNEY TO WORK. *Social Forces 1976 55(1): 166-181.* This paper investigates the accuracy of theory and research suggesting that higher-status workers are more likely than other workers to maximize travel distance because of disagreeable features of the area around worksites. Our evidence suggests that higher-status white, male workers have relatively long commuting distances in old metropolitan areas while this is less true of new metropolitan areas. Journey to work patterns thus seem to explain some of the differences in residential structure between new and old metropolitan areas.   J

1666. Gurak, Douglas T. and Kritz, Mary M. DOMINICAN AND COLOMBIAN WOMEN IN NEW YORK CITY: HOUSEHOLD STRUCTURE AND EMPLOYMENT PATTERNS. *Migration Today 1982 10(3-4): 14-21.* Analyzes the social and economic situation of Dominican- and Colombian-American women in New York City.

1667. Haas, Jack. THE STAGES OF THE HIGH-STEEL IRON-WORKER APPRENTICE CAREER. *Sociol. Q. 1974 15(1): 93-108.* "This paper describes the contingencies and stages of the ironworker apprentice career. The analysis of nine months of participant observation data, most of which was collected by observing ironworkers throughout the construction of a twenty-one story office building, indicates four critical career stages that ironworker apprentices must successfully negotiate in their movement towards acceptance as trusted co-workers. Each of the career stages—sponsorship, 'punking,' initiative taking, and 'getting scale'—involves the work group or its representatives testing and assessing apprentices. These evaluations are communicated to the apprentice and other ironworkers and provide the apprentice a basis for assessing his progress and gauging his suitability for more responsible and often times more risky demonstrations of competence. Ironworkers perceive their work as extremely perilous and their danger increases while working with inexperienced neophytes. The workers must rely on the coordinated and trustworthy actions of co-workers and the ever-present threats to their safety lead them to develop and enforce processes of continuous surveillance, testing, and evaluation of all workers. These processes are most stringently applied to apprentices but apply through-out the ironworker career."   J

1668. Hamilton, Mary Agnes. ON-THE-JOB LEARNING. *Society 1982 19(6): 48-54.* The organization and administration of work experience programs have not been successful because the classroom teacher has not been involved in the process.

1669. Hamilton, Mary Townsend. SEX AND INCOME INEQUALITY AMONG THE EMPLOYED. *Ann. of the Am. Acad. of Pol. and Social Sci. 1973 (409): 42-52.* "Discrimination in the labor market has received considerable attention in the last two decades. Racial aspects have been a primary concern, but the question of discrimination against females has assumed an increasing importance. Despite statements of alleged discrimination against women, there is a paucity of empirical evidence. For the most part, the evidence cited— including that in governmental studies—is based upon comparisons of gross earnings by sex obtained from census studies or studies of particular industries. The purpose of this study is to isolate pure measures of wage discrimination on the basis of sex, within narrowly defined occupations. The measures are pure in that factors other than sex, to which wage differentials might be attributed, are taken into account. The results of the analysis of wages in four narrowly defined occupations clearly suggest that wage discrimination has a sex dimension. A sex variable is consistently powerful in explaining wage dispersion. Moreover, the estimated sex differentials generally exceed those related to color, often by considerable amounts. This finding poses obvious theoretical questions. If the wage for labor is determined under free market conditions, the continued existence of discrimination seems implausible in the absence of real differences in productivity among sex and color groups. This suggests that there are differences in the supply and demand curves relating to different groups of labor which arise out of subjective, rather than objective, factors."   J

1670. Hanagan, Michael and Stephenson, Charles. THE SKILLED WORKER AND WORKING-CLASS PROTEST. *Social Sci. Hist. 1980 4(1): 5-14.* This editor's introduction to a special issue devoted to skilled workers and worker protest emphasizes the growing appreciation among labor historians for the positive role of the skilled worker in the general labor movement. 2 notes.   L. K. Blaser

1671. Hanlon, Martin D. PRIMARY GROUP ASSISTANCE DURING UNEMPLOYMENT. *Human Organization 1982 41(2): 156-161.* Discusses the nature of primary group support—the support during a life crisis provided by friends, neighbors, and relatives—as it is revealed in a period of unemployment following layoff from a job, using data collected in 1976 and 1977.

1672. Hannan, Michael T.; Tuma, Nancy Brandon; and Groeneveld, Lyle P. INCOME AND INDEPENDENCE EFFECTS ON MARITAL DISSOLUTION: RESULTS FROM THE SEATTLE AND DENVER INCOME MAINTENANCE EXPERIMENTS. *Am. J. of Sociol. 1978 84(3): 611-633.*

1673. Hanson, Sandra L. THE EFFECTS OF RURAL RESIDENCE ON THE SOCIO-ECONOMIC ATTAINMENT PROCESS OF MARRIED FEMALES. *Rural Sociol. 1982 47(1): 91-113.* Compares the earnings and relative socioeconomic status of married women with rural backgrounds and urban women on the basis of a series of studies and interviews conducted in Pennsylvania from 1947 to 1971; examines the generally higher financial and social standing of urban women; discusses the variables, including education, responsible for this.

1674. Harper, Dean; Mills, Bobby; and Parris, Ronald. EXPLOITATION IN MIGRANT LABOUR CAMPS. *British J. of Sociol. 1974 25(3): 283-295.* Examines the exploitation of migrant farm workers in US labor camps during the 1970's. Describes life in the camps, analyzing the nature of exploitation as a recurring social phenomenon, with special reference to Marx's theory of exploitation. Secondary sources, 13 notes.   R. G. Neville

1675. Harris, Richard J. REWARDS OF MIGRATION FOR INCOME CHANGE AND INCOME ATTAINMENT: 1968-1973. *Social Sci. Q. 1981 62(2): 275-293.* Shows that community size did not itself provide an adequate framework to evaluate the benefits of migration from 1968-73, although migrants did obtain significant benefits by moving from low to high wage areas and from high to low unemployment areas.

1676. Harrison, Bennett. WELFARE PAYMENTS AND THE REPRODUCTION OF LOW-WAGE WORKERS AND SECONDARY JOBS. *Rev. of Radical Pol. Econ. 1979 11(2): 1-16.* Surveys and analyzes welfare households in the United States in order to determine 1) if welfarism is a permanent classification based on necessity, and 2) the role of welfarism in radical politics. A survey of 2,700 welfare households revealed that 50% claimed one working member each year, and 92% claimed at least one during a five-year period. Low and uncertain welfare payments are desired by industry, to create a labor pool available for low-paying and temporary jobs. American welfarism has progressed beyond that point; recipients need not work, and thus are ripe for exploitation in order to agitate for higher wages and better working conditions. 2 tables, 2 fig., 13 notes, appendix.   V. L. Human

1677. Hayghe, Howard. HUSBANDS AND WIVES AS EARNERS: AN ANALYSIS OF FAMILY DATA. *Monthly Labor Rev. 1981 104(2): 46-59.* Provides a broad base of information on the increasingly prevalent dual-earner family type (especially their demographic and economic characteristics), compares dual-earner families with traditional families, and lists recent studies dealing with dual-earner families and their unique problems.

1678. Hedges, Janice Neipert. YOUTH UNEMPLOYMENT IN THE 1974-75 RECESSION. *Monthly Labor Rev. 1976 99(1): 49-56.* Unemployment during the 1974-75 recession seemed to hit hardest teenagers and men in their 20's.

1679. Henderson, Eric. SKILLED AND UNSKILLED BLUE COLLAR NAVAJO WORKERS: OCCUPATIONAL DIVERSITY IN AN AMERICAN INDIAN TRIBE. *Social Sci. J. 1979 16(2): 63-80.* Surveys attitudinal, lifestyle, economic, and occupational differences in Navajo Indian workers, skilled and unskilled, at the Navajo Generating Station in Page, Arizona, 1973-75. One of seven articles in this issue on the social impact of energy development.

1680. Hill, Martha S. and Corcoran, Mary. UNEMPLOYMENT AMONG FAMILY MEN: A 10-YEAR LONGITUDINAL STUDY. *Monthly Labor Rev. 1979 102(11): 19-23.* Surveys unemployment, 1967-76, based on a sample of 1,251 men age 35-64, as of 1976, who were household heads and employed in every year of the survey. Shows that one-third of the group were unemployed at some point during the period, while the chronic joblessness of 5% accounted for more than half the group's total worktime lost to unemployment.

1681. Hirschman, Charles and Wong, Morrison G. TRENDS IN SOCIOECONOMIC ACHIEVEMENT AMONG IMMIGRANT AND NATIVE-BORN ASIAN-AMERICANS, 1960-1976. *Sociol. Q. 1981 22(4): 495-514.* Analyzes changes in the socioeconomic status of immigrant and native-born Asian Americans, examining their educational achievements, their representation in professional occupations, and earnings in the context of the changing structural conditions and opportunities of Asians in US society.

1682. Hotchkiss, Lawrence; Curry, Evans; Haller, Archibald O.; and Widaman, Keith. THE OCCUPATIONAL ASPIRATION SCALE: AN EVALUATION AND ALTERNATE FORM FOR FEMALES. *Rural Sociol. 1979 44(1): 95-118.* Provides a comparison of occupation aspirations among black females, white females, white males, and black males of high school age living in the midwest based on data collected in 1971.

1683. Howard, Robert. SECOND CLASS IN SILICON VALLEY. *Working Papers Mag. 1981 8(5): 20-31.* Describes the "holistic" workplace concept of the electronics industry in Santa Clara County called Silicon Valley, and what it has provided for the engineers and computer scientists who are 25% of the workforce, and then compares those conditions with those of unskilled production workers.

1684. Hunt, Janet G. and Hunt, Larry L. THE DUALITIES OF CAREERS AND FAMILIES: NEW INTEGRATIONS OR NEW POLARIZATIONS? *Social Problems 1982 29(5): 499-510.* The living patterns of men and women in "dual career families" are not radically different from those in "conventional sex-roles," but their careers do threaten, contrary to the literature, family life.

1685. Hunt, Larry L. and Hunt, Janet G. BLACK CATHOLICISM AND OCCUPATIONAL STATUS IN NORTHERN CITIES. *Social Sci. Q. 1978 58(4): 657-670.* The relationship between black Catholicism and occupational status in northern cities is examined using 1968 data for 15 cities. Multiple regression analysis shows that a modest nationwide Catholic advantage in occupational attainment is attributable to opposite trends in eastern and midwestern cities. Suggests that Catholic affiliation implies a status advantage only where it facilitates contact with whites and/or is a minority affiliation that can symbolize a distinctive lifestyle.   J

1686. Hyman, Herbert H.; Stokes, Janet; and Strauss, Helen M. OCCUPATIONAL ASPIRATIONS AMONG THE TOTALLY BLIND. *Social Forces 1973 51(4): 403-416.* Fundamental problems in social psychology are being explored through a program of research among the totally blind. This article presents comparative findings on the occupational aspirations of children and adults, both Negro and white, all of whom have been blind from birth or early childhood, plus collateral findings on the parents and sighted siblings of the blind children. Neither ignorance and fantasy nor the sense that they have been labeled and consigned to a brutish existence—both plausible hypotheses—have, in fact, shaped their approach to a career. The burdens of class and race that weigh heavily upon ordinary aspirants are unexpectedly lightened for them, and special processes of socialization within the family and of communication lead to the setting of high but not unrealistic goals.   J

1687. Iglehart, Alfreda P. WIVES, HUSBANDS, AND SOCIAL CHANGE: THE ROLE OF SOCIAL WORK. *Social Service Rev. 1982 56(1): 27-38.* Examines the social change that accompanies the increasing participation of wives in the US labor force, and discusses the importance of understanding this trend for social workers as well as sociologists, demographers, and economists in the 1980's.

1688. Ives, Edward D. A MANUAL FOR FIELD WORKERS. *Northeast Folklore 1974 15: 7-76.* The author, director of the Northeast Archives of Folklore and Oral History, discusses the mechanics of field interviews and the accession of materials for the archives. Comments are directed toward his students, but many of them apply to anyone interested in oral history. Discusses equipment, how to prepare for interviews, the type of questions to ask, releases, photographs, the journal, how to choose a topic, and the followup procedures of editing and transcribing the tapes. Reproduces a sample interview and its transcription, along with the forms used by the Northeast Archives. Illus., biblio., appendixes.   D. R. Jamieson

1689. Jaco, D. E. and Wilber, G. L. ASIAN AMERICANS IN THE LABOR MARKET. *Monthly Labor Rev. 1975 98(7): 33-38.* Discusses the recent success of Americans of Japanese, Chinese, and Filipino descent in the job market, and their higher overall labor force participation in comparison to whites.

1690. Janson, Philip and Martin, Jack K. JOB SATISFACTION AND AGE: A TEST OF TWO VIEWS. *Social Forces 1982 60(4): 1089-1102.* Previous impressionistic treatments of the sources of worker satisfaction have identified a stable, positive relationship between job satisfaction and age. Tests two explanations commonly found in this literature: that the relationship between age and satisfaction is the result of generational differences in education and value systems (i.e., a cohort explanation) and that this relationship is simply a function of older workers having moved into better jobs across their careers (i.e., a life-cycle explanation). Neither explanation is adequate, leaving the question of what accounts for higher levels of satisfaction of older workers unresolved. Based on the 1973 Quality of Employment Survey.   J/S

1691. Job, Barbara Cottman. HOW LIKELY ARE INDIVIDUALS TO ENTER THE LABOR FORCE? *Monthly Labor Rev. 1979 102(9): 28-34.* Of people not employed or seeking work in the first half of 1976 (a period of rising employment), one in five was a member of the labor force a year later; attempts to identify contributing factors to future participation for nonparticipants in general.

1692. Johnson, Beverly L. MARITAL AND FAMILY CHARACTERISTICS OF THE LABOR FORCE, MARCH 1979. *Monthly Labor Rev. 1980 103(4): 48-52.* Presents data on the reasons for the increase in multiearner families during the 1970's, particularly the rise in the number of working wives, mothers, and one-parent families, both black and white.

1693. Johnson, J. Myron. IS 65+ OLD?? *Social Policy 1976 7(3): 9-12.* Examines the correlation between aging and the ability to work, especially mandatory retirement ages and obsolescence on the job, 1970's.

1694. Jones, Caroline R. BLACK WOMEN IN THE ARMY: WHERE THE JOBS ARE. *Crisis 1975 82(5): 175-177.* Black women are joining the US Army in increasing numbers. They are attracted by out-of-the-ordinary job opportunities, acceptance by men into the service, and the fair treatment received in the service. Women are doing interesting work and getting the same pay, equal benefits, and same responsibilities as men. Equal opportunity also extends to education in the Army.   A. G. Belles

1695. Jones, Elise F. THE IMPACT OF WOMEN'S EMPLOYMENT ON MARITAL FERTILITY IN THE U.S. 1970-1975. *Population Studies [Great Britain] 1981 35(2): 161-174.* The 1975 National Fertility Study concluded that employment reduced intended and unintended female fertility.

1696. Jones, Elise F. WAYS IN WHICH CHILDBEARING AFFECTS WOMEN'S EMPLOYMENT: EVIDENCE FROM THE U.S. 1975 NATIONAL FERTILITY STUDY. *Population Studies [Great Britain] 1982 36(1): 5-14.*

1697. Jones, Lamar B. and Rice, G. Randolph. AGRICULTURAL LABOR IN THE SOUTHWEST: THE POST BRACERO YEARS. *Social Sci. Q. 1980 61(1): 86-94.* Examines the wage and employment effects of excluding temporary Mexican farm workers from the agricultural labor market in Texas, California, New Mexico, and Arizona. Utilizing a simple time trend model, the authors detect no significant improvement in agricultural wages from 1965, the year braceros were excluded, to 1977. The effect of exclusion on employment is inconclusive due to the increasing number of illegal aliens following termination of the Mexican Bracero Program. Based on Department of Agriculture and Department of Labor data; 4 tables, 8 notes, biblio.   L. F. Velicer

1698. Judkins, Bennett M. OCCUPATIONAL HEALTH AND THE DEVELOPING CLASS CONSCIOUSNESS OF SOUTHERN TEXTILE WORKERS: THE CASE OF THE BROWN LUNG ASSOCIATION. *Maryland Hist. 1982 13(1): 55-71.* Traces the history of the Southern Brown Lung Association to test the validity of conflicting movement theories. Traditionalists stress that movement membership and leaders emerge from basic grievances and shared values, while modernists emphasize professional cadres leading self-interested members. The Brown Lung Association's experience supports the traditionalist theory, but cadres provided initial impetus. Based on participant observation, interviews, content analysis, and published sources; 27 notes.   G. O. Gagnon

1699. Kagan, Robert William. GOD & MAN AT YALE—AGAIN. *Commentary 1982 73(2): 48-51.* Discusses intellectual pluralism at Yale University regarding the tenure evaluation of Thomas Pangle, who was denied tenure in 1979 because of his intellectual convictions.

1700. Kahne, Hilda and Kohen, Andrew I. ECONOMIC PERSPECTIVES ON THE ROLES OF WOMEN IN THE AMERICAN ECONOMY. *J. of Econ. Literature 1975 13(4): 1249-1292.* Bibliographical survey of recent economic literature on the economic role of women since 1940.

1701. Kahne, Hilda. ECONOMIC RESEARCH ON WOMEN AND FAMILIES. *Signs 1978 3(3): 652-665.* Reviews literature on the productive roles of women in the market and family, based on Wellesley's bibliography, "Recent Economic Research: A Compilation of Articles, Delivered Papers, Manuscripts, Mid 1975-76." Suggests that radical economic theories be used to analyze continuing occupational segregation and that women's migration patterns be studied more fully. Notes the preoccupation of researchers with family studies in a time when women are demanding treatment as individuals and when some women are not accepting traditional family roles. Secondary sources; 35 notes.   S. P. Conner

1702. Kaplan, H. Roy and Tausky, Curt. THE MEANING OF WORK AMONG THE HARD-CORE UNEMPLOYED. *Pacific Sociol. Rev. 1974 17(2): 185-198.*

1703. Kelly, Gail P. SCHOOLING, GENDER, AND THE RESHAPING OF OCCUPATIONAL AND SOCIAL EXPECTATIONS: THE CASE OF VIETNAMESE IMMIGRANTS TO THE UNITED STATES. *Int. J. of Women's Studies [Canada] 1978 1(4): 323-335.* In American refugee camps, 1975, Vietnamese women were given virtually no role models for assimilation into American society; men were prepared to work at lower class occupations and to assume total power in the household, thus receiving power in exchange for loss of wealth and social status in their cultural transition.

1704. Kin, Kwang Chung; Kim, Hei Chu, and Hurh, Won Moo. JOB INFORMATION DEPRIVATION IN THE UNITED STATES: A CASE STUDY OF KOREAN IMMIGRANTS. *Ethnicity 1981 8(2): 219-232.* A study of Chicago Koreans indicates that job information was usually received from personal contacts. Since most personal contacts were in turn from fellow Koreans this tended to create a closed circle with most job information inaccessible. 6 tables, note, biblio.   T. W. Smith

1705. Klein, Deborah Pisetzner and Whipple, Daniel S. EMPLOYMENT IN AGRICULTURE: A PROFILE. *Monthly Labor Rev. 1974 97(4): 28-32.* Analyzes the characteristics of agricultural workers in the

United States, using principally material from 1972-73, showing that they are predominantly male, self-employed, and working long hours.

1706. Kluegel, James R. and Smith, Eliot R. WHITES' BELIEFS ABOUT BLACKS' OPPORTUNITY. *Am. Sociol. Rev. 1982 47(4): 518-532.* Data from a recent national survey show that whites tend to perceive widespread reverse discrimination, to see blacks' opportunity as having greatly improved in recent years, and in general to deny structural limits to blacks' opportunity. These perceptions are, in part, the product of the prevailing beliefs about stratification held by the American public. Empirical analysis shows that whites' beliefs about blacks' opportunity are significantly influenced by persons' perceptions of their own opportunity, by stratification ideology explaining opportunity in general, and by feelings of relative deprivation.   J

1707. Kolko, Gabriel. WORKING WIVES: THEIR EFFECTS ON THE STRUCTURE OF THE WORKING CLASS. *Sci. and Soc. 1978 42(3): 257-277.* The expanding numbers of women in the American work force has been preconditioned by such factors as increased life expectancy for women and mechanical conveniences in the home, but the immediate cause has been economic need. This increase in female workers has provided capitalism with expanded markets for consumer goods and alternative sources for profit other than the results of military spending. The entry of working wives has added to the size of the working class rather than providing upward class mobility since the women invariably enter at low rungs of the income ladder and do not provide sufficient earning power to enable families to transcend their class. Women tend to enter the labor market in times of economic stagnation pushed by increasing inflation, constant real income, and the general unemployment picture existing since 1965. Working wives constitute a precarious basis for capitalist prosperity which is gradually becoming undermined by eroding economic conditions.   N. Lederer

1708. Kornblum, William and Williams, Terry M. YOUTH'S RIGHT TO WORK. *Social Policy 1981 12(1): 44-48.* Case-studies of inner-city adolescents show that America's "youth unemployment problem" is real; it is caused not by the existence of minimum wage requirements nor by minority group cultural factors but by the absence of training and subsidized work experiences.

1709. Latkiewicz, John and Anderson, Colette. INDUSTRIES' REACTIONS TO THE INDOCHINESE REFUGEES AS EMPLOYEES. *Migration Today 1983 11(2-3): 14-20.* Recent interviews with employers regarding the employment of Southeast Asian refugees revealed both positive and negative perceptions.

1710. Leigh, J. Paul. EDUCATION, WORKING CONDITIONS, AND WORKERS' HEALTH. *Social Sci. J. 1983 20(2): 99-107.* Studies of health factors of blue collar workers show that working conditions have as much to do with health as do diet and education, 1975-82.

1711. Leiter, Jeffrey. CONTINUITY AND CHANGE IN THE LEGITIMATION OF AUTHORITY IN SOUTHERN MILL TOWNS. *Social Problems 1982 29(5): 540-550.* A survey of workers' attitudes in a North Carolina mill town indicates that paternalism still binds J. P. Stevens and Company and its employees; worker loyalty is due in part to the company's market power, the high proportion of women and the growing proportion of Negroes in the work force, and the workers' extreme localism.

1712. Leroy, H. Craig. YOUTH EMPLOYMENT IN THE LABOR MARKET OF THE 1980S. *Urban Rev. 1983 15(2): 119-129.* Looks at the unemployment among youth in the 1970's. Concludes that the youth population is declining and youth will have to come to the work force with better academic preparation than previously needed.   R. J. Wechman

1713. Leuthold, Jane H. THE EFFECT OF TAXATION ON THE HOURS WORKED BY MARRIED WOMEN. *Industrial and Labor Relations Rev. 1978 31(4): 520-527.* Examines the effect of taxation on the labor supply of married working women, 1967-71.

1714. Levitan, Sar A. and Taggart, Robert. EMPLOYMENT PROBLEMS OF DISABLED PERSONS. *Monthly Labor Rev. 1977 100(3): 3-13.* Discusses the work disability of mentally or physically handicapped persons, analyzes the particular employment problems of the disabled, and talks about vocational rehabilitation programs and objectives.

1715. Levitan, Sar A. and Belous, Richard S. WORKING WIVES AND MOTHERS: WHAT HAPPENS TO FAMILY LIFE? *Monthly Labor Rev. 1981 104(9): 26-30.* Presents statistics on the working patterns and family-related obligations of women in the labor force; traditional ideas about what constitutes a family and what work roles should be no longer are realities, 1970's.

1716. Lewis, Lionel S. WORKING AT LEISURE. *Society 1982 19(5): 27-32.* From 1957 to 1959 *Fortune* magazine reported that leisure was an extension of work and emphasized the work ethic, while in the 1967-69 issues leisure became more important in its own right, it was even more important in the 1977-79 issues.

1717. Long, James E. and Jones, Ethel B. MARRIED WOMEN IN PART-TIME EMPLOYMENT. *Industrial and Labor Relations Rev. 1981 34(3): 413-425.* Deals with three aspects of the part-time employment pattern of working wives: 1) the wives' characteristics, 2) the level and structure of their earnings in part-time jobs, and 3) the duration of their employment when part-time jobs are available to them and concludes that part-time work opportunities appear to increase the length of the working life of married women.   J/S

1718. Long, Larry H. WOMEN'S LABOR FORCE PARTICIPATION AND THE RESIDENTIAL MOBILITY OF FAMILIES. *Social Forces 1974 52(3): 342-348.* Families in which the wife works are more likely to undertake short-distance moving and slightly less likely to undertake long-distance migration than families in which the wife does not work. The effect of the wife's employment is greater in raising the family's local mobility rates than in lowering migration rates. The reasons behind these findings are explored, along with the implied consequences. It is concluded that the migration of husbands interferes substantially with career development among wives and in this way contributes to explaining why women earn less than men at the same age, occupation, and educational level.   J

1719. Lovell-Troy, Lawrence A. ETHNIC OCCUPATIONAL STRUCTURES: GREEKS IN THE PIZZA BUSINESS. *Ethnicity 1981 8(1): 82-95.* Two ethnic groups, the Italians and the Greeks, dominate the pizza business in Connecticut. The Greek participation is seen as an extension of their historic involvement in restaurants. Greek Americans tend to establish shops outside the ethnic community, choosing locations free of competition. 4 tables, 8 notes, biblio.
T. W. Smith

1720. Luxenberg, Stan. EDUCATION AT AT&T. *Change 1978/79 10(11): 26-35.* Discusses the growing role of education at the American Telephone and Telegraph Company, from the tentative liberal arts programs of the 1950's to the tightly organized, sophisticated programs emerging from the present $700 million yearly education budget.

1721. Lynd, Staughton. WORKER'S CONTROL IN A TIME OF DIMINISHED WORKER'S RIGHTS. *Radical Am. 1976 10(5): 4-19.* Recent court decisions imply that workers receiving the recognition of their unions should in effect be amenable to giving up most of the rights they exerted to bring their union into being. This judicial trend in the restriction of workers' rights will probably continue into the future. Any movement for workers' control over the workplace should concentrate on removing from collective bargaining agreements clauses dealing with management prerogatives, nostrike provisions, and binding arbitration statements. Based primarily on legal documentation.   N. Lederer

1722. Lyon, Larry and Rector-Owen, Holley. LABOR MARKET MOBILITY AMONG YOUNG BLACK AND WHITE WOMEN. *Social Sci. Q. 1981 62(1): 64-78.* A National Longitudinal survey (1968-71) of 5,159 women, ages 14-24, suggests that white women bring to the labor market many individual advantages over their black counterparts. Secondary literature, survey data; 6 tables, 12 notes.
M. Mtewa

1723. Lyson, Thomas A. STABILITY AND CHANGE IN FARMING PLANS: RESULTS FROM A LONGITUDINAL STUDY OF YOUNG ADULTS. *Rural Sociol. 1982 47(3): 544-556.* Examines

farming plans in high school and actual attainment of farm jobs, showing that farming plans of high school seniors poorly predict actual attainment of a farm job and that previous exposure to farming relates strongly to farming plans and/or farm job attainment.

1724. Maccoby, Michael. CHANGING WORK: THE BOLIVAR PROJECT. *Working Papers for a New Soc. 1975 3(2): 43-56.* The Harman International Industries, makers of automobile mirrors in Bolivar, Tennessee, developed a program of worker self-management.
S

1725. Mann, Dale. CHASING THE AMERICAN DREAM: JOBS, SCHOOLS, AND EMPLOYMENT TRAINING PROGRAMS IN NEW YORK STATE. *Teachers Coll. Record 1982 83(3): 341-376.* A survey of over 3,000 New York youths in areas with employment problems revealed that two-thirds were either in school or working full time. Minority youths were more likely to be both in school and employed, but held a disproportionate number of low-paying, dead-end jobs. Although most youths want to work, few have been assisted by government employment programs. These tend to target aid to the most trainable and employable. Among minorities, Hispanics are the poorest and the worst-served by job programs. Such programs should focus on the least skilled, be targeted more specifically to minorities, and be more closely tied to local school systems. Based on the author's survey; 7 charts, 6 notes.   E. Bailey

1726. Martin, Philip L. and Richards, Alan. INTERNATIONAL MIGRATION OF LABOR: BOON OR BANE? *Monthly Labor Rev. 1980 103(10): 4-9.* "Surveys contemporary labor migrations, assesses their impacts on the areas which send and receive them, and explores future trends in international labor flows," focusing on illegal aliens to the United States, the guest worker program in Western Europe, foreign workers in the Middle East, and black labor in South Africa; 1942-80.

1727. Martineau, William H. and MacQueen, Rhoda Sayres. OCCUPATIONAL DIFFERENTIATION AMONG THE OLD ORDER AMISH. *Rural Sociol. 1977 42(3): 383-397.* Examines occupational differentiation among the Old Order Amish living in Lancaster County, Pennsylvania, in terms of their resistance to social change and internal sources of change and stability, 1970's.

1728. Martinez, Vilma S. ILLEGAL IMMIGRATION AND THE LABOR FORCE: AN HISTORICAL AND LEGAL VIEW. *Am. Behavioral Scientist 1976 19(3): 335-363.* Discusses illegal immigration into the United States by Mexican nationals, from a legal standpoint, and also from the perspective of Mexican Americans, showing the effect of this immigration on the contemporary US labor force.

1729. Massey, Douglas S. and Schnabel, Kathleen. BACKGROUND AND CHARACTERISTICS OF UNDOCUMENTED HISPANIC MIGRANTS TO THE U.S. *Migration Today 1983 11(1): 6-13.* Finds that undocumented Hispanic migrants to the United States are 60% Mexican, male, and usually between the ages of 15 and 39; also finds that due to the decreasing birthrate in the United States, immigrants will be needed for the low-skill labor market for many years.

1730. Maurer, Harry. NOT WORKING. *Antioch Rev. 1980 38(1): 68-90.* Several people discuss why they are unemployed, the kinds of work performed before unemployment, and how they are coping with joblessness, 1960's-70's.

1731. McEaddy, Beverly Johnson. WOMEN WHO HEAD FAMILIES: A SOCIOECONOMIC ANALYSIS. *Monthly Labor Rev. 1976 99(6): 3-9.* Analyzes the results of a Special Labor Force Report (1975), detailing the increase of families headed by women since 1960, giving characteristics of age, marital status, and labor force participation.

1732. McGahey, Rick. IN SEARCH OF THE UNDESERVING POOR. *Working Papers Mag. 1981 8(6): 62-64.* Questions three common ideas about America's "underclass:" a new black middle class has caused the black "underclass" to remain in poverty, the working "underclass" is stuck in low-paying jobs because of a lack of education, and the "underclass" breeds new generations of chronic poor, "the debate on urban poverty should direct our attention to the profound changes occurring in the economy, and to the need for fundamental changes in labor market structure" rather than to race and class as sources of the problem.

1733. McIver, John P. UNEMPLOYMENT AND PARTISANSHIP: A SECOND OPINION. *Am. Pol. Q. 1982 10(4): 439-451.* The Schlozman and Verba hypothesis that unemployment leads to abandonment of affiliation with the incumbent party is questioned in light of the Niemi critique of partisan recall data. The 1974-76 Center for Political Studies National Election Panel provides more appropriate data for testing the hypothesis. Support is not as strong as Schlozman and Verba's analysis would suggest. However, the panel data do lend some credence to the proposition that job loss will lead to erosion of political support for the incumbent party.   J/S

1734. Miller, Joanne; Schooler, Carmi; Kohn, Melvin L.; and Miller, Karen A. WOMEN AND WORK: THE PSYCHOLOGICAL EFFECTS OF OCCUPATIONAL CONDITIONS. *Am. J. of Sociol. 1979 85(1): 66-94.* Examines the effects of working conditions on the psychological functioning of working women, based on 1964 and 1974 studies.

1735. Miller, Marc. WORKERS' OWNED. *Southern Exposure 1980 8(4): 12-21.* Discusses the idea for a black community-owned company which was first voiced in the early 1960's and eventually became reality in the form of the Workers' Owned Sewing Company, which was founded in 1979, from what was originally Bertie Industries in Bertie County, North Carolina.

1736. Mills, Nicolaus. BROWN-LUNG COTTON-MILL BLUES. *Dissent 1978 25(1): 8-11.* Discusses the suppression of information on brown-lung, the occupational disease of cotton-mill workers, throughout the history of the American textile industry, and the progress in the late 1970's by the Carolina Brown Lung Association to eradicate the disease and bring the industry under control.

1737. Mjøset, Lars and Petersen, Trond. CLASS AND GENDER: A NOTE ON CLASS STRUCTURE IN NORWAY AND USA. *Acta Sociol. [Finland] 1983 26(1): 49-60.* Women have been more likely than men to be lower-level rather than managerial workers, and being a woman is in itself a disadvantage to advancement in the capitalist hierarchy of control.

1738. Moffett, W. A. THE ACADEMIC JOB CRISIS: A UNIQUE OPPORTUNITY, OR BUSINESS AS USUAL. *Coll. and Res. Lib. 1973 34(3): 191-194.* Considers the viability of hiring for academic library positions those individuals who possess Ph.D.'s but who for various reasons cannot secure employment in their subject field as teachers. Offers reasons for the selectivity of applicants, but argues that the library profession would be enhanced by including subject specialists who have had classroom experience. Based on primary and secondary sources; 4 notes.   E. R. McKinstry

1739. Moore, Kristin A. and Hofferth, Sandra L. WOMEN AND THEIR CHILDREN. Smith, Ralph E., ed. *The Subtle Revolution: Women at Work* (Washington: Urban Inst., 1979): 125-157. Discusses the issues that have arisen over the care of children, traditionally women's responsibility, since women began entering the labor market in large numbers, focusing on statistics on changes in childbearing patterns from 1890-1977 and day care from 1970-77, considering the effects of working mothers and day care on children and families.

1740. Morgan, Barrie S. OCCUPATIONAL SEGREGATION IN METROPOLITAN AREAS IN THE UNITED STATES, 1970. *Urban Studies [Great Britain] 1980 17(1): 63-69.* Examines the evolution of occupational segregation in eight categories—1) professionals, 2) managers and administrators, 3) salesmen, 4) clerical workers, 5) craftsmen, 6) operatives, 7) nonhousehold service workers, and 8) nonfarm laborers—for 32 major cities, 1950-70. Laborers have become less segregated from higher status groups, but the extent of white-collar and labor desegregation "seems to contradict all the theory relating residential structure and social structure." 4 tables, ref.   S

1741. Morrison, Malcolm H. THE AGING OF THE U.S. POPULATION: HUMAN RESOURCE IMPLICATIONS. *Monthly Labor Rev. 1983 106(5): 13-19.* Discusses the implications of recent demographic

and labor force trends for the future employment possibilities of older workers.

1742. Mortimer, Jeylan T. and Kumka, Donald. A FURTHER EXAMINATION OF THE "OCCUPATIONAL LINKAGE HYPOTHESIS." *Sociol. Q. 1982 23(1): 3-16.* Examines the occupational linkage hypothesis, which specifies the ways by which a father's occupation influences the psychological attributes of his sons.

1743. Myers, George C. MIGRATION AND THE LABOR FORCE. *Monthly Labor Rev. 1974 97(9): 12-16.* A review article prompted by five books dealing with migration of labor in the United States and western Europe: Ellen M. Bussey, *The Flight from Rural Poverty—How Nations Cope* (Lexington, Mass.: D. C. Heath, 1973), Stephen Castles and Godula Kosack, *Immigrant Workers and Class Structure in Western Europe* (London: Oxford U. Pr., 1973), Gerald Rosenblum, *Immigrant Workers: Their Impact on American Labor Radicalism* (New York: Basic Books, 1973), Lyle and Magdaline Shannon, *Minority Migrants in the Urban Community: Mexican-American and Negro Adjustments to Industrial Society* (Beverly Hills, Calif.: Sage Publications, 1973), and Michael Mann, *Workers on the Move: The Sociology of Relocation* (New York: Cambridge U. Pr., 1973).

1744. Myers, Samuel L., Jr. and Phillips, Kenneth E. HOUSING SEGREGATION AND BLACK EMPLOYMENT: ANOTHER LOOK AT THE GHETTO STRATEGY. *Am. Econ. Rev. 1979 69(2): 298-302.* The empirical evidence is unclear in the 10-year-old debate over ghetto dispersal v. ghetto development policy. Both techniques have contributed to the massive dislocation of poor blacks. Pocket ghettos in the suburban communities are developing. This article offers no definable conclusion. 9 ref.   D. K. Pickens

1745. Nackenoff, Carol. ECONOMIC DUALISM AND WHAT IT MEANS TO AMERICAN LABOR FORCE PARTICIPANTS. *J. of Pol. 1983 45(1): 110-142.* Those employed in the peripheral economy were no less attached to the political system and traditional values and norms than were those employed in core industries, despite their generally less favorable incomes and prospects for advancement. Expansion of the core industries had ended by 1947, and employment gains since then have occurred in government service and the periphery. Women, minorities, the poorly educated, young, and old have not been excluded from core employment, but it was primarily in that sector that job insecurity has been experienced in the 1970's. Class and socioeconomic status appear more important than sector in determining life changes and work-force experiences. %HD Based on the 1972-1977 General Social Surveys of the National Opinion Research Center; 3 illus., 5 tables, 19 notes, biblio., appendix.   A. W. Novitsky

1746. Nelson, Charmeynne D. MYTHS ABOUT BLACK WOMEN WORKERS IN MODERN AMERICA. *Black Scholar 1975 6(6): 11-15.* Explores myths about Negro women workers, 1969-75, emphasizing those regarding employment and heads of families.

1747. Newman, Dale. WORK AND COMMUNITY LIFE IN A SOUTHERN TEXTILE TOWN. *Labor Hist. 1978 19(2): 204-225.* Studies a rural-industrial county in Piedmont North Carolina. White cotton mill operatives experienced less control over their daily activities and work than did blacks. White mill workers felt degraded when forced into mill work; blacks did not. Union activity originated with blacks in the 1970's. Although the effort failed, it reflected the values and heritage brought to the mill by black operatives. Based on interviews; 77 notes.
                                                              L. L. Athey

1748. Newman, Jerry M. DISCRIMINATION IN RECRUITMENT: AN EMPIRICAL ANALYSIS. *Industrial and Labor Relations Rev. 1978 32(1): 15-23.* Analyzes discrimination in recruitment between black and white applicants, based on fictitious résumés.

1749. Newman, Morris J. THE LABOR MARKET EXPERIENCE OF BLACK YOUTH, 1954-78. *Monthly Labor Rev. 1979 102(10): 19-27.* Reveals that the poor employment situation of black youth is part of a long-term deterioration, which is independent of economic trends.

1750. Newman, Morris J. A PROFILE OF HISPANICS IN THE U.S. WORK FORCE. *Monthly Labor Rev. 1978 101(12): 3-14.*

Focuses on Mexicans, Puerto Ricans, Cubans, and internal migration; covers 1973-77.

1751. Niemi, Albert W., Jr. OCCUPATIONAL/EDUCATIONAL DISCRIMINATION AGAINST BLACK MALES. *J. of Black Studies 1978 9(1): 87-92.* Computation of a coefficient of discrimination against black males in jobs requiring from 11 years or less education to 17 years or more education reveals that black males made substantial gains in obtaining jobs in all except the lowest category during 1960-70. In 1970 black males with four years of college found it most difficult to find jobs commensurate with their education because the extreme discrimination at this level in the South lowered the national average. Regional differences in discrimination at all other levels were small in 1970. Census data and secondary sources; 2 tables, 3 notes, biblio.
R. G. Sherer

1752. Niemi, Beth and Lloyd, Cynthia B. FEMALE LABOR SUPPLY IN THE CONTEXT OF INFLATION. *Am. Econ. Rev. 1981 71(2): 70-75.* Because of inflation during 1968-79, more women have found it an economic necessity to be gainfully employed. The terms of employment are long-term career commitment and professional advancement. The possibility of increased inflation has strengthened this commitment and contributed to enduring two-wage earner families. 3 tables, biblio.
D. K. Pickens

1753. Northrup, Herbert R.; Wilson, James T.; and Rose, Karen M. THE TWELVE-HOUR SHIFT IN THE PETROLEUM AND CHEMICAL INDUSTRIES. *Industrial and Labor Relations Rev. 1979 32(3): 312-336.* This article reports the results of a 1977 field survey of managers in fifty plants in the United States and Canada that have recently instituted twelve-hour shifts in continuous operation situations in the chemical and petroleum industries. The authors reports that in all the plants studied the shift change has significantly improved morale without impairing efficiency, job safety, or workers' health. The drawbacks of this work schedule include the difficulty that some older workers have in adjusting to it; the possibility that it might not be feasible in industries in which the work is more arduous; and the general opposition of unions—which were present in only three of the fifty plants—to any lengthening of the workday.
J

1754. Oates, Mary J. and Williamson, Susan. WOMEN'S COLLEGES AND WOMEN ACHIEVERS. *Signs 1978 3(4): 795-806.* Adds further information to the growing bibliography on women's colleges. Using *Who's Who in America*, 38th edition, as the data base, suggests that future analyses should divide colleges into three categories: seven sisters, nonseven sisters, and coeducational institutions. In doing so, the seven sisters surpassed all other groups in the production of women achievers. In categorizing occupations, type of college bore little influence in the arts; in other fields, there were distinctions which should be analyzed every 10 years. Challenges the view that women's colleges have a monopoly on training women for nontraditional careers. Secondary sources; 6 tables, 30 notes, appendix.
S. P. Conner

1755. O'Farrell, Brigid and Harlan, Sharon L. CRAFTWORKERS AND CLERKS: THE EFFECT OF MALE CO-WORKER HOSTILITY ON WOMEN'S SATISFACTION WITH NON-TRADITIONAL JOBS. *Social Problems 1982 29(3): 252-265.* Assesses the effect of male hostility on women working in non-traditional blue-collar jobs by comparing women in traditionally male craft jobs with women in traditionally female clerical jobs, using five dimensions of job satisfaction: pay, work content, promotion opportunities, supervisors and co-workers; challenges traditional assumptions about women's priorities in the workplace and supports the feminist argument that male workers play an important role in perpetrating job segregation.

1756. O'Leary, Jeanne M. LABOR FORCE CHARACTERISTICS OF NONMETROPOLITAN WOMEN. *J. of NAL Assoc. 1977 2(2): 22-27.* Discusses the differences in the labor force participation of urban and rural (not necessarily farm) women; rural women's participation traditionally has been lower than that of urban women, but between 1960 and 1970 employment of rural women resulted in 94% of the growth in nonmetropolitan labor, while in metropolitan areas women were responsible for only 60% of the total growth of the metropolitan labor force.

1757. O'Neill, June. A TIME-SERIES ANALYSIS OF WOMEN'S LABOR FORCE PARTICIPATION. *Am. Econ. Rev. 1981 71(2): 76-80.* Regardless of decline in women's real earnings, women's number in the labor force increased during 1947-77, influenced in part by a slowdown in husbands' total income and the increase in marital instability and divorce. 2 tables, biblio.
D. K. Pickens

1758. Oppenheimer, Valerie Kincaide. STRUCTURAL SOURCES OF ECONOMIC PRESSURE FOR WIVES TO WORK: AN ANALYTICAL FRAMEWORK. *J. of Family Hist. 1979 4(2): 177-197.* Finds 1) that young males have much lower income than older males during the best of times, 2) that since the Great Depression cohort and other effect have increased this difference, 3) that as a result more women have been drawn into the labor force to supplement family incomes, and 4) that both the enlarged difference in income and high level of female employment will continue. 2 tables, fig., 18 notes, biblio.
T. W. Smith

1759. Ossofsky, Jack. RETIREMENT PREPARATION: A NEEDED ADDITION TO THE PENSION PLAN. *Urban and Social Change Rev. 1977 10(2): 22-26.* Examines educational programs designed for employees nearing retirement age to prepare them for living on retirement incomes and to assure maximum exploitation of pension benefits; covers 1964-74.

1760. Osterman, Paul. UNDERSTANDING YOUTH UNEMPLOYMENT. *Working Papers for a New Soc. 1978 6(1): 58-63.* Desire for part-time employment, infrequent previous work experience, and duration of unemployment among youths 16-19 makes unemployment for teenagers different from that of adults, and hence makes legislative necessities different.

1761. O'Toole, James. THE RESERVE ARMY OF THE UNDEREMPLOYED: I-THE WORLD OF WORK. *Change 1975 7(4): 26-33, 63.* Expectations of young, highly educated workers are rising while the number of good jobs declines. An expert on work patterns discusses the alarming implications for society.
J

1762. O'Toole, James. THANK GOD, IT'S MONDAY. *Wilson Q. 1980 4(1): 126-137.* Surveys new approaches to work reform during the 1970's, especially the move on the part of employers to design work in order to conform to the need of the employee to achieve what psychologist Abraham Maslow calls "self-actualization."

1763. Palmer, R. W. A DECADE OF WEST INDIAN MIGRATION TO THE UNITED STATES, 1962-1972: AN ECONOMIC ANALYSIS. *Social and Econ. Studies [Jamaica] 1974 23(4): 571-587.* Examines migration of Jamaicans to the United States. Because of US immigration law and wage differences, many of the migrants are skilled personnel. With the exception of remittances, this is a loss for Jamaica which will continue as long as the wage difference exists. Figs., 16 notes.
E. S. Johnson

1764. Pampel, Fred C. and Weiss, Jane A. ECONOMIC DEVELOPMENT, PENSION POLICIES, AND THE LABOR FORCE PARTICIPATION OF AGED MALES: A CROSS-NATIONAL, LONGITUDINAL APPROACH. *Am. J. of Sociol. 1983 89(2): 350-372.* The greatest decline in labor force participation by older men has occurred in the most developed countries, where retirement has become fully institutionalized; but this decline is more a result of occupational changes in industrial economies than of changes in government structures and policies that involve social welfare and pension programs.

1765. Parrish, John B. WOMEN IN PROFESSIONAL TRAINING. *Monthly Labor Rev. 1974 97(5): 41-43.* Between 1960 and 1973 American women entered professional training in increasing numbers, suggesting a greater share in high-level occupations in the future.

1766. Parsons, Donald O. THE DECLINE IN MALE LABOR FORCE PARTICIPATION. *J. of Pol. Econ. 1980 88(1): 117-134.* The decline of male workers between the ages of 45 and 54 in the United States from 1948 to 1976 is primarily attributable to the Social Security disability program.

1767. Parsons, Donald O. THE MALE LABOUR FORCE PARTICIPATION DECISION: HEALTH, REPORTED HEALTH AND ECONOMIC INCENTIVES. *Economica [Great Britain] 1982 49(193): 81-91.* Most frequently, health problems are offered by men between the ages of 25 and 54 to explain their inability to participate in the labor force. Since the increase in this phenomenon corresponds to an equal expansion in the Social Security disability program, declaration of poor health is an economic matter that "makes difficult the estimation of the responsiveness of adult labor supply to economic mechanisms, particularly to parameters of alternate welfare systems of interest to social planners." Discussed here is the choice environment in which the male labor force decision is made. "A strong work disincentive effect of the Social Security replacement ratio (potential benefits relative to market wage)" exists that is *not* apparent when self-rated health is used as the health index." Consequently, economic factors must be considered when accounting for claims of poor health. 2 tables, biblio., appendix.
D. H. Murdoch

1768. Passent, Daniel. O ROBOTNIKU AMERYKANSKIM [About the American worker]. *Nowe Drogi [Poland] 1975 (8): 126-136.* Surveys the US working class with reference to the workers' conditions, political attitudes, reaction to the Vietnam War, which emphasizes the important fact that the Communist Party of the United States is becoming a working-class party.

1769. Perrucci, Carolyn C. and Targ, Dena B. EARLY WORK ORIENTATION & LATER SITUATIONAL FACTORS AS ELEMENTS OF WORK COMMITMENT AMONG MARRIED WOMEN COLLEGE GRADUATES. *Sociol. Q. 1978 19(2): 266-280.* Using Becker's theory of commitment, national longitudinal data on 1961 college graduates are analyzed to determine the effects of early work orientation and the situational attributes of full-time work experience, husband's attitude and income, and number of children on the probability of 1968 employment among white married women.   J

1770. Peterson, James L. WORK AND SOCIOECONOMIC LIFE CYCLES: AN AGENDA FOR LONGITUDINAL RESEARCH. *Monthly Labor Rev. 1979 102(2): 23-27.* Summarizes the findings of the National Longitudinal Survey pertaining to variables in labor force participation—attachment to work, occupational achievement, and meaning attached to work—as they apply to and vary with different life cycle stages, 1966-77.

1771. Pfeffer, Max. CHANGING CHARACTERISTICS OF FARM WORKERS AND THE LABOUR PROCESS: HARVEST MECHANIZATION IN CALIFORNIA. *Development and Change [Netherlands] 1981 12(2): 215-236.* Compares tomato and lettuce production in California to show that "harvest mechanization is resisted by growers as long as a farm work force suited to the needs of the labor-intensive crop harvest is available"; and "growers resist harvest mechanization but their tendency to do so is linked to characteristics in the production of particular commodities and the effect of those characteristics on the farm work force."

1772. Philliber, William W. WIFE'S ABSENCE FROM THE LABOR FORCE AND LOW INCOME AMONG APPALACHIAN MIGRANTS. *Rural Sociol. 1982 47(4): 705-710.* Analysis of Appalachian families living in Cincinnati, Ohio, shows that one reason for lower than average income is that the husband is the sole provider.

1773. Pincus, Fred L. ON THE HIGHER VOC-ED IN AMERICA. *Social Policy 1970 10(1): 34-40.* Analyzes the economic effects in the 1970's of vocational education in junior colleges; concludes that, contrary to standard opinion, such education is not a means to financial security or social mobility.

1774. Poitras, Guy. THROUGH THE REVOLVING DOOR: CENTRAL AMERICAN MANPOWER IN THE UNITED STATES. *Inter-Am. Econ. Affairs 1983 36(4): 63-78.* Examines the movement of urban workers from Central America to the United States since the 1970's, noting that the workers come from diverse social and economic backgrounds and usually participate in US labor markets for only a short time before returning to their native countries.

1775. Portes, Alejandro. LABOR FUNCTIONS OF ILLEGAL ALIENS. *Society 1977 14(6): 31-37.* General examination of the subject of illegal aliens, especially those entering across the border from Mexico; examines political and economic impact as well as the effect which the aliens have on the unskilled labor market, 1970's.

1776. Presser, Harriet B. and Baldwin, Wendy. CHILD CARE AS A CONSTRAINT ON EMPLOYMENT: PREVALENCE, CORRELATES, AND BEARING ON THE WORK AND FERTILITY NEXUS. *Am. J. of Sociol. 1980 85(5): 1202-1213.* Women with small children, especially the young, black, single, poor, or poorly educated, are constrained from seeking or taking employment because of the lack of child care facilities.

1777. Rachleff, Peter. WORKING THE FAST LANE: JOBS, TECHNOLOGY AND SCIENTIFIC MANAGEMENT IN THE US POSTAL SERVICE. *Radical Am. 1982 16(1-2): 79-97.* The struggle to push the postal service toward greater efficiency and productivity, more speed, and fewer errors has been marked by mechanization of processes and by relocation of major centers. All this has not improved delivery speed or reduced error. On the contrary, it has managed to increase management's control over postal workers by reducing the work force through attrition, by relocating plants further from the urban, and largely black, work force in major city post offices, by severing work groups, and by preventing integration of postal workers into immediate neighborhoods by picking isolated sites. In short, the strike in 1970 that brought forth calls for modernization seems only to have provoked racism and union-busting tactics. Based on general research including interviews with numerous postal workers; note, 8 illus.
C. M. Hough

1778. Randall, Donna M. and Short, James F., Jr. WOMEN IN TOXIC WORK ENVIRONMENTS: A CASE STUDY OF SOCIAL PROBLEM DEVELOPMENT. *Social Problems 1983 30(4): 410-424.* Considers the 1975 controversy in Kellogg, Idaho, when the Bunker Hill Company refused to hire fertile females unless they were sterilized; company officials feared later legal problems if these women were allowed to work in areas involving exposure to lead.

1779. Rank, Mark R. and Voss, Paul R. OCCUPATIONAL MOBILITY AND ATTAINMENT AMONG MIGRANTS ENTERING THE UPPER GREAT LAKES REGION. *Rural Sociol. 1982 47(3): 512-528.* People who moved into nonmetropolitan counties of the Upper Great Lakes Region (northern Minnesota, Wisconsin, and Michigan) more often than not experienced greater upward mobility.

1780. Rasmus, Jack. JOB CONTROL . . . NOT JOB ENRICHMENT. *Can. Dimension 1974 10(3): 23-31.* Management sees job enrichment as the answer to worker discontent while labor prefers job control.
S

1781. Rasmus, Jack. WORKERS AND THE ENERGY CRISIS: A PROGRAM OF ACTION. *Int. Socialist Rev. 1974 35(6): 16-21, 38-42.*

1782. Reichert, Josh and Massey, Douglas S. PATTERNS OF U.S. MIGRATION FROM A MEXICAN SENDING COMMUNITY: A COMPARISON OF LEGAL AND ILLEGAL MIGRANTS. *Int. Migration Rev. 1979 13(4): 599-623.* Analyzes the differences between legal and illegal Mexican migration to the United States by the migrant population of a mestizo town in Michoacán, Mexico, 1977-78.

1783. Rhee, Jong Mo. THE REDISTRIBUTION OF THE BLACK WORK FORCE IN THE SOUTH BY INDUSTRY. *Phylon 1974 35(3): 293-300.* Explores the remarkable shift in the distribution of the black workers in the South. As a proportion of the total number of employees in the South, black workers have declined markedly in the years since 1940. By 1970 there were 1.5 million fewer blacks in agriculture and personal services. The 1960's were years of accelerated change when considerable gains were made in every industrial area except mining for black laborers. The black males had left agriculture, the black females had left personal services. However, black females managed to upgrade themselves more than black males. Based on primary and secondary sources; 3 tables, 7 notes.
B. A. Glasrud

1784. Riesman, David. THE DREAM OF ABUNDANCE RECONSIDERED. *Public Opinion Q. 1981 45(3): 285-302.* Problems of postindustrial America include the use of leisure time, waste and spending, the restructuring of the workday and workweek, and nuclear war. Presented at the third of the Paul F. Lazarsfeld Lectures, Center for the Social Sciences of Columbia University, 13 February, 1981.

J. Powell

1785. Ripley, Randall B. and Franklin, Grace A. THE PRIVATE SECTOR IN PUBLIC EMPLOYMENT AND TRAINING PROGRAMS. *Policy Studies Rev. 1983 2(4): 695-714.* Two decades have shown that the nature of the program is more important than its sponsorship, public or private, in getting people employed; there are inherent tensions in private sector involvement.

1786. Rist, Ray C. PLAYING ON THE MARGIN. *Society 1982 19(6): 15-18.* The schools could help alleviate the problem of unemployment among youth through innovative programs linking education and work experience.

1787. Rizzo, Ann-Marie. PERCEPTIONS OF MEMBERSHIP AND WOMEN IN ADMINISTRATION: IMPLICATIONS FOR PUBLIC ORGANIZATIONS. *Administration & Soc. 1978 10(1): 33-48.* Examines female administrators' perceptions of membership within the work group, sense of efficacy, impact on the organization, and participation in the public sector, 1960's-77.

1788. Robbins, Albert. DISSENT IN THE CORPORATE WORLD: WHEN DOES AN EMPLOYEE HAVE THE RIGHT TO SPEAK OUT? *Civil Liberties Rev. 1978 5(3): 6-10.* Describes the 1st National Seminar on Individual Rights in the Corporation, sponsored by *The Civil Liberties Review* and the Arthur Garfield Hays Civil Liberties Program of New York University Law School in 1978, which was concerned with the right of employees to speak out against their employer in the public interest.

1789. Roberts, Markley. A LABOR VIEW OF MANPOWER REVENUE SHARING. *New Generation 1974 56(1): 20-24.*

1790. Rones, Philip L. THE LABOR MARKET PROBLEMS OF OLDER WORKERS. *Monthly Labor Rev. 1983 106(5): 3-12.* During 1968-81, workers over 55 years old did not have particularly high unemployment rates, but, once unemployed, were less able than younger workers to find jobs and were more likely to leave the work force in discouragement.

1791. Rones, Philip L. OLDER MEN: THE CHOICE BETWEEN WORK AND RETIREMENT. *Monthly Labor Rev. 1978 101(11): 3-10.* Discusses the reasons for the increased job market status of older people during 1967-77; specifically, the factors contributing to the decision of older men to remain on the job.

1792. Rooney, James F. EMPLOYMENT AND SOCIAL INTEGRATION AMONG THE SKID ROW POPULATION. *Sociol. Inquiry 1977 47(2): 109-118.* Employment among skid row residents had no significant independent association with measures of social integration: number of friends, frequency of visiting, basic conceptions of friendship, helping friends, or to any reference group measure, but retained significance with the percentage of friends in skid row, and intimacy to close friends. The lack of association with reference group measures indicates that working patterns and group identification have become independent phenomena, constituting a partial shift from the former economic functions of skid row. The theory of the disaffiliating effects of skid row living was upheld only for loss of friends outside the area, and acceptance of skid row as one's place of permanent residence. There was no association of residence in skid row and change in the qualitative components of friendship.   J

1793. Root, Norman and Daley, Judy R. ARE WOMEN SAFER WORKERS? A NEW LOOK AT THE DATA. *Monthly Labor Rev. 1980 103(9): 3-10.* Investigates women's work-related injuries and illnesses by occupation, type of industry, injury, and accident, using data compiled from reports made to state workers' compensation agencies in 1977.

1794. Rosen, Corey and Klein, Katherine. JOB-CREATING PERFORMANCE OF EMPLOYEE-OWNED FIRMS. *Monthly Labor Rev. 1983 106(8): 15-19.* Data from 43 employee-owned firms from 1973-82 show that such ownership is associated with superior performance and job creation three times faster than conventional firms.

1795. Rosenbaum, James E. ORGANIZATIONAL CAREER MOBILITY: PROMOTION CHANCES IN A CORPORATION DURING PERIODS OF GROWTH AND CONTRACTION. *Am. J. of Sociol. 1979 85(1): 21-48.* Analyzes the chances for promotion in a large corporation based on age of employees at different levels in the corporation's hierarchy, and periods of company growth and contraction, 1962-72.

1796. Rosenblum, Marc J. HARD TIMES HIT THE OLD HARDEST. *Social Policy 1976 7(3): 43-47.* Because of the reduction in labor force participation and generally widespread unemployment among the aged, as well as small social security stipends, the elderly are the most effected by adverse economic conditions.

1797. Rubin, Marilyn. DEBUNKING THE MYTH: WORKING WOMEN IN SUBURBIA. *New York Affairs 1979 5(4): 78-83.* Briefly traces the rise of American suburbs since the 1920's, describes the typical suburban family consisting of working-supporting husband and father, and stay-at-home housewife-mother, and debunks the myth of the non-working suburban woman based on data since the 1950's on female labor force participation.

1798. Ruggiero, Mary; Greenberger, Ellen; and Steinberg, Laurence D. OCCUPATIONAL DEVIANCE AMONG ADOLESCENT WORKERS. *Youth & Soc. 1982 13(4): 423-448.* Adolescents in Orange County, California, were more likely to steal from their employers, come to work intoxicated, or commit other occupational deviancies when they worked "at menial and technically unsophisticated tasks," experienced stressful conditions at the workplace, for lack of training were supervised closely and had few opportunities for decisionmaking, experienced work settings "characterized by low levels of social support," and received "monetary compensation perceived to be low."

1799. Rumberger, Russell W. THE CHANGING SKILL REQUIREMENTS OF JOBS IN THE U.S. ECONOMY. *Industrial and Labor Relations Rev. 1981 34(4): 578-590.* The analysis reveals that between 1960 and 1976 changes in the distribution of employment have favored more skilled jobs, while changes in the skill requirements of individual occupations have tended to narrow the distribution of job skills. Overall, the average skill requirements of jobs increased in this period, but at a slower rate than in earlier periods.   J/S

1800. Ryan, Sheila. CHAMBERMAIDS: A PROFILE OF SOME WOMEN'S WORK. *Social Policy 1977 7(5): 36-40.* Personal experience, interviews, and statistics indicate how chambermaids who perform a menial service for minimum wage are exploited by management and ignored by the predominantly middle-class women's movement—a "graphic illustration of the many inequities experienced by women in all low-pay service jobs."

1801. Rytina, Nancy F. THE ECONOMIC STATUS OF MIGRANT WIVES: AN APPLICATION OF DISCRIMINANT ANALYSIS. *Sociol. and Social Res. 1981 65(2): 142-152.* Views the labor force behavior of wives who experience migration in terms of economic status. The lower work rate of migrant wives after moving is a function not only of moving for husbands' job opportunities, but being in the childrearing stage of the life cycle. However, the socioeconomic characteristics are lower for nonworking than for migrant wives, and migrant wives who work have higher levels of education and higher status jobs prior to and after moving than nonmigrants. Based on data for 1970.   J/S

1802. Rytina, Nancy F. OCCUPATIONAL CHANGES AND TENURE, 1981. *Monthly Labor Rev. 1982 105(9): 29-33.* Various statistics that illustrate the numbers of people who changed their occupations during 1980-81 and their reasons for doing so.

1803. St. Marie, S. M. and Bednarzik, R. W. EMPLOYMENT AND UNEMPLOYMENT DURING 1975. *Monthly Labor Rev. 1976 99(2): 11-20.* During 1974-75 unemployment was the highest during the postwar era, hitting assembly line workers and construction workers hardest.

1804. Sanchez, Juan J. and Solache, Saul. YEMENI AGRICULTUR-AL WORKERS IN CALIFORNIA: MIGRATION IMPACT. *J. of Ethnic Studies 1980 8(1): 85-94.* The Yemeni immigration to the United States is the most recent of Arab migrations. The Yemeni in California are principally engaged in migrant labor. Most have come as sojourners. They are young, unmarried men who expect to return to Yemen after making their fortune. A major expense for them is sending money to their families in Yemen. Much of their social interaction is with Mexican Americans. 6 notes, biblio.   S

1805. Sanders, Wayne. FREE SPEECH FOR THE PRIVATE EM-PLOYEE: WILL STATE ACTION RULINGS BRING THE CON-STITUTION TO THE WORKPLACE? *Southern Speech Communication J. 1981 46(4): 397-410.* Discusses whether or not private sector employees should have First Amendment free speech protections at the workplace by presenting "a rationale for free speech in private organizations, a review of free speech cases argued on state action grounds, and an assessment of the effectiveness of the state action strategy in seeking free speech protection"; 1968-80.

1806. Schulz, James H.; Leavitt, Thomas D.; and Kelly, Leslie. PRIVATE PENSIONS FALL FAR SHORT OF PRERETIREMENT INCOME LEVELS. *Monthly Labor Rev. 1979 102(2): 28-32.* Study of 989 private pension funds, 1974-78 indicates that retirement salaries equal one-fifth of final-year for $15,000-a-year 30-year employees.

1807. Schweitzer, Stuart O. and Smith, Ralph E. THE PERSIS-TENCE OF THE DISCOURAGED WORKER EFFECT. *Industrial and Labor Relations Rev. 1974 27(2): 249-260.* "The memory of past failure in the labor market may influence subsequent labor force participation decisions, creating a persistent 'scar effect.' If so, the discouraged worker effect is more serious than indicated by analyses that measure only the relationship between unemployment and participation rates in the same period of time. Using data from the University of Michigan Income Dynamics Panel, this study demonstrates that signifi-cant negative relationships do exist between current participation and both current and past unemployment."   J

1808. Scully, Gerald W. PAY AND PERFORMANCE IN MAJOR LEAGUE BASEBALL. *Am. Econ. Rev. 1974 64(6): 915-930.* A rough measure of the economic loss to professional baseball players as a consequence of the reserve clause. The institutional characteristics of the labor market are subjected to a model of marginal revenue product and salary determination. Results verify that ballplayers lose heavily. Possible reforms include adoption of an option year, long-term con-tracts, and an entirely free market, none of which would be fatal to the game. 2 tables, 18 notes, biblio.   V. L. Human

1809. Sell, Ralph R. MARKET AND DIRECT ALLOCATION OF LABOR THROUGH MIGRATION. *Sociol. Q. 1983 24(1): 93-105.* Recent research has shown that while fewer migrations are job related, more of the remaining job-related migrations are occupational reloca-tions.

1810. Shaiken, Harley. NUMERICAL CONTROL: THE MACHIN-IST'S DAYS ARE NUMBERED. *Can. Dimension [Canada] 1981 15(8)-16(1): 26-30.* Examines the detrimental effects that current and future computerized automation will have on machinists, especially those employed in the metal-working industries.

1811. Shapiro, David and Crowley, Joan E. ASPIRATIONS AND EXPECTATIONS OF YOUTH IN THE UNITED STATES: PART 2. EMPLOYMENT ACTIVITY. *Youth & Soc. 1982 14(1): 33-58.* Contin-ued from a previous article (see entry 20A:2251). Examines and analyzes the employment aspirations of youth through national surveys, finding them to have a strong orientation toward higher-status, white collar jobs.

1812. Shapiro, David and Shaw, Lois B. GROWTH IN THE LABOR FORCE ATTACHMENT OF MARRIED WOMEN: ACCOUNTING FOR CHANGES IN THE 1970'S. *Southern Econ. J. 1983 50(2): 461-473.* The presence of 30 to 34-year-old married women in the work force is a function of the husband's income, pre-school children in the household, education, and wages.

1813. Shostak, Arthur B. HIGH TECH, HIGH TOUCH, AND LABOR. *Social Policy 1983 13(3): 20-23.* Discusses 1982 developments in corporate and public policy regarding unemployment caused by automation in factories and offices.

1814. Smith, Elsie J. REFERENCE GROUP PERSPECTIVES OF MIDDLE-CLASS BLACK WORKERS AND COLLEGE BOUND BLACK YOUTH. *J. of Negro Educ. 1979 48(4): 479-487.* Using objective socioeconomic data and tests that purportedly measure reference group perspectives (i.e., commonly shared outlooks of identifi-able groups) and views of the social opportunity structure, compares blacks from middle class occupations with lower class black college bound youths. The author found that the students had reference group perspectives that were more middle class than the middle class black workers to whose status these lower class students aspired. Original test data and secondary sources; 25 notes.   R. E. Butchart

1815. Smith, James P. and Welch, Finis R. BLACK-WHITE MALE WAGE RATIOS: 1960-70. *Am. Econ. Rev. 1977 67(3): 323-338.* Authors are optimistic about the race toward wage parity during the last decade. Earnings for blacks have increased relative to whites but recently have done so at a slower rate. Envisions full racial parity by the end of the 20th century but there is the real possibility of a slower rate of economic growth for all workers, white or black. 6 tables.   D. K. Pickens

1816. Smith, Patrick. THE PROBLEM OF MIGRANT WORKERS. *Contemporary Rev. [Great Britain] 1973 223(1291): 57-62.* A compar-ative survey of the problems encountered by successive waves of migrant labor in Europe and North America since 1945.

1817. Staines, Graham L. and Quinn, Robert P. AMERICAN WORKERS EVALUATE THE QUALITY OF THEIR JOBS. *Month-ly Labor Rev. 1979 102(1): 3-12.* Discusses a 1977 survey which provides an overview of working conditions and employee satisfaction with jobs.

1818. Stein, Barry N. OCCUPATIONAL ADJUSTMENT OF REF-UGEES: THE VIETNAMESE IN THE UNITED STATES. *Int. Migration Rev. 1979 13(1): 25-45.* Examines the plight of Vietnamese refugees in the United States during the 1970's and the difficulty they encounter in trying to adjust to economic and occupational experiences in the United States, compared to Nazi, Hungarian, Cuban, and other immigrant refugees.

1819. Steinberg, Laurence D.; Greenberger, Ellen; Vaux, Alan; and Ruggiero, Mary. EARLY WORK EXPERIENCE: EFFECTS ON ADOLESCENT OCCUPATIONAL SOCIALIZATION. *Youth & Soc. 1981 12(4): 403-422.* Examines the correlates and apparent conse-quences of part-time employment among high school students. Findings support two conflicting theories: early work enhances their futures in the job market, and early work makes them more cynical and alienated from that market.   J/S

1820. Stevens, Gillian and Boyd, Monica. THE IMPORTANCE OF MOTHER: LABOR FORCE PARTICIPATION AND INTERGEN-ERATIONAL MOBILITY OF WOMEN. *Social Forces 1980 59(1): 186-199.* Previous research concerning the linkages between women's occupational origins and destinations has applied models developed for the study of men's intergenerational occupational mobility. In this paper, we use an approach that incorporates two unique aspects of women's occupational experiences. First, we consider housework to be a possible occupational outcome for women. Second, we consider the occupations of mothers as well as those of fathers in the portrayal of women's occupational origins. We show that this approach more fully displays the influences of occupational origins on women's subsequent occupational activities. In particular, we find that women whose mothers worked are themselves more likely to join the labor force, and their occupations are likely to resemble their mother's.   J

1821. Stevenson, Wayne. YOUTH EMPLOYMENT STATUS AND SUBSEQUENT LABOR MARKET EXPERIENCE. *Social Sci. J. 1982 19(4): 35-45.* Unemployment during youth affects the earning potential of later employment because it subjects the jobless to a lack of experience.

1822. Stillman, Don. THE DEVASTATING IMPACT OF PLANT RELOCATIONS. *Working Papers for a New Soc. 1978 6(4): 42-53.* Discusses the relocation and closure of industrial plants in the northern and midwestern states in the 1970's, the benefits to the corporations from state and federal tax breaks associated with the moves, the havoc created for the large numbers of workers laid off, and actual and possible regulatory legislation.

1823. Stinson, John F., Jr. VIETNAM VETERANS IN THE LABOR MARKET OF THE 1970'S. *Monthly Labor Rev. 1979 102(11): 3-11.* While the overall employment situation of Vietnam veterans improved steadily during 1970-78, the unemployment rate among younger veterans remained higher than that among nonveterans of the same age.

1824. Stolzenberg, Ross M. OCCUPATIONS: LABOR MARKETS AND THE PROCESS OF WAGE ATTAINMENT. *Am. Sociol. Rev. 1975 40(5): 645-665.* A key problem in sociology, as in economics, is explaining why some workers earn more money than others. Sociological models of earnings have stressed the role of a worker's occupation and have tended to ignore the conditions of the labor market in which he finds work. Economic models have stressed labor market functioning at the expense of considering the role of a worker's occupation in determining his wages. In this paper, I attempt to combine sociological models of earnings with (a) economic models of earning and (b) concepts and findings from the sociology of occupations and professions. I argue theoretically and empirically that some similar conclusions about the processes governing individual earnings attainment can be drawn by examining occupations in terms of labor markets and by analysis of labor markets from the standpoint of occupations. These conclusions are: (a) that government markets tend to be fragmented along occupational lines, (b) that the processes governing wage attainment vary from one occupation to another and (c) that occupational differences in these processes can be predicted from and explained in terms of the forces which lead to occupational segmentation of labor markets. I discuss some useful implications of my analyses for the study of the relationship between worker age and worker earnings, and I perform some empirical and theoretical analyses of occupational differences in the age-wage relationship. Data are drawn from the U.S. Censuses of 1960 and 1970 and from publications of the U.S. Bureau of Labor Statistics.   A

1825. Stone, Julia E. AGE DISCRIMINATION IN EMPLOYMENT ACT: A REVIEW OF RECENT CHANGES. *Monthly Labor Rev. 1980 103(3): 32-36.* Discusses amendments to and administration of the Age Discrimination in Employment Act (US, 1967), from 1979 the responsibility of the Equal Employment Opportunity Commission.

1826. Stover, Ed. INFLATION AND THE FEMALE LABOR FORCE. *Monthly Rev. 1975 26(8): 50-58.* Inflation has increased the number of women in the labor force and diminished family production while increasing family consumption and turning the housewife into a person directly exploited by capitalism.

1827. Sum, Andrew M. WOMEN IN THE LABOR FORCE: WHY PROJECTIONS HAVE BEEN TOO LOW. *Monthly Labor Rev. 1977 100(7): 18-24.* The underestimate of the female civilian labor force resulted from erroneous projections of the participation rate of women rather than from underestimates of the number of women in the population.

1828. Sutton, John R. SOME DETERMINANTS OF WOMEN'S TRADE UNION MEMBERSHIP. *Pacific Sociol. Rev. 1980 23(4): 377-391.* Studies data from the 1972-73 Quality of Employment Survey of the University of Michigan's Institute for Social Research and concludes that sex in itself is a major, irreducible determinant of union membership.

1829. Tannen, Michael B. VOCATIONAL EDUCATION AND EARNINGS FOR WHITE MALES: NEW EVIDENCE FROM LONGITUDINAL DATA. *Southern Econ. J. 1983 50(2): 369-384.* Vocational training in secondary school, or shortly thereafter, does not increase the earning prospects of noncollege white men.

1830. Tarr-Whelan, Linda. WOMEN WORKERS AND ORGANIZED LABOR. *Social Policy 1978 9(1): 13-17.* Collective bargaining

in organized labor is critical for the reduction of sex-stereotyping of women in the work force, 1950-78.

1831. Taub, Elwood. MANPOWER AND MANPOWER REVENUE SHARING. *New Generation 1974 56(1): 15-19.*

1832. Terry, Sylvia Lazos. WORK EXPERIENCE OF THE POPULATION IN 1979. *Monthly Labor Rev. 1981 104(6): 48-53.* Examines those who worked or sought work in 1979 in terms of age, sex, race, and extent of employment; and explores changes which have occurred in Americans' work experience during the 1970's.

1833. Thompson, Duane E. and Borglum, Richard P. A CASE STUDY OF EMPLOYEE ATTITUDES AND LABOR UNREST. *Industrial and Labor Relations Rev. 1973 27(1): 74-83.* This study exploits the fortuitous circumstance than an employee attitude survey was completed in a multiplant company shortly before the outbreak of a long strike in three of the company's five plants and the occurrence of other forms of unrest in all five plants. The authors compare the variations among plants in labor unrest—measured by the criterion of strike-no strike and a ranking along other dimensions of unrest by several company executives—with interplant variations in scores on the attitude survey. They concluded that survey techniques can provide the manager and scholar with a basis for predicting labor unrest and a vehicle for initiating the changes needed to head off such unrest.   J

1834. Thompson, Wayne E. LABOR-MANAGEMENT FOCUS: IMPROVING GOVERNMENT PRODUCTIVITY. *Natl. Civic Rev. 1975 64(7): 335-338.* There are two fundamental goals at the heart of public labor-management relations: to provide more effective and efficient services to the taxpayers and consumers, i.e., increase productivity, and to provide fair benefits to the government worker. The two are inextricably related and, fortunately, not mutually exclusive.   J

1835. Tideman, T. Nicolaus. DEFINING AREA DISTRESS IN UNEMPLOYMENT. *Public Policy 1973 21(4): 441-492.*

1836. Toscano, David J. EMPLOYEE OWNERSHIP AND DEMOCRACY IN THE WORKPLACE. *Social Policy 1981 12(1): 16-23.* Analyzes three types of employee ownerships: 1) the mock-conventional firm, which is a direct employee ownership, 2) the employee stock ownership plans, and 3) the producer cooperatives, which combine employee ownership of capital with workers' control. Although employee ownership is not yet an alternative to capitalism, it does provide a way by which workers can maintain their jobs, while access to capital offers the means for transforming the social relations of the workplace.

1837. Treas, Judith. U.S. INCOME STRATIFICATION: BRINGING FAMILIES BACK IN. *Sociol. and Social Res. 1982 66(3): 231-251.* A research focus on family income, as opposed to individual earnings, affords insights into the behavioral underpinnings of economic inequalities generated by family members' coordinated efforts of income-getting from disparate sources. After reviewing issues of conceptualization and measurement of family income inequality, this paper discusses the distributional effects of postwar demographic trends, labor force changes and social welfare developments.   J

1838. Tschetter, John and Lukasiewicz, John. EMPLOYMENT CHANGES IN CONSTRUCTION: SECULAR, CYCLICAL, AND SEASONAL. *Monthly Labor Rev. 1983 106(3): 11-17.* Chronicles changes in the construction industry during 1950-80, demonstrating patterns of employment; projects future trends.

1839. Tyrie, Andrea and Treas, Judith. THE OCCUPATIONAL AND MARITAL MOBILITY OF WOMEN. *Am. Sociol. Rev. 1974 39(3): 293-302.* Comparison of male and female occupational and marital mobility, 1955-71, indicates that occupational mobility of men and women is different, but that similar patterns guide men and women from their origins to the status of the male head of household.

1840. Villemez, Wayne J. GEMEINSCHAFT, NONECONOMIC DISTINCTIONS, AND THE MIGRANT WORKER: FROM THE INSIDE LOOKING OUT. *Pacific Sociol. Rev. 1975 18(4): 463-482.* Evidence gathered in Palm Beach County, Florida, during the 1970's indicates that differences in economic conditions do not account for the differences in behavior patterns observed in the various neighborhoods of migrant laborers.

1841. Waite, Linda J.; Suter, Larry E.; and Shortlidge, Richard L., Jr. CHANGES IN CHILD CARE ARRANGEMENTS OF WORKING WOMEN FROM 1965 TO 1971. *Social Sci. Q. 1977 58(2): 302-311.* Indicates that the location of care by nonrelatives shifted from inside to outside the child's home, but that women prefer to use personal friends or family rather than formal day care centers. Concludes that trends in women's employment and living patterns may be adding pressure for formal day care arrangements, but any future increases in the use of such arrangements may be determined as much by their supply as by demand for them.   J/S

1842. Waite, Linda J. WORKING WIVES: 1940-1960. *Am. Sociol. Rev. 1976 41(1): 65-80.* Changes since 1940 in the rates and patterns of labor force participation of married women are examined using retrospective work histories of wives taken from the 1960 Growth of American Families Study. The effects of certain predictor variables, such as income of the husband, wage potential of the wife and number of children under six, on the probability of a woman working are determined for life cycle stages. Changes since 1940 in the effects of these predictors are examined using a single-equation, additive linear model and analysis of covariance techniques. The major hypothesis tested in this research is that significant changes have occurred since 1940 in the effects of the factors influencing working by wives. The reseach supports this hypothesis for the early stages of marriage and childbearing only. No changes in either probability of work activity between births or the effects of all predictors when these are considered together on this activity are found for wives with three or more children. When each causal variable is considered separately, a significant decrease is noted in the effects of those factors which tend to inhibit wives' working. Among these are the presence of children under six, the age of the wife and her educational level. The factors which tend to facilitate working, past labor force activity and wife's earning power, have tended to increase in effect or have remained strongly positive influences.   J

1843. Waldman, Elizabeth and McEaddy, Beverly J. WHERE WOMEN WORK: AN ANALYSIS BY INDUSTRY AND OCCUPATION. *Monthly Labor Rev. 1974 97(5): 3-13.* Examines figures on the employment of women in American industry between 1940 and 1970. Although more women joined the work force, the pattern of women's employment changed little, with women concentrated in the rapidly growing service industries.

1844. Wallace, Michael and Kalleberg, Arne L. INDUSTRIAL TRANSFORMATION AND THE DECLINE OF CRAFT: THE DECOMPOSITION OF SKILL IN THE PRINTING INDUSTRY, 1931-1978. *Am. Sociol. Rev. 1982 47(3): 307-324.* Printers have long been considered the epitome of the skilled blue-collar craftsmen. Recently, however, all this has been changing. The steady decline of industrial profit margins after World War II has led many large printing establishments to introduce more sophisticated printing technologies, particularly computerized typesetting processes, which have routinized work tasks and led to a decline of skill among printing craftsmen. Gives substantive and empirical evidence for these processes and supports the theory of industrial transformation. Skill levels in the industry have declined largely due to the shift to capital-intensive printing techniques. Social relations of production between employers and employees influence the nature of technology utilized in an industry.   J/S

1845. Weaver, Charles N. WORKERS' EXPECTATIONS ABOUT LOSING AND REPLACING THEIR JOBS. *Monthly Labor Rev. 1980 103(4): 53-54.* Discusses 1977 and 1978 surveys of worker job security and job replacement confidence which remain high despite high unemployment.

1846. Wegmann, Robert G. GROUP JOB SEARCH TRAINING FOR YOUTH. *Youth & Soc. 1983 14(3): 320-334.* Reports the successful efforts of the national Job Factory for Youth during 1979-81, and the Job Track program in San Francisco during 1980, in decreasing youth unemployment.

1847. Wellman, David. BAY AREA LONGSHOREMEN. *Society 1980 17(3): 63-67.* A photo essay, supported by brief explanations, about the work of longshoremen in the San Francisco Bay Area, California, 1980.

1848. Westcott, Diane. THE YOUNGEST WORKERS: 14-AND 15-YEAR-OLDS. *Monthly Labor Rev. 1981 104(2): 65-69.* Despite child labor and school attendance laws, approximately 1.6 million young teens held jobs in 1979 and the labor force participation rate of girls is fast approaching that of boys, although the latter are employed in more varied occupations.

1849. Westin, Alan F. PRIVACY AND PERSONNEL RECORDS: A LOOK AT EMPLOYEE ATTITUDES. *Civil Liberties Rev. 1978 4(5): 28-34.* Presents a survey on workers' concern about how personnel records are collected and used, employees' rights of access to their records, and confidentiality.

1850. Willits, Fern K.; Bealer, Robert C.; and Crider, Donald M. MIGRANT STATUS AND SUCCESS: A PANEL STUDY. *Rural Sociol. 1978 43(3): 387-402.* The traditional American success ideal is based on actively sought out personal achievement; deals specifically with internal migration as it is related to higher income and occupational prestige; covers 1947-71.

1851. Wise, David A. ACADEMIC ACHIEVEMENT AND JOB PERFORMANCE. *Am. Econ. Rev. 1975 65(3): 350-366.* Discovers that a relation exists between academic achievement and job performance by means of a strong statistical methodology. Stresses that measures of ability and academic achievement used in the selection and certification process in higher education are related to the college graduate's productivity, and that college education contributed to productivity ability. Charts.   D. K. Pickens

1852. Wolkinson, Benjamin W. and Barton, David. ARBITRATION AND THE RIGHTS OF MENTALLY HANDICAPPED WORKERS. *Monthly Labor Rev. 1980 103(4): 41-47.* Discusses the rights and protections of mentally disabled workers from 1947 to the Rehabilitation Act (US, 1973), until 1978, during which time "restraints on management's ability to penalize workers afflicted by mental illness" have been established.

1853. Woodworth, Warner. WORKERS AS BOSSES. *Social Policy 1981 11(4): 40-45.* Discusses the rise of worker-owned industries in America between 1970 and 1981 as a response to the industrial decline in the Northeast and Midwest of the nation; and illustrates this trend with the experience of the Rath Packing Company in Waterloo, Iowa, which in 1979 became worker-owned.

1854. Wool, Harold. COAL INDUSTRY RESURGENCE ATTRACTS VARIETY OF NEW WORKERS. *Monthly Labor Rev. 1981 104(1): 3-8.* Reports on recent trends in employment in the coal industry characterized by an influx of younger men, higher educational levels among laborers and an increase in women employees both underground and on the surface since 1970 despite dangerous working conditions.

1855. Wright, James and Hamilton, Richard. BLUE COLLARS, CAP & GOWN. *Dissent 1978 25(2): 219-223.* The appearance of a college-educated segment within the blue-collar working class is unique to the last half of the 20th century in the United States.

1856. Wright, James D. and Hamilton, Richard F. WORK SATISFACTION AND AGE: SOME EVIDENCE FOR THE "JOB CHANGE" HYPOTHESIS. *Social Forces 1978 56(4): 1140-1158.* Previous research on work satisfaction has consistently shown that older people are more satisfied with their jobs than younger people. The present paper addresses three possible explanations for this tendency: 1) the "now generation" of workers subscribes to a set of post-material values that contradict the demands of the industrial system and cause greater work discontent; 2) the standards of the old are systematically eroded by their years in the system, such that they learn to be satisfied with less; and 3) older workers simply have better jobs. A decisive choice among these hypotheses cannot be made without longitudinal data; nonetheless, the bulk of the evidence presented here (for economically active, salaried white males, drawn from the University of

Michigan's 1972-73 Quality of Employment survey) clearly favors the last hypothesis.   J

1857. Wright, Michael J. REPRODUCTIVE HAZARDS AND "PROTECTIVE" DISCRIMINATION. *Feminist Studies 1979 5(2): 302-309.* It is discriminatory to remove women workers from heavy industries due to exposure to dangerous substances that can damage a fetus, while allowing men workers to continue working even though exposure may be just as harmful to them as to unborn children. Focuses on specific substances. Also lists the demands on behalf of workers by organized labor, and women's and equal rights groups for a policy which protects both women and men workers.   G. Smith

1858. Yellowitz, Irwin. AMERICAN JEWISH LABOR: HISTORIO-GRAPHICAL PROBLEMS AND PROSPECTS. *Am. Jewish Hist. Q. 1976 65(3): 203-213.* Although the history of American Jewish labor has been a subject of inquiry for over half a century, the major problems in concept and method have not been resolved. The boundaries of American Jewish labor as distinguished from that of the American Jewish labor *movement* should be defined by the influence of Jewish identity and concerns upon leaders and institutions, and the impact of these major figures and their organizations upon the Jewish community. The complex interaction of Jewish, American, trade union, and socialist concerns deserves further study (e.g., Samuel Gompers or Meyer London as Jewish rather than American Labor leaders) as well as considerations of events and persons outside New York City. 34 notes.
F. Rosenthal

1859. Young, Anne McDougall. LABOR FORCE PATTERNS OF STUDENTS, GRADUATES, AND DROPOUTS, 1981. *Monthly Labor Rev. 1982 105(9): 39-42.* Four tables that chart the employment status of persons 16-24 years old, by sex and race, and by school enrollment status, 1981.

1860. Young, Anne McDougall. LABOR MARKET EXPERIENCE OF RECENT COLLEGE GRADUATES. *Monthly Labor Rev. 1974 97(10): 33-40.* Examines the job status in October 1972 of college graduates of 1971, their job hunting methods, and their earnings levels.

1861. Young, Anne McDougall. RECENT TRENDS IN LABOR FORCE ACTIVITY AND HIGHER EDUCATION. *Monthly Labor Rev. 1983 106(3): 39-41.* Despite a sluggish economy in 1982, higher education continues to provide workers with a considerable advantage in the job market.

1862. Young, Anne McDougall. WORK EXPERIENCE OF THE POPULATION IN 1972. *Monthly Labor Rev. 1974 97(2): 48-56.* A March 1973 survey of the work experience of the population in the United States shows that the proportion of workers employed full-time year-round increased in 1972, mainly because of expansion in service industries.

1863. Young, Anne McDougall. WORK EXPERIENCE OF THE POPULATION IN 1978. *Monthly Labor Rev. 1980 103(3): 43-47.* Analyzes replies to the March 1979 Current Population Survey question regarding work experience in the preceding year and compares them to earlier surveys.

1864. Young, Anne McDougall. YOUTH LABOR FORCE MARKED TURNING POINT IN 1982. *Monthly Labor Rev. 1983 106(8): 29-32.* The 16-to-24-year-old labor force has dropped significantly since its peak in 1979, particularly between October 1981 and October 1982, but unemployment in this group remains high.

1865. Zeisel, Rose N. MODERNIZATION AND MANPOWER IN TEXTILE MILLS. *Monthly Labor Rev. 1973 96(6): 18-25.* Discusses the influence of technological change in the production level of skilled labor in textile mill industries in the 1960's and 70's.

1866. Zimmerman, Diana. AMERICA'S NOMADS. *Migration Today 1981 9(3): 24-32, (4-5): 34-38.* Part 1. Examines the deplorable economic, housing, education, health, and child labor conditions for migrant farm workers, who are mostly Chicano and black, since Edward R. Murrow's 1959 documentary, *Harvest of Shame;* farm conditions have not improved since Murrow's expose. Part 2. The National Labor Relations Act of 1938, the Fair Standards Labor Act of 1938, and the

Social Security Act of 1935 have hurt migrant farm workers; the federal government, the producers, the industry, and consumers all benefit from these unprotected workers.

1867. Zinn, Maxine Baca. EMPLOYMENT AND EDUCATION OF MEXICAN-AMERICAN WOMEN: THE INTERPLAY OF MODERNITY AND ETHNICITY IN EIGHT FAMILIES. *Harvard Educ. Rev. 1980 50(1): 47-62.* Examines and compares the role of outside employment and education on conjugal power and ethnicity in Mexican American women from eight families, 1970's.

1868. Zwerdling, Daniel. BEYOND BOREDOM: A LOOK AT WHAT'S NEW ON THE ASSEMBLY LINE. *Washington Monthly 1973 5(5/6): 80-92.*

1869. Zwerdling, Daniel. SAVING JOBS BY BUYING THE PLANT: EMPLOYEE OWNERSHIP: HOW WELL IS IT WORKING? *Working Papers for a New Soc. 1979 7(1): 14-27.* Discusses recent accomplishments and mistakes in worker and community take-overs of factories dumped by corporations, beginning in 1977, in order to save jobs; uses the efforts of the Mahoning Valley community in Ohio to purchase the Campbell plant of the Youngstown Sheet and Tube Co. steel mill as a primary example.

1870. —. [THE HAWTHORNE RELAY EXPERIMENT: REINTERPRETING THE DATA]. *Am. Sociol. Rev. 1980 45(6): 995-1027.*
Schlaifer, Robert. THE RELAY ASSEMBLY TEST ROOM: AN ALTERNATIVE STATISTICAL INTERPRETATION (COMMENT ON FRANKE AND KAUL, ASR OCTOBER 1978), *pp. 995-1005.* Richard Herbert Franke and James D. Kaul's 1978 statistical analysis (see entry in this bibliography) of data from the first relay experiment, the most prolonged of the 1927-33 Hawthorne experiments, found production improving in two abrupt jumps over the first three years of the experiment and attributed the jumps to managerial discipline, economic depression, and scheduled rest time; further analysis, however, supports the original Hawthorne researchers' observation of a continuous, inexplicable growth in productivity over the first three years, a growth the original researchers attributed to improved social relations.
Franke, Richard Herbert. WORKER PRODUCTIVITY AT HAWTHORNE (REPLY TO SCHLAIFER), *pp. 1006-1027.* Robert Schlaifer's models confound rather than explain the behavior in the experiment; a reappraisal of the data supports the 1978 conclusion that the main factors in increasing productivity were managerial discipline, the economic depression, and the provision of rest pauses.

1871. —. IMMIGRATION ISSUES IN AN ERA OF UNSANCTIONED MIGRATION: A SYMPOSIUM. *Industrial and Labor Relations Rev. 1980 33(3): 295-314.*
Fogel, Walter. UNITED STATES IMMIGRATION POLICY AND UNSANCTIONED MIGRANTS, *pp. 295-311.* After providing an introduction to the symposium as a whole, this paper argues that basic changes are needed in this country's immigration policy to cope with the large flow of migrants who have entered the United States illegally in recent years. Fogel attacks the position, described best in Michael J. Piore's recent study, *Birds of Passage,* that most illegal immigrants fill only those jobs that native workers will not take and intend their stay in the United States to be temporary, not permanent. Fogel disputes both of those claims and argues that alternate forms of adjustment to labor shortages are available and preferable. He favors an immigration policy that would make our society less heavily dependent on rapid economic growth and, by reducing the number of migrants permitted to enter this country, would increase the relative wage of low-skilled indigenous workers. He recommends particularly the adoption of a law prohibiting the employment of illegal aliens and levying civil or criminal penalties on employers who violate that law. 47 notes.

Piore, Michael J. COMMENT, *pp. 312-314.* This comment presents a brief response to Fogel's criticism of the author's position on immigration policy. Piore summarizes his recent study, *Birds of Passage,* as arguing in part that most undocumented migration to this country in recent years has been initiated by employers with jobs to fill that native workers shun; that most migrants originally intended their stay to be temporary; and that severe problems resulted when this migration, like many others, failed to remain temporary in nature. The author recommends that public policy should focus less on controlling the supply of foreign labor than on controlling the demand for such labor, through improving the terms and enforcement of minimum wage and similar laws.   J

1872. —. [JOB SATISFACTION AND WORKING WOMEN].
Andrisani, Paul J. JOB SATISFACTION AMONG WORKING WOMEN. *Signs 1978 3(3): 588-607.* Between 1967 and 1972, job satisfaction among American women declined, but there is no evidence to prove that levels of satisfaction were extremely low. In no year surveyed were more than 3% of the women dissatisfied. The measurable decline from "highly satisfied" to "somewhat satisfied" among the national sample of 5,000 women may be attributed to a changing work ethic which places more emphasis on "intrinsic" aspects. Black women are less satisfied than whites, and a husband's attitude about his wife's career is more important than the psychological strains of preschool children. Based on National Longitudinal Survey personal interviews, US Department of Labor research, and secondary sources; 5 tables, 31 notes, appendix.
Ferber, Marianne A. COMMENT ON PAUL ANDRISANI'S "JOB SATISFACTION AMONG WORKING WOMEN." *Signs 1978 4(1): 196-199.* Questions Andrisani's hypothesis that job satisfaction means a successful adjustment to the working world. Because job satisfaction is influenced by career aspirations, women who advance may still be dissatisfied if the advancements do not meet their aspirations. Husbands' attitudes may be less important than Andrisani thinks, because they are influenced by the wife's pursuits.
Andrisani, Paul J. REPLY TO FERBER. *Signs 1978 4(1): 199-200.* Aspirations and measures of job satisfaction cannot be considered absolute measures, but job dissatisfaction is increasing. There is 'potential pathology' in the problem which cannot be dismissed.   S. P. Conner

1873. —. TEN YEARS ON THE ASSEMBLY LINE. *Progressive Labor 1973 8(6): 63-68.* "This interview with a veteran auto worker brings into sharp focus the question of the life-and-death character of the class struggle. Working for the big auto moguls, or any boss, is not simply a matter of 'bringing home the bacon' every week. It is a question of workers and bosses locked in a death battle."   J

1874. —. WHAT A LIFE: TODAY'S COWBOY AT WORK. *Colorado Heritage 1981 (1): 68-100.* Provides a briefly annotated pictorial presentation of cowboys and cattle raising in Colorado. Depicted and described are such activities as branding, calving, dehorning, dipping, earmarking, feeding, herding, rounding-up, spraying, vaccination and watering of cattle. Ranching is a modern business and benefits from technology, but "the contemporary cowboy's life is not all that different from his counterparts of a century ago." 55 photos.
O. H. Zabel

The Labor Movement

1875. Androsov, V. P. NOVYE IAVLENIIA V RABOCHEM DVI-ZHENII SSHA [New phenomena in the American workers' movement]. *Novaia i Noveishaia Istoriia [USSR] 1973 (3): 19-31.* The American economic crisis has caused even greater contradictions within the capitalist system leading to a radical regrouping of social and political forces. Details problems over manning levels, pay, and unemployment. The alliance of trade union bureaucrats with government and capitalists worked against proletarian interests. Realizing this, workers struck more often, and even government employees went on strike. Progressive workers of different races worked together against the racist policies of the workers' aristocracy. Lower-paid workers began to unionize themselves. The rank and file were beginning to assert themselves against the trade unions' alliance with the two-party bourgeois system. The logic of class warfare will lead to greater struggles. Based on contemporary newspaper and documentary sources; 40 notes.   D. N. Collins

1876. Åsard, Erik. AMERICAN UNIONS AND INDUSTRIAL DEMOCRACY: THE "BUSINESS UNIONISM" THESIS REEXAMINED. *Statsvetenskaplig Tidskrift [Sweden] 1982 85(3): 155-164.* Examines some alternatives to traditional business unionism that have recently been considered by trade union leaders in the United States.

1877. Barbash, Jack. THE LABOR MOVEMENT AFTER WORLD WAR II. *Monthly Labor Rev. 1976 99(11): 34-37.* Discusses factors in the growth of the labor movement in industry from 1946-70's, emphasizing strikes, the AFL-CIO merger, the Taft-Hartley Act, and collective bargaining.

1878. Bendiner, Burton B. A LABOR RESPONSE TO THE MULTI-NATIONALS. *Monthly Labor Rev. 1978 101(7). 9-13.* Established in 1966 in response to the development of multinational corporations, the World Auto Councils coordinate assistance and cooperation among the world's auto unions.

1879. Benson, H. W. LABOR LEADERS, INTELLECTUALS, AND FREEDOM IN THE UNIONS. *Dissent 1973 20(2): 206-210.* Successful revolt of Miners for Democracy within the United Mine Workers of America.

1880. Berney, Barbara. THE RISE AND FALL OF THE UMW FUND. *Southern Exposure 1978 6(2): 95-102.* The United Mine Workers of America Health and Retirement Fund, created in 1946, was one of the most innovative health care delivery systems in America. Beginning with a royalty of five cents per ton of coal mined, which was later raised to 40 cents per ton, the Fund collected revenues from mine operators which were used to establish a series of hospitals in the coal regions and partially to subsidize health clinics and rehabilitation services for disabled miners. The decline of the coal industry during 1950's-early 1960's caused a revenue decline resulting in the sale of the hospitals in 1962. Incompetent and even criminal mismanagement of the Fund under the leadership of Anthony Boyle created further problems of revenue flow. Under the 1977 contract the burden of health insurance was shifted to the coal operators, with miners having to pay part of the cost to subsidize health clinics.   N. Lederer

1881. Blake, David H. LABOR'S MULTINATIONAL OPPORTU-NITIES. *Foreign Policy 1973 (12): 132-143.* Points to trends toward a new sense of internationalism in labor movements in response to effects of multinational corporations.

1882. Block, Richard N. UNION ORGANIZING AND THE ALLO-CATION OF UNION RESOURCES. *Industrial and Labor Relations Rev. 1980 34(1): 101-113.* This study examines the propensity of unions to allocate resources to organizing activity. The author hypothesizes that as a union increases its extent of organization, the need of its members for organizing services declines relative to their need for representation services and also the costs of organizing are more likely to exceed its benefits. Consequently, the percentage of a union's resources devoted to organizing is expected to vary inversely with the extent to which the union has organized its primary jurisdiction. Data limitations prevent a direct test of this hypothesis, but a model based on this reasoning is used to predict differences across labor unions in the number of NLRB representation elections per 1000 union members. An analysis of relevant data for 1972-78 tends to support the model.   J

1883. Bolton, Lena W. BARGAINING AHEAD: MAJOR CON-TRACTS EXPIRING IN 1974. *Monthly Labor Rev. 1973 96(12): 43-51.* Discusses labor union leadership and collective bargaining negotiations in the steel, aluminum, aerospace, and coal mining industries in 1973, including likely prospects for 1974.

1884. Burlington, Bo. COMMUNITY UNION. *Working Papers for a New Soc. 1977 4(4): 20-22.* Discusses the organizational growth of the Rhode Island Workers Association due to its obtaining contractual reforms for workers from management, 1974-75.

1885. Chaison, Gary N. FEDERATION EXPULSIONS AND UNION MERGERS IN THE UNITED STATES. *Relations Industrielles/Industrial Relations [Canada] 1973 28(2): 343-361.* "While the frequency of mergers among unions in the United States has only recently increased, mergers have played a major role in the affairs of unions expelled from federations (AFL, CIO, and AFL-CIO) since 1949. An examination of the seventeen expelled unions indicates that only two have entirely disbanded and only one has returned directly to its federation. The remaining expelled unions merged with or into either their rival affiliates or other expelled unions. It is suggested that this high incidence of mergers was the result of the manner in which isolation induced exiles to merge while also reducing previously formidable barriers."   J

1886. Chapman, Frank. NEW CHALLENGE TO LABOR RIGHTS. *Freedomways 1979 19(3): 137-142.* Reviews antilabor sentiments since the 1930's as expressed in the Taft-Hartley Act, the New Deal's use of labor to bail out big business during the Depression, the strong-arm strikebreaking methods of such companies as US Steel and General Motors, the Landrum-Griffin Act, the antiunion stance of the J. P. Stevens Company, etc., and calls for vigilance by the labor unions and resistance to antilabor movements.

1887. Cooke, William N. DETERMINANTS OF THE OUTCOMES OF UNION CERTIFICATION ELECTIONS. *Industrial and Labor Relations Rev. 1983 36(3): 402-414.* Analyzes determinants of union election outcomes at the level of the work unit. Considers social psychology of groups, the economic and sociopolitical environment, National Labor Relations Board procedures, and the extent of union organization of the industry. A negative relationship exists between unit size and union victories in units of fewer than 65 workers, but no relationship exists in larger units. Also negatively related to union victories are delays between petition and election dates, elections held in southern states having right-to-work laws, and elections involving the Teamsters. In contrast, workers are more likely to vote for representation as unemployment levels and the proportion of consent elections rise and as the rate of unionization in their industry rises to 35%. Based on NLRB election records.   J/S

1888. Cox, Robert W. LABOR AND HEGEMONY. *Int. Organization 1977 31(3): 385-424.* The United States' notice of withdrawal from the ILO is to be understood in terms of hegemonic power relations. "Tripartism" is an ideology based upon a dominant historical tendency, namely the emergence of a corporative form of state in both developed and underdeveloped countries. The AFL-CIO has participated in the construction of the corporative state in the United States and has supported its hegemonic role in the world in concert with American business interests and the CIA. Neither the ILO nor international trade union organizations (especially the ICFTU) has enjoyed a stable relationship with the center of hegemonic power in the labor field, since the AFL-CIO has conducted a unilateral foreign policy. The functionalist strategy of executive leadership asserting the autonomy of an international organization through task expansion in technical fields has been almost totally irrelevant to the issue. Nor has the ILO found an alternative counter-hegemonic base of support, e.g., in the Third World. The existing hegemony has reasserted itself through the ILO program and ideology even as the United States has withdrawn material support. Hegemony, which no longer operates through majority votes in international organizations, works instead through bureaucratic controls. This structure of power has prevented the ILO from confronting effectively the real social issues of employment-creation, land reform, marginality, and poverty in general. Initiatives that have been taken to deal with such issues have all ultimately been diverted into programs consistent with the hegemonic ideology and power relations.   J

1889. Fisher, Robert W. LABOR IN A YEAR OF ECONOMIC STABILIZATION. *Monthly Labor Rev. 1973 96(1): 17-26.* Discusses employment recovery, inflation, collective bargaining, and labor law as they affected labor unions in 1972.

1890. Fraser, Douglas A. BUSINESS WAGES CLASS WARFARE: WILL LABOR FOLLOW SUIT? *Radical Hist. Rev. 1978 (18): 117-121.* Reprints the resignation letter of United Automobile Workers of America President Douglas A. Fraser from the Labor-Management

Group, a committee of eight corporate leaders and eight labor leaders, on 19 July 1978.

1891. Freeman, Richard B. UNIONISM AND THE DISPERSION OF WAGES. *Industrial and Labor Relations Rev. 1980 34(1): 3-23.* This study examines the effect of trade unionism on the dispersion of wages among male wage and salary workers in the private sector in the United States. It finds that the application of union wage policies designed to standardize rates within and across establishments significantly reduces wage dispersion among workers covered by union contracts and that unions further reduce wage dispersion by narrowing the white-collar/blue-collar differential within establishments. These effects dominate the more widely studied impact of unionism on the dispersion of average wages across incustries, so that on net unionism appears to reduce rather than increase wage dispersion or inequality in the United States.   J

1892. Freeman, Richard L. and Medoff, James L. THE TWO FACES OF UNIONISM. *Public Interest 1979 (57): 69-93.* The view that unions are organizations whose chief function is to raise wages is seriously misleading. In addition to raising wages, unions have important nonwage effects that influence modern industrial life. Workers have been provided a voice at work and in the political arena, so unions have positively influenced the economic and social systems. Such union influenced areas as efficiency, personnel practices and employee benefits, race, and corruption are examined according to the two responses to unionism, the negative "monopoly view" and the positive "collective voice/institutional response view." 4 tables, 6 notes.   S. Harrow

1893. Gamm, Sara. THE ELECTION BASE OF NATIONAL UNION EXECUTIVE BOARDS. *Industrial and Labor Relations Rev. 1979 32(3): 295-311.* This article analyzes the effect of the election base of executive boards on the internal political life of national unions, especially the capacity of such unions to support opposition to incumbent members of the board. An examination of the constitutions of nearly all American unions with a membership of over 25,000 in 1975 indicates that the great majority of national unions elect board members on an at-large basis, a system, the author argues, that tends to discourage dissent within unions and to prevent effective representation of local interests. In contrast, the majority of unions that select board members by regional election include those that have experienced successful "revolts" in recent years, such as the Steelworkers and Mine Workers.   J

1894. Gilpin, Toni. ORGANIZING AGAINST CONCESSIONS. *Int. Labor and Working Class Hist. 1983 (23): 51-57.* Examines union strategies to combat the recent trend toward concessions bargaining, in which corporations demand that workers either give up wage increases and benefits or face unemployment through layoffs or plant closings, as discussed at the 1982 "Organizing against Concessions" conference in Detroit, Michigan.

1895. Godson, Roy. THE AFL FOREIGN POLICY MAKING PROCESS FROM THE END OF WORLD WAR II TO THE MERGER. *Labor Hist. 1975 16(3): 325-337.* Contrary to traditional interpretation, a close examination of the American Federation of Labor decisionmaking processes reveals that its foreign policy was made independently of the US government. The most important policymaking body was the Free Trade Union Committee, composed of Matthew Woll, David Dubinsky, George Meany, and William Green, who were largely autonomous in foreign policy. Based on the AFL and FTUC archives and personal interviews; 28 notes.   L. L. Athey

1896. Godson, Roy. NONGOVERNMENTAL ORGANIZATIONS IN WORLD POLITICS: THE AMERICAN FEDERATION OF LABOR IN FRANCE, 1945-1952. *World Affairs 1973/74 136(3): 208-231.*

1897. Gray, Lois S. UNIONS IMPLEMENTING MANAGERIAL TECHNIQUES. *Monthly Labor Rev. 1981 104(6): 3-13.* Focuses upon the tendency of American labor unions to adopt two personnel practices characteristic of business and government in the United States: searching for outside talent and personnel training, describing how the political structure of labor unions stands as an obstacle to this trend; 1970-81.

1898. Haslam, Gerald. *THE LAST HURRAH* AND AMERICAN BOSSISM. *Rendezvous 1973 8(1): 33-44.* Discusses the depiction of political bossism, ward heelers, and union leaders in Edwin O'Connor's novel *The Last Hurrah* , 1956.

1899. Hendricks, Wallace E. and Kahn, Lawrence M. COST-OF-LIVING CLAUSES IN UNION CONTRACTS: DETERMINANTS AND EFFECTS. *Industrial and Labor Relations Rev. 1983 36(3): 447-460.* Both union bargaining power and inflation uncertainty positively affected the probability that a cost-of-living adjustment clause was adopted as well as the strength of the clause adopted. Negatively influencing the incidence and strength of adjustment clauses were unanticipated changes in an industry's prices. Wage inflation was greater under contracts with uncapped adjustments than under all other contracts, a result that also was positively influenced by the amount of unanticipated inflation. Covers 1969-81.   J/S

1900. Hodgson, James D. THE LABOR MOVEMENT ISN'T WHAT IT USED TO BE. *Center Mag. 1973 6(5): 56-60.*

1901. Holloway, Harry. INTEREST GROUPS IN THE POSTPARTISAN ERA: THE POLITICAL MACHINE OF THE AFL-CIO. *Pol. Sci. Q. 1977 94(1): 117-133.* Argues that the weakening of political parties has been accompanied by the rise of interest group political activity and that the political machine created by the AFL-CIO federation embodies such activity on an unusual scale.   J

1902. Howard, Robert. SOLIDARITY BEGINS AT HOME. *Working Papers Mag. 1982 9(1): 18-27.* Over the past 30 years, unionists have neglected the concept that they are a social force with the result that younger members are apathetic and not willing to make sacrifices.

1903. Humphreys, James. MILLER VS BOYLE: REVOLT IN THE COAL FIELDS. *New South 1973 28(1): 34-42.* How Arnold Miller defeated United Mine Workers of America president Tony Boyle.

1904. Janus, Charles J. UNION MERGERS IN THE 1970'S: A LOOK AT THE REASONS AND THE RESULTS. *Monthly Labor Rev. 1978 101(10): 13-23.* Explores 21 mergers in trade unions, professional groups, and the public sector.

1905. Johnson, Ronald W. ORGANIZED LABOR'S POSTWAR RED SCARE: THE UE IN ST. LOUIS. *North Dakota Q. 1980 48(1): 28-39.* Discusses the antiradical attacks on District 8 of the United Electrical, Radio and Machine Workers of America (UE) in St. Louis, Missouri, as an example of the antiradical, anti-Communist conflicts within the Congress of Industrial Organizations (CIO) during the late 1940's by liberal and right-wing people in organized labor.

1906. Keitel, Robert S. THE MERGER OF THE INTERNATIONAL UNION OF MINE, MILL AND SMELTER WORKERS INTO THE UNITED STEEL WORKERS OF AMERICA. *Labor Hist. 1974 15(1): 36-43.* Contends that a politically radical union can not survive if removed from economic realities. Provides the merger of the Mine-Mill workers into the United Steelworkers as a case study illustrating the thesis. Based on publications of the Mine-Mill Union and newspapers. 26 notes.   L. L. Athey

1907. Koch, Lene. ANTI-COMMUNISM IN THE AMERICAN LABOR MOVEMENTS. REFLECTIONS ON THE COMMUNIST EXPULSIONS IN 1949-1950. *Am. Studies in Scandinavia [Norway] 1981 13(2): 93-110.* The Congress of Industrial Organizations (CIO) developed a consistent political stance closely allied with the Democratic Party's position. This position evolved partially in response to the Communists within the CIO and partly as a result of the ouster of the Communists from the CIO in 1949 and 1950. 37 notes.
                                                       E. E. Krogstad

1908. Kupferberg, Seth. AFSCME: PROFILE OF A UNION. *Working Papers for a New Soc. 1979 6(6): 44-54.* Describes the merger between the Civil Service Employees Association (CSEA) and the American Federation of State, County and Municipal Employees (AFSCME) in April 1978, and the problems that a union with one million members faces in light of the relationship among today's economy, public employees, and politicians in the United States.

1909. Lapitski, M. PROFSOIUZNOE DVIZHENIE V SSHA: TENDENTSII RAZVITIIA [The trade union movement in the USA: tendencies of its development]. *Mirovaia Ekonomika i Mezhdunarodnye Otnosheniia [USSR] 1975 (7): 109-115.* Recent growth of "progressive" forces in the lower levels of American trade unions has resulted in intensification of industrial disputes and the politicization of the organized workers' movement.

1910. Mostovets, N. V. NOVYE CHERTY RABOCHEGO DVIZHENIIA I DEIATEL'NOSTI KOMPARTII SSHA [New characteristics of the workers' movement and activity of the Communist Party in the USA]. *Voprosy Istorii [USSR] 1977 (12): 51-63.* Reviews the American political and economic scene, 1977, based on American periodical sources, and stemming from remarks by Brezhnev at the 25th Party Congress. (This coincided with the US Bicentennial celebrations.) The new characteristics appear to lie in the strengthening of trade union activities.

1911. Okuneva, M. A. LENINSKAIA KRITIKA TRED-IUNIONIZMA I POLITIKA AFT-KPP V LATINSKOI AMERIKE [Lenin's criticism of reformist trade-union ideology and the AFL-CIO policy in Latin America]. *Voprosy Istorii [USSR] 1973 (10): 96-110.* Imperialism's unceasing attempts to bring the working-class movement in Latin America under its influence represent a new phenomenon in contemporary neo-colonialist policies. Among the various means most frequently used to achieve this purpose, particular importance attaches to reformist trade union ideology which was trenchantly criticized by V. I. Lenin. The article graphically shows the wide-scale "trade union expansion" launched by the reactionary AFL-CIO leadership with the aim of introducing trade unionist doctrines in the working-class movement of Latin America. Its chief instrument is the American Institute for Free Labor Development, which is chiefly oriented on professional trade union leaders who mould the labour aristocracy to serve as a vehicle of influencing the entire proletariat. This "trade union expansion" on the part of the AFL-CIO is encountering mounting resistance from the progressive forces of Latin America.   J

1912. Olsen, David. LABOR'S STAKE IN WORKER CONTROL. *Working Papers for a New Soc. 1981 8(2): 12-16.* Although American unions have largely shunned the responsibilities of management and economic leadership because of their perception of worker participation in these spheres as a management device to undermine unions, this article advances a variety of reasons for the fresh appeal of democratic management as a partial remedy for the nearly universal problems of worker discontent, economic stagnation, and declining productivity.

1913. Peterson, Mark. THE MULTINATIONAL CORPORATION. *Freeman 1974 24(1): 18-23.* Argues against the AFL-CIO's position that multinational corporations cause unemployment in the United States.

1914. Powell, Daniel A. PAC TO COPE: THIRTY-TWO YEARS OF SOUTHERN LABOR IN POLITICS. Fink, Gary M. and Reed, Merl E., eds. *Essays in Southern Labor History: Selected Papers, Southern Labor History Conference, 1976.* (Westport, Conn.; London, England: Greenwood Pr., 1977): 244-255. A narrative of 1943-75 relative to southern labor's entry into politics, and an evaluation of its effect. With labor at an all-time low the CIO's organization of its Political Action Committee (PAC) in 1943 was of epochal significance; likewise AFL's organization of its Labor's League for Political Education (LLPE). With the merger of the parent organizations these also merged to form the Committee on Political Education (COPE) in 1955. The race issue's emergence to a major place in southern politics slowed up COPE's effectiveness, sidetracking interest from the authentic issues. The situation has been improved significantly in recent years, and it is anticipated that COPE will become increasingly effective.
                                                       R. V. Ritter

1915. Raphael, Edna E. WORKING WOMEN AND THEIR MEMBERSHIP IN LABOR UNIONS. *Monthly Labor Rev. 1974 97(5): 27-33.* Between 1966 and 1970 the proportion of American women workers who were members of labor unions declined, although earnings differentials between men and women were less for women who were union members.

1916. Redburn, Thomas. GOVERNMENT UNIONS: THE NEW BULLIES ON THE BLOCK. *Washington Monthly 1974 6(10): 19-27.* Charts the growth and victories of government labor organizations, 1961-74, illustrating how their votes, money, and resistance to external evaluation make public employees the most powerful and dangerous force in today's labor movement.

1917. Reynolds, Morgan O. THE INTELLECTUAL MUDDLE OVER LABOR UNIONS. *J. of Social and Pol. Studies 1979 4(3): 269-281.* Economic analysis of labor unions reveals that they retard the optimum performance of the American economic system and that, after 40 years of experience, they lack an intellectual constituency for their defense.

1918. "Rusticus". THE SADLOWSKI CAMPAIGN. *Radical Am. 1977 11(1): 75-78.* Ed Sadlowski's campaign for the presidency of the United Steelworkers of America creates problems for the steelworker rank-and-file. His promises are reminiscent of those made by I. W. Abel in his campaign and then repudiated. Sadlowski's demagoguery and reformism raise suspicion. The rank-and-file have not organized to any extent to support Sadlowski, nor have they been welcome at Sadlowski's headquarters to occupy meaningful roles in the campaign. Sadlowski and McBride have raised radical demands in the campaign, including the right of a worker accused of work rule infraction to remain on the job until the matter is settled. The issue of job security is deeply felt among the union membership. N. Lederer

1919. Savel'eva, I. M. SOVREMENNYE NEOLIBERAL'NYE KONTSEPTSII AMERIKANSKOGO TRED-IUNIONIZMA [The contemporary neo-liberal conceptions of American trade unionism]. *Voprosy Istorii [USSR] 1974 (4): 77-90.* "Analyzes the views of the ideologists of American neo-liberalism on the character and functions of the trade union movement. The author formulates the basic principles of neo-liberal ideology: state regulation of socio-economic relations, flexible social manoeuvring and the positive view on the trade unions. Under the impact of far-reaching changes in America's socio-political life, the mounting strike movement, the powerful manifestations of the Negro population and students, and due to the activization of the extreme Right and Left trends of bourgeois thought ('firm individualists' and the 'New Left'), the neo-liberals in the 1960's-70's put forward a new conception of trade unionism. The neo-liberals' class aim consists in the striving to rely on the assistance of trade unions in implementing bourgeois-reformist programmes and at the same time preventing the possibility of their being transformed into a force capable of undermining the pillars of capitalism. By advocating the 'social activity' of the trade unions, the neo-liberals are seeking to confine their political activity to the narrow bounds of the two-party system." J

1920. Schmid, Alex P. DIE AUSSENPOLITISCHE ROLLE DER GEWERKSCHAFTEN (AFL-CIO) DER VEREINIGTEN STAATEN [The foreign policy of trade unions (AFL-CIO) of the United States]. *Zeitgeschichte [Austria] 1975 3(1): 8-14.* Most US labor unions have never been concerned with international workers' movements. Occasionally interest surfaced when foreign labor markets posed a threat to American workers. Arthur W. Calhoun, in 1928, felt American laborers would benefit most by supporting US industry's expansion into the world economy. After World War II, the AFL and the CIO actively supported foreign and military assistance programs which provided millions of jobs for Americans. Further involvement is likely only in an expanding economy. Based on primary and secondary sources; 40 notes. G. H. Libbey

1921. Scott, Joan W. L'HISTOIRE DU MONDE OUVRIER AUX ÉTATS-UNIS DEPUIS 1960 [The history of the labor world in the United States since 1960]. *Mouvement Social [France] 1977 July-Sept.(100): 121-131.* Studies information in historical research orientation in the United States after 1960. Historians have reversed their perspective on the labor movement, from a previous emphasis on economic history to an emphasis on social history. The change in methodology which resulted from this reversal was evident in research published in the early 1970's. The new methodology is influenced by three factors: 1) the New Left trend of local militant groups which express class conflict outside established organizations, calling for reinterpretation of class struggle and class consciousness concepts, 2) the influence of the social sciences and especially sociology on labor

history, calling for research into the causes of social agitation and instability, such as urban violence and labor unrest, and 3) the new availability of statistical analysis and scientific method in research, permitting the historian to take into account certain quantitative data never before considered. The new research orientation also considers aspects of culture rather than ideology in the labor movement, leading to studies on ethnic background, family life, professional mobility, and cultural political movements, such as those led by blacks and women. Based on published works; 12 notes. S. Sevilla

1922. Sexton, Patricia Cayo. ORGANIZING A LABOR COLLEGE. *Dissent 1973 20(3): 349-352.*

1923. Sharman, Ben. A TRADE UNIONIST VIEW OF MULTINATIONAL CORPORATIONS. *WorldView 1975 18(11): 31-35.* Discusses employee-employer relations and labor unions' views toward multinational corporations in the 1970's, including wages and job security.

1924. Shenfield, Arthur. TRADE UNION POWER AND THE LAW. *Modern Age 1980 24(3): 260-265.* Compares the activity of business cartels, which are illegal within the United States, and unions, which are legal. Unions should have a legal corporate existence, and be subject to rules that would make them peaceful. Based mainly on secondary sources; 2 notes. J. Powell

1925. Stieber, Jack. THE FUTURE OF PUBLIC EMPLOYEE UNIONISM IN THE UNITED STATES. *Industrial Relations [Canada] 1974 29(4): 825-839.* The author makes an evaluation of the significant features of collective bargaining in the United States' public sector. He deals successively with the forms of organization of public employee unionism, the impact of legislation on employee organization, the rivalries existing between various unions, associations, and professional organizations and also with more specific issues such as: the status of supervisors, union security, the strike, political activity and minority participation. J

1926. Weir, Stan. DOUG FRASER'S MIDDLE CLASS COALITION. *Radical Am. 1979 13(1): 18-29.* United Automobile Workers of America President Douglas Fraser resigned from the Labor Management Group, a nongovernmental committee of representatives from labor and management, in 1978 and urged unions and liberal and leftist organizations to organize an umbrella group of liberals to fight business; this will be ineffective because the coalition does not include the ranks of labor.

1927. Withorn, Ann. THE DEATH OF CLUW. *Radical Am. 1976 10(2): 47-51.* The Coalition of Labor Union Women has been divided in membership and purpose since its founding in 1973, between women in the upper levels of the trade union bureaucracy and women from various segments of the political Left. As described by a CLUW member, this division resulted in the ending of the organization as a viable group for all practical purposes at its first constitutional convention in December, 1975. The forces of conflict within the body included trade union women using the CLUW for upward mobility within union ranks, the internal divisions of the Left, the economic crisis, and the nature of American trade unionism. N. Lederer

1928. —. LIBERALS WIN IN UMW—WILL MINERS LOSE? *Progressive Labor 1973 9(1): 11-13.* This article unravels the false facade of liberalism in the trade union movement. Can the workers win if the big liberal politicians like Kennedy, et al., are supporting certain forces who they would like to see control the unions. The bosses would like to see workers in the usual bind, 'heads we win-tails you lose'. J

Professional, Technical, and White Collar Workers

1929. Alexander, Sharon Josephs. PIECE WORK IN THE UNIVERSITY, 1970'S STYLE. *Frontiers 1980 5(1): 56-58.* Discusses the reasons California state universities hire employees on a piecework basis, the advantages to the administration, and why employees choose to work part-time on a piecework basis, focusing on the Women's Studies

Program at California State University, Sacramento, which is entirely staffed by part-time workers whose job security is secure semester-by-semester; 1979.

1930. Alutto, Joseph A. and Belasco, James A. DETERMINANTS OF ATTITUDINAL MILITANCY AMONG NURSES AND TEACHERS. *Industrial and Labor Relations Rev. 1974 27(2): 216-227.* Although the increase in union activity among white-collar workers has been widespread, it is apparent that differences in militancy still exist among these workers. This study explores these differences by means of a questionnaire survey that measured the attitudes of approximately nine hundred nurses and teachers toward subjects such as collective bargaining and strikes by professional workers. The results demonstrate that attitudinal militancy does vary between these occupations and also within each occupation, according to the nature of the employing institution and the age, seniority, and certain personal characteristics of individual nurses and teachers.   J

1931. American Association of University Professors. THE ANNUAL REPORT ON THE ECONOMIC STATUS OF THE PROFESSION, 1982-83. *Acad.: Bull. of the AAUP 1983 69(4): 1-75.* Reports salary levels, tenure status, and fringe benefits for university faculty members.

1932. Antos, Joseph R. UNION EFFECTS ON WHITE-COLLAR COMPENSATION. *Industrial and Labor Relations Rev. 1983 36(3): 461-479.* Nonunion wages and total compensation are more responsive than union pay levels to worker productivity differences, such as education and work experience. Also, large firms pay 10-15% more to their white-collar employees than small firms in the nonunion sector but only 5% or less in the union sector. Overall, the white-collar union wage differential appears to be 3.5-4%, rising to 7.1% when fringe benefits are included in the dependent variable. Finds significant spillovers to nonunion white-collar workers.   J/S

1933. Atkin, J. Myron. WHO WILL TEACH IN HIGH SCHOOL? *Hist. Teacher 1982 15(2): 225-242.* The kind of people who will teach in public schools should be a matter of national concern. Many factors currently tend to discourage the most qualified students from teaching careers. These include poor pay, limited job prospects, limited advancement possibilities and a general pessimism on the part of society toward public education. Education departments in colleges and universities are faced with a series of problems that compound these difficulties. Note.
L. K. Blaser

1934. Bartol, Kathryn M. and Bartol, Robert A. WOMEN IN MANAGERIAL AND PROFESSIONAL POSITIONS: THE UNITED STATES AND THE SOVIET UNION. *Industrial & Labor Relations Rev. 1975 28(4): 524-534.* This study compares the employment of women in professional and managerial positions in the Soviet Union and the United States. The results indicate that women in the Soviet Union have made considerably greater progress than American women in the attainment of professional positions, but differences are less dramatic in managerial occupations. The data also suggest that many employment problems persist for Soviet women workers and that the USSR perhaps has been overrated as a model of employment equality.   J

1935. Barton, Paul E. HUMAN RESOURCES, THE CHANGING LABOR MARKET, AND UNDERGRADUATE EDUCATION. *Liberal Educ. 1975 61(2): 275-284.* While the number of college graduates has increased during the 1970's, the number of jobs requiring college degrees has decreased.

1936. Bartosik, Jerzy. EMIGRACJA EUROPEJSKA WYSOKO KWALIFIKOWANEJ SIŁY ROBOCZEJ DO USA [The European emigration of a highly qualified labor force to the USA]. *Przegląd Zachodni [Poland] 1968 24(4): 455-458.* Discusses the "brain drain", particularly from Western Europe to America which reached such alarming proportions during 1963-66. It is estimated that annually 10,000 specialists (40% of those from Europe) emigrate to the United States.

1937. Blumberg, Paul and Murtha, James M. COLLEGE GRADUATES AND THE AMERICAN DREAM. *Dissent 1977 24(1): 45-53.* Summarizes studies which point to decreased opportunities for college

graduates in the 1970's with attendant lowering of real income and increased unemployment among the college-educated.

1938. Braito, Rita and Powers, Edward A. WHAT THE OTHER HALF THINKS: THE IMPLICATIONS OF FEMALE PERCEPTIONS FOR WORK DEMANDS. *Sociol. Inquiry 1977 47(1): 59-64.* Surveys 353 female registered nurses in a northwestern urban center in 1968 and finds that the women believed that their husbands would not be threatened if theirs were the greater income, and that they saw a greater need for money than did their husbands.

1939. Brown, Ralph S. REPORT ON THE CONFERENCE. *Acad.: Bull. of the AAUP 1983 69(1): 4-9.* Summarizes major issues discussed at the American Association of University Professors Conference on Faculty and Higher Education in Hard Times, 20-22 May 1982, in Washington, D.C.: planning, reduction in size of faculty, financial exigency and tenure abrogation, program reduction, and affirmative action claims.

1940. Byrnes, Robert F. THE ACADEMIC LABOR MARKET: WHERE DO WE GO FROM HERE? *Slavic Rev. 1977 36(2): 286-291.* A review essay: Allen M. Cartter's, *Ph.D.'s and the Academic Labor Market* (New York: McGraw-Hill, 1976). The book is a thorough study of Ph.D. programs in American universities in relation to the labor market, especially in the academic world where there is a glut of trained specialists. New emphasis should be placed on undergraduate programs, with improved quality and more saturation regarding Eastern Europe. Graduate programs should come second and be reevaluated and improved where retained, with a new emphasis on self reliance rather than subsidy.   R. V. Ritter

1941. Carter, Michael J. and Carter, Susan Boslego. WOMEN'S RECENT PROGRESS IN THE PROFESSIONS OR, WOMEN GET A TICKET TO RIDE AFTER THE GRAVY TRAIN HAS LEFT THE STATION. *Feminist Studies 1981 7(3): 477-504.* Challenges the view that women are making increasing progress in the professions. Greater stratification is emerging in the professions as the number of practitioners grows and the power of traditional professional organizations declines before government regulation. The number of top spots has not increased, but competition for them is growing. Women, often impeded by domestic responsibilities, are disproportionately found in the lower ranks, with low pay, little autonomy and least chance for mobility. Among new PhD's, MD's and lawyers, women are more likely than men to be in community colleges, on hospital staffs, or in legal clinics. 80 notes.   S. Hildenbrand

1942. Chait, Richard P. and Ford, Andrew T. BEYOND TRADITIONAL TENURE—EXTENDED PROBATIONARY PERIODS AND SUSPENSION OF "UP-OR-OUT" RULE. *Change 1982 14(5): 44-54.* Discusses policies designed to defer the tenure decision, especially in extended probationary periods, noting how various colleges and universities developed tenure policies during 1970-81.

1943. Cheng, Charles W.; Hamer, Irving; and Barron, Melanie. A FRAMEWORK FOR CITIZEN INVOLVEMENT IN TEACHER NEGOTIATIONS. *Educ. and Urban Soc. 1979 11(2): 219-240.* Discusses the need since the 1960's for the structure of teacher collective bargaining to be changed in order to achieve more participation in educational decisionmaking by parents and citizens.

1944. Clinton, Charles A. THE ANTHROPOLOGIST AS HIRED HAND. *Human Organization 1975 34(2): 197-204.* Explores the new role of anthropologists as a "minor functionary in a research bureaucracy."   S

1945. Delon, Floyd G. THE CONTROL OF TEACHER CONDUCT: IMPACTS ON SCHOOL SOCIAL CLIMATE. *Educ. and Urban Soc. 1982 14(2): 235-254.* Discusses teachers' rights in public schools since 1960, including federal and state court decisions, civil rights legislation, and collective bargaining.

1946. Doyle, Philip. MUNICIPAL PENSION PLANS: PROVISIONS AND PAYMENTS. *Monthly Labor Rev. 1977 100(11): 24-31.* Surveys pensions offered to municipal employees across the United States, including discussion of benefits, age and service requirements, pension escalators, and similar plans provided by the federal government.

1947. Dreijmanis, John. POLITICAL SCIENCE IN THE UNITED STATES: AN UNCERTAIN VOCATION. *Politico [Italy] 1980 45(4): 649-658.* The post-World War II period witnessed an unprecedented increase in enrollment in all institutions of higher education in the United States. At this time the American economy was also rapidly expanding. Thus in the 1950's and 1960's most of the graduates were absorbed into jobs in accordance with their career expectations. In the 1970's, the situation for university graduates worsened dramatically, especially for those holding doctorates. This situation was also true of those with doctorates in political science. Table, 59 notes.   J. Powell

1948. Dresch, Stephen P. THE WEAKENING OF ACADEMIC LABOR MARKET AND THE POLITICIZATION OF ACADEME. *PS 1983 16(3): 527-531.* Discusses the transition from market- to politically-determined faculty salaries since 1949, a development that has led to the growth of faculty unionization.

1949. Egger, Rowland. CIVIL SERVANTS AT MID-CAREER: MANAGEMENT TRAINING IN AMERICAN UNIVERSITIES. *Public Administration [Great Britain] 1976 54(1): 83-98.* Discusses the effects of the Training Act (1958) in creating management training programs for civil service employees at colleges and universities.

1950. Eisinger, Peter K. BLACK EMPLOYMENT IN MUNICIPAL JOBS: THE IMPACT OF BLACK POLITICAL POWER. *Am. Pol. Sci. Rev. 1982 76(2): 380-392.* An analysis of affirmative action data regarding levels of black employment in the civil service of 43 US cities indicates that observed variations are mainly a function of the size of the black population and the presence of a black mayor. By interpreting the size of the black population as an indicator of potential bloc voting power and by making explicit the links between the mayor's office and the personnel system, the authors conclude that civil service hiring represents one tangible benefit of black political power.   J/S

1951. Falk, William W.; Grimes, Michael D.; and Lord, George F., III. PROFESSIONALISM AND CONFLICT IN A BUREAUCRATIC SETTING: THE CASE OF A TEACHERS' STRIKE. *Social Problems 1982 29(5): 551-560.* A survey of teachers' attitudes in a Southern city during a strike in 1979 reveals that strikers are more professionally oriented than nonstrikers, and they are unhappy in their jobs and want greater authority over them.

1952. Fannin, Patricia M. THE CAREERS OF PROFESSIONAL WOMEN. *Teachers Coll. Record 1981 82(4): 689-693.* Reviews Alice M. Yohalen's *The Careers of Professional Women: Commitment and Conflict* (1979), a followup to the study described in Eli Ginzberg's *Lifestyles of Educated Women* (1966). Both studies reveal that most professional women experienced some dissatisfaction with either their professional or their family lives, often caused by employment discontinuity or job discrimination. 7 notes.   E. C. Bailey, Jr.

1953. Faulkner, Peter. WHISTLE BLOWER: PETER FAULKNER, NUCLEAR ENGINEER. *Civil Liberties Rev. 1978 5(3): 41-49.* Peter Faulkner, systems application engineer for the Nuclear Services Corp., submitted confidential documents and a criticism of the engineering deficiencies in atomic power systems to Senate Subcommittee's Energy Research and Development Administration hearing in 1974, this resulted in his dismissal by his employers.

1954. Felzan, Jill. RETOOLING THE HISTORY PH.D.: CAREERS IN BUSINESS PROGRAMS. *Public Hist. 1981 3(3): 132-136.* Discusses the Careers in Business program started in the late 1970's at the Graduate School of Business Administration at New York University for people with doctorates in the humanities and social sciences.

1955. Fenn, Donna. WHITE SLAVES. *Washington Monthly 1981 13(9): 21-28.* Reports on the current status of nurses and nursing suggesting that health care and hospital practices produce unsafe working conditions, an underpaid and undertrained staff, and a general feeling of second class status, 1970's.

1956. Fiorito, Jack. THE SCHOOL-TO-WORK TRANSITION OF COLLEGE GRADUATES. *Industrial and Labor Relations Rev. 1981 35(1): 103-114.* The lag between curriculum choice and degree attainment generally ensures a mismatch between new labor supply and employer requirements, even if students are quite responsive to labor market conditions. The author hypothesizes that adjustment to that lag is primarily a function of market conditions and the technical compatibility of possible combinations of college majors and occupations. The author's model explains a large proportion of the differences in that probability across majors and occupations. Covers 1965-78.   J/S

1957. Fisher, Berenice. THE PERILS OF SUCCESS: WOMEN AND ORGANIZATIONAL LEADERSHIP. *Hist. of Educ. Q. 1983 23(1): 113-122.* Reviews *Women and Educational Leadership* (1980), edited by Sari Knapp Biklen and Marilyn Brannigan, and *Outsiders on the Inside: Women and Organizations* (1981), edited by Barbara L. Forisha and Barbara Goldman, which examine the problems and contradictions faced by women entering leadership positions in government and industry.   J. T. Holton

1958. Gier, Nicholas. THE PHENOMENAL RISE OF FACULTY UNIONS. *Rendezvous 1978 13(1): 23-32.* While union membership in traditional areas is declining, faculty and teacher unions are growing dramatically. In 28 states allowing faculty bargaining, 28% of higher education faculty and staff are represented by unions, and a large majority of professors nationwide support collective bargaining. Educators' unionization is moving from the experimental stage to solid achievement, with all major organizations accepting a traditional "union" role. Positive attitudes about collective bargaining are gradually overcoming widespread resistance. Secondary sources; 7 tables, 16 notes.   L. K. Blaser

1959. Gorden, William I.; Tengler, Craig D.; and Infante, Dominic A. WOMEN'S CLOTHING PREDISPOSITIONS AS PREDICTORS OF DRESS AT WORK, JOB SATISFACTION, AND CAREER ADVANCEMENT. *Southern Speech Communication J. 1982 47(4): 422-434.* Data from women employees in the West, South, and Midwest confirms the hypothesis that female office employees whose clothing predispositions indicated higher clothing-consciousness, practicality, and lower exhibitionism, dressed more conservatively and experienced more career advancement and job satisfaction; discusses the implications in terms of organizational dress expectations and the price paid for violating such expectations.

1960. Gordon, Margaret S. THE LABOR MARKET AND THE STUDENT INTERESTS. *Liberal Educ. 1975 61(2): 149-160.* A job market crisis foreshadowed for college graduates during the 1980's could be averted with counseling programs at colleges and universities.

1961. Greenbaum, Joan. DIVISION OF LABOR IN THE COMPUTER FIELD. *Monthly Rev. 1976 28(3): 40-55.* Over the past twenty years computer related jobs have ". . . been transformed by capitalism to suit its needs, through carefully planned division of labor." What had been a dynamic new craft comprised of talented generalists became a rigid, hierarchical system of labor marked by narrowly defined job responsibilities, artificially restrained wages, and lack of opportunity for advancement. The recent oversupply of trained personnel has intensified these developments. 26 notes.   M. R. Yerburgh

1962. Haber, Sheldon E. THE MOBILITY OF PROFESSIONAL WORKERS AND FAIR HIRING. *Industrial and Labor Relations Rev. 1981 34(2): 257-264.* Analyzes data from the 1970 Census Public Use Sample to determine spatial mobility by occupation. Formulates a model which takes spatial mobility into account in estimating the proportion that blacks were expected to comprise of the labor pool available to employers in New York City and Philadelphia. When the model's estimates are compared with data, the results show that not only are local area data less appropriate for professionals than for blue-collar workers but national data can also be misleading when applied to professionals. The proportion of blacks among professionals available to a firm often lies somewhere between the estimates derived from local and national data.   J/S

1963. Hansen, W. Lee. THE DECLINE OF FACULTY SALARIES IN THE 1970S. *Q. Rev. of Econ. and Business 1981 21(4): 7-11.* Reviews the declining real wages and economic status of college professors; causes include the formula for faculty salary changes, which inhibit salary increases, and the decreasing social priority for higher education, which limits the funds allocated to higher education.

1964. Harrington, Michael. OLD WORKING CLASS, NEW WORKING CLASS. *Dissent 1974 21(2): 328-343.* Discusses the social and political implications of the new working class, which consists of skilled professional and technical workers in public sectors, and its relationship to the old working class, the blue-collar workers in industry. First published in the Winter 1972 *Dissent.*   S

1965. Holder, Todd and Hicks, Laurabeth. INCREASING THE COMPETENCIES OF TEACHERS AND COUNSELORS WITH SYSTEMATIC INTERPERSONAL SKILLS TRAINING. *J. of Negro Educ. 1977 46(4): 419424.* Results of a program designed to increase teacher and counselor competence through training in Robert Carkhuff's Human Resource Development model. The program netted significant growth in interpersonal functioning. Secondary sources and data from original project; 19 notes.   R. E. Butchart

1966. Holly, Susan. WOMEN IN MANAGEMENT OF WEEKLIES. *Journalism Q. 1979 56(4): 810-815.* A 1977 study of the status of women in the weekly newspaper industry tends to confirm earlier research which showed that women had greater opportunities on weeklies than in other areas of the industry. However, this study also shows that while women are in the majority among employees, they are not as likely as men to be in management. Further, their wages are lower than those for men, and they generally report having less control over operations. 3 tables, 20 notes.   J. S. Coleman

1967. Hornburger, Jane M. REFLECTIONS ON TEACHER TRAINING PROGRAMS. *J. of Negro Educ. 1977 46(4): 425-429.* Criticizes teacher training programs and demands new approaches to the problem. Discusses possible reforms. Biblio.   R. E. Butchart

1968. Jaffe, A. J. and Froomkin, Joseph. OCCUPATIONAL OPPORTUNITIES FOR COLLEGE-EDUCATED WORKERS, 1950-75. *Monthly Labor Rev. 1978 101(6): 15-21.* While 1975 data indicates a decrease of college educated persons entering lucrative positions from 1950, they still retain an advantage over high school educated persons whose unemployment rate remains consistently higher.

1969. James, Tom. SEEKING THE LIMITS OF BARGAINING. *Compact 1975 9(3): 13-16.* At federal and state levels, teachers are seeking legislation to permit collective bargaining and an increased role in educational policy.

1970. Johnson, Susan Moore. TEACHER UNIONS IN SCHOOLS: AUTHORITY AND ACCOMMODATION. *Harvard Educ. Rev. 1983 53(3): 309-326.* Examination of six school districts in which teachers' unions have employed collective bargaining indicates that quality of administrative leadership, the students' needs, and staff allegiance to schools are more important than unionization in determining labor relations.

1971. Jones, Arnita A. HUMANITIES LABOR FORCE: WOMEN HISTORIANS AS A SPECIAL CASE. *Hist. Teacher 1982 15(3): 363-376.* Surveys the labor market for historians over the last two decades, with a focus on current trends. Issues covered include availability of employment, academic versus nonacademic employment, full-time and part-time jobs, promotion and advancement, comparison of history with other humanities disciplines, and a comparison of women and men in the professional history labor market. 21 notes.
L. K. Blaser

1972. Josephine, Helen. ALL THINGS BEING EQUAL: PAY EQUITY FOR LIBRARY WORKERS. *Wilson Lib. Bull. 1982 57(4): 300-303.* Examines the problem of low pay for US and Canadian women library workers and their rights in federal legislation and judicial cases, 1977-82.

1973. Kassalow, Everett M. WHITE-COLLAR UNIONS AND THE WORK HUMANIZATION MOVEMENT. *Monthly Labor Rev. 1977 100(5): 9-13.* Increasing labor organization among white-collar workers indicates concern with job satisfaction in industrialized countries, 1945-76.

1974. Kerchner, Charles T. THE IMPACT OF COLLECTIVE BARGAINING ON SCHOOL GOVERNANCE. *Educ. and Urban Soc. 1979 11(2): 181-207.* Assesses the impact of teacher collective bargaining on school administrations and managerial work based on studies done in the 1960's and 1970's.

1975. Kerr, Donna H. TEACHING COMPETENCE AND TEACHER EDUCATION IN THE UNITED STATES. *Teachers Coll. Record 1983 84(3): 525-552.* Because of a pervasive lack of commitment to quality education, American society has failed to attract its best and brightest to teaching careers. Teacher education, which has changed little in the past 50 years, has been largely confined to underfunded, intellectually barren undergraduate programs. Accreditation agencies have been content to maintain the status quo. Improvement might be achieved by creating rigorous doctoral programs to train master teachers, by requiring all teacher training to be graduate level, and by adjusting accreditation and hiring policies to insure that the best available people are hired. 7 notes, biblio.   E. C. Bailey, Jr.

1976. Kuechle, David. YESHIVA SHOCK WAVES. *Harvard Educ. Rev. 1982 52(3): 267-279.* Discusses the Supreme Court decision in *National Labor Relations Board* v. *Yeshiva University* (US, 1980) in which the Court ruled that faculty members at Yeshiva University were managers and thus did not have the right to collective bargaining protection under the National Labor Relations Act; examines its impact on related cases since that decision.

1977. Ladd, Everett Carll, Jr. and Lipset, Seymour Martin. UNIONIZING THE PROFESSORIATE. *Change 1973 5(6): 38-44.* The trade-union movement is spreading to college and university teachers in increasingly pervasive forms, and will irrevocably change the world of learning. The coauthors, long-time students of American academic life, chronicle the present growth of unionization and its conflicts and conjecture on its future directions.   J

1978. Latta, Geoffrey W. UNION ORGANIZATION AMONG ENGINEERS: A CURRENT ASSESSMENT. *Industrial and Labor Relations Rev. 1981 35(1): 29-42.* Studies campaigns since 1968 by unions seeking to organize professional engineers. The results of interviews with union and management representatives describe four major causes of the relative failure of unions on this front: employer opposition, the attitudes and values of engineers, the lack of bargaining power of engineers, and union attitudes and organizing policies. Strong resistance to unionization by employers can draw on a value system in the United States that is not supportive of unionization.   J/S

1979. Lattimore, Dan L. and Nayman, Oguz B. PROFESSIONALISM OF COLORADO'S DAILY NEWSMEN: A COMMUNICATOR ANALYSIS. *Gazette [Netherlands] 1974 20(1): 1-10.* A survey of 184 editorial department employees of Colorado's 26 daily newspapers in 1972 indicates a desire for greater professionalism, voice in editorial policy, and widening of the scope of local news reporting and editorializing.

1980. Lee, Patrick C. MALE AND FEMALE TEACHERS IN ELEMENTARY SCHOOLS: AN ECOLOGICAL ANALYSIS. *Teachers Coll. Record 1973 75(1): 79-98.* Studies the preponderance of female teachers in elementary education, and the socializing impact on students.

1981. Little, Craig B. TECHNICAL-PROFESSIONAL UNEMPLOYMENT: MIDDLE-CLASS ADAPTABILITY TO PERSONAL CRISIS. *Sociol. Q. 1976 17(2): 262-274.* Previous research generally indicates that unemployment is damaging to self-esteem and morale with attendant economic deprivations. Research among the middle-class unemployed is quite rare and is inconclusive as to the specific impact of unemployment on members of this stratum. In this study, interviews with one hundred unemployed male technical-professionals during the aerospace-defense-electronics recession of early 1972 revealed that for many, unemployment was less stressful than expected. The expression of a positive attitude toward job loss by 48 percent of the sample became a subject of special interest. The reason most frequently given for having a positive attitude toward job loss was that it represented an opportunity to escape from an undesirable job. Being laid off apparently made a decision that many unemployed men had considered but had not brought themselves to make prior to the layoff. Additional variables which might help to explain the high percentage of men expressing a positive attitude toward job loss are discussed. Especially important are factors which taken together enchance the adaptability of these middle-class professionals to their unemployment by softening its financial impact.   J

1982. Luce, Sally R. and Ostling, Kristen. WOMEN AND WHITE COLLAR UNIONS: AN ANNOTATED BIBLIOGRAPHY. *Resources for Feminist Res. [Canada] 1981 10(2): 95-106.* An annotated bibliography of books and articles containing information or commentary, pertinent to the topic of women and white-collar unions, and usually published since 1975.

1983. Mantell, Edmund H. DISCRIMINATION BASED ON EDUCATION IN THE LABOR MARKET FOR ENGINEERS. *Rev. of Econ. and Statistics 1974 56(2): 158-166.*

1984. Marshall, Joan L. THE EFFECTS OF COLLECTIVE BARGAINING ON FACULTY SALARIES IN HIGHER EDUCATION. *J. of Higher Educ. 1979 50(3): 310-322.* The effects of collective bargaining on faculty salaries are examined. Thirty institutions with collective bargaining agreements are matched with similar institutions without such agreements, and faculty salaries are compared prior to and following unionization. Collective bargaining agreements are found to have little effect upon increases in faculty salaries.   J

1985. Martindale, Don. KING OF THE HOBOES: PORTRAIT OF AN INTERNATIONAL CULTURAL WORKMAN. *Int. J. of Contemporary Sociol. 1979 16(1-2): 222-242.* Examines the overabundance of PhD's produced by the American graduate school system in the 1960's and 1970's, focusing upon the growth of a large number of nontenured instructors who shift from one temporary position to another, and provides a case study of this phenomenon involving the career of Joseph Roucek (b. 1902), an American sociologist.

1986. Marzolf, Marion. THE WOMAN JOURNALIST: COLONIAL PRINTER TO CITY DESK, PART II. *Journalism Hist. 1975 2(1): 24-27, 32.* Considers some female journalists since 1939 and the general success of women in becoming professional journalists.

1987. McDonnell, Lorraine M. and Pascal, Anthony H. NATIONAL TRENDS IN TEACHER COLLECTIVE BARGAINING. *Educ. and Urban Soc. 1979 11(2): 129-151.* Discusses the data collected from a National Institute of Education study done in 1970 and 1974 examining the consequences of noneconomic issues in teacher collective bargaining on school districts.

1988. Moore, Kathryn M. and Sagaria, Mary Ann D. DIFFERENTIAL JOB CHANGE AND STABILITY AMONG ACADEMIC ADMINISTRATORS. *J. of Higher Educ. 1982 53(5): 501-513.* Job change patterns of academic administrators were studied, focusing on trends for different groups of administrators. The prevalent pattern was for persons to assume their current positions from within institutions. However, job change within and across colleges and universities differed based on personal and career characteristics including gender and position type.   J

1989. Nash, Al. THE UNIVERSITY LABOR EDUCATOR: A MARGINAL OCCUPATION. *Industrial and Labor Relations Rev. 1978 32(1): 40-55.* This study reviews the university labor educator as a semiprofessional who acts as a ridge between the worlds of higher education and organized labor but is not fully accepted in either. Using data from a survey of individuals listed in the 1976 directory of the University and College Labor Education Association (UCLEA) and from reports published by the UCLEA, the author analyzes the determinants of the status of this occupation, the facets of its marginality, and its progress as an emerging profession.   J

1990. Nelson, Lynn R. SOCIAL STUDIES TEACHERS: THEIR VIEW OF THEIR PROFESSION. *Social Educ. 1981 45(6): 418-420.* Discusses social studies teachers' satisfaction with their jobs and concludes that the majority enjoy their jobs and are proud to be teachers, a third would leave teaching if a better opportunity arose, and most are not members of a professional organization other than the National Education Association or American Federation of Teachers;

teachers find that "intrinsic rewards in teaching are more important than tangible items such as salary."

1991. Nixon, Howard L., II. FACULTY SUPPORT OF TRADITIONAL LABOR TACTICS ON CAMPUS. *Sociology of Educ. 1975 48(3): 276-286.* Examines the relationship among faculty status, academic field, and attitudinal support of traditional labor tactics on campus.

1992. Oppenheimer, Martin. THE UNIONIZATION OF THE PROFESSIONAL. *Social Policy 1975 5(5): 34-40.* Explores the increasing numbers of white-collar, technical, and professional workers who are becoming unionized.

1993. Parrish, John B. and Duff, Franklin L. JOB EXPERIENCE OF COLLEGE GRADUATES: A CASE STUDY. *Q. Rev. of Econ. and Business 1975 15(4): 25-36.* College graduates in 1973 made a reasonably satisfactory transition to the job market by 1974 despite recession, if survey findings of one major institution are representative. This overall finding, however, needs to be interpreted with caution because extreme variations were reported among bachelor's degree graduates in 69 disciplines. Graduates in accountancy, the engineering specialties, physiology and biophysics, and agricultural economics experienced few job difficulties. In contrast, graduates had serious job difficulties in such fields as the languages, classics, speech communication, philosophy, psychology, sociology, anthropology, history, and political science. In the light of these findings, academic institutions may wish to make students more aware of the variation in job market success of graduates in the various disciplines.   J

1994. Parrish, John B. UNIONIZATION AND EDUCATION: LESSONS FROM THE ILLINOIS SCHOOLROOMS. *J. of Social, Pol. and Econ. Studies 1981 6(3): 235-267.* Discusses the problems, issues, and implications of the formation of teacher unions in the United States from 1960 to 1981, commenting on the history and goals of the National Education Association and the American Federation of Teachers, and analyzes the impact of unionization on parents, students, and the quality of US education with reference to the experience of the Illinois school system.

1995. Pashigian, B. Peter. OCCUPATIONAL LICENSING AND THE INTERSTATE MOBILITY OF PROFESSIONALS. *J. of Law and Econ. 1979 22(1): 1-26.* While personal investment of time in learning state-specific law and procedures is seen as a cause of low interstate mobility among lawyers, greater influence is felt from the effects of licensing and the limitations on the use of reciprocity; 1950's-70's.

1996. Pernia, Ernesto M. THE QUESTION OF THE BRAIN DRAIN FROM THE PHILIPPINES. *Int. Migration Rev. 1976 10(1): 63-72.* Discusses the emigration of physicians, scientists, and engineers from the Philippines to the United States, 1962-70.

1997. Ponak, Allen M. UNIONIZED PROFESSIONALS AND THE SCOPE OF BARGAINING: A STUDY OF NURSES. *Industrial and Labor Relations Rev. 1981 34(3): 396-407.* Examines the common assumption that unionized professionals will seek to expand the scope of negotiations to include issues reflecting distinctly professional concerns and shows that the nurses questioned differentiated professional from traditional goals and attached more importance to the former.   J/S

1998. Powell, Douglas H. and Driscoll, Paul F. MIDDLE-CLASS PROFESSIONALS FACE UNEMPLOYMENT. *Society 1973 10(2): 18-26.*

1999. Roemer, Robert E. and Schnitz, James E. ACADEMIC EMPLOYMENT AS DAY LABOR: THE DUAL LABOR MARKET IN HIGHER EDUCATION. *J. of Higher Educ. 1982 53(5): 514-531.* In recent years the labor market has been divided into tenure track and nontenure track positions. This division of the academic labor market is interpreted by means of dual labor market theory. Consequences of a dual labor market for both institutions of higher education and individual academicians are suggested.   J

2000. Russo, John B. CHANGES IN BARGAINING STRUCTURES: THE IMPLICATIONS OF THE SERRANO DECISION.

Educ. and Urban Soc. 1979 11(2): 208-218. Discusses the effects of *Serrano* v. *Priest* (1971), handed down by the California Supreme Court, on teacher collective bargaining.

2001. Sawicki, Robert L. THE UNIONIZATION OF PROFESSORS AT THE UNIVERSITY OF DELAWARE. *Liberal Educ. 1974 60(4): 449-460.* Describes the circumstances that led University of Delaware faculty to decide in favor of collective bargaining during the years 1965-73.

2002. Schlachter, Gail. QUASI UNIONS AND ORGANIZATIONAL HEGEMONY WITHIN THE LIBRARY FIELD. *Lib. Q. 1973 43(3): 185-198.* A tightening labor market has made it increasingly difficult for professional employees to rely upon their scarcity and uniqueness to guarantee favorable bargaining positions. As a result, many professionals have considered joining collective bargaining associations, and unions have had success among these traditionally hard-to-organize workers. When faced with successful union membership drives, several professional societies have turned themselves into *quasi unions:* associations which add an employee orientation to their original professional base. In so doing, they have consistently succeeded in thwarting unionization and preserving organizational leadership within their profession. In the library field, union-related, social, technological, economic, and legislative factors have been contributing to union membership growth. Recent limited research indicates, however, that if librarians had a choice, they would prefer to affiliate with a professional association turned quasi union rather than a traditional labor organization. These findings correspond to the industrial relations theory that professional societies can and will be viable alternatives to traditional labor organizations. Thus, based on historical precedent and current theory, the assumption seems reasonable that the American Library Association will succeed in maintaining organizational hegemony among librarians only if it responds to increasing union activity by evolving into a quasi union.   J

2003. Scott, Charles E. THE MARKET FOR PH.D. ECONOMISTS: THE ACADEMIC SECTOR. *Am. Econ. Rev. 1979 69(2): 137-142.* After an elaborate statistical display, concludes that future academic opportunities for economists are dismal. This knowledge is conventional wisdom to anyone associated with higher education. 3 tables, 19 ref.
                                                              D. K. Pickens

2004. Sekscenski, Edward S. THE HEALTH SERVICES INDUSTRY: A DECADE OF EXPANSION. *Monthly Labor Rev. 1981 104(5): 9-16.* Examines the growth of the health services industry during the 1970's which was accompanied by an increased work force and a need for more highly skilled workers whose wages remained below the overall work force; despite shorter work weeks, absences surpassed national averages.

2005. Shanas, Bert. ALBERT SHANKER: THE POLITICS OF CLOUT. *New York Affairs 1978 5(1): 3-22.* Discusses Albert Shanker, president of the American Federation of Teachers, executive vice president of the New York State United Teachers, and president of the New York City United Federation of Teachers, and the political clout he wields on city, state, and national levels, specifically his ability to negotiate teachers' labor contracts.

2006. Smith, Bruce L. R. THE BRAIN DRAIN RE-EMERGENT: FOREIGN MEDICAL GRADUATES IN AMERICAN MEDICAL SCHOOLS. *Minerva [Great Britain] 1979 17(4): 483-503.* The governments of poor countries resent the desertion of nationals who leave to study in advanced countries, and subsequently remain; the United States, by encouraging the migration of physicians through special incentives, has exacerbated this brain drain, but Congress recently dealt with the problem by abruptly swinging towards autarchy, which would eliminate access to US biomedical training.

2007. Strom, David. TEACHER UNIONISM: AN ASSESSMENT. *Educ. and Urban Soc. 1979 11(2): 152-167.* Provides a history of teacher collective bargaining and activism since the mid-19th century and assesses teacher unionism and the results of teachers' demands in the 1960's and 1970's.

2008. Tucker, John T. GOVERNMENT EMPLOYMENT: AN ERA OF SLOW GROWTH. *Monthly Labor Rev. 1981 104(10): 19-25.* The federal payroll rate of growth has been decreasing since 1975 as state and local government sector payrolls have increased.

2009. Volz, William H. LEGAL LIABILITY IN UNIVERSITY PROMOTION, TENURE, AND RETENTION DECISIONS: JUDICIALLY COMPELLED DISCLOSURE AND ACADEMIC FREEDOM. *Michigan Acad. 1983 15(2): 159-177.* Examines judicial decisions since the 1960's regarding the conflict between universities' needs for confidentiality in decisionmaking on faculty promotion, tenure, and retention; and the necessity for violating that confidentiality when universities' decisions are alleged to be unlawfully discriminatory.

2010. Wallace, Roger L. COMMENTS ON THE IMPACT OF COLLECTIVE BARGAINING ON ADMINISTRATIVE AND FACULTY ROLES IN ACADEME. *Michigan Acad. 1976 9(1): 7-14.* Discusses the issue of faculty unions in four-year colleges and universities in the United States today, giving historical background since World War II, and discussing the rapid increase in collective bargaining in the universities since that time, with arguments for and against faculty unionization.

2011. Ward, Dwayne. LABOR MARKET ADJUSTMENTS IN ELEMENTARY AND SECONDARY TEACHING: THE REACTION TO THE "TEACHER SURPLUS." *Teachers Coll. Record 1975 77(2): 189-218.* Several government and private studies of trends in teacher supply and demand prove that the teacher surplus is real, although demand varies by subject and location. States have taken little action on the problem, preferring at most the initiation of planning. Little information is available on the reaction of schools to the surplus. Students, however, seem to be turning dramatically away from teaching as a prospective career. More detailed study is needed. Primary and secondary sources; 8 tables, 41 notes.
                                                              E. Bailey

2012. Williams, Richard C. THE IMPACT OF COLLECTIVE BARGAINING ON THE PRINCIPAL: WHAT DO WE KNOW? *Educ. and Urban Soc. 1979 11(2): 168-180.* Critiques four studies which assessed the impact of teacher collective bargaining on the principal's leadership and role as administrator, 1970's.

2013. Zainaldin, Jamil S. AAUP RELEASES REPORT ON ECONOMIC STATUS OF THE TEACHING PROFESSION. *AHA Perspectives 1982 20(9): 10-12.* Discusses the increase in faculty salaries between 1976-77 and 1981-82, demonstrating that history faculty as a group demonstrated a relative loss in income over the five-year period and a drop in relative ranking among all academic faculty.

2014. —. BLACKS IN LEADING LAW FIRMS. *Change 1979 11(7): 42.* Charts the paucity of black lawyers in 50 major law firms during 1979.

2015. —. CAREERS IN BUSINESS PROGRAMS. *Public Hist. 1981 3(3): 137-143.* Describes the careers in business programs sponsored by numerous universities directed at students with doctorates in the humanities, social sciences, and physical sciences who wish to consider careers in business; institutions offering these programs include the University of Virginia, the University of Texas, the Wharton School of the University of Pennsylvania, New York University, the Institute for Research in History, and the Maine Council on Economic Education.

2016. —. [FACULTY ROLES IN HIGHER EDUCATION]. *Acad.: Bull. of the AAUP 1983 69(1): 10-16.*
Strohm, Paul. FACULTY ROLES TODAY AND TOMORROW, *pp. 10-15.* Discusses the importance of the faculty in institutional planning processes, the importance of program review and personnel strategies, cost cutting techniques, and reactions to financial exigency.
Dunathan, Harmon C. WHEN JUDGMENTS ARE MADE, *pp. 15-16.* Claims that the effectiveness of faculty participation in institutional planning is linked to the degree of stringency-exigency of the institution.

Keller, George. THE COURAGE TO PLAN, *p. 16.* The faculty needs to be more active and decisive in stringency planning; college teachers already have played some role; they sometimes underestimate the seriousness of the situation; and they must be more cognizant of newer methods of planning.

2017. —. HARRY BRAVERMAN'S WORLD OF WORK. *Can. Dimension [Canada] 1979 14(3): 20-24.* Harry Braverman's *Labor and Monopoly Capital* (Monthly Rev. Pr.) traces the growth of scientific management and its effects on the labor process; applies these management techniques to modern-day white-collar workers; 20th century.

2018. —. [THE NEW HISTORIAN]. *Maryland Hist. 1979 10(1): 3-5, 7-19, 21-28.*

Jones, Arnita and Pomeroy, Robert. INTRODUCTION: HISTORY CAREERS IN A CHANGING MARKETPLACE, *pp. 3-5.* Introduces articles by historians who have nonfaculty careers and briefly summarizes the genesis (in 1976) of the National Coordinating Committee for the Promotion of History (NCC). NCC's purpose is to meet the crisis caused by the paucity of faculty positions for historians.

Bruser, Lawrence. RESEARCH AND PUBLIC AFFAIRS, *pp. 7-10.* Describes career as a public affairs researcher for Mitsui Corporation. Explains similarities to and divergences from academia, and stresses compatible social values. Offers advice to historians who wish to explore business positions.

Miller, Roberta. URBAN POLICY, *pp. 11-12.* Indicates a wide range of opportunities in the private and public sectors for historians to exercise their skills. Statistics, computer, and theoretical analysis skills must be acquired in graduate school. Provides guidelines for Urban Policy job seekers.

Swiger, Ernest. CONSULTING, *pp. 13-14.* Combines job search tips with a description of the consulting business.

Mendelsohn, Johanna. PUBLIC INTEREST GROUPS, *pp. 15-19.* Lengthy discourse on the author's use of her graduate school skills for public interest organization. Chides her mentors and graduate schools in general for not helping her prepare for a nonfaculty position.

Anderson, Harold. BANK HISTORY AND ARCHIVES, *pp. 21-24.* Describes his movement to a position with Wells Fargo Bank and stresses that some adjustment to working in a corporation is necessary but that "Freedom's fetters are the same, whether you are in academia or in the business world."

Langley, Harold. MUSEUMS AND THE HISTORIAN, *pp. 25-28.* Urges historians to do as the author did, work to capitalize on an increasing interest by the public in history as seen through objects. Opportunities exist in public museums and in the private sector.   G. O. Gagnon

Individual Locals, Strikes, and Lockouts

2019. Ackermann, John A. THE IMPACT OF THE COAL STRIKE OF 1977-1978. *Industrial and Labor Relations Rev. 1979 32(2): 175-188.* In an effort to determine whether the 109-day-long coal strike of 1977-78 constituted a national emergency within the meaning of the Taft-Hartley Act, this study examines, among other sources, the results of weekly surveys by the BLS of both the actual and expected effects of the strike on large employers in 11 coal-dependent states. The study finds that employer predictions of strike effects proved to be consistently exaggerated; those effects probably never constituted an actual emergency; and in fact the strike's economic impact was diminishing when President Carter finally invoked Taft-Hartley in response to growing political pressures.   J

2020. Alter, Jonathan. FEATHERBEDDING IN THE TOWER: HOW THE CONTROLLERS LET THE CAT OUT OF THE BAG. *Washington Monthly 1981 13(8): 22-27.* When the 19,000 air traffic controllers and their supervisors went on strike in 1981, they were replaced by 9,000 people who handled 75% of the normal air traffic, which suggests that the US government is overstaffed; focuses on the Professional Air Traffic Controllers Organization's over-compensation for the controllers' bad working conditions; 1950's-81.

2021. Andrew, William D. FACTIONALISM AND ANTI-COMMUNISM: FORD LOCAL 600. *Labor Hist. 1979 20(2): 227-255.* The House Committee on Un-American Activities hearings of 1952 provided a powerful rationale for the United Auto Workers to create an administratorship for Ford Local 600, but the history of the local reveals that factionalism and anti-Reuther activities in the local were important elements in the decision. Based on UAW proceedings, newspapers, and HUAC hearings; 70 notes.   L. L. Athey

2022. Bailey, Richard. THE STARR COUNTY STRIKE. *Red River Valley Hist. Rev. 1979 4(1): 42-61.* Describes the labor dispute of 1966-67 in Rio Grande City, Texas, involving farms, strikers, growers, police, and Texas Rangers in Starr County.

2023. Barnum, Darold T. and Helburn, I. B. INFLUENCING THE ELECTORATE: EXPERIENCE WITH REFERENDA ON PUBLIC EMPLOYEE BARGAINING. *Industrial and Labor Relations Rev. 1982 35(3): 330-342.* Develops a model of the factors influencing public opinion on labor relations issues and tests the model with data from local referenda, each determining whether a community would adopt the Fire and Police Employee Relations Act (Texas, 1973) and thereby allow local police and firefighters to bargain collectively. Tests for such variables as income levels, unionization rates, and the number and nature of opposing and supporting groups.   J/S

2024. Batzer, Arild. LA HUELGA, LANDARBEIDEREN OG CESAR CHAVEZ [The strike, farmworkers, and Cesar Chavez]. *Samtiden [Norway] 1970 79(10): 649-662.* Describes Cesar Chavez (founder of the United Farm Workers Union) and the strike by California grape pickers, 1965-70.   M. A. Bott

2025. Becker, Bill. CHALLENGING THE "RIGHT-TO-WORK-FOR-LESS". *Southern Exposure 1976 4(1-2): 88-89.* Arkansans for Progress, a labor group, is attempting to repeal the state's right-to-work laws in order to work for more easily negotiated union security agreements, 1975-76.

2026. Becker, Eugene H. STEELWORKERS LAUD IMPORT CURB, BAN OUTSIDERS' ELECTION CONTRIBUTIONS. *Monthly Labor Rev. 1978 101(12): 65-69.* Outlines the proceedings of the United Steelworkers of America convention of 18-22 September 1978.

2027. Bensman, David. J. P. STEVENS: WHAT'S BEHIND THE BOYCOTT. *Working Papers for a New Soc. 1977 5(2): 20-29.* Because of the organizational work during the last ten years of the Amalgamated Clothing and Textile Workers Union (ACTWU), the unfair labor practices of the J. P. Stevens textile manufacturers in Roanoke, North Carolina, have been countered by an effective consumer boycott.

2028. Bensman, David. WORK AND WORKERS IN THE 1980S: MINDING ITS OWN BUSINESS: A LOCAL TRADE UNION IN ACTION. *Dissent 1982 29(3): 330-335.* Profiles Republic Lodge 1987 of the International Association of Machinists and Aerospace Workers at Fairchild Republic, aircraft manufacturers in Farmingdale, New York since 1950.

2029. Benson, H. W. GROWTH OF REFORM AMONG THE TEAMSTERS. *Dissent 1979 26(2): 153-157.* Describes two reform groups that have recently arisen in the Teamsters Union to fight against corruption within the Union, and gives examples from several books published in the 1970's on the Teamsters.

2030. Bernard, Jacqueline. ORGANIZING HOSPITAL WORKERS. *Working Papers for a New Soc. 1976 4(3): 53-59.* Discusses the United Mine Workers of America's and the National Labor Relations Board's roles in the attempt to unionize hospital workers in Pikeville and Prestonsburg, Kentucky, 1973-76.

2031. Betheil, Richard. THE ENA IN PERSPECTIVE: THE TRANSFORMATION OF COLLECTIVE BARGAINING IN THE BASIC STEEL INDUSTRY. *Rev. of Radical Pol. Econ. 1978 10(2): 1-24.* An account of the attempt by management to impose a "wages productivity deal" on unions in the steel industry during 1946-73 and the manner in which collective bargaining led to the Experimental Negotiating Agreement of 1973.

2032. Bethell, Thomas N. THE UMW: NOW MORE THAN EVER. *Washington Monthly 1978 10(1): 12-23.* Discusses the goals and activities of the United Mine Workers since 1890 as a background to the coal strike of 1977-78.

2033. Bethell, Tom. THE GRAVY TRAIN. *Washington Monthly 1976 8(3): 6-11.* Discusses economic and contractual disputes among railroads, labor unions and federal government in railroad construction by the Consolidated Railroad Corporation in the Delmarva Peninsula of Delaware, 1973-76.

2034. Bethell, Tom and Hall, Bob. 1974: THE BROOKSIDE STRIKE. *Southern Exposure 1976 4(1-2): 114-123.* Coal miners who wished to join the United Mine Workers of America struck a Duke Power Company subsidiary's mine in Harlan County, Kentucky, in 1974.

2035 Beyer, Janice M.; Trice, Harrison M.; and Hunt, Richard E. THE IMPACT OF FEDERAL SECTOR UNIONS ON SUPERVISORS' USE OF PERSONNEL POLICIES. *Industrial and Labor Relations Rev. 1980 33(2): 212-231.* The results of our analysis provided strongest support for Hypotheses 5 and 6. Supervisors' awareness of the union's positions on both policies was found to be related to their use of the policies, and this awareness was found to be related, in turn, to the power of the union. Hypothesis 7, however, which predicted that unions would be perceived as supportive to the policy when the contract included a specific provision on that policy, had no support at all. Hypothesis 1 received partial support for the alcoholism policy but no support for [Equal Employment Opportunity] EEO. A larger proportion of supervisors in unionized installations had used the alcoholism policy in the past, giving some support to the top portion of our model (Figure 1) for the alcoholism policy. Results for Hypothesis 2 were rather mixed, providing stronger support for the alcoholism than for the EEO policy. The most positive predictors of policy use among indicators of union power were the number of grievance and arbitration provisions in the contract and contract administration activities by the union. Other indicators of union power, especially union characteristics, had negative or mixed effects on supervisors' use of the policies. Support for Hypothesis 3 was limited; only a specific provision on the EEO policy affected expected future use of that policy. For Hypothesis 4 results differed for the two policies: The alcoholism policy was used more where less-skilled employees were represented by the union, but the EEO policy was used more where unions represented more-skilled employees. Since the results for Hypothesis 1 and 2 were given limited or no support for the EEO policy, we were forced to conclude that the general pattern of our findings supported the model proposed in Figure 1 only for the alcoholism policy. These results were explored further using qualitative data.   J

2036. Bisanz, Charles F. THE ANATOMY OF A MASS PUBLIC PROTEST ACTION: A SHUTDOWN BY INDEPENDENT TRUCK DRIVERS. *Human Organization 1977 36(1): 62-65.* Examines truck driver culture and the use of mass public protest which culminated in freeway blockages in Ohio, Pennsylvania, and several other states in 1973.

2037. Bloch, Ed. PCB, UE, AND GE. *Monthly Rev. 1981 33(5): 17-24.* Discusses how General Electric Company in 1975 was forced to clean up its use of polychlorinated biphenyl at the Fort Edward and Hudson Falls plants in New York, and the role of the United Electrical, Radio, and Machine Workers of America Local 332 in backing up General Electric in order to protect jobs.

2038. Blume, Norman. CONTROL AND SATISFACTION AND THEIR RELATION TO RANK-AND-FILE SUPPORT FOR UNION POLITICAL ACTION. *Western Pol. Q. 1973 26(1): 51-63.* Analyzes data gathered in 1967 from Local 12 of the United Automobile Workers of America Union in Toledo, Ohio, in order to determine how control of union decisionmaking processes and members' satisfaction with their shop stewards and jobs are related to worker support for union political activities.   S

2039. Bornstein, Leon. INDUSTRIAL RELATIONS IN 1977: HIGHLIGHTS OF KEY DEVELOPMENTS. *Monthly Labor Rev. 1978 101(2): 24-31.* Improved job and income security were major issues in collective bargaining in the United States in 1977; the United Steelworkers of America negotiated plans described as a start toward its goal of "lifetime job security."

2040. Branscome, James. THROUGH MINE DISASTER CARNAGE AND THE YABLONSKI MURDERS EMERGES ARNOLD MILLER, A HIGH SCHOOL DROPOUT AND COAL-FIELD VETERAN, TO REFORM AND LEAD THE VOLATILE UMW AT A TIME WHEN THE NATION NEEDS COAL. *Southern Voices 1974 1(1): 66-70.*

2041. Brett, Jeanne M. and Goldberg, Stephen B. WILDCAT STRIKES IN BITUMINOUS COAL MINING. *Industrial and Labor Relations Rev. 1979 32(4): 465-483.* Investigates wildcat strikes in bituminous coal mines, finding that high-strike mines resemble low-strike mines in working conditions, age of work force, and area standard of living. In low-strike mines, however, management is more accessible to labor and they have a problem-solving relationship.   J/S

2042. Bryant, Pat. A LONG TIME COMING: MULTIRACIAL ORGANIZING FOR WORK, LAND AND EQUALITY IN PLAQUEMINES PARISH, LOUISIANA. *Southern Exposure 1982 10(3): 83-89.* Led by community organizer, Ronald Chisom, the poor, black members of the Fishermen and Concerned Citizens Association, initially opposed imposition of oystering regulations that favored the corporations over the small oysterer; the success of the organization on this issue encouraged it to challenge the dominance of the Perez family machine and seek other social reforms.

2043. Capozzola, John M. PUBLIC EMPLOYEE STRIKES: MYTHS AND REALITIES. *Natl. Civic Rev. 1979 68(4): 178-188.* The strike remains the most controversial and confused issue of public employment. From 1958 through 1976, 7,950 work stoppages occurred, involving more than 4 million public employees. Should they have the right to strike? More sensible questions are what can be done to minimize the number, and what constitutes an appropriate management response to those that do occur?   J

2044. Carlson, Richard J. and Sedwick, Thomas. COLLECTIVE BARGAINING IN THE PUBLIC SECTOR: A FOCUS ON STATE GOVERNMENT. *State Government 1977 50(3): 145-151.* Assesses administrative aspects of collective bargaining (negotiation of contracts, decisionmaking, and training programs) among state government employees, 1962-76.

2045. Cesari, Laurent. LE SYNDICAT "UNITED AUTOMOBILE WORKERS OF AMERICA" ET L'AUTOMATION (1945-1977) [The United Automobile Workers of America and automation, 1945-77]. *Mouvement Social [France] 1981 (117): 53-76.* The leadership of the United Automobile Workers (UAW) maintained a policy based on the theories drawn by Keynes that stressed automation and growth of productivity. The UAW wanted the full benefits of technological progress for the automobile workers. All the opponents to the union leaders fought on the same battlefield: they stated that the UAW leaders were poor bargainers, able only to get bits and pieces from the automobile companies. Thus technological progress is the latest avatar of the American dream.   J/S

2046. Chavez, Cesar. THE CALIFORNIA FARM WORKERS' STRUGGLE. *Black Scholar 1976 7(9): 16-19.* Reprints an article from the *Los Angeles Times*, 8 April 1976. The author, who is president of the United Farm Workers of America, AFL-CIO, discusses the present struggle of the farm workers to obtain an effective farm labor law in California.   B. D. Ledbetter

2047. Chernow, Ron. GREY FLANNEL GOONS: THE LATEST IN UNION BUSTING. *Working Papers for a New Soc. 1981 8(1): 18-25.* Professional union-busters, including industrial psychologists, personnel managers, and labor lawyers, beginning in the late 1970's, have used tactics unlike the violence of Pinkerton detectives; focuses on professional antiunionism at IBM, Polaroid, Texas Instruments, McDonald's, Procter & Gamble, Dupont, Delta, and Eastman Kodak, etc.

2048. Choi, Yearn H. COLLECTIVE BARGAINING IN THE PUBLIC SECTOR: WHERE ARE WE? *State Government 1978 51(4):*

225-229. Offers suggestions for handling negotiations between the public, government management, and employees; 1968-78.

2049. Clarke, Carlene A. THE *YESHIVA* CASE: AN ANALYSIS AND AN ASSESSMENT OF ITS POTENTIAL IMPACT ON PUBLIC UNIVERSITIES. *J. of Higher Educ. 1981 52(5): 449-469.* The impact on public universities of the Supreme Court's *Yeshiva* decision regarding faculty collective bargaining is clarified through analysis of the case's meaning for the University of California, Berkeley. A review of the literature on the relationship between collective bargaining and academic governance is provided as background to the court decision.   J

2050. Coffin, Tom. BUSTED BY LAW: ORGANIZING IN THE CONSTRUCTION INDUSTRY. *Southern Exposure 1980 8(1): 26-34.* A first-person account of an engineering technician in the construction industry who attempted to organize for the International Union of Operating Engineers, Local 926, at a branch of the Law Engineering Testing Company, Inc., in Atlanta, Georgia. He did not enter the company to become a labor organizer, but after a year he saw the union shop as the only viable way to upgrade wages and the classification of laborers. He was fired in 1978 because of his attempts to form a union. His appeal to the National Labor Relations Board (NLRB) was denied, he claimed, on the basis of a false, backdated company memo. 9 photos.   H. M. Parker, Jr.

2051. Copozzola, John M. THE IMPACT OF GOVERNMENT EMPLOYEE UNIONS. *Pro. of the Acad. of Pol. Sci. 1981 34(2): 153-166.* Focuses on the bargaining taking place in state and local agencies. The strike issue illustrates the need for reevaluating the concept of sovereignty and the notion that public sector employees have special obligations. 3 notes.   T. P. Richardson

2052. Corralejo, Jorge. REPORT ON PROPOSITION 14: FARM-WORKERS VS. BIG GROWERS, BIG MONEY AND BIG LIES. *Radical Am. 1977 11(2): 74-78.* Proposition 14 on the California ballot in 1976 represented an effort by the United Farmworkers to place into the state constitution the essence of the legislation contained in the California Agriculture Labor Relations Act (1975). Agribusiness campaigned against the proposition and raised the myth of protecting the rights of the yeoman farmer and the individual against the group. The union employed its considerable boycott staff and its liberal-left-clergy coalition of supporters in the unsuccessful fight to enact the proposition. The campaign strengthened the existing law by calling needed attention to it and familiarizing many with its provisions. The struggle also may have pushed the union closer to acting more and more as a traditional trade union.   N. Lederer

2053. Davis, Pearce and Pati, Gopal C. ELAPSED TIME PATTERNS IN LABOR GRIEVANCE ARBITRATION: 1942-1972. *Arbitration J. 1974 29(1): 15-27.* Suggests ways unions and companies can shorten delay between filing of grievance and final award.   S

2054. Dawson, Irving O. NEW DEVELOPMENTS AND PROBLEMS IN LABOR RELATIONS IN THE FEDERAL CIVIL SERVICE. *Rocky Mountain Social Sci. J. 1974 11(3): 91-101.* Reviews some problems of transferring collective bargaining to governments and focuses on problems of militant unionism in the public sector in the 1970's.   S

2055. Dertouzos, James N. and Pencavel, John H. WAGE AND EMPLOYMENT DETERMINATION UNDER TRADE UNION-ISM: THE INTERNATIONAL TYPOGRAPHICAL UNION. *J. of Pol. Econ. 1981 89(6): 1162-1181.* Examines wage and employment data from 1946 to 1965 to determine if these fulfilled the objectives of the International Typographical Union.

2056. Devereux, Sean. THE REBEL IN ME. *Southern Exposure 1976 4(1-2): 4-15.* Interviews Selina Burch on her labor organizing with the Communications Workers of America, 1945-73.

2057. Dunbar, Tony and Hall, Bob. UNION BUSINESS: WHO, WHERE, WHEN, HOW & WHY. *Southern Exposure 1980 8(2): 27-43.* Exposes the new breed of union busters: trained lawyers and consultants. Using barely legal practices, they seek to intimidate, exasperate, or manipulate workers into rejecting a union. They rely on several common themes in their propaganda: the theme of union lies, union greed, the fear of job loss, and the misery of the inevitable long-term strike. They also conduct seminars in order to train management in these union-busting techniques and rely upon an elaborate right-wing net of antiunion organizations. 6 illus., fig.   S

2058. Ehrenreich, John and Ehrenreich, Barbara. HOSPITAL WORKERS: A CASE STUDY IN THE "NEW WORKING CLASS." *Monthly Rev. 1973 24(8): 12-27.* Describes working conditions in the hospital industry, emphasizing problems of worker organization and hospital reform.

2059. Eisele, C. Frederick. ORGANIZATION SIZE, TECHNOLO-GY, AND FREQUENCY OF STRIKES. *Industrial and Labor Relations Rev. 1974 27(4): 560-571.* It is often assumed that strikes tend to occur more frequently in large firms than in small, and that among firms of the same size, strikes will occur most frequently in those employing assembly-line techniques or other forms of technology associated with repetitive tasks and presumably worker discontent. This study tests these assumptions with survey data describing the technology, size, and strike experience during the 1950-69 period of 282 manufacturing plants in fourteen states. This evidence shows very little relationship between type of technology and strike frequency and a stronger, but still mixed, relationship between plant size and frequency of strikes.   J

2060. Ershov, S. A. and Makarenko, N. A. ZABASTOVOCHNOE DVIZHENIE RABOCHEGO KLASSA V STRANAKH KAPITALA V 70-X GODAKH [The strike movement of the working class in capitalist countries in the 1970's]. *Novaia i Noveishaia Istoriia [USSR] 1980 (3): 21-38.* Deals with strikes, pointing out, in particular, the causes of the growth in scale of open class battles, with attending shifts in the social base of the workers' movement.   J/S

2061. Farris, Carl and Hall, Leon. A CALL TO ACTION ON THE J. P. STEVENS CAMPAIGN. *Freedomways 1977 17(3): 135-142.* Leaders of the Amalgamated Clothing and Textile Workers Union (ACT-WU) are using the boycott tactics of the civil rights movement to organize the 44,000 textile workers employed by the J. P. Stevens Co. of Roanoke Rapids, North Carolina.

2062. Fedler, Fred and Taylor, Phillip. REPORTERS AND THE NEWSPAPER GUILD: MEMBERSHIP ATTITUDES AND SALA-RIES. *Journalism Q. 1981 58(1): 83-88.* In light of the fact that reporters have historically been reluctant to join unions, this study surveyed attitudes toward unions and the effects of union membership on wages. It was found that unions have a greater effect on salary at smaller newspapers. Additionally, reporters who indicated that they were satisfied with their job were twice as likely to say that they would not join a union. Based on a questionnaire and secondary sources; 7 notes.   J. S. Coleman

2063. Feldman, Roger and Scheffler, Richard. THE UNION IM-PACT ON HOSPITAL WAGES AND FRINGE BENEFITS. *Industrial and Labor Relations Rev. 1982 35(2): 196-206.* Uses 1977 data from a national probability sample of 1,200 hospitals to estimate the effect of unions on wages and fringe benefits in four occupations: registered nurses, practical nurses, secretaries and housekeepers. The results show that unionization has a significant impact on wages that increases with the length of time collective bargaining has been in effect at the individual hospital. The overall wage effect of unions is about 8% for both types of nurses and 11% to 12% for secretaries and housekeepers employed in hospitals.   J

2064. Finger, Bill. VICTORIA SOBRE FARAH. *Southern Exposure 1976 4(1-2): 45-49.* During 1972-74 garment workers, mostly Mexican Americans, successfully struck the Farah Company's El Paso, Texas, Gateway plant in order to join the Amalgamated Clothing Workers Union of America.

2065. Fink, Leon and Greenberg, Brian. ORGANIZING MONTEF-IORE: LABOR MILITANCY MEETS A PROGRESSIVE HEALTH CARE EMPIRE. Reverby, Susan and Rosner, David, ed. *Health Care in America: Essays in Social History* (Philadelphia: Temple U. Pr., 1979): 226-244. Relates the successful unionization of Montefiore Hospital in New York City in 1959 after three failures at organization during the previous decade. Factors leading to the successful effort included administration attempts to improve efficiency and increase productivity, the success of the Retail Drug Employees, Local 1199, in tailoring appeals to each hospital department and minority group, and the union's ability to transfer the sense of its collective strength to hospital employees and recruit exceptionally motivated organizers. 11 notes.   S

2066. Fink, Leon. UNION POWER, SOUL POWER: THE STORY OF 1199B AND LABOR'S SEARCH FOR A SOUTHERN STRATEGY. *Southern Changes 1983 5(2): 9-20.* In 1969, black hospital workers in Charleston, South Carolina, organized as Local 1199B, Retail Drug and Hospital Employees Affiliate of the International Retail, Wholesale and Department Store Union and staged a strike that was supported by the Southern Christian Leadership Conference and other civil rights and labor organizations; the intervention of the federal government produced concessions for the strikers but failed to secure for them union representation.

2067. Fischer, Ben. THE STEEL INDUSTRY'S EXPEDITED ARBITRATION: A JUDGMENT AFTER TWO YEARS. *Arbitration J. 1973 28(3): 185-191.* About two years ago, ten major steel producers and the United Steelworkers of America, AFL-CIO, established an expedited system of arbitration designed to produce quicker, less expensive, decisions in cases which, both sides agreed, did not need the 'full treatment' which had become customary in labor-management arbitration generally. The author, for many years in charge of the union's arbitration work nationally, believes that the system works very well, not only in achieving the objectives it was specifically designed for, but in creating a better attitude on the part of grievants and supervisors who, in the past, have often felt remote from the process. Critics of the plan have warned that the quality of decisions would deteriorate as a result of procedures which emphasized brief decisions, with little or no accompanying opinions. This has not been the case in the 'routine cases' which parties refer to expedited arbitration. On the contrary, quality remains high ('Some goof—as do the best and most experienced arbitrators') and new arbitrators are acquiring the experience and exposure they need for full time work in the profession.   J

2068. Flanagan, Leo Nelson. THE UNIONIZATION OF LIBRARY SUPPORT STAFFS. *Wilson Lib. Bull. 1974 48(6): 491-499.* Discusses the problems of library support staffs (the nonprofessionals) and their attempts to unionize in order to obtain better pay, status, and benefits.

2069. Franklin, William S. A COMPARISON OF FORMALLY AND INFORMALLY TRAINED JOURNEYMEN IN CONSTRUCTION. *Industrial and Labor Relations Rev. 1973 26(4): 1086-1094.* "In the controversy over the admission policies of construction unions, few facts have been available for appraising the effectiveness of the various methods of learning a construction trade. This study draws upon pension and welfare-fund records in six crafts and six cities to compare the employment experience of formally and informally trained journeymen. The author finds that, on the average, journeymen with apprenticeship training suffer less unemployment and are more likely to become supervisors than journeymen who are trained informally."   J

2070. Friedland, William H. and Thomas, Robert J. PARADOXES OF AGRICULTURAL UNIONISM IN CALIFORNIA. *Society 1974 11(4): 54-62.* Analyzes Cesar Chavez' revitalization of the grape and lettuce boycott, and discusses the paradox of Teamsters and United Farm Workers competing for workers' allegiance; one of five articles on "State Politics and Public Interests."

2071. Fritsch, Johann. LAGE UND KAMPF DER LANDARBEITER DER USA IN DEN SIEBZIGER JAHREN: ZUR GRÜNDUNG DER UNITED FARM WORKERS UNION [Conditions and struggle of the farm workers in the USA in the seventies: on the founding of the United Farm Workers]. *Zeitschrift für Geschichtswissenschaft [East Germany] 1976 24(12): 1414-1423.* After initial success in organizing farm workers in the 1930's, the farm labor movement fell victim to McCarthyism in subsequent decades. In the 1960's the movement was revived in California, America's leading agricultural state. With the Delano strike in 1965, the United Farm Workers Union became the leading agricultural union in the US, and after defeating a challenge by the reactionary Teamsters' Union, it attained legal recognition of

agricultural workers' unions in California. The UFWU has played a leading role in the struggle against racism. Primary and secondary sources; 32 notes.   J. T. Walker

2072. Fugita, Stephen S. A PERCEIVED ETHNIC FACTOR IN CALIFORNIA'S FARM LABOR CONFLICT: THE NISEI FARMER. *Explorations in Ethnic Studies 1978 1(1): 50-72.* Examines the conflict between the Nisei Farmers League and the United Farm Workers Union in California's San Joaquin Valley over agricultural labor, 1971-77.

2073. Fuller, Varden and Mason, Bert. FARM LABOR. *Ann. of the Am. Acad. of Pol. and Social Sci. 1977 (429): 63-80.* Farm population estimates indicate that the massive off-farm exodus is approaching its termination; during 1970-74 the rate of farm population decline fell to an average 1.2 percent per year. Estimates of farm occupations for 1974 imply that the nation's agriculture is dominantly a self-employment industry, though multiple job holding is widespread. The aggregate of persons doing some farm wagework is extremely heterogeneous and the market for hired farm labor is characterized by casual employment relationships. Farm labor in the United States lacks market structure and is seldom a chosen life-time occupation. Of nearly 2 3/4 million who did some farm work in 1974, it was the chief activity for only 693,000. Contrary to popular conception, hired farm labor is not dominated by migrants; in 1974, about 8 percent of the farm work force was migratory. Evidence on labor force participation, daily and annual earnings, and hourly wages illustrates that the hired farm labor market is dominantly a ready-access, casual market for the salvage of low opportunity cost time. Recent developments in federal policies indicate that farm workers are likely to receive federal protection equal to nonagricultural workers. Since 1967, hired workers on large farms have been covered by Fair Labor Standards Act minimum wage requirements, and agricultural minimum wages will be increased to general industry levels by 1978. Agricultural workers remain excluded from the federal unemployment insurance program and National Labor Relations Act. Farm worker unionization is prominent only on large-scale industrialized farms but will apparently continue to be exceptional nationally.   J

2074. Glaberman, Martin. BLACK CATS, WHITE CATS, WILDCATS: AUTO WORKERS IN DETROIT. *Radical Am. 1975 9(1): 25-29.* Gives a short history of auto workers in Detroit 1941 to present, including the influx of new workers during the war years, the years of Walter Reuther's career, and the Detroit rebellion of 1967.

2075. Goldfield, Michael. THE DECLINE OF ORGANIZED LABOR: NLRB UNION CERTIFICATION ELECTION RESULTS. *Pol. & Soc. 1982 11(2): 167-209.* Analyzes statistics from the National Labor Relations Board and other data that cast doubts on the generally accepted notion of a decline in organized labor during the 1970's. The unevenness of the decline demonstrated by the data challenges and makes suspect the conventional explanations offered: employer offensives against unions; regional differences in the acceptance of unionization, especially in the South; the changing composition of the labor force in recent years; a lessening in the aggressive stance of unions and their bureaucratization; and the differing economic conditions facing the various unions. Based on data provided by the NLRB Data Systems Division and Labor Department statistics; 20 tables, 3 graphs, 59 notes.
                                                             D. G. Nielson

2076. Goldstein, Joyce. CEDAR GROVE, W. VA.: WHO WILL PAY THE BILL? *Southern Exposure 1978 6(2): 89-92.* The community health facility at Cedar Grove, like its counterparts throughout the coal region, will probably have to close due to the termination of financial support from the United Mine Workers of America Health and Retirement Fund. The transfer of health care delivery payments to a fee-for-service reimbursement of physicians will cut off income formerly going to clinics and clinic-based health care workers. The Health Service Act introduced into Congress by Ronald Dellums (D-California) would reestablish the viability of such health clinics by setting up funding for community-based health care delivery services controlled by the populations involved.   N. Lederer

2077. Granof, Eugene B. and Moe, Stephen A. GRIEVANCE ARBITRATION IN THE U.S. POSTAL SERVICE: THE POSTAL SERVICE VIEW. *Arbitration J. 1974 29(1): 1-14.* The US Postal

Service established an experimental arbitration system, based on a rotating panel of arbitrators, to expedite grievance settlement.

2078. Green, Jim. HOLDING THE LINE: MINERS' MILITANCY AND THE STRIKE OF 1978. *Radical Am. 1978 12(3): 3-27.* Although commonly viewed as a defeat for the mine workers, the long strike of 1977-78 actually represents a partly successful rank and file struggle to minimize the defeats which the coal operators, with the acquiescence of the United Mine Workers of America leadership, sought to impose on the union members. The miners were desperately endeavoring to preserve as many of their earlier hard-won gains as possible, including health and medical benefits, with a special emphasis on free clinical care. Increase in miners' pensions also was a major issue. The strikers also upheld the tradition of waging local wildcat strikes to gain safety and other improvements. Left-wing political groups, most notably the Miners Right to Strike Committee, sought to politicize the struggle.   N. Lederer

2079. Grubbs, Donald H. PRELUDE TO CHAVEZ: THE NATIONAL FARM LABOR UNION IN CALIFORNIA. *Labor Hist. 1975 16(4): 453-469.* Examines the activities of the National Farm Labor Union and the strike against the Di Giorgio Fruit Co. in Kern County, California, as a prelude to the success of Cesar Chavez. The NFLU used secondary boycotts during the two-and-one-half year strike, but they were defeated by court injunction and a House Committee on Education and Labor investigation dominated by Congressman Richard Nixon. Only after the bracero problem waned did farm workers organize effectively. Based on records of the NFLU and the Southern Tenant Farmers' Union Papers; 38 notes.   L. L. Athey

2080. Gunn, Christopher. THE FRUITS OF RATH: A NEW MODEL OF SELF-MANAGEMENT. *Working Papers for a New Soc. 1981 8(2): 17-21.* Records the success of Local 46 of the Amalgamated Meat Cutters in taking over management of the Rath Packing Company in Vinton, Iowa, by a series of economic maneuvers; the workers' equity capital secured a federal loan to revitalize the financially failing firm, and Rath became the first large-scale employee stock ownership trust to exercise control by one-worker, one-vote.

2081. Hartman, Paul T. and Franke, Walter H. THE CHANGING BARGAINING STRUCTURE IN CONSTRUCTION: WIDE-AREA AND MULTICRAFT. *Industrial and Labor Relations Rev. 1980 33(2): 170-184.* Examines changes in the bargaining structure of the construction industry, using interview data mostly from the Midwest, accepting the opinion that multicraft bargaining at the local level is a possible alternative to the union-management problem in the construction industry. Wide-area bargaining and structural changes strengthen the union. Governmental interest in responsible leadership coincided with the top union officers' interest in strengthening their own roles. 37 notes.   G. E. Pergl

2082. Hendricks, Wallace and Kahn, Lawrence M. THE DETERMINANTS OF BARGAINING STRUCTURE IN U.S. MANUFACTURING INDUSTRIES. *Industrial and Labor Relations Rev. 1982 35(2): 181-195.* Estimates the determinants of collective bargaining structure in the manufacturing sector. Industry concentration and plant size are strongly associated with single firm as opposed to multifirm agreements. Among multiplant firms with single firm agreements, however, concentration and plant size strongly increase the probability of firmwide agreements. In addition, union rivalry tends to lead to decentralized bargaining units and labor intensity of production to centralized units.   J/S

2083. Henle, Peter. REVERSE COLLECTIVE BARGAINING? A LOOK AT SOME UNION CONCESSION SITUATIONS. *Industrial and Labor Relations Rev. 1973 26(3): 956-968.* "This article examines several bargaining relationships that have recently attracted attention because the unions involved have agreed to radical revisions in existing contracts in order to save jobs. The author notes that each of these cases has centered on one plant in a relatively successful multiplant firm, in which labor costs have been clearly above those of competitors, and there is a history of mutual trust and confidence between the parties."   J

2084. Hentoff, Nat. A LABOR ODYSSEY: THE UNIONIZATION OF *THE VILLAGE VOICE. Social Policy 1978 8(5): 47-49.* Traces events leading to the unionization of New York City's *Village Voice* newspaper in 1977.

2085. Hoffman, Eileen B. RESOLVING LABOR-MANAGEMENT DISPUTES: A NINE-COUNTRY COMPARISON. *Arbitration J. 1974 29(3): 185-204.* Every industrialized country is preoccupied with ways to minimize the losses resulting from unresolved labor conflicts. And specialists in each country look to others for guidance in avoiding particular kinds of disputes. This report examines and compares current practices in nine countries—Argentina, Australia, the Federal Republic of Germany, Israel, Italy, Japan, Sweden, the United Kingdom, and the United States. It first appeared as a special report of The Conference Board, and major excerpts are reprinted here, with permission.   J

2086. Howell, Frances Baseden. A SPLIT LABOR MARKET: MEXICAN FARM WORKERS IN THE SOUTHWEST. *Sociol. Inquiry 1982 52(2): 132-140.* The split-labor-market theory explains importation of foreign contract workers, passage of farm labor legislation, development and implementation of mechanized equipment, expansion of the "runaway shop," and decrease in the number of independent farmers concurrent with an increase in large-scale corporate farms; the farm worker movement, the United Farm Workers and the Arizona Farm Workers being two of the most familiar examples, also has a major impact.

2087. Hughes, Jonathan. THE GREAT STRIKE AT NUSHAGAK STATION, 1951: INSTITUTIONAL GRIDLOCK. *J. of Econ. Hist. 1982 42(1): 1-20.* In the summer of 1951 the Bering Sea fishermen's union strike against the Bristol Bay salmon packers signaled the end of old-time industrial labor relations there. The issues of the strike and its conduct offer a case study of deteriorating symbiosis in industrial relations, which is not untypical elsewhere in American industry. Events in 1951-52 at a remote cannery site on the Nushagak River serve as a partial microcosm of larger evolutionary consequences in American industry.   J

2088. Hurd, Richard W. ORGANIZING THE WORKING POOR—THE CALIFORNIA GRAPE STRIKE EXPERIENCE. *Rev. of Radical Pol. Econ. 1974 6(1): 50-75.* Examines the development of the United Farm Workers Union from the early 1960's, particularly during the California grape strikes (1966-70). The manner in which community and union organizing were combined to achieve grass roots participation, the emphasis upon non-violence, and the successful use of boycott tactics suggest important lessons for future organizers. Secondary and primary materials, especially newspapers; 109 notes.   P. R. Shergold

2089. Ichniowski, Casey. ECONOMIC EFFECTS OF THE FIREFIGHTERS' UNION. *Industrial and Labor Relations Rev. 1980 33(2): 198-211.* Using more observations and a larger set of variables than previous studies, concludes that the International Association of Fire Fighters had little effect on fire fighters' wages in 1966 and 1976. It had more influence on fringe benefits and total compensation. Significant differences in the economic environment also appeared, suggesting the need for more detailed study. Primary research; 5 tables, 29 notes.   G. E. Pergl

2090. James, Edgar. SADLOWSKI AND THE STEELWORKERS: NOTES FOR NEXT TIME. *Working Papers for a New Soc. 1977 5(1): 32-41.* Ed Sadlowski's unsuccessful bid in 1976-77 for the United Steelworkers of America presidency was due to some mistakes in his campaign and to his being unsanctioned by the AFL-CIO hierarchy.

2091. Jenkins, J. Craig and Perrow, Charles. INSURGENCY OF THE POWERLESS: FARM WORKER MOVEMENTS (1946-1972). *Am. Sociol. Rev. 1977 42(2): 249-268.* Drawing on the perspective developed in recent work by Oberschall (1973), Tilly (1975) and Gamson (1975), authors analyze the political process centered around farm worker insurgencies. Comparing the experience of two challenges, they argue that the factors favored in the classical social movement literature fail to account for either the rise or outcome of insurgency. Instead, the important variables pertain to social resources—in this case, sponsorship by established organizations. Farm workers themselves are powerless; as an excluded group, their demands tend to be systematically ignored. But powerlessness may be overridden if the national political elite is neutralized and members of the polity contribute resources and attack insurgent targets. To test the argument, entries in the *New York Times Annual Index* are content coded and statistically analyzed, demonstrating how the political environment surrounding insurgent efforts alternatively contains them or makes them successful.   J

2092. Kashner, Frank. A RANK & FILE STRIKE AT GE. *Radical Am. 1978 12(6): 42-60.* The author traces the development of his radicalism since the mid-1960's, his employment at the Lynn, Massachusetts, General Electric Co. River Works Plant in 1971, the rank-and-file strike over industrial safety there in which he participated in 1975, and later union organizing.

2093. Kaufman, Bruce E. BARGAINING THEORY, INFLATION, AND CYCLICAL STRIKE ACTIVITY IN MANUFACTURING. *Industrial and Labor Relations Rev. 1981 34(3): 333-355.* Presents a theoretical and empirical analysis of cyclical movements in strike activity and shows that inflation has been responsible for much of the increase in strike rates experienced in manufacturing in the 1970's.
                                                                J/S

2094. Keisling, Phil. MONEY OVER WHAT REALLY MATTERED: WHERE THE AIR TRAFFIC CONTROLLERS WENT WRONG. *Washington Monthly 1983 15(6): 10-18.* By ignoring the largest problem, that of arbitrary and unresponsive management in the Federal Aviation Administration, the Professional Air Traffic Controllers Organization made a fatal mistake when it went on strike in 1981 over publicly unpopular salary demands instead.

2095. Kochan, Thomas A. and Baderschneider, Jean. DEPENDENCE ON IMPASSE PROCEDURES: POLICE AND FIREFIGHTERS IN NEW YORK STATE. *Industrial and Labor Relations Rev. 1978 31(4): 431-449.* Presents a model of the determinants of reliance on impasse procedures in public collective bargaining and tests it with the experiences of New York police and firefighters, 1968-76.

2096. Kornblum, William. WHY THE INSURGENTS LOST IN STEEL. *Dissent 1977 24(2): 135-137.* Discusses dissent in the United Steelworkers of America in terms of the unsuccessful 1976-77 insurgent campaign of Ed Sadlowski against Lloyd McBride; until insurgent demands are satisfied, dissent will continue.

2097. Koziara, Karen S.; Bradley, Mary I.; and Pierson, David A. BECOMING A UNION LEADER: THE PATH TO LOCAL OFFICE. *Monthly Labor Rev. 1982 105(2): 44-46.* Examines more general hypotheses about the officer selection process in unions suggested by earlier studies of the 1950's and early 1960's; people who eventually become union officers become active in union administration early in their tenure with the union and then progress up the administrative hierarchy.

2098. Lewin, David and McCormick, Mary. COALITION BARGAINING IN MUNICIPAL GOVERNMENT: THE NEW YORK CITY EXPERIENCE. *Industrial and Labor Relations Rev. 1981 34(2): 175-190.* Analyzes the emergence and development of two-tier coalition bargaining in the municipal government of New York City from the late 1960's through the 1980 negotiations. The fiscal crisis of the mid-1970's provided a major thrust to the adoption of this type of bargaining structure. Through it, management and union officials were able not only to reach master and subsidiary agreements covering wages and conditions of employment, but to bargain broader fiscal rescue agreements with representatives of the federal and state governments.   J/S

2099. Lippert, John. FLEETWOOD WILDCAT: ANATOMY OF A WILDCAT STRIKE. *Radical Am. 1977 11(5): 7-37.* The wildcat strike at Fleetwood Fisher Body plant in Detroit on 26 August 1976 embodied several lessons for the radical working class movement. The United Automobile Workers of America failed to support the strikers in their grievances against management and was unable, or unwilling, to restore jobs to those fired because of their role in leading the workers off the job. The walkout was supported by only a minority of the labor force at the plant and achieved little if anything. The episode raised serious doubts about the health of the auto industry, the viable future of the UAW, and the forms that worker militancy should take in the future in

order to achieve meaningful gains on the plant level. Based on the memoirs of a young worker participant in the walkout.   N. Lederer

2100. Lippert, John. SHOPFLOOR POLITICS AT FLEETWOOD. *Radical Am. 1978 12(4): 52-69.* At the Fleetwood Fisher Body Plant in Detroit, Michigan, two groups of Cadillac assembly line workers differ over how to contend about the amount of labor the workers are willing to perform; late 1970's.

2101. Liubimova, V. STACHECHNAIA BOR'BA TRUDIASH-CHIKHSIA V KAPITALISTICHESKIKH STRANAKH (1959-1960 GG.) [The workers' strike in the capitalist countries, 1959-60]. *Mirovaia Ekonomika i Mezhdunarodnye Otnosheniia [USSR] 1960 (5): 117-125.* Notes the increasing use of the strike as a weapon in capitalist countries, and reviews the strikes that have taken place in various areas.
                                                            J. S. S. Charles

2102. Lozier, John. AMBIVALENCE TOWARD PROMOTION AMONG APPALACHIAN COAL MINERS: THE LEGEND OF LARRY HARPER. *Appalachian J. 1975 2(2): 111-115.* Investigates the 1953 suicide of Larry Harper, an Appalachian coal miner whose promotion to foreman created distance between him and the labor unions.

2103. Lunsford, Everett P., Jr. OUR MERCHANT MARINERS AND THEIR UNIONS. *US Naval Inst. Pro. 1975 101(5): 66-85.* Over the years US merchant marine seafaring has greatly changed and has now fallen on hard times. The federal government, the unions, and the companies must share the blame for this state of affairs. Largely through the efforts of the National Maritime Council, the industry is showing signs of improving, although "it is regretted that the industry had to decline as far as it did before action was taken, and that government pressure and initiative was needed to turn it around." The seamen themselves, their unions, their employers, and their politicians "will have to do better than those who have gone before them." 10 photos, 6 notes.
                                                            A. N. Garland

2104. Martin, James E. JOINT UNION-MANAGEMENT COMMITTEES: A COMPARATIVE LONGITUDINAL STUDY. *Administration & Soc. 1983 15(1): 49-74.* The effectiveness of joint union-management committees in six federal government facilities in a large midwestern city during 1972-76 was closely related to the labor relations climate in which the committees operated.

2105. May, James W., Jr. ATLANTA TRANSIT STRIKE, 1949-1950, PRELUDE TO SALE. Fink, Gary M. and Reed, Merl E., eds. *Essays in Southern Labor History: Selected Papers, Southern Labor History Conference, 1976.* (Westport, Conn.; London, England: Greenwood Pr., 1977): 208-219. Studies the years of disagreements and negotiations between labor and management which preceded the Atlanta transit strike, longest in the city's history. Unable to break the deadlock with Division 732 of the Amalgamated Association of Street, Electric Railway and Motor Coach Employees of America, the Georgia Power Company sold its recently modernized Atlanta transit properties to the locally controlled Atlanta Transit Company. In forcing this sale Division 732 had "successfully challenged Atlanta's traditionally impervious power structure." 42 notes.   R. V. Ritter

2106. McConville, Ed. OLIVER HARVEY: "GOT TO TAKE SOME RISKS." *Southern Exposure 1978 6(2): 24-28.* Harvey was involved for many years in the effort to organize a union of health service workers at the Duke University Medical Center in Durham, North Carolina. Despite poor working conditions at Duke, unionization was an uphill battle given to the hostile attitude of the power establishment in Durham and the intransigent anti-union attitude of the Duke Hospital administration. Harvey also became involved in local civil rights agitation during the 1960's. The fight for union recognition at Duke, including the demand for a minimum wage of $1.60 per hour, culminated in a strike supported by students and faculty in 1968. The union finally came to Duke as a result of a NLRB election in 1972. Oliver Harvey, now retired, continues to work for the betterment of health service workers on an unofficial basis. Based on oral interviews.   N. Lederer

2107. McDonald, Joseph A. UNION ATTITUDES AND CLASS CONSCIOUSNESS: THE CASE OF THE TUFTED TEXTILE IN-

DUSTRY. *Appalachian J. 1981 9(1): 37-49.* Analyzes the reasons why tufted textile workers in Dalton, Georgia, as in many areas in the South, have been slow to unionize.

2108. McLean, Robert A. COALITION BARGAINING AND STRIKE ACTIVITY IN THE ELECTRICAL EQUIPMENT INDUS-TRY, 1950-1974. *Industrial and Labor Relations Rev. 1977 30(3): 356-363.* Some critics of coalition bargaining have predicted that it will lead to an increase in strike activity. This study tests that claim through an analysis of strike activity in the electrical equipment industry before and after 1966, when coalition bargaining was initiated at General Electric and Westinghouse. Concludes that strike activity has indeed increased in that industry since 1966 but for reasons other than the introduction of coalition bargaining. J

2109. Medoff, James L. LAYOFFS AND ALTERNATIVES UN-DER TRADE UNIONS IN U.S. MANUFACTURING. *Am. Econ. Rev. 1979 69(3): 380-395.* Trade unions shape the structure of layoffs via seniority and similar programs; nonunion firms use quits and new hires to adjust employment. Covers 1958-79. 3 tables, 44 ref.
D. K. Pickens

2110. Mills, Nicolaus. THE WHIP AND THE BEE: DIARY FROM THE GRAPE STRIKE. *Dissent 1973 20(2): 200-205.*

2111. Nash, Al. LOCAL 1707, CSAE: FACETS OF A UNION IN THE NON-PROFIT FIELD. *Labor Hist. 1979 20(2): 256-277.* The author participated in the development of Local 1707, Community and Social Agency Employees Union, in New York City during 1958-63. Discusses the differences between professional unions and blue-collar unions, struggles for leadership, and the role of state agencies and private agencies as employers. 5 notes. L. L. Athey

2112. Navarro, Peter. UNION BARGAINING POWER IN THE COAL INDUSTRY, 1945-1981. *Industrial and Labor Relations Rev. 1983 36(2): 214-229.* The level of coal consumption has had a consistently strong effect on the balance of bargaining power throughout the postwar period and industry profits have also influenced settlements, but to a lesser extent. In recent negotiations, the most important power factor has been the sharp decline in the percentage of coal produced by mines covered by UMW contracts. In addition, not only has pre-strike stockpiling by major consumers blunted the union's strike weapon, but also the weakness of union leadership in recent years has helped to precipitate and prolong strikes. Only the evidence on the union's democratic contract ratification procedure, adopted in 1973, is mixed: although providing a slight strategic advantage to the union on occasion, it has also led to confusion at the bargaining table and contributed to the weakness of the leadership. The author also illustrates the importance of including rule changes in measuring union power. J

2113. Neumann, George R. THE PREDICTABILITY OF STRIKES: EVIDENCE FROM THE STOCK MARKET. *Industrial and Labor Relations Rev. 1980 33(4): 525-535.* Discussions of strike activity, and in particular of the costs of strike activity, generally ignore the existence of capital markets. If strikes are costly and if they are predictable, the presence of capital markets limits the losses that can be imposed on firms. This paper examines the effect of strikes on the value of the firm as measured by the stock market. The results indicate that strikes do have a negative effect on the value of the firm, although not a very large one, and that the stock market predicts the occurrence of strikes efficiently. J

2114. Nocera, Joseph. SAVING OUR SCHOOLS FROM THE TEACHERS' UNIONS. *Washington Monthly 1979 11(3): 12-22.* Discusses the Washington Teachers Union strike of March, 1979 in Washington, D.C., notable because the group was protesting a roll-back in wages and working conditions recommended by the school board, rather than making demands for increases in benefits.

2115. Northrup, Herbert R. THE NEW EMPLOYEE-RELATIONS CLIMATE IN AIRLINES. *Industrial and Labor Relations Rev. 1983 36(2): 167-181.* Examines recent developments in the air transport industry and assesses the extent to which deregulation has been a compelling factor of change. Among the problems examined are the entry of nonunion carriers into the market, the flight controllers' strike,

the decline of traffic during the recent recession, and particularly the differing union approaches to the industry's problems, as exemplified by those of the Air Line Pilots Association and the International Associa-tion of Machinists and Aerospace Workers. Concludes that the impact of deregulation has been significant and is likely to reduce union power permanently in this industry, but recent ventures in union-management cooperation may not survive the end of the recession and the lifting of competitive restrictions imposed as a result of the flight controllers' strike. J/S

2116. Nyden, Paul J. AS THE COAL BUSINESS BOOMS, TUR-MOIL HITS THE MINEWORKERS. *Working Papers for a New Soc. 1977 4(4): 46-53, 108.* Discusses the administration, factions, and strikes of the United Mine Workers of America 1972-76; considers its activities under the leadership of Arthur Miller.

2117. Orr, John A. THE RISE AND FALL OF STEEL'S HUMAN RELATIONS COMMITTEE. *Labor Hist. 1973 14(1): 69-82.* Traces the origins, history, operation, and decline of the United Steelworkers of America's Human Relations Committee 1960-65. The committee had four major impacts upon steel labor relations: 1) better understanding between labor and management, 2) better focusing on problems, 3) attuning agreements to needs of steel, and 4) reducing the government's role. Yet the attitudes were more important than the committee for harmonious relations in the 1960's. Based on periodicals and a doctoral dissertation; 11 notes. L. L. Athey

2118. Paulson, Darryl and Stiff, Janet. AN EMPTY VICTORY: THE ST. PETERSBURG SANITATION STRIKE, 1968. *Florida Hist. Q. 1979 57(4): 421-433.* A sanitation workers' strike in May 1968 began as a nonviolent movement but became violent by midsummer. After four months the workers returned to their jobs without pay raises and with a loss of seniority. The city suffered some $400,000 worth of damage plus the cost of overtime wages. It did gain with the promotion of integration, a fair housing ordinance, and redistricting. Primary and secondary sources; 2 photos, 42 notes. N. A. Kuntz

2119. Pellet, Gail. THE MAKING OF *HARLAN COUNTY, U.S.A.:* AN INTERVIEW WITH BARBARA KOPPLE. *Radical Am. 1977 11(2): 33-42.* The film was originally subsidized by the rank and file organization, Miners for Democracy, to be a history of this group. Instead it became documentary of the strike in 1973 by a newly formed local of the United Mine Workers of America in Kentucky against the Brookside Mine owners who refused to recognize the union. The makers of the film were able to win the trust of the striking miners. This resulted in graphic footage of various aspects of the strike, including courtroom scenes and violence. Miner's wives play an important role in the film as they did in the strike. The film's funding and distribution largely came from volunteer effort. Based on an oral interview with Barbara Kopple, producer and director of the film. N. Lederer

2120. Perry, Charles R. TEACHER BARGAINING: THE EXPERI-ENCE IN NINE SYSTEMS. *Industrial and Labor Relations Rev. 1979 33(1): 3-17.* This study appraises the impact of the collective bargaining process on the allocation of resources and on policy control in public schools through an analysis of the bargaining experience over more than a decade in nine diverse school systems. Collective bargaining is not radically different in public education and in the private sector. J/S

2121. Perry, James L. and Berkes, Leslie J. PREDICTING LOCAL GOVERNMENT STRIKE ACTIVITY: AN EXPLORATORY ANALYSIS. *Western Pol. Q. 1977 30(4): 513-527.* Strikes among public employees are strongly affected by nonrandom variables (especial-ly union influence and fiscal effort), may be manipulatable through public policy, and are subject to influence from cyclical shifts in unemployment; 1977.

2122. Peterson, Andrew A. DETERRING STRIKES BY PUBLIC EMPLOYEES: NEW YORK'S TWO-FOR-ONE SALARY PENAL-TY AND THE 1979 PRISON GUARD STRIKE. *Industrial and Labor Relations Rev. 1981 34(4): 545-562.* Focuses on the Taylor Law's requirement that New York State strikers lose two days' salary for each day they are on strike. Particular emphasis is placed on the litigation that occurred in the aftermath of the statewide strike by prison guards in 1979, when the guards' union challenged several aspects of the two-for-one penalty. The author concludes that the act's current provision governing payment of the penalty imposes a major hardship on participants in a long strike, and he recommends the act be amended in a way that he believes will not undermine the deterrent purposes of the penalty.   J/S

2123. Rada, Stephen E. MANIPULATING THE MEDIA: A CASE STUDY OF A CHICANO STRIKE IN TEXAS. *Journalism Q. 1977 54(1): 109-113.* Studies the strike by Chicano workers against the Economy Furniture Factory of Austin, Texas, from 1968-72, and shows how the workers had to struggle to gain access to the media in order to promote their cause.

2124. Raynor, Bruce. UNIONISM IN THE SOUTHERN TEXTILE INDUSTRY: AN OVERVIEW. Fink, Gary M. and Reed, Merl E., eds. *Essays in Southern Labor History: Selected Papers, Southern Labor History Conference, 1976.* (Westport, Conn.; London, England: Greenwood Pr., 1977): 80-99. Textile unionization in the South has come on hard times; total disorganization and discouragement after losing ground for 25 years, is the order of the day. Studies some of the sources of past frustration in textile organizing, assesses the current state of labor relations in the industry, and projects future trends in textile unionism. The failures may be attributed to: 1) the effective (if illegal) antiunion tactics employed by mill owners, 2) a hostile political climate, and 3) the nature of the southern labor force. There have been, however, a sufficient number of significant changes in the labor situation and personnel to justify some optimism for the future. 31 notes.
                                                                R. V. Ritter

2125. Read, Leonard E. PILOT ERRORS. *Freeman 1973 23(4): 207-210.* Unions are a product of the new economics' lust for power. Appointment of union men to federal departments and commissions "is but an acknowledgment of their overpowering influence" on government. Note.   D. A. Yanchisin

2126. Rehmus, Charles M. and Kerner, Benjamin A. THE AGENCY SHOP AFTER *ABOOD:* NO FREE RIDE, BUT WHAT'S THE FARE? *Industrial and Labor Relations Rev. 1980 34(1): 90-100.* In *Abood* v. *Detroit Board of Education,* the US Supreme Court ruled in 1977 that nonmembers of public employee unions might constitutionally be required to pay an agency shop or fair share fee to their bargaining representative, provided that such fees are used only to pay for the union's costs of collective bargaining and contract administration and not for its political expenditures. Thus far, seven states have grappled with the problem of attempting to define what kinds of union expenditures fall on one or the other side of this dividing line. This study shows that each state has approached the problem differently, developing varying answers to the procedural and substantive issues involved. The authors argue that these differences arise from the mistaken belief that the two types of union expenditures—political and bargaining—are for fundamentally different purposes and thus different rules should be applied to each. They contend that union-management relations in the public sector are inescapably political and, therefore, at least nonpartisan political expenditures should be charged against all bargaining unit members.   J

2127. Reverby, Susan. HOSPITAL ORGANIZING IN THE 1950'S: AN INTERVIEW WITH LILLIAN ROBERTS. *Signs 1976 1(4): 1053-1063.* Little unionizing of hospital personnel occurred in the United States until the late 1950's, when the racial makeup of nonprofessionals changed to black, Puerto Rican, and Chicano, and job issues became linked to civil rights. Lillian Roberts, a black nurse's aide who became a union organizer, attempted to unionize Mt. Sinai Hospital in Chicago. The ensuing strike for union recognition got no support from other unions or the public. The strikes, mostly southern blacks who had migrated to Chicago, were ineffective in gaining union recognition, but they did acquire a wage increase and better working conditions. Based on an oral interview; 2 notes.   J. Gammage

2128. Rinaldi, Matthew. DISSENT IN THE BROTHERHOOD: ORGANIZING IN THE TEAMSTERS UNION. *Radical Am. 1977 11(4): 43-55.* Indicates that forces within the Teamsters union seeking change are small in numbers and influence, owing to fear, apathy and alienation among the membership. The authoritarian internal structure of the union, and its strong ties to organized crime and to the American

ruling establishment, also aid in determining that no mass insurgent movement within the organization can exist. However, factions continue to operate, especially in the San Francisco Bay area, through the work of Teamsters for a Democratic Union (TDU) and UPSurge. These present sources of organized discontent are held together through *The Fifth Wheel,* a newspaper originally founded to support the efforts of an earlier oppositional group, the Teamsters Rank and File (TURF).
                                                                N. Lederer

2129. Robbins, Lynn A. NAVAJO WORKERS AND LABOR UNIONS. *Southwest Econ. and Soc. 1978 3(3): 4-23.* Traces the formation of voluntary labor organizations among the Navajo Indians in the Southwest and their relationship with national labor unions, 1958-78.

2130. Ruben, George. ORGANIZED LABOR IN 1981: A SHIFTING OF PRIORITIES. *Monthly Labor Rev. 1982 105(1): 21-28.* Discusses organized labor's woes during 1981 due to wage and benefit concessions and decreased employment; notes new labor laws.

2131. Russell, James. LETTER FROM SAN FRANCISCO: RANK-AND-FILE UNION VICTORY. *Radical Am. 1978 12(5): 70-74.* In an election of San Francisco's Local 2 of the Hotel and Restaurant Employees and Bartenders International Union in 1978, a rank-and-file group campaigned against and defeated a powerful union official it considered corrupt.

2132. Schoeplein, Robert N. SECULAR CHANGES IN THE SKILL DIFFERENTIAL IN MANUFACTURING, 1952-1973. *Industrial and Labor Relations Rev. 1977 30(3): 314-324.* Shows that the skill differential in manufacturing, when measured on the national level, has remained surprisingly stable over the 1952-73 period, in spite of its history of narrowing throughout the first half of the century and the severe pressures of inflation during the years since 1965. At the level of individual cities, however, this skill differential is shown to be moving toward convergence at one of two points, with differentials tending to be considerably wider in less unionized cities than in more unionized cities.
                                                                J

2133. Seltzer, Curtis. THE UNIONS—HOW MUCH CAN A GOOD MAN DO. *Washington Monthly 1974 6(4): 7-24.* The economics of the energy industries threaten Arnold Miller's United Mine Workers of America.   S

2134. Seroka, James H. LOCAL PUBLIC EMPLOYEE UNIONIZATION. *Policy Studies J. 1979 8(3): 430-437.* Summarizes fiscal, managerial, and socioeconomic changes in local government that have influenced labor relations for municipal and county government, and discusses their implications for bargaining, unionization, legal status of public employee unions, and disruption of local service.

2135. Shannon, Stephen C. WORK STOPPAGE IN GOVERNMENT: THE POSTAL STRIKE OF 1970. *Monthly Labor Rev. 1978 101(7): 14-22.* Gives the background behind the postal strike of 1970, discussing union negotiations, the radicalism of New York City postal workers, and the subsequent passage of the Postal Reorganization Act (1970).

2136. Shearer, Derek. FOR THE UFW, A BAD DAY AT THE POLLS: BUT DOES IT MATTER? *Working Papers for a New Soc. 1977 4(4): 12-13.* Discusses Cesar Chavez and the United Farm Workers Union's loss of the Proposition 14 (1976) initiative in California. Considers corporate agriculture's opposition (1975-76) to the measure that would have compelled growers to allow union organizers in their fields.

2137. Sklar, Susan. AN EXPERIMENT IN WORKER OWNERSHIP. *Dissent 1982 29(1): 61-70.* Describes the small but growing movement for worker ownership, such as that at the Rath Pork Packing Company of Waterloo, Iowa, despite the deterring effect of Ronald Reagan's administration.

2138. Sloan, Cliff and Hall, Bob. "IT'S GOOD TO BE HOME IN GREENVILLE"... BUT IT'S BETTER IF YOU HATE UNIONS. *Southern Exposure 1979 7(1): 82-93.* Describes the efforts of labor organizers in the antiunion city of Greenville, South Carolina, in the

1970's, home of Michelin Tire Corporation and J.P. Stevens & Company, among others, and gives a brief history of the area's industry since 1873.

2139. Smith, Russell L. and Hopkins, Anne H. PUBLIC EMPLOYEE ATTITUDES TOWARD UNIONS. *Industrial and Labor Relations Rev. 1979 32(4): 484-495.* This study investigates the attitudes toward unions of public sector employees in five states. Analyzing responses to questionnaires sent to 2000 state employees, the authors find that as in the private sector, attitudes toward unions are more favorable among employees in large organizations and with work situation dissatisfactions, lower occupational status, negative life experiences, and less involvement with the organization. In contrast to previous studies of private sector employees, however, the authors report that work situation dissatisfactions are most important in predicting attitudes toward unionization only among union members; among nonmembers, prework and life experiences were better predictors.   J

2140. Straussman, Jeffrey D. and Rodgers, Robert. PUBLIC SECTOR UNIONISM AND TAX BURDENS. *Policy Studies J. 1979 83(3): 438-448.* Cross-section analysis questions the belief that public unions have been a major cause of state and local fiscal problems, at least in terms of the impact of strikes and collective bargaining legislation.

2141. Sulzner, George T. POLITICS, LABOR RELATIONS, AND PUBLIC PERSONNEL MANAGEMENT: RETROSPECT AND PROSPECT. *Policy Studies J. 1982 11(2): 279-289.* Discusses the impact of public collective bargaining on public service personnel administration, with special attention to personnel administration-union representative relations, and the demands for smaller work forces and increased productivity during the 1980's.

2142. Taniguchi, Chad. THE FIRST TIME: 1979 HAWAII UNITED PUBLIC WORKERS STRIKE. *Amerasia J. 1980 7(2): 1-28.* Discusses the background of the 1979 public workers' strike in Hawaii, impressions of the strikers, and results of the strike. Concludes that cultural and job differences within the union, and poor public relations and leadership, reduced the effectiveness of the strike. Based on interviews and secondary sources; 81 notes.   E. S. Johnson

2143. Ullman, Robert. GM AND THE AUTO WORKERS: OSHA RESHUFFLES THE DECK. *Working Papers for a New Soc. 1978 6(3): 50-54.* Regulations of the Occupational Safety and Health Administration, 1971-78, have reduced health and safety hazards in General Motors' Pontiac (Michigan) automobile plant and have strengthened union-management relations by allowing unprecedented control over working conditions by the United Automobile Workers of America.

2144. Vázquez, Mario F. THE ELECTION DAY IMMIGRATION RAID AT LILLI DIAMOND ORIGINALS AND THE RESPONSE OF THE ILGWU. Mora, Magdalena and DelCastillo, Adelaida R., ed. *Mexican Women in the United States: Struggles Past and Present* (Los Angeles: U. of California Chicano Studies Res. Center, 1980): 145-148. Documents the conflict between management and labor at the Lilli Diamond Originals garment plant in Los Angeles, California. On 26 October 1976, the Western States Region Organizing Department of the International Ladies' Garment Workers' Union was informed that workers at the plant wanted to unionize. On election day, 14 January 1977, immigration officials arrested some of the strike supporters who were illegal aliens.   J. Powell

2145. Vroman, Susan. THE DIRECTION OF WAGE SPILLOVERS IN MANUFACTURING. *Industrial and Labor Relations Rev. 1982 36(1): 102-112.* Supports the traditional view that union wage behavior influences or spills over into nonunion wage changes but not vice versa. Covers 1960-78.   J/S

2146. Wagner, Dave and Buhle, Paul. WORKER CONTROL AND THE NEWS: THE MADISON, WISCONSIN, *PRESS CONNECTION. Radical Am. 1980 14(4): 7-20.* The story (1978-80) of a newspaper run by striking newspaper employees, its role in Madison's political scene, and its struggle to overcome undercapitalization as a worker-controlled, community-owned daily in a town with two monopoly-owned dailies. Describes the *Press Connection's* financial struggle and competition with the major dailies while implementing (or attempting to

implement) cooperative production, control, and ownership. Internal difficulties and the lack of money proved too much for those involved to continue. 10 illus.   C. M. Hough

2147. Walsh, Edward and Craypo, Charles. UNION OLIGARCHY AND THE GRASS ROOTS: THE CASE OF THE TEAMSTERS' DEFEAT IN FARMWORKER ORGANIZING. *Sociol. and Social Res. 1979 63(2): 269-293.* Inflexibility in the internal structure of the International Brotherhood of Teamsters combined with refusal to acknowledge the voice of the farmworkers in choosing a representative led to the failure of the IBT to organize the workers and marked the end of a grass roots support campaign already being squelched by internal power struggles, 1975-77.

2148. Wardell, Mark L.; Vaught, Charles; and Edwards, John N. STRIKES: A POLITICAL ECONOMY APPROACH. *Social Sci. Q. 1982 63(3): 409-427.* Assesses various theoretical approaches to strike resolution in America and examines strikes in the coal industry during 1976-78.

2149. Weir, Stan. WORK IN AMERICA: ENCOUNTERS ON THE JOB. *Radical Am. 1974 8(4): 99-108.* Examples of labor disputes on the local level.

2150. Wex, J. H. and McGee, W. S. UNIONIZATION OF COURT EMPLOYEES HAS RAISED LEGAL, PRACTICAL QUESTIONS. *Monthly Labor Rev. 1979 102(8): 20-24.* Efforts by judicial employees to organize had succeeded in 17 states by 1977; strikes have been few, not impairing court operations. The court, however, must balance claims of the employees' right to organize and strike against the defendant's right to a fair and speedy trail; courts may have to adjudicate contempt of court proceedings against their own employees.

2151. Wheeler, Hoyt N. IS COMPROMISE THE RULE IN FIRE FIGHTER ARBITRATION? *Arbitration J. 1974 29(3): 176-184.* "According to a popular view, the prospect of compulsory arbitration of contract terms inhibits bargaining, in that it causes parties, expecting a 'compromise' at the hands of the arbitrator or factfinder, to maintain intransigent positions. The author tests this hypothesis by studying 38 arbitration and factfinding decisions involving fire fighters—public employees who were subject to the kind of compulsory third-party procedures that were supposed to put a 'chill' on bargaining. His conclusion was that arbitrators did not commonly adopt 'intermediate' positions. The union or public negotiator, it would seem, would be wise to proceed on a case-by-case basis, attempting to reach the best bargain he can, without risking a decision by an arbitrator which accepts the other side's position in its entirety."   J

2152. Widick, B. J. NEW TRENDS IN THE UNIONS. *Dissent 1973 20(3): 281-283.*

2153. Windmuller, John P. CONCENTRATION TRENDS IN UNION STRUCTURE: AN INTERNATIONAL COMPARISON. *Industrial and Labor Relations Rev. 1981 35(1): 43-57.* The structure of unionism in nine Western countries became on the whole more concentrated during 1957-78, as indicated by a reduction in the number of national unions affiliated with major federations and an increase in the relative size of the largest unions. The reasons for the trend, which has implications for the internal life of unions and for collective bargaining, are linked to the efforts of unions to adapt their structure to changes in the environments in which they operate, often reinforced by pro-merger pressures from the central labor federations. The trend toward greater concentration may be expected to continue, especially in countries in which the major trade union federations are still composed of substantial numbers of affiliated unions.   J

2154. Witney, Fred. FINAL-OFFER ARBITRATION: THE INDIANAPOLIS EXPERIENCE. *Monthly Labor Rev. 1973 96(5): 20-25.* Discusses and evaluates the use of final-offer arbitration in a public sector labor dispute, specifically referring to the case of the city of Indianapolis and the American Federation of State, County, and Municipal Employees, with negotiations lasting from September 1971 through February 1972.

2155. Wolman, Philip J. THE OAKLAND GENERAL STRIKE OF 1946. *Southern California Q. 1975 57(2): 147-178.* Examines the causes and events concerning the general strike in Oakland, California, 3-5 December 1946. Part of a nationwide series of strikes in 1946, the Oakland incident involved most city workers whole-heartedly endorsing a strike which for 54 hours shut down most economic activity in the city. Essential facilities were maintained at minimum levels while city leaders and national union officials worked to end the strike, but its official termination neither resolved smoldering issues nor penetrated worker discontent. In the 1947 municipal election a labor slate of candidates defeated the incumbents. Suggests that the general strike was occasioned by an emotional outburst against business' failure to effect long-postponed social changes. Primary sources, including personal interviews, and secondary studies; 99 notes.   A. Hoffman

2156. Wynne, John M., Jr. UNIONS AND BARGAINING AMONG EMPLOYEES OF STATE PRISONS. *Monthly Labor Rev. 1978 101(3): 10-16.* Unionization of employees during the 1970's in state prisons has improved employee economic benefits and working conditions through collective bargaining and lobbying, but gains for employees have not necessarily improved the penal institutions (because of resultant conflict and restrictions on prison authorities).

2157. Zager, Robert. THE PROBLEM OF JOB OBSOLESCENCE: WORKING IT OUT AT RIVER WORKS. *Monthly Labor Rev. 1978 101(7): 29-32.* Discusses why the International Federation of Professional and Technical Engineers has cooperated with management despite technological advances and threatened job obsolescence since 1970 in General Electric's River Works engine plant.

2158. Zaitseva, N. Ia. DVIZHENIE RIADOVYKH I BOR'BA ZA SMENU RUKOVODSTVA V PROFSOIUZE GORNIAKOV S.SH.A. (1969-1974 GG.) [The movement of the rank and file and the struggle for replacement of the leadership in the United Mine Workers of America (1969-74)]. *Vestnik Moskovskogo U., Seriia 8: Istoriia [USSR] 1980 (6): 29-39.* During 1965-67, 40 of 186 unions replaced their leadership. Social unionism, the interest in political struggle, became important. In the Mine Workers, the struggle of Joseph A. Yablonsky against Tony Boyle represented this new movement. The reactionary press saw in the murder of Yablonsky proof of the evils of unions. Boyle's corrupt practices and secret agreements with mine owners led to his ouster in 1972 by Arnold Miller. A new tendency in the union movement in the United States had appeared. 73 notes.   D. Balmuth

2159. Zieger, Gay P. and Zieger, Robert H. UNIONS ON THE SILVER SCREEN: A REVIEW-ESSAY ON *F.I.S.T., BLUE COLLAR,* AND *NORMA RAE. Labor Hist. 1982 23(1): 67-78.* Reviews three American motion pictures of the late 1970's that focus on unions in the United States: *Blue Collar* (1978), *F.I.S.T.* (1978), and *Norma Rae* (1979). *Blue Collar* depicts union corruption and the alienation of the work place. *F.I.S.T.* concentrates on the labor movements' mixed legacy of militancy and venality, while *Norma Rae* deals with the tenacity of social conflict and the idealism surrounding union organizing. A number of labor documentaries made during the same time period, however, may have a more permanent impact on labor history than the three films reviewed. 8 notes, biblio.   L. F. Velicer

2160. Zimmer, Lynn and Jacobs, James B. CHALLENGING THE TAYLOR LAW: PRISON GUARDS ON STRIKE. *Industrial and Labor Relations Rev. 1981 34(4): 531-544.* In analyzing the 1979 strike by nearly all of the prison guards in New York, focuses on the social organization of the prison environment and the guards' changing occupational role as critical causes of the New York State prison guard strike. Collective bargaining is not well suited to resolving those problems, and in fact the bargaining system may have aggravated them. It was the state's use of National Guard troops and the application of Taylor Law sanctions, rather than any bargaining strategy by either party, that brought the guards back to work.   J/S

2161. —. [HARLAN COUNTY, USA]. *Dissent 1977 24(3): 307-310.*
Mills, Nicolaus. "HARLAN COUNTY, U.S.A.," *pp. 307-309.* Reviews the movie *Harlan County, U.S.A.* dealing with a mining strike in Kentucky recorded on film by Barbara Kopple; discussion combines scenarios from the documentary film and semi-critical review of Kopple's work.

Howe, Irving. ANOTHER VIEW OF "HARLAN COUNTY, U.S.A.," *pp. 309-310.* Sees evasions and failures in the Kopple film, especially bias, including reticence on the crookedness of John L. Lewis, lack of specifics which the coal miners requested in their contract, and the fact that Kopple skirting of the issue that scab laborers are not imports but rather locals who refused to join the strike.
Mills, Nicolaus. NICOLAUS MILLS REPLIES, *p. 310.* Responds to Howe, maintaining that for the perspective she took, Kopple could not have adequately covered the opposition to the strike within the same movie.

2162. —. AN INTERVIEW WITH RAY ROGERS. *Working Papers Mag. 1982 9(1): 48-57.* Union organizer Ray Rogers describes his campaign to force the J. P. Stevens Company to sign a contract.

2163. —. MINORITY MEMBERSHIP IN APPRENTICESHIP PROGRAMS IN THE CONSTRUCTION TRADES. *Industrial & Labor Relations Rev. 1973 27(1): 93-102.*
Strauss, George. MINORITY MEMBERSHIP PROGRAMS IN THE CONSTRUCTION TRADES: COMMENT, pp. 93-99. In "Minority Membership Programs in the Construction Trades" (see abstract 10:3414), Alex Maurizi argued that shortening the length of apprentice training "may be a far more successful means for achieving an increased participation of nonwhites in the construction trades than the current antidiscrimination efforts." Strauss argues that the extent of minority participation in construction apprenticeship programs is far more significantly influenced by factors other than the length of the training period and that, historically, minorities have been excluded from higher-status (longer training length) trades. 3 tables, 19 notes.
Maurizi, Alex. REPLY, pp. 100-102. Strauss's hypothesis that "status" is an independent factor in the analysis must be rejected: the sign of the coefficient of the status variable is positive, not negative. "The fact that nonwhite apprentices are older could be one reason that there are fewer nonwhites in the longer training program. It is this difference in their average ages that requires explanation, and it is the importance of kinship in the choice of apprentices that appears to be the explanation." 2 tables, 6 notes.
D. D. Cameron

2164. —. A NATIONAL SCANDAL: A CONVERSATION WITH ANTHONY MAZZOCCHI. *WorldView 1975 18(11): 26-30.* Presents an interview with Anthony Mazzocchi, Director of the Citizen Legislative Department of the Oil, Chemical, and Atomic Workers Union, dealing with occupational safety and health hazards of industrial workers in the 1970's.

2165. —. ON THE LINE IN AUTO. *Progressive Labor 1974 9(4): 45-55.* Auto workers lead the way in fighting back against bosses' attack on all workers. [Leonard] Woodcock and other labor leaders are an obstacle. They must be swept aside.   J

2166. —. PHILADELPHIA, 1973: WHY THE SPECTER OF A GENERAL STRIKE LOOMED FROM THE TEACHERS' FIGHT. *Progressive Labor 1973 9(2): 17-25.* The courageous 8-week strike battle waged by the Philadelphia Federation of Teachers has written a stirring chapter in the history of the international working class. The general strike which was threatened and planned by almost every major union in the city overwhelmed at that moment every enemy of the working class.   J

2167. —. SADLOWSKI'S STEEL. *Can. Dimension [Canada] 1977 12(3): 16-18.* Focuses on the new breed of US union leaders, exemplified by Ed Sadlowski's challenge for leadership of the United Steelworkers of America against Lloyd McBride in 1976-77.

2168. —. STEEL PLANTS: BOSSES INFERNO. *Progressive Labor 1974 9(4): 8-24.* Steel mills are graveyards for workers. In these plants the sharpest forms of bosses oppression take place. Unsafe conditions kill. It is at the point of production that the class struggle is often the sharpest. Today's graveyards for workers will become the burial ground for the ruling class allowing life to flourish and develop under working class leadership.   J

2169. —. WE WALK THE LINE: THE STRUGGLE AT PRE-TERM. *Radical Am. 1979 13(2): 8-24.* Account of the 44 female workers' strike against Preterm, Boston's largest abortion clinic, from November 1976 until summer 1977; describes Preterm from its founding as a gynecological center in 1972, to its current operation.

Government Programs, Policies, and Politics

2170. Abraham, Steven E. NLRB JURISDICTION OF SECOND-ARY BOYCOTTS: *ILA* V. *ALLIED INTERNATIONAL, INC.,* A MISSED OPPORTUNITY FOR THE SUPREME COURT TO REEVALUATE *MOBILE. New York U. J. of Int. Law and Pol. 1983 15(2): 395-434.* The International Longshoremen's case (1982), rising out of the boycott of Soviet goods following the invasion of Afghanistan, dismissed the union's claim that the boycott was beyond the jurisdiction of the National Labor Relations Board because the issue was not "in commerce" but involved foreign nations and foreign relations; this countered the decision of *American Radio Association* v. *Mobile Steamship Association, Inc.* (US, 1974), but the legal reasoning in the case was based on a narrow interpretation.

2171. Ashenfelter, Orley and Smith, Robert S. COMPLIANCE WITH THE MINIMUM WAGE LAW. *J. of Pol. Econ. 1979 87(2): 333-350.* Examination of extent and pattern of compliance with federal minimum wage guidelines during 1973-75 indicates that enforcement by the federal government does have some impact.

2172. Azevedo, Ross E. PHASE III—A STABILIZATION PRO-GRAM THAT COULD NOT WORK. *Q. Rev. of Econ. and Business 1976 16(1): 7-22.* In January 1973, then-President Richard Nixon abandoned administered wage and price controls for Phase III, a program based on voluntary cooperation and self-enforcement. Unfortunately, from its very inception, Phase III was doomed to be a failure as a stabilization effort. This article details the administrative difficulties and substantive problems associated with the implementation and operation of Phase III and indicates the manner in which they led to its ultimate demise. The article links these difficulties to the costs and frustrations imposed on the business community by Phase III, providing strategic suggestions for future stabilization programs.   J

2173. Baker, David G. and Colby, David C. THE POLITICS OF MUNICIPAL EMPLOYMENT POLICY: A COMPARATIVE STUDY OF U.S. CITIES. *Am. J. of Econ. and Sociol. 1981 40(3): 249-263.* Municipal employment policy has been partially ignored in urban research, perhaps because of the implicit assumption that employment policy parallels expenditure and taxation policy. However, a strong relationship is found between municipal employment levels and the specified socioeconomic environment. Relationships between that environment and employment policy deviate considerably from expenditure policy. Although expenditure policy is more directly related to municipal economic environment, public employment policy is related to the sociopolitical environment.   J/S

2174. Ball, Robert. LABOR AND MATERIALS REQUIRED FOR HIGHWAY CONSTRUCTION. *Monthly Labor Rev. 1973 96(6): 40-45.* Discusses employment opportunities created by federal government-sponsored highway construction projects from 1958-70, emphasizing production costs.

2175. Barnes, Peter. JOBS: PROSPECTS FOR FULL EMPLOY-MENT. *Working Papers for a New Soc. 1975 3(3): 49-58.* Discusses whether the federal government should guarantee jobs for the unemployed in the 1970's.

2176. Barton, Paul E. VOCATIONAL EDUCATION: FEDERAL POLICIES FOR THE 1980S. *Educ. and Urban Soc. 1981 14(1): 83-102.* Because the federal government sponsored the Smith-Hughes Act (US, 1917), creating vocational education at the high school level, presents seven policies for the federal government to pursue during the 1980's, concluding that industry and education should work more closely together.

2177. Bassi, Laurie J. CETA—DID IT WORK? *Policy Studies J. 1983 12(1): 106-118.* The Comprehensive Employment and Training Act (US, 1973) did employ people but was not cost-effective in increasing marketable skills.

2178. Batten, Michael D. and Kestenbaum, Sara. OLDER PEOPLE, WORK, AND FULL EMPLOYMENT. *Social Policy 1976 7(3): 30-33.* Examines the effects of the Comprehensive Employment and Training Act (1973) on the employment and career gains of aging persons, 1973-76.

2179. Bell, Carolyn. IMPLEMENTING SAFETY AND HEALTH REGULATIONS FOR WOMEN IN THE WORKPLACE. *Feminist Studies 1979 5(2): 286-301.* Discusses whether the Occupational Safety and Health Act (US, 1970), designed to assure workers of uniform health and safety protection, has protected or restricted workers, particularly women, in the labor force, the topic of a conference among students and faculty at Smith College in 1976. Briefly discusses the regulatory policies of the Environmental Protection Agency (EPA) and the Equal Employment Opportunity Commission (EEOC) as well as OSHA, focusing on OSHA's standards for certain dangerous chemicals and the problems of implementing policy standards of the nearly 70,000 chemicals, with 2,000 added each year, used in the workplace.

G. Smith

2180. Bell, Winifred. FEDERAL SOCIAL WELFARE PROGRAMS: 1945-1968. *Current Hist. 1973 65(383): 15-19, 39-40.* Discusses federal public welfare programs dealing specifically with housing, urban development, employment, health care, and nutrition.

2181. Bendick, Marc, Jr. THE ROLE OF PUBLIC PROGRAMS AND PRIVATE MARKETS IN REEMPLOYING DISPLACED WORKERS. *Policy Studies Rev. 1983 2(4): 715-733.* Most workers affected by economic change have not experienced unacceptable reemployment difficulties; those experiencing difficulties have done so because of such private labor market failures as geographic immobility and inefficient labor exchanges; consequently public policy aimed at redressing these problems will be more effective than programs attacking the problem of declining industries.

2182. Berkowitz, Edward. GROWTH OF THE U. S. SOCIAL WELFARE SYSTEM IN THE POST-WORLD WAR II ERA: THE UMW REHABILITATION, AND THE FEDERAL GOVERN-MENT. *Res. in Econ. Hist. 1980 5: 233-247.* The fact that government social welfare expenditures tripled between 1945 and 1956 contradicts the implicit assertion of political historians that those years were marked by conservatism and inactivity. The relationship between the federal government and the UMW's [United Mine Workers of America] Welfare and Retirement Fund was one source of the growth of federal expenditures which is often overlooked. Federal officials helped create the fund in 1946, and many federal officials worked for the fund after 1946. One focus of the fund's efforts was rehabilitation. A special relationship between the fund and the vocational rehabilitation program resulted in favored treatment of coal miners by the program and increased appropriations for the program. This relationship influenced the passage of three major pieces of federal social welfare legislation in the 1950's, including disability insurance.   J

2183. Best, Fred and Mattesich, James. SHORT-TIME COMPENSA-TION SYSTEMS IN CALIFORNIA AND EUROPE. *Monthly Labor Rev. 1980 103(7): 13-22.* Examines the concept of short-time compensation programs under which "employees on reduced workweeks would be partially reimbursed for lost earnings and workers would not lose their jobs" in the United States, particularly the 18-month Work Sharing Unemployment Insurance program in California which began in mid-1978 and was extended in mid-1979 for two more years, and compares it to similar programs in Europe which have been used since the 1920's.

2184. Bezdek, Roger H. and Cook, William N. SOME QUESTIONS CONCERNING CERTIFICATION OF THE DISADVANTAGED UNDER THE EMERGENCY EMPLOYMENT ACT. *Urban and Social Change Rev. 1973 6(2): 64-68.*

2185.   Bingham, Barbara J. U.S. CIVIL WORKS CONSTRUCTION SHOWS DECREASE IN REQUIRED LABOR. *Monthly Labor Rev. 1978 101(10): 24-30.* Increase in offsite employee-hours in the Army Corps of Engineers land and dredging projects has been offset by a decrease in onsite employee-hours, 1960-72.

2186.   Boden, Les and Wegman, David. INCREASING OSHA'S CLOUT: SIXTY MILLION NEW INSPECTORS. *Working Papers for a New Soc. 1978 6(3): 43-49.* The Occupational Safety and Health Administration would be more effective if more inspectors were hired and if current regulations were more strictly adhered to.

2187.   Bond, Deborah T. STATE LABOR LEGISLATION ENACTED IN 1975. *Monthly Labor Rev. 1976 99(1): 17-29.* Reviews 1975 labor legislation state by state, noting that Virginia became the 43rd government to pass a minimum wage law and that California and nine other states moved to aid farm workers.

2188.   Booth, Philip. UNEMPLOYMENT INSURANCE AND PUBLIC WELFARE: II. PROBLEMS AND OPPORTUNITIES. *Public Welfare 1976 34(1): 14-20.* Discusses the present system of unemployment insurance, indicating problems in coverage and recommending further steps the federal government might take to better help displaced workers and their families; one of three articles on this subject in this issue.

2189.   Borjas, George J. WAGE DETERMINATION IN THE FEDERAL GOVERNMENT: THE ROLE OF CONSTITUENTS AND BUREAUCRATS. *J. of Pol. Econ. 1980 88(6): 1110-1147.* Analysis of income differential among so-called similar individuals in 21 federal agencies indicates that agencies with small and well-organized constituencies and with bureaucracies sharing a common interest generally receive higher wages; 1961-76.

2190.   Borus, Michael E. INDICATORS OF CETA PERFORMANCE. *Industrial and Labor Relations Rev. 1978 32(1): 3-14.* Attempts to validate 19 current indices of long-run program impact in the Comprehensive Employment and Training Act (US, 1973).

2191.   Boskin, Michael J. THE EFFECTS OF GOVERNMENT EXPENDITURES AND TAXES ON FEMALE LABOR. *Am. Econ. Rev. 1974 64(2): 251-256.*

2192.   Brightman, Carol. THE CETA FACTOR. *Working Papers for a New Soc. 1978 6(3): 34-42.* The Comprehensive Employment and Training Act (1973), a federal program intended to provide employment for municipal workers and youth, has been a blend of political patronage and grass roots activism.

2193.   Bulmer, Charles and Carmichael, John L., Jr. TOIL AND TROUBLE: THE REFORM OF THE LABOR LAW. *Policy Studies J. 1979 8(3): 400-406.* Examines problems with current labor law, such as the proliferation of court appeals, and the provisions of the Labor Reform Act (US, 1977).

2194.   Buttel, Frederick H. and Larson, Oscar W., III. POLITICAL IMPLICATIONS OF MULTIPLE JOBHOLDING IN U.S. AGRICULTURE: AN EXPLORATORY ANALYSIS. *Rural Sociol. 1982 47(2): 272-294.* Compares a previous study on research about the involvement of part-time farmers in agrarian protest based on 1960's data from a National Farmers Organization study, and a study from 1979 of New York farmers, to test "the proposition that part-time or multiple jobholding farm operators are a progressive element in agricultural politics," and concludes "that part- or full-time farmers do not exhibit dramatic socioeconomic differentials and that both groups are equally well integrated into the society and rural community."

2195.   Calavita, Kitty. THE DEMISE OF THE OCCUPATIONAL SAFETY AND HEALTH ADMINISTRATION: A CASE STUDY IN SYMBOLIC ACTION. *Social Problems 1983 30(4): 437-448.* Examines the current attempt by the Reagan administration to deregulate the Occupational Safety and Health Administration; finds that the agency, whose creation was a symbolic action, has been a vehicle for "real material and ideological gains by labor," 1970-83.

2196.   Cardoso, Lawrence A. "WETBACKS" AND "SLAVES": RECENT ADDITIONS TO THE LITERATURE. *J. of Am. Ethnic Hist. 1982 1(2): 68-71.* Reviews *Operation Wetback: The Mass Deportation of Mexican Undocumented Workers in 1954* (1980) by Juan Ramon García and *Slave Trade Today: American Exploitation of Illegal Aliens* (1980) by Sasha G. Lewis.   N. C. Burckel

2197.   Carmichael, John R., Jr. and Bulmer, Charles. LABOR AND EMPLOYMENT POLICY: A BIBLIOGRAPHY. *Policy Studies J. 1978 7(1): 165-167.* Bibliography of books published 1960's-70's pertaining to federal policy on labor and unemployment.

2198.   Carpenter, Linda J. WORKERS' COMPENSATION AND THE SCHOLARSHIP ATHLETE. *J. of Higher Educ. 1982 53(4): 448-459.* According to Supreme Court decisions, scholarship athletes may be eligible for workmen's compensation benefits for injuries and disabilities incurred as a result of sports participation. The potential for workers' compensation eligibility exists regardless of the athletes' purportedly amateur, nonemployee status. This could have massive financial impact on both intercollegiate athletic programs and their sponsoring universities.   J/S

2199.   Carroll, Thomas M. RIGHT TO WORK LAWS DO MATTER. *Southern Econ. J. 1983 50(2): 494-509.* Unions are weaker, wages are lower, and unemployment rates are higher in states having right to work laws.

2200.   Cebula, Richard J. A NOTE ON THE IMPACT OF RIGHT-TO-WORK LAWS ON THE COST OF LIVING IN THE UNITED STATES. *Urban Studies [Great Britain] 1982 19(2): 193-195.* Investigates whether and to what extent regional differences in the cost of living in the United States can be attributed to right to work laws prohibiting the "union shop." Suggests the laws lower the overall cost of living by roughly 8% in metropolitan areas. The existence of right to work laws implies less union power and thus less labor market pressure to increase labor costs. There is likely to be a tendency for final product prices to be lower, all other things being equal, though in practice numerous other factors are also involved. Based on secondary sources; 2 tables, biblio., note.   D. J. Nicholls

2201.   Cimbala, Stephen J. and Stout, Robert L. THE ECONOMIC REPORT OF THE PRESIDENT: BEFORE AND AFTER THE FULL EMPLOYMENT AND BALANCED GROWTH ACT OF 1978. *Presidential Studies Q. 1983 13(1): 50-61.* Examines the economic and political characteristics of the *Economic Report of the President* before and after the 1978 Humphrey-Hawkins Act. This legislation, committing each administration to move toward full employment and reasonable price stability within a specific time period, has had the effect of making the economic report highly political in nature, as well as highly unreliable and inaccurate over the standard two or five year projection periods. 4 tables, 14 notes.   D. H. Cline

2202.   Clinton, Lawrence; Chadwick, Bruce A.; and Bahr, Howard M. VOCATIONAL TRAINING FOR INDIAN MIGRANTS: CORRELATES OF "SUCCESS" IN A FEDERAL PROGRAM. *Human Organization 1973 32(1): 17-27.* Uses records from the Adult Vocational Training Program of the Bureau of Indian Affairs' office in Portland to determine the factors that lead to successful completion of the program. Males are more likely to complete the program than are females. Successful previous employment was the most important correlate for male completion, while off-reservation living experience was the most important for females. Abstracts in English, French, and Spanish. Tables, 2 notes, biblio.   E. S. Johnson

2203.   Cohen, Eli E. REVENUE SHARING AND YOUTH MANPOWER PROGRAMS. *New Generation 1974 56(1): 25-28.*

2204.   Conyers, John, Jr. THE ECONOMY IS THE ISSUE: PLANNING FOR FULL EMPLOYMENT. *Freedomways 1977 17(2): 71-78.* The author, in this speech before the National Coalition to Fight Inflation and Unemployment, 15 May 1977, called for mass political organization to achieve national economic planning for full employment in the United States.

2205.   Cooke, William N. and Gautschi, Frederick H., III. POLITICAL BIAS IN NLRB UNFAIR LABOR PRACTICE DECISIONS.

Industrial and Labor Relations Rev. 1982 35(4): 539-549. Previous research has suggested that US presidents appoint members to the National Labor Relations Board who reflect the administration's own union-management predilections. No adequate empirical evidence has yet been reported, however, to show that, once appointed, board members act in a biased manner. The present study develops and tests a choice model of Board member decisions in selected unfair labor practice cases, 1954-77. The evidence strongly supports the popular belief that board decisions are heavily dependent upon shifting political winds.   J

2206. Corman, James C. UNEMPLOYMENT INSURANCE AND PUBLIC WELFARE: III. REFORM AND COORDINATION. *Public Welfare 1976 34(1): 21-26.* Congressman Corman (California) discusses reforms of the unemployment insurance system, including the generation of more jobs that pay adequate wages, uniformity of benefits and qualifications nationwide, and the development of improved and expanded support programs for those who can not work or earn enough; one of three articles on this subject in this issue.

2207. Couturier, Jean J. PUBLIC INVOLVEMENT IN GOVERN-MENT LABOR RELATIONS: A MENAGE À TROIS? *Natl. Civic Rev. 1978 67(7): 312-315.* What is the "public interest" in public labor relations? If it exists, how is it defined? How is it expressed? How influential is the expression? The answers to these questions were sought through studies of the bargaining process in Milwaukee, Philadelphia, Memphis and Berkeley. None of the answers were entirely clear. The process needs to be defined and delineated.   J

2208. Cowen, Peter. WHY JOHNNY CAN'T WORK: THE ROB-BERY FACTOR. *Washington Monthly 1974 6(9): 29-34.* Investigates the questionable practices of some private vocational training institutions and criticizes the state system for failing to provide training for jobs.

2209. Dahm, Margaret M. UNEMPLOYMENT INSURANCE AND PUBLIC WELFARE: I. BASIC PHILOSOPHY AND TODAY'S SYSTEM. *Public Welfare 1976 34(1): 6-13.* Discusses the concept of unemployment insurance based on payroll taxes, and distinguishes this from welfare, analyzing the present unemployment insurance system and making recommendations for the future; one of three articles on this subject in this issue.

2210. Davis, Otto A.; Joseph, Myron L.; Perry, Wayne D.; and Niles, John S. AN EMPIRICAL STUDY OF THE NAB-JOBS PROGRAM. *Public Policy 1973 21(2): 235-262.* Vocational education program.

2211. DeMarco, John J. and Nigro, Lloyd G. IMPLEMENTING PERFORMANCE APPRAISAL REFORM IN THE UNITED STATES CIVIL SERVICE. *Public Administration [Great Britain] 1983 61(1): 45-57.* Reactions to job performance appraisal procedures required by the Civil Service Reform Act (US, 1978), as implemented at four Department of the Navy research and development laboratories, are generally favorable, but the new procedures may face serious long-term problems.

2212. Derber, Milton; Jennings, Ken; McAndrew, Ian; and Wagner, Martin. BARGAINING AND BUDGET MAKING IN ILLINOIS PUBLIC INSTITUTIONS. *Industrial and Labor Relations Rev. 1973 27(1): 49-62.* This study of the relationship between collective bargaining and the budget-making process in the public sector is largely based on interviews in thirty public institutions in Illinois, with almost 100 management and union representatives. The authors found that although the expiration dates of most contracts in these relationships are tied to fiscal year or budget adoption dates, settlements frequently come several weeks after these deadlines. The reasons for the looseness of this relationship are explained, and information is also provided on the attitudes of negotiators toward the use of budget information in bargaining, the availability of such information to union representatives, and labor's use of the 'end run' to influence bargaining and budgets.   J

2213. Doeringer, Peter B. and Piore, Michael J. UNEMPLOYMENT AND THE "DUAL LABOR MARKET." *Public Interest 1975 (38): 67-79.* Points out that much current unemployment occurs in the secondary labor sector where jobs are unattractive and notes changes in public policy to deal with this.

2214. Donnelly, Patrick G. THE ORIGINS OF THE OCCUPA-TIONAL SAFETY AND HEALTH ACT OF 1970. *Social Problems 1982 30(1): 13-25.* The Occupational Safety and Health Act (US, 1970) emerged because of the influence of protesting workers on the two main political parties, resulting in better working conditions with regard to safety and health.

2215. Dressel, Paula L. POLICY SOURCES OF WORKER DISSAT-ISFACTIONS: THE CASE OF HUMAN SERVICE WORKERS IN AGING. *Social Service Rev. 1982 56(3): 406-423.* Dissatisfaction among workers associated with services established by the Older Americans Act (US, 1965) is largely due to policies of the act itself, such as "the symbolic nature of legislation, policy ambiguities, universal entitlement, and calculated fragmentation."

2216. Eames, Patricia E. AT WORK IN 1934. *Civil Liberties Rev. 1974 1(4): 129-131.* Discusses shortcomings of the National Labor Relations Board during the 1960's and 70's and the ways liberals and labor could stimulate the board to pursue a more vigorous law enforcement policy.   S

2217. Edgell, David L. and Wandner, Stephen A. UNEMPLOY-MENT INSURANCE: ITS ECONOMIC PERFORMANCE. *Monthly Labor Rev. 1974 97(4): 33-40.* The unemployment insurance program in the United States provided income for the jobless and helped stabilize the economy between 1945 and 1973.

2218. Elder, Peyton. THE 1974 AMENDMENTS TO THE FEDER-AL MINIMUM WAGE LAW. *Monthly Labor Rev. 1974 97(7): 33-37.* Amendments to the federal minimum wage law in 1974 raised the minimum wage and covered domestic service workers and more public employees for the first time.

2219. Elder, Peyton. THE 1977 AMENDMENTS TO THE FEDER-AL MINIMUM WAGE LAW. *Monthly Labor Rev. 1978 101(1): 9-11.* Amendments to the Fair Labor Standards Act increased the minimum wage to $2.65 an hour on 1 January 1978, and included modifications in the law's coverage.

2220. Elliot, Ralph D. DO RIGHT TO WORK LAWS HAVE AN IMPACT ON UNION ORGANIZING ACTIVITIES? *J. of Social and Pol. Studies 1979 4(1): 81-93.* Using variables from 1950, 1960, and 1970 data, tests the relationship between the level of union organizing activity and the presence of right to work laws and concludes that these laws do not significantly affect union organizing, and therefore are not the cause of any union weakness.

2221. Elson, Martin W. and Burton, John F., Jr. WORKER'S COMPENSATION INSURANCE: RECENT TRENDS IN COSTS. *Monthly Labor Rev. 1981 104(3): 45-50.* Presents estimates of employers' costs of workmen's compensation insurance purchased from private carriers or state funds in 47 jurisdictions as of 1 July 1978 as a first step in determining whether the variations in premiums are great enough to influence where businesses locate and whether recent trends in premium levels indicate any reluctance by states to boost program benefits and costs, for fear of losing employers to lower cost jurisdictions.

2222. Enger, Thomas P. FOREIGN TRADE POLICY OF AMERI-CAN LABOUR. *J. of World Trade Law [Switzerland] 1973 7(4): 449-460.* The American labor unions have traditionally supported free trade initiatives in Congress. Since 1969, however, they have adopted a protectionist attitude to trade policy. The thesis of this article is that this change is due to structural changes in the U.S. economy, and labor will therefore not reverse its protectionist attitude to trade once the recession ends and employment rises.   J

2223. Epstein, Edwin M. CORPORATIONS AND LABOR UNIONS IN ELECTORAL POLITICS. *Ann. of the Am. Acad. of Pol. and Social Sci. 1976 425: 33-58.* Federal prohibitions of corporate and union contributions have been motivated by two objectives: to reduce or eliminate domination of the electoral process by business and labor through their aggregated wealth; and to protect stockholders and union members from having their organizations' funds used for political purposes of which they do not approve. Federal regulations have been largely ineffective in preventing corporate and union monies from reaching political candidates and parties both legally and illegally. Recent developments, including passage of the Federal Election Campaign Act of 1971 as amended in 1974, important decisions by the Supreme Court since 1972, and rulings by the Federal Election Commission, have widened the area of legal campaign-related activities in which corporations and labor organizations can engage, particularly through political action committees. The liberalization of previous restrictions, together with more rigorous and effective electoral disclosure requirements, and widespread public suspicion concerning the political activities of "special interests" make it likely that business corporations and labor unions will be quite circumspect in their election involvements during 1976. However, several legal and political issues which could affect corporate and union campaign activities in 1976 and beyond remain unresolved.   J

2224. Fasman, Zachary D. and Clark, R. Theodore, Jr. NON-DISCRIMINATORY DISCRIMINATION: AN OVERVIEW OF THE DISCRIMINATION PROBLEM. *J. of Intergroup Relations 1974 3(2): 25-44.* Reviews the problems of the goals and achievements of the Civil Rights Act of 1964 (Title VII) concerning employment discrimination.   S

2225. Flanagan, Robert J. THE NATIONAL ACCORD AS A SOCIAL CONTRACT. *Industrial and Labor Relations Rev. 1980 34(1): 35-50.* In September 1979 the Carter administration and the AFL-CIO issued the text of a National Accord, which discussed general principles to be followed in several areas of economic and social policy. In combining discussions of pay-price policy and other economic and social issues, the accord resembles "social contract" arrangements in several Western European countries. This invited paper assesses the viability of the National Accord as a social contract by examining three interrelated issues: the suitability of the accord as an institutional mechanism to secure wage and price restraint, given the characteristics of the underlying wage-determination process in this country; the breadth of institutional representation in the negotiations leading to the accord; and the ability of the negotiators to deliver on their commitments. The author concludes that the accord fails on all those counts to be an effective social contract, but he also argues that any social contract approach to wage and price restraint is unlikely to be successful in this country.   J

2226. Fleming, Thomas F., Jr. MANPOWER IMPACT OF PURCHASES BY STATE AND LOCAL GOVERNMENTS. *Monthly Labor Rev. 1973 96(6): 33-39.* Discusses employment opportunities created by state government and local government 1959-71, emphasizing the patterns of growth of the gross national product.

2227. Fontham, Michael R. THE PROPOSED EEOC GUIDELINES: LEGALIZATION OF EMPLOYMENT DISCRIMINATION AGAINST WHITE MALES. *J. of Intergroup Relations 1978 6(4): 30-39.* Analyzes the effects of the proposed Equal Employment Opportunity Commission alterations in the enforcement of Title VII of the Civil Rights Act of 1964.

2228. Fox, Daniel M. and Stone, Judith F. BLACK LUNG: MINER'S MILITANCY AND MEDICAL UNCERTAINTY, 1968-1972. *Bull. of the Hist. of Medicine 1980 54(1): 43-63.* The passage of the Coal Mine Health and Safety Act (US, 1969; amended, 1972) resulted from strikes and demonstrations by miners who persuaded public officials to accept theirs, rather than medical men's, definition of disease. The curtailment of the United Mine Workers of America health care and pension system was a threat to miners, as were the decline of the coal industry and periodic mine disasters. After three weeks of wildcat strikes in February 1969, the West Virginia legislature accepted the miners' demands for recognition of black lung disease as a compensable occupational disease. The federal law of 1969 resulted from the miners' strength as well as the shrewd political stance of the mine operators. In this case, decisions were not medical but political. Sources include government documents and interviews; 54 notes.   M. Kaufman

2229. Frenkel, Richard L.; Priest, Curtiss W.; and Ashford, Nicholas A. OCCUPATIONAL SAFETY AND HEALTH: A REPORT ON WORKER PERCEPTIONS. *Monthly Labor Rev. 1980 103(9): 11-14.*

Summarizes some of the data emerging from the Quality of Employment Surveys, sponsored by the Department of Labor in 1977, pertaining to relationships between aspects of work and worker satisfaction.

2230. Galbraith, James K. WHY WE HAVE NO FULL EMPLOYMENT POLICY. *Working Papers for a New Soc. 1978 6(2): 26-33.* Full employment would entail massive control over taxation, government expenditures and costs, and would doubtless entail indirect control over wages and prices in the private sector, as well as lending added strength to labor unions, all of which would require a major reordering of political power (based on economic controls) which the present power structure would not tolerate.

2231. Gallagher, Daniel G. and Pegnetter, Richard. IMPASSE RESOLUTION UNDER THE IOWA MULTISTEP PROCEDURE. *Industrial and Labor Relations Rev. 1979 32(3): 327-338.* This study examines the first two years of impasse experience under the Iowa Public Employment Relations Act to determine the effectiveness of a three-step procedure that uses mediation, factfinding, and issue-by-issue final-offer arbitration for all classifications of public employees. The authors conclude that the Iowa procedure compares favorably with other procedures in minimizing the proportion of disputes going to arbitration; that factfinding with recommendations prior to arbitration reduces both the tendency to use arbitration and the number of issues taken to arbitration; and that a provision allowing the arbitrator to select the recommendation of the factfinder instead of one of the parties' offers has produced some convergence of the final offers of the parties.   J

2232. Gartaganis, Arthur J. TRENDS IN FEDERAL EMPLOYMENT, 1958-72. *Monthly Labor Rev. 1974 97(10): 17-25.* The US government civilian work force grew from 2.2 million in 1958 to 2.4 million in 1965; then, primarily because of increased defense spending during the Vietnam War, it peaked at 2.7 million in 1967, before dropping to 2.6 million in 1972.

2233. Gaston, Leonard. UNEMPLOYMENT IN INFLATIONARY TIMES. *Colorado Q. 1976 24(3): 341-349.* Discusses methods to be used by the federal government to limit unemployment in inflationary times, notably in 1976.

2234. Gates, Margaret J. OCCUPATIONAL SEGREGATION AND THE LAW. *Signs 1976 1(3, Part 2): 61-74.* Past and present laws and judicial attitudes directly or indirectly contribute to occupational segregation. Twenty-six states require limiting certain job categories to one sex; discriminatory laws touch policing, veterans' preferences, military service, and serving liquor. Protective legislation and domestic relations laws contribute to sex segregation in employment. Laws and decisions since 1964 offer remedies for gender-related barriers in the work force, but it is still early to judge the results of these, except in police patrol where women have increased markedly. Based on court decisions; 36 notes.   S. E. Kennedy

2235. Gatling, Wade S. EQUAL OPPORTUNITY IN THE AIR FORCE. *Crisis 1976 83(7): 250-252.* The Air Force is actively working to eliminate institutional impediments to upward mobility of minorities and women by insuring equal opportunity for all members of the Air Force. Recruitment, training, and promotion are all parts of the affirmative action plan of the Air Force Equal Opportunity Program.   A. G. Belles

2236. Gliatta, Stephen. KEEPING UP WITH THE JONES ACT: THE EFFECT OF U.S. BASED STOCK OWNERSHIP ON THE APPLICABILITY OF THE JONES ACT TO FOREIGN SEAMEN. *New York U. J. of Int. Law and Pol. 1982 15(1): 141-168.* Discusses the applicability of the Merchant Marine Act (US, 1920), which provides that a seaman who is injured in the course of work may bring civil action for damages against his employer when the employer's negligence is at fault, to cases involving foreign sailors working for foreign companies that do business with the United States.

2237. Goldsmith, Frank. CONTROLLING OCCUPATIONAL HAZARDS. *Pro. of the Acad. of Pol. Sci. 1977 32(3): 106-120.* Studies the developing awareness of the seriousness of occupational hazards both those contributing to accidents and those contributing to chronic illnesses. The intervention of federal government and other governmental agencies has had a significant effect in achieving protective legislation against workplace hazards. Yet there are no authoritative data to determine whether the workplace has become safer and healthier. 3 notes.   R. V. Ritter

2238. Goldstein, Morris and Smith, Robert S. THE ESTIMATED IMPACT OF THE ANTIDISCRIMINATION PROGRAM AIMED AT FEDERAL CONTRACTORS. *Industrial and Labor Relations Rev. 1976 29(4): 523-543.* Examines two executive orders aimed at improving the economic status of minorities and women in the realm of federal contracts, 1965-76.

2239. Goodrich, James A. OPTIMIZING UNDER CETA: PROGRAM DESIGN, IMPLEMENTATION PROBLEMS, AND LOCAL AGENCIES. *Policy Studies J. 1980 8(7): 1119-1126.* Surveys the functioning of CETA (Comprehensive Employment and Training Act (US, 1973)) since 1975, the roles of the federal and local agencies, and argues that incentives at the local level will help to optimize functioning.

2240. Green, Philip. AFFIRMATIVE ACTION AND THE INDIVIDUALIST PRINCIPLE. *Social Policy 1981 11(5): 14-20.* Reviews arguments used against the policy of affirmative action, most of which are based upon the individualist principle or the merit system, describes the debate concerning the Civil Rights Act (US 1964), and suggests that arguments against affirmative action are essentially arguments for maintaining the status quo.

2241. Greenberg, Deborah M. PUBLIC POLICY ISSUES IN THE QUOTA CONTROVERSY. *Educ. and Urban Soc. 1975 8(1): 73-85.* Discusses the pros and cons of affirmative action programs. Notes that in many situations there would be no improvement without quotas, that society benefits from the perspective brought to positions filled by minority candidates, and that in no other way will a united society be created. Argues that the courts have not ruled that unqualified individuals be selected for positions to fill quotas and that job-related tests may make quotas unnecessary. 2 notes.   C. A. D'Aniello

2242. Greene, Richard. GEOGRAPHIC WAGE INDEXING FOR CETA AND MEDICARE. *Monthly Labor Rev. 1980 103(9): 15-19.* Discusses the current procedures for indexing the federal Comprehensive Employment and Training Act (US, 1973) and Medicare programs, in an attempt to allocate funds more efficiently by accounting for differences in local labor-market conditions.

2243. Grodin, Joseph R. ARBITRATION OF PUBLIC SECTOR LABOR DISPUTES: THE NEVADA EXPERIMENT. *Industrial and Labor Relations Rev. 1974 28(1): 89-102.*

2244. Gross, Bertram M. JOB RIGHTS UNDER AMERICAN CAPITALISM. *Social Policy 1975 5(5): 20-33.* Examines 30 years of full employment legislation, from the Full Employment Bill of 1944 to the proposed "Equal Opportunity and Full Employment Act of 1976," with comments on the relations between genuine full employment and modern capitalism.   S

2245. Grossman, Jonathan. FAIR LABOR STANDARDS ACT: MAXIMUM STRUGGLE FOR A MINIMUM WAGE. *Monthly Labor Rev. 1978 101(6): 22-30.* The Fair Labor Standards Act (1938) guaranteed a minimum wage and a maximum number of working hours a week; chronicles amendments during 1949-77.

2246. Gunderson, Morley. THE CASE FOR GOVERNMENT SUPPORTED TRAINING PROGRAM. *Industrial Relations [Canada] 1974 29(4): 709-725.* Concepts of Public Expenditure Economics are applied to the operation of labor markets in general and training programs in particular to see if the free market provides a socially optimal amount of training. The case for government supported training is discussed when there exist market imperfections and equity considerations, as well as market failure due to externalities, high risk and uncertainty, and merit goods.   J

2247. Guttman, Robert. JOB TRAINING PARTNERSHIP ACT: NEW HELP FOR THE UNEMPLOYED. *Monthly Labor Rev. 1983 106(3): 3-10.* Discusses the problems of the Comprehensive Employment and Training Act (US, 1973) and the enactment of the Job Training Partnership Act (US, 1983), covering inter-governmental

relations, business and local government relations, and programmatic issues; summarizes the provisions of the act.

2248. Haggard, Thomas R. RIGHT TO WORK: WHAT IS IT? WHO HAS IT? *Reason 1979 11(1): 34-37.* Defines and reviews right-to-work laws, concluding that reform of federal labor law is necessary to make the law consistent with the notion of a truly free society, and active support of right-to-work laws is required to expose the underlying coerciveness of collective bargaining agreements and the federal laws that facilitate them.

2249. Hahn, Andrew B. [THE FEDERAL YOUTH EMPLOYMENT INITIATIVES]. *Youth & Soc. 1979 11(2): 237-261; 1980 12(2): 221-246.* PART 1. TAKING STOCK OF YEDPA. Summarizes the various parts of the Youth Employment and Demonstrations Project Act (US, 1977) (YEDPA). It differs from earlier job programs in its focus on disadvantaged youth, and in its mandate to approach the problem from several directions at the same time. These sponsored programs facilitate the collection of research data. PART 2. EARLY THEMES OF YEDPA. Although YEDPA is the largest collection of social experiments on a single issue, its record as employer is mixed. It did not reach a high proportion of women or school dropouts, had limited success in improving youth employability or educational attainment, and did not increase private sector jobs. It only provided low-level deadend jobs. However, it did show that large-scale public job creation can be done rapidly, that youth who finish the programs can benefit, and that the costs per youth could be low.   J. H. Sweetland

2250. Hale, George E. THE POLITICAL IMPLICATIONS OF AMERICAN NATIONAL MANPOWER POLICY. *Am. Behavioral Scientist 1974 17(4): 555-571.* The weaknesses of the national manpower policy developed in the 1960's may be institutionalized in the 1970's.

2251. Halpin, Terrence C. THE EFFECT OF UNEMPLOYMENT INSURANCE ON SEASONAL FLUCTUATIONS IN EMPLOYMENT. *Industrial and Labor Relations Rev. 1979 32(3): 353-362.* Despite long interest in the employment stabilization effects of the experience-rated unemployment insurance tax, no empirical test has been done to see if rating actually induces firms to smooth their employment fluctuations. This study examines differences among states in seasonal variations in employment within each of three industries to see if those differences are linked to state differences in the strength of experience rating, defined as the extent to which firms balance their UI tax payments and expected benefit withdrawals. Rating strength is measured in several ways, such as the ratio of taxable wages to total covered wages in each state. The results of regression analysis indicate that experience rating has been effective in reducing seasonal employment fluctuations in two of the three industries studied.   J

2252. Hardy, Richard J. and McCrone, Donald J. THE IMPACT OF THE CIVIL RIGHTS ACT OF 1964 ON WOMEN. *Policy Studies J. 1978 7(2): 240-243.* Attempts to determine if the relative income of black women has improved systematically since the implementation of Title 7 of the Civil Rights Act of 1964.

2253. Harrison, Bennett. INFLATION AND UNEMPLOYMENT: JOBS ABOVE ALL. *Social Policy 1975 5(6): 36-42.* Inflation, caused by monopolies and a lack of federal economic planning, can be reduced without inducing deflation and unemployment.   S

2254. Haveman, Robert H. TOWARD EFFICIENCY AND EQUITY THROUGH DIRECT JOB CREATION. *Social Policy 1980 11(1): 41-50.* Defines the concept of direct job creation, surveys major governmental policies in this area during the 1970's, and discusses reasons for this shift from programs designed to change the productivity of individual workers.

2255. Heins, Marjorie. THE FOURTEEN-YEAR FUROR OVER EQUAL EMPLOYMENT. *Working Papers for a New Soc. 1978 6(4): 61-5.* Discusses progress to end employment discrimination against women and minorities since the Civil Rights Act (1964, Title VII); cites court cases.

2256. Henderson, Lenneal J. THE IMPACT OF THE EQUAL EMPLOYMENT OPPORTUNITY ACT OF 1972 ON EMPLOYMENT OPPORTUNITIES FOR WOMEN AND MINORITIES IN

MUNICIPAL GOVERNMENT. *Policy Studies J. 1978 7(2): 234-239.* Examines the effect of agencies which attempt to assess the position of women and minorities in city government following implementation of the Equal Employment Opportunity Act (US, 1972).

2257. Henle, Peter and Schmitt, Raymond. PENSION REFORM: THE LONG, HARD ROAD TO ENACTMENT. *Monthly Labor Rev. 1974 97(11): 3-12.* Examines the genesis of the Employment Retirement Income Security Act (US, 1974), and some of its implications for workers and companies.

2258. Hero, Rodney E. MINORITIES AND PUBLIC EMPLOY-MENT: A COMPARISON BASED ON EVIDENCE FROM THE GENERAL REVENUE SHARING LEGISLATION. *State Government 1983 56(1): 8-13.* Discusses revenue-sharing legislation in the 1970's, specifically evaluating the nondiscrimination provisions and their effects on employment in the Sunbelt region.

2259. Herrink, Ruth J. SHOULD HEARING OFFICERS REPLACE OCCUPATIONAL-PROFESSIONAL BOARDS? *State Government 1978 51(1): 65-67.* Based on the experience of the Virginia state legislature which replaced occupational and professional licensing and review boards with hearing officers, recommends the gradual deregulation (based on the needs of individual professions) of professions in order to lessen bureaucracy and slowly do away with outmoded and outdated professional regulation.

2260. Hickey, Joseph A. CHANGES IN STATE UNEMPLOY-MENT INSURANCE LEGISLATION. *Monthly Labor Rev. 1974 97(1): 39-46.* In 1973, many state legislatures in the United States eliminated provisions in their unemployment insurance laws that discriminated on the basis of sex, and others extended coverage to state and local government employees previously excluded.

2261. Hickey, Joseph A. STATE UNEMPLOYMENT INSURANCE LAWS: STATUS REPORT. *Monthly Labor Rev. 1973 96(1): 37-44.* Discusses workers' maximum weekly benefits in state unemployment insurance laws in 1972.

2262. Hickey, Joseph A. UNEMPLOYMENT INSURANCE—STATE CHANGES IN 1975. *Monthly Labor Rev. 1976 99(1): 37-41.* Reviews state improvements and extensions of unemployment benefits in 1975 with additional emergency federal aid in the form of loans to 15 states.

2263. Hicks, Alexander; Friedland, Roger; and Johnson, Edwin. CLASS POWER AND STATE POLICY: THE CASE OF LARGE BUSINESS CORPORATIONS, LABOR UNIONS AND GOVERN-MENTAL REDISTRIBUTION IN THE AMERICAN STATES. *Am. Sociol. Rev. 1978 43(3): 302-315.* This paper investigates the impact of business and labor organizations upon governmental redistribution to the poor, or the extent to which government expenditures and revenues redistribute income to poor households. A cross-sectional analysis of 48 American states circa 1960 supports the propositions that large business corporations negatively affect governmental redistribution and that labor unions positively affect governmental redistribution. The analysis also supports past findings relating socioeconomic development, poverty, and the interaction of redistribution. Findings suggest that redistribution to the poor by American state governments is a class issue, partially determined by conflicting class forces.

2264. Hill, Herbert. THE POSTPONEMENT OF ECONOMIC EQUALITY. *Black Scholar 1977 9(1): 18-23.* Despite the NAACP's struggle during 1964-77 to force adherence to the Civil Rights Act (US, 1964), a Supreme Court ruling which let stand seniority systems in effect before 1965 (systems which traditionally exclude women and blacks) has blocked economic equality.

2265. Hoachlander, E. Gareth. CONSIDERING DEREGULATION IN EDUCATION: EXPERIENCE WITH THE VOCATIONAL ED-UCATION ACT. *Educ. and Urban Soc. 1982 14(4): 425-441.* Examines the case for deregulating vocational education, now legislated by the Vocational Education Act (US, 1963).

2266. Holloway, Wilfred B. DEVELOPING COMPETENCE. *Society 1982 19(6): 40-47.* Traditionally youth participation in an adult culture has been limited; an attempt to create an opportunity for youth to learn competence in adult roles was initiated under the Youth Employment and Demonstration Projects Act (US, 1977) through programs in which young people made "meaningful contributions to their communities."

2267. Horton, Raymond D. ARBITRATION, ARBITRATORS, AND THE PUBLIC INTEREST. *Industrial & Labor Relations Rev. 1975 28(4): 497-507.* This article raises several questions about the desirability of the growing reliance on interest arbitration in the public sector. The author argues that arbitrators are inescapably "political actors" and therefore may be less objective than often assumed; that the lawyers who dominate the arbitration profession are seldom trained in the economic analysis required in most interest arbitration cases; and that decisions in such cases often have more far-reaching effects than the average arbitrator may realize. To meet these problems, the author recommends limiting the use of interest arbitration by legalizing some public employee strikes and improving the arbitration process by selecting arbitrators on a random basis and instituting qualifying exams for arbitrators.   J

2268. Howards, Irving and Brehm, Henry. THE IMPOSSIBLE DREAM: THE NATIONALIZATION OF WELFARE? A LOOK AT DISABILITY INSURANCE & STATE INFLUENCE OVER THE FEDERAL GOVERNMENT. *Polity 1978 11(1): 7-26.* State participation has not prevented the national disability insurance program (enacted in 1956) from becoming a public assistance program; emphasizes the continued power of the states in the federal system.

2269. Howe, Charles. THE COMPREHENSIVE EMPLOYMENT AND TRAINING ACT. *New Generation 1974 56(1): 2-11.*

2270. Hribal, Amy S. and Minor, G. M. WORKERS' COMPENSA-TION—1975 ENACTMENTS. *Monthly Labor Rev. 1976 99(1): 30-36.* In 1975 no state had yet fully complied with federal workers' compensation coverage, benefits, and program administration.

2271. Isbell, Florence. CARTER'S CIVIL SERVICE REFORM: 35 PERCENT IFS, BUTS AND MAYBES. *Civil Liberties Rev. 1978 5(1): 6-15.* Analyzes the major principles of President Jimmy Carter's proposed Civil Service Reform Act, his chief legislative goal for 1978.

2272. Jacobs, David. ON THE DETERMINANTS OF CLASS LEG-ISLATION: AN ECOLOGICAL STUDY OF POLITICAL STRUG-GLES BETWEEN WORKERS AND MANAGEMENT. *Sociol. Q. 1978 19(3): 469-480.* Examines the social conditions which lead to the political decisions regarding the conflict between labor and management in the United States based on several studies done during the 1940's-70's.

2273. Jacobs, James B. THE ROLE OF MILITARY FORCES IN PUBLIC SECTOR LABOR RELATIONS. *Industrial and Labor Relations Rev. 1982 35(2): 163-180.* Examines the use of military forces as replacements in public sector strikes, a practice employed in over 40 cases since President Nixon established the modern precedent by deploying troops in the 1970 postal strike. Despite the dubious legality of Nixon's action, legal constraints on the president and particularly on the governors in this context are very weak. Political and philosophical qualms about breaking strikes with military replacements may have more vitality as constraints, but they are subject to erosion if the appropriate role of military forces in public sector labor relations does not become a subject of public debate. The use of troops as strike replacements is primarily a political rather than legal problem.   J/S

2274. Jauffret-Epstein, Sophie. LE DEVOIR DE NEGOCIER DE BONNE FOI EN DROIT DU TRAVAIL AMERICAIN [The role of fair negotiations in American labor laws]. *Rev. Int. de Droit Comparé [France] 1982 34(4): 1123-1152.* Describes the role of the National Labor Relations Board in maintaining an equilibrium in the duties and powers both of industry and labor; offers several recent case histories.

2275. Johnson, Florence C. CHANGES IN WORKMEN'S COM-PENSATION LAWS IN 1973. *Monthly Labor Rev. 1974 97(1): 32-38.* A record number of amendments to workmen's compensation laws were adopted by state legislatures in the United States and Puerto Rico in 1973, with occupational diseases, flexibility and levels of benefits, medical care, and farm workers' coverage receiving most attention.

2276. Johnson, Florence C. CHANGES IN WORKMEN'S COMPENSATION LAWS IN 1972. *Monthly Labor Rev. 1973 96(1): 45-49.* Discusses current maximum benefits for disabled workers in state workmen's compensation laws, emphasizing the influence of the 1970 Report of the National Commission on State Workers' Compensation Laws.

2277. Johnston, Michael. PATRONS AND CLIENTS, JOBS AND MACHINES: A CASE STUDY OF THE USES OF PATRONAGE. *Am. Pol. Sci. Rev. 1979 73(2): 385-398.* How are patronage rewards allocated within a political machine? This article studies the distribution of 675 CETA Title I jobs within a New Haven machine. Data suggest that the jobs were used as patronage, but that patronage allocations did not follow conventionally assumed patterns of organization maintenance. Ethnic particularism overshadowed, and in fact redefined, considerations of vote-maximization and recruitment of workers. Questionnaire data suggest that those hired were not highly active politically, either before or after hiring, a finding contrary to normal suppositions about patronage recipients. The seemingly anomalous (and perhaps even counterproductive) patronage allocations become understandable, however, viewed in light of some problems and contradictions inherent in patron-client politics. These involve the inflexibility of job-based incentive systems, qualifications on assumptions of reciprocity, and the "aging" of the organization.   J

2278. Jones, Benjamin. PUBLIC EMPLOYEE LABOR ARBITRATION AND THE DELEGATION OF GOVERNMENTAL POWERS. *State Government 1978 51(2): 109-114.* Discusses the use of arbitration, the legal concept of the delegation of powers (in compulsory arbitration), its judicial application, and the statutory and constitutional options for state governments; 1960's-70's.

2279. Jones, Ralph T. ADMINISTERING PUBLIC SECTOR LABOR RELATIONS: THE NEED FOR POLITICAL ANALYSIS. *Policy Studies J. 1975 3(4): 381-385.* Discusses issues and problems of formulating and administering labor relations policy in the public sector.
                                                                            S

2280. Jump, Bernard, Jr. STATE AND LOCAL EMPLOYEE PENSIONS: AN ASSESSMENT OF THEIR ADEQUACY. *Policy Studies J. 1982 11(2): 328-342.* A sample of 100 large state and local government pension plans indicates that the common criticism charging that state and local pension plans are too liberal with respect to income replacement rates and with regard to age and length of service requirements for eligibility is only partly justified in light of the lower wages that public employees earn compared to the private sector.

2281. Kasarda, John D. NEW SKILLS FOR NEW ROLES. *Society 1982 19(3): 26-29.* *Urban America in the Eighties,* a report by the President's Commission for a National Agenda for the Eighties, aroused political controversy and much criticism and demonstrated the need for new strategies to deal with unemployment and urban areas.

2282. Kasper, Daniel M. AN ALTERNATIVE TO WORKMEN'S COMPENSATION. *Industrial & Labor Relations Rev. 1975 28(4): 535-548.* Using criteria established by the National Commission on State Workmen's Compensation Laws, this study appraises a model common law negligence system and the commission's own model workmen's compensation system. The author concludes that both of those models are deficient in certain respects and proposes an alternative system, combining universal insurance and the common law method of determining negligence, that he argues better meets all of the commission's criteria.   J

2283. Katz, Harry C. THE MUNICIPAL BUDGETARY RESPONSE TO CHANGING LABOR COSTS: THE CASE OF SAN FRANCISCO. *Industrial and Labor Relations Rev. 1979 32(4): 506-519.* Reveals San Francisco city government's budget adjustments in response to changing labor costs, 1945-76.   J/S

2284. Kazis, Richard and Sabonis, Peter. CETA AND THE PRIVATE SECTOR IMPERATIVE. *Social Policy 1980 10(4): 6-12.* Examines the need for large and small businesses to make a commitment to hiring unemployed and unskilled workers since CETA public service employment programs cannot provide sufficient job opportunities for

them, and discusses the federal government's strategy to encourage private business to get involved since the Area Redevelopment Act of 1961.

2285. Kenski, Henry C. THE IMPACT OF UNEMPLOYMENT ON CONGRESSIONAL ELECTIONS 1958-1974: A CROSS-SECTIONAL ANALYSIS. *Am. Pol. Q. 1979 7(2): 147-154.* Bivariate tabulations uncover relationships between the high rates of change in and high rates of unemployment and the percentage of states experiencing gains in the U.S. House Democratic percentage vote during the period 1958-1974. Efforts to establish linear relationships between these unemployment measures and either the percentage of the Democratic vote or the interelection change in the Democratic vote produced null results. The failure to discover consistent and meaningful relationships through these modes of analysis suggests that the political impact of unemployment may not be linear. Reasons are advanced as to why unemployment, while not unimportant, appears to have been less potent in more recent elections than previously assumed.   J

2286. Kirstein, Peter N. AGRIBUSINESS, LABOR, AND THE WETBACKS: TRUMAN'S COMMISSION ON MIGRATORY LABOR. *Historian 1978 40(4): 650-667.* Demands for labor by agribusiness and railroad industries in the early 1940's led to the adoption of the bracero program of labor importation from Mexico. By 1950, however, divergent attitudes between organized labor and agribusiness over the use of alien labor and immigration led President Harry S. Truman to appoint a President's Commission on Migratory Labor. Examines the relationship between the problem-plagued bracero program and the Truman commission's investigation of social, economic, health, and educational conditions among migratory workers. Another focus of the study dealt with the extent of illegal migration into the United States and with means to eliminate it. Although the investigation was thorough and significant proposals were advanced, none of the recommendations were adopted. Concludes that "a quarter of a century after the commission's report, virtually nothing has been achieved in ameliorating the plight of domestic and Mexican national migratory labor in America."
                                                            M. S. Legan

2287. Lamb, Charles M. EQUAL EMPLOYMENT OPPORTUNITY AND THE CARTER ADMINISTRATION. *Policy Studies J. 1979 8(3): 377-383.* Examines why President Jimmy Carter shifted some Equal Employment Opportunity programs from the Civil Service Commission to the Labor Department.

2288. Lapidus, Gail Warshofsky. OCCUPATIONAL SEGREGATION AND PUBLIC POLICY: A COMPARATIVE ANALYSIS OF AMERICAN AND SOVIET PATTERNS. *Signs 1976 1(3, Part 2): 119-136.* Soviet experience since 1917 shows that economic participation does not necessarily mean equality of status and authority for women. Although cultural norms, educational efforts, and public policy support high levels of female employment, authority in the USSR remains hierarchical, stratified, and paternalistic, with declining proportions of women at successively higher levels of the hierarchy even in occupations they dominate. Greater change in cultural values and institutional arrangements which contribute to occupational segregation would require reciprocal redefinition of male and female roles. Makes comparisons with the United States throughout. Based on Soviet statistical and English-language secondary sources; 4 tables, 32 notes.
                                                            S. E. Kennedy

2289. Lee, Robert D., Jr. PARTICIPANTS IN THE PUBLIC PERSONNEL MANAGEMENT PROCESS. *Policy Studies J. 1982 11(2): 261-270.* Discusses the role of government, labor, business, and other types of pressure groups and government agencies in determining personnel policy.

2290. Lehne, Richard. EMPLOYMENT EFFECTS OF GRANT-IN-AID EFFECTS. *Publius 1975 5(3): 101-109.* Discusses the political uses and economic implications of federal governmental grants-in-aid 1957-72.

2291. Levine, Arthur. "I GOT MY JOB THROUGH CREEP." *Washington Monthly 1974 6(9): 35-46.* Discusses how Civil Service posts were filled during the Nixon administration, 1969-74.

2292. Levitan, Sar A. JOB CORPS EXPERIENCE WITH MANPOWER TRAINING. *Monthly Labor Rev. 1975 98(10): 3-11.* Discusses the efforts of the Job Corps, created under the Economic Opportunity Act (1964), to improve employment prospects of disadvantaged youth.

2293. Levitan, Sar A. THE 1975 MANPOWER BUDGET. *New Generation 1974 56(1): 12-14.*

2294. Levy, David A. STATE LABOR LEGISLATION ENACTED IN 1973. *Monthly Labor Rev. 1974 97(1): 22-31.* A review of state labor legislation in the United States in 1973 shows that most attention was given to higher minimum wage rates, improved occupational safety, collective bargaining procedures for public employees, elimination of discrimination in employment, and updating of child labor standards.

2295. Levy, Frank and Wiseman, Michael. AN EXPANDED PUBLIC-SERVICE EMPLOYMENT PROGRAM: SOME DEMAND AND SUPPLY CONSIDERATIONS. *Public Policy 1975 23(1): 105-134.* Uses the Office of Economic Opportunity's *Survey of Economic Opportunity* for 1967 to create a profile of potential male applicants for public service jobs. Surveys of existing municipal employment in San Francisco and Oakland to discover what kinds of jobs the applicants might obtain, and analysis of the results showed how many of these jobs might be created in the near future. Both cities could use 10 to 15% more low-skilled positions without creating "useless" or "make-work" jobs. The supply of low-skilled workers is sufficient to meet the demand for public service workers. Also estimates the costs involved. Based on original research and secondary materials; 29 notes.
J. M. Herrick

2296. Lewin, David. LOCAL GOVERNMENT LABOR RELATIONS IN TRANSITION: THE CASE OF LOS ANGELES. *Labor Hist. 1976 17(2): 191-213.* Provides a case study in public sector labor relations. During 1966-71 labor relations became more formal, but multiple sources of authority and bargaining continued. The civil service system was not reduced, public employee unions remained diverse in character and impact, government was spurred by unions into consideration of management functions, and "longitudinal methodology" as a model for study of the public sector proved important. Based on Los Angeles city and county records and publications; 38 notes.
L. L. Athey

2297. Lieske, Joel A. MANPOWER AND THE NEW FEDERALISM: THE TRANSITION TO CETA. *Publius 1978 8(4): 129-151.* Describes an early attempt at assessing CETA, the Comprehensive Employment and Training Act (US, 1973). Analysis was based on field site visits to six midwest prime sponsors and data collected by the Department of Labor. The program was developed on the premise that decentralization and decategorization will result in comprehensive manpower programs. The study identifies three emerging patterns: centralized political control, a classic or pork barrel approach, and an in-between pattern of decisionmaking. Indicates that community participation reinforces the values, goals, objectives, and major philosophies of the sponsors. Concludes that the record of CETA is mixed, the chief advantage being the concept itself. 4 tables, 37 notes.
R. S. Barnard

2298. MacLaury, Judson. THE JOB SAFETY LAW OF 1970: ITS PASSAGE WAS PERILOUS. *Monthly Labor Rev. 1981 104(3): 18-24.* Traces the history of governmental legislation concerning workplace hazards from the first factory inspection law (Massachusetts, 1877) down to the Occupational Safety and Health Act (US, 1970) and then describes the three-year battle before Congress passed the 1970 act.

2299. Margolis, Richard J. THE LIMITS OF LOCALISM. *Working Papers Mag. 1981 8(4): 32-39.* Study of 75 migrant farmworker camps under the auspices of the National Migrant Farmworker Housing Coalition shows that the plight of the farmworker is as terrible as it ever was and shows how local control, which the Reagan Administration has touted as a way of ignoring social ills, breeds poverty and hunger; also includes a brief history of migrant labor during the 20th century.

2300. Marvel, Mary K. IMPLEMENTATION AND SAFETY REGULATION: VARIATIONS IN FEDERAL AND STATE ADMINISTRATION UNDER OSHA. *Administration & Soc. 1982 14(1): 15-33.* Concludes that the only way to avoid ineffective implementation of the Occupational Safety and Health Act (US, 1970) is "to forge links between policy formulation and implementation," and to provide "a more prominent role for the policy analyst in program formulation."

2301. Masters, W. Frank. THE ARBITRABILITY ISSUE IN MICHIGAN PUBLIC SCHOOL DISPUTES. *Arbitration J. 1973 28(2): 119-131.* "Even the most casual reader of arbitration awards in public school systems must be aware of the high incidence of arbitrability issues. Many reasons have been put forward to explain this phenomenon. The most obvious, of course, is the newness of the process for both school administrators and teacher organization representatives. This may account for many of the 'procedural arbitrability' issues—the failure of the grieving party to proceed in a timely manner or to exhaust all steps of grievance procedure. Another reason is that many of the subjects of arbitration are also covered by statute, raising questions as to whether arbitration of those issues is required by the collective agreements. The author studied arbitration cases following the passage of the Michigan Public Employment Relations Act, and concludes that though arbitrability is still a serious problem, it appears that, in time, the arbitration process in the public sector 'will look very much like its private sector counterpart.' "
J

2302. Mead, Lawrence M. EXPECTATIONS AND WELFARE WORK: WIN IN NEW YORK CITY. *Policy Studies Rev. 1983 2(4): 648-662.* A study of the Work Incentive Program (WIN) showed that the success of the program was closely correlated with administrators' expectation that the recipients would find work.

2303. Medoff, Marshall H. THE EQUAL RIGHTS AMENDMENT: AN EMPIRICAL ANALYSIS OF SEXUAL DISCRIMINATION. *Econ. Inquiry 1980 18(3): 367-379.* Census data for 1970 and the period from 1960 to 1970 indicate that women in states which have ratified the Equal Rights Amendment suffer more discrimination in the job market than women in unratified states: although women in ratified states are more likely to work at jobs commensurate with their ability, they receive less pay than their male counterparts; and although unemployment is less among women in ratified states, this is at least partly because those who discriminate more by paying low wages are less likely to discriminate in the number of women hired; finally, between 1960 and 1970, women in ratified states suffered a 12% decline in their relative wages as well as a decrease in their relative occupational positions compared to women in unratified states.

2304. Meier, Kenneth J. CONSTRAINTS ON AFFIRMATIVE ACTION. *Policy Studies J. 1978 7(2): 208-213.* Studies the effect of three environmental constraints: economic, political, and administrative/labor pool, on affirmative action programs in state and local government bureaucracies, 1960's-70's.

2305. Mills, James R. LEISURE SHARING: ITS TIME HAS COME. *State Government 1979 52(2): 75-79.* Examines the operation of California legislation on leisure sharing, a program whereby employed persons are given time off so unemployed persons might have part-time work; 1979.

2306. Milward, H. Brinton and Swanson, Cheryl. THE IMPACT OF AFFIRMATIVE ACTION ON ORGANIZATION BEHAVIOR. *Policy Studies J. 1978 7(2): 201-207.* Analyzes the motivations behind the implementation of affirmative action employment of women and minorities at high levels of an organization, but the lack thereof at lower, core levels of the same organization, 1970's.

2307. Minor, Gerri. WORKERS' COMPENSATION LAWS: KEY STATE AMENDMENTS OF 1978. *Monthly Labor Rev. 1979 102(1): 43-50.*

2308. Minow, Nell. A SELECTION OF FINE WHINES: SOUR GRAPES ARE SPOILING THE FEDERAL ANTI-DISCRIMINATION SYSTEM. *Washington Monthly 1981 13(4): 18-24.* Describes the system for dealing with discrimination complaints filed with an unnamed federal agency's Office of Civil Rights (OCR), focusing on the many illegitimate complaints, particularly by OCR employees against the OCR itself, which force legitimate complaints to wait; and suggests changes to simplify the backlog.

2309. Mitchell, Daniel J. B. and Weber, Arnold R. WAGES AND THE PAY BOARD. *Am. Econ. Rev. 1974 64(2): 88-92.* Describes the success of Federal Pay Board wage stabilization policies in 1971-72.

2310. Moore, Thomas Gale. THE BENEFICIARIES OF TRUCKING REGULATION. *J. of Law and Econ. 1978 21(2): 327-343.* Discusses the benefits to labor and the holders of public convenience and necessity "carrying commodity" certificates deriving from the Interstate Commerce Commission (ICC)'s regulation of the trucking industry, 1938-76.

2311. Moore, William Howard. WAS ESTES KEFAUVER "BLACKMAILED" DURING THE CHICAGO CRIME HEARINGS?: A HISTORIAN'S PERSPECTIVE. *Public Hist. 1982 4(1): 4-28.* Narrates Seymour Hersh and Jeff Gerth's questionable 1976 *New York Times* exposé, which claimed that in 1950 Chicago labor lawyer Sidney R. Korshak, assisted by underworld acquaintances, blackmailed Senator Estes Kefauver, head of the Senate committee investigating organized crime, in an attempt to end the investigation.

2312. Moore, William J.; Newman, Robert J.; and Thomas, R. William. DETERMINANTS OF THE PASSAGE OF RIGHT-TO-WORK LAWS: AN ALTERNATIVE INTERPRETATION. *J. of Law and Econ. 1974 17(1): 197-211.* Using multiple discriminant analysis, reanalyzes data originally presented in Neil A. and Catherine A. Palomba's article and suggests that degree of unionization, blue-collar composition of the labor force, South geographic region, level of agricultural employment, and population density are important in distinguishing non-RTW and RTW states.

2313. Mounts, Gregory J. LABOR AND THE SUPREME COURT: SIGNIFICANT DECISIONS OF 1977-78. *Monthly Labor Rev. 1979 102(1): 51-57.*

2314. Mounts, Gregory J. LABOR AND THE SUPREME COURT: SIGNIFICANT DECISIONS OF 1978-79. *Monthly Labor Rev. 1980 103(1): 14-21.* Surveys the decisions of the term, emphasizing the Supreme Court's approval of voluntary efforts to eliminate the effects of discrimination, its rejection of NLRB attempts at balancing conflicting interests, and its strengthening of public employers' rights.

2315. Mounts, Gregory J. LABOR AND THE SUPREME COURT: SIGNIFICANT DECISIONS OF 1979-80. *Monthly Labor Rev. 1981 104(4): 13-22.* Views recent Supreme Court decisions as a return to private sector emphasis insofar as a series of cases expanded the flexibility of private sector employers and unions while limiting that of public sector employers.

2316. Mounts, Gregory J. LABOR AND THE SUPREME COURT: SIGNIFICANT DECISIONS OF 1976-77. *Monthly Labor Rev. 1978 101(1): 12-17.* Supreme Court decisions interpreted employment discrimination narrowly, limited the unions' "work preservation" doctrine, and upheld public employees' agency shops.

2317. Moye, William T. PRESIDENTIAL LABOR-MANAGEMENT COMMITTEES: PRODUCTIVE FAILURES. *Industrial and Labor Relations Rev. 1980 34(1): 51-66.* Over the last quarter-century, six presidents have sought to encourage labor-management-government collaboration through the creation of advisory committees. This study describes how these committees have grappled with such crucial topics as wage-price stabilization, fiscal and monetary policy, and the employment problems created by technological change. Each of these committees eventually expired for a number of reasons: some presidents ignored them and others viewed them as an exercise in public relations; business and labor representatives sooner or later disagreed with presidential policies and with each other; and those representatives could not speak for all American employers and workers. Nonetheless, the author concludes, the committees produced some concrete achievements, such as recommending or providing important support for certain programs, and they also provided a needed forum in which labor and business leaders could discuss issues of mutual concern.   J

2318. Naismith, Rachael. THE MOVEABLE LIBRARY: SERVING MIGRANT FARM WORKERS. *Wilson Lib. Bull. 1983 57(7): 571-575.* Several communities in California during the 1970's had some type of "bookmobile" program for the migrant farmworker, but these valuable services have been ended or cut since the advent of Proposition 13; details the needs and benefits of library availability for migrant labor.

2319. Nelson, Richard R. STATE LABOR LEGISLATION ENACTED IN 1979. *Monthly Labor Rev. 1980 103(1): 22-39.* Surveys labor law for 1979, state-by-state, noting the passage of bans on employment discrimination, relaxed child labor and mandatory retirement requirements, and other changes.

2320. Nelson, Richard R. STATE LABOR LEGISLATION ENACTED IN 1980. *Monthly Labor Rev. 1981 104(1): 21-34.* State by state synopsis of labor legislation enacted during 1980, which was characterized by a lack of clear trends but focusing on new interests such as sexual harassment and lie detector tests for jobs rather than on wages and labor relations.

2321. Nelson, Richard R. STATE LABOR LEGISLATION ENACTED IN 1982. *Monthly Labor Rev. 1983 106(1): 44-56.* Details state by state the significant labor legislation from 1982; these included traditional employment concerns as well as equal pay for jobs of comparable worth and the impact of plant closings or relocations.

2322. Nelson, Richard R. STATE LABOR LEGISLATION ENACTED IN 1981. *Monthly Labor Rev. 1982 105(1): 29-42.* Examines labor legislation enacted during 1981 in a state-by-state synopsis.

2323. Nelson, Richard R. STATE LABOR LEGISLATION ENACTED IN 1978. *Monthly Labor Rev. 1979 102(1): 26-42.* State labor laws passed in 1978 included wages, child labor, and occupational safety.

2324. Neumann, George R. and Nelson, Jon P. SAFETY REGULATION AND FIRM SIZE: EFFECTS OF THE COAL MINE HEALTH AND SAFETY ACT OF 1969. *J. of Law & Econ. 1982 25(2): 183-199.* While the number of fatal accidents and output per miner have both decreased since the passage of the act, the significance of the act cannot be accurately gauged because of the many factors involved, including the closing of small mines, which have greater fatality rates, 1950-76.

2325. Nichols, Albert L. and Zeckhauser, Richard. GOVERNMENT COMES TO THE WORKPLACE: AN ASSESSMENT OF OSHA. *Public Interest 1977 (49): 39-69.* Congress passed the Occupational Safety and Health Act (1970) "to assure so far as possible . . . safe and healthful working conditions" for all workers. While imposing significant economic costs, the act has accomplished little. OSHA has failed because it has focused on job safety rather than on occupational health, and has employed direct regulation rather than an incentive approach. 9 notes.   S. Harrow

2326. North, David S. and Martin, Philip L. IMMIGRATION AND EMPLOYMENT: A NEED FOR POLICY COORDINATION. *Monthly Labor Rev. 1980 103(10): 47-50.* Discusses the objectives of immigration and employment policies, how they interact, what could be done to change the situation, and important issues to deal with as immigration and employment officials face the possibility that immigrants may constitute 45% of labor force growth.

2327. North, David S. NONIMMIGRANT WORKERS: VISITING LABOR FORCE PARTICIPANTS. *Monthly Labor Rev. 1980 103(10): 26-30.* Summarizes the five programs enabling visiting nonimmigrants in the United States to work: students; temporary workers of distinguished merit and ability; other temporary workers; exchange visitors; and intracompany transferees; and discusses how these temporary visitors interact with the US labor market; based on 1978 data from the Immigration and Naturalization Service.

2328. Norton, Eleanor Holmes. A CRITICAL YEAR FOR EQUAL EMPLOYMENT: NEW STRUCTURES, APPROACHES, DIRECTIONS. *J. of Intergroup Relations 1978 6(4): 3-10.* Discusses the importance of *Regents of the University of California* v. *Allan Bakke* (US, 1978) for affirmative action programs and civil rights law enforcement.

2329. Nyporenko, Iu. I. ANTYNARODNE ZAKONODAVSTVO SSHA: INSTRUMENT NASTUPU NA HROMADYANS'KI PRAVA TRUDYASHCHUKH (1945-1977) [The antinational legislation of the United States: an instrument of attack against the social rights of workers (1945-77)]. *Ukrains'kyi Istorychnyi Zhurnal [USSR] 1977 (7): 67-75.* After World War II the government of the United States launched a campaign against workers' rights, on which millions of dollars have been expended; details this exploitation.

2330. O'Boyle, Edward J. THE PROBLEM OF EVALUATING INSTITUTIONAL TRAINING UNDER THE MANPOWER DEVELOPMENT AND TRAINING ACT. *R. of Social Econ. 1974 32(1): 32-48.*

2331. O'Cleireacain, Carol. GETTING SERIOUS ABOUT PENSION FUNDS. *Working Papers Mag. 1981 8(4): 17-21.* Discusses the ownership of pension-fund capital by American workers with control of the money not in the hands of workers but under the control of labor and management under the 1947 Taft-Hartley amendments to the National Labor Relations Act or under the management of banks or money managers based on a requirement of the Employment Retirement Income Security Act (ERISA) of 1974.

2332. O'Kelly, Charlotte G. THE "IMPACT" OF EQUAL EMPLOYMENT LEGISLATION ON WOMEN'S EARNINGS: LIMITATIONS OF LEGISLATIVE SOLUTIONS TO DISCRIMINATION IN THE ECONOMY. *Am. J. of Econ. and Sociol. 1979 38(4): 419-430.* Although a strong legal basis now exists for equal opportunity in employment for women, women's earnings have actually dropped relative to men's. This holds true even when experience on the job, life-time work experience, and education are similar. Females are also still twice as likely as males to be below the poverty line. The impact of low female earnings may be of even greater significance today because of the increase in female-headed families. Equal opportunity legislation has not been sufficient to end economic sexism. [Covers 1960's-70's]. 8 tables, 13 notes.   J

2333. Ortiz, Isidro D. THE POLITICS OF COLLECTIVE BARGAINING. *Policy Studies J. 1978 6(4): 510-513.* California's Agricultural Labor Relations Act (1975), which guaranteed farm workers the right to name which union was to represent them in labor-management collective bargaining, was nullified and the board created to administer the law was rendered inoperative in 1977, due to lack of funds. One of 16 articles in this issue on agricultural policy.

2334. Oshinsky, David M. WISCONSIN LABOR AND THE CAMPAIGN OF 1952. *Wisconsin Mag. of Hist. 1972/73 56(2): 109-118.* Examines the role of organized labor in the senatorial primary and election of 1952 in Wisconsin. Although Labor did not significantly affect the Republican primary which renominated Joseph McCarthy, labor leaders lavishly used money and organizing to try to elect Democrat Thomas E. Fairchild and to portray McCarthy as an anti-New Dealer whose legislative record assaulted labor's recent economic gains. For most urban blue-collar workers, McCarthy's support of the Taft-Hartley Act and his economic views generally negated any of his anticommunist appeal. 3 illus., 5 tables, 49 notes.   N. C. Burckel

2335. Osterman, Paul. THE POLITICS AND ECONOMICS OF CETA PROGRAMS. *J. of the Am. Planning Assoc. 1981 47(4): 434-446.* Reports on the results of field observation of several youth programs in two prime sponsors, providing both an analysis of the workings of the Comprehensive Employment and Training Act (CETA) system and an evaluation of youth programs. The article reports the results of the programs and explains the discouraging outcomes by examining the administrative and political implementation of the programs. A great deal can be explained from this perspective, but purely administrative reforms are incomplete because they pay inadequate attention to the substantive rationale of the program. The article makes this point by examining the historical experience of youth programs, presents a brief explanation of the problem of youth employment, examines the implicit theories of the programs, and shows how the success or failure of particular programs can be explained by relationship of the implicit theory to the real problem.   J/S

2336. Padilla, Arthur. THE UNEMPLOYMENT INSURANCE SYSTEM: ITS FINANCIAL STRUCTURE. *Monthly Labor Rev. 1981 104(12): 32-37.* Discusses the federal-state system of financing unemployment insurance, focusing on the extended benefits program of 1970

and the federal supplemental benefits program of 1974, which, along with less reliance on employer state taxes to pay for benefits, means a larger role for the federal government.

2337. Pegusheva, L. V. AFT-KPP V LATINSKOI AMERIKE [AFT-KPP in Latin America]. *Novaia i Noveishaia Istoriia [USSR] 1970 (4): 56-66.* The activities of the American Institute for the Development of Free Trade Union Movement reveal how the American government tried in the 1960's to utilize Latin American labor unions for its own ends. The history of the Institute is traced from its inception in the 1940's. It was anti-Communist and reformist, based on a theory of class cooperation. Indirect attempts by ex-members of the Institute to divert the labor unions to a moderate path were frustrated by rank and file members in many countries. Based on newspapers and secondary accounts; 47 notes.
                                                        D. N. Collins

2338. Perry, Charles S. GOVERNMENT REGULATION OF COAL MINE SAFETY: EFFECTS OF SPENDING UNDER STRONG AND WEAK LAW. *Am. Pol. Q. 1982 10(3): 303-314.* Federal government spending on mine health and safety has strongly reduced bituminous coal mine fatalities when safety law has been strong but not when law has been weak.   J

2339. Pettus, Beryl E. OSHA INSPECTION COSTS, COMPLIANCE COSTS, AND OTHER OUTCOMES: THE FIRST DECADE. *Policy Studies Rev. 1982 1(3): 596-614.* Despite the common criticism of the Occupational Safety and Health Act (US, 1970) that it has greatly increased the cost of operation of the regulated industries while providing few benefits, the program still has the potential to change working conditions and practices, particularly in industrial technology and innovation, labor-management relations, preventive industrial medicine, and other important areas.

2340. Phelps, Richard. FACILITATING THE INTERSTATE MIGRATION OF UNEMPLOYED WORKERS. *Public Hist. 1982 4(2): 57-69.* Discusses federal efforts to help unemployed workers move to states with jobs available, particularly during the depression, and considers the feasibility of another such project, given the geographic variations in labor requirements.

2341. Pichler, Joseph A. and Fitch, H. Gordon. AND WOMEN MUST WEEP: THE NLRB AS FILM CRITIC. *Industrial and Labor Relations Rev. 1975 28(3): 395-410.* Discusses the use of the anti-union film *And Women Must Weep* during the 1950's-70's, and the 1974 decision by the National Labor Relations Board that this use does not constitute an unfair labor practice by employers.

2342. Pincus, Ann. HOW TO GET A GOVERNMENT JOB. *Washington Monthly 1976 8(4): 22-27.* Paints a bleak canvas of employment opportunities and advancement possibilities in the Civil Service in the District of Columbia due primarily to the "buddy" referral system among bureaucrats, 1976.

2343. Pohlmann, Marcus D. and Crisci, George S. SUPPORT FOR ORGANIZED LABOR IN THE HOUSE OF REPRESENTATIVES: THE 89TH AND 95TH CONGRESSES. *Pol. Sci. Q. 1982-83 97(4): 639-652.* Support for organized labor in the House of Representatives is measured in the 86th and 95th congresses by a labor legislation support score giving the percentage of key labor votes as supported by individual representatives. An increase in "New Democrats" during the 95th Congress, along with demographic shifts to the Sunbelt and the suburbs show no neat relationship to labor support. On the other hand, labor support remained closely tied to liberal ideology, party unity, and presidential support among congressional Democrats in the 95th Congress. The distribution of labor support shifted from more controversial bills to more moderate ones, having little effect on average labor support scores and the number of prolabor representatives. Liberalism, party unity, and presidential support declined among House Democrats during the 95th Congress. Based on Labor Legislation Support Scores from the *Congressional Quarterly Almanac* for 1965, 1966, 1977, and 1978; 6 tables, 2 fig., 25 notes, appendix.   J. Powell

2344. Rein, Mildred. WORK IN WELFARE: PAST FAILURES AND FUTURE STRATEGIES. *Social Service Rev. 1982 56(2): 211-229.* Discusses the unsuccessful work programs such as the Work

Incentive Program (WIN), the "thirty and one-third" exemption, and social services that have been promoted by the federal government since 1967 to reduce Aid to Families with Dependent Children costs and caseloads.

2345. Reubens, Edwin P. ALIENS, JOBS, AND IMMIGRATION POLICY. *Public Interest 1978 (51): 113-134.* Concerning the economic importance of aliens to the United States and their home countries, new information is available from official reports and commissioned studies, journalistic accounts, and the author's own field trips to the southern and western borders of the United States, Mexico, and other countries. An industrial and occupational breakdown of alien workers shows only a limited area of competition with Americans, although the presence of these aliens probably does hinder unionization. Aliens do not figure importantly in the rendering of public services, nor do they add a large increment to the US population. Few countries consider the migration of professionals to the United States a serious problem because they have a surplus of these individuals. The big problem with which the present system is unable to cope concerns illegal entrants. Following an evaluation of several public policy proposals to deal with this difficulty, including that of the Carter Administration, recommends an informal legitimization of aliens now here, with tighter border controls and a flexible program for authorizing temporary work. Table.   S. Harrow

2346. Richter, Irving. AMERICAN LABOR. *Center Mag. 1979 12(3): 34-43.* Excerpt from Irving Richter's upcoming book which is a political survey of labor in America from 1945 to 1977. Concludes with a discussion among Richter and several scholars and researchers which occurred in 1979.

2347. Rist, Ray C. BEYOND THE QUANTITATIVE CUL-DE-SAC: A QUALITATIVE PERSPECTIVE ON YOUTH EMPLOY-MENT PROGRAMS. *Policy Studies J. 1982 10(3): 522-538.* Presents a policy evaluation strategy for youth employment programs based on a qualitative analysis of on-site observations at 47 locations in 31 states.

2348. Robbins, Albert and Krieger, Lois. RETALIATORY FIRING UNDER OSHA: ROBERT ELLIOT, PILE DRIVER. *Civil Liberties Rev. 1978 5(3): 37-41.* Robert Elliot, pile driver foreman for the P & Z Company in California, was fired in 1975 because of his complaint to the Metro Insurance Administration about unsafe working conditions, resulting in a successful Occupational Safety and Health Administration suit against the company.

2349. Roberts, Alden E. MIGRATION, LABOR MOBILITY, AND RELOCATION ASSISTANCE: THE CASE OF THE AMERICAN INDIAN. *Social Service Rev. 1977 51(3): 464-473.* Of nonmigrant Indian families, those in areas not receiving assistance from the Bureau of Indian Affairs and those in urban areas where BIA funds are available, the latter group has a better relative and absolute standard of living; assistance needs a broader base.

2350. Robinson, Donald Allen. TWO MOVEMENTS IN PURSUIT OF EQUAL EMPLOYMENT OPPORTUNITY. *Signs 1979 4(3): 413-433.* After passage in 1964, Title VII of the Civil Rights Act made only "statutory promises" to women. Because of the strange coalition formed by woman's rights advocate Martha Griffiths and southern obstructionist Howard "Judge" Smith, the word "sex" had been added successfully to the bill. Little was done for women until the volume of complaints to the Equal Employment Opportunity Commission reached over 25% and feminist action groups exerted pressure. Between 1968 and 1971, the EEOC began to make important policy decisions, creating a "magna carta" of the working woman. By 1974, however, limited resources divided between blacks and women and ineffective leadership plagued the Commission. Based on US government sources and on personal correspondence with participants; 69 notes.   S. P. Conner

2351. Robles, Tom E. THE EEOC MODEL OFFICE EXPERI-ENCE. *J. of Intergroup Relations 1978 6(4): 18-22.* With a systematic program, the Dallas Equal Employment Opportunity Commission office has handled employment discrimination complaints.

2352. Rogulev, Iu. N. POLITIKA ADMINISTRATSII TRUMANA V OBLASTI TRUDOVYKH OTNOSHENII V GODY VOINY V KOREE [The politics of the Truman administration in the sphere of labor relations at the time of the Korean War]. *Vestnik Moskovskogo U., Seriia 9: Istoriia [USSR] 1974 29(6): 15-30.* At the time of the Korean War the Truman administration attempted to control wages through the Wage Stabilization Board. In the interest of national unity the anti-communist leaders of the AFL-CIO joined businessmen and government officials on the board. Rising prices and rising profits caused the labor representatives to resign in February 1951, but conciliationist union leaders prevented a permanent split. In the face of working-class pressure the administration agreed in December 1952 to permit wage increases and the business representatives resigned. The incoming Eisenhower administration quickly ended wage regulation. Primary sources; 91 notes.   C. J. Read

2353. Roomkin, Myron. A QUANTITATIVE STUDY OF UNFAIR LABOR PRACTICE CASES. *Industrial and Labor Relations Rev. 1981 34(2): 245-256.* The number of charges of unfair labor practices filed with the National Labor Relations Board has grown steadily. This article analyzes the incidence of case filings since 1952 as a function of economic variables. The study finds that, contrary to the assumptions of national labor policy, the board's activities themselves may be an important determinant of union and employer demands for regulatory intervention. The model proves less satisfactory, however, in explaining the filing behavior of individuals.   J/S

2354. Rosen, Sumner M. CETA: SOME CASE STUDIES. *Social Policy 1975 6(3): 44-48.* Discusses implications of the Comprehensive Employment and Training Act for the health care industry during the 1970's and suggests improvements for the present system of preventive care.

2355. Rosenbloom, David H. THE CIVIL SERVICE COMMIS-SION'S DECISION TO AUTHORIZE THE USE OF GOALS AND TIMETABLES IN THE FEDERAL EQUAL EMPLOYMENT OP-PORTUNITY PROGRAM. *Western Pol. Q. 1973 26(2): 236-251.* Discusses the Civil Service Commission's decision in 1971 to adopt the Equal Employment Opportunity Program policy of using goals and timetables to promote the hiring of minorities.   S

2356. Rosenthal, Albert J. EMPLOYMENT DISCRIMINATION AND THE LAW. *Ann. of the Am. Acad. of Pol. and Social Sci. 1973 (407): 91-101.* While there have been prohibitions, by the federal, state, and local governments, against racial discrimination in employment since the 1940s, the major legal weapon against such discrimination has been Title VII of the Civil Rights Act of 1964. The largest part of the burden of enforcing this statute has not been borne by the federal government, but rather by civil rights organizations, whose resources have been limited. A remarkable record of favorable judicial decisions has been achieved in cases brought under this statue. Nevertheless, the disparities between blacks and whites in average income and in proportionate unemployment have not been markedly reduced. Stronger legislation and a greater commitment on the part of all branches of government as well as the public seem necessary if there is to be more significant progress toward truly fair employment practices.   J

2357. Runner, Diana. LEGISLATIVE REVISIONS OF UNEM-PLOYMENT INSURANCE IN 1980. *Monthly Labor Rev. 1981 104(1): 35-39.* State by state synopsis of revisions of unemployment insurance during 1980, characterized by few changes except in Alaska and Pennsylvania.

2358. Runner, Diana. STATE UNEMPLOYMENT INSURANCE: CHANGES DURING 1978. *Monthly Labor Rev. 1979 102(2): 13-16.* Offers statistics on changes in coverage, benefits, financing, disqualifica-tion, and eligibility to state unemployment insurance in 26 states made during 1978.

2359. Runner, Diana. UNEMPLOYMENT INSURANCE LAWS: LEGISLATIVE REVISIONS IN 1982. *Monthly Labor Rev. 1983 106(1): 38-43.* The Tax Equity and Fiscal Responsibility Act (US, 1982) provided extension of unemployment benefits beyond the maxi-mum of 39 weeks through establishment of a federal supplemental compensation program; most states entered agreements with the Depart-ment of Labor for participation in the program by the end of 1982.

2360. Saks, Daniel H. and Smith, Ralph E. YOUTH WITH POOR JOB PROSPECTS. *Educ. and Urban Soc. 1981 14(1): 15-32.* Unemployment of teenagers was 18% in 1980; discusses such strategies for youth employment as the Vocational Education Act (US, 1963) and the Job Corps.

2361. Sandler, Mark. EQUAL EMPLOYMENT OPPORTUNITY CONSCIOUSNESS AMONG ARKANSAS PUBLIC SCHOOL DISTRICTS. *J. of Negro Educ. 1982 51(4): 412-424.* Title Seven of the Civil Rights Act (US, 1964) and subsequent legislation to promote equal employment mandated that employment procedures must not discriminate because of race, sex, religion, or age. An investigation of the application forms from school districts in Arkansas demonstrates that two-thirds of the sample reflect no awareness of the federal guidelines.
A. G. Belles

2362. Schiller, Bradley R. WELFARE: REFORMING OUR EXPECTATIONS. *Public Interest 1981 (62): 55-65.* Public welfare programs have promised much yet delivered little since the 1930's. Despite such innovations as the Work Incentive Program (WIN), welfare rolls have not declined. Contemporary welfare reform proposals aim to provide employment for all able-bodied recipients based on the erroneous assumption that those receiving welfare are lazy "chiselers." Recent programs aim to provide job and work-experience opportunities for recipients without many of the counseling, training, and educational services offered in the early days of WIN. Early results indicate provision of jobs alone will not satisfy the goal of decreasing the welfare rolls. While the welfare system has helped millions of people, it has not substantially decreased welfare rolls. We must abandon our unrealistic expectations for welfare reform. Secondary sources; 2 notes.
J. M. Herrick

2363. Seidman, Joel and Staudohar, Paul D. THE HAWAII PUBLIC EMPLOYMENT RELATIONS ACT: A CRITICAL ANALYSIS. *Industrial and Labor Relations Rev. 1973 26(3): 919-937.* "The Hawaii Public Employment Relations Act is known best for its grant of the right to strike to government employees, except those involved in a stoppage that has been determined through investigation to present a danger to public health or safety. This study describes the legislative intent of this and other novel features of the Hawaii law, including an automatic agency shop, a tripartite administrative board, and statewide bargaining units. The authors also point out the political forces that shaped this law and appraise its record through 1972." J

2364. Shapiro, Walter. THE INTRACTABLES. *Washington Monthly 1976 8(3): 12-18.* Discusses labor unions' attitudes toward Democratic Party presidential candidate Jimmy Carter in 1976, emphasizing issues involving the AFL-CIO and public welfare.

2365. Shils, Edward B. THE STATE GOVERNMENT DILEMMA: CIVIL SERVICE VS. COLLECTIVE BARGAINING LAWS. *Int. Social Sci. Rev. 1982 57(3[i.e., 4]): 210-225.* State and local unionism rose sharply in the 1960's and 70's, and collective bargaining statutes were enacted in a majority of states, often without amending existing civil service laws. A conflict of laws rose with intense pressures on the legislatures for accommodation statutes. Such statutes would have spelled out the legal relationship of civil service to collective bargaining. When these were not forthcoming, the courts entered the picture and judicial accommodation decisions developed. Conflict of laws still exists in great measure and gray areas abound, causing frustration to government, unions, personnel, and labor practitioners. J/S

2366. Simeral, Margaret H. THE IMPACT OF THE PUBLIC EMPLOYMENT PROGRAM ON SEX-RELATED WAGE DIFFERENTIALS. *Industrial and Labor Relations Rev. 1978 31(4): 509-519.* Tests the potential of a public service program for improving the status of women in the labor market by examining the experience of 2,289 participants in the Public Employment Program, 1971.

2367. Slyck, Philip van. WILL PROTECTION FROM IMPORTS SAVE U.S. JOBS? *Freedom At Issue 1973 (20): 11-12, 23.*

2368. Smith, Arthur B., Jr. THE IMPACT ON COLLECTIVE BARGAINING OF EQUAL EMPLOYMENT OPPORTUNITY REMEDIES. *Industrial and Labor Relations Rev. 1975 28(3): 376-394.*

Discusses the impact of Title VII of the Civil Rights Act of 1964 and Executive Order 11246 on employment discrimination.

2369. Smith, Arthur B., Jr. THE LAW AND EQUAL EMPLOYMENT OPPORTUNITY: WHAT'S PAST SHOULD NOT BE PROLOGUE. *Industrial and Labor Relations Rev. 1980 33(4): 493-505.* This article explores the debate over the role of law in insuring equal employment opportunity. The author describes the constant change in judicial and administrative regulation on this subject that has resulted, he believes, from the absence of consensus on whether the goal of public policy should be to promote equal treatment or equal achievement in the workplace. He argues that the overlapping and conflicting regulations, inconsistent results, and general confusion produced by the past encounters between the law and discriminatory employment practices should not be the model for future development of policy. J

2370. Smith, J. Clay, Jr. APPRENTICESHIPS AND AGE DISCRIMINATION. *J. of Intergroup Relations 1980-81 8(4): 52-72.* Dissents from the Equal Employment Opportunity Commission's decision to remove the apprenticeship exemption from regulations implementing the Age Discrimination in Employment Act (US, 1980) on the grounds that opening apprenticeship programs to all age groups can only decrease the number of apprenticeship positions which the youth will receive.

2371. Smith, James F. REFLECTIONS OF A RESPONDENT ATTORNEY. *J. of Intergroup Relations 1978 6(4): 40-48.* Reorganizational changes in the Equal Employment Opportunity Commission allow it to enforce equal opportunity laws more effectively.

2372. Smith, Joseph Burkholder. LIFE WITHOUT BADGES: THE COST OF COVER IN THE CIA. *Washington Monthly 1978 10(3): 44-48.* Examines negative aspects of employment in the Central Intelligence Agency—inability to flaunt status due to the secret nature of the work, infighting within the organization, and the tendency toward insularity among CIA employees and their families; covers 1950's-70's.

2373. Smith, William M. FEDERAL PAY PROCEDURES AND THE COMPARABILITY SURVEY. *Monthly Labor Rev. 1976 99(8): 27-31.* Discusses the concept of comparability of federal and private-sector salaries, established by Government Pay Acts (1962, 1970), examining the process of developing comparability information and detailing the results of the recent survey on pay adjustment, the National Survey of Professional, Administrative, Technical, and Clerical Pay, conducted by the Bureau of Labor Statistics to comply with the 1970 law.

2374. Spector, William D. THE DILEMMA OF ERISA: A CLOSER LOOK AT PENSION PLANS AND BENEFITS. *Urban and Social Change Rev. 1977 10(2): 19-21.* Reviews the history of pension reform, 1940's-74, and assesses the expected impact of the Employee Retirement Income Security Act (1974) which seeks to assure equitable and sound financial bases for private pensions and protection for anticipated employee and beneficiary benefits.

2375. Sunshine, Jonathan. DISABILITY PAYMENTS STABILIZING AFTER ERA OF ACCELERATING GROWTH. *Monthly Labor Rev. 1981 104(5): 17-22.* After a 25 year period of rapid growth in both private and government plans, disability benefits since 1975 have stopped increasing.

2376. Szerszen, Carol; Hendricks, Wallace; and Feuille, Peter. REGULATION, DEREGULATION, AND COLLECTIVE BARGAINING IN AIRLINES. *Industrial and Labor Relations Rev. 1980 34(1): 67-81.* To test the hypothesis that government regulation of an industry's product market increases union power in that industry, this study first compares earning and the "scores" of union contracts in airlines and manufacturing, and then compares negotiated wage rates and union contract scores in the more regulated and the less regulated segments of air transportation. The results, while not definitive because of data limitations, consistently support the hypothesis for the period prior to the recent deregulation of airlines. The authors nevertheless predict that deregulation will have little effect on union power in this industry, arguing that the industry and union characteristics that have developed over the 40 years of regulation have created a bargaining environment that will not change significantly in the near future.   J

2377. Tabb, William. ZAPPING LABOR. *Marxist Perspectives 1980 3(1): 64-77.* The Trilateral Commission seeks to create space in which to transform the economy of the United States by forcing down real wages and cutting social services.

2378. Thompson, Joel A. IMPLEMENTING WORKMEN'S COMPENSATION PROGRAMS IN THE STATES. *Administration & Soc. 1982 14(2): 237-260.* Organizational characteristics are important in determining performance, but performance is not significant "in explaining policy impact."

2379. Thompson, Joel A. OUTPUTS AND OUTCOMES OF STATE WORKMEN'S COMPENSATION LAWS. *J. of Pol. 1981 43(4): 1129-1132.* Between 1910 and 1921, 42 states adopted various workmen's compensation laws. In the 1970's, increased interest paralleled the increased production and utilization of hazardous chemicals, toxins, and nuclear materials as well as the increased awareness of their long-term effects. The Occupational Safety and Health Act of 1970 established a National Commission on State Workmen's Compensation Laws, which made 84 specific recommendations. Compliance with these recommendations in 1976 was primarily determined by the wealth of the individual states and the involvement of concerned interest groups. Labor organizations were positively and business and insurance groups were negatively related to comprehensive legislation. Partisanship was not significantly related. 3 illus., table, 56 notes.   A. W. Novitsky

2380. Thompson, Joel A. STATE COMPLIANCE WITH WORKMEN'S COMPENSATION RECOMMENDATIONS. *Policy Studies J. 1979 8(3): 417-430.* Determines state compliance with recommendations proposed by the National Commission on State Workmen's Compensation Laws in 1972.

2381. Thompson, Joel A. WORKERS' COMPENSATION: ARE THE STATES MEETING THE CHALLENGE? *State Government 1980 53(2): 94-98.* Compares state workers' compensation laws during 1972-80, and examines the degree of compliance each state has reached on 19 essential recommendations produced by the National Commission on State Workmen's Compensation Laws.

2382. Tinsley, LaVerne C. WORKERS' COMPENSATION IN 1982: SIGNIFICANT LEGISLATION ENACTED. *Monthly Labor Rev. 1983 106(1): 57-63.* Benefits and services for work-related injuries were improved, and 18 states modified their coverage to extend to previously uncovered occupations or to volunteer workers; rehabilitation services also were expanded.

2383. Tollefson, John O. and Pichler, Joseph A. A COMMENT ON RIGHT-TO-WORK LAWS: A SUGGESTED ECONOMIC RATIONALE. *J. of Law and Econ. 1974 17(1): 193-196.* Reanalysis of data originally presented in Neil A. and Catherine A. Palomba's article suggests that unionization is the most important predictor of a state's right-to-work status.

2384. Topel, Robert and Welch, Finis. UNEMPLOYMENT INSURANCE: SURVEY AND EXTENSIONS. *Economica [Great Britain] 1980 47(187): 351-380.* Investigates some of the major theoretical and empirical issues indicating causal links between the provision of unemployment insurance and unemployment, with particular reference to the role of systems of unemployment insurance financing. Based on empirical background data from the United States for 1973-76, with other data from 1938-76; 9 tables, 39 notes, biblio.   D. H. Murdoch

2385. VanDeWater, Peter E. THE WORKERS' EDUCATION SERVICE. *Michigan Hist. 1976 60(2): 99-113.* In 1943 the University of Michigan began the Workers' Education Service (WES) to train workers to be better citizens. An instant success, WES soon faced challenges from management which felt threatened by its program. In 1948 General Motors surreptitiously investigated it and Governor Kim Sigler made it a focus of his anti-Communist crusade. Although University administrators remained supportive the Regents were pressured by General Motors and dismissed WES director Arthur Elder. This led labor to boycott WES classes. By 1949 the controversial program ended. Primary sources; illus., 3 photos, 44 notes.   D. W. Johnson

2386. Vroman, Susan and Vroman, Wayne. MONEY WAGE CHANGES: BEFORE, DURING AND AFTER CONTROLS. *Southern Econ. J. 1979 45(4): 1172-1187.* Traces the changes in money wages in manufacturing before, during, and after President Nixon's Economic Stabilization Program, from 1969 to 1975.

2387. Wachter, Michael L. UNEMPLOYMENT POLICIES. *Pro. of the Acad. of Pol. Sci. 1979 33(3): 176-189.* Reviews the unemployment problem and considers policy options, 1960-79.   K. N. T. Crowther

2388. Weber, Arnold R. MAKING WAGE CONTROLS WORK. *Public Interest 1973 (30): 28-40.* Discusses the problems associated with wage stabilization from the 1940's-73, especially the difficulties encountered by the Nixon administration's Pay Board.

2389. Weissbrodt, Sylvia. CHANGES IN STATE LABOR LAWS IN 1972. *Monthly Labor Rev. 1973 96(1): 27-36.* Discusses issues in occupational safety, employment discrimination, wages, child labor, and agricultural labor.

2390. Williams, Walter E. THE NEW JIM CROW LAWS. *Reason 1978 10(4): 16-23, 38.* Excesses in federal regulation of wage laws, licensing restrictions, labor legislation, and education distribution are responsible for current economic difficulties of Negroes; reduction in government control could resolve the problem.

2391. Wiltberger, Heather. CREDITING WORK EXPERIENCE. *Society 1982 19(6): 55-61.* Although the Youth Employment and Demonstration Projects Act (US, 1977) addressed the unemployment problems of youth by attempting to involve both education and labor in youth training programs, implementation of those goals has been affected by economic conditions and child labor laws.

2392. Youngdahl, James E. EEOC: MANDATE FOR LABOR. *Southern Exposure 1976 4(1-2): 70-74.* Examines the Equal Employment Opportunity Commission's role in southern labor disputes specifically over discrimination, 1930's-70's.

2393. —. [MINIMUM WAGE].
Silberman, Jonathan I. and Durden, Garey C. DETERMINING LEGISLATIVE PREFERENCES ON THE MINIMUM WAGE: AN ECONOMIC APPROACH. *J. of Pol. Econ. 1976 84(2): 317-329.* Empirically investigates voting patterns on the Fair Labor Standards Act (amendment, 1973) by the use of an economic model.
Kau, James B. and Rubin, Paul H. VOTING ON MINIMUM WAGES: A TIME-SERIES ANALYSIS. *J. of Pol. Econ. 1978 86(2, part 1): 337-342.* Using probit analysis, undertakes a time-series study of the economic determinants of passage of minimum wage legislation in the period 1938-74. In contrast with a study by Silberman and Durden, finds higher wages were associated with voting for minimum wages and that blacks voting after 1964 were negatively and sometimes significantly associated with voting for minimum wages. Table, 4 notes, ref.   J. Tull

Racial, Ethnic, and Sex Discrimination

2394. Abel, Emily. COLLECTIVE PROTEST AND THE MERITOCRACY: FACULTY WOMEN AND SEX DISCRIMINATION LAWSUITS. *Feminist Studies 1981 7(3): 505-538.* Surveys 20 women who began legal actions under Title VII of the Civil Rights Act of 1964. These actions pitted the highly individualistic legal and meritocratic university systems against collectivist principles of reform politics. A pattern is evident among the women surveyed. Some remained loyal to the individualistic principles, claiming to struggle for individual justice only. Others, adhering to the more political view, claimed to work for an improvement of opportunity for all women. Although the costs were enormous, all expressed satisfaction at having undertaken action in defense of their rights, even though the outcomes were not all clearcut victories. Interviews; 62 notes.   S. Hildenbrand

2395. Adams, William and Albin, Suzanne. PUBLIC INFORMATION ON SOCIAL CHANGE: TV COVERAGE OF WOMEN IN THE WORKFORCE. *Policy Studies J. 1980 8(5): 717-734.* Analyzes US network news stories on sex discrimination in employment, 1968-78.

2396. Aldrich, Howard E. EMPLOYMENT OPPORTUNITIES FOR BLACKS IN THE BLACK GHETTO: THE ROLE OF WHITE-OWNED BUSINESSES. *Am. J. of Sociol. 1973 78(6): 1403-1425.* Black-white relations in economic institutions are important determinants of the life chances of blacks. Black leaders and civil rights groups argue that white ownership of businesses in black communities retards the economic and political achievement of blacks. This paper explores the empirical basis for such arguments using a panel study of small businesses in Boston, Chicago, and Washington, D.C. The following propositions are supported: (1) white-owned businesses are much larger than black businesses and dominate the labor market of the ghetto, (2) white owners are more likely than black owners to hire 'outsiders,' and (3) white owners hire white employees in greater proportions than the racial composition of the ghetto population would imply. Ghetto economic development is often seen as a solution to the problems of the black community, but this research points out several important limitations of a development strategy. J

2397. Allen, Walter R. FAMILY ROLES, OCCUPATIONAL STATUSES, AND ACHIEVEMENT ORIENTATIONS AMONG BLACK WOMEN IN THE UNITED STATES. *Signs 1979 4(4): 670-686.* Because black women belong to two minority groups, they are excellent subjects for "research into the dynamics of discrimination, motivation, and occupational achievement." Black female achievement orientations differ substantially from other sex-race groups. During 1964-74, the greatest number of black women changed from service work to other professions, with increased entry into white-collar work. They remain in the least prestigious positions, however. Based on the National Longitudinal Study of the High School Class of 1972, the Bureau of Census and Bureau of Labor statistics, and secondary sources; 6 tables, 28 notes. S. P. Conner

2398. Almquist, Elizabeth M. WOMEN IN THE LABOR FORCE. *Signs 1977 2(4): 843-855.* Review essay of selected periodical and book-length material (1970's) on working women indicates that while women are participating in the labor force to a greater extent, changes in occupational mobility, job status, pay increases, and discrimination have changed very little, 1950's-70's.

2399. Anderson, Bernard E. and Wallace, Phyllis A. PUBLIC POLICY AND BLACK ECONOMIC PROGRESS: A REVIEW OF THE EVIDENCE. *Am. Econ. Rev. 1975 65(2): 47-52.* Summarizes and evaluates economic evidence used to explain the patterns and causes of change in employment and income of Negroes during the 1960's. There is a lack of consensus among economists on the degree of influence exerted by various public policies on employment and income levels. S

2400. Anderson, Marion. BOMBS OR BREAD: BLACK UNEMPLOYMENT AND THE PENTAGON BUDGET. *Black Scholar 1983 14(1): 2-11.* Industries in which blacks were involved and states where blacks resided were the hardest hit by the massive unemployment and inflation that resulted from increased military spending, 1970-78.

2401. Antos, Joseph R.; Chandler, Mark; and Mellow, Wesley. SEX DIFFERENCES IN UNION MEMBERSHIP. *Industrial and Labor Relations Rev. 1980 33(2): 162-169.* Primary research indicates that differences in industrial and occupational status account for a significant portion of the large male-female unionization differential. It is not precisely clear what the figures imply for the issue of sex discrimination in union membership. Increasing female unionization would probably diminish only modestly the present male-female wage differential. Based on documents; 13 notes. G. E. Pergl

2402. Baker, Sally Hillsman and Levenson, Bernard. JOB OPPORTUNITIES OF BLACK AND WHITE WORKING-CLASS WOMEN. *Social Problems 1975 22(4): 510-533.* Examines entry employment of black, Puerto Rican, and white female graduates of a New York City vocational school—High School of Fashion Industry—and shows that job referral and placement depend more on race than on vocational

training. Minority women have restricted access to white-collar jobs and are channeled into industries characterized by minimum advancement opportunities. Also, women in general are prepared for low-level, sex-typed occupations. Training alone is not the answer for economic inequality, but job search networks must be broadened for all groups that suffer discrimination. Notes, biblio. A. M. Osur

2403. Barrett, Nancy S. WOMEN IN THE JOB MARKET: UNEMPLOYMENT AND WORK SCHEDULES. Smith, Ralph E., ed. *The Subtle Revolution: Women at Work* (Washington: Urban Inst., 1979): 63-98. "Analyzes some of the factors behind female joblessness and the relatively high propensity of women to work part time," using statistics; 1950-77.

2404. Bayles, Michael D. COMPENSATORY REVERSE DISCRIMINATION IN HIRING. *Social Theory and Practice 1973 2(3): 301-312.* Discusses ethical questions posed by the problem of reverse discrimination, the preferential hiring of minorities and women in the 1970's.

2405. Beck, E. M.; Horan, Patrick M.; and Tolbert, Charles M., II. INDUSTRIAL SEGMENTATION AND LABOR MARKET DISCRIMINATION. *Social Problems 1980 28(2): 113-130.* Investigates two elements of economic structure which cause earnings discrimination against minorities in the United States: the differential allocation of minority labor to different segments of the industrial economy, and the differential evaluation of minority credentials within different industrial segments; and on the basis of the 1976 Current Population Survey argues that the latter mechanism accounts for most of the discriminatory practices at play in the labor market.

2406. Beck, E. M. LABOR UNIONISM AND RACIAL INCOME INEQUALITY: A TIME SERIES ANALYSIS OF THE POST-WORLD WAR II PERIOD. *Am. J. of Sociol. 1980 85(4): 791-814.* Labor union activity in the United States, 1947-74, has increased between-race inequality in family income and reduced within-race inequality.

2407. Becker, Henry Jay. RACIAL SEGREGATION AMONG PLACES OF EMPLOYMENT. *Social Forces 1980 58(3): 761-776.* Indices of racial segregation in employment are presented for black and non-Hispanic white workers in the same occupational category. Controlling on the availability of blacks in each category, the most racially segregated groups are laborers and service workers. At each occupational level, women are more racially segregated from one another than are men, although differential employment in high- and low-segregation industries accounts for some of these differences. The racial composition of an establishment's work-force in one occupation is strongly related to its racial composition in other occupations, particularly though, within the blue collar and white collar subgroups. The black proportions of sales workers and clerical workers are higher the more the total establishment's employment is concentrated in that occupation. Further research directions are suggested. 5 tables, 7 notes, biblio. J

2408. Bergmann, Barbara R. and Adelman, Irma. THE 1973 REPORT OF THE PRESIDENT'S COUNCIL OF ECONOMIC ADVISERS: THE ECONOMIC ROLE OF WOMEN. *Am. Econ. Rev. 1973 63(4): 509-514.* Considers Chapter 4 of the 1973 Economic Report of the President as giving "creditable coverage" to the economic role of women in the United States. There is not only sex discrimination in employment but also job segregation; the authors' own tabulations based on the 1960-70 censuses show that more than 70% of women workers were employed in occupations in which women were overrepresented. Quit rates, layoff rates, and unemployment are all higher for women. The bleak picture of economic facts painted in the report still "tends to underestimate the possibilities and need for social change." Table, 8 notes. C. W. Olson

2409. Bergquist, Virginia A. WOMEN'S PARTICIPATION IN LABOR ORGANIZATIONS. *Monthly Labor Rev. 1974 97(10): 3-9.* The expansion of women's participation in American labor unions between 1968 and 1972 was not matched by an increase in leadership positions.

2410. Berman, Gerald S. and Haug, Marie R. OCCUPATIONAL AND EDUCATIONAL GOALS AND EXPECTATIONS: THE EFFECTS OF RACE AND SEX. *Social Problems 1975 23(2): 166-181.*

The authors surveyed undergraduate students at two large urban campuses in a midwestern city in 1970 to determine the relationship between educational and occupational expectations and aspirations as affected by sex and race. Aspiration refers to a goal that a person would like to achieve, while expectation refers to a goal that one intends or expects to attain. "These findings indicate that societal changes in the opportunity structure have had some limited impact on black men, but have not yet materially affected women." 8 tables, ref.　　　A. M. Osur

2411. Blau, Francine D. and Jusenius, Carol L. ECONOMISTS' APPROACHES TO SEX SEGREGATION IN THE LABOR MARKET: AN APPRAISAL. *Signs 1976 1(3, Part 2): 181-199.* Neoclassical economists have made a major contribution to the study of sex segregation and pay differentials between men and women by suggesting plausible reasons for these pay differentials. But they offer less satisfactory tools for understanding the linkage between such pay differentials and sex segregation. Institutional labor-market economics may offer more fruitful leads and deserve further attention, although it has not yet been incorporated into neoclassical models to any great extent. Based on secondary sources; 41 notes.　　　S. E. Kennedy

2412. Blount, Alma; Gonzalez, Martin; and Petrow, Steven. LOST IN THE STREAM. *Southern Exposure 1980 8(4): 67-76.* Discusses the hardships of migrant laborers, specifically the conditions of Jamaican cane cutters in South Florida with photographs of Mexican American and black farmworkers in Florida; 1980.

2413. Blumrosen, Alfred W. LABOR ARBITRATION AND DISCRIMINATION: THE SITUATION AFTER GRIGGS AND RIOS. *Arbitration J. 1973 28(3): 145-158.* To the proverbial man on the street, race discrimination is a matter of evil intent. But the Supreme Court has made it clear in the Griggs case that the target of the Civil Rights Act of 1964 is not the deliberate wrongdoer or racist alone, but the whole body of attitudes and practices that even well-intentioned individuals may exhibit. Thus, 'the law has focused over the years on reforming systems which discriminate,' the author points out. On the basis of his study of published awards three years ago, he concluded that arbitrators have dealt effectively with discriminatory practices which also constituted contractual violations. But where the contract was inherently discriminatory, arbitrators had felt obliged to uphold the agreement, at whatever cost to the statutory rights of employees. Now, three years later, he finds some improvement, based upon 'consciousness raising experience,' particularly in cases involving discrimination against women. But if arbitration awards are to be deferred to, in the manner anticipated by the Fifth Circuit decision in the Rios case, it might become advisable for parties to broaden the scope of arbitral authority so as to permit them to strike down provisions that are clearly repugnant to the purpose of the Civil Rights Act.　　　J

2414. Borjas, George J. THE SUBSTITUTABILITY OF BLACK, HISPANIC, AND WHITE LABOR. *Econ. Inquiry 1983 21(1): 93-106.* Analyzes labor market competition among blacks, Hispanic Americans, and whites, 1976.

2415. Bose, Christine E. and Rossi, Peter H. GENDER AND JOBS: PRESTIGE STANDINGS OF OCCUPATIONS AS AFFECTED BY GENDER. *Am. Sociol. Rev. 1983 48(3): 316-330.* Attempts to measure prestige for the full range of men's and women's occupations and gender incumbency effects on prestige. Household and college sample respondents each rate 110 occupations using standard NORC prestige methods and metrics. Findings support the theoretical assumption that incumbent prestige ratings represent achieved occupational status as modified by ascribed sex of incumbent, rather than as some more equal mix of gender prestige and occupational prestige. Occupation remains the major contributor to prestige. Sex of incumbent affects householders' ratings, while college students do not make this differentiation. Sex composition influences female and high-status raters in each sample. However, the near equity in subjective occupational repute is unrelated to the actual resources of jobs.　　　J/S

2416. Brauer, Carl M. WOMEN ACTIVISTS, SOUTHERN CONSERVATIVES, AND THE PROHIBITION OF SEX DISCRIMINATION IN TITLE VII OF THE 1964 CIVIL RIGHTS ACT. *J. of Southern Hist. 1983 49(1): 37-57.* An amendment to prohibit sex discrimination was added to the 1964 Civil Rights bill, legislation originally intended to ban just racial discrimination. The National Women's Party and some congresswomen sponsored the amendment. Because opponents of the bill in the House of Representatives adopted a legislative strategy of ridicule, supporters in the Senate wanted to pass the bill quickly and avoid obstruction. They, consequently, were unwilling to challenge the inclusion of women in this bill. Based on the National Women's Party Papers, various other manuscript holdings, interviews, newspapers, journals, and printed primary sources; 37 notes.　　　T. D. Schoonover

2417. Brecher, Charles. THE MISMATCH MISUNDERSTANDING. *New York Affairs 1977 4(1): 6-12.* The principal cause of unemployment among Negroes in cities and suburbs is racial discrimination rather than a disparity between Negroes' job skills and employment opportunities; discusses the implications of the increasing number of white women workers in the labor force since 1965.

2418. Brewer, Marilynn B. FURTHER BEYOND NINE TO FIVE: AN INTEGRATION AND FUTURE DIRECTIONS. *J. of Social Issues 1982 38(4): 149-157.* Some of the findings of the studies reported in this issue are reviewed, with particular attention to conclusions regarding perceptions of the nature of sexual harassment and the possible differential effects of status and power on responses to incidents of social-sexual behavior in the workplace. In addition, some suggestions are made for further research in the area, with emphasis on the dyadic nature of sexual harassment and its relation to differential socialization of males and females, 1960's-82.　　　J/S

2419. Bunzel, John H. TO EACH ACCORDING TO HER WORTH? *Public Interest 1982 (67): 77-93.* The doctrine of equal pay for equal work has been expanded by recent court decisions, and in 1981 San Jose, California, negotiated a comparable worth settlement with the American Federation of State, County, and Municipal Employees. The settlement ignored marketplace factors. Many argue that the marketplace inherently discriminates against women, and it is not possible to show that in occupations demanding similar knowledge and responsibility equal wages will be paid when there is no discrimination. Other variables may produce this effect. Reviews the concept of comparable worth and cases involving academic employers. 7 notes.　　　J. M. Herrick

2420. Burris, Val and Wharton, Amy. SEX SEGREGATION IN THE U.S. LABOR FORCE. *Rev. of Radical Pol. Econ. 1982 14(3): 43-56.* Some tendency for female employment in predominantly male occupations to decline has been offset by a concentration of women workers in exclusively female occupations. Sex segregation has declined in middle-class occupations, such as professional, technical, and managerial fields, while it has remained stable in working-class—blue-collar and lower white-collar—occupations. Causes for this virtual stasis are males' self-protection and divisive tactics by employers. Secondary sources; 5 tables, 16 notes, 62 ref.　　　D. R. Stevenson

2421. Burstein, Paul. EQUAL EMPLOYMENT OPPORTUNITY LEGISLATION AND THE INCOME OF WOMEN AND NON-WHITES. *Am. Sociol. Rev. 1979 44(3): 367-391.* Examines the impact of federal legislation on white and nonwhite women's and nonwhite men's income relative to white men's income nationally since the 1940's. Discusses law enforcement in detail.　　　J/S

2422. Burstein, Paul and MacLeod, Margo W. PROHIBITING EMPLOYMENT DISCRIMINATION: IDEAS AND POLITICS IN THE CONGRESSIONAL DEBATE OVER EQUAL EMPLOYMENT OPPORTUNITY LEGISLATION. *Am. J. of Sociol. 1980 86(3): 512-533.* Discusses proposals in Congress for prohibiting discrimination in employment from 1942 until Congress passed the Civil Rights Act of 1964, especially Title VII, amended in 1972.

2423. Cayer, N. Joseph and Schaefer, Roger C. AFFIRMATIVE ACTION AND MUNICIPAL EMPLOYEES. *Social Sci. Q. 1981 62(3): 487-494.* Examines the attitudes of rank-and-file employees of a municipality in Texas toward equal opportunity and affirmative action programs, compares employee attitudes to those of managers, and comments on the need to educate employees about the meaning and impact of the Equal Employment Opportunity Act of 1972.

2424. Clarke, Garvey E. ENGINEERING: A PROFESSION OF OPPORTUNITY. *Crisis 1979 86(5): 155-157.* In 1979, blacks represent only 1.1% of engineers in America. At the same time, engineering offers greater opportunities for good salaries and advancements than many other professions. Engineers' training to analyze and solve problems equips them for the future, in industry, education, or social service.   A. G. Belles

2425. Coats, Warren L., Jr. THE ECONOMICS OF DISCRIMINATION. *Modern Age 1974 18(1): 64-70.* Describes racial and sexual discrimination in the labor market, citing in particular several studies on the reasons for the limited economic participation of blacks and women in the United States.

2426. Colt, Cristine. SEX DISCRIMINATION: CRISTINE COLT, ADVERTISING SALESPERSON. *Civil Liberties Rev. 1978 5(3): 28-37.* Cristine Colt, advertising salesperson for Dow Jones Co., publishers of *Barron's* and the *Wall Street Journal*, describes her 1975-77 protest against her employer's refusal to promote her to a deserved sales management position.

2427. Comanor, William S. RACIAL DISCRIMINATION IN AMERICAN INDUSTRY. *Economica [Great Britain] 1973 40(160): 363-378.* Analyzes statistically the pattern of racial discrimination in employment in US metropolitan areas and investigates the relationship between discrimination and industry profit rates.

2428. Conyers, John, Jr. THE ECONOMIC CRISIS: THE POLITICS OF UNEMPLOYMENT: LOST—ANOTHER GENERATION OF BLACK YOUTH. *Freedomways 1975 15(3): 153-160.*

2429. Cooney, Rosemary Santana. CHANGING LABOR FORCE PARTICIPATION OF MEXICAN AMERICAN WIVES: A COMPARISON WITH ANGLOS AND BLACKS. *Social Sci. Q. 1975 56(2): 252-261.* Data on Mexican American married women, aged 15-54, in the Southwest in 1960 and 1970 and data on comparable Anglo and black females substantiate the importance of socioeconomic factors for explaining interethnic variations in female labor force participation, but are also consistent with the hypothesis that the importance of familism for the Mexican American population has declined.   J

2430. Cooney, Rosemary Santana and Warren, Alice E. Colón. DECLINING FEMALE PARTICIPATION AMONG PUERTO RICAN NEW YORKERS: A COMPARISON WITH NATIVE WHITE NONSPANISH NEW YORKERS. *Ethnicity 1979 6(3): 281-297.* Every cultural and racial group identified by the census except Puerto Ricans have increased women's participation in the New York labor force during the 1960's. Comparison with white women indicates that education is the major reason for this anomaly. Puerto Ricans are not as well educated as are other groups. Consequently though the number of jobs has increased the number of jobs requiring higher levels of education have increased more rapidly, reducing the opportunities for Puerto Ricans. Puerto Rican women who have acquired better educations move from the city. Based on US censuses; biblio.   S

2431. Cooney, Rosemary Santana and Ortiz, Vilma. NATIVITY, NATIONAL ORIGIN, AND HISPANIC FEMALE PARTICIPATION IN THE LABOR FORCE. *Social Sci. Q. 1983 64(3): 510-523.* Integration into the work force by Puerto Rican, Mexican, and Cuban women is more influenced by their place of birth (United States or foreign) than their national origin, and when national origin is an important factor, it has a larger effect on foreign-born women.

2432. Corcoran, Mary. THE STRUCTURE OF FEMALE WAGES. *Am. Econ. Rev. 1978 68(2): 165-170.* Given the sociobiological realities of marriage and children for many women, certain assumptions or stereotypes have emerged regarding the earning power of women. Apparently timing (availability of a job at the time of seeking said job) is a key factor in determining what job a woman currently holds. Unemployment does not lessen a woman's job skills. Many women experience interruptions in work careers, but the interruptions never significantly lowered their wages. 2 ref.   D. K. Pickens

2433. Coser, Rose Laub. WOMEN AND WORK. *Dissent 1980 27(1): 51-55.* Surveys working conditions for women in the 1970's and argues

that the division of labor should be based on social skills rather than on sex.

2434. Craft, James A. RACIAL AND OCCUPATIONAL ASPECTS OF PUBLIC EMPLOYMENT SERVICE PLACEMENTS. *Q. Rev. of Econ. and Business 1973 13(3): 53-60.* Data from the Employment Security Automated Reporting System is used to examine traditional criticisms of US Employment Service placement activity. A correlation analysis is employed to determine the degree of similarity between the occupational structure of USES placements and that of the economy, and the similarity between the relative importance of occupations for black and white placements. The findings indicate that, in general, the past criticisms of USES placements tend to be borne out. This study helps to evaluate quantitatively the validity and extent of the problem.   J

2435. Cramer, M. Richard. RACE AND SOUTHERN WHITE WORKERS' SUPPORT FOR UNIONS. *Phylon 1978 39(4): 311-321.* Examines the connection of the racial attitudes of southern whites and their attitudes toward unionization, based on studies during the 1960's and 1970's, and concludes that prejudiced southern white workers are resistant to unionization efforts.

2436. Crowe, Patricia Ward. COMPLAINANT REACTIONS TO THE MASSACHUSETTS COMMISSION AGAINST DISCRIMINATION. *Law and Soc. Rev. 1978 12(2): 217-235.* The Massachusetts Commission Against Discrimination (MCAD) is charged with hearing complaints of discrimination on grounds of race, color, sex, age, and ethnic background. Complainants report mixed attitudes with respect to its procedures and rewards. Reactions to MCAD are largely determined by symbolic and emotional issues rather than by actual outcomes. Based on interviews of complainants; 2 tables, 37 notes.   H. R. Mahood

2437. Cummings, Scott. RACIAL PREJUDICE AND POLITICAL ORIENTATIONS AMONG BLUE-COLLAR WORKERS. *Social Sci. Q. 1977 57(4): 907-920.* Under certain economic conditions and contrary to neo-Marxist theory, racial prejudice is a manifestation of, rather than an obstacle to, white working class militancy. Analyzes recent survey data that measure prejudice toward blacks and three types of political orientation. Union affiliation, region of the country, and craft versus noncraft occupations were control variables. Historical evidence from early industrial development in the United States supports the conclusions drawn from these data and suggests several reasons why there is no systematic connection between racial prejudice, class militancy, and efforts to organize. Based on data from the 1972 Survey Research Center's national election survey and secondary sources; 2 tables, 6 notes, biblio.   W. R. Hively

2438. Davis, Howard. EMPLOYMENT GAINS OF WOMEN BY INDUSTRY, 1968-78. *Monthly Labor Rev. 1980 103(6): 3-9.* Demonstrates that the employment of women increased most in the service sector during this period, although noticeable gains were made in the traditionally male-dominated industries of construction and mining.

2439. Davis, Walter G. THE BLACK WORKER IN AMERICA. *Crisis 1976 83(2): 56-62.* Discusses the role of blacks in organized labor. Racial discrimination has prevented them from meaningful participation in labor unions. The black worker, labor, and management must be brought together to provide a more optimistic future in the world of work.   A. G. Belles

2440. Deckard, Barbara and Sherman, Howard. MONOPOLY POWER AND SEX DISCRIMINATION. *Pol. and Soc. 1974 4(4): 475-482.* Criticizes conservative and liberal explanations of the dilemma presented by capitalist maximizing-of-profits theory and the reality of sex discrimination against female workers. Presents an outline of an interdisciplinary model which shows the dilemma to be more apparent than real. Based on secondary sources; 16 notes.   D. G. Nielson

2441. Deere, Carmen Diana. RURAL WOMEN'S SUBSISTENCE PRODUCTION IN THE CAPITALIST PERIPHERY. *Rev. of Radical Pol. Econ. 1976 8(1): 9-17.* Argues that division of labor in rural agricultural markets contributes to the low value placed on labor during capital accumulation.

2442. DeFichy, Wendy. AFFIRMATIVE ACTION: EQUAL OP-
PORTUNITY FOR WOMEN IN LIBRARY MANAGEMENT. *Coll.
and Res. Lib. 1973 34(3): 194-201.* Urges the establishment of affirmative action programs to admit more women into library management.
Discusses strategies for Affirmative Action Committees, including the
endorsement and support of national women's organizations such as the
National Organization for Women. Considers suggestions on securing
full cooperation from top management personnel and the role of library
schools. Hopefully, "an equal opportunity library will influence employment practices within the community at large." Based on primary and
secondary sources; 21 notes.   E. R. McKinstry

2443. Dunne, Faith. OCCUPATIONAL SEX-STEREOTYPING
AMONG RURAL YOUNG WOMEN AND MEN. *Rural Sociol. 1980
45(3): 396-415.* Delineates some major issues influencing the status
attainment process of young rural women in comparison with that of
young men, focusing on occupational sex-stereotyping, using data taken
from a survey in 1977-78.

2444. Dye, Thomas R. and Renick, James. POLITICAL POWER
AND CITY JOBS: DETERMINANTS OF MINORITY EMPLOY-
MENT. *Social Sci. Q. 1981 62(3): 475-486.* Examines the impact of
minority representation on city councils and the size and percentage of
minority populations on the employment of blacks, Hispanics, and
women in administrative, professional, and protective jobs in municipal
government.

2445. Dye, Thomas R. and Strickland, Julie. WOMEN AT THE TOP:
A NOTE ON INSTITUTIONAL LEADERSHIP. *Social Sci. Q. 1982
63(2): 333-341.* Discusses the percentage of women in top leadership
positions and concludes that of the less than 5% of leaders who are
women, most are younger and better educated than their male counterparts, and their experience is in university or government rather than
corporate leadership.

2446. Epstein, Cynthia Fuchs. SEPARATE AND UNEQUAL:
NOTES ON WOMEN'S ACHIEVEMENT. *Social Policy 1976 6(5):
17-23.* Discusses sociological factors in employment discrimination
against women in the 1970's.

2447. Exum, William H. CLIMBING THE CRYSTAL STAIR:
VALUES, AFFIRMATIVE ACTION AND MINORITY FACULTY.
Social Problems 1983 30(4): 383-399. Discusses the number of available minority faculty members, the demand for them at colleges and
universities, and the failure, after 15 years of affirmative action, to
achieve the desired change.

2448. Ferber, Marianne A. and Green, Carole A. TRADITIONAL
OR REVERSE SEX DISCRIMINATION? A CASE STUDY OF A
LARGE PUBLIC UNIVERSITY. *Industrial and Labor Relations Rev.
1982 35(4): 550-564.* Multiple regression analysis of data on all full-
time faculty members hired during the academic years 1975-76 through
1978-79 at the University of Illinois, Urbana-Champaign, shows that
women are paid an average of $2,200 less than men when such criteria as
highest degree, experience, number of publications, honors, and field are
held constant. Evidence does not show that this gap closes over time.
Furthermore, women are less likely to be hired in tenure-track positions.
Articles published is the largest contributing factor to high academic
rank, but sex is also a significant factor. The evidence shows no effective
affirmative action in faculty employment.   J/S

2449. Ferber, Marianne A. and Lowry, Helen M. WOMEN: THE
NEW RESERVE ARMY OF THE UNEMPLOYED. *Signs 1976 1(3,
Part 2): 213-232.* Direct, indirect, and differential discrimination causes
some, and perhaps most, of the disadvantaged situation of women in the
labor market. The relatively high overt and disguised unemployment
rate for women results in part from women's behavior including high
turnover, less time spent on job search, less inclination to adjust
domicile to job availability, crowding into a few occupations, and
leaving the labor market when conditions are unfavorable. Discrimination *per se* does not explain why women are segregated, but discrimination does tend to cause career interruptions, and women seek
occupations where interruptions are not severely penalized. Based on
published government statistics and secondary sources; graph, 3 tables,
39 notes.   S. E. Kennedy

2450. Flanders, Dwight P. and Anderson, Peggy Engelhardt. SEX
DISCRIMINATION IN EMPLOYMENT: THEORY AND PRAC-
TICE. *Industrial and Labor Relations Rev. 1973 26(3): 938-955.* The
authors of this study first employ microeconomic theory to illustrate the
choices an employer faces in deciding on the male-female mix of his
labor force. They then test several hypotheses suggested by economic
theory, using a sample of 337 males and 106 females employed in four
managerial levels within the personnel departments of sixty-one firms.
Variations in the male-female employment mix are measured against
variations in salary, education work experience, age, size of firm, and the
sex mix of each firm's total labor force.   J

2451. Fossett, Mark and Swicegood, Gray. REDISCOVERING CITY
DIFFERENCES IN RACIAL OCCUPATIONAL INEQUALITY.
Am. Sociol. Rev. 1982 47(5): 681-689. City differences in racial
occupational inequality are of sufficient magnitude to warrant sustained
empirical and theoretical analysis.   J/S

2452. Frank, Robert H. WHY WOMEN EARN LESS: THE THEO-
RY AND ESTIMATION OF DIFFERENTIAL OVERQUALIFICA-
TION. *Am. Econ. Rev. 1978 68(3): 360-373.* Recognizing two social
facts: that the average wage rate for females in the United States is 2/3 of
the average wage for males and that 58% of all women in the labor force
are married, indicates that one mate (usually the female) takes a job with
less income because rarely is it possible for both spouses to have high
income jobs in the same geographical area. For reasons of cultural value
or a social norm, the husband, therefore, takes the better paying job. The
differential degree of compromise manifests itself in the wage structure.
20 notes, ref.

2453. Freeman, Richard. BLACK ECONOMIC PROGRESS SINCE
1964. *Public Interest 1977 (52): 52-68.* Analyzes statistics on black
employment and education since 1964, finding impressive gains attributable to prolonged antidiscrimination efforts. Still, the effects of family
structure, social origins and past discrimination cannot be altered by the
Civil Rights Act. Concludes with a number of questions and suggestions
on this and related problems. 5 tables, note.   J. Tull

2454. Freeman, Richard B. DISCRIMINATION IN THE ACA-
DEMIC MARKETPLACE. Sowell, Thomas, ed. *Essays and Data on
American Ethnic Groups* (Washington, D.C.: Urban Inst. Pr., 1978):
167-201. Qualitative variables that are elusive in other fields are more
tangible in academia because level of training is indicated by degree and
by the ranking of the various institutions. Gross annual income
differences were examined by race, as were variables that determined
income such as degree level and amount of publication from the 1950's
to the 1970's, the era of affirmative action. Concludes that the demand
for minority faculty has increased except in the case of Orientals, who
had been well represented in academia before affirmative action
programs were initiated. Primary and secondary sources; 14 tables, fig.,
6 notes.   K. A. Talley

2455. Fuchs, Victor R. WOMEN'S EARNINGS: RECENT TRENDS
AND LONG-RUN PROSPECTS. *Monthly Labor Rev. 1974 97(5):
23-26.* Discusses the factors accounting for differences in earnings
between white women and men in the United States between 1959 and
1970, with particular reference to role differentiation.

2456. Gabin, Nancy. "THEY HAVE PLACED A PENALTY ON
WOMANHOOD": WOMEN AUTO WORKERS IN THE DE-
TROIT-AREA UAW LOCALS, 1945-1947. *Feminist Studies 1982 8(2):
373-398.* Challenges the view that women workers returned quietly to
their homes after World War II, by describing the efforts of some
women in the auto industry to keep their jobs in the postwar period
despite massive discrimination. Women who protested discriminatory
treatment by management and the United Automobile Workers of
America designed to reduce the number of women in the auto industry
to the prewar figure met hostility from male workers and the general
public. Based on materials at the Wayne State University Archives of
Labor History and Urban Affairs; 47 notes.   S. Hildenbrand

2457. Gabin, Nancy. WOMEN WORKERS AND THE UAW IN
THE POST-WORLD WAR II PERIOD: 1945-1954. *Labor Hist. 1980
21(1): 5-30.* Discusses the experience of women in the United Automobile Workers of America, 1945-54. Women were discriminated against

by not only management but also by locals appeals committees, and the International Executive Board, which systematically upheld agreements prohibiting the employment of married women, providing unequal hiring and wage rates on similar jobs, and disallowing women's seniority rights. These practices conflicted with UAW policies, but they were deeply rooted in social ideology of male union members. Based on the Emil Mazey collection of the Archives of Labor History and Urban Affairs, Wayne State U.; 41 notes.   L. L. Athey

2458. Garcia, Jose Z.; Clark, Cal; and Clark, Janet. POLICY IM-PACTS ON CHICANOS AND WOMEN: A STATE CASE STUDY. *Policy Studies J. 1978 7(2): 251-257.* Studies the changes of status of Mexican Americans and women in the New Mexico state government work force during 1971-78.

2459. Garcia, Philip. AN EVALUATION OF UNEMPLOYMENT AND EMPLOYMENT DIFFERENCES BETWEEN MEXICAN AMERICANS AND WHITES: THE SEVENTIES. *Social Sci. J. 1983 20(1): 51-62.* Unemployment rates for Mexican Americans are higher than for Anglos and are more sensitive to changes in the demand for labor.

2460. Garcia, Philip. TRENDS IN THE RELATIVE INCOME POSITION OF MEXICAN-ORIGIN WORKERS IN THE U.S.: THE EARLY SEVENTIES. *Sociol. and Social Res. 1982 66(4): 467-483.* Lower incomes among Mexican Americans are highly related to lower job statuses. Mexican immigrants experience unique obstacles to earnings. Mexican-white differences in annual income widen during the periods of high national employment.   J/S

2461. Georgakas, Dan and Surkin, Marvin. NIGGERMATION IN AUTO: COMPANY POLICY AND THE RISE OF BLACK CAU-CUSES. *Radical Am. 1975 9(1): 31-57.* Since 1968 several cases of company policy in the automobile industry have been challenged by ELRUM, the Detroit unit of the League of Revolutionary Black Workers.

2462. Geschwender, James A. THE LEAGUE OF REVOLUTION-ARY BLACK WORKERS: PROBLEMS OF CONFRONTING BLACK MARXIST-LENINIST ORGANIZATIONS. *J. of Ethnic Studies 1974 2(3): 1-23.* Analyzes the five-year career of the Detroit-based League of Revolutionary Black Workers, formed by the integra-tion of the Dodge Revolutionary Union Movement at the Hamtramck Assembly Plant with the component Ford and Eldon Avenue Move-ments in 1968; it was designed to fight racism and the oppression of Negroes in the automobile industry. Led by John Watson, General G. Baker, Jr., Luke S. Tripp, Jr., and using their periodical, *The Inner City Voice* , they called wildcat strikes, sought to raise black worker consciousness of their economic power, and organized the Detroit Branch of the Black Panther Party. Control of the Wayne State University student paper, and cooperation with the National Black Economic Development Conference followed. Ideological disagreements between adherents of a capitalist exploitation model, with socialist revolution as its goal, and the colonial model favoring a black separatist state led to the League's demise, but the stimulus it provided has not been lost. Based largely on first-hand newspaper accounts, interviews with participants; 70 notes.   G. J. Bobango

2463. Geschwender, James A. MARXIST-LENINIST ORGANIZA-TION: PROGNOSIS AMONG BLACK WORKERS. *J. of Black Studies 1978 8(3): 279-298.* The rise and fall (1968-71) of the League of Revolutionary Black Workers in the Detroit automobile industry provides a model for predicting possible future developments in Marxist-Leninist black workers' organizations in the United States. Most actual or potential black industrial workers share the characteristics of the league's members, except their history of radicalism. From a 1972 peak, black workers' groups declined to token levels by 1976 because of the discriminatory discharge of black workers in a declining national economy. When the economy revives, black workers' organizations can thrive by combining Marxist class theory with black nationalism. Based on published government documents and secondary sources; 2 tables, biblio.   R. G. Sherer

2464. Gillespie, J. David and Mitchell, Michael L. *BAKKE, WEBER,* AND RACE IN EMPLOYMENT. *Policy Studies J. 1979 8(3): 383-391.*

Applies quantitative methodology to informed public opinion to deter-mine the linkage between the *Bakke* decision (1978) and the discretion-ary use of race in private employment, noting the legal parallel of Title 6 of the Civil Rights Act (US, 1964) as applied to *Bakke* and Title 7 as used in the *Weber* decision (1979) and other cases.

2465. Gilroy, Curtis L. BLACK AND WHITE UNEMPLOYMENT: THE DYNAMICS OF THE DIFFERENTIAL. *Monthly Labor Rev. 1974 97(2): 38-47.* Analysis of black and white unemployment rates in the United States between 1954 and 1973 shows how blacks are affected relatively more than whites by changes in the demand for labor.

2466. Gilroy, Curtis L. INVESTMENT IN HUMAN CAPITAL AND BLACK-WHITE UNEMPLOYMENT. *Monthly Labor R. 1975 98(7): 13-21.* Discusses differences in quantity and quality of education which accounts for much of the unemployment differential from 1960 to 1970.   S

2467. Glacel, Barbara Pate. THE STATUS OF EQUAL EMPLOY-MENT OPPORTUNITY FOR WOMEN IN THE FEDERAL GOV-ERNMENT. *J. of Intergroup Relations 1976 5(1): 15-30.* Discusses sex discrimination against women in federal employment in the 1970's.

2468. Goering, John M. and Kalachek, Edward. PUBLIC TRANS-PORTATION AND BLACK UNEMPLOYMENT. *Society 1973 10(5): 39-42.*

2469. Goldman, Alan H. LIMITS TO THE JUSTIFICATION OF REVERSE DISCRIMINATION. *Social Theory and Practice 1975 3(3): 289-306.* Discusses questions of justice involved in reverse discrimina-tion in hiring for jobs in the 1970's.

2470. Gonzalez, Rosalinda M. and Fernandez, Raul A. U.S. IMPERI-ALISM AND MIGRATION: THE EFFECTS ON MEXICAN WOM-EN AND FAMILIES. *Rev. of Radical Pol. Econ. 1979 11(4): 112-124.* Illegal Mexican immigration into the United States is a consequence of US imperialism. Having destroyed the economy of Mexico, US capital-ists have acted to keep the Mexican people as a reserve force of cheap labor. Especially exploited are women and children, who will labor for less money and are less skilled at demanding their rights. At present, the all-powerful capitalists are striving to shut off illegal immigration on the one hand, in order to prevent having to pay higher wages, and to keep those who have entered in a position of second-class persons without rights for the same purpose. 34 notes.   V. L. Human

2471. Gould, William B. BLACK WORKERS INSIDE THE HOUSE OF LABOR. *Ann. of the Am. Acad. of Pol. and Social Sci. 1973 (407): 78-90.* While both construction and industrial unions have made some efforts to remedy racial discrimination in employment, their failure to come to grips with systematic practices of discrimination has made the federal judiciary the main forum for the resolution of such disputes. Institutional practices that can have a discriminatory impact upon black workers and racial minorities remain in effect. Contrary to public belief about rank and file and local union resistance to national union policies that promote civil rights, it is the official policy of the American Federation of Labor and Congress of Industrial Organizations (AFL-CIO) not to alter such procedures which are negotiated in the collective bargaining process—and which screen out blacks disproportionately to whites. Even unions with a substantial black membership continue to have lily-white executive boards at the national level. More blacks are moving into leadership positions—especially in the United Auto Work-ers (UAW) and some of the public employee unions. However, in the interim the phenomenon of black workers in white-led unions is bound to produce discontent, black worker organizations, and, in some instances, industrial strife.   J

2472. Gray, David M. DISCRIMINATION PROBLEMS OF WORKING-CLASS WHITES. *J. of Intergroup Relations 1974 3(4): 19-25.* Discusses discrimination against working class whites primarily by psychologists, illustrating that social class discrimination functions similarly to other forms of discrimination.

2473. Gurin, Patricia and Gaylord, Carolyn. EDUCATIONAL AND OCCUPATIONAL GOALS OF MEN AND WOMEN AT BLACK COLLEGES. *Monthly Labor Rev. 1976 99(6): 10-16.* Discusses the results of surveys conducted in 1964-65 and again in 1970 among students at black colleges, finding that sex-role influences inhibited the educational and career goals of black women in ways similar to findings among white women.

2474. Haber, Sheldon E.; Lamas, Enrique J.; and Green, Gordon. A NEW METHOD FOR ESTIMATING JOB SEPARATIONS BY SEX AND RACE. *Monthly Labor Rev. 1983 106(6): 20-27.* During 1977, women were as likely or less likely than men to separate from employers; blacks of both sexes were less likely than whites to separate from employers.

2475. Haddock, Wilbur. BLACK WORKERS LEAD THE WAY. *Black Scholar 1973 5(3): 43-48.* Black and minority labor, as part of the civil and human rights movement of the 1960's, is a driving force in the labor struggles of the 1970's.

2476. Hall, Bob. BUCKING THE SYSTEM: THE SUCCESS AND SURVIVAL OF ORGANIZED WORKERS IN RURAL, ANTI-UNION NORTH CAROLINA. *Southern Exposure 1982 10(5): 66-73.* Profiles the triracial politics of Robeson County, North Carolina, involving Lumbee Indians, blacks, whites, and various attempts at unionization within the county.

2477. Hall, Grace and Saltzstein, Alan. EQUAL EMPLOYMENT OPPORTUNITY FOR MINORITIES IN MUNICIPAL GOVERNMENT. *Social Sci. Q. 1977 57(4): 864-872.* Newly available data from 26 Texas cities reveal unexpectedly complex employment patterns for blacks and Mexican Americans in municipal government. Indices which consider both a minority group's representation and its distribution across salary levels demonstrate that blacks are more disadvantaged than Spanish surnamed individuals. Mexican American employment is related more strongly to the professional and educational characteristics of that population than is the case for blacks. Urbanization has not affected the hiring of both groups equally; black employment potential seems to increase in rapidly growing central cities. Based on Equal Employment Opportunity statistics and secondary sources; 3 tables, 3 notes, biblio.
W. R. Hively

2478. Hamburger, Robert. A STRANGER IN THE HOUSE. *Southern Exposure 1977 5(1): 22-31.* While domestic service by black women in northern cities has declined rapidly in recent years, this occupation as late as 1965 was engaged in by nearly one million black workers, about one-third of all black working women. Oral interviews with two black women, Roena Bethune and Rose Marie Hairston, reveal the poor working conditions of domestic servants.
N. Lederer

2479. Hanushek, Eric. ETHNIC INCOME VARIATIONS: MAGNITUDES AND EXPLANATIONS. Sowell, Thomas, ed. *Essays and Data on American Ethnic Groups* (Washington, D.C.: Urban Inst. Pr., 1978): 139-166. Discusses income determination as influenced by factors of ethnic background, divided by Standard Metropolitan Statistical Areas (SMSA). For example, blacks who, on the whole, earn less than whites, have less schooling and are concentrated in the South. Uses a variation of the human capital model which views education and training as an investment and concludes that there is a high return on postsecondary education, decreasing by ethnic group and economic region. Primary sources; 13 tables, 23 notes.
K. A. Talley

2480. Hedges, Janice Neipert and Bemis, Stephen E. SEX STEREOTYPING: ITS DECLINE IN SKILLED TRADES. *Monthly Labor Rev. 1974 97(5): 14-22.* Examines the movement of women into skilled jobs in the United States between 1960 and 1973 with the decline of social, legal, economic, and psychological barriers.

2481. Height, Dorothy I. THE NEW BLACK WOMAN. *J. of Ecumenical Studies 1979 16(1): 166-169.* Surveys the economic situation of black American women since 1940. As victims of both sexism and racism, black American women are still found in service-oriented jobs, many are still the sole wage-earners in the family, and more black women than white women are on welfare; but more black women than black men have received baccalaureate degrees, and small but significant gains have been made in the numbers of black women elected or appointed to public office. Table.
S

2482. Hill, Herbert. THE AFL-CIO AND THE BLACK WORKER: TWENTY-FIVE YEARS AFTER THE MERGER. *J. of Intergroup Relations 1982 10(1): 5-61.* Finds that 25 years after the American Federation of Labor (AFL) and the Congress of Industrial Organizations (CIO) merged, the basic goals of improving the lot of blacks in labor unions, ending the militant racism in the workplace and increasing the numbers of minorities in union leadership positions, have not been achieved.

2483. Hill, Robert. THE ILLUSION OF BLACK PROGRESS. *Black Scholar 1978 10(2): 18-24, 49-52.* Persistent unemployment within the black community is due to the lack of available jobs for Negroes, not to their unsuitability for jobs, 1970's.

2484. Hopkins, Elaine B. UNEMPLOYED! AN ACADEMIC WOMAN'S SAGA. *Change 1973/74 5(10): 49-53.* "The experience of losing her university teaching position because she did not possess a doctorate led this teacher to a more thorough study of women in academe and policies she believes discriminate against them. 'Allowing women permanent places in the ivory tower will require revolutionary changes,' she concludes, but such changes could humanize the university."
J

2485. Hughes, Chip. A NEW TWIST FOR TEXTILES. *Southern Exposure 1976 3(4): 73-79.* Labor organization and membership among employees of southern textile mills began to grow with the advent of civil rights legislation and the hiring of blacks; membership and pressure in the unions grew through the 1960's and promises to be a major point of contention for mill workers in the 1970's.

2486. Ichniowski, Casey. HAVE ANGELS DONE MORE? THE STEEL INDUSTRY CONSENT DECREE. *Industrial and Labor Relations Rev. 1983 36(2): 182-198.* Analyzes the consent decree of 1974 that reformed plant seniority systems in basic steel to resolve problems of equal employment opportunity. The major factors leading to the negotiation of this industrywide decree were the large number of plant-level suits being filed against the parties and the influence of the *Bethlehem Steel* decision of June 1971. The decree provided in part for the replacement of departmental seniority by plantwide seniority in most promotion, transfer, layoff, and recall decisions; the retention of pay rates after transfer to a position that provides a lower pay rate than the previous position; the establishment of goals for minority representation in skilled jobs; and a back-pay settlement. Minority representation in skilled jobs increased in the four-year period after the decree more rapidly than pre-1974 employment trends would have predicted; but in 1978, considerable underutilization of blacks in those jobs still existed.
J

2487. Iden, George. THE LABOR FORCE EXPERIENCE OF BLACK YOUTH: A REVIEW. *Monthly Labor Rev. 1980 103(8): 10-16.* The high unemployment rate among black male youths during the 1970's can be attributed to the job market and the minimum wage; discusses prospects based on actions taken in 1978 to alleviate the situation.

2488. Jenness, Linda. FEMINISM AND THE WOMAN WORKER. *Int. Socialist Rev. 1974 35(3): 4-7.* Statistical analysis of working women.

2489. Johnson, Beverly L. WOMEN WHO HEAD FAMILIES, 1970-77: THEIR NUMBERS ROSE, INCOME LAGGED. *Monthly Labor Rev. 1978 101(2): 32-37.* Between 1970 and 1977 there was a large increase in the number of American families in which women had the main economic and social responsibilities, but their incomes lagged behind those of other families, with the incidence of poverty especially high among black and Hispanic families.

2490. Johnson, William G. and Lambrinos, James. EMPLOYMENT DISCRIMINATION. *Society 1983 20(3): 47-50.* Discusses the effectiveness of current public policy regarding employment for the disabled, focusing on the Rehabilitation Act (US, 1973).

2491. Kane, Tim D. CHICANO EMPLOYMENT PATTERNS: AN ANALYSIS OF THE EFFECTS OF DECLINING ECONOMIC GROWTH RATES IN CONTEMPORARY AMERICA. *Aztlán 1979 10: 15-29.* Analyzes employment patterns for Chicanos from full employment in 1969 to severe recession in 1975. Real income of Chicano families declined, the recession forced Chicanos into employment with poorer wages and potential, and Chicanos failed to share in expected

relative wage increases. Mexican Americans were more adversely affected by the recession than were Anglo workers. 9 tables, 7 notes.
A. Hoffman

2492. Kelley, Maryellen R. DISCRIMINATION IN SENIORITY SYSTEMS: A CASE STUDY. *Industrial and Labor Relations Rev. 1982 36(1): 40-55.* According to the 1977 Supreme Court decision in *Teamsters* v. *United States,* seniority systems that have disparate impacts on women and black workers as compared to white men are not necessarily illegal. This paper uses a case study to examine what constitutes illegally discriminatory treatment in a seniority system in light of the *Teamsters* decision and subsequent rulings by federal courts. The empirical findings strongly suggest that as of 1976, at least with respect to promotions, the seniority system in the plant studied illegally discriminated against white women and black workers. J/S

2493. Kessler-Harris, Alice. WOMEN'S WAGE WORK AS MYTH AND HISTORY. *Labor Hist. 1978 19(2): 287-307.* A review article prompted by recent publications on women's wage work. Questions traditional assumptions about the determining influence of women's home and child care roles on their labor market behavior. The need now is to probe how labor market roles have reinforced the cultural patterns and values of sex role discrimination. 25 notes. L. L. Athey

2494. Kilson, Martin. THE BLACK BOURGEOISIE REVISITED: FROM E. FRANKLIN FRAZIER TO THE PRESENT. *Dissent 1983 30(1): 85-96.* The dramatic expansion of the black middle class since the publication of E. Franklin Frazier's *Black Bourgeoisie* (1957) is characterized by occupational differentiation and employment in national job markets.

2495. Krzykała, Franciszek. KSZTAŁTOWANIE SIĘ STOSUN-KÓW SPOŁECZNYCH, OCEN I KARIER ZAWODOWYCH PRA-COWNIKÓW ZATRUDNIONYCH W PRZEMYŚLE SAMOCHODOWYM USA NA PRZYKŁADZIE GENERAL MO-TORS I CHRYSLER CORPORATION W DETROIT (HAM-TRAMCK) W 1972 ROKU [Social relationships, assessments, and careers of US motor industry employees exemplified by the General Motors and Chrysler Corporations in Detroit (Hamtramck) in 1972]. *Przegląd Socjologiczny [Poland] 1977 29: 81-100.* Gives some results of three investigations of Detroit automobile companies: the conflicts between white workers and black ones in a given firm, the division of labor into "formal" and "informal," and employees' attitudes to technical and organizational innovations.

2496. Lattin, Patricia Hopkins. ACADEMIC WOMEN, AFFIRMA-TIVE ACTION, AND MID-AMERICA IN THE EIGHTIES. *Women's Studies Int. Forum 1983 6(2): 223-230.* Experience as an affirmative action official at a public university in the Midwest had led the author to believe that women in the academic world are much better off today than they were 10 years ago, but that problems still exist.

2497. Laudicina, Eleanor V. TOWARDS NEW FORMS OF LIBER-ATION: A MILDLY UTOPIAN PROPOSAL. *Social Theory and Practice 1973 2(3): 275-288.* Discusses recent trends and issues in the women's liberation movement, including occupational equality, sex roles, and child rearing responsibilities.

2498. Laws, Judith Long. WORK ASPIRATION OF WOMEN: FALSE LEADS AND NEW STARTS. *Signs 1976 1(3, Part 2): 33-49.* In contrast to much literature on the sociology of occupations, which has its roots in class centrism and sexism, the author shows work motivation as dynamic and responsive to events in the work life, with contemporaneous environment more important than static attributes of the individual. Focus on the work environment emphasizes opportunities and incentives available to working women and directs attention to positive and negative contacts with role partners to modify perceived possibilities and incentives. Women need better occupational maps and better occupational options. Based on secondary sources; 26 notes.
S. E. Kennedy

2499. Leavitt, Jacqueline. THE HISTORY, STATUS, AND CON-CERNS OF WOMEN PLANNERS. *Signs 1980 5(3): supplement 226-230.* The planning profession expanded radically during the 1950's and 1960's, but few women were included in that expansion because the

planning profession was sexually stereotyped as a male profession. Less than one year old, the American Planning Association's technical division on planning and women is now studying the relationship of women to issues of poverty, transportation, and the nonnuclear family. Based on reports of planning organizations and on secondary sources; 12 notes.
S. P. Conner

2500. Levinson, Richard M. SEX DISCRIMINATION AND EM-PLOYMENT PRACTICES: AN EXPERIMENT WITH UNCON-VENTIONAL JOB INQUIRIES. *Social Problems 1975 22(4): 533-543.* Examines discriminatory acts in occupational recruitment based on job inquiries in response to 256 different classified advertisements in Atlanta, Georgia. Discrimination by sex was found in more than one-third of the inquiries, with men experiencing greater discrimination. The sex of an individual is very important for jobs associated with women, and male callers are seen as deviant or abnormal for applying for such jobs. Notes, biblio.
A. M. Osur

2501. Li, Peter S. OCCUPATIONAL ACHIEVEMENT AND KIN-SHIP ASSISTANCE AMONG CHINESE IMMIGRANTS IN CHI-CAGO. *Sociol. Q. 1977 18(4): 478-489.* Building on the basic model of Blau and Duncan, this paper explores the process of stratification among Chinese immigrants in Chicago, and examines the effects of kinship assistance on the career cycle. It was found that while kinship assistance is an important resource to some immigrants during and after migration, it frequently obligates the immigrants to remain in the ethnic business, and thereby hinders their upward mobility. This study suggests the usefulness as well as the limitations of kinship assistance in the stratification process of ethnic minorities. J

2502. Lieberson, Stanley. A RECONSIDERATION OF THE IN-COME DIFFERENCES FOUND BETWEEN MIGRANTS AND NORTHERN-BORN BLACKS. *Am. J. of Sociol. 1978 83(4): 940-966.* Compares income differences between Northern-born and Northern-migrating Negroes, finding that educational attainment and original impetus of migration figure greatly in the success and tenacity of the two groups during the 1970's.

2503. Lingle, R. Christopher and Jones, Ethel B. WOMEN'S IN-CREASING UNEMPLOYMENT: A CROSS-SECTIONAL ANALY-SIS. *Am. Econ. Rev. 1978 68(2): 84-89.* Since 1945, female rates of unemployment have tended to exceed the male rates of joblessness. Due to marriage and children, women experience discontinuity in employment which tends to force downward their wages. Unfortunately there is a cyclical characteristic of women's unemployment behavior. Table, ref.
D. K. Pickens

2504. Livingston, Joy A. RESPONSES TO SEXUAL HARASS-MENT ON THE JOB: LEGAL, ORGANIZATIONAL, AND INDI-VIDUAL ACTIONS. *J. of Social Issues 1982 38(4): 5-22.* Remedial actions to curtail and prevent sexual harassment in the workplace have focused on providing victims with legal redress, establishing employers' responsibilities, and encouraging employees to resist harassment. First, the development of judicial and legal criteria defining harassment as illegal behavior and establishing parameters of employer responsibilities are reviewed. Then, the discussion examines actions employers have taken to meet their responsibilities (e.g., issuing policy statements). Secondary analyses of data collected from 3,139 women who reported experiences of sexual harassment are used to explore individual responses to harassment, and potential determinants of those responses. Finally, support services provided by women's organizations are discussed, and some conclusions are drawn about the impact of remedial actions on the prevention of sexual harassment on the job, 1974-81. J

2505. Lloyd, Cynthia B. and Niemi, Beth. SEX DIFFERENCES IN LABOR SUPPLY ELASTICITY: THE IMPLICATIONS OF SECTO-RAL SHIFTS IN DEMAND. *Am. Econ. Rev. 1978 68(2): 78-83.* Examines employment of women in the context of labor supply theory and the business cycle. Interestingly, in recent recessions, the number of women withdrawing from the labor market has declined. In the long run, the implications are not pleasant. For despite favorable growth in traditional female employment, the gap between women's part in total employment and what it would be if their numbers in all industries remained constant has increased in recent years. Tables, ref.

D. K. Pickens

2506. Loeb, Jane W.; Ferber, Marianne A.; and Lowry, Helen M. THE EFFECTIVENESS OF AFFIRMATIVE ACTION FOR WOMEN. *J. of Higher Educ. 1978 49(3): 218-230.* A comparison of salary and rank by sex at a major institution [the University of Illinois] before and after initiation of an approved affirmative action program suggests that required programs are more costly than effective. Rather than the current regulatory approach, federal incentives and greater attention to results than procedures are recommended.   J

2507. Long, James E. PRODUCTIVITY, EMPLOYMENT DISCRIMINATION, AND THE RELATIVE ECONOMIC STATUS OF SPANISH ORIGIN MALES. *Social Sci. Q. 1977 58(3): 357-373.* Concludes that both employment discrimination and low productivity have contributed to the inferior economic status of Spanish origin males compared with white males. The data also suggest that recent efforts to upgrade their economic status have not been very successful.   J

2508. Lyon, Larry and Abell, Troy. MALE ENTRY INTO THE LABOR FORCE: ESTIMATES OF OCCUPATIONAL REWARDS AND LABOR MARKET DISCRIMINATION. *Sociol. Q. 1980 21(1): 81-92.* Black male workers, while experiencing notable upward mobility, still remain far behind their white counterparts in income and prestige; draws from causal models developed from the National Longitudinal Surveys of Labor Market Experience of 1966 and 1971.

2509. Lyon, Larry; Abell, Troy; Jones, Elizabeth; and Rector-Owen, Holly. THE NATIONAL LONGITUDINAL SURVEYS DATA FOR LABOR MARKET ENTRY: EVALUATING THE SMALL EFFECTS OF RACIAL DISCRIMINATION AND THE LARGE EFFECTS OF SEXUAL DISCRIMINATION. *Social Problems 1982 29(5): 524-539.* A study that estimates the effects of racial and sexual discrimination on differences in income and prestige for people performing their first full-time job in the 1970's finds that traditional measures of discrimination are not useful, except to demonstrate that differences according to gender are considerable.

2510. Madden, Janice Fanning. WHY WOMEN WORK CLOSER TO HOME. *Urban Studies [Great Britain] 1981 18(2): 181-194.* Differences in work status, household composition, and household roles explain why women in the United States work closer to home. While sex differences in job tenure, work hours, and wages are in themselves sufficient to account fully for sex differences in the distance between workplace and residence, sex differences in household roles and responses to husbands' work patterns are of even greater importance in influencing women to work closer to home, 1976. Based on the 1976 Panel Survey of Income Dynamics; 5 tables, biblio., 23 notes.

D. J. Nicholls

2511. Malkiel, Burton G. and Malkiel, Judith A. MALE-FEMALE PAY DIFFERENTIALS IN PROFESSIONAL EMPLOYMENT. *Am. Econ. Rev. 1973 63(4): 693-705.* Analyzes salary differentials of professional employees of a single corporation to determine 1) if education, experience, and productivity explain the salary structure, and 2) if there is discrimination against women. Education, experience, and productivity variables do explain over three-fourths of the salary variance for both men and women. And, at equal job levels, with the same characteristics, men and women do get equal pay. But the answer is "No" to the question, "Do men and women, with equal characteristics, get equal pay?" The difference is explained by the fact that "women with the same training, experience, etc. as men tend to be assigned to lower job levels." There is no absence of discrimination, merely a different method by which it occurs. 7 tables, 12 notes.   C. W. Olson

2512. Marable, Manning. THE CRISIS OF THE BLACK WORKING CLASS: AN ECONOMIC AND HISTORICAL ANALYSIS. *Sci. & Soc. 1982 46(2): 130-161.* Massive black unemployment in the old-line industries and their preemption in the new growth industries are evidences of a profound crisis for black labor in America. 52 notes.

L. V. Eid

2513. Markusen, Ann R. CITY SPATIAL STRUCTURE, WOMEN'S HOUSEHOLD WORK, AND NATIONAL URBAN POLICY. *Signs*

1980 5(3): supplement 23-44. Of the two types of urban space, household reproduction of labor power is more complex and less understood than wage-labor production. The nuclear, patriarchal family type in the United States has defined most modern space utilization, but the household is not simply a "passive consumption unit." Because of that belief, however, women are caught in conflicting roles. Because the Carter administration policy is aimed at business incentives to change employment patterns, women will not be helped. Encouraging day-care facilities and discouraging discrimination must become the central aims of national urban policy. Secondary sources; table, 29 notes.

S. P. Conner

2514. Mbatia, O. L. E. THE ECONOMIC EFFECTS OF FAIR EMPLOYMENT LAWS ON OCCUPATIONS: THE APPLICATION OF INFORMATION THEORY TO EVALUATE PROGRESS OF BLACK AMERICANS, 1954-1972. *J. of Black Studies 1978 8(3): 259-278.* Uses patterns of occupational distribution to measure black Americans' economic progress during 1954-72. Concepts of information theory, especially indices of racial entropy and empirical regression analysis, are more useful in understanding minority employment patterns than are numbers or percentages of persons employed. Most Negroes remain in unskilled or semiskilled occupations, but they did make economic progress, 1954-72, decreasing their representation in unskilled jobs and increasing their share in professional and managerial occupations. Fair Employment Practices "laws have a long way to go before they can effectively deal with racist employment practices." Based on published government documents and secondary sources; 4 tables, 11 notes, biblio.   R. G. Sherer

2515. McDonagh, Eileen L. TO WORK OR NOT TO WORK: THE DIFFERENTIAL IMPACT OF ACHIEVED AND DERIVED STATUS UPON THE POLITICAL PARTICIPATION OF WOMEN, 1956-1976. *Am. J. of Pol. Sci. 1982 26(2): 280-297.* Measures of achieved status, based on the occupational prestige of one's own job and only applicable to employed men and women, and derived status, based on the occupational prestige of one's spouse's job and applicable to housewives, were used to examine the interaction effects of social status and employment. Results show that social status variables, rather than employment, are the important determinants for women's political participation.   J/S

2516. McKay, Roberta V. AMERICANS OF SPANISH ORIGIN IN THE LABOR FORCE: AN UPDATE. *Monthly Labor Rev. 1976 99(9): 3-6.* Analyzes unemployment of workers of Spanish origin and compares these to whites and blacks during the 1974-75 recessions.

2517. Mennerick, Lewis A. ORGANIZATIONAL STRUCTURING OF SEX ROLES IN A NONSTEREOTYPED INDUSTRY. *Administrative Sci. Q. 1975 20(4): 570-586.* Analyzes the sex structuring which occurs in the travel agency industry in New York City based on industry data for 1974, indicating that male agents tend to hold management positions and female agents tend to hold sales positions.

2518. Miller, Baila. MECHANISMS OF DISCRIMINATION. *Peace and Change 1980 6(3): 33-39.* Describes three social control mechanisms that are considered standard business practices that discriminate against women and minorities despite Civil Rights legislation passed in 1964: circumscribed recruitment procedures, arbitrary job qualifications, and work segregation patterns, based on 30 random cases heard by the Federal Court of Appeals between 1969 and 1975.

2519. Mills, Kay. FIGHTING SEXISM ON THE AIRWAVES. *J. of Communication 1974 24(2): 150-155.* Discusses sexism in public broadcasting, both in content and in employment practices, citing statistics and suggesting strategies for women to persuade the FCC and the National Association of Broadcasters to change their sexist policies.

2520. Mindiola, Tatcho. THE COST OF BEING A MEXICAN FEMALE WORKER IN THE 1970 HOUSTON LABOR MARKET. *Aztlán 1980 11(2): 231-247.* Statistical analysis of the employment discrimination experienced by Mexican women in Houston, Texas. The percent of discrimination was determined through measurement of the difference between Anglo male income and the income of Mexican female workers, along with the income of Anglo females, Mexican males, and black males and females, discounting differences due to education, age, marital status, and other background factors. A clear cut pattern of discrimination existed, with Mexican women encountering the most discrimination in sales occupations and the least in government employment. Census Bureau data and published studies; biblio.

A. Hoffman

2521. Mindiola, Tatcho, Jr. AGE AND INCOME DISCRIMINATION AGAINST MEXICAN AMERICANS AND BLACKS IN TEXAS, 1960 AND 1970. *Social Problems 1979 27(2): 196-208.* Estimates discrimination in income for Mexican Americans and Negroes in Texas in 1960 and 1970, showing that younger groups experienced less discrimination and that blacks suffered greater discrimination than Mexican Americans, but, while discrimination against blacks declined, that against Mexicans increased.

2522. Mogull, Robert G. UNEMPLOYMENT AMONG BLACKS. *Indiana Social Studies Q. 1972/73 25(3): 32-36.* A disproportionate share of total unemployment is experienced by the nonwhite sector of the labor force. Uses the terms Negro, black, and nonwhite interchangeably. Nonwhites account for a large share of the long-term and very long-term unemployed. Nonwhites suffer disproportionately from unemployment, part-time or underemployment, and hidden unemployment. Based on secondary sources; 6 tables, 4 notes.

M. L. Frey

2523. Moore, William J. THE IMPACT OF CHILDREN AND DISCRIMINATION ON THE HOURLY WAGE RATES OF BLACK AND WHITE WIVES. *Q. Rev. of Econ. and Business 1977 17(3): 43-64.* This article develops a postschooling investment model of human capital to isolate the influence of the number of children on the current wage rates of married women who work full time. Ordinary-least-squares regression analysis showed that the number of children had a small but significant negative influence on the earnings of married women with their spouses present, holding a number of other factors such as experience, education, race, and so on. Also, through decomposition analysis, it was found that the number of children depresses the wages of white married women more than black married women.

2524. Mosley, Myrtis Hall. BLACK WOMEN ADMINISTRATORS IN HIGHER EDUCATION: AN ENDANGERED SPECIES. *J. of Black Studies 1980 10(3): 295-310.* Questionnaires returned by 120 black women administrators in white higher education in 1975 revealed their bleak prospect. Only 5% had training in higher education or related fields. Their salaries were below those of black men, and white women and men. Neither the women's movement nor federal affirmative action programs have appreciably helped them in salary, promotion, or participation in policy formulation. Personal contact was more important than traditional advertising in their recruitment. Many felt conflict or competition with black men. Based on 120 questionnaires of black women administrators and other primary sources; fig., biblio.

R. G. Sherer

2525. Nanjundappa, G. OCCUPATIONAL DIFFERENTIALS AMONG BLACK MALE CROSS-REGIONAL MIGRANTS FROM AND TO THE SOUTH. *Phylon 1981 42(1): 52-59.* The 1967 Survey of Economic Opportunity of 1967 offers investigators a chance to study the occupational differentials among black male cross-regional migrants. Under study were men who either moved out of or into the South. More than two-thirds of those who moved out were semiskilled or unskilled blue collar workers or farmers. Less than one-third were highly skilled or white collar. As a whole, the South sustained a net loss of 878,000 workers.

A. G. Belles

2526. Neuse, Steven M. SEX EMPLOYMENT PATTERNS IN STATE GOVERNMENT. *State Government 1979 52(2): 52-57.* Examines eight Texas state agencies for employment patterns, job characteristics, and key job values; indicates that, despite legal and political pressures applied throughout the 1970's, women are still underrepresented in government.

2527. Ng, Wing-cheung. AN EVALUATION OF THE LABOR MARKET STATUS OF CHINESE AMERICANS. *Amerasia J. 1977 4(2): 101-122.* Investigation using the Dual Labor Market hypothesis shows that Chinese American males are split between the Primary Labor Market (marked by favorable wages, working conditions, job stability, etc.) and the Secondary Labor Market (which exhibits less desirable characteristics). Chinese American females mostly are confined to the Secondary Labor Market. Chinese Americans and white Americans differ significantly in occupation concentrations. The Double Labor Market hypothesis is not verified completely by this study, but "could be a useful conceptual framework" if revised to take into account the differing responses of different ethnic minorities to discrimination. 4 tables, 29 notes.

T. L. Powers

2528. Niemi, Albert W., Jr. SEXIST EARNINGS DIFFERENCES: THE COST OF FEMALE SEXUALITY. *Am. J. of Econ. and Sociol. 1977 36(1): 33-40.* Comparison of male and female earnings by education, race, sex and age during 1960-70 and analysis of the differences indicate that discrimination against women is very costly to females, White and Black, especially those with a college education.

J

2529. Niemi, Beth and Lloyd, Cynthia. SEX DIFFERENTIALS IN EARNINGS AND UNEMPLOYMENT RATES. *Feminist Studies 1975 2(2/3): 194-201.* Discusses the ways sex discrimination affects wage and unemployment differentials between women and men. "As female labor-force participation rises, the occupational segregation of women both depresses their relative wages and raises their unemployment rate." Table, 13 notes.

J. D. Falk

2530. Parham, T. D., Jr. BLACK JOB EXPECTATION: A COMPARATIVE ANALYSIS. *J. of Black Studies 1978 8(3): 299-307.* Advantaged, socially differentiated black communities such as Tuskegee (Alabama), Groveton (Virginia) and Durham (North Carolina) best provide data for "a favorable report on occupational opportunities for the emerging work force." In these cities, black high school seniors based their job preferences primarily on the extent to which jobs were open to them, but white high school seniors' job preferences were more closely related to their attitudes and values. This pattern was more pronounced in job expectation than in job aspiration. Blacks scoring low (whites, high) in humanitarianism expected to enter helpful and military occupations. Whites scoring low in humanitarianism preferred intrinsic reward jobs, low scoring blacks did not. Based on responses from 229 white, 412 black, 13 "other" students; 3 tables, note.

R. G. Sherer

2531. Parlin, Bradley W. IMMIGRANT, EMPLOYERS, AND EXCLUSION. *Society 1977 14(6): 23-26.* Discusses employment difficulties encountered by immigrants to the United States, especially their precarious legal standing, tendencies toward discrimination or exclusion, and their overall employability, 1960's-70's.

2532. Parsons, Donald O. RACIAL TRENDS IN MALE LABOR FORCE PARTICIPATION. *Am. Econ. Rev. 1980 70(5): 911-920.* In exploring the relationship between black and white male employment, the favorable benefits of Social Security, and the least favorable labor market opportunities, the result for blacks was 6.1% in 1958, to 16.6% in 1976, for an actual rate of increase in unemployment; for whites in those years, the figures rose from 3.4% to 7.5%. "The decline in labor force participation, particularly among blacks, is the result of increasingly attractive alternatives to work." 2 tables, fig., 10 notes, biblio.

D. K. Pickens

2533. Peake, Charles F. NEGRO OCCUPATION-EMPLOYMENT PARTICIPATION IN AMERICAN INDUSTRY: HISTORICAL PERSPECTIVE, IMPROVEMENTS DURING THE 1960'S, AND RECENT PLATEAUING. *Am. J. of Econ. and Sociol. 1975 34(1): 67-86.* Examines participation by Negroes in certain occupations and industries in the United States during 1920-70. Multiple regression analysis indicates that wages, labor turnover, and competition are important factors in influencing the ratios of Negro participation in different industries. Secondary sources; 4 tables, 28 notes.

W. L. Marr

2534. Porter, James N. RACE, SOCIALIZATION, AND MOBILITY IN EDUCATIONAL AND EARLY OCCUPATIONAL ATTAINMENT. *Am. Sociol. Rev. 1974 39(3): 303-316.* Social organizational and sociopsychological differences in the socialization of white and black men account for two separate systems of educational and occupational mobility.

2535. Poston, Dudley L., Jr.; Martin, Walter T.; and Goodman, Jerry D. EARNINGS DIFFERENCES BETWEEN OLD AND NEW U.S. IMMIGRANTS. *Pacific Sociol. Rev. 1982 25(1): 97-106.* Compares the economic position of recent immigrants to the United States from Asian and Latin American countries with that of immigrants from European nations; recent immigrants from the Third World generally earn less than European immigrants. Based on the 1970 Census.

2536. Poston, Dudley L., Jr. and Alvírez, David. ON THE COST OF BEING A MEXICAN AMERICAN WORKER. *Social Sci. Q. 1973 33(4): 697-709.* "Compares the incomes of Anglos with those of Mexican Americans among full-time male workers in the southwestern United States in 1960 .... more than half of the difference in average income relates to occupational and educational differences, but a substantial residual remains which is interpreted as resulting from minority status." J

2537. Rabkin, Peggy A. "AFFIRMATIVE ACTION AND REVERSE DISCRIMINATION: THE IMPLICATIONS OF HERBERT HILL'S *BLACK LABOR AND THE AMERICAN LEGAL SYSTEM,* AND WILLIAM B. GOULD'S *BLACK WORKERS IN WHITE UNIONS.*" *Afro-Americans in New York Life and Hist. 1979 3(2): 69-78.* Review article prompted by Herbert Hill's *Black Labor and the American Legal System* (Bureau of National Affairs, Inc., 1977) and William B. Gould's *Black Workers in White Unions* (Cornell U. Pr., 1977), which call into question the reasoning behind recent Supreme Court decisions on seniority disputes between management and black workers.

2538. Ramsbotham, Ann and Farmer, Pam. WOMEN WORKING: THE BUILDING TRADES BEGIN TO OPEN UP. *Southern Exposure 1980 8(1): 35-39.* Women have been unrepresented in many occupations, but it is the trades, including the building trades, from which they have been most consistently excluded. Women today still comprise only 3% of all skilled craft workers. In construction work they earn an average of 68% of the wages of their male counterparts. Those who succeed in entering the construction trades often face resistance, hostility, and harassment from those who feel that the jobs belong rightfully to men. Interviews with four women (a plumber, two carpenters, and an owner-secretary of a sheet metal business) demonstrate that women can make and take their place in the construction world as wage laborers, in a democratic collective, as owner-builders, as teachers, as bosses. Their experiences defy those who maintain that construction work cannot be done by women. 7 photos.
H. M. Parker, Jr.

2539. Raymond, Richard D. and Sesnowitz, Michael. LABOR MARKET DISCRIMINATION AGAINST MEXICAN AMERICAN COLLEGE GRADUATES. *Southern Econ. J. 1983 49(4): 1122-1136.* Surveying the 1975 wages of Mexican American graduates from the Pan American University, Rio Grande Valley, Texas, 1966-74, finds that there is more discrimination in the private than in the public sector (though real wages were higher), and that discrimination takes the form of lower salary increments, rather than lower starting salaries.

2540. Roach, Jack L. and Roach, Janet K. DISUNITY AND UNITY OF THE WORKING CLASS: REPLY TO PIVEN AND CLOWARD. *Social Problems 1979 26(3): 267-270.* Response to Frances Fox Piven and Richard A. Cloward's article (see entry in this bibliography). Describes the oppression and inequities suffered by US minority groups, chiefly blacks, since the 1950's, and how, in spite of gains in the past two decades, the gaps between minorities and organized labor appear to have widened, causing a weakening of their ability to force acceptance of separate demands.

2541. Robbins, Lynn A. NAVAJO LABOR AND THE ESTABLISHMENT OF A VOLUNTARY WORKERS ASSOCIATION. *J. of Ethnic Studies 1978 6(3): 97-112.* As a result of a series of actions initiated by Navajo workers in 1971 at the Navajo Project near Page, Arizona, rectifications of employment discrimination and irregularities in hiring and firing practices were effected. Associations between the Navajo Nation, international unions, and major contracting companies were altered, a factor which has become a landmark in Navajo labor relations and has had a profound effect on other tribes involved in major energy projects. Events of the past decade have seen Navajo worker

independence institutionalized in the Office of Navajo Labor Relations, and the one labor movement which had genuine grass-roots vitality has produced the Navajo Construction Workers Associations. From interviews of workers and union officials, Navajo Nation reports, and *The Navajo Times;* 5 notes, biblio.
G. J. Bobango

2542. Rogers, David L. and Goudy, Willis J. COMMUNITY STRUCTURE AND OCCUPATIONAL SEGREGATION 1960 AND 1970. *Rural Sociol. 1981 46(2): 263-281.* Examines the impact of community structure on occupational segregation according to sex between 1960 and 1970, focusing on the status of women in small communities, where the number of women employed has risen, although women remain concentrated in a small number of occupations due to economic factors and class structure.

2543. Rowbotham, Sheila. THE CARROT, THE STICK, AND THE MOVEMENT. *Radical Am. 1973 7(4/5): 73-79.* Deals with Women's Liberation and the search for adequate jobs and pay in a capitalistic society in the 1950's-60's. S

2544. Ryan, Vernon D. and Warland, Rex H. RACE AND THE EFFECT OF FAMILY STATUS AMONG MALE AGRICULTURAL LABORERS. *Rural Sociol. 1978 43(3): 335-347.* Questions Daniel P. Moynihan's 1965 thesis that low-income blacks experience high divorce rates due to the man's weakening position in the family as a result of his inability to provide economic security; Moynihan's study fails to consider other causes of high divorce rates.

2545. Safier, Gwendolyn. "I SENSED THE CHALLENGES" LEADERS AMONG CONTEMPORARY U.S. NURSES. *Oral Hist. Rev. 1975: 30-58.* Examines the changes in American nursing since World War II through interviews with 16 recognized leaders in the profession. Their comments expose the sexist basis of American life and the problems encountered by professional women before the feminist drive for equal rights. Illus., 43 notes.
D. A. Yanchisin

2546. Sánchez, Rosaura. THE CHICANA LABOR FORCE. Sánchez, Rosaura and Martinez Cruz, Rosa, eds. *Essays on la Mujer* (Los Angeles, Ca.: Chicano Studies Center Publ., 1977): 3-15. Emphasizes the importance of class differences among women when considering the interests and aims of Mexican Americans. The shift from rural areas to an urban environment in this century has changed important social characteristics of the Chicano family. Women are more likely to work outside the home and make contacts outside the family unit, but they are also freer to be exploited by employers. The majority of the 40% of Chicanas who are employed work in clerical jobs, as operatives, or in service occupations, and their average annual income was $2,682 in 1974 (the average income for white women was $6,770 that same year). The upward social mobility and the higher education of some Chicanas cannot erase their largely working class backgrounds and it is essential that these women "recognize the low economic status of the majority of Chicano women and identify with their struggle rather than with middle class feminist aspirations." Bureau of Census reports, newspaper articles, and secondary sources; 5 tables.
M. T. Wilson

2547. Sansbury, Gail Gregory. "NOW, GIRLS, WHAT'S THE MATTER WITH YOU GIRLS?": CLERICAL WORKERS ORGANIZE. *Radical Am. 1980 14(6): 67-75.* Clerical workers at the University of Rhode Island who had joined the American Federation of State, County and Municipal Employees felt they were not being adequately represented by the male-dominated state employees Council 22, shifted their affiliation to the National Education Association, and won a contract that improved their situation markedly. Details the particular circumstances and strategies, which make this a lesson for female-dominated collective bargaining units. The local union and the NEA became much more adept at small group meetings held at convenient times, and the workers had the advantage of typewriters, telephones, family connections, and somewhat flexible hours. Based on an oral history project at the University of Rhode Island; 2 illus., 2 notes.
C. M. Hough

2548. Santos, Richard. EARNINGS AMONG SPANISH-ORIGIN MALES IN THE MIDWEST. *Social Sci. J. 1982 19(2): 51-59.* Analyzes the incomes of Spanish-origin males in Illinois, Indiana, Michigan, Ohio, and Wisconsin, concluding that they earn approximately one-fifth less than a comparable group of white males.

2549. Sawhill, Isabel. DISCRIMINATION AND POVERTY AMONG WOMEN WHO HEAD FAMILIES. *Signs 1976 1(3, Part 2): 201-211.* Labor market discrimination by sex and race as well as occupational segregation contribute to the lack of income which characterizes families headed by women (which have grown at twice the rate of two-parent families in the past decade). Changes in attitudes regarding sex roles in families and end of racial discrimination would be helpful in alleviating this situation, but the elimination of sex discrimination alone would improve the economic status of these women and their families. Based on government census documents, published official statistics, and secondary sources; 3 tables, 22 notes.   S. E. Kennedy

2550. Sawyer, Jack and Senn, David J. INSTITUTIONAL RACISM AND THE AMERICAN PSYCHOLOGICAL ASSOCIATION. *J. of Social Issues 1973 29(1): 67-80.* "Institutional racism—institutional practice that perpetuates racial inequality—does not require individual prejudice or institutional intent, but is a by-product of business as usual. Psychologists for Social Action showed how APA practices institutional racism by condoning employment practices of Lancaster Press, APA's major printer. In May 1969, the Press employed one black person ('wash-up man') out of 300 employees, though Lancaster's 63,000 population included over 15 percent blacks and Puerto Ricans. Both the Press and the APA Central Office attributed this to low educational level. The authors met with representatives of Lancaster minority communities and together with them influenced the Press to hire 9 black persons out of 18 new employees between October 1, 1969 and September 30, 1970. A May 1973 postscript documents APA's continued hesitancy to influence its suppliers toward equal employment practices. [One of seven articles in this issue on 'The White Researcher in Black Society.'].''   J

2551. Schlein, Lisa. LOS ANGELES GARMENT DISTRICT SEWS A CLOAK OF SHAME. Mora, Magdalena and DelCastillo, Adelaida R., ed. *Mexican Women in the United States: Struggles Past and Present* (Los Angeles: U. of California Chicano Studies Res. Center, 1980): 113-116. Focuses on the exploitation of workers, the majority of which are Spanish-speaking women. Labor code violations, dispersion of production processes, and runaway shops enhance their exploitability and frustrate efforts to organize them.   J. Powell

2552. Schneider, Beth E. CONSCIOUSNESS ABOUT SEXUAL HARASSMENT AMONG HETEROSEXUAL AND LESBIAN WOMEN WORKERS. *J. of Social Issues 1982 28(4): 75-97.* Discusses the ways in which a woman's sexual identity affects her experiences and interpretation of interactions at work as sexual harassment. Finds that women have a great many physical and sexual experiences at work most of which they dislike; there is substantial recognition of the problem among working women. However, there is a gap between experiencing and disliking the phenomenon and applying the term sexual harassment in describing it. Further, women vary in the use of the label sexual harassment by the degree of social and economic inequality and powerlessness each experiences at her workplace; as a group, lesbians are more likely than heterosexuals to employ the terms. Covers 1972-82.   J/S

2553. Schreiber, Mark E. CIVIL LIBERTIES IN THE GREEN MACHINE. *Civil Liberties Rev. 1976 3(2): 34-47.* Discusses civil rights issues in the military, especially discrimination against Negroes in terms of housing, jobs, and promotions, and discrimination against women, especially those who have children.

2554. Schwartz, Harvey. A UNION COMBATS RACISM: THE ILWU'S JAPANESE-AMERICAN "STOCKTON" INCIDENT OF 1945. *Southern California Q. 1980 62(2): 161-176.* Describes how the leaders of the International Longshoremen's and Warehousemen's Union responded to the refusal of its Local 6 Stockton Unit to work with a Japanese American in May 1945. The ILWU had taken a strong position against discrimination. When unit leaders refused to affirm the ILWU's constitutional stand forbidding discrimination, they were suspended. Hearings were held and the unit leaders were expelled from the local. The ILWU's swift response to the challenge demonstrated to its multiracial Hawaiian local that the union's position was consistent and honorable, despite the incident in California. Photos, 41 notes.   A. Hoffman

2555. Sexton, Patricia Cayo. WORKERS (FEMALE) ARISE! *Dissent 1974 21(3): 380-396.* Discusses sex discrimination and the need for women to form labor organizations in the 1970's.

2556. Shannon, Lyle W. MEASURING CHANGES IN OCCUPATION AND INCOME: SOME PROBLEMS WITH A COHORT OF MEXICAN-AMERICANS, NEGROES AND ANGLOS. *Pacific Sociol. R. 1976 19(1): 3-19.* Compares occupational mobility of Mexican Americans, Negroes, and Anglos in the 1960's and 70's.

2557. Shover, Michele. MARRIED ACADEMIC WOMEN: "GO TO THE END OF THE LINE." *Frontiers 1978 3(1): 56-61.* Discusses employment discrimination of married women in higher education and the importance of having women as role models and intellectuals in the academic environment.

2558. Siu, Bobby. UNDEREMPLOYMENT OF INDOCHINESE REFUGEES: U.S.A. AND CANADA. Adelman, Howard, ed. *The Indochinese Refugee Movement: The Canadian Experience* (Toronto: Operation Lifeline, 1980): 147-150. Underemployment, poor wages, and improper use of professional and technical skills plagues Indochinese refugees, but while older refugees find the economic situation difficult to accept, younger ones assume that suffering now will bring prosperity later; 1970's.

2559. Small, Sylvia. BLACK WORKERS IN LABOR UNIONS: A LITTLE LESS SEPARATE, A LITTLE MORE EQUAL. *Ethnicity 1976 3(2): 174-196.* Despite complaints of unequal treatment, especially in admission to unions, Labor Bureau statistics show that representative proportions of both blacks and whites are found in labor organizations, as of March 1971. Comparative analysis of statistics shows that there is still disparity in job functions and to some extent in pay, but that overall, wages for blacks who are union members are higher (for both males and females) than for nonunion blacks. Concludes that wage parity can best be accomplished through black participation in labor unions, which explains continued black membership.   G. A. Hewlett

2560. Smith, Catherine Begnoche. INFLUENCE OF INTERNAL OPPORTUNITY STRUCTURE AND SEX OF WORKER ON TURNOVER PATTERNS. *Administrative Sci. Q. 1979 24(3): 362-381.* Examines the impact of structural limits on advancement opportunity and worker characteristics on the quitting and replacement rate in a state civil service organization; 1969-77.

2561. Smith, Elsie J. THE CAREER DEVELOPMENT OF YOUNG BLACK FEMALES: THE FORGOTTEN GROUP. *Youth & Soc. 1981 12(3): 277-312.* A review of the scanty literature on black female career development shows conflicting results. Black adolescents and college women show little awareness of occupational opportunities, choosing sex-role stereotyped careers. They seem to have no higher aspirations than white women of the same age, and seem no more socialized for higher job and educational aspirations than black men. Since the mid-1960's, education and career aspirations of Southern black women seem to have declined. Biblio.   J. H. Sweetland

2562. Smith, Elsie J. REGIONAL ORIGIN AND MIGRATION: IMPACT ON BLACK WORKERS. *J. of Black Studies 1978 8(3): 309-320.* Studies of American urban racial problems have blamed black unemployment and low income on the migration of poorly educated Negroes from the South. Most studies during 1967-73, which specifically compare poorly educated black migrants with resident blacks, show that migrants have higher levels of income and employment, although second- and third-generation migrants tend to decline economically. More studies are needed of the regional origin and migrational history of black workers. This research should develop a conceptual framework, such as reference group theory, for analyzing the relationships among migration, education, and employment. Based on published government documents and secondary sources; biblio.   R. G. Sherer

2563. Smith, James P. THE IMPROVING ECONOMIC STATUS OF BLACK AMERICANS. *Am. Econ. Rev. 1978 68(2): 171-177.* Using cohort convergence, regression results, and the vintage hypothesis, argues that because younger blacks are more similar to whites in marketable skills, these blacks therefore are not located in careers with

little growth potential. Their status has greatly improved. Tables, ref.
D. K. Pickens

2564. Snyder, David; Hayward, Mark D.; and Hudis, Paula M. THE LOCATION OF CHANGE IN THE SEXUAL STRUCTURE OF OCCUPATIONS, 1950-1970: INSIGHTS FROM LABOR MARKET SEGMENTATION THEORY. *Am. J. of Sociol. 1978 84(3): 706-717.* Analyzes trends in sex discrimination in the US labor market during 1950-70.

2565. Steele, James. BLACK YOUTH: WHAT DOES THE BICENTENNIAL OFFER? *Freedomways 1975 15(3): 171-177.* Calls for a youth movement of Negroes to fight for jobs and rights denied them.

2566. Stevenson, Mary. WOMEN'S WAGES AND JOB SEGREGATION. *Pol. and Soc. 1973 4(1): 83-96.* Charges that economic discrimination may be the direct product of sex discrimination in the occupational structure and asserts that economists have been remiss in examining the female worker in her economic role. Central to the examination of this charge are the ambiguities that exist in the division of labor by sex which have been further confounded by technological advancements. Suggests an alternative way of classifying occupations that avoids prior shortcomings and which provides an index of discrimination on the basis of sex. Secondary sources; table, 28 notes.
D. G. Nielson

2567. Strauss, Robert P. and Horvath, Francis W. WAGE RATE DIFFERENCES BY RACE AND SEX IN THE US LABOUR MARKET: 1960-1970. *Economica [Great Britain] 1976 43(171): 287-298.* Analyzes wage rate discrimination between blacks and whites and men and women in the United States, using data for 1960, 1967, and 1970. Describes measurement problems in testing for such discrimination when using Census data, analyzes problems when inferring discriminations with various statistical models, and presents tested results. These show that if industry and occupation are properly stratified for estimating purposes, and analysis made with each homogeneous group, in the majority of groups "blacks earn the same as whites, work as many weeks and earn the same hourly rate . . . observed differences by race may be due primarily to adverse employment distributions." For women, however, wage rate discrimination is still prevalent. 5 tables, ref.
D. H. Murdoch

2568. Szafran, Robert F. WHAT KINDS OF FIRMS HIRE AND PROMOTE WOMEN AND BLACKS? A REVIEW OF THE LITERATURE. *Sociol. Q. 1982 23(2): 171-190.* Covers 1967-80.

2569. Szymanski, Albert. THE GROWING ROLE OF SPANISH SPEAKING WORKERS IN THE U.S. ECONOMY. *Aztlán 1978 9: 177-208.* Examines and sustains the Marxist theory that capitalism's need of an exploitable group of laborers to do dirty work causes the oppression of national minorities. A new wave of predominantly Latin American immigrants is entering the market with this function, thereby displacing the blacks, who, in turn, are advancing economically and socially. Based primarily on statistics provided by the US Census; 20 tables, 9 notes, biblio.
R. V. Ritter

2570. Szymanski, Albert. RACIAL DISCRIMINATION AND WHITE GAIN. *Am. Sociol. Rev. 1976 41(3): 403-414.* The question of whether or not whites gain economically from economic discrimination against third world people is examined with evidence from the 1970 U.S. census. The impact of racial discrimination is measured by the percentage of the population of third world origin in each state and by the ratio of black to white male earnings for those who work full time. White gain is measured by the level of white male earnings in each state and the Gini coefficient of earnings inequality among white males. If whites gain economically from racism, we would expect to find that the greater the percentage of the population of a state that is third world and the lower the ratio of black/white earnings then the higher the level of white earnings and the less the inequality in white earnings. The basic relationships were examined controlling for percentage of the population that is urban, percentage of the economically active population in manufacturing, level of personal income, region and percentage of the population that is third world. It is found that whites do *not* gain from economic discrimination; on the contrary, white working people actually lose economically from such discrimination. It is argued that racism is a divisive force which undermines the economic and political strength of working people and acts to worsen the economic position of white workers in the most racist areas. In support of this interpretation, data on the strength of unions is examined.
J

2571. Szymanski, Albert. RACISM AND SEXISM AS FUNCTIONAL SUBSTITUTES IN THE LABOR MARKET. *Sociol. Q. 1976 17(1): 65-73.* The returns from the 1970 U.S. census are used to examine whether racial and sexual discrimination tend to vary together or whether they are functional substitutes for one another in the labor market, i.e., whether they operate in the same manner to produce the same results. The impact of racial discrimination is measured by both the percentage of the population of a state that is of third world origin and the ratio of black to white male annual earnings. Sexual discrimination is measured by the ratio of white female to white male earnings and urban female to urban male earnings. The values of each of these indicators is compared for the 50 U.S. states. The effect of the percentage of the population that is urban, the percentage of the economically active population in manufacturing, the level of personal income, region, and percentage of the population that is third world is controlled for. The results show that sexual discrimination can be seen as a functional substitute for racial discrimination in the labor market. Where racial discrimination is the most significant, sexual discrimination is the least. This supports the argument that the capitalist economic system needs a specially oppressed group of menial laborers to perform its most menial and low-paying tasks. Either white women or third world people (men and women) can fill these jobs. When third world people are available, white working women do not have to be pressed into them to the same extent. However, when third world people are not present, or are not especially discriminated against, then white working women tend more to perform the "dirty work" jobs and are consequently less likely to be found in the "better" jobs.
J

2572. Taylor, Daniel E. EDUCATION, ON-THE-JOB TRAINING, AND THE BLACK-WHITE PAY GAP. *Monthly Labor Rev. 1981 104(4): 28-34.* While the incomes of black men have increased faster than those of white men, blacks still earn less than whites, but their monetary returns for each year of education are as high as those for white men, although on-the-job training does not pay off as well for blacks.

2573. Thomas, Gail E. and Scott, Will B. BLACK YOUTH AND THE LABOR MARKET: THE UNEMPLOYMENT DILEMMA. *Youth and Soc. 1979 11(2): 163-189.* Regardless of educational level, black youth have consistently higher unemployment rates than whites. The human capital thesis, assuming that such differences are due to differences in value to employer, was the basis of Lyndon Johnson's Great Society programs of education. More recent explanations based on Karl Marx or the dual market thesis refer to membership in an exploited group. The problem can only be eliminated by improving social networks and developing sponsorship groups for blacks, thus changing the structure of the labor market. Based on secondary sources, especially the work of R. H. Turner; 3 tables, note, biblio.
J. H. Sweetland

2574. Thompson, Frank J. BUREAUCRATIC RESPONSIVENESS IN THE CITIES: THE PROBLEM OF MINORITY HIRING. *Urban Affairs Q. 1974 10(1): 40-68.* Summarizes minority hiring practices of the Oakland, California city government. Department and personnel officials faced federal and minority pressures to hire more minority workers. Job opportunity publicity was altered to attract more minority applicants. More minority candidates responded than before, but did not gain employment, because they failed written tests. 2 tables, notes, biblio.
P. J. Woehrmann

2575. Thompson, Frank J. CIVIL SERVANTS AND THE DEPRIVED: SOCIO-POLITICAL AND OCCUPATIONAL EXPLANATIONS OF ATTITUDES TOWARD MINORITY HIRING. *Am. J. of Pol. Sci. 1978 22(2): 325-347.* This essay focuses on the attitudes of public administrators toward one politically important issue, minority hiring. The central hypothesis is that the receptivity of civil servants to hiring minorities will be more a function of their occupational concerns and of certain of their socio-political characteristics than of their perceptions of public sentiment and external group pressure. The data provide some support for this hypothesis and thereby raise an important question. Since the sampled administrators do not adjust their attitudes toward minority hiring in response to what groups outside the bureaucracy want, what, if anything, prevents these officials from acting in ways which provoke tension between government agencies and segments of society? The author considers some implications of the data for an answer to this question.   J

2576. Thurow, Lester. NOT MAKING IT IN AMERICA: THE ECONOMIC PROGRESS OF MINORITY GROUPS. *Social Policy 1976 6(5): 5-11.* Discusses unemployment and incomes of minorities, particularly Negroes, in the 1960's and 70's.

2577. Tienda, Marta. NATIONALITY AND INCOME ATTAINMENT AMONG NATIVE AND IMMIGRANT HISPANIC MEN IN THE UNITED STATES. *Sociol. Q. 1983 24(2): 253-272.* Data from 1976 indicate that Hispanics earned less than whites, partly due to discrimination, and that the presence of too many other Hispanics in an area diluted earning power.

2578. Tolchin, Susan. THE EXCLUSION OF WOMEN FROM THE JUDICIAL PROCESS. *Signs 1977 2(4): 877-887.* Inequity in appointments of women to the judiciary remains a fact, but the increase in the number of female law students and the greater percentage of lawyers entering politics may herald an increase of women as judges.

2579. Tomkins, Adrienne. SEX DISCRIMINATION: ADRIENNE TOMKINS, STENOGRAPHER. *Civil Liberties Rev. 1978 5(3): 19-23.* Adrienne Tomkins, stenographer for Public Service Electric and Gas Co. in New Jersey since 1971, describes her successful protest against sexual harassment by her supervisor.

2580. Tsonc, Peter Z. W. CHANGING PATTERNS OF LABOR FORCE PARTICIPATION RATES OF NONWHITES IN THE SOUTH. *Phylon 1974 35(3): 301-312.* Many significant changes have taken place recently in the population of the labor force by age, sex, and color in the South. For example, the proportion of young people in the labor force in the South declined in various sex-color groups. Among males, the proportion of old people declined as well. Only the young were smaller proportions of the labor force among white and nonwhite females. Other age groups assumed larger proportions. By 1970 the South was less dependent than previously on nonwhite men, young and old white males, and young nonwhite females. Based on primary sources; 4 tables, 4 graphs.   B. A. Glasrud

2581. Vail, David. WOMEN AND SMALL FARM REVIVAL: THE DIVISION OF LABOR AND DECISION-MAKING ON MAINE'S ORGANIC FARMS. *Rev. of Radical Pol. Econ. 1982 13(4): 19-32.* Evidence from a survey of small commercial organic farms suggests that most women face a double, and some a triple, burden of farm, household, and off-farm labor. This suggests that farms in the new agrarian movement are likely to end or transform traditional male domination that characterizes both capitalism and petty commodity production. 9 tables, 55 ref., 17 notes.   D. R. Stevenson

2582. Villemez, Wayne J. and Wiswell, Candace Hinson. THE IMPACT OF DIMINISHING DISCRIMINATION ON THE INTERNAL SIZE DISTRIBUTION OF BLACK INCOME: 1954-74. *Social Forces 1978 56(4): 1019-1034.* A number of studies have sought to ascertain the scope of black economic gains in the last two decades. The extent of these gains is still under debate, but observers agree that some gains have been made. The locus of these gains in the black sector has not been adequately demonstrated. This paper examines income data for males from 1954-74 to determine the pattern of reduction in black-white inequality and the concomitant variation of those reductions with changes in the size distribution of black income. Findings show that, in the industrial non-South, decreasing black-white inequality has been accompanied by increasing inequality among blacks, and there are indications that most black economic gains have occurred at the top of the black distribution. The data argue against the possibility of long-range improvements in the coeconomic status of blacks as a group. The theoretical and policy implications of these findings are discussed.   J

2583. Weir, Angela and Wilson, Elisabeth. WOMEN'S LABOR, WOMEN'S DISCONTENT. *Radical Am. 1973 7(4/5): 80-94.* A discussion of Selma James' pamphlet *Women, the Unions and Work, or What is Not to be Done* involves an analysis of the "social formations

which produce the conditions of capitalism" at a particular time (1972-73), and the "particular contradictions of capitalism."   S

2584. Welch, Finis. BLACK-WHITE DIFFERENCES IN RETURNS TO SCHOOLING. *Am. Econ. Rev. 1973 63(5): 893-907.* Attempts to identify some of the components responsible for the rapid rise of income for blacks in the United States during 1959-66. In 1959 white high school graduates worked 15-20% more weeks than blacks; this figure had fallen to 2% by 1966. The tight labor market explains this. The school completion level (up 9.2% for blacks while up only 0.2% for whites with 13-25 years work experience) coupled with the quality of education received are vastly different from earlier periods. Finally, and data cannot identify this, there is the downward drift in market discrimination. 7 tables, 10 notes.   C. W. Olson

2585. Welch, Susan. RECRUITMENT OF WOMEN TO PUBLIC OFFICE: A DISCRIMINANT ANALYSIS. *Western Pol. Q. 1978 31(3): 372-380.* This paper tests the proposition that an important reason for female exclusion from public office is their severe underrepresentation in the "eligible pool" of the population from which candidates for public office are drawn. This eligible pool is determined on the basis primarily of educational and occupational status. The proposition is tested using data from the population and the legislature of twelve midwestern states. Discriminant analysis is utilized to predict female legislative membership in state legislatures on the basis of factors found to be important in predicting male membership. A very substantial proportion of the difference between actual female membership and that predicted by female proportions in the population can be explained by this eligible pool proposition.   J

2586. Westcott, Diane Nilsen. BLACKS IN THE 1970'S: DID THEY SCALE THE JOB LADDER? *Monthly Labor Rev. 1982 105(6): 29-38.* Employment gains for Negroes during the 1970's increased slowly due to three recessions, as opposed to rapid gains during the 1960's caused by social change and favorable economic conditions; focuses on the sharp gains for blacks in professional and technical, managerial and administrative, sales, and clerical occupations; although they did not get the higher salary white-collar positions, they made gains in higher salary blue-collar positions.

2587. Whalen, Eileen and Lawrence, Ken. AMERICAN WORKERS AND LIBERATION STRUGGLES IN SOUTHERN AFRICA: THE BOYCOTT OF COAL AND CHROME. *Radical Am. 1975 9(3): 1-16.* Discusses the need for labor reform in the 1960's and 1970's and calls for solidarity of black workers through economic boycotts to rid the United Mine Workers of America of racism and to promote anti-imperialism in Southern Africa.

2588. Williamson, Jane. THE STRUGGLE AGAINST SEX DISCRIMINATION. *Wilson Lib. Bull. 1982 57(4): 304-307.* Discusses federal legislation and test cases during 1963-81 protecting working women from unfair treatment because of their gender.

2589. Wright, Erik Olin. RACE, CLASS AND INCOME INEQUALITY. *Am. J. of Sociol. 1978 83(6): 1368-1397.* Discusses the idea that class, based on the Marxist definition, and race differences are related to income returns to education.

2590. Wright, James R. AFFIRMATIVE ACTION: A PLAN FOR AMERICA. *Freedomways 1977 17(1): 30-34.* Discusses affirmative action needs in the realm of employment for women and minorities, 1970's.

2591. —. [DIFFERENTIATING BETWEEN THE LIVING STANDARDS OF HUSBANDS AND WIVES IN TWO-WAGE-EARNER FAMILIES, 1968 AND 1979]. *J. of Econ. Hist. 1983 43(1): 231-242.*

Spalter-Roth, Roberta M. DIFFERENTIATING BETWEEN THE LIVING STANDARDS OF HUSBANDS AND WIVES IN TWO-WAGE-EARNER FAMILIES, 1968 AND 1979, *pp. 231-240*. Applies a feminist analysis to the measurement of living standards during the 1970's. Widely made assumptions of homogeneous pooling and redistribution of income, labor, and expenditures within families mask inequalities and uneven changes in the living standards of wage-working husbands and wives. Findings show differential living standards between husbands and wives when assumptions of homogeneous pooling and redistribution are not made. The suggested rough indicators are useful for the measurement of living standards.
Cain, Louis P. DISCUSSION, *pp. 241-242*.   J/S

2592. —. [DISCRIMINATION AGAINST WOMEN]. *Am. J. of Econ. and Sociol. 1979 38(3): 287-292.*
Davis, J. C. and Hubbard, Carl M. ON THE MEASUREMENT OF DISCRIMINATION AGAINST WOMEN, *pp. 287-291*. Socioeconomic *measurements* implicitly invite individuals and governments to base decisions on them. We attempt to show that estimates of *discrimination* represent poor guides to decision-making when discrimination is defined too broadly, when *earnings differentials* are not properly adjusted for changes in relative *productivity,* and when the *present-value method* used is not well-suited to the problem.
Niemi, Albert W., Jr. DISCRIMINATION AGAINST WOMEN RECONSIDERED, *pp. 291-292*. Sexist *earnings* differences must not be confused with *wage discrimination;* wage discrimination against females is only one source of the large sexist earnings gap. The author agrees that his calculations of adjusted *earnings ratios* do not capture all changes in relative *productivity* between *male* and *female workers* . His *present value estimates* compared male and female earnings during entire productive lives, from labor market entrance to retirement. Hence they do reflect earnings variations at all age levels and thus the average experience of females with comparable educational attainment.   J

2593. —. [EFFECTS OF CHILD-CARE PROGRAMS ON WOMEN'S WORK EFFORT]. *J. of Pol. Econ. 1974 82(2, part II): 136-169.*
Heckman, James J. EFFECTS OF CHILD-CARE PROGRAMS ON WOMEN'S WORK EFFORT, pp. 136-163.
Rosen, Sherwin. COMMENT, pp. 164-169.

Economics and Statistics of Labor

2594. Alba, Francisco. INDUSTRIALIZACIÓN SUSTITUTIVA Y MIGRACIÓN INTERNACIONAL: EL CASO DE MÉXICO [Import substitution industrialization and international migration: the Mexican case]. *Foro Int. [Mexico] 1978 18(3): 464-479*. Migration of Mexican labor to the United States is a function of Mexican imports substitution industrialization, concomitant structural unemployment, and a reflection of the general world trend of labor moving from the periphery to centers of growth. Based on newspaper articles and secondary sources; 31 notes.   D. A. Franz

2595. Aldrich, Howard and Weiss, Jane. DIFFERENTIATION WITHIN THE UNITED STATES CAPITALIST CLASS: WORKFORCE SIZE AND INCOME DIFFERENCES. *Am. Sociol. Rev. 1981 46(3): 279-290*. A particularly important source of differentiation in the capitalist class is the amount of economic resources capitalists control, especially the number of workers they employ. Workforce size is a major dimension of stratification within the business population and in the capitalist class. Analysis of income determination among 468 small business owners demonstrates the usefulness of a continuous rather than a categorical conceptualization of fractions within the capitalist class. Workforce size is a more powerful predictor of income than other variables traditionally used in studies of economic inequality.   J

2596. Alterman, Jack. THE UNITED STATES ECONOMY IN 1985: AN OVERVIEW OF BLS PROJECTIONS. *Monthly Labor Rev. 1973 96(12): 3-7*. Discusses current Bureau of Labor Statistics projections of economic trends for 1985, including work hours, gross national product, and size of the labor force.

2597. Alves, Wayne M. and Rossi, Peter H. WHO SHOULD GET WHAT? FAIRNESS JUDGMENTS OF THE DISTRIBUTION OF EARNINGS. *Am. J. of Sociol. 1978 84(3): 541-564.*

2598. Annable, James E., Jr. and Fruitman, Frederick H. AN EARNINGS FUNCTION FOR HIGH-LEVEL MANPOWER. *Industrial and Labor Relations Rev. 1973 26(4): 1107-1121*. "This paper develops an analytical framework to explain interpersonal variations in income, resulting in an equilibrium model allowing only for differences in worker quality and nonpecuniary conditions of employment, and a disequilibrium model that also allows for market lags and imperfections. The authors then test their models, using data collected in a detailed survey of over 1,300 alumni of the Massachusetts Institute of Technology. The disequilibrium model proves to have more explanatory power than the equilibrium earnings function, as many of the forty-two variables tested show significant relationships."   J

2599. Armknecht, Paul A., Jr. JOB VACANCIES IN MANUFACTURING, 1969-73. *Monthly Labor Rev. 1974 97(8): 27-33*. The job vacancy survey program of 1969-73 in the United States, while an imperfect measure of unmet labor demand, held its own as an economic indicator.

2600. Ascheim, Joseph. PRICE-LEVEL STABILITY AT FULL EMPLOYMENT: RECENT AMERICAN EXPERIENCE. *Oxford Econ. Papers [Great Britain] 1955 7(3): 265-271*. In the years following World War II, especially during 1951-53, the United States enjoyed a combination of stability in prices and high-level employment.

2601. Babeau, André. LE RAPPORT MACRO-ECONOMIQUE DU PATRIMOINE AU REVENU DES MENAGES [The macroeconomic wealth-income ration of households]. *Rev. Econ. [France] 1983 34(1): 64-123*. Provides a simple formula expressing the wealth-income ratio as a function of factors such as indebtment behavior and influence of inflation on the variation of nominal income and on capital gains. Shows, using data from France and the United States, that the provided relationship is a useful tool for analyzing the observed evolution of the ratio.   J/S

2602. Barrett, Nancy S.; Gerardi, Geraldine; and Hart, Thomas P. A FACTOR ANALYSIS OF QUARTERLY PRICE AND WAGE BEHAVIOR FOR U.S. MANUFACTURING. *Q. J. of Econ. 1974 88(3): 385-408*. Identifies the main economic variables associated with movements of quarterly price and wage statistics for US manufacturing.   S

2603. Barsky, C. B. and Personick, M. E. MEASURING WAGE DISPERSION: PAY RANGES REFLECT INDUSTRY TRAITS. *Monthly Labor Rev. 1981 104(4): 35-41*. Attributes differences in wage dispersions among industries to characteristics such as degree of unionization, geographic location, occupational mix, and methods of wage payment: greatest wage dispersion occurs in industries with broad occupational staffing or with much incentive pay; high-paying industries, often heavily unionized, show less variation in earnings and a penchant for single job rates.

2604. Bednarzik, Robert W.; Hewson, Marillyn A.; and Urquhart, Michael A. THE EMPLOYMENT SITUATION IN 1981: NEW RECESSION TAKES ITS TOLL. *Monthly Labor Rev. 1982 105(3): 3-14*. Presents statistics showing the 1981 recession's negative effects on employment, the housing and automobile industries, and related industries.

2605. Bednarzik, Robert W. INVOLUNTARY PART-TIME WORK AND EDUCATIONAL ATTAINMENT. *J. of General Educ. 1976 28(2): 135-143*. An analysis of the distribution of involuntary part-time work reveals that its incidence varies inversely with educational attainment. Since 1968 involuntary part-time employment has increased among higher-educated members of the labor force due to the search for "least-cost" employees and to the upgrading of the workforce faster than appropriate employment opportunities are created. However, once a job is obtained, educational qualifications decrease the chances of a reduced workweek. Based on secondary sources; 13 notes.   N. A. Williamson

2606. Bednarzik, Robert W. LAYOFFS AND PERMANENT JOB LOSSES: WORKERS' TRAITS AND CYCLICAL PATTERNS. *Monthly Labor Rev. 1983 106(9): 3-12.* Unemployment and rehiring data taken from 1968-82 indicate that among those laid off but not terminated, only those looking for work and without a recall date should be considered unemployed.

2607. Bell, Donald and Wiatrowski, William. DISABILITY BENE-FITS FOR EMPLOYEES IN PRIVATE PENSION PLANS. *Monthly Labor Rev. 1982 105(8): 36-40.* A 1980 survey from the Bureau of Labor Statistics indicates a high incidence of pension plans in medium and large private sector establishments containing disability retirement features; analyzes the eligibility requirements and typical benefits in these plans.

2608. Bender, Lloyd D. and Parcels, Larry C. STRUCTURAL DIFFERENCES AND THE TIME PATTERN OF BASIC EMPLOY-MENT. *Land Econ. 1983 59(2): 220-234.* Uses data from 345 rural counties, 1962-67, to construct a regression model that attempts to explain the changes in employment and population in rural areas. Finds that rural areas can absorb rather large employment increases without a population increase and that previous economic growth or decline will influence the impact of current employment changes. Based on second-ary sources; 3 fig., 4 tables, 9 notes, 19 ref.   E. S. Johnson

2609. Betsey, Charles L. DIFFERENCES IN UNEMPLOYMENT EXPERIENCE BETWEEN BLACKS AND WHITES. *Am. Econ. Rev. 1978 68(2): 192-197.* Blacks constitute 12% of the working population, but they provided 24% of the 6.9 million unemployed in August 1977. Their spells of unemployment are longer and the spells start earlier in the business cycle. The task for an equitable social policy is to reduce the length of the spells of unemployment. Tables, ref.

2610. Birch, David L. WHO CREATES JOBS? *Public Interest 1981 (65): 3-14.* Little knowledge about how individual firms create jobs prompted the Massachusetts Institute of Technology Program on Neighborhood and Regional Change to analyze data for insight into the process of job creation. When a firm leaves an area it does not drastically alter the existing job base. All areas in the United States lose jobs at about the same rate. The most successful areas for creating employment opportunities are those with the highest rates of innovation and business failure. The American economy is characterized by high job turnover. Small businesses are the greatest job replacers. Businesses whose well-being fluctuates are the most vital and effective job creators. The government ought to create an environment which promotes the growth of new service-oriented smaller businesses. Based on primary sources; 5 tables, 2 notes.   J. M. Herrick

2611. Bishop, Christine E. HEALTH EMPLOYMENT AND THE NATION'S HEALTH. *Current Hist. 1977 72(427): 207-210, 227-228.* "Trends in the training and employment of health workers and trends in their earnings do much to determine the availability and quality of health care for Americans, and the cost of that care."

2612. Blumberg, Paul. ANOTHER DAY, ANOTHER $3,000: EXEC-UTIVE SALARIES IN AMERICA. *Dissent 1978 25(2): 157-168.* The range of income inequality in the United States is illustrated by comparison of the top corporate executives and of the average blue-collar worker, 1960's-70's.

2613. Borum, Joan D. WAGE INCREASES IN 1980 OUTPACED BY INFLATION. *Monthly Labor Rev. 1981 104(5): 55-57.* Presents statistics showing that the increase in wages for American workers during 1980 was high but less than the increase in consumer prices, and compares 1980 figures with 1979 statistics.

2614. Borum, Joan D. WAGE INCREASES OF 1978 ABSORBED BY INFLATION. *Monthly Labor Rev. 1979 102(6): 10-13.* Provides statistics on the absorption of wage increases by rapid inflation in 1978, and glances at the situation for 1979.

2615. Bowers, Norman. EMPLOYMENT ON THE RISE IN THE FIRST HALF OF 1983. *Monthly Labor Rev. 1983 106(8): 8-13.* During mid-1981-83, employment in the United States increased and unemployment was down, consistent with other indicators of economic health.

2616. Bowers, Norman. HAVE EMPLOYMENT PATTERNS IN RECESSIONS CHANGED? *Monthly Labor Rev. 1981 104(2): 15-28.* Shows, through a survey of postwar recessions, that the increasing proportion of service sector jobs has moderated overall employment declines and points out that women in nontraditional jobs, blacks, and youths bear a disproportionate share of job losses.

2617. Bowers, Norman. YOUTH LABOR FORCE ACTIVITY: AL-TERNATIVE SURVEYS COMPARED. *Monthly Labor Rev. 1981 104(3): 3-17.* Studies four surveys of employment among young workers, 1966-79, in order to account for differences between survey measures of current labor force status which might take their rise in methodological, design, or questionnaire differences among the surveys.

2618. Bowles, Samuel. THE INTEGRATION OF HIGHER EDU-CATION INTO THE WAGE LABOR SYSTEM. *Rev. of Radical Pol. Econ. 1974 6(1): 100-133.* American education history reveals two main functions of schooling: to expand the forces of production, and to reproduce the social relations of production. But there exists a basic contradiction between those two ends, and tensions have been exacerbat-ed as new groups of workers have entered the wage system. In response the educational structure has been forced to change. Within this historically based framework the implications of the Carnegie Commis-sion on Higher Education (1967-73) are analyzed, and alternative scenarios for future student unrest postulated. Secondary materials; 59 notes.   P. R. Shergold

2619. Boyd, Monica. OCCUPATIONS OF FEMALE IMMI-GRANTS AND NORTH AMERICAN IMMIGRATION STATIS-TICS. *Int. Migration Rev. 1976 10(1): 73-80.* Discusses labor force potential and occupations of women immigrants to the United States and Canada, 1964-71.

2620. Bradshaw, T. F. and Stinson, J. F. TRENDS IN WEEKLY EARNINGS: AN ANALYSIS. *Monthly Labor Rev. 1975 98(8): 22-32.* Discusses existing weekly wage gaps between whites and Negroes and between men and women.

2621. Brand, Horst and Huffstutler, Clyde. PRODUCTIVITY IN THE PUMP AND COMPRESSOR INDUSTRY. *Monthly Labor Rev. 1982 105(12): 38-45.* Output per employee hour rose 2.1% annually between 1958 and 1980, with productivity highest during 1958-68 and lowest during 1973-80; employment rose 2.7% annually.

2622. Brand, Horst. PRODUCTIVITY IN THE PHARMACEUTI-CAL INDUSTRY. *Monthly Labor Rev. 1974 97(3): 9-14.* Productivi-ty in the pharmaceutical industry in the United States from 1963 to 1972 has risen consistently, reflecting growth in demand and changes in the technology of quality control.

2623. Braverman, Harry. WORK AND UNEMPLOYMENT. *Month-ly Rev. 1975 27(2): 18-31.* Discusses philosophical and sociological aspects of labor and how they relate to unemployment in the 1970's.

2624. Bronfenbrenner, Martin. SOME REACTIONARY SUGGES-TIONS ON THE LABOR FRONT. *South Atlantic Q. 1975 74(2): 237-243.* A plea for reform of American labor laws. The present system, rigged in favor of labor unions, is primarily responsible for the wage-price spiral that will eventually destroy the economy. Unions should be put into two groups: Class A, which would compel arbitration of disputes and permit lawsuits for illegal strikes; and Class B, which would allow strikes but remove the protections of unions which have been built into the law. The reform has no prospect of adoption at present, but its discussion does serve to point out that inflation is not necessarily automatic and that labor unions need not be above the law. 10 notes.   V. L. Human

2625. Buckley, John E. DO AREA WAGES REFLECT AREA LIVING COSTS? *Monthly Labor Rev. 1979 102(11): 24-29.* Compares data on 1977 wage and living-cost ratios in US metropolitan areas to results of a 1966-67 survey, and shows no significant change in the ratio.

2626. Capdevielle, Patricia; Alvarez, Donato; and Cooper, Brian. INTERNATIONAL TRENDS IN PRODUCTIVITY AND LABOR COSTS. *Monthly Labor Rev. 1982 105(12): 3-14.* Indexes of relative trends in manufacturing productivity as related to hourly compensation in 1981 and in unit labor costs in the 1974-75 and 1980-81 recessions increased in most European countries, Canada, Japan, and the United States.

2627. Capdevielle, Patricia and Neef, Arthur. PRODUCTIVITY AND UNIT LABOR COSTS IN THE U.S. AND ABROAD. *Monthly Labor Rev. 1975 98(7): 28-32.* Unit labor costs in manufacturing rose sharply in the United States and abroad with only minor productivity gains in 1974.

2628. Carey, Max L. EVALUATING THE 1975 OCCUPATIONAL EMPLOYMENT PROJECTIONS. *Monthly Labor Rev. 1980 103(6): 10-21.* Analyzes the 1975 Bureau of Labor Statistics industry-occupation matrix projects and concludes that although staffing patterns were error prone, the projections were comparatively superior.

2629. Carter, Keith A. INADEQUACIES OF THE TRADITIONAL LABOR FORCE FRAMEWORK FOR RURAL AREAS: A LABOR UTILIZATION FRAMEWORK APPLIED TO SURVEY DATA. *Rural Sociol. 1982 47(3): 459-474.* A study of Florida's Gadsden, St. Lucie, and Washington counties indicates that available labor force estimates for rural areas are inaccurate; unemployment rates during the 1970's were greater than official figures indicated, and more workers were underutilized than officially evident.

2630. Chiswick, Barry R. IMMIGRANT EARNINGS PATTERNS BY SEX, RACE, AND ETHNIC GROUPINGS. *Monthly Labor Rev. 1980 103(10): 22-25.* Summarizes data on earnings and occupational mobility of immigrants in the United States, based on data from the 1970 census; immigrant men reach earnings equal to earnings of native-born men, while for women earnings vary by racial and ethnic group.

2631. Chiswick, Barry R. SONS OF IMMIGRANTS: ARE THEY AT AN EARNINGS DISADVANTAGE? *Am. Econ. Rev. 1977 67(1): 376-380.* Nativeborn white males have a small income advantage over second-generation male Americans. Income disadvantages appear to result from other factors such as class, intelligence, and motivation. 3 tables, 4 references.   D. K. Pickens

2632. Clark, Don P. THE PROTECTION OF UNSKILLED LABOR IN THE UNITED STATES MANUFACTURING INDUSTRIES: FURTHER EVIDENCE. *J. of Pol. Econ. 1980 88(6): 1249-1254.* Based on empirical data from the 1970's, establishes a positive relationship between nominal and effective tariff protection rates and unskilled labor intensity in US manufacturing industries.

2633. Clark, Gordon L. and Ballard, Kenneth P. THE DEMAND AND SUPPLY OF LABOR AND INTERSTATE RELATIVE WAGES: AN EMPIRICAL ANALYSIS. *Econ. Geog. 1981 57(2): 95-112.* Covers 1958-75.

2634. Clark, Kim B. THE IMPACT OF UNIONIZATION ON PRODUCTIVITY: A CASE STUDY. *Industrial and Labor Relations Rev. 1980 33(4): 451-469.* This study examines the effect of unionization on productivity through the use of time-series data on selected establishments in the U.S. cement industry. The analysis combines statistical estimation of the union impact and interviews with union and management officials to forge a link between econometric estimation and the traditional institutional analysis of union policy and management practice. The econometric analysis deals primarily with the problem of controlling for interfirm differences in variables such as the quality of management and also for the possible union impact on labor quality. The case studies are designed to show the specific ways in which unionization affects productivity. The empirical results indicate that unionization leads to productivity gains, deriving in large part from a series of extensive changes in management personnel and procedures.   J

2635. Clarke, James J. AN ANALYSIS OF UNEMPLOYMENT ACROSS INDUSTRIAL SECTORS, 1965-1977. *Rev. of Social Econ. 1981 39(2): 197-203.*

2636. Cohen, Malcolm S. and Schwartz, Arthur R. U.S. LABOR TURNOVER: ANALYSIS OF A NEW MEASURE. *Monthly Labor Rev. 1980 103(11): 9-13.* The new method for estimating labor turnover in the United States uses "employee earnings information submitted by employers to the Social Security Administration" in all sectors of the economy; the old method used data from the Bureau of Labor Statistics' Labor Turnover Survey to show labor turnover in manufacturing only.

2637. Cooke, William N. THE BEHAVIOR OF UNEMPLOYMENT INSURANCE RECIPIENTS UNDER ADVERSE MARKET CONDITIONS. *Industrial and Labor Relations Rev. 1981 34(3): 386-395.* Examines the effect on job search behavior of changes in unemployment insurance (UI) provisions and in labor market conditions and concludes that extended benefit programs during periods of high unemployment do not cause recipients to ignore the realities of the market.   J/S

2638. Cutright, Phillips. THE CIVILIAN EARNINGS OF WHITE AND BLACK DRAFTEES AND NONVETERANS. *Am. Sociol. Rev. 1974 39(3): 317-327.* Controlling for race, region of employment, academic achievement, and years of education, and nonveterans, 1950's-64, indicates draftees' incomes equal or are below incomes of nonveterans.

2639. Daly, Patricia A. AGRICULTURAL EMPLOYMENT: HAS THE DECLINE ENDED? *Monthly Labor Rev. 1981 104(11): 11-17.* Based on data from the monthly *Current Population survey* and its yearly Hired Farm Working Force study, concludes that although the sharp decrease in farm employment continued during the 1950's and 1960's, it has moderated during 1976-80.

2640. Davies, David G. UNEMPLOYMENT, INFLATION, AND PUBLIC POLICY. *South Atlantic Q. 1974 73(4): 460-474.* Analyzes the causes and potential cures of the present unemployment and inflation. Economic theory in vogue is not convincing. Unemployment is caused by minimum wages, unemployment benefits, working women, and monopoly power, as well as by lesser factors. No cure will be effected until these causes are attacked. The major problem is lack of knowledge: no one understands the American economy. Table, 46 notes.   V. L. Human

2641. Davies, Margery and Brodhead, Frank. LABOR AND MONOPOLY CAPITAL: A REVIEW. *Radical Am. 1975 9(2): 79-94.* Reviews *Labor and Monopoly Capital: The Degradation of Work in the Twentieth Century* by Harry Braverman (New York: Monthly R. Press, 1974).   S

2642. Davis, Harry E. MULTIEMPLOYER PENSION PLAN PROVISIONS IN 1973. *Monthly Labor Rev. 1974 97(10): 10-16.* Multiemployer pension plan coverage in the United States increased sevenfold between 1950 and 1973, primarily due to the development of jointly administered negotiated plans in industries with multiemployer collective bargaining agreements.

2643. Davis, Howard. HOURS AND EARNINGS OF PRODUCTION OR NONSUPERVISORY WORKERS, 1968-78. *Monthly Labor Rev. 1980 103(4): 54-56.* Discusses the patterns in the rise of hourly wages of production or nonsupervisory workers, and the drop in average weekly hours, between 1968 and 1978.

2644. Defina, Catherine C. LABOR AND THE ECONOMY DURING 1975. *Monthly Labor Rev. 1976 99(1): 3-16.* The year 1975 saw progress against both inflation and unemployment, though unemployment was higher than in 1974.

2645. Defina, Catherine C. LABOR AND THE ECONOMY IN 1973. *Monthly Labor Rev. 1974 97(1): 9-21.* 1973 was a moderate year for pay raises in the United States, despite large price increases; and employment grew at an unprecedented rate, but by December both a higher rate of inflation and a higher unemployment rate were widely predicted.

2646. Devens, Richard M. THE AVERAGE WORKWEEK: TWO SURVEYS COMPARED. *Monthly Labor Rev. 1978 101(7): 3-8.* Compares the seasonal, cyclical, and secular trends of the average workweek for manufacturing, construction, transportation, and public utilities during 1956-77, as surveyed in the Current Employment Statistics Program and the Current Population Survey.

2647. Devens, Richard M. UNEMPLOYMENT AMONG RECIPI-ENTS OF FOOD STAMPS AND AFDC. *Monthly Labor Rev. 1979 102(3): 47-52.* Statistics, 1975-79, indicate that the majority of food stamp and Aid to Families with Dependent Children recipients are outside the labor force.

2648. DiPrete, Thomas A. UNEMPLOYMENT OVER THE LIFE CYCLE: RACIAL DIFFERENCES AND THE EFFECT OF CHANGING ECONOMIC CONDITIONS. *Am. J. of Sociol. 1981 87(2): 286-307.* Analyzes the unemployment experience of white and nonwhite male heads of household, showing that nonwhites differ in unemployment experience from whites mostly at low tenure levels.

2649. Douty, H. M. THE SLOWDOWN IN REAL WAGES: A POSTWAR PROSPECTIVE. *Monthly Labor Rev. 1977 100(8): 7-12.* Examines the effects of productivity and price changes on real wages 1947-62 and 1962-76, concluding that small strides in productivity and high inflation cast doubts on whether real earnings will regain the rate of increase which characterized the 1947-62 period.

2650. DuBoff, Richard B. FULL EMPLOYMENT: THE HISTORY OF A RECEDING TARGET. *Pol. and Soc. 1977 7(1): 1-25.* The meaning of "full employment" has changed radically since World War II. There are many explanations for abandoning full employment goals and instead seeking "high" employment and a "natural rate" of unemployment. Inflation and the changing composition of the labor force provide the rationale in most instances. These macroeconomic explanations do not fit the American economic system. Primary and secondary sources; 74 notes.   D. G. Nielson

2651. Duke, John and Huffstutler, Clyde. PRODUCTIVITY IN SAWMILLS INCREASES AS LABOR INPUT DECLINES. *Monthly Labor Rev. 1977 100(4): 33-37.* Analyzes relations among sawmill productivity, technological change, and labor input during 1958-75.

2652. Easterlin, Richard A.; Wachter, Michael L. and Wachter, Susan M. DEMOCRACY AND FULL EMPLOYMENT: THE CHANG-ING IMPACT OF POPULATION SWINGS ON THE AMERICAN ECONOMY. *Pro. of the Am. Phil. Soc. 1978 122(3): 119-130.* Discussses the causes of simultaneous unemployment and inflation. This new phenomenon is a product of fluctuating population swings, of which declining birth rates, rather than changing immigration patterns, are the dominant causal factor. The postwar baby boom's members have reached the age of employability and have surfeited the market, while producing few children and thereby reducing demand for the products of labor. The government has moved to make up the difference by means of welfare payments, thereby spending monies not created by production. 4 tables, 5 fig., 9 notes, biblio.   V. L. Human

2653. Ehrenberg, Ronald G. MUNICIPAL GOVERNMENT STRUCTURE, UNIONIZATION, AND THE WAGES OF FIRE FIGHTERS. *Industrial and Labor Relations Rev. 1973 27(1): 36-48.* This study tests the hypothesis that labor costs in municipal government are influenced by the structure of 'management'—whether the chief operating officer is a professional manager or elected official—as well as by the strength of organization among employees. Using fire fighters as a test group, the author constructs a model to explain the variation among cities in the demand for and supply of firemen and applies this model to data for 1969 and a sample of 270 cities. He concludes that unionism does have a significant wage effect in cities that have agreed to a formal labor contract, but the structure of city government appears to have only a minor impact on wages.   J

2654. Eldridge, Donald P. and Saunders, Norman C. EMPLOYMENT AND EXPORTS, 1963-72. *Monthly Labor Rev. 1973 96(8): 16-27.* Employment related to agricultural exports in the United States fluctuated during 1963-72, while, in general, other export-related jobs rose steadily.

2655. Fain, T. Scott. SELF-EMPLOYED AMERICANS: THEIR NUMBER HAS INCREASED. *Monthly Labor Rev. 1980 103(11): 3-8.* The number of self-employed Americans increased during 1972-79, especially during 1976-79; data indicate that self-employed workers put in a shorter workweek, were younger than other workers, made less than other workers, and were more likely to be women than in the past.

2656. Falaris, Evangelos M. MIGRATION AND REGIONAL WAGES. *Southern Econ. J. 1982 48(3): 670-686.* Applies a multiple choice conditional logic model to migration, based on interviews with nonblack men when they were 12th graders and periodically since then until 1971, finding that restricted wages are more relevant than unrestricted wages in explaining interregional migration.

2657. Farber, Samuel. MATERIAL AND NON-MATERIAL WORK INCENTIVES AS IDEOLOGIES AND PRACTICES OF ORDER. *Rev. of Radical Pol. Econ. 1982 14(4): 29-39.* Work incentives constitute ideologies and practices of order. Studies of the United States and the USSR demonstrate that these incentives presuppose a basic harmony of interests between workers and managers, and they ignore fundamental conflicts of interest. There is no reason that either harmony or conflict is necessary and unchangeable. Secondary works; 68 notes.   D. R. Stevenson

2658. Fearn, Robert M. CYCLICAL, SEASONAL, AND STRUC-TURAL FACTORS IN AREA UNEMPLOYMENT RATES. *Industrial and Labor Relations Rev. 1975 28(13): 424-431.*

2659. Ferleger, Louis. A CRITIQUE OF CONVENTIONAL EX-PLANATIONS OF LABOR MARKET CONDITIONS FOR EM-PLOYED BLACKS. *Policy Studies J. 1982 10(3): 539-555.* Examines the importance of the service sector in explaining the structure of black employment over the past two decades, and the failure of neo-classical and segmentation analysis to properly credit this phenomenon.

2660. Finlay, William. ONE OCCUPATION, TWO LABOR MAR-KETS: THE CASE OF LONGSHORE CRANE OPERATORS. *Am. Sociol. Rev. 1983 48(3): 306-315.* A case study of a single (new) occupation within a single (old) industry—longshore crane operators. Argues that because the labor market is the arena of negotiation between firms and workers, analysis should focus on both labor market outcomes and labor market formation. In this case the labor market outcome has been the fragmentation of the occupation into two labor markets, the one providing workers an advantaged status, the other providing workers a disadvantaged status. This is related to technological changes in the industry, and to the conflict among employer goals, union principles, and individual worker interests.   J

2661. Fisk, Donald M. MODEST PRODUCTIVITY GAINS IN STATE UNEMPLOYMENT INSURANCE SERVICE. *Monthly Labor Rev. 1983 106(1): 24-27.* Gains in productivity averaged 1.9% during 1966-78; unemployment caused wide fluctuations in year-to-year data.

2662. Flaim, Paul O. THE EFFECT OF DEMOGRAPHIC CHANG-ES ON THE NATION'S JOBLESS RATE. *Monthly Labor Rev. 1979 102(3): 13-23.* Examines the impact of demographic, definitional and computational, social and institutional, and legislative changes on the unemployment rate in the United States, 1959-79.

2663. Fogel, Walter. OCCUPATIONAL EARNINGS: MARKET AND INSTITUTIONAL INFLUENCES. *Industrial and Labor Relations Rev. 1979 33(1): 24-35.* This study investigates various influences on occupational earnings by estimating a standard human capital equation across 175 detailed occupational classifications, using the mean 1969 earnings of full-year male workers in each occupation as the dependent variable. The equation accounts for two-thirds of the earnings variations, but that fraction overstates the equation's explanatory value. Occupations with the largest positive residuals ("high paid") included a number of manager and self-employed groups and those with the largest negative residuals ("low paid") included several service and female-oriented occupations.   J

2664. Foley, John W. TRENDS, DETERMINANTS AND POLICY IMPLICATIONS OF INCOME INEQUALITY IN U.S. COUNTIES. *Sociol. and Social Res. 1977 61(4): 441-461.* This paper reviews earlier research and presents new analytical findings regarding the trends, determinants and public policy implications of income inequality. Using the Gini Coefficient measured at three points in time, a 20-year trend in income inequality is presented for 300 US counties. The distribution of income was found to have been increasingly more equally distributed in these counties since 1950 with the exception of SMSA counties. Income inequality declined within the SMSA counties from 1950 to 1960, however, subsequently this trend has been reversed. Investigating the determinants of income inequality, a five-variable model explained more than half the variance within these counties in income inequality as measured by the Gini Coefficient. The variables used were indicators of Growth Rate, Resource Level, Racial Cleavage, Maturity of Local Economy, and Population Density. To explore these findings an additional measure of income distribution was regressed on this five-variable set, and the original dependent variable was regressed on cases representing heuristic subsets of these counties. Areas that are fast growing, sparsely populated, wealthy, and largely white were found to be low in income inequality. Income inequality as it related to the provision of public services and social control was also examined. Strongly positive relationships are observed in SMSA counties between level of inequality and public spending for police, welfare, public hospitals, etc., but not in non-SMSA counties. This suggests that where income inequality is high and most visible it engenders rival claims for increased public expenditures.   J

2665. Foran, Terry G. UNIONISM AND WAGE DIFFEREN-TIALS. *Southern Econ. J. 1973 40(2): 269-278.*

2666. Fuchs, Victor R. RECENT TRENDS AND LONG-RUN PROSPECTS FOR FEMALE EARNINGS. *Am. Econ. Rev. 1974 64(2): 236-242.* Discusses the trends in income earned by women during 1960-70, and predicts future trends.

2667. Fulco, Lawrence J. PRODUCTIVITY REPORTS. *Monthly Labor Rev. 1979 102(10): 57-61.* Reports that labor productivity declined the first quarter of 1979 and compares that to the productivity changes in the United States, 1967-78.

2668. Fusfeld, Daniel R. A LIVING WAGE. *Ann. of the Am. Acad. of Pol. and Social Sci. 1973 (409): 34-41.* The only effective way to eliminate poverty in the United States is to pay all workers a living wage, defined as one that would enable a worker to maintain an urban family of four in health and decency. In 1972 that implied a minimum wage of 3.50 dollars per hour. Such a minimum wage would have important repercussions on the low wage industries and the workers they employ. The impact on business firms can be eased by special tax and loan programs. The most important problems will arise from loss of jobs as the low wage industries adapt to the high minimum wage. A three-pronged program is called for: (1) full employment, (2) public service employment and (3) education and training. A sharply accelerated equal opportunity employment program will also be needed, because many low wage workers are Blacks, Latins and women. This program implies a redistribution of income in favor of the low wage worker that could be negated by wage increases for other workers, triggering price increases throughout the economy. Reduced income taxes for workers with annual incomes above 7,000 dollars and up to perhaps 15,000 dollars will be needed to overcome that effect. The net result would be an end to poverty and to many of its social evils.   J

2669. Garfinkel, Irwin and Plotnick, Robert D. POVERTY, UNEM-PLOYMENT, AND THE CURRENT RECESSION. *Public Welfare 1975 33(3): 10-17.* Provides statistics on poverty and unemployment trends from 1959 to 1975, and discusses the relationship between poverty and unemployment in the 1975 recession in the United States.

2670. Gauzner, N. BEZRABOTITSA: PROBLEMY I PERSPEK-TIVY [Unemployment: problems and perspectives]. *Mirovaia Ekonomi-ka i Mezhdunarodnye Otnosheniia [USSR] 1975 (11): 49-60.* The postwar growth of unemployment in the United States and other Western nations is an example of the failure of Keynesianism.

2671. Gauzner, N. KAPITALISTICHESKAIA RATSIONALI-ZATSIIA I EKSTENSIVNYE GRANITSY TRUDA [Capitalist ratio-nalization and new forms of exploitation of labor]. *Mirovaia Ekonomika i Mezhdunarodnye Otnosheniia [USSR] 1981 (7): 26-39.* Examines the changes in working hours in the developed capitalist countries, showing that there have been no essential changes in favor of leisure time under capitalism, and considers the impact of work sharing, overtime, part-time, and shift work, and flexible time schemes on the working class.

2672. Gellner, Christopher G. REGIONAL DIFFERENCES IN EMPLOYMENT AND UNEMPLOYMENT, 1957-72. *Monthly Labor Rev. 1974 97(3): 15-24.* Examines salient changes; the Northeast and North Central States were more sensitive to economic downturns, while the unemployment rate in the West rose above the national average.

2673. Gerking, Shelby D. and Mutti, John H. COSTS AND BENE-FITS OF ILLEGAL IMMIGRATION: KEY ISSUES FOR GOV-ERNMENT POLICY. *Social Sci. Q. 1980 61(1): 71-85.* Examines the effects of illegal Mexican immigration on output and income distribution in the southwestern United States. Workers who possess skills similar to illegal alien laborers suffer lower wages when the rate of illegal immigration rises. The effects of increased immigration on the rest of the labor force and the owners of capital, however, are ambiguous. A general equilibrium model highlights the results. Based on Immigration and Naturalization Service data and on secondary works; 2 fig., 19 notes, biblio.   L. F. Velicer

2674. Gilroy, Curtis L. and Bradshaw, Thomas F. EMPLOYMENT AND UNEMPLOYMENT: A REPORT ON 1973. *Monthly Labor Rev. 1974 97(2): 3-14.* Keeping pace with the growth in the economy, the job market in the United States showed substantial improvement in 1973; total employment showed the largest percentage increase since 1955; and the number of jobless dropped to 4.3 million.

2675. Ginzberg, Eli and Horowitz, Irving Louis. PLANNING FULL EMPLOYMENT. *Society 1976 13(4): 57-64.* Discusses income distri-bution, employment policies, black employment, and other economic matters under various presidents since 1945.

2676. Givens, Harrison, Jr. AN EVALUATION OF MANDATORY RETIREMENT. *Ann. of the Am. Acad. of Pol. and Social Sci. 1978 438: 50-58.* This paper discusses the issues raised by mandatory retirement, the meaning of the new law, the law's specifics, and the uncertainties still ahead. The new law, prohibiting mandatory retirement before age 70 in the private sector, and altogether for most federal employment, is in form an amendment to the Age Discrimination in Employment Act of 1967, or ADEA. The pros and cons of mandatory retirement at any fixed age are reviewed, including the changing financial and demographic considerations affecting the retirement decision. The paper then discusses the likely effects of mandatory retirement on employees and employers and on the composition of the work force. About 90 percent of both men and women have in recent years retired before age 65, and those few working to age 65 have generally stopped well before 70. Nevertheless, the sure opportunity to work to 70, and a developing perception of the great erosion of financial security caused by continuing substantial inflation, may well lead to significant shifts in retirement decisions. Uncertainties arise from the independent operation of state laws and the likelihood of extensive dispute requiring judicial resolution.   J

2677. Grandjean, Burke D. HISTORY AND CAREER IN A BU-REAUCRATIC LABOR MARKET. *Am. J. of Sociol. 1981 86(5): 1057-1092.* A cohort analysis of socioeconomic achievement in the US civil service, a representative bureaucratic labor market (BLM), 1963-77, indicates the importance both of entry ports and career lines and of being in the right cohort (i.e. in the right place at the right time); however, it also indicates that education, age, occupation, minority group membership, and sex—important factors in the non-BLM—are not irrelevant to career success in a BLM.

2678. Green, Gloria P.; Devens, Richard M.; and Whitmore, Bob. EMPLOYMENT AND UNEMPLOYMENT: TRENDS DURING 1977. *Monthly Labor Rev. 1978 101(2): 12-23.* The overall job situation in the United States improved in 1977, as strong employment growth accompanied fairly substantial reductions in unemployment, with the jobless rate falling to 6.4%, the lowest in more than three years.

2679. Gregory, Karl D. SOME ALTERNATIVES FOR REDUCING THE BLACK-WHITE UNEMPLOYMENT RATE DIFFEREN-TIAL. *Am. Econ. Rev. 1976 66(2): 324-328.* Over the last 20 years, the gap between the unemployed rates has ranged from 2.9 to 6.8 percent while the gap for all teenagers has been progressively wider. Despite faster economic growth, the gap via black/white unemployment rates remains between 3.9 and 4.9 percent. Regardless of the alternatives, the future is not promising.   D. K. Pickens

2680. Gross, Bertram and Moses, Stanley. 120 MILLION JOBS: HOW? *Social Policy 1982 13(2): 8-10.* Discusses the problems and outlook for full employment of the work force in 1982.

2681. Grossman, Allyson Sherman. THE EMPLOYMENT SITUA- TION FOR MILITARY WIVES. *Monthly Labor Rev. 1981 104(2): 60-64.* During the 1970's the labor force participation rate of military wives advanced by 20% (now at 50%, it equals that of civilian wives); attributes this rise to rapidly increasing prices, low military pay, diminished benefits, and greater societal acceptance of working wives and mothers.

2682. Grossman, Allyson Sherman. WORKING MOTHERS AND THEIR CHILDREN. *Monthly Labor Rev. 1981 104(5): 49-54.* Discuss- es statistics related to the increasing number of working mothers during 1970-80, including racial differences, family income, the costs of child- rearing, day-care centers, changing family patterns and the proportion of children with working mothers.

2683. Grossman, Herschel I. THE CYCLIC PATTERN OF UNEM- PLOYMENT AND WAGE INFLATION. *Economica [Great Britain] 1974 41(164): 403-413.* Earlier studies have indicated that in Britain, Europe, and the United States 1) a decreasing unemployment rate was accompanied by an increasing rate of wage inflation, leading to a further decrease in the unemployment rate, 2) accelerating wage inflation produced an initial increase in unemployment, followed by a decline, and decelerating inflation produced a short decrease in unemployment before an increase. Since World War II, however, the cyclical pattern seems to have changed, so that at the end of accelerating inflation, unemployment has increased, and at the end of decelerating inflation, unemployment has decreased. This change is the result of factors identified by use of a model, modified by dynamic considerations (partial adjustment and adaptive expectations). Results show that the dominant factors are speed of adjustment of unemployment and the speed of adjustment of inflationary expectations, either or both of which have apparently increased. 2 fig., ref.   D. H. Murdoch

2684. Hamermesh, Daniel S. ENTITLEMENT EFFECTS, UNEM- PLOYMENT INSURANCE AND EMPLOYMENT DECISIONS. *Econ. Inquiry 1979 17(3): 317-332.* Empirically shows that for US married women in 1971 the entitlement effects of social insurance programs offset the employment disincentive effects of unemployment benefits and cause a slight increase in employment for that study group.

2685. Hamermesh, Daniel S. WHO "WINS" IN WAGE BARGAIN- ING? *Industrial and Labor Relations Rev. 1973 26(4): 1146-1149.* This study tests the 'split the difference' bargaining model by examining data on the parties' opening and final positions with respect to wages in forty- three recent negotiations. The author finds that final settlements usually fall closer to the employer's initial offer than to the union's initial demand, but the difficulty of interpreting these results demonstrates, in his opinion, the severe problems involved in any empirical test of bargaining theory.   J

2686. Harker, John. TRADE UNIONS AND A CODE OF CON- DUCT FOR MULTINATIONALS. *Can. Labour [Canada] 1977 22(1): 8-11.* Discusses the principal bases for the commitment of trade unions to the development of and enforcement of a code of conduct for multinational corporations, and describes the evolution of code guide- lines by the Organization for Economic Cooperation and Development (OECD).

2687. Haworth, Joan Gustafson; Gwartney, James; and Haworth, Charles. EARNINGS, PRODUCTIVITY, AND CHANGES IN EM- PLOYMENT DISCRIMINATION DURING THE 1960'S. *Am. Econ. Rev. 1975 65(1): 158-168.* The authors found that people with more years of schooling made the largest gains in relative earnings, and that these people were primarily young and lived in the North. Suggests that progress was made during the 1960's toward breaking the poverty cycle resulting from discriminatory employment practices.   D. K. Pickens

2688. Hayghe, Howard. MARITAL AND FAMILY PATTERNS OF WORKERS: AN UPDATE. *Monthly Labor Rev. 1982 105(5): 53-56.*

Statistics for the 12 months ending March 1981 on labor force changes due to the large number of married women with children re-entering the labor force; focuses on marital status, ethnic background, median income, and poverty level and percentages.

2689. Hedges, J. N. and Gallogly, S. J. FULL AND PART TIME: A REVIEW OF DEFINITIONS. *Monthly Labor Rev. 1977 100(3): 21-28.* Discusses the definition of full and part-time employment used by the Current Population Survey and suggests alternative definitions, particu- larly in light of recent changes in the hours of work.

2690. Hedges, J. N. and Mellor, E. F. WEEKLY AND HOURLY EARNINGS OF U.S. WORKERS, 1967-78. *Monthly Labor Rev. 1979 102(8): 31-41.* Real earnings of all workers increased 7% in 11 years; the black-white earnings gaps narrowed, particularly among women, while median earnings of all women remained about 60% of those of all men.

2691. Hedges, Janice Neipert. LONG WORKWEEKS AND PREMI- UM PAY. *Monthly Labor Rev. 1976 99(4): 7-12.* "Long hours have declined since 1973, primarily in goods-producing industries; still, one- quarter of all full-time workers worked more than 40 hours a week in May 1975."

2692. Hedges, Janice Neipert and Taylor, Daniel E. RECENT TRENDS IN WORKTIME: HOURS EDGE DOWNWARD. *Monthly Labor Rev. 1980 103(3): 3-11.* Changing composition of the labor force, union contracts, federal laws, and increased vacations and holidays contributed to a reduction in hours during 1968-79.

2693. Henle, Peter and Ryscavage, Paul. THE DISTRIBUTION OF EARNED INCOME AMONG MEN AND WOMEN, 1958-77. *Monthly Labor Rev. 1980 103(4): 3-10.* Data shows that income inequality among men continues but the trend is slowing; income inequality among women is more unequal than among men, and women's income in general continues to be substantially lower than men's.

2694. Henry, James S. HALLELUJAH I'M A BUM: THE NEW CONSERVATIVE THEORIES OF UNEMPLOYMENT. *Working Papers for a New Soc. 1979 6(6): 71-79.* Describes the high rate of unemployment in the United States in the past 10 years and the trend of reviving conservative theories of unemployment from the 1920's.

2695. Henry, James S. LAZY, YOUNG, FEMALE, AND BLACK: THE NEW CONSERVATIVE THEORIES OF UNEMPLOYMENT. *Working Papers for a New Soc. 1978 6(3): 55-65.* Recession has caused conservative economic theories that unemployment figures are high because of unemployed people's reluctance to seek jobs.

2696. Herzog, Henry W. Jr. and Schlottmann, Alan M. LABOR FORCE MIGRATION AND ALLOCATIVE EFFICIENCY IN THE UNITED STATES: THE ROLES OF INFORMATION AND PSY- CHIC COSTS. *Econ. Inquiry 1981 19(3): 459-475.* Examines the relative importance of information, and psychic and other costs of relocation as mitigating factors offsetting the attractiveness of earnings differentials within the migration decision.

2697. Hibbs, Douglas A., Jr. THE MASS PUBLIC AND MACRO- ECONOMIC PERFORMANCE: THE DYNAMICS OF PUBLIC OPINION TOWARD UNEMPLOYMENT AND INFLATION. *Am. J. of Pol. Sci. 1979 23(4): 705-731.* In every year since 1972 more than 70 percent of the mass public identified an economic issue, principally inflation or unemployment, as "the most important problem facing this country today." This study is motivated by the belief that public opinion toward salient economic issues is an important part of the domestic political environment influencing macroeconomic policy. The first few sections of the article review data on the public's relative aversion to inflation and unemployment in the 1970's in the context of recent macroeconomic history and the objective and subjective costs associated with rising prices and low employment. Most of the ideas discussed are embodied in a dynamic model of short-run opinion fluctuations introduced in the main parts of the paper. The final section considers the political implications of the estimation results.   J

2698. Hilaski, Harvey J. and Wang, Chao Ling. HOW VALID ARE ESTIMATES OF OCCUPATIONAL ILLNESS? *Monthly Labor Rev. 1982 105(8): 27-35.* Bureau of Labor Statistics giving rates of occupational diseases exclude chronic illnesses and diseases whose fatal consequences are latent; other studies supplement the bureau survey, but they are often inadequate.

2699. Hill, C. Russell. MIGRANT-NONMIGRANT EARNINGS DIFFERENTIALS IN A LOCAL LABOR MARKET. *Industrial and Labor Relations Rev. 1975 28(3): 411-423.* Compares the wages of migrant labor with nonmigrant in Detroit, Michigan, 1962-67.

2700. Hirsch, Barry T. THE DETERMINANTS OF UNIONIZATION: AN ANALYSIS OF INTERAREA DIFFERENCES. *Industrial and Labor Relations Rev. 1980 33(2): 147-161.* Utilizes two previously unused data sources on unionization to examine the determinants of union membership and collective bargaining coverage across SMSAs. Develops an economic framework in which equilibrium levels of unionization are determined by demand and supply. The model is robust when using either dependent variable, thus increasing confidence in the appropriateness of an economic framework. Unionization levels are positively related to an area's earnings level and negatively to its percentage of white-collar workers. The industry structure in an area is also a significant determinant, but interarea differences in the sex and racial composition of the labor force, and population growth appear to affect unionization to a lesser degree. Region also has only a small effect after accounting for other determinants of unionization. Finally, the results indicate that while RTW laws have little, if any, effect on the extent of collective bargaining coverage across SMSAs, such laws do appear to decrease the level of union membership.   J/S

2701. Hirschman, Charles and Blankenship, Kim. THE NORTH-SOUTH EARNINGS GAP: CHANGES DURING THE 1960S AND 1970S. *Am. J. of Sociol. 1981 87(2): 388-403.* Tests the convergence hypothesis by examining the trend in the earnings gap between workers living in the South and the North (the non-South) of the United States from 1960 to 1976, showing some convergence for advantaged workers but also a substantial regional difference for black workers, blue collar workers, and workers with lower educational attainment.

2702. Hodgens, Evan L. KEY CHANGES IN MAJOR PENSION PLANS. *Monthly Labor Rev. 1975 98(7): 22-27.* Examines how benefits in 144 pension plans increased substantially from 1970 to 1974, but failed to keep pace with the cost of living.

2703. Horvath, Francis W. FORGOTTEN UNEMPLOYMENT: RECALL BIAS IN RETROSPECTIVE DATA. *Monthly Labor Rev. 1982 105(3): 40-43.* Discusses the discrepancies in data obtained from the Current Population Survey (CPS), conducted by the Census Bureau for the Bureau of Labor Statistics on a monthly basis, compared to the data obtained from the Work Experience Supplement to the Current Population Survey.

2704. Houff, James N. IMPROVING AREA WAGE SURVEY INDEXES. *Monthly Labor Rev. 1973 96(1): 52-57.* Discusses the Bureau of Labor Statistics' attempts to improve the accuracy of area wage survey indexes of wage rate changes by eliminating industry turnovers and employment shifts in 1972.

2705. Husby, Ralph D. WORK INCENTIVES AND THE COST EFFECTIVENESS OF INCOME MAINTENANCE PROGRAMS. *Q. Rev. of Econ. and Business 1973 13(1): 7-14.* This empirical study examines the budgetary costs of some basic income maintenance plans with different tax rates. Because of the unsettled question of the impact of such plans on work incentives, a range of assumptions on labor supply is considered. Insights are provided into the question of whether tax rates should be kept low to minimize adverse effects on labor supply or high to minimize 'leakages' of benefits to higher-income families.   J

2706. Jackson, Mark and Jones, E. B. UNEMPLOYMENT AND OCCUPATIONAL WAGE CHANGES IN LOCAL LABOR MARKETS. *Industrial and Labor Relations Rev. 1973 26(4): 1135-1145.* This study is one of the few that have investigated the Phillips curve at the level of the local labor market, and it is the first to employ occupational wage rates as a measure of the price of labor. An analysis of

ten occupations in twenty local markets reveals several different wage-unemployment relationships, leading the authors to question the stability of a Phillips curve at the economywide level.   J

2707. Jencks, Christopher. THE MINIMUM WAGE CONTROVERSY. *Working Papers for a New Soc. 1978 6(2): 12-14.* Discusses the pros and cons of minimum wages, asserting that since the basic concept stems from the desire to protect incomes (especially those supporting families) from the competitive economic system, alternative plans to determine wages by a public employee's number of dependents or by subsidies for private employees who are the sole means of support for a family should be considered.

2708. Jenkins, J. Craig. THE DEMAND FOR IMMIGRANT WORKERS: LABOR SCARCITY OR SOCIAL CONTROL? *Int. Migration Rev. 1978 12(4): 514-535.* Analyzes the economic role of Mexican immigrant workers in the United States since the 1950's, based on the labor scarcity and social control arguments.

2709. Job, Barbara Cottman. THE BLACK LABOR FORCE DURING THE 1975-78 RECOVERY. *Monthly Labor Rev. 1979 102(5): 3-7.* Describes recent trends in labor force participation, employment and unemployment among black workers, and the impacts of the 1973-75 recession on black and white workers.

2710. Job, Barbara Cottman. EMPLOYMENT AND PAY TRENDS IN THE RETAIL TRADE INDUSTRY. *Monthly Labor Rev. 1980 103(3): 40-43.* Covers 1968-78.

2711. Johnson, Thomas and Hebein, Frederick J. INVESTMENTS IN HUMAN CAPITAL AND GROWTH IN PERSONAL INCOME 1956-1966. *Am. Econ. Rev. 1974 64(4): 604-615.* Econometric study of personal income growth derived from investments in education and on-the-job training between 1956 and 1966.

2712. Johnston, Denis F. THE UNITED STATES ECONOMY IN 1985: POPULATION AND LABOR FORCE PROJECTIONS. *Monthly Labor Rev. 1973 96(12): 8-17.* Discusses 1960-72 Bureau of Labor Statistics projections for size of labor force and population distribution by age and sex for 1980 and 1985.

2713. —. [THE FULL-TIME WORKWEEK IN THE UNITED STATES]. *Industrial and Labor Relations Rev. 1980 33(3): 379-389.* Jones, Ethel B. THE FULL-TIME WORKWEEK IN THE UNITED STATES, 1900-1970: COMMENT, pp. 379-384. Statistical rejection of Thomas J. Kniesner's computation of the work week. (See abstract #390).
Kniesner, Thomas J. REPLY, pp. 385-389.

2714. Kahn, Lawrence M. THE EFFECT OF UNIONS ON THE EARNINGS OF NONUNION WORKERS. *Industrial and Labor Relations Rev. 1978 31(2): 205-216.* This study examines the indirect impact of unions on the real annual wages of nonunion workers, using data from the 1967 Survey of Economic Opportunity. Earnings functions are constructed to compare wages of workers in San Francisco and Los Angeles—which differ significantly in their labor history and extent of union organization—within relatively unorganized industries and occupations, and within an occupation that is highly organized in one of those cities but not in the other. The data suggests that the net indirect union effect across industries and occupations is to lower the earnings of nonunion workers.   J

2715. Keyserling, Leon H. THE PROBLEM OF HIGH UNEMPLOYMENT. *Policy Studies J. 1979 8(3): 349-358.* Government economic policy has assumed that inflation can be inhibited by a rise in the unemployment rate, but actually the inflation rate increases as unused capacity increases.

2716. Killingsworth, Charles C. HOW MUCH UNEMPLOYMENT DO WE NEED? *Dissent 1976 23(4): 415-423.* Analyzes unemployment since the 1950's, which emphasizes how much unemployment there is, as of June 1976, what is the outlook for unemployment, what is being done about unemployment, and what should be done.

2717. Kohler, Daniel. EMPLOYMENT COST INDEX UP 7.7 PERCENT IN 1978. *Monthly Labor Rev. 1979 102(7): 28-31.*

2718. LaGory, Mark and Magnani, Robert J. STRUCTURAL COR-RELATES OF BLACK-WHITE OCCUPATIONAL DIFFERENTI-ATION: WILL U.S. REGIONAL DIFFERENCES IN STATUS REMAIN? *Social Problems 1979 27(2): 157-169.* Assesses data gathered between 1965 and 1979 on black-white educational, occupational and income attainment in the United States, depending on such factors as metropolitan size, occupational distribution, the impact of black population growth on local income markets, and school segregation.

2719. Leffler, Keith B. MINIMUM WAGES, WELFARE, AND WEALTH TRANSFERS TO THE POOR. *J. of Law and Econ. 1978 21(2): 345-358.* Because of the positive relationship of higher minimum wage to lowered costs of establishing eligibility for public welfare programs, an increase in minimum wages does not adversely affect the poor through increased disemployment, 1950-76.

2720. Leggett, John C. and Gioglio, Jerry. BREAK OUT THE DOUBLE DIGIT: MASS UNEMPLOYMENT IN THE CITY OF NEW BRUNSWICK. *Rev. of Radical Pol. Econ. 1978 10(1): 32-46.* Seeks to demonstrate that the Bureau of Labor Statistics systematically produced inaccurate figures on the scale of unemployment in New Brunswick, New Jersey, in 1975-76.

2721. Leon, Carol. EMPLOYMENT AND UNEMPLOYMENT IN THE FIRST HALF OF 1979. *Monthly Labor Rev. 1979 102(8): 3-7.* After 15 quarters of consecutive increases, total employment held steady in the second quarter of 1979. The number of employees on nonfarm payrolls rose rapidly in the first quarter, but grew slowly in the spring, and all sectors except government experienced employment gains at the beginning of the year; by midyear, however, many had slight declines. Unemployment, which had declined 14 quarters, was virtually unchanged at 5.7% during the first half of the year, although labor force participation rates were down by midyear after growing rapidly in the first quarter.

2722. Leon, Carol and Bednarzik, Robert W. A PROFILE OF WOMEN ON PART-TIME SCHEDULES. *Monthly Labor Rev. 1978 101(10): 3-12.* Discusses earnings, educational attainment, family/marital status, and work performance of women employed in part-time employment, 1940-70.

2723. Leon, Carol Boyd. EMPLOYED BUT NOT AT WORK: A REVIEW OF UNPAID ABSENCES. *Monthly Labor Rev. 1981 104(11): 18-22.* Provides statistics on employees who are absent from their jobs for various reasons, focusing on who the workers are, why they are absent, the industries that employ them, and the differences between male and female workers.

2724. Leon, Carol Boyd. THE EMPLOYMENT-POPULATION RA-TIO: ITS VALUE IN LABOR FORCE ANALYSIS. *Monthly Labor Rev. 1981 104(2): 36-45.* Describes the differences in the fluctuations in 1960-80 of the employment-population ratio, the employment level, the labor force participation rate, and the unemployment rate, and demonstrates the use of the employment-population ratio in secular and cyclical analyses and for interarea comparisons.

2725. Leon, Carol Boyd. OCCUPATIONAL WINNERS AND LOS-ERS: WHO THEY WERE DURING 1972-80. *Monthly Labor Rev. 1982 105(6): 18-28.* Although employment increased in most occupations, almost half of the increases were in 20 of 235 occupations surveyed, particularly professional and technical workers followed by managers and administrators, service workers, and craft and kindred workers, while farmworkers and private household workers declined.

2726. Linneman, Peter. THE ECONOMIC IMPACTS OF MINI-MUM WAGE LAWS: A NEW LOOK AT AN OLD QUESTION. *J. of Pol. Econ. 1982 90(3): 443-469.* Analyzes the socioeconomic characteristics of those members of the US population during 1974-75 who earned less than the minimum wage established by the 1974 amendment to the Fair Labor Standards Act (FLSA) and compares the post-1974 status of this group (composed primarily of women, blacks, nonveterans, and non-union members) to the employment rate and hours worked of people who earned more than the minimum wage in order to determine the economic impact of the FLSA amendment.

2727. Lipsky, David B. and Drotning, John E. THE INFLUENCE OF COLLECTIVE BARGAINING ON TEACHERS' SALARIES IN NEW YORK STATE. *Industrial and Labor Relations Rev. 1973 27(1): 18-35.* This study tests a model of teacher salary determination with data describing several aspects of all school districts in New York state, outside of New York City. The authors find that collective bargaining is not significant in explaining variations in 1968 teacher salaries among all school districts, but bargaining did have a significant effect among small districts and on the rate of salary change from 1967 to 1968. On the whole, however, the authors conclude that the results of this and other studies show that bargaining has had a surprisingly minor effect on teacher salaries.   J

2728. Long, James E. THE EFFECT OF AMERICANIZATION ON EARNINGS: SOME EVIDENCE FOR WOMEN. *J. of Pol. Econ. 1980 88(3): 620-629.* Presents statistical data on earnings of foreign-born women and compares these to statistics offered earlier for native-and foreign-born men; 1969-70.

2729. Lopreato, Sally Cook and Poston, Dudley L., Jr. DIFFER-ENCES IN EARNINGS AND EARNINGS ABILITY BETWEEN BLACK VETERANS AND NONVETERANS IN THE UNITED STATES. *Social Sci. Q. 1977 57(4): 750-766.* Military life provides job training, racial integration, and experience with bureaucracies. It may serve as a bridging environment which allows black veterans to convert their civilian education into earnings more effectively than nonveterans can. A regression analysis supports this conclusion for black male workers, between the ages of 25 and 54, who have at least 8 years of education, excluding Vietnam veterans. When the sample is disaggregated into three age groups and four regional-metropolitan categories, and the educational level is controlled, veterans retain their earnings advantage in all but one instance. Based on a one-percent sample of the 1970 US Census and on secondary sources; 3 tables, 7 notes, biblio.   W. R. Hively

2730. Luksetich, William A. MARKET POWER AND DISCRIMI-NATION IN WHITE-COLLAR EMPLOYMENT: 1969-1975. *Rev. of Social Econ. 1981 39(2): 145-164.* Examines the empirical evidence that indicates a relationship between measures of market power and the white-collar employment opportunities of minorities and women.

2731. MacRae, C. Duncan and Yezer, Anthony M. J. THE PERSON-AL INCOME TAX AND FAMILY LABOR SUPPLY. *Southern Econ. J. 1976 43(1): 783-792.* Discusses labor supply functions in families in the presence of a progressive income tax in the 1970's, including the influence of wages.

2732. Mantell, Edmund H. THE LABOR MARKET FOR ENGI-NEERS: A HARMONIZING OF METHODOLOGIES. *Industrial and Labor Relations Rev. 1973 27(1): 63-73.* This study analyzes a large sample of engineers for whom data are available concerning several dimensions of ability, together with a history of their education and earnings during the 1943-70 period. A model incorporating these variables accounts for about 65 percent of the variation in annual earnings within four of the five educational groupings of the engineers studied. The author also compares the internal rates of return to education among these engineers with rates of return among members of other professions and concludes that over the long run, the labor market has tended to produce an equilibrium between the supply of and demand for engineers of similar ability and education.   J

2733. Martin, Philip L. and Mamer, John. THE FARM LABOR MARKET. *Pro. of the Acad. of Pol. Sci. 1982 34(3): 223-234.* Although public and private reforms have transformed the farm labor market in several areas of the United States, illegal aliens impede the diffusion of modern labor practices and threaten to undo progress already made. If the current pool of low-skilled domestic and foreign labor shrinks, production of some labor-intensive crops will be reduced. The more efficient farmers may buy out their less efficient neighbors. If the farm labor pool is replenished, the gap between industrial and agricultural labor markets will widen, making it more difficult to equalize conditions. Based on primary and secondary sources; 2 notes.   T. P. Richardson

2734. Mellos, Koula. DEVELOPMENTS IN ADVANCED CAPITALIST IDEOLOGY. *Can. J. of Pol. Sci. [Canada] 1978 11(4): 829-861.* The new developments are an increased incidence of government intervention in the economy and science-technology as a force of production. These result in replacing the competitive basis of interaction by a cooperative basis of social interaction. A new form of class struggle appears, fought almost entirely within the institution of collective bargaining which allows the working class to pursue and acquire a greater share of the surplus and obtain better working conditions. Primary and secondary sources; 71 notes.   G. P. Cleyet

2735. Mitchell, Daniel J. B. PHASE II WAGE CONTROLS. *Industrial and Labor Relations Rev. 1974 27(3): 351-375.* This study provides a comprehensive summary of Pay Board standards during Phase II and assesses the effectiveness of those controls by a variety of tests, using data from internal Pay Board records among other sources. The author concludes that Phase II controls did have a significant impact on wage increases in new union agreements, but they had less effect on deferred increases and nonunion wages and little if any effect on aggregate income shares. The impact of Phase II on the nonwage aspects of industrial relations is also examined through an analysis of data on contract duration, strike activity, and NLRB election results.   J

2736. Mortimer, Jeylan T. and Lorence, Jon. WORK EXPERIENCE AND OCCUPATIONAL VALUE SOCIALIZATION: A LONGITUDINAL STUDY. *Am. J. of Sociol. 1979 84(6): 1361-1385.* Examines selection and socialization hypotheses with respect to the development of assessments of the importance of different rewards offered by work, using data gathered from male graduates of the University of Michigan, from 1966, 1967, and 1976.

2737. Moshenskii, M. ZARABOTNAIA PLATA V USLOVIIAKH GOSUDARSTVENNO-MONOPOLISTICHESKOGO KAPITALIZMA: FORMY, PROTIVORECHIIA [Wages under the conditions of state monopoly capitalism: forms and contradictions]. *Mirovaia Ekonomika i Mezhdunarodnye Otnosheniia [USSR] 1975 (11): 24-37.* Analyzes wages and income policy in the United States, Great Britain, and elsewhere.

2738. Mount, R. I. and Bennett, R. E. ECONOMIC AND SOCIAL FACTORS IN INCOME INEQUALITY. *Am. J. of Econ. and Sociol. 1975 34(2): 161-174.* The economic and social factors in wage differentials are examined for US data in 1969. Possession of an academic degree, and a person's sex, are important determinants of these differentials. Based on secondary sources; 4 tables, 6 notes.
W. L. Marr

2739. Murphey, Janice D. WAGE GAINS IN 1975: A SUMMARY ANALYSIS. *Monthly Labor Rev. 1976 99(4): 3-6.* "Examines wage changes in 1975 in the economy as a whole and under collective bargaining contracts, and offers a brief look at prospects for 1976."

2740. Murphy, Janice D. WAGE GAINS SMALLER DURING 1976. *Monthly Labor Rev. 1977 100(4): 3-6.* Analyzes factors affecting wages in 1976.

2741. Newman, Robert J. DYNAMIC PATTERNS IN REGIONAL WAGE DIFFERENTIALS. *Southern Econ J. 1982 49(1): 246-254.* A statistical study of differences in wages earned between the South and other regions shows some narrowing of the traditional difference in wages excluding nonwhites during the 1960's; this change caused a greater demand for short-term labor, which may be a temporary phenomenon.

2742. Niemi, A. W. THE IMPACT OF RECENT CIVIL RIGHTS LAWS. *Am. J. of Econ. and Sociol. 1974 33(2): 137-144.* Presents employment and income data on southern and northern white and nonwhite labor forces for the period 1960-70. Concludes that only for northern Negro women has occupational and income structure moved toward equality with whites over this decade in the United States. Secondary sources; 7 tables, 9 notes.   W. L. Marr

2743. Nikitin, S. AMERIKANSKII KAPITALIZM I PROIZVODITEL'NOST' TRUDA: UROKI 70-KH GODOV [American capitalism and labor productivity: lessons of the 1970's]. *Mirovaia Ekonomika i Mezhdunarodnye Otnosheniia [USSR] 1980 (4): 56-69.* In the framework of international comparisons, American productivity deteriorated during the 1970's compared with the previous 20 years' growth, growth partly based on achievements in science, education, and management, rather than on improved capital-labor ratios; the deterioration in the 1970's may be ascribed to factors such as the low efficiency of the State-Monopoly regulator, lower research and development expenditures, and legal pollution-abatement measures.

2744. Norsworthy, J. R. and Fulco, L. J. PRODUCTIVITY AND COSTS IN THE PRIVATE ECONOMY, 1973. *Monthly Labor Rev. 1974 97(6): 3-9.* Output per man-hour in the private economy in the United States increased at a lower rate in 1973 than in 1972; analysis of the 1967-73 period shows that part of the productivity slowdown is accounted for by employment shifts.

2745. Norwood, Janet L. LABOR MARKET CONTRASTS: UNITED STATES AND EUROPE. *Monthly Labor Rev. 1983 106(8): 3-7.* A review of demographic factors and data from 1970 indicates that the employment future is better in the United States than in Europe as of 1983.

2746. Olson, Laura Katz. THE POLITICAL ECONOMY OF WORKER PENSION FUNDS. *Policy Studies J. 1979 8(3): 406-416.* Worker pension funds have become a major source of capital that has increased the power of financial institutions and promoted the growth of corporate profits; but they have not been used for socially useful projects and have created or sustained antiworker practices, inhibiting, for example, unionization through the support of corporate enterprises that have antiunion tendencies.

2747. Osterman, Paul. AN EMPIRICAL STUDY OF LABOR MARKET SEGMENTATION. *Industrial & Labor Relations Rev. 1975 28(4): 508-523.* This study tests a refined version of the dual labor market theory which hypothesizes that the labor force is segmented in three groups: secondary jobs as usually defined, plus a primary sector consisting of upper tier jobs in which workers enjoy a high degree of autonomy and a personal participation in the work process, and lower tier jobs providing little autonomy and participation. Using data from the 1967 Survey of Economic Opportunity, the author shows that the determinants of annual earnings differ substantially among the three segments. Human capital characteristics explain the variance in individuals' earnings very well in the upper tier and moderately well in the lower tier of the primary sector, but in the secondary sector only the amount of time worked proved to be a significant determinant of earnings.   J

2748. Owen, John D. WORKWEEKS AND LEISURE: AN ANALYSIS OF TRENDS, 1948-75. *Monthly Labor Rev. 1976 99(8): 3-8.* Discusses trends since the end of World War II in the American labor market, showing that the postwar period marked a shift in the composition of the working class, with larger proportions of women and students in the working force, and offering a hypothesis for the postwar leveling-off of working hours.

2749. Paldam, Martin and Pedersen, Peder J. THE MACROECONOMIC STRIKE MODEL: A STUDY OF SEVENTEEN COUNTRIES, 1948-1975. *Industrial and Labor Relations Rev. 1982 35(4): 504-521.* Analyzes data on industrial conflict (strikes and lockouts) in seventeen OECD countries, 1948-75. A number of models are tested, including the major elements of the Ashenfelter and Johnson model. Contrary to Ashenfelter and Johnson's results for the United States, this study finds for most countries a positive relationship between the number of conflicts and the rate of increase in real wages in manufacturing. Further, the increase in nominal wages produces stronger results in all models tested than the increase in real wages; the effect of unemployment is unstable across countries; and only one of two political variables yields even modest results. Relations between changes in the wage structure and changes in the level of conflict might explain these findings.   J/S

2750. Pampel, Fred C. CHANGES IN LABOR FORCE PARTICIPATION AND INCOME OF THE AGED IN THE UNITED STATES, 1947-1976. *Social Problems 1979 27(2): 125-142.* Shows how elderly men and women, though their participation in the labor market declined between 1947 and 1976, received a higher income due to raised retirement benefits and cohort growth.

2751. Pampel, Fred C.; Land, Kenneth C.; and Felson, Marcus. A SOCIAL INDICATOR MODEL OF CHANGES IN THE OCCUPATIONAL STRUCTURE OF THE UNITED STATES: 1947-1974. *Am. Sociol. Rev. 1977 42(6): 951-964.* This paper presents a ten-equation dynamic structural equation model that shows how aggregate changes in the occupational structure of the United States affect each other and are affected by economic, technological and institutional changes. The model postulates a recursive flow of causation from changes in sectorial (agricultural, manufacturing, services) demand and productivity to changes in the distribution of occupations by sector, bureaucratization and status level. Model equations are estimated on annual national data from 1947 to 1972 and are used to make conditional forecasts of the endogenous variables for 1973 and 1974. The equations fit the observed data well, lack demonstrable autocorrelation of disturbances, and forecast the 1973 and 1974 values with considerable accuracy. Empirically, the model facilitates the quantitative estimation of the relative effects of economic growth and technological change on expansion of the service economy, bureaucratization of jobs, and growth of high-status occupations. In particular, when combined with recent findings on the sources of intergenerational occupational mobility in twentieth-century American society by Hauser et al. (1975), the model shows how changes in the pattern of economic growth and productivity from that which has prevailed for most of the post-World War II period may imply a decline in the rates of upward occupational mobility in the absence of other counterbalancing structural changes.   J

2752. Parnes, Herbert S. INFLATION AND EARLY RETIREMENT: RECENT LONGITUDINAL FINDINGS. *Monthly Labor Rev. 1981 104(7): 27-30.* Examines the data from the 1978 National Longitudinal Survey (NLS) of middle-aged and older men, which focuses on the retirement status and expectations of a national sample between 1976 and 1978 and which gave quite different results from the 1978 Louis Harris poll that reported a reversal in the trend toward earlier retirement; the NLS findings show that basically the trend toward early retirement seems to be continuing.

2753. Parnes, Herbert S. and Sheets, Carol T. THE NATIONAL LONGITUDINAL SURVEYS DATA FILES: CONTENT AND STRUCTURE. Raben, Joseph and Marks, Gregory, ed. *Data Bases in the Humanities and Social Sciences* (Amsterdam: North-Holland Publ., 1980): 15-20. In 1965 the US Department of Labor contracted with the Center for Human Resource Research of Ohio State University to prepare the National Longitudinal Surveys of Labor Market Behavior, a continuing study of the labor market experience of men 45 to 59 years of age, women 30 to 44 years of age, and young people between 14 and 24 years of age.

2754. Perlo, Victor. THE FALSE CLAIM OF DECLINING PRODUCTIVITY AND ITS POLITICAL USE. *Sci. & Soc. 1982 46(3): 284-327.* The highly publicized deflated value productivity indexes of the Bureau of Labor Statistics are seriously flawed, and for the past decade give a completely false picture of stagnant and declining productivity. The statistics are influenced, to a major degree, by the trend of real wages, which have stagnated and declined since 1972. While the statistics seem to portray an alarming decline in worker productivity, they do not measure the actual trend in physical output per man-hour. Printed primary sources; 56 notes.   L. V. Eid

2755. Perrone, Luca and Wright, Erik Olin. CLASSI SOCIALI, SCUOLA, OCCUPAZIONE E REDDITO IN U.S.A.: UNA ANALISI QUANTITATIVA SULLE DISEGUAGLIANZE SOCIALI IN UNA SOCIETÀ POST-INDUSTRIALE [Social classes, schooling, employment, and income in the United States: a quantitative analysis of social inequalities in a postindustrial society]. *Quaderni di Sociologia [Italy] 1975 24(1-2): 55-91.* In evaluating the relevance of Marxist conceptions of social class, analyzes the effect of social class background on income in the United States, showing that income differences closely correspond to social classes, even when such variables as education level, job tenure, occupational prestige, race, and sex are taken into account.

2756. Perrucci, Carolyn Cummings. INCOME ATTAINMENT OF COLLEGE GRADUATES: A COMPARISON OF EMPLOYED

WOMEN AND MEN. *Sociol. and Social Res. 1978 62(3): 361-386.* In the prediction of 1964 income for a national sample of 1961 college graduates, there are significant gender effects, and marital status interactions for women but not for men. Employed women, both married and single, have lower incomes than men, and relatively little of the income difference between the sexes can be accounted for by differences in personal resources (e.g., education). Marriage is the best single predictor of income for men, and little of the income advantage enjoyed by married men is due to superior personal resources. Conversely, marriage entails a small "cost" for women. The following predictor variables positively influence income of both men and women: graduate educational attainment, occupational status, years of work experience, age, hours worked weekly, college selectivity, grades, and valuation of pecuniary success. Social origins and marital fertility have little effect on income during the early careers of either men or women college graduates.   J

2757. Perry, Charles S. THE RATIONALIZATION OF U.S. FARM LABOR: TRENDS BETWEEN 1956 AND 1979. *Rural Sociol. 1982 47(4): 670-691.* Discusses the trends of an increasing proportion of workers being hired for a longer duration and for family labor declining at a faster rate than hired labor.

2758. Personick, Valerie A. and Sylvester, Robert A. EVALUATION OF BLS 1970 ECONOMIC AND EMPLOYMENT PROJECTIONS. *Monthly Labor Rev. 1976 99(8): 13-26.* Analyzes the projections of 1970 economic and employment data published by the Bureau of Labor Statistics in 1966, examining the data and the underlying assumptions which resulted in errors in industry output and employment estimates.

2759. Phelps, Edmund S. ECONOMIC POLICY AND UNEMPLOYMENT IN THE 1960'S. *Public Interest 1974 (34): 30-46.* Reflects on macroeconomic programs which attempted to "create an environment of greater job opportunities and higher employment" and on microeconomic ones which invested in "low-income workers for the purpose of raising their relative earning power."

2760. Piore, Michael J. ECONOMIC FLUCTUATION, JOB SECURITY, AND LABOR-MARKET DUALITY IN ITALY, FRANCE, AND THE UNITED STATES. *Pol. & Soc. 1980 9(4): 379-407.* Comparative case studies offer several explanations of the origins of dualism in the French, Italian, and American labor markets. The human capital perspective tends to dictate the explanation for particular jobs of the secondary sector being filled by particular groups of workers. 50 notes.   D. G. Nielson

2761. Pollnac, Ricard B.; Gersuny, Carl; and Poggie, John J., Jr. ECONOMIC GRATIFICATION PATTERNS OF FISHERMEN AND MILLWORKERS IN NEW ENGLAND. *Human Organization 1975 34(1): 1-7.* Describes a 1972 study of economic gratification orientations, concluding that they "are related to occupation, temporal perspective, and ethnicity."

2762. Porter, Felice and Keller, Richard L. PUBLIC AND PRIVATE PAY LEVELS: A COMPARISON IN LARGE LABOR MARKETS. *Monthly Labor Rev. 1981 104(7): 22-26.* Examines data collected during a survey between summer of 1974 and fall of 1980 of wages of city government employees and compares the wages of city government workers, workers in private industry, and federal government workers in selected US cities.

2763. Portes, Alejandro and Bach, Robert L. IMMIGRANT EARNINGS: CUBAN AND MEXICAN IMMIGRANTS IN THE UNITED STATES. *Int. Migration Rev. 1980 14(3): 315-341.* Studies the applicability of the determinants of earnings for these two groups, interviewed upon arrival in 1973 and then again in 1976, to recent perspectives on income.

2764. Prier, Robert J. LABOR AND MATERIAL REQUIREMENTS FOR FEDERALLY AIDED HIGHWAYS. *Monthly Labor Rev. 1979 102(12): 29-34.* Labor requirements in hours per $1,000 on federally aided highway construction rose 0.6% per year, 1973-76, after a long decline.

2765. Prybyla, Jan S. THE UNEMPLOYMENT PROBLEM IN THE UNITED STATES. *Australian Q. [Australia] 1961 33(3): 26-34.* Identifies the structural causes of postwar unemployment.

2766. Reagan, Barbara B. STOCKS AND FLOWS OF ACADEMIC ECONOMISTS. *Am. Econ. Rev. 1979 69(2): 143-147.* The use of the stock-flow method as an indicator of discrimination also simplifies measuring the effect of affirmative action regarding women with the Ph.D. degree. Fig., 6 ref.   D. K. Pickens

2767. Reed, Leonard. THE GREAT FEDERAL GRAVY TRAIN ROBBERY. *Washington Monthly 1980 11(12): 39-45.* Briefly traces the federal employee pay scale since 1962, and discusses the controversy over the 1979 recommendations for federal employees' pay raises. President Carter originally requested a 5.5% raise (later changed to 7%) while the committee known as the Pay Agent requested a 9.8% raise; the figure decided upon was 11%.

2768. Rees, Albert. H. GREGG LEWIS AND THE DEVELOPMENT OF ANALYTICAL LABOR ECONOMICS. *J. of Pol. Econ. 1976 84(4, 2), S3-S8.* Records the contributions of H. Gregg Lewis during his long career as a teacher at the University of Chicago.

2769. Reid, Frank. CONTROL AND DECONTROL OF WAGES IN THE UNITED STATES: AN EMPIRICAL ANALYSIS. *Am. Econ. Rev. 1981 71(1): 108-120.* Without fiscal and monetary restrictions, controls have limited effectiveness. Also, both wages and prices must be equally affected. The historical experience in this area, however, is not encouraging. The Nixon policy did not work. 3 tables, 28 ref., 8 notes.   D. K. Pickens

2770. Reid, Frank. THE RESPONSE OF WAGES TO THE REMOVAL OF CONTROLS: THE AMERICAN EXPERIENCE. *Industrial Relations [Canada] 1977 32(4): 621-627.* Assesses the format of wage and price controls, 1971-74, developing a model to explain the rate of wage change and the effect of the controls.

2771. Reynolds, Craig A. EMPLOYMENT AND THE INCOME GAP. *Crisis 1981 88(4): 185-191.* In 1980, black unemployment was over twice as high as white, and the black median income was less than 60% of white family median income. The causes for income differences in the last 30 years can be partially explained by credentialism and immigration. Discrimination against blacks often has been on the basis of qualifications higher than actually required in order to screen out blacks. In addition, waves of illegal immigrants have provided employers with cheaper labor, displacing black workers.   A. G. Belles

2772. Rittenoure, R. Lynn. MEASURING FAIR EMPLOYMENT PRACTICES: THE SEARCH FOR A "FIGURE OF MERIT." *Am. J. of Econ. and Sociol. 1978 37(2): 113-128.* Quantitative measures of equal employment opportunity in the bureaucracy are of quite recent vintage, even though data have been collected on minority employment since the early 1960s. Such measures as have been developed are useful in the sense that they are simple and easy to comprehend. Concentrating as they do on integration alone, however, they do not capture a sufficiently wide variety of personnel practices to truly assess equal employment opportunity. This paper presents a new measure which retains the basic simplicity required of a figure of merit but expands the dimensions of former measures to include an index of the occupational distribution of minorities within an organization. The measure presented implies a policy goal of income parity for minority groups within the bureaucracy and assorgesses progress toward that goal. It is argued that a worthy figure of merit can promote cost-effective implementation of public policy with regard to fair employment within the civil service.   J

2773. Roberts, Markley. WAGE-PRICE CONTROLS AND INCOME DISTRIBUTION. *Policy Studies J. 1975 4(1): 15-19.* An examination of US wage-price policies during 1960-74 indicates that economic controls on income must be pursued within a social and political context.

2774. Robinson, Joan. EMPLOYMENT AND INFLATION. *Q. Rev. of Econ. and Business 1979 19(3): 7-16.* In the 1930's growing unemployment was accompanied by falling prices. Now we suffer from stagflation. There are two types of price formation—demand and supply

in commodity markets and administered prices for manufactures. Inflation, properly speaking, is not due to "demand pull" which causes real output to rise, but to rising rates of pay. The attempt to combat inflation by monetary restrictions reduces employment and real output without stopping the rise of prices.   J

2775. Roepke, Howard G. and Freudenberg, David A. THE EMPLOYMENT STRUCTURES OF NONMETROPOLITAN COUNTIES. *Ann. of the Assoc. of Am. Geog. 1981 71(4): 580-592.* Analyzes economic base structures of nonmetropolitan, urban-centered counties; the counties experienced significant economic growth and change during the 1960's.

2776. Rogers, David L.; Pendleton, Brian F.; Goudy, Willis J.; and Richards, Robert O. INDUSTRIALIZATION, INCOME BENEFITS, AND THE RURAL COMMUNITY. *Rural Sociol. 1978 43(2): 250-264.* Examines the impact (1960-70) of industrialization on income levels and distributions in Iowa towns with populations of 2,500 to 10,000.

2777. Rojek, Andrzej. PRZYCZYNY ZMIAN WYDAJNOŚCI PRACY W GOSPODARCE AMERYKAŃSKIEJ W LATACH 1965-1979 [Causes of changes in labor productivity in the American economy, 1965-79]. *Ekonomista [Poland] 1982 (1-2): 169-179.*

2778. Rones, P. L. and Leon, C. EMPLOYMENT AND UNEMPLOYMENT DURING 1978: AN ANALYSIS. *Monthly Labor Rev. 1979 102(2): 3-12.* With the drop of the unemployment rate to 5.8%, 59% of all Americans of working age were employed at the end of 1978.

2779. Rones, Philip L. MOVING TO THE SUN: REGIONAL JOB GROWTH, 1968 TO 1978. *Monthly Labor Rev. 1980 103(3): 12-19.* Federal spending and favorable economic conditions combined to make the economies of the states of the South and West grow fastest, 1968-78.

2780. Rones, Philip L. THE RETIREMENT DECISION: A QUESTION OF OPPORTUNITY? *Monthly Labor Rev. 1980 103(11): 14-17.* Discusses retirement trends in the United States, 1950-79.

2781. Rosen, Richard. IDENTIFYING STATES AND AREAS PRONE TO HIGH AND LOW UNEMPLOYMENT. *Monthly Labor Rev. 1980 103(3): 20-24.* Unemployment rate increases during the 1974-75 recession were highest in state and metropolitan areas with heavy concentrations of manufacturing employment.

2782. Rosenfeld, Carl and Brown, Scott Campbell. THE LABOR FORCE STATUS OF OLDER WORKERS. *Monthly Labor Rev. 1979 102(11): 12-18.* Statistics on employment, 1950-78, show a sharp decline among men age 60 to 64 compared to stable rates for women in this age group.

2783. Rosenthal, Neal H. THE UNITED STATES ECONOMY IN 1985: PROJECTED CHANGES IN OCCUPATIONS. *Monthly Labor Rev. 1973 96(12): 18-26.* Discusses current Bureau of Labor Statistics projections for occupational trends and job openings for white collar, blue collar and farm workers in 1985.

2784. Ross, Robert and Trachte, Kent. GLOBAL CITIES AND GLOBAL CLASSES: THE PERIPHERALIZATION OF LABOR IN NEW YORK CITY. *Rev. (Fernand Braudel Center) 1983 6(3): 393-431.* The internationalization of capital considerably weakens labor organizations by the threat to move elsewhere. The acceleration of international capital flowing away from the core regions and towards the periphery will erode the bargaining power and ultimately the standard of living of the formerly privileged labor in global cities. Analysis of industrial and human trends in New York City since the 1960's shows that being a "global city" does not entail a privileged working class status. 9 tables, biblio.   L. V. Eid

2785. Ruben, George. COLLECTIVE BARGAINING IN 1982: RESULTS DICTATED BY ECONOMY. *Monthly Labor Rev. 1983 106(1): 28-37.* Economic conditions created an unfavorable atmosphere for demands from labor as unemployment rose to its highest level since 1940, business failures occurred at a higher rate than any year since the Great Depression, and factory use was at its lowest level in 35 years.

2786. Ryscavage, Paul M. ANNUAL EARNINGS OF HOUSE-HOLD HEADS. *Monthly Labor Rev. 1975 98(8): 14-21.* Examines the effects of inflation on the gross income of production and nonsupervisory workers.

2787. Ryscavage, Paul. TWO DIVERGENT MEASURES OF PURCHASING POWER. *Monthly Labor Rev. 1979 102(8): 25-30.* Disposable income grew by 2.5% per year during 1970-78, while spendable earnings rose by 0.3%, much of the difference caused by growth rates in groups covered in both series.

2788. Rytina, Nancy F. EARNINGS OF MEN AND WOMEN: A LOOK AT SPECIFIC OCCUPATIONS. *Monthly Labor Rev. 1982 105(4): 25-31.* Occupations in which women workers dominate tend to rank lower in terms of earnings; men dominate higher paid occupations.

2789. Rytina, Nancy F. TENURE AS A FACTOR IN THE MALE-FEMALE EARNINGS GAP *Monthly Labor Rev. 1982 105(4): 32-34.* Women have fewer years in their current occupations than men, a factor which affects the earnings disparity.

2790. Safa, Helen I. LA PARTICIPACIÓN DIFERENCIAL DE MUJERES EMIGRANTES DE AMÉRICA LATINA EN LA FUERZA DE TRABAJO DE LOS ESTADOS UNIDOS [The participation differential of Latin American emigrant women in the US labor force]. *Demografía y Economía [Mexico] 1978 12(1): 113-128.* Discusses the impact of women of Latin American origin in the labor market in New York City, 1970's.

2791. —. [SIZE DISTRIBUTION OF FAMILY INCOME].
Sale, Tom S., III. INTERSTATE ANALYSIS OF THE SIZE DISTRIBUTION OF FAMILY INCOME, 1950-1970. *Southern Econ. J. 1974 40(3): 434-441.* Size distribution of family income, when measured by the Gini ratio for 48 states, indicates that income has become more equally distributed while rates of decrease appear to be slowing.
Fromby, John P. and Seaks, Terry G. COMMENT. *Southern Econ. J. 1978 45(2): 615-621.* Errors in Sale's article affected new regressions; examines the stability of regressions through time.
Singh, S. K. and Sale, Tom S., III. REPLY. *Southern Econ. J. 1978 45(2): 622-629.* Corrects data errors, deriving an improved economic model which incorporates time as a variable and separates secular and cyclical effects.

2792. Salkever, David S. EFFECTS OF CHILDREN'S HEALTH ON MATERNAL HOURS OF WORK: A PRELIMINARY ANALYSIS. *Southern Econ. J. 1980 47(1): 156-166.* Data analyzed with a basic labor supply model indicate that children's disabilities and health problems negatively affect maternal working hours; 1972.

2793. Scaggs, Mary Beth W. RECENT EMPLOYMENT TRENDS IN THE LUMBER AND WOOD PRODUCTS INDUSTRY. *Monthly Labor Rev. 1983 106(8): 20-24.* Low prices for Canadian lumber and a weak housing market have had a particularly depressing effect on West Coast producers since 1979; focuses on economic conditions since 1979 and the effects on employment and hours in the industry.

2794. Schoepfle, Gregory K. IMPORTS AND DOMESTIC EMPLOYMENT: IDENTIFYING AFFECTED INDUSTRIES. *Monthly Labor Rev. 1982 105(8): 13-26.* Identifies some of the problems in measuring the domestic market share dominated by imports and indicates that 25% of manufacturing groups are affected by increased market penetration by imports.

2795. Schriver, William R.; Bowlby, Roger L.; and Pursell, Donald E. EVALUATION OF TRADE READJUSTMENT ASSISTANCE TO WORKERS: A CASE STUDY. *Social Sci. Q. 1976 57(3): 547-556.* Examines the subsequent work experience of a redundant work force that was eligible for trade readjustment assistance under the Trade Expansion Act of 1962. *Evaluation of Trade Readjustment Assistance to Workers: A Case Study* indicates that although TRA benefits prolonged the potential job search period they did not lead to a wage advantage even when the benefits included training, nor did the benefits mitigate alienation associated with the layoff.   J

2796. Schwenk, Albert E. EARNINGS DIFFERENCES IN MACHINERY MANUFACTURING. *Monthly Labor Rev. 1974 97(7): 38-47.* An econometric analysis of 22 labor markets in the United States in 1970-71, exploring the reasons for differing wage rates for the same occupation in the machinery manufacturing industry.

2797. Schwenk, Albert E. PROFIT RATES AND NEGOTIATED WAGE CHANGES. *Q. Rev. of Econ. and Business 1980 20(1): 63-75.* This article analyzes the relationship between profitability and negotiated wage changes. Two hypotheses are tested: 1) the impact of profit rates on wage changes is stronger for unconcentrated industries than for concentrated ones; and 2) the appropriate profits measure for cross-section wage-change analysis is not the reported profit rate, but that rate relative to the "normal" profit rate for the firm or industry. Support for the hypotheses is provided by OLS regression analysis of two data sets, one covering wage settlements in 13 firms over the 1954-71 period, and the other covering settlements in a number of manufacturing industries during 1967-69. 3 tables, 6 notes, biblio., 3 appendixes.   J

2798. Scully, Gerald W. and Gallaway, Lowell E. A SPECTRAL ANALYSIS OF THE DEMOGRAPHIC STRUCTURE OF AMERICAN UNEMPLOYMENT. *J. of Business 1973 46(1): 87-102.* An analysis covering demographic aspects of the structure of unemployment through the use of spectral or cross-spectral analysis, illustrating basic structural differences between labor subgroups and the prime group (white adult males). There is little evidence to suggest that unemployment rates for demographic subgroups behave cyclically differently than the prime group. The first-fired-last-hired mechanism does operate in the labor market with the greatest impact being against nonwhites. Based on secondary sources; 5 figs., 8 tables, 14 notes.

C. A. Gallacci

2799. Sehgal, Ellen and Vialet, Joyce. DOCUMENTING THE UNDOCUMENTED: DATA, LIKE ALIENS, ARE ELUSIVE. *Monthly Labor Rev. 1980 103(10): 18-21.* Gathering statistics concerning illegal aliens in the United States, particularly their number and their role in the labor market, is extremely difficult.

2800. Sekscenski, Edward S. WOMEN'S SHARE OF MOONLIGHTING NEARLY DOUBLES DURING 1969-79. *Monthly Labor Rev. 1980 103(5): 36-39.* Analyzes moonlighting employment nationally during this period, discussing all sectors and groups of the economy.

2801. Sell, Ralph R. and Johnson, Michael P. INCOME AND OCCUPATIONAL DIFFERENCES BETWEEN MEN AND WOMEN IN THE UNITED STATES. *Sociol. and Social Res. 1977 62(1): 1-20.* According to the U.S. Bureau of Census the median income in 1974 for men aged 25 and older working year-round full-time was $12,786; the comparable income for women was $7,370. This paper describes several of the dimensions of this income differential through: 1) a description of the American occupational structure by sex as it existed in 1970 and 1960; 2) a description of the associated reward structure for these occupations in 1969; and 3) a decomposition of this 1969 income differential into components which may be attributed to: a) differences in the opportunity structure of women as indicated by major occupation, education, and number of weeks worked, and b) a residual amount attributed to unanalyzed differences. The results suggest that structural differences is the predominant factor promoting income differences by sex.   J

2802. Shahidsaless, Shahin; Gillis, William; and Shaffer, Ron. COMMUNITY CHARACTERISTICS AND EMPLOYMENT MULTIPLIERS IN NONMETROPOLITAN COUNTIES, 1950-1970. *Land Econ. 1983 59(1): 84-93.* Uses data from 264 nonmetropolitan counties to construct a regression model in order to evaluate the effect of economic base multipliers. Finds that specific community characteristics have a strong influence on the magnitude of the economic base multipliers. The findings suggest any community attempting to expand should have a comprehensive community development strategy. Secondary sources; 2 tables, 9 notes, 28 ref.   E. S. Johnson

2803. Sheifer, Victor J. COST-OF-LIVING ADJUSTMENT: KEEPING UP WITH INFLATION? *Monthly Labor Rev. 1979 102(6): 14-17.* Discusses the inclusion of escalator clauses since 1948 in union contracts which automatically provide periodic cost-of-living raises in order to keep up with inflation.

2804. Sheifer, Victor J. EMPLOYMENT COST INDEX: MEASURE OF CHANGE IN "PRICE OF LABOR." *Monthly Labor Rev. 1975 98(7): 3-12.* Examines new statistics which will provide comprehensive data on changes in the rate of hourly wages.

2805. Sheiman, I. EFFEKTIVNOST' TRUDA V SFERE USLUG [The effectiveness of labor in service industries]. *Mirovaia Ekonomika i Mezhdunarodnye Otnosheniia [USSR] 1982 (3): 80-91.* Evaluates the economic and social effectiveness of service industries in the West, particularly the United States, and finds that this important economic sector, whose stable growth is the principle feature of postwar US economic history, has achieved a high degree of coordination among the various branches of the economy, but, as is to be expected under conditions of private enterprise, service industries exhibit numerous conflicting tendencies.

2806. Shelley, Edwin F. and Shelley, Florence D. A RETIREMENT INDEX? *Social Policy 1976 7(3): 52-54.* Suggests an index for retirement based on years of work completed, age, health, income in retirement, possibility or preference for new careers, future happiness, and personal preference, in order to do away with mandatory retirement ages, 1970's.

2807. Sheppard, Harold L. THE ISSUE OF MANDATORY RE-TIREMENT. *Ann. of the Am. Acad. of Pol. and Social Sci. 1978 438: 40-49.* The issue of mandatory retirement is complicated, not as easily resolved as it may first appear. Part of the issue has to do with whether there ought to be any age at which employees must retire; another is, given mandatory retirement, is there an appropriate age for it? The newest federal legislation addresses the issue by using age 70 (with some exceptions) as the earliest age at which employers may legitimately require their employees to retire. This paper investigates whether a problem actually exists with respect to a mandatory retirement age. It discusses evidence from a national survey dealing with hiring and firing practices and points out the need to distinguish between functional and chronological age. Some research and policy issues are discussed, and, finally, the relationship of mandatory retirement to the young in the work force is considered. The paper concludes by noting that the emerging issue will center on costs to the total economy of early retirement for a growing population whose life expectancy is continuing to rise and what the alternative solutions to those costs might be, including the alternative of reversing the trend toward early retirement.
J

2808. Shiskin, Julius and Stein, R. L. PROBLEMS IN MEASURING UNEMPLOYMENT. *Monthly Labor Rev. 1975 98(8): 3-10.* Examines the issues and problems raised by the Bureau of Labor Statistics study of the intensity of job searching by the unemployed.

2809. Shultz, George P. and Dam, Kenneth W. REFLECTIONS ON WAGE AND PRICE CONTROLS. *Industrial and Labor Relations Rev. 1977 30(2): 139-151.* This article appraises the controls program of 1971-74 in the context of a general analysis of all such programs. The authors suggest, among other ideas, that wage and price control programs have a "life cycle" that is both inevitable and remarkably short in duration, that the tendency of such programs to concentrate on the largest firms and unions is based on a faulty analysis of how the economy operates, and that one of the most difficult problems faced by control programs is dealing with the unending interaction of controls with other public programs as well as with private actions. The authors conclude that the principal lesson of the 1971-74 experience is that wage and price controls are not an effective method for dealing with inflation.
J

2810. Sieling, Mark S. CLERICAL PAY DIFFERENTIALS IN METROPOLITAN AREAS. 1961-80. *Monthly Labor Rev. 1982 105(7): 10-14.* Traces the trends in the wages of office clerical workers from 1961-80, and concludes that, in general, salaries are higher in large urban areas and in north central and western areas; differences narrowed during the 1960's and widened during the 1970's.

2811. Smith, Patricia B. THE EMPLOYMENT COST INDEX IN 1980: A FIRST LOOK AT TOTAL COMPENSATION. *Monthly Labor Rev. 1981 104(6): 22-26.* Analyzes the Employment Cost Index (ECI) in 1980, when it first measured total compensation change; the ECI includes both increased wages and salaries and compensation for employees in the nonfarm, private sector, and examines differing rates for white-collar, blue-collar, and service workers.

2812. Smith, Shirley J. NEW WORKLIFE ESTIMATES REFLECT CHANGING PROFILE OF LABOR FORCE. *Monthly Labor Rev. 1982 105(3): 15-20.* Because worklife expectancies of men leveled off between 1970 and 1977, and that of women increased, a new model known as the increment-decrement working life table was established rendering the conventional model obsolete.

2813. Solberg, Eric J. and Langille, Frederick. THE WAGE RATE, POTENTIAL WORK INCENTIVES, AND BENEFIT PAYMENT REDUCTION IN THE *AFDC* PROGRAM. *Q. R. of Econ. and Business 1974 14(2): 85-100.* Argues that potential work incentive effects and benefit payment reductions from the disregard provision in the AFDC program are largely dependent on the wage rate. A main contribution is an explicit comparison of the effects on both disposable income of the AFDC recipient and the AFDC benefit payment from either increases in the market wage rate or decreases in the marginal tax rate. It is clear that substantial reductions in welfare costs can be realized if employable recipients can find suitable employment. It also becomes clear that employment at *low* wage rates may actually increase program costs.
J

2814. Sollogoub, Michel. LA COMPARAISON DE L'INÉGALITÉ DANS LA RÉPARTITION PERSONNELLE DES REVENUS: NOTE SUR L'ÉTUDE DE L'O.C.D.E. ET SUR LES CAS FRANÇAIS ET AMÉRICAIN (1962-1970) [Comparison of inequality in personal distribution of income: note on the study of the OECD and on the French and American cases, 1962-70]. *Rev. d'Écon. Pol. [France] 1980 90(3): 286-306.* A comparative statistical analysis of the distribution of average incomes by age in the United States and France, with the use of Paglin-Gini and Paglin-Atkinson coefficients of inequality measurements.

2815. Sommers, Dixie. OCCUPATIONAL RANKINGS FOR MEN AND WOMEN BY EARNINGS. *Monthly Labor Rev. 1974 97(8): 34-51.* Analyzes the US census of 1970, confirming that skill, sex, and age are likely to determine the worker's position on the pay ladder.

2816. Sorrentino, Constance. INTERNATIONAL COMPARISONS OF LABOR FORCE PARTICIPATION, 1960-81. *Monthly Labor Rev. 1983 106(2): 23-36.* Compares rates of labor force activity since 1960 among nine industrial nations, showing the effects of trends in work force composition by age and sex; US labor force activity has increased largely because of greater participation by women and youth.

2817. Sproat, Kezia. USING NATIONAL LONGITUDINAL SURVEYS TO TRACK YOUNG WORKERS. *Monthly Labor Rev. 1979 102(10): 28-33.* Summarizes recent findings and ongoing research by the National Longitudinal Surveys of Labor Force Experience (NLS) on the youth labor market, focusing on the effects of the family and education on employment, 1960's-70's.

2818. Squires, Gregory D. EDUCATION, JOBS AND INEQUALITY: FUNCTIONAL AND CONFLICT MODELS OF SOCIAL STRATIFICATION IN THE UNITED STATES. *Social Problems 1977 24(4): 436-450.* Examines two competing interpretations of the relationship between formal education and occupational structure, and the dynamics of American social stratification, 1960-75.

2819. Staller, Jerome M. and Solnick, Loren M. EFFECTS OF ESCALATORS ON WAGES IN MAJOR CONTRACTS EXPIRING IN 1974. *Monthly Labor Rev. 1974 97(7): 27-32.* Wage increases in the United States under escalated three-year contracts expiring in 1974 were higher than increases under other contracts, possibly reflecting the unexpected flare-up of inflation and union bargaining strength.

2820. Stamas, George D. REAL AFTER-TAX ANNUAL EARN-INGS FROM THE CURRENT POPULATION SURVEY. *Monthly Labor Rev. 1979 102(8): 42-45.* Median annual earnings of production and nonsupervisory workers and their spouses increased substantially, 1973-77, whether measured before or after subtracting federal income and social security taxes. When adjusted for changes in consumer prices, however, after-tax earnings of most groups of workers were about the same in 1977 as those reported for 1973.

2821. Stein, Robert L. and Ryscavage, Paul M. MEASURING ANNUAL EARNINGS BY HOUSEHOLD HEADS IN PRODUCTION JOBS. *Monthly Labor Rev. 1974 97(4): 3-11.* Data on median annual earnings of family heads in production jobs in the United States from 1963 to 1972 show an average annual increase of 5.3% or 1.6% after tax.

2822. Stein, Robert L. NATIONAL COMMISSION RECOMMENDS CHANGES IN LABOR FORCE STATISTICS. *Monthly Labor Rev. 1980 103(4): 11-21.* Discusses recommendations of the National Commission on Employment and Unemployment Statistics established in 1976 by Congress, and the Secretary of Labor's response on the ways to implement the findings of the Commission presented in 1979, which suggest that employment and unemployment data needs to be expanded and refined.

2823. Steinnes, Donald N. CAUSALITY AND MIGRATION: A STATISTICAL RESOLUTION OF THE "CHICKEN OR EGG FOWL-UP." *Southern Econ. J. 1978 45(1): 218-226.* Does migration follow jobs, or do jobs follow migration? Study of data, 1947-63, indicates that causality is unidirectional and that migration follows employment.

2824. Stelluto, George L. FEDERAL PAY COMPARABILITY: FACTS TO TEMPER THE DEBATE. *Monthly Labor Rev. 1979 102(6): 18-28.* Describes the process by which the amount of the pay raises of federal white collar employees is decided.

2825. Stiglitz, Joseph E. APPROACHES TO THE ECONOMICS OF DISCRIMINATION. *Am. Econ. Rev. 1973 63(2): 287-295.* Discusses economic theories which explain causes of wage discrimination in the labor market (1972).

2826. Stoddard, Ellwyn R. A CONCEPTUAL ANALYSIS OF THE "ALIEN INVASION": INSTITUTIONALIZED SUPPORT OF ILLEGAL MEXICAN ALIENS IN THE U.S. *Int. Migration Rev. 1976 10(2): 157-189.* Discusses economic factors in patterns of immigration of illegal aliens from Mexico in the 1960's and 70's, including the role of quota systems and the Bracero Program.

2827. Straussman, Jeffrey D. THE "RESERVE ARMY" OF UNEMPLOYED REVISITED. *Society 1977 14(3): 40-45.* Examines the theoretical origins of the federal government's apparent preference for job rationing over full employment, 1944-70's; considers the economic theory of labor supply.

2828. Stryker, Robin. RELIGIO-ETHNIC EFFECTS ON ATTAINMENTS IN THE EARLY CAREER. *Am. Sociol. Rev. 1981 46(2): 212-231.* Tests a cultural explanation for religioethnic effects on attainments by a structural equation model applied to a sample of white males who were seniors in Wisconsin high schools in 1957.   J/S

2829. Talbot, Joseph E., Jr. A REVIEW OF WAGE GAINS IN 1973. *Monthly Labor Rev. 1974 97(4): 17-20.* Wage increases in the United States in 1973 averaged only slightly above those in 1972, despite sharp increases in consumer prices.

2830. Taylor, Amy K. GOVERNMENT HEALTH POLICY AND HOSPITAL LABOR COSTS: THE EFFECTS OF WAGE AND PRICE CONTROL ON HOSPITAL WAGE RATES AND EMPLOYMENT. *Public Policy 1979 27(2): 203-226.* Examination of the rapid growth of hospitals' wage rates and employment levels, 1968-78, indicates that wage-price controls functioned to reduce real hospital wages and employment levels below what they would have been without controls.

2831. Ulman, Lloyd. COLLECTIVE BARGAINING AND COMPETITIVE BARGAINING. *Scottish J. of Pol. Econ. [Great Britain] 1974 21(2): 97-109.* Queries whether the inflationary potential of an economy is affected by the degree to which its collective bargaining

system is centralized and whether a centralized bargaining system is more amenable than a decentralized system to official pressures for wage restraint. The author builds two models. Model A, the form in the United States, involves the negotiation of wages, fringes, and some work conditions between the company and one or more national unions. Model B, the European form, is characterized by wider separation of the centers of decision-making and by greater overlap in the determination of pay. Model A is less inflationary because the settlements are the outcome of hard bargaining on both sides. Biblio.   J. D. Neville

2832. Ulmer, Melville J. FULL EMPLOYMENT WITHOUT INFLATION. *Social Policy 1975 5(5): 7-12.* Presents theoretical reasons for, and practical problems in, achievement of full employment without inflation.   S

2833. Villemez, Wayne J. and Kasarda, John D. THE ECOLOGICAL IMPACT OF REGIONAL DESTINATION ON BLACK MIGRANT INCOME. *Social Sci. Q. 1977 57(4): 767-783.* The more educated black migrants leaving the South tend to go West where they are better rewarded than in the North. However, the western economy penalizes less educated migrants; and, on the whole, western migrants earn less than northern migrants. Subjective images of a better social or physical environment may partially explain these results. Despite a greater income return on education in the West and the greater likelihood of western migrants to occupy higher status jobs, black migrants to the West earn less, proportional to whites, than do black migrants to the North. Based on the 1972 Neighborhood Characteristics Public Use Sample of the 1970 US Census and on secondary works; 5 tables, 4 notes, biblio.   W. R. Hively

2834. Villemez, Wayne J. THE FUNCTIONAL SUBSTITUTABILITY OF BLACKS AND FEMALES IN THE LABOR MARKET: A CLOSER LOOK. *Sociol. Q. 1977 18(4): 548-563.* The interrelationship between labor market discrimination against black males and white females—as reflected in the respective size distributions of their full-time income—is examined for states in the U.S. Employing previously used data, conclusions opposite those of other researchers are reached. The hypothesis of a simple negative association between the two forms of discrimination is rejected, along with the implication of that association that blacks and females are functional substitutes in a capitalist economy. More adequate measurement and analysis shows that the presumed relationship is largely spurious, and caused primarily by the sexual specificity of labor demand as well as supply.   J

2835. Waldman, Elizabeth; Grossman, Allyson Sherman; Hayghe, Howard; and Johnson, Beverly L. WORKING MOTHERS IN THE 1970'S: A LOOK AT THE STATISTICS. *Monthly Labor Rev. 1979 102(10): 39-49.* Analyzes the trends in the increasing number of working mothers during the 1970's in two-earner families and families maintained by women, focusing on later marriages and fewer children.

2836. Wang, Chao Ling and Hilaski, Harvey J. THE SAFETY AND HEALTH RECORD IN THE CONSTRUCTION INDUSTRY. *Monthly Labor Rev. 1978 101(3): 3-9.* Statistics collected under the Occupational Safety and Health Act (1970) indicate that injuries and fatalities have dropped, 1972-75, in construction, the most dangerous major industry.

2837. Weiss, Yoram and Lillard, Lee A. EXPERIENCE, VINTAGE, AND TIME EFFECTS IN THE GROWTH OF EARNINGS: AMERICAN SCIENTISTS, 1960-1970. *J. of Pol. Econ. 1978 86(3): 427-448.* Analysis of longitudinal earning data indicates higher earnings growth for scientists of the same experience but more recent vintage. Theoretical justification for such a relation is suggested, and the implied biases in cross-section data are noted. Because of a basic identification problem, an alternative interpretation, time-experience interaction, is also considered. The general conclusion is that earning growth is not uniform or neutral. There is no simple mechanical method by which lifetime profiles can be inferred from single cross-section data.   J

2838. Wells, Miriam J. SOCIAL CONFLICT, COMMODITY CONSTRAINTS, AND LABOR MARKET STRUCTURE IN AGRICULTURE. *Comparative Studies in Soc. and Hist. [Great Britain] 1981 23(4): 679-704.* The very nature of the strawberry industry in California has diminished employer control over the allocation and cost of labor. The labor market structure is influenced by social conflict. The underlying social dynamic is shaped by the level of organization and the tension among social classes. Labor market structure plays a key role in shaping the social relationships between labor and capital. Differences in the organization of work have both social and economic causes and consequences. Ref., 14 notes, table.   S. A. Farmerie

2839. Westcott, D. N. and Bednarzik, R. W. EMPLOYMENT AND UNEMPLOYMENT: A REPORT ON 1980. *Monthly Labor Rev. 1981 104(2): 4-14.* Reports that at the onset of 1980 the nation entered a recession; employment fell sharply but recouped in the fourth quarter, except in the hard-hit housing and auto industries; unemployment rose faster than at any time since the 1974-75 recession, peaked at midyear, and was well above prerecession levels at year-end.

2840. White, Ann Dryden. EARNINGS AND JOBS OF EX-OF-FENDERS: A CASE STUDY. *Monthly Labor Rev. 1976 99(12): 31-39.* Explores labor market activities in a sample of work release program prisoners in North Carolina from 1969-71 which demonstrates that while prisoners' wages initially were below preincarceration levels, they experienced more success than those who did not participate in the programs.

2841. White, Rudolph A. HAS BLS UNDERESTIMATED BUSI-NESS PH.D. DEMAND? *Monthly Labor Rev. 1979 102(9): 42-46.* Available statistics (1975-78) clearly disprove the conclusion in Bureau of Labor Statistics studies that business is the field with the greatest relative oversupply of PhD's; there is no clear signal that the market is near a balance.

2842. Williams, J. Allen, Jr.; Beeson, Peter G.; and Johnson, David R. SOME FACTORS ASSOCIATED WITH INCOME AMONG MEXI-CAN AMERICANS. *Social Sci. Q. 1973 53(4): 710-715.* Their study replicates Duncan's 1969 contrast of income-producing effects of status inheritance with those of discrimination using a sample of Mexican Americans. The findings suggest that status inheritance and education explain more of the income discrepancy between Anglos and Mexican Americans than was found to be true between Anglos and blacks in the Duncan study.   J

2843. York, James D. PRODUCTIVITY GROWTH IN PLASTICS LOWER THAN ALL MANUFACTURING. *Monthly Labor Rev. 1983 106(9): 17-21.* Despite strong growth and the introduction of improved technology in the plastics industry, annual labor productivity grew at a rate of 1.4% compared with 1.8% for all industry during 1972-81.

2844. Young, Anne McDougall. THE DIFFERENCE A YEAR MAKES IN THE NATION'S YOUTH WORK FORCE. *Monthly Labor Rev. 1979 102(10): 34-38.* Describes the changes in the US youth work force, October 1977-October 1978, focusing on student and teenage employment with respect to sex, race, and family income.

2845. Ziegler, Martin. EFFORTS TO IMPROVE ESTIMATES OF STATE AND LOCAL UNEMPLOYMENT. *Monthly Labor Rev. 1977 100(11): 12-18.* Discusses the methods for keeping statistics developed by the State Employment Security Agencies under the auspices of the Labor Statistics Bureau and examines improved methods of reporting on those receiving unemployment insurance according to county of residence, eligibility, coverage, disqualification provisions, benefits, and forgiveness of earnings, to aid in distribution of federal funds to state and local aid agencies.

2846. —. THE ANNUAL REPORT ON THE ECONOMIC STA-TUS OF THE PROFESSION, 1981-1982. *Acad.: Bull. of the AAUP 1982 68(4): 2-80.* Discusses academic salaries in the United States during 1981-82 (comparing them with salaries in the 1970's), academic market outlook, salary differences by state and by discipline, and turnover.

2847. —. BEZRABOTITSA V STRANAKH KAPITALIZMA [Un-employment in capitalist countries]. *Mirovaia Ekonomika i Mezhdunar-odnye Otnosheniia [USSR] 1982 (12): 141-143.* Describes the effect of the recession in the capitalist countries on the labor market and presents statistics illustrating the growth of unemployment.

2848. —. BLACK AMERICANS. Sowell, Thomas, ed. *Essays and Data on American Ethnic Groups* (Washington, D.C.: Urban Inst. Pr., 1978): 278-295. Statistical data on black Americans' personal income by age, education, and sex; personal earnings by occupation, education, and sex; family income distribution by number of income earners per family; family income by age, education, and sex of family head; family earnings by number of income earners, education, and sex of family head; and fertility rates by woman's education and family income. From 1970 US Census Public Use Sample; 6 tables.   K. A. Talley

2849. —. CHINESE AMERICANS. Sowell, Thomas, ed. *Essays and Data on American Ethnic Groups* (Washington, D.C.: Urban Inst. Pr., 1978): 296-313. Statistics on Chinese Americans' personal income by age, education, and sex; personal earnings by occupation, education, and sex; family income distribution by number of income earners per family; family income by age, education, and sex of family head; family earning by number of income earners, education, and sex of family head; and fertility rates by woman's education and family education. From 1970 US Census Public Use Sample; 5 tables.   K. A. Talley

2850. —. FACTS WE DARE NOT FORGET: EXCERPTS FROM A NEGLECTED GOVERNMENT REPORT ON POVERTY AND UNEMPLOYMENT TO WHICH THE NEW ADMINISTRATION WILL SURELY PAY NO ATTENTION. *Dissent 1981 28(2): 164-172.* Presents selections from the 12th report of the National Advisory Council on Economic Opportunity, presented in 1980 to President Carter, dealing with the impact of poverty and unemployment upon health, infant mortality, crime rates, family life, suicide, and child abuse; analyzes the effect of social welfare programs upon poverty and the social problems caused by it; 1960-80.

2851. —. FILIPINO AMERICANS. Sowell, Thomas, ed. *Essays and Data on American Ethnic Groups* (Washington, D.C.: Urban Inst. Pr., 1978): 314-331. Statistics of Filipino Americans' personal income by age, education, and sex; personal earnings by occupation, education, and sex; family income distribution by number of income earners per family; family income by age, education, and sex of family head; family earnings by number of income earners, education, and sex of family head; and fertility rates by woman's education and family income. From the 1970 US Census Public Use Sample; 5 tables.   K. A. Talley

2852. —. GERMAN AMERICANS. Sowell, Thomas, ed. *Essays and Data on American Ethnic Groups* (Washington, D.C.: Urban Inst. Pr., 1978): 332-335. Statistics on German Americans by personal income distribution by sex; family income distribution; occupational distribution by sex; and education by age. From US Bureau of the Census, *Current Population Reports,* Series P-20, Nos. 221, 249; 3 tables.

     K. A. Talley

2853. —. INCOME, MEDIAN AGE, OCCUPATION AND FER-TILITY BY ETHNIC GROUPS. Sowell, Thomas, ed. *Essays and Data on American Ethnic Groups* (Washington, D.C.: Urban Inst. Pr., 1978): 257-259. A table dividing statistics on income, median age, occupation and fertility in 13 different ethnic groups in the United States. Statistics are from the 1970 Census Public Use Sample and from *Current Population Reports,* Series P-20.   K. A. Talley

2854. —. IRISH AMERICANS. Sowell, Thomas, ed. *Essays and Data on American Ethnic Groups* (Washington, D.C.: Urban Inst. Pr., 1978): 336-339. Statistics on Irish Americans' personal income distribution by sex; family income distribution; occupational distribution by sex; and education by age. From US Bureau of the Census, *Current Population Reports,* Series P-20, Nos. 221, 249; 3 tables.   K. A. Talley

2855. —. ITALIAN AMERICANS. Sowell, Thomas, ed. *Essays and Data on American Ethnic Groups* (Washington, D.C.: Urban Inst. Pr., 1978): 340-343. Statistics on Italian Americans' personal income distribution by sex; family income distribution; occupational distribution by sex; and education by age. From US Bureau of the Census, *Current Population Reports,* Series P-20, Nos. 221, 249; 3 tables.

     K. A. Talley

2856. —. JAPANESE AMERICANS. Sowell, Thomas, ed. *Essays and Data on American Ethnic Groups* (Washington, D.C.: Urban Inst. Pr., 1978): 344-361. Statistics on Japanese Americans' personal income by age, education, and sex; personal earnings by occupation, education, and sex; family income distribution by number of income earners per family; family income by age, education, and sex of family head; family earnings by number of income earners, education, and sex of family head; and fertility rates by woman's education and family income. From the 1970 US Census Public Use Sample; 5 tables. K. A. Talley

2857. —. JEWISH AMERICANS. Sowell, Thomas, ed. *Essays and Data on American Ethnic Groups* (Washington, D.C.: Urban Inst. Pr., 1978): 362-373. Statistics on Jewish American family income distribution by number of income earners per family; family income by age, education, and sex of family head; family income by number of income earners, education, and sex of family head; and number of children in the household by woman's education and family income. From National Jewish Population Study, 1969; 3 tables. K. A. Talley

2858. —. MEXICAN AMERICANS. Sowell, Thomas, ed. *Essays and Data on American Ethnic Groups* (Washington, D. C.: Urban Inst. Pr., 1978): 374-375. Statistics on Mexican Americans' family income distribution; family income distribution by age of family head; occupational distribution; and educational distribution by age. From the US Bureau of the Census, *Current Population Reports,* Series P-20, Nos. 213, 224; 4 tables. K. A. Talley

2859. —. MONOPSONY AND TEACHERS' SALARIES: SOME CONTRARY EVIDENCE. *Industrial and Labor Relations Rev. 1975 28(4): 574-577.*
Thornton, Robert J. MONOPSONY AND TEACHERS' SALARIES: SOME CONTRARY EVIDENCE: COMMENT, *pp. 574-575.*
Baird, Robert N. and Landon, John H. REPLY, *pp. 576-577.*

2860. —. POLISH AMERICANS. Sowell, Thomas, ed. *Essays and Data on American Ethnic Groups* (Washington, D.C.: Urban Inst. Pr., 1978): 376-379. Statistics on Polish Americans' personal income distribution by sex; family income distribution; occupational distribution by sex; and educational distribution by age. From US Bureau of the Census *Current Population Reports,* Series P-20, Nos. 221, 249.
K. A. Talley

2861. —. PUERTO RICANS. Sowell, Thomas, ed. *Essays and Data on American Ethnic Groups* (Washington, D.C.: Urban Inst. Pr., 1978): 380-397. Statistics on Puerto Ricans' personal income by age, education, and sex; personal earnings by occupation, education, and sex; family income distribution by number of income earners per family; family income by age, education, and sex of family head; family earnings by number of income earners, education, and sex of family head; and fertility rates by woman's education and family income. From 1970 US Census Public Use Sample and *Current Population Reports,* Series P-20, Nos. 213, 244; 5 tables. K. A. Talley

2862. —. [QUALITY OF EDUCATION AND WAGE DIFFERENCES]. *Am. Econ. Rev. 1980 70(1): 186-203.*
Akin, John S. and Garfinkel, Irv. THE QUALITY OF EDUCATION AND COHORT VARIATION IN BLACK-WHITE EARNINGS DIFFERENTIAL: COMMENT, *pp. 186-191.* In response to Finis Welch's contention that the quality of education is the critical factor in wage differences, this article finds that when adjustments are made for this factor, large wage differences still exist between the races. 3 tables, 9 ref.
Welch, Finis. REPLY, *pp. 192-195.* Critiques Akin's and Garfinkel's conclusion by arguing that expenditures are not complete explanations because the major problem remains: how educational quality can be measured. 2 tables, 5 ref.
Link, Charles; Ratledge, Edward, and Lewis, Kenneth. REPLY, *pp. 196-203.* Rejects Akin's and Garfinkel's findings and accepts Welch's conclusions. 5 tables, 8 ref. D. K. Pickens

2863. —. REVIEW OF THE MONTH: CAPITALISM AND UNEMPLOYMENT. *Monthly Rev. 1975 27(2): 1-14.* The editors of the *Monthly Review* discuss economic aspects of unemployment in a capitalist society during the 1970's.

2864. —. [WAGE CONTROLS]. *Industrial and Labor Relations Rev. 1978 31(2): 149-160.*
Weber, Arnold R. and Mitchell, Daniel J. B. FURTHER REFLECTIONS ON WAGE CONTROLS, *pp. 149-158.* Comments on a previous article by Schultz and Dam. Wage controls can have far fewer disadvantages than price controls. Denies that the wage segment of controls severely impaired the allocation of labor, significantly weakened collective bargaining, or produced excessive wage increases when controls were removed. Primary and secondary sources; table, 21 notes.
Schultz, George P. and Dam, Kenneth W. REPLY, *pp. 159-160.* Wage controls without price controls are politically infeasible.
L. W. Van Wyk

2865. —. WEST INDIANS. Sowell, Thomas, ed. *Essays and Data on American Ethnic Groups* (Washington, D.C.: Urban Inst. Pr., 1978): 398-415. Statistics on West Indians' personal income by age, education, and sex; personal earnings by occupation, education and sex; family income distribution by number of income earners per family; family income by age, education, and sex of family head; family earnings by number of income earners, education, and sex of family head; fertility rates by woman's education and family income. From the 1970 US Census Public Use Sample; 5 tables. K. A. Talley

SUBJECT INDEX

Subject Profile Index (ABC-Spindex) carries both generic and specific index terms. Begin a search at the general term but also look under more specific or related terms. This index includes numerous selective cross-references.

Each string of index descriptors is intended to present a profile of a cited article; however, no particular relationship between any two terms in the profile is implied. Terms within the profile are listed alphabetically after the leading term. The variety of punctuation and capitalization reflects production methods and has no intrinsic meaning, e.g., there is no difference in the meaning between "Labor, skilled" and "Labor (skilled)."

Cities, towns, and counties are listed following their respective states, e.g., "Massachusetts (Lowell)."

Note that "United States" is not used as a leading index term; if no country is mentioned, the index entry refers to the United States alone. When an entry refers to both Canada and the United States, both "Canada" and "USA" appear in the string of index descriptors, but "USA" is not a leading term.

In order to preserve both the established idiom of labor history and the intellectual distinctions among related terms in this special subject bibliography, the editors chose not to subsume a number of key subject headings under any single adjectival form. Thus, for example, users will find pertinent material cited under the following related, but not synonymous, terms: "Employee Turnover" and "Job Satisfaction"; "Manpower," "Labor Force," and "Personnel"; "Occupational Hazards" and "Working Conditions."

The chronology of the abstract follows the subject index terms. In the chronology, "c" stands for "century," e.g., "19c" means "19th century."

The last number in the index string, in italics, refers to the abstract number.

A

Abolition. Freedmen. Labor market, split. Race relations. Slavery, extension of. 1830-63. *547*

Abolition Movement *See also* Emancipation.

—. Attitudes. Competition. Economic Structure. Evangelism. Poverty. ca 1830-60. *579*

Abood v. *Detroit Board of Education* (US, 1977). Agency shop fees. Collective Bargaining. Politics. Public Employees. 1977-80. *2126*

Abortion. Massachusetts (Boston). Preterm Institute. Strikes. Women. 1972-77. *2169*

Abortion clinics. Braverman, Harry. Labor. Profit motive. Women. 1973-77. *1463*

Absenteeism. 1950-80. *2723*

Academic achievement. Children. Mothers. North Central States. Occupations. 1977. *1566*

—. College graduates. Employment. Job performance. 1975. *1851*

Academic Degrees. See Degrees, Academic.

Accident Insurance *See also* Workers' Compensation.

—. Judicial process. Management. New England. 1890-1910. *75*

Accidents *See also* Industrial Accidents.

—. California. Industrial safety. Tanneries. Working Conditions. 1901-80. *222*

—. Coal Mines and Mining. Disaster relief. Mabey, Charles R. Palmer, Annie. Social work. Utah (Castle Gate). 1924-36. *959*

—. Courts. Federal Employers' Liability Act (US, 1908). Management. Railroads. Safety Appliances Act (US, 1893). Working Conditions. 1890-1913. *334*

—. Industry. Legislation. Occupational Safety and Health Act (US, 1970). 1877-1970. *2298*

—. Industry. Occupational Safety and Health Act (US, 1970). Working Conditions. 1964-79. *1601*

Acculturation *See also* Assimilation.

—. Chinese Americans. Discrimination. Georgia (Augusta). 1865-1980. *339*

—. Immigration. Polish Americans. 1860-1960. *175*

—. Jews. Women. 1901-30's. *999*

ACLU. *See* American Civil Liberties Union.

Acocella, Giuseppe (review article). France. Germany. Labor Unions and Organizations. Political Participation. 1920-78. *260*

Adams, Mary. Apprenticeship. Letters. New Hampshire (Derry). Tailoring. 1833-35. *528*

Addams, Jane. Education. Hull House. Illinois (Chicago). Working class. 1890's. *705*

Adolescence *See also* Youth.

—. Agriculture. Attitudes. Employment. 1970's. *1723*

—. Blacks. Employment. Recessions. Women. 1945-81. *2616*

—. Child labor. Occupations. 1979. *1848*

Adventists. Labor unions and organizations. 1877-1903. *668*

Advertising *See also* Marketing; Propaganda; Publicity.

—. Colt, Cristine C. (account). Dow Jones Co. Sex discrimination. 1975-78. *2426*

—. Consumers. Wages. Working hours. 1919-76. *375*

—. Employment. War Advertising Council. Women. World War II. 1941-45. *1401*

Advisory committees. Industrial Relations. Presidents. 1955-80. *2317*

Aeronautics *See also* Air Lines.

—. Eastern Airlines. Gellert, Dan. L-1011 (aircraft). Occupational Safety. Working Conditions. 1972-78. *1647*

AFDC. *See* Aid to Families with Dependent Children.

Affirmative Action *See also* Equal Opportunity; Quotas.

—. Air Force Equal Opportunity Program. Minorities. Social Mobility. Women. 1976. *2235*

—. Attitudes. Cities. Public Employees. Texas. 1978. *2423*

—. Bakke, Allan. Civil rights. Discrimination. Employment. Equal opportunity. Law enforcement. *Regents of the University of California* v. *Allan Bakke* (US, 1978). 1978. *2328*

—. Blacks. Cities. Civil service. Employment. Political power. 1970-78. *1950*

—. Blacks. Discrimination (review article). Gould, William B. Hill, Herbert. Labor Unions and Organizations. Seniority. Supreme Court. 1970's. *2537*

—. Blacks. Quotas. 1920's-78. *363*

—. Civil Rights Act (US, 1964). Individualism. 1964-81. *2240*

—. Civil Rights Act (US, 1964; Titles VI, VII). Employment. *Kaiser Aluminum and Chemical Company* v. *Weber* (US, 1979). Race. *Regents of the University of California* v. *Allan Bakke* (US, 1978). Supreme Court. 1970's. *2464*

—. College Teachers. Discrimination. Income. 1950's-70's. *2454*

—. College teachers. Minorities. 1965-80. *2447*

—. Colleges and Universities. Women. 1982. *2496*

—. Degrees, Academic. Discrimination. Economists. Employment. Women. 1950-78. *2766*

—. Economic Conditions. Local government. Public Employees. State Government. 1960's-70's. *2304*

—. Employment. Minorities. Organizational Theory. Women. 1970's. *2306*

—. Employment. Minorities. Women. 1970's. *2590*

—. Equal opportunity. Ideology. Middle Classes. 17c-1981. *99*

—. Equal opportunity. Library management. Women. 1973. *2442*

—. Hiring practices. Minorities. Women. 1970's. *2404*

—. Illinois, University of. Women. 1960's-70's. *2506*

—. Justice. 1970's. *2469*

Affirmative action programs. Employment. Public policy. Quotas. 1975. *2241*

AFL. *See* American Federation of Labor.

AFL-CIO. American Institute for Free Labor Development. Latin America. Neocolonialism. 1960's-70's. *1911*

—. Attitudes. Manpower. Revenue sharing. 1974. *1789*

—. Blacks. Leadership. Racism. 1955-79. *2482*

—. Carter, Jimmy. Democratic Party. Labor Unions and Organizations. Public welfare. 1976. *2364*

—. Carter, Jimmy (administration). Economic policy. National Accord (document). Wages. 1979. *2225*

—. Collective bargaining. Industry. Labor Unions and Organizations. Mergers. Strikes. Taft-Hartley Act (US, 1947). 1946-70's. *1877*

—. Economic growth. Employment. Expansionism. Foreign policy. Multinational corporations. 1880's-1970's. *257*

—. Employment. Imports. Protectionism. 1973. *2367*

—. Foreign policy. International Labor Organization. Social Problems. 1970's. *1888*

—. Foreign Policy. Internationalism. Labor Unions and Organizations. 1886-1975. *1920*

—. Interest groups. Political parties. 1970's. *1901*

—. Labor. 1935-77. *264*

—. Labor Unions and Organizations. 1881-1982. *263*

—. Multinational corporations. Unemployment. USA. 1970-74. *1913*

AFL-CIO (Committee on Political Education). Political Action Committees. South. 1943-75. *1914*

AFL-CIO (expulsions). Labor Unions and Organizations. Mergers. 1949-73. *1885*

Africa *See also* Pan-Africanism.

—. Attitudes. Blacks. Cherokee Indians. Colonization. Indian Territory. Slavery. 1830-60. *618*

—. Industrial arts education. Pan-Africanism. Racism. South. 1879-1940. *364*

Africa, Southern. Blacks. Boycotts. Labor reform. United Mine Workers of America. USA. 1960's-74. *2587*

African crops. Agriculture. Slaves. South Carolina. 17c-18c. *640*

AFSCME. *See* American Federation of State, County, and Municipal Employees.

Age. Blacks. Discrimination. Income. Mexican Americans. Texas. 1960-70. *2521*

—. Coal Mines and Mining. Management. Standard of living. Strikes, wildcat. Working conditions. 1970's. *2041*

—. Ethnic groups. Fertility. Income. Occupations. 1969-70. *2853*

—. Job Satisfaction. 1972-73. *1856*

—. Job satisfaction. Working Class. 1973. *1690*

—. Labor force. 1953-78. *1517*

—. Retirement. 1970's. *1693*

Age Discrimination in Employment Act (US, 1967). Equal Employment Opportunity Commission. 1967-80. *1825*

Age Discrimination in Employment Act (US, 1967; amended, 1978). Law and Society. Retirement, mandatory. 1970's. *2676*

Age Discrimination in Employment Act (US, 1980). Apprenticeship. Discrimination. 1980. *2370*

Aged *See also* Pensions; Public Welfare.

—. Comprehensive Employment and Training Act (US, 1973). Employment. 1973-76. *2178*

—. Economic Structure. Employment. Men. Pensions. Western Nations. 1950-75. *1764*

—. Employment. 1982. *1741*
—. Employment. Industry. Management. Retirement, mandatory. Social Reform. 1850-1900. *696*
—. Employment. Men. 1967-77. *1791*
—. Employment. Men. Women. 1950-78. *2782*
—. Income. Labor Market. 1947-76. *2750*
—. Indexes. Retirement. 1970's. *2806*
—. Labor force. Unemployment. 1970's. *1796*
—. Retirement. Unemployment. 1966-73. *1584*
—. Unemployment. 1968-81. *1790*
Agency shop fees. *Abood* v. *Detroit Board of Education* (US, 1977). Collective Bargaining. Politics. Public Employees. 1977-80. *2126*
Agrarians. Populism. Radicals and Radicalism. Wisconsin. Working class. 19c. *864*
Agricultural Adjustment Administration. Depressions. Labor Unions and Organizations. Sharecroppers. Southern Tenant Farmers' Union. ca 1930's. *1266*
Agricultural Commodities *See also* Crops.
—. Family. Great Plains. Marxism. Wages. 1920. *381*
Agricultural Cooperatives. Colorado Co-operative Company. Depressions. Labor Exchange. Midwest. 1890-1905. *851*
—. DeBernardi, Giovanni Battista. Depressions. Labor Exchange. Self-help. 1889-1910. *808*
—. Farmers Educational and Cooperative Union of America (Local 11). Labor Unions and Organizations. North Dakota (Burleigh County; Still). 1913-78. *1275*
Agricultural Industry. California. Elections. Proposition 14 (1976). United Farm Workers Union. 1976. *2052*
Agricultural Labor *See also* Farm Workers; Farmers; Migrant Labor.
—. 1956-79. *2757*
—. Agricultural Reform. Diffusion. Labor Market. Undocumented Workers. 1850-1981. *2733*
—. Alabama. Attitudes. Chinese Americans. Keffer, John C. Reconstruction. Smith, William H. 1869. *713*
—. Attitudes. Bracero Program. Labor Unions and Organizations. Mexico. Undocumented Workers. 1943-74. *1511*
—. Behavior. Mexican Americans. Mexico. Social Customs. USA. 16c-20c. *208*
—. Blacks. Discrimination. South. Wages. 1898-1902. *879*
—. Blacks. Divorce. Men. Moynihan, Daniel P. ("The Negro Family"). 1965-78. *2544*
—. Blacks. Logan, Frenise A. North Carolina Bureau of Labor Statistics. Wages. Whites. 1887. *891*
—. Boycotts. Labor Unions and Organizations. Race relations. South Carolina. 1886-95. *872*
—. California. Contract labor. Leasing. 1900-10. *953*
—. California. Elections. Labor Unions and Organizations. National Labor Relations Act (US, 1935). 1975-76. *1358*
—. California. Labor Unions and Organizations. Migration, Internal. "Okies". 1930's. *994*
—. California. Labor Unions and Organizations. National Industrial Recovery Act (US, 1933). 1933-34 *1298*
—. California. Mexican Americans. United Cannery, Agricultural, Packing and Allied Workers of America. 1937-40. *1213*
—. California. Sikhs. 1904-82. *198*
—. California. Social conflict. Strawberry industry. 20c. *2838*
—. California (Colusa County). Farms. Mexican Americans. 1950-69. *1519*
—. California (Salinas). Filipino Labor Union. Lettuce. Strikes. 1934. *1136*
—. California, southern. Depressions. Steinbeck, John *(In Dubious Battle)*. Strikes. 1933. *1104*
—. California (Stockton; Chinatown). Discrimination. Filipino Americans. Immigration. 1920-39. *1398*
—. California (Wheatland). Photographs. Riots. 1913. *1261*
—. California Women Farmworkers Project. Oral history. Women. 1870's-1970's. *206*
—. Capital, fixed. Economic development. Farmers. Slavery. South. ca 1840-80. *578*
—. Coffee. Ethnic groups. Hawaii. 1813-1978. *172*
—. Cotton. Productivity. Quantitative methods. South. 1850's-1900's. 1958-78. *895*
—. Economic Conditions. 1950's-80. *2639*
—. Economic Development. Wages. 1800-60. *428*
—. Economic Structure. Freedmen. Racism. Reconstruction. Texas. 1865-74. *737*

—. Employment. 1972-73. *1705*
—. Family. Indiana. Mexicans. Migrant Labor. 1930's-83. *237*
—. Farmers. Industrial Workers of the World. Labor Disputes. Ranchers. Washington (Yakima Valley). 1910-36. *1216*
—. Farms. 1970-74. *2073*
—. Georgia (Glynn County). Occupations. Slavery. 1790-1860. *616*
—. Hawaii. Russians. 1900-10. *931*
—. Illinois. Indiana. Ohio. Westward Movement. 1850-70. *475*
—. Industrial labor. Puerto Rican Americans. 1942-51. *203*
—. Industrial Relations. Management. Production. Western states. World War I. 1913-18. *935*
—. Industrialization. Labor force (sectoral distribution). Regional change. Research. 1850-80. 1970's. *145*
—. Industrialization. Models. Slavery. South. 1800's. *571*
—. Italy, northern. Slavery. South. ca 1800-60. 1876-81. *604*
—. Labor, division of. Production, subsistence. Women. 20c. *2441*
—. Slavery. Substitutability. 1850-60. *626*
—. South. Tenancy. Wages. 1930-60. *3*
Agricultural Labor (free). Crops (staple). Economic Conditions. Slavery. 1850's-60's. *565*
Agricultural Labor Relations Act (1975). California. Collective bargaining. Politics. 1975-77. *2333*
—. California. Emergency Farm Labor Supply Program. Labor law. New Deal. ca 1930-79. *320*
Agricultural Labor (white). Louisiana. Slavery. 1790-1820. *606*
Agricultural Organizations. Farmers' Alliance. North Carolina. ca 1888-91. *823*
—. Farmers, tenant. Southern Tenant Farmers' Union. 1934-70. *306*
Agricultural Production. Productivity. Slavery. South. 1850-60. *572*
Agricultural Reform *See also* Land Reform.
—. Agricultural Labor. Diffusion. Labor Market. Undocumented Workers. 1850-1981. *2733*
—. Arkansas. Colored Farmers' Alliance. Cotton pickers. Humphrey, R. M. Strikes. 1891. *810*
Agriculture *See also* Agricultural Labor; Agricultural Organizations; Dairying; Farms; Forests and Forestry; Land; Plantations; Rural Development.
—. Adolescence. Attitudes. Employment. 1970's. *1723*
—. African crops. Slaves. South Carolina. 17c-18c. *640*
—. Behavior. Employment. Woman's Land Army. Women. World War I. 1917-20. *1416*
—. Blacks. Economic Conditions. *One Kind of Freedom* (book). Ransom, Roger. South. Sutch, Richard. 1860's-80's. 1977-78. *885*
—. Boycotts. California. Chavez, Cesar. Labor Unions and Organizations. Teamsters, International Brotherhood of. United Farm Workers Union. 1962-74. *2070*
—. Bracero program. Mexico. President's Commission on Migratory Labor. Truman, Harry S. Undocumented workers. 1950. *2286*
—. California. Chavez, Cesar. Elections. Proposition 14 (1976). United Farm Workers Union. 1975-76. *2136*
—. California. Farm Workers. Mechanization. 1964-80. *1771*
—. Economic Conditions. Farms (tenant). Productivity. South. 1850's-90's. *662*
—. Economic Conditions. Industry. Labor. Land. Productivity. 1869-99. *893*
—. Employment. Exports. 1963-72. *2654*
—. Europe. Industrialization. Market economy. North America. Peasant movements (colloquium). ca 1875-1975. *12*
—. Family. Great Plains. Sweden. Women. 18c-19c. *5*
—. Great Plains. Labor casualization. Mechanization. Wheat. 1865-1902. *643*
—. Productivity. Slavery. South. 1800's-60. 1974-79. *585*
—. Research. Slave narratives. South. 1850's-65. *590*
Agriculture Department. Alabama. Blacks. Campbell, Thomas M. Social Conditions. South. ca 1883-1956. *1407*
Ah Quin. California Southern Railroad. Chinese Americans. Construction. Diaries. 1868-1914. *695*

Ah-Choi. California. Chinese. Occupations. Prostitution. Women. 1840's-50's. *442*
Aid to Families with Dependent Children. Employment (incentives toward). Public Welfare. Wages. 1972-74. *2813*
—. Food stamps. Unemployment. 1975-79. *2647*
—. Public Welfare. 1967-82. *2344*
Air Force Equal Opportunity Program. Affirmative action. Minorities. Social Mobility. Women. 1976. *2235*
Air Lines. Collective bargaining. Deregulation. Federal Regulation. 1958-78. *2376*
—. Deregulation. Labor Unions and Organizations. Transportation, Commercial. 1978-82. *2115*
Air traffic controllers. Federal Government. Professional Air Traffic Controllers Organization. Strikes. Working conditions. 1950's-81. *2020*
Airplane Industry and Trade. California (Los Angeles). Women. Working Conditions. World War II. 1941-81. *951*
—. Fairchild Republic (corporation). International Association of Machinists and Aerospace Workers (Lodge 1987). Labor Unions and Organizations. New York (Farmingdale). 1950-82. *2028*
—. Labor Unions and Organizations. Militancy. Nash, Al (reminiscences). New York (Long Island City). Political factions. World War II. 1940-44. *1209*
ALA. *See* American Library Association.
Alabama *See also* South Central and Gulf States.
—. Agricultural labor. Attitudes. Chinese Americans. Keffer, John C. Reconstruction. Smith, William H. 1869. *713*
—. Agriculture Department. Blacks. Campbell, Thomas M. Social Conditions. South. ca 1883-1956. *1407*
—. Blacks. Industrial Arts Education. Tuskegee Institute. Washington, Booker T. 1870's-90's. *708*
—. Blacks. Labor Union of Alabama. National Negro Labor Union. Politics. Rapier, James T. Reconstruction. 1837-75. *880*
—. Bureau of Refugees, Freedmen, and Abandoned Lands. Freedmen. Reconstruction. 1865-67. *612*
—. Child labor movement. Episcopal Church, Protestant. Murphy, Edgar Gardner. 1890-1907. *679*
—. Coal Miners. Kilby, Thomas E. Strikes. United Mine Workers of America. 1890-1929. *1260*
—. Freedmen. Plantations. Sharecropping (origins). 1865-67. *596*
—. Kentucky. Labor Unions and Organizations (development). United Mine Workers of America. 1932-33. *1176*
—. Mims, Shadrach (letter). Pratt, Daniel. Textile Industry. Williams, Price. Working Conditions. 1854. *455*
—. Poor. Whites. 1870-1950. *687*
Alabama (Gadsden). Goodyear Tire and Rubber Company. House, John D. Rubber. United Rubber Workers. 1941. *1210*
—. Labor Unions and Organizations. 1930-43. *1056*
Alabama (Jefferson County; Coalburg). Blacks. Coal Miners. Convict labor. Mortality. Parke, Thomas D. Sloss-Sheffield coal mine. Working conditions. 1895. *745*
Alabama (Mobile). Blacks. Fair Employment Practices Commission. Shipyards. South. World War II. 1938-45. *1351*
Alaska *See also* Far Western States.
—. Asian Americans. Canning industry. Contracts. Labor Disputes. Salmon. 1880-1937. *301*
—. Canneries. Filipino Americans. Labor Unions and Organizations. Salmon. 1920-38. *1198*
—. Elections. Miners. Public Opinion. Strikes. Western Federation of Miners. 1905-08. *1155*
Alaska (Anchorage). Labor Unions and Organizations. Lewis, Lena Morrow. Railroads. Socialist Party. World War I. 1916-18. *1187*
Alaska (Douglas Island). Labor Unions and Organizations. Miners. Strikes. Treadwell Mines. Western Federation of Miners. 1905-10. *1154*
Alaska (Nome). American Federation of Labor. Industrial Workers of the World. Labor Unions and Organizations. 1905-20. *1152*
Alaska (Nushagak River). Canneries. Fishermen. Strikes. 1951-52. *2087*
Alcohol. Working Conditions. 1972. *1629*
Alcoholism *See also* Skid Rows; Temperance Movements.

Andre, Rae. Domesticity. Hayden, Delores. Wives (review article). Wright, Gwendolyn. 20c. *66*

Andry plantation. Louisiana Territory. Slave revolts. 1801-12. *564*

Anthony, Lucy. Employment. Equal opportunity. Feminism. Shaw, Anna Howard. 1865-1919. *685*

Anthracite. Child Labor. Miners. Pennsylvania. Strikes. Working conditions. ca 1880-1903. *1107*

Anthropologists. Bureaucracies. Employment. Research. 1974. *1944*

Anti-Communist Movements. Conflict. Congress of Industrial Organizations. Missouri (St. Louis). United Electrical, Radio, and Machine Workers of America. 1946-49. *1905*

—. Congress of Industrial Organizations. Democratic Party. Labor Unions and Organizations. 1945-50. *1907*

—. General Motors Corporation. Michigan, University of. Workers' Education Service. 1943-49. *2385*

Antietam Woolen Manufacturing Company. Attitudes. Delaware. Duplanty, McCall and Company. Maryland (Funkstown). Textile Industry. Working Conditions. 1814-19. *477*

Antiforeign sentiment. Coal Miners. Strikes. Utah (Carbon County). Utah Fuel Company. 1902-04. *1230*

Antitrust. Congress. Courts. Management. Sports. 1950's-70's. *1646*

Antiunionization. Business. Consultants. Labor Unions and Organizations. Lawyers. 1979-80. *2057*

—. Industrial Relations. ca 1976-80. *2047*

—. Industry. Labor Unions and Organizations. South Carolina (Greenville). 1873-1979. *2138*

Antiwar Sentiment *See also* Peace Movements.

—. Labor Unions and Organizations. Socialism. World War I. 1914-17. *1034*

Appalachia. American Federation of Labor. Industrial Relations. Public Employees. Tennessee Valley Authority. 1933-78. *1324*

—. Copper Mines and Mining. Cornish Americans. 1830-90. *147*

—. Leftism. Mountaineers. Music. Resettlement Administration (music program). Seeger, Charles. Social Organization. 1935-37. *1368*

Appalachians. Income. Migration. Ohio (Cincinnati). Wives. 1975. *1772*

Appointments to office. Confirmation. National Labor Relations Board. Presidents. Senate. 1935-78. *316*

—. National Labor Relations Board. Politics. Unfair Labor Practices. 1954-77. *2205*

Apprenticeship. Adams, Mary. Letters. New Hampshire (Derry). Tailoring. 1833-35. *528*

—. Age Discrimination in Employment Act (US, 1980). Discrimination. 1980. *2370*

—. Arts and Crafts. Journeymen. Maryland (Baltimore). Slavery. Wealth. 1790-1820. *536*

—. Construction industry. Maurizi, Alex. Minorities. 1959-72. *2163*

—. Indentured servants. Law. Tennessee. 1800-60. *506*

—. Ironworkers. Steel Industry. 1974. *1667*

—. New York (Geneva). *People v. Fisher* (New York, 1832). Shoe industry. Strikes. 1825-36. *522*

Arbitration. American Federation of State, County, and Municipal Employees. Indiana (Indianapolis). Labor Disputes. 1971-72. *2154*

—. Delegation of powers. Law. Public Employees. State Government. 1960's-70's. *2278*

—. Fire Fighters. Public Employees. 1966-73. *2151*

—. Iowa Public Employment Relations Act (1974). Public employees. 1970's. *2231*

—. Labor disputes. Nevada. Public Employees. 1970's. *2243*

—. Labor Disputes. Postal Reorganization Act (1970). Postal Service. 1970-74. *2077*

—. Michigan. Public Employment Relations Act (Michigan). Public Schools (employees). 1970-73. *2301*

—. Political Reform. Public Employees. Strikes. 1968-75. *2267*

Arbitration, grievance. Labor Disputes. 1942-72. *2053*

Arbitration, Industrial *See also* Collective Bargaining; Strikes.

—. Discrimination. *Griggs vs. Duke Power Company (1971). Rios vs. Reynolds Metals Company (1972).* 1964-73. *2413*

—. Fire fighters. Georgia Railroad. Race Relations. Smith, Hoke. Strikes. 1909. *1418*

—. Great Britain. Industrial Disputes Act (Great Britain). Labor Disputes. USA. 1973. *295*

—. Industrialized Countries. Labor Disputes. 1962-74. *2085*

—. Labor Disputes. Public safety services. 1973. *294*

—. Steel industry. United Steelworkers of America. 1971-73. *2067*

Arbitration, Industrial (criteria). Public sector. 1973. *327*

Arbitration, mercantile. Law. New Netherland. Women. 1662. *409*

Archival Catalogs and Inventories. Cornell University (New York State School of Labor and Industrial Relations; Martin P. Catherwood Library). 1982. *123*

—. Dubinsky, David. International Ladies' Garment Workers' Union (Archives). Labor Unions and Organizations. 1982. *104*

—. Georgia State University (Southern Labor Archives). Labor Unions and Organizations. South. 1966-82. *52*

—. Immigrants. Minnesota, University of, St. Paul (Immigration History Research Center). 20c. *136*

—. Labor Unions and Organizations. Maryland, University of, College Park (archives). 1982. *259*

—. Labor Unions and Organizations. Michigan, University of, Ann Arbor (Labadie Collection). Radicals and Radicalism. 1911-82. *141*

—. Labor Unions and Organizations. New York University (Robert F. Wagner Labor Archives, Tamiment Institute/Ben Josephson Library). 1906-82. *129*

—. Labor Unions and Organizations. Ohio. Ohio Historical Society. 1975-82. *59*

—. Labor Unions and Organizations. Pennsylvania State University (Pennsylvania Historical Collections and Labor Archives). 1982. *68*

—. Labor Unions and Organizations. State Historical Society of Wisconsin (Archives Division). Wisconsin. 1982. *111*

—. Labor Unions and Organizations. Temple University (Urban Archives). 1982. *71*

—. Labor Unions and Organizations. Texas, University of, Arlington (Texas Labor Archives). 1982. *73*

—. Labor Unions and Organizations. Wayne State University (Walter P. Reuther Library; Archives of Labor and Urban Affairs). 1982. *108*

Archives *See also* Documents.

—. American Civil Liberties Union. Besig, Ernest. California, northern. Civil Rights. 1915-80. *64*

—. Employment. Information Storage and Retrieval Systems. Pullman Palace Car Company. 1890-1967. *398*

—. Labor. Labor history. 1950-80. *109*

—. Methodology. Northeast Archives of Folklore and Oral History. Oral history. 1974. *1688*

Archives, local. Economic History. Historiography. Phillips, Ulrich Bonnell. Slave prices. Texas (Harrison County). 1849-60. *552*

Archives of the Jewish Labor Bund. Europe. Immigration. Jews. Labor movement. New York City. 20c. *286*

Arizona (Bisbee). Industrial Workers of the World. Labor Unions and Organizations. Mining. Strikes. 1917. *1119*

—. Industrial Workers of the World. Shattuck Mine. Strikes. 1917. *1270*

—. Miners. Western Federation of Miners (Local #106). 1893-1909. *302*

Arizona (Globe). Copper Miners. Strikes. Western Federation of Miners. 1917. *1239*

—. Copper Mines and Mining. Strikes. Western Federation of Miners. World War I. 1917. *1224*

Arizona (Page). Discrimination. Indians. Industrial Relations. Navajo Construction Workers Associations. Office of Navajo Labor Relations. 1971-77. *2541*

—. Indians. Navajo Indians. Occupations. Social Status. 1973-75. *1679*

Arkansans for Progress. Labor Unions and Organizations. Right-to-work laws. 1975-76. *2025*

Arkansas *See also* South Central and Gulf States.

—. Agricultural Reform. Colored Farmers' Alliance. Cotton pickers. Humphrey, R. M. Strikes. 1891. *810*

—. Attitudes. Discrimination. Employment. Equal opportunity. Public Schools. 1980. *2361*

Arkansas (Cushing). Manganese. Miners. Social Conditions. 1849-1959. *233*

Arkansas (Elaine). Farmers, tenant. Race Relations. Sharecroppers. Violence. 1919. *1449*

Arkansas (Greenwood). Heartsill, Willie Blount Wright. Knights of Labor (Local 239). Labor disputes. Mining. 1892-96. *750*

Arkansas (Yell County). Farmers. Slavery. 1840-60. *617*

Armaments Industry. Blacks. Crosswaith, Frank R. Employment. Labor Reform. Negro Labor Committee. New York City (Harlem). World War II. 1939-45. *1447*

Armed Forces. *See* Military.

Armies *See also* National Guard.

—. American Federation of Labor. Industrial Workers of the World. Labor Disputes. Nevada (Goldfield). Western Federation of Miners. 1904-08. *1273*

—. American Federation of Labor. Police. Streetcars. Strikes. Tennessee (Knoxville). 1919-20. *1118*

—. Blacks. Equal Opportunity. Women. 1975. *1694*

—. Blacks. Freedmen's Bureau. Mississippi (Natchez district). Sharecropping. 1860's. *681*

—. Buffington, A. R. Documents. Illinois. Rock Island Arsenal. Strikes. 1897-99. *809*

—. Railroads. Strikes. Values. 1877. 1894. *788*

Arms. *See* Ordnance; Weapons.

Army Corps of Engineers. Construction. Working Hours. 1960-72. *2185*

—. Florida (Pensacola). Gulf Coast. Navy Yard. Slavery. 1826-62. *563*

Army personnel. Attitudes. Social Change. World War II. 1940's-70's. *227*

Aronowitz, Stanley (views). Class consciousness. Economic Structure. Industrial Relations. Radicals and Radicalism. Working class. 1960-76. *1556*

Art and State. New Deal. New Jersey. Public Works of Art Project. 1932-40. *1371*

Arthur, Chester A. Labor, commissioner of. Wright, Carroll. 1884-1905. *859*

Artisans. Attitudes. Capitalism. Working Class. 18c-19c. 1970's. *525*

—. Economic conditions. Industrialization. Occupational structure. Pennsylvania (Germantown). Production networks. 1767-91. *540*

—. New Jersey (Newark). Pennsylvania (Lancaster). 1820-80. *539*

Artists. Buildings, public. Federal Programs. New Deal. 1930's. *1348*

Arts and Crafts. Apprenticeship. Journeymen. Maryland (Baltimore). Slavery. Wealth. 1790-1820. *536*

—. Pennsylvania (Lancaster). 18c. *447*

—. Pennsylvania (Philadelphia). 1820-50. *521*

—. Slavery. 1619-1865. *614*

Asian Americans *See also* Chinese Americans; Filipino Americans; Indochinese Americans; Japanese Americans; Korean Americans.

—. Alaska. Canning industry. Contracts. Labor Disputes. Salmon. 1880-1937. *301*

—. Labor market. 1970. *1689*

—. Social Mobility. 1960-76. *1681*

Assembly line workers. Automobile Industry and Trade. Working Conditions. 1900-33. *981*

—. Construction workers. Unemployment. 1974-75. *1803*

—. Working Conditions. 1972-73. *1868*

Assimilation *See also* Acculturation; Integration.

—. Attitudes. Bilingualism. New York City. Puerto Ricans. Working class. 1979. *1560*

—. Cities. Immigrants. Labor force. Northeastern or North Atlantic States. 1870-1930. *39*

—. Clecak, Peter (account). Educators. 19c-20c. *34*

—. Coal Miners. Iowa. Italian Americans. 1890-1920. *226*

—. Education. Jews. Labor movement. Socialism. 1880's-1945. *291*

—. Occupations. Refugees. Sex roles. Social status. Vietnamese. 1975. *1703*

Associated Silk Workers Union. American Civil Liberties Union. Freedom of Assembly. Freedom of Speech. New Jersey (Paterson). Strikes. 1924. *1159*

Athletics. *See* Physical Education and Training; Sports.

Atlanta Transit Company. Georgia Power Company. Street, Electric Railway and Motor Coach Employees of America. Strikes. 1946-50. *2105*

Atomic energy. Employment. Federal Government. Private sector. 1963-73. *1522*

—. Conservatism. Economic Theory. Recessions. Unemployment. 1978. *2695*

—. Machines. Management, scientific. Production. 1870-1920. *716*

—. Movie theaters. Ushers. Youth. 1920-29. *941*

—. Self-perception. Women. Working conditions. 1964-79. *1734*

Behavior patterns. Economic conditions. Florida (Palm Beach County). Migrant labor. 1970-74. *1840*

Belgian Americans. French Canadian Americans. Independent Textile Workers. Rhode Island (Woonsocket). Working Class. 1931-50's. *1157*

Bell, Daniel. Braverman, Harry. Industrialization. Legislation. Models. Wages. Working Hours. 1900-70. *397*

Bell Telephone System. Company unions. Labor Unions and Organizations. Telephone Workers. 1919-37. *1248*

Beltrame, Ed. Fishermen. Florida (Cortez). Knowlton, Bob. Labor Unions and Organizations. United Packinghouse Workers of America. 1930-58. *1163*

Bentley, William. Cabinetmaking. Diaries. Furniture. Massachusetts (Salem). 1784-1819. *503*

Berkeley Guidance Study. California. Depressions. Employment. Family. Women. 1930-70. *1379*

Berkin, Carol R. Degler, Carl N. Dublin, Thomas. Kennedy, Susan. Lovett, Clara M. Women (review article). 1770's-1980. *118*

Berry, George L. Illinois (Chicago). Newspapers. Strikes. 1912-14. *1265*

Berry pickers. California (El Monte). Farm workers. Foreign Relations. Japan. Mexico. Strikes. 1933. *1170*

Bertie Industries. Blacks. Employee-community ownership. North Carolina (Bertie County). Workers' Owned Sewing Company. 1960-80. *1735*

Besig, Ernest. American Civil Liberties Union. Archives. California, northern. Civil Rights. 1915-80. *64*

Bethlehem Steel Corporation. Daily Life. Depressions. Labor Unions and Organizations. Pennsylvania. Working conditions. 1910-50's. *309*

—. Executive Behavior. Management, scientific. Pennsylvania. Taylor, Frederick W. 1898-1901. *721*

Bethune, Mary McLeod. Blacks. Equal opportunity. National Youth Administration. Public Policy. Youth. 1935-44. *1441*

Bibliographies. American Federation of Labor. Historiography. Industrial Workers of the World. 1905-69. *1013*

—. American Studies. Labor history. 20c. *140*

—. Business. Exposes. Government. 1967-83. *1586*

—. Chaff, Sandra L. Physicians. Walsh, Mary Roth. Women. 1835-1977. *350*

—. Chinese. Discrimination. Industrial Workers of the World. Knights of Labor. Labor. Newspapers. Washington. 1885-1919. *119*

—. Dangerous substances. Fertility. Men. Occupational safety. Women. 1970-78. *1600*

—. Dissertations. 18c-20c. 1971-79. *101*

—. Economic structure. Sex Roles. Women. 1940-75. *1700*

—. Employment. Federal policy. 1960's-70's. *2197*

—. Folklore. Industry. Occupations. 1888-1978. *80*

—. Government. Industrial relations. 19c-20c. 1981. *103*

—. Historiography. Hobsbawn, Eric. Labor. Thompson, E. P. 1960's-70's. *1551*

—. Industrial Workers of the World. Labor Unions and Organizations. Local history. 20c. *1058*

—. Labor history. 17c-1973. *124*

—. Labor history. 17c-1975. *126*

—. Labor history. 17c-1979. *127*

—. Labor history. 17c-1980. *125*

—. Labor history. 17c-1981. *128*

—. Labor history. 1974. *1541*

—. Labor history. 1976. *1540*

—. Labor history. South. 1900-75. *146*

—. Labor Unions and Organizations. 1963-77. *273*

—. Labor Unions and Organizations. Working class. 1940's. *174*

—. Labor Unions and Organizations (white-collar). Women. 1975-80. *1982*

—. Maine. Women. Working Class. 1975. *202*

—. South. Strikes. Textile industry. 1929-76. *1284*

Bicentennial celebrations. Communist Party. Economic Conditions. Labor Unions and Organizations. Politics. 1976-77. *1910*

Biklen, Sari Knapp. Brannigan, Marilyn. Employment. Forisha, Barbara L. Goldman, Barbara. Leadership. Organizations. Women (review article). 1940-80. *1957*

Bilbo, Theodore G. Employment. Fair Employment Practices Commission. Filibusters. Mississippi. Racism. Senate. 1941-46. *1290*

Bilingualism. Assimilation. Attitudes. New York City. Puerto Ricans. Working class. 1979. *1560*

Birth Rate *See also* Fertility; Population.

—. Inflation. Public Welfare. Unemployment. 1945-77. *2652*

Black lung disease. Coal Mine Health and Safety Act (US, 1969; amended, 1972). Coal Miners. Medicine. Strikes, wildcat. United Mine Workers of America. Workers' Compensation. 1968-72. *2228*

Blacklisting. Bureaucracies. Chicago, Burlington & Quincy Railroad. Employment. North Central States. Railroads. 1877-92. *779*

—. California (Hollywood). Film industry. Letters. Trumbo, Dalton. 1940's-60's. *1606*

Blackmail. Crime and Criminals (organized). Illinois (Chicago). Kefauver, Estes. Korshak, Sidney R. Senate Committee to Investigate Organized Crime. 1950-76. *2311*

Blacks. Adolescence. Employment. Recessions. Women. 1945-81. *2616*

—. Affirmative Action. Cities. Civil service. Employment. Political power. 1970-78. *1950*

—. Affirmative action. Discrimination (review article). Gould, William B. Hill, Herbert. Labor Unions and Organizations. Seniority. Supreme Court. 1970's. *2537*

—. Affirmative Action. Quotas. 1920's-78. *363*

—. AFL-CIO. Leadership. Racism. 1955-79. *2482*

—. Africa. Attitudes. Cherokee Indians. Colonization. Indian Territory. Slavery. 1830-60. *618*

—. Africa, Southern. Boycotts. Labor reform. United Mine Workers of America. USA. 1960's-74. *2587*

—. Age. Discrimination. Income. Mexican Americans. Texas. 1960-70. *2521*

—. Agricultural Labor. Discrimination. South. Wages. 1898-1902. *879*

—. Agricultural Labor. Divorce. Men. Moynihan, Daniel P. ("The Negro Family"). 1965-78. *2544*

—. Agricultural labor. Logan, Frenise A. North Carolina Bureau of Labor Statistics. Wages. Whites. 1887. *891*

—. Agriculture. Economic Conditions. *One Kind of Freedom* (book). Ransom, Roger. South. Sutch, Richard. 1860's-80's. 1977-78. *885*

—. Agriculture Department. Alabama. Campbell, Thomas M. Social Conditions. South. ca 1883-1956. *1407*

—. Alabama. Industrial Arts Education. Tuskegee Institute. Washington, Booker T. 1870's-90's. *708*

—. Alabama. Labor Union of Alabama. National Negro Labor Union. Politics. Rapier, James T. Reconstruction. 1837-75. *880*

—. Alabama (Jefferson County; Coalburg). Coal Miners. Convict labor. Mortality. Parke, Thomas D. Sloss-Sheffield coal mine. Working conditions. 1895. *745*

—. Alabama (Mobile). Fair Employment Practices Commission. Shipyards. South. World War II. 1938-45. *1351*

—. Aluminum Company of America. Labor. Tennessee (Alcoa). 1919-39. *1431*

—. American Agricultural Chemical Community. Company towns. Daily life. Diggs, Paul. Florida (Pierce). Social organization. 1938. *966*

—. American Federation of Labor. Brotherhood of Sleeping Car Porters. "George" stereotype. Randolph, A. Philip. 1867-1935. *1421*

—. American Order of Fascisti. Employment. Georgia. White supremacy. 1930-33. *1417*

—. Armaments Industry. Crosswaith, Frank R. Employment. Labor Reform. Negro Labor Committee. New York City (Harlem). World War II. 1939-45. *1447*

—. Armies. Equal Opportunity. Women. 1975. *1694*

—. Armies. Freedmen's Bureau. Mississippi (Natchez district). Sharecropping. 1860's. *681*

—. Attitudes. Chinese. Democracy. Discrimination. Exclusion Act (US, 1882). Immigration. 1850-1910. *701*

—. Attitudes. Immigrants. South. 1865-1910. *700*

—. Attitudes. Social Organization. Whites. 1960's-70's. *1706*

—. Auto Workers. Labor Disputes. Michigan (Detroit). 1941-75. *2074*

—. Automobile Industry and Trade. Communism. League of Revolutionary Black Workers. Michigan (Detroit). 1968-76. *2463*

—. Automobile industry and Trade. Labor Unions and Organizations. League of Revolutionary Black Workers. Michigan (Detroit). 1968-73. *2462*

—. Automobile Industry and Trade. Michigan (Detroit). Migration, Internal. 1910-30. *1432*

—. Baseball. Discrimination. Editors and Editing. *Pittsburgh Courier-Journal*. Smith, Wendell. 1933-45. *1448*

—. Bertie Industries. Employee-community ownership. North Carolina (Bertie County). Workers' Owned Sewing Company. 1960-80. *1735*

—. Bethune, Mary McLeod. Equal opportunity. National Youth Administration. Public Policy. Youth. 1935-44. *1441*

—. Bondage systems. South. 1865-1940. *678*

—. Bossism. Fishermen and Concerned Citizens Association. Louisiana (Plaquemines Parish). Perez family. Pressure Groups. Social reform. 1979-82. *2042*

—. Brotherhood of Sleeping Car Porters. March on Washington Movement. National Negro Congress. Randolph, A. Philip. 1925-41. *1166*

—. Buses. Missouri (St. Louis). Public transportation. Unemployment. 1973. *2468*

—. Business Cycles. Unemployment. Youth. 1954-78. *1749*

—. Businesses, white-owned. Employment opportunities. Ghettos. 1973. *2396*

—. California (Los Angeles). Employment. Housing. Segregation. Transportation. 1941-45. *1440*

—. California (Sausalito). Discrimination. International Brotherhood of Boilermakers, Iron Shipbuilders and Helpers of America. *James v. Marinship* (California, 1945). Shipbuilding. 1940-48. *1450*

—. Capitalism. Households. Income. Labor history. Pennsylvania (Philadelphia). South Africa. Steel Industry. 19c-20c. *138*

—. Catholic Church. Cities. North. Occupations. Social Status. 1968. *1685*

—. Cattle Raising. Cowboys. Rodeos. 1880's-1970's. *143*

—. Chesapeake Bay area. Immigration. Population. 1619-1712. *410*

—. Children. Discrimination. Wages. Whites. Wives. Women. 1967. *2523*

—. Children. Freedmen's Bureau. Indentured servants. Law. North Carolina. 1865-68. *731*

—. Christian, Marcus B. Dillard University. Federal Writers' Project. Historiography. Louisiana. Works Progress Administration. 1930's-79. *1406*

—. Cities. Discrimination. Employment. Unemployment. Women. 1960's-70's. *2417*

—. Cities. Domestics. North. Women. Working conditions. 20c. *2478*

—. Cities. Ewen, Linda Ann. Greer, Edward. Industrial Relations (review article). Meier, August. Rudwick, Elliott. 1900-81. *353*

—. Cities. Hispanic Americans. Public Employees. Women. 1977. *2444*

—. City Government. Equal opportunity. Mexican Americans. Texas. Urbanization. 1973. *2477*

—. City Life. Migration. Occupations. Pennsylvania (Pittsburgh). Polish Americans. 1900-30. *1382*

—. City Politics. Elections, municipal. Knights of Labor. Political Reform. Virginia (Richmond). 1886-88. *869*

—. Civil rights. Discrimination. Military. Women. 1976. *2553*

—. Civil rights. Employment. Income. Legislation. Women. 1960-70. *2742*

—. Civil Rights. Labor Unions and Organizations. South. Textile industry. 1950's-70's. *2485*

—. Civil Rights Act (US, 1964; Title VIII). Discrimination. Employment. Income. Women. 1964-70's. *2252*

—. Civilian Conservation Corps. Discrimination. New York. 1933-42. *1433*

—. Coal mines and mining. Immigrants. West Virginia. 1880-1917. *9*

—. Coal Mines and Mining. Oregon Improvement Company. Strikebreakers. Washington (King County). 1891. *883*

—. Colleges and Universities. Education. Occupational goals. Sex Roles. Women. 1964-70. *2473*

Burawoy, Michael. Canada. Capitalism. Edwards, Richard. Pfeffer, Richard M. USA. Working Class (review article). Zimbalist, Andrew. 1945-70's. *1497*

Burch, Selina (interview). Communications Workers of America. Labor unions and organizations. 1945-73. *2056*

Bureau of Indian Affairs. Indians. Occupational mobility. Public Welfare. Standard of living. 1970. *2349*

—. Oregon (Portland). Training programs. Vocational education. 1964-66. *2202*

Bureau of Labor Statistics. *See* Labor Department (Bureau of Labor Statistics).

Bureau of Refugees, Freedmen, and Abandoned Lands. Alabama. Freedmen. Reconstruction. 1865-67. *612*

Bureaucracies. Anthropologists. Employment. Research. 1974. *1944*

—. Blacklisting. Chicago, Burlington & Quincy Railroad. Employment. North Central States. Railroads. 1877-92. *779*

—. Bureaucratic Labor Market. Civil service. 1963-77. *2677*

—. Business. Public welfare. Social services. 1900-40. *1374*

—. Civil Service. Federal Government. Legislation. Pensions. Retirement. 1897-1920. *1308*

—. Constituencies. Federal government. Wages. 1961-76. *2189*

Bureaucratic Labor Market. Bureaucracies. Civil service. 1963-77. *2677*

Bureaucratization. Conservatism. Labor Unions and Organizations. Radicals and Radicalism. 1930's-70's. *254*

Burgess, Ernest W. Central Business District. Housing. Models. Occupations. Pennsylvania (Philadelphia). 1920-60. *62*

Burlington Industries, Inc. Brown Lung Association. Brown lung disease. Cotton. Liberty Mutual Insurance Co. Occupational diseases. South. 1970's. *1609*

Buses. Blacks. Missouri (St. Louis). Public transportation. Unemployment. 1973. *2468*

Business *See also* Advertising; Banking; Consumers; Corporations; Management; Manufactures; Marketing; Multinational Corporations; Private Sector.

—. Antiunionization. Consultants. Labor Unions and Organizations. Lawyers. 1979-80. *2057*

—. Bibliographies. Exposes. Government. 1967-83. *1586*

—. Bureaucracies. Public welfare. Social services. 1900-40. *1374*

—. California (San Francisco). Construction. Eight-hour day. Law and Order Committee. Strikes. 1916-17. *1190*

—. Connecticut. Ethnic groups. Greek Americans. Occupations. Pizza. 1900-75. *1719*

—. Costs. State Government. Workers' compensation. 1978-81. *2221*

—. Degrees, doctoral. Labor Department (Bureau of Labor Statistics). Statistics. 1975-79. *2841*

—. Discrimination. Minorities. Social control. Women. 1969-75. *2518*

—. Employee ownership. Productivity. 1970-82. *1794*

—. Employee Ownership. South. 1979-82. *1607*

—. Fraser, Douglas. Industrial Relations. Labor-Management Group. Letters. United Automobile Workers of America. 1978. *1890*

—. Income. 1966-68. *2595*

—. Labor Unions and Organizations. New Deal. Taft-Hartley Act (US, 1947). Wagner Act (US, 1935). World War II. 1935-47. *1293*

—. New York City. Women. 1660-1775. *446*

Business Cycles *See also* Depressions; Recessions.

—. Blacks. Unemployment. Youth. 1954-78. *1749*

—. Current Population Survey. Work sharing. 1950's-79. *1574*

—. Economic Policy. Inflation. Phillips curve. Prices. Wages. 1890-1976. *402*

—. Employment. Labor Supply. Women. 1956-76. *2505*

—. Europe. Inflation. Unemployment. Wages. 1945-70. *2683*

—. Unemployment. 1960's-70's. *2658*

—. Unemployment. 1967-79. *1632*

—. Unemployment. Women. 1945-78. *2503*

Business Education. Colleges and Universities. Historians. New York University (Graduate School of Business Administration). 1977-80. *1954*

—. Colleges and Universities. Occupations. 1969-81. *2015*

Business (family). Employment. Family. 1950-81. *1614*

Business, Small. Economic Conditions. Employment. Neighborhoods. Regions. 1969-80. *2610*

Business Unionism. Labor Unions and Organizations. 1970-80. *1876*

Businesses, white-owned. Blacks. Employment opportunities. Ghettos. 1973. *2396*

Butler, Benjamin F. (papers). Elections (presidential). People's Party. Third Parties. 1884. *857*

C

Cabinetmaking. Bentley, William. Diaries. Furniture. Massachusetts (Salem). 1784-1819. *503*

California *See also* Far Western States.

—. Accidents. Industrial safety. Tanneries. Working Conditions. 1901-80. *222*

—. Agricultural Industry. Elections. Proposition 14 (1976). United Farm Workers Union. 1976, *2052*

—. Agricultural Labor. Contract labor. Leasing. 1900-10. *953*

—. Agricultural Labor. Elections. Labor Unions and Organizations. National Labor Relations Act (US, 1935). 1975-76. *1358*

—. Agricultural labor. Labor Unions and Organizations. Migration, Internal. "Okies". 1930's. *994*

—. Agricultural Labor. Labor Unions and Organizations. National Industrial Recovery Act (US, 1933). 1933-34. *1298*

—. Agricultural Labor. Mexican Americans. United Cannery, Agricultural, Packing and Allied Workers of America. 1937-40. *1213*

—. Agricultural labor. Sikhs. 1904-82. *198*

—. Agricultural Labor. Social conflict. Strawberry industry. 20c. *2838*

—. Agricultural Labor Relations Act (1975). Collective bargaining. Politics. 1975-77. *2333*

—. Agricultural Labor Relations Act (1975). Emergency Farm Labor Supply Program. Labor law. New Deal. ca 1930-79. *320*

—. Agriculture. Boycotts. Chavez, Cesar. Labor Unions and Organizations. Teamsters, International Brotherhood of. United Farm Workers Union. 1962-74. *2070*

—. Agriculture. Chavez, Cesar. Elections. Proposition 14 (1976). United Farm Workers Union. 1975-76. *2136*

—. Agriculture. Farm Workers. Mechanization. 1964-80. *1771*

—. Ah-Choi. Chinese. Occupations. Prostitution. Women. 1840's-50's. *442*

—. American Railway Union. Illinois (Pullman). Strikes. 1893-94. *829*

—. Berkeley Guidance Study. Depressions. Employment. Family. Women. 1930-70. *1379*

—. Bulosan, Carlos (autobiography). Filipino Americans. Labor Unions and Organizations. Leftism. 1934-38. *1117*

—. Catholic Church. Indians. Missions and Missionaries. 1775-1805. *411*

—. Chavez, Cesar. Farm workers. Labor law. 1965-76. *2046*

—. Chavez, Cesar. Farm Workers. Mexican Americans. Strikes. United Farm Workers Union. 1965-70. *2024*

—. Chinese. Constitutions, State. Federal Regulation. International Workingmen's Association. Labor reform. 1877-82. *865*

—. Chinese. Economic Structure. Family. Prostitution. Women. 1849-1925. *185*

—. Chinese Americans. City Life. Laundry. 1848-90. *724*

—. Collective bargaining. *Serrano v. Priest* (1971). Supreme courts, state. Teachers. 1970's. *2000*

—. Elliot, Robert. Lawsuits. Occupational Safety and Health Administration. P & Z Company. Working conditions. 1975-77. *2348*

—. Europe. Short-time compensation programs. Unemployment Insurance. Work Sharing Unemployment Insurance program. 1920's-80. *2183*

—. Farm Workers. Grape industry. Labor Unions and Organizations. Strikes. United Farm Workers Union. 1966-70. *2088*

—. Farm workers. Labor law. Law. Minimum wage. State Government. Virginia. 1975. *2187*

—. Farm Workers. Mexican Americans. Migrant labor. Yemeni. 1950-70. *1804*

—. Farm workers. Migrant labor. Miners. South Africa. ca 1890-1975. *1593*

—. Farm Workers. United Farm Workers Union. 1960's-76. *2071*

—. Farmers, tenant. Japanese Americans. 1890-1909. *955*

—. Federal Policy. Indian-White Relations. Mexican War. Military Government. 1846-49. *443*

—. Labor force. Mexican Americans. Texas. Women. 1969-74. *1557*

—. Labor Unions and Organizations. Lobbying. Progressives. 1900-19. *1008*

—. Leisure. State Legislatures. Unemployment. 1979. *2305*

—. Libraries. Migrant Labor. 1970-80. *2318*

—. Lundeberg, Harry. Preservation. San Francisco Maritime Museum. Ships. 1945-55. *98*

California (Colusa County). Agricultural Labor. Farms. Mexican Americans. 1950-69. *1519*

California (Delano). Chavez, Cesar. Grape industry. Strikes. 1967-70. *2110*

California (El Monte). Berry pickers. Farm workers. Foreign Relations. Japan. Mexico. Strikes. 1933. *1170*

California (Fresno). Clyde, Edward M. Freedom of Speech. Industrial Workers of the World. 1911. *1045*

—. Freedom of Speech. Industrial Workers of the World. 1910-11. *1026*

California (Grass Valley). British Americans. Coad, John. Gold Miners. Letters. 1858-60. *430*

California (Hollywood). Blacklisting. Film industry. Letters. Trumbo, Dalton. 1940's-60's. *1606*

California (Inglewood). Communist Party. North American Aviation. Strikes. United Automobile Workers of America. 1941. *1233*

California (Kern County). DiGiorgio Fruit Co. Farm Workers. National Farm Labor Union. Strikes. 1947-49. *2079*

California (Los Angeles). Airplane Industry and Trade. Women. Working Conditions. World War II. 1941-81. *951*

—. American Federation of Labor. Bombings. Labor movement. *Los Angeles Times*. McNamara case. Progressives. 1910-14. *1360*

—. Blacks. Employment. Housing. Segregation. Transportation. 1941-45. *1440*

—. Clothing Industry. Mexican Americans. Women. Working Conditions. 1970-79. *2551*

—. Communist Party. Labor Unions and Organizations. Mexicans. Radicals and Radicalism. 1930-39. *1203*

—. Congress of Industrial Organizations. Labor Unions and Organizations. Mexican Americans. 1938-50. *1004*

—. Employment. Industry. Mexican Americans. Women (interviews). 1928. *1446*

—. Immigration and Naturalization Service. Industrial Relations. International Ladies' Garment Workers' Union. Lilli Diamond Originals. Mexican Americans. Raids. 1976-77. *2144*

—. Industrial relations. Local government. Public Employees. 1966-74. *2296*

—. International Ladies' Garment Workers' Union. Mexican Americans. Women. Working Conditions. 1933-39. *1204*

—. Mexican Americans. Pacific Electric Railroad. Strikes. 1900-03. *1277*

—. Mexican Americans. Working class. 1820-1920. *31*

—. Mexicans. Migration. Undocumented Workers. 1979. *1561*

California (Los Angeles, San Francisco). Labor (nonunion, union). Wages. 1960's. *2714*

California, northern. American Civil Liberties Union. Archives. Besig, Ernest. Civil Rights. 1915-80. *64*

California (Oakland). City government. Employment. Minorities. 1965-73. *2574*

—. General Strikes. Social change. 1946-47. *2155*

California (Orange County). Deviant Behavior. Working Conditions. Youth. 1981. *1798*

California (Salinas). Agricultural Labor. Filipino Labor Union. Lettuce. Strikes. 1934. *1136*

California (San Diego). Freedom of Speech. Industrial Workers of the World. Mexico (Tijuana). 1911-12. *1069*

California (San Francisco). Babow, Irving. Palace Hotel. Personal Narratives. Working Conditions. 1925-29. *923*

—. Bombings. City Government. Law and Order Committee. McDevitt, William. Rolph, James J. Socialism. 1916. *1328*

—. Budgets. City government. Costs. 1945-76. *2283*

—. Business. Construction. Eight-hour day. Law and Order Committee. Strikes. 1916-17. *1190*

—. Chinese Americans. Discrimination. 1850-80. *723*

—. Class consciousness. International Workingmen's Association. Social mobility. 1880's. *756*

—. Diaries. Immigrants. Irish Americans. Ironworkers. Roney, Frank. 1875-76. *733*

—. General strikes. National Guard. Ports. 1934. *1172*

—. General strikes. Personal narratives. Photographs. 1934. *1122*

—. Hotel and Restaurant Employees and Bartenders International Union. Labor Unions and Organizations. 1975-78. *2131*

—. Hughes, Charles Evans. Labor. Political Campaigns (presidential). Republican Party. 1916. *1327*

—. Job Factory for Youth. Job Track (program). Unemployment. Youth. 1979-81. *1846*

—. Labor market. Longshoremen. Strikes. 1934-39. *1178*

—. Men. Public schools. Wages. Women. 1879. *897*

—. Modernization. Reform. Social Conditions. Workingmen's Party of California. 1870-80. *734*

California (San Francisco Bay area). Domestic service. Japanese Americans. Women. Working conditions. 1905-40. *1394*

—. Longshoremen. 1980. *1847*

California (San Francisco, Oakland). Employment program. Public service jobs. 1960-75. *2295*

California (San Joaquin Valley). Farm Workers. Japanese Americans. Labor Disputes. Mexican Americans. Nisei Farmers League. United Farm Workers Union. 1971-77. *2072*

California (San Jose). Comparable Worth. Sex Discrimination. Wages. 1960-81. *2419*

California (Santa Barbara). Fleischmann, Max. Philanthropy. Relief work. Unemployment. 1930-32. *1342*

California (Santa Clara County). Economic Conditions. Electronics industry. Environment. Social problems. 1950's-70's. *1532*

—. Electronics industry. Working Conditions. 1972-81. *1683*

California (Sausalito). Blacks. Discrimination. International Brotherhood of Boilermakers, Iron Shipbuilders and Helpers of America. *James v. Marinship* (California, 1945). Shipbuilding. 1940-48. *1450*

California, southern. Agricultural Labor. Depressions. Steinbeck, John *(In Dubious Battle)*. Strikes. 1933. *1104*

—. Cities. Employment. Mexican Americans. 1900-39. *1424*

California Southern Railroad. Ah Quin. Chinese Americans. Construction. Diaries. 1868-1914. *695*

California State University, Sacramento. Employment (part-time). Women's Studies. 1979. *1929*

California (Stockton). Discrimination. Hawaii. International Longshoremen's and Warehousemen's Union. Japanese Americans. 1945. *2554*

California (Stockton; Chinatown). Agricultural Labor. Discrimination. Filipino Americans. Immigration. 1920-39. *1398*

California, University of, Berkeley. Collective bargaining. College teachers. *National Labor Relations Board* v. *Yeshiva University* (US, 1980). Supreme Court. 1960-80. *2049*

California (Wheatland). Agricultural Labor. Photographs. Riots. 1913. *1261*

—. Industrial Workers of the World. Migrant Labor. State Government. Strikes. Trials. 1913-17. *1133*

California Women Farmworkers Project. Agricultural Labor. Oral history. Women. 1870's-1970's. *206*

Callahan, Patrick Henry. Industrial Relations. Kentucky. Louisville Varnish Company. Profit sharing. 1908-40. *942*

"Calling" (concept). Equality. Great Chain of Being (theme). Labor, dignity of. Puritans. 17c-18c. *418*

Calumet and Hecla Mining Company. Copper Mines and Mining. Labor Unions and Organizations. Social Change. 1840-1968. *51*

Cambodia. Economic conditions. Employment. Laos. Refugee Act (US, 1980). Vietnam, South. 1975-79. *1563*

Campaign Finance. Corporations. Federal regulation. Labor Unions and Organizations. 1971-76. *2223*

Campaigns, Political. *See* Political Campaigns.

Campbell, Thomas M. Agriculture Department. Alabama. Blacks. Social Conditions. South. ca 1883-1956. *1407*

Canada *See also* British North America; North America.

—. American Federation of Labor. Gompers, Samuel. Labor. USA. 1881. *766*

—. Burawoy, Michael. Capitalism. Edwards, Richard. Pfeffer, Richard M. USA. Working Class (review article). Zimbalist, Andrew. 1945-70's. *1497*

—. Chemical Industry. Oil Industry and Trade. Twelve-hour day. USA. Working Conditions. 1977. *1753*

—. Computers. Industry. Robots. Unemployment. USA. 1964-81. *1479*

—. Decentralization. Europe. Industrial relations. Labor (participation). USA. 1960's-70's. *1546*

—. Employment. Indochinese. Refugees. USA. 1970-79. *2558*

—. Finns. Immigrants. Labor Unions and Organizations. Radicals and Radicalism. USA. 1918-26. *965*

—. Labor. Provincial government. Public employment bureaus. Social Reform. State government. Unemployment. USA. 1890-1916. *1356*

—. Libraries. Library workers. USA. Wages. Women. 1977-82. *1972*

—. Manufacturing. Productivity. USA. 1974-81. *2626*

—. Models. Strikes. USA. 1900-71. *310*

Cancer. New Jersey, northern. Painting. Radium dials. 1917-24. *990*

Canneries. Alaska. Filipino Americans. Labor Unions and Organizations. Salmon. 1902-38. *1198*

—. Alaska (Nushagak River). Fishermen. Strikes. 1951-52. *2087*

Canning industry. Alaska. Asian Americans. Contracts. Labor Disputes. Salmon. 1880-1937. *301*

—. Migrant Labor. New York State Factory Investigating Commission. Polish Americans. 1900-35. *960*

Cannon, Joseph Gurney. Gompers, Samuel. House of Representatives. Illinois (Danville). Labor Unions and Organizations. Voting and Voting Behavior. 1906-08. *1063*

Cantor, Milton. Dublin, Thomas. Foner, Philip. Katzman, David. Laurie, Bruce. Tentler, Leslie Woodcock. Women (review article). Work. 17c-20c. *231*

Capital *See also* Banking; Capitalism; Investments; Labor; Monopolies.

—. Cotton. Textile Industry. Wages. 1880-1930. *406*

—. Immigration restrictions. Labor, foreign. Legislation. 1870's-1920's. *137*

Capital, fixed. Agricultural Labor. Economic development. Farmers. Slavery. South. ca 1840-80. *578*

Capitalism *See also* Capital; Socialism.

—. Artisans. Attitudes. Working Class. 18c-19c. 1970's. *525*

—. Behavior. Family. Massachusetts (Lowell). Sex roles. 1860. *427*

—. Blacks. Households. Income. Labor history. Pennsylvania (Philadelphia). South Africa. Steel Industry. 19c-20c. *138*

—. Braverman, Harry (review article). Labor. Marxism. 20c. *135*

—. Braverman, Harry (review article). Monopolies. 20c. *2641*

—. Burawoy, Michael. Canada. Edwards, Richard. Pfeffer, Richard M. USA. Working Class (review article). Zimbalist, Andrew. 1945-70's. *1497*

—. Children. Mexico. Undocumented Workers. Women. ca 1950-79. *2470*

—. Collective bargaining. Government. Ideology. Intervention. 1978. *2734*

—. Computers. Labor, division of. Wages. 1960-70's. *1961*

—. Domestics. Economic Structure. 1970-73. *1649*

—. Dublin, Thomas. Family. Great Britain. Levine, David. Massachusetts (Lowell). Population. Working Class (review article). 1550-1869. *444*

—. Economic performance. Industrialization. Statistics. Unemployment. 19c-1976. *379*

—. Economic Policy. Federal Government. Wages. 1970's. *2737*

—. Economic Policy. Kentucky. Labor policies. Politicians. 1787-1890's. *10*

—. Economics. Unemployment. 1970-75. *2863*

—. Economy. Engerman, Stanley L. Fogel, Robert William. Genovese, Eugene D. Slavery (review article). 1831-61. 1974. *635*

—. Employment. Equal Opportunity and Full Employment Act of 1976 (proposed). Full Employment Bill of 1944. 1944-74. *2244*

—. Employment. Norway. Sex Discrimination. Social Classes. USA. 1973-80. *1737*

—. Employment. Wages. Women's Liberation Movement. 1950's-60's. *2543*

—. Federal Regulation. Productivity. Technology. 1950-80. *2743*

—. Fiction. Ideology. Women. 1830's-50's. *436*

—. Household production. Women. ca 1790-1910. *188*

—. Ideology. Slavery. South. 19c. *632*

—. Industrialization. Social Organization. Women. 19c-1978. *163*

—. Industrialized countries. Monopolies. Work, degradation of. 1900-73. *20*

—. James, Selma (pamphlet). Social Conditions. Women. Working Conditions. 1972-73. *2583*

—. Labor market. Production. 1890-1975. *380*

—. Labor movement. 1860-1920. *112*

—. Leisure. Social Organization. 1890-1920's. *77*

—. Occupations. Patriarchy. Segregation. Sex Discrimination. Women. ca 1700-1970's. *346*

—. Political Leadership. Working class. 1890-1976. *238*

—. Racism. 1978. *360*

—. Unemployment. 1975-82. *2847*

—. Working Conditions. 20c. *19*

—. Working hours. 1960-80. *2671*

Capitalist countries. Strikes. Working class. 1970-80. *2060*

Capitol Building. Construction. Federal government. Labor policy. 1850's. *456*

Carbon County Coal Strike (1933). National Miners Union. Strikes. United Mine Workers of America. Utah. 1900-39. *1225*

Carden, Georgiana. Education, Compulsory. Elementary education. Mexican Americans. Migrant Labor. 1920's. *1400*

Career Satisfaction. *See* Job Satisfaction.

Careers. *See* Occupations.

Caribbean Region. *See* West Indies.

Carkhuff, Robert. Counselors. Human Resource Development. Models. Teachers. 1976. *1965*

Carmody, John. American Federation of Labor. Civil Works Administration. New Deal. Work relief. 1933-34. *1357*

Carnegie, Andrew. Bond issues. Homestead Strike. Libraries. Ohio Valley Trades and Labor Assembly. West Virginia (Wheeling). 1892-1911. *811*

—. Higher education. Pensions. Retirement. 1901-18. *1087*

Carnegie Commission on Higher Education. Higher education. Student unrest. Wage labor system. 1967-73. *2618*

Carnegie Steel Company. Amalgamated Association of Iron and Steel Workers. Fitch, John A. (report). Homestead Strike. Pennsylvania (Pittsburgh). Steel industry. Strikes. 1892-1909. *787*

—. Amalgamated Association of Iron and Steel Workers. Pennsylvania (Homestead). Republicanism. Steel Industry. Strikes. 1892. *832*

Carpenters. Brotherhood of Carpenters and Joiners of America. District of Columbia. Knights of Labor. 1881-96. *803*

—. Labor unions and organizations. McGuire, Peter J. Socialism. United Brotherhood of Carpenters and Joiners of America. 1881-1902. *799*

Carranza, Venustiano. American Federation of Labor. Gompers, Samuel. Mexico (Carrizal). Prisoners. USA. 1916. *1079*

Carriage and wagon industry. Habakkuk, H. J. Labor supply hypothesis. Manufactures. Ohio (Cincinnati). 1850-1900. *648*

Cartels *See also* Monopolies.

—. Labor Unions and Organizations. Law. 1980. *1924*

Carter, Jimmy. AFL-CIO. Democratic Party. Labor Unions and Organizations. Public welfare. 1976. *2364*

—. Civil Service. Equal Opportunity. Labor Department. 1977-78. *2287*

Collective Bargaining *See also* Arbitration, Industrial; Bargaining Theory; Labor Unions and Organizations; Strikes.

—. *Abood* v. *Detroit Board of Education* (US, 1977). Agency shop fees. Politics. Public Employees. 1977-80. *2126*

—. AFL-CIO. Industry. Labor Unions and Organizations. Mergers. Strikes. Taft-Hartley Act (US, 1947). 1946-70's. *1877*

—. Agricultural Labor Relations Act (1975). California. Politics. 1975-77. *2333*

—. Air Lines. Deregulation. Federal Regulation. 1958-78. *2376*

—. California. *Serrano* v. *Priest* (1971). Supreme courts, state. Teachers. 1970's. *2000*

—. California, University of, Berkeley. College teachers. *National Labor Relations Board* v. *Yeshiva University* (US, 1980). Supreme Court. 1960-80. *2049*

—. Capitalism. Government. Ideology. Intervention. 1978. *2734*

—. Citizen participation. Educational Policy. Public Schools. Teachers. 1960's-70's. *1943*

—. City Government. Coalitions. New York City. Public Employees. 1975-80. *2098*

—. Civil rights. Courts. Public schools. Teachers. 1960-82. *1945*

—. Civil Rights Act (US, 1964; Title VII). Discrimination. Employment. Executive Order 11246. 1964-74. *2368*

—. Civil service. Labor Unions and Organizations. Strikes. 1960-72. *2054*

—. College Teachers. Delaware, University of. 1965-73. *2001*

—. College Teachers. Higher education. Wages. 1970's. *1984*

—. College teachers. *National Labor Relations Board* v. *Yeshiva University* (US, 1980). Supreme Court. Yeshiva University. 1973-81. *1976*

—. Colleges and universities. Labor Unions and Organizations. 1945-76. *2010*

—. Construction. Leadership. North Central States. 1970-79. *2081*

—. Contracts. Industry. Labor Unions and Organizations. Leadership. 1973-74. *1883*

—. Contracts. Labor Unions and Organizations. 1973. *2083*

—. Corporations. Unemployment. Wages. 1982. *1894*

—. Court of Industrial Relations. Nebraska. Public employees. 1919-76. *1366*

—. Decisionmaking. Industrial democracy. Labor Unions and Organizations. 1920's-70's. *1478*

—. Economic analysis. Industry. Profits. Wages. 1954-71. *2797*

—. Economic Conditions. Unemployment. 1940-82. *2785*

—. Economic Conditions. Wages. 1975. *2739*

—. Educational Administration. Public Schools. Teachers. 1960's-70's. *1974*

—. Educational policy. Teachers. 1975. *1969*

—. Educators. Higher education. 1960-78. *1958*

—. Europe. Inflation. USA. 1974. *2831*

—. Experimental Negotiating Agreement. Steel industry. 1946-73. *2031*

—. Federal Government. Labor law. Right to work. 1979. *2248*

—. Fire and Police Employee Relations Act (Texas, 1973). Public Employees. Referendum. Texas. 1973-81. *2023*

—. Fire fighters. Impasse procedures. Models. New York. Police. 1968-76. *2095*

—. France. Great Britain. USA. 18c-20c. *287*

—. Government. Public Opinion. 1970's. *2207*

—. Illinois. Public institutions (budgets). 1973. *2212*

—. Industrial democracy. Sweden. USA. ca 1968-77. *279*

—. Industrial Relations. 1978. *1464*

—. Industry. Manufacturing. 1975. *2082*

—. Labor Unions and Organizations. 1972-73. *1900*

—. Labor Unions and Organizations. Legislation. Public employees. 1974. *1925*

—. Labor unions and organizations. Sex roles. Stereotypes. Women. 1950-78. *1830*

—. Monopsony. Public Schools. Teachers. Wages. 1960's-70's. *2859*

—. New York. Teachers. Wages. 1967-68. *2727*

—. Nurses and Nursing. Professionals. 1955-77. *1997*

—. Pensions (multiemployer). 1950-73. *2642*

—. Principals. Teachers. 1970's. *2012*

—. Public Administration. Public Employees. 1960-80. *2141*

—. Public Employees. 1968-78. *2048*

—. Public Employees. State government. 1960's-70's. *2365*

—. Public Employees. State government. 1962-76. *2044*

—. Public schools. Teachers. 1970's. *2120*

—. Teachers. 1850's-1970's. *2007*

—. Teachers. 1970's. *1987*

Collective bargaining rights. Court decisions. Labor unions and organizations. 1970's. *1721*

College graduates. Academic achievement. Employment. Job performance. 1975. *1851*

—. Attitudes. Employment. Women. 1961-68. *1769*

—. Counseling programs. Labor market. 1975-80's. *1960*

—. Curricula. Employment. Models. Occupations. 1965-78. *1956*

—. Discrimination. Mexican Americans. Wages. 1966-74. *2539*

—. Employment. Higher Education. Wages. 1950-75. *1968*

—. Employment. Income. 1971-72. *1860*

—. Employment experience. 1973-74. *1993*

—. Family. Human Relations. Wellesley College. Women. 1880-1910. *6*

—. Income. Men. Women. 1960's. *2756*

—. Income. Unemployment. 1970's. *1937*

—. Job satisfaction (expectations). Men. Women. 1970's. *1659*

—. Occupations. 1970's. *1935*

—. Working class. 1950-78. *1855*

College Teachers. Affirmative action. Discrimination. Income. 1950's-70's. *2454*

—. Affirmative action. Minorities. 1965-80. *2447*

—. American Association of University Professors (conference). 1982. *1939*

—. California, University of, Berkeley. Collective bargaining. *National Labor Relations Board* v. *Yeshiva University* (US, 1980). Supreme Court. 1960-80. *2049*

—. Collective bargaining. Delaware, University of. 1965-73. *2001*

—. Collective bargaining. Higher education. Wages. 1970's. *1984*

—. Collective bargaining. *National Labor Relations Board* v. *Yeshiva University* (US, 1980). Supreme Court. Yeshiva University. 1973-81. *1976*

—. Confidentiality. Courts. Decisionmaking. 1960's-81. *2009*

—. Educational Administration. Planning. 1982. *2016*

—. Employment. 1981. *1999*

—. Employment, temporary. Roucek, Joseph. Tenure. 1960-79. *1985*

—. Higher education. Labor. University and College Labor Education Association. 1976. *1989*

—. Illinois, University of, Urbana-Champaign. Sex discrimination. 1975-79. *2448*

—. Income. 1982-83. *1931*

—. Labor Unions and Organizations. 1967-72. *1991*

—. Labor Unions and Organizations. 1973. *1977*

—. Labor Unions and Organizations. Wages. 1949-79. *1948*

—. Pangle, Thomas. Tenure. Yale University. 1979-80. *1699*

—. Sex discrimination. Trials. Women. 1964-82. *2394*

—. Social Conditions. Wages. 1969-80. *1963*

—. Wages. 1976-82. *2013*

—. Wages. 1981-82. *2846*

Colleges and Universities *See also* names of individual institutions; Degrees, Academic; Higher Education; Junior Colleges; Scholarships, Fellowships, etc.; Students.

—. Affirmative action. Women. 1982. *2496*

—. Blacks. Education. Occupational goals. Sex Roles. Women. 1964-70. *2473*

—. Brookwood Labor College. Labor. New York (Katonah). 1921-37. *1044*

—. Business Education. Historians. New York University (Graduate School of Business Administration). 1977-80. *1954*

—. Business Education. Occupations. 1969-81. *2015*

—. Cartter, Allen M. (review article). Employment. Graduate Programs. Scholars. ca 1950-75. *1940*

—. Civil service. Management. Training Act (1958). Training programs. 1958-70's. *1949*

—. Collective bargaining. Labor Unions and Organizations. 1945-76. *2010*

—. Educational administrators. Occupational changes. 1981. *1988*

—. Educational programs. Labor Unions and Organizations. Rutgers University. 1930-76. *1481*

—. Employment. Libraries. 1973. *1738*

—. Labor colleges. New Rochelle College. New York. 1972. *1922*

—. Labor education. Labor Unions and Organizations. Tyler, Gus (views). 1928-78. *133*

—. Occupations. Women. 1920-75. *1754*

—. Scholarships, Fellowships, etc. Sports. Workers' compensation. 1953-77. *2198*

—. Sex Discrimination. Women. 1973-74. *2484*

—. Tenure. 1970's-81. *1942*

Colombian Americans. Dominican Americans. Employment. Family. Immigrants. New York City. Women. 1981. *1666*

—. Employment. Immigrants. New York City. 1970's. *1652*

Colonization. Africa. Attitudes. Blacks. Cherokee Indians. Indian Territory. Slavery. 1830-60. *618*

Colorado *See also* Western States.

—. Ammons, Elias. Coal Miners. Federal government. Intervention. Strikes. Wilson, Woodrow. 1914. *1175*

—. Cattle raising. Cowboys. 1980. *1874*

—. Coal Mines and Mining. Industrial Workers of the World. Strikes. 1927. *1199*

—. Newspapers. Professionalism. 1972. *1979*

Colorado Co-operative Company. Agricultural Cooperatives. Depressions. Labor Exchange. Midwest. 1890-1905. *851*

Colorado (Denver). Divorce. Economic Conditions. Income. Washington (Seattle). 1970's. *1672*

—. Employment. Geographic mobility. Social Mobility. 1870-92. *740*

—. Frontier and Pioneer Life. Saloons. Social mobility. 1858-85. *722*

Colorado Fuel and Iron Company. Coal Miners. Ludlow Massacre. National Guard. Strikes. 1913-14. *1141*

Colorado (Las Animas, Huerfano counties). Coal miners. Strikes. United Mine Workers of America. 1904-14. *1263*

Colorado River. Boulder Canyon project. Hoover Dam. Industrial Workers of the World. Nevada. Strikes. 1931. *1241*

Colorado (San Juan area). King, Alfred Castner. Literature. Mining. Nason, Frank Lewis. 1898-1907. *992*

Colorado (San Luis Valley). Mexican Americans. Migrant Labor. 1973. *1469*

Colored Farmers' Alliance. Agricultural Reform. Arkansas. Cotton pickers. Humphrey, R. M. Strikes. 1891. *810*

—. Blacks. Farmers. South. ca 1886-95. *656*

—. Blacks. Humphrey, R. M. Labor Unions and Organizations. South. Strikes. 1876-91. *868*

Colored National Labor Union *See also* National Colored Labor Union.

—. Blacks. Florida. Labor unions and organizations. National Negro Labor Union. Race Relations. Reconstruction. 1865-75. *881*

Colt, Cristine C. (account). Advertising. Dow Jones Co. Sex discrimination. 1975-78. *2426*

Commerce *See also* Banking; Business; International Trade; Monopolies; Prices; Retail Trade; Statistics; Stock Exchange; Tariff; Trade; Transportation.

—. Maryland. Slavery. Woolfolk, Austin. 1819-30's. *550*

Commons, John R. Brody, David. Dawley, Alan. Historians. Labor history. Montgomery, David. Perlman, Selig. 1910-80. *115*

—. Conservatism. Institutions. Labor history. 1884-1935. *95*

Communications Behavior. Employment. Illinois (Chicago). Korean Americans. 1970-79. *1704*

Communications Workers of America. Burch, Selina (interview). Labor unions and organizations. 1945-73. *2056*

Communism *See also* Anarchism and Anarchists; Anti-Communist Movements; Leftism; Maoism; Marxism; Socialism.

—. Anarchism and Anarchists. Ethnic Groups. Historiography. 1880's-1920's. *28*

—. Automobile Industry and Trade. Blacks. League of Revolutionary Black Workers. Michigan (Detroit). 1968-76. *2463*

—. Employment. Family. 1968-79. *1677*

Demonstrations *See also* Riots; Youth Movements.

—. Communism. Films. Strikes. Workers' Film and Photo League. 1930-38. *902*

Department stores. Industrial Relations. Sales. Women. 1900-40. *1380*

—. Management. Sales. Women. Work culture. 1890-1960. *151*

Deportation *See also* Repatriation.

—. Immigrants. Justice Department. Labor Department. Palmer, A. Mitchell. Post, Louis F. Red Scare. Wilson, William B. 1919-20. *1305*

—. Immigrants. Labor Unions and Organizations. Mexican Americans. New Deal. 1930's. *1300*

Depressions *See also* Recessions.

—. Agricultural Adjustment Administration. Labor Unions and Organizations. Sharecroppers. Southern Tenant Farmers' Union. ca 1930's. *1266*

—. Agricultural Cooperatives. Colorado Co-operative Company. Labor Exchange. Midwest. 1890-1905. *851*

—. Agricultural Cooperatives. DeBernardi, Giovanni Battista. Labor Exchange. Self-help. 1889-1910. *808*

—. Agricultural Labor. California, southern. Steinbeck, John *(In Dubious Battle)*. Strikes. 1933. *1104*

—. American Federation of Labor. Coal Miners. New Mexico (Gallup). Strikes. 1933. *1246*

—. Anderson, Karen. Social Change. Wandersee, Winifred D. Ware, Susan. Women (review article). World War II. 1920-45. *1410*

—. Attitudes. Great Britain. Law. Poor. USA. Vagrancy. 14c-1939. *939*

—. Banditry. New Deal. Working class. 1929-39. *913*

—. Berkeley Guidance Study. California. Employment. Family. Women. 1930-70. *1379*

—. Bethlehem Steel Corporation. Daily Life. Labor Unions and Organizations. Pennsylvania. Working conditions. 1910-50's. *309*

—. Brucker, Wilber M. Federal Aid. Michigan. Murphy, Frank. Unemployment. 1929-33. *1345*

—. Causeways. Civilian Conservation Corps (co. 796). Missouri River. South Dakota (Farm Island). 1934. *1375*

—. Civil Works Administration. Louisiana. 1932-34. *1338*

—. Coal Miners. Hevener, John W. Kentucky (Harlan County). Labor Unions and Organizations. 1930's. *1162*

—. DeBernardi, Giovanni Battista. Freedom Colony. Kansas. Labor Exchange. Utopias. 1894-1905. *654*

—. Discrimination. Indiana (Gary). Mexican Americans. Nativism. Repatriation. 1920's-30's. *1381*

—. Employment. Federal Emergency Relief Administration. 1933-40. *1367*

—. Employment. Federal Programs. 1934-41. *1454*

—. Ethnicity. Historiography. Labor. 1930's. 1970-82. *914*

—. Europe, western. Unemployment. USA. 1929-41. *948*

—. Farmer-Labor Party. New Deal. Oregon Commonwealth Federation. Political Factions. 1933-38. *1334*

—. Federal Emergency Relief Administration. Hopkins, Harry L. Letters. Public Welfare. Rhode Island. 1934. *1347*

—. Federal Theatre Project. Flanagan, Hallie. Hopkins, Harry L. Politics. Theater. Works Progress Administration. 1935-39. *1295*

—. Kentucky (Louisville). Labor disputes. Violence. 1877. *844*

—. Labor force. Middle Classes. Values. Women. 1930's. *929*

—. Labor force. Segregation. Women. 1930's. *1423*

—. Labor market. Pennsylvania (Pittsburgh). Wages. 1908. *1459*

—. Labor unions and organizations. Michigan (Detroit). Radicals and Radicalism. 1920's-30's. *908*

—. Liberalism. New Deal. Political activism. Socialist Party. Unemployment. 1929-36. *1354*

—. Liberalism. Psychology. Society for the Psychological Study of Social Issues. 1930's. *1086*

—. Mass Media. Professionalism. Women. 1930's. *1094*

—. Mecklenburg, George H. Minnesota (Minneapolis). Organized Unemployed, Inc. Poor. Self-help. Unemployment. 1932-35. *916*

—. Mexico. Migrant Labor. Obregón, Álvaro (administration). Repatriation. 1920-23. *1385*

—. Professionals. Unemployment. 1929-35. *1093*

—. Radicals and Radicalism. Unemployed councils. 1929-33. *1065*

—. Self-perception. Unemployment. Working Class. 1920's-30's. *995*

Deregulation. Air Lines. Collective bargaining. Federal Regulation. 1958-78. *2376*

—. Air Lines. Labor Unions and Organizations. Transportation, Commercial. 1978-82. *2115*

—. Licenses. State Legislatures. Virginia. 1974-78. *2259*

—. Occupational Safety and Health Administration. Reagan, Ronald. 1970-83. *2195*

Dermatosis. Labor. Occupational diseases. 1976-78. *1599*

Detente. Meany, George. Working Class. 1976. *1515*

Developing Nations *See also* Industrialized Countries.

—. Brain drain. Medical Education. USA. 1970's. *2006*

—. Great Britain. Japan. Manufacturing. Subcontracting. Unemployment. USA. 1966-76. *1535*

Deverall, Richard Lawrence-Grace. Coal Mines and Mining. Documents. Ickes, Harold. Strikes. United Mine Workers of America. West Virginia (Welch). 1943. *1235*

Deviant Behavior. California (Orange County). Working Conditions. Youth. 1981. *1798*

Dewey, John. Education. Industry. Prosser, Charles. Snedden, David. 20c. *251*

Diaries. Ah Quin. California Southern Railroad. Chinese Americans. Construction. 1868-1914. *695*

—. Bentley, William. Cabinetmaking. Furniture. Massachusetts (Salem). 1784-1819. *503*

—. California (San Francisco). Immigrants. Irish Americans. Ironworkers. Roney, Frank. 1875-76. *733*

—. Coal Miners. Medrick, George. Pennsylvania, western. Strikes. United Mine Workers of America. 1927. *1146*

—. Massachusetts (Beverly). Shoe Industry. Trask, Sarah E. Women. Working Class. 1849-51. *412*

—. Sex roles. Westward Movement. Women. 19c. *223*

Dick, William M. American Federation of Labor. Gompers, Samuel. Labor Unions and Organizations. Socialism. 1880-1910. *772*

—. Gompers, Samuel. Labor Unions and Organizations (review article). Laslett, John. Socialism. 1881-1924. *765*

Diet. *See* Food Consumption.

Diffusion. Agricultural Labor. Agricultural Reform. Labor Market. Undocumented Workers. 1850-1981. *2733*

Diggs, Paul. American Agricultural Chemical Community. Blacks. Company towns. Daily life. Florida (Pierce). Social organization. 1938. *966*

DiGiorgio Fruit Co. California (Kern County). Farm Workers. National Farm Labor Union. Strikes. 1947-49. *2079*

Dillard University. Blacks. Christian, Marcus B. Federal Writers' Project. Historiography. Louisiana. Works Progress Administration. 1930's-79. *1406*

Dillon, Francis. Automobile Industry and Trade. Michigan. Motor Products Corporation. Strikes. United Automobile Workers of America. 1933-39. *1110*

Disability. Labor force. Men. Social Security. 1948-76. *1766*

—. Pensions. Private sector. Retirement. 1980. *2607*

Disadvantaged. Employers. Labor market. Vocational Education. 1962-74. *1638*

Disaster relief. Accidents. Coal Mines and Mining. Mabey, Charles R. Palmer, Annie. Social work. Utah (Castle Gate). 1924-36. *959*

Disasters. Coal Mines and Mining. Fire. Illinois (Cherry). 1909. *840*

Discharging. *See* Dismissals.

Discipline. Factories. Family. Massachusetts (Webster). Rhode Island (Slatersville). 1790-1840. *482*

Discrimination *See also* Civil Rights; Minorities; Racism; Segregation; Sex Discrimination.

—. Acculturation. Chinese Americans. Georgia (Augusta). 1865-1980. *339*

—. Affirmative action. Bakke, Allan. Civil rights. Employment. Equal opportunity. Law enforcement. *Regents of the University of California v. Allan Bakke* (US, 1978). 1978. *2328*

—. Affirmative action. College Teachers. Income. 1950's-70's. *2454*

—. Affirmative action. Degrees, Academic. Economists. Employment. Women. 1950-78. *2766*

—. Age. Blacks. Income. Mexican Americans. Texas. 1960-70. *2521*

—. Age Discrimination in Employment Act (US, 1980). Apprenticeship. 1980. *2370*

—. Agricultural Labor. Blacks. South. Wages. 1898-1902. *879*

—. Agricultural Labor. California (Stockton; Chinatown). Filipino Americans. Immigration. 1920-39. *1398*

—. American Federation of Labor. Fair Employment Practices Commission. Federal Government. Labor Unions and Organizations. Shipbuilding. West Coast Master Agreement. World War II. 1939-46. *1313*

—. Arbitration, Industrial. *Griggs vs. Duke Power Company (1971)*. *Rios vs. Reynolds Metals Company (1972)*. 1964-73. *2413*

—. Arizona (Page). Indians. Industrial Relations. Navajo Construction Workers Associations. Office of Navajo Labor Relations. 1971-77. *2541*

—. Arkansas. Attitudes. Employment. Equal opportunity. Public Schools. 1980. *2361*

—. Attitudes. Blacks. Chinese. Democracy. Exclusion Act (US, 1882). Immigration. 1850-1910. *701*

—. Attitudes. Complaints. Law and Society. Massachusetts Commission Against Discrimination. 1971-72. *2436*

—. Automobile Industry and Trade. United Automobile Workers of America. Women. World War II. 1942-45. *1422*

—. Baseball. Blacks. Editors and Editing. *Pittsburgh Courier-Journal*. Smith, Wendell. 1933-45. *1448*

—. Bibliographies. Chinese. Industrial Workers of the World. Knights of Labor. Labor. Newspapers. Washington. 1885-1919. *119*

—. Blacks. California (Sausalito). International Brotherhood of Boilermakers, Iron Shipbuilders and Helpers of America. *James v. Marinship* (California, 1945). Shipbuilding. 1940-48. *1450*

—. Blacks. Children. Wages. Whites. Wives. Women. 1967. *2523*

—. Blacks. Cities. Employment. Unemployment. Women. 1960's-70's. *2417*

—. Blacks. Civil rights. Military. Women. 1976. *2553*

—. Blacks. Civil Rights Act (US, 1964; Title VIII). Employment. Income. Women. 1964-70's. *2252*

—. Blacks. Civilian Conservation Corps. New York. 1933-42. *1433*

—. Blacks. Communist Party. Fair Employment Practices Commission. Labor Unions and Organizations. New York City. Pennsylvania (Philadelphia). Transport Workers Union. 1934-44. *1420*

—. Blacks. Education. Employment. South. 1960-70. *1751*

—. Blacks. Employment. 1959-80. *2771*

—. Blacks. Employment. Ghettos. Housing. Social Policy. Suburbs. 1969-79. *1744*

—. Blacks. Employment. Gould, William B. Hill, Herbert. Labor Law. 19c-1977. *338*

—. Blacks. Employment. Labor. Women. World War II. 1941-45. *1378*

—. Blacks. Employment. Labor market. 1890-1970. *342*

—. Blacks. Employment. Recruitment. Whites. 1970's. *1748*

—. Blacks. Employment. Women. 1950-74. *2425*

—. Blacks. Employment (review article). Fulmer, William E. Rubin, Lester. Wrong, Elaine Gale. 1865-1973. *357*

—. Blacks. Fair Employment Practices Commission. Railroads. Southeastern Carriers Conference. World War II. 1941-45. *1399*

—. Blacks. Georgia Railroad. Railroads. Strikes. 1909. *1397*

—. Blacks. Ideology. Socialism. Working class. 19c-20c. *367*

—. Blacks. Income. Men. Social Mobility. 1937-80. *2508*

—. Blacks. Indiana (Gary). US Steel Corporation. 1906-74. *344*

Duke University Medical Center. Civil rights. Harvey, Oliver. Labor Unions and Organizations. North Carolina (Durham). 1930's-70's. *2106*

Duplanty, McCall and Company. Antietam Woolen Manufacturing Company. Attitudes. Delaware. Maryland (Funkstown). Textile Industry. Working Conditions. 1814-19. *477*

DuPont, E. I. and Company. Brandywine River Valley. Delaware. Documents. Economic growth. Industrialization. Pennsylvania. Standard of living. 1800-60. *408*

—. Delaware. Savings. Wages. 1813-60. *407*

Durnford, Andrew. Blacks. Louisiana (Plaquemines Parish). Planter class. 1820-60. *620*

Dutch West India Company. Civil Rights. New Netherland (New Amsterdam). Sailors. 1628-63. *487*

—. New Netherland. Slavery. 1646-64. *580*

Dye, Nancy Schrom. Greenwald, Maurine Weiner. Labor Unions and Organizations. New York. Women (review article). World War I. 1870-1920. *371*

E

Eastern Airlines. Aeronautics. Gellert, Dan. L-1011 (aircraft). Occupational Safety. Working Conditions. 1972-78. *1647*

Econometrics. Economic theory. Exploitation. Pigou, A. C. 1930-65. *395*

Economic analysis. Collective Bargaining. Industry. Profits. Wages. 1954-71. *2797*

Economic Conditions *See also* terms beginning with Economic; Business Cycles; Statistics.

—. Affirmative action. Local government. Public Employees. State Government. 1960's-70's. *2304*

—. Agricultural Labor. 1950's-80. *2639*

—. Agricultural Labor (free). Crops (staple). Slavery. 1850's-60's. *565*

—. Agriculture. Blacks. *One Kind of Freedom* (book). Ransom, Roger. South. Sutch, Richard. 1860's-80's. 1977-78. *885*

—. Agriculture. Farms (tenant). Productivity. South. 1850's-90's. *662*

—. Agriculture. Industry. Labor. Land. Productivity. 1869-99. *893*

—. American Federation of Labor. New York City. Socialist Labor Party. Working class. 1890-96. *773*

—. American Federation of State, County, and Municipal Employees. Civil Service Employees Association. Politics. Public Employees. 1978-79. *1908*

—. American Revolution. 1774-81. *417*

—. Artisans. Industrialization. Occupational structure. Pennsylvania (Germantown). Production networks. 1767-91. *540*

—. Attitudes. Labor. 1982. *1526*

—. Attitudes. Labor Unions and Organizations. Law Reform. South. Southwest. 1940-80. *266*

—. Behavior patterns. Florida (Palm Beach County). Migrant labor. 1970-74. *1840*

—. Bicentennial celebrations. Communist Party. Labor Unions and Organizations. Politics. 1976-77. *1910*

—. Blacks. Employment. 1920-70. *2533*

—. Blacks. Employment. Equal opportunity. Law. Occupations. 1954-72. *2514*

—. Blacks. Federal regulation. 1960's-77. *2390*

—. Blacks. Georgia, central. Labor agents. Migration, Internal. 1899-1900. *657*

—. Blacks. Income. Philanthropy. 1944-74. *1616*

—. Blacks. Women. 1940-79. *2481*

—. Business, Small. Employment. Neighborhoods. Regions. 1969-80. *2610*

—. California (Santa Clara County). Electronics industry. Environment. Social problems. 1950's-70's. *1532*

—. Cambodia. Employment. Laos. Refugee Act (US, 1980). Vietnam, South. 1975-79. *1563*

—. Chinese Americans. Far Western States. Immigration. Labor market, split. Race Relations. 1848-82. 1970's. *184*

—. Civilian Conservation Corps. New Deal. Vermont. 1933-42. *1363*

—. Clerical workers. District of Columbia. Federal government. Women. 1862-90. *672*

—. Coal Mines and Mining. Ethnic Groups. Pennsylvania (Daisytown). Social Mobility. 1910-40. *924*

—. Coal Mines and Mining. Strikes. 1977-78. *2019*

—. Collective bargaining. Unemployment. 1940-82. *2785*

—. Collective bargaining. Wages. 1975. *2739*

—. Colorado (Denver). Divorce. Income. Washington (Seattle). 1970's. *1672*

—. Conyers, John, Jr. (views). Employment, full. Planning (national). 1977. *2204*

—. Discrimination. Freedmen. Property. ca 1880-1920. *682*

—. Divorce. Social Classes. 1880-1920. *205*

—. Edwards, P. K. Politics. Snyder, David. Strikes. 1900-48. *1254*

—. Employment. 1981-83. *2615*

—. Employment. 1982. *2680*

—. Employment. Federal Government. South. Western States. 1968-78. *2779*

—. Employment. Higher education. 1970-82. *1861*

—. Employment. Housing. Lumber and Lumbering. 1979-83. *2793*

—. Employment. Immigrants. New York City. 1979-82. *1641*

—. Employment. Skills. 1960-76. *1799*

—. Employment. Social Change. 1960-82. *2816*

—. Employment, full. Federal Policy. Politics. 1978. *2230*

—. Employment projections. Labor Department (Bureau of Labor Statistics). 1966-70. *2758*

—. Engerman, Stanley L. Fogel, Robert William. Slavery (review article). 1840-60. 1974. *567*

—. Exclusion policy. Filipinos. Immigration. Split labor market theory. 1927-34. *1387*

—. Federal government. Inflation. Unemployment. 1976. *2233*

—. Federal Regulation. Industrial Mobility. Legislation. North. North Central States. 1970's. *1822*

—. Historiography. Slavery. South. 17c-1865. 1974. *574*

—. Immigration. 1890-1914. *385*

—. Immigration. Labor scarcity. Mexico. Social control. 1950's-70's. *2708*

—. Income. Inequality. Social Conditions. 1969. *2738*

—. Industrial Revolution. Slavery. South. ca 1800-60. *591*

—. Inflation. Labor Law. Reform. Wages. 1930-75. *2624*

—. Inflation. Price controls. Wages. 1971-74. *2809*

—. Inflation. Unemployment. 1973. *2645*

—. International Trade. Labor Unions and Organizations. Protectionism. 1969-73. *2222*

—. Iron industry. Wages. 1800-30. *498*

—. Junior colleges. Vocational education. 1946-79. *1773*

—. Labor. 1970's-81. *1588*

—. Labor Force. Social Mobility. Wives. Women. Working class. 1960's-78. *1707*

—. Labor history. Mexican Americans. 1850-1976. *7*

—. Labor Unions and Organizations. 1972. *1889*

—. Legislation. Retirement, mandatory. 20c. *2807*

—. Life cycles. National Longitudinal Surveys. Occupations. Social Organization. 1966-77. *1770*

—. Manufacturing. Natural resource products. Substitution. 1960's-70's. *387*

—. Manufacturing. Prices. Wages. 1953-70. *2602*

—. Marxism. Slavery. Social Organization. South. 17c-1860. *570*

—. National Recovery Administration. New Deal. Supreme Court. Virginia. 1933-35. *1316*

—. Occupational segregation. Social Organization. Women. 1960-70. *2542*

—. Occupations. Refugees. Vietnamese Americans. 1970's. *1818*

—. Population. Social Organization. Suburban Life. 1970's. *1538*

—. Racism. Whites. Working Class. 1970. *2570*

—. Slavery. 18c-19c. *545*

—. Slavery (review article). South. ca 1800-60. *566*

—. Social Conditions. Unemployment. Wages. Working class. 1921-29. *996*

—. Unemployment. 1950-76. *2716*

—. Unemployment insurance. 1945-73. *2217*

—. Wages. 1976. *2740*

—. Wages. World War II. 1939-50. *1456*

Economic development. Agricultural Labor. Capital, fixed. Farmers. Slavery. South. ca 1840-80. *578*

—. Agricultural Labor. Wages. 1800-60. *428*

—. Brazil. Slavery. South. 19c. *581*

—. Coal Miners. Europeans. Immigrants. Kansas. 1870-1940. *307*

—. Corporations. Public Policy. South. 1979. *1513*

—. Employment. Public Works Administration. Texas. 1933-34. *1369*

—. Employment. Rural Development. Towns. 1950-70. *2802*

—. Employment. Women. 1950-67. *1580*

—. Labor Unions and Organizations. 1979. *1917*

—. Mexican Americans. Midwest. Migrant Labor. 1900-30. *993*

—. Mexican Americans. Southwest. Working class. 1603-1900. *78*

—. New York City. Unemployment. 1962-73. *1530*

Economic Growth *See also* Economic History; Economic Policy; GNP; Industrialization; Modernization.

—. AFL-CIO. Employment. Expansionism. Foreign policy. Multinational corporations. 1880's-1970's. *257*

—. Blacks. Men. Wages. Whites. 1960-77. *1815*

—. Brandywine River Valley. Delaware. Documents. DuPont, E. I. and Company. Industrialization. Pennsylvania. Standard of living. 1800-60. *408*

—. Cities. Occupational mobility. Pennsylvania. 19c. *142*

—. Counties. Employment. Urbanization. 1960's. *2775*

—. Employment. Mexican Americans. 1969-75. *2491*

—. Housework. Values. Women. 1800-1930. *27*

—. Labor force. New England. Population. 17c. *479*

—. Labor Unions and Organizations. 1918-62. *271*

—. Slavery. South. 1840-60. *577*

—. Social change. Technology. 1790's-1860's. *466*

Economic History. Archives, local. Historiography. Phillips, Ulrich Bonnell. Slave prices. Texas (Harrison County). 1849-60. *552*

—. Engerman, Stanley L. Fogel, Robert William. Slavery (review article). 1800-60. 1974. *558*

—. Sharecropping. South. 1870-1900. *726*

—. Slavery (review article). ca 1800-60. 1960's-70's. *568*

Economic history, comparative. ca 1920-75. *377*

Economic Opportunity Act (1964). Job Corps. Vocational Education. Youth, disadvantaged. 1964-75. *2292*

Economic performance. Capitalism. Industrialization. Statistics. Unemployment. 19c-1976. *379*

Economic Planning *See also* City Planning; Planning.

—. Employment, full. Labor market. 1972. *403*

—. Income distribution. Wage-price controls. 1960-74. *2773*

—. Wage-price controls. 1971-74. *2864*

Economic planning, federal. Inflation. Monopolies. Unemployment. 1971-74. *2253*

Economic Policy *See also* Budgets; Industrialization; International Trade; Modernization; Protectionism; Tariff.

—. AFL-CIO. Carter, Jimmy (administration). National Accord (document). Wages. 1979. *2225*

—. Business Cycles. Inflation. Phillips curve. Prices. Wages. 1890-1976. *402*

—. Capitalism. Federal Government. Wages. 1970's. *2737*

—. Capitalism. Kentucky. Labor policies. Politicians. 1787-1890's. *10*

—. Inflation. Public opinion. Unemployment. 1972-76. *2697*

—. Inflation. Unemployment. 1953-78. *2715*

—. Nixon administration (Pay Board). Wage controls. 1940's-73. *2388*

—. Unemployment. 1960's. *2759*

—. Unemployment. 1960-79. *2387*

Economic Reform. Congress on Labor. Illinois. Labor. World's Columbian Exposition (Chicago, 1893). 1893. *757*

Economic Regulations *See also* Federal Regulation.

—. Bakeries. New York City. Strikes. 1801-13. *469*

—. Wage-price controls. 1960-74. *2769*

Economic Report of the President. Employment. Full Employment and Balanced Growth Act (US, 1978). Presidents. Prices. 1974-81. *2201*

Economic stabilization. Nixon, Richard M. (administration). Phase III (1973). Wage-price controls. 1970-73. *2172*

Economic Stabilization Program. Manufacturing. Wage-price controls. 1969-75. *2386*

Economic Status. Blacks. Employment. 1960-77. *2563*

—. Contracts, federal. Executive orders. Minorities. Women. 1965-76. *2238*

—. Discrimination. Hispanic Americans. Men. Productivity. 1960's-70's. *2507*

—. Constitutions. Labor Unions and Organizations. Leadership. 1975. *1893*

—. Labor Unions and Organizations. 1979. *1887*

—. Labor Unions and Organizations. Leadership. Sadlowski, Ed. United Steelworkers of America. 1976-77. *1918*

—. Labor Unions and Organizations. Leadership. Sadlowski, Ed. United Steelworkers of America. 1976-77. *2096*

—. Labor Unions and Organizations. Membership. 1972-79. *2075*

—. Labor Unions and Organizations. National Labor Relations Board. Wages. Working Conditions. 1970-75. *1628*

—. McKinley, William. Ohio. Republican Party. Working class. 1891-93. *863*

—. Morgan, Thomas John. Socialism. United Labor Party (platform). 1886-96. *861*

Elections, congressional. Democratic Party. Unemployment. 1958-74. *2285*

Elections, municipal. Blacks. City Politics. Knights of Labor. Political Reform. Virginia (Richmond). 1886-88. *869*

—. Knights of Labor. Political Parties. Reform. Virginia (Lynchburg). Working Class. 1881-90. *862*

Elections (presidential). Butler, Benjamin F. (papers). People's Party. Third Parties. 1884. *857*

—. Congress of Industrial Organizations. Labor Non-Partisan League. Pennsylvania. Roosevelt, Franklin D. 1936. *1362*

—. Domestic Policy. Foreign policy. Lewis, John L. Roosevelt, Franklin D. 1936-40. *1355*

Elections (senatorial). Labor Unions and Organizations. State Politics. Wisconsin. 1952. *2334*

Electric power. Natural gas. Occupations. Technology. 1960-77. *1610*

Electrical equipment industry. Coalition bargaining. General Electric Company. Strikes. Westinghouse Electric Corporation. 1950-74. *2108*

Electrical industry. Banking. Labor Unions and Organizations. Public Employees. White collar workers. 1940's. *1090*

Electrical Workers, International Brotherhood of. Industry. Labor Unions and Organizations. New York City. Personal Narratives. Pessen, Edward. World War II. 1940-44. *980*

Electronic equipment. Marketing. Retail Trade. Wages. Working Conditions. 1970's. *1528*

Electronics industry. California (Santa Clara County). Economic Conditions. Environment. Social problems. 1950's-70's. *1532*

—. California (Santa Clara County). Working Conditions. 1972-81. *1683*

Elementary education. Carden, Georgiana. Education, Compulsory. Mexican Americans. Migrant Labor. 1920's. *1400*

—. Children. Sex roles. Socialization. Teachers. Women. 1959-71. *1980*

Elites *See also* Decisionmaking; Social Classes; Social Status.

—. American Revolution (antecedents). Sons of Liberty. Working Class. 1763-87. *434*

—. Farm Workers. Labor Disputes. Political Participation. 1946-72. *2091*

Ellender, Allen J. Conservatism. Hall, Covington. Louisiana. Radicals and Radicalism. 1871-1972. *751*

Elliot, Robert. California. Lawsuits. Occupational Safety and Health Administration. P & Z Company. Working conditions. 1975-77. *2348*

Ellsworth, James William. Coal Miners. Industrial Relations. Pennsylvania (Ellsworth). Strikes. 1900-06. *1174*

Emancipation *See also* Freedmen.

—. Domestic Service. Slavery. South. 1865-67. *630*

Emergency Employment Act (1971). Certification. Employment. Federal Government. Handicapped. 1971-73. *2107*

Emergency Farm Labor Supply Program. Agricultural Labor Relations Act (1975). California. Labor law. New Deal. ca 1930-79. *320*

Emerson, Arthur L. Brotherhood of Timber Workers. Industrial Workers of the World. Labor Disputes. Louisiana, western. Lumber and Lumbering. Texas, eastern. 1900-16. *1022*

Emigration *See also* Demography; Immigration; Population; Race Relations; Refugees.

—. Documents. Exports. Industry. Labor. Mexico. 1945-46. *1553*

—. Intellectuals. Jews. Labor movement. Russia. USA. 1880's. *770*

Employee Ownership. Amalgamated Meat Cutters. Iowa (Vinton). Labor Unions and Organizations. Rath Pork Packing Company. 1970-81. *2080*

—. Attitudes. Productivity. 1976-78. *1608*

—. Business. Productivity. 1970-82. *1794*

—. Business. South. 1979-82. *1607*

—. Corporations. Factories. Ohio (Mahoning Valley). Youngstown Sheet and Tube Company. 1977-79. *1869*

—. Decisionmaking. Job satisfaction. Pacific Northwest. Plywood manufacturing. 1977-79. *1661*

—. Industry. 1970's. *1836*

—. Industry. Public policy. 1970's. *1579*

—. Industry. Spain (Mondragon). USA. 1943-78. *1548*

—. Iowa (Waterloo). Rath Pork Packing Company. 1970-81. *1853*

—. Iowa (Waterloo). Rath Pork Packing Company. Reagan, Ronald (administration). 1970's-80's. *2137*

Employee representation. Corporations. Hoover, Herbert C. Labor Unions and Organizations. 1919-29. *1373*

Employee Retirement Income Security Act (US, 1974). Pensions. Reform. 1940's-74. *2374*

Employee turnover. Social Security Administration. Statistics. 1974-80. *2636*

Employee Turnover patterns. Civil service. Equal Opportunity. Sex. State Government. 1969-77. *2560*

Employee-community ownership. Bertie Industries. Blacks. North Carolina (Bertie County). Workers' Owned Sewing Company. 1960-80. *1735*

Employees *See also* terms beginning with Labor, Occupational, Personnel, Vocational, and Worker.

—. Alcoholism. Chicago, Burlington & Quincy Railroad. Law Enforcement. Management. Railroads. 1876-1902. *677*

—. Attitudes. Older Americans Act (US, 1965; amended 1973). Social services. 1982. *2215*

—. Attitudes. Personnel records. Privacy, right to. 1978. *1849*

—. Civil Liberties. *Civil Liberties Review.* Corporations. Freedom of Speech. National Seminar on Individual Rights in the Corporation, 1st. 1978. *1788*

—. Corporations. Freedom of Speech. 1971-74. *1625*

Employers *See also* Management.

—. Attitudes. Indochinese Americans. Refugees. 1982. *1709*

—. Coal Mines and Mining. Mitchell, John. United Mine Workers of America. 1897-1907. *807*

—. Disadvantaged. Labor market. Vocational Education. 1962-74. *1638*

—. Engineering. Great Britain. Technical education. 1890-1914. *219*

—. Fringe benefits. Life insurance. 1971-80. *1581*

Employment *See also* Occupations; Unemployment.

—. 1976-79. *1691*

—. Academic achievement. College graduates. Job performance. 1975. *1851*

—. Adolescence. Agriculture. Attitudes. 1970's. *1723*

—. Adolescence. Blacks. Recessions. Women. 1945-81. *2616*

—. Advertising. War Advertising Council. Women. World War II. 1941-45. *1401*

—. Affirmative action. Bakke, Allan. Civil rights. Discrimination. Equal opportunity. Law enforcement. *Regents of the University of California v. Allan Bakke* (US, 1978). 1978. *2328*

—. Affirmative Action. Blacks. Cities. Civil service. Political power. 1970-78. *1950*

—. Affirmative Action. Civil Rights Act (US, 1964; Titles VI, VII). *Kaiser Aluminum and Chemical Company v. Weber* (US, 1979). Race. *Regents of the University of California v. Allan Bakke* (US, 1978). Supreme Court. 1970's. *2464*

—. Affirmative action. Degrees, Academic. Discrimination. Economists. Women. 1950-78. *2766*

—. Affirmative action. Minorities. Organizational Theory. Women. 1970's. *2306*

—. Affirmative action. Minorities. Women. 1970's. *2590*

—. Affirmative action programs. Public policy. Quotas. 1975. *2241*

—. AFL-CIO. Economic growth. Expansionism. Foreign policy. Multinational corporations. 1880's-1970's. *257*

—. AFL-CIO. Imports. Protectionism. 1973. *2367*

—. Aged. 1982. *1741*

—. Aged. Comprehensive Employment and Training Act (US, 1973). 1973-76. *2178*

—. Aged. Economic Structure. Men. Pensions. Western Nations. 1950-75. *1764*

—. Aged. Industry. Management. Retirement, mandatory. Social Reform. 1850-1900. *696*

—. Aged. Men. 1967-77. *1791*

—. Aged. Men. Women. 1950-78. *2782*

—. Agricultural Labor. 1972-73. *1705*

—. Agriculture. Behavior. Woman's Land Army. Women. World War I. 1917-20. *1416*

—. Agriculture. Exports. 1963-72. *2654*

—. American Dream. Massachusetts. Radicals and Radicalism. Youth. 1977. *1620*

—. American Order of Fascisti. Blacks. Georgia. White supremacy. 1930-33. *1417*

—. Anthony, Lucy. Equal opportunity. Feminism. Shaw, Anna Howard. 1865-1919. *685*

—. Anthropologists. Bureaucracies. Research. 1974. *1944*

—. Archives. Information Storage and Retrieval Systems. Pullman Palace Car Company. 1890-1967. *398*

—. Arkansas. Attitudes. Discrimination. Equal opportunity. Public Schools. 1980. *2361*

—. Armaments Industry. Blacks. Crosswaith, Frank R. Labor Reform. Negro Labor Committee. New York City (Harlem). World War II. 1939-45. *1447*

—. Atomic energy. Federal Government. Private sector. 1963-73. *1522*

—. Attitudes. 1970-81. *1602*

—. Attitudes. Blind. Education. Pennsylvania (Pittsburgh). Workshop for the Blind. 19c-1939. *911*

—. Attitudes. College Graduates. Women. 1961-68. *1769*

—. Attitudes. Ethnic Groups. Family. Rhode Island. Women. 1968-69. *1624*

—. Attitudes. Minorities. Public Employees. 1960's-70's. *2575*

—. Attitudes. Teachers (surplus). 1950-74. *2011*

—. Automobile Industry and Trade. Housing. Recessions. Unemployment. 1980. *2839*

—. Berkeley Guidance Study. California. Depressions. Family. Women. 1930-70. *1379*

—. Bibliographies. Federal policy. 1960's-70's. *2197*

—. Biklen, Sari Knapp. Brannigan, Marilyn. Forisha, Barbara L. Goldman, Barbara. Leadership. Organizations. Women (review article). 1940-80. *1957*

—. Bilbo, Theodore G. Fair Employment Practices Commission. Filibusters. Mississippi. Racism. Senate. 1941-46. *1290*

—. Blacklisting. Bureaucracies. Chicago, Burlington & Quincy Railroad. North Central States. Railroads. 1877-92. *779*

—. Blacks. 1960-80. *2659*

—. Blacks. California (Los Angeles). Housing. Segregation. Transportation. 1941-45. *1440*

—. Blacks. Cities. Discrimination. Unemployment. Women. 1960's-70's. *2417*

—. Blacks. Civil rights. Income. Legislation. Women. 1960-70. *2742*

—. Blacks. Civil Rights Act (US, 1964; Title VIII). Discrimination. Income. Women. 1964-70's. *2252*

—. Blacks. Commuting. Illinois (Chicago). Suburbanization. 1960-70. *1622*

—. Blacks. Construction. Ickes, Harold. Public Works Adminstration. Quotas. 1933-40. *1413*

—. Blacks. Discrimination. 1959-80. *2771*

—. Blacks. Discrimination. Education. South. 1960-70. *1751*

—. Blacks. Discrimination. Ghettos. Housing. Social Policy. Suburbs. 1969-79. *1744*

—. Blacks. Discrimination. Gould, William B. Hill, Herbert. Labor Law. 19c-1977. *338*

—. Blacks. Discrimination. Labor. Women. World War II. 1941-45. *1378*

—. Blacks. Discrimination. Labor market. 1890-1970. *342*

—. Blacks. Discrimination. Recruitment. Whites. 1970's. *1748*

—. Blacks. Discrimination. Women. 1950-74. *2425*

—. Blacks. Economic Conditions. 1920-70. *2533*

—. Blacks. Economic Conditions. Equal opportunity. Law. Occupations. 1954-72. *2514*

—. Blacks. Economic Status. 1960-77. *2563*

Environmental Protection Agency. Equal Employment Opportunity Commission. Occupational Safety and Health Act (US, 1970). Women. 1970-76. *2179*

Episcopal Church, Protestant. Alabama. Child labor movement. Murphy, Edgar Gardner. 1890-1907. *679*

Equal Employment Opportunity Act (US, 1972). City government. Federal Policy. Minorities. Public Employees. Women. 1972-78. *2256*

Equal Employment Opportunity Commission. Age Discrimination in Employment Act (US, 1967). 1967-80. *1825*

—. Civil Rights Act (US, 1964; Title VII). Discrimination. Employment. Law Enforcement (proposed). Men. Whites. 1978. *2227*

—. Congress. Feminism. Sex Discrimination. 1964-74. *2350*

—. Discrimination. Employment. Labor disputes. South. 1930's-70's. *2392*

—. Discrimination. Employment. Law Enforcement. 1978. *2371*

—. Discrimination. Employment. Texas (Dallas). 1970's. *2351*

—. Environmental Protection Agency. Occupational Safety and Health Act (US, 1970). Women. 1970-76. *2179*

Equal Employment Opportunity Program. Civil Service Commission. Employment. Federal Policy. Minorities. 1970-71. *2355*

Equal Opportunity *See also* Affirmative Action.

—. Affirmative action. Bakke, Allan. Civil rights. Discrimination. Employment. Law enforcement. *Regents of the University of California* v. *Allan Bakke* (US, 1978). 1978. *2328*

—. Affirmative action. Ideology. Middle Classes. 17c-1981. *99*

—. Affirmative action. Library management. Women. 1973. *2442*

—. Alcoholism. Federal Government. Labor Unions and Organizations. Personnel policies. Public Employees. 1971-77. *2035*

—. American Psychological Association. Lancaster Press. Psychologists for Social Action. Racism, institutional. 1969-73. *2550*

—. Anthony, Lucy. Employment. Feminism. Shaw, Anna Howard. 1865-1919. *685*

—. Arkansas. Attitudes. Discrimination. Employment. Public Schools. 1980. *2361*

—. Armies. Blacks. Women. 1975. *1694*

—. Bethune, Mary McLeod. Blacks. National Youth Administration. Public Policy. Youth. 1935-44. *1441*

—. Blacks. City Government. Mexican Americans. Texas. Urbanization. 1973. *2477*

—. Blacks. Economic Conditions. Employment. Law. Occupations. 1954-72. *2514*

—. Blacks. Employment. Labor Department (Division of Negro Economics). World War I. 1917-21. *1311*

—. Carter, Jimmy. Civil Service. Labor Department. 1977-78. *2287*

—. Civil Rights Act (US, 1964). Employment. NAACP. Seniority. Supreme Court. 1964-77. *2264*

—. Civil Rights Act (US, 1964; Title VII). Courts. Discrimination. Employment. 1964-78. *2255*

—. Civil Rights Act (US, 1964; Title VII, amended 1972). Congress. Discrimination. Employment. Politics. 1942-72. *2422*

—. Civil service. Employee Turnover patterns. Sex. State Government. 1969-77. *2560*

—. Civil service. Employment. Minorities. Public policy. Quantitative Methods. 1960's-70's. *2772*

—. Consent decrees. Employment. Seniority. Steel industry. 1974-78. *2486*

—. Discrimination. Employment. Law. Public policy. 1964-72. *2369*

—. Discrimination. Employment. Legislation. Wages. Women. 1960's-70's. *2332*

—. Employment. Federal Policy. Income. Law enforcement. Legislation. Race. Sex. 1940's-76. *2421*

—. Federal government. Public Employees. Sex discrimination. Women. 1970's. *2467*

—. Mexican Americans. New Mexico. Public Employees. State government. Women. 1971-78. *2458*

Equal Opportunity and Full Employment Act of 1976 (proposed). Capitalism. Employment. Full Employment Bill of 1944. 1944-74. *2244*

Equal Rights Amendment. Employment. Sex Discrimination. Women. 1960-70. *2303*

Equality. Blacks. Employment. Marriage. Sex roles. Whites. 1976. *1572*

—. *Boston Daily Evening Voice* (newspaper). Labor Unions and Organizations. Massachusetts. Race Relations. Working Class. 1864-67. *870*

—. "Calling" (concept). Great Chain of Being (theme). Labor, dignity of. Puritans. 17c-18c. *418*

—. Catholic Worker Movement. Human Rights. Public policy. 1933-78. *288*

—. Child rearing. Employment. Sex roles. Women's liberation movement. 1970's. *2497*

ERISA. *See* Employee Retirement Income Security Act.

Esval, Orland E. (reminiscences). Farms. Montana (Peerless). Threshing crew. 1921. *943*

Ethnic Groups *See also* Minorities.

—. Age. Fertility. Income. Occupations. 1969-70. *2853*

—. Agricultural labor. Coffee. Hawaii. 1813-1978. *172*

—. Anarchism and Anarchists. Communism. Historiography. 1880's-1920's. *28*

—. Attitudes. Employment. Family. Rhode Island. Women. 1968-69. *1624*

—. Blacks. Industrial relations. Models. 1960's-70's. *1578*

—. Business. Connecticut. Greek Americans. Occupations. Pizza. 1900-75. *1719*

—. Class consciousness. Historiography. Labor movement. 1963-82. *54*

—. Coal Miners. Industrialization. Pennsylvania (Scranton). Urbanization. Working Class. 1855-85. *743*

—. Coal Mines and Mining. Economic Conditions. Pennsylvania (Daisytown). Social Mobility. 1910-40. *924*

—. Copper Miners. Discrimination. Michigan. Wages. 1860-1913. *697*

—. Cost of living. Employment. Income. Pennsylvania (Philadelphia). Poverty. 1880. *889*

—. Education. Income. Training. 1970's. *2479*

—. Employment. Immigrants. Pennsylvania (Philadelphia). 1900-35. *973*

—. Georgia (Atlanta). Labor force. Louisiana (New Orleans). Texas (San Antonio). Women. 1930-40. *926*

—. High schools. Occupations. Religion. Wisconsin. 1957-78. *2828*

—. Immigrants. Industry. Job status. Pennsylvania (Philadelphia). 1850-80. *102*

—. Immigrants. Occupations. Race. Sex. Wages. 1970. *2630*

—. Indiana (Indianapolis). Occupations. Social Mobility. 1850-60. *439*

—. New Mexico. Occupations. Population. Social Organization. 1790. *481*

—. Occupational mobility. Pennsylvania (Pittsburgh). Residential patterns. 1880-1920. *249*

—. Pennsylvania (Philadelphia). Women. Working Class. 1910-30. *1412*

—. Retail Trade. Skills. Wages. Women. 1903-15. *1445*

Ethnicity. Aurant, Harold V. Labor Unions and Organizations (review article). Roseblum, Gerald. Socialism. 1869-1920. *659*

—. Depressions. Historiography. Labor. 1930's. 1970-82. *914*

—. Education. Employment. Family. Mexican Americans. Women. 1970's. *1867*

—. Irish Americans. Land League. Radicals and Radicalism. Reform. Working class. 1880-83. *758*

—. Jewish Labor Bund. Socialism. 1897-1980. *275*

—. Missouri (St. Louis). Politics. Socialist Labor Party. Working class. 1876-81. *858*

Europe. Agriculture. Industrialization. Market economy. North America. Peasant movements (colloquium). ca 1875-1975. *12*

—. Archives of the Jewish Labor Bund. Immigration. Jews. Labor movement. New York City. 20c. *286*

—. Business Cycles. Inflation. Unemployment. Wages. 1945-70. *2683*

—. California. Short-time compensation programs. Unemployment Insurance. Work Sharing Unemployment Insurance program. 1920's-80. *2183*

—. Canada. Decentralization. Industrial relations. Labor (participation). USA. 1960's-70's. *1546*

—. Collective bargaining. Inflation. USA. 1974. *2831*

—. Employment. 1970-82. *2745*

—. Immigration history. Labor history. 1980. *1500*

—. Labor force. Sex roles. Social Organization. Women. 18c-1979. *213*

—. Migrant labor. North America. 1945-73. *1816*

—. USA. Working Conditions. 1972. *1495*

Europe, Western. Brain drain. Immigration. Labor. 1963-66. *1936*

—. Budgets. Family. Income. Life cycles. 1889-90. *890*

—. Depressions. Unemployment. USA. 1929-41. *948*

—. Immigrants. Labor. Middle East. South Africa. USA. 1942-80. *1726*

—. Immigrants. Labor. USA. 1973. *1743*

—. Japan. Public services. Trilateral Commission. Wages. 1973-79. *2377*

Europeans. Coal Miners. Economic Development. Immigrants. Kansas. 1870-1940. *307*

Evangelism. Abolition Movement. Attitudes. Competition. Economic Structure. Poverty. ca 1830-60. *579*

Evans, Herndon J. Coal Miners. Editors and Editing. Kentucky (Harlan County). Pineville *Sun* (newspaper) Strikes. 1929-32. *1264*

Everett Mill. Massachusetts (Lawrence). Polish Americans. Radicals and Radicalism. Strikes. Textile Industry. Women. 1912. *1219*

Ewen, Linda Ann. Blacks. Cities. Greer, Edward. Industrial Relations (review article). Meier, August. Rudwick, Elliott. 1900-81. *353*

Exclusion Act (US, 1882). Attitudes. Blacks. Chinese. Democracy. Discrimination. Immigration. 1850-1910. *701*

Exclusion policy. Economic conditions. Filipinos. Immigration. Split labor market theory. 1927-34. *1387*

Executive Behavior. Bethlehem Steel Corporation. Management, scientific. Pennsylvania. Taylor, Frederick W. 1898-1901. *721*

Executive Order 11246. Civil Rights Act (US, 1964; Title VII). Collective bargaining. Discrimination. Employment. 1964-74. *2368*

Executive orders. Contracts, federal. Economic status. Minorities. Women. 1965-76. *2238*

Executives. Corporations. Decisionmaking. Dissent. 1960's-77. *1626*

Exhibits and Expositions. Bread and Roses (project). Laborer (image). National Union of Hospital and Health Care Employees (District 1199). New York City. Painting. 1980. *1555*

—. Davis, Katharine Bement. Housing. Illinois. Working Class. World's Columbian Exposition (Chicago, 1893). 1893. *674*

Expansionism *See also* Imperialism.

—. AFL-CIO. Economic growth. Employment. Foreign policy. Multinational corporations. 1880's-1970's. *257*

Experimental Negotiating Agreement. Collective bargaining. Steel industry. 1946-73. *2031*

Experimental Schools. *See* Education, Experimental Methods; Free Schools.

Exploitation. Econometrics. Economic theory. Pigou, A. C. 1930-65. *395*

—. Farm workers. Marxism. Migrant Labor. 1970's. *1674*

Exports. Agriculture. Employment. 1963-72. *2654*

—. Documents. Emigration. Industry. Labor. Mexico. 1945-46. *1553*

—. Employment. Imports. Manufactures. 1964-75. *1462*

Exposes. Bibliographies. Business. Government. 1967-83. *1586*

F

Factionalism. Communism. Martin, Homer. Michigan. United Automobile Workers of America. 1937-39. *1182*

—. Communist Party. Ford Motor Company. House Committee on Un-American Activities. Reuther, Walter P. United Automobile Workers of America (Local 600). 1944-52. *2021*

—. Great Britain. Labor Unions and Organizations. Organizational Theory. USA. 20c. *139*

—. Militancy. United Automobile Workers of America. 1937-41. *1109*

Factories. Christianity. Slavery (urban). Social Organization. Tobacco. Virginia (Richmond). ca 1820-65. *615*

—. Corporations. Employee Ownership. Ohio (Mahoning Valley). Youngstown Sheet and Tube Company. 1977-79. *1869*

—. Discipline. Family. Massachusetts (Webster). Rhode Island (Slatersville). 1790-1840. *482*

—. Engerman, Stanley L. Historiography. Slavery (review article). 19c. 1974. *576*

—. Engerman, Stanley L. Quantitative methods. Slavery (review article). South. 1830-60's. 1974. *621*

—. Engerman, Stanley L. Slavery (review article). 1790-1860. *598*

—. Engerman, Stanley L. Slavery (review article). 1840-60. *619*

Folk songs. Merchant Marine. Sea shanties. 19c. *225*

Folklore *See also* Folk Songs.

—. Bibliographies. Industry. Occupations. 1888-1978. *80*

—. Blacks. Laundry. South. Women. 17c-20c. *153*

—. Joe Magarac (mythical character). Pennsylvania, western. Slavs. Steelworkers. Surnames. 19c-1970's. *308*

—. Korson, George. Miners. Pennsylvania. 1920's-60's. *76*

Foner, Eric (review article). Civil War. Ideology. Reconstruction. Social Organization. 1860-76. 1980. *14*

Foner, Philip. Cantor, Milton. Dublin, Thomas. Katzman, David. Laurie, Bruce. Tentler, Leslie Woodcock. Women (review article). Work. 17c-20c. *231*

Food Consumption. Education. Health. Working conditions. 1975-82. *1710*

Food stamps. Aid to Families with Dependent Children. Unemployment. 1975-79. *2647*

Ford Motor Company. Americanization Program. Industrial Relations. 1914-21. *972*

—. Attitudes. Labor. Wages. 1890-1915. *969*

—. Communist Party. Factionalism. House Committee on Un-American Activities. Reuther, Walter P. United Automobile Workers of America (Local 600). 1944-52. *2021*

Foreign Policy *See also* Defense Policy; Detente.

—. AFL-CIO. Economic growth. Employment. Expansionism. Multinational corporations. 1880's-1970's. *257*

—. AFL-CIO. International Labor Organization. Social Problems. 1970's. *1888*

—. AFL-CIO. Internationalism. Labor Unions and Organizations. 1886-1975. *1920*

—. American Federation of Labor. Decisionmaking. 1945-57. *1895*

—. American Federation of Labor. Labor delegation. USSR. 1926-27. *1042*

—. Domestic Policy. Elections (presidential). Lewis, John L. Roosevelt, Franklin D. 1936-40. *1355*

—. Import restrictions. International Steel Cartel. Steel Workers Organizing Committee. US Steel Corporation. 1937. *1325*

—. International Labor Organization. Isolationism. New Deal. Perkins, Frances. Roosevelt, Franklin D. 1921-34. *1346*

—. Labor Unions and Organizations. Latin America. USA. 20c. *331*

Foreign Relations *See also* Detente; Tariff.

—. American Federation of Labor. France. Nongovernmental organizations. USA. 1945-52. *1896*

—. Berry pickers. California (El Monte). Farm workers. Japan. Mexico. Strikes. 1933. *1170*

—. Mexico. Migrant labor. Texas. 1942-47. *1419*

Foreign Trade. *See* Trade.

Forest and Farm Workers Union. Hall, Covington. Labor Unions and Organizations. Louisiana. Lumber and Lumbering. Socialism. 1907-16. *1126*

Forests and Forestry *See also* Lumber and Lumbering.

—. Blacks. Florida. Labor. Reconstruction. 1860-1900. *628*

—. Florida. Labor, forced. Peonage. 1870's-1950. *229*

Forisha, Barbara L. Biklen, Sari Knapp. Brannigan, Marilyn. Employment. Goldman, Barbara. Leadership. Organizations. Women (review article). 1940-80. *1957*

Fortune. Leisure. Periodicals. 1957-79. *1716*

Foster, Frank K. Comte, Auguste. Gompers, Samuel. Ideology. Labor Unions and Organizations. McGregor, Hugh. Spencer, Herbert. 1876-1900. *755*

Fowler-Gallagher, Susan. Domestic service (review article). Hamburger, Robert. Katzman, David. Middle Classes. Women. 1870-1920. 1978. *57*

France. Acocella, Giuseppe (review article). Germany. Labor Unions and Organizations. Political Participation. 1920-78. *260*

—. American Federation of Labor. Foreign Relations. Nongovernmental organizations. USA. 1945-52. *1896*

—. Centennial Exposition of 1876. Labor delegation. Pennsylvania (Philadelphia). 1876. *688*

—. Collective Bargaining. Great Britain. USA. 18c-20c. *287*

—. Economic theory (dualism). Italy. Labor market. 1960-79. *2760*

—. Farmers. Germany. Politics. Social History (review article). White Collar Workers. 1890-20c. *89*

—. Households. Income. Wealth. 1948-80. *2601*

—. Income. 1962-70. *2814*

—. Industrial Relations. Italy. Strikes. USA. 1876-1970. *311*

Franklin, Benjamin. International Typographical Union. Pennsylvania (Philadelphia). Printing. Strikes. Wages. 1754-1852. *531*

Fraser, Douglas. Business. Industrial Relations. Labor-Management Group. Letters. United Automobile Workers of America. 1978. *1890*

—. Labor Unions and Organizations. Liberalism. 1978. *1926*

Frazier, E. Franklin (*Black Bourgeoisie*). Blacks. Employment. Middle Classes. 1957-82. *2494*

Free enterprise. Blacks. Florida. Labor, forced. 1940-50. *361*

Free love. Feminism. Speeches. Stanton, Elizabeth Cady. 1868-70. *647*

Freedmen. Abolition. Labor market, split. Race relations. Slavery, extension of. 1830-63. *547*

—. Agricultural Labor. Economic Structure. Racism. Reconstruction. Texas. 1865-74. *737*

—. Alabama. Bureau of Refugees, Freedmen, and Abandoned Lands. Reconstruction. 1865-67. *612*

—. Alabama. Plantations. Sharecropping (origins). 1865-67. *596*

—. Authority. South. Teachers. Women. 1865-70. *703*

—. Convict lease system. Dale Coal Company. Georgia. LeConte, Lancaster. Letters. 1887-89. *739*

—. Discrimination. Economic Conditions. Property. ca 1880-1920. *682*

—. Labor. Motte, J. Rhett. Plantations. Reconstruction. Share wages. South Carolina (St. John's Parish). 1867. *882*

Freedmen's Bureau. Armies. Blacks. Mississippi (Natchez district). Sharecropping. 1860's. *681*

—. Blacks. Children. Indentured servants. Law. North Carolina. 1865-68. *731*

—. Blacks. Mississippi. 1865-67. *702*

—. Contracts. Planters. Sharecropping. South. 1865-68. *732*

Freedom Colony. DeBernardi, Giovanni Battista. Depressions. Kansas. Labor Exchange. Utopias. 1894-1905. *654*

Freedom of Assembly *See also* Freedom of Speech; Riots.

—. American Civil Liberties Union. Associated Silk Workers Union. Freedom of Speech. New Jersey (Paterson). Strikes. 1924. *1159*

Freedom of Speech. American Civil Liberties Union. Associated Silk Workers Union. Freedom of Assembly. New Jersey (Paterson). Strikes. 1924. *1159*

—. California (Fresno). Clyde, Edward M. Industrial Workers of the World. 1911. *1045*

—. California (Fresno). Industrial Workers of the World. 1910-11. *1026*

—. California (San Diego). Industrial Workers of the World. Mexico (Tijuana). 1911-12. *1069*

—. Civil Liberties. *Civil Liberties Review.* Corporations. Employees. National Seminar on Individual Rights in the Corporation, 1st. 1978. *1788*

—. Corporations. Employees. 1971-74. *1625*

—. Fiske, Harold B. Industrial Workers of the World. Kansas. Labor Unions and Organizations. Trials. 1923-27. *1014*

—. Industrial Workers of the World. Political Protest. Pratt, N. S. Washington (Spokane). 1909-10. *1113*

—. Oklahoma. Political Repression. Vigilantes. World War I. 1914-17. *1303*

—. Private Sector. Supreme Courts, State. Working Conditions. 1968-80. *1805*

Freeway blockages. Civil Disturbances. Ohio. Pennsylvania. Truck driver culture. 1973. *2036*

French Canadian Americans. Belgian Americans. Independent Textile Workers. Rhode Island (Woonsocket). Working Class. 1931-50's. *1157*

French Canadians. Child labor. Family. Massachusetts (Lowell). Migration. Standard of living. 1870's. *649*

—. Farmers. Kansas. Mennonites. Swedish Americans. 1875-1925. *110*

—. Massachusetts (Lowell). Occupational mobility. Quebec. Working Class. 1870-80. *683*

Friedlander, Peter (review article). Michigan (Detroit). United Automobile Workers of America. Working Class. 1936-39. 1975. *1112*

Friendship. Cities. Employment. Skid rows. 1970's. *1792*

Fringe benefits. Employers. Life insurance. 1971-80. *1581*

—. Fire fighters. International Association of Fire Fighters. Labor Unions and Organizations. Wages. 1966-76. *2089*

—. Hospitals. Labor Unions and Organizations. Occupations. Wages. 1977. *2063*

—. Income. Social Security. 1950-81. *1470*

Frontier and Pioneer Life *See also* Cowboys.

—. Census. Employment. Iowa. Women. 1833-70. *467*

—. Census. Illinois (Pike County). Occupations. Towns. 1820-60. *489*

—. Colorado (Denver). Saloons. Social mobility. 1858-85. *722*

—. Construction. Oklahoma (Muskogee, Tahlequah). Personal narratives. Vogel, Henry. 1887-1900. *671*

—. Men. Overland Journeys to the Pacific. Wagon trains. Women. 1840's-50's. *433*

—. Teachers. Western States. Women. 1848-54. *448*

Full Employment and Balanced Growth Act (US, 1978). *Economic Report of the President.* Employment. Presidents. Prices. 1974-81. *2201*

Full Employment Bill of 1944. Capitalism. Employment. Equal Opportunity and Full Employment Act of 1976 (proposed). 1944-74. *2244*

Fuller, Amy. Massachusetts (Berkshire County; Dalton). Occupational choice. Paper Industry. Women. ca 1840-90. *453*

Fullerton, Samuel Holmes. Gulf Lumber Company. Louisiana. Lumber and Lumbering. 1906-27. *933*

Fulmer, William E. Blacks. Discrimination. Employment (review article). Rubin, Lester. Wrong, Elaine Gale. 1865-1973. *357*

Furniture. Bentley, William. Cabinetmaking. Diaries. Massachusetts (Salem). 1784-1819. *503*

G

Galenson, David. Economics. Immigration. Indentured Servants (review article). Maryland. Virginia. West Indies. 1654-1776. *533*

García, Juan Ramon. Lewis, Sasha G. Mexicans. Undocumented Workers (review article). Working Conditions. 1954-80. *2196*

Garden Homes. Cooperatives. Public housing. Wisconsin (Milwaukee). 1918-25. *1288*

Gardner, Vernon O. Banking. Brotherhood of Railway Telegraphers. Manion, Edward J. Missouri (St. Louis). Telegraphers National Bank. 1922-42. *1171*

Garment Industry. *See* Clothing Industry.

Garraty, John A. (review article). Economic Theory. Intellectuals. Poverty. Public Policy. Unemployment. 17c-1978. *107*

Gaventa, John. Macintyre, Stuart. Politics. Radicals and Radicalism (review article). Working Class. ca 1880-1940. *93*

Gellert, Dan. Aeronautics. Eastern Airlines. L-1011 (aircraft). Occupational Safety. Working Conditions. 1972-78. *1647*

General Electric Company. Coalition bargaining. Electrical equipment industry. Strikes. Westinghouse Electric Corporation. 1950-74. *2108*

—. Labor Unions and Organizations. Leadership. Massachusetts. New York. Pennsylvania. Westinghouse Electric Corporation. 1933-37. *1249*

—. Labor Unions and Organizations. New York (Fort Edward, Hudson Falls). Occupational Hazards. Pollution. Polychlorinated biphenyl. United Electrical, Radio, and Machine Workers of America. 1975. *2037*

General Electric Company (River Works Plant). Industrial safety. Kashner, Frank (account). Labor Unions and Organizations. Massachusetts (Lynn). Radicals and Radicalism. Strikes, wildcat. 1960's-77. *2092*

—. International Federation of Professional and Technical Engineers. Massachusetts (Everett, Lynn). Occupations. Technology. 1970-78. *2157*

General Motors Corporation. Anti-Communist Movements. Michigan, University of. Workers' Education Service. 1943-49. *2385*

—. Attitudes. Auto Workers. Chrysler Corporation. Michigan (Detroit, Hamtramck). Race Relations. 1972. *2495*

—. Contracts. Cost of Living. United Automobile Workers of America. Wages. 1919-74. *392*

—. Films. Strikes. *United Action Means Victory* (film). United Automobile Workers of America. 1938-40. *1244*

—. Georgia (Atlanta). Strikes. United Automobile Workers of America. 1936. *1167*

—. *Great Sitdown* (film). Historiography. Strikes. United Automobile Workers of America. *With Babies and Banners* (film). 1937. 1976-79. *1188*

—. Lewis, John L. Strikes, sit-down. 1936-37. *1148*

—. Michigan (Flint). Strikes (sit-down). United Automobile Workers of America. 1936-37. *1251*

—. Michigan (Pontiac). Occupational Safety and Health Administration. United Automobile Workers of America. Working conditions. 1971-78. *2143*

General strikes. American Distillery Company. American Federation of Labor. Illinois (Pekin). 1934-36. *1114*

—. California (Oakland). Social change. 1946-47. *2155*

—. California (San Francisco). National Guard. Ports. 1934. *1172*

—. California (San Francisco). Personal narratives. Photographs. 1934. *1122*

—. Cigar industry. Florida (Tampa). 1901-11. *1232*

—. Communist Party. Washington (Seattle). 1919. *1085*

Generations. Employment. Immigrants. Income. 1970. *2631*

—. Occupational Mobility. Women. 1960-79. *1820*

—. Occupations. 1966-76. *1742*

Genovese, Eugene D. Capitalism. Economy. Engerman, Stanley L. Fogel, Robert William. Slavery (review article). 1831-61. 1974. *635*

—. David, Paul A. Engerman, Stanley L. Fogel, Robert William. Gutman, Herbert G. Slavery (review article). 19c. *569*

—. Economic Theory. Engerman, Stanley L. Fogel, Robert William. Slavery (review article). 1831-61. 1974. *639*

Genovese, Eugene D. (review article). Slavery. South. 19c. 1974. *607*

Geographic distribution. Comprehensive Employment and Training Act (US, 1973). Federal funds. Medicare. Wage indexing. 1978-80. *2242*

Geographic Mobility *See also* Migration, Internal.

—. Blacks. Education. Income. 1965-70. *2833*

—. Colorado (Denver). Employment. Social Mobility. 1870-92. *740*

—. Family. Labor force. Women. 1970's. *1718*

—. Lawyers. Licenses. State Government. 1950's-70's. *1995*

Geographic proximity. Employment. Sex roles. Women. 1976. *2510*

Geographic space. Cities. Employment. Family. Federal Policy. Households. Women. 1977-80. *2513*

Geology. Coal mines and mining. Federal regulation. 1969-77. *1539*

George, Henry *(Progress and Poverty)*. Land. Monopolies. Political economy. Taxation. Working class. 1858-94. *664*

"George" stereotype. American Federation of Labor. Blacks. Brotherhood of Sleeping Car Porters. Randolph, A. Philip. 1867-1935. *1421*

George's Creek Coal and Iron Company. Chesapeake and Ohio Canal. Iron Mining. Maryland (Lonaconing area). 1837-40. *440*

Georgia. American Order of Fascisti. Blacks. Employment. White supremacy. 1930-33. *1417*

—. Blacks. Cooperative Workers of America. Hoover, Hiram F. Secret Societies. South Carolina. 1886-87. *873*

—. Convict lease system. Dale Coal Company. Freedmen. LeConte, Lancaster. Letters. 1887-89. *739*

—. Indentured servants. Military Strategy. Slavery. 1732-73. *512*

—. National Recovery Administration. State Government. Strikes. Talmadge, Eugene. Textile industry. 1934. *1095*

—. Plantations. Rice. Slaves. 1820-80. *543*

Georgia (Atlanta). Blacks. Family. Social Mobility. 1870-80. *699*

—. Coffin, Tom. Construction. International Union of Operating Engineers, Local 926. Labor Unions and Organizations. Law Engineering Testing Company. National Labor Relations Board. 1973-78. *2050*

—. Educational reform. Illinois (Chicago). New York City. Progressivism. Teachers. 1890-1920. *243*

—. Employment. Job inquiries. Men. Recruitment. Sex discrimination. 1975. *2500*

—. Ethnic Groups. Labor force. Louisiana (New Orleans). Texas (San Antonio). Women. 1930-40. *926*

—. General Motors Corporation. Strikes. United Automobile Workers of America. 1936. *1167*

Georgia (Augusta). Acculturation. Chinese Americans. Discrimination. 1865-1980. *339*

—. Strikes. Textile mills. Working conditions. 1886. *830*

Georgia, central. Blacks. Economic Conditions. Labor agents. Migration, Internal. 1899-1900. *657*

Georgia (Dalton). Attitudes. Labor Unions and Organizations. Textile industry. 1920-81. *2107*

Georgia (Glynn County). Agricultural labor. Occupations. Slavery. 1790-1860. *616*

Georgia Power Company. Atlanta Transit Company. Street, Electric Railway and Motor Coach Employees of America. Strikes. 1946-50. *2105*

Georgia Railroad. Arbitration, Industrial. Fire fighters. Race Relations. Smith, Hoke. Strikes. 1909. *1418*

—. Blacks. Discrimination. Railroads. Strikes. 1909. *1397*

Georgia State University (Southern Labor Archives). Archival Catalogs and Inventories. Labor Unions and Organizations. South. 1966-82. *52*

German Americans. Bakeries. Illinois (Chicago). Labor Unions and Organizations. 1880-1910. *814*

—. Census. Illinois (Chicago). Immigrants. Newspapers. Working Class. 1850-1910. *706*

—. Education. Family. Income. Occupations. 1969-70. *2852*

Germany. Acocella, Giuseppe (review article). France. Labor Unions and Organizations. Political Participation. 1920-78. *260*

—. Farmers. France. Politics. Social History (review article). White Collar Workers. 1890-20c. *89*

—. Labor force. Propaganda. Public opinion. Sex roles. USA. Women. World War II. 1939-45. *1437*

Germer, Adolph. Coal miners. Illinois (Virden). Socialism. Strikes. United Mine Workers of America. 1893-1900. *785*

Ghettos. Blacks. Businesses, white-owned. Employment opportunities. 1970's. *2396*

—. Blacks. Discrimination. Employment. Housing. Social Policy. Suburbs. 1969-79. *1744*

Gilbert, James B. Industrialization. Intellectuals. Labor (review article). Rodgers, Daniel T. Values. 1850-1920. 1974-77. *55*

Gilman, Daniel Spencer. Labor Unions and Organizations. Letters. Massachusetts (Lowell). Working Conditions. 1844-46. *505*

Girls. Domestic service. Female Charitable Society. Industrialization. Massachusetts (Salem). 1800-40. *451*

—. High schools. Labor market. 1890-1928. *158*

Glaberman, Martin. Blacks. Communist Party. Keeran, Roger R. Labor Unions and Organizations. Meier, August. Rudwick, Elliott. United Automobile Workers of America (review article). 1930's-40's. *1191*

Glacier National Park. Civilian Conservation Corps. Montana. 1933-42. *1343*

Glasscock, William E. Coal Miners. Martial law. National Guard. United Mine Workers of America. Violence. West Virginia (Cabin Creek, Paint Creek). 1912-13. *1101*

GNP. Economic trends. Labor Department (Bureau of Labor Statistics; projections). Work hours. 1973. 1985. *2596*

—. Employment opportunities. Local government. State government. 1959-71. *2226*

Gold Miners. British Americans. California (Grass Valley). Coad, John. Letters. 1858-60. *430*

—. Crime and Criminals. Labor Unions and Organizations. Nevada (Goldfield). 1904-08. *1125*

Golden Hill (battle). Nassau Street Riots. New York City. Riots. 1770. *413*

Goldin, Claudia Dale (review article). Cities. Slavery. South. 1820-60. 1976. *548*

Goldman, Barbara. Biklen, Sari Knapp. Brannigan, Marilyn. Employment. Forisha, Barbara L. Leadership. Organizations. Women (review article). 1940-80. *1957*

Gompers, Samuel. American Federation of Labor. Brotherhood of Painters and Decorators. Rank-and-file movements. Voluntarism. 1894-1900. *759*

—. American Federation of Labor. Canada. Labor. USA. 1881. *766*

—. American Federation of Labor. Carranza, Venustiano. Mexico (Carrizal). Prisoners. USA. 1916. *1079*

—. American Federation of Labor. Dick, William M. Labor Unions and Organizations. Socialism. 1880-1910. *772*

—. American Federation of Labor. Fascism. Immigration. Jingoism. Racism. 1850-1924. *1425*

—. American Federation of Labor. Iglesias Pantin, Santiago. Labor Unions and Organizations. Puerto Rico. 1897-1920's. *903*

—. American Federation of Labor. Labor party (concept). Socialism. 1893-95. *848*

—. American Federation of Labor. Labor Unions and Organizations. Military preparedness policies. Rank-and-file movements. Wilson, Woodrow. 1914-17. *1041*

—. Brandeis, Louis D. Judaism. Kogan, Michael S. Labor Unions and Organizations. 1880's-1975. *292*

—. Cannon, Joseph Gurney. House of Representatives. Illinois (Danville). Labor Unions and Organizations. Voting and Voting Behavior. 1906-08. *1063*

—. Communism. Pan American Federation of Labor. Political Attitudes. 1920's. *1075*

—. Comte, Auguste. Foster, Frank K. Ideology. Labor Unions and Organizations. McGregor, Hugh. Spencer, Herbert. 1876-1900. *755*

—. Dick, William M. Labor Unions and Organizations (review article). Laslett, John. Socialism. 1881-1924. *765*

—. Intervention. Labor Unions and Organizations. Latin America. Pan American Federation of Labor. Revolution. World War I. 1918-27. *1074*

—. Lenin, V. I. Socialists. USA. 1912-18. *1036*

Gompers, Samuel (papers). History. Literature. 1860's-20c. *767*

Goodyear Tire and Rubber Company. Alabama (Gadsden). House, John D. Rubber. United Rubber Workers. 1941. *1210*

Gordon, Jean. Child Labor Law (Louisiana, 1908). Louisiana (New Orleans). New York. Theatrical Syndicate. 1908-12. *1315*

Gordon, Max (account). Communist Party. Labor Party. Politics. Popular Front. ca 1930-39. *1376*

Gould, Jay. Knights of Labor. Missouri (Sedalia). Modernization. Railroads. Strikes. 1885-86. *754*

Gould, William B. Affirmative action. Blacks. Discrimination (review article). Hill, Herbert. Labor Unions and Organizations. Seniority. Supreme Court. 1970's. *2537*

—. Blacks. Discrimination. Employment. Hill, Herbert. Labor Law. 19c-1977. *338*

Government *See also* City Government; Civil Service; Constitutions; County Government; Federal Government; Legislative Bodies; Local Government; Military Government; Political Science; Politics; Provincial Government; Public Administration; Public Employees; State Government.

—. Attitudes. Unemployment. 18c-1978. *74*

—. Bibliographies. Business. Exposes. 1967-83. *1586*

—. Bibliographies. Industrial relations. 19c-20c. 1981. *103*

—. Capitalism. Collective bargaining. Ideology. Intervention. 1978. *2734*

—. Collective Bargaining. Public Opinion. 1970's. *2207*

—. Comprehensive Employment and Training Act (US, 1973). Employment. Job Training Partnership Act (US, 1983). 1982. *2247*

—. Discrimination. Employment. LaGuardia, Fiorello. New York City. Private sector. World War II. 1941-43. *1296*

—. Economic Theory. Labor market, operation of. Training programs. Vocational Education. 1974. *2246*

—. Labor Unions and Organizations. Public employees. 1961-74. *1916*

—. Railroads. Strikes. 1877. *797*

Government Employees. *See* Civil Service; Public Employees.

Government expenditures. Labor force. Taxation. Women. 1970's. *2191*

Government Pay Acts (1962, 1970). Comparability, concept of. Wages. 1962-76. *2373*

Government regulation. Illinois. Kelley, Florence. Working Conditions. 1892-93. *843*

—. Legislation. Occupational Safety. Workers' Compensation. 19c-20c. *1291*

Governors. Hoadly, George. National guard. Ohio (Hocking Valley). Strikes. 1884-85. *778*

Graduate Programs. Cartter, Allen M. (review article). Colleges and Universities. Employment. Scholars. ca 1950-75. *1940*

Grady, John. Defections. Haywood, William Dudley. Industrial Workers of the World. Letters. Schuyler, Mont. USA. USSR. 1921-22. *1062*

Graham, Barney. Coal miners. Davidson-Wilder Strike of 1932. Strikes. Tennessee, eastern. United Mine Workers of America. 1932-33. *1096*

Granite industry. Bodwell Granite Company. Maine (Vinalhaven). 1851-1919. *655*

Granite workers. Cerasoli, Mose (memoir). Labor Disputes. Vermont. 1913-38. *987*

Grape industry. California. Farm Workers. Labor Unions and Organizations. Strikes. United Farm Workers Union. 1966-70. *2088*

—. California (Delano). Chavez, Cesar. Strikes. 1967-70. *2110*

Great Britain. Allen, V. L. Industrial Relations. 1935-54. *258*

—. Arbitration, Industrial. Industrial Disputes Act (Great Britain). Labor Disputes. USA. 1973. *295*

—. Attitudes. Depressions. Law. Poor. USA. Vagrancy. 14c-1939. *939*

—. British North America. Immigration. Indenture, length of. 1718-59. *509*

—. Capitalism. Dublin, Thomas. Family. Levine, David. Massachusetts (Lowell). Population. Working Class (review article). 1550-1869. *444*

—. Class consciousness. Feminism. Labor Unions and Organizations. USA. Women's Trade Union League. 1890-1925. *1404*

—. Coal Miners. Immigration. 1860-70. *694*

—. Coal Mines and Mining. Illinois. Labor Unions and Organizations. Legislation. Lobbying. 1861-72. *850*

—. Collective Bargaining. France. USA. 18c-20c. *287*

—. Cotton. Plantations. Slavery. South. 17c-19c. *593*

—. Developing nations. Japan. Manufacturing. Subcontracting. Unemployment. USA. 1966-76. *1535*

—. Economic Theory. Labor Unions and Organizations. Wages. 1920-79. *394*

—. Employers. Engineering. Technical education. 1890-1914. *219*

—. Employment. Japan. Wages. ca 1873-1981. *382*

—. Factionalism. Labor Unions and Organizations. Organizational Theory. USA. 20c. *139*

—. Historiography. Ideology. Labor history. USA. ca 1940's-74. *90*

—. Labor Unions and Organizations. Political Change. Socialism. USA. World War I. 1914-25. *1070*

—. Labor Unions and Organizations. Steel industry. USA. 1888-1912. *270*

—. Labor Unions and Organizations (review article). Women. 18c-1980. *230*

—. Leisure. Sports. Work. 1830-60. *493*

—. Novels (Victorian). Sex Discrimination. Wages. Women (image). 19c-20c. *366*

Great Britain (Bristol). Immigration. Indentured servants. North America. West Indies. Working Class. 17c. *535*

Great Britain (London). British North America. Indentured servitude. 1718-59. *508*

Great Chain of Being (theme). "Calling" (concept). Equality. Labor, dignity of. Puritans. 17c-18c. *418*

Great Northern Railway Company. Contract labor. Immigration. Japan. Northern Pacific Railroad. 1898-1907. *957*

—. Minnesota (St. Paul). Northern Pacific Railroad. Working Conditions. 1915-21. *1000*

Great Plains. Agricultural Commodities. Family. Marxism. Wages. 1920. *381*

—. Agriculture. Family. Sweden. Women. 18c-19c. *5*

—. Agriculture. Labor casualization. Mechanization. Wheat. 1865-1902. *643*

—. Indians. Sex roles. Social organization. Women. 19c. *181*

Great Sitdown (film). General Motors Corporation. Historiography. Strikes. United Automobile Workers of America. *With Babies and Banners* (film). 1937. 1976-79. *1188*

Greek Americans. Business. Connecticut. Ethnic groups. Occupations. Pizza. 1900-75. *1719*

—. Labor Unions and Organizations. Western States. Working class. 1897-1924. *977*

—. Western States. Working Class. ca 1900-30. *978*

Green Corn Rebellion, 1917. Oklahoma. Radicals and Radicalism. Working Class Union. 1914-17. *1269*

Green, James. Brody, David. Working Class (review article). 20c. *45*

Greenback Labor Party. Monetary Systems. Pennsylvania (Pittsburgh). Political Protest. Railroads. Strikes. 1877. *849*

Greenback Party. Labor Reform Party. New Hampshire. 1870-78. *860*

Greenwald, Maurine Weiner. Dye, Nancy Schrom. Labor Unions and Organizations. New York. Women (review article). World War I. 1870-1920. *371*

Greer, Edward. Blacks. Cities. Ewen, Linda Ann. Industrial Relations (review article). Meier, August. Rudwick, Elliott. 1900-81. *353*

Grenell, Judson. Knights of Labor. Labadie, Joseph. Michigan (Detroit). Socialist Labor Party. 1877-86. *771*

Griggs vs. Duke Power Company (1971). Arbitration, Industrial. Discrimination. *Rios vs. Reynolds Metals Company (1972).* 1964-73. *2413*

Gross, Edward. Occupational differentiation. Sex Discrimination. Women. 1975. *370*

Gross National Product. *See* GNP.

Growth of American Families Study. Employment. Wives. Women. 1940-60. *1842*

Gulf Coast. Army Corps of Engineers. Florida (Pensacola). Navy Yard. Slavery. 1826-62. *563*

Gulf Lumber Company. Fullerton, Samuel Holmes. Louisiana. Lumber and Lumbering. 1906-27. *933*

Gutman, Herbert G. David, Paul A. Engerman, Stanley L. Fogel, Robert William. Genovese, Eugene D. Slavery (review article). 19c. *569*

—. Engerman, Stanley L. Fogel, Robert William. Quantitative Methods. Slavery (review article). 1840-60. 1974-75. *641*

—. Labor history. Working Class. 1970-79. *22*

Gutman, Herbert G. (review article). Industrialization. 18c-1976. *58*

H

Habakkuk, H. J. Carriage and wagon industry. Labor supply hypothesis. Manufactures. Ohio (Cincinnati). 1850-1900. *648*

Haber, William. Michigan. National Youth Administration. Public Welfare. Works Progress Administration. 1930's. *1336*

Hall, Covington. Conservatism. Ellender, Allen J. Louisiana. Radicals and Radicalism. 1871-1972. *751*

—. Forest and Farm Workers Union. Labor Unions and Organizations. Louisiana. Lumber and Lumbering. Socialism. 1907-16. *1126*

Hamburger, Robert. Domestic service (review article). Fowler-Gallagher, Susan. Katzman, David. Middle Classes. Women. 1870-1920. *57*

Hamilton Manufacturing Company. Cotton. Labor Disputes. Massachusetts (Lowell). Social mobility. Textile Industry. Women. 1836-60. *425*

Handicapped *See also* Blind; Mental Illness.

—. Certification. Emergency Employment Act (1971). Employment. Federal Government. 1971-73. *2184*

—. Discrimination. Public policy. Rehabilitation Act (US, 1973). 1973-82. *2490*

—. Employment. Vocational rehabilitation. 1965-75. *1714*

Handicrafts. *See* Arts and Crafts.

Hanraty, Pete. Coal Miners. Oklahoma. Strikes. United Mine Workers of America. 1899-1903. *1102*

Hard, Herbert. Amlie, Thomas. Farmer-Labor Party. New Deal. Ohio Farmer-Labor Progressive Federation. Third Parties. 1930-40. *1333*

Harlan County, U.S.A. (film). Coal Mines and Mining. Kentucky. Kopple, Barbara. Strikes. United Mine Workers of America. 1973-74. *2161*

—. Coal Mines and Mining. Kentucky. Kopple, Barbara (interview). Strikes. United Mine Workers of America. 1973-76. *2119*

Harman International Industries. Labor Reform. Tennessee (Bolivar). Worker self-management. 1974-75. *1724*

Harper, Larry. Coal Miners. Labor Unions and Organizations. Promotions. Suicide. West Virginia (Stony Creek). 1940's-54. *2102*

Harris, Howell John. Industrial Relations (review article). 1940's. *131*

Harris, William H. Blacks. Racism (review article). 1865-1982. *369*

Harvard University, Graduate School of Business. Environment. Western Electric Company. Working Conditions. 1924-33. *1002*

Harvey, Oliver. Civil rights. Duke University Medical Center. Labor Unions and Organizations. North Carolina (Durham). 1930's-70's. *2106*

Hat industry. Employment. Iowa. Milliners. Social Customs. Women. 1870-80. *680*

—. Industrial Relations. Milliners. Pennsylvania (Philadelphia). Stetson Company. 1870-1929. *44*

Hawaii *See also* Far Western States.

—. Agricultural labor. Coffee. Ethnic groups. 1813-1978. *172*

—. Agricultural Labor. Russians. 1900-10. *931*

—. California (Stockton). Discrimination. International Longshoremen's and Warehousemen's Union. Japanese Americans. 1945. *2554*

—. China (Fukien; Amoy). Contract labor. 1852. *502*

—. China (Fukien; Amoy). Contract labor. 1852. *511*

—. Contract labor. Poles. Working Conditions. 1896-99. *689*

—. Public Employees. Strikes. 1979. *2142*

—. Unemployment. 1930's. *1457*

Hawaii Public Employment Relations Act. Public Employees. Strikes. 1960's-72. . *2363*

Hawthorne experiments. Human Relations. Illinois (Chicago). Western Electric Company. 1924-33. 1977. *945*

Hawthorne relay experiment. Productivity. 1927-39. 1978. 1978. *1870*

Hayden, Delores. Andre, Rae. Domesticity. Wives (review article). Wright, Gwendolyn. 20c. *66*

Haywood, William Dudley. Defections. Grady, John. Industrial Workers of the World. Letters. Schuyler, Mont. USA. USSR. 1921-22. *1062*

—. Labor Unions and Organizations. Socialism. 1890-1928. *199*

Heads of Households. *See* Household Heads.

Health. Attitudes. Coal Miners. Occupational Safety. 19c. *41*

—. Children. Women. Working hours. 1972. *2792*

—. Education. Food Consumption. Working conditions. 1975-82. *1710*

—. Employment. Men. Social Security. 1977. *1767*

Health care industry. Comprehensive Employment and Training Act (US, 1973). Employment. Preventive care. 1970's. *2354*

Health hazards. Women. Working Conditions. 1869-1979. *187*

Health Services *See also* Medical Care.

—. Income. White Collar Workers. 1970-79. *2004*

Heartsill, Willie Blount Wright. Arkansas (Greenwood). Knights of Labor (Local 239). Labor disputes. Mining. 1892-96. *750*

Hellier, Thomas. Confessions. Documents. Domestic Servants. Murder. Virginia (Charles City County). Williams, Paul. Williamson, Cuthbert (family). 1650-70. *500*

Hentoff, Nat (account). Labor Unions and Organizations. New York City. *Village Voice* (newspaper). 1958-77. *2084*

Heterosexuals. Attitudes. Lesbians. Sexual harassment. Women. Working Conditions. 1972-82. *2552*

Hevener, John W. Coal Miners. Depressions. Kentucky (Harlan County). Labor Unions and Organizations. 1930's. *1162*

High School of Fashion Industry. Minorities. New York City. Sex Discrimination. Vocational Education. Women. 1975. *2402*

High Schools. Blacks. Midwest. Occupational Goals. Whites. Women. 1971. *1682*

—. Blacks. Occupational goals. South. Whites. 1970's. *2530*

—. Boys. Occupational knowledge. Washington. 1958-72. *1617*

—. Child labor. Curricula. Labor reform. Photographs. ca 1908. *920*

—. Curricula. Labor education. Teaching. 1972-82. *36*

—. Ethnic Groups. Occupations. Religion. Wisconsin. 1957-78. *2828*

—. Federal Policy. Smith-Hughes Act (US, 1917). Vocational education. 1917-80's. *2176*

—. Finnish Americans. Labor College Movement. Minnesota (Duluth, Minneapolis). Radicals and Radicalism. Work People's College. 1903-37. *921*

—. Girls. Labor market. 1890-1928. *158*

—. Occupations. Teaching. 1950-81. *1933*

Higher Education *See also* Colleges and Universities; Junior Colleges; Technical Education.

—. Blacks. Educational administrators. Women. 1975. *2524*

—. Carnegie, Andrew. Pensions. Retirement. 1901-18. *1087*

—. Carnegie Commission on Higher Education. Student unrest. Wage labor system. 1967-73. *2618*

—. Collective bargaining. College Teachers. Wages. 1970's. *1984*

—. Collective bargaining. Educators. 1960-78. *1958*

—. College Graduates. Employment. Wages. 1950-75. *1968*

—. College Teachers. Labor. University and College Labor Education Association. 1976. *1989*

—. Discrimination. Employment. Wives. Women. 1970's. *2557*

—. Economic Conditions. Employment. 1970-82. *1861*

—. Economists. Employment. 1960-76. *2003*

—. Occupations (expectations). Race. Sex. Students. 1970. *2410*

Highways. Construction. Costs. Federal Government. 1958-76. *2764*

—. Construction projects. Employment. Federal government. 1958-70. *2174*

Hill, Herbert. Affirmative action. Blacks. Discrimination (review article). Gould, William B. Labor Unions and Organizations. Seniority. Supreme Court. 1970's. *2537*

—. Blacks. Discrimination. Employment. Gould, William B. Labor Law. 19c-1977. *338*

Hiring Practices *See also* Job Placements; Recruitment.

—. Affirmative Action. Minorities. Women. 1970's. *2404*

—. Blacks. Wages. 1945-73. *354*

Hiring system. Slavery. Virginia (Elizabeth City County). 1782-1810. *588*

Hirsch, Susan E. New Jersey (Newark). New York (Cohoes, Troy). Walkowitz, Daniel J. Working Class (review article). 1800-84. 1978. *32*

Hispanic Americans *See also* Cuban Americans; Mexican Americans; Puerto Rican Americans, etc.

—. Blacks. Cities. Public Employees. Women. 1977. *2444*

—. Blacks. Competition. Labor. Whites. 1976. *2414*

—. Cities. Immigrants. Labor. Northeastern or North Atlantic States. 1970. *1531*

—. Discrimination. Economic Status. Men. Productivity. 1960's-70's. *2507*

—. Discrimination. Income. Men. Whites. 1976. *2577*

—. Economic Structure. Immigration. Labor market. Minorities. ca 1950-70. *2569*

—. Employment. New York City. Women. 1970's. *2790*

—. Employment. Women. 1970-82. *2431*

—. Income. Men. 1975-78. *1582*

—. Income. North Central States. 1970. *2548*

—. Labor force. Migration, internal. 1973-77. *1750*

—. Recessions. Unemployment. 1974-75. *2516*

Historians. Brody, David. Commons, John R. Dawley, Alan. Labor history. Montgomery, David. Perlman, Selig. 1910-80. *115*

—. Business Education. Colleges and Universities. New York University (Graduate School of Business Administration). 1977-80. *1954*

—. Employment. Women. 1958-81. *1971*

—. Labor Unions and Organizations. Massachusetts (West Lynn). Radicals and Radicalism. Saturday Workshop (conference). Shoeworkers. 1979. *16*

—. Occupations. ca 1976-79. *2018*

Historiography *See also* Historians; Quantitative Methods.

—. American Federation of Labor. Bibliographies. Industrial Workers of the World. 1905-69. *1013*

—. Anarchism and Anarchists. Communism. Ethnic Groups. 1880's-1920's. *28*

—. Archives, local. Economic History. Phillips, Ulrich Bonnell. Slave prices. Texas (Harrison County). 1849-60. *552*

—. Bibliographies. Hobsbawn, Eric. Labor. Thompson, E. P. 1960's-70's. *1551*

—. Blacks. Christian, Marcus B. Dillard University. Federal Writers' Project. Louisiana. Works Progress Administration. 1930's-79. *1406*

—. Brissenden, Paul F. Industrial Workers of the World. 20c. *1012*

—. Class consciousness. Ethnic Groups. Labor movement. 1963-82. *54*

—. Depressions. Ethnicity. Labor. 1930's. 1970-82. *914*

—. Economic Conditions. Slavery. South. 17c-1865. 1974. *574*

—. Economics (research). Engerman, Stanley L. Fogel, Robert William. Slavery (review article). South. ca 1820-1974. *633*

—. Engerman, Stanley L. Fogel, Robert William. Quantitative methods. Slavery. Social Mobility. 1800's-50's. 1930's-70's. *623*

—. Engerman, Stanley L. Fogel, Robert William. Slavery (review article). 19c. 1974. *576*

—. General Motors Corporation. *Great Sitdown* (film). Strikes. United Automobile Workers of America. *With Babies and Banners* (film). 1937. 1976-79. *1188*

—. Great Britain. Ideology. Labor history. USA. ca 1940's-74. *90*

—. Industry. Labor Unions and Organizations. World War II. 1941-45. *1024*

—. Iron Industry. James, Thomas. Maramec Iron Works. Massey, Samuel. Missouri. Slavery. 1828-50. 1950's-70's. *582*

—. Jews. Labor. 20c. *1858*

—. Labor. Mexican Americans. Oral history. 1920's-30's. *917*

—. Labor. South. 19c-20c. *69*

—. Labor Unions and Organizations. Socialism. 1890-1930. *289*

—. Marxism. Research. Sex roles. Women. 19c. 1970's. *190*

—. Methodology. 19c-1940's. 1950-78. *23*

—. Research. Working class. 19c-20c. *49*

—. Slavery. South. 17c-19c. 1918-77. *573*

—. Slavery. South. 1800-60. 1956-79. *629*

—. USA. USSR. 1976. *122*

History *See also* particular branches of history, e.g. business history, oral history, psychohistory, science, history of.

—. Data bases. Knights of Labor. 1880's. 1973. *762*

—. Gompers, Samuel (papers). Literature. 1860's-1920's. *767*

—. Labor Unions and Organizations. 1980. *33*

History Teaching. Brown University. Labor history. Taft, Philip. 1957-68. *85*

—. Curricula. Labor education. 1975. *92*

—. Labor history. Perlman, Selig (*Theory of the Labor Movement*). Working class. 1928-78. *48*

Hoadly, George. Coal Mines and Mining. Ohio (Hocking Valley). Strikes. 1884-85. *819*

—. Governors. National guard. Ohio (Hocking Valley). Strikes. 1884-85. *778*

Hobsbawn, Eric. Bibliographies. Historiography. Labor. Thompson, E. P. 1960's-70's. *1551*

Hocking Valley. Coal Miners. Lewis, John L. Ohio, southeastern. Strikes. United Mine Workers of America. 1927. *1258*

Hodgdon, Elizabeth. Hodgdon, Sarah. Letters. Massachusetts (Lowell). New Hampshire (Rochester). Textile Industry. 1830-40. *421*

Hodgdon, Sarah. Hodgdon, Elizabeth. Letters. Massachusetts (Lowell). New Hampshire (Rochester). Textile Industry. 1830-40. *421*

Holidays. Labor Day. 1882-94. *854*

Homans, George C. (theory). Industry. Social organization. Work group (environmental change). 1974. *1504*

Homeownership. Children. Education. Rhode Island (Providence). Schooling. Working class. 1880-1925. *214*

Homestead Strike. Amalgamated Association of Iron and Steel Workers. Carnegie Steel Company. Fitch, John A. (report). Pennsylvania (Pittsburgh). Steel industry. Strikes. 1892-1909. *787*

—. Bond issues. Carnegie, Andrew. Libraries. Ohio Valley Trades and Labor Assembly. West Virginia (Wheeling). 1892-1911. *811*

—. National Guard (16th Regiment). Pennsylvania. Windsor, Fred E. 1892. *822*

Homicide. See Murder.

Honorary Degrees. See Degrees, Academic.

Hoover Dam. Boulder Canyon project. Colorado River. Industrial Workers of the World. Nevada. Strikes. 1931. *1241*

—. Boulder Canyon Project. Industrial Workers of the World. Nevada. Six Companies, Inc. Strikes. 1931. *1240*

Hoover, Herbert C. Corporations. Employee representation. Labor Unions and Organizations. 1919-29. *1373*

—. Dix, I. F. Local politics. Self-help. Unemployed Citizens' League. Washington (Seattle). 1931-32. *1340*

—. Hopkins, Harry L. Lewis, John L. Wallace, Henry A. 1930-49. *330*

Hoover, Hiram F. Blacks. Cooperative Workers of America. Georgia. Secret Societies. South Carolina. 1886-87. *873*

Hopkins, Harry L. Depressions. Federal Emergency Relief Administration. Letters. Public Welfare. Rhode Island. 1934. *1347*

—. Depressions. Federal Theatre Project. Flanagan, Hallie. Politics. Theater. Works Progress Administration. 1935-39. *1295*

—. Hoover, Herbert C. Lewis, John L. Wallace, Henry A. 1930-49. *330*

Hormel, George A., and Company. Labor Unions and Organizations. Minnesota (Austin). Olson, Floyd B. Strikes. 1933. *1142*

Horses. Drivers. Lumber and Lumbering. Pennsylvania (Forest, Warren counties). Personal narratives. Wheeler and Dusenberry Lumber Company. 1885-1930. *195*

Horton, Myles (interview). Moyers, Bill. Radicals and Radicalism. Tennessee (Chattanooga area). 1932-81. *284*

Hospital industry. Labor Reform. Medical professions. Working conditions. 1950's-73. *2058*

Hospital Workers. Illinois (Chicago). Labor Unions and Organizations. Minorities. Mt. Sinai Hospital. Roberts, Lillian (interview). 1950's. *2127*

—. Kentucky (Pikeville, Prestonsburg). Labor Unions and Organizations. National Labor Relations Board. United Mine Workers of America. 1973-76. *2030*

Hospitalization. Employment. Mental Illness. New York (Buffalo). 1914-55. *1737*

Hospitals *See also* Health Care Industry; Medical Professions.

—. Blacks. Federal government. Labor Unions and Organizations. South Carolina (Charleston). 1969. *2066*

—. Employment. Federal Government. Wage-price controls. 1968-78. *2830*

—. Fringe benefits. Labor Unions and Organizations. Occupations. Wages. 1977. *2063*

—. Labor Unions and Organizations. Montefiore Hospital. New York City. Retail Drug Employees, Local 1199. 1948-59. *2065*

—. Management, scientific. Nurses and Nursing. 1873-1959. *218*

Hotel and Restaurant Employees and Bartenders International Union. California (San Francisco). Labor Unions and Organizations. 1975-78. *2131*

House Committee on Un-American Activities. Communist Party. Factionalism. Ford Motor Company. Reuther, Walter P. United Automobile Workers of America (Local 600). 1944-52. *2021*

House, John D. Alabama (Gadsden). Goodyear Tire and Rubber Company. Rubber. United Rubber Workers. 1941. *1210*

Indochinese Americans. Attitudes. Employers.
Refugees. 1982. 1709
Industrial accidents. Massachusetts (Lowell).
Occupational Safety. 1890-1905. 690
Industrial Arts Education See also Technical
Education.
—. Africa. Pan-Africanism. Racism. South.
1879-1940. 364
—. Alabama. Blacks. Tuskegee Institute.
Washington, Booker T. 1870's-90's. 708
Industrial Conference, 1st. Ideology. Labor Unions
and Organizations. Management. Wilson,
Woodrow. 1919. 1322
Industrial Conference, 2d. Company unions.
Industrial democracy. Labor Reform. Wilson,
Woodrow. 1919-20. 1292
Industrial Democracy See also Employee
Ownership; Worker Participation; Worker Self-
Management.
—. Collective bargaining. Decisionmaking. Labor
Unions and Organizations. 1920's-70's. 1478
—. Collective bargaining. Sweden. USA. ca
1968-77. 279
—. Company unions. Industrial Conference, 2d.
Labor Reform. Wilson, Woodrow. 1919-20.
1292
—. Labor Unions and Organizations. Scandinavia.
ca 1950-77. 278
Industrial Disputes Act (Great Britain).
Arbitration, Industrial. Great Britain. Labor
Disputes. USA. 1973. 295
Industrial districts. Maryland (Baltimore).
1830's-60's. 458
Industrial labor. Agricultural labor. Puerto Rican
Americans. 1942-51. 203
Industrial Location. Labor. Piedmont Plateau.
Textile Industry. 1880-1900. 748
Industrial Mobility. Clothing industry. Working
class. 1950-74. 1552
—. Economic Conditions. Federal Regulation.
Legislation. North. North Central States.
1970's. 1822
Industrial production. Manpower, use of. Models
(economic). 1960-74. 1527
Industrial Rayon Corporation. Strikes. Textile
Workers Organizing Committee. Virginia
(Covington). 1937-38. 1156
Industrial Relations See also Arbitration,
Industrial; Collective Bargaining; General
Strikes; Labor Unions and Organizations;
Strikes.
—. Advisory committees. Presidents. 1955-80. 2317
—. Agricultural Labor. Management. Production.
Western states. World War I. 1913-18. 935
—. Allen, V. L. Great Britain. 1935-54. 258
—. American Federation of Labor. Appalachia.
Public Employees. Tennessee Valley Authority.
1933-78. 1324
—. Americanization Program. Ford Motor
Company. 1914-21. 972
—. And Women Must Weep (Film). Films. Labor
Unions and Organizations. National Labor
Relations Board. 1950's-74. 2341
—. Antiunionization. ca 1976-80. 2047
—. Arizona (Page). Discrimination. Indians.
Navajo Construction Workers Associations.
Office of Navajo Labor Relations. 1971-77.
2541
—. Aronowitz, Stanley (views). Class
consciousness. Economic Structure. Radicals
and Radicalism. Working class. 1960-76. 1556
—. Bibliographies. Government. 19c-20c. 1981. 103
—. Blacks. Ethnic Groups. Models. 1960's-70's.
1578
—. Blacks. Migration, Internal. Pine industry.
South. Working conditions. ca 1912-26. 900
—. Boston Associates. Company towns.
Massachusetts (Lowell). Textile Industry.
Women. 1810-60. 450
—. Business. Fraser, Douglas. Labor-Management
Group. Letters. United Automobile Workers of
America. 1978. 1890
—. California (Los Angeles). Immigration and
Naturalization Service. International Ladies'
Garment Workers' Union. Lilli Diamond
Originals. Mexican Americans. Raids. 1976-77.
2144
—. California (Los Angeles). Local government.
Public Employees. 1966-74. 2296
—. Callahan, Patrick Henry. Kentucky. Louisville
Varnish Company. Profit sharing. 1908-40. 942
—. Canada. Decentralization. Europe. Labor
(participation). USA. 1960's-70's. 1546
—. Christianity. Massachusetts (Lawrence).
Scudder, Vida Dutton. Social reform. Women.
1912. 1132

—. Clothing industry. Dress and Waist
Manufacturers' Association. International
Ladies' Garment Workers' Union. Moskowitz,
Belle. New York City. Protocols. 1913-16.
1227
—. Coal Miners. Ellsworth, James William.
Pennsylvania (Ellsworth). Strikes. 1900-06.
1174
—. Collar Laundry Union. Irish Americans. New
York (Troy). Women. 1864-69. 538
—. Collective Bargaining. 1978. 1464
—. Current Population Survey. Employment
(definitions). 1940-76. 2689
—. Department stores. Sales. Women. 1900-40.
1380
—. Federal government. Midwest. 1972-76. 2104
—. Federal Government. Public Employees. 1975.
1834
—. France. Italy. Strikes. USA. 1876-1970. 311
—. Hat industry. Milliners. Pennsylvania
(Philadelphia). Stetson Company. 1870-1929.
44
—. Howland, William Dillwyn. Massachusetts
(New Bedford). Textile Industry. 1880-97. 660
—. Industrial Workers of the World. 1920's. 1027
—. Industry. Working Conditions. 1970's. 67
—. Inflation. Recessions. 1980. 1529
—. Institutes. Labor Disputes. 1945-48. 1489
—. International Harvester Company. Minorities.
Race relations. 1831-1976. 337
—. Iron furnace. Pennsylvania (Hopewell Village).
1800-50. 488
—. J. P. Stevens & Company, Inc. North
Carolina. 1945-81. 1711
—. Job Security. 1977. 2039
—. Job security. Labor unions and organizations.
Multinational corporations. Wages. 1970's.
1923
—. Knights of Labor. Politics. Rhode Island.
1880's. 753
—. Labor Law. Social conditions. State
Legislatures. 1940's-70's. 2272
—. Manufacturing. Nicholson, John. Pennsylvania
(Philadelphia). 1793-97. 473
—. Mining. Strikes. Utah (Eureka). 1886-97. 804
—. Mining. Western states. 1892-1904. 827
—. Motivation theories. 1900-73. 389
—. Pennsylvania. Steel industry. 1800-1959. 312
—. Phase II (1971). Wage controls. 1971. 2735
—. Political analysis. Public Policy. 1950-75. 2279
—. Taylor, Frederick W. 20c. 100
—. United Steelworkers of America's Human
Relations Committee. 1960-65. 2117
—. USSR. Work incentives. 20c. 2657
Industrial Relations (review article). Blacks. Cities.
Ewen, Linda Ann. Greer, Edward. Meier,
August. Rudwick, Elliott. 1900-81. 353
—. Harris, Howell John. 1940's. 131
—. Ramirez, Bruno. Rodgers, Daniel T. Work
ethic. 1850-1920. 70
Industrial Revolution. Economic Conditions.
Slavery. South. ca 1800-60. 591
—. Labor Disputes. Miners. West. 1860-1910. 845
—. Massachusetts (Lynn). Morality. Social Classes.
1826-60. 431
Industrial Safety See also Occupational Safety.
—. Accidents. California. Tanneries. Working
Conditions. 1901-80. 222
—. Brown Lung Association. Class consciousness.
South. Textile Industry. 1970-80. 1698
—. Child labor. Illinois. Kelley, Florence. Labor
Reform. Women. 1891-1900. 698
—. Coal Mine Health and Safety Act (US, 1969).
Federal Regulation. 1950-76. 2324
—. Coal Miners. Federal Regulation. 1942-79.
2338
—. Diseases. Labor Department (Bureau of Labor
Statistics). Statistics. 1975-80. 2698
—. General Electric Company (River Works
Plant). Kashner, Frank (account). Labor
Unions and Organizations. Massachusetts
(Lynn). Radicals and Radicalism. Strikes,
wildcat. 1960's-77. 2092
—. Labor (satisfaction). Quality of Employment
Surveys. Working Conditions. 1977. 2229
—. Occupational Safety and Health Act (US,
1970). Pressure Groups. 1970. 2214
—. Women. 1977. 1793
Industrial Technology. Factory system (welfare
work). Labor Disputes. National Cash Register
Company. 1895-1913. 1211
—. Printing. Working Class. 1931-78. 1844
Industrial Workers of the World. Agricultural
Labor. Farmers. Labor Disputes. Ranchers.
Washington (Yakima Valley). 1910-36. 1216

—. Alaska (Nome). American Federation of
Labor. Labor Unions and Organizations.
1905-20. 1152
—. Alexander, Moses. Idaho. Labor reform.
1914-17. 1193
—. American Federation of Labor. Armies. Labor
Disputes. Nevada (Goldfield). Western
Federation of Miners. 1904-08. 1273
—. American Federation of Labor. Bibliographies.
Historiography. 1905-69. 1013
—. American Federation of Labor. Congress of
Industrial Organizations. Management,
Scientific. Taylor, Frederick W. 1900-13. 1017
—. American Federation of Labor. Disque, Brice
P. Federal government. Lumber and
Lumbering. Oregon. Strikes. Washington.
1917-18. 1021
—. American Federation of Labor. Louisiana.
Marine Transport Workers. Sailors' Union.
Strikes. United Fruit Company. 1913. 1127
—. American Federation of Labor. One Big Union
movement. Washington. 1919. 1007
—. Arizona (Bisbee). Labor Unions and
Organizations. Mining. Strikes. 1917. 1119
—. Arizona (Bisbee). Shattuck Mine. Strikes. 1917.
1270
—. Bibliographies. Chinese. Discrimination.
Knights of Labor. Labor. Newspapers.
Washington. 1885-1919. 119
—. Bibliographies. Labor Unions and
Organizations. Local history. 20c. 1058
—. Blacks. Crime and Criminals. Fletcher,
Benjamin Harrison. Labor. Longshoremen.
1910-33. 1067
—. Boulder Canyon project. Colorado River.
Hoover Dam. Nevada. Strikes. 1931. 1241
—. Boulder Canyon Project. Hoover Dam.
Nevada. Six Companies, Inc. Strikes. 1931.
1240
—. Brissenden, Paul F. Historiography. 20c. 1012
—. Brotherhood of Timber Workers. Emerson,
Arthur L. Labor Disputes. Louisiana, western.
Lumber and Lumbering. Texas, eastern.
1900-16. 1022
—. Brotherhood of Timber Workers. Louisiana.
Lumber and Lumbering. Race Relations.
Texas. 1910-13. 1164
—. California (Fresno). Clyde, Edward M.
Freedom of Speech. 1911. 1045
—. California (Fresno). Freedom of Speech.
1910-11. 1026
—. California (San Diego). Freedom of Speech.
Mexico (Tijuana). 1911-12. 1069
—. California (Wheatland). Migrant Labor. State
Government. Strikes. Trials. 1913-17. 1133
—. Cigar industry. Pennsylvania (McKees Rocks,
Pittsburgh). Pressed Steel Car Company. Steel
Industry. Strikes. 1909-13. 1194
—. Class Consciousness. "New unionism".
1909-20. 1003
—. Coal Mines and Mining. Colorado. Strikes.
1927. 1199
—. County jails. Kansas. Prisons. Reform.
1915-20. 1037
—. Courts. Riots. Washington (Everett). 1916.
1111
—. Criminal syndicalism acts. Idaho. Labor Law.
State Government. 1917-33. 1071
—. Davis, David W. Idaho. Nonpartisan League.
Public opinion. Red Scare. Socialist Party.
1919-26. 1053
—. Defections. Grady, John. Haywood, William
Dudley. Letters. Schuyler, Mont. USA. USSR.
1921-22. 1062
—. DeLeon, Daniel. Socialism. Working class.
1905-13. 1020
—. Documentaries. Films. Labor Disputes.
Theater. 1905-18. 1018
—. Documentaries. Films. Labor Disputes.
Wobblies (film). 1905-18. 1980. 1028
—. Domestics. Labor Unions and Organizations.
Letters. Street, Jane. Women. 1917. 1032
—. Farmers. Orchards. Strikes. Washington
(Yakima Valley). 1933. 1215
—. Federal Bureau of Investigation. Labor
Disputes. Ohio (Toledo). Radicals and
Radicalism. 1918-20. 1010
—. Films. Labor history. Leftism. Northern Lights
(film). Wobblies (film). ca 1900-17. 1978-79.
50
—. Fiske, Harold B. Freedom of speech. Kansas.
Labor Unions and Organizations. Trials.
1923-27. 1014
—. Freedom of Speech. Political Protest. Pratt, N.
S. Washington (Spokane). 1909-10. 1113

—. Archives. Employment. Pullman Palace Car Company. 1890-1967. 398
—. Labor market experience. National Longitudinal Surveys of Labor Market Behavior. Statistics. 1965-80. 2753
Inland Steel Company. Immigration. Indiana (East Chicago; Indiana Harbor). Lake Michigan. Mexican Americans. Social Conditions. 1919-32. 937
Institute for Labor Education and Research. Labor Unions and Organizations. New Jersey. New York. Socialism. Teaching. 1976-77. 1516
Institutes See also Libraries; Museums.
—. Industrial Relations. Labor Disputes. 1945-48. 1489
Institutions. Commons, John R. Conservatism. Labor history. 1884-1935. 95
—. Immigration. Labor. Mexicans. Southwest. Texas. Undocumented workers. 1821-1975. 235
Insurance. Coal Miners. Investments. Occupational Safety. Slavery. Virginia, eastern. 1780-1865. 599
Integration See also Assimilation.
—. British Commonwealth. Military. USA. Women. World War I. World War II. 1900-78. 240
—. Employment. Revenue sharing. South. Southwest. 1970-80. 2258
Intellectuals. Economic Theory. Garraty, John A. (review article). Poverty. Public Policy. Unemployment. 17c-1978. 107
—. Emigration. Jews. Labor movement. Russia. USA. 1880's. 770
—. Gilbert, James B. Industrialization. Labor (review article). Rodgers, Daniel T. Values. 1850-1920. 1974-77. 55
—. Job satisfaction. Social status. Work, institution of. Working Class. 1960's-70's. 1510
Interest Groups See also Political Factions; Pressure Groups.
—. AFL-CIO. Political parties. 1970's. 1901
—. Economic Structure. Inflation. Labor force. Minimum wage. 1960-79. 1507
Intergovernmental Relations. Federal government. Public Welfare. State Government. Workers' Compensation. 1956-78. 2268
—. Labor Department. Public Administration. World War I. 1917-18. 1297
Internal Migration. See Migration, Internal.
International Association of Bridge and Structural Iron Workers. Films. Martyr to His Cause (film). McNamara, James B. McNamara, John J. 1907-11. 1150
International Association of Fire Fighters. Fire fighters. Fringe benefits. Labor Unions and Organizations. Wages. 1966-76. 2089
International Association of Machinists and Aerospace Workers (Lodge 1987). Airplane Industry and Trade. Fairchild Republic (corporation). Labor Unions and Organizations. New York (Farmingdale). 1950-82. 2028
International Brotherhood of Boilermakers, Iron Shipbuilders and Helpers of America. Blacks. California (Sausalito). Discrimination. James v. Marinship (California, 1945). Shipbuilding. 1940-48. 1450
International Brotherhood of Pulp, Sulphite, and Paper Mill Workers. American Federation of Labor. Labor Unions and Organizations. Militancy. Paper workers. 1933-35. 1280
—. Blacks. Immigrants. Pacific Northwest. South. Women. 1909-40. 1281
—. Labor Unions and Organizations. Paper Industry. Virginia (Covington). West Virginia Pulp and Paper Company. 1933-52. 1282
International Brotherhood of Teamsters. See Teamsters, International Brotherhood of.
International Federation of Professional and Technical Engineers. General Electric Company (River Works Plant). Massachusetts (Everett, Lynn). Occupations. Technology. 1970-78. 2157
International Harvester Company. Industrial relations. Minorities. Race relations. 1831-1976. 337
International Juridical Association. International Labor Defense. King, Carol Weiss. Legal aid. Working Class. 1921-52. 1158
International Labor Defense. International Juridical Association. King, Carol Weiss. Legal aid. Working Class. 1921-52. 1158
International Labor Organization. AFL-CIO. Foreign policy. Social Problems. 1970's. 1888
—. Foreign Policy. Isolationism. New Deal. Perkins, Frances. Roosevelt, Franklin D. 1921-34. 1346

International Ladies' Garment Workers' Union. American Federation of Labor. Jews. Labor Unions and Organizations. 1930's. 1005
—. California (Los Angeles). Immigration and Naturalization Service. Industrial Relations. Lilli Diamond Originals. Mexican Americans. Raids. 1976-77. 2144
—. California (Los Angeles). Mexican Americans. Women. Working Conditions. 1933-39. 1204
—. Class consciousness. Cohn, Fannia. Newman, Pauline. Pesotta, Rose. Women. 1900-35. 1185
—. Clothing industry. Dress and Waist Manufacturers' Association. Industrial Relations. Moskowitz, Belle. New York City. Protocols. 1913-16. 1227
—. Clothing industry. Texas. Women. 1933-50. 1168
International Ladies' Garment Workers' Union (Archives). Archival Catalogs and Inventories. Dubinsky, David. Labor Unions and Organizations. 1982. 104
International Law. International Telecommunication Union. Labor Unions and Organizations. Telecommunications. 1932-74. 1503
International Longshoremen's and Warehousemen's Union. California (Stockton). Discrimination. Hawaii. Japanese Americans. 1945. 2554
—. Far Western States. International Longshoremen's Association. Labor Unions and Organizations. 1934-37. 1108
International Longshoremen's Association. Far Western States. International Longshoremen's and Warehousemen's Union. Labor Unions and Organizations. 1934-37. 1108
—. Race relations. South Central and Gulf States. 1866-1920. 1195
International Longshoremen's Association v. Allied International, Inc. (US, 1982). Boycotts. International Trade. National Labor Relations Board. 1974-82. 2170
International Steel Cartel. Foreign policy. Import restrictions. Steel Workers Organizing Committee. US Steel Corporation. 1937. 1325
International Telecommunication Union. International Law. Labor Unions and Organizations. Telecommunications. 1932-74. 1503
International Trade. Boycotts. International Longshoremen's Association v. Allied International, Inc. (US, 1982). National Labor Relations Board. 1974-82. 2170
—. Economic Conditions. Labor Unions and Organizations. Protectionism. 1969-73. 2222
—. Labor content. 1965-70. 1518
International Typographical Union. Employment. Income. Labor Unions and Organizations. 1946-65. 2055
—. Franklin, Benjamin. Pennsylvania (Philadelphia). Printing. Strikes. Wages. 1754-1852. 531
International Union of Operating Engineers, Local 926. Coffin, Tom. Construction. Georgia (Atlanta). Labor Unions and Organizations. Law Engineering Testing Company. National Labor Relations Board. 1973-78. 2050
International Workingmen's Association. Boston Eight Hour League. Labor Unions and Organizations. Marxism. McNeill, George. New York. Steward, Ira. 1860-89. 760
—. California. Chinese. Constitutions, State. Federal Regulation. Labor reform. 1877-82. 865
—. California (San Francisco). Class consciousness. Social mobility. 1880's. 756
—. Marxism. Railroads. Strikes. 1877. 802
—. Railroads. Strikes. 1877. 801
Internationalism. AFL-CIO. Foreign Policy. Labor Unions and Organizations. 1886-1975. 1920
Interpersonal Relations See also Human Relations.
—. Social Customs. Unemployment. 1976-77. 1671
Interstate Commerce Commission. Federal Regulation. Trucks and Trucking. 1938-76. 2310
Intervention. Ammons, Elias. Coal Miners. Colorado. Federal government. Strikes. Wilson, Woodrow. 1914. 1175
—. Capitalism. Collective bargaining. Government. Ideology. 1978. 2734
—. Debs, Eugene V. Federal government. Illinois (Blue Island). Pullman Palace Car Company. Strikes. Strikes. 1894. 813
—. Gompers, Samuel. Labor Unions and Organizations. Latin America. Pan American Federation of Labor. Revolution. World War I. 1918-27. 1074

Interviews. Auto Workers. Class Consciousness. Massachusetts (Framingham). 1973. 1645
—. Income. Social conditions. Working class. 1973-76. 1590
—. Occupations. Terkel, Studs (Working). 1970. 1477
Inventions See also Industrial Technology.
—. Cotton scrapers. Mississippi. Ned, slave. Patent laws. Slavery. Stuart, Oscar J. E. ca 1850. 575
Investments See also Stock Exchange.
—. Coal Miners. Insurance. Occupational Safety. Slavery. Virginia, eastern. 1780-1865. 599
Iowa See also North Central States.
—. Assimilation. Coal Miners. Italian Americans. 1890-1920. 226
—. Census. Employment. Frontier and Pioneer Life. Women. 1833-70. 467
—. Domesticity. Photographs. Women. ca 1890-1910. 150
—. Employment. Hat industry. Milliners. Social Customs. Women. 1870-80. 680
—. Income. Industrialization. Rural areas. Towns. 1960-70. 2776
—. Men. Teachers. ca 1860-99. 717
—. Murals. New Deal. 1934-42. 1341
Iowa (Muscatine). Industrialization. Pearl button factories. Strikes. 1911-12. 1245
Iowa Public Employment Relations Act (1974). Arbitration. Public employees. 1970's. 2231
Iowa (Vinton). Amalgamated Meat Cutters. Employee Ownership. Labor Unions and Organizations. Rath Pork Packing Company. 1970-81. 2080
Iowa (Waterloo). Employee Ownership. Rath Pork Packing Company. 1970-81. 1853
—. Employee Ownership. Rath Pork Packing Company. Reagan, Ronald (administration). 1970's-80's. 2137
Ireland. Irish Americans. Labor movement. League of Nations controversy. Massachusetts. 1918-19. 905
Irish. Discrimination. Labor market. Massachusetts (Waltham). 1850-90. 691
Irish Americans. Attitudes. Labor movement. Leadership. 19c. 283
—. Boycotts. New York City. Working Conditions. 1880-86. 806
—. California (San Francisco). Diaries. Immigrants. Ironworkers. Roney, Frank. 1875-76. 733
—. Coal Miners. Ownership. Pennsylvania. Terrorism. Working Conditions. 1850-70. 707
—. Collar Laundry Union. Industrial Relations. New York (Troy). Women. 1864-69. 538
—. Construction. Massachusetts. Population. Railroads. Towns. Western Railroad. 1833-42. 465
—. Education. Family. Income. Occupations. 1969-70. 2854
—. Ethnicity. Land League. Radicals and Radicalism. Reform. Working class. 1880-83. 758
—. Immigrants. Industry. Labor boycotts. New York City. 1880-86. 653
—. Immigration. New York. Women. 1840-60. 176
—. Ireland. Labor movement. League of Nations controversy. Massachusetts. 1918-19. 905
—. Labor Unions and Organizations. Molly Maguires. Myths and Symbols. Nativism. Pennsylvania. Philadelphia and Reading Railroad. Violence. 1860's-78. 1098
Iron furnace. Industrial relations. Pennsylvania (Hopewell Village). 1800-50. 488
Iron Industry See also Steel Industry.
—. Blacks. Immigrants. Pennsylvania (Reading). Recruitment. Robesonia Iron Company. 1915-23. 928
—. Blacks. Migration, internal. Pennsylvania (Pittsburgh). Steel Industry. 1916-30. 952
—. Chesapeake Bay area. Slavery. 1619-1783. 602
—. Chesapeake Bay area. Slavery. 1716-83. 601
—. Economic Conditions. Wages. 1800-30. 498
—. Finnish Americans. Labor Unions and Organizations. Minnesota (Mesabi Range). Radicals and Radicalism. 1914-17. 1222
—. Historiography. James, Thomas. Maramec Iron Works. Massey, Samuel. Missouri. Slavery. 1828-50. 1950's-70's. 582
—. Maryland (Baltimore County). Northampton Iron Works. Police. Values. 1780-1820. 537
—. New York (Troy). Social Customs. Statistics. Working Class. 1860-80. 744
—. Oxford Iron Works. Ross, David. Slavery, industrial. Virginia (Lynchburg). 1775-1817. 561

—. Agriculture. Boycotts. California. Chavez, Cesar. Teamsters, International Brotherhood of. United Farm Workers Union. 1962-74. *2070*

—. Air Lines. Deregulation. Transportation, Commercial. 1978-82. *2115*

—. Airplane Industry and Trade. Fairchild Republic (corporation). International Association of Machinists and Aerospace Workers (Lodge 1987). New York (Farmingdale). 1950-82. *2028*

—. Airplane Industry and Trade. Militancy. Nash, Al (reminiscences). New York (Long Island City). Political factions. World War II. 1940-44. *1209*

—. Alabama (Gadsden). 1930-43. *1056*

—. Alaska. Canneries. Filipino Americans. Salmon. 1902-38. *1198*

—. Alaska (Anchorage). Lewis, Lena Morrow. Railroads. Socialist Party. World War I. 1916-18. *1187*

—. Alaska (Douglas Island). Miners. Strikes. Treadwell Mines. Western Federation of Miners. 1905-10. *1154*

—. Alaska (Nome). American Federation of Labor. Industrial Workers of the World. 1905-20. *1152*

—. Alcoholism. Equal Opportunity. Federal Government. Personnel policies. Public Employees. 1971-77. *2035*

—. Aluminum Company of America. Aluminum Workers' Union. Pennsylvania (New Kensington). 1900-71. *305*

—. Amalgamated Association of Street and Electric Railway Employees of America. Local Government. Louisiana. New Orleans Public Service Inc. Public utilities. 1894-1929. *1143*

—. Amalgamated Meat Cutters. Employee Ownership. Iowa (Vinton). Rath Pork Packing Company. 1970-81. *2080*

—. American Federation of Labor. Chicago Newspaper Guild. Illinois. White collar workers. 1933-40. *1089*

—. American Federation of Labor. Communist Party. Radicals and Radicalism. Trade Union Unity League. 1933-35. *1016*

—. American Federation of Labor. Dick, William M. Gompers, Samuel. Socialism. 1880-1910. *772*

—. American Federation of Labor. Discrimination. Fair Employment Practices Commission. Federal Government. Shipbuilding. West Coast Master Agreement. World War II. 1939-46. *1313*

—. American Federation of Labor. Federation of Organized Trades and Labor Unions. Knights of Labor. Ohio (Columbus). 1881-86. *763*

—. American Federation of Labor. Gompers, Samuel. Iglesias Pantin, Santiago. Puerto Rico. 1897-1920's. *903*

—. American Federation of Labor. Gompers, Samuel. Military preparedness policies. Rank-and-file movements. Wilson, Woodrow. 1914-17. *1041*

—. American Federation of Labor. International Brotherhood of Pulp, Sulphite, and Paper Mill Workers. Militancy. Paper workers. 1933-35. *1280*

—. American Federation of Labor. International Ladies' Garment Workers' Union. Jews. 1930's. *1005*

—. American Federation of Labor. World War I. Zionism. 1917-18. *1064*

—. American Institute for Free Labor Development. Latin America. 1942-68. *2337*

—. American Labor Museum. Botto, Maria. Botto, Pietro (residence). Houses. Museums. New Jersey (Haledon). Textile industry. 1907-81. *904*

—. American Library Association. Library workers, nonprofessional. 1935-73. *2068*

—. Americanization. Indiana (Gary). Polish Americans. US Steel Corporation. 1906-20. *925*

—. *And Women Must Weep* (Film). Films. Industrial Relations. National Labor Relations Board. 1950's-74. *2341*

—. Anderson, Mary. Illinois (Chicago). Nestor, Agnes. Robins, Margaret Dreier. Women. Women's Trade Union League. Working conditions. 1903-20. *1389*

—. Anti-Communist Movements. Congress of Industrial Organizations. Democratic Party. 1945-50. *1907*

—. Antiunionization. Business. Consultants. Lawyers. 1979-80. *2057*

—. Antiunionization. Industry. South Carolina (Greenville). 1873-1979. *2138*

—. Antiwar sentiment. Socialism. World War I. 1914-17. *1034*

—. Archival Catalogs and Inventories. Dubinsky, David. International Ladies' Garment Workers' Union (Archives). 1982. *104*

—. Archival Catalogs and Inventories. Georgia State University (Southern Labor Archives). South. 1966-82. *52*

—. Archival Catalogs and Inventories. Maryland, University of, College Park (archives). 1982. *259*

—. Archival Catalogs and Inventories. Michigan, University of, Ann Arbor (Labadie Collection). Radicals and Radicalism. 1911-82. *141*

—. Archival Catalogs and Inventories. New York University (Robert F. Wagner Labor Archives, Tamiment Institute/Ben Josephson Library). 1906-82. *129*

—. Archival Catalogs and Inventories. Ohio. Ohio Historical Society. 1975-82. *59*

—. Archival Catalogs and Inventories. Pennsylvania State University (Pennsylvania Historical Collections and Labor Archives). 1982. *68*

—. Archival Catalogs and Inventories. State Historical Society of Wisconsin (Archives Division). Wisconsin. 1982. *111*

—. Archival Catalogs and Inventories. Temple University (Urban Archives). 1982. *71*

—. Archival Catalogs and Inventories. Texas, University of, Arlington (Texas Labor Archives). 1982. *73*

—. Archival Catalogs and Inventories. Wayne State University (Walter P. Reuther Library; Archives of Labor and Urban Affairs). 1982. *108*

—. Arizona (Bisbee). Industrial Workers of the World. Mining. Strikes. 1917. *1119*

—. Arkansans for Progress. Right-to-work laws. 1975-76. *2025*

—. Attitudes. Economic conditions. Law Reform. South. Southwest. 1940-80. *266*

—. Attitudes. Georgia (Dalton). Textile industry. 1920-81. *2107*

—. Attitudes. Immigrants. Jews. 1900-20. *1083*

—. Attitudes. Individualism. South. Working conditions. 1970's. *1514*

—. Attitudes. Militancy. Nurses and Nursing. Teachers. 1974. *1930*

—. Attitudes. Public Employees. 1970's. *2139*

—. Attitudes. Reporters and Reporting. Wages. 1978. *2062*

—. Auto Workers (skilled). Congress of Industrial Organizations. Social Conditions. 1940-76. *171*

—. Automation. Unemployment. 1800-40's. 1960's-70's. *1523*

—. Automobile industry and Trade. Blacks. League of Revolutionary Black Workers. Michigan (Detroit). 1968-73. *2462*

—. Automobile Industry and Trade. Coulthard, Stan. Dairying. Michigan (Detroit). 1922-35. *1040*

—. Automobile Industry and Trade. Industrialization. Politicization. USA. 1960's-74. *1637*

—. Automobile Workers Union. Communist Party. Michigan (Detroit). 1920's-1935. *1234*

—. Bakeries. German Americans. Illinois (Chicago). 1880-1910. *814*

—. Banking. 1920-31. *915*

—. Banking. Electrical industry. Public Employees. White collar workers. 1940's. *1090*

—. Bell Telephone System. Company unions. Telephone Workers. 1919-37. *1248*

—. Beltrame, Ed. Fishermen. Florida (Cortez). Knowlton, Bob. United Packinghouse Workers of America. 1930-58. *1163*

—. Bethlehem Steel Corporation. Daily Life. Depressions. Pennsylvania. Working conditions. 1910-50's. *309*

—. Bibliographies. 1963-77. *273*

—. Bibliographies. Industrial Workers of the World. Local history. 20c. *1058*

—. Bibliographies. Working class. 1940's. *174*

—. Bicentennial celebrations. Communist Party. Economic Conditions. Politics. 1976-77. *1910*

—. Blacks. Civil Rights. South. Textile industry. 1950's-70's. *2485*

—. Blacks. Colored Farmers' Alliance. Humphrey, R. M. South. Strikes. 1876-91. *868*

—. Blacks. Colored National Labor Union. Florida. National Negro Labor Union. Race Relations. Reconstruction. 1865-75. *881*

—. Blacks. Communist Party. Discrimination. Fair Employment Practices Commission. New York City. Pennsylvania (Philadelphia). Transport Workers Union. 1934-44. *1420*

—. Blacks. Communist Party. Glabermann, Martin. Keeran, Roger R. Meier, August. Rudwick, Elliott. United Automobile Workers of America (review article). 1930's-40's. *1191*

—. Blacks. Construction. 1870-1980. *356*

—. Blacks. Cotton. North Carolina. Textile Industry. Whites. 1908-74. *1747*

—. Blacks. Discrimination. 1970's. *2439*

—. Blacks. Discrimination. 1973. *2471*

—. Blacks. Discrimination. National Colored Labor Union. National Labor Union. 1866-72. *866*

—. Blacks. Discrimination. Working Class. 1950-79. *2540*

—. Blacks. Federal government. Hospitals. South Carolina (Charleston). 1969. *2066*

—. Blacks. Indians. Lumbee Indians. North Carolina (Robeson County). Politics. Whites. 1970-82. *2476*

—. Blacks. Johnson, Henry. Personal Narratives. Politics. 1900-37. *1384*

—. Blacks. Journalism. Marxism. Political protest. Randolph, A. Philip. ca 1911-75. *106*

—. Blacks. Knights of Labor. South. 1880-87. *871*

—. Blacks. Wages. 1971. *2559*

—. *Blue Collar* (film). Films. *F.I.S.T.* (film). *Norma Rae* (film). 1978-79. *2159*

—. Bossism. O'Connor, Edwin (*The Last Hurrah*). Political Leadership. 1956. *1898*

—. *Boston Daily Evening Voice* (newspaper). Equality. Massachusetts. Race Relations. Working Class. 1864-67. *870*

—. Boston Eight Hour League. International Workingmen's Association. Marxism. McNeill, George. New York. Steward, Ira. 1860-89. *760*

—. Boyce, Edward. Mining. Western Federation of Miners. 1896-1902. *800*

—. Boyle, Tony. Miller, Arnold. United Mine Workers of America. 1919-72. *1903*

—. Brandeis, Louis D. Gompers, Samuel. Judaism. Kogan, Michael S. 1880's-1975. *292*

—. Brewing industry. United States Brewers' Association. Workers' compensation. 1910-12. *899*

—. Brookwood Labor College. New York. 1926-36. *907*

—. Brown, Ronald C. Miners (review article). Social Conditions. Western States. Wyman, Mark. 1860-1920. *21*

—. Bulosan, Carlos (autobiography). California. Filipino Americans. Leftism. 1934-38. *1117*

—. Burch, Selina (interview). Communications Workers of America. 1945-73. *2056*

—. Bureaucratization. Conservatism. Radicals and Radicalism. 1930's-70's. *254*

—. Business. New Deal. Taft-Hartley Act (US, 1947). Wagner Act (US, 1935). World War II. 1935-47. *1293*

—. Business Unionism. 1970-80. *1876*

—. California. Farm Workers. Grape industry. Strikes. United Farm Workers Union. 1966-70. *2088*

—. California. Lobbying. Progressives. 1900-19. *1008*

—. California (Los Angeles). Communist Party. Mexicans. Radicals and Radicalism 1930-39. *1203*

—. California (Los Angeles). Congress of Industrial Organizations. Mexican Americans. 1938-50. *1004*

—. California (San Francisco). Hotel and Restaurant Employees and Bartenders International Union. 1975-78. *2131*

—. Calumet and Hecla Mining Company. Copper Mines and Mining. Michigan (Keweenaw Peninsula). Social Change. 1840-1968. *51*

—. Campaign Finance. Corporations. Federal regulation. 1971-76. *2223*

—. Canada. Finns. Immigrants. Radicals and Radicalism. USA. 1918-26. *965*

—. Cannon, Joseph Gurney. Gompers, Samuel. House of Representatives. Illinois (Danville). Voting and Voting Behavior. 1906-08. *1063*

—. Carpenters. McGuire, Peter J. Socialism. United Brotherhood of Carpenters and Joiners of America. 1881-1902. *799*

—. Cartels. Law. 1980. *1924*

—. Cement industry. Productivity. 1920-80. *378*

—. Cement industry. Productivity. 1953-76. *2634*

—. Central Labor Union. Eight-hour day. Knights of Labor. Massachusetts (Boston). Strikes. 1886. *817*

—. Chicago Board of Education. Chicago Teachers' Federation. Corporations. Education, Finance. Illinois. Teachers. 1898-1934. *1092*

—. Chinese. Knights of Labor. Oregon. Political Protest. Unemployment. Washington. 1880's. *836*

—. Christianity. Church and Social Problems. Socialism. 1880-1913. *255*

—. Chrysler Corporation (Kercheval-Jefferson plant). Michigan (Detroit). United Automobile Workers of America (Local 7). 1937-78. *1208*

—. Cities. Manufactures. Skill differential. 1952-73. *2132*

—. City Government. Fire fighters. Management (structure). 1969-73. *2653*

—. Civil rights. Duke University Medical Center. Harvey, Oliver. North Carolina (Durham). 1930's-70's. *2106*

—. Civil service. Collective bargaining. Strikes. 1960-72. *2054*

—. Class consciousness. Feminism. Great Britain. USA. Women's Trade Union League. 1890-1925. *1404*

—. Clerical Workers. Rhode Island, University of. Women. 1974-77. *2547*

—. Clerical workers. Women's Trade Union League. 1900-30. *1144*

—. Coal Miners. Company towns. New Mexico (Dawson). 1920-50. *303*

—. Coal Miners. Depressions. Hevener, John W. Kentucky (Harlan County). 1930's. *1162*

—. Coal Miners. Harper, Larry. Promotions. Suicide. West Virginia (Stony Creek). 1940's-54. *2102*

—. Coal Miners. Illinois (Macoupin, Montgomery Counties). Radicals and Radicalism. United Mine Workers of America. Virden Massacre. ca 1870-1939. *297*

—. Coal miners. Strikes. 1881-94. *749*

—. Coal Miners. Texas (Thurber). 1880's-1920's. *1197*

—. Coal miners. United Mine Workers of America. Violence. West Virginia (Logan, Mingo Counties). 1921-22. *1228*

—. Coal Mines and Mining. 1945-81. *2112*

—. Coal Mines and Mining. Great Britain. Illinois. Legislation. Lobbying. 1861-72. *850*

—. Coal Mines and Mining. Leadership. Miller, Arnold. United Mine Workers of America. 1972-74. *2040*

—. Coalition of Labor Union Women. Leftism. Women. 1973-75. *1927*

—. Code of conduct. Multinational corporations. Organization for Economic Cooperation and Development. 1966-76. *2686*

—. Coffin, Tom. Construction. Georgia (Atlanta). International Union of Operating Engineers, Local 926. Law Engineering Testing Company. National Labor Relations Board. 1973-78. *2050*

—. Collections and services. Libraries, public. 1967-76. *94*

—. Collective Bargaining. 1972-73. *1900*

—. Collective bargaining. Colleges and universities. 1945-76. *2010*

—. Collective bargaining. Contracts. 1973. *2083*

—. Collective bargaining. Contracts. Industry. Leadership. 1973-74. *1883*

—. Collective bargaining. Decisionmaking. Industrial democracy. 1920's-70's. *1478*

—. Collective bargaining. Legislation. Public employees. 1974. *1925*

—. Collective bargaining. Sex roles. Stereotypes. Women. 1950-78. *1830*

—. Collective bargaining rights. Court decisions. 1970's. *1721*

—. College Teachers. 1967-72. *1991*

—. College teachers. 1973. *1977*

—. College teachers. Wages. 1949-79. *1948*

—. Colleges and Universities. Educational programs. Rutgers University. 1930-76. *1481*

—. Colleges and Universities. Labor education. Tyler, Gus (views). 1928-78. *133*

—. Communism. Congress of Industrial Organizations. Levenstein, Harvey A. (review article). 1930's-40's. *1084*

—. Communist Party. Congress of Industrial Organizations. Minnesota, northern. 1936-49. *269*

—. Communist Party. Mexico. 1935-39. *1043*

—. Communist Party. Ohio (Youngstown). Steel Workers Organizing Committee. Steuben, John. 1936. *1161*

—. Company unions. 1900-37. *1061*

—. Comte, Auguste. Foster, Frank K. Gompers, Samuel. Ideology. McGregor, Hugh. Spencer, Herbert. 1876-1900. *755*

—. Conference for Progressive Political Action. Elections. Railroads. 1919-25. *1344*

—. Congress of Industrial Organizations. Democratic Party. Elections. Michigan (Detroit). 1937. *1052*

—. Congress of Industrial Organizations. Management. National Industrial Recovery Act (US, 1933). National Labor Relations Act (US, 1935). South. Textile Industry. 1933-41. *1081*

—. Constitutions. Editorials. New Deal. Periodicals. Supreme Court. 1935-37. *1302*

—. Constitutions. Elections. Leadership. 1975. *1893*

—. Construction. Journeymen. Training. 1973. *2069*

—. Construction industry. Skill differential. Undocumented workers. Wages. 1907-72. *393*

—. Contracts. Cost of Living Clauses. Inflation. Wages. 1969-81. *1899*

—. Contracts. Rhode Island Workers Association. 1974-75. *1884*

—. Corporations. Employee representation. Hoover, Herbert C. 1919-29. *1373*

—. Corporations. Income. Social Classes. State government. ca 1960. *2263*

—. Cost of living. Right-to-work laws. 1981. *2200*

—. County government. Local government. Public Employees. 1970's. *2134*

—. Courts. Public Employees. 1970's. *2150*

—. Crime and Criminals. Gold Miners. Nevada (Goldfield). 1904-08. *1125*

—. Decisionmaking. Ohio (Toledo). Political Participation. United Automobile Workers of America. 1967. *2038*

—. Defense industries. Industry. Personal Narratives. World War II. 1930-47. *918*

—. Defense Policy. Federal Policy. Industry. World War II. 1939-41. *1361*

—. DeLeon, Daniel. Leadership. 1893-1908. *1068*

—. Deportation. Immigrants. Mexican Americans. New Deal. 1930's. *1300*

—. Depressions. Michigan (Detroit). Radicals and Radicalism. 1920's-30's. *908*

—. Discrimination. Employment. Public employees. Supreme Court. 1976-77. *2316*

—. Discrimination. Mexican Americans. North Central States. Steel workers. 1919-45. *1243*

—. Domestics. Industrial Workers of the World. Letters. Street, Jane. Women. 1917. *1032*

—. Dye, Nancy Schrom. Greenwald, Maurine Weiner. New York. Women (review article). World War I. 1870-1920. *371*

—. Economic conditions. 1972. *1889*

—. Economic Conditions. International Trade. Protectionism. 1969-73. *2222*

—. Economic Development. 1979. *1917*

—. Economic growth. 1918-62. *271*

—. Economic structure, international. 1976. *1550*

—. Economic Theory. Great Britain. Wages. 1920-79. *394*

—. Elections. 1979. *1887*

—. Elections. Leadership. Sadlowski, Ed. United Steelworkers of America. 1976-77. *1918*

—. Elections. Leadership. Sadlowski, Ed. United Steelworkers of America. 1976-77. *2096*

—. Elections. Membership. 1972-79. *2075*

—. Elections. National Labor Relations Board. Wages. Working Conditions. 1970-75. *1628*

—. Elections. Sadlowski, Ed. United Steelworkers of America. 1976-77. *2090*

—. Elections (senatorial). State Politics. Wisconsin. 1952. *2334*

—. Electrical Workers, International Brotherhood of. Industry. New York City. Personal Narratives. Pessen, Edward. World War II. 1940-44. *980*

—. Employment. Income. International Typographical Union. 1946-65. *2055*

—. Employment. Occupational Mobility. Resignations. Working conditions. 1970's. *1486*

—. Employment. Professionals. ca 1960-74. *1992*

—. Energy industries. Miller, Arnold. United Mine Workers of America. 1950's-74. *2133*

—. Engineers. 1968-80. *1978*

—. Factionalism. Great Britain. Organizational Theory. USA. 20c. *139*

—. Family. Income. Race Relations. 1947-74. *2406*

—. Family. Massachusetts (Lowell). Textile Industry. Women. 1830-60. *423*

—. Family. Women. 20c. *244*

—. Far Western States. International Longshoremen's and Warehousemen's Union. International Longshoremen's Association. 1934-37. *1108*

—. Federal government. Merchant marine. National Maritime Council. 1945-75. *2103*

—. Federal Government (appointments). 1970-73. *2125*

—. Federal policy. Undocumented Workers. 1979-82. *1520*

—. Feminism. Lobbying. Middle Classes. Women's Trade Union League. ca 1903-20. *1405*

—. *Fifth Wheel* (newspaper). Rank-and-File movements. Teamsters, International Brotherhood of. 1977. *2128*

—. Finnish Americans. Imatra I (association). New York City (Brooklyn). 1890-1921. *277*

—. Finnish Americans. Iron Industry. Minnesota (Mesabi Range). Radicals and Radicalism. 1914-17. *1222*

—. Fire fighters. Fringe benefits. International Association of Fire Fighters. Wages. 1966-76. *2089*

—. Fiscal Policy. Local Government. Public Employees. State Government. Taxation. 1960-71. *2140*

—. Fiske, Harold B. Freedom of speech. Industrial Workers of the World. Kansas. Trials. 1923-27. *1014*

—. Foreign policy. Latin America. USA. 20c. *331*

—. Forest and Farm Workers Union. Hall, Covington. Louisiana. Lumber and Lumbering. Socialism. 1907-16. *1126*

—. Fraser, Douglas. Liberalism. 1978. *1926*

—. Fringe benefits. Hospitals. Occupations. Wages. 1977. *2063*

—. General Electric Company. Leadership. Massachusetts. New York. Pennsylvania. Westinghouse Electric Corporation. 1933-37. *1249*

—. General Electric Company. New York (Fort Edward, Hudson Falls). Occupational Hazards. Pollution. Polychlorinated biphenyl. United Electrical, Radio, and Machine Workers of America. 1975. *2037*

—. General Electric Company (River Works Plant). Industrial safety. Kashner, Frank (account). Massachusetts (Lynn). Radicals and Radicalism. Strikes, wildcat. 1960's-77. *2092*

—. Gilman, Daniel Spencer. Letters. Massachusetts (Lowell). Working Conditions. 1844-46. *505*

—. Gompers, Samuel. Intervention. Latin America. Pan American Federation of Labor. Revolution. World War I. 1918-27. *1074*

—. Government. Public employees. 1961-74. *1916*

—. Great Britain. Political Change. Socialism. USA. World War I. 1914-25. *1070*

—. Great Britain. Steel industry. USA. 1888-1912. *270*

—. Greek Americans. Western States. Working class. 1897-1924. *977*

—. Haywood, William Dudley. Socialism. 1890-1928. *199*

—. Hentoff, Nat (account). New York City. *Village Voice* (newspaper). 1958-77. *2084*

—. Historians. Massachusetts (West Lynn). Radicals and Radicalism. Saturday Workshop (conference). Shoeworkers. 1979. *16*

—. Historiography. Industry. World War II. 1941-45. *1024*

—. Historiography. Socialism. 1890-1930. *289*

—. History. 1980. *33*

—. Hormel, George A., and Company. Minnesota (Austin). Olson, Floyd B. Strikes. 1933. *1142*

—. Hospital Workers. Illinois (Chicago). Minorities. Mt. Sinai Hospital. Roberts, Lillian (interview). 1950's. *2127*

—. Hospital workers. Kentucky (Pikeville, Prestonsburg). National Labor Relations Board. United Mine Workers of America. 1973-76. *2030*

—. Hospitals. Montefiore Hospital. New York City. Retail Drug Employees, Local 1199. 1948-59. *2065*

—. House of Representatives. Voting and Voting Behavior. 1965-78. *2343*

—. Idaho (Coeur d'Alene River area). Miners. Silver mining. 1887-1900. *789*

—. Ideology. Industrial Conference, 1st. Management. Wilson, Woodrow. 1919. *1322*

—. Ideology. *National Workman* (newspaper). New York City. 19c. *781*

—. Ideology. Neoliberalism. 1960's-70's. *1919*

—. Illinois. Teachers. 1960-81. *1994*

—. Illinois (Belleville). Political Change. Trades and Labor Assembly. 1902-18. *1072*

—. Gompers, Samuel. Intervention. Labor Unions and Organizations. Pan American Federation of Labor. Revolution. World War I. 1918-27. *1074*

Latinos. *See* Hispanic Americans.

Laundry. Blacks. Folklore. South. Women. 17c-20c. *153*

—. California. Chinese Americans. City Life. 1848-90. *724*

Laurie, Bruce. Cantor, Milton. Dublin, Thomas. Foner, Philip. Katzman, David. Tentler, Leslie Woodcock. Women (review article). Work. 17c-20c. *231*

—. Pennsylvania (Philadelphia). Working Class (review article). 1800-50. 1980. *457*

Law *See also* Courts; International Law; Judges; Judicial Administration; Judicial Process; Lawyers; Legislation; Legislative Bodies; Martial Law; Police.

—. Apprenticeship. Indentured servants. Tennessee. 1800-60. *506*

—. Arbitration. Delegation of powers. Public Employees. State Government. 1960's-70's. *2278*

—. Arbitration, mercantile. New Netherland. Women. 1662. *409*

—. Attitudes. Depressions. Great Britain. Poor. USA. Vagrancy. 14c-1939. *939*

—. Attitudes. Labor. Sexual harassment. Women. 1974-81. *2504*

—. Blacks. Children. Freedmen's Bureau. Indentured servants. North Carolina. 1865-68. *731*

—. Blacks. Economic Conditions. Employment. Equal opportunity. Occupations. 1954-72. *2514*

—. Blacks (free). Delaware (Kent County). Slavery. 1790-1830. *587*

—. California. Farm workers. Labor law. Minimum wage. State Government. Virginia. 1975. *2187*

—. Cartels. Labor Unions and Organizations. 1980. *1924*

—. Child labor. Illinois. Women. 1890-1920. *321*

—. Discrimination. Employment. Equal opportunity. Public policy. 1964-72. *2369*

—. Employment. Racism. 1964-73. *2356*

—. Florida. Labor, forced. Tabert, Martin. Turpentine camps. 1923-50. *362*

—. Immigration, illegal. Labor force. Mexican Americans. Undocumented Workers. 1976. *1728*

—. Occupational segregation. Sex Discrimination. Women. 20c. *2234*

—. Puerto Rico. State legislatures. Workers' compensation. 1973. *2275*

—. State Government. Unemployment insurance. 1972. *2261*

—. State Government. Workers' compensation. 1907-72. *2276*

—. State legislatures. Unemployment insurance. 1973. *2260*

Law and Order Committee. Bombings. California (San Francisco). City Government. McDevitt, William. Rolph, James J. Socialism. 1916. *1328*

—. Business. California (San Francisco). Construction. Eight-hour day. Strikes. 1916-17. *1190*

Law and Society. Age Discrimination in Employment Act (US, 1967; amended, 1978). Retirement, mandatory. 1970's. *2676*

—. Attitudes. Complaints. Discrimination. Massachusetts Commission Against Discrimination. 1971-72. *2436*

Law enforcement. Affirmative action. Bakke, Allan. Civil rights. Discrimination. Employment. Equal opportunity. *Regents of the University of California* v. *Allan Bakke* (US, 1978). 1978. *2328*

—. Alcoholism. Chicago, Burlington & Quincy Railroad. Employees. Management. Railroads. 1876-1902. *677*

—. Baldwin-Felts Detectives. Coal Mines and Mining. West Virginia (southern). 1890's-1935. *296*

—. Discrimination. Employment. Equal Employment Opportunity Commission. 1978. *2371*

—. Employment. Equal opportunity. Federal Policy. Income. Legislation. Race. Sex. 1940's-76. *2421*

—. Employment. Immigrants. State Government. Women. Working Hours. 1920. *1414*

—. Farm Workers. Strikes. Texas (Rio Grande City). 1966-67. *2022*

—. Immigration. Mexico. 1924-29. *1320*

—. Labor movement. Liberals. National Labor Relations Board. 1960's-70's. *2216*

Law Enforcement (proposed). Civil Rights Act (US, 1964; Title VII). Discrimination. Employment. Equal Employment Opportunity Commission. Men. Whites. 1978. *2227*

Law Engineering Testing Company. Coffin, Tom. Construction. Georgia (Atlanta). International Union of Operating Engineers, Local 926. Labor Unions and Organizations. National Labor Relations Board. 1973-78. *2050*

Law Reform. Attitudes. Economic conditions. Labor Unions and Organizations. South. Southwest. 1940-80. *266*

—. Congress. Labor Law. Minimum wage. 1977. *2219*

—. Federal Government. Minimum wage. 1974. *2218*

Lawsuits. California. Elliot, Robert. Occupational Safety and Health Administration. P & Z Company. Working conditions. 1975-77. *2348*

—. Liability. Merchant Marine Act (US, 1920). Sailors. 1920-82. *2236*

Lawyers *See also* Judges.

—. Antiunionization. Business. Consultants. Labor Unions and Organizations. 1979-80. *2057*

—. Blacks. Employment. 1979. *2014*

—. Geographic Mobility. Licenses. State Government. 1950's-70's. *1995*

—. Judges. Politics. Sex Discrimination. Women. 1970's. *2578*

Layoffs. *See* Dismissals.

Lead. Bunker Hill Company. Fertility. Idaho (Kellogg). Occupational Hazards. Women. 1975-81. *1778*

Leadership *See also* Political Leadership.

—. AFL-CIO. Blacks. Racism. 1955-79. *2482*

—. Attitudes. Irish Americans. Labor movement. 19c. *283*

—. Auto workers. United Automobile Workers of America. 1974. *2165*

—. Bagley, Sarah G. Female Labor Reform Association. Labor Reform. Massachusetts (Lowell). Women. 1806-48. *541*

—. Behavior. Cigar Makers' International Union of America. Death and Dying. Strasser, Adolph. Wills. 1910-39. *1128*

—. Biklen, Sari Knapp. Brannigan, Marilyn. Employment. Forisha, Barbara L. Goldman, Barbara. Organizations. Women (review article). 1940-80. *1957*

—. Boyle, Tony. Labor Reform. Miller, Arnold. Rank-and-file movements. United Mine Workers of America. Yablonsky, Joseph A. 1969-74. *2158*

—. Coal Mines and Mining. Labor Unions and Organizations. Miller, Arnold. United Mine Workers of America. 1972-74. *2040*

—. Collective Bargaining. Construction. North Central States. 1970-79. *2081*

—. Collective bargaining. Contracts. Industry. Labor Unions and Organizations. 1973-74. *1883*

—. Constitutions. Elections. Labor Unions and Organizations. 1975. *1893*

—. DeLeon, Daniel. Labor Unions and Organizations. 1893-1908. *1068*

—. Elections. Labor Unions and Organizations. Sadlowski, Ed. United Steelworkers of America. 1976-77. *1918*

—. Elections. Labor Unions and Organizations. Sadlowski, Ed. United Steelworkers of America. 1976-77. *2096*

—. General Electric Company. Labor Unions and Organizations. Massachusetts. New York. Pennsylvania. Westinghouse Electric Corporation. 1933-37. *1249*

—. Labor Unions and Organizations. 1950's-60's. *2097*

—. Labor Unions and Organizations. New Deal. 1933-40. *1046*

—. Women. 1970's. *2445*

League of Nations controversy. Ireland. Irish Americans. Labor movement. Massachusetts. 1918-19. *905*

League of Revolutionary Black Workers. Automobile Industry and Trade. Blacks. Communism. Michigan (Detroit). 1968-76. *2463*

—. Automobile industry and Trade. Blacks. Labor Unions and Organizations. Michigan (Detroit). 1968-73. *2462*

—. Blacks. Labor Disputes. Michigan (Detroit). 1968-75. *2461*

League to Enforce Peace. American Federation of Labor. World War I. 1914-20. *1030*

Leasing. Agricultural Labor. California. Contract labor. 1900-10. *953*

Leather industry. Massachusetts (Lynn). Social Organization. Strikes. 1890. *792*

Leatherworkers. Massachusetts (Lynn). Social Organization. Strikes. 1890. *793*

LeConte, Lancaster. Convict lease system. Dale Coal Company. Freedmen. Georgia. Letters. 1887-89. *739*

Lector (reader), function. Cubans. Florida (Tampa). Labor Disputes. Perez, Louis A., Jr. (reminiscences). Tobacco workers. ca 1925-35. *979*

Left. DeCaux, Len. Labor Movement (review essay). Mortimer, Wyndham. Saxton, Alexander. Zinn, Howard. 19c-1971. *1650*

—. Labor. Socialism (review article). ca 1870-1929. 1978-79. *117*

Leftism *See also* Communism; New Left; Radicals and Radicalism; Socialism.

—. American Federation of Labor. American Labor Union. Washington. Western Federation of Miners. 1880's-1920. *1066*

—. Appalachia. Mountaineers. Music. Resettlement Administration (music program). Seeger, Charles. Social Organization. 1935-37. *1368*

—. Bulosan, Carlos (autobiography). California. Filipino Americans. Labor Unions and Organizations. 1934-38. *1117*

—. Coalition of Labor Union Women. Labor Unions and Organizations. Women. 1973-75. *1927*

—. Congress of Industrial Organizations. Isolationism. Pacific Northwest. USSR. 1937-41. *1051*

—. Films. Industrial Workers of the World. Labor history. *Northern Lights* (film). *Wobblies* (film). ca 1900-17. 1978-79. *50*

—. Labor history. 20c. *81*

—. Labor Unions and Organizations. Political Participation. 1970's. *1909*

Legal aid. International Juridical Association. International Labor Defense. King, Carol Weiss. Working Class. 1921-52. *1158*

Legal Status. Discrimination. Employment. Immigrants. 1960's-70's. *2531*

Legislation *See also* Congress; Law; Legislative Bodies.

—. Accidents. Industry. Occupational Safety and Health Act (US, 1970). 1877-1970. *2298*

—. Bell, Daniel. Braverman, Harry. Industrialization. Models. Wages. Working Hours. 1900-70. *397*

—. Blacks. Civil rights. Employment. Income. Women. 1960-70. *2742*

—. Bureaucracies. Civil Service. Federal Government. Pensions. Retirement. 1897-1920. *1308*

—. Capital. Immigration restrictions. Labor, foreign. 1870's-1920's. *137*

—. Civil Rights. Workers' rights. 1945-77. *2329*

—. Class Struggle. Labor Reform (review article). Steinberg, Ronnie. 1920's-70's. *317*

—. Coal Mines and Mining. Great Britain. Illinois. Labor Unions and Organizations. Lobbying. 1861-72. *850*

—. Collective bargaining. Labor Unions and Organizations. Public employees. 1974. *1925*

—. Discrimination. Employment. Equal opportunity. Wages. Women. 1960's-70's. *2332*

—. Economic Conditions. Federal Regulation. Industrial Mobility. North. North Central States. 1970's. *1822*

—. Economic Conditions. Retirement, mandatory. 20c. *2807*

—. Employment. Equal opportunity. Federal Policy. Income. Law enforcement. Race. Sex. 1940's-76. *2421*

—. Fair Labor Standards Act (US, 1938; amended, 1973). Minimum wage. Models. Roll-call Voting. 1938-74. *2393*

—. Federal government. Occupational hazards. Working Conditions. 1960-77. *2237*

—. Federal government. Public Welfare. United Mine Workers of America Health and Retirement Fund. 1945-70's. *2182*

—. Government regulation. Occupational Safety. Workers' Compensation. 19c-20c. *1291*

—. Illinois. Reform. Wages. Women. Working Conditions. 1893-1917. *318*

—. Labor Law. State Government. 1981. *2322*

—. Labor Law. State Government. 1982. *2321*

—. Labor movement. Labor Unions and Organizations. Voluntarism. 1890's-1930's. *901*

—. Labor Non-Partisan League. Political representation. Working conditions. 1936-38. *1365*

—. Minimum wage. State government. Washington. 1913-25. *1364*

—. National Commission on State Workmen's Compensation Laws. State Government. Workers' Compensation. 1972-80. *2381*

—. Population. Unemployment. 1959-79. *2662*

—. State Government. Unemployment insurance. 1980. *2357*

—. Unemployment. Youth. 1950-75. *1760*

—. Workers' compensation. 1982. *2382*

Legislation (state). Labor. Models. National Commission on State Workmen's Compensation Laws. Workers' compensation, alternative to. 1970-75. *2282*

Legislative Bodies *See also* Congress; House of Representatives; Senate; State Legislatures.

—. Recruitment. Sex Discrimination. Women. 1970's. *2585*

Leisure *See also* Recreation.

—. California. State Legislatures. Unemployment. 1979. *2305*

—. Capitalism. Social Organization. 1890-1920's. *77*

—. Family. Farmers. Sex roles. 1920-55. *246*

—. *Fortune*. Periodicals. 1957-79. *1716*

—. Great Britain. Sports. Work. 1830-60. *493*

—. Industrialization. Values. 19c-20c. *18*

—. Labor market. Working class. 1948-75. *2748*

—. Massachusetts (Worcester). Middle Classes. Parks. Working class. 1870-1910. *728*

Lenin, V. I. Gompers, Samuel. Socialists. USA. 1912-18. *1036*

Lesbians. Attitudes. Heterosexuals. Sexual harassment. Women. Working Conditions. 1972-82. *2552*

Letters. Adams, Mary. Apprenticeship. New Hampshire (Derry). Tailoring. 1833-35. *528*

—. American Railway Union. Illinois (Chicago). Lincoln, Robert Todd. Pullman Palace Car Company. Strikes. 1894. *786*

—. Blacklisting. California (Hollywood). Film industry. Trumbo, Dalton. 1940's-60's. *1606*

—. Blacks. Labor. Riley, William R. Tennessee. United Mine Workers of America. 1892-95. *876*

—. British Americans. California (Grass Valley). Coad, John. Gold Miners. 1858-60. *430*

—. Business. Fraser, Douglas. Industrial Relations. Labor-Management Group. United Automobile Workers of America. 1978. *1890*

—. Civil War. Louisiana, northeastern. Overseers. Plantations. Thigpen, Henry A. 1862-65. *589*

—. Convict lease system. Dale Coal Company. Freedmen. Georgia. LeConte, Lancaster. 1887-89. *739*

—. Dall, Caroline. Farley, Harriet. Feminism. Working Class. 1850. *426*

—. Defections. Grady, John. Haywood, William Dudley. Industrial Workers of the World. Schuyler, Mont. USA. USSR. 1921-22. *1062*

—. DeLeon, Daniel. Socialist Labor Party. 1896-1904. *332*

—. Depressions. Federal Emergency Relief Administration. Hopkins, Harry L. Public Welfare. Rhode Island. 1934. *1347*

—. Domestics. Industrial Workers of the World. Labor Unions and Organizations. Street, Jane. Women. 1917. *1032*

—. Gilman, Daniel Spencer. Labor Unions and Organizations. Massachusetts (Lowell). Working Conditions. 1844-46. *505*

—. Hodgdon, Elizabeth. Hodgdon, Sarah. Massachusetts (Lowell). New Hampshire (Rochester). Textile Industry. 1830-40. *421*

—. Indentured servants, former. Maryland (Anne Arundel County). Roberts, William. Tenancy. Working Class. 1756-69. *515*

—. Massachusetts (Lowell). Robinson, Harriet Hanson. Women. Working Class. 1845-46. *494*

Letters to the editor. Illinois (Chicago). Immigrants. *Italia* (newspaper). Padrone system. 1886. *720*

Lettuce. Agricultural Labor. California (Salinas). Filipino Labor Union. Strikes. 1934. *1136*

Levenstein, Harvey A. (review article). Communism. Congress of Industrial Organizations. Labor Unions and Organizations. 1930's-40's. *1084*

Levine, David. Capitalism. Dublin, Thomas. Family. Great Britain. Massachusetts (Lowell). Population. Working Class (review article). 1550-1869. *444*

Levison, Andrew (review article). Industrialists. Labor Unions and Organizations. Radicals and Radicalism. Social change. 1930's-70's. *1506*

Lewis, H. Gregg. Chicago, University of. Economic Theory. Labor economics, analytical. 1940-76. *2768*

Lewis, John L. Coal Miners. Hocking Valley. Ohio, southeastern. Strikes. United Mine Workers of America. 1927. *1258*

—. Coal Miners. United Mine Workers of America. 1880-1920. *1173*

—. Domestic Policy. Elections (presidential). Foreign policy. Roosevelt, Franklin D. 1936-40. *1355*

—. General Motors Corporation. Strikes, sit-down. 1936-37. *1148*

—. Hoover, Herbert C. Hopkins, Harry L. Wallace, Henry A. 1930-49. *330*

—. Labor Unions and Organizations. Power (abuses of). United Mine Workers of America. 1880-1972. *1029*

—. Labor Unions and Organizations. Reorganized United Mine Workers of America. United Mine Workers of America. 1920-33. *1011*

Lewis, Lena Morrow. Alaska (Anchorage). Labor Unions and Organizations. Railroads. Socialist Party. World War I. 1916-18. *1187*

Lewis, Sasha G. García, Juan Ramon. Mexicans. Undocumented Workers (review article). Working Conditions. 1954-80. *2196*

Liability. Lawsuits. Merchant Marine Act (US, 1920). Sailors. 1920-82. *2236*

Liberalism. Depressions. New Deal. Political activism. Socialist Party. Unemployment. 1929-36. *1354*

—. Depressions. Psychology. Society for the Psychological Study of Social Issues. 1930's. *1086*

—. Fraser, Douglas. Labor Unions and Organizations. 1978. *1926*

—. United Mine Workers of America. 1972-73. *1928*

Liberals. Labor movement. Law enforcement. National Labor Relations Board. 1960's-70's. *2216*

Liberty Mutual Insurance Co. Brown Lung Association. Brown lung disease. Burlington Industries, Inc. Cotton. Occupational diseases. South. 1970's. *1609*

Librarians. American Library Association. Labor Unions and Organizations (white-collar). Quasi unions. 1970-73. *2002*

Libraries *See also* names of individual libraries; Archives; Museums.

—. Bond issues. Carnegie, Andrew. Homestead Strike. Ohio Valley Trades and Labor Assembly. West Virginia (Wheeling). 1892-1911. *811*

—. California. Migrant Labor. 1970-80. *2318*

—. Canada. Library workers. USA. Wages. Women. 1977-82. *1972*

—. Colleges and Universities. Employment. 1973. *1738*

Libraries, public. Collections and services. Labor Unions and Organizations. 1967-76. *94*

—. Labor Unions and Organizations. Women. 1917-20. *1091*

Library management. Affirmative action. Equal opportunity. Women. 1973. *2442*

Library workers. Canada. Libraries. USA. Wages. Women. 1977-82. *1972*

Library workers, nonprofessional. American Library Association. Labor Unions and Organizations. 1935-73. *2068*

Licenses. Deregulation. State Legislatures. Virginia. 1974-78. *2259*

—. Geographic Mobility. Lawyers. State Government. 1950's-70's. *1995*

Life and Labor (periodical). Labor Unions and Organizations. Women's Trade Union League. 1911-21. *1408*

Life and Times of Rosie the Riveter (film). Employment. Films. Women. World War II. 1940-45. *1411*

Life cycles. Budgets. Europe, Western. Family. Income. 1889-90. *890*

—. Economic Conditions. National Longitudinal Surveys. Occupations. Social Organization. 1966-77. *1770*

Life insurance. Employers. Fringe benefits. 1971-80. *1581*

—. North Carolina. Slavery. Virginia. 1840-65. *624*

Lilli Diamond Originals. California (Los Angeles). Immigration and Naturalization Service. Industrial Relations. International Ladies' Garment Workers' Union. Mexican Americans. Raids. 1976-77. *2144*

Lincoln, Robert Todd. American Railway Union. Illinois (Chicago). Letters. Pullman Palace Car Company. Strikes. 1894. *786*

Linen. Employment. Massachusetts (Boston). Poverty. Textile Industry. United Society for Manufactures and Importation. Women. 1735-60. *459*

Literacy. Children. Employment. Income. Wives. Women. 1901. *946*

Literacy tests. American Federation of Labor. Immigration restrictions. 1890's. *768*

Literature *See also* Fiction; Journalism; Novels; Poetry.

—. Bulosan, Carlos. Labor. Marxism. 1931-56. *988*

—. Colorado (San Juan area). King, Alfred Castner. Mining. Nason, Frank Lewis. 1898-1907. *992*

—. Delaware (Kent County). Pennsylvania (Philadelphia). Political history. Quantitative Methods. Race. Social Classes. 1760-1830. 1979. *441*

—. Federal Writers' Project. New Deal. Penkower, Monty Noam (review article). 1930's. 1977. *1353*

—. Gompers, Samuel (papers). History. 1860's-1920's. *767*

Lobbying *See also* Interest Groups; Political Factions.

—. California. Labor Unions and Organizations. Progressives. 1900-19. *1008*

—. Coal Mines and Mining. Great Britain. Illinois. Labor Unions and Organizations. Legislation. 1861-72. *850*

—. Consumers League of New York. New York (Albany). Perkins, Frances. State Legislatures. 1911. *1335*

—. Feminism. Labor Unions and Organizations. Middle Classes. Women's Trade Union League. ca 1903-20. *1405*

—. Labor Department. 1864-1913. *323*

—. Labor Unions and Organizations. New York. Workers' compensation. 1876-1910. *847*

Local Government *See also* Local Politics; Public Administration.

—. Affirmative action. Economic Conditions. Public Employees. State Government. 1960's-70's. *2304*

—. Amalgamated Association of Street and Electric Railway Employees of America. Labor Unions and Organizations. Louisiana. New Orleans Public Service Inc. Public utilities. 1894-1929. *1143*

—. California (Los Angeles). Industrial relations. Public Employees. 1966-74. *2296*

—. Comprehensive Employment and Training Act (US, 1973). Federal Government. Public Administration. 1975-79. *2239*

—. County government. Labor Unions and Organizations. Public Employees. 1970's. *2134*

—. Employment opportunities. GNP. State government. 1959-71. *2226*

—. Farm Workers. Housing. Migrant labor. 20c. *2299*

. Federal government. Pensions. Public Employees. 1977. *1946*

—. Fiscal Policy. Labor Unions and Organizations. Public Employees. State Government. Taxation. 1960-71. *2140*

—. Labor Unions and Organizations. Public Employees. State Government. 1880-1980. *2051*

—. Pensions. Public employees. State Government. 1982. *2280*

—. Public employees. Strikes. Unemployment. 1977. *2121*

Local history. Bibliographies. Industrial Workers of the World. Labor Unions and Organizations. 20c. *1058*

Local Politics *See also* Local Government.

—. Dix, I. F. Hoover, Herbert C. Self-help. Unemployed Citizens' League. Washington (Seattle). 1931-32. *1340*

—. Missouri. Racism. Radical Republicanism. St. Louis *Daily Press* (newspaper). 1864-66. *663*

Logan, Frenise A. Agricultural labor. Blacks. North Carolina Bureau of Labor Statistics. Wages. Whites. 1887. *891*

London, Jack (article). Australia (Sydney). Strikes. USA. 1908-09. *1205*

Longitudinal data. Attitudes. Labor (manual). Middle Classes. Research. 1956-75. *1597*

Longshore crane operators. Labor market. Technology. 1981. *2660*

Longshoremen. Blacks. Crime and Criminals. Fletcher, Benjamin Harrison. Industrial Workers of the World. Labor. 1910-33. *1067*

—. California (San Francisco). Labor market. Strikes. 1934-39. *1178*

—. California (San Francisco Bay Area). 1980. *1847*

—. Christianity. Oxford Group movement. Strikes. Washington (Seattle). 1921-34. *1268*

Los Angeles Times. American Federation of Labor. Bombings. California (Los Angeles). Labor movement. McNamara case. Progressives. 1910-14. *1360*

Losche, Peter (review article). Congress of Industrial Organizations. 1930's-40's. 1975. *1039*

Louisiana *See also* South Central and Gulf States.

—. Agricultural Labor (white). Slavery. 1790-1820. *606*

—. Amalgamated Association of Street and Electric Railway Employees of America. Labor Unions and Organizations. Local Government. New Orleans Public Service Inc. Public utilities 1894-1929. *1143*

—. American Federation of Labor. Industrial Workers of the World. Marine Transport Workers. Sailors' Union. Strikes. United Fruit Company. 1913. *1127*

—. Blacks. Christian, Marcus B. Dillard University. Federal Writers' Project. Historiography. Works Progress Administration. 1930's-79. *1406*

—. Blacks. Immigrants. Italians. Race Relations. Sugar cane. 1880-1910. *729*

—. Brotherhood of Timber Workers. Industrial Workers of the World. Lumber and Lumbering. Race Relations. Texas. 1910-13. *1164*

—. Civil Works Administration. Depressions. 1932-34. *1338*

—. Civil Works Administration. Federal Programs. Public Health. Sanitation. 1933-34. *1337*

—. Conservatism. Ellender, Allen J. Hall, Covington. Radicals and Radicalism. 1871-1972. *751*

—. Forest and Farm Workers Union. Hall, Covington. Labor Unions and Organizations. Lumber and Lumbering. Socialism. 1907-16. *1126*

—. Fullerton, Samuel Holmes. Gulf Lumber Company. Lumber and Lumbering. 1906-27. *933*

—. Labor disputes. Lumber and Lumbering. Texas, eastern. 1906-16. *1145*

—. Medical care. Plantations (rice, sugar). Slaves. South Carolina. 1810-60. *637*

—. Oil Industry and Trade. Strikes. Texas. 1917-18. *1196*

—. Profitability model. Slave investments. Sugar industry. ca 1830's-1860's. *638*

Louisiana (Germantown). Country stores. Slaves. 1851-61. *597*

Louisiana (Lafourche Parish). Labor, forced. Prisoners of war, German. Sugar cane fields. 1943-44. *934*

Louisiana (New Orleans). Child Labor Law (Louisiana, 1908). Gordon, Jean. New York. Theatrical Syndicate. 1908-12. *1315*

—. Crime and Criminals. Prohibition. 1918-33. *1323*

—. Ethnic Groups. Georgia (Atlanta). Labor force. Texas (San Antonio). Women. 1930-40. *926*

—. Kendig, Bernard. Slave trade. 1850-60. *631*

—. Prices. Slavery. 1804-62. *595*

—. Public opinion. Street, Electric Railway and Motor Coach Employees of America. Strikes. 1929-30. *1120*

Louisiana, northeastern. Civil War. Letters. Overseers. Plantations. Thigpen, Henry A. 1862-65. *589*

Louisiana (Plaquemines Parish). Blacks. Bossism. Fishermen and Concerned Citizens Association. Perez family. Pressure Groups. Social reform. 1979-82. *2042*

—. Blacks. Durnford, Andrew. Planter class. 1820-60. *620*

Louisiana Territory. Andry plantation. Slave revolts. 1801-12. *564*

Louisiana, western. Brotherhood of Timber Workers. Emerson, Arthur L. Industrial Workers of the World. Labor Disputes. Lumber and Lumbering. Texas, eastern. 1900-16. *1022*

—. Brotherhood of Timber Workers. Lumber and Lumbering. Race Relations. Southern Lumber Operators' Association. Texas, eastern. 1911-13. *1165*

Louisville Varnish Company. Callahan, Patrick Henry. Industrial Relations. Kentucky. Profit sharing. 1908-40. *942*

Lovett, Clara M. Berkin, Carol R. Degler, Carl N. Dublin, Thomas. Kennedy, Susan. Women (review article). 1770's-1980. *118*

Lowell Female Labor Reform Association. Labor reform. New England. Textile Industry. Women. 1845-47. *429*

Lubin, Isador. Labor Department (Bureau of Labor Statistics). New Deal. Perkins, Frances. Statistics. Unemployment. 1920-49. *1452*

Ludlow Massacre. Coal Miners. Colorado Fuel and Iron Company. National Guard. Strikes. 1913-14. *1141*

Lukens Iron Works. Authority. Paternalism. Pennsylvania (Coatesville). Profits. Strikes. 1886. *839*

—. Paternalism. Pennsylvania (Coatesville). Strikes. 1886. *838*

Lumbee Indians. Blacks. Indians. Labor Unions and Organizations. North Carolina (Robeson County). Politics. Whites. 1970-82. *2476*

Lumber and Lumbering. American Federation of Labor. Disque, Brice P. Federal government. Industrial Workers of the World. Oregon. Strikes. Washington. 1917-18. *1021*

—. Blacks. Michigan. 1864-1922. *196*

—. Brotherhood of Timber Workers. Emerson, Arthur L. Industrial Workers of the World. Labor Disputes. Louisiana, western. Texas, eastern. 1900-16. *1022*

—. Brotherhood of Timber Workers. Industrial Workers of the World. Louisiana. Race Relations. Texas. 1910-13. *1164*

—. Brotherhood of Timber Workers. Louisiana, western. Race Relations. Southern Lumber Operators' Association. Texas, eastern. 1911-13. *1165*

—. Drivers. Horses. Pennsylvania (Forest, Warren counties). Personal narratives. Wheeler and Dusenberry Lumber Company. 1885-1930. *195*

—. Economic Conditions. Employment. Housing. 1979-83. *2793*

—. Forest and Farm Workers Union. Hall, Covington. Labor Unions and Organizations. Louisiana. Socialism. 1907-16. *1126*

—. Fullerton, Samuel Holmes. Gulf Lumber Company. Louisiana. 1906-27. *933*

—. Japanese Americans. Oregon (Toledo). Pacific Spruce Corporation. Riots. 1925-26. *1444*

—. Labor disputes. Louisiana. Texas, eastern. 1906-16. *1145*

—. Labor Unions and Organizations. Washington. Workers' compensation. 1911. *1461*

—. Michigan (Upper Peninsula). Strikes. 1937. *1105*

Lumbermen. Community Participation. Michigan (Bay City, Saginaw). Strikes. 1880's. *816*

Lundeberg, Harry. California. Preservation. San Francisco Maritime Museum. Ships. 1945-55. *98*

Lunn, George. New York (Schenectady). Socialist Party. Voting and Voting Behavior. Working Class. 1911-16. *1304*

Luther, Seth. Reform. Rhode Island. 1795-1863. *510*

Lykins, Johnston. Baptists. Indians. Kansas. Pottawatomi Indians. Pottawatomie Baptist Manual Labor Training School. 1846-67. *11*

Lynd, Alice. Lynd, Staughton. Methodology. Militancy (review article). Oral history. 20c. 1973. *25*

Lynd, Staughton. Lynd, Alice. Methodology. Militancy (review article). Oral history. 20c. 1973. *25*

L-1011 (aircraft). Aeronautics. Eastern Airlines. Gellert, Dan. Occupational Safety. Working Conditions. 1972-78. *1647*

M

Mabey, Charles R. Accidents. Coal Mines and Mining. Disaster relief. Palmer, Annie. Social work. Utah (Castle Gate). 1924-36. *959*

—. Strikes. United Mine Workers of America. Utah (Carbon County). 1922. *1231*

Machine shops. Labor, unskilled. Steel Industry. 1880-1915. *173*

Machine tools. Automation. Labor. Management. Science and Society. Technology. 1950-78. *1524*

Machinery manufacturing industry. Labor market. Wages. 1970-71. *2796*

Machines *See also* Mechanization.

—. Behavior. Management, scientific. Production. 1870-1920. *716*

Machinists. Computers. 1977-82. *1810*

—. Pennsylvania (Carbondale, Scranton). Powderly, Terence V. Working Class. 1866-77. *742*

Macintyre, Stuart. Gaventa, John. Politics. Radicals and Radicalism (review article). Working Class. ca 1880-1940. *93*

Madison *Press Connection*. Newspapers. Strikes. Wisconsin. Worker self-management. 1978-80. *2146*

Magazines. *See* Periodicals.

Maine *See also* New England; Northeastern or North Atlantic States.

—. Bibliographies. Women. Working Class. 1975. *202*

—. Farms. Labor. Women. 1940-80. *2581*

Maine (Auburn, Lewiston). Shoe industry. Strikes. United Shoe Workers of America. 1937. *1124*

Maine (Vinalhaven). Bodwell Granite Company. Granite industry. 1851-1919. *655*

Malkiel, Theresa Serber. Jews. Labor Unions and Organizations. New York City. Socialist Party. Women. 1900's-14. *1059*

Management *See also* Arbitration, Industrial; Collective Bargaining; Employers; Executive Behavior; Industrial Relations; Industrialists.

—. Accident Insurance. Judicial process. New England. 1890-1910. *75*

—. Accidents. Courts. Federal Employers' Liability Act (US, 1908). Railroads. Safety Appliances Act (US, 1893). Working Conditions. 1890-1913. *334*

—. Age. Coal Mines and Mining. Standard of living. Strikes, wildcat. Working conditions. 1970's. *2041*

—. Aged. Employment. Industry. Retirement, mandatory. Social Reform. 1850-1900. *696*

—. Agricultural Labor. Industrial Relations. Production. Western states. World War I. 1913-18. *935*

—. Alcoholism. Chicago, Burlington & Quincy Railroad. Employees. Law Enforcement. Railroads. 1876-1902. *677*

—. Antitrust. Congress. Courts. Sports. 1950's-70's. *1646*

—. Automation. Labor. Machine tools. Science and Society. Technology. 1950-78. *1524*

—. Blue collar workers. Corporations. Wages. 1960's-70's. *2612*

—. Civil service. Colleges and universities. Training Act (1958). Training programs. 1958-70's. *1949*

—. Congress of Industrial Organizations. Labor Unions and Organizations. National Industrial Recovery Act (US, 1933). National Labor Relations Act (US, 1935). South. Textile Industry. 1933-41. *1081*

—. Decisionmaking. Democracy. Psychology, humanistic. Worker participation. 1960's-75. *84*

—. Department stores. Sales. Women. Work culture. 1890-1960. *151*

—. Educational reform. Industry. Working Conditions. 1880-1920. *60*

—. Employment. Mental illness. Rehabilitation Act (US, 1973). 1947-78. *1852*

—. Ideology. Industrial Conference, 1st. Labor Unions and Organizations. Wilson, Woodrow. 1919. *1322*

—. Jews. Labor. Massachusetts (Lynn). Shoe industry. 1900-55. *927*

—. Job enrichment. Job Satisfaction. Worker self-management. 1971-74. *1780*

—. Labor Unions and Organizations. Mechanization. Postal service. Technology. 1970's. *1777*

—. Newspapers (weekly). Wages. Women. 1977. *1966*

—. Worker Self-Management. 1970's-82. *1619*

Management, participation in. Productivity. Profit sharing. 1970's. *374*

Management, Scientific. American Federation of Labor. Congress of Industrial Organizations. Industrial Workers of the World. Taylor, Frederick W. 1900-13. *1017*

—. Behavior. Machines. Production. 1870-1920. *716*

—. Bethlehem Steel Corporation. Executive Behavior. Pennsylvania. Taylor, Frederick W. 1898-1901. *721*

—. Braverman, Harry (review article). White Collar Workers. 20c. *2017*

Massachusetts (Everett, Lynn). General Electric Company (River Works Plant). International Federation of Professional and Technical Engineers. Occupations. Technology. 1970-78. *2157*

Massachusetts (Fall River). Howard, Robert. Labor Disputes. Textile Industry. 1880's. *736*

—. Howard, Robert. Labor Disputes. Textile industry. 19c. *476*

—. Immigrants (new, old). Labor Unions and Organizations. Textile industry. 1890-1905. *735*

Massachusetts (Fall River, Lynn). Industrialization. Social Organization. Working class. 1850-1930. *43*

Massachusetts (Framingham). Auto Workers. Class Consciousness. Interviews. 1973. *1645*

Massachusetts (Haverhill). Shoe Industry. Strikes. Women. 1895. *780*

Massachusetts Institute of Technology. Construction workers. Disequilibrium model. Income. 1973. *2598*

Massachusetts (Lawrence). Christianity. Industrial Relations. Scudder, Vida Dutton. Social reform. Women. 1912. *1132*

—. Everett Mill. Polish Americans. Radicals and Radicalism. Strikes. Textile Industry. Women. 1912. *1219*

Massachusetts (Lowell). Bagley, Sarah G. Female Labor Reform Association. Labor Reform. Leadership. Women. 1806-48. *541*

—. Behavior. Capitalism. Family. Sex roles. 1860. *427*

—. Boston Associates. Company towns. Industrial Relations. Textile Industry. Women. 1810-60. *450*

—. Boston Manufacturing Company. Textile workers. Women. 1813-50. *495*

—. Capitalism. Dublin, Thomas. Family. Great Britain. Levine, David. Population. Working Class (review article). 1550-1869. *444*

—. Child labor. Family. French Canadians. Migration. Standard of living. 1870's. *649*

—. Community, sense of. Strikes. Values. Women. 1820-50. *422*

—. Cotton. Hamilton Manufacturing Company. Labor Disputes. Social mobility. Textile Industry. Women. 1836-60. *425*

—. Dublin, Thomas. Kennedy, Susan. Social Organization. Women (review article). Working Class. 1600-1978. *207*

—. Family. Labor Unions and Organizations. Textile Industry. Women. 1830-60. *423*

—. French Canadians. Occupational mobility. Quebec. Working Class. 1870-80. *683*

—. Gilman, Daniel Spencer. Labor Unions and Organizations. Letters. Working Conditions. 1844-46. *505*

—. Hodgdon, Elizabeth. Hodgdon, Sarah. Letters. New Hampshire (Rochester). Textile Industry. 1830-40. *421*

—. Industrial accidents. Occupational Safety. 1890-1905. *690*

—. Labor Disputes. Social Organization. Textile Industry. Values. Women. 1836-40's. *424*

—. Letters. Robinson, Harriet Hanson. Women. Working Class. 1845-46. *494*

—. Mills. *The Operatives' Magazine.* Periodicals. Women. 1841-45. *419*

—. Mills, woolen and cotton. Textile Industry. Women. 1833-57. *480*

Massachusetts (Lynn). Casson, Herbert N. Labor Church. Socialism. Working class. 1893-98. *747*

—. Factory system. Mechanization. Shoe industry. 1852-83. *497*

—. Family. Methodology. Poverty. Working Class. 1915-40. *940*

—. General Electric Company (River Works Plant). Industrial safety. Kashner, Frank (account). Labor Unions and Organizations. Radicals and Radicalism. Strikes, wildcat. 1960's-77. *2092*

—. Housing. Shoe Industry. Working class. 1915. *985*

—. Industrial Revolution. Morality. Social Classes. 1826-60. *431*

—. Industrialization. Knights of St. Crispin. Radicals and Radicalism. Shoe industry. Working Class. 1820-90. *46*

—. Industrialization. Morality. Shoe industry. Social Classes. 1826-60. *432*

—. Jews. Labor. Management. Shoe industry. 1900-55. *927*

—. Labor Unions and Organizations. Shoe industry. Women. 1833-60. *523*

—. Labor Unions and Organizations. Shoe Industry. Working class. 1895-1925. *791*

—. Leather industry. Social Organization. Strikes. 1890. *792*

—. Leatherworkers. Social Organization. Strikes. 1890. *793*

—. Public Opinion. Shoe Industry. Strikes. 1860. *516*

Massachusetts (Marlboro). Public Opinion. Shoe Industry. Strikes. 1898-99. *795*

Massachusetts (New Bedford). Howland, William Dillwyn. Industrial Relations. Textile Industry. 1880-97. *660*

Massachusetts (Salem). Bentley, William. Cabinetmaking. Diaries. Furniture. 1784-1819. *503*

—. Domestic service. Female Charitable Society. Girls. Industrialization. 1800-40. *451*

Massachusetts (Springfield). Blacks. Occupations. Property. Social Mobility. 1868-80. *714*

Massachusetts (Waltham). Discrimination. Irish. Labor market. 1850-90. *691*

Massachusetts (Webster). Discipline. Factories. Family. Rhode Island (Slatersville). 1790-1840. *482*

—. Methodism. Textile industry. Working class. 1820's-50's. *483*

Massachusetts (West Lynn). Historians. Labor Unions and Organizations. Radicals and Radicalism. Saturday Workshop (conference). Shoeworkers. 1979. *16*

Massachusetts (Worcester). Leisure. Middle Classes. Parks. Working class. 1870-1910. *728*

Massey, Samuel. Historiography. Iron Industry. James, Thomas. Maramec Iron Works. Missouri. Slavery. 1828-50. 1950's-70's. *582*

Mathews, Henry M. Baltimore and Ohio Railroad. Railroads. Strikes. West Virginia (Martinsburg, Berkeley County). 1877. *796*

Maurizi, Alex. Apprenticeship. Construction industry. Minorities. 1959-72. *2163*

Mazzocchi, Anthony (interview). Industry. Labor Unions and Organizations. Occupational safety. Oil, Chemical, and Atomic Workers Union. 1970's. *2164*

McBride, Lloyd. Sadlowski, Ed. United Steelworkers of America. 1976-77. *2167*

McDevitt, William. Bombings. California (San Francisco). City Government. Law and Order Committee. Rolph, James J. Socialism. 1916. *1328*

McDonald, Duncan. Jones, Mary Harris. Personal narratives. 1830-1930. 1936. *314*

McGregor, Hugh. Comte, Auguste. Foster, Frank K. Gompers, Samuel. Ideology. Labor Unions and Organizations. Spencer, Herbert. 1876-1900. *755*

McGuire, Peter J. Carpenters. Labor unions and organizations. Socialism. United Brotherhood of Carpenters and Joiners of America. 1881-1902. *799*

McKinley, William. Elections. Ohio. Republican Party. Working class. 1891-93. *863*

—. Labor disputes. Murphy, S. W. (letter). Railroads and State. West Virginia. 1893. *842*

McNamara case. American Federation of Labor. Bombings. California (Los Angeles). Labor movement. *Los Angeles Times.* Progressives. 1910-14. *1360*

McNamara, James B. Films. International Association of Bridge and Structural Iron Workers. *Martyr to His Cause* (film). McNamara, John J. 1907-11. *1150*

McNamara, John J. Films. International Association of Bridge and Structural Iron Workers. *Martyr to His Cause* (film). McNamara, James B. 1907-11. *1150*

McNeill, George. Boston Eight Hour League. International Workingmen's Association. Labor Unions and Organizations. Marxism. New York. Steward, Ira. 1860-89. *760*

Meany, George. Detente. Working Class. 1976. *1515*

Measurements *See also* Methodology.

—. Employment cost index. Wages. 1975. *2804*

Meatpacking industry. Illinois (Chicago). Muckraking. Reform. Sinclair, Upton *(Jungle).* 1904-06. *989*

Mechanization *See also* Automation; Machines.

—. Agriculture. California. Farm Workers. 1964-80. *1771*

—. Agriculture. Great Plains. Labor casualization. Wheat. 1865-1902. *643*

—. Automobile Industry and Trade. Job satisfaction. 1970's. *1636*

—. Factory system. Massachusetts (Lynn). Shoe industry. 1852-83. *497*

—. Ideology. Occupations. Social status. Wages. Working Class. 1880-1914. *47*

—. Labor Unions and Organizations. Lasters. Shoe industry. 1890-1900. *846*

—. Labor Unions and Organizations. Management. Postal service. Technology. 1970's. *1777*

—. Massachusetts (Berkshire County). Paper industry. Women. Working conditions. 1820-55. *454*

—. Productivity. Worker self-management. 19c-20c. *209*

Mecklenburg, George H. Depressions. Minnesota (Minneapolis). Organized Unemployed, Inc. Poor. Self-help. Unemployment. 1932-35. *916*

Medical Care *See also* Health Services; Hospitals.

—. Coal Mines and Mining. United Mine Workers of America Health and Retirement Fund. 1946-78. *1880*

—. Louisiana. Plantations (rice, sugar). Slaves. South Carolina. 1810-60. *637*

Medical Care (costs). Coal Mines and Mining. United Mine Workers of America Health and Retirement Fund. West Virginia (Cedar Grove). 1970's. *2076*

—. Employment. Wages. 1965-76. *2611*

Medical Education. Brain drain. Developing Nations. USA. 1970's. *2006*

—. Nurses and Nursing. Pennsylvania Hospital Training School for Nurses. Walker, Lucy. 1895-1907. *241*

—. Physicians. Preston, Ann. Women. 1813-72. *435*

Medical Professions *See also* Health Services; Nurses and Nursing; Physicians.

—. Hospital industry. Labor Reform. Working conditions. 1950's-73. *2058*

Medicare. Comprehensive Employment and Training Act (US, 1973). Federal funds. Geographic distribution. Wage indexing. 1978-80. *2242*

Medicine *See also* headings beginning with the word medical.

—. American Medical Association. Sex Discrimination. 1847-1910. *189*

—. Black lung disease. Coal Mine Health and Safety Act (US, 1969; amended, 1972). Coal Miners. Strikes, wildcat. United Mine Workers of America. Workers' Compensation. 1968-72. *2228*

Medrick, George. Coal Miners. Diaries. Pennsylvania, western. Strikes. United Mine Workers of America. 1927. *1146*

Meier, August. Blacks. Cities. Ewen, Linda Ann. Greer, Edward. Industrial Relations (review article). Rudwick, Elliott. 1900-81. *353*

—. Blacks. Communist Party. Glabermann, Martin. Keeran, Roger R. Labor Unions and Organizations. Rudwick, Elliott. United Automobile Workers of America (review article). 1930's-40's. *1191*

Membership. Elections. Labor Unions and Organizations. 1972-79. *2075*

—. Labor Unions and Organizations. 1834-36. *526*

—. Labor Unions and Organizations. Sex Discrimination. Wages. 1979. *2401*

Membership (perceived). Public Administration. Women. 1960's-77. *1787*

Memoirs. Bands (dance). Clark, Earl. Ohio (Columbus). 1920's. *1473*

—. Immigration. Labor. Mánsson, Evelina. Swedish Americans. 1901-07. *974*

Men *See also* Boys.

—. Aged. Economic Structure. Employment. Pensions. Western Nations. 1950-75. *1764*

—. Aged. Employment. 1967-77. *1791*

—. Aged. Employment. Women. 1950-78. *2782*

—. Agricultural Labor. Blacks. Divorce. Moynihan, Daniel P. ("The Negro Family"). 1965-78. *2544*

—. Americanization. Immigration. Income. 1970. *1603*

—. Bibliographies. Dangerous substances. Fertility. Occupational safety. Women. 1970-78. *1600*

—. Blacks. Discrimination. Income. Social Mobility. 1937-80. *2508*

—. Blacks. Economic growth. Wages. Whites. 1960-77. *1815*

—. Blacks. Employment. Resignations. Whites. Women. 1977. *2474*

—. Blacks. Migration, Internal. Occupations. South. 1967. *2525*

—. Blacks. Wages. Whites. Women. 1950-74. *2620*

—. California (San Francisco). Public schools. Wages. Women. 1879. *897*

—. Blacks. Income. North. 1970's. *2502*
—. Blacks. Industrial Relations. Pine industry. South. Working conditions. ca 1912-26. *900*
—. Blacks. Iron Industry. Pennsylvania (Pittsburgh). Steel Industry. 1916-30. *952*
—. Blacks. Johnson, D. W. Personal Narratives. Recruitment. 1917-22. *1403*
—. Blacks. Men. Occupations. South. 1967. *2525*
—. Employment. 1982. *1809*
—. Employment. Statistics. 1947-63. *2823*
—. Farm workers. New Mexico (North Central). Social Change. 1930-50. *964*
—. Federal Programs. Unemployment. 1930's-81. *2340*
—. Hispanic Americans. Labor force. 1973-77. *1750*
—. Income. 1968-73. *1675*
—. Income. Occupations. Social Status. Success ideal. 1947-71. *1850*
—. Labor force. 1955-70. *2696*
—. Regionalism. Wages, real. 1851-80. *887*
Militancy. Airplane Industry and Trade. Labor Unions and Organizations. Nash, Al (reminiscences). New York (Long Island City). Political factions. World War II. 1940-44. *1209*
—. American Federation of Labor. International Brotherhood of Pulp, Sulphite, and Paper Mill Workers. Labor Unions and Organizations. Paper workers. 1933-35. *1280*
—. Attitudes. Labor Unions and Organizations. Nurses and Nursing. Teachers. 1974. *1930*
—. Automobile Industry and Trade. Michigan (Detroit). Production standards. United Automobile Workers of America. Working Conditions. World War II. 1937-55. *276*
—. Factionalism. United Automobile Workers of America. 1937-41. *1109*
Militancy (review article). Lynd, Alice. Lynd, Staughton. Methodology. Oral history. 20c. 1973. *25*
Military *See also* Armies; Civil-Military Relations; Defense Policy; Navies; Veterans; War.
—. Blacks. Civil rights. Discrimination. Women. 1976. *2553*
—. British Commonwealth. Integration. USA. Women. World War I. World War II. 1900-78. *240*
—. Employment. Wives. 1970-80. *2681*
—. Public Employees. Strikes. 1970-81. *2273*
Military Expenditures. Blacks. Inflation. Unemployment. 1970-78. *2400*
Military Government *See also* Military Occupation.
—. California. Federal Policy. Indian-White Relations. Mexican War. 1846-49. *443*
Military Occupation. Japan. Labor movement. 1945-52. *1534*
Military preparedness policies. American Federation of Labor. Gompers, Samuel. Labor Unions and Organizations. Rank-and-file movements. Wilson, Woodrow. 1914-17. *1041*
Military Service. Blacks. Education. Income. Veterans. 1940-70. *2729*
—. Income. 1950's-64. *2638*
Military Strategy. Georgia. Indentured servants. Slavery. 1732-73. *512*
Militia. Illinois (Chicago). Police. Riots. Strikes. 1877. *833*
Mill, John Stuart. Economic Theory. Income, distribution of. Marx, Karl. Smith, Adam. Spencer, Herbert. 18c-1971. *405*
Miller, Arnold. Boyle, Tony. Labor Reform. Leadership. Rank-and-file movements. United Mine Workers of America. Yablonsky, Joseph A. 1969-74. *2158*
—. Boyle, Tony. Labor Unions and Organizations. United Mine Workers of America. 1919-72. *1903*
—. Coal Mines and Mining. Labor Unions and Organizations. Leadership. United Mine Workers of America. 1972-74. *2040*
—. Coal Mines and Mining. Strikes. United Mine Workers of America. 1972-76. *2116*
—. Energy industries. Labor Unions and Organizations. United Mine Workers of America. 1950's-74. *2133*
Milliners. Employment. Hat industry. Iowa. Social Customs. Women. 1870-80. *680*
—. Hat industry. Industrial Relations. Pennsylvania (Philadelphia). Stetson Company. 1870-1929. *44*
Mills. Massachusetts (Lowell). *The Operatives' Magazine.* Periodicals. Women. 1841-45. *419*
Mills, woolen and cotton. Massachusetts (Lowell). Textile Industry. Women. 1833-57. *480*

Millworkers. Attitudes. Fishermen. New England. Wages. 1972. *2761*
Mims, Shadrach (letter). Alabama. Pratt, Daniel. Textile Industry. Williams, Price. Working Conditions. 1854. *455*
Mine, Mill and Smelter Workers, International Union of. Labor Unions and Organizations. Radicals and Radicalism. United Steelworkers of America. 1950-67. *1906*
Miners. Alaska. Elections. Public Opinion. Strikes. Western Federation of Miners. 1905-08. *1155*
—. Alaska (Douglas Island). Labor Unions and Organizations. Strikes. Treadwell Mine. Western Federation of Miners. 1905-10. *1154*
—. Anthracite. Child Labor. Pennsylvania. Strikes. Working conditions. ca 1880-1903. *1107*
—. Arizona (Bisbee). Western Federation of Miners (Local #106). 1893-1909. *302*
—. Arkansas (Cushing). Manganese. Social Conditions. 1849-1959. *233*
—. California. Farm workers. Migrant labor. South Africa. ca 1890-1975. *1593*
—. Chinese Americans. Western States. 1849-90. *727*
—. Folklore. Korson, George. Pennsylvania. 1920's-60's. *76*
—. Idaho (Coeur d'Alene River area). Labor Unions and Organizations. Silver mining. 1887-1900. *789*
—. Industrial revolution. Labor Disputes. West. 1860-1910. *845*
—. Industrial Workers of the World. Labor Disputes. Nevada (Goldfield, Tonopah). 1901-22. *1242*
—. Labor Unions and Organizations. Western Federation of Miners. 1893-1920. *1153*
Miners for Democracy. Labor Unions and Organizations. Rank-and-file movements. United Mine Workers of America. 1972. *1879*
Miners' Magazine. Editorials. Poetry. Songs. Western Federation of Miners. 1900-07. *1283*
Miners (review article). Brown, Ronald C. Labor Unions and Organizations. Social Conditions. Western States. Wyman, Mark. 1860-1920. *21*
Mingo War. Coal Miners. Labor Disputes. United Mine Workers of America. Violence. West Virginia (southern). 1919-22. *1177*
Minimum wage. California. Farm workers. Labor law. Law. State Government. Virginia. 1975. *2187*
—. Congress. Labor Law. Law Reform. 1977. *2219*
—. Economic Structure. Inflation. Interest groups. Labor force. 1960-79. *1507*
—. Employment. Income (redistribution). Minorities. Poverty. 1972-73. *2668*
—. Fair Labor Standards Act (US, 1938). 1938-77. *2245*
—. Fair Labor Standards Act (US, 1938; amended, 1973). Legislation. Models. Roll-call Voting. 1938-74. *2393*
—. Fair Labor Standards Act (US, 1938; amended, 1974). 1974-75. *2726*
—. Federal government. 1973-75. *2171*
—. Federal Government. Law Reform. 1974. *2218*
—. Income. 1970's. *2707*
—. Legislation. State government. Washington. 1913-25. *1364*
—. Poor. Public welfare. 1950-76. *2719*
Mining *See also* Common types of mining, e.g., Copper Mines and Mining, and specific mining occupations, e.g., Gold Miners; Miners.
—. Arizona (Bisbee). Industrial Workers of the World. Labor Unions and Organizations. Strikes. 1917. *1119*
—. Arkansas (Greenwood). Heartsill, Willie Blount Wright. Knights of Labor (Local 239). Labor disputes. 1892-96. *750*
—. Boyce, Edward. Labor Unions and Organizations. Western Federation of Miners. 1896-1902. *800*
—. City Planning. Company towns. Corporations. North Central States. 19c-20c. *2*
—. Colorado (San Juan area). King, Alfred Castner. Literature. Nason, Frank Lewis. 1898-1907. *992*
—. Cornish Americans. Western States. 19c. *166*
—. Industrial Relations. Strikes. Utah (Eureka). 1886-97. *804*
—. Industrial relations. Western states. 1892-1904. *827*
—. Kansas (Cherokee County). Labor Unions and Organizations. Missouri (Jasper, Newton counties). Oklahoma (Ottawa County). Tri-State Union. 1848-1960's. *950*
Minnesota *See also* North Central States.

—. Boosterism. 1851. *490*
—. Michigan. Migration. Occupational Mobility. Rural areas. Wisconsin. 1970's. *1779*
—. Workers' Compensation. 1909-13. *1286*
Minnesota (Austin). Hormel, George A., and Company. Labor Unions and Organizations. Olson, Floyd B. Strikes. 1933. *1142*
Minnesota (Duluth, Minneapolis). Finnish Americans. High Schools. Labor College Movement. Radicals and Radicalism. Work People's College. 1903-37. *921*
Minnesota (Mesabi Range). Finnish Americans. Iron Industry. Labor Unions and Organizations. Radicals and Radicalism. 1914-17. *1222*
Minnesota (Minneapolis). Boardinghouses. Women. Women's Christian Association. 1880's-1979. *746*
—. Depressions. Mecklenburg, George H. Organized Unemployed, Inc. Poor. Self-help. Unemployment. 1932-35. *916*
Minnesota, northern. Communist Party. Congress of Industrial Organizations. Labor Unions and Organizations. 1936-49. *269*
Minnesota (St. Paul). Great Northern Railway Company. Northern Pacific Railroad. Working Conditions. 1915-21. *1000*
Minnesota (Smithville). Finnish Americans. Immigrants. Labor movement. Socialism. Work People's College. 1900-20. *962*
Minnesota State Federation of Labor. Radicals and Radicalism. Reform. Workers' compensation. 1910-33. *1287*
Minnesota, University of, St. Paul (Immigration History Research Center). Archival Catalogs and Inventories. Immigrants. 20c. *136*
Minorities *See also* Discrimination; Ethnic Groups; Population; Racism; Segregation.
—. Affirmative action. Air Force Equal Opportunity Program. Social Mobility. Women. 1976. *2235*
—. Affirmative action. College teachers. 1965-80. *2447*
—. Affirmative action. Employment. Organizational Theory. Women. 1970's. *2306*
—. Affirmative action. Employment. Women. 1970's. *2590*
—. Affirmative Action. Hiring practices. Women. 1970's. *2404*
—. Apprenticeship. Construction industry. Maurizi, Alex. 1959-72. *2163*
—. Attitudes. Employment. Public Employees. 1960's-70's. *2575*
—. Blacks. Income. Unemployment. 1960's-70's. *2576*
—. Business. Discrimination. Social control. Women. 1969-75. *2518*
—. California (Oakland). City government. Employment. 1965-73. *2574*
—. City government. Equal Employment Opportunity Act (US, 1972). Federal Policy. Public Employees. Women. 1972-78. *2256*
—. Civil service. Employment. Equal opportunity. Public policy. Quantitative Methods. 1960's-70's. *2772*
—. Civil Service Commission. Employment. Equal Employment Opportunity Program. Federal Policy. 1970-71. *2355*
—. Contracts, federal. Economic status. Executive orders. Women. 1965-76. *2238*
—. Discrimination. Economic structure. Employment. Industry. Wages. 1976. *2405*
—. Discrimination. Fair Employment Practices Commission. South. World War II. 1941-45. *1435*
—. Discrimination. Women. 20c. *345*
—. Economic Structure. Hispanic Americans. Immigration. Labor market. ca 1950-70. *2569*
—. Employment. Income (redistribution). Minimum wage. Poverty. 1972-73. *2668*
—. Employment. South. Women. 1920-70. *242*
—. High School of Fashion Industry. New York City. Sex Discrimination. Vocational Education. Women. 1975. *2402*
—. Hospital Workers. Illinois (Chicago). Labor Unions and Organizations. Mt. Sinai Hospital. Roberts, Lillian (interview). 1950's. *2127*
—. Industrial relations. International Harvester Company. Race relations. 1831-1976. *337*
—. Unemployment. Youth. 18c-20c. *157*
—. Vocational education. Women. 1979-81. *1576*
—. White Collar Workers. Women. 1969-75. *2730*
Mintz, Sidney. Americas (North and South). Slavery (review article). 18c-19c. *559*
Missions and Missionaries. California. Catholic Church. Indians. 1775-1805. *411*

—. American Labor Museum. Botto, Maria. Botto, Pietro (residence). Houses. Labor Unions and Organizations. New Jersey (Haledon). Textile industry. 1907-81. *904*

Music. Appalachia. Leftism. Mountaineers. Resettlement Administration (music program). Seeger, Charles. Social Organization. 1935-37. *1368*

Musicians. American Federation of Musicians. Petrillo, James Caesar. Strikes. 1942-44. *1100*

—. Danz, John. Strikes. Washington (Seattle). 1921-35. *1135*

Muste, Abraham J. Radicals and Radicalism. Unemployed Leagues. 1932-36. *912*

Myths and Symbols. Irish Americans. Labor Unions and Organizations. Molly Maguires. Nativism. Pennsylvania. Philadelphia and Reading Railroad. Violence. 1860's-78. *1098*

N

NAACP. Civil Rights Act (US, 1964). Employment. Equal opportunity. Seniority. Supreme Court. 1964-77. *2264*

Nardella, Luigi (interview). Rhode Island. Strikes. Textile Industry. 1922. *1116*

Nash, Al (account). Community and Social Agency Employees Union (Local 1707). New York City. Nonprofit organizations. 1958-63. *2111*

Nash, Al (reminiscences). Airplane Industry and Trade. Labor Unions and Organizations. Militancy. New York (Long Island City). Political factions. World War II. 1940-44. *1209*

Nason, Frank Lewis. Colorado (San Juan area). King, Alfred Castner. Literature. Mining. 1898-1907. *992*

Nassau Street Riots. Golden Hill (battle). New York City. Riots. 1770. *413*

National Accord (document). AFL-CIO. Carter, Jimmy (administration). Economic policy. Wages. 1979. *2225*

National Advisory Council on Economic Opportunity (12th report). Poverty. Social problems. Unemployment. 1960-80. *2850*

National Alliance of Businessmen. Unemployment. Vocational education. 1968-71. *2210*

National Association of Drug Clerks. Labor Unions and Organizations. Mandabach, Peter A. Pharmacists. 1910-34. *1252*

National Brotherhood of Operative Potters. Potters. Strikes. Tariff. 1894. *837*

National Cash Register Company. Factory system (welfare work). Industrial Technology. Labor Disputes. 1895-1913. *1211*

—. Ohio (Dayton). Patterson, John H. Physical Education and Training. Working Conditions. 1890-1915. *667*

National Colored Labor Union *See also* Colored National Labor Union; National Negro Labor Union.

—. Blacks. Discrimination. Labor Unions and Organizations. National Labor Union. 1866-72. *866*

National Commission on Employment and Unemployment Statistics. Employment. Statistics. 1976-79 *2822*

National Commission on State Workmen's Compensation Laws. Labor. Legislation (state). Models. Workers' compensation, alternative to. 1970-75. *2282*

—. Labor Law. State Government. Workers' compensation. 1972-79. *2380*

—. Legislation. State Government. Workers' Compensation. 1972-80. *2381*

National Farm Labor Union. California (Kern County). DiGiorgio Fruit Co. Farm Workers. Strikes. 1947-49. *2079*

National Farmers Organization. Farmers (multiple jobholding). New York. Politics. 1960's. 1979. *2194*

National Guard *See also* Militia.

—. California (San Francisco). General strikes. Ports. 1934. *1172*

—. Coal Miners. Colorado Fuel and Iron Company. Ludlow Massacre. Strikes. 1913-14. *1141*

—. Coal Miners. Glasscock, William E. Martial law. United Mine Workers of America. Violence. West Virginia (Cabin Creek, Paint Creek). 1912-13. *1101*

—. Coal Miners. Ohio. Strikes. White, George. 1932. *1218*

—. Davey, Martin L. Ohio. Steel Industry. Strikes. 1937. *1253*

—. Governors. Hoadly, George. Ohio (Hocking Valley). Strikes. 1884-85. *778*

National Guard (16th Regiment). Homestead strike. Pennsylvania. Windsor, Fred E. 1892. *822*

National Industrial Recovery Act (US, 1933). Agricultural Labor. California. Labor Unions and Organizations. 1933-34. *1298*

—. Congress of Industrial Organizations. Labor Unions and Organizations. Management. National Labor Relations Act (US, 1935). South. Textile Industry. 1933-41. *1081*

National Labor Relations Act (US, 1935). Agricultural Labor. California. Elections. Labor Unions and Organizations. 1975-76. *1358*

—. Congress of Industrial Organizations. Labor Unions and Organizations. Management. National Industrial Recovery Act (US, 1933). South. Textile Industry. 1933-41. *1081*

—. Contracts. Dismissals. Labor Law. 1930's-70's. *1634*

National Labor Relations Act (US, 1935, Section 9a). Labor Unions and Organizations. 1935-82. *1339*

National Labor Relations Board. *And Women Must Weep* (Film). Films. Industrial Relations. Labor Unions and Organizations. 1950's-74. *2341*

—. Appointments to office. Confirmation. Presidents. Senate. 1935-78. *316*

—. Appointments to office. Politics. Unfair Labor Practices. 1954-77. *2205*

—. Boycotts. *International Longshoremen's Association v. Allied International, Inc.* (US, 1982). International Trade. 1974-82. *2170*

—. Coffin, Tom. Construction. Georgia (Atlanta). International Union of Operating Engineers, Local 926. Labor Unions and Organizations. Law Engineering Testing Company. 1973-78. *2050*

—. Elections. Labor Unions and Organizations. Wages. Working Conditions. 1970-75. *1628*

—. Hospital workers. Kentucky (Pikeville, Prestonsburg). Labor Unions and Organizations. United Mine Workers of America. 1973-76. *2030*

—. Labor law. 1930's-81. *2274*

—. Labor movement. Law enforcement. Liberals. 1960's-70's. *2216*

National Labor Relations Board (cases). Unfair labor practices. 1952-79. *2353*

National Labor Relations Board v. Yeshiva University (US, 1980). California, University of, Berkeley. Collective bargaining. College teachers. Supreme Court. 1960-80. *2049*

—. Collective bargaining. College teachers. Supreme Court. Yeshiva University. 1973-81. *1976*

National Labor Tribune (newspaper; letters, editorials). Immigrants. Strikebreakers. 1878-85. *798*

National Labor Union. Blacks. Discrimination. Labor Unions and Organizations. National Colored Labor Union. 1866-72. *866*

National Longitudinal Surveys. Economic Conditions. Life cycles. Occupations. Social Organization. 1966-77. *1770*

—. Labor Market. Racism. Sex Discrimination. 1970-80. *2509*

National Longitudinal Surveys of Labor Force Experience. Education. Employment. Family. Youth. 1960's-70's. *2817*

National Longitudinal Surveys of Labor Market Behavior. Information Storage and Retrieval Systems. Labor market experience. Statistics. 1965-80. *2753*

National Maritime Council. Federal government. Labor Unions and Organizations. Merchant marine. 1945-75. *2103*

National Maritime Union. Blacks. Communist Party. Racism. United Electrical, Radio, and Machine Workers of America. World War II. 1941-45. *1391*

National Miners Union. Blacks. Pennsylvania, western. United Mine Workers of America. 1925-31. *1429*

—. Carbon County Coal Strike (1933). Strikes. United Mine Workers of America. Utah. 1900-39. *1225*

National Negro Congress. Blacks. Brotherhood of Sleeping Car Porters. March on Washington Movement. Randolph, A. Philip. 1925-41. *1166*

National Negro Labor Union. Alabama. Blacks. Labor Union of Alabama. Politics. Rapier, James T. Reconstruction. 1837-75. *880*

—. Blacks. Colored National Labor Union. Florida. Labor unions and organizations. Race Relations. Reconstruction. 1865-75. *881*

National Recovery Administration. Economic Conditions. New Deal. Supreme Court. Virginia. 1933-35. *1316*

—. Georgia. State Government. Strikes. Talmadge, Eugene. Textile industry. 1934. *1095*

National Seminar on Individual Rights in the Corporation, 1st. Civil Liberties. *Civil Liberties Review.* Corporations. Employees. Freedom of Speech. 1978. *1788*

National Textile Workers Union. North Carolina (Gastonia). Strikes. Textile Industry. Weisbord, Vera Buch (reminiscence). 1929. *1272*

National Union of Hospital and Health Care Employees (District 1199). Bread and Roses (project). Exhibits and Expositions. Laborer (image). New York City. Painting. 1980. *1555*

National Women's Party. Civil Rights Act (US, 1964, Title VII). Congress. Women. 1963-64. *2416*

National Women's Trade Union League. Labor Unions and Organizations. Women. 1903-59. 1982. *335*

National Workman (newspaper). Ideology. Labor Unions and Organizations. New York City. 19c. *781*

National Youth Administration. Bethune, Mary McLeod. Blacks. Equal opportunity. Public Policy. Youth. 1935-44. *1441*

—. Civilian Conservation Corps. North Dakota. 1930-45. *1319*

—. Employment, part-time. New Deal. South Dakota. Struble, Anna C. Youth. 1935-43. *1318*

—. Haber, William. Michigan. Public Welfare. Works Progress Administration. 1930's. *1336*

Nationalization. Labor Unions and Organizations. Plumb, Glenn Edward. Railroads. 1917-20. *1192*

Nativism. Depressions. Discrimination. Indiana (Gary). Mexican Americans. Repatriation. 1920's-30's. *1381*

—. Immigrants. Labor unions and organizations. 1880-1920. *293*

—. Irish Americans. Labor Unions and Organizations. Molly Maguires. Myths and Symbols. Pennsylvania. Philadelphia and Reading Railroad. Violence. 1860's-78. *1098*

Natural gas. Electric power. Occupations. Technology. 1960-77. *1610*

Natural resource products. Economic Conditions. Manufacturing. Substitution. 1960's-70's. *387*

Navajo Construction Workers Associations. Arizona (Page). Discrimination. Indians. Industrial Relations. Office of Navajo Labor Relations. 1971-77. *2541*

Navajo Indians. Arizona (Page). Indians. Occupations. Social Status. 1973-75. *1679*

—. Indians. Labor Unions and Organizations. Southwest. 1958-78. *2129*

Naval Construction. See Shipbuilding.

Navies *See also* Military; Shipbuilding.

—. Civil service. 1981-82. *2211*

—. Merchant marine. Shipping. 1974. *1493*

Navy Yard. Army Corps of Engineers. Florida (Pensacola). Gulf Coast. Slavery. 1826-62. *563*

Near East. See Middle East.

Nebraska *See also* Western States.

—. Collective bargaining. Court of Industrial Relations. Public employees. 1919-76. *1366*

—. Industrial Workers of the World. Justice Department. Labor Unions and Organizations. Public opinion. World War I. 1915-20. *1077*

—. Industrial Workers of the World. Labor Unions and Organizations. 1914-20. *1076*

Nebraska (Omaha). Migrant Labor. Tramps. 1887-1913. *224*

Ned, slave. Cotton scrapers. Inventions. Mississippi. Patent laws. Slavery. Stuart, Oscar J. E. ca 1850. *575*

Negligence, contributory. New England. Textile mills. Workers' compensation. 1895-1916. *949*

Negro Labor Committee. Armaments Industry. Blacks. Crosswaith, Frank R. Employment. Labor Reform. New York City (Harlem). World War II. 1939-45. *1447*

Negroes. See Blacks.

Neighborhoods. Business, Small. Economic Conditions. Employment. Regions. 1969-80. *2610*

Neocolonialism. AFL-CIO. American Institute for Free Labor Development. Latin America. 1960's-70's. *1911*

Neoliberalism. Ideology. Labor Unions and
Organizations. 1960's-70's. *1919*

Nestor, Agnes. Anderson, Mary. Illinois (Chicago).
Labor Unions and Organizations. Robins,
Margaret Dreier. Women. Women's Trade
Union League. Working conditions. 1903-20.
1389

Nevada *See also* Far Western States.

—. Arbitration. Labor disputes. Public Employees.
1970's. *2243*

—. Boulder Canyon project. Colorado River.
Hoover Dam. Industrial Workers of the
World. Strikes. 1931. *1241*

—. Boulder Canyon Project. Hoover Dam.
Industrial Workers of the World. Six
Companies, Inc. Strikes. 1931. *1240*

Nevada (Goldfield). American Federation of
Labor. Armies. Industrial Workers of the
World. Labor Disputes. Western Federation of
Miners. 1904-08. *1273*

—. Crime and Criminals. Gold Miners. Labor
Unions and Organizations. 1904-08. *1125*

Nevada (Goldfield, Tonopah). Industrial Workers
of the World. Labor Disputes. Miners.
1901-22. *1242*

New Deal. Agricultural Labor Relations Act
(1975). California. Emergency Farm Labor
Supply Program. Labor law. ca 1930-79. *320*

—. American Federation of Labor. Carmody,
John. Civil Works Administration. Work relief.
1933-34. *1357*

—. American Federation of Labor. Third Parties.
1920's-30's. *1054*

—. Amlie, Thomas. Farmer-Labor Party. Hard,
Herbert. Ohio Farmer-Labor Progressive
Federation. Third Parties. 1930-40. *1333*

—. Art and State. New Jersey. Public Works of
Art Project. 1932-40. *1371*

—. Artists. Buildings, public. Federal Programs.
1930's. *1348*

—. Attitudes. Roper, Elmo. Socialism. Working
class. 1939. *997*

—. Automobile Industry and Trade. Indiana.
Ohio. Politics. United Automobile Workers of
America. 1935-40. *1331*

—. Banditry. Depressions. Working class. 1929-39.
913

—. Blacks. Labor Department. Perkins, Frances.
1933-45. *1310*

—. Business. Labor Unions and Organizations.
Taft-Hartley Act (US, 1947). Wagner Act (US,
1935). World War II. 1935-47. *1293*

—. Civil Works Administration. Work relief
programs. 1933-39. *1294*

—. Civilian Conservation Corps. Economic
Conditions. Vermont. 1933-42. *1363*

—. Coal industry. Congress. Supreme Court.
1932-40. *1329*

—. Congress. Roosevelt, Franklin D. Social
Security Act (US, 1935). Unemployment
insurance. 1934-35. *1289*

—. Congress of Industrial Organizations. Labor
Disputes. Newspapers. South. 1930-39. *1082*

—. Constitutions. Editorials. Labor unions and
organizations. Periodicals. Supreme Court.
1935-37. *1302*

—. Deportation. Immigrants. Labor Unions and
Organizations. Mexican Americans. 1930's.
1300

—. Depressions. Farmer-Labor Party. Oregon
Commonwealth Federation. Political Factions.
1933-38. *1334*

—. Depressions. Liberalism. Political activism.
Socialist Party. Unemployment. 1929-36. *1354*

—. Economic Conditions. National Recovery
Administration. Supreme Court. Virginia.
1933-35. *1316*

—. Employment, part-time. National Youth
Administration. South Dakota. Struble, Anna
C. Youth. 1935-43. *1318*

—. Farmer-Labor Party. Michigan. State Politics.
1933-37. *1330*

—. Federal Writers' Project. Literature. Penkower,
Monty Noam (review article). 1930's. 1977.
1353

—. Foreign Policy. International Labor
Organization. Isolationism. Perkins, Frances.
Roosevelt, Franklin D. 1921-34. *1346*

—. Iowa. Murals. 1934-42. *1341*

—. Labor Department (Bureau of Labor
Statistics). Lubin, Isador. Perkins, Frances.
Statistics. Unemployment. 1920-49. *1452*

—. Labor Unions and Organizations. Leadership.
1933-40. *1046*

—. Labor unions and organizations. Radicals and
Radicalism. Working class. 1930's. *1321*

New England *See also* individual states;
Northeastern or North Atlantic States.

—. Accident Insurance. Judicial process.
Management. 1890-1910. *75*

—. Attitudes. Fishermen. Millworkers. Wages.
1972. *2761*

—. Cotton. South. Technology. Textile Industry.
1890-1970. *65*

—. Economic Growth. Labor force. Population.
17c. *479*

—. Industrialization. Politics. Working Class
(review article). 1780-1950. *82*

—. Labor reform. Lowell Female Labor Reform
Association. Textile Industry. Women. 1845-47.
429

—. Mortality. Textile Industry. 1905-12. *919*

—. Negligence, contributory. Textile mills.
Workers' compensation. 1895-1916. *949*

—. Productivity. Textile industry. 1830-60. *463*

—. Textile industry. Women. 1827-48. *464*

New Hampshire *See also* New England;
Northeastern or North Atlantic States.

—. Employment. Massachusetts (Essex County).
Social Classes. Women. 1650-1750. *484*

—. Greenback Party. Labor Reform Party.
1870-78. *860*

New Hampshire (Berlin). Congress of Industrial
Organizations. Nonpartisan League. Political
Parties. 1932-36. *1299*

New Hampshire (Derry). Adams, Mary.
Apprenticeship. Letters. Tailoring. 1833-35. *528*

New Hampshire (Manchester). Amoskeag
Manufacturing Company. Family. Working
Class. 1900-24. *954*

New Hampshire (Rochester). Hodgdon, Elizabeth.
Hodgdon, Sarah. Letters. Massachusetts
(Lowell). Textile Industry. 1830-40. *421*

New Jersey *See also* Northeastern or North
Atlantic States.

—. Art and State. New Deal. Public Works of
Art Project. 1932-40. *1371*

—. Chinese. Labor Disputes. Passaic Steam
Laundry. Strikebreakers. 1870-95. *644*

—. Institute for Labor Education and Research.
Labor Unions and Organizations. New York.
Socialism. Teaching. 1976-77. *1516*

—. Manufacturing. Pennsylvania. Sex
Discrimination. Wages. 1900-50. *358*

—. Public Service Electric and Gas Company.
Sexual harassment. Tomkins, Adrienne
(account). 1971-77. *2579*

New Jersey (Bayonne). Polish Americans. Standard
Oil Company of New Jersey. Strikes. 1915-16.
1137

New Jersey (Haledon). American Labor Museum.
Botto, Maria. Botto, Pietro (residence).
Houses. Labor Unions and Organizations.
Museums. Textile industry. 1907-81. *904*

New Jersey (New Brunswick). Labor Department
(Bureau of Labor Statistics). Statistics.
Unemployment. 1975-76. *2720*

New Jersey (Newark). Artisans. Pennsylvania
(Lancaster). 1820-80. *539*

—. Hirsch, Susan E. New York (Cohoes, Troy).
Walkowitz, Daniel J. Working Class (review
article). 1800-84. 1978. *32*

New Jersey, northern. Cancer. Painting. Radium
dials. 1917-24. *990*

New Jersey (Passaic). Strikes. Textile industry.
Working conditions. 1875-1926. *1140*

New Jersey (Paterson). American Civil Liberties
Union. Associated Silk Workers Union.
Freedom of Assembly. Freedom of Speech.
Strikes. 1924. *1159*

—. Immigrants. Industrial Workers of the World.
Strikes. Textile Industry. Violence. 1913. *1223*

—. Industrial Workers of the World. Strikes.
1913-19. *1160*

—. Silk industry. Strikes. 1913-24. *1149*

New Left *See also* Communism; Leftism; Radicals
and Radicalism; Socialism.

—. Blacks. Labor history. Models. 1865-1978. *365*

—. Labor movement. Research. Social sciences.
1960-75. *1921*

New Mexico *See also* Western States.

—. Equal opportunity. Mexican Americans. Public
Employees. State government. Women.
1971-78. *2458*

—. Ethnic Groups. Occupations. Population. Social
Organization. 1790. *481*

New Mexico (Albuquerque). Daily Life. Social
mobility. Trade. 1706-90. *468*

New Mexico (Dawson). Coal Miners. Company
towns. Labor Unions and Organizations.
1920-50. *303*

New Mexico (Gallup). American Federation of
Labor. Coal Miners. Depressions. Strikes.
1933. *1246*

New Mexico (North Central). Farm workers.
Migration, Internal. Social Change. 1930-50.
964

New Netherland *See also* New York.

—. Arbitration, mercantile. Law. Women. 1662.
409

—. Dutch West India Company. Slavery. 1646-64.
580

New Netherland (New Amsterdam). Civil Rights.
Dutch West India Company. Sailors. 1628-63.
487

New Orleans Public Service Inc. Amalgamated
Association of Street and Electric Railway
Employees of America. Labor Unions and
Organizations. Local Government. Louisiana.
Public utilities. 1894-1929. *1143*

New Rochelle College. Colleges and Universities.
Labor colleges. New York. 1972. *1922*

"New unionism". Class Consciousness. Industrial
Workers of the World. 1909-20. *1003*

New York *See also* Northeastern or North
Atlantic States.

—. Blacks. Civilian Conservation Corps.
Discrimination. 1933-42. *1433*

—. Blacks. Farms. Jamaicans. Migrant Labor.
Social mobility. 1960's-70's. *1635*

—. Boston Eight Hour League. International
Workingmen's Association. Labor Unions and
Organizations. Marxism. McNeill, George.
Steward, Ira. 1860-89. *760*

—. Brookwood Labor College. Labor Unions and
Organizations. 1926-36. *907*

—. Child Labor Law (Louisiana, 1908). Gordon,
Jean. Louisiana (New Orleans). Theatrical
Syndicate. 1908-12. *1315*

—. Collective bargaining. Fire fighters. Impasse
procedures. Models. Police. 1968-76. *2095*

—. Collective bargaining. Teachers. Wages.
1967-68. *2727*

—. Colleges and Universities. Labor colleges. New
Rochelle College. 1972. *1922*

—. Dye, Nancy Schrom. Greenwald, Maurine
Weiner. Labor Unions and Organizations.
Women (review article). World War I.
1870-1920. *371*

—. Education. Labor Force. Puerto Rican
Americans. Women. 1960's. *2430*

—. Employment. Puerto Rican Americans.
Women. 1920's-40's. *961*

—. Employment. Schools. Training. Youth.
1977-81. *1725*

—. Farmers (multiple jobholding). National
Farmers Organization. Politics. 1960's. 1979.
2194

—. General Electric Company. Labor Unions and
Organizations. Leadership. Massachusetts.
Pennsylvania. Westinghouse Electric
Corporation. 1933-37. *1249*

—. Immigration. Irish Americans. Women.
1840-60. *176*

—. Institute for Labor Education and Research.
Labor Unions and Organizations. New Jersey.
Socialism. Teaching. 1976-77. *1516*

—. Labor movement. O'Reilly, Leonora. Social
reform. Women's Trade Union League.
1870-1927. *783*

—. Labor Unions and Organizations. Lobbying.
Workers' compensation. 1876-1910. *847*

—. Labor Unions and Organizations. Political
Leadership. Shanker, Albert. Teachers. 1978.
2005

—. Labor Unions and Organizations. Women.
1900-20. *1439*

—. Labor Unions and Organizations. Women's
Trade Union League. ca 1903-10. *1019*

—. Prison guards. Public employees. Strikes.
Wages. 1979. *2122*

—. Prison guards. Strikes. 1979. *2160*

New York (Albany). Consumers League of New
York. Lobbying. Perkins, Frances. State
Legislatures. 1911. *1335*

New York (Auburn, Syracuse). Immigrants. Labor
Forward Movement. Labor Unions and
Organizations. Revivals. 1913. *1151*

New York (Buffalo). Construction, nonunion.
Labor market. 1973. *1485*

—. Employment. Hospitalization. Mental Illness.
1914-55. *967*

—. Industrialists. Police reports. Research sources.
Strikes. 1890-1913. *853*

New York City. American Federation of Labor.
Economic conditions. Socialist Labor Party.
Working class. 1890-96. *773*

—. Archives of the Jewish Labor Bund. Europe. Immigration. Jews. Labor movement. 20c. *286*

—. Assimilation. Attitudes. Bilingualism. Puerto Ricans. Working class. 1979. *1560*

—. Bakeries. Economic Regulations. Strikes. 1801-13. *469*

—. Blacks. Communist Party. Discrimination. Fair Employment Practices Commission. Labor Unions and Organizations. Pennsylvania (Philadelphia). Transport Workers Union. 1934-44. *1420*

—. Boycotts. Irish Americans. Working Conditions. 1880-86. *806*

—. Bread and Roses (project). Exhibits and Expositions. Laborer (image). National Union of Hospital and Health Care Employees (District 1199). Painting. 1980. *1555*

—. Business. Women. 1660-1775. *446*

—. City Government. Coalitions. Collective Bargaining. Public Employees. 1975-80. *2098*

—. Clothing industry. Dress and Waist Manufacturers' Association. Industrial Relations. International Ladies' Garment Workers' Union. Moskowitz, Belle. Protocols. 1913-16. *1227*

—. Clothing industry. Labor (protests). Women. 1831-69. *445*

—. Colombian Americans. Dominican Americans. Employment. Family. Immigrants. Women. 1981. *1666*

—. Colombian Americans. Employment. Immigrants. 1970's. *1652*

—. Community and Social Agency Employees Union (Local 1707). Nash, Al (account). Nonprofit organizations. 1958-63. *2111*

—. Discrimination. Employment. Government. LaGuardia, Fiorello. Private sector. World War II. 1941-43. *1296*

—. Economic Conditions. Employment. Immigrants. 1979-82. *1641*

—. Economic development. Unemployment. 1962-73. *1530*

—. Educational reform. Georgia (Atlanta). Illinois (Chicago). Progressivism. Teachers. 1890-1920. *243*

—. Electrical Workers, International Brotherhood of. Industry. Labor Unions and Organizations. Personal Narratives. Pessen, Edward. World War II. 1940-44. *980*

—. Employment. Hispanic Americans. Women. 1970's. *2790*

—. Employment. Italians. Jews. Women. 1880-1905. *709*

—. Employment. Public Welfare. Work Incentive Program. 1977-79. *2302*

—. Employment. Training programs. 1970-78. *1480*

—. Employment program. Youth. 1974-76. *1651*

—. Golden Hill (battle). Nassau Street Riots. Riots. 1770. *413*

—. Hentoff, Nat (account). Labor Unions and Organizations. *Village Voice* (newspaper). 1958-77. *2084*

—. High School of Fashion Industry. Minorities. Sex Discrimination. Vocational Education. Women. 1975. *2402*

—. Hospitals. Labor Unions and Organizations. Montefiore Hospital. Retail Drug Employees, Local 1199. 1948-59. *2065*

—. Ideology. Labor Unions and Organizations. *National Workman* (newspaper). 19c. *781*

—. Immigrants. Industry. Irish Americans. Labor boycotts. 1880-86. *653*

—. Immigrants. Italians. Jews, Russian. Social Mobility. 1880-1935. *194*

—. Jews. Labor Unions and Organizations. Malkiel, Theresa Serber. Socialist Party. Women. 1900's-14. *1059*

—. Jews. Social Classes. Socialism. United Hebrew Trades. 1877-1926. *774*

—. Labor Unions and Organizations. Student activism. Travel accounts. Violence. 1968-79. *1533*

—. Occupational Mobility. Pennsylvania (Philadelphia). Professionals. 1970. *1962*

—. Postal Service. Public Employees. Strikes. 1970. *2135*

—. Sex roles. Travel agency industry. 1974. *2517*

—. Standard of living. Working class. 1960's-82. *2784*

New York City (Brooklyn). Finnish Americans. Imatra I (association). Labor Unions and Organizations. 1890-1921. *277*

New York City (Harlem). Armaments Industry. Blacks. Crosswaith, Frank R. Employment. Labor Reform. Negro Labor Committee. World War II. 1939-45. *1447*

New York (Cohoes, Troy). Hirsch, Susan E. New Jersey (Newark). Walkowitz, Daniel J. Working Class (review article). 1800-84. 1978. *32*

New York (Farmingdale). Airplane Industry and Trade. Fairchild Republic (corporation). International Association of Machinists and Aerospace Workers (Lodge 1987). Labor Unions and Organizations. 1950-82. *2028*

New York (Fort Edward, Hudson Falls). General Electric Company. Labor Unions and Organizations. Occupational Hazards. Pollution. Polychlorinated biphenyl. United Electrical, Radio, and Machine Workers of America. 1975. *2037*

New York (Geneva). Apprenticeship. *People* v. *Fisher* (New York, 1832). Shoe industry. Strikes. 1825-36. *522*

New York (Katonah). Brookwood Labor College. Colleges and Universities. Labor. 1921-37. *1044*

New York (Little Falls). Immigrants. Industrial Workers of the World. Strikes. Textile Industry. Women. 1912. *1256*

—. Industrial Workers of the World. Labor Reform. Strikes. Textile Industry. Women. 1912. *1255*

New York (Long Island City). Airplane Industry and Trade. Labor Unions and Organizations. Militancy. Nash, Al (reminiscences). Political factions. World War II. 1940-44. *1209*

New York (Poughkeepsie). Blacks. Daily Life. Oral history. 1880-1980. *349*

New York (Rochester). Labor. Socialism. 1917-19. *958*

New York (Schenectady). Lunn, George. Socialist Party. Voting and Voting Behavior. Working Class. 1911-16. *1304*

New York State Factory Investigating Commission. Canning industry. Migrant Labor. Polish Americans. 1900-35. *960*

New York (Troy). Collar Laundry Union. Industrial Relations. Irish Americans. Women. 1864-69. *538*

—. Iron Industry. Social Customs. Statistics. Working Class. 1860-80. *744*

—. Ironworkers. Social Customs. Statistics. Working Class. 1860-80. *898*

New York University (Graduate School of Business Administration). Business Education. Colleges and Universities. Historians. 1977-80. *1954*

New York University (Robert F. Wagner Labor Archives, Tamiment Institute/Ben Josephson Library). Archival Catalogs and Inventories. Labor Unions and Organizations. 1906-82. *129*

New York (Yonkers). Alexander Smith and Sons Carpet Company. Rug and Carpet Industry. Strikes. Women. 1884-86. *818*

Newman, Pauline. Class consciousness. Cohn, Fannia. International Ladies' Garment Workers' Union. Pesotta, Rose. Women. 1900-35. *1185*

Newspapers *See also* Journalism; Periodicals; Press; Reporters and Reporting.

—. Berry, George L. Illinois (Chicago). Strikes. 1912-14. *1265*

—. Bibliographies. Chinese. Discrimination. Industrial Workers of the World. Knights of Labor. Labor. Washington. 1885-1919. *119*

—. Census. German Americans. Illinois (Chicago). Immigrants. Working Class. 1850-1910. *706*

—. Colorado. Professionalism. 1972. *1979*

—. Congress of Industrial Organizations. Labor Disputes. New Deal. South. 1930-39. *1082*

—. Idaho (Pocatello). Pullman Palace Car Company. Railroads. Strikes. 1894. *782*

—. Madison *Press Connection*. Strikes. Wisconsin. Worker self-management. 1978-80. *2146*

—. Russian Americans. Socialists. *Znamia*. 1889-90. *665*

Newspapers (weekly). Management. Wages. Women. 1977. *1966*

Nicholson, John. Industrial Relations. Manufacturing. Pennsylvania (Philadelphia). 1793-97. *473*

Nisei Farmers League. California (San Joaquin Valley). Farm Workers. Japanese Americans. Labor Disputes. Mexican Americans. United Farm Workers Union. 1971-77. *2072*

Nissen, Bruce. Labor Unions and Organizations. Social change. 1930-80. *1490*

Nixon administration (Pay Board). Economic Policy. Wage controls. 1940's-73. *2388*

Nixon, Richard M. (administration). Civil Service. 1969-74. *2291*

—. Economic stabilization. Phase III (1973). Wage-price controls. 1970-73. *2172*

NLRB. *See* National Labor Relations Board.

Nongovernmental organizations. American Federation of Labor. Foreign Relations. France. USA. 1945-52. *1896*

Nonpartisan League. Congress of Industrial Organizations. New Hampshire (Berlin). Political Parties. 1932-36. *1299*

—. Davis, David W. Idaho. Industrial Workers of the World. Public opinion. Red Scare. Socialist Party. 1919-26. *1053*

—. Documentaries. Films. North Dakota. *Northern Lights* (film). 1915-16. *1139*

Nonprofit organizations. Community and Social Agency Employees Union (Local 1707). Nash, Al (account). New York City. 1958-63. *2111*

Norma Rae (film). *Blue Collar* (film). Films. *F.I.S.T.* (film). Labor Unions and Organizations. 1978-79. *2159*

North. Blacks. Catholic Church. Cities. Occupations. Social Status. 1968. *1685*

—. Blacks. Cities. Domestics. Women. Working conditions. 20c. *2478*

—. Blacks. Income. Migration, Internal. 1970's. *2502*

—. Economic Conditions. Federal Regulation. Industrial Mobility. Legislation. North Central States. 1970's. *1822*

—. South. Wages. 1960-76. *2701*

North America. Agriculture. Europe. Industrialization. Market economy. Peasant movements (colloquium). ca 1875-1975. *12*

—. Europe. Migrant labor. 1945-73. *1816*

—. Great Britain (Bristol). Immigration. Indentured servants. West Indies. Working Class. 17c. *535*

—. Immigrants. Occupations. Statistics. Women. 1964-71. *2619*

North American Aviation. California (Inglewood). Communist Party. Strikes. United Automobile Workers of America. 1941. *1233*

North Carolina. Agricultural Organizations. Farmers' Alliance. ca 1888-91. *823*

—. Blacks. Children. Freedmen's Bureau. Indentured servants. Law. 1865-68. *731*

—. Blacks. Cotton. Labor Unions and Organizations. Textile Industry. Whites. 1908-74. *1747*

—. Blacks. Farmers. Knights of Labor. Race Relations. 1889. *878*

—. Immigrants. Labor scarcity. South Carolina. 1815-1925. *130*

—. Industrial Relations. J. P. Stevens & Company, Inc. 1945-81. *1711*

—. Labor market. Prisoners. Wages. Work release program. 1969-71. *2840*

—. Life insurance. Slavery. Virginia. 1840-65. *624*

North Carolina (Bertie County). Bertie Industries. Blacks. Employee-community ownership. Workers' Owned Sewing Company. 1960-80. *1735*

North Carolina Bureau of Labor Statistics. Agricultural labor. Blacks. Logan, Frenise A. Wages. Whites. 1887. *891*

North Carolina (Carrboro). Childhood. Personal narratives. Quinney, Valerie. Sex Roles. 1900-14. *1434*

North Carolina (Durham). Civil rights. Duke University Medical Center. Harvey, Oliver. Labor Unions and Organizations. 1930's-70's. *2106*

North Carolina (Gastonia). National Textile Workers Union. Strikes. Textile Industry. Weisbord, Vera Buch (reminiscence). 1929. *1272*

North Carolina (Onslow County). Secession. Slavery. Turpentine industry. 1790-1861. *546*

North Carolina (Roanoke Rapids). Amalgamated Clothing and Textile Workers Union. Boycotts. J. P. Stevens & Company, Inc. Textile Industry. 1963-77. *2061*

—. Amalgamated Clothing and Textile Workers Union. Boycotts. J. P. Stevens & Company, Inc. Textile industry. 1965-75. *2027*

North Carolina (Robeson County). Blacks. Indians. Labor Unions and Organizations. Lumbee Indians. Politics. Whites. 1970-82. *2476*

North Carolina (Salem). Attitudes. Moravians. Slavery. 1771-1851. *542*

—. Methodology. Northwest Women's History Project. Oregon (Portland). Shipbuilding. Washington (Vancouver). Women. World War II. 1940-82. *1409*

Orchards. Farmers. Industrial Workers of the World. Strikes. Washington (Yakima Valley). 1933. *1215*

Oregon *See also* Far Western States.

—. American Federation of Labor. Disque, Brice P. Federal government. Industrial Workers of the World. Lumber and Lumbering. Strikes. Washington. 1917-18. *1021*

—. Chinese. Knights of Labor. Labor Unions and Organizations. Political Protest. Unemployment. Washington. 1880's. *836*

—. Mexicans. Migrant labor. Photographs. Washington. 1943-47. *1392*

Oregon Commonwealth Federation. Depressions. Farmer-Labor Party. New Deal. Political Factions. 1933-38. *1334*

Oregon (Hood River Valley). Mexicans. Migrant Labor. Undocumented Workers. Wages. 1978. *1611*

Oregon Improvement Company. Blacks. Coal Mines and Mining. Strikebreakers. Washington (King County). 1891. *883*

Oregon (Portland). Bureau of Indian Affairs. Training programs. Vocational education. 1964-66. *2202*

—. Methodology. Northwest Women's History Project. Oral history. Shipbuilding. Washington (Vancouver). Women. World War II. 1940-82. *1409*

Oregon (Toledo). Japanese Americans. Lumber and Lumbering. Pacific Spruce Corporation. Riots. 1925-26. *1444*

Oregon (Umatilla County). Indians. Unemployment. 1970's. *1598*

O'Reilly, Leonora. Labor movement. New York. Social reform. Women's Trade Union League. 1870-1927. *783*

O'Reilly, Mary. Clothing Industry. Illinois (Chicago). Socialist Party. Strikes. Women. Zeh, Nellie M. 1910. *1115*

Organization for Economic Cooperation and Development. Code of conduct. Labor Unions and Organizations. Multinational corporations. 1966-76. *2686*

Organizational Theory *See also* Public Administration.

—. Affirmative action. Employment. Minorities. Women. 1970's. *2306*

—. Factionalism. Great Britain. Labor Unions and Organizations. USA. 20c. *139*

—. Labor force. Occupations. Social Change. 1945-79. *1505*

Organizations *See also* specific organizations by name.

—. Biklen, Sari Knapp. Brannigan, Marilyn. Employment. Forisha, Barbara L. Goldman, Barbara. Leadership. Women (review article). 1940-80. *1957*

Organized Unemployed, Inc. Depressions. Mecklenburg, George H. Minnesota (Minneapolis). Poor. Self-help. Unemployment. 1932-35. *916*

Organizing. Labor Unions and Organizations. 1972-78. *1882*

Organizing Tactics. Cloward, Richard. Labor Movement. Piven, Frances Fox. Poor. Pressure Groups. 1960-78. *1554*

OSHA. *See* Occupational Safety and Health Administration.

Overland Journeys to the Pacific. Frontier and Pioneer Life. Men. Wagon trains. Women. 1840's-50's. *433*

Overseers. Civil War. Letters. Louisiana, northeastern. Plantations. Thigpen, Henry A. 1862-65. *589*

Ownership. Coal Miners. Irish Americans. Pennsylvania. Terrorism. Working Conditions. 1850-70. *707*

Oxford Group movement. Christianity. Longshoremen. Strikes. Washington (Seattle). 1921-34. *1268*

Oxford Iron Works. Iron industry. Ross, David. Slavery, industrial. Virginia (Lynchburg). 1775-1817. *561*

P

P & Z Company. California. Elliot, Robert. Lawsuits. Occupational Safety and Health Administration. Working conditions. 1975-77. *2348*

Pacific Electric Railroad. California (Los Angeles). Mexican Americans. Strikes. 1900-03. *1277*

Pacific Northwest. American Federation of Labor. Knights of Labor. Radicals and Radicalism. Socialism. 1871-1912. *775*

—. Blacks. Immigrants. International Brotherhood of Pulp, Sulphite, and Paper Mill Workers. South. Women. 1909-40. *1281*

—. Congress of Industrial Organizations. Isolationism. Leftism. USSR. 1937-41. *1051*

—. Decisionmaking. Employee Ownership. Job satisfaction. Plywood manufacturing. 1977-79. *1661*

Pacific Spruce Corporation. Japanese Americans. Lumber and Lumbering. Oregon (Toledo). Riots. 1925-26. *1444*

Padrone system. Construction. Florida East Coast Railway. Immigrants. Italian Americans. Railroads. Recruitment. ca 1890-1901. *828*

—. Illinois (Chicago). Immigrants. *Italia* (newspaper). Letters to the editor. 1886. *720*

—. Italian Americans. Labor Unions and Organizations. Personal Narratives. Rizzo, Saverio. Triangle fire. 1900-30. *963*

Paint Creek-Cabin Creek Strike. *Socialist and Labor Star* (newspaper). Strikes. Thompson, Wyatt Hamilton. West Virginia. 1912-13. *1131*

Painting *See also* Murals.

—. Bread and Roses (project). Exhibits and Expositions. Laborer (image). National Union of Hospital and Health Care Employees (District 1199). New York City. 1980. *1555*

—. Cancer. New Jersey, northern. Radium dials. 1917-24. *990*

Palace Hotel. Babow, Irving. California (San Francisco). Personal Narratives. Working Conditions. 1925-29. *923*

Palmer, A. Mitchell. Deportation. Immigrants. Justice Department. Labor Department. Post, Louis F. Red Scare. Wilson, William B. 1919-20. *1305*

Palmer, Annie. Accidents. Coal Mines and Mining. Disaster relief. Mabey, Charles R. Social work. Utah (Castle Gate). 1924-36. *959*

Pan American Federation of Labor. Communism. Gompers, Samuel. Political Attitudes. 1920's. *1075*

—. Gompers, Samuel. Intervention. Labor Unions and Organizations. Latin America. Revolution. World War I. 1918-27. *1074*

Pan-Africanism. Africa. Industrial arts education. Racism. South. 1879-1940. *364*

Pangle, Thomas. College teachers. Tenure. Yale University. 1979-80. *1699*

Paper Industry. Fuller, Amy. Massachusetts (Berkshire County; Dalton). Occupational choice. Women. ca 1840-90. *453*

—. International Brotherhood of Pulp, Sulphite, and Paper Mill Workers. Labor Unions and Organizations. Virginia (Covington). West Virginia Pulp and Paper Company. 1933-52. *1282*

—. Massachusetts (Berkshire County). Mechanization. Women. Working conditions. 1820-55. *454*

Paper workers. American Federation of Labor. International Brotherhood of Pulp, Sulphite, and Paper Mill Workers. Labor Unions and Organizations. Militancy. 1933-35. *1280*

Parke, Thomas D. Alabama (Jefferson County; Coalburg). Blacks. Coal Miners. Convict labor. Mortality. Sloss-Sheffield coal mine. Working conditions. 1895. *745*

Parks. Leisure. Massachusetts (Worcester). Middle Classes. Working class. 1870-1910. *728*

Parochial Schools. *See* Church Schools.

Parties, Political. *See* Political Parties.

Passaic Steam Laundry. Chinese. Labor Disputes. New Jersey. Strikebreakers. 1870-95. *644*

Patent laws. Cotton scrapers. Inventions. Mississippi. Ned, slave. Slavery. Stuart, Oscar J. E. ca 1850. *575*

Paternalism. Authority. Lukens Iron Works. Pennsylvania (Coatesville). Profits. Strikes. 1886. *839*

—. Lukens Iron Works. Pennsylvania (Coatesville). Strikes. 1886. *838*

Paternalism, corporate. Company towns. Planning. Wisconsin (Kohler). 1905-70's. *1*

Patriarchy. Capitalism. Occupations. Segregation. Sex Discrimination. Women. ca 1700-1970's. *346*

Patronage. Comprehensive Employment and Training Act (US, 1973). Connecticut (New Haven). 1973-75. *2277*

Patterson, John H. National Cash Register Company. Ohio (Dayton). Physical Education and Training. Working Conditions. 1890-1915. *667*

Payroll taxes. Public welfare. Unemployment insurance. 1976. *2209*

Peace Movements *See also* Antiwar Sentiment.

—. Labor Unions and Organizations. Lanfersiek, Walter. Socialist Party. 1895-1962. *267*

Pearl button factories. Industrialization. Iowa (Muscatine). Strikes. 1911-12. *1245*

Peasant movements (colloquium). Agriculture. Europe. Industrialization. Market economy. North America. ca 1875-1975. *12*

Pedagogy. *See* Education; Teaching.

Penkower, Monty Noam (review article). Federal Writers' Project. Literature. New Deal. 1930's. 1977. *1353*

Pennsylvania *See also* Northeastern or North Atlantic States.

—. Anthracite. Child Labor. Miners. Strikes. Working conditions. ca 1880-1903. *1107*

—. Bethlehem Steel Corporation. Daily Life. Depressions. Labor Unions and Organizations. Working conditions. 1910-50's. *309*

—. Bethlehem Steel Corporation. Executive Behavior. Management, scientific. Taylor, Frederick W. 1898-1901. *721*

—. Brandywine River Valley. Delaware. Documents. DuPont, E. I. and Company. Economic growth. Industrialization. Standard of living. 1800-60. *408*

—. Cities. Economic growth. Occupational mobility. 19c. *142*

—. Civil Disturbances. Freeway blockages. Ohio. Truck driver culture. 1973. *2036*

—. Coal industry. Strikes. United Mine Workers of America. ca 1895-1925. *815*

—. Coal Miners. Irish Americans. Ownership. Terrorism. Working Conditions. 1850-70. *707*

—. Coal Miners. Social status. 1901-20. *1099*

—. Coal Miners. Strikes. United Mine Workers of America. 1922-23. *1180*

—. Coal Mines and Mining. Federal government. Roosevelt, Theodore. Strikes. 1902. *1309*

—. Coal Mines and Mining. Self-employment. 1920-44. *922*

—. Congress of Industrial Organizations. Elections (presidential). Labor Non-Partisan League. Roosevelt, Franklin D. 1936. *1362*

—. Davis, James John. Labor, Secretaries of. Political Leadership. Republican Party. 1873-1947. *1372*

—. Family. Indentured servants. Religion. Women. 18c. *518*

—. Folklore. Korson, George. Miners. 1920's-60's. *76*

—. General Electric Company. Labor Unions and Organizations. Leadership. Massachusetts. New York. Westinghouse Electric Corporation. 1933-37. *1249*

—. Homestead strike. National Guard (16th Regiment). Windsor, Fred E. 1892. *822*

—. Indentured servants. 1785-90. *527*

—. Industrial Relations. Steel industry. 1800-1959. *312*

—. Irish Americans. Labor Unions and Organizations. Molly Maguires. Myths and Symbols. Nativism. Philadelphia and Reading Railroad. Violence. 1860's-78. *1098*

—. Manufacturing. New Jersey. Sex Discrimination. Wages. 1900-50. *358*

—. Rural-Urban Studies. Social Classes. Wives. Women. 1947-71. *1673*

Pennsylvania (Allegheny-Kiskiminetas Valley). Steel Industry. Strikes. 1919. *1200*

Pennsylvania (Berks County; Joanna Furnace). Iron Industry. Women. 1881-1925. *200*

Pennsylvania (Carbondale, Scranton). Machinists. Powderly, Terence V. Working Class. 1866-77. *742*

Pennsylvania (Coatesville). Authority. Lukens Iron Works. Paternalism. Profits. Strikes. 1886. *839*

—. Lukens Iron Works. Paternalism. Strikes. 1886. *838*

Pennsylvania (Cornwall). Attitudes. Working Class. 1900-20. *975*

Pennsylvania (Daisytown). Coal Mines and Mining. Economic Conditions. Ethnic Groups. Social Mobility. 1910-40. *924*

Pennsylvania (Ellsworth). Coal Miners. Ellsworth, James William. Industrial Relations. Strikes. 1900-06. *1174*

Pennsylvania (Forest, Warren counties). Drivers. Horses. Lumber and Lumbering. Personal narratives. Wheeler and Dusenberry Lumber Company. 1885-1930. *195*

Pennsylvania (Germantown). Artisans. Economic conditions. Industrialization. Occupational structure. Production networks. 1767-91. *540*

Pennsylvania (Homestead). Amalgamated Association of Iron and Steel Workers. Carnegie Steel Company. Republicanism. Steel Industry. Strikes. 1892. *832*

—. Catholic Church. Church Schools. Teacher Training. 1888-1921. *178*

Pennsylvania (Hopewell Village). Industrial relations. Iron furnace. 1800-50. *488*

Pennsylvania Hospital Training School for Nurses. Medical Education. Nurses and Nursing. Walker, Lucy. 1895-1907. *241*

Pennsylvania (Lancaster). Artisans. New Jersey (Newark). 1820-80. *539*

—. Arts and Crafts. 18c. *447*

Pennsylvania (Lancaster County). Amish, Old Order. Occupations. Social change. 1970's. *1727*

—. Iron industry. 1850-1900. *658*

—. Iron industry. Protectionism. Strikes. Wages. 1840-1900. *300*

Pennsylvania (McKees Rocks, Pittsburgh). Cigar industry. Industrial Workers of the World. Pressed Steel Car Company. Steel Industry. Strikes. 1909-13. *1194*

Pennsylvania (New Kensington). Aluminum Company of America. Aluminum Workers' Union. Labor Unions and Organizations. 1900-71. *305*

Pennsylvania (Philadelphia). 1730-1820. *471*

—. Arts and Crafts. 1820-50. *521*

—. Blacks. Capitalism. Households. Income. Labor history. South Africa. Steel Industry. 19c-20c. *138*

—. Blacks. Communist Party. Discrimination. Fair Employment Practices Commission. Labor Unions and Organizations. New York City. Transport Workers Union. 1934-44. *1420*

—. Burgess, Ernest W. Central Business District. Housing. Models. Occupations. 1920-60. *62*

—. Census. Public Schools. Teachers. 1865-90. *686*

—. Centennial Exposition of 1876. France. Labor delegation. 1876. *688*

—. Children. Cities. Family. Income. 1880. *693*

—. Cost of living. Employment. Ethnic Groups. Income. Poverty. 1880. *889*

—. Delaware (Kent County). Literature. Political history. Quantitative Methods. Race. Social Classes. 1760-1830. 1979. *441*

—. Employment. Ethnic Groups. Immigrants. 1900-35. *973*

—. Ethnic groups. Immigrants. Industry. Job status. 1850-80. *102*

—. Ethnic Groups. Women. Working Class. 1910-30. *1412*

—. Franklin, Benjamin. International Typographical Union. Printing. Strikes. Wages. 1754-1852. *531*

—. Hat industry. Industrial Relations. Milliners. Stetson Company. 1870-1929. *44*

—. Income. Occupations (hierarchy). Social Change. 1789-1969. *134*

—. Indentured servants. 1745-1800. *532*

—. Indentured servants. Marketing. 1771-73. *514*

—. Indentured servants. Women. 1769-1800. *472*

—. Industrial Relations. Manufacturing. Nicholson, John. 1793-97. *473*

—. Industrialization. Textile Industry. Working Conditions. 1787-1820. *474*

—. Laurie, Bruce. Working Class (review article). 1800-50. 1980. *457*

—. New York City. Occupational Mobility. Professionals. 1970. *1962*

—. Occupations. Sociology. Working Class. 1754-1800. *478*

—. Philadelphia Federation of Teachers. Strikes. 1973. *2166*

—. Pilots, Ship. Strikes. Wages. 1792. *449*

—. Slavery. 1684-1775. *613*

—. Standard of living. Working class. 1780's-90's. *896*

Pennsylvania (Pittsburgh). Amalgamated Association of Iron and Steel Workers. Carnegie Steel Company. Fitch, John A. (report). Homestead Strike. Steel industry. Strikes. 1892-1909. *787*

—. Attitudes. Blind. Education. Employment. Workshop for the Blind. 19c-1939. *911*

—. Attitudes. Death and Dying. Working class. 1890's. *710*

—. Blacks. City Life. Migration. Occupations. Polish Americans. 1900-30. *1382*

—. Blacks. Iron Industry. Migration, internal. Steel Industry. 1916-30. *952*

—. Depressions. Labor market. Wages. 1908. *1459*

—. Ethnic groups. Occupational mobility. Residential patterns. 1880-1920. *249*

—. Greenback Labor Party. Monetary Systems. Political Protest. Railroads. Strikes. 1877. *849*

—. Industry. Skills. Wage differentials. 1889-1914. *1458*

—. Jews. Working Class. 1890-1930. *228*

—. Social Change. Technology. Women. Working class. 1870-1900. *711*

—. Social Conditions. Technology. Women. Working class. 1870-1900. *712*

—. Steel Industry. Strikes. 1919. *1097*

Pennsylvania (Reading). Blacks. Immigrants. Iron Industry. Recruitment. Robesonia Iron Company. 1915-23. *928*

Pennsylvania (Scranton). Coal Miners. Ethnic Groups. Industrialization. Urbanization. Working Class. 1855-85. *743*

Pennsylvania State University (Pennsylvania Historical Collections and Labor Archives). Archival Catalogs and Inventories. Labor Unions and Organizations. 1982. *68*

Pennsylvania (Steelton). Blacks. Immigration, new. Occupational mobility. 1880-1920. *156*

Pennsylvania, western. Blacks. National Miners Union. United Mine Workers of America. 1925-31. *1429*

—. Coal Miners. Diaries. Medrick, George. Strikes. United Mine Workers of America. 1927. *1146*

—. Folklore. Joe Magarac (mythical character). Slavs. Steelworkers. Surnames. 19c-1970's. *308*

Pension funds. Corporations. Labor. 1970's. *2746*

—. Drucker, Peter F. (review article). Socialism. 1949-70's. *88*

Pension plans. Cost of living. 1970-74. *2702*

Pensions *See also* Aged.

—. Aged. Economic Structure. Employment. Men. Western Nations. 1950-75. *1764*

—. Bureaucracies. Civil Service. Federal Government. Legislation. Retirement. 1897-1920. *1308*

—. Carnegie, Andrew. Higher education. Retirement. 1901-18. *1087*

—. Disability. Private sector. Retirement. 1980. *2607*

—. Educational programs. Retirement. 1964-74. *1759*

—. Employee Retirement Income Security Act (US, 1974). Reform. 1940's-74. *2374*

—. Employment Retirement Income Security Act (US, 1974). 1974. *2257*

—. Federal government. Local Government. Public Employees. 1977. *1946*

—. Income. Private Sector. 1974-78. *1806*

—. Labor. 1965-80. *2331*

—. Local government. Public employees. State Government. 1982. *2280*

—. Massachusetts. Social workers. 1920's. *1088*

—. Social Policy. State Government. Teachers. 1891-1930. *322*

Pensions (multiemployer). Collective bargaining. 1950-73. *2642*

Peonage. Blacks. South. 1903-25. *1386*

—. Florida. Forests and Forestry. Labor, forced. 1870's-1950. *229*

Peonage, legal. South Carolina. 1880-1907. *684*

People v. Fisher (New York, 1832). Apprenticeship. New York (Geneva). Shoe industry. Strikes. 1825-36. *522*

People's Institute of Applied Religion. Labor Unions and Organizations. Religious leaders. South. Williams, Claude. Williams, Joyce. 1940-75. *290*

People's Party. Butler, Benjamin F. (papers). Elections (presidential). Third Parties. 1884. *857*

Perez family. Blacks. Bossism. Fishermen and Concerned Citizens Association. Louisiana (Plaquemines Parish). Pressure Groups. Social reform. 1979-82. *2042*

Perez, Louis A., Jr. (reminiscences). Cubans. Florida (Tampa). Labor Disputes. *Lector* (reader). function. Tobacco workers. ca 1925-35. *979*

Periodicals *See also* Newspapers; Press.

—. Constitutions. Editorials. Labor unions and organizations. New Deal. Supreme Court. 1935-37. *1302*

—. *Fortune.* Leisure. 1957-79. *1716*

—. Immigration. Industrialization. Morality. Muckraking. 1900-09. *983*

—. Massachusetts (Lowell). Mills. *The Operatives' Magazine.* Women. 1841-45. *419*

—. Rhode Island (Saylesville). Sayles Finishing Plants. Social Organization. Textile Industry. 1920's-30's. *1138*

Perkins, Frances. Blacks. Labor Department. New Deal. 1933-45. *1310*

—. Consumers League of New York. Lobbying. New York (Albany). State Legislatures. 1911. *1335*

—. Foreign Policy. International Labor Organization. Isolationism. New Deal. Roosevelt, Franklin D. 1921-34. *1346*

—. Labor Department (Bureau of Labor Statistics). Lubin, Isador. New Deal. Statistics. Unemployment. 1920-49. *1452*

Perlman, Selig. Brody, David. Commons, John R. Dawley, Alan. Historians. Labor history. Montgomery, David. 1910-80. *115*

Perlman, Selig *(Theory of the Labor Movement).* History Teaching. Labor history. Working class. 1928-78. *48*

Personal Narratives. Babow, Irving. California (San Francisco). Palace Hotel. Working Conditions. 1925-29. *923*

—. Blacks. Johnson, D. W. Migration, Internal. Recruitment. 1917-22. *1403*

—. Blacks. Johnson, Henry. Labor Unions and Organizations. Politics. 1900-37. *1384*

—. California (San Francisco). General strikes. Photographs. 1934. *1122*

—. Childhood. North Carolina (Carrboro). Quinney, Valerie. Sex Roles. 1900-14. *1434*

—. Clothing industry. Missouri (St. Louis). Photographic essays. Strikes. Women. ca 1930-39. *1390*

—. Construction. Frontier and Pioneer Life. Oklahoma (Muskogee, Tahlequah). Vogel, Henry. 1887-1900. *671*

—. Defense industries. Industry. Labor Unions and Organizations. World War II. 1930-47. *918*

—. Drivers. Horses. Lumber and Lumbering. Pennsylvania (Forest, Warren counties). Wheeler and Dusenberry Lumber Company. 1885-1930. *195*

—. Electrical Workers, International Brotherhood of. Industry. Labor Unions and Organizations. New York City. Pessen, Edward. World War II. 1940-44. *980*

—. Italian Americans. Labor Unions and Organizations. Padrone system. Rizzo, Saverio. Triangle fire. 1900-30. *963*

—. J. P. Stevens & Company, Inc. Rogers, Ray. Strikes. 1976. *2162*

—. Jones, Mary Harris. McDonald, Duncan. 1830-1930. 1936. *314*

—. Labor. Montana. Railroads. 1910-50. *971*

Personal narratives (review article). Banks, Ann. Working class. 1925-40. *1349*

Personnel. Labor Unions and Organizations. Recruitment. 1970-81. *1897*

Personnel policies *See also* Specific kinds of policies, e.g., Dismissals; Hiring; Promotions; Recruitment.

—. Alcoholism. Equal Opportunity. Federal Government. Labor Unions and Organizations. Public Employees. 1971-77. *2035*

Personnel records. Attitudes. Employees. Privacy, right to. 1978. *1849*

Pesotta, Rose. Class consciousness. Cohn, Fannia. International Ladies' Garment Workers' Union. Newman, Pauline. Women. 1900-35. *1185*

Pessen, Edward. Electrical Workers, International Brotherhood of. Industry. Labor Unions and Organizations. New York City. Personal Narratives. World War II. 1940-44. *980*

Petrillo, James Caesar. American Federation of Musicians. Musicians. Strikes. 1942-44. *1100*

Petroleum. *See* specific terms beginning with "Oil."

Pfeffer, Richard M. Burawoy, Michael. Canada. Capitalism. Edwards, Richard. USA. Working Class (review article). Zimbalist, Andrew. 1945-70's. *1497*

Pharmacists. Labor Unions and Organizations. Mandabach, Peter A. National Association of Drug Clerks. 1910-34. *1252*

Phase II (1971). Industrial relations. Wage controls. 1971. *2735*

Phase III (1973). Economic stabilization. Nixon, Richard M. (administration). Wage-price controls. 1970-73. *2172*

Philadelphia and Reading Railroad. Irish Americans. Labor Unions and Organizations. Molly Maguires. Myths and Symbols. Nativism. Pennsylvania. Violence. 1860's-78. *1098*

Philadelphia Federation of Teachers. Pennsylvania (Philadelphia). Strikes. 1973. *2166*

Philanthropy. Blacks. Economic Conditions. Income. 1944-74. *1616*

—. California (Santa Barbara). Fleischmann, Max. Relief work. Unemployment. 1930-32. *1342*

Philippines. Brain drain. Immigration. USA. 1962-70. *1996*

Phillips curve. Business Cycles. Economic Policy. Inflation. Prices. Wages. 1890-1976. *402*

—. Labor markets, local. Unemployment. Wages. 1973. *2706*

Phillips, Ulrich Bonnell. Archives, local. Economic History. Historiography. Slave prices. Texas (Harrison County). 1849-60. *552*

Photographic essays. Clothing industry. Missouri (St. Louis). Personal narratives. Strikes. Women. ca 1930-39. *1390*

Photographs. Agricultural Labor. California (Wheatland). Riots. 1913. *1261*

—. California (San Francisco). General strikes. Personal narratives. 1934. *1122*

—. Child labor. Curricula. High Schools. Labor reform. ca 1908. *920*

—. Domesticity. Iowa. Women. ca 1890-1910. *150*

—. Employment. Women. 20c. *191*

—. Mexicans. Migrant labor. Oregon. Washington. 1943-47. *1392*

Photography *See also* Films.

—. Occupations. Rhode Island. Women. 1880-1925. *162*

Physical Education and Training *See also* Sports.

—. National Cash Register Company. Ohio (Dayton). Patterson, John H. Working Conditions. 1890-1915. *667*

Physicians. Bibliographies. Chaff, Sandra L. Walsh, Mary Roth. Women. 1835-1977. *350*

—. Medical education. Preston, Ann. Women. 1813-72. *435*

Piedmont Plateau. Industrial Location. Labor. Textile Industry. 1880-1900. *748*

—. Labor Unions and Organizations. Textile industry. 1901-32. *1217*

Pigou, A. C. Econometrics. Economic theory. Exploitation. 1930-65. *395*

Pilots, Ship. Pennsylvania (Philadelphia). Strikes. Wages. 1792. *449*

Pinchot, Gifford. Coal Miners. Strikes. United Mine Workers of America. 1925-26. *1179*

Pine industry. Blacks. Industrial Relations. Migration, Internal. South. Working conditions. ca 1912-26. *900*

Pineville *Sun* (newspaper). Coal Miners. Editors and Editing. Evans, Herndon J. Kentucky (Harlan County). Strikes. 1929-32. *1264*

Pittsburgh Courier-Journal. Baseball. Blacks. Discrimination. Editors and Editing. Smith, Wendell. 1933-45. *1448*

Piven, Frances Fox. Cloward, Richard. Labor Movement. Organizing Tactics. Poor. Pressure Groups. 1960-78. *1554*

Pizza. Business. Connecticut. Ethnic groups. Greek Americans. Occupations. 1900-75. *1719*

Planning *See also* City Planning; Economic Planning; Urbanization.

—. American Planning Association. Women. 1950-79. *2499*

—. College teachers. Educational Administration. 1982. *2016*

—. Company towns. Paternalism, corporate. Wisconsin (Kohler). 1905-70's. *1*

Planning (national). Conyers, John, Jr. (views). Economic Conditions. Employment, full. 1977. *2204*

Plantations. Alabama. Freedmen. Sharecropping (origins). 1865-67. *596*

—. Civil War. Letters. Louisiana, northeastern. Overseers. Thigpen, Henry A. 1862-65. *589*

—. Cotton. Great Britain. Slavery. South. 17c-19c. *593*

—. Freedmen. Labor. Motte, J. Rhett. Reconstruction. Share wages. South Carolina (St. John's Parish). 1867. *882*

—. Georgia. Rice. Slaves. 1820-80. *543*

Plantations (rice, sugar). Louisiana. Medical care. Slaves. South Carolina. 1810-60. *637*

Planter class. Blacks. Durnford, Andrew. Louisiana (Plaquemines Parish). 1820-60. *620*

Planters. Contracts. Freedmen's Bureau. Sharecropping. South. 1865-68. *732*

Plastics industry. Productivity. 1972-81. *2843*

Plumb, Glenn Edward. Labor Unions and Organizations. Nationalization. Railroads. 1917-20. *1192*

Plywood manufacturing. Decisionmaking. Employee Ownership. Job satisfaction. Pacific Northwest. 1977-79. *1661*

Poale Zion. Labor Unions and Organizations. Zeire Zion. Zionism. 1920's. *1023*

Poetry. Editorials. *Miners' Magazine*. Songs. Western Federation of Miners. 1900-07. *1283*

Poland. Immigration. Polish Americans. Socialists. 1883-1914. *177*

Poles. Contract labor. Hawaii. Working Conditions. 1896-99. *689*

Police *See also* Crime and Criminals; Law Enforcement; Prisons.

—. American Federation of Labor. Armies. Streetcars. Strikes. Tennessee (Knoxville). 1919-20. *1118*

—. Collective bargaining. Fire fighters. Impasse procedures. Models. New York. 1968-76. *2095*

—. Illinois (Chicago). Militia. Riots. Strikes. 1877. *833*

—. Iron Industry. Maryland (Baltimore County). Northampton Iron Works. Values. 1780-1820. *537*

—. Labor Disputes. Social Democratic Party. Wisconsin (Milwaukee). Working class. 1900-15. *1312*

—. Missouri (St. Louis). Promotions. 1899-1975. *248*

—. Women. 1905-75. *247*

Police reports. Industrialists. New York (Buffalo). Research sources. Strikes. 1890-1913. *853*

Polish Americans. Acculturation. Immigration. 1860-1960. *175*

—. Americanization. Indiana (Gary). Labor Unions and Organizations. US Steel Corporation. 1906-20. *925*

—. Blacks. City Life. Migration. Occupations. Pennsylvania (Pittsburgh). 1900-30. *1382*

—. Blacks. Employment. Illinois (Chicago). Industry. Stereotypes. Violence. 1890-1919. *359*

—. Bohemian Americans. British Americans. Cleveland Rolling Mill Company. Human Relations. Ohio. Strikes. 1882-85. *874*

—. Canning industry. Migrant Labor. New York State Factory Investigating Commission. 1900-35. *960*

—. Education. Family. Income. Occupations. 1969-70. *2860*

—. Everett Mill. Massachusetts (Lawrence). Radicals and Radicalism. Strikes. Textile Industry. Women. 1912. *1219*

—. Immigrants. Labor Unions and Organizations. Press. Silesia. 1880-99. *661*

—. Immigration. Poland. Socialists. 1883-1914. *177*

—. Krzycki, Leo. Labor Unions and Organizations. Radicals and Radicalism. Socialist Party. 1900's-66. *281*

—. New Jersey (Bayonne). Standard Oil Company of New Jersey. Strikes. 1915-16. *1137*

Political Action Committees. AFL-CIO (Committee on Political Education). South. 1943-75. *1914*

Political activism. Depressions. Liberalism. New Deal. Socialist Party. Unemployment. 1929-36. *1354*

—. Labor Unions and Organizations. 1950's-82. *1902*

Political analysis. Industrial relations. Public Policy. 1950-75. *2279*

Political Attitudes. Communism. Gompers, Samuel. Pan American Federation of Labor. 1920's. *1075*

—. Communist Party. Vietnam War. Working class. Working Conditions. ca 1960-74. *1768*

—. Labor Unions and Organizations. Racism. Working class. 1830-1972. *2437*

Political Campaigns (presidential). California (San Francisco). Hughes, Charles Evans. Labor. Republican Party. 1916. *1327*

Political change. Civil service. 19c-20c. *329*

—. Class conflict. Vermont (Rutland). Working Class. 1880-96. *650*

—. Great Britain. Labor Unions and Organizations. Socialism. USA. World War I. 1914-25. *1070*

—. Illinois (Belleville). Labor Unions and Organizations. Trades and Labor Assembly. 1902-18. *1072*

Political Corruption *See also* Elections; Lobbying; Political Reform.

—. Coal Miners. Kentucky (Harlan, Bell counties). Labor Disputes. 1920-39. *1121*

Political Economy *See also* Economics.

—. George, Henry (*Progress and Poverty*). Land. Monopolies. Taxation. Working class. 1858-94. *664*

Political Factions *See also* Interest Groups; Lobbying.

—. Airplane Industry and Trade. Labor Unions and Organizations. Militancy. Nash, Al (reminiscences). New York (Long Island City). World War II. 1940-44. *1209*

—. Depressions. Farmer-Labor Party. New Deal. Oregon Commonwealth Federation. 1933-38. *1334*

Political history. Delaware (Kent County). Literature. Pennsylvania (Philadelphia). Quantitative Methods. Race. Social Classes. 1760-1830. 1979. *441*

Political Imprisonment. Cuba. Education. Occupations. Refugees. 1973-80. *1564*

Political Leadership. Bossism. Labor Unions and Organizations. O'Connor, Edwin (*The Last Hurrah*). 1956. *1898*

—. Capitalism. Working class. 1890-1976. *238*

—. Davis, James John. Labor, Secretaries of. Pennsylvania. Republican Party. 1873-1947. *1372*

—. Labor Unions and Organizations. New York. Shanker, Albert. Teachers. 1978. *2005*

Political Participation. Acocella, Giuseppe (review article). France. Germany. Labor Unions and Organizations. 1920-78. *260*

—. American Revolution. 1760's-80's. *507*

—. American Revolution. Social Conditions. 1760-80. *492*

—. Decisionmaking. Labor Unions and Organizations. Ohio (Toledo). United Automobile Workers of America. 1967. *2038*

—. Elites. Farm Workers. Labor Disputes. 1946-72. *2091*

—. Employment. Social status. Women. 1956-76. *2515*

—. Labor Unions and Organizations. Leftism. 1970's. *1909*

Political Parties *See also* names of political parties, e.g., Democratic Party, Republican Party, etc.; Campaign Finance; Elections; Political Campaigns; Third Parties.

—. AFL-CIO. Interest groups. 1970's. *1901*

—. Congress of Industrial Organizations. New Hampshire (Berlin). Nonpartisan League. 1932-36. *1299*

—. Elections (municipal). Knights of Labor. Reform. Virginia (Lynchburg). Working Class. 1881-90. *862*

Political parties, incumbent. Unemployment. Voting and Voting Behavior. 1974-76. *1733*

Political power. Affirmative Action. Blacks. Cities. Civil service. Employment. 1970-78. *1950*

Political program. Class struggle. Reform. Standard of living. Working class. 1950's-73. *1471*

Political Protest *See also* Civil Disturbances; Demonstrations; Revolution; Riots; Youth Movements.

—. Beatty, James H. Coxey, Jacob S. Idaho. Trials. 1894. *835*

—. Blacks. Human rights. Labor Disputes. 1960's-70's. *2475*

—. Blacks. Journalism. Labor Unions and Organizations. Marxism. Randolph, A. Philip. ca 1911-75. *106*

—. Chinese. Knights of Labor. Labor Unions and Organizations. Oregon. Unemployment. Washington. 1880's. *836*

—. Coxey's Army. Missouri River. Montana. Unemployment. 1894. *834*

—. Freedom of Speech. Industrial Workers of the World. Pratt, N. S. Washington (Spokane). 1909-10. *1113*

—. Greenback Labor Party. Monetary Systems. Pennsylvania (Pittsburgh). Railroads. Strikes. 1877. *849*

Political Reform *See also* names of reform movements, e.g. Progressivism, etc.; Lobbying; Political Corruption.

—. Arbitration. Public Employees. Strikes. 1968-75. *2267*

—. Blacks. City Politics. Elections, municipal. Knights of Labor. Virginia (Richmond). 1886-88. *869*

Political representation. Labor Non-Partisan
League. Legislation. Working conditions.
1936-38. *1365*

Political Repression. Freedom of speech.
Oklahoma. Vigilantes. World War I. 1914-17.
1303

Political Science *See also* Democracy; Government;
Imperialism; Law; Legislation; Politics; Public
Administration; Revolution; Utopias.

—. Degrees, Academic. Employment. 1950-80.
1947

Political Speeches. Marx, Eleanor. Rhode Island
(Providence). Socialism. 1886. *805*

Political Stratification. Self-employment. Social
Status. Working Class. 1968-73. *1484*

Politicians. Capitalism. Economic Policy.
Kentucky. Labor policies. 1787-1890's. *10*

Politicization. Automobile Industry and Trade.
Industrialization. Labor Unions and
Organizations. USA. 1960's-74. *1637*

Politics *See also* headings beginning with the word
political; City Politics; Elections; Government;
Intergovernmental Relations; Legislative Bodies;
Lobbying; Local Politics; Presidents; State
Politics.

—. *Abood v. Detroit Board of Education* (US,
1977). Agency shop fees. Collective Bargaining.
Public Employees. 1977-80. *2126*

—. Agricultural Labor Relations Act (1975).
California. Collective bargaining. 1975-77. *2333*

—. Alabama. Blacks. Labor Union of Alabama.
National Negro Labor Union. Rapier, James
T. Reconstruction. 1837-75. *880*

—. American Federation of State, County, and
Municipal Employees. Civil Service Employees
Association. Economic Conditions. Public
Employees. 1978-79. *1908*

—. Appointments to office. National Labor
Relations Board. Unfair Labor Practices.
1954-77. *2205*

—. Automobile Industry and Trade. Indiana. New
Deal. Ohio. United Automobile Workers of
America. 1935-40. *1331*

—. Bicentennial celebrations. Communist Party.
Economic Conditions. Labor Unions and
Organizations. 1976-77. *1910*

—. Blacks. Indians. Labor Unions and
Organizations. Lumbee Indians. North Carolina
(Robeson County). Whites. 1970-82. *2476*

—. Blacks. Johnson, Henry. Labor Unions and
Organizations. Personal Narratives. 1900-37.
1384

—. Child care. Public Welfare. 1940-45. *1301*

—. Cities. Employment. Public Policy. Social
Conditions. 1966-70. *2173*

—. Civil Rights Act (US, 1964; Title VII,
amended 1972). Congress. Discrimination.
Employment. Equal opportunity. 1942-72. *2422*

—. Communist Party. Gordon, Max (account).
Labor Party. Popular Front. ca 1930-39. *1376*

—. Comprehensive Employment and Training Act
(US, 1973). Public Welfare. Youth. 1977-79.
2335

—. Depressions. Federal Theatre Project.
Flanagan, Hallie. Hopkins, Harry L. Theater.
Works Progress Administration. 1935-39. *1295*

—. Economic conditions. Edwards, P. K. Snyder,
David. Strikes. 1900-48. *1254*

—. Economic Conditions. Employment, full.
Federal Policy. 1978. *2230*

—. Ethnicity. Missouri (St. Louis). Socialist Labor
Party. Working class. 1876-81. *858*

—. Farmers. France. Germany. Social History
(review article). White Collar Workers.
1890-20c. *89*

—. Farmers (multiple jobholding). National
Farmers Organization. New York. 1960's.
1979. *2194*

—. Gaventa, John. Macintyre, Stuart. Radicals
and Radicalism (review article). Working
Class. ca 1880-1940. *93*

—. Industrial Relations. Knights of Labor. Rhode
Island. 1880's. *753*

—. Industrialization. New England. Working Class
(review article). 1780-1950. *82*

—. Judges. Lawyers. Sex Discrimination. Women.
1970's. *2578*

—. Labor. 1945-79. *2346*

—. Labor movement. Northeastern or North
Atlantic States. 1881-94. *752*

—. Labor Unions and Organizations. Mooney,
Tom. Socialism. 1917-42. *1055*

—. Reform (review article). 1890-1930. *333*

—. Working Class. 19c-20c. *105*

Polls. *See* Social Surveys.

Pollution. General Electric Company. Labor
Unions and Organizations. New York (Fort
Edward, Hudson Falls). Occupational Hazards.
Polychlorinated biphenyl. United Electrical,
Radio, and Machine Workers of America.
1975. *2037*

Polychlorinated biphenyl. General Electric
Company. Labor Unions and Organizations.
New York (Fort Edward, Hudson Falls).
Occupational Hazards. Pollution. United
Electrical, Radio, and Machine Workers of
America. 1975. *2037*

Poor *See also* Poverty.

—. Alabama. Whites. 1870-1950. *687*

—. Attitudes. Depressions. Great Britain. Law.
USA. Vagrancy. 14c-1939. *939*

—. Blacks. Labor Market. Working class. 1975-80.
1732

—. Cloward, Richard. Labor Movement.
Organizing Tactics. Piven, Frances Fox.
Pressure Groups. 1960-78. *1554*

—. Depressions. Mecklenburg, George H.
Minnesota (Minneapolis). Organized
Unemployed, Inc. Self-help. Unemployment.
1932-35. *916*

—. Employment initiatives. Federal Programs.
Youth Employment and Demonstration
Projects Act (US, 1977). 1977-80. *2249*

—. Minimum wage. Public welfare. 1950-76. *2719*

Popular Front. Communist Party. Gordon, Max
(account). Labor Party. Politics. ca 1930-39.
1376

Population *See also* names of ethnic or racial
groups, e.g., Jews, Blacks, etc.; Aged; Birth
Rate; Census; Demography; Fertility;
Migration, Internal; Mortality.

—. Blacks. Chesapeake Bay area. Immigration.
1619-1712. *410*

—. Capitalism. Dublin, Thomas. Family. Great
Britain. Levine, David. Massachusetts (Lowell).
Working Class (review article). 1550-1869. *444*

—. Construction. Irish Americans. Massachusetts.
Railroads. Towns. Western Railroad. 1833-42.
465

—. Economic Conditions. Social Organization.
Suburban Life. 1970's. *1538*

—. Economic Growth. Labor force. New England.
17c. *479*

—. Economic theory. Employment. 1930's-70's.
404

—. Employment. 1970-79. *1832*

—. Employment. Rural areas. 1962-67. *2608*

—. Ethnic Groups. New Mexico. Occupations.
Social Organization. 1790. *481*

—. Legislation. Unemployment. 1959-79. *2662*

Population distribution. Labor Department (Bureau
of Labor Statistics; projections). Labor force.
1960-72. 1908-85. *2712*

Populism. Agrarians. Radicals and Radicalism.
Wisconsin. Working class. 19c. *864*

—. Judicial Administration. Labor. Supreme
Courts, State. Western States. 1893-1902. *856*

Porter, William Sydney. *See* Henry, O.

Ports. American Seamen's Friend Society.
Merchant Marine. Protestantism. 1828-38. *504*

—. California (San Francisco). General strikes.
National Guard. 1934. *1172*

Post, Charles William. Labor Disputes. Michigan
(Battle Creek). Open shop movement.
1895-1920. *1057*

Post, Louis F. Deportation. Immigrants. Justice
Department. Labor Department. Palmer, A.
Mitchell. Red Scare. Wilson, William B.
1919-20. *1305*

Postal Reorganization Act (1970). Arbitration.
Labor Disputes. Postal Service. 1970-74. *2077*

Postal Service. Arbitration. Labor Disputes. Postal
Reorganization Act (1970). 1970-74. *2077*

—. Labor Unions and Organizations. Management.
Mechanization. Technology. 1970's. *1777*

—. New York City. Public Employees. Strikes.
1970. *2135*

Pottawatomi Indians. Baptists. Indians. Kansas.
Lykins, Johnston. Pottawatomie Baptist
Manual Labor Training School. 1846-67. *11*

Pottawatomie Baptist Manual Labor Training
School. Baptists. Indians. Kansas. Lykins,
Johnston. Pottawatomi Indians. 1846-67. *11*

Potters. National Brotherhood of Operative
Potters. Strikes. Tariff. 1894. *837*

Poverty *See also* Economic Conditions; Poor;
Public Welfare.

—. Abolition Movement. Attitudes. Competition.
Economic Structure. Evangelism. ca 1830-60.
579

—. Cost of living. Employment. Ethnic Groups.
Income. Pennsylvania (Philadelphia). 1880. *889*

—. Discrimination. Education (influence of).
Employment. Employment. Income. 1960's.
2687

—. Economic Theory. Garraty, John A. (review
article). Intellectuals. Public Policy.
Unemployment. 17c-1978. *107*

—. Employment. Income (redistribution).
Minimum wage. Minorities. 1972-73. *2668*

—. Employment. Linen. Massachusetts (Boston).
Textile Industry. United Society for
Manufactures and Importation. Women.
1735-60. *459*

—. Family. Household heads. Income. Women.
1970-77. *2489*

—. Family. Massachusetts (Lynn). Methodology.
Working Class. 1915-40. *940*

—. Household heads. Labor market. Sex
discrimination. Women. ca 1950-70's. *2549*

—. Landlords and Tenants. Maryland. Social
Conditions. Stiverson, Gregory A. (review
article). 18c. 1978. *534*

—. Mexican Americans. Texas (El Paso). Women.
1880-1920. *167*

—. National Advisory Council on Economic
Opportunity (12th report). Social problems.
Unemployment. 1960-80. *2850*

—. Recessions. Unemployment. 1959-75. *2669*

Powderly, Terence V. Knights of Labor.
Temperance Movements. 1878-93. *776*

—. Machinists. Pennsylvania (Carbondale,
Scranton). Working Class. 1866-77. *742*

Power (abuses of). Labor Unions and
Organizations. Lewis, John L. United Mine
Workers of America. 1880-1972. *1029*

Prairie States. *See* individual states by name;
Great Plains; Midwest.

Pratt, Daniel. Alabama. Mims, Shadrach (letter).
Textile Industry. Williams, Price. Working
Conditions. 1854. *455*

Pratt, N. S. Freedom of Speech. Industrial
Workers of the World. Political Protest.
Washington (Spokane). 1909-10. *1113*

Pregnancy Discrimination Act (US, 1978).
Employment. Sex discrimination. 1908-78. *348*

Presbyterian Church. Labor. Sermons. Sunday,
William Ashley ("Billy"). Virtue. Women.
1915. *970*

Prescott, Charles (account). Massachusetts.
Montana. Railroads. 1873-1932. *182*

Preservation. California. Lundeberg, Harry. San
Francisco Maritime Museum. Ships. 1945-55.
98

Presidents *See also* names of individual presidents.

—. Advisory committees. Industrial Relations.
1955-80. *2317*

—. Appointments to office. Confirmation. National
Labor Relations Board. Senate. 1935-78. *316*

—. *Economic Report of the President.*
Employment. Full Employment and Balanced
Growth Act (US, 1978). Prices. 1974-81. *2201*

President's Commission for a National Agenda for
the Eighties *(Urban America in the Eighties).*
Cities. Domestic Policy. Unemployment.
1970-80. *2281*

President's Commission on Migratory Labor.
Agriculture. Bracero program. Mexico.
Truman, Harry S. Undocumented workers.
1950. *2286*

Press *See also* Journalism; Newspapers; Periodicals;
Reporters and Reporting.

—. Immigrants. Labor Unions and Organizations.
Polish Americans. Silesia. 1880-99. *661*

—. Labor disputes. Norway. Thrane, Marcus.
USA. 1886-94. *777*

Pressed Steel Car Company. Cigar industry.
Industrial Workers of the World. Pennsylvania
(McKees Rocks, Pittsburgh). Steel Industry.
Strikes. 1909-13. *1194*

Pressure Groups *See also* Interest Groups.

—. Blacks. Bossism. Fishermen and Concerned
Citizens Association. Louisiana (Plaquemines
Parish). Perez family. Social reform. 1979-82.
2042

—. Cloward, Richard. Labor Movement.
Organizing Tactics. Piven, Frances Fox. Poor.
1960-78. *1554*

—. Industrial safety. Occupational Safety and
Health Act (US, 1970). 1970. *2214*

—. Public Employees. Public Policy. 1978. *2289*

Prestige. Attitudes. Occupations. Sex roles. 1970.
2415

Preston, Ann. Medical education. Physicians.
Women. 1813-72. *435*

Psychologists for Social Action. American Psychological Association. Equal opportunity. Lancaster Press. Racism, institutional. 1969-73. *2550*

Psychology *See also* Social Psychology.

—. Depressions. Liberalism. Society for the Psychological Study of Social Issues. 1930's. *1086*

Psychology, humanistic. Decisionmaking. Democracy. Management. Worker participation. 1960's-75. *84*

Public Administration *See also* Bureaucracies; Civil Service; Civil-Military Relations; Government.

—. Collective bargaining. Public Employees. 1960-80. *2141*

—. Comprehensive Employment and Training Act (US, 1973). Federal Government. Local Government. 1975-79. *2239*

—. Intergovernmental Relations. Labor Department. World War I. 1917-18. *1297*

—. Membership (perceived). Women. 1960's-77. *1787*

—. Occupational Safety and Health Act (US, 1970). 1970-78. *2300*

Public Employees *See also* Civil Service.

—. 1975-80. *2008*

—. *Abood* v. *Detroit Board of Education* (US, 1977). Agency shop fees. Collective Bargaining. Politics. 1977-80. *2126*

—. Affirmative action. Attitudes. Cities. Texas. 1978. *2423*

—. Affirmative action. Economic Conditions. Local government. State Government. 1960's-70's. *2304*

—. Alcoholism. Equal Opportunity. Federal Government. Labor Unions and Organizations. Personnel policies. 1971-77. *2035*

—. American Federation of Labor. Appalachia. Industrial Relations. Tennessee Valley Authority. 1933-78. *1324*

—. American Federation of State, County, and Municipal Employees. Civil Service Employees Association. Economic Conditions. Politics. 1978-79. *1908*

—. Arbitration. Delegation of powers. Law. State Government. 1960's-70's. *2278*

—. Arbitration. Fire fighters. 1966-73. *2151*

—. Arbitration. Iowa Public Employment Relations Act (1974). 1970's. *2231*

—. Arbitration. Labor disputes. Nevada. 1970's. *2243*

—. Arbitration. Political Reform. Strikes. 1968-75. *2267*

—. Attitudes. Employment. Minorities. 1960's-70's. *2575*

—. Attitudes. Labor Unions and Organizations. 1970's. *2139*

—. Banking. Electrical industry. Labor Unions and Organizations. White collar workers. 1940's. *1090*

—. Blacks. Cities. Hispanic Americans. Women. 1977. *2444*

—. California (Los Angeles). Industrial relations. Local government. 1966-74. *2296*

—. Central Intelligence Agency. 1950's-70's. *2372*

—. City Government. Coalitions. Collective Bargaining. New York City. 1975-80. *2098*

—. City government. Equal Employment Opportunity Act (US, 1972). Federal Policy. Minorities. Women. 1972-78. *2256*

—. City government. Federal government. Private sector. Wages. 1974-80. *2762*

—. City Government. Florida (St. Petersburg). Sanitation. Strikes. 1968. *2118*

—. Collective bargaining. 1968-78. *2048*

—. Collective bargaining. Court of Industrial Relations. Nebraska. 1919-76. *1366*

—. Collective Bargaining. Fire and Police Employee Relations Act (Texas, 1973). Referendum. Texas. 1973-81. *2023*

—. Collective bargaining. Labor Unions and Organizations. Legislation. 1974. *1925*

—. Collective bargaining. Public Administration. 1960-80. *2141*

—. Collective bargaining. State government. 1960's-70's. *2365*

—. Collective bargaining. State government. 1962-76. *2044*

—. County government. Labor Unions and Organizations. Local government. 1970's. *2134*

—. Courts. Labor Unions and Organizations. 1970's. *2150*

—. Discrimination. Employment. Labor Unions and Organizations. Supreme Court. 1976-77. *2316*

—. Equal opportunity. Federal government. Sex discrimination. Women. 1970's. *2467*

—. Equal opportunity. Mexican Americans. New Mexico. State government. Women. 1971-78. *2458*

—. Federal Government. 1958-72. *2232*

—. Federal Government. Industrial relations. 1975. *1834*

—. Federal government. Local Government. Pensions. 1977. *1946*

—. Federal Government. Wages. 1962-79. *2767*

—. Fiscal Policy. Labor Unions and Organizations. Local Government. State Government. Taxation. 1960-71. *2140*

—. Government. Labor Unions and Organizations. 1961-74. *1916*

—. Hawaii. Strikes. 1979. *2142*

—. Hawaii Public Employment Relations Act. Strikes. 1960's-72. . *2363*

—. Labor Unions and Organizations. Local Government. State Government. 1880-1980. *2051*

—. Labor Unions and Organizations. Prisons. Working conditions. 1970's. *2156*

—. Local government. Pensions. State Government. 1982. *2280*

—. Local government. Strikes. Unemployment. 1977. *2121*

—. Military. Strikes. 1970-81. *2273*

—. New York. Prison guards. Strikes. Wages. 1979. *2122*

—. New York City. Postal Service. Strikes. 1970. *2135*

—. Pressure groups. Public Policy. 1978. *2289*

—. Private sector. Training programs. 1960's-80's. *1785*

—. Strikes. 1958-76. *2043*

—. Wages. 1970's. *2824*

Public employment bureaus. Canada. Labor. Provincial government. Social Reform. State government. Unemployment. USA. 1890-1916. *1356*

Public Employment Program. Wages. Women. 1971. *2366*

Public Employment Relations Act (Michigan). Arbitration. Michigan. Public Schools (employees). 1970-73. *2301*

Public Health *See also* Diseases; Hospitals; Medicine; Pollution; Sanitation.

—. Civil Works Administration. Federal Programs. Louisiana. Sanitation. 1933-34. *1337*

Public housing. Cooperatives. Garden Homes. Wisconsin (Milwaukee). 1918-25. *1288*

Public institutions (budgets). Collective bargaining. Illinois. 1973. *2212*

Public Opinion *See also* Propaganda.

—. Alaska. Elections. Miners. Strikes. Western Federation of Miners. 1905-08. *1155*

—. Amalgamated Association of Street and Electric Railway Employees of America. Streetcars. Strikes. Texas (Houston). 1897-1905. *1279*

—. Collective Bargaining. Government. 1970's. *2207*

—. Davis, David W. Idaho. Industrial Workers of the World. Nonpartisan League. Red Scare. Socialist Party. 1919-26. *1053*

—. Economic Policy. Inflation. Unemployment. 1972-76. *2697*

—. Germany. Labor force. Propaganda. Sex roles. USA. Women. World War II. 1939-45. *1437*

—. Industrial Workers of the World. Justice Department. Labor Unions and Organizations. Nebraska. World War I. 1915-20. *1077*

—. Jews. Labor movement. Stereotypes. 1880's-1915. *343*

—. Louisiana (New Orleans). Street, Electric Railway and Motor Coach Employees of America. Strikes. 1929-30. *1120*

—. Massachusetts (Lynn). Shoe Industry. Strikes. 1860. *516*

—. Massachusetts (Marlboro). Shoe Industry. Strikes. 1898-99. *795*

Public policy. Affirmative action programs. Employment. Quotas. 1975. *2241*

—. Aliens. Immigration. 1970's. *2345*

—. Automation. Unemployment. 1982. *1813*

—. Bethune, Mary McLeod. Blacks. Equal opportunity. National Youth Administration. Youth. 1935-44. *1441*

—. Blacks. Economic Theory. Employment. Income. 1960's. *2399*

—. Catholic Worker Movement. Equality. Human Rights. 1933-78. *288*

—. Cities. Employment. Politics. Social Conditions. 1966-70. *2173*

—. Civil service. Employment. Equal opportunity. Minorities. Quantitative Methods. 1960's-70's. *2772*

—. Corporations. Economic development. South. 1979. *1513*

—. Counties. Income. Inequality. 1950-70's. *2664*

—. Discrimination. Employment. Equal opportunity. Law. 1964-72. *2369*

—. Discrimination. Handicapped. Rehabilitation Act (US, 1973). 1973-82. *2490*

—. Economic Theory. Garraty, John A. (review article). Intellectuals. Poverty. Unemployment. 17c-1978. *107*

—. Economic theory. Inflation. Unemployment. ca 1945-72. *2640*

—. Employee Ownership. Industry. 1970's. *1579*

—. Employment. Immigration. 1968-79. *2326*

—. Employment. Job creation. Productivity. 1970-79. *2254*

—. Employment. Labor. 1970's. *1468*

—. Employment. Youth. 1978-80. *2347*

—. Industrial relations. Political analysis. 1950-75. *2279*

—. Occupational segregation. USA. USSR. Women. 1917-70's. *2288*

—. Pressure groups. Public Employees. 1978. *2289*

—. Unemployment. 1970's-83. *2181*

—. Unemployment. 1975. *2213*

Public safety services. Arbitration, Industrial. Labor Disputes. 1973. *294*

Public Schools *See also* Schools.

—. Arkansas. Attitudes. Discrimination. Employment. Equal opportunity. 1980. *2361*

—. California (San Francisco). Men. Wages. Women. 1879. *897*

—. Census. Pennsylvania (Philadelphia). Teachers. 1865-90. *686*

—. Citizen participation. Collective bargaining. Educational Policy. Teachers. 1960's-70's. *1943*

—. Civil rights. Collective bargaining. Courts. Teachers. 1960-82. *1945*

—. Collective bargaining. Educational Administration. Teachers. 1960's-70's. *1974*

—. Collective bargaining. Monopsony. Teachers. Wages. 1960's-70's. *2859*

—. Collective bargaining. Teachers. 1970's. *2120*

Public Schools (employees). Arbitration. Michigan. Public Employment Relations Act (Michigan). 1970-73. *2301*

Public Schools (review article). Feinberg, Walter. Rosemont, Henry, Jr. Social control. Violas, Paul C. Working Class. 1880-20c. *4*

Public sector. Arbitration, Industrial (criteria). 1973. *327*

Public Service Electric and Gas Company. New Jersey. Sexual harassment. Tomkins, Adrienne (account). 1971-77. *2579*

Public service jobs. California (San Francisco, Oakland). Employment program. 1960-75. *2295*

Public services. Employment. US Employment Service. 1890-1933. *325*

—. Europe, Western. Japan. Trilateral Commission. Wages. 1973-79. *2377*

Public Transportation *See also* Buses.

—. Blacks. Buses. Missouri (St. Louis). Unemployment. 1973. *2468*

Public Utilities *See also* Corporations; Electric Power; Railroads; Railroads and State; Telephone.

—. Amalgamated Association of Street and Electric Railway Employees of America. Labor Unions and Organizations. Local Government. Louisiana. New Orleans Public Service Inc. 1894-1929. *1143*

Public Welfare *See also* Children; Hospitals; Social Security; Social Work.

—. AFL-CIO. Carter, Jimmy. Democratic Party. Labor Unions and Organizations. 1976. *2364*

—. Aid to Families with Dependent Children. 1967-82. *2344*

—. Aid to Families with Dependent Children. Employment (incentives toward). Wages. 1972-74. *2813*

—. Birth rate. Inflation. Unemployment. 1945-77. *2652*

—. Bureau of Indian Affairs. Indians. Occupational mobility. Standard of living. 1970. *2349*

—. Bureaucracies. Business. Social services. 1900-40. *1374*

—. Child care. Politics. 1940-45. *1301*

—. Comprehensive Employment and Training Act (US, 1973). Politics. Youth. 1977-79. *2335*

—. Corman, James C. Reform. Unemployment Insurance. 1976. *2206*

—. Depressions. Federal Emergency Relief Administration. Hopkins, Harry L. Letters. Rhode Island. 1934. *1347*

—. Employment. New York City. Work Incentive Program. 1977-79. *2302*

—. Employment. Radicals and Radicalism. 1968-79. *1676*

—. Federal government. Intergovernmental Relations. State Government. Workers' Compensation. 1956-78. *2268*

—. Federal government. Legislation. United Mine Workers of America Health and Retirement Fund. 1945-70's. *2182*

—. Federal government. Unemployment Insurance. 1976. *2188*

—. Federal Programs. 1945-68. *2180*

—. Haber, William. Michigan. National Youth Administration. Works Progress Administration. 1930's. *1336*

—. Minimum wage. Poor. 1950-76. *2719*

—. Payroll taxes. Unemployment insurance. 1976. *2209*

—. Reform. Welfare State. 1935-80. *2362*

—. Transfer payments. Work ethic. 1976. *1492*

Public Welfare (rejectees). Ohio (Cuyahoga County). Unemployment. 1974-75. *1655*

Public Works Administration. Economic Development. Employment. Texas. 1933-34. *1369*

Public Works Adminstration. Blacks. Construction. Employment. Ickes, Harold. Quotas. 1933-40. *1413*

Public Works and Economics Development Act (1965). Regionalism. Unemployment. 1965-73. *1835*

Public Works of Art Project. Art and State. New Deal. New Jersey. 1932-40. *1371*

Publicity *See also* Advertising; Propaganda.

—. Civil-Military Relations. Labor force. War Manpower Commission. Women. World War II. 1942-45. *1442*

Puerto Rican Americans. Agricultural labor. Industrial labor. 1942-51. *203*

—. Education. Labor Force. New York. Women. 1960's. *2430*

—. Employment. New York. Women. 1920's-40's. *961*

Puerto Ricans. Assimilation. Attitudes. Bilingualism. New York City. Working class. 1979. *1560*

—. Education. Family. Fertility. Income. Occupations. 1969-70. *2861*

Puerto Rico. American Federation of Labor. Gompers, Samuel. Iglesias Pantín, Santiago. Labor Unions and Organizations. 1897-1920's. *903*

—. Law. State legislatures. Workers' compensation. 1973. *2275*

Pullman, George M. Illinois (Pullman). Labor Unions and Organizations. Railroads. Strikes. 1880-94. *821*

Pullman Palace Car Company. American Railway Union. Illinois (Chicago). Letters. Lincoln, Robert Todd. Strikes. 1894. *786*

—. Archives. Employment. Information Storage and Retrieval Systems. 1890-1967. *398*

—. Debs, Eugene V. Federal government. Illinois (Blue Island). Intervention. Strikes. Strikes. 1894. *813*

—. Idaho (Pocatello). Newspapers. Railroads. Strikes. 1894. *782*

Pump and compressor industry. Productivity. 1958-80. *2621*

Purchasing power. Income. 1970-78. *2787*

Puritans. "Calling" (concept). Equality. Great Chain of Being (theme). Labor, dignity of. 17c-18c. *418*

Q

Quality control. Drug trade. Productivity. Technology. 1963-72. *2622*

Quality of Employment Surveys. Industrial safety. Labor (satisfaction). Working Conditions. 1977. *2229*

Quantitative Methods *See also* Methodology.

—. Agricultural Labor. Cotton. Productivity. South. 1850's-1900's. 1958-78. *895*

—. Civil service. Employment. Equal opportunity. Minorities. Public policy. 1960's-70's. *2772*

—. Coal Miners. Illinois. Socialist Party. Voting and Voting Behavior. 1900-40. *1370*

—. Delaware (Kent County). Literature. Pennsylvania (Philadelphia). Political history. Race. Social Classes. 1760-1830. 1979. *441*

—. Engerman, Stanley L. Fogel, Robert William. Gutman, Herbert G. Slavery (review article). 1840-60. 1974-75. *641*

—. Engerman, Stanley L. Fogel, Robert William. Historiography. Slavery. Social Mobility. 1800's-50's. 1930's-70's. *623*

—. Engerman, Stanley L. Fogel, Robert William. Slavery (review article). South. 1830-60's. 1974. *621*

—. Massachusetts (Boston). Migration. Thernstrom, Stephan. Working Class. 1880-90. *892*

—. Sex Discrimination. Wages. Women. 1960's. *2592*

Quasi unions. American Library Association. Labor Unions and Organizations (white-collar). Librarians. 1970-73. *2002*

Quebec. Construction. Indians. Iroquois Indians (Mohawk). Social Organization. 1860-1974. *154*

—. French Canadians. Massachusetts (Lowell). Occupational mobility. Working Class. 1870-80. *683*

Quinney, Valerie. Childhood. North Carolina (Carrboro). Personal narratives. Sex Roles. 1900-14. *1434*

Quotas. Affirmative Action. Blacks. 1920's-78. *363*

—. Affirmative action programs. Employment. Public policy. 1975. *2241*

—. Blacks. Construction. Employment. Ickes, Harold. Public Works Adminstration. 1933-40. *1413*

—. Bracero Program. Immigration, patterns of. Mexico. Undocumented workers. USA. 1960's-70's. *2826*

R

Race. Affirmative Action. Civil Rights Act (US, 1964; Titles VI, VII). Employment. *Kaiser Aluminum and Chemical Company v. Weber* (US, 1979). *Regents of the University of California v. Allan Bakke* (US, 1978). Supreme Court. 1970's. *2464*

—. Cities. Occupations. 1931-81. *2451*

—. Delaware (Kent County). Literature. Pennsylvania (Philadelphia). Political history. Quantitative Methods. Social Classes. 1760-1830. 1979. *441*

—. Discrimination. Employment. Sex. 1950-78. *2834*

—. Discrimination. Occupational attainment. Sex. 1890-1910. *894*

—. Discrimination. Sex. Wages. 1960-70. *2567*

—. Education. Income. Social Classes. 1978. *2589*

—. Education. Men. Occupational Mobility. Socialization. 1960-65. *2534*

—. Employment. Equal opportunity. Federal Policy. Income. Law enforcement. Legislation. Sex. 1940's-76. *2421*

—. Employment Service. Job Placements. 1973. *2434*

—. Ethnic Groups. Immigrants. Occupations. Sex. Wages. 1970. *2630*

—. Higher Education. Occupations (expectations). Sex. Students. 1970. *2410*

—. Men. Unemployment. 1980. *2648*

—. Unemployment (demographic structure). 1973. *2798*

Race Relations *See also* Acculturation; Discrimination; Emigration; Human Relations; Immigration; Indian-White Relations.

—. Abolition. Freedmen. Labor market, split. Slavery, extension of. 1830-63. *547*

—. Agricultural labor. Boycotts. Labor Unions and Organizations. South Carolina. 1886-95. *872*

—. Arbitration, Industrial. Fire fighters. Georgia Railroad. Smith, Hoke. Strikes. 1909. *1418*

—. Arkansas (Elaine). Farmers, tenant. Sharecroppers. Violence. 1919. *1449*

—. Attitudes. Auto Workers. Chrysler Corporation. General Motors Corporation. Michigan (Detroit, Hamtramck). 1972. *2495*

—. Blacks. Colored National Labor Union. Florida. Labor unions and organizations. National Negro Labor Union. Reconstruction. 1865-75. *881*

—. Blacks. Farmers. Knights of Labor. North Carolina. 1889. *878*

—. Blacks. Immigrants. Italians. Louisiana. Sugar cane. 1880-1910. *729*

—. Blacks. Labor force. Social Change. Tobacco. Virginia. 1660-1710. *414*

—. Blacks. Labor market. Whites. 1865-1920. *715*

—. *Boston Daily Evening Voice* (newspaper). Equality. Labor Unions and Organizations. Massachusetts. Working Class. 1864-67. *870*

—. Brotherhood of Timber Workers. Industrial Workers of the World. Louisiana. Lumber and Lumbering. Texas. 1910-13. *1164*

—. Brotherhood of Timber Workers. Louisiana, western. Lumber and Lumbering. Southern Lumber Operators' Association. Texas, eastern. 1911-13. *1165*

—. Chinese Americans. Economic Conditions. Far Western States. Immigration. Labor market, split. 1848-82. 1970's. *184*

—. Coal Mines and Mining. Knights of Labor. United Mine Workers of America. West Virginia, southern. 1880-94. *867*

—. Employment. Segregation. 1970's. *2407*

—. Family. Income. Labor Unions and Organizations. 1947-74. *2406*

—. Industrial relations. International Harvester Company. Minorities. 1831-1976. *337*

—. Industrialization. Labor Unions and Organizations (black). 19c-20c. *368*

—. International Longshoremen's Association. South Central and Gulf States. 1866-1920. *1195*

—. Knights of Labor. South. 1880-87. *877*

—. Labor Unions and Organizations. Unemployment. 1910-50's. *1383*

—. Labor Unions and Organizations. Working conditions. 1969-73. *1509*

Racial protest. Civil Rights Act (US, 1964; Title VII). Courts. Labor Disputes. Self-help. Taft-Hartley Act (US, 1947). 1968-71. *1307*

Racism. AFL-CIO. Blacks. Leadership. 1955-79. *2482*

—. Africa. Industrial arts education. Pan-Africanism. South. 1879-1940. *364*

—. Agricultural Labor. Economic Structure. Freedmen. Reconstruction. Texas. 1865-74. *737*

—. American Federation of Labor. Fascism. Gompers, Samuel. Immigration. Jingoism. 1850-1924. *1425*

—. Bilbo, Theodore G. Employment. Fair Employment Practices Commission. Filibusters. Mississippi. Senate. 1941-46. *1290*

—. Blacks. Communist Party. National Maritime Union. United Electrical, Radio, and Machine Workers of America. World War II. 1941-45. *1391*

—. Capitalism. 1978. *360*

—. Coal Miners. Strikes. United Mine Workers of America. 1894-1920. *1259*

—. Discrimination. Employment. Industry. Metropolitan areas. Profits. 1973. *2427*

—. Economic Conditions. Whites. Working Class. 1970. *2570*

—. Employment. Law. 1964-73. *2356*

—. Federal Policy. Immigration. Labor. Mexican Americans. 1920's. *1436*

—. Labor Market. National Longitudinal Surveys. Sex Discrimination. 1970-80. *2509*

—. Labor market. Sex Discrimination. 1960's-70's. *2571*

—. Labor Unions and Organizations. Political Attitudes. Working class. 1830-1972. *2437*

—. Labor Unions and Organizations. South. 1960's-70's. *2435*

—. Local Politics. Missouri. Radical Republicanism. St. Louis *Daily Press* (newspaper). 1864-66. *663*

Racism, institutional. American Psychological Association. Equal opportunity. Lancaster Press. Psychologists for Social Action. 1969-73. *2550*

Racism (review article). Blacks. Harris, William H. 1865-1982. *369*

Radical Republicanism. Local Politics. Missouri. Racism. St. Louis *Daily Press* (newspaper). 1864-66. *663*

Radicals and Radicalism *See also* Leftism; Political Reform; Revolution; Social Reform.

—. Agrarians. Populism. Wisconsin. Working class. 19c. *864*

—. Alienation. Technology, structure of. 1970's. *1466*

—. American Dream. Employment. Massachusetts. Youth. 1977. *1620*

—. American Federation of Labor. Communist Party. Labor Unions and Organizations. Trade Union Unity League. 1933-35. *1016*

—. American Federation of Labor. Knights of Labor. Pacific Northwest. Socialism. 1871-1912. *775*

—. Archival Catalogs and Inventories. Labor Unions and Organizations. Michigan, University of, Ann Arbor (Labadie Collection). 1911-82. *141*

—. Aronowitz, Stanley (views). Class consciousness. Economic Structure. Industrial Relations. Working class. 1960-76. *1556*

—. Bureaucratization. Conservatism. Labor Unions and Organizations. 1930's-70's. *254*

—. California (Los Angeles). Communist Party. Labor Unions and Organizations. Mexicans. 1930-39. *1203*

—. Canada. Finns. Immigrants. Labor Unions and Organizations. USA. 1918-26. *965*

—. Coal Miners. Illinois (Macoupin, Montgomery Counties). Labor Unions and Organizations. United Mine Workers of America. Virden Massacre. ca 1870-1939. *297*

—. Conservatism. Ellender, Allen J. Hall, Covington. Louisiana. 1871-1972. *751*

—. Copper Mines and Mining. Finnish Americans. Labor force. Michigan. 1890-1920. *168*

—. Depressions. Labor unions and organizations. Michigan (Detroit). 1920's-30's. *908*

—. Depressions. Unemployed councils. 1929-33. *1065*

—. Employment. Public Welfare. 1968-79. *1676*

—. Ethnicity. Irish Americans. Land League. Reform. Working class. 1880-83. *758*

—. Everett Mill. Massachusetts (Lawrence). Polish Americans. Strikes. Textile Industry. Women. 1912. *1219*

—. Federal Bureau of Investigation. Industrial Workers of the World. Labor Disputes. Ohio (Toledo). 1918-20. *1010*

—. Finnish Americans. High Schools. Labor College Movement. Minnesota (Duluth, Minneapolis). Work People's College. 1903-37. *921*

—. Finnish Americans. Iron Industry. Labor Unions and Organizations. Minnesota (Mesabi Range). 1914-17. *1222*

—. Finnish Americans. Socialism. 1903-14. *1221*

—. Fleetwood Fisher Body plant. Michigan (Detroit). Strikes (wildcat). United Automobile Workers of America. 1976. *2099*

—. General Electric Company (River Works Plant). Industrial safety. Kashner, Frank (account). Labor Unions and Organizations. Massachusetts (Lynn). Strikes, wildcat. 1960's-77. *2092*

—. Green Corn Rebellion, 1917. Oklahoma. Working Class Union. 1914-17. *1269*

—. Historians. Labor Unions and Organizations. Massachusetts (West Lynn). Saturday Workshop (conference). Shoeworkers. 1979. *16*

—. Horton, Myles (interview). Moyers, Bill. Tennessee (Chattanooga area). 1932-81. *284*

—. Industrial Workers of the World. Kansas. Red Scare. Trials. 1917-19. *1038*

—. Industrialists. Labor Unions and Organizations. Levison, Andrew (review article). Social change. 1930's-70's. *1506*

—. Industrialization. Knights of St. Crispin. Massachusetts (Lynn). Shoe industry. Working Class. 1820-90. *46*

—. Italian Americans. Italy. 1916-26. *1015*

—. Italian Americans. Rhode Island. 1905-30. *932*

—. Jones, Mary Harris. Labor Unions and Organizations. *Mother Jones* (periodical). Socialism. 1850's-1920's. 1970's. *120*

—. Krzycki, Leo. Labor Unions and Organizations. Polish Americans. Socialist Party. 1900's-66. *281*

—. Labor Unions and Organizations. Mine, Mill and Smelter Workers, International Union of. United Steelworkers of America. 1950-67. *1906*

—. Labor unions and organizations. New Deal. Working class. 1930's. *1321*

—. Minnesota State Federation of Labor. Reform. Workers' compensation. 1910-33. *1287*

—. Muste, Abraham J. Unemployed Leagues. 1932-36. *912*

Radicals and Radicalism (review article). Gaventa, John. Macintyre, Stuart. Politics. Working Class. ca 1880-1940. *93*

Radium dials. Cancer. New Jersey, northern. Painting. 1917-24. *990*

Raids. California (Los Angeles). Immigration and Naturalization Service. Industrial Relations. International Ladies' Garment Workers' Union. Lilli Diamond Originals. Mexican Americans. 1976-77. *2144*

Railroads. Accidents. Courts. Federal Employers' Liability Act (US, 1908). Management. Safety Appliances Act (US, 1893). Working Conditions. 1890-1913. *334*

—. Alaska (Anchorage). Labor Unions and Organizations. Lewis, Lena Morrow. Socialist Party. World War I. 1916-18. *1187*

—. Alcoholism. Chicago, Burlington & Quincy Railroad. Employees. Law Enforcement. Management. 1876-1902. *677*

—. Armies. Strikes. Values. 1877. 1894. *788*

—. Baltimore and Ohio Railroad. Mathews, Henry M. Strikes. West Virginia (Martinsburg, Berkeley County). 1877. *796*

—. Blacklisting. Bureaucracies. Chicago, Burlington & Quincy Railroad. Employment. North Central States. 1877-92. *779*

—. Blacks. Discrimination. Fair Employment Practices Commission. Southeastern Carriers Conference. World War II. 1941-45. *1399*

—. Blacks. Discrimination. Georgia Railroad. Strikes. 1909. *1397*

—. Conference for Progressive Political Action. Elections. Labor Unions and Organizations. 1919-25. *1344*

—. Consolidated Railroad Corporation. Construction. Delaware (Delmarva Peninsula). Federal government. Labor disputes. 1973-76. *2033*

—. Construction. Florida East Coast Railway. Immigrants. Italian Americans. Padrone system. Recruitment. ca 1890-1901. *828*

—. Construction. Illinois Central Railroad. 1850-56. *452*

—. Construction. Irish Americans. Massachusetts. Population. Towns. Western Railroad. 1833-42. *465*

—. Gould, Jay. Knights of Labor. Missouri (Sedalia). Modernization. Strikes. 1885-86. *754*

—. Government. Strikes. 1877. *797*

—. Greenback Labor Party. Monetary Systems. Pennsylvania (Pittsburgh). Political Protest. Strikes. 1877. *849*

—. Idaho (Pocatello). Newspapers. Pullman Palace Car Company. Strikes. 1894. *782*

—. Illinois (Pullman). Labor Unions and Organizations. Pullman, George M. Strikes. 1880-94. *821*

—. Indiana (Terre Haute). Strikes. 1870-90. *831*

—. Industry. Strikes. 1877. *841*

—. International Workingmen's Association. Marxism. Strikes. 1877. *802*

—. International Workingmen's Association. Strikes. 1877. *801*

—. Labor. Montana. Personal Narratives. 1910-50. *971*

—. Labor disputes. Management, Scientific. Working class. 1903-22. *910*

—. Labor Unions and Organizations. Mexico. USA. 1880-1933. *282*

—. Labor Unions and Organizations. Nationalization. Plumb, Glenn Edward. 1917-20. *1192*

—. Massachusetts. Montana. Prescott, Charles (account). 1873-1932. *182*

—. Strikes. Violence. Working class. 1877. *794*

—. Women. World War I. 1917-30. *1396*

Railroads and State See also Railroads.

—. Labor disputes. McKinley, William. Murphy, S. W. (letter). West Virginia. 1893. *842*

Railroads (branch lines). Missouri-Kansas-Texas Railroad. Oklahoma. Texas. 1906-75. *956*

Ramirez, Bruno. Industrial Relations (review article). Rodgers, Daniel T. Work ethic. 1850-1920. *70*

Ranchers. Agricultural Labor. Farmers. Industrial Workers of the World. Labor Disputes. Washington (Yakima Valley). 1910-36. *1216*

Randolph, A. Philip. American Federation of Labor. Blacks. Brotherhood of Sleeping Car Porters. "George" stereotype. 1867-1935. *1421*

—. Blacks. Brotherhood of Sleeping Car Porters. March on Washington Movement. National Negro Congress. 1925-41. *1166*

—. Blacks. Journalism. Labor Unions and Organizations. Marxism. Political protest. ca 1911-75. *106*

Rank-and-file movements. American Federation of Labor. Brotherhood of Painters and Decorators. Gompers, Samuel. Voluntarism. 1894-1900. *759*

—. American Federation of Labor. Gompers, Samuel. Labor Unions and Organizations. Military preparedness policies. Wilson, Woodrow. 1914-17. *1041*

—. Boyle, Tony. Labor Reform. Leadership. Miller, Arnold. United Mine Workers of America. Yablonsky, Joseph A. 1969-74. *2158*

—. *Fifth Wheel* (newspaper). Labor Unions and Organizations. Teamsters, International Brotherhood of. 1977. *2128*

—. Labor Unions and Organizations. Miners for Democracy. United Mine Workers of America. 1972. *1879*

Ransom, Roger. Agriculture. Blacks. Economic Conditions. *One Kind of Freedom* (book). South. Sutch, Richard. 1860's-80's. 1977-78. *885*

Rapier, James T. Alabama. Blacks. Labor Union of Alabama. National Negro Labor Union. Politics. Reconstruction. 1837-75. *880*

Rath Pork Packing Company. Amalgamated Meat Cutters. Employee Ownership. Iowa (Vinton). Labor Unions and Organizations. 1970-81. *2080*

—. Employee Ownership. Iowa (Waterloo). 1970-81. *1853*

—. Employee Ownership. Iowa (Waterloo). Reagan, Ronald (administration). 1970's-80's. *2137*

Reagan, Ronald. Deregulation. Occupational Safety and Health Administration. 1970-83. *2195*

Reagan, Ronald (administration). Automation. Computers. Corporations. Labor. 1981-82. *1549*

—. Employee Ownership. Iowa (Waterloo). Rath Pork Packing Company. 1970's-80's. *2137*

Reapportionment. See Apportionment.

Recessions See also Business Cycles; Depressions.

—. Adolescence. Blacks. Employment. Women. 1945-81. *2616*

—. Automobile Industry and Trade. Employment. Housing. Unemployment. 1980. *2839*

—. Behavior. Conservatism. Economic Theory. Unemployment. 1978. *2695*

—. Blacks. Labor force. 1975-78. *2709*

—. Employment, Part-time. Working Conditions. 1982. *1573*

—. Hispanic Americans. Unemployment. 1974-75. *2516*

—. Industrial relations. Inflation. 1980. *1529*

—. Manufactures. Metropolitan areas. States. Unemployment. 1974-75. *2781*

—. Men. Unemployment. Youth. 1974-75. *1678*

—. Poverty. Unemployment. 1959-75. *2669*

Reconstruction See also Emancipation; Freedmen.

—. Agricultural labor. Alabama. Attitudes. Chinese Americans. Keffer, John C. Smith, William H. 1869. *713*

—. Agricultural Labor. Economic Structure. Freedmen. Racism. Texas. 1865-74. *737*

—. Alabama. Blacks. Labor Union of Alabama. National Negro Labor Union. Politics. Rapier, James T. 1837-75. *880*

—. Alabama. Bureau of Refugees, Freedmen, and Abandoned Lands. Freedmen. 1865-67. *612*

—. Blacks. Colored National Labor Union. Florida. Labor unions and organizations. National Negro Labor Union. Race Relations. 1865-75. *881*

—. Blacks. Florida. Forests and Forestry. Labor. 1860-1900. *628*

—. Chattahoochee Penitentiary. Convict lease system. Florida. Martin, Malachi. 1868-77. *652*

—. Civil War. Foner, Eric (review article). Ideology. Social Organization. 1860-76. 1980. *14*

—. Freedmen. Labor. Motte, J. Rhett. Plantations. Share wages. South Carolina (St. John's Parish). 1867. *882*

Recreation See also Leisure; Sports.

—. Cities. Family. Social Change. Working conditions. 1830-90. *215*

Recruitment See also Job Placement; Hiring.

—. Blacks. Discrimination. Employment. Whites. 1970's. *1748*

—. Blacks. Immigrants. Iron Industry. Pennsylvania (Reading). Robesonia Iron Company. 1915-23. *928*

—. Blacks. Johnson, D. W. Migration, Internal. Personal Narratives. 1917-22. *1403*

—. Construction. Florida East Coast Railway. Immigrants. Italian Americans. Padrone system. Railroads. ca 1890-1901. *828*

—. Employment. Georgia (Atlanta). Job inquiries. Men. Sex discrimination. 1975. *2500*

—. Labor Unions and Organizations. Personnel. 1970-81. *1897*

—. Legislative Bodies. Sex Discrimination. Women. 1970's. *2585*

Rhode Island (Woonsocket). Belgian Americans. French Canadian Americans. Independent Textile Workers. Working Class. 1931-50's. *1157*

Rhode Island Workers Association. Contracts. Labor Unions and Organizations. 1974-75. *1884*

Rice. Ball plantation. Fertility. Slavery. South Carolina (Cooper River district). 1735-1865. *556*

—. Georgia. Plantations. Slaves. 1820-80. *543*

—. Slave drivers. South Carolina. 1820-65. *555*

Rice, Hazel F. (account). North Dakota Workmen's Compensation Bureau. Transportation. Working conditions. 1919-22. *1352*

Richmond Typographical Union. Baughman Brothers (company). Boycotts. Knights of Labor. Virginia. 1886-88. *784*

Right to work. Collective bargaining. Federal Government. Labor law. 1979. *2248*

Right-to-work laws. Arkansans for Progress. Labor Unions and Organizations. 1975-76. *2025*

—. Cost of living. Labor Unions and Organizations. 1981. *2200*

—. Labor Unions and Organizations. 1950-70. *2220*

—. Labor Unions and Organizations. States. 1974. *2383*

—. Labor unions and organizations. Unemployment. Wages. 1964-78. *2199*

—. States. 1974. *2312*

Riley, William R. Blacks. Labor. Letters. Tennessee. United Mine Workers of America. 1892-95. *876*

Rios vs. Reynolds Metals Company (1972). Arbitration, Industrial. Discrimination. *Griggs vs. Duke Power Company (1971)*. 1964-73. *2413*

Riots *See also* Civil Disturbances; Demonstrations; Strikes.

—. Agricultural Labor. California (Wheatland). Photographs. 1913. *1261*

—. Courts. Industrial Workers of the World. Washington (Everett). 1916. *1111*

—. Golden Hill (battle). Nassau Street Riots. New York City. 1770. *413*

—. Illinois (Chicago). Militia. Police. Strikes. 1877. *833*

—. Japanese Americans. Lumber and Lumbering. Oregon (Toledo). Pacific Spruce Corporation. 1925-26. *1444*

Rizzo, Saverio. Italian Americans. Labor Unions and Organizations. Padrone system. Personal Narratives. Triangle fire. 1900-30. *963*

Roberts, Lillian (interview). Hospital Workers. Illinois (Chicago). Labor Unions and Organizations. Minorities. Mt. Sinai Hospital. 1950's. *2127*

Roberts, William. Indentured servants, former. Letters. Maryland (Anne Arundel County). Tenancy. Working Class. 1756-69. *515*

Robesonia Iron Company. Blacks. Immigrants. Iron Industry. Pennsylvania (Reading). Recruitment. 1915-23. *928*

Robins, Margaret Dreier. Anderson, Mary. Illinois (Chicago). Labor Unions and Organizations. Nestor, Agnes. Women. Women's Trade Union League. Working conditions. 1903-20. *1389*

Robinson, Harriet Hanson. Letters. Massachusetts (Lowell). Women. Working Class. 1845-46. *494*

Robots. Canada. Computers. Industry. Unemployment. USA. 1964-81. *1479*

Rock Island Arsenal. Armies. Buffington, A. R. Documents. Illinois. Strikes. 1897-99. *809*

Rodeos. Blacks. Cattle Raising. Cowboys. 1880's-1970's. *143*

Rodgers, Daniel T. Gilbert, James B. Industrialization. Intellectuals. Labor (review article). Values. 1850-1920. 1974-77. *55*

—. Industrial Relations (review article). Ramirez, Bruno. Work ethic. 1850-1920. *70*

Rogers, John R. Kansas. Land Reform. Union Labor Party. 1838-1901. *855*

Rogers, Ray. J. P. Stevens & Company, Inc. Personal narratives. Strikes. 1976. *2162*

Roll-call Voting. Fair Labor Standards Act (US, 1938; amended, 1973). Legislation. Minimum wage. Models. 1938-74. *2393*

Rolph, James J. Bombings. California (San Francisco). City Government. Law and Order Committee. McDevitt, William. Socialism. 1916. *1328*

Roman Catholic Church. *See* Catholic Church.

Roney, Frank. California (San Francisco). Diaries. Immigrants. Irish Americans. Ironworkers. 1875-76. *733*

Roosevelt, Franklin D. Congress. New Deal. Social Security Act (US, 1935). Unemployment insurance. 1934-35. *1289*

—. Congress of Industrial Organizations. Elections (presidential). Labor Non-Partisan League. Pennsylvania. 1936. *1362*

—. Domestic Policy. Elections (presidential). Foreign policy. Lewis, John L. 1936-40. *1355*

—. Foreign Policy. International Labor Organization. Isolationism. New Deal. Perkins, Frances. 1921-34. *1346*

Roosevelt, Franklin D. (administration). Civil rights. Congress. Discrimination. Fair Employment Practices Commission. World War II. 1941-46. *1428*

—. Industry. Labor Unions and Organizations. War Manpower Commission. War Production Board. World War II. 1939-45. *906*

Roosevelt, Theodore. Coal Mines and Mining. Federal government. Pennsylvania. Strikes. 1902. *1309*

Roper, Elmo. Attitudes. New Deal. Socialism. Working class. 1939. *997*

Roseblum, Gerald. Aurant, Harold V. Ethnicity. Labor Unions and Organizations (review article). Socialism. 1869-1920. *659*

Rosemont, Henry, Jr. Feinberg, Walter. Public Schools (review article). Social control. Violas, Paul C. Working Class. 1880-20c. *4*

Ross, David. Iron industry. Oxford Iron Works. Slavery, industrial. Virginia (Lynchburg). 1775-1817. *561*

Roucek, Joseph. College Teachers. Employment, temporary. Tenure. 1960-79. *1985*

Rubber. Alabama (Gadsden). Goodyear Tire and Rubber Company. House, John D. United Rubber Workers. 1941. *1210*

Rubber industry. Industrial Workers of the World. Ohio (Akron). Strikes. 1913. *1278*

—. Ohio (Akron). Strikes, sit-down. 1934-38. *1212*

Rubin, Lester. Blacks. Discrimination. Employment (review article). Fulmer, William E. Wrong, Elaine Gale. 1865-1973. *357*

Rudwick, Elliott. Blacks. Cities. Ewen, Linda Ann. Greer, Edward. Industrial Relations (review article). Meier, August. 1900-81. *353*

—. Blacks. Communist Party. Glabermann, Martin. Keeran, Roger R. Labor Unions and Organizations. Meier, August. United Automobile Workers of America (review article). 1930's-40's. *1191*

Rug and Carpet Industry. Alexander Smith and Sons Carpet Company. New York (Yonkers). Strikes. Women. 1884-86. *818*

Rumberger, Russell W. Education. Employment (review article). 1960-76. *1570*

Rural areas. Employment. Florida (Gadsden, St. Lucie, Washington counties). 1970-80. *2629*

—. Employment. Metropolitan Areas. Women. 1960-70. *1756*

—. Employment. Population. 1962-67. *2608*

—. Income. Industrialization. Iowa. Towns. 1960-70. *2776*

—. Michigan. Migration. Minnesota. Occupational Mobility. Wisconsin. 1970's. *1779*

—. Socialism. Wisconsin (Milwaukee). 1910-20. *1050*

Rural Development. Economic Development. Employment. Towns. 1950-70. *2802*

Rural market. Cities. Labor. 1870-1900. *888*

Rural Settlements. Industry. Michigan (Belding). Silk industry. Women. Working Conditions. 1885-1932. *87*

Rural-Urban Studies. Commuting. Illinois. Industry. 1970's. *1605*

—. Occupations. Sex. Social Status. Stereotypes. 1977-78. *2443*

—. Pennsylvania. Social Classes. Wives. Women. 1947-71. *1673*

Russia *See also* USSR.

—. Emigration. Intellectuals. Jews. Labor movement. USA. 1880's. *590*

—. Serfdom. Slavery. USA. 18c-1860's. *586*

Russian Americans. Newspapers. Socialists. *Znamia*. 1889-90. *665*

Russians. Agricultural Labor. Hawaii. 1900-10. *931*

Rutgers University. Colleges and Universities. Educational programs. Labor Unions and Organizations. 1930-76. *1481*

S

Saddlemakers. Western States. 1865-1920. *197*

Sadlowski, Ed. Elections. Labor Unions and Organizations. Leadership. United Steelworkers of America. 1976-77. *1918*

—. Elections. Labor Unions and Organizations. Leadership. United Steelworkers of America. 1976-77. *2096*

—. Elections. Labor Unions and Organizations. United Steelworkers of America. 1976-77. *2090*

—. McBride, Lloyd. United Steelworkers of America. 1976-77. *2167*

Safety Appliances Act (US, 1893). Accidents. Courts. Federal Employers' Liability Act (US, 1908). Management. Railroads. Working Conditions. 1890-1913. *334*

Sailors. Civil Rights. Dutch West India Company. New Netherland (New Amsterdam). 1628-63. *487*

—. Lawsuits. Liability. Merchant Marine Act (US, 1920). 1920-82. *2236*

Sailors' Union. American Federation of Labor. Industrial Workers of the World. Louisiana. Marine Transport Workers. Strikes. United Fruit Company. 1913. *1127*

St. Louis *Daily Press* (newspaper). Local Politics. Missouri. Racism. Radical Republicanism. 1864-66. *663*

St. Louis Transit Company. Mass Transit. Missouri. Modernization. Monopolies. Strikes. 1900. *1229*

Salaries. *See* Wages.

Sales. Department stores. Industrial Relations. Women. 1900-40. *1380*

—. Department stores. Management. Women. Work culture. 1890-1960. *151*

Salmon. Alaska. Asian Americans. Canning industry. Contracts. Labor Disputes. 1880-1937. *301*

—. Alaska. Canneries. Filipino Americans. Labor Unions and Organizations. 1902-38. *1198*

Saloons. Colorado (Denver). Frontier and Pioneer Life. Social mobility. 1858-85. *722*

San Francisco Maritime Museum. California. Lundeberg, Harry. Preservation. Ships. 1945-55. *98*

Sanders, Dobbie (reminiscences). South. Steel mills. Working Class. 1922-59. *116*

Sanitation *See also* Pollution; Public Health.

—. City Government. Florida (St. Petersburg). Public Employees. Strikes. 1968. *2118*

—. Civil Works Administration. Federal Programs. Louisiana. Public Health. 1933-34. *1337*

Saturday Workshop (conference). Historians. Labor Unions and Organizations. Massachusetts (West Lynn). Radicals and Radicalism. Shoeworkers. 1979. *16*

Savings. Delaware. DuPont, E. I. and Company. Wages. 1813-60. *407*

Sawmills. Productivity. Technology. 1958-75. *2651*

Saxton, Alexander. DeCaux, Len. Labor Movement (review essay). Left. Mortimer, Wyndham. Zinn, Howard. 19c-1971. *1650*

Sayles Finishing Plants. Periodicals. Rhode Island (Saylesville). Social Organization. Textile Industry. 1920's-30's. *1138*

Scandinavia. Industrial democracy. Labor Unions and Organizations. ca 1950-77. *278*

Scholars *See also* Degrees, Academic.

—. Cartter, Allen M. (review article). Colleges and Universities. Employment. Graduate Programs. ca 1950-75. *1940*

Scholarships, Fellowships, etc. Colleges and Universities. Sports. Workers' compensation. 1953-77. *2198*

School boards. District of Columbia. Strikes. Teachers. Wages. Washington Teachers Union. Working conditions. 1979. *2114*

Schooling. Children. Education. Homeownership. Rhode Island (Providence). Working class. 1880-1925. *214*

Schools *See also* Church Schools; Colleges and Universities; Education; Junior Colleges; Public Schools; Students; Teaching.

—. Crime and Criminals. Employment. Housing. Metropolitan areas. Transportation. 1970's. *1474*

—. Employment. New York. Training. Youth. 1977-81. *1725*

—. Labor Unions and Organizations. Teachers. 1979-80. *1970*

Schools (attendance). Illinois (Chicago). Working Class. 1880-1930. *91*

Schools, summer. Labor movement. Middle classes. South. Women. 1927-41. *947*

Schuyler, Mont. Defections. Grady, John. Haywood, William Dudley. Industrial Workers of the World. Letters. USA. USSR. 1921-22. *1062*

Science and Society. Automation. Labor. Machine tools. Management. Technology. 1950-78. *1524*

Scientific management. *See* Management, scientific.
Scientists *See also* names of individual scientists.
—. Professionalization. Self-image. 19c-20c. *212*
—. Wages. 1960-70. *2837*

Scots Americans. Immigration. Indentured servants. 17c-18c. *530*

Scudder, Vida Dutton. Christianity. Industrial Relations. Massachusetts (Lawrence). Social reform. Women. 1912. *1132*

Sea Islands. Blacks. Labor. South Carolina. Tourism. 1960-80. *1543*

Sea shanties. Folk songs. Merchant Marine. 19c. *225*

Secession. North Carolina (Onslow County). Slavery. Turpentine industry. 1790-1861. *546*

Secret Societies. Blacks. Cooperative Workers of America. Georgia. Hoover, Hiram F. South Carolina. 1886-87. *87J*

Security. Labor Unions and Organizations. World War II. 1941-45. *1047*

Sedition. Jones Family (group). Oklahoma (Cleveland, Pottawatomie counties). Trials. Working Class Union. World War I. 1917. *1206*

Seeger, Charles. Appalachia. Leftism. Mountaineers. Music. Resettlement Administration (music program). Social Organization. 1935-37. *1368*

Segregation *See also* Discrimination; Minorities.
—. Blacks. California (Los Angeles). Employment. Housing. Transportation. 1941-45. *1440*
—. Capitalism. Occupations. Patriarchy. Sex Discrimination. Women. ca 1700-1970's. *346*
—. Depressions. Labor force. Women. 1930's. *1423*
—. Employment. Race Relations. 1970's. *2407*

Self-actualization. Working Conditions. 1970-80. *1762*

Self-employment. 1972-79. *2655*
—. Coal Mines and Mining. Pennsylvania. 1920-44. *922*
—. Political Stratification. Social Status. Working Class. 1968-73. *1484*

Self-help. Agricultural Cooperatives. DeBernardi, Giovanni Battista. Depressions. Labor Exchange. 1889-1910. *808*
—. Civil Rights Act (US, 1964; Title VII). Courts. Labor Disputes. Racial protest. Taft-Hartley Act (US, 1947). 1968-71. *1307*
—. Depressions. Mecklenburg, George H. Minnesota (Minneapolis). Organized Unemployed, Inc. Poor. Unemployment. 1932-35. *916*
—. Dix, I. F. Hoover, Herbert C. Local politics. Unemployed Citizens' League. Washington (Seattle). 1931-32. *1340*

Self-image. Professionalization. Scientists. 19c-20c. *212*

Self-perception. Behavior. Women. Working conditions. 1964-79. *1734*
—. Depressions. Unemployment. Working Class. 1920's-30's. *995*

Senate *See also* House of Representatives; Legislation.
—. Appointments to office. Confirmation. National Labor Relations Board. Presidents. 1935-78. *316*
—. Atomic power plants. Dismissals. Engineering. Faulkner, Peter. Nuclear Services Corp. 1973-77. *1953*
—. Bilbo, Theodore G. Employment. Fair Employment Practices Commission. Filibusters. Mississippi. Racism. 1941-46. *1290*
—. Kern, John W. Labor Law. Workman's Compensation Act (1916). 1908-17. *1314*

Senate Committee to Investigate Organized Crime. Blackmail. Crime and Criminals (organized). Illinois (Chicago). Kefauver, Estes. Korshak, Sidney R. 1950-76. *2311*

Seniority. Affirmative action. Blacks. Discrimination (review article). Gould, William B. Hill, Herbert. Labor Unions and Organizations. Supreme Court. 1970's. *2537*
—. Blacks. Discrimination. Women. 1976-77. *2492*
—. Civil Rights Act (US, 1964). Employment. Equal opportunity. NAACP. Supreme Court. 1964-77. *2264*
—. Consent decrees. Employment. Equal opportunity. Steel industry. 1974-78. *2486*

Serfdom. Russia. Slavery. USA. 18c-1860's. *586*

Serials. *See* Periodicals.
Sermons. Labor. Presbyterian Church. Sunday, William Ashley ("Billy"). Virtue. Women. 1915. *970*
Serrano v. *Priest* (1971). California. Collective bargaining. Supreme courts, state. Teachers. 1970's. *2000*
Service industries. 1950-77. *2805*
Servants. *See* Domestic service; Indentured servants.
Sex *See also* Men; Women.
—. Child Labor. Cotton. Occupational segregation. Textile industry. 1910. *968*
—. Civil service. Employee Turnover patterns. Equal Opportunity. State Government. 1969-77. *2560*
—. Discrimination. Employment. Race. 1950-78. *2834*
—. Discrimination. Occupational attainment. Race. 1890-1910. *894*
—. Discrimination. Race. Wages. 1960-70. *2567*
—. Employment. Equal opportunity. Federal Policy. Income. Law enforcement. Legislation. Race. 1940's-76. *2421*
—. Employment. Occupations. 1920-40. 1950-70. *121*
—. Ethnic Groups. Immigrants. Occupations. Race. Wages. 1970. *2630*
—. Higher Education. Occupations (expectations). Race. Students. 1970. *2410*
—. Occupations. Rural-Urban Studies. Social Status. Stereotypes. 1977-78. *2443*
Sex discrimination. Advertising. Colt, Cristine C. (account). Dow Jones Co. 1975-78. *2426*
—. American Medical Association. Medicine. 1847-1910. *189*
—. Auto Workers. Michigan (Detroit). United Automobile Workers of America. Women. 1945-47. *2456*
—. Boycotts, consumer. District of Columbia. Employment. Women. World War II. 1941-46. *1451*
—. Broadcasting. Women. 1974. *2519*
—. California (San Jose). Comparable Worth. Wages. 1960-81. *2419*
—. Capitalism. Employment. Norway. Social Classes. USA. 1973-80. *1737*
—. Capitalism. Occupations. Patriarchy. Segregation. Women. ca 1700-1970's. *346*
—. Clerical workers. Wages. 1880-1980. *355*
—. Clothing industry. Textile Industry. Wages. Women. 1910-70. *351*
—. College teachers. Illinois, University of, Urbana-Champaign. 1975-79. *2448*
—. College teachers. Trials. Women. 1964-82. *2394*
—. Colleges and Universities. Women. 1973-74. *2484*
—. Congress. Equal Employment Opportunity Commission. Feminism. 1964-74. *2350*
—. Construction. Occupations. Women. 1980. *2538*
—. Council of Economic Advisers (report). Employment. Women. 1960-73. *2408*
—. Economic Theory. Monopolies. 1974. *2440*
—. Economists. Methodology. Wages. 1970's. *2411*
—. Employment. 1973. *2450*
—. Employment. Equal Rights Amendment. Women. 1960-70. *2303*
—. Employment. Federal Regulation. Women. 1963-81. *2588*
—. Employment. Georgia (Atlanta). Job inquiries. Men. Recruitment. 1975. *2500*
—. Employment. Pregnancy Discrimination Act (US, 1978). 1908-78. *348*
—. Employment. Social Classes. 1950-79. *2420*
—. Equal opportunity. Federal government. Public Employees. Women. 1970's. *2467*
—. Fertility. Industry. Occupational hazards. Women. 1970's. *1857*
—. Great Britain. Novels (Victorian). Wages. Women (image). 19c-20c. *366*
—. Gross, Edward. Occupational differentiation. Women. 1970's. *370*
—. High School of Fashion Industry. Minorities. New York City. Vocational Education. Women. 1975. *2402*
—. Household heads. Labor market. Poverty. Women. ca 1950-70's. *2549*
—. Imperialism. Mexican Americans. Mexico. Migration. Southwest. Working class. 1850-1982. *53*
—. Income. Labor market. 1960's-73. *1669*
—. Judges. Lawyers. Politics. Women. 1970's. *2578*
—. Labor Market. National Longitudinal Surveys. Racism. 1970-80. *2509*

—. Labor market. Racism. 1960's-70's. *2571*
—. Labor Unions and Organizations. Membership. Wages. 1979. *2401*
—. Labor unions and organizations. Women. 1970's. *2555*
—. Law. Occupational segregation. Women. 20c. *2234*
—. Legislative Bodies. Recruitment. Women. 1970's. *2585*
—. Manufacturing. New Jersey. Pennsylvania. Wages. 1900-50. *358*
—. Men. Professionals. Wage differentials. Women. 1966-71. *2511*
—. Nurses and Nursing. Professionals. Women. 1941-75. *2545*
—. Occupational Segregation. Wages. Women. 1945-73. *2566*
—. Occupations. Social Change. 1950-70. *2564*
—. Quantitative Methods. Wages. Women. 1960's. *2592*
—. Unemployment. Wages. Women. 1947-73. *2529*
—. United Automobile Workers of America. 1945-54. *2457*
—. Wages. Women. 1960-70. *2528*
—. Women. 1970's. *2446*

Sex roles. Assimilation. Occupations. Refugees. Social status. Vietnamese. 1975. *1703*
—. Attitudes. Occupations. Prestige. 1970. *2415*
—. Behavior. Capitalism. Family. Massachusetts (Lowell). 1860. *427*
—. Bibliographies. Economic structure. Women. 1940-75. *1700*
—. Blacks. Colleges and Universities. Education. Occupational goals. Women. 1964-70. *2473*
—. Blacks. Employment. Equality. Marriage. Whites. 1976. *1572*
—. Child rearing. Employment. Equality. Women's liberation movement. 1970's. *2497*
—. Childhood. North Carolina (Carrboro). Personal narratives. Quinney, Valerie. 1900-14. *1434*
—. Childhood. Socialization. 1979. *250*
—. Children. Elementary education. Socialization. Teachers. 1959-71. *1980*
—. Collective bargaining. Labor unions and organizations. Stereotypes. Women. 1950-78. *1830*
—. Cuban Americans. Employment. Family. Women. 1960's-70's. *1630*
—. Diaries. Westward Movement. Women. 19c. *223*
—. Discrimination. Employment (review article). Women. 1978. *2493*
—. Employment. Geographic proximity. Women. 1976. *2510*
—. Employment. Marriage. Women. 1890-1978. *186*
—. Europe. Labor force. Social Organization. Women. 18c-1979. *213*
—. Family. Farmers. Leisure. 1920-55. *246*
—. Germany. Labor force. Propaganda. Public opinion. USA. Women. World War II. 1939-45. *1437*
—. Great Plains. Indians. Social organization. Women. 19c. *181*
—. Historiography. Marxism. Research. Women. 19c. 1970's. *190*
—. Labor force. Michigan. Women. World War II. 1941-45. *1388*
—. Labor (skilled). Stereotypes. Women. 1960-73. *2480*
—. Men. Printing. Women. 1850-80. *675*
—. Men. Wages. Whites. Women. 1959-70. *2455*
—. New York City. Travel agency industry. 1974. *2517*
—. Occupations. Rhode Island. Women. 1900-40. *1443*
—. Slavery. South. 18c-1865. *636*

Sexual harassment. Attitudes. 1960's-82. *2418*
—. Attitudes. Heterosexuals. Lesbians. Women. Working Conditions. 1972-82. *2552*
—. Attitudes. Labor. Law. Women. 1974-81. *2504*
—. Blue collar workers. Job Satisfaction. Women. Working Conditions. 1970's. *1755*
—. New Jersey. Public Service Electric and Gas Company. Tomkins, Adrienne (account). 1971-77. *2579*
—. Women. 18c-1978. *340*

Shanker, Albert. Labor Unions and Organizations. New York. Political Leadership. Teachers. 1978. *2005*

Share wages. Freedmen. Labor. Motte, J. Rhett. Plantations. Reconstruction. South Carolina (St. John's Parish). 1867. *882*

—. Davis, David W. Idaho. Industrial Workers of the World. Nonpartisan League. Public opinion. Red Scare. 1919-26. *1053*

—. Depressions. Liberalism. New Deal. Political activism. Unemployment. 1929-36. *1354*

—. Jews. Labor Unions and Organizations. Malkiel, Theresa Serber. New York City. Women. 1900's-14. *1059*

—. Krzycki, Leo. Labor Unions and Organizations. Polish Americans. Radicals and Radicalism. 1900's-66. *281*

—. Labor Unions and Organizations. Lanfersiek, Walter. Peace movements. 1895-1962. *267*

—. Lunn, George. New York (Schenectady). Voting and Voting Behavior. Working Class. 1911-16. *1304*

—. Woman suffrage. Working Class. 1901-12. *1306*

Socialists. Gompers, Samuel. Lenin, V. I. USA. 1912-18. *1036*

—. Immigration. Poland. Polish Americans. 1883-1914. *177*

—. Newspapers. Russian Americans. *Znamia.* 1889-90. *665*

Socialization. Blind. Occupational goals. 1973. *1686*

—. Childhood. Sex roles. 1979. *250*

—. Children. Elementary education. Sex roles. Teachers. Women. 1959-71. *1980*

—. Education. Men. Occupational Mobility. Race. 1960-65. *2534*

—. Employment, part-time. Youth. 1980. *1819*

—. Occupations. Values. 1966-76. *2736*

Socialization differences. Blacks. Labor force. South. Whites. Women. 1870. 1880. *692*

Society for the Psychological Study of Social Issues. Depressions. Liberalism. Psychology. 1930's. *1086*

Society of Jesus. *See* Jesuits.

Sociology *See also* Cities; Emigration; Family; Immigration; Labor; Marriage; Population; Race Relations; Slavery; Social Classes; Social Conditions; Social Organization; Social Problems; Social Surveys.

—. Labor market. Models. Occupations. Wages. 1960-75. *1824*

—. Occupations. Pennsylvania (Philadelphia). Working Class. 1754-1800. *478*

—. Occupations. Research. 1976-82. *1494*

—. Research. Working class. 1930's-70's. *72*

Songs. Editorials. *Miners' Magazine.* Poetry. Western Federation of Miners. 1900-07. *1283*

—. Industrial Workers of the World. Rhetoric. 1906-17. *1009*

Sons of Liberty. American Revolution (antecedents). Elites. Working Class. 1763-87. *434*

Sorge, Friedrich A. Labor movement. Marxism. 1866-76. *651*

South. AFL-CIO (Committee on Political Education). Political Action Committees. 1943-75. *1914*

—. Africa. Industrial arts education. Pan-Africanism. Racism. 1879-1940. *364*

—. Agricultural Labor. Blacks. Discrimination. Wages. 1898-1902. *879*

—. Agricultural Labor. Capital, fixed. Economic development. Farmers. Slavery. ca 1840-80. *578*

—. Agricultural Labor. Cotton. Productivity. Quantitative methods. 1850's-1900's. 1958-78. *895*

—. Agricultural labor. Industrialization. Models. Slavery. 1800's. *571*

—. Agricultural Labor. Italy, northern. Slavery. ca 1800-60. 1876-81. *604*

—. Agricultural Labor. Tenancy. Wages. 1930-60. *3*

—. Agricultural Production. Productivity. Slavery. 1850-60. *572*

—. Agriculture. Blacks. Economic Conditions. *One Kind of Freedom* (book). Ransom, Roger. Sutch, Richard. 1860's-80's. 1977-78. *885*

—. Agriculture. Economic Conditions. Farms (tenant). Productivity. 1850's-90's. *662*

—. Agriculture. Productivity. Slavery. 1800's-60. 1974-79. *585*

—. Agriculture. Research. Slave narratives. 1850's-65. *590*

—. Agriculture Department. Alabama. Blacks. Campbell, Thomas M. Social Conditions. ca 1883-1956. *1407*

—. Alabama (Mobile). Blacks. Fair Employment Practices Commission. Shipyards. World War II. 1938-45. *1351*

—. Archival Catalogs and Inventories. Georgia State University (Southern Labor Archives). Labor Unions and Organizations. 1966-82. *52*

—. Attitudes. Blacks. Immigrants. 1865-1910. *700*

—. Attitudes. Economic conditions. Labor Unions and Organizations. Law Reform. Southwest. 1940-80. *266*

—. Attitudes. Individualism. Labor unions and organizations. Working conditions. 1970's. *1514*

—. Attitudes. Professionalism. Strikes. Teachers. 1979. *1951*

—. Authority. Freedmen. Teachers. Women. 1865-70. *703*

—. Bibliographies. Labor history. 1900-75. *146*

—. Bibliographies. Strikes. Textile industry. 1929-76. *1284*

—. Blacks. Bondage systems. 1865-1940. *678*

—. Blacks. Civil Rights. Labor Unions and Organizations. Textile industry. 1950's-70's. *2485*

—. Blacks. Colored Farmers' Alliance. Farmers. ca 1886-95. *656*

—. Blacks. Colored Farmers' Alliance. Humphrey, R. M. Labor Unions and Organizations. Strikes. 1876-91 *868*

—. Blacks. Cotton. Farmers. Marketing. Social change. Social Classes. Whites. 1865-1940. *884*

—. Blacks. Discrimination. Education. Employment. 1960-70. *1751*

—. Blacks. Folklore. Laundry. Women. 17c-20c. *153*

—. Blacks. High Schools. Occupational goals. Whites. 1970's. *2530*

—. Blacks. Immigrants. International Brotherhood of Pulp, Sulphite, and Paper Mill Workers. Pacific Northwest. Women. 1909-40. *1281*

—. Blacks. Industrial Relations. Migration, Internal. Pine industry. Working conditions. ca 1912-26. *900*

—. Blacks. Industry. Labor force. 1940-70. *1783*

—. Blacks. Knights of Labor. Labor Unions and Organizations. 1880-87. *871*

—. Blacks. Labor. Textile Industry. 1941-81. *1640*

—. Blacks. Labor force. 1940-70. *2580*

—. Blacks. Labor force. Socialization differences. Whites. Women. 1870. 1880. *692*

—. Blacks. Men. Migration, Internal. Occupations. 1967. *2525*

—. Blacks. Peonage. 1903-25. *1386*

—. Brazil. Economic development. Slavery. 19c. *581*

—. Brown Lung Association. Brown lung disease. Burlington Industries, Inc. Cotton. Liberty Mutual Insurance Co. Occupational diseases. 1970's. *1609*

—. Brown Lung Association. Brown lung disease. Occupational Diseases. Textile industry. Workers' Compensation. 1970's. *1736*

—. Brown Lung Association. Class consciousness. Industrial safety. Textile Industry. 1970-80. *1698*

—. Business. Employee Ownership. 1979-82. *1607*

—. Capitalism. Ideology. Slavery. 19c. *632*

—. Children. Slavery. Textile Industry. Women. 1790-1860. *609*

—. China. Chinese Americans. Cuba. Federal Policy. Labor problems. 1865-70. *645*

—. Cities. Goldin, Claudia Dale (review article). Slavery. 1820-60. 1976. *548*

—. Congress of Industrial Organizations. Labor Disputes. New Deal. Newspapers. 1930-39. *1082*

—. Congress of Industrial Organizations. Labor Unions and Organizations. Management. National Industrial Recovery Act (US, 1933). National Labor Relations Act (US, 1935). Textile Industry. 1933-41. *1081*

—. Contracts. Freedmen's Bureau. Planters. Sharecropping. 1865-68. *732*

—. Corporations. Economic development. Public Policy. 1979. *1513*

—. Costs. Textile Industry. Wages. 1800-80. *670*

—. Cotton. Great Britain. Plantations. Slavery. 17c-19c. *593*

—. Cotton. New England. Technology. Textile Industry. 1890-1970. *65*

—. Cotton production. Profitability. Slavery. 1860. *634*

—. DeBow, James Dunwoody Brownson. Economic Theory. Proslavery Sentiments. 1800-67. *583*

—. Discrimination. Employment. Equal Employment Opportunity Commission. Labor disputes. 1930's-70's. *2392*

—. Discrimination. Fair Employment Practices Commission. Minorities. World War II. 1941-45. *1435*

—. Domestic Service. Emancipation. Slavery. 1865-67. *630*

—. Economic conditions. Employment. Federal Government. Western States. 1968-78. *2779*

—. Economic Conditions. Historiography. Slavery. 17c-1865. 1974. *574*

—. Economic Conditions. Industrial Revolution. Slavery. ca 1800-60. *591*

—. Economic Conditions. Marxism. Slavery. Social Organization. 17c-1860. *570*

—. Economic Conditions. Slavery (review article). ca 1800-60. *566*

—. Economic growth. Slavery. 1840-60. *577*

—. Economic History. Sharecropping. 1870-1900. *726*

—. Economic theory. Engerman, Stanley L. Fogel, Robert William. Methodology. Slavery (review article). ca 1974. *557*

—. Economics (research). Engerman, Stanley L. Fogel, Robert William. Historiography. Slavery (review article). ca 1820-1974. *633*

—. Employment. Integration. Revenue sharing. Southwest. 1970-80. *2258*

—. Employment. Minorities. Women. 1920-70. *242*

—. Engerman, Stanley L. Fogel, Robert William. Quantitative methods. Slavery (review article). 1830-60's. 1974. *621*

—. Genovese, Eugene D. (review article). Slavery. 19c. 1974. *607*

—. Historiography. Labor. 19c-20c. *69*

—. Historiography. Slavery. 17c-19c. 1918-77. *573*

—. Historiography. Slavery. 1800-60. 1956-79. *629*

—. Industrialization. Slavery. 1800-50. *594*

—. Ironworkers. Slavery. Working conditions. 1820's-65. *562*

—. Knights of Labor. ca 1885-88. *769*

—. Knights of Labor. Race relations. 1880-87. *877*

—. Labor. Women (review article). 19c-1977. *201*

—. Labor movement. Middle classes. Schools, summer. Women. 1927-41. *947*

—. Labor movement. Social change. 19c-20c. *30*

—. Labor Unions and Organizations. 1920's-74. *265*

—. Labor Unions and Organizations. People's Institute of Applied Religion. Religious leaders. Williams, Claude. Williams, Joyce. 1940-75. *290*

—. Labor Unions and Organizations. Racism. 1960's-70's. *2435*

—. Labor Unions and Organizations. Textile industry. 1918-40. *944*

—. Labor Unions and Organizations. Textile industry. ca 1949-75. *2124*

—. Market forces, competitive. Profit motive. Slavery. 1800-60. *554*

—. North. Wages. 1960-76. *2701*

—. Sanders, Dobbie (reminiscences). Steel mills. Working Class. 1922-59. *116*

—. Sex roles. Slavery. 18c-1865. *636*

—. Slave drivers, black. 19c. *610*

—. Slavery. 1800-60. *584*

—. Slaves, quasifree. Tennessee (Nashville). Thomas, James P. 1818-82. *627*

—. Textile industry. Women. Working conditions. 1908-52. *984*

South Africa. Blacks. Capitalism. Households. Income. Labor history. Pennsylvania (Philadelphia). Steel Industry. 19c-20c. *138*

—. California. Farm workers. Migrant labor. Miners. ca 1890-1975. *1593*

—. Europe, Western. Immigrants. Labor. Middle East. USA. 1942-80. *1726*

South Carolina. African crops. Agriculture. Slaves. 17c-18c. *640*

—. Agricultural labor. Boycotts. Labor Unions and Organizations. Race relations. 1886-95. *872*

—. Blacks. Cooperative Workers of America. Georgia. Hoover, Hiram F. Secret Societies. 1886-87. *873*

—. Blacks. Labor. Sea Islands. Tourism. 1960-80. *1543*

—. Immigrants. Labor scarcity. North Carolina. 1815-1925. *130*

—. Louisiana. Medical care. Plantations (rice, sugar). Slaves. 1810-60. *637*

—. Peonage, legal. 1880-1907. *684*

—. Rice. Slave drivers. 1820-65. *555*

South Carolina (Charleston). Blacks. Federal government. Hospitals. Labor Unions and Organizations. 1969. *2066*

South Carolina (Cooper River district). Ball
plantation. Fertility. Rice. Slavery. 1735-1865.
556
South Carolina (Edgefield County). Labor, low-
skilled. Social Status. Textile industry. 1850-60.
496
South Carolina (Greenville). Antiunionization.
Industry. Labor Unions and Organizations.
1873-1979. *2138*
South Carolina (St. John's Parish). Freedmen.
Labor. Motte, J. Rhett. Plantations.
Reconstruction. Share wages. 1867. *882*
South Central and Gulf States *See also* individual
states.
—. International Longshoremen's Association. Race
relations. 1866-1920. *1195*
—. Ironworkers. Slave Revolts (anticipated). 1856.
560
South Dakota *See also* Western States.
—. Civilian Conservation Corps. Employment.
Environment. 1933-42. *1317*
—. Employment, part-time. National Youth
Administration. New Deal. Struble, Anna C.
Youth. 1935-43. *1318*
South Dakota (Farm Island). Causeways. Civilian
Conservation Corps (co. 796). Depressions.
Missouri River. 1934. *1375*
Southeastern Carriers Conference. Blacks.
Discrimination. Fair Employment Practices
Commission. Railroads. World War II.
1941-45. *1399*
Southern Lumber Operators' Association.
Brotherhood of Timber Workers. Louisiana,
western. Lumber and Lumbering. Race
Relations. Texas, eastern. 1911-13. *1165*
Southern Tenant Farmers' Union. Agricultural
Adjustment Administration. Depressions. Labor
Unions and Organizations. Sharecroppers. ca
1930's. *1266*
—. Agricultural Organizations. Farmers, tenant.
1934-70. *306*
Southwest *See also* individual states; Far Western
States.
—. Attitudes. Economic conditions. Labor Unions
and Organizations. Law Reform. South.
1940-80. *266*
—. Blacks. Labor Force. Mexican Americans.
Whites. Women. 1950-70. *2429*
—. Bracero Program. Employment. Farm Workers.
Wages. 1954-77. *1697*
—. Economic Development. Mexican Americans.
Working class. 1603-1900. *78*
—. Employment. Integration. Revenue sharing.
South. 1970-80. *2258*
—. Farm Workers. Mexican Americans. Mexicans.
1971-81. *2086*
—. Immigration. Income. Undocumented Workers.
1960-80. *2673*
—. Immigration. Institutions. Labor. Mexicans.
Texas. Undocumented workers. 1821-1975. *235*
—. Imperialism. Mexican Americans. Mexico.
Migration. Sex Discrimination. Working class.
1850-1982. *53*
—. Income. Mexican Americans. 1960. *2536*
—. Indians. Labor Unions and Organizations.
Navajo Indians. 1958-78. *2129*
—. Mexican Americans. 1896-1915. *936*
Spain (Mondragon). Employee Ownership.
Industry. USA. 1943-78. *1548*
Special Interest Groups. *See* Interest Groups;
Lobbying; Political Factions; Pressure Groups.
Speeches. Feminism. Free love. Stanton, Elizabeth
Cady. 1868-70. *647*
Spencer, Herbert. Comte, Auguste. Foster, Frank
K. Gompers, Samuel. Ideology. Labor Unions
and Organizations. McGregor, Hugh.
1876-1900. *755*
—. Economic Theory. Income, distribution of.
Marx, Karl. Mill, John Stuart. Smith, Adam.
18c-1971. *405*
Split labor market theory. Economic conditions.
Exclusion policy. Filipinos. Immigration.
1927-34. *1387*
Sports. Antitrust. Congress. Courts. Management.
1950's-70's. *1646*
—. Colleges and Universities. Scholarships,
Fellowships, etc. Workers' compensation.
1953-77. *2198*
—. Great Britain. Leisure. Work. 1830-60. *493*
Stampp, Kenneth. Bancroft, Frederic. Missouri
(Boone County). Slavery. 1820-65. *605*
Standard of Living *See also* Cost of Living.
—. Age. Coal Mines and Mining. Management.
Strikes, wildcat. Working conditions. 1970's.
2041

—. Brandywine River Valley. Delaware.
Documents. DuPont, E. I. and Company.
Economic growth. Industrialization.
Pennsylvania. 1800-60. *408*
—. Bureau of Indian Affairs. Indians.
Occupational mobility. Public Welfare. 1970.
2349
—. Child labor. Family. French Canadians.
Massachusetts (Lowell). Migration. 1870's. *649*
—. Class struggle. Political program. Reform.
Working class. 1950's-73. *1471*
—. Employment. Family. Women. 1950-73. *1545*
—. Housework. Mass production. Social status.
Technology. 1900-70. *245*
—. Husbands. Income. Men. Wives. Women. 1968.
1979. *2591*
—. New York City. Working class. 1960's-82.
2784
—. Pennsylvania (Philadelphia). Working class.
1780's-90's. *896*
Standard Oil Company of New Jersey. New Jersey
(Bayonne). Polish Americans. Strikes. 1915-16.
1137
Stanton, Elizabeth Cady. Feminism. Free love.
Speeches. 1868-70. *647*
State Department (Foreign Service). Family.
Occupational mobility. Wives. Women. 1974.
1565
State Employment Security Agencies. Labor
Department (Bureau of Labor Statistics).
Statistics. Unemployment insurance. 1977-78.
2845
State Government *See also* Constitutions, State;
Governors; State Legislatures; State Politics.
—. Affirmative action. Economic Conditions. Local
government. Public Employees. 1960's-70's.
2304
—. Arbitration. Delegation of powers. Law. Public
Employees. 1960's-70's. *2278*
—. Business. Costs. Workers' compensation.
1978-81. *2221*
—. California. Farm workers. Labor law. Law.
Minimum wage. Virginia. 1975. *2187*
—. California (Wheatland). Industrial Workers of
the World. Migrant Labor. Strikes. Trials.
1913-17. *1133*
—. Canada. Labor. Provincial government. Public
employment bureaus. Social Reform.
Unemployment. USA. 1890-1916. *1356*
—. Civil service. Employee Turnover patterns.
Equal Opportunity. Sex. 1969-77. *2560*
—. Coal miners. Convict labor. Labor Disputes.
Tennessee. Violence. 1891-93. *646*
—. Coal miners. Convict labor. Strikes. Tennessee.
1891-93. *642*
—. Coal Mines and Mining. Strikes. United Mine
Workers of America. West Virginia (Paint
Creek). 1912-13. *1257*
—. Collective bargaining. Public Employees.
1960's-70's. *2365*
—. Collective bargaining. Public Employees.
1962-76. *2044*
—. Corporations. Income. Labor Unions and
Organizations. Social Classes. ca 1960. *2263*
—. Criminal syndicalism acts. Idaho. Industrial
Workers of the World. Labor Law. 1917-33.
1071
—. Employment. Immigrants. Law Enforcement.
Women. Working Hours. 1920. *1414*
—. Employment. Texas. Women. 1970's. *2526*
—. Employment opportunities. GNP. Local
government. 1959-71. *2226*
—. Equal opportunity. Mexican Americans. New
Mexico. Public Employees. Women. 1971-78.
2458
—. Federal aid. Unemployment insurance. 1975.
2262
—. Federal government. Intergovernmental
Relations. Public Welfare. Workers'
Compensation. 1956-78. *2268*
—. Federal Government. Unemployment insurance.
1970-81. *2336*
—. Fiscal Policy. Labor Unions and Organizations.
Local Government. Public Employees.
Taxation. 1960-71. *2140*
—. Geographic Mobility. Lawyers. Licenses.
1950's-70's. *1995*
—. Georgia. National Recovery Administration.
Strikes. Talmadge, Eugene. Textile industry.
1934. *1095*
—. Labor Law. 1972. *2389*
—. Labor Law. 1978. *2323*
—. Labor Law. 1979. *2319*
—. Labor Law. 1980. *2320*
—. Labor Law. Legislation. 1981. *2322*

—. Labor Law. Legislation. 1982. *2321*
—. Labor Law. National Commission on State
Workmen's Compensation Laws. Workers'
compensation. 1972-79. *2380*
—. Labor Law. Workers' compensation. 1970's.
2379
—. Labor Law (amended). Workers'
Compensation. 1978. *2307*
—. Labor Unions and Organizations. Local
Government. Public Employees. 1880-1980.
2051
—. Law. Unemployment insurance. 1972. *2261*
—. Law. Workers' compensation. 1907-72. *2276*
—. Legislation. Minimum wage. Washington.
1913-25. *1364*
—. Legislation. National Commission on State
Workmen's Compensation Laws. Workers'
Compensation. 1972-80. *2381*
—. Legislation. Unemployment insurance. 1980.
2357
—. Local government. Pensions. Public employees.
1982. *2280*
—. Pensions. Social Policy. Teachers. 1891-1930.
322
—. Productivity. Unemployment insurance.
1966-78. *2661*
—. Unemployment insurance. 1978. *2358*
—. Vocational Education. 1974. *2208*
—. Workers' compensation. 1970's. *2378*
State Government (compliance). Federal
Regulation. Workers' Compensation. 1975.
2270
State Historical Society of Wisconsin (Archives
Division). Archival Catalogs and Inventories.
Labor Unions and Organizations. Wisconsin.
1982. *111*
State Legislatures. California. Leisure.
Unemployment. 1979. *2305*
—. Consumers League of New York. Lobbying.
New York (Albany). Perkins, Frances. 1911.
1335
—. Deregulation. Licenses. Virginia. 1974-78. *2259*
—. Industrial Relations. Labor Law. Social
conditions. 1940's-70's. *2272*
—. Labor Law. 1973. *2294*
—. Law. Puerto Rico. Workers' compensation.
1973. *2275*
—. Law. Unemployment insurance. 1973. *2260*
State Politics *See also* Elections; Governors;
Political Campaigns; Political Parties; State
Government.
—. Elections (senatorial). Labor Unions and
Organizations. Wisconsin. 1952. *2334*
—. Farmer-Labor Party. Michigan. New Deal.
1933-37. *1330*
States. Labor Unions and Organizations. Right-to-
work laws. 1974. *2383*
—. Manufactures. Metropolitan areas. Recessions.
Unemployment. 1974-75. *2781*
—. Right-to-work laws. 1974. *2312*
Statistics *See also* Social Surveys.
—. Business. Degrees, doctoral. Labor Department
(Bureau of Labor Statistics). 1975-79. *2841*
—. Capitalism. Economic performance.
Industrialization. Unemployment. 19c-1976. *379*
—. Census. Occupations. Women. 1890-1940. *37*
—. Current Employment Statistics Program.
Current Population Survey. Labor. Workweek.
1956-77. *2646*
—. Diseases. Industrial safety. Labor Department
(Bureau of Labor Statistics). 1975-80. *2698*
—. Domestic service. Women. 1870-1980. *383*
—. Employee turnover. Social Security
Administration. 1974-80. *2636*
—. Employment. Migration, Internal. 1947-63.
2823
—. Employment. National Commission on
Employment and Unemployment Statistics.
1976-79. *2822*
—. Immigrants. North America. Occupations.
Women. 1964-71. *2619*
—. Industry. Labor Department (Bureau of Labor
Statistics). Occupations. 1975. *2628*
—. Information Storage and Retrieval Systems.
Labor market experience. National
Longitudinal Surveys of Labor Market
Behavior. 1965-80. *2753*
—. Iron Industry. New York (Troy). Social
Customs. Working Class. 1860-80. *744*
—. Ironworkers. New York (Troy). Social
Customs. Working Class. 1860-80. *898*
—. Labor Department (Bureau of Labor
Statistics). Lubin, Isador. New Deal. Perkins,
Frances. Unemployment. 1920-49. *1452*

—. Blacks. Colored Farmers' Alliance. Humphrey, R. M. Labor Unions and Organizations. South. 1876-91. *868*

—. Blacks. Discrimination. Georgia Railroad. Railroads. 1909. *1397*

—. Bohemian Americans. British Americans. Cleveland Rolling Mill Company. Human Relations. Ohio. Polish Americans. 1882-85. *874*

—. Boulder Canyon project. Colorado River. Hoover Dam. Industrial Workers of the World. Nevada. 1931. *1241*

—. Boulder Canyon Project. Hoover Dam. Industrial Workers of the World. Nevada. Six Companies, Inc. 1931. *1240*

—. Business. California (San Francisco). Construction. Eight-hour day. Law and Order Committee. 1916-17. *1190*

—. California. Chavez, Cesar. Farm Workers. Mexican Americans. United Farm Workers Union. 1965-70. *2024*

—. California. Farm Workers. Grape industry. Labor Unions and Organizations. United Farm Workers Union. 1966-70. *2088*

—. California (Delano). Chavez, Cesar. Grape industry. 1967-70. *2110*

—. California (Inglewood). Communist Party. North American Aviation. United Automobile Workers of America. 1941. *1233*

—. California (Kern County). DiGiorgio Fruit Co. Farm Workers. National Farm Labor Union. 1947-49. *2079*

—. California (Los Angeles). Mexican Americans. Pacific Electric Railroad. 1900-03. *1277*

—. California (San Francisco). Labor market. Longshoremen. 1934-39. *1178*

—. California (Wheatland). Industrial Workers of the World. Migrant Labor. State Government. Trials. 1913-17. *1133*

—. Canada. Models. USA. 1900-71. *310*

—. Capitalist countries. Working class. 1970-80. *2060*

—. Carbon County Coal Strike (1933). National Miners Union. United Mine Workers of America. Utah. 1900-39. *1225*

—. Central Labor Union. Eight-hour day. Knights of Labor. Labor Unions and Organizations. Massachusetts (Boston). 1886. *817*

—. Christianity. Longshoremen. Oxford Group movement. Washington (Seattle). 1921-34. *1268*

—. Cigar Industry. Florida (Tampa). 1899. *825*

—. Cigar industry. Industrial Workers of the World. Pennsylvania (McKees Rocks, Pittsburgh). Pressed Steel Car Company. Steel Industry. 1909-13. *1194*

—. City Government. Florida (St. Petersburg). Public Employees. Sanitation. 1968. *2118*

—. Civil service. Collective bargaining. Labor Unions and Organizations. 1960-72. *2054*

—. Class conflict. Rhode Island (Pawtucket). Textile Industry. 1790-1824. *519*

—. Class Struggle. Immigration. Sweden. 1879-1906. *239*

—. Clothing industry. Illinois (Chicago). Men. 1910-11. *1271*

—. Clothing Industry. Illinois (Chicago). O'Reilly, Mary. Socialist Party. Women. Zeh, Nellie M. 1910. *1115*

—. Clothing industry. Missouri (St. Louis). Personal narratives. Photographic essays. Women. ca 1930-39. *1390*

—. Coal industry. Pennsylvania. United Mine Workers of America. ca 1895-1925. *815*

—. Coal Miners. Colorado Fuel and Iron Company. Ludlow Massacre. National Guard. 1913-14. *1141*

—. Coal miners. Colorado (Las Animas, Huerfano counties). United Mine Workers of America. 1904-14. *1263*

—. Coal miners. Convict labor. State Government. Tennessee. 1891-93. *642*

—. Coal miners. Davidson-Wilder Strike of 1932. Graham, Barney. Tennessee, eastern. United Mine Workers of America. 1932-33. *1096*

—. Coal Miners. Davis, Thomas Boyd. Martial law. West Virginia. 1912-22. *1123*

—. Coal Miners. Debs, Eugene V. Socialist Party. West Virginia. 1912-14. *1129*

—. Coal Miners. Diaries. Medrick, George. Pennsylvania, western. United Mine Workers of America. 1927. *1146*

—. Coal Miners. Duke Power Company. Kentucky (Harlan County; Brookside). United Mine Workers of America. 1973-74. *2034*

—. Coal Miners. Editors and Editing. Evans, Herndon J. Kentucky (Harlan County). Pineville *Sun* (newspaper). 1929-32. *1264*

—. Coal Miners. Ellsworth, James William. Industrial Relations. Pennsylvania (Ellsworth). 1900-06. *1174*

—. Coal miners. Germer, Adolph. Illinois (Virden). Socialism. United Mine Workers of America. 1893-1900. *785*

—. Coal Miners. Hanraty, Pete. Oklahoma. United Mine Workers of America. 1899-1903. *1102*

—. Coal Miners. Hocking Valley. Lewis, John L. Ohio, southeastern. United Mine Workers of America. 1927. *1258*

—. Coal Miners. Kentucky (Harlan County; Evarts). United Mine Workers of America. 1931. *1106*

—. Coal miners. Labor Unions and Organizations. 1881-94. *749*

—. Coal Miners. National Guard. Ohio. White, George. 1932. *1218*

—. Coal Miners. Pennsylvania. United Mine Workers of America. 1922-23. *1180*

—. Coal Miners. Pinchot, Gifford. United Mine Workers of America. 1925-26. *1179*

—. Coal Miners. Racism. United Mine Workers of America. 1894-1920. *1259*

—. Coal Miners. United Mine Workers of America. 1977-78. *2078*

—. Coal Mines and Mining. 1976-78. *2148*

—. Coal Mines and Mining. Colorado. Industrial Workers of the World. 1927. *1199*

—. Coal Mines and Mining. Deverall, Richard Lawrence-Grace. Documents. Ickes, Harold. United Mine Workers of America. West Virginia (Welch). 1943. *1235*

—. Coal Mines and Mining. Economic Conditions. 1977-78. *2019*

—. Coal Mines and Mining. Federal government. Pennsylvania. Roosevelt, Theodore. 1902. *1309*

—. Coal Mines and Mining. *Harlan County, U.S.A.* (film). Kentucky. Kopple, Barbara. United Mine Workers of America. 1973-74. *2161*

—. Coal Mines and Mining. *Harlan County, U.S.A.* (film). Kentucky. Kopple, Barbara (interview). United Mine Workers of America. 1973-76. *2119*

—. Coal Mines and Mining. Hoadly, George. Ohio (Hocking Valley). 1884-85. *819*

—. Coal Mines and Mining. Miller, Arnold. United Mine Workers of America. 1972-76. *2116*

—. Coal Mines and Mining. State Government. United Mine Workers of America. West Virginia (Paint Creek). 1912-13. *1257*

—. Coal Mines and Mining. United Mine Workers of America. 1890-1978. *2032*

—. Coalition bargaining. Electrical equipment industry. General Electric Company. Westinghouse Electric Corporation. 1950-74. *2108*

—. Communism. Demonstrations. Films. Workers' Film and Photo League. 1930-38. *902*

—. Community Participation. Lumbermen. Michigan (Bay City, Saginaw). 1880's. *816*

—. Community, sense of. Massachusetts (Lowell). Values. Women. 1820-50. *422*

—. Company towns. Congress of Industrial Organizations. Ohio. Steel Industry. 1937. *1103*

—. Connecticut Railway and Lighting Company. Connecticut (Waterbury). Streetcars. 1903. *1250*

—. Copper Miners. Michigan. Montana (Butte). Western Federation of Miners (Local No. 1). 1913-14. *1267*

—. Corporations. Costs. Stock Exchange. 1967-71. 1974-75. *2113*

—. Courts. Jackson, John Jay, Jr. Jones, Mary Harris. United Mine Workers of America. West Virginia. 1902. *1262*

—. Cowboys. Western States. Working conditions. 1870-90. *820*

—. Danz, John. Musicians. Washington (Seattle). 1921-35. *1135*

—. Davey, Martin L. National Guard. Ohio. Steel Industry. 1937. *1253*

—. Debs, Eugene V. Federal government. Illinois (Blue Island). Intervention. Pullman Palace Car Company. Strikes. 1894. *813*

—. Debs, Eugene V. Federal government. Illinois (Blue Island). Intervention. Pullman Palace Car Company. Strikes. 1894. *813*

—. Democratic Party. Republican Party. Rhode Island. Textile industry. 1934. *1147*

—. District of Columbia. School boards. Teachers. Wages. Washington Teachers Union. Working conditions. 1979. *2114*

—. Documentaries. Films. Michigan (Flint). United Automobile Workers of America. *With Babies and Banners* (film). Women. 1937. *1238*

—. Economic conditions. Edwards, P. K. Politics. Snyder, David. 1900-48. *1254*

—. Economy Furniture Factory. Mass Media. Mexican Americans. Texas (Austin). 1968-72. *2123*

—. Everett Mill. Massachusetts (Lawrence). Polish Americans. Radicals and Radicalism. Textile Industry. Women. 1912. *1219*

—. Farm Workers. Law Enforcement. Texas (Rio Grande City). 1966-67. *2022*

—. Farmers. Industrial Workers of the World. Orchards. Washington (Yakima Valley). 1933. *1215*

—. Farmers. North Dakota. Prices. 1932. *1236*

—. Federal Aviation Administration. Professional Air Traffic Controllers Organization. 1960's-82. *2094*

—. Films. General Motors Corporation. *United Action Means Victory* (film). United Automobile Workers of America. 1938-40. *1244*

—. Fire Fighters. Tennessee (Memphis). Voluntary Associations. 1858-60. *517*

—. France. Industrial Relations. Italy. USA. 1876-1970. *311*

—. Franklin, Benjamin. International Typographical Union. Pennsylvania (Philadelphia). Printing. Wages. 1754-1852. *531*

—. General Motors Corporation. Georgia (Atlanta). United Automobile Workers of America. 1936. *1167*

—. General Motors Corporation. *Great Sitdown* (film). Historiography. United Automobile Workers of America. *With Babies and Banners* (film). 1937. 1976-79. *1188*

—. Georgia. National Recovery Administration. State Government. Talmadge, Eugene. Textile industry. 1934. *1095*

—. Georgia (Augusta). Textile mills. Working conditions. 1886. *830*

—. Gould, Jay. Knights of Labor. Missouri (Sedalia). Modernization. Railroads. 1885-86. *754*

—. Government. Railroads. 1877. *797*

—. Governors. Hoadly, George. National guard. Ohio (Hocking Valley). 1884-85. *778*

—. Greenback Labor Party. Monetary Systems. Pennsylvania (Pittsburgh). Political Protest. Railroads. 1877. *849*

—. Hawaii. Public Employees. 1979. *2142*

—. Hawaii Public Employment Relations Act. Public Employees. 1960's-72. . *2363*

—. Hormel, George A., and Company. Labor Unions and Organizations. Minnesota (Austin). Olson, Floyd B. 1933. *1142*

—. Idaho (Pocatello). Newspapers. Pullman Palace Car Company. Railroads. 1894. *782*

—. Illinois (Chicago). Militia. Police. Riots. 1877. *833*

—. Illinois (Pullman). Labor Unions and Organizations. Pullman, George M. Railroads. 1880-94. *821*

—. Immigrants. Industrial Workers of the World. New Jersey (Paterson). Textile Industry. Violence. 1913. *1223*

—. Immigrants. Industrial Workers of the World. New York (Little Falls). Textile Industry. Women. 1912. *1256*

—. Indiana (Gary). Martial law. Steel industry. 1919. *1201*

—. Indiana (Terre Haute). Railroads. 1870-90. *831*

—. Industrial Rayon Corporation. Textile Workers Organizing Committee. Virginia (Covington). 1937-38. *1156*

—. Industrial Relations. Mining. Utah (Eureka). 1886-97. *804*

—. Industrial Workers of the World. Labor Reform. New York (Little Falls). Textile Industry. Women. 1912. *1255*

—. Industrial Workers of the World. Labor Unions and Organizations. Washington (Yakima Valley). 1933. *1134*

—. Industrial Workers of the World. New Jersey (Paterson). 1913-19. *1160*

—. Industrial Workers of the World. Ohio (Akron). Rubber industry. 1913. *1278*

—. Industrialists. New York (Buffalo). Police reports. Research sources. 1890-1913. *853*

—. Industrialization. Iowa (Muscatine). Pearl button factories. 1911-12. *1245*

—. Industry. Railroads. 1877. *841*

—. Inflation. Manufacturing. 1954-75. *2093*

—. International Workingmen's Association. Marxism. Railroads. 1877. *802*

—. International Workingmen's Association. Railroads. 1877. *801*

—. Iron industry. Pennsylvania (Lancaster County). Protectionism. Wages. 1840-1900. *300*

—. J. P. Stevens & Company, Inc. Personal narratives. Rogers, Ray. 1976. *2162*

—. Labor Unions and Organizations. Mexican Americans. Texas. 1920-40. *1427*

—. Leather industry. Massachusetts (Lynn). Social Organization. 1890. *792*

—. Leatherworkers. Massachusetts (Lynn). Social Organization. 1890. *793*

—. Local government. Public employees. Unemployment. 1977. *2121*

—. Louisiana. Oil Industry and Trade. Texas. 1917-18. *1196*

—. Louisiana (New Orleans). Public opinion. Street, Electric Railway and Motor Coach Employees of America. 1929-30. *1120*

—. Lukens Iron Works. Paternalism. Pennsylvania (Coatesville). 1886. *838*

—. Lumber and Lumbering. Michigan (Upper Peninsula). 1937. *1105*

—. Mabey, Charles R. United Mine Workers of America. Utah (Carbon County). 1922. *1231*

—. Madison *Press Connection.* Newspapers. Wisconsin. Worker self-management. 1978-80. *2146*

—. Maine (Auburn, Lewiston). Shoe industry. United Shoe Workers of America. 1937. *1124*

—. Manufacturing. Models. Wages. 1948-75. *2749*

—. Manufacturing. Technology. 1950-69. *2059*

—. Mass Transit. Missouri. Modernization. Monopolies. St. Louis Transit Company. 1900. *1229*

—. Massachusetts (Haverhill). Shoe Industry. Women. 1895. *780*

—. Massachusetts (Lynn). Public Opinion. Shoe Industry. 1860. *516*

—. Massachusetts (Marlboro). Public Opinion. Shoe Industry. 1898-99. *795*

—. Mexican Americans. Sheep Shearers' Union. Texas (western). 1934. *1189*

—. Military. Public Employees. 1970-81. *2273*

—. Missouri (St. Louis). Streetcars. 1900. *1247*

—. Models. 1900-77. *299*

—. Nardella, Luigi (interview). Rhode Island. Textile Industry. 1922. *1116*

—. National Brotherhood of Operative Potters. Potters. Tariff. 1894. *837*

—. National Textile Workers Union. North Carolina (Gastonia). Textile Industry. Weisbord, Vera Buch (reminiscence). 1929. *1272*

—. New Jersey (Bayonne). Polish Americans. Standard Oil Company of New Jersey. 1915-16. *1137*

—. New Jersey (Passaic). Textile industry. Working conditions. 1875-1926. *1140*

—. New Jersey (Paterson). Silk industry. 1913-24. *1149*

—. New York. Prison guards. 1979. *2160*

—. New York. Prison guards. Public employees. Wages. 1979. *2122*

—. New York City. Postal Service. Public Employees. 1970. *2135*

—. Paint Creek-Cabin Creek Strike. *Socialist and Labor Star* (newspaper). Thompson, Wyatt Hamilton. West Virginia. 1912-13. *1131*

—. Pennsylvania (Allegheny-Kiskiminetas Valley). Steel Industry. 1919. *1200*

—. Pennsylvania (Philadelphia). Philadelphia Federation of Teachers. 1973. *2166*

—. Pennsylvania (Philadelphia). Pilots, Ship. Wages. 1792. *449*

—. Pennsylvania (Pittsburgh). Steel Industry. 1919. *1097*

—. Public employees. 1958-76. *2043*

—. Railroads. Violence. Working class. 1877. *794*

—. Rhode Island. Streetcars. 1890's-1904. *1202*

Strikes, sit-down. General Motors Corporation. Lewis, John L. 1936-37. *1148*

—. General Motors Corporation. Michigan (Flint). United Automobile Workers of America. 1936-37. *1251*

—. Ohio (Akron). Rubber industry. 1934-38. *1212*

Strikes, wildcat. Age. Coal Mines and Mining. Management. Standard of living. Working conditions. 1970's. *2041*

—. Black lung disease. Coal Mine Health and Safety Act (US, 1969; amended, 1972). Coal Miners. Medicine. United Mine Workers of America. Workers' Compensation. 1968-72. *2228*

—. Fleetwood Fisher Body plant. Michigan (Detroit). Radicals and Radicalism. United Automobile Workers of America. 1976. *2099*

—. General Electric Company (River Works Plant). Industrial safety. Kashner, Frank (account). Labor Unions and Organizations. Massachusetts (Lynn). Radicals and Radicalism. 1960's-77. *2092*

Strong, Anna Louise. China. Maoism. USA. USSR. 1919-70. *161*

Struble, Anna C. Employment, part-time. National Youth Administration. New Deal. South Dakota. Youth. 1935-43. *1318*

Stuart, Oscar J. E. Cotton scrapers. Inventions. Mississippi. Ned, slave. Patent laws. Slavery. ca 1850. *575*

Student activism. Labor Unions and Organizations. New York City. Travel accounts. Violence. 1968-79. *1533*

Student unrest. Carnegie Commission on Higher Education. Higher education. Wage labor system. 1967-73. *2618*

Students *See also* Colleges and Universities; Schools.

—. Higher Education. Occupations (expectations). Race. Sex. 1970. *2410*

Subcontracting. Developing nations. Great Britain. Japan. Manufacturing. Unemployment. USA. 1966-76. *1535*

Substitutability. Agricultural labor. Slavery. 1850-60. *626*

Substitution. Economic Conditions. Manufacturing. Natural resource products. 1960's-70's. *387*

Suburban Life *See also* Cities; Housing.

—. Economic Conditions. Population. Social Organization. 1970's. *1538*

Suburbanization. Blacks. Commuting. Employment. Illinois (Chicago). 1960-70. *1622*

Suburbs. Blacks. Discrimination. Employment. Ghettos. Housing. Social Policy. 1969-79. *1744*

—. Labor force. Women. 1920's-70's. *1797*

Success ideal. Income. Migration, internal. Occupations. Social Status. 1947-71. *1850*

Sugar cane. Blacks. Immigrants. Italians. Louisiana. Race Relations. 1880-1910. *729*

Sugar cane fields. Labor, forced. Louisiana (Lafourche Parish). Prisoners of war, German. 1943-44. *934*

Sugar industry. Louisiana. Profitability model. Slave investments. ca 1830's-1860's. *638*

Suicide. Coal Miners. Harper, Larry. Labor Unions and Organizations. Promotions. West Virginia (Stony Creek). 1940's-54. *2102*

Sullivan, Anna (interview). Massachusetts. Oral history. Textile Workers Union of America. Women. 1918-76. *1220*

Sunday, William Ashley ("Billy"). Labor. Presbyterian Church. Sermons. Virtue. Women. 1915. *970*

Supreme Court. Affirmative action. Blacks. Discrimination (review article). Gould, William B. Hill, Herbert. Labor Unions and Organizations. Seniority. 1970's. *2537*

—. Affirmative Action. Civil Rights Act (US, 1964; Titles VI, VII). Employment. *Kaiser Aluminum and Chemical Company* v. *Weber* (US, 1979). Race. *Regents of the University of California* v. *Allan Bakke* (US, 1978). 1970's. *2464*

—. California, University of, Berkeley. Collective bargaining. College teachers. *National Labor Relations Board* v. *Yeshiva University* (US, 1980). 1960-80. *2049*

—. Civil Rights Act (US, 1964). Employment. Equal opportunity. NAACP. Seniority. 1964-77. *2264*

—. Coal industry. Congress. New Deal. 1932-40. *1329*

—. Collective bargaining. College teachers. *National Labor Relations Board* v. *Yeshiva University* (US, 1980). Yeshiva University. 1973-81. *1976*

—. Constitutions. Editorials. Labor unions and organizations. New Deal. Periodicals. 1935-37. *1302*

—. Discrimination. Employment. Labor Unions and Organizations. Public employees. 1976-77. *2316*

—. Economic Conditions. National Recovery Administration. New Deal. Virginia. 1933-35. *1316*

—. Labor Law. 1977-78. *2313*

—. Labor Law. 1978-79. *2314*

—. Labor Law. Private sector. 1979-80. *2315*

Supreme courts, state. California. Collective bargaining. *Serrano* v. *Priest* (1971). Teachers. 1970's. *2000*

—. Freedom of Speech. Private Sector. Working Conditions. 1968-80. *1805*

—. Judicial Administration. Labor. Populism. Western States. 1893-1902. *856*

Surnames. Folklore. Joe Magarac (mythical character). Pennsylvania, western. Slavs. Steelworkers. 19c-1970's. *308*

Survey of Economic Opportunity, 1967. Labor market segmentation. Wages (determinants of). 1967-75. *2747*

Sutch, Richard. Agriculture. Blacks. Economic Conditions. *One Kind of Freedom* (book). Ransom, Roger. South. 1860's-80's. 1977-78. *885*

Sweden *See also* Scandinavia.

—. Agriculture. Family. Great Plains. Women. 18c-19c. *5*

—. Class Struggle. Immigration. Strikes. 1879-1906. *239*

—. Collective bargaining. Industrial democracy. USA. ca 1968-77. *279*

Swedish Americans. Farmers. French Canadians. Kansas. Mennonites. 1875-1925. *110*

—. Immigration. Labor. Månsson, Evelina. Memoirs. 1901-07. *974*

T

Tabert, Martin. Florida. Labor, forced. Law. Turpentine camps. 1923-50. *362*

Taft, Philip. Brown University. History Teaching. Labor history. 1937-68. *85*

—. Labor Unions and Organizations. 1928-76. *24*

Taft, Philip (reminiscences). Labor history. 1902-28. *909*

Taft-Hartley Act (US, 1947). AFL-CIO. Collective bargaining. Industry. Labor Unions and Organizations. Mergers. Strikes. 1946-70's. *1877*

—. Business. Labor Unions and Organizations. New Deal. Wagner Act (US, 1935). World War II. 1935-47. *1293*

—. Civil Rights Act (US, 1964; Title VII). Courts. Labor Disputes. Racial protest. Self-help. 1968-71. *1307*

Tailoring. Adams, Mary. Apprenticeship. Letters. New Hampshire (Derry). 1833-35. *528*

Talmadge, Eugene. Georgia. National Recovery Administration. State Government. Strikes. Textile industry. 1934. *1095*

Tanneries. Accidents. California. Industrial safety. Working Conditions. 1901-80. *222*

Tariff *See also* Protectionism.

—. Labor, unskilled. Manufactures. 1970-79. *2632*

—. National Brotherhood of Operative Potters. Potters. Strikes. 1894. *837*

Tax Equity and Fiscal Responsibility Act (US, 1982). Unemployment insurance. 1982. *2359*

Tax rates. Income maintenance programs (cost-effectiveness). Labor supply. Work incentives. 1973. *2705*

Taxation *See also* Income Tax; Tariff.

—. Fiscal Policy. Labor Unions and Organizations. Local Government. Public Employees. State Government. 1960-71. *2140*

—. George, Henry (*Progress and Poverty*). Land. Monopolies. Political economy. Working class. 1858-94. *664*

—. Government expenditures. Labor force. Women. 1970's. *2191*

—. Income. Prices. 1973-77. *2820*

—. Wives. Women. Working Hours. 1967-71. *1713*

Taylor, Frederick W. American Federation of Labor. Congress of Industrial Organizations. Industrial Workers of the World. Management, Scientific. 1900-13. *1017*

—. Bethlehem Steel Corporation. Executive Behavior. Management, scientific. Pennsylvania. 1898-1901. *721*

—. Factory coordination. Industry. Management, scientific. Management, systematic. 1880-1915. *113*

—. Industrial Relations. 20c. *100*

Taylor, Paul S. (*Mexican Labor in the United States*). Labor. Mexican Americans. Research. 1926-34. *1453*

Teacher Training. Catholic Church. Church Schools. Pennsylvania (Homestead). 1888-1921. *178*

—. Educational Reform. 1977. *1967*

—. Employment. 1930-83. *1975*

Teachers *See also* Educators; Teaching.

—. American Federation of Teachers. Women's Liberation Movement. 1916-73. *234*

—. Attitudes. Labor Unions and Organizations. Militancy. Nurses and Nursing. 1974. *1930*

—. Attitudes. Professionalism. South. Strikes. 1979. *1951*

—. Attitudes. Social studies. 1980-81. *1990*

—. Authority. Freedmen. South. Women. 1865-70. *703*

—. California. Collective bargaining. *Serrano v. Priest* (1971). Supreme courts, state. 1970's. *2000*

—. Carkhuff, Robert. Counselors. Human Resource Development. Models. 1976. *1965*

—. Census. Pennsylvania (Philadelphia). Public Schools. 1865-90. *686*

—. Chicago Board of Education. Chicago Teachers' Federation. Corporations. Education, Finance. Illinois. Labor Unions and Organizations. 1898-1934. *1092*

—. Children. Elementary education. Sex roles. Socialization. Women. 1959-71. *1980*

—. Citizen participation. Collective bargaining. Educational Policy. Public Schools. 1960's-70's. *1943*

—. Civil rights. Collective bargaining. Courts. Public schools. 1960-82. *1945*

—. Collective bargaining. 1850's-1970's. *2007*

—. Collective bargaining. 1970's. *1987*

—. Collective bargaining. Educational Administration. Public Schools. 1960's-70's. *1974*

—. Collective bargaining. Educational policy. 1975. *1969*

—. Collective bargaining. Monopsony. Public Schools. Wages. 1960's-70's. *2859*

—. Collective bargaining. New York. Wages. 1967-68. *2727*

—. Collective bargaining. Principals. 1970's. *2012*

—. Collective bargaining. Public schools. 1970's. *2120*

—. District of Columbia. School boards. Strikes. Wages. Washington Teachers Union. Working conditions. 1979. *2114*

—. Educational reform. Georgia (Atlanta). Illinois (Chicago). New York City. Progressivism. 1890-1920. *243*

—. Frontier and Pioneer Life. Western States. Women. 1848-54. *448*

—. Illinois. Labor Unions and Organizations. 1960-81. *1994*

—. Iowa. Men. ca 1860-99. *717*

—. Labor Unions and Organizations. New York. Political Leadership. Shanker, Albert. 1978. *2005*

—. Labor Unions and Organizations. Schools. 1979-80. *1970*

—. Labor Unions and Organizations. Wages. 1897-1960. *313*

—. Pensions. Social Policy. State Government. 1891-1930. *322*

Teachers (surplus). Attitudes. Employment. 1950-74. *2011*

Teaching *See also* Education; History Teaching; Schools; Teachers.

—. Curricula. High Schools. Labor education. 1972-82. *36*

—. High Schools. Occupations. 1950-81. *1933*

—. Institute for Labor Education and Research. Labor Unions and Organizations. New Jersey. New York. Socialism. 1976-77. *1516*

—. Labor Unions and Organizations. Shoe industry. 1830-1972. *304*

—. Women. 1850's-20c. *35*

Teamsters, International Brotherhood of. Agriculture. Boycotts. California. Chavez, Cesar. Labor Unions and Organizations. United Farm Workers Union. 1962-74. *2070*

—. Farm Workers. 1975-77. *2147*

—. *Fifth Wheel* (newspaper). Labor Unions and Organizations. Rank-and-File movements. 1977. *2128*

—. Labor Reform. 1970's. *2029*

Technical Education *See also* Vocational Education.

—. Employers. Engineering. Great Britain. 1890-1914. *219*

Technology *See also* Engineering; Industrial Technology; Inventions; Manufactures; Technical Education.

—. American Federation of Labor. Working Class. 1920's. *1025*

—. Attitudes. Blue collar workers. Connecticut. 1950-80. *1558*

—. Automation. Labor. Machine tools. Management. Science and Society. 1950-78. *1524*

—. Capitalism. Federal Regulation. Productivity. 1950-80. *2743*

—. Clerical workers. Employment. Women. 1870-1930. *220*

—. Cotton. New England. South. Textile Industry. 1890-1970. *65*

—. Drug trade. Productivity. Quality control. 1963-72. *2622*

—. Economic Growth. Social change. 1790's-1860's. *466*

—. Education. Labor, division of. 1974. *79*

—. Electric power. Natural gas. Occupations. 1960-77. *1610*

—. General Electric Company (River Works Plant). International Federation of Professional and Technical Engineers. Massachusetts (Everett, Lynn). Occupations. 1970-78. *2157*

—. Housework. Mass production. Social status. Standard of Living. 1900-70. *245*

—. Labor. Productivity. Skills. Telecommunications industry. 1970's. *1482*

—. Labor market. Longshore crane operators. 1981. *2660*

—. Labor, skilled. Productivity. Textile industry. 1960's-70's. *1865*

—. Labor Unions and Organizations. Management. Mechanization. Postal service. 1970's. *1777*

—. Manufacturing. Strikes. 1950-69. *2059*

—. Pennsylvania (Pittsburgh). Social Change. Women. Working class. 1870-1900. *711*

—. Pennsylvania (Pittsburgh). Social Conditions. Women. Working class. 1870-1900. *712*

—. Productivity. Sawmills. 1958-75. *2651*

—. Telephone. Working Conditions. 1968-79. *1501*

Technology, structure of. Alienation. Radicals and Radicalism. 1970's. *1466*

Telecommunications. International Law. International Telecommunication Union. Labor Unions and Organizations. 1932-74. *1503*

Telecommunications industry. Labor. Productivity. Skills. Technology. 1970's. *1482*

Telegraphers National Bank. Banking. Brotherhood of Railway Telegraphers. Gardner, Vernon O. Manion, Edward J. Missouri (St. Louis). 1922-42. *1171*

Telephone. Technology. Working Conditions. 1968-79. *1501*

Telephone Workers. Bell Telephone System. Company unions. Labor Unions and Organizations. 1919-37. *1248*

Television. Discrimination. Employment. Reporters and Reporting. Women. 1968-78. *2395*

Temperance Movements *See also* Alcoholism.

—. Knights of Labor. Powderly, Terence V. 1878-93. *776*

—. Massachusetts (Boston). Social Customs. Values. Working class. 1838-40. *420*

Temple University (Urban Archives). Archival Catalogs and Inventories. Labor Unions and Organizations. 1982. *71*

Tenancy. Agricultural Labor. South. Wages. 1930-60. *3*

—. Indentured servants, former. Letters. Maryland (Anne Arundel County). Roberts, William. Working Class. 1756-69. *515*

Tennessee *See also* South Central and Gulf States.

—. Apprenticeship. Indentured servants. Law. 1800-60. *506*

—. Blacks. Labor. Letters. Riley, William R. United Mine Workers of America. 1892-95. *876*

—. Coal miners. Convict labor. Labor Disputes. State Government. Violence. 1891-93. *646*

—. Coal miners. Convict labor. State Government. Strikes. 1891-93. *642*

—. Convict lease system. O'Connor, Thomas. 1871-83. *718*

Tennessee (Alcoa). Aluminum Company of America. Blacks. Labor. 1919-39. *1431*

—. Hultquist, Victor J. Smith, Arthur B. 1919-39. *1226*

Tennessee (Bolivar). Harman International Industries. Labor Reform. Worker self-management. 1974-75. *1724*

Tennessee (Chattanooga area). Horton, Myles (interview). Moyers, Bill. Radicals and Radicalism. 1932-81. *284*

Tennessee, eastern. Coal miners. Davidson-Wilder Strike of 1932. Graham, Barney. Strikes. United Mine Workers of America. 1932-33. *1096*

Tennessee (Knoxville). American Federation of Labor. Armies. Police. Streetcars. Strikes. 1919-20. *1118*

Tennessee (Memphis). Fire Fighters. Strikes. Voluntary Associations. 1858-60. *517*

Tennessee (Nashville). Slaves, quasifree. South. Thomas, James P. 1818-82. *627*

Tennessee Valley Authority. American Federation of Labor. Appalachia. Industrial Relations. Public Employees. 1933-78. *1324*

Tentler, Leslie Woodcock. Cantor, Milton. Dublin, Thomas. Foner, Philip. Katzman, David. Laurie, Bruce. Women (review article). Work. 17c-20c. *231*

Tenure. College Teachers. Employment, temporary. Roucek, Joseph. 1960-79. *1985*

—. College teachers. Pangle, Thomas. Yale University. 1979-80. *1699*

—. Colleges and universities. 1970's-81. *1942*

Terkel, Studs *(Working)*. Interviews. Occupations. 1970. *1477*

Terrorism *See also* Crime and Criminals.

—. Coal Miners. Irish Americans. Ownership. Pennsylvania. Working Conditions. 1850-70. *707*

Texas *See also* South Central and Gulf States.

—. Affirmative action. Attitudes. Cities. Public Employees. 1978. *2423*

—. Age. Blacks. Discrimination. Income. Mexican Americans. 1960-70. *2521*

—. Agricultural Labor. Economic Structure. Freedmen. Racism. Reconstruction. 1865-74. *737*

—. Blacks. City Government. Equal opportunity. Mexican Americans. Urbanization. 1973. *2477*

—. Brotherhood of Timber Workers. Industrial Workers of the World. Louisiana. Lumber and Lumbering. Race Relations. 1910-13. *1164*

—. California. Labor force. Mexican Americans. Women. 1969-74. *1557*

—. Clothing industry. International Ladies' Garment Workers' Union. Women. 1933-50. *1168*

—. Collective Bargaining. Fire and Police Employee Relations Act (Texas, 1973). Public Employees. Referendum. 1973-81. *2023*

—. Congress of Industrial Organizations. Oil Industry and Trade. World War II. 1942-43. *1035*

—. Economic Development. Employment. Public Works Administration. 1933-34. *1369*

—. Employment. State government. Women. 1970's. *2526*

—. Foreign Relations. Mexico. Migrant labor. 1942-47. *1419*

—. Immigration. Institutions. Labor. Mexicans. Southwest. Undocumented workers. 1821-1975. *235*

—. Labor force. Mexican Americans. Mexico. Migration. 1960's-70's. *1587*

—. Labor Unions and Organizations. Mexican Americans. Socialism. 1900-20. *1001*

—. Labor Unions and Organizations. Mexican Americans. Strikes. 1920-40. *1427*

—. Labor Unions and Organizations. Mexican Americans. United Cannery, Agricultural, Packing and Allied Workers of America. 1935-50. *1214*

—. Louisiana. Oil Industry and Trade. Strikes. 1917-18. *1196*

—. Missouri-Kansas-Texas Railroad. Oklahoma. Railroads (branch lines). 1906-75. *956*

Texas (Austin). Economy Furniture Factory. Mass Media. Mexican Americans. Strikes. 1968-72. *2123*

Texas (Dallas). Discrimination. Employment. Equal Employment Opportunity Commission. 1970's. *2351*

Texas, eastern. Brotherhood of Timber Workers. Emerson, Arthur L. Industrial Workers of the World. Labor Disputes. Louisiana, western. Lumber and Lumbering. 1900-16. *1022*

—. Brotherhood of Timber Workers. Louisiana, western. Lumber and Lumbering. Race Relations. Southern Lumber Operators' Association. 1911-13. *1165*

—. Labor disputes. Louisiana. Lumber and Lumbering. 1906-16. *1145*

—. Civil service. Colleges and universities. Management. Training Act (1958). 1958-70's. *1949*

—. Economic Theory. Government. Labor market, operation of. Vocational Education. 1974. *2246*

—. Employment. New York City. 1970-78. *1480*

—. Private sector. Public employees. 1960's-80's. *1785*

—. Professionals. Women. 1960-73. *1765*

Training programs (evaluation). Employment. Manpower Development and Training Act (1962). 1962-70. *2330*

Tramps. Migrant Labor. Nebraska (Omaha). 1887-1913. *224*

Transfer payments. Public welfare. Work ethic. 1976. *1492*

Transport Workers Union. Blacks. Communist Party. Discrimination. Fair Employment Practices Commission. Labor Unions and Organizations. New York City. Pennsylvania (Philadelphia). 1934-44. *1420*

Transportation *See also* names of transportation vehicles, e.g. Automobiles, Ships, Buses, Trucks, Railroads, etc.; Aeronautics; Commerce; Mass Transit; Merchant Marine; Postal Service; Public Transportation; Shipping.

—. Blacks. California (Los Angeles). Employment. Housing. Segregation. 1941-45. *1440*

—. Commuting. Kentucky. 1979. *1644*

—. Crime and Criminals. Employment. Housing. Metropolitan areas. Schools. 1970's. *1474*

—. North Dakota Workmen's Compensation Bureau. Rice, Hazel F. (account). Working conditions. 1919-22. *1352*

Transportation, Commercial. Air Lines. Deregulation. Labor Unions and Organizations. 1978-82. *2115*

Trask, Sarah E. Diaries. Massachusetts (Beverly). Shoe Industry. Women. Working Class. 1849-51. *412*

Travel. Employment. Women. 1970's-82. *1639*

Travel accounts. Labor Unions and Organizations. New York City. Student activism. Violence. 1968-79. *1533*

Travel agency industry. New York City. Sex roles. 1974. *2517*

Treadwell Mines. Alaska (Douglas Island). Labor Unions and Organizations. Miners. Strikes. Western Federation of Miners. 1905-10. *1154*

Trials *See also* Crime and Criminals.

—. Beatty, James H. Coxey, Jacob S. Idaho. Political Protest. 1894. *835*

—. California (Wheatland). Industrial Workers of the World. Migrant Labor. State Government. Strikes. 1913-17. *1133*

—. College teachers. Sex discrimination. Women. 1964-82. *2394*

—. Fiske, Harold B. Freedom of speech. Industrial Workers of the World. Kansas. Labor Unions and Organizations. 1923-27. *1014*

—. Industrial Workers of the World. Kansas. Radicals and Radicalism. Red Scare. 1917-19. *1038*

—. Industrial Workers of the World. Kansas (Wichita). Labor Unions and Organizations. Oil Industry and Trade. *United States v. C. W. Anderson et al.* (US, 1919). World War I. 1917-19. *1078*

—. Jones Family (group). Oklahoma (Cleveland, Pottawatomie counties). Sedition. Working Class Union. World War I. 1917. *1206*

Triangle fire. Italian Americans. Labor Unions and Organizations. Padrone system. Personal Narratives. Rizzo, Saverio. 1900-30. *963*

Trilateral Commission. Europe, Western. Japan. Public services. Wages. 1973-79. *2377*

Tri-State Union. Kansas (Cherokee County). Labor Unions and Organizations. Mining. Missouri (Jasper, Newton counties). Oklahoma (Ottawa County). 1848-1960's. *950*

Truck driver culture. Civil Disturbances. Freeway blockades. Ohio. Pennsylvania. 1973. *2036*

Trucks and Trucking. Federal Regulation. Interstate Commerce Commission. 1938-76. *2310*

Truman, Harry S. Agriculture. Bracero program. Mexico. President's Commission on Migratory Labor. Undocumented workers. 1950. *2286*

Truman, Harry S. (administration). Wage Stabilization Board. Wages. 1950-53. *2352*

Trumbo, Dalton. Blacklisting. California (Hollywood). Film industry. Letters. 1940's-60's. *1606*

Turpentine camps. Florida. Labor, forced. Law. Tabert, Martin. 1923-50. *362*

Turpentine industry. North Carolina (Onslow County). Secession. Slavery. 1790-1861. *546*

Tuskegee Institute. Alabama. Blacks. Industrial Arts Education. Washington, Booker T. 1870's-90's. *708*

Twelve-hour day. American Iron and Steel Institute. Steel industry. Working conditions. 1890's-1923. *1207*

—. Canada. Chemical Industry. Oil Industry and Trade. USA. Working Conditions. 1977. *1753*

—. Labor Reform. Steel industry. 1887-1923. *1169*

Tyler, Gus (views). Colleges and Universities. Labor education. Labor Unions and Organizations. 1928-78. *133*

U

UAW. *See* United Automobile Workers of America.

UFWA. *See* United Farm Workers of America.

UMWA. *See* United Mine Workers of America.

Undocumented Workers. Agricultural Labor. Agricultural Reform. Diffusion. Labor Market. 1850-1981. *2733*

—. Agricultural Labor. Attitudes. Bracero Program. Labor Unions and Organizations. Mexico. 1943-74. *1511*

—. Agriculture. Bracero program. Mexico. President's Commission on Migratory Labor. Truman, Harry S. 1950. *2286*

—. Bracero Program. Immigration, patterns of. Mexico. Quotas. USA. 1960's-70's. *2826*

—. California (Los Angeles). Mexicans. Migration. 1979. *1561*

—. Capitalism. Children. Mexico. Women. ca 1950-79. *2470*

—. Construction industry. Labor Unions and Organizations. Skill differential. Wages. 1907-72. *393*

—. Federal policy. Labor unions and organizations. 1979-82. *1520*

—. Immigrants. Mexico (Michoacán). 1977-78. *1782*

—. Immigration. Income. Southwest. 1960-80. *2673*

—. Immigration. Institutions. Labor. Mexicans. Southwest. Texas. 1821-1975. *235*

—. Immigration, illegal. Labor force. Law. Mexican Americans. 1976. *1728*

—. Immigration policy. Labor force. 1950's-70's. *1871*

—. Labor. Mexican Americans. Social mobility. 1970-80. *1562*

—. Labor market. Mexico. USA. 1970's. *1775*

—. Labor market. Statistics. 1968-80. *2799*

—. Labor Unions and Organizations. Mexico. 1867-1977. *8*

—. Mexicans. 1970's. *1729*

—. Mexicans. 20c. *1595*

—. Mexicans. Migrant Labor. Oregon (Hood River Valley). Wages. 1978. *1611*

—. Mexico. 1973. *1596*

—. Mexico. Research. 1930-76. *42*

Undocumented Workers (review article). García, Juan Ramon. Lewis, Sasha G. Mexicans. Working Conditions. 1954-80. *2196*

Unemployed Citizens' League. Dix, I. F. Hoover, Herbert C. Local politics. Self-help. Washington (Seattle). 1931-32. *1340*

Unemployed councils. Depressions. Radicals and Radicalism. 1929-33. *1065*

Unemployed Leagues. Muste, Abraham J. Radicals and Radicalism. 1932-36. *912*

Unemployment *See also* Employment; Unemployment Insurance.

—. 1946-61. *2765*

—. 1946-80. *1542*

—. 1950-70. *1487*

—. 1981. *2604*

—. AFL-CIO. Multinational corporations. USA. 1970-74. *1913*

—. Aged. 1968-81. *1790*

—. Aged. Labor force. 1970's. *1796*

—. Aged. Retirement. 1966-73. *1584*

—. Aid to Families with Dependent Children. Food stamps. 1975-79. *2647*

—. Assembly line workers. Construction workers. 1974-75. *1803*

—. Attitudes. 1960's-70's. *1730*

—. Attitudes. 1969-70. *1702*

—. Attitudes. Government. 18c-1978. *74*

—. Attitudes. Job Security. Social Surveys. 1977-78. *1845*

—. Attitudes. Labor force. 1973. *1807*

—. Attitudes. Middle Classes. Professionals. 1972. *1981*

—. Attitudes. Occupational flexibility. Social Psychology. 1962. *1567*

—. Automation. Labor Unions and Organizations. 1800-40's. 1960's-70's. *1523*

—. Automation. Public policy. 1982. *1813*

—. Automobile Industry and Trade. Employment. Housing. Recessions. 1980. *2839*

—. Behavior. Conservatism. Economic Theory. Recessions. 1978. *2695*

—. Birth rate. Inflation. Public Welfare. 1945-77. *2652*

—. Blacks. 1948-72. *2522*

—. Blacks. 1970's. *2483*

—. Blacks. Buses. Missouri (St. Louis). Public transportation. 1973. *2468*

—. Blacks. Business Cycles. Youth. 1954-78. *1749*

—. Blacks. Cities. Discrimination. Employment. Women. 1960's-70's. *2417*

—. Blacks. Education. 1960-70. *2466*

—. Blacks. Income. Minorities. 1960's-70's. *2576*

—. Blacks. Industry. 1955-81. *2512*

—. Blacks. Inflation. Military Expenditures. 1970-78. *2400*

—. Blacks. Johnson, Lyndon. Labor market. Marx, Karl. Youth. 1950-80. *2573*

—. Blacks. Methodology. Whites. 1910's-70's. *1430*

—. Blacks. Social policy. Whites. 1964-77. *2609*

—. Blacks. Whites. 1954-73. *2465*

—. Blacks. Youth. 1970's-80. *2487*

—. Blacks. Youth. 1975. *2428*

—. Brucker, Wilber M. Depressions. Federal Aid. Michigan. Murphy, Frank. 1929-33. *1345*

—. Business Cycles. 1960's-70's. *2658*

—. Business Cycles. 1967-79. *1632*

—. Business Cycles. Europe. Inflation. Wages. 1945-70. *2683*

—. Business Cycles. Women. 1945-78. *2503*

—. California. Leisure. State Legislatures. 1979. *2305*

—. California (San Francisco). Job Factory for Youth. Job Track (program). Youth. 1979-81. *1846*

—. California (Santa Barbara). Fleischmann, Max. Philanthropy. Relief work. 1930-32. *1342*

—. Canada. Computers. Industry. Robots. USA. 1964-81. *1479*

—. Canada. Labor. Provincial government. Public employment bureaus. Social Reform. State government. USA. 1890-1916. *1356*

—. Capitalism. 1975-82. *2847*

—. Capitalism. Economic performance. Industrialization. Statistics. 19c-1976. *379*

—. Capitalism. Economics. 1970-75. *2863*

—. Chinese. Knights of Labor. Labor Unions and Organizations. Oregon. Political Protest. Washington. 1880's. *836*

—. Cities. Domestic Policy. President's Commission for a National Agenda for the Eighties (*Urban America in the Eighties*). 1970-80. *2281*

—. Cities. Youth. 1970's. *1708*

—. Collective Bargaining. Corporations. Wages. 1982. *1894*

—. Collective bargaining. Economic Conditions. 1940-82. *2785*

—. College graduates. Income. 1970's. *1937*

—. Conservatism. Economic Theory. 1920's. 1970's. *2694*

—. Coxey's Army. Missouri River. Montana. Political Protest. 1894. *834*

—. Current Population Survey. 1967-79. *2703*

—. Democratic Party. Elections, congressional. 1958-74. *2285*

—. Depressions. Europe, western. USA. 1929-41. *948*

—. Depressions. Liberalism. New Deal. Political activism. Socialist Party. 1929-36. *1354*

—. Depressions. Mecklenburg, George H. Minnesota (Minneapolis). Organized Unemployed, Inc. Poor. Self-help. 1932-35. *916*

—. Depressions. Professionals. 1929-35. *1093*

—. Depressions. Self-perception. Working Class. 1920's-30's. *995*

—. Developing nations. Great Britain. Japan. Manufacturing. Subcontracting. USA. 1966-76. *1535*

—. Discrimination. Employment. Women. 1940's-70's. *2449*

—. Dismissals. 1968-82. *2606*

—. Economic Conditions. 1950-76. *2716*

—. Economic Conditions. Federal government. Inflation. 1976. *2233*

—. Economic Conditions. Inflation. 1973. *2645*

—. Economic Conditions. Social Conditions. Wages. Working class. 1921-29. *996*

—. Coal miners. Colorado (Las Animas, Huerfano counties). Strikes. 1904-14. *1263*
—. Coal miners. Davidson-Wilder Strike of 1932. Graham, Barney. Strikes. Tennessee, eastern. 1932-33. *1096*
—. Coal Miners. Diaries. Medrick, George. Pennsylvania, western. Strikes. 1927. *1146*
—. Coal Miners. Discrimination. Japanese Americans. Mitchell, John. Wyoming. 1886-1910. *1402*
—. Coal Miners. Duke Power Company. Kentucky (Harlan County; Brookside). Strikes. 1973-74. *2034*
—. Coal miners. Germer, Adolph. Illinois (Virden). Socialism. Strikes. 1893-1900. *785*
—. Coal Miners. Glasscock, William E. Martial law. National Guard. Violence. West Virginia (Cabin Creek, Paint Creek). 1912-13. *1101*
—. Coal Miners. Hanraty, Pete. Oklahoma. Strikes. 1899-1903. *1102*
—. Coal Miners. Hocking Valley. Lewis, John L. Ohio, southeastern. Strikes. 1927. *1258*
—. Coal Miners. Illinois (Macoupin, Montgomery Counties). Labor Unions and Organizations. Radicals and Radicalism. Virden Massacre. ca 1870-1939. *297*
—. Coal Miners. Keeney, Frank. West Virginia. 1916-31. *1130*
—. Coal Miners. Kentucky (Harlan County; Evarts). Strikes. 1931. *1106*
—. Coal Miners. Labor Disputes. Mingo War. Violence. West Virginia (southern). 1919-22. *1177*
—. Coal miners. Labor Unions and Organizations. Violence. West Virginia (Logan, Mingo Counties). 1921-22. *1228*
—. Coal Miners. Lewis, John L. 1880-1920. *1173*
—. Coal Miners. North Dakota (Wilton). Washburn Lignite Coal Company. 1900-30's. *1276*
—. Coal Miners. Pennsylvania. Strikes. 1922-23. *1180*
—. Coal Miners. Pinchot, Gifford. Strikes. 1925-26. *1179*
—. Coal Miners. Racism. Strikes. 1894-1920. *1259*
—. Coal Miners. Strikes. 1977-78. *2078*
—. Coal Mines and Mining. Deverall, Richard Lawrence-Grace. Documents. Ickes, Harold. Strikes. West Virginia (Welch). 1943. *1235*
—. Coal Mines and Mining. Employers. Mitchell, John. 1897-1907. *807*
—. Coal Mines and Mining. *Harlan County, U.S.A.* (film). Kentucky. Kopple, Barbara. Strikes. 1973-74. *2161*
—. Coal Mines and Mining. *Harlan County, U.S.A.* (film). Kentucky. Kopple, Barbara (interview). Strikes. 1973-76. *2119*
—. Coal Mines and Mining. Knights of Labor. Race Relations. West Virginia, southern. 1880-94. *867*
—. Coal Mines and Mining. Labor Unions and Organizations. Leadership. Miller, Arnold. 1972-74. *2040*
—. Coal Mines and Mining. Miller, Arnold. Strikes. 1972-76. *2116*
—. Coal Mines and Mining. State Government. Strikes. West Virginia (Paint Creek). 1912-13. *1257*
—. Coal Mines and Mining. Strikes. 1890-1978. *2032*
—. Conflicts of interest. Finance. Mitchell, John (1870-1919). 1899-1908. *1060*
—. Courts. Jackson, John Jay, Jr. Jones, Mary Harris. Strikes. West Virginia. 1902. *1262*
—. Energy industries. Labor Unions and Organizations. Miller, Arnold. 1950's-74. *2133*
—. Hospital workers. Kentucky (Pikeville, Prestonsburg). Labor Unions and Organizations. National Labor Relations Board. 1973-76. *2030*
—. Labor Unions and Organizations. Lewis, John L. Power (abuses of). 1880-1972. *1029*
—. Labor Unions and Organizations. Lewis, John L. Reorganized United Mine Workers of America. 1920-33. *1011*
—. Labor Unions and Organizations. Miners for Democracy. Rank-and-file movements. 1972. *1879*
—. Liberalism. 1972-73. *1928*
—. Mabey, Charles R. Strikes. Utah (Carbon County). 1922. *1231*
United Mine Workers of America Health and Retirement Fund. Coal Mines and Mining. Medical care. 1946-78. *1880*
—. Coal Mines and Mining. Medical Care (costs). West Virginia (Cedar Grove). 1970's. *2076*

—. Federal government. Legislation. Public Welfare. 1945-70's. *2182*
United Packinghouse Workers of America. Beltrame, Ed. Fishermen. Florida (Cortez). Knowlton, Bob. Labor Unions and Organizations. 1930-58. *1163*
United Rubber Workers. Alabama (Gadsden). Goodyear Tire and Rubber Company. House, John D. Rubber. 1941. *1210*
United Shoe Workers of America. Maine (Auburn, Lewiston). Shoe industry. Strikes. 1937. *1124*
United Society for Manufactures and Importation. Employment. Linen. Massachusetts (Boston). Poverty. Textile Industry. Women. 1735-60. *459*
United States. *See* entries beginning with the word American or US; North America; states; regions, e.g. New England, Western States, etc.; British North America; also names of government agencies and departments, e.g. Bureau of Indian Affairs, State Department.
United States Brewers' Association. Brewing industry. Labor Unions and Organizations. Workers' compensation. 1910-12. *899*
United States v. *C. W. Anderson et al.* (US, 1919). Industrial Workers of the World. Kansas (Wichita). Labor Unions and Organizations. Oil Industry and Trade. Trials. World War I. 1917-19. *1078*
United Steelworkers of America. Arbitration, Industrial. Steel industry. 1971-73. *2067*
—. Conventions. 1978. *2026*
—. Elections. Labor Unions and Organizations. Leadership. Sadlowski, Ed. 1976-77. *1918*
—. Elections. Labor Unions and Organizations. Leadership. Sadlowski, Ed. 1976-77. *2096*
—. Elections. Labor Unions and Organizations. Sadlowski, Ed. 1976-77. *2090*
—. Labor Unions and Organizations. Mine, Mill and Smelter Workers, International Union of. Radicals and Radicalism. 1950-67. *1906*
—. McBride, Lloyd. Sadlowski, Ed. 1976-77. *2167*
United Steelworkers of America's Human Relations Committee. Industrial relations. 1960-65. *2117*
Universities. *See* Colleges and Universities; Higher Education.
University and College Labor Education Association. College Teachers. Higher education. Labor. 1976. *1989*
Urbanization *See also* City Planning; Modernization; Rural-Urban Studies.
—. Blacks. City Government. Equal opportunity. Mexican Americans. Texas. 1973. *2477*
—. Coal Miners. Ethnic Groups. Industrialization. Pennsylvania (Scranton). Working Class. 1855-85. *743*
—. Counties. Economic growth. Employment. 1960's. *2775*
US Employment Service. Employment. Public services. 1890-1933. *325*
US Steel Corporation. Americanization. Indiana (Gary). Labor Unions and Organizations. Polish Americans. 1906-20. *925*
—. Blacks. Discrimination. Indiana (Gary). 1906-74. *344*
—. Foreign policy. Import restrictions. International Steel Cartel. Steel Workers Organizing Committee. 1937. *1325*
Ushers. Behavior. Movie theaters. Youth. 1920-29. *941*
USSR *See also* Russia.
—. American Federation of Labor. Foreign policy. Labor delegation. 1926-27. *1042*
—. China. Maoism. Strong, Anna Louise. USA. 1919-70. *161*
—. Congress of Industrial Organizations. Isolationism. Leftism. Pacific Northwest. 1937-41. *1051*
—. Defections. Grady, John. Haywood, William Dudley. Industrial Workers of the World. Letters. Schuyler, Mont. USA. 1921-22. *1062*
—. Historiography. USA. 1976. *122*
—. Industrial Relations. Work incentives. 20c. *2657*
—. Managers. Professionals. USA. Women. 1917-70. *1934*
—. Occupational segregation. Public policy. USA. Women. 1917-70's. *2288*
Utah *See also* Far Western States.
—. Carbon County Coal Strike (1933). National Miners Union. Strikes. United Mine Workers of America. 1900-39. *1225*
—. Employment. Women. 1896-1940. *1426*
—. Labor Unions and Organizations. Mormons. 1850-96. *262*

—. Women. 1900-76. *148*
Utah (Carbon County). Antiforeign sentiment. Coal Miners. Strikes. Utah Fuel Company. 1902-04. *1230*
—. Mabey, Charles R. Strikes. United Mine Workers of America. 1922. *1231*
Utah (Castle Gate). Accidents. Coal Mines and Mining. Disaster relief. Mabey, Charles R. Palmer, Annie. Social work. 1924-36. *959*
Utah, eastern. Coal fields. Immigrants. Labor movement. Strikebreakers. 1875-1929. *826*
Utah (Eureka). Industrial Relations. Mining. Strikes. 1886-97. *804*
Utah Fuel Company. Antiforeign sentiment. Coal Miners. Strikes. Utah (Carbon County). 1902-04. *1230*
Utah Gazetteer, 1892-93. Employment. Utah (Salt Lake City). Women. 1892-93. *719*
Utah (Salt Lake City). Employment. *Utah Gazetteer, 1892-93.* Women. 1892-93. *719*
Utah (Willard). Convict labor camp. 1911-30. *982*
Utilities. *See* Public Utilities.
Utopias. DeBernardi, Giovanni Battista. Depressions. Freedom Colony. Kansas. Labor Exchange. 1894-1905. *654*

V

Vagrancy. Attitudes. Depressions. Great Britain. Law. Poor. USA. 14c-1939. *939*
Values *See also* Attitudes; Public Opinion.
—. Armies. Railroads. Strikes. 1877. 1894. *788*
—. Community, sense of. Massachusetts (Lowell). Strikes. Women. 1820-50. *422*
—. Depressions. Labor force. Middle Classes. Women. 1930's. *929*
—. Economic growth. Housework. Women. 1800-1930. *27*
—. Economic Structure. Employment. 1972-77. *1745*
—. Fairness (concept). Income. 1970's. *2597*
—. Gilbert, James B. Industrialization. Intellectuals. Labor (review article). Rodgers, Daniel T. 1850-1920. 1974-77. *55*
—. Industrialization. Leisure. 19c-20c. *18*
—. Iron Industry. Maryland (Baltimore County). Northampton Iron Works. Police. 1780-1820. *537*
—. Labor Disputes. Massachusetts (Lowell). Social Organization. Textile Industry. Women. 1836-40's. *424*
—. Massachusetts (Boston). Social Customs. Temperance movements. Working class. 1838-40. *420*
—. Occupations. Socialization. 1966-76. *2736*
Vermont *See also* New England; Northeastern or North Atlantic States.
—. Cerasoli, Mose (memoir). Granite workers. Labor Disputes. 1913-38. *987*
—. Civilian Conservation Corps. Economic Conditions. New Deal. 1933-42. *1363*
—. Massachusetts (Clinton). Textile workers. 1851. *415*
Vermont (Rutland). Class conflict. Political Change. Working Class. 1880-96. *650*
Verona (vessel). Industrial Workers of the World. Violence. Washington (Everett). 1916. *1274*
Veterans. Blacks. Education. Income. Military Service. 1940-70. *2729*
—. Employment. Vietnam War. 1970-78. *1823*
—. Employment. Vietnam War. 1973-74. *1660*
Vietnam, South. Cambodia. Economic conditions. Employment. Laos. Refugee Act (US, 1980). 1975-79. *1563*
Vietnam War. Communist Party. Political attitudes. Working class. Working Conditions. ca 1960-74. *1768*
—. Employment. Veterans. 1970-78. *1823*
—. Employment. Veterans. 1973-74. *1660*
Vietnamese. Assimilation. Occupations. Refugees. Sex roles. Social status. 1975. *1703*
Vietnamese Americans. Economic Conditions. Occupations. Refugees. 1970's. *1818*
Vigilantes. Freedom of speech. Oklahoma. Political Repression. World War I. 1914-17. *1303*
Village Voice (newspaper). Hentoff, Nat (account). Labor Unions and Organizations. New York City. 1975-77. *2084*
Violas, Paul C. Feinberg, Walter. Public Schools (review article). Rosemont, Henry, Jr. Social control. Working Class. 1880-20c. *4*
Violence. Arkansas (Elaine). Farmers, tenant. Race Relations. Sharecroppers. 1919. *1449*

—. Blacks. Employment. Illinois (Chicago). Industry. Polish Americans. Stereotypes. 1890-1919. *359*

—. Coal miners. Convict labor. Labor Disputes. State Government. Tennessee. 1891-93. *646*

—. Coal Miners. Glasscock, William E. Martial law. National Guard. United Mine Workers of America. West Virginia (Cabin Creek, Paint Creek). 1912-13. *1101*

—. Coal Miners. Labor Disputes. Mingo War. United Mine Workers of America. West Virginia (southern). 1919-22. *1177*

—. Coal miners. Labor Unions and Organizations. United Mine Workers of America. West Virginia (Logan, Mingo Counties). 1921-22. *1228*

—. Coal Mines and Mining. Ohio (Hocking Valley). Strikebreakers. 1884-85. *790*

—. Depressions. Kentucky (Louisville). Labor disputes. 1877. *844*

—. Immigrants. Industrial Workers of the World. New Jersey (Paterson). Strikes. Textile Industry. 1913. *1223*

. Industrial Workers of the World. *Verona* (vessel). Washington (Everett). 1916. *1274*

—. Irish Americans. Labor Unions and Organizations. Molly Maguires. Myths and Symbols. Nativism. Pennsylvania. Philadelphia and Reading Railroad. 1860's-78. *1098*

—. Labor Unions and Organizations. New York City. Student activism. Travel accounts. 1968-79. *1533*

—. Railroads. Strikes. Working class. 1877. *794*

Virden Massacre. Coal Miners. Illinois (Macoupin, Montgomery Counties). Labor Unions and Organizations. Radicals and Radicalism. United Mine Workers of America. ca 1870-1939. *297*

Virginia. Baughman Brothers (company). Boycotts. Knights of Labor. Richmond Typographical Union. 1886-88. *784*

—. Blacks. Labor force. Race relations. Social Change. Tobacco. 1660-1710. *414*

—. California. Farm workers. Labor law. Law. Minimum wage. State Government. 1975. *2187*

—. Church of England. Clergy (recruitment). 1726-76. *438*

—. Deregulation. Licenses. State Legislatures. 1974-78. *2259*

—. Economic Conditions. National Recovery Administration. New Deal. Supreme Court. 1933-35. *1316*

—. Economics. Galenson, David. Immigration. Indentured Servants (review article). Maryland. West Indies. 1654-1776. *533*

—. Indentured servitude. Maryland. Slavery. 1620-1720. *608*

—. Iron industry. Slavery. 1720-1865. *603*

—. Life insurance. North Carolina. Slavery. 1840-65. *624*

Virginia (Charles City County). Confessions. Documents. Domestic Servants. Hellier, Thomas. Murder. Williams, Paul. Williamson, Cuthbert (family). 1650-70. *500*

Virginia (Covington). Industrial Rayon Corporation. Strikes. Textile Workers Organizing Committee. 1937-38. *1156*

—. International Brotherhood of Pulp, Sulphite, and Paper Mill Workers. Labor Unions and Organizations. Paper Industry. West Virginia Pulp and Paper Company. 1933-52. *1282*

Virginia, eastern. Coal Miners. Insurance. Investments. Occupational Safety. Slavery. 1780-1865. *599*

Virginia (Elizabeth City County). Hiring system. Slavery. 1782-1810. *588*

Virginia (Lynchburg). Elections (municipal). Knights of Labor. Political Parties. Reform. Working Class. 1881-90. *862*

—. Iron industry. Oxford Iron Works. Ross, David. Slavery, industrial. 1775-1817. *561*

Virginia (Richmond). Blacks. City Politics. Elections, municipal. Knights of Labor. Political Reform. 1886-88. *869*

—. Christianity. Factories. Slavery (urban). Social Organization. Tobacco. ca 1820-65. *615*

Virtue. Labor. Presbyterian Church. Sermons. Sunday, William Ashley ("Billy"). Women. 1915. *970*

Vocational Education *See also* Technical Education; Training Programs.

—. Bureau of Indian Affairs. Oregon (Portland). Training programs. 1964-66. *2202*

—. Disadvantaged. Employers. Labor market. 1962-74. *1638*

—. Economic Conditions. Junior colleges. 1946-79. *1773*

—. Economic Opportunity Act (1964). Job Corps. Youth, disadvantaged. 1964-75. *2292*

—. Economic Theory. Government. Labor market, operation of. Training programs. 1974. *2246*

—. Employment. Youth Employment and Demonstration Projects Act (US, 1977). 1977-82. *2391*

—. Federal Policy. High Schools. Smith-Hughes Act (US, 1917). 1917-80's. *2176*

—. High School of Fashion Industry. Minorities. New York City. Sex Discrimination. Women. 1975. *2402*

—. Men. Wages. Whites. 1961-71. *1829*

—. Minorities. Women. 1979-81. *1576*

—. National Alliance of Businessmen. Unemployment. 1968-71. *2210*

—. State Government. 1974. *2208*

—. Work Experience Programs. 1980. *1668*

Vocational Education Act (US, 1963). Federal Regulation. 1963-80. *2265*

Vocational rehabilitation. Employment. Handicapped. 1965-75. *1714*

Vogel, Henry. Construction. Frontier and Pioneer Life. Oklahoma (Muskogee, Tahlequah) Personal narratives. 1887-1900. *671*

Voluntarism. American Federation of Labor. Brotherhood of Painters and Decorators. Gompers, Samuel. Rank-and-file movements. 1894-1900. *759*

—. Labor movement. Labor Unions and Organizations. Legislation. 1890's-1930's. *901*

Voluntary Associations. Community participation. Missouri (St. Louis; Carondelet). Social Organizations. Women. Working Class. 1970's. *1612*

—. Fire Fighters. Strikes. Tennessee (Memphis). 1858-60. *517*

—. Idaho (Pocatello). Women. World War I. 1917-18. *986*

Voting and Voting Behavior *See also* Elections.

—. Cannon, Joseph Gurney. Gompers, Samuel. House of Representatives. Illinois (Danville). Labor Unions and Organizations. 1906-08. *1063*

—. Coal Miners. Illinois. Quantitative Methods. Socialist Party. 1900-40. *1370*

—. House of Representatives. Labor Unions and Organizations. 1965-78. *2343*

—. Lunn, George. New York (Schenectady). Socialist Party. Working Class. 1911-16. *1304*

—. Political parties, incumbent. Unemployment. 1974-76. *1733*

W

Wage controls. Economic Policy. Nixon administration (Pay Board). 1940's-73. *2388*

—. Industrial relations. Phase II (1971). 1971. *2735*

—. Labor law. Massachusetts Bay Colony. 1630-60. *461*

Wage differentials. Industry. Pennsylvania (Pittsburgh). Skills. 1889-1914. *1458*

—. Labor Unions and Organizations. 1933-73. *2665*

—. Men. Occupational structure. Women. 1960-77. *2801*

—. Men. Professionals. Sex Discrimination. Women. 1966-71. *2511*

Wage indexing. Comprehensive Employment and Training Act (US, 1973). Federal funds. Geographic distribution. Medicare. 1978-80. *2242*

Wage labor system. Carnegie Commission on Higher Education. Higher education. Student unrest. 1967-73. *2618*

Wage Stabilization Board. Truman, Harry S. (administration). Wages. 1950-53. *2352*

Wage stabilization policies. Federal Pay Board. 1971-72. *2309*

Wage survey indexes. Employment. Industry. Labor Department (Bureau of Labor Statistics). 1972. *2704*

Wage-price controls *See also* Price controls; Wage controls.

—. 1914-71. *396*

—. Economic Planning. 1971-74. *2864*

—. Economic planning. Income distribution. 1960-74. *2773*

—. Economic Regulations. 1960-74. *2769*

—. Economic stabilization. Nixon, Richard M. (administration). Phase III (1973). 1970-73. *2172*

—. Economic Stabilization Program. Manufacturing. 1969-75. *2386*

—. Employment. Federal Government. Hospitals. 1968-78. *2830*

—. Models. 1971-74. *2770*

—. War. 20c. *400*

Wages *See also* Cost of Living; Fringe benefits; Income; Minimum Wage; Prices.

—. 1973. *2829*

—. Advertising. Consumers. Working hours. 1919-76. *375*

—. AFL-CIO. Carter, Jimmy (administration). Economic policy. National Accord (document). 1979. *2225*

—. Agricultural Commodities. Family. Great Plains. Marxism. 1920. *381*

—. Agricultural Labor. Blacks. Discrimination. South. 1898-1902. *879*

—. Agricultural labor. Blacks. Logan, Frenise A. North Carolina Bureau of Labor Statistics. Whites. 1887. *891*

—. Agricultural Labor. Economic Development. 1800-60. *428*

—. Agricultural Labor. South. Tenancy. 1930-60. *3*

—. Aid to Families with Dependent Children. Employment (incentives toward). Public Welfare. 1972-74. *2813*

—. Attitudes. Fishermen. Millworkers. New England. 1972. *2761*

—. Attitudes. Ford Motor Company. Labor. 1890-1915. *969*

—. Attitudes. Labor Unions and Organizations. Reporters and Reporting. 1978. *2062*

—. Bargaining theory. 1973. *2685*

—. Bell, Daniel. Braverman, Harry. Industrialization. Legislation. Models. Working Hours. 1900-70. *397*

—. Blacks. Children. Discrimination. Whites. Wives. Women. 1967. *2523*

—. Blacks. Economic growth. Men. Whites. 1960-77. *1815*

—. Blacks. Education. Whites. 1967-74. *2862*

—. Blacks. Employment. 1972-80. *2586*

—. Blacks. Hiring practices. 1945-73. *354*

—. Blacks. Labor Unions and Organizations. 1971. *2559*

—. Blacks. Men. Whites. Women. 1950-74. *2620*

—. Blue collar workers. Corporations. Management. 1960's-70's. *2612*

—. Bracero Program. Employment. Farm Workers. Southwest. 1954-77. *1697*

—. Bureaucracies. Constituencies. Federal government. 1961-76. *2189*

—. Business Cycles. Economic policy. Inflation. Phillips curve. Prices. 1890-1976. *402*

—. Business Cycles. Europe. Inflation. Unemployment. 1945-70. *2683*

—. California (Los Angeles, San Francisco). Labor (nonunion, union). 1960's. *2714*

—. California (San Francisco). Men. Public schools. Women. 1879. *897*

—. California (San Jose). Comparable Worth. Sex Discrimination. 1960-81. *2419*

—. Canada. Libraries. Library workers. USA. Women. 1977-82. *1972*

—. Capital. Cotton. Textile Industry. 1880-1930. *406*

—. Capitalism. Computers. Labor, division of. 1960-70's. *1961*

—. Capitalism. Economic Policy. Federal Government. 1970's. *2737*

—. Capitalism. Employment. Women's Liberation Movement. 1950's-60's. *2543*

—. Census. Men. Occupations. Women. 1969-70. *2815*

—. Child Care. Employment. Women. 1971-72. *2593*

—. City government. Federal government. Private sector. Public Employees. 1974-80. *2762*

—. Clark, John M. Economic Theory. 20c. *373*

—. Clerical workers. Metropolitan areas. 1961-80. *2810*

—. Clerical workers. Occupations. Women. 1870's-1982. *217*

—. Clerical workers. Sex Discrimination. 1880-1980. *355*

—. Clothing industry. Sex Discrimination. Textile Industry. Women. 1910-70. *351*

—. Collective bargaining. College Teachers. Higher education. 1970's. *1984*

—. Collective Bargaining. Corporations. Unemployment. 1982. *1894*

—. Collective Bargaining. Economic analysis. Industry. Profits. 1954-71. *2797*

—. Collective bargaining. Economic Conditions. 1975. *2739*

—. Collective bargaining. Monopsony. Public Schools. Teachers. 1960's-70's. *2859*

—. Collective bargaining. New York. Teachers. 1967-68. *2727*

—. College graduates. Discrimination. Mexican Americans. 1966-74. *2539*

—. College Graduates. Employment. Higher Education. 1950-75. *1968*

—. College teachers. 1976-82. *2013*

—. College teachers. 1981-82. *2846*

—. College teachers. Labor Unions and Organizations. 1949-79. *1948*

—. College Teachers. Social Conditions. 1969-80. *1963*

—. Comparability, concept of. Government Pay Acts (1962, 1970). 1962-76. *2373*

—. Construction. Davis-Bacon Act (US, 1931). Federal Government. 1931-81. *319*

—. Construction industry. Labor Unions and Organizations. Skill differential. Undocumented workers. 1907-72. *393*

—. Contracts. Cost of Living. General Motors Corporation. United Automobile Workers of America. 1919-74. *392*

—. Contracts. Cost of living. Inflation. 1948-78. *2803*

—. Contracts. Cost of Living Clauses. Inflation. Labor Unions and Organizations. 1969-81. *1899*

—. Contracts, escalated. Inflation. 1970-74. *2819*

—. Copper Miners. Discrimination. Ethnic Groups. Michigan. 1860-1913. *697*

—. Costs. South. Textile Industry. 1800-80. *670*

—. Delaware. DuPont, E. I. and Company. Savings. 1813-60. *407*

—. Depressions. Labor market. Pennsylvania (Pittsburgh). 1908. *1459*

—. Discrimination. Economic structure. Employment. Industry. Minorities. 1976. *2405*

—. Discrimination. Economic Theory. Labor market. 1972. *2825*

—. Discrimination. Employment. Equal opportunity. Legislation. Women. 1960's-70's. *2332*

—. Discrimination. Employment. Men. Whites. Women. 1970's. *1592*

—. Discrimination. Occupations. Women. 1907-08. *1377*

—. Discrimination. Race. Sex. 1960-70. *2567*

—. Discrimination. Women. 1890-1911. *341*

—. District of Columbia. School boards. Strikes. Teachers. Washington Teachers Union. Working conditions. 1979. *2114*

—. Douglas, Paul H. Economic Theory. Labor supply. 1918-48. *1455*

—. Economic Conditions. 1976. *2740*

—. Economic Conditions. Inflation. Labor Law. Reform. 1930-75. *2624*

—. Economic Conditions. Inflation. Price controls. 1971-74. *2809*

—. Economic Conditions. Iron industry. 1800-30. *498*

—. Economic Conditions. Manufacturing. Prices. 1953-70. *2602*

—. Economic Conditions. Social Conditions. Unemployment. Working class. 1921-29. *996*

—. Economic Conditions. World War II. 1939-50. *1456*

—. Economic Theory. Great Britain. Labor Unions and Organizations. 1920-79. *394*

—. Economists. Methodology. Sex Discrimination. 1970's. *2411*

—. Elections. Labor Unions and Organizations. National Labor Relations Board. Working Conditions. 1970-75. *1628*

—. Electronic equipment. Marketing. Retail Trade. Working Conditions. 1970's. *1528*

—. Employment. 1978. *2717*

—. Employment. Great Britain. Japan. ca 1873-1981. *382*

—. Employment. Industry. Working hours. 1975. *2691*

—. Employment. Medical Care (costs). 1965-76. *2611*

—. Employment. Regions. 1960's. *2741*

—. Employment. Retail trade. 1968-78. *2710*

—. Employment cost index. Measurements. 1975. *2804*

—. Employment Cost Index. Private sector. 1980. *2811*

—. Ethnic Groups. Immigrants. Occupations. Race. Sex. 1970. *2630*

—. Ethnic Groups. Retail Trade. Skills. Women. 1903-15. *1445*

—. Europe, Western. Japan. Public services. Trilateral Commission. 1973-79. *2377*

—. Family. Income tax, progressive. Labor supply. 1970's. *2731*

—. Family. Women. 1959-79. *2452*

—. Family. Women, single. Working conditions. 1870-1920. *170*

—. Federal Government. Public Employees. 1962-79. *2767*

—. Fire fighters. Fringe benefits. International Association of Fire Fighters. Labor Unions and Organizations. 1966-76. *2089*

—. Franklin, Benjamin. International Typographical Union. Pennsylvania (Philadelphia). Printing. Strikes. 1754-1852. *531*

—. Fringe benefits. Hospitals. Labor Unions and Organizations. Occupations. 1977. *2063*

—. Great Britain. Novels (Victorian). Sex Discrimination. Women (image). 19c-20c. *366*

—. Household heads. Production. 1963-72. *2821*

—. Ideology. Mechanization. Occupations. Social status. Working Class. 1880-1914. *47*

—. Illinois. Legislation. Reform. Women. Working Conditions. 1893-1917. *318*

—. Immigrants. 1970. *2535*

—. Immigration. Jamaicans. USA. 1962-72. *1763*

—. Industrial Relations. Job security. Labor unions and organizations. Multinational corporations. 1970's. *1923*

—. Industry. Labor Unions and Organizations. Occupations. 1973-78. *2603*

—. Inflation. 1978-79. *2614*

—. Inflation. Labor. World War I. 1914-26. *1460*

—. Inflation. Prices. 1979-80. *2613*

—. Iron industry. Pennsylvania (Lancaster County). Protectionism. Strikes. 1840-1900. *300*

—. Labor. Manufactures. Mexico (border zone). USA. 1965-74. *1544*

—. Labor market. Machinery manufacturing industry. 1970-71. *2796*

—. Labor market. Models. Occupations. Sociology. 1960-75. *1824*

—. Labor market. North Carolina. Prisoners. Work release program. 1969-71. *2840*

—. Labor markets, local. Phillips curve. Unemployment. 1973. *2706*

—. Labor, supply and demand. 1958-75. *2633*

—. Labor Unions and Organizations. 1968-77. *1488*

—. Labor Unions and Organizations. 1970. *1499*

—. Labor Unions and Organizations. Manufacturing. 1960-78. *2145*

—. Labor Unions and Organizations. Membership. Sex Discrimination. 1979. *2401*

—. Labor Unions and Organizations. Men. 1946-78. *1891*

—. Labor unions and organizations. Right-to-work laws. Unemployment. 1964-78. *2199*

—. Labor Unions and Organizations. Teachers. 1897-1960. *313*

—. Labor Unions and Organizations. White Collar Workers. 1976-79. *1932*

—. Labor Unions and Organizations. Women. 1966-70. *1915*

—. Management. Newspapers (weekly). Women. 1977. *1966*

—. Manufacturing. Models. Strikes. 1948-75. *2749*

—. Manufacturing. New Jersey. Pennsylvania. Sex Discrimination. 1900-50. *358*

—. Maryland. Prices. 1750-1850. *372*

—. Men. Sex roles. Whites. Women. 1959-70. *2455*

—. Men. Vocational education. Whites. 1961-71. *1829*

—. Metropolitan areas. 1966-77. *2625*

—. Mexicans. Migrant Labor. Oregon (Hood River Valley). Undocumented Workers. 1978. *1611*

—. Michigan (Detroit). Migrant Labor. 1962-67. *2699*

—. Migration. 1960-71. *2656*

—. New York. Prison guards. Public employees. Strikes. 1979. *2122*

—. North. South. 1960-76. *2701*

—. Occupational Segregation. Sex discrimination. Women. 1945-73. *2566*

—. Occupations. 1969. *2663*

—. Pennsylvania (Philadelphia). Pilots, Ship. Strikes. 1792. *449*

—. Production. Working Hours. 1968-78. *2643*

—. Public Employees. 1970's. *2824*

—. Public Employment Program. Women. 1971. *2366*

—. Quantitative Methods. Sex Discrimination. Women. 1960's. *2592*

—. Scientists. 1960-70. *2837*

—. Sex Discrimination. Unemployment. Women. 1947-73. *2529*

—. Sex Discrimination. Women. 1960-70. *2528*

—. Textile Industry. Women. 1910-70. *253*

—. Truman, Harry S. (administration). Wage Stabilization Board. 1950-53. *2352*

—. Women. 1970-78. *2432*

Wages (determinants of). Labor market segmentation. Survey of Economic Opportunity, 1967. 1967-75. *2747*

Wages, real. Inflation. Prices. Productivity. 1947-76. *2649*

—. Migration, Internal. Regionalism. 1851-80. *887*

Wagner Act (US, 1935). Business. Labor Unions and Organizations. New Deal. Taft-Hartley Act (US, 1947). World War II. 1935-47. *1293*

Wagon trains. Frontier and Pioneer Life. Men. Overland Journeys to the Pacific. Women. 1840's-50's. *433*

Walker, Lucy. Medical Education. Nurses and Nursing. Pennsylvania Hospital Training School for Nurses. 1895-1907. *241*

Walkowitz, Daniel J. Hirsch, Susan E. New Jersey (Newark). New York (Cohoes, Troy). Working Class (review article). 1800-84. 1978. *32*

Wallace, Henry A. Hoover, Herbert C. Hopkins, Harry L. Lewis, John L. 1930-49. *330*

Walsh, Mary Roth. Bibliographies. Chaff, Sandra L. Physicians. Women. 1835-1977. *350*

Wandersee, Winifred D. Anderson, Karen. Depressions. Social Change. Ware, Susan. Women (review article). World War II. 1920-45. *1410*

War *See also* names of wars, battles, etc., e.g. American Revolution, Gettysburg (battle), etc.; Antiwar Sentiment; Civil War; International Law; Military; Military Strategy; Prisoners of War; Refugees.

—. Wage-price controls. 20c. *400*

War Advertising Council. Advertising. Employment. Women. World War II. 1941-45. *1401*

War Manpower Commission. Civil-Military Relations. Labor force. Publicity. Women. World War II. 1942-45. *1442*

—. Industry. Labor Unions and Organizations. Roosevelt, Franklin D. (administration). War Production Board. World War II. 1939-45. *906*

War Production Board. Industry. Labor Unions and Organizations. Roosevelt, Franklin D. (administration). War Manpower Commission. World War II. 1939-45. *906*

Ware, Susan. Anderson, Karen. Depressions. Social Change. Wandersee, Winifred D. Women (review article). World War II. 1920-45. *1410*

Washburn Lignite Coal Company. Coal Miners. North Dakota (Wilton). United Mine Workers of America. 1900-30's. *1276*

Washington *See also* Far Western States.

—. American Federation of Labor. American Labor Union. Leftism. Western Federation of Miners. 1880's-1920. *1066*

—. American Federation of Labor. Disque, Brice P. Federal government. Industrial Workers of the World. Lumber and Lumbering. Oregon. Strikes. 1917-18. *1021*

—. American Federation of Labor. Industrial Workers of the World. One Big Union movement. 1919. *1007*

—. Bibliographies. Chinese. Discrimination. Industrial Workers of the World. Knights of Labor. Labor. Newspapers. 1885-1919. *119*

—. Boys. High schools. Occupational knowledge. 1958-72. *1617*

—. Chinese. Knights of Labor. Labor Unions and Organizations. Oregon. Political Protest. Unemployment. 1880's. *836*

—. Labor Unions and Organizations. Lumber and Lumbering. Workers' compensation. 1911. *1461*

—. Legislation. Minimum wage. State government. 1913-25. *1364*

—. Mexicans. Migrant labor. Oregon. Photographs. 1943-47. *1392*

Washington, Booker T. Alabama. Blacks. Industrial Arts Education. Tuskegee Institute. 1870's-90's. *708*

Washington (Everett). Courts. Industrial Workers of the World. Riots. 1916. *1111*

—. Industrial Workers of the World. *Verona* (vessel). Violence. 1916. *1274*

Washington (King County). Blacks. Coal Mines and Mining. Oregon Improvement Company. Strikebreakers. 1891. *883*

Washington (Seattle). Christianity. Longshoremen. Oxford Group movement. Strikes. 1921-34. *1268*

—. Colorado (Denver). Divorce. Economic Conditions. Income. 1970's. *1672*

—. Communist Party. General Strikes. 1919. *1085*

—. Danz, John. Musicians. Strikes. 1921-35. *1135*

—. Dix, I. F. Hoover, Herbert C. Local politics. Self-help. Unemployed Citizens' League. 1931-32. *1340*

Washington (Spokane). Freedom of Speech. Industrial Workers of the World. Political Protest. Pratt, N. S. 1909-10. *1113*

Washington Teachers Union. District of Columbia. School boards. Strikes. Teachers. Wages. Working conditions. 1979. *2114*

Washington (Vancouver). Methodology. Northwest Women's History Project. Oral history. Oregon (Portland). Shipbuilding. Women. World War II. 1940-82. *1409*

Washington (Yakima Valley). Agricultural Labor. Farmers. Industrial Workers of the World. Labor Disputes. Ranchers. 1910-36. *1216*

—. Farmers. Industrial Workers of the World. Orchards. Strikes. 1933. *1215*

—. Industrial Workers of the World. Labor Unions and Organizations. Strikes. 1933. *1134*

Wayne State University (Walter P. Reuther Library; Archives of Labor and Urban Affairs). Archival Catalogs and Inventories. Labor Unions and Organizations. 1982. *108*

Wealth. Apprenticeship. Arts and Crafts. Journeymen. Maryland (Baltimore). Slavery. 1790-1820. *536*

—. France. Households. Income. 1948-80. *2601*

Weisbord, Vera Buch (reminiscence). National Textile Workers Union. North Carolina (Gastonia). Strikes. Textile Industry. 1929. *1272*

Welfare. See Public Welfare.

Welfare State. Public welfare. Reform. 1935-80. *2362*

Wellesley College. College graduates. Family. Human Relations. Women. 1880-1910. *6*

WES. See Worker' Education Service.

West. Industrial revolution. Labor Disputes. Miners. 1860-1910. *845*

West Coast Master Agreement. American Federation of Labor. Discrimination. Fair Employment Practices Commission. Federal Government. Labor Unions and Organizations. Shipbuilding. World War II. 1939-46. *1313*

West Indians. Education. Family. Fertility. Income. Occupations. 1969-70. *2865*

West Indies. Economics. Galenson, David. Immigration. Indentured Servants (review article). Maryland. Virginia. 1654-1776. *533*

—. Great Britain (Bristol). Immigration. Indentured servants. North America. Working Class. 17c. *535*

West Virginia. Blacks. Coal mines and mining. Immigrants. 1880-1917. *9*

—. Coal Miners. Davis, Thomas Boyd. Martial law. Strikes. 1912-22. *1123*

—. Coal Miners. Debs, Eugene V. Socialist Party. Strikes. 1912-14. *1129*

—. Coal Miners. Keeney, Frank. United Mine Workers of America. 1916-31. *1130*

—. Courts. Jackson, John Jay, Jr. Jones, Mary Harris. Strikes. United Mine Workers of America. 1902. *1262*

—. Labor disputes. McKinley, William. Murphy, S. W. (letter). Railroads and State. 1893. *842*

—. Paint Creek-Cabin Creek Strike. *Socialist and Labor Star* (newspaper). Strikes. Thompson, Wyatt Hamilton. 1912-13. *1131*

West Virginia (Cabin Creek, Paint Creek). Coal Miners. Glasscock, William E. Martial law. National Guard. United Mine Workers of America. Violence. 1912-13. *1101*

West Virginia (Cedar Grove). Coal Mines and Mining. Medical Care (costs). United Mine Workers of America Health and Retirement Fund. 1970's. *2076*

West Virginia (Logan, Mingo Counties). Coal miners. Labor Unions and Organizations. United Mine Workers of America. Violence. 1921-22. *1228*

West Virginia (Martinsburg, Berkeley County). Baltimore and Ohio Railroad. Mathews, Henry M. Railroads. Strikes. 1877. *796*

West Virginia (Ohio County). Industrialization. Labor Unions and Organizations. Ohio Valley Trades and Labor Assembly. 1882-1914. *812*

West Virginia (Paint Creek). Coal Mines and Mining. State Government. Strikes. United Mine Workers of America. 1912-13. *1257*

West Virginia Pulp and Paper Company. International Brotherhood of Pulp, Sulphite, and Paper Mill Workers. Labor Unions and Organizations. Paper Industry. Virginia (Covington). 1933-52. *1282*

West Virginia (southern). Baldwin-Felts Detectives. Coal Mines and Mining. Law Enforcement. 1890's-1935. *296*

—. Coal Miners. Labor Disputes. Mingo War. United Mine Workers of America. Violence. 1919-22. *1177*

—. Coal Mines and Mining. Knights of Labor. Race Relations. United Mine Workers of America. 1880-94. *867*

West Virginia State Federation of Labor. Nugent, John. Socialism. 1901-14. *1006*

West Virginia (Stony Creek). Coal Miners. Harper, Larry. Labor Unions and Organizations. Promotions. Suicide. 1940's-54. *2102*

West Virginia (Welch). Coal Mines and Mining. Deverall, Richard Lawrence-Grace. Documents. Ickes, Harold. Strikes. United Mine Workers of America. 1943. *1235*

West Virginia (Wheeling). Bond issues. Carnegie, Andrew. Homestead Strike. Libraries. Ohio Valley Trades and Labor Assembly. 1892-1911. *811*

Western Electric Company. Environment. Harvard University, Graduate School of Business. Working Conditions. 1924-33. *1002*

—. Hawthorne experiments. Human Relations. Illinois (Chicago). 1924-33. 1977. *945*

Western Federation of Miners. Alaska. Elections. Miners. Public Opinion. Strikes. 1905-08. *1155*

—. Alaska (Douglas Island). Labor Unions and Organizations. Miners. Strikes. Treadwell Mines. 1905-10. *1154*

—. American Federation of Labor. American Labor Union. Leftism. Washington. 1880's-1920. *1066*

—. American Federation of Labor. Armies. Industrial Workers of the World. Labor Disputes. Nevada (Goldfield). 1904-08. *1273*

—. Arizona (Globe). Copper Miners. Strikes. 1917. *1239*

—. Arizona (Globe). Copper Mines and Mining. Strikes. World War I. 1917. *1224*

—. Boyce, Edward. Labor Unions and Organizations. Mining. 1896-1902. *800*

—. Editorials. *Miners' Magazine.* Poetry. Songs. 1900-07. *1283*

—. Labor Unions and Organizations. Miners. 1893-1920. *1153*

Western Federation of Miners (Local No. 1). Copper Miners. Michigan. Montana (Butte). Strikes. 1913-14. *1267*

Western Federation of Miners (Local #106). Arizona (Bisbee). Miners. 1893-1909. *302*

Western Nations See also Industrialized Countries.

—. Aged. Economic Structure. Employment. Men. Pensions. 1950-75. *1764*

—. Keynesianism. Unemployment. 1945-70's. *2670*

—. Labor Unions and Organizations. 1957-78. *2153*

Western Railroad. Construction. Irish Americans. Massachusetts. Population. Railroads. Towns. 1833-42. *465*

Western States See also individual states; Far Western States; Southwest.

—. Agricultural Labor. Industrial Relations. Management. Production. World War I. 1913-18. *935*

—. Basque Americans. Sheepherders. ca 1870-1980. *160*

—. Brown, Ronald C. Labor Unions and Organizations. Miners (review article). Social Conditions. Wyman, Mark. 1860-1920. *21*

—. Chinese Americans. Miners. 1849-90. *727*

—. Cornish Americans. Mining. 19c. *166*

—. Cowboys. Strikes. Working conditions. 1870-90. *820*

—. Economic conditions. Employment. Federal Government. South. 1968-78. *2779*

—. Frontier and Pioneer Life. Teachers. Women. 1848-54. *448*

—. Greek Americans. Labor Unions and Organizations. Working class. 1897-1924. *977*

—. Greek Americans. Working Class. ca 1900-30. *978*

—. Industrial relations. Mining. 1892-1904. *827*

—. Judicial Administration. Labor. Populism. Supreme Courts, State. 1893-1902. *856*

—. Saddlemakers. 1865-1920. *197*

Westinghouse Electric Corporation. Coalition bargaining. Electrical equipment industry. General Electric Company. Strikes. 1950-74. *2108*

—. General Electric Company. Labor Unions and Organizations. Leadership. Massachusetts. New York. Pennsylvania. 1933-37. *1249*

Westward Movement See also Cowboys; Frontier and Pioneer Life.

—. Agricultural labor. Illinois. Indiana. Ohio. 1850-70. *475*

—. Diaries. Sex roles. Women. 19c. *223*

Wheat. Agriculture. Great Plains. Labor casualization. Mechanization. 1865-1902. *643*

Wheeler and Dusenberry Lumber Company. Drivers. Horses. Lumber and Lumbering. Pennsylvania (Forest, Warren counties). Personal narratives. 1885-1930. *195*

White collar workers See also Clerical Workers; Professionals.

—. American Federation of Labor. Chicago Newspaper Guild. Illinois. Labor Unions and Organizations. 1933-40. *1089*

—. Banking. Electrical industry. Labor Unions and Organizations. Public Employees. 1940's. *1090*

—. Blue collar workers. Social Change. Working Class. 1969-72. *1964*

—. Braverman, Harry (review article). Management, scientific. 20c. *2017*

—. Farmers. France. Germany. Politics. Social History (review article). 1890-20c. *89*

—. Health services. Income. 1970-79. *2004*

—. Industrialized countries. Labor Unions and Organizations. Work humanization movement. 1945-76. *1973*

—. Labor Unions and Organizations. Wages. 1976-79. *1932*

—. Minorities. Women. 1969-75. *2730*

White, George. Coal Miners. National Guard. Ohio. Strikes. 1932. *1218*

White supremacy. American Order of Fascisti. Blacks. Employment. Georgia. 1930-33. *1417*

Whites. Agricultural labor. Blacks. Logan, Frenise A. North Carolina Bureau of Labor Statistics. Wages. 1887. *891*

—. Alabama. Poor. 1870-1950. *687*

—. Attitudes. Blacks. Social Organization. 1960's-70's. *1706*

—. Blacks. Children. Discrimination. Wages. Wives. Women. 1967. *2523*

—. Blacks. Competition. Hispanic Americans. Labor. 1976. *2414*

—. Blacks. Cotton. Farmers. Marketing. Social change. Social Classes. South. 1865-1940. *884*

—. Blacks. Cotton. Labor Unions and Organizations. North Carolina. Textile Industry. 1908-74. *1747*

—. Blacks. Discrimination. Employment. Recruitment. 1970's. *1748*

—. Blacks. Economic growth. Men. Wages. 1960-77. *1815*

—. Blacks. Education. Income. 1959-66. *2584*

—. Blacks. Education. Income. Occupations. 1965-79. *2718*

—. Blacks. Education. Income. Training. 1960-80. *2572*

—. Blacks. Education. Wages. 1967-74. *2862*

—. Blacks. Employment. 1955-75. *2532*

—. Blacks. Employment. Equality. Marriage. Sex roles. 1976. *1572*

—. Blacks. Employment. Family (one-parent). Women. 1970's. *1692*

—. Blacks. Employment. Men. Resignations. Women. 1977. *2474*

—. Blacks. Employment. Women. Youth. 1968-71. *1722*

—. Blacks. Family. Income. Moynihan, Daniel P. ("The Negro Family"). Women. 1965-77. *1583*

—. Blacks. High Schools. Midwest. Occupational Goals. Women. 1971. *1682*

—. Blacks. High Schools. Occupational goals. South. 1970's. *2530*

—. Blacks. Income. Mexican Americans. Occupational mobility. 1960's-70's. *2556*

—. Blacks. Indians. Labor Unions and Organizations. Lumbee Indians. North Carolina (Robeson County). Politics. 1970-82. *2476*

—. Blacks. Labor Force. Mexican Americans. Southwest. Women. 1950-70. *2429*

—. Blacks. Labor force. Socialization differences. South. Women. 1870. 1880. *692*

—. Blacks. Labor market. Race Relations. 1865-1920. *715*

—. Blacks. Men. Wages. Women. 1950-74. *2620*

—. Banks, Ann. Personal narratives (review article). 1925-40. *1349*

—. Belgian Americans. French Canadian Americans. Independent Textile Workers. Rhode Island (Woonsocket). 1931-50's. *1157*

—. Bibliographies. Labor Unions and Organizations. 1940's. *174*

—. Bibliographies. Maine. Women. 1975. *202*

—. Blacks. Discrimination. Ideology. Socialism. 19c-20c. *367*

—. Blacks. Discrimination. Labor Unions and Organizations. 1950-79. *2540*

—. Blacks. Labor Market. Poor. 1975-80. *1732*

—. Blue collar workers. Social Change. White collar workers. 1969-72. *1964*

—. *Boston Daily Evening Voice* (newspaper). Equality. Labor Unions and Organizations. Massachusetts. Race Relations. 1864-67. *870*

—. California (Los Angeles). Mexican Americans. 1820-1920. *31*

—. Capitalism. Political Leadership. 1890-1976. *238*

—. Capitalist countries. Strikes. 1970-80. *2060*

—. Casson, Herbert N. Labor Church. Massachusetts (Lynn). Socialism. 1893-98. *747*

—. Census. German Americans. Illinois (Chicago). Immigrants. Newspapers. 1850-1910. *706*

—. Children. Education. Homeownership. Rhode Island (Providence). Schooling. 1880-1925. *214*

—. Civil Rights. Domesticity. Knights of Labor. Women. 1870-90. *875*

—. Class conflict. Political Change. Vermont (Rutland). 1880-96. *650*

—. Class struggle. Political program. Reform. Standard of living. 1950's-73. *1471*

—. Clothing industry. Industrial Mobility. 1950-74. *1552*

—. Coal Miners. Ethnic Groups. Industrialization. Pennsylvania (Scranton). Urbanization. 1855-85. *743*

—. College graduates. 1950-78. *1855*

—. Communist Party. Political attitudes. Vietnam War. Working Conditions. ca 1960-74. *1768*

—. Community participation. Missouri (St. Louis; Carondelet). Social Organizations. Voluntary Associations. Women. 1970's. *1612*

—. Dall, Caroline. Farley, Harriet. Feminism. Letters. 1850. *426*

—. Davis, Katharine Bement. Exhibits and Expositions. Housing. Illinois. World's Columbian Exposition (Chicago, 1893). 1893. *674*

—. DeLeon, Daniel. Industrial Workers of the World. Socialism. 1905-13. *1020*

—. Depressions. Self-perception. Unemployment. 1920's-30's. *995*

—. Detente. Meany, George. 1976. *1515*

—. Diaries. Massachusetts (Beverly). Shoe Industry. Trask, Sarah E. Women. 1849-51. *412*

—. Discrimination. Psychologists. Whites. 1974. *2472*

—. Dublin, Thomas. Kennedy, Susan. Massachusetts (Lowell). Social Organization. Women (review article). 1600-1978. *207*

—. Economic conditions. Labor Force. Social Mobility. Wives. Women. 1960's-78. *1707*

—. Economic Conditions. Racism. Whites. 1970. *2570*

—. Economic Conditions. Social Conditions. Unemployment. Wages. 1921-29. *996*

—. Economic Development. Mexican Americans. Southwest. 1603-1900. *78*

—. Elections. McKinley, William. Ohio. Republican Party. 1891-93. *863*

—. Elections (municipal). Knights of Labor. Political Parties. Reform. Virginia (Lynchburg). 1881-90. *862*

—. Employment. Feminism. Massachusetts (Boston). 1974-75. *1631*

—. Ethnic Groups. Pennsylvania (Philadelphia). Women. 1910-30. *1412*

—. Ethnicity. Irish Americans. Land League. Radicals and Radicalism. Reform. 1880-83. *758*

—. Ethnicity. Missouri (St. Louis). Politics. Socialist Labor Party. 1876-81. *858*

—. Family. Immigration. 1890-1940. *17*

—. Family. Massachusetts (Lynn). Methodology. Poverty. 1915-40. *940*

—. Feinberg, Walter. Public Schools (review article). Rosemont, Henry, Jr. Social control. Violas, Paul C. 1880-20c. *4*

—. French Canadians. Massachusetts (Lowell). Occupational mobility. Quebec. 1870-80. *683*

—. Friedlander, Peter (review article). Michigan (Detroit). United Automobile Workers of America. 1936-39. 1975. *1112*

—. Gaventa, John. Macintyre, Stuart. Politics. Radicals and Radicalism (review article). ca 1880-1940. *93*

—. George, Henry (*Progress and Poverty*). Land. Monopolies. Political economy. Taxation. 1858-94. *664*

—. Great Britain (Bristol). Immigration. Indentured servants. North America. West Indies. 17c. *535*

—. Greek Americans. Labor Unions and Organizations. Western States. 1897-1924. *977*

—. Greek Americans. Western States. ca 1900-30. *978*

—. Gutman, Herbert G. Labor history. 1970-79. *22*

—. Historiography. Research. 19c-20c. *49*

—. History Teaching. Labor history. Perlman, Selig (*Theory of the Labor Movement*). 1928-78. *48*

—. Housing. Massachusetts (Lynn). Shoe Industry. 1915. *985*

—. Ideology. Mechanization. Occupations. Social status. Wages. 1880-1914. *47*

—. Illinois (Chicago). Schools (attendance). 1880-1930. *91*

—. Immigrants. Jews. Maryland (Baltimore). Social Mobility. 1895-1916. *704*

—. Imperialism. Mexican Americans. Mexico. Migration. Sex Discrimination. Southwest. 1850-1982. *53*

—. Income. Interviews. Social conditions. 1973-76. *1590*

—. Indentured servants, former. Letters. Maryland (Anne Arundel County). Roberts, William. Tenancy. 1756-69. *515*

—. Industrial Technology. Printing. 1931-78. *1844*

—. Industrialization. 1820's-20c. *29*

—. Industrialization. Knights of St. Crispin. Massachusetts (Lynn). Radicals and Radicalism. Shoe Industry. 1820-90. *46*

—. Industrialization. Labor history. 1865-1950. *401*

—. Industrialization. Massachusetts (Fall River, Lynn). Social Organization. 1850-1930. *43*

—. Intellectuals. Job satisfaction. Social status. Work, institution of. 1960's-70's. *1510*

—. International Juridical Association. International Labor Defense. King, Carol Weiss. Legal aid. 1921-52. *1158*

—. Iron Industry. New York (Troy). Social Customs. Statistics. 1860-80. *744*

—. Ironworkers. New York (Troy). Social Customs. Statistics. 1860-80. *898*

—. Jews. Pennsylvania (Pittsburgh). 1890-1930. *228*

—. Knights of Labor Centennial Symposium. Labor Unions and Organizations. Social Change. 1879-1979. *315*

—. Labor disputes. Management, Scientific. Railroads. 1903-22. *910*

—. Labor Disputes. Police. Social Democratic Party. Wisconsin (Milwaukee). 1900-15. *1312*

—. Labor history. 1982. *83*

—. Labor history. Social history. United Automobile Workers of America (review article). ca 1900-40. 1968-76. *144*

—. Labor market. Leisure. 1948-75. *2748*

—. Labor movement. Labor Unions and Organizations. 20c. *285*

—. Labor Unions and Organizations. Massachusetts (Lynn). Shoe Industry. 1895-1925. *791*

—. Labor unions and organizations. New Deal. Radicals and Radicalism. 1930's. *1321*

—. Labor Unions and Organizations. Political Attitudes. Racism. 1830-1972. *2437*

—. Labor Unions and Organizations. Socialism. 1916-19. *1049*

—. Leisure. Massachusetts (Worcester). Middle Classes. Parks. 1870-1910. *728*

—. Letters. Massachusetts (Lowell). Robinson, Harriet Hanson. Women. 1845-46. *494*

—. Lunn, George. New York (Schenectady). Socialist Party. Voting and Voting Behavior. 1911-16. *1304*

—. Machinists. Pennsylvania (Carbondale, Scranton). Powderly, Terence V. 1866-77. *742*

—. Massachusetts (Boston). Migration. Quantitative Methods. Thernstrom, Stephan. 1880-90. *892*

—. Massachusetts (Boston). Social Customs. Temperance movements. Values. 1838-40. *420*

—. Massachusetts (Webster). Methodism. Textile industry. 1820's-50's. *483*

—. New York City. Standard of living. 1960's-82. *2784*

—. Occupations. Pennsylvania (Philadelphia). Sociology. 1754-1800. *478*

—. Pennsylvania (Philadelphia). Standard of living. 1780's-90's. *896*

—. Pennsylvania (Pittsburgh). Social Change. Technology. Women. 1870-1900. *711*

—. Pennsylvania (Pittsburgh). Social Conditions. Technology. Women. 1870-1900. *712*

—. Political Stratification. Self-employment. Social Status. 1968-73. *1484*

—. Politics. 19c-20c. *105*

—. Railroads. Strikes. Violence. 1877. *794*

—. Research. Sociology. 1930's-70's. *72*

—. Sanders, Dobbie (reminiscences). South. Steel mills. 1922-59. *116*

—. Socialist Party. Woman suffrage. 1901-12. *1306*

Working Class (review article). Brody, David. Class Struggle. Montgomery, David. 20c. *56*

—. Brody, David. Green, James. 20c. *45*

—. Burawoy, Michael. Canada. Capitalism. Edwards, Richard. Pfeffer, Richard M. USA. Zimbalist, Andrew. 1945-70's. *1497*

—. Capitalism. Dublin, Thomas. Family. Great Britain. Levine, David. Massachusetts (Lowell). Population. 1550-1869. *444*

—. Hirsch, Susan E. New Jersey (Newark). New York (Cohoes, Troy). Walkowitz, Daniel J. 1800-84. 1978. *32*

—. Industrialization. New England. Politics. 1780-1950. *82*

—. Laurie, Bruce. Pennsylvania (Philadelphia). 1800-50. 1980. *457*

Working Class Union. Green Corn Rebellion, 1917. Oklahoma. Radicals and Radicalism. 1914-17. *1269*

—. Jones Family (group). Oklahoma (Cleveland, Pottawatomie counties). Sedition. Trials. World War I. 1917. *1206*

Working Conditions *See also* Eight-Hour Day; Hours of Work; Twelve-Hour Day.

—. Accidents. California. Industrial safety. Tanneries. 1901-80. *222*

—. Accidents. Courts. Federal Employers' Liability Act (US, 1908). Management. Railroads. Safety Appliances Act (US, 1893). 1890-1913. *334*

—. Accidents. Industry. Occupational Safety and Health Act (US, 1970). 1964-79. *1601*

—. Aeronautics. Eastern Airlines. Gellert, Dan. L-1011 (aircraft). Occupational Safety. 1972-78. *1647*

—. Age. Coal Mines and Mining. Management. Standard of living. Strikes, wildcat. 1970's. *2041*

—. Air traffic controllers. Federal Government. Professional Air Traffic Controllers Organization. Strikes. 1950's-81. *2020*

—. Airplane Industry and Trade. California (Los Angeles). Women. World War II. 1941-81. *951*

—. Alabama. Mims, Shadrach (letter). Pratt, Daniel. Textile Industry. Williams, Price. 1854. *455*

—. Alabama (Jefferson County; Coalburg). Blacks. Coal Miners. Convict labor. Mortality. Parke, Thomas D. Sloss-Sheffield coal mine. 1895. *745*

—. Alcohol. 1972. *1629*

—. Alienation. Social Problems. 1959. *13*

—. American Iron and Steel Institute. Steel industry. Twelve-hour day. 1890's-1923. *1207*

—. Anderson, Mary. Illinois (Chicago). Labor Unions and Organizations. Nestor, Agnes. Robins, Margaret Dreier. Women. Women's Trade Union League. 1903-20. *1389*

—. Anthracite. Child Labor. Miners. Pennsylvania. Strikes. ca 1880-1903. *1107*

—. Antietam Woolen Manufacturing Company. Attitudes. Delaware. Duplanty, McCall and Company. Maryland (Funkstown). Textile Industry. 1814-19. *477*

—. Assembly line workers. 1972-73. *1868*

—. Assembly line workers. Automobile Industry and Trade. 1900-33. *981*

—. Attitudes. Heterosexuals. Lesbians. Sexual harassment. Women. 1972-82. *2552*

—. Attitudes. Individualism. Labor unions and organizations. South. 1970's. *1514*

—. Attitudes. Working Hours. 1960-78. *1496*

—. Automobile Industry and Trade. Fleetwood Fisher Body Plant. Michigan (Detroit). 1978. *2100*

—. Automobile Industry and Trade. Michigan (Detroit). Militancy. Production standards. United Automobile Workers of America. World War II. 1937-55. *276*

—. Babow, Irving. California (San Francisco). Palace Hotel. Personal Narratives. 1925-29. *923*

—. Behavior. Self-perception. Women. 1964-79. *1734*

—. Bethlehem Steel Corporation. Daily Life. Depressions. Labor Unions and Organizations. Pennsylvania. 1910-50's. *309*

—. Blacks. Cities. Domestics. North. Women. 20c. *2478*

—. Blacks. Florida. Jamaican Americans. Mexican Americans. Migrant labor. 1980. *2412*

—. Blacks. Industrial Relations. Migration, Internal. Pine industry. South. ca 1912-26. *900*

—. Blue collar workers. Job Satisfaction. Sexual Harassment. Women. 1970's. *1755*

—. Boycotts. Irish Americans. New York City. 1880-86. *806*

—. California. Elliot, Robert. Lawsuits. Occupational Safety and Health Administration. P & Z Company. 1975-77. *2348*

—. California (Los Angeles). Clothing Industry. Mexican Americans. Women. 1970-79. *2551*

—. California (Los Angeles). International Ladies' Garment Workers' Union. Mexican Americans. Women. 1933-39. *1204*

—. California (Orange County). Deviant Behavior. Youth. 1981. *1798*

—. California (San Francisco Bay area). Domestic service. Japanese Americans. Women. 1905-40. *1394*

—. California (Santa Clara County). Electronics industry. 1972-81. *1683*

—. Canada. Chemical Industry. Oil Industry and Trade. Twelve-hour day. USA. 1977. *1753*

—. Capitalism. 20c. *19*

—. Capitalism. James, Selma (pamphlet). Social Conditions. Women. 1972-73. *2583*

—. Chambermaids. Middle Classes. Women's liberation movement. 1970's. *1800*

—. Cities. Family. Recreation. Social Change. 1830-90. *215*

—. Civil Liberties. 1960's-70's. *1627*

—. Class struggle. Occupational Safety. Steel industry. 1974. *2168*

—. Coal Miners. Irish Americans. Ownership. Pennsylvania. Terrorism. 1850-70. *707*

—. Communist Party. Political attitudes. Vietnam War. Working class. ca 1960-74. *1768*

—. Contract labor. Hawaii. Poles. 1896-99. *689*

—. Costs. Federal Regulation. Industry. Occupational Safety and Health Act (US, 1970). 1971-81. *2339*

—. Cowboys. Strikes. Western States. 1870-90. *820*

—. District of Columbia. School boards. Strikes. Teachers. Wages. Washington Teachers Union. 1979. *2114*

—. Education. Food Consumption. Health. 1975-82. *1710*

—. Educational reform. Industry. Management. 1880-1920. *60*

—. Elections. Labor Unions and Organizations. National Labor Relations Board. Wages. 1970-75. *1628*

—. Electronic equipment. Marketing. Retail Trade. Wages. 1970's. *1528*

—. Employment. Labor Unions and Organizations. Occupational Mobility. Resignations. 1970's. *1486*

—. Employment, Part-time. Recessions. 1982. *1573*

—. Environment. Harvard University, Graduate School of Business. Western Electric Company. 1924-33. *1002*

—. Europe. USA. 1972. *1495*

—. Family. Slavery. Women. 1830-60. *592*

—. Family. Wages. Women, single. 1870-1920. *170*

—. Farm Workers. Federal policy. Migrant Labor. 1959-80. *1866*

—. Federal government. Legislation. Occupational hazards. 1960-77. *2237*

—. Federal Regulation. Occupational Safety and Health Act (US, 1970). 1970-76. *2325*

—. Freedom of Speech. Private Sector. Supreme Courts, State. 1968-80. *1805*

—. García, Juan Ramon. Lewis, Sasha G. Mexicans. Undocumented Workers (review article). 1954-80. *2196*

—. General Motors Corporation. Michigan (Pontiac). Occupational Safety and Health Administration. United Automobile Workers of America. 1971-78. *2143*

—. Georgia (Augusta). Strikes. Textile mills. 1886. *830*

—. Gilman, Daniel Spencer. Labor Unions and Organizations. Letters. Massachusetts (Lowell). 1844-46. *505*

—. Government regulation. Illinois. Kelley, Florence. 1892-93. *843*

—. Great Northern Railway Company. Minnesota (St. Paul). Northern Pacific Railroad. 1915-21. *1000*

—. Health hazards. Women. 1869-1979. *187*

—. Hospital industry. Labor Reform. Medical professions. 1950's-73. *2058*

—. Illinois. Legislation. Reform. Wages. Women. 1893-1917. *318*

—. Industrial relations. Industry. 1970's. *67*

—. Industrial safety. Labor (satisfaction). Quality of Employment Surveys. 1977. *2229*

—. Industrialization. Pennsylvania (Philadelphia). Textile Industry. 1787-1820. *474*

—. Industry. Michigan (Belding). Rural Settlements. Silk industry. Women. 1885-1932. *87*

—. Ironworkers. Slavery. South. 1820's-65. *562*

—. Job Satisfaction. Social Surveys. 1977. *1817*

—. Job Stress. 1920-80. *1658*

—. Labor disputes. 1974. *2149*

—. Labor history. 1966-81. *165*

—. Labor movement. Women. 1840's. *486*

—. Labor Non-Partisan League. Legislation. Political representation. 1936-38. *1365*

—. Labor (protests). Red baiting. Socialist influence. 1871-1920. *298*

—. Labor Unions and Organizations. Prisons. Public Employees. 1970's. *2156*

—. Labor Unions and Organizations. Race Relations. 1969-73. *1509*

—. Massachusetts. Social Classes. 1620-1776. *460*

—. Massachusetts (Berkshire County). Mechanization. Paper industry. Women. 1820-55. *454*

—. National Cash Register Company. Ohio (Dayton). Patterson, John H. Physical Education and Training. 1890-1915. *667*

—. New Jersey (Passaic). Strikes. Textile industry. 1875-1926. *1140*

—. North Dakota Workmen's Compensation Bureau. Rice, Hazel F. (account). Transportation. 1919-22. *1352*

—. Nurses and nursing. 1970-80. *1955*

—. Reporters and Reporting. 1880-1900. *738*

—. Self-actualization. 1970-80. *1762*

—. South. Textile industry. Women. 1908-52. *984*

—. Technology. Telephone. 1968-79. *1501*

—. Unemployment. Women. 1950-77. *2403*

—. Women. 1955-80. *2433*

Working hours *See also* Eight-Hour Day; Twelve-Hour Day; Workweek.

—. 1968-79. *2692*

—. Advertising. Consumers. Wages. 1919-76. *375*

—. Army Corps of Engineers. Construction. 1960-72. *2185*

—. Attitudes. Working Conditions. 1960-78. *1496*

—. Bell, Daniel. Braverman, Harry. Industrialization. Legislation. Models. Wages. 1900-70. *397*

—. Capitalism. 1960-80. *2671*

—. Children. Health. Women. 1972. *2792*

—. Employment. Immigrants. Law Enforcement. State Government. Women. 1920. *1414*

—. Employment. Industry. Wages. 1975. *2691*

—. Production. Wages. 1968-78. *2643*

—. Taxation. Wives. 1967-71. *1713*

Working Hours (night shifts). Occupational Hazards. 1981. *1633*

Workingmen's Party of California. California (San Francisco). Modernization. Reform. Social Conditions. 1870-80. *734*

Worklife expectancy. Men. Women. 1970. *1642*

Workmen's Compensation. *See* Workers' Compensation

Workmen's Compensation Act (1916). Kern, John W. Labor Law. Senate. 1908-17. *1314*

Works Progress Administration. Blacks. Christian, Marcus B. Dillard University. Federal Writers' Project. Historiography. Louisiana. 1930's-79. *1406*

—. Depressions. Federal Theatre Project. Flanagan, Hallie. Hopkins, Harry L. Politics. Theater. 1935-39. *1295*

—. Haber, William. Michigan. National Youth Administration. Public Welfare. 1930's. *1336*

Workshop for the Blind. Attitudes. Blind. Education. Employment. Pennsylvania (Pittsburgh). 19c-1939. *911*

Workweek. Current Employment Statistics Program. Current Population Survey. Labor. Statistics. 1956-77. *2646*

Workweek, full-time. Models. Social Conditions. 1900-70. *390*

—. Models. Social Conditions. 1900-70. *2713*

World Auto Councils. Labor Unions and Organizations. Multinational corporations. 1966-78. *1878*

World War I. Agricultural Labor. Industrial Relations. Management. Production. Western states. 1913-18. *935*

—. Agriculture. Behavior. Employment. Woman's Land Army. Women. 1917-20. *1416*

—. Alaska (Anchorage). Labor Unions and Organizations. Lewis, Lena Morrow. Railroads. Socialist Party. 1916-18. *1187*

—. American Federation of Labor. Labor Unions and Organizations. Zionism. 1917-18 *1064*

—. American Federation of Labor. League to Enforce Peace. 1914-20. *1030*

—. Antiwar sentiment. Labor Unions and Organizations. Socialism. 1914-17. *1034*

—. Arizona (Globe). Copper Mines and Mining. Strikes. Western Federation of Miners. 1917. *1224*

—. Blacks. Employment. Equal opportunity. Labor Department (Division of Negro Economics). 1917-21. *1311*

—. British Commonwealth. Integration. Military. USA. Women. World War II. 1900-78. *240*

—. Dye, Nancy Schrom. Greenwald, Maurine Weiner. Labor Unions and Organizations. New York. Women (review article). 1870-1920. *371*

—. Freedom of speech. Oklahoma. Political Repression. Vigilantes. 1914-17. *1303*

—. Gompers, Samuel. Intervention. Labor Unions and Organizations. Latin America. Pan American Federation of Labor. Revolution. 1918-27. *1074*

—. Great Britain. Labor Unions and Organizations. Political Change. Socialism. USA. 1914-25. *1070*

—. Idaho (Pocatello). Voluntary Associations. Women. 1917-18. *986*

—. Industrial Workers of the World. Justice Department. Labor Unions and Organizations. Nebraska. Public opinion. 1915-20. *1077*

—. Industrial Workers of the World. Kansas (Wichita). Labor Unions and Organizations. Oil Industry and Trade. Trials. *United States v. C. W. Anderson et al.* (US, 1919). 1917-19. *1078*

—. Inflation. Labor. Wages. 1914-26. *1460*

—. Intergovernmental Relations. Labor Department. Public Administration. 1917-18. *1297*

—. Jones Family (group). Oklahoma (Cleveland, Pottawatomie counties). Sedition. Trials. Working Class Union. 1917. *1206*

—. Railroads. Women. 1917-30. *1396*

World War II. Advertising. Employment. War Advertising Council. Women. 1941-45. *1401*

—. Airplane Industry and Trade. California (Los Angeles). Women. Working Conditions. 1941-81. *951*

—. Airplane Industry and Trade. Labor Unions and Organizations. Militancy. Nash, Al (reminiscences). New York (Long Island City). Political factions. 1940-44. *1209*

—. Alabama (Mobile). Blacks. Fair Employment Practices Commission. Shipyards. South. 1938-45. *1351*

—. American Federation of Labor. Discrimination. Fair Employment Practices Commission. Federal Government. Labor Unions and Organizations. Shipbuilding. West Coast Master Agreement. 1939-46. *1313*

—. Anderson, Karen. Depressions. Social Change. Wandersee, Winifred D. Ware, Susan. Women (review article). 1920-45. *1410*

—. Armaments Industry. Blacks. Crosswaith, Frank R. Employment. Labor Reform. Negro Labor Committee. New York City (Harlem). 1939-45. *1447*

—. Army personnel. Attitudes. Social Change. 1940's-70's. *227*

—. Automobile Industry and Trade. Discrimination. United Automobile Workers of America. Women. 1942-45. *1422*

Y

Z

AUTHOR INDEX

A

Abbott, Collamer M. 147
Abel, Emily 2394
Abell, Troy 2508 2509
Abraham, Steven E. 2170
Ackermann, John A. 2019
Adams, Donald R., Jr. 372
407 408 498
Adams, William 2395
Adelman, Howard 2558
Adelman, Irma 2408
Africa, Philip 542
Agnew, Brad 671
Aho, C. M. 1462
Aiken, John R. 409
Akin, John S. 2862
Alanen, Arnold R. 1 2
Alba, Francisco 2594
Albelda, Randy 1377
Albin, Suzanne 2395
Aldrich, Howard 2396 2595
Aldrich, Mark 886 919 1377
Alexander, Mary 920
Alexander, Sharon Josephs
1929
Allen, John E. 1095
Allen, Walter R. 2397
Almquist, Elizabeth M. 2398
Alston, Lee J. 3
Altenbaugh, Richard J. 4
921
Alter, George 102
Alter, Jonathan 2020
Alterman, Jack 2596
Alutto, Joseph A. 1930
Alvarez, Donato 2626
Alves, Wayne M. 2597
Alvírez, David 2536
American Association of
University Professors
1931
Ammerman, David L. 501
Amsden, Jon 749
Amsterdam, Susan 335
Andersen, Arlow W. 777
Anderson, Bernard E. 2399
Anderson, Colette 1709
Anderson, Harold 2018
Anderson, Karen Tucker
1378
Anderson, Marion 2400
Anderson, Peggy Engelhardt
2450
Anderson, Ralph V. 578
Anderson, Terry L. 410 479
Andrew, William D. 2021
Andrisani, Paul J. 1872
Androsov, V. P. 1875
Ankarloo, Bengt 5
Annable, James E., Jr. 2598
Ansley, Fran 642 1096
Antler, Joyce 6
Antos, Joseph R. 1932 2401
Applen, Allen G. 643
Archibald, Katherine 1451
Archibald, Robert R. 411
Aries, Nancy R. 1463
Armknecht, Paul A., Jr.
2599
Armstrong, Thomas F. 543
Aron, Cindy S. 672
Aronowitz, Stanley 254 1556
Arroyo, Laura E. 1557
Arroyo, Luis Leobardo 7
1004
Åsard, Erik 1876
Ascheim, Joseph 2600
Ashenfelter, Orley 2171
Asher, Robert 293 847 1005
1097 1286 1287 1558
Ashford, Nicholas A. 2229
Askol'dova, S. M. 255
Atchley, Robert C. 1559
Atkin, J. Myron 1933
Attinasi, John J. 1560
Attoe, Wayne 1288
Aufhauser, R. Keith 544
Aurand, Harold W. 673 922
1098 1099

Austin, Mary 1100
Azevedo, Ross E. 2172

B

Babeau, André 2601
Babow, Irving 923
Babu, B. Ramesh 1289
Baca, Reynaldo 1561 1562
Bach, Jennifer B. 1563
Bach, Robert L. 8 1563
1564 2763
Baderschneider, Jean 2095
Bahr, Howard M. 148 1598
2202
Bailey, Kenneth R. 9 1101
Bailey, Richard 2022
Bailey, Robert J. 1290
Baird, Robert N. 2859
Baker, David G. 2173
Baker, Katharine Gratwick
1565
Baker, Mary Holland 1566
Baker, Ross K. 336
Baker, Sally Hillsman 2402
Baldwin, Wendy 1776
Ball, Robert 2174
Ballard, Kenneth P. 2633
Banks, Alan J. 10
Banks, Carol M. 866
Barbash, Jack 256 1877
Barkey, Fred A. 1006
Barnes, Joseph W. 674
Barnes, Peter 2175
Barnes, William F. 1567
Barnhill, John 1102
Barnum, Darold T. 2023
Baron, Ava 675
Barr, Thomas P. 11
Barral, Pierre 12
Barrera, Mario 337
Barrett, Nancy S. 1568 2403
2602
Barron, Hal Seth 1046
Barron, Melanie 1943
Barsky, C. B. 2603
Bartlett, Robin L. 1569
Bartol, Kathryn M. 1934
Bartol, Robert A. 1934
Barton, David 1852
Barton, Josef J. 149
Barton, Paul E. 1935 2176
Bartosik, Jerzy 1936
Barzel, Yoram 545
Baskett, Thomas S., Jr. 750
Bassett, W. Bruce 1570
Bassi, Laurie J. 2177
Batten, Michael D. 2178
Batzer, Arild 2024
Baughman, James L. 1103
Bauman, John F. 924
Baxandall, Rosalyn 676
Bayles, Michael D. 2404
Bealer, Robert C. 1850
Beck, E. M. 2405 2406
Beck, Scott H. 1571
Becker, Bill 2025
Becker, Eugene H. 2026
Becker, Henry Jay 2407
Beckett, Joyce O. 1572
Becnel, Thomas 751
Bednarzik, R. W. 1573 1574
1803 2604 2605 2606
2722 2839
Beeson, Peter G. 2842
Beeten, Neil 925
Belasco, James A. 1930
Bell, Brenda 642 1096
Bell, Carolyn 1575 2179
Bell, Daniel 13
Bell, Donald 2607
Bell, Mary Lou 1659
Bell, Winifred 2180
Bellamy, Donnie D. 546
Belous, Richard S. 1715
Bemis, Stephen E. 2480
Bender, Lloyd D. 2608
Bendick, Marc, Jr. 2181
Bendiner, Burton B. 1878
Benedict, Michael Les 14

Benjamin, Daniel K. 1367
Bennett, Mary 150
Bennett, R. E. 2738
Bennett, Sari J. 752
Bennett, Sheila Kishler 1379
Bensman, David 2027 2028
Benson, Charles S. 1576
Benson, H. W. 1879 2029
Benson, Jackson J. 1104
Benson, Susan Porter 151
499 1380
Benz, George A. 373
Berch, Bettina 15
Bercuson, David Jay 1007
Berger, Brigitte 1577
Berger, Harriet F. 316
Berger, Henry W. 257
Bergmann, Barbara R. 2408
Bergquist, Virginia A. 2409
Berkes, Leslie J. 2121
Berkin, Carol Ruth 442 538
1437
Berkowitz, Edward D. 1374
2182
Berkowitz, Monroe 258 1291
Berman, Gerald S. 2410
Bernard, Jacqueline 2030
Bernard, Jessie 152
Berney, Barbara 1880
Bernhardt, Debra 1105
Best, Fred 2183
Best, Gary Dean 1292
Best, Laura 897
Betheil, Richard 2031
Bethell, Thomas N. 2032
2033 2034
Betsey, Charles L. 2609
Betten, Neil 1381
Beyer, Janice M. 2035
Bezdek, Roger H. 2184
Bingham, Barbara J. 2185
Biola, Heather 153
Birch, David L. 2610
Birtle, Andrew 778
Bisanz, Charles F. 2036
Bishop, Bill 1106
Bishop, Christine E. 2611
Black, Paul V. 677 779
Blackwelder, Julia Kirk 926
Blackwell, James E. 1578
Blair, John D. 227
Blake, David H. 1881
Blanchard, David 154
Blankenship, Kim 2701
Blasi, Joseph R. 1579
Blatt, Martin 16 927
Blatz, Perry K. 1107
Blau, Francine D. 2411
Blewett, Mary H. 412 497
780
Blitz, Rudolph C. 155 1580
Bloch, Ed 2037
Bloch, Herman D. 866
Block, Richard N. 1882
Blostin, Allan P. 1581
Blount, Alma 2412
Blumberg, Paul 1937 2612
Blume, Norman 2038
Blumrosen, Alfred W. 2413
Boardman, Anthony E. 142
Boccaccio, Mary 259
Boden, Les 2186
Bodnar, John 17 156 928
1382
Bolin, Winifred D.
Wandersee 929
Bolton, Lena W. 1883
Bombardini, Lorenzino 781
Bonacich, Edna 547 1383
1430
Bond, Deborah T. 2187
Bonney, Richard J. 782
Bonthius, Andrew 1108
Boone, Richard W. 157
Booth, Philip 2188
Borglum, Richard P. 1833
Borisiuk, V. I. 1293
Borjas, George J. 1582 2189
2414
Bornstein, Leon 1464 2039

Borum, Joan D. 2613 2614
Borus, Michael E. 2190
Boryczka, Ray 1109 1110
Bose, Christine E. 2415
Boskin, Joseph 338
Boskin, Michael J. 2191
Botting, David C., Jr. 1111
Bould, Sally 1583 1584
Bourg, Carroll J. 18
Bowers, Mollie H. 294
Bowers, Norman 1465 1585
2615 2616 2617
Bowlby, Roger L. 2795
Bowles, Samuel 1466 2618
Bowman, James S. 1586
Boyd, Marjorie 374
Boyd, Monica 1820 2619
Boyer, Lee R. 413
Brack, John 375
Bradley, Mary I. 2097
Bradshaw, Benjamin Spencer
1587
Bradshaw, T. F. 2620 2674
Braito, Rita 1938
Brand, H. 1588
Brand, Horst 317 2621 2622
Brandes, Joseph 930
Brandwein, Larry 94
Branscome, James 2040
Brauer, Carl M. 2416
Braverman, Harry 19 20
2623
Braverman, Miriam 1589
Brecher, Charles 2417
Brecher, Jeremy 1590
Breen, T. H. 414 500
Brehm, Henry 2268
Bremer, William W. 1294
Brett, Jeanne M. 2041
Brewer, Marilynn B. 2418
Briar, Katherine Hooper
1591
Brier, Stephen 749 867 1384
Briggs, Vernon M., Jr. 1467
Brigham, Loriman S. 415
Brightman, Carol 2192
Bringhurst, Newell G. 21
Brinkerhoff, David B. 250
Brodhead, Frank 2641
Brodski, R. M. 931
Brody, David 22 23 24 25
1112
Brody, Ralph 1655
Bronfenbrenner, Martin 2624
Brown, Catherine 339
Brown, Gary D. 1592
Brown, Lorraine 1295
Brown, Ralph S. 1939
Brown, Scott Campbell 1621
2782
Browning, Harley L. 26
1536
Brownlee, W. Elliot, Jr. 27
548
Broyles, Glen J. 1113
Brune, Lester H. 1114
Bruser, Lawrence 2018
Brush, Ted 644
Bryan, Dexter 1561 1562
Bryant, Pat 2042
Buckley, John E. 2625
Buckman, Rilma O. 1655
Buhle, Mari Jo 1115
Buhle, Paul 28 753 932 1116
2146
Bularzik, Mary 340 783
Bulmer, Charles 1468 2193
2197
Bulosan, Carlos 1117
Bunzel, John H. 2419
Burawoy, Michael 1593
Burkhauser, Richard V. 376
Burki, Mary Ann Mason
1008
Burlington, Bo 1884
Burnham, Dorothy 549
Burns, Anna C. 933
Burran, James A. 1118
Burris, Val 2420
Burstein, Paul 2421 2422

Burton, John F., Jr. 2221
Bustamante, Jorge 1594 1595
1596
Butler, Joseph T., Jr. 934
Buttel, Frederick H. 2194
Byrkit, James W. 1119
Byrne, J. J. 1642
Byrnes, Robert F. 1940

C

Cacciatore, Giuseppe 260
Cain, Louis P. 2591
Calavita, Kitty 2195
Calderhead, William 550
Calvi, Giulia 935
Cameron, Rondo 377
Campbell, Randolph 551 552
553
Canarella, Giorgio 554
Candela, Joseph L., Jr. 318
Cannon, Lynn Weber 1597
Cantor, Milton 29 46 424
432 520 521 736 743
744 792 806 1551
Capdevielle, Patricia 2626
2627
Capeci, Dominic J., Jr. 1296
Capozzola, John M. 2043
Cardoso, Lawrence A. 1385
2196
Carey, Max L. 2628
Carlson, Alvar W. 1469
Carlson, Leonard A. 748
Carlson, Richard J. 2044
Carmichael, John L., Jr.
1468 2193 2197
Caroli, Betty Boyd 709
Carpenter, Gerald 1120
Carpenter, Linda J. 2198
Carper, N. Gordon 1386
Carr, Joe Daniel 1121
Carr, Lois Green 501
Carroll, Thomas M. 2199
Carter, David A. 1009
Carter, Keith A. 2629
Carter, Michael J. 1941
Carter, Susan B. 158 1941
Carvalho, Joseph, III 784
Cary, Lorin Lee 785 1010
1011
Casillas, Mike 936
Cassity, Michael J. 30 754
Castillo, Pedro 31
Cayer, N. Joseph 2423
Cebula, Richard J. 2200
Celenza, James 1116
Cesari, Laurent 2045
Chadwick, Bruce A. 1598
2202
Chaison, Gary N. 261 1885
Chait, Richard P. 1942
Chambers-Schiller, Lee 416
Chandler, Mark 2401
Chao Ling Wang 1599
Chapin, John R. 786
Chapman, Frank 1886
Char, Tin-Yuke 502
Char, Wai Jane 502
Chavez, Cesar 2046
Chavkin, Wendy 1600
Chelius, James R. 1601
Chelte, Anthony F. 1602
Chen, Yung-Ping 1470
Cheng, Charles W. 1943
Chernow, Ron 2047
Cherry, Robert 1471
Childress, Marilyn 920
Chiles, Frederic 1122
Chinloy, Peter 1472
Chiswick, Barry R. 1603
1604 2630 2631
Choi, Yearn H. 2048
Christiansen, John B. 1387
Chudacoff, Howard P. 32
Cimbala, Stephen J. 2201
Ciporen, Marvin 33
Ciro, Sepulveda 937
Clark, Cal 2458
Clark, Don P. 2632

Garfinkel, Irv 2862
Garfinkel, Irwin 2669
Garkovich, Lorraine 1644
Garlock, Jonathan 761 762
Garraty, John A. 74 948
Garson, G. David 1645
Gartaganis, Arthur J. 2232
Garvey, Edward R. 1646
Gasinski, Tadeusz Z. 689
Gaston, Leonard 2233
Gates, Margaret J. 2234
Gatling, Wade S. 2235
Gautschi, Frederick H., III 2205
Gauzner, N. 2670 2671
Gaylord, Carolyn 2473
Gedicks, Al 168
Gellert, Dan 1647
Gellner, Christopher G. 2672
Gengarelly, W. Anthony 1305
Genini, Ronald 1026
Georgakas, Dan 2461
Gerardi, Geraldine 2602
Gerking, Shelby D. 2673
Gerson, Kathleen 1648
Gerstein, Ira 1649
Gerstle, Gary 1157
Gersuny, Carl 75 510 690 805 949 2761
Geschwender, James A. 2462 2463
Ghetti, Sandra 1027
Gibson, Arrell Morgan 950
Gier, Nicholas 1958
Gildemeister, Glen A. 763
Gillespie, Angus K. 76
Gillespie, J. David 2464
Gillis, William 2802
Gilman, Amy 436
Gilpin, Toni 1894
Gilroy, Curtis L. 2465 2466 2674
Ginger, Ann Fagan 1158
Ginger, Ray 1650
Gintis, Herbert 1466
Ginzberg, Eli 1651 2675
Gioglio, Jerry 2720
Giraldo, Fernando Urrea 1652
Gitelman, H. M. 496 691
Givens, Harrison, Jr. 2676
Glaberman, Martin 651 1653 2074
Glacel, Barbara Pate 2467
Glanz, Rudolph 343
Glaser, Martha 1159
Glassberg, Eudice 889
Glenn, Evelyn Nakano 169 1394
Glenn, Norval D. 1654
Gliatta, Stephen 2236
Glick, Clarence E. 511
Glickstein, Jonathan A. 579
Gluck, Sherna Berger 951
Godson, Roy 1895 1896
Goering, John M. 2468
Goldberg, Joseph P. 764 1452
Goldberg, Stephen B. 2041
Goldblatt, Louis 1490
Goldfield, Michael 2075
Goldin, Claudia 170 437 692 693 885
Goldman, Alan H. 2469
Goldman, Robert 77
Goldsmith, Frank 2237
Goldstein, Joyce 2076
Goldstein, Morris 2238
Goldstein, Neal 1655
Golin, Steve 1160
Gomez, Joseph A. 1028
Gómez-Quiñones, Juan 78
Gonzalez, Martin 2412
Gonzalez, Rosalinda M. 1656 2470
Goode, Bill 171
Goodfriend, Joyce D. 580
Goodman, Jerry D. 2535
Goodman, Walter 1029
Goodrich, James A. 2239
Gorden, William I. 1959
Gordon, Linda 676 1306

Gordon, Lynn 321
Gordon, Margaret S. 1960
Gordon, Max 1161 1376
Gordon, Michael A. 653 806
Gordon, Robert J. 382
Gordon, Suzanne 1657 1658
Gottlieb, Amy Zahl 694 850
Gottlieb, David 1659
Gottlieb, Peter 952 1162
Gotto, Baron 172
Goudy, Willis J. 2542 2776
Gould, William B. 295 1307 2471
Gover, Kathryn R. 1660
Gowaskie, Joseph M. 807
Graebner, William 322 1087 1308
Graham, Richard 581
Grandjean, Burke D. 79 2677
Granof, Eugene B. 2077
Grant, H. Roger 654 808 851
Grant, Jim 265
Gratton, Brian 1088
Gray, David M. 2472
Gray, Lois S. 1897
Gray, Ralph 512
Graziosi, Andrea 173
Green, Archie 80
Green, Barbara L. 582
Green, Ben 1163
Green, Carole A. 2448
Green, George 73 266
Green, Gloria P. 2678
Green, Gordon 2474
Green, James 81 174 1003 1164
Green, Jim 16 82 83 1165 2078
Green, Philip 2240
Greenbaum, Joan 1961
Greenberg, Brian 2065
Greenberg, Deborah M. 2241
Greenberg, Edward S. 84 1661
Greenberger, Ellen 1798 1819
Greene, Rebecca S. 1395
Greene, Richard 1491 1662 2242
Greene, Victor 175
Greene, William H. 1663
Greenwald, Maureen 1396
Greer, Edward 344
Gregory, Karl D. 2679
Griego, Andrew 695
Grimes, Michael D. 1951
Grindle, Roger L. 655
Grodin, Joseph R. 2243
Groeneveld, Lyle P. 1672
Groneman, Carol 176
Groniowski, Krzysztof 177
Gross, Bertram 2244 2680
Grossman, Allyson Sherman 383 2681 2682 2835
Grossman, Herschel I. 2683
Grossman, Jonathan 323 852 1309 2245
Grover, Mary Anne 178
Groves, Paul A. 458
Grubbs, Donald H. 2079
Grubbs, Frank L., Jr. 1030
Gudelunas, William 1098
Guest, Avery M. 1613 1664 1665
Guimary, Donald 301
Guimary, Donald L. 1198
Gundersen, Joan R. 438
Gunderson, Morley 2246
Gunn, Christopher 2080
Gurak, Douglas T. 1666
Gurin, Patricia 2473
Guttman, Robert 2247
Guzda, Henry P. 324 325 1310 1311
Gwartney, James 2687

H

Haas, Jack 1667
Haber, Carole 696

Haber, Sheldon 384 1962 2474
Haddock, Wilbur 2475
Hadsell, Richard M. 296
Haggard, Thomas R. 2248
Hahn, Andrew B. 2249
Hailstones, Thomas J. 1492
Haines, Michael R. 890
Haines, Randall A. 267
Hale, George E. 2250
Hall, Bob 2034 2057 2138 2476
Hall, Grace 2477
Hall, Leon 2061
Hall, Mark 583
Hall, Paul 1493
Hall, Richard H. 1494
Hallagan, William S. 953
Haller, Archibald O. 1682
Halpin, Terrence C. 2251
Hamburger, Robert 2478
Hamer, Irving 1943
Hamermesh, Daniel S. 2684 2685
Hamilton, Mary Agnes 1668
Hamilton, Mary Townsend 1669
Hamilton, Richard F. 1855 1856
Hamilton, Stephen F. 179
Hammett, Hugh B. 1397
Hanagan, Michael 1670
Hancock, Harold B. 513
Hanlon, Martin D. 1671
Hannan, Michael T. 1672
Hannon, Joan Underhill 697
Hansen, W. Lee 1963
Hanson, Sandra L. 1673
Hanushek, Eric 2479
Harahan, Joseph P. 809
Harap, Louis 268
Hardy, Charles, III 44
Hardy, Melissa A. 439
Hardy, Richard J. 2252
Hareven, Tamara K. 954
Harker, John 2686
Harlan, Sharon L. 1755
Harmon, Sandra D. 698
Harper, C. W. 584
Harper, Dean 1674
Harring, Sidney L. 853 1312
Harrington, Michael 1964
Harris, Richard J. 1675
Harris, William 699 1166 1313
Harrison, Bennett 1676 2253
Harrison, William B. 385
Hart, Thomas P. 2602
Hartland-Thonberg, Penelope 85
Hartley, Shirley Foster 345
Hartman, Paul T. 2081
Hartmann, Heidi I. 180 346
Hartmann, Susan M. 181
Harvey, Donald G. 182
Harvey, Katherine A. 440
Haskell, Thomas L. 585
Haslam, Gerald 1898
Haug, Marie 1578 2410
Haughton, Virginia 1314
Haveman, Robert H. 2254
Havira, Barbara S. 86 87
Hawes, Joseph M. 247
Haworth, Charles 2687
Haworth, Joan Gustafson 2687
Hayghe, Howard 386 1677 2688 2835
Haynes, John E. 269
Hayward, Mark D. 2564
Head, Faye E. 1315
Heavner, Robert O. 514
Hebein, Frederick J. 2711
Heck, Tom R. 396
Heckman, James J. 2593
Hedges, Janice Neipert 1495 1496 1678 2480 2689 2690 2691 2692
Height, Dorothy I. 2481
Heinemann, Ronald L. 1316
Heins, Marjorie 2255
Helburn, I. B. 2023
Helfand, Barry 1031

Hellwig, David J. 700 701
Hemminger, Carol 1398
Henderson, Alexa B. 1399
Henderson, Eric 1679
Henderson, Lenneal J. 2256
Hendrick, Irving G. 1400
Hendricks, Wallace 1899 2082 2376
Hendrickson, Kenneth E., Jr. 1317 1318 1319
Henle, Peter 2083 2257 2693
Henretta, James A. 441
Henretta, John C. 1525
Henry, James 88 2694 2695
Hentoff, Nat 2084
Herbst, John 904
Herbst, Jurgen 89
Hero, Rodney E. 2258
Heron, Craig 1497
Herring, Neill 1167
Herrink, Ruth J. 2259
Hershberg, Theodore 102
Herzog, Henry W. Jr. 2696
Hewson, Marillyn A. 2604
Hibbs, Douglas A., Jr. 2697
Hicken, Victor 297
Hickey, Joseph A. 2260 2261 2262
Hicks, Alexander 2263
Hicks, Laurabeth 1965
Hield, Melissa 1168
Higgs, Robert 879 891 955
Hilaski, Harvey J. 2698 2836
Hildebrand, George H. 1498
Hill, Ann Corinne 347
Hill, C. Russell 2699
Hill, Charles 1169
Hill, Herbert 2264 2482
Hill, Martha S. 1680
Hill, Peter J. 183
Hill, Robert 2483
Hilton, Mike 184
Hine, William C. 586
Hirata, Lucie Cheng 185 442
Hirsch, Barry T. 1499 2700
Hirsch, Susan 398
Hirschman, Charles 1681 2701
Hoachlander, E. Gareth 2265
Hobby, Daniel T. 1032
Hobsbawm, E. J. 90
Hodgens, Evan L. 2702
Hodgson, James D. 1900
Hoerder, Dirk 491 1500
Hofferth, Sandra L. 186 1739
Hoffman, Abraham 1170 1320 1453
Hoffman, Alice 68
Hoffman, Eileen B. 2085
Hoffman, Ronald 428
Hofsommer, Donovan L. 956
Hogan, David 91
Hogeboom, Willard L. 92
Holder, Todd 1965
Holloway, Harry 1901
Holloway, Wilfred B. 326 2266
Holly, Susan 1966
Holmes, Joseph J. 298
Holmes, William F. 656 657 810
Holt, James 270 765
Homsey, Elizabeth Moyne 587
Honey, Maureen 1401
Hopkins, Anne H. 2139
Hopkins, Elaine B. 2484
Horan, Patrick M. 2405
Horn, James P. P. 515
Hornburger, Jane M. 1967
Horowitz, Irving Louis 2675
Horstman, Ronald 1171
Horton, Raymond D. 2267
Horvath, Francis W. 2567 2703
Hotchkiss, Lawrence 1682
Houff, James N. 2704
Hough, Leslie S. 52
Howard, Robert 1501 1683 1902
Howards, Irving 2268
Howe, Carolyn 1502

Howe, Charles 2269
Howe, Irving 2161
Howell, David 93
Howell, Frances Baseden 2086
Howlett, Charles F. 1033
Hribal, Amy S. 2270
Hubbard, Carl M. 2592
Huckle, Patricia 348
Hudis, Paula M. 2564
Hudson, James J. 1172
Huffstutler, Clyde 2621 2651
Hughes, Chip 2485
Hughes, Jonathan 2087
Hughes, Sarah S. 588
Humphrey, David Burras 387
Humphrey, George D. 702
Humphreys, James 1903
Hunt, Janet G. 1684 1685
Hunt, Larry L. 1684 1685
Hunt, Richard E. 2035
Hunt, Richard P. 854
Hunt, Vilma R. 187
Hurd, Richard W. 1321 2088
Hurh, Won Moo 1704
Hurt, R. Douglas 855 856
Hurtado, Albert L. 443
Hurwitz, Haggai 1322
Husby, Ralph D. 2705
Huston, James L. 516
Hutchinson, John 1173
Huzel, James P. 444
Hyclak, Thomas 253
Hyman, Herbert H. 1686
Hyser, Raymond M. 1174

I

Ichioka, Yuji 957 1402
Ichniowski, Casey 2089 2486
Ickowitz, Allan 1503
Iden, George 2487
Iglehart, Alfreda P. 1687
Imhoff, Clem 1403
Imhoff, Kathleen 94
Infante, Dominic A. 1959
Isbell, Florence 2271
Isserman, Maurice 95 958
Ives, Edward D. 1688

J

Jackson, Harvey H. 589
Jackson, Joy J. 1323
Jackson, Mark 2706
Jaco, D. E. 1689
Jacobs, David 2272
Jacobs, Donald M. 590
Jacobs, James B. 2160 2273
Jacoby, Robin Miller 1404 1405
Jaffe, A. J. 1968
James, Edgar 2090
James, Edward T. 857
James, John A. 388
James, Tom 1969
Janiewski, Dolores 445
Janson, Philip 1690
Janus, Charles J. 1904
Jauffret-Epstein, Sophie 2274
Javersak, David T. 96 811 812
Jebsen, Harry, Jr. 813
Jeffreys-Jones, Rhodri 97 905
Jemnitz, János 1034
Jencks, Christopher 2707
Jenkins, J. Craig 2091 2708
Jenness, Linda 2488
Jennings, Ken 2212
Jensen, Billie Barnes 1175
Jensen, Joan M. 188
Jentz, John 706
Jentz, John B. 814
Job, Barbara Cottman 1691 2709 2710
Johnson, Beverly L. 1692 2489 2835
Johnson, Clyde 1035
Johnson, David R. 2842
Johnson, Doyle P. 1504

LIST OF PERIODICALS

A

Academe: Bulletin of the AAUP
Acta Sociologica [Finland]
Actualité Economique [Canada]
Administration & Society
Administrative Science Quarterly
Adventist Heritage
Agricultural History
AHA Perspectives
Alabama Historical Quarterly
Alabama Review
Alaska Journal (ceased pub 1980)
Amerasia Journal
American Behavioral Scientist
American Economic Review
American Heritage
American Historical Review
American History Illustrated
American Jewish Archives
American Jewish Historical Quarterly (see
    American Jewish History)
American Jewish History
American Journal of Economics and Sociology
American Journal of Political Science
American Journal of Sociology
American Literature
American Neptune
American Political Science Review
American Politics Quarterly
American Quarterly
American Scholar
American Sociological Review
American Studies in Scandinavia [Norway]
American Studies International
American Studies (Lawrence, KS)
American Studies (Washington, DC) (see
    American Studies International)
American West
Americas: A Quarterly Review of Inter-American
    Cultural History (Academy of American
    Franciscan History)
Amerikanskii Ezhegodnik [Union of Soviet
    Socialist Republic]
Annales Canadiennes d'Histoire (see Canadian
    Journal of History = Annales Canadiennes
    d'Histoire) [Canada]
Annali della Facoltà di Scienze Politiche: Materiali
    di Storia [Italy]
Annals of Iowa
Annals of the American Academy of Political and
    Social Science
Annals of the Association of American
    Geographers
Antioch Review
Appalachian Journal
Arbitration Journal
Årbog for Arbejderbevaegelsens Historie
    [Denmark]
Arkansas Historical Quarterly
Armed Forces and Society
Asian & Pacific Quarterly of Cultural and Social
    Affairs [South Korea]
Atlantic Community Quarterly
Atlantis: A Women's Studies Journal [Canada]
Australian Quarterly [Australia]
Aztlán

B

Black Scholar
Boletín del Archivo General de la Nación
    [Mexico]
Brigham Young University Studies
British Journal of Sociology [Great Britain]
Bulletin de la Société d'Histoire Moderne [France]
Bulletin of the History of Medicine
Business History [Great Britain]
Business History Review
Byzantine and Modern Greek Studies [Great
    Britain]

C

Cahiers des Amériques Latines [France]
Cahiers d'Etudes Africaines [France]
Cahiers Internationaux d'Histoire Economique et
    Sociale [Italy]
California Historical Quarterly (see California
    History)

California History
Canadian Dimension [Canada]
Canadian Journal of History = Annales
    Canadiennes d'Histoire [Canada]
Canadian Journal of History of Sport = Revue
    Canadienne de l'Histoire des Sports [Canada]
Canadian Journal of Political Science = Revue
    Canadienne de Science Politique [Canada]
Canadian Labour [Canada]
Canadian Review of American Studies [Canada]
Capitol Studies (see Congressional Studies)
Caribbean Review
Cato Journal
Center Magazine
Change
Chicago History
Chronicles of Oklahoma
Cincinnati Historical Society Bulletin
Civil Liberties Review (ceased pub 1979)
Civil War History
College and Research Libraries
Colorado Heritage
Colorado Quarterly
Columbia Journal of Transnational Law
Commentary
Communications Historiques (see Historical Papers
    = Communications Historiques) [Canada]
Compact
Comparative Studies in Society and History [Great
    Britain]
Congress & the Presidency: A Journal of Capitol
    Studies
Congressional Studies (see Congress & the
    Presidency)
Connecticut History
Contemporary Review [Great Britain]
Crisis
Current History

D

Dacca University Studies Part A [Bangladesh]
Delaware History
Democracy
Demografía y Economía [Mexico]
Development and Change [Netherlands]
Diplomatic History
Dissent
Durham University Journal [Great Britain]

E

East Tennessee Historical Society's Publications
Economic Development and Cultural Change
Economic Geography
Economic Inquiry
Economic Journal [Great Britain]
Economica [Great Britain]
Education and Urban Society
Ekonomista [Poland]
Encounter
Environmental Review
Essex Institute Historical Collections
Ethnic Groups
Ethnicity (ceased pub 1981)
Explorations in Economic History
Explorations in Ethnic Studies

F

Feminist Studies
Film and History
Filson Club History Quarterly
Florida Historical Quarterly
Foreign Affairs
Foreign Policy
Foreign Service Journal
Foro Internacional [Mexico]
Frankfurter Hefte [German Federal Republic]
Freedom at Issue
Freedomways
Freeman
Frontiers

G

Gateway Heritage
Gazette: International Journal for Mass
    Communication Studies [Netherlands]
Geographical Review

Georgia Historical Quarterly
Great Plains Quarterly

H

Harvard Educational Review
Hawaiian Journal of History
Historia Mexicana [Mexico]
Historian
Historical Journal [Great Britain]
Historical Journal of Massachusetts
Historical Journal of Western Massachusetts (see
    Historical Journal of Massachusetts)
Historical Magazine of the Protestant Episcopal
    Church
Historical Methods
Historical Methods Newsletter (see Historical
    Methods)
Historical New Hampshire
Historical Papers = Communications Historiques
    [Canada]
Historical Social Research = Historische
    Sozialforschung [German Federal Republic]
Historische Sozialforschung (see Historical Social
    Research = Historische Sozialforschung)
    [German Federal Republic]
Historisk Tidskrift [Sweden]
Historisk Tidsskrift [Denmark]
History and Theory
History of Education Quarterly
History of Education Review [Australia]
History Teacher
History Today [Great Britain]
History Workshop Journal [Great Britain]
Human Organization

I

Idaho Yesterdays
Indiana Magazine of History
Indiana Social Studies Quarterly
Industrial and Labor Relations Review
Industrial Relations = Relations Industrielles
    [Canada]
Inter-American Economic Affairs
International Journal of Contemporary Sociology
International Journal of Oral History
International Journal of Women's Studies [Canada]
International Labor and Working Class History
International Migration Review
International Organization
International Review of Social History
    [Netherlands]
International Social Science Review
International Socialist Review
Irish Historical Studies [Republic of Ireland]
Istoriia SSSR [Union of Soviet Socialist Republic]
Italia Contemporanea [Italy]
Italian Americana

J

Jewish Social Studies
Journal of African-Afro-American Affairs
Journal of American Ethnic History
Journal of American History
Journal of American Studies [Great Britain]
Journal of Arizona History
Journal of Asian and African Studies
    [Netherlands]
Journal of Black Studies
Journal of Business
Journal of Communication
Journal of Developing Areas
Journal of Economic History
Journal of Economic Literature
Journal of Ecumenical Studies
Journal of Ethnic Studies
Journal of Family History: Studies in Family,
    Kinship, and Demography
Journal of Forest History
Journal of General Education
Journal of Higher Education
Journal of Historical Geography
Journal of Interdisciplinary History
Journal of Intergroup Relations
Journal of Law & Economics
Journal of Library History, Philosophy, &
    Comparative Librarianship
Journal of Mexican American History

Journal of Mississippi History
Journal of NAL Associates
Journal of Negro Education
Journal of Negro History
Journal of Peasant Studies [Great Britain]
Journal of Political and Military Sociology
Journal of Political Economy
Journal of Politics
Journal of Popular Culture
Journal of Presbyterian History
Journal of San Diego History
Journal of Social and Political Studies (see Journal
   of Social, Political and Economic Studies)
Journal of Social History
Journal of Social Issues
Journal of Social, Political and Economic Studies
Journal of Southern History
Journal of Sport History
Journal of the American Institute of Planners (see
   Journal of the American Planning Association)
Journal of the American Planning Association
Journal of the Hellenic Diaspora: Critical
   Thoughts on Greek and World Issues
Journal of the History of Ideas
Journal of the History of Medicine and Allied
   Sciences
Journal of the History of the Behavioral Sciences
Journal of the Illinois State Historical Society
Journal of the Lancaster County Historical Society
Journal of the University of Bombay [India]
Journal of the West
Journal of the West Virginia Historical
   Association
Journal of Urban History
Journal of World Trade Law [Switzerland]
Journalism History
Journalism Quarterly

K

Kansas Historical Quarterly (superseded by Kansas
   History)
Kansas History
Keystone Folklore
Kyklos [Switzerland]

L

Labor History
Labour = Travailleur [Canada]
Labour History [Australia]
Land Economics
Latin American Perspectives
Law & Society Review
Liberal Education
Library Quarterly
Literature and History [Great Britain]
Louisiana History
Louisiana Studies (see Southern Studies: An
   Interdisciplinary Journal of the South)

M

Maine Historical Society Quarterly
Mankind
Marxist Perspectives (ceased pub 1980)
Maryland Historian
Maryland Historical Magazine
Michigan Academician
Michigan History
Mid-America
Midwest Quarterly
Migration Today
Military Affairs
Milwaukee History
Minerva: A Review of Science, Learning and
   Policy [Great Britain]
Minnesota History
Mirovaia Ekonomika i Mezhdunarodnye
   Otnosheniia [Union of Soviet Socialist
   Republic]
Missouri Historical Review
Missouri Historical Society. Bulletin (superseded
   by Gateway)
Mita Gakkai Zasshi [Japan]
Modern Age
Modernist Studies: Literature and Culture
   1920-1940 (ceased pub 1980) [Canada]
Montana: Magazine of Western History
Monthly Labor Review
Monthly Review
Mouvement Social [France]
Movimento Operaio e Socialista [Italy]

N

National Civic Review
Nebraska History
Negro History Bulletin
Nevada Historical Society Quarterly
New England Quarterly
New Generation
New Jersey History
New Left Review [Great Britain]
New Mexico Historical Review
New Scholar
New South (superseded by Southern Voices)
New York Affairs
New York History
New York University Journal of International Law
   and Politics
New-England Galaxy
New York Historical Society Quarterly (suspended
   pub 1979)
North Carolina Historical Review
North Dakota History
North Dakota Quarterly
North Jersey Highlander
North Louisiana Historical Association Journal
Northeast Folklore
Northwest Ohio Quarterly: a Journal of History
   and Civilization
Novaia i Noveishaia Istoriia [Union of Soviet
   Socialist Republic]
Nowe Drogi [Poland]
Nuestro Tiempo (IHE) [Spain]
Nuova Rivista Storica [Italy]

O

Ohio History
Old Northwest
Oral History Review
Oregon Historical Quarterly
Oxford Economic Papers [Great Britain]

P

Pacific Historian
Pacific Historical Review
Pacific Northwest Quarterly
Pacific Northwesterner
Pacific Sociological Review (see Sociological
   Perspectives)
Paedagogica Historica [Belgium]
Palimpsest
Párttörténeti Közlemények [Hungary]
Past and Present [Great Britain]
Peace and Change
Pennsylvania Folklife
Pennsylvania Heritage
Pennsylvania History
Pennsylvania Magazine of History and Biography
Pensiero Politico [Italy]
Permian Historical Annual
Pharmacy in History
Phylon
Policy Studies Journal
Policy Studies Review
Polish American Studies
Polish Review
Political Science Quarterly
Political Studies [Great Britain]
Politico [Italy]
Politics [Australia]
Politics & Society
Polity
Ponte [Italy]
Population Studies [Great Britain]
Present Tense
Presidential Studies Quarterly
Proceedings of the Academy of Political Science
Proceedings of the American Philosophical Society
Proceedings of the South Carolina Historical
   Association
Progressive Labor
Prologue: the Journal of the National Archives
Przegląd Socjologiczny [Poland]
Przegląd Zachodni [Poland]
PS
Public Administration [Great Britain]
Public Historian
Public Interest
Public Opinion Quarterly
Public Policy
Public Welfare

Publius

Q

Quaderni di Sociologia [Italy]
Quarterly Journal of Economics
Quarterly Journal of Speech
Quarterly Journal of the Library of Congress
Quarterly Review of Economics and Business

R

Radical America
Radical History Review
Railroad History
Reason
Red River Valley Historical Review
Register of the Kentucky Historical Society
Relations Industrielles (see Industrial Relations =
   Relations Industrielles) [Canada]
Rendezvous
Research in Economic History
Research Studies
Resources for Feminist Research = Documentation
   sur la Recherche Féministe [Canada]
Review (Fernand Braudel Center)
Review of Economics and Statistics
Review of Politics
Review of Radical Political Economics
Review of Social Economy
Reviews in American History
Revista de Ciencias Sociales [Puerto Rico]
Revista de Economía Política [Spain]
Revista Mexicana de Ciencia Política (see Revista
   Mexicana de Ciencias Políticas y Sociales)
   [Mexico]
Revista Mexicana de Ciencias Políticas y Sociales
   [Mexico]
Revista/Review Interamericana [Puerto Rico]
Revue Canadienne de l'Histoire des Sports (see
   Canadian Journal of History of Sport = Revue
   Canadienne de l'Histoire des Sports) [Canada]
Revue Canadienne de Science Politique (see
   Canadian Journal of Political Science = Revue
   Canadienne de Science Politique) [Canada]
Revue Economique [France]
Revue Française d'Etudes Américaines [France]
Revue Historique [France]
Revue Internationale de Droit Comparé [France]
Rhode Island History
Rochester History
Rocky Mountain Social Science Journal (see Social
   Science Journal)
RQ
Rural Sociology

S

Samtiden [Norway]
Scandinavian Journal of History [Sweden]
Scandinavian Review
Science and Society
Scottish Journal of Political Economy [Great
   Britain]
Sea History
Signs: Journal of Women in Culture and Society
Slavic Review: American Quarterly of Soviet and
   East European Studies
Smithsonian
Social and Economic Studies [Jamaica]
Social Education
Social Forces
Social History [Great Britain]
Social History = Histoire Sociale [Canada]
Social Policy
Social Problems
Social Science History
Social Science Journal
Social Science Quarterly
Social Service Review
Social Studies
Social Studies of Science [Great Britain]
Social Theory and Practice
Societas
Society
Sociological Analysis
Sociological Inquiry
Sociological Perspectives
Sociological Quarterly
Sociology and Social Research
Sociology of Education
Sotsiologicheskie Issledovaniia [Union of Soviet
   Socialist Republic]

Soundings (Nashville, TN)
South Atlantic Quarterly
South Carolina Historical Magazine
South Dakota History
Southern California Quarterly
Southern Changes
Southern Economic Journal
Southern Exposure
Southern Speech Communication Journal
Southern Studies: An Interdisciplinary Journal of
    the South
Southern Voices (ceased pub 1974)
Southwest Economy and Society
Southwestern Historical Quarterly
Spiegel Historiael [Netherlands]
State Government
Statsvetenskaplig Tidskrift [Sweden]
Studi Storici [Italy]
Studies in History and Society (suspended pub
    1977)
Swedish Pioneer Historical Quarterly (see Swedish-
    American Historical Quarterly)
Swedish American Historical Quarterly
Synthesis

T

Tampa Bay History
Teachers College Record
Technology and Culture
Tennessee Folklore Society Bulletin
Tennessee Historical Quarterly
Tijdschrift voor Geschiedenis [Netherlands]
Travailleur (see Labour = Travailleur) [Canada]
Trends in History

Turun Historiallinen Arkisto [Finland]

U

UCLA Historical Journal
Ukrains'kyi Istorychnyi Zhurnal [Union of Soviet
    Socialist Republic]
United States Naval Institute Proceedings
University of Turku, Institute of General History.
    Publications (ceased pub 1977) [Finland]
Upper Midwest History
Upper Ohio Valley Historical Review
Urban Affairs Quarterly
Urban and Social Change Review
Urban Review
Urban Studies [Great Britain]
Urbanism Past and Present
Utah Historical Quarterly

V

Vermont History
Vestnik Moskovskogo Universiteta, Seriia 8:
    Istoriia [Union of Soviet Socialist Republic]
Vestnik Moskovskogo Universiteta, Seriia 9:
    Istoriia (superseded by Vestnik Moskovskogo
    Universiteta, Seriia 8: Istoriia) [Union of
    Soviet Socialist Republic]
Virginia Magazine of History and Biography
Voprosy Istorii [Union of Soviet Socialist
    Republic]

W

Washington Monthly

West Georgia College Studies in the Social
    Sciences
West Tennessee Historical Society Papers
West Texas Historical Association Year Book
West Virginia History
Western Folklore
Western Historical Quarterly
Western Illinois Regional Studies
Western Pennsylvania Historical Magazine
Western Political Quarterly
Western States Jewish Historical Quarterly
William and Mary Quarterly
Wilson Library Bulletin
Wilson Quarterly
Wisconsin Magazine of History
Women's Studies International Forum
Working Papers for a New Society (see Working
    Papers Magazine)
Working Papers from the Regional Economic
    History Center
Working Papers Magazine
World Affairs
Worldview

Y

Yivo Annual of Jewish Social Science
Youth and Society

Z

Z Pola Walki [Poland]
Zeitgeschichte [Austria]
Zeitschrift für Geschichtswissenschaft [German
    Democratic Republic]

LIST OF ABSTRACTERS

A

Aimone, A. C.
Alvis, R.
Anderson, B. P.
Andrew, J.
Athey, L. L.

B

Bailey, E. C.
Bailey, E. C.
Balmuth, D.
Bamber, J.
Banker, J. R.
Barnard, R. S.
Bassett, T. D. S.
Beaber, P. A.
Beck, P. J.
Bedford, W. B.
Belles, A. G.
Billigmeier, J. C.
Blaser, L. K.
Blum, G. P.
Bobango, G. J.
Bolton, G. A.
Bott, M. A.
Bowers, D. E.
Bradford, J. C.
Broussard, J. H.
Brown, R. T.
Burckel, N. C.
Buschen, J. J.
Bushnell, D.
Butchart, R. E.

C

Cameron, D. D.
Campbell, E. R.
Carp, E. W.
Carr, S. P.
Chard, D. F.
Charles, J. S. S.
Cleyet, G. P.
Cline, D. H.
Coleman, J. S.
Coleman, P. J.
Collins, D. N.
Conner, S. P.
Coutinho, J. V.
Crapster, B. L.
Crowther, K. N. T.
Curtis, G. H.

D

D'Aniello, C. A.
Davis, G. H.
Davison, S. R.
Dejevsky, N.
Dewees, A. C.
Dietz, J. L.

E

Eads, O. W.

Egerton, F. N.
Eid, L. V.
Eminhizer, E. E.
Erlebacher, A.
Evans, H. M.

F

Fahl, R. J.
Falk, J. D.
Farmerie, S. A.
Fenske, B. L.
Findling, J. E.
Fitzgerald, C. B.
Ford, K. E.
Franz, D. A.
Frenkley, N.
Frey, M. L.
Fulton, R. T.

G

Gagnon, G. O.
Gallacci, C. A.
Gammage, J.
Garland, A. N.
Gilmont, K. E.
Glasrud, B. A.
Grant, C. L.
Griswold del Castillo, R.
Groves, J. V.
Gunter, C. R.

H

Harahan, J. P.
Hardacre, P. H.
Harling, F. F.
Harrow, S.
Hartigan, F. X.
Harvey, C. L.
Hazelton, J. L.
Hegstad, P. A.
Herrick, J. M.
Herstein, S. R.
Hewlett, G. A.
Hidas, P. I.
Hildenbrand, S.
Hilliker, J. F.
Hively, W. R.
Hobson, W. K.
Hoffman, A.
Holton, J. T.
Homan, G. D.
Hough, C. M.
Howell, R.
Human, V. L.
Hunley, J. D.
Hurt, R. D.

J

Jamieson, D. R.
Johnson, D. W.
Johnson, E. S.
Johnson, L. F.
Jones, G. H. G.

K

Kalinowski, L.
Kascus, M. A.
Kaufman, M.
Kearns, W. A.
Keller, R. A.
Kennedy, S. E.
Keyser, E. L.
Koppel, T.
Krenkel, J. H.
Krogstad, E. E.
Kuntz, N. A.

L

Lake, G. L.
Lambert, D. K.
Larson, A. J.
Ledbetter, B. D.
Lederer, N.
Lee, J. M.
Leedom, J. W.
Legan, M. S.
Levy, D.
Lewis, J. A.
Libbey, G. H.
Linkfield, T. P.
Lokken, R. N.
Lovin, H. T.
Lowitt, R.
Lucas, M. B.

M

Mahood, H. R.
Marks, H. S.
Marr, W. L.
Marshall, P. C.
Marti, D. B.
McCarthy, J. M.
McGeoch, L. A.
McGinnis, D.
McGinty, G. W.
McKinney, G. B.
McKinstry, E. R.
McLaughlin, P. L.
McNeill, C. A.
Migliazzo, A. C.
Miller, R. M.
Moen, N. W.
Mtewa, M.
Mulligan, W. H.
Munro, G. E.
Murdoch, D. H.
Myers, J. P. H.
Myers, R. C.
Myres, S. L.

N

Neville, G. L.
Neville, J. D.
Neville, R. G.
Newhouse, N. A.
Newton, C. A.
Nicholls, D. J.

Nielson, D. G.
Noble, R. E.
Novitsky, A. W.

O

Oaks, R. F.
Ohrvall, C. W.
Olson, C. W.
Olson, G. L.
Osur, A. M.

P

Parker, H. M.
Paul, B. J.
Paul, J. F.
Pergl, G. E.
Petersen, P. L.
Pickens, D. K.
Piersen, W. D.
Pliska, S. R.
Porter, B. S.
Powell, J.
Powell, L. N.
Powers, T. L.
Puffer, K. J.
Pusateri, C. J.

R

Raife, L. R.
Read, C. J.
Reed, J. B.
Reichardt, O. H.
Richardson, T. P.
Riles, R.
Ritter, R. V.
Ritter, R. V.
Rosenthal, F.
Ruffo-Fiore, S.
Russell, L. A.
Ryan, E. E.

S

Sapper, N. G.
Savitt, T. L.
Schoonover, T. D.
Schroeder, G. R.
Schulz, C. B.
Selleck, R. G.
Sevilla, S.
Shaw, F. J.
Sherer, R. G.
Shergold, P. R.
Simmerman, T.
Sirriyeh, E. M.
Sliwoski, R. S.
Smith, C. O.
Smith, D. L.
Smith, G.
Smith, J. D.
Smith, L. D.
Smith, L. C.
Smith, M.
Smith, T. W.

Smoot, J. G.
Snow, K. C.
Solomon, S. L.
Souby, A. R.
Sprague, S. S.
Stack, R. E.
Stevenson, D. R.
Stickney, E. P.
Street, J. B.
Street, N. J.
Strom, S. C.
Summers, N.
Sussman, B.
Sweetland, J. H.
Swift, D. C.

T

Talley, K. A.
Tate, M. L.
Taylorson, P. J.
Thacker, J. W.
Tharaud, B. C.
Thomson, H. F.
Tomlinson, R. H.
Touchstone, D. B.
Trickey, D. J.
Tull, J.

V

Vance, M. M.
Van Wyk, L.
Velicer, L. F.
Vivian, J. F.

W

Walker, J. T.
Walton, P. D.
Ward, H. M.
Wasson, G. V.
Watson, C. A.
Wechman, R. J.
Wendel, T. H.
Wentworth, M. J.
Whitham, W. B.
Wiederrecht, A. E.
Williamson, N. A.
Wilson, M. T.
Woehrmann, P. J.
Woodward, R. L.
Woolfe, L.

Y

Yanchisin, D. A.
Yerburgh, M. R.

Z

Zabel, O. H.
Ziewacz, L. E.
Zornow, W. F.